INTERVENTIONS

for Achievement and Behavior Problems
in a Three-Tier Model Including RTI

INTERVENTIONS

for Achievement and Behavior Problems in a Three-Tier Model Including RTI

Edited by

Mark R. Shinn, PhD
Hill M. Walker, PhD

NASP

From the NASP Publications Board Operations Manual

The content of this document reflects the ideas and positions of the authors. The responsibility lies solely with the authors and does not necessarily reflect the position or ideas of the National Association of School Psychologists.

Copies may be ordered from:
NASP Publications
4340 East West Highway, Suite 402
Bethesda, MD 20814
(301) 657-0270
(301) 657-0275, fax
(866) 331-NASP, Toll Free
e-mail: *publications@naspweb.org*
www.nasponline.org

ISBN 978-0-932955-68-5

Printed in the United States of America

14 15 16 17   10 9 8 7 6 5 4 3 2

DEDICATION

To Seth, a fine writer, and to Ronnie Detrich, Steve Forness, Mike Epstein, and Frank Gresham, for all their efforts in promoting evidence-based practices in our field.

—H.M.W.

My career outcomes are the product of a family of five, starting with Michelle and completed by our three boys—Peter, Dominic, and Matteo—and of the serendipitous opportunities that have been provided to me by good teachers and great mentors, including Stan Deno, Jim Ysseldyke, Hill Walker, Wes Becker, Randy Sprick, and the many students and colleagues and friends at the University of Oregon, Oregon Social Learning Center and the Oregon Research Institute. My students have taught me more than I ever taught them, so I try to make it up to them with the Interventions series. Three is the charm, so the next edition will have a new team, with what I know will be a commitment to evidence-based practices.

—M.R.S.

TABLE OF CONTENTS

FOREWORD

Thinking of Yellow Brick Roads, Emerald Cities, and Wizards

Gary Germann
Retired Special Education Director

INTRODUCTION

The editors and authors in the chapters to follow describe nothing less than a new assessment model and special education delivery system, one consistent with the spirit, intent, and language of IDEA 2004. In the model proposed by the title of this book, school psychologists are first involved primarily in developing interventions directed at students' achievement and behavior problems. Second, the interventions are delivered across three tiers that begin in the general education classroom, evolve to a modified general education program, and finally are intensified and individualized and may include special education. Third, the model is framed and supported by a legally sanctioned educational problem-solving process called RTI (*response to intervention*). RTI is characterized by the following core features:

- High-quality, research-based instruction and behavioral support in general education.
- Universal (school-wide or district-wide) screening of academics and behavior to determine which students need closer monitoring or additional interventions.
- Multiple tiers of increasingly intense scientific, research-based interventions that are matched to student need.
- Use of a collaborative approach by school staff for development, implementation, and monitoring of the intervention process.
- Continuous monitoring of student progress during the interventions, using objective information to determine if students are meeting goals.
- Follow-up measures providing information that the intervention was implemented as intended and with appropriate consistency.

Please relay feedback to the primary author, Gary Germann, via the following e-mail address: gary.germann@edformation.com.

- Documentation of parent involvement throughout the process.
- Documentation that any special education evaluation timelines specified in IDEA 2004 and in the state regulations are followed unless both the parents and the school team agree to an extension.

Most school psychologists would be uncomfortable in eliminating any of the components described in the above delivery approach. In fact, parents and practitioners should insist on the implementation of such a model in schools. However, even given the model's apparent benefits and its alignment with best assessment practices, successful implementation remains uncertain. Policy makers, when reauthorizing IDEA in 2004, gave practitioners a *choice* to (a) adopt the assessment and problem-solving model described in this book, (b) continue with the current model, or (c) do both. Which choice represents the "Yellow Brick Road" that will direct school psychologists toward the Emerald City of Oz? If children benefit when the educational system adopts the first option *a*, who benefits from options *b* and *c*?

> **Dorothy**: [*asking her little dog, Toto*] Now which way do we go?
> **Scarecrow**: Pardon me, this way is a very nice way.
> **Dorothy**: Who said that?
> [*Toto barks at scarecrow*]
> **Dorothy**: Don't be silly, Toto. Scarecrows don't talk.
> **Scarecrow**: [*points other way*] It's pleasant down that way, too.
> **Dorothy**: That's funny. Wasn't he pointing the other way?
> **Scarecrow**: [*points both ways*] Of course, some people do go both ways.

It is possible that 50 years of practice have created a system that will not or cannot embrace a new legally sanctioned model (RTI) because of the self-interest of those who benefit from the continuation of the current assessment model. Is it possible, as Pogo said: "We have met the enemy and he is us"?

> It must be remembered that there is nothing more difficult to plan, more doubtful of success, nor more dangerous to manage than the creation of a new system. For the initiator has the enmity of all who would profit by the preservation of the old institution and merely lukewarm defenders in those who would gain by the new ones. (Machiavelli, *The Prince*, 1513)

As I write this it is the winter of 2009, and in an effort to answer these questions, I find myself thinking back 30 years to 1979 when my special education cooperative made the decision to choose option *a*, RTI. At that time the Yellow Brick Road wasn't so much a road as a minefield. The challenge was not to follow the road. Rather, the challenge was to build it. I am also reminded of a bet I made long ago with Stan Deno (professor of special education programs, University of Minnesota). It is time for me to concede its loss. A bit of history will clarify and explain.

BUILDING THE YELLOW BRICK ROAD

Professor Marvel: Better get under cover, Sylvester. There's a storm blowin' up, a whopper. Just speakin' the vernacular of the peasantry.

My experience in education dates back to 1966 when I graduated with an undergraduate degree in speech and hearing science. The country was engaged in the civil rights movement with its primary emphasis on race and gender. The rights of those with special education needs were caught up in the movement, giving birth to an already evolving and exciting profession. Primary responsibility for ensuring the opportunity for equal education for those with special education needs was left up to individual states. State laws had evolved at different times and with different requirements, causing confusion among providers and inconsistencies in service options. During this time I worked in K–12 as a special educator, attained various degrees, and taught graduate courses at an institution of higher education. Something new and exciting was happening and I was right in the middle of it!

In 1975, the Education for All Handicapped Children Act (EAHCA) was enacted. This landmark legislation represented the original federal special education law and guaranteed the right to a free and appropriate public education in the least restrictive environment (LRE) to all children with disabilities. At this time I was a young director of special education in the Pine County Special Education Cooperative (now the St. Croix River Education District, Minnesota), with just 3 years of experience. I joined a growing legion of energized special educators who vigorously advocated for students whose achievement and behavior problems required specially designed instructional modifications. Energized by young, newly trained and dedicated teachers, inspired by the good intentions of parent advocate groups, and enabled by concerned policy makers, our growing legion of educators championed the special education cause and dramatically increased the number and kinds of services, resulting in new educational opportunities for millions of students. New special teachers taught in special places to special kids using special materials. Our vision was clear, our mission was right, and our will was strong. It was the best of times.

Beware the Potholes

No one, including myself, can question the promise or intent of EAHCA, nor can the motivations of those who struggled to implement it in those early years, or now, be characterized as anything but well intended. However, the foundational beliefs on which that law was written have had a profound, and often negative, influence on special education over the past 34 years in terms of research, training, and practice. What should have heralded a revolution of innovation, resulting in improved instruction and increased achievement, instead turned into a quagmire of rules, processes, testing, and regulation focused on controlling *entitlement*, not improving instruction.

Although righteous in the cause and sincere in motives, the enthusiastic and zealous advocates for special education were charting a path that would have critical unintended consequences. It is ironic that, in the evolution of special education, two trends are markedly and paradoxically divergent. First is the systematic *integration* of children with special "needs" into school environments. Second is the systematic *separation* of the structures designed to manage and deliver "special" instruction and related services. It is a classic case of unintended consequences caused by actions based on good intentions. If students with special instructional needs are to continue to become *a part of* general education, then special education must stop building service delivery structures that are *apart from* general education. Why would special educators now expect general educators to embrace them as service partners when for 34 years they have charted their own "special" path without them? How did this happen?

> **Scarecrow**: Come along, Dorothy. You don't want any of those apples.
> **Apple Tree**: Are you hinting my apples aren't what they ought to be?
> **Scarecrow**: Oh, no! It's just that she doesn't like little green worms!

I argue that the potholes that have impeded our progress are attributable to the underpinnings of EACHA, and of the act's subsequent reauthorizations, that are based on a set of fundamental beliefs, not empirically derived conclusions.

A *belief* is something regarded as true. Belief systems act like filters. By editing our reality, belief systems cause us to see and act in particular ways. Values and ethics evolve from belief systems. Nations fight wars over belief systems. "Reading wars" are fought by practitioners because of fundamental beliefs about how to define and measure reading. The science of evolution is challenged by the belief in intelligent design. Our country's penal system is designed around the belief that punishment, not retribution and rehabilitation, should guide practice. Belief systems influence values, symbols, language, interpretations, and perspectives that distinguish members of one category of people from another, resulting in unique cultures. Not surprisingly, beliefs are slow to respond to science and data.

The entire modern special education system has created a culture based on the following set of foundational beliefs. The extent to which these beliefs are empirically correct determines the extent to which an efficient and effective service delivery system can be built. The following beliefs are statements of what is valued, and what is valued is what is implemented in practice.

- Children are born "constitutionally broken" or acquire pathology, illness, impairment, disorder, and/or disability.
- Disabilities result from an intrinsic physical condition, and identification requires a diagnosis of the illness or disability.
- Internalized disabling conditions cause educational disadvantage that handicaps educational performance.

- Disabilities can be grouped into distinct diagnostic categories or classifications based on a set of common unique attributes identifiable and differentiated through the use of modern assessment tools, or psychometrics.
- There is a known and unique set of treatment–aptitude interactions to each disability that can be used to guide and direct instruction.
- Only children whose poor school performance is the result of identified disabilities are entitled to "specially" designed and funded instruction and related services.

Laws based on the above set of beliefs lead to the following questions in our schools. The *referring* question is: Does the child have a disability? The *assessment* question is: Does the child meet the disability eligibility criteria for special education entitlement?

A Separate and Unequal System

What are the consequences, intended and unintended, of a federal entitlement system based on these beliefs? Certainly a partial answer is that a special education system is created, flourishes, and is systematically separated from general education. The following are some examples of this separation:

- *A separate and unique classification system based on medical pathology is imposed* on an institution designed to deliver *educational* services. At the time of this writing, the number of disabilities, impairments, disorders, disturbances, or injuries is 13. These are just the major categories. Dozens of subcategories also exist, and various other descriptors number in the hundreds.
- *Separate earmarked fiscal entitlements are provided* to serve children with disabilities.
- *Separate and specific rules and processes are promulgated*, defining in minute detail the types of disabilities entitled to be served, by whom, when, where, and how.
- *Separate administrative "special" education bureaucracies are established* at the federal, state, and local district level to monitor implementation by policing process and punishing violations.
- *Separate remedial, general education, and special education systems are encouraged* to ensure funding is not commingled or misappropriated.
- *Children, teachers, and services are labeled* according to disability categories.
- *Separate "due process" rules are promulgated*, ensuring that parents are given every possible opportunity to object to the special assessment, label, service, and entitlement.
- *Compliance with statutes is based on administrative process, not student outcomes.* Bureaucratic entitlement and compliance needs (i.e., a paper trail) take precedence over student needs and performance outcomes.
- *A separate and special individual education plan (IEP) is required*, with general education's passive involvement.

- *Separate and related types of services are mandated* but not defined, expanding the depth and breadth of special education.
- *A separate teacher licensing mechanism is created* that defines, restricts, and certifies competence according to the type of disability the teacher can serve, not the instructional services he or she can deliver.
- *Separate teacher training departments are organized* according to categorical disabilities and train teachers to meet the new teacher certification requirements.
- *A separate special education publishing industry is created* to provide the necessary special materials for students whose disabilities cause them to learn differently and therefore require instruction uniquely designed to fit their instructional needs and learning styles.
- *A separate test publishing industry is created and responds* with hundreds of new tests and assessment tools designed to document and certify disability eligibility criteria. School psychologists are overwhelmed with "testing for eligibility" and are effectively removed from the problem-solving effort.
- *A separate network of advocate groups is created*, representing disability categories.
- *New special education vocabulary and/or jargon are developed* within the education establishment, separating special and general education.
- *Separate professional organizations directed at specific disability areas are created*, with their own conferences, journals, membership, and dues.

In summary, the above actions, values, symbols, language, interpretations, and perspectives, which distinguished members of one category of people from another (special and general educators), created two distinct cultures: one a separate and unequal special education system that was a parallel educational universe that existed in a different dimension from general education. More than three decades of implementation inertia now drives this system consisting of two groups with conflicting interests for whom student outcomes are an afterthought. The system has a life of its own, and any efforts to change it are viewed as a threat and are resisted.

QUESTIONS ANSWERED AND ANSWERS QUESTIONED

Wizard of Oz: You, my friend, are a victim of disorganized thinking.

From the very beginning it was obvious to some of us in the field of special education that what was being assessed at the point of referral and what the referrer was asking to be assessed were not the same. Teachers were referring students for special education services because of achievement and/or behavior problems. The problem from their perspective, and that of the child, was not a disability caused by presumed pathology; rather, it was a discrepancy between the progress they *expected* in achievement or behavior and the child's *actual* progress. Teachers were referring achievement problems or behavior problems or both and asking the assessment to answer the following questions:

- For which students do I need to individualize instruction or find more intensive instructional programs?
- How do I organize my classroom for instructional grouping?
- How do I set measurable goals for student progress in the short term (months) versus the long term (years)?
- How do I clearly communicate educational need and progress in nontechnical language to parents and other professional colleagues?
- How do I determine instructional needs of new students as they constantly arrive at our school door?
- How do I provide information on educational needs, goals, and progress for those students who may need remedial programs like special education?
- Most important, how do I know that my teaching is working for each student so that I can make changes in instruction when necessary?

Instead of giving teachers the answers to their questions, the assessment gave teachers what the law required—answers to two entitlement questions: Does the child have a disability, and does the child meet the disability eligibility criteria for special education entitlement?

It was also immediately evident that eligibility criteria based on mild intellectual disability (MID), specific learning disability (SLD), and emotional–behavioral disability (EBD) were the tails wagging the special education dog. Whereas sensory, motor, and severe developmental problems were diagnosed by evident pathology discovered during ancillary testing, these three high-incidence disabilities (MID, SLD, and EBD) were actually diagnosed based on the student's achievement and/or behavior, with no genuine pathology cited or observed at the time of referral. The "nine-to–three" disabled children (i.e., students whose disabilities only became obvious when they entered school in the morning and were gone when they left school in the afternoon) were overwhelming the system. In fact, if we remove speech and language students from the population, more than 85% of special education students fell within these three disability categories, and the vast majority of these students were experiencing reading and/or behavior problems.

Enormous amounts of human resources were being expended at great cost to answer questions that were not asked by the referrer, nor were the answers necessary or relevant for educational problem-solving. This situation was not something that could be fixed by tweaking the system.

> **Scarecrow**: I could while away the hours/conferrin' with the flowers/consultin' with the rain/And my head I'd be scratchin'/While my thoughts were busy hatchin'/If I only had a brain.

By the late 1970s it was clear that adopting one of the many new assessment tools designed to identify presumed pathology was not an answer. The tools, in fact, represented the problem! An appropriate response to students' achievement and behavior problems identified by the referral question required nothing less than a new assessment and decision-making paradigm—a difficult task, made even more difficult by at least the following obstacles:

- School psychologists were the assessment experts, and they had to manage and implement a new system. This was not possible when 75% of their time was being used to implement the deviant status disability model, in which eligibility for services is based on a label of deviance.
- Any attempts at innovation were probably going to be interpreted as a violation of law by the state department of education and result in loss of funding.
- Special education administrators had no money to pay for costs associated with a major innovation.
- An evaluation of the system required monitoring the process, not student outcomes, resulting in a system overwhelmed with a process in which student outcomes received only secondary consideration.
- The largest and fastest-growing classification of disabilities (SLD and EBD) could not be reliably identified.
- Needs perceived by the general education system and parents outweighed available special education resources.
- Due process requirements were unmanageable, undecipherable, and invitations for conflict.
- Parent advocacy was viewed with suspicion, and relationships were becoming adversarial, as parents turned to a growing industry of attorneys, poised and ready to exploit a system in distress.
- Special education advocates were communicating with general educators using a new vocabulary they did not understand ("IDEA mandates we provide IEPs to children with ADHD and SLD in the LRE").
- Costs were soaring, and traditional educational boundaries were expanding into new and poorly understood therapies, treatments, assessments, and interventions that lacked supporting evidence and were prohibitively expensive.
- The search for pathology and the case for entitlement consumed inordinate amounts of resources.
- Children were being labeled with stereotypical descriptors that created a negative and disempowering caricature of the child.
- Reacting to a referred problem resulted in a "wait to fail" delivery model as opposed to a model focused on proactive early identification and response.
- Services and teachers were labeled according to their disability categories, not by their areas of instructional expertise. Teachers became LD teachers or MID teachers as opposed to teachers who taught reading or math.
- The primary evaluation question was "Did the student learn?" as opposed to "Is the student learning?"
- The primary assessment question was: "What is wrong with the child?"
- And finally, and most important, although the problems were understood, a solution was not apparent.

On the other hand, the thought of continuing with this seriously flawed system was not an acceptable option. The lack of resources and an appropriate delivery model were more than overcome by a certain "audacity of hope."

Over the years I have attempted to summarize the plight of overwhelmed educators through the use of short metaphors. Readers might find themselves relating to any of the following: First, "When you are up to your neck in alligators, it is hard to remember that your mission is to drain the swamp!" Second, "We are so busy being what we are, that we don't have time to become what we should be!" Third, "It's hard to build an airplane while you're flying it." Finally, "If you don't like what you been gittin', then you gotta stop doin' what you been doin'; because if you keep on doin' what you been doin', then you're goin' to keep gittin' what you been gittin'."

SPECIAL EDUCATION AS A PROBLEM-SOLVING MODEL

> **Auntie Em**: Why don't you find a place where there isn't any trouble?
> **Dorothy**: A place where there isn't any trouble. Do you suppose there is such a place, Toto? There must be. It's not a place you can get to by a boat or a train. It's far, far away. Behind the moon, beyond the rain.

Unknown to me, Stan Deno and Phyllis Mirkin, both at the University of Minnesota, had described a different type of educational problem-solving and decision-making system in their book, *Data-Based Program Modification – A Manual* (Deno & Mirkin, 1977). At the same time (1977) an Institute for Research on Learning Disabilities (IRLD) was created at the University of Minnesota. Its principal investigator was Jim Ysseldyke. Phyllis Mirkin was associate director and Stan Deno was the lead researcher.

The purpose of the IRLD was to study the assessment and decision-making process that leads to the placement of students in special education programs. By 1979 Stan and Phyllis, along with a remarkable group of graduate students, were carefully laying the research foundation for curriculum-based measurement (CBM) as an approach to monitoring individual students' academic progress and teachers' instructional effectiveness. At the same time, Jim Ysseldyke was focusing on the problems associated with the existing methodology for assessing and identifying SLD.[1]

> **Wizard of Oz**: I am the great and powerful . . . [*steps out from behind the curtain*] Wizard of Oz.

The Internet gave birth to Google, every person's wizard. But prior to the Internet, it was customary to seek out wisdom and advice from the literature and

---

[1] The graduate students included Lynn Fuchs, Vanderbilt University; Karen Wesson-King, University of Wisconsin/Milwaukee and now deceased; Doug Marston, Minneapolis Public Schools; Mark Shinn, formerly at the University of Oregon and now at National-Louis University and coeditor of this book; and Jerry Tindal, University of Oregon. As a graduate student, then as a doctoral intern, and finally as an employee of the Pine County Cooperative, Jerry Tindal provided the necessary bridge between training, research, and practice. His contributions to the development of the original Pine County model were fundamentally critical and essential.

experts. I wish I could credit personal sagacity as the reason for calling Stan Deno sometime in the winter of 1979. Accident and serendipity are better explanations. I remember the call well. It went like this:

> **Me**: Hi, I am the director of the Pine County Special Education Cooperative and I am interested in implementing a data-based program modification system modeled after the one described in your manual. Would you be interested in working in partnership with us?
>
> **Stan**: Say what? Can you meet Phyllis and me for lunch?
>
> **Me**: How about 12:30?
>
> **Stan**: See you then. You're buying, right? Bye.

Over the next several weeks an informal partnership was agreed to that outlined basic responsibilities. Stan, Phyllis, and the University of Minnesota's IRLD would provide the Cooperative with its intellectual and developmental capital; the graduate students' time and energy; and the supporting science necessary to create a comprehensive intervention- and outcome-based education problem-solving system modeled after Stan and Phyllis's data-based program modification (DBPM) system.

The Cooperative would provide two school psychologists (Chris McHugh and Jeff Menigo) to manage the implementation effort, an unbelievable group of willing teachers, a supportive group of principals, and the nervous approval of the superintendents. I would provide leadership, implementation and design management, developmental oversight, resources, damage control, and the necessary reality-based perspective. In addition, the Cooperative and schools would provide 5 days of teacher training prior to the upcoming school year (1979–1980) and an additional half day of training every other week during the first year. This was possible because I had convinced my board that we should use our new EAHCA entitlement to make ourselves *better*, not bigger. Finally, the Cooperative's members would provide the IRLD a school-based research and training laboratory. Sometime during this planning process Stan reminded me that in the future I should remember that his job as a university professor was to "admire" problems, and my job, as a school administrator, was to "solve" problems. The significance and relevancy of the statement was not apparent at the time.

The Data-Based Program Modification (DBPM) Model—A Different Paradigm

> **Dorothy**: Oh, thank you so much! We've been gone such a long time and we feel so messy . . . What kind of a horse is that? I've never seen a horse like that before!
>
> **Guardian of the Emerald City Gates**: And never will again, I fancy. There's only one of him and he's it. He's the Horse of a Different Color you've heard tell about.

Beginning in the fall of 1979 the Pine County Special Education Cooperative implemented a special education system conceptualized by Stan Deno and Phyllis Mirkin in their *DBPM Manual*.[2] The actual problem-solving system was necessarily modified as we developed practice and learned from our experience and research. However, the four basic imperatives described in the *DBPM Manual*, and the related implications about instruction of children whose achievement and/or behavior are educationally handicapping, were never compromised. The four imperatives are described in Table 1.

> **Cowardly Lion**: All right, I'll go in there for Dorothy. Wicked Witch or no Wicked Witch, guards or no guards, I'll tear them apart. I may not come out alive, but I'm going in there. There's only one thing I want you fellows to do.
> **Tin Woodsman, Scarecrow**: What's that?
> **Cowardly Lion**: Talk me out of it.

It is easy to understand why a deviant status disability model is popular with general educators. A model that blames the child's achievement and/or behavior failures on the child's disability and allows adults to abdicate their instructional responsibility is one that is easy to love. Couple this with the user-friendliness of the system to general education—that is, the problem is the disability, not the instruction; general education teachers refer children, special education teachers serve them; general education teachers are not a part *of* the problem, they are apart *from* the problem; don't ask general education teachers to change a system that serves them so well and was championed by special education for so many years; and if special education wants general education to serve children with disabilities, give general education the money. It is helpful to remember that when teachers refer a child for special education, they are asking to have two problems solved: first, solve the teacher's problem by assuming the responsibility for expected progress, and second, solve the student's problem by increasing actual progress.

On the other hand, a model predicated on the following assumptions is easy for general education to question or reject. The assumptions are that (a) the child's lack of progress can be solved by modifying the instructional program; (b) a modification may or may not work; (c) teachers will need to frequently, directly, and continuously monitor the effects of the modification; (d) the program may have to be modified again if it is not successful; (e) this process begins in the general education classroom; and (f) interventions begin early in an effort to prevent referral to special education. This model requires a cultural change!

The Pine County Special Education Cooperative Model

During the next several school years, our partnership between the Cooperative and the university created, developed, nurtured, and improved an intervention-based,

---

[2]In 1990 the Pine County Special Education Cooperative was expanded to include additional schools and its name was changed to the St. Croix River Education District.

Table 1. Education Problem-Solving Imperatives and Delivery Implications

Imperative	Implication
1. The program goals for all students, regardless of the nature of their handicaps, must be derived from an analysis of those behaviors that are necessary to function in a less restrictive environment.	In a practical sense, this imperative means that teachers at any level of the Cascade [Evelyn Deno's Cascade of Services] should determine the behaviors that are necessary for the children to function at the next higher level, and they should direct their instruction toward those behaviors. To do so at level 2, for example, would eliminate the setting of auditory and visual processing tasks as educational objectives unless the value of the tasks for level 1 performance could be demonstrated.
2. Placement of a pupil in an educational setting should be determined by their present repertoire of behaviors rather than heir diagnostic label (e.g., learning disabled, dyslexic, minimally brain damaged, neurologically impaired, or emotionally disturbed).	Present assumptions are that labels may be necessary to justify the use of program resources but not, generally, to make instructional program decisions. Further, it is generally believed that labeling has had detrimental effects on individual development; for that reason alone, they should be avoided.
3. The success of instructional programs should be based on the rate at which the program moves the pupil toward functioning in more normal environments.	At the level of instruction, this imperative means that evidence must be presented that the pupil is making progress along a sequence of approximations to normality. If a "special" education program cannot demonstrably improve a child's rate of development, it is indefensible as a service. We are critical of defining quality of service in terms of time, program, or teacher–pupil ratio.
4. Whenever possible, special educational services for handicapped students should be brought to the individual rather than bringing the individual to the services.	In effect, this imperative means that revision in either instructional objectives or instructional treatments should occur within the natural environment (i.e., home, school, and community) rather than in one that is foreign to the child (i.e., special class, school, or residential center). In practical terms, this imperative has produced the need to retrain regular school personnel so that they can individualize instructional programs and, thereby, increase classroom tolerance for behavioral diversity.

Note. Reprinted from *Data-Based Program Modification: A Manual*, by S. L. Deno & P. Mirkin, 1977, Minneapolis, MN: University of Minnesota. A publication of the Leadership Training Institute/Special Education, University of Minnesota, under a grant from the Exceptional Child Program, Bureau of Adult and Occupational Education, U.S. Office of Education, Dept. of Health, Education, and Welfare.

problem-solving model built on direct, frequent, and continuous monitoring of students' achievement and behavior. The model included a tiered system that systematically provided data for guiding and justifying more intensive instruction in more restrictive environments (Tindal, Wesson, & Deno, 1985).

From the very beginning the partnership targeted special education services based on three goals: increase student achievement, improve teacher instruction, and report success. To achieve these goals curriculum-based measurement (CBM) was used to assess—frequently, directly, and continuously—where the student was at any given time relative to his or her norm group and criterion and also in terms of his or her rate of progress. The student's school support team examined the data and determined if the current intervention was generating the appropriate progress. If the student was falling behind in achievement, the intervention was changed in an attempt to improve instruction. Finally, progress was reported to relevant stakeholders using computer applications that our Cooperative designed and wrote.

To assist in this data-based decision-making process, starting in 1981, the Cooperative began benchmarking student basic skills three times each year using CBM probes. Students with skill discrepancies were monitored on a more frequent basis.

Measurement of general outcomes in the basic skill areas of reading, spelling, writing, and math for all students, as well as measurement for early literacy skills for nonreaders, was done three times a year. This benchmark testing had several purposes, including the following:

- To regularly monitor the progress of each student in the school.
- To establish school and district reading benchmarks, or norms.
- To call immediate attention to students who were having difficulty.
- To aid communication between teachers, parents, and other professionals.
- To provide information on effectiveness of educational programming.
- To place new students in the appropriate course or instructional setting.
- To focus instruction for new students.
- To monitor growth in students' achievement over time.
- To determine student proficiency related to the district's graduation standards.
- To screen students for Title 1 eligibility, special education services, and gifted programs.

Students of concern included any special education or Title 1 students, as well as any other student any teacher or parent was concerned about. The progress of students of concern was monitored frequently. Data were displayed graphically to all stakeholders on a software program called the Progress Monitoring Program. Frequent monitoring of students of concern had several purposes, including the following:

- To provide a basis for evaluating instructional programming for individual students with difficulties, as it was occurring.
- To provide information to help teachers make decisions about goals, materials, levels, and groups.
- To document progress of students' with IEPs. This documentation was necessary for periodic and annual reviews.

In the late 1970s and early 1980s, desktop computing was just beginning to demonstrate its usefulness to educators. Although not sophisticated by today's standards (e.g., AIMSweb), the Cooperative managed benchmark data and reported the data to teachers and principals using computer spreadsheet applications. In addition, Cooperative staff developed several proprietary computer applications. First were a group of continuous assessment programs (CAPs) for the Apple IIe computer that created random equivalent lists of nonsense words, letters of the alphabet for letter naming and letter sound fluency, spelling lists, math computation problems, and isolated and nonsense word lists. Second, a software program was written that charted individual students' progress over time, computed slope of improvement, marked program modifications, and red-flagged the lack of student improvement.

Finally, the Cooperative's entire special education system essentially eliminated the use of "disability" descriptors for teachers, resources, and students. Instead of labeling children according to disabilities, our labels described children's educational problems as they related to the areas in which performance was discrepant, that is, children with any combination of skill discrepancies, whether academic, motor, social, communication, vocational or transition, or adaptive living. Instead of labeling services according to disabilities, our labels described special education services as they related to *functions*, that is, assessment services, program modification services (academic, social, communication, vocational or transition, motor, and adaptive living), general education consultation services, training services, and education support and related services.

Pine County Special Education Cooperative Beliefs

Dorothy: We must be over the rainbow!

If new possibilities are to be created, then dominant belief structures must be challenged, because if the beliefs are not true, then the consequences will be predictably troublesome. Poor student outcomes are a seriously troublesome consequence! *Beliefs* about the causes of student variance influence how resources are organized to deal with those variances. This is best understood by examining SLD eligibility. If one believes that some children are born with a specific learning disability and that the disability manifests itself in a discrepancy between the child's ability and his or her achievement, then you organize your assessment and decision-making resources accordingly. Because students' entitlement to services is based on the psychometrics used to make eligibility decisions, the assessment process becomes focused on *which instruments* can be used to establish eligibility, their reliability and validity, and the specific criteria that represent a statistically significant internal discrepancy. If the basic belief is not true, then the assessment and problem-solving web that is woven can indeed become very tangled and might even last for years.

The foundational belief of DBPM and the Pine County Special Education Cooperative was that disability is *never* the problem. The handicap or problem is always the *discrepancy* between the student's actual progress and the expected progress. It is this progress discrepancy that is the basis of the teacher's referral and concern. It is this discrepancy the teacher is requesting to be assessed. It is this discrepancy they want targeted for reduction or elimination in the IEP. It is the reduction of this discrepancy they want periodically reviewed, and ultimately, it is the elimination or reduction of the discrepancy that certifies the referring problem's solution.

In a problem-solving model the purpose of assessment is not to determine the cause of the variance; it is to determine the extent of the discrepancy and the instructional factors that may be contributing to its existence. Assessment becomes a process whereby a database of student progress becomes the basis to form and direct instruction. A problem-solving model modifies instruction *a posteriori* (dependent on experience) to the process of assessing, as opposed to attempting to predict *a priori* (independent of experience) the instructional modifications that will be effective. Table 2 describes the process.

> **Dorothy**: Somewhere over the rainbow, bluebirds fly. Birds fly over the rainbow. Why then, oh why can't I? If happy little bluebirds fly beyond the rainbow, why oh why can't I?

NOW ABOUT THAT BET I LOST TO STAN DENO

> **Wizard of Oz**: [*preparing to leave the Emerald City on a hazardous journey*] To confer, converse, and otherwise hob-nob with my brother wizards.

It was sometime in the early to mid-1980s. Stan Deno and I were driving back to Minneapolis, Minnesota, from Des Moines, Iowa, where we had provided the initial training to Iowa teachers on the intervention and outcome-based education problem-solving system the partnership had developed in Pine County, Minnesota.

Stan and I and some of the previously mentioned graduate students, now working in various universities and locations, were training and consulting with Jeff Grimes (at that time the manager of the School Psychology Services division in the Iowa State Department of Public Instruction) and Iowa school staff members to implement what was known as project RE-AIM (Relevant Educational Assessment and Intervention Model). The project was written by the State Department of Public Instruction and was designed to train 500 Iowa special educators in the use of an intervention model that consisted of (a) behavioral consultation, (b) curriculum-based measurement, and (c) referral question consultative decision-making.

Stan and I were excited by the reaction to our just-completed training event and were contrasting Iowa's acceptance of our model to Minnesota's complete rejection and repudiation of the model.

Table 2. Pine County Special Education Cooperative Beliefs

Problem-Solving Phase	Decision Question	Beliefs
Problem Selection	What are the problem(s) requiring program modifications?	1. It is the child's performance on mainstream tasks that results in a child's being viewed as successful or unsuccessful by the teacher. 2. Assessments should be directed to specific areas of difficulty in the school curriculum and/or environment. 3. Special education service eligibility should be related to the severity of the discrepancy between the referred child's performance on functional district curriculum tasks and his/her peers' performance on the same tasks. 4. The primary focus of assessment should be on variables that can be manipulated in the environment. 5. Provision of special education services should be determined by the student's present repertoire of behaviors.
Program Selection	What plan is likely to be least restrictive and yet effective in solving the problem?	6. For an individual student, on the basis of assessment data, the regular classroom program is the most effective educational alternative. 7. Given the above, the IEP is a guess about what might be helpful to the student rather than a plan that will help. 8. Given the above, we have no alternative but to continuously evaluate the effectiveness of our IEP using time series data and modify it when it is not working. 9. No a priori assumption should be made that the optimal program for any student will simply occur as a result of matching student disability with teacher certification.
Program Operationalization	Is the agreed-upon program modification being implemented as planned?	10. IEPs should be specific with regard to the following: skills or behaviors for which special education services are being provided, the person(s) responsible for delivering services, the measurable annual short-term goals for each discrepancy, location of service, time allocated for the service, and the measurement system to be used to monitor the effectiveness of the service. 11. Since a plan is only good if implemented, implementation of the IEP component in number 10 should be continuously monitored.

Table 2. (*continued*)

Problem-Solving Phase	Decision Question	Beliefs

Program Improvement	Does the program modification implemented appear to be solving the problem?	12. Time-series student performance data should be the primary data when monitoring programs to determine if they are working or should be changed.
		13. The measurement system (materials) used to monitor program improvement, if truly practical and useful, should do the following:
		  a. Be immediately *sensitive* to the effects of relatively small adjustments made in (a) instructional methods and materials, (b) motivational techniques, and (c) administrative arrangements (e.g., adjustments in group, setting for instruction, teacher/tutor, time of instruction).
		  b. Be easy for the teacher, parent, and student *to administer*.
		  c. Be *easy to include* many parallel forms that are frequently administered (daily), if necessary, to the same student.
		  d. Be *time-efficient*.
		  e. Be *unobtrusive* with respect to routine instruction.
		  f. Be *inexpensive* to produce.
		  g. Be *simple* to teach.

Program Certification	Should the program as presently planned and implemented be terminated?	14. It is the student's performance that ultimately certifies the program as successful. 15. Time-series data on IEP goals are the primary indicator of program completion. 16. If a special education program cannot demonstrably improve a student's rate of performance, it is indefensible as a service.

Auntie Em: I saw you tinkering with that contraption, Hickory. Now you and Hunk get back to that wagon.

Hickory: All right, Mrs. Gale. But someday, they're going to erect a statue to me in this town.

Auntie Em: Well, don't start posing for it now.

We were taken by the irony of the contrast between Minnesota and Iowa. Three examples will clarify. First, Iowa was *re-aiming* their efforts to our problem-solving model and away from an "internal discrepancy" model they had endorsed and developed, which had actually become known as the Iowa Discrepancy Model. At the same time, Minnesota's state special education department was embracing that same internal discrepancy model despite Iowa's experiences and a growing body of research questioning the science of psychometrics and the validity of the SLD construct (e.g., the IRLD at the University of Minnesota). It was particularly frustrating because the IRLD had just completed its 5-year research effort and published its findings. Among the conclusions of Ysseldyke et al. (1983) were the following:

- There are no reliable psychometric differences on norm-referenced tests between students with learning disabilities and their low-achieving peers.
- There are technically adequate norm-referenced tests, but no technically adequate measures of the psychological processes and abilities that assessors were required to use to identify deficiencies.
- Curriculum-based measurement is a technically adequate alternative to the lengthy assessments that are currently administered.
- Student results are better when teachers gather data on student performance and use the data to adapt instruction. However, it is difficult to get them to do so.
- Clear and consistent differences exist in the performance of learning disability resource room students and regular classroom students on 1-minute samples using simple measures of reading, spelling, and written expression. Given that these measures reliably differentiate students, they also are useful for referral and assessment (eligibility) decisions.

It is amazing that after 25 years of failed practice and conflicting science how mired our profession remains in the dialectic of entitlement and disability, in particular as it relates to SLD.

The second example was that Iowa was embracing CBM as valid and reliable for identifying academic discrepancies and monitoring interventions and their effects. At the same time, Minnesota was rejecting the use of CBM in Pine County's intervention-based problem-solving model. Eventually this rejection resulted in a position paper by the Minnesota State Department of Education's Special Education Monitoring Section stating, among other things, that the use of CBM to determine eligibility was highly inappropriate, in violation of state and federal requirements and, in their opinion, an outrageous example of poor assessment practice as these procedures were currently used in Minnesota (Lombard, 1988).

> **Dorothy:** Weren't you frightened?
> **Wizard of Oz:** Frightened? Child, you're talking to a man who's laughed in the face of death, sneered at doom, and chuckled at catastrophe... I was petrified.

Third, Iowa was using their federal special education allocations to pay Stan and myself to train them on a problem-solving model, and at the same time the Minnesota Special Education Monitoring Section had just taken away a significant amount of the Cooperative's school district's federal allocation and a portion of state special education funding for developing and implementing the same system in Pine County schools! I was reminded of Stan's observation about my job being to solve problems and his being to admire them, as I stood alone and told my superintendents that, despite a foundation of scientific evidence, enthusiastic staff support, strong parent satisfaction, and demonstrated student growth, they were losing most of their federal and state special education funding.

What was done in Minnesota was punished, and when done in Iowa it was rewarded. There are two lessons to be learned here. First, when science contradicts practice, innovation is a better response than entrenchment. Second, if you are in a hole, stop digging!

> **Auntie Em:** Almira Gulch. Just because you own half the town doesn't mean that you have the power to run the rest of us. For twenty-three years I've been dying to tell you what I thought of you! And now... well, being a Christian woman, I can't say it!

As part of my Iowa presentation I had provided the audience the following written summary:

> In no other environment is human variance so obvious as in our schools. When a child's actual achievement is severely discrepant from the expected, they find themselves handicapped within the school environment. For too long, special educators have searched within the child for pathology in the hopes that such knowledge would direct their instruction, as well as provide justification for political action. We now recognize that answers to learning problems are not to be found within the child, but are explained only through an analysis of the instructional program. This increased understanding of student variance in addition to an expanding knowledge regarding the contributions of the environment on students' achievement, make it increasingly unnecessary to identify inferred "mentalistic constructs" in order to engage in educational problem-solving. The call for entrenchment through the continuation of past assessment practices, the maintenance of strict and narrowly defined eligibility criteria and the addition of regulation and process no longer suggest the solutions but best state the problem. The solution requires fundamental reform and restructuring of the educational system. Within this system, children will no longer receive special education because they are "broken" but because their diversity, without regard to causation, requires a greater degree of accommodation than is currently available. The special educator's primary function will be to expand the capacity for accommodation via an effective problem-solving model.

Buoyed by our Iowa reception, Stan and I were expressing our hope that special education practice would ultimately be guided and persuaded by science, and that the "disability treatment" model would evolve into an educational DBPM/Pine County problem-solving model characterized by data-based interventions targeted at achievement and behavior discrepancies and guided by positive student outcomes.

As an academic, trainer, and scientist, Stan was optimistic that a growing and substantial database of scientific evidence would soon result in a fundamental shift in the current assessment paradigm and delivery model. I shared the "audacity" of his hope, but questioned the rationale for his optimism. From my perspective, special education eligibility and entitlement were about resource allocation and were best answered by politicians, not educators. Therefore, change would occur only when the system's inefficient entitlement decisions caused it to become economically bankrupt, necessitating political action. Only then would the bright sunshine of science, research, data, and evidence lead policy makers toward a more enlightened and, of course, more cost-effective entitlement system.

At that time, I bet that a shift to an *all school* intervention and outcome-based problem-solving system represented by the Pine County model would not occur in my lifetime. Stan, ever vigilant where money is concerned, recognized that this was a bet he liked, since I would have to be dead for him to lose, and of course I would be unable to accept his payment. The bet was wagered.

With the reauthorization of IDEA in 2004 and the publication of this book, the loss of the bet is conceded. I am alive and so is an education problem-solving model (response to intervention).

NO RIGHT WAY TO DO A WRONG THING

Allocating educational services based on a deviant-status classification system is wrong. The disability is never, never, ever, ever the educational problem requiring an instructional solution. This perspective results in the wrong labels, identified with the wrong instruments, given for the wrong purposes, by people trained in the wrong methodology and implementing the wrong interventions. It creates an administrative bureaucracy (i.e., special education) that is separate from the general education system in terms of its funding, administration, staffing, licensing, rules, curriculum, locations, and language. Use of a deviant-status classification system focuses attention on process, not progress, to the detriment of all. It perpetuates a model that blames the child for instructional failure, with the unintended consequence of delaying instructional improvements in the general education programs. The problem, from an educator's perspective is always the discrepancy between a set of expectations for progress and performance and the child's actual progress and performance. The purpose of assessment is to identify this discrepancy as the problem, measure and quantify it, and measure the response to instruction intended to reduce or eliminate the discrepancy.

What a shame it will be, and what an opportunity lost, if RTI becomes just another way to define SLD or is defined as a prereferral intervention strategy! RTI is a new paradigm for educational problem solving, not a new way of identifying SLD! There aren't any better psychometric solutions for identifying SLD. Trying to identify SLD as an internal, child-centered disability is the problem, not the solution. The basic reality educators face each day is the natural diversity found in a classroom. When public policy requires the identification of pathology to justify program modification, it lessens general education's need to create instructional programs designed to deal with this natural diversity. We need to stop trying to answer political resource allocation and entitlement questions using psychometric models. Who is learning disabled is not a question answered by educators, it is one answered by politicians. If the purpose of determining eligibility is to improve instruction and increase achievement, then the best assessment would measure academic and social skills and the response to instruction, not pathology. If the purpose of determining eligibility is to justify entitlement, it is a question of resource allocation and best answered by politicians. Eligibility for SLD is not, has never been, nor will ever be a question answered by testing for pathology.

SUMMARY—THE PROMISE OF RTI

> **Scarecrow**: The sum of the square roots of any two sides of an isosceles triangle is equal to the square root of the remaining side. Oh joy! Rapture! I got a brain! How can I ever thank you enough?
> **Wizard of Oz**: You can't.

In a field whose self-identity since the beginning has been defined by a deviant status disability model—in which eligibility for services is based on a label of deviance—RTI is long overdue.

Response to intervention is an educational problem-solving process characterized by systematic and universal screening of all students; early response with high-quality and evidence-based instruction and behavior interventions; team decision making based on and matched to individual student needs; and frequent, direct, and continuous assessment of progress that is applied to individual educational decisions within a formative evaluation model. RTI requires all school resources to be aligned and allocated to provide effective and efficient interventions for the purpose of improving child outcomes. The provision of instructional and behavioral interventions is not limited to those who have a *disability*. The existence of disability is removed from the equation and all students are served on the basis of their *need*, without regard to causality. Just as medicine does not make treatment to patients with cancer available, or not available, based on whether the patient's cancer is primarily caused by genetic or environmental reasons, educators should not make instructional interventions available to students based on the presumed etiology of the problem.

A child reading six words correctly in first-grade materials at the end of Grade 1 is "educationally handicapped" to the same degree regardless of what is causing the discrepancy. In an RTI model, instruction is provided along a continuum of least restrictive alternatives, in which special education and its related and supportive services are operationally defined and provided to those students demonstrating a need for the services. Movement along the continuum is based on team decisions formed with data collected from an all-school assessment process using valid and reliable measures and reported on a direct, frequent, and continuous basis.

RTI provides a delivery vehicle—now sanctioned by law, consistent with best practice, and based on science—that provides an opportunity to chart a new path and create a new history for special education. Given the manner in which the 2004 IDEA reauthorization dealt with RTI, it is unclear what path will be taken. The authorization to identify special education needs using an RTI process is strong evidence that special education has arrived at a redefining moment in its educational evolution. The idea that students can receive individualized and special instruction based solely on their needs has never been more than a remote eventuality. But with the inclusion of RTI in IDEA 2004, the idea is no longer relegated to a distant future. It is possible today.

RTI's authorization is, to be certain, a significant milestone, but it remains unclear as to where the marker is going to be posted. If it becomes just another procedure to identify SLD, then it too will be relegated to the problem pile, not a part of the solution. I am hopeful that RTI is not an isolated event but, rather, marks a significant event in the politics of dealing with student variance. RTI represents the first step—and a potentially important one—in an evolution that will eventually lead to a more enlightened approach to helping those students with achievement and behavior problems.

As powerful as the separate components of RTI are, the concept of RTI is so much more than the sum of its parts. Long ago I concluded that if teachers experienced the diversity of student performance identified through an all-school assessment system and the challenge of providing instruction matched to all students' needs, disability classification would cease to be an important issue. As schools became accustomed to dealing with all student variance, disability would vanish as a concern. Have we finally arrived at a point where disability, even though it may remain a potent factor in entitlement decisions in the near future, will not be relevant to the process of solving children's achievement and behavior problems?

Scarecrow: I've got a way to get us in there, and you're gonna lead us.

Science claims to be a search for truth, and that would seem to protect it from conservatism and the irrationality of belief. Science represents a culture of innovation. Yet when Charles Darwin published his ideas of evolution, he faced fiercer opposition from his fellow scientists than from religious authorities. His theories challenged too many fixed ideas and too many strongly held beliefs. Jonas Salk ran into the same wall with his radical innovations in immunology, as did Max Planck with his revolutionizing of physics. Planck later wrote of the scientific opposition he faced: "A new scientific truth does not triumph by convincing its opponents and making them see the light, but rather because its opponents eventually die, and a new generation grows up that is familiar with it."

This book is written for this new generation of school psychologists. A better future will not be achieved by continuing the practices of the past. Will you lead or will you follow?

> **Dorothy**: [as the Wizard's balloon goes off without her] Come back! Come back! Don't leave without me! Come back!
>
> **Wizard of Oz**: I can't come back! I don't know how it works! Good-bye folks!

REFERENCES

Deno, E. (1970). Special education as developmental capital. *Exceptional Children, 37,* 229–237.

Deno, S. L., & Mirkin, P. (1977). *Data-based program modification: A manual.* Minneapolis, MN: University of Minnesota.

Education for All Handicapped Children Act (EAHCA), Pub. L. No 94–142 (1975).

Lombard, T. (1988). *Curriculum-based measurement: Megatesting or mctesting.* Roseville: Minnesota State Department of Education.

Tindal, G., Wesson, C., & Deno, S. (1985). The Pine County model for special education delivery: A data-based system. In T. Kratochwill (Ed.), *Advances in school psychology* (Vol. IV, pp. 223–250). Hillsdale, NJ: Erlbaum.

Ysseldyke, J., Thurlow, M., Graden, J., Wesson, C., Algozzine, B., & Deno, S. L. (1983). Generalizations from five years of research on assessment and decision-making: The University of Minnesota Institute. *Exceptional Education Quarterly, 4,* 75–93.

PREFACE

Hill M. Walker, PhD
University of Oregon

Mark R. Shinn, PhD
National-Louis University

This book is a compendium of chapters on state-of-the-art innovations and approaches for those professionals who are attempting to educate all who come through the schoolhouse door. Aside from a host of societal risk factors to which they can be exposed, today's students represent an enormous diversity of histories, backgrounds, ethnicities, languages, and cultural attitudes. Effectively educating this body of students severely challenges the skills and accommodation capacities of schools and the personnel who operate them. However, concurrent with these developments have come some impressive advances in assessment tools, diagnostic precision, and interventions for academic and social–behavioral problems. These improved methods, if applied with integrity, make it possible for a substantial majority of students to achieve school success. A very important goal of this book is to make this information available to administrators, school psychologists, special educators, behavioral and mental health specialists, early interventionists, and general educators in user-friendly forms that they can use effectively.

The continuing gap between what we in the profession know and what we practice, however, remains a major obstacle to realizing this outcome (Rogers, 1995; Walker, 2004). In educational fields, as in so many fields, the lag time between the development of important new innovations and their incorporation into routine practices and treatment regimens can be vast (Schoenwald & Hoagwood, 2001). In medical practice, this delay is particularly excruciating and has likely plagued the field of education since its inception. Rogers provides a compelling example of the nettlesome difficulties and terrible consequences of failing to adopt a proven innovation—even when the stakes for not doing so are very high. In the mid-1700s, scurvy frequently devastated merchant and naval crews to such an extent that ships often would have to return to port because they lacked sufficient crew to continue the voyage. At the time, a surgeon in the British Royal Navy (James Lind) discovered the dietary cure for scurvy, yet despite this important discovery, it took another 100 years before this simple dietary cure was fully implemented in the British naval and merchant fleets! The lag time between the development and adoption of innovative practices in mental health in schools is estimated by many experts to be 20 years.

The first edition of this book (Stoner, Shinn, & Walker, 1991) attempted to provide school professionals with access to the best, and most up-to-date, scientifically based interventions by content experts at preschool, elementary, and secondary school levels. Our second version (Shinn, Walker, & Stoner, 2002) expanded on the original conception of scientifically based practices and was an attempt to *encourage* the development and delivery of early intervention approaches within a conceptual framework of primary, secondary, and tertiary forms of prevention. A number of chapters in the second edition were written from a prevention perspective, but given the lack of cohesion in the knowledge base regarding schools as an important platform for prevention at the turn of the century, many of the book's chapters did not address this critical issue.

Although the second edition was published less than a decade ago, the available knowledge base and societal context for the third edition have both changed. The body of knowledge now available as to what works, and what doesn't work, has expanded remarkably in the past 10 years. This is especially the case with school-based practices designed for students who face behavioral and academic challenges. In the years since the second edition, as societal problems reflected in the schools have continued to worsen, we have witnessed a concurrent effort by researchers, professionals, legislators, policy makers, and the public to commit to *prevention* and *early intervention* approaches to address the social–emotional–behavioral challenges and academic needs of children in this country. For example, we saw the passage of the No Child Left Behind (NCLB) Act in 2001, which provides the means for *all* children to get off to a healthy start in school and become competent readers by the end of third grade. We saw the reauthorization of IDEA in 2004, with the passage of the Individuals with Disabilities Education Improvement Act. IDEA 2004 set forth the national priority that all students have a right to a high-quality, appropriate general education accompanied by the necessary accommodations and supports that would help prevent the need for special education. Finally, we have seen the emergence of consensually validated practice guides in which state-of-the-art information on critically important topics has been made available to educational consumers, free of charge. These practice guides, produced by the U.S. Department of Education's Institute of Education Sciences (IES), are a signal development in reducing the gap between available knowledge and current practices in preventing school dropout, reducing behavior problems in the elementary classroom, and organizing instruction to improve student learning.

This third edition (Shinn & Walker, in press) builds on the themes and content from the first and second editions and sustains our ongoing commitment to scientifically based practices. We believe that the educational system's commitment to scientifically based practices should be part of a larger societal mission to ensure that each individual receives an appropriate, effective education. Access to interventions that meet an evidence-based standard in this regard has recently been characterized by Detrich, Keyworth, and States (2008) as a consumer protection issue—a position with which we are in total agreement.

These themes of scientifically based practices and evidence-based approaches are reflected in each of this edition's chapters. Further, the introductory chapter makes the case that interventions must be *explicitly* and *proactively* designed and implemented across multiple tiers of increasing intensity.

REFERENCES

Detrich, R., Keyworth, R., & States, J. (2008). *Advances in evidence-based education: A roadmap to evidence-based education.* Oakland, CA: The Wing Institute.

Rogers, E. M. (1995). *Diffusion of innovations* (4th ed.). New York: The Free Press.

Schoenwald, S. K., & Hoagwood, K. (2001). Effectiveness, Transportability, and Dissemination of Interventions: What Matters When? *Psychiatric Services, 52,* 1190–1197.

Shinn, M. R., & Walker, H. M. (Eds.). (in press). *Interventions for achievement and behavior in a three-tier model including RTI* (3rd ed.). Bethesda, MD: National Association of School Psychologists.

Shinn, M. R., Walker, H. M., & Stoner, G. (2002). *Interventions for Academic and Behavior Problems II: Preventive and Remedial Approaches.* Bethesda, MD: National Association of School Psychologists.

Stanovich, K. E. (1986). Matthew effects in reading: Some consequences of individual differences in the acquisition of literacy. *Reading Research Quarterly, 21,* 360–406.

Stanovich, K. E. (2000). Reading disability: Are reforms based on evidence possible? In K. E. Stanovich (Ed.), *Progress in understanding reading: Scientific foundations and new frontiers* (pp. 323–337). New York: Guilford.

Stoner, G., Shinn, M. R., & Walker, H. M. (Eds.). (1991). *Interventions for academic and behavior problems* (1st ed.). Silver Spring, MD: National Association of School Psychologists.

INTERVENTIONS
for Achievement and Behavior Problems in a Three-Tier Model Including RTI

CHAPTER 1

Systemic, Evidence-Based Approaches for Promoting Positive Student Outcomes Within a Multitier Framework: Moving From Efficacy to Effectiveness

Hill M. Walker
University of Oregon

Mark R. Shinn
National-Louis University

INTRODUCTION

Schools today are perhaps more stressed, but certainly are as stressed, as they have ever been in their history. Most of the myriad pressures and stressors currently impinging on the approximately 125,000 U.S. schools are not self-imposed; rather, they stem mainly from problems endemic to the larger society and reflect a set of expectations for educators that are both unrealistic and unachievable, given current societal attitudes, conditions, and available resources. As we have noted numerous times in our prior work, schools are unfairly held accountable for many negative or disappointing student outcomes that are not principally of their making. However, schools *are* expected to compensate and correct for these outcomes and, moreover, to overcome the lack of school preparedness caused by institutionalized poverty. Schools are pressured to produce world-class outcomes while alleviating the effects of weak and dysfunctional parenting that damages many at-risk students' ability to absorb the normalizing and protective benefits of schooling. Other social toxins that spill over into the schooling process, and that hamstring the ability of educators to effectively teach and socialize our youth, include violence, fear for one's personal safety, society's refusal to support schools fiscally as well as politically, rampant child abuse and neglect, the Balkanization of our culture, class conflicts, racial discrimination, and a general animus toward others in ordinary social relations.

Please relay feedback to the primary author, Hill M. Walker, at the following e-mail address: hwalker@uoregon.edu.

This list is by no means exhaustive, but all of the above can be classified as problems arising within the larger society and nurtured by it. These conditions put the future of our children and youth in jeopardy and negatively color their perceptions of the world in which they live. Although schools can ameliorate to some extent the damaging impacts of long-term exposure to risk, we need to look at our society and not solely at our schools to discover the root causes and ultimate solutions to these conditions that are so destructive to our way of life.

Given all these constraints, schools are doing relatively well in fulfilling their primary mission of preparing youth for life in the 21st century (Walker, Ramsey, & Gresham, 2004). Despite the gloomy picture that is so often painted by critics of the U.S. educational enterprise, we are in the midst of the largest school reform effort of the past 30 years. This reform is driven and sustained by a number of seismic shifts in thinking about school improvements, including (a) applications of increased knowledge, (b) a willingness to consider prevention versus a remediation approach, (c) recognition of the importance of early intervention, (d) acceptance that general education teachers cannot do it all, and (e) understanding that special education is not the sole solution to every problem that general education identifies.

MAKING A SOCIETAL COMMITMENT TO A MULTITIER MODEL

In the second edition of this book (Shinn, Walker, & Stoner, 2002), we made the case that the state of society required a strong *commitment* to the concepts of prevention and the powerful interventions necessary to promote positive youth development. At the turn of this century, our country made one such societal commitment to address the development of America's reading needs. The No Child Left Behind Act of 2001 (NCLB) set forth the standard that all students should receive scientifically based reading instruction to enable them to be successful readers by the end of Grade 3, when they move beyond reading mastery and begin to use reading as a tool for learning. NCLB put in motion a set of legally mandated requirements for school systems as well as targeted funds for intervening with those students who were at risk and not making adequate yearly progress.

NCLB was based on the acknowledgement of a body of science showing that some children, notably those from low-income backgrounds, typically entered schools well behind their counterparts in important reading prerequisites, such as language experience. For example, low-income 5-year-old children are estimated to lag behind their high-income counterparts by more than 30 million words in language experience (Hart & Risley, 1995). When these students are provided with "standard" reading instruction (i.e., undifferentiated instruction and/or reading programs or philosophies that are not scientifically based), this gap actually *increases* with continued schooling (Hirsch, 2003; Stanovich, 1986, 2000). NCLB attempted to reduce or eliminate this gap by requiring that schools use scientifically based reading programs instead of standard reading programs. Notably, from a research perspective (Torgesen, 2001,

2002) and from early evaluations of the Reading First program that was part of NCLB (National Center for Education Evaluation and Regional Assistance, 2008), it was discovered that this gap *could* be reduced using scientifically based instruction. However, despite demonstration of a gap *reduction*, the achievement gap remained substantial.

A remedy proposed to reduce the remaining gap has been the promotion of multitiered interventions of increasing intensity (e.g., a three-tier model) matched to student needs as determined by universal screening and progress monitoring (Batsche et al., 2005; Burdette, 2007; Torgesen, 2005; Torgesen, Houston, Rissman, & Kosanovich, 2007; Vaughn & Linan-Thompson, 2004). In our chapter in the second edition of this book (Walker & Shinn, 2002), we included the multitiered interventions model shown in Figure 1. Our goal was to graphically represent efforts to build multitiered services for a single type of problem (i.e., students at risk for antisocial, violent, and/or destructive behavior). In contrast with Figure 1, the Figure 2 developed by Horner and his colleagues (Sugai, Horner, & Gresham, 2002) and disseminated widely by the National State Directors of Special Education, developed a multitier model with tiers for academics *and* social behavior, reflecting the need to build a service delivery system that is *comprehensive* rather than problem-specific (Batsche et al., 2005).

Figure 1. Preventing violent and destructive behavior in schools: Primary, secondary, and tertiary systems of interventions.

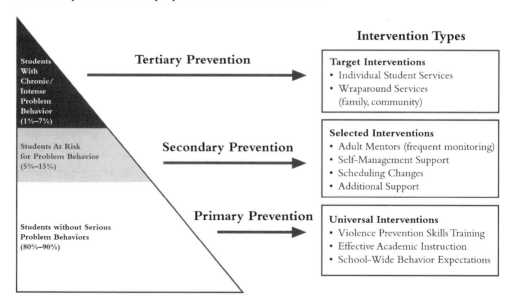

Note. From "Integrated approaches to preventing antisocial behavior patterns among school-age children and youth," by H. M. Walker, R. H. Horner, G. Sugai, M. Bullis, J. R. Sprague, D. Bricker, & M. J. Kaufman, 1996, *Journal of Emotional and Behavioral Disorders*, 4, pp. 194–209. Copyright 1996 by SAGE. Reprinted with permission.

Figure 2. **Multitiered services and parallel interventions for academic and behavioral systems.**

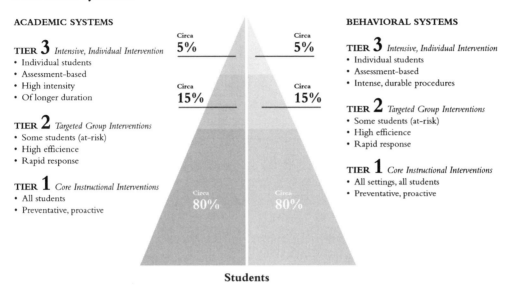

ACADEMIC SYSTEMS

TIER 3 *Intensive, Individual Intervention*
• Individual students
• Assessment-based
• High intensity
• Of longer duration

TIER 2 *Targeted Group Interventions*
• Some students (at-risk)
• High efficiency
• Rapid response

TIER 1 *Core Instructional Interventions*
• All students
• Preventative, proactive

BEHAVIORAL SYSTEMS

TIER 3 *Intensive, Individual Intervention*
• Individual students
• Assessment-based
• Intense, durable procedures

TIER 2 *Targeted Group Interventions*
• Some students (at-risk)
• High efficience
• Rapid response

TIER 1 *Core Instructional Interventions*
• All settings, all students
• Preventative, proactive

Circa 5%   Circa 5%
Circa 15%   Circa 15%
Circa 80%   Circa 80%

Students

Note. From "Behaviorally Effective School Environments," by G. Sugai, R. H. Horner, & F. Gresham, 2002, in M. R. Shinn, H. M. Walker, & G. Stoner (Eds.), *Interventions for Academic and Behavior Problems II: Preventive and Remedial Approaches*, p. 320, Bethesda, MD: National Association of School Psychologists. Copyright 2002 by National Association of School Psychologists. Reprinted with permission.

In the past 7 years, a number of variations on Figure 2 have been broadly disseminated that represent a multitude of permutations of tiers and conceptualizations. Nearly all the variations we have seen specify a set of numbers within each tier (e.g., 80%, 15%, 5%). What do these numbers mean? For some school personnel, these numbers represent the expected outcomes of successful implementation of a multitier model. Others see the numbers representing an *evaluative standard* by which they can compare outcomes of their current service delivery system. For example, we have heard a district administrator say that because they were only serving 10% of their students in Title 1 programs, a common Tier 2 intervention, they were underserving at-risk students. In another instance, a low-income school district essentially gave up on reform efforts because their Tier 3 percentages were 40% instead of 5%.

We consider the explicit listing of percentages in each tier to be problematic at best and misleading at worst if used as evaluative criteria or primary drivers of policy as noted in the examples above. To avoid problems with reification (i.e., the percentages taking on a life of their own), we suggest treating the tiers and the percentages within any multitier model as *heuristics* only. According to Merriam-Webster's Collegiate Dictionary, a heuristic is defined as "involving or serving as an aid to learning, discovery, or problem-solving." A heuristic, then, can *guide thinking,* but it is not a formula, a blueprint for action, or an instruction manual.

The heuristic represented by the tiers and their respective percentages provides a conceptual roadmap for allocating resources, defining populations, and differentiating types of interventions that can be coordinated with each other (Walker et al., 1996). When we distill the common elements of the myriad graphic representations of a multitier model and treat them as a set of implicit and explicit heuristics, we find the following interrelated and overarching "big" ideas.

1. No single tier solves all problems.
2. A well-designed multitiered system will have hierarchal tiers of increasing intensity.
3. Effective interventions at a lower-level tier reduce the need for interventions at subsequent tiers; however, some students require continuing intervention at more than one level.

We propose two sets of descriptors that should be kept in mind in understanding the multitier model as a heuristic. The first set of descriptors—*most, some,* and *few*—relate to the commonly cited percentages of students (e.g., 80%, 15%, 5%) presented in Figures 1 and 2. The percentages are not specific numbers but rather are a general concept. Tier 1 interventions, if designed and delivered well, should meet the needs of *most* students. However, even with an effective Tier 1 intervention, *some* students will still need more intensive interventions and may require Tier 2 intervention. If Tiers 1 and 2 are designed and delivered well, there will still be a *few* students who need Tier 3 interventions. Again, the value of treating these numbers as a set of heuristics, rather than empirical criteria, is that it allows for thinking about *how* multitiered services are structured and *what the intended effect* would be.

The second set of descriptors is *least, more,* and *most*. These descriptors refer to the intensity of provided interventions. Tier 1 intervention should be scientifically based and appropriately intensive, with the goal of promoting positive development and preventing problems. Of the three tiers, it is the *least* intensive. Tier 2 is characterized by *more* intensive intervention. Tier 3 is the *most* intensive intervention. One feature of increased intensity is additional intervention time. A theme of this book and of best practices in general is that to reduce the gap and meet the needs of students, more intensive interventions include dimensions beyond just more instructional time, such as explicitness, opportunities to respond, types of corrective feedback, powerful motivational programs, and so on. Tier 2 and 3 interventions, as exemplified by the chapters in this book, specify a variety of specific instructional and/or curriculum features that make an intervention more intensive.

No Single Tier Solves All Problems

In 1989, Deno laid out a set of general assumptions that have long formed the basis for multitiered early-intervening services. Among them were two key ideas. First, general education alone cannot meet the needs of all students. This statement was not intended to be a blaming one; rather, it was a realistic assessment of basic capacity that was designed to communicate that the variability in students' needs exceeded the capacity of any general education teacher to address those needs with 100% success. Second, as a corollary to the first statement, Deno noted that some students needed *more* intervention than was provided by general education alone for them to learn what was expected. School *systems* were obligated to design and deliver additional services that provided something more. These two statements form the basis for the heuristic that a general educational environment, no matter how successful it is for *most* students, will not be successful for *all*, and that our responsibility is to design systems that ensure universal success by building more options. In order to do so, more than one tier will be required.

The Hierarchy of Multiple Tiers May Need to Be Revisited

If more than one tier is needed, then who decides how many? Although many multitiered early-intervening service models feature three tiers, there is no uniform position regarding the specific number of tiers needed. Tier 1 consists of the general education curriculum or interventions delivered to all students through core programs (e.g., reading, social studies, school-wide behavior support). For example, in chapter 18 by Denton and Vaughn, the key to students' success in general education reading is the need for an effective core reading program taught by teachers who are able to deliver differentiated instruction. Classwide peer tutoring, discussed in chapter 24 by Greenwood, Seals, and Kamps, is just one example of how Tier 1 general education instruction can be differentiated. Similarly, Frey, Lingo, and Nelson, in chapter 16, stress effective school-wide positive behavior support as the key to creating a school climate that ensures personal safety and is characterized by academic achievement and social competence.

Tier 2 typically is composed of interventions for students who are at risk (see Walker et al., 1996). Tier 2 interventions may constitute remedial programs currently in place, such as Title 1, or they may be newly designed programs delivered to a small group of students who share certain intervention needs or, in some circumstances, to at-risk individual students.

Tier 3 is composed of intensive interventions for individual students with chronic or severe long-standing problems that exceed the capacity of Tier 1 or Tier 2 interventions to satisfactorily resolve their problems. In most conceptions, Tier 3 is *not* considered special education, but rather is a set of *most* intensive general education interventions. The obvious implication of this view is that, if special education is not a Tier 3 intervention and students need more than general education can provide, then there must be an ongoing need for more than three tiers.

If the conception represented by Figure 2 and other similar figures is taken as a literal blueprint, then determining where special education fits in relation to the three tiers creates problems. In theory, special education is neither a tier nor a place but a specially designed program to meet a student's unique needs. Is it a fourth tier or is it Tier 3.5? Is there a fifth tier? In chapter 23 of this book, Schumaker and Deshler present a multitier model consisting of five tiers. Is their model consistent or inconsistent with the general conception of multitiered interventions as intended in this book? We submit that there is ample room for professionals to offer permutations on a multitiered conception that fit their world view and service delivery realities. In our view, the overarching, big idea should be that schools need to be *proactive* in their design (and fleshing out) of tiered interventions to meet the needs of (a) all students, (b) students who are more at risk, and (c) students with chronic, long-standing problems. The specific mechanisms for doing this can vary based on a number of variables, including available resources, severity of needs for the whole school context, staffing patterns and skill levels, and developmental level (i.e., preschool, elementary, secondary).

Effective Intervention at a Lower Level Tier Reduces the Need at Subsequent Tiers

A final big idea is that the more effective the interventions are at a lower tier, the fewer the number of students who will need more intensive intervention at subsequent tiers. For example, a powerful scientifically based Tier 1 core reading intervention that meets the needs of 75% of all students clearly reduces the number of students who require more intensive tiered interventions, compared with a Tier 1 reading program that is successful with only 50% of students. This heuristic stresses that interventions are dependent on effective, powerful interventions being delivered across all tiers with high levels of integrity.

RTI IN A MULTITIER MODEL: A MEANS TO WHAT ENDS?

Up to this point, we have avoided referring to the development and implementation of multitiered service delivery systems as "response to intervention" (RTI). We have done this intentionally because of what we believe has been confusion as to the *means* and *ends*. In the Individuals with Disabilities Education Improvement Act of 2004 (IDEA 2004), federal law provided local education agencies (LEAs) the option of no longer using the ability–achievement discrepancy approach to identifying a student with specific learning disabilities (SLD). Instead, IDEA 2004 allowed LEAs to use as the cornerstone of the SLD entitlement process a system that determines whether a student responded to appropriate instruction in reading and math. This approach became known as *response to intervention*. The scientific and legal basis for this radical shift in SLD identification practice is described in more detail in chapter 3 by Gresham, Reschly, and Shinn.

As with any innovation that requires departure from traditional practices, RTI has been the subject of myriad interpretations, conceptualizations, controversies, and conundrums among educational and related services professionals. RTI has become a ubiquitous term that seems to have taken on a life of its own, serving as a sort of professional "projective test"; it means different things to different people.

RTI as the Means to the Ends of Special Education Entitlement

For many educators, RTI is primarily the *means* to identify some students as SLD. A multitier model is adopted by educators to enable the use of RTI as the core of the SLD entitlement process (see, for example, Pericola Case, Speece, & Eddy Molloy, 2003; Vaughn & Fuchs, 2003). The implicit goal, or *end*, in this approach is to use RTI for SLD diagnosis by moving students through tiers as necessary. Distinguishing features of this approach involve deciding how long a student should fail at Tier 2 before receiving Tier 3 supports and instruction and deciding between a standard treatment protocol or a problem-solving approach (e.g., Wanzek & Vaughn, 2007). In practice, using RTI as a means to diagnose SLD typically is reactive and idiographic. That is, a teacher identifies a student about whom there are concerns, usually by making a referral to a team, and then the team develops an intervention for that specific student. If the intervention fails, the student is "moved" to a more intensive tier (Shinn, 2007).

This interpretation of RTI as primarily entitlement is understandable, given the language of IDEA 2004 and a long-standing national interest in using entitlement approaches such as prereferral intervention (e.g., Graden, Christenson, & Casey, 1985) to reduce the need for special education because of an insufficient number of effective options in general education. Additionally, this conception of RTI fits with almost 30 years of school practice that has focused more on disability identification than on effective treatment.

RTI as the Means to the Ends of Significant School Improvement Using Evidence-Based Practices

Although it is easy to understand the view of RTI as a means of determining SLD entitlement, RTI is also a generic term (i.e., professional shorthand) for what we describe in this volume as a multitiered service delivery system based on evidence-based practices. In this use of the term, RTI is a means of building a more comprehensive, coordinated, and effective service delivery system that is based on the *proactive* foundational practices of (a) prevention, (b) evidence-based interventions across tiers, (c) data-based decision making, and (d) early intervention that uses universal screening rather than referral (see Brown-Chidsey, Bronaugh, & McGraw, 2009; Fletcher & Vaughn, 2009).

This use of the term was the implicit focus of the National Association of State Directors of Special Education (NASDSE) in their widely disseminated document, *Response to Intervention: Policy Considerations and Implementation* (Batsche et al., 2005). The explicit goal was to use RTI to ensure that *all* students receive effective interventions for academics and behavior. This latter approach incorporates several fundamental and long-standing core principles and adapts the U.S. Public Health Service classification of prevention types (i.e., primary, secondary, and tertiary) to the school setting through a multitier model (Walker et al., 1996). The goal of Tier 1 (i.e., primary prevention) is to promote positive development and prevent problems from emerging. The goal of Tier 2 (i.e., secondary prevention) is to reverse the effects of prior risk exposure or harm. The goal of Tier 3 (i.e., tertiary prevention) is to reduce harm from such exposure. The broad adoption of this RTI model by educators has resulted in at-risk students being identified earlier, receiving more timely services that are tailored to their needs, being exposed to evidence-based interventions and procedures, and achieving reductions in duplications of service and more efficient use of limited resources (Glover, Diperna, & Vaughn, 2007).

Distinguishing features of this RTI approach involve questions such as "Is our core reading program meeting the needs of our students?" and "What are our screening criteria for immediate delivery of Tier 2 or Tier 3 interventions?" In practice, this approach typically is proactive; that is, effective interventions are selected based on the needs of groups of students such as at-risk readers or students with chronic long-standing behavioral difficulties. *After* effective interventions of appropriate intensity are selected by school professionals and a service delivery approach is adopted (e.g., how Tier 2 will be provided), *then* students are identified. This process is driven by universal screening, in which all students are tested at one time and then aligned to the tier with interventions that meet their instructional or behavioral needs. If the intervention fails, the approach emphasizes evaluating the effectiveness of the intervention and improving it *within the tier* instead of moving the student to a more intensive tier. Thus, the failure to respond initially results in an *intervention improvement decision*.

Our conception of the heuristic of the three-tier model reflects the big ideas inherent in previous versions. In Figure 3 we have flipped the triangle figure to convey our emphasis on Tier 1 and prevention, rather than on Tier 3, which we believe continues to unintentionally direct the focus toward special education.

Throughout this book, we make every effort to *not* treat RTI as a term that connotes SLD entitlement as the overarching goal. Instead, we focus on using the term RTI to designate a service delivery system operating across multiple tiers, which incorporates scientifically based practices that increase in intensity as the needs of students become more severe. Whatever one's perspective on this set of issues, it is important to recognize the power and positive impact that a heuristic such as the three-tiered model can have across such a broad set of professional practices. We agree with Merrell and Buchanan's (2006) observation that the adaptation of the U.S. Public Health Service model to the creation and delivery of school-based interventions remains one of the most significant developments in our field's history.

MULTITIER MODELS THAT EMBRACE THE USE OF EVIDENCE-BASED APPROACHES

In the past decade, enormous public and professional pressures have evolved for the adoption and use of *evidence-based practices*, that is, practices that have been validated by a

Figure 3. The three-tier model conceptualized by Walker and Shinn.

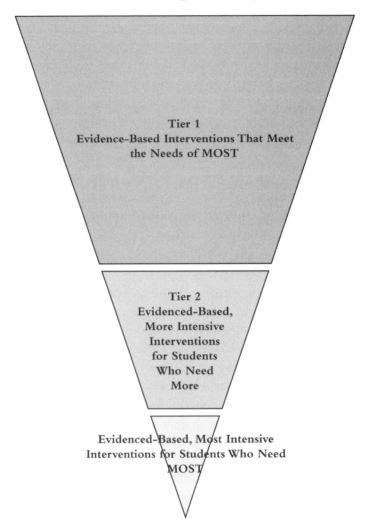

Tier 1
Evidence-Based Interventions That Meet
the Needs of MOST

Tier 2
Evidenced-Based,
More Intensive
Interventions
for Students
Who Need
More

Evidenced-Based, Most Intensive
Interventions for Students Who Need
MOST

sound body of scientific evidence developed using randomized controlled trials and other types of research designs (e.g., single subject, quasi-experimental, and so on). Some key characteristics of evidence-based practices include the following:

1. An acceptable magnitude of treatment outcome.
2. Outcomes that are replicated when implemented by others.
3. Gains that are maintained over time.

Large numbers of lists of vetted, evidence-based practices and interventions have been compiled and distributed in the past decade. However, for educators seeking access to effective educational programs and practices, we recommend the *What Works Clearinghouse*, the website of the Institute of Education Sciences within the U.S.

Department of Education, as a solid source of information. The What Works system collects, screens, and identifies studies of the effectiveness of educational interventions (e.g., programs, products, practices, and policies) in which educational consumers can have trust and confidence. IES staff and professional experts have established rigorous standards and criteria for this purpose.

The most effective program or practice will not yield the expected outcomes in the absence of a high-quality application (referred to as *high-fidelity implementation* or *treatment fidelity*). In one highly recommended resource, Fixsen, Naoom, Blase, Friedman, and Wallace (2005) have contributed an excellent and comprehensive synthesis of the research literature on treatment integrity within educational and child mental health domains.

Efficacy Versus Effectiveness

An important distinction regarding evidence-based approaches has to do with *efficacy* (how well an intervention actually works under idealized conditions) versus *effectiveness* (how well it works under normal, routine conditions of usage). The true test of an intervention or practice is its effectiveness in applications that are not influenced by its developers. Hoagwood and associates have written extensively about what she refers to as the "transportability" issue, which involves bridging the chasm that exists between efficacy and effectiveness (e.g., Burns & Hoagwood, 2002; Schoenwald & Hoagwood, 2001). She notes that large numbers of promising school mental health interventions fall through the cracks and end up at the bottom of the chasm, where they are not used because they do not fit in with the normal routines and operations of schools. These mental health interventions may be efficacious but not effective. It is very important to take steps to ensure not only that a practice or intervention program "works" but also that it works in the context of normal school routines. In our view, this is the essence of effectiveness.

An equally important consideration refers to the *acceptability* of an innovation or practice to educational consumers (e.g., general and special education teachers). Teachers typically evaluate a new approach in terms of the trade-off between the perceived effort required to apply the approach and the benefit or gain that will be realized as a result of its application. Huge numbers of programs fail this simple cost–benefit test. Given our long experience with developing, implementing, and disseminating interventions for academic and behavioral problems in schools, we believe the following consumer issues strongly influence an intervention's acceptability and ultimate use:

- It fits seamlessly into school routines.
- It is consistent with school and educator values.
- It solves a high-priority issue or problem.
- Time and effort costs are reasonable.
- The teacher perceives that she or he has the skills and resources to apply the practice effectively.

- The necessary supports and technical assistance are available to ensure that the practice can be effective.

We would nominate the model of positive behavior interventions and supports as an example of practices that are evidence-based and pass the test provided by these consumer issues.

Evidence-Based Education

Detrich, Keyworth, and States (2008) have developed an excellent conceptual model governing the application of evidence-based practices within school contexts. In *Advances in Evidence-Based Education: A Roadmap to Evidence-Based Education,* their heuristic representing the roadmap's key elements is presented graphically (see Figure 4). The four elements of efficacy, effectiveness, monitoring, and implementation form the core of an evidence-based school culture that supports effective innovations that can substantially improve schooling outcomes, especially for at-risk students. Detrich et al. (2008) justifiably assign great importance to *high quality implementation* and *progress monitoring with sensitive tools* as necessary requirements in matching proven interventions and practices to the needs of students. Their work and thinking are highly recommended to those seeking to transform school cultures into positive host environments for effective practices.

THE SOCIAL AND ECONOMIC IMPERATIVES OF QUALITY EARLY CHILDHOOD DEVELOPMENT PROGRAMS

The Economic Policy Institute of Washington, DC has published a comprehensive analysis of the economic, fiscal, and social benefits of investing in high-quality early childhood development (ECD) programs (see Lynch, 2004). Four exemplary ECD programs having a strong empirical base were analyzed in terms of their cost-effectiveness: the Perry Preschool, the Prenatal/Early Infancy Program, the Abecedarian Program, and the Chicago Child–Parent Center Program. For each of these programs, Lynch calculated the cost–benefit ratio that represents the dollars returned for every dollar invested in the ECD program in inflation-adjusted costs. The dollar benefits for the four programs were, respectively, $8.40, $5.06, $3.78, and $7.14 for every dollar invested. Such returns represent a stellar public investment that is well worth the attention of federal and state legislators and policy makers. The results speak to the power of quality preschool programs and early intervention in achieving important prevention goals as well as longer-term positive outcomes.

Similar findings regarding the effectiveness of early intervention were reported by Strain and Timm (2001), based on a 25-year longitudinal follow-up study of graduates of the Regional Intervention Program (RIP). This program is an example of

Figure 4. **Roadmap for conceptualizing empirical approaches within school contexts.**

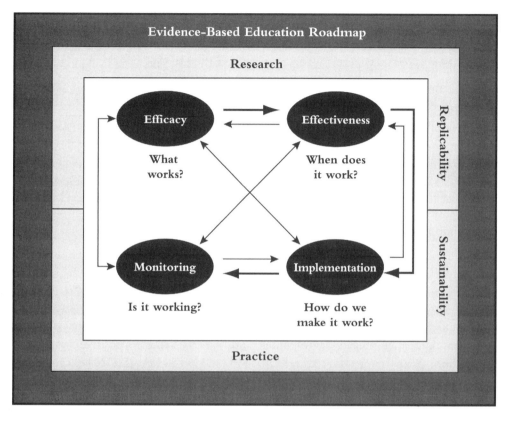

Note. From "*A Roadmap to evidence-based Education: Building an Evidence-Based Culture*" by R. Detrich, R. Keyworth, and J. States, 2007, *Journal of Evidence-Based Practices for Schools*, 8(1), p. 30. Copyright 2007 by Rowman & Littlefield Education. Adapted with permission.

a high-quality early childhood intervention and development program for severely at-risk 3- to 6-year-olds. The outcomes of this investigation were truly remarkable in terms of documenting the long-term benefits of the RIP. Society's systematic investment in such high-quality programs would provide even the most severely at-risk children with a solid opportunity to achieve enduring school success and would do much to reduce adolescent delinquency and other destructive outcomes at this developmental level (see Zigler, Taussig, & Black, 1992).

Understanding The Role of Risk and Protective Factors

Larger and larger numbers of children are exposed to powerful and multiple risk factors in their lives prior to beginning their school careers due to the social "toxins" that operate in our society and culture. The cumulative effects of these risks are often manifested in very poor school readiness levels that prevent at-risk children from succeeding in school and can ultimately lead to school failure and dropout. Protective factors that offset and buffer the destructive effects of risk exposure are frequently lacking in the lives of these children. However, compelling research by Hawkins, Catalano, Kosterman, Abbott, and Hill (1999) and Hawkins, Kosterman, Catalano, Hill, and Abbott (2008) demonstrates that high quality early intervention for at-risk student populations, delivered at the beginning of their school careers, that targets the *child, peers, teachers, and parents* in a coordinated fashion, produces strong protections against a host of negative outcomes in adolescence. Their intervention offered protection against: (a) *violent delinquent acts,* (b) *heavy drinking,* (c) *adolescent pregnancy,* (d) *multiple sex partners,* (e) *behavioral episodes at school,* and (f) *academic underachievement.* Hawkins et al. (1999) concluded that full engagement and attachment to schooling served as a strong protective factor in accounting for these impressive outcomes. Thus, while schools are generally unable to control or influence risk factors that are external to the school setting, they have the potential to implement preschool and proven early intervention programs that can buffer, offset, and sometimes prevent long term, destructive outcomes.

In a thoughtful review and analysis, Crews et al. (2007) contributed a meta-analytic synthesis of risk and protective factors in the domain of emotional–behavioral disorders at child and adolescent levels. They argue that professionals need to understand the role of risk and protective factors for at least three reasons: (a) Substantial numbers of today's students experience negative outcomes and fail to achieve positive outcomes; (b) Current policy imperatives dictate that risk and protective factors be considered as prevention strategies where possible; and (c) Risk and protective factor exposure affects the response of children and youth to intervention.

The Crews et al. (2007) synthesis examined the findings of a series of meta-analyses for risk and protective factors reported in the literature. These authors were able to successfully identify those risk and protective factors that were associated respectively with *externalizing and internalizing* behavior disorders. This review substantially enhances our understanding of the specific risk and protective factors that can be used as a foundation in designing interventions to buffer and offset externalizing and internalizing disorders in the context of schooling.

SELECTING EVIDENCE-BASED INTERVENTIONS THAT MATCH CONTEXT AND TARGET BEHAVIORS OF CONCERN

There is a strong and continuing need in educational practice for decision-making processes and tools that allow practitioners to compare, contrast, and select from available promising or proven interventions that match up well with both the intervention context and the target behaviors of concern. Merrell and Buchanan (2006) have presented an interesting conceptual model for facilitating this process that combines the U.S. Public Health Service's rubric of prevention (primary, secondary, and tertiary; see Gordon, 1983) with the RE-AIM (reach, efficacy, adoption, implementation, and maintenance) framework for selecting, implementing, and evaluating interventions (Glasgow, 2002; Glasgow, Vogt, & Boles, 1999). The Glasgow et al. RE-AIM model is not the same as the RE-AIM model popularized in the literature based on what subsequently became Iowa's problem-solving model (Reschly & Grimes, 1991).

The goal of the Merrell and Buchanan model is to assist systems in identifying appropriate prevention and intervention approaches for their respective settings while accounting for both efficacy and effectiveness, available resources, and other critical issues in the delivery-implementation process. To date, the RE-AIM model has provided perhaps the clearest specification of the essential elements and processes that define a path from discovery research to satisfactory application of a practice based upon sound evidence.

The five dimensions of the RE-AIM model combine to determine the overall population–based impact of an intervention. *Reach* refers to the participation rate among a known population and to characteristics of participants versus nonparticipants. *Efficacy* pertains to the results of the intervention for specified outcome criteria, when the intervention is implemented as intended. *Adoption* operates at the setting level and focuses on the percentage and representativeness of organizations that adopt a given program. *Implementation* refers to intervention integrity, or the quality and consistency of practice application when the program is delivered in real-world settings. Finally, *maintenance* operates at both the individual and setting levels and refers to sustainability over time. At the individual level, maintenance refers to how well behavior-change efforts hold up in the long term. At the organization level, it refers to the extent to which practice or policy becomes institutionalized or functions as a routine part of the cultural practices of an organization.

The cumulative impact of the five RE-AIM dimensions provides a powerful conceptual base for determining the overall public health impact of an intervention. If any of the five RE-AIM dimensions have sufficiently low values, the overall impact and consumer acceptance of the intervention or practice may be so weak as to be of little consequence.

In the RE-AIM framework, a key barrier preventing the successful impact of effective interventions involves the very characteristics of the environment used to demonstrate intervention efficacy in a clinical trial. That is, homogeneous samples of highly motivated clients, adherence to highly standardized protocols, and delivery within specialized environments by skilled interventionists having adequate implementation support are not present in the real world settings where the intervention is to be adopted, implemented, and maintained. Further, as noted earlier, Schoenwald and Hoagwood (2001) have asserted that a critical determinant of adoption failure and limited usage by target consumers is the failure of many developers to ensure that their intervention is carefully integrated into the *ongoing routines* of the proposed intervention setting. Some program developers have attempted to address these problems and constraints by confining the research and development of an intervention, from beginning to end, within the target practice setting (see Fantuzzo et al., 2007).

Merrell and Buchanan's (2006) review of the RE-AIM framework and the U.S. Public Health Service's prevention framework is an important contribution to successful implementation of multitiered early-intervention systems. It addresses the nettlesome issues involved in specifying how key elements can be hypothetically specified in the decision-making process for intervention evaluation and selection. As they note, the combined frameworks provide a heuristic for facilitating decision making by educational leaders. However, data collection protocols and correlated decision criteria for operationalizing these elements remain to be developed, validated, and applied successfully. Field-based consumers need specific tools that allow them to achieve the RE-AIM goals. This lack of operational decision-making tools is not unique to the RE-AIM framework. Currently, there are few tools to support decision makers in the selection and monitoring of intervention programs that fit the populations, settings, and target behaviors relevant to the service domain in which the programs will be implemented. This problem exists in any context where it is necessary to organize the collective decisions of individuals charged with using evidence-based practices to influence publicly valued outcomes in one or more service settings. However, these types of decision-making tools are increasingly becoming available. The work of Joseph Torgesen, in reading, is a good example. Among the decision-making tools Torgesen has made available for reviewing and selecting evidence-based interventions are ones for (a) selection of school-wide reading interventions (Torgesen, 2006), (b) middle and high school literacy instruction (Torgesen, Houston, & Rissman, 2007), and (c) development of a plan for comprehensive reading assessment (Florida Center for Reading Research, 2007). In the area of behavioral health, decision-making tools for comparing and evaluating interventions have had limited availability, especially relating to procedures for matching up interventions with *both* target behaviors and implementation contexts.

SUPPORTING EFFECTIVE SERVICES: THE DECISION SUPPORT SYSTEM FOR YOUTH WELL-BEING

Examples of intervention decision-making tools increasingly can also be found in publicly funded social service settings, including prisons, group care facilities, treatment centers for adjudicated youth, schools, mental health treatment centers, hospitals, and community health clinics. One promising tool has been developed by Deschutes Research Inc. and the Oregon Research Institute, both of Eugene, Oregon. *The Decision Support System for Youth Well-Being* provides a structured, Web-based decision process for individuals responsible for identifying, implementing, and tracking the use of evidence-based programs intended to influence the prevalence of healthy and harmful adolescent behaviors in school and community settings (see http://www.youthwellbeing.com). This decision system is subscriber supported and provides an integrated set of easy-to-use functions that enable individuals and groups to spend limited resources in an accountable, responsible, and sustainable fashion. It is aimed at subscribers who (a) must comply with mandates to adopt evidence-based programs; (b) don't have time to search for and compare evidence-based programs; (c) must plan for, and document the effects of, the use of programs that target the prevalence of specific healthy and harmful behaviors for specified groups of youth; or (d) must maintain the continuity of their efforts across time in the face of changes in those responsible for managing intervention efforts. Typical users are state education agencies, district superintendents, school principals, prevention specialists in education service districts, and ad hoc health promotion teams. The system has substantial applicability in the context of evaluating and selecting interventions for use in educational settings.

Primary Features of the Decision Support System

The DSS has been used successfully by decision makers to assess the well-being of a group of adolescents for whom they are responsible. The system allows them to choose target behaviors they wish to influence, compare and select programs relevant to the behaviors of interest, and produce and maintain a plan that documents the consequences of these decisions across time. The system brings together all the necessary supports for these decisions within a feedback loop, in which outputs resulting from the actions of a control component are fed back to adjust inputs to the system. The effect is to stabilize the system by triggering actions that minimize the difference between a reference value and the actual output of the system. When working in the DSS website, decision makers adjust the selection and implementation of evidence-based programs in light of a selected program's influence on the prevalence of behaviors deemed important for a specified group of students. Components of the feedback loop, accessed using tabs at the top of each Web page, enable subscribers to explore measures of the prevalence of healthy and harmful behaviors for a chosen group. In the best possible world, decision makers have access to a database containing repeated measures of the prevalence of healthy and harmful behaviors, which they could use to assess the well-being of the youth for whom they choose intervention programs. Databases of this type are available for monitoring individual academic progress (e.g., the Oregon TESA/OAKS database, http://www.oaks.k12.or.us), but they do not exist for measures of physical and social well-being upon which the success of academic instruction often depends. If these databases existed, then decision makers could use the measures to examine the actual history of each behavior's prevalence and the results of interventions chosen to influence it. Unfortunately, repeated measures often do not exist at levels congruent with the group to be influenced by chosen programs (i.e., not at the school district or school level). In these cases, the decision makers have to rely on their professional judgment to choose behaviors to influence. This may entail reliance on cross-sectional assessments such as the Youth Risk

Behavior Surveillance System (YBRSS; http://www.cdc.gov/HealthyYouth/yrbs/ index.htm) or sporadically collected measures of well-being (e.g., Oregon's Center for Health Statistics, http://www.dhs.state.or.us/dhs/ph/chs/youthsurvey/index.shtml), which rarely provide measures of prevalence for small units of intervention (e.g., a single school).

Choose Behaviors to Change and Set Targets for the Degree of Change Desired

This feature of the Decision Support System for Youth Well-Being supports the creation of action plans by users for a specified group of youth. Plans are scale independent; that is, groups may be defined at any level, from a few students in a single grade in a single school to all the students in a service district, county, state, or community. This flexibility reflects the fact that organizational frameworks for intervention management decisions vary widely across user organizations. Once the group is specified, the system offers the user a built-in set of some 30 behaviors to include in the plan. These behaviors (23 harmful, 7 healthy) were derived from analyses of the interrelationships of these behaviors using 2 years of Oregon Healthy Teen data (Boles, Biglan, & Smolkowski, 2006). They are organized under 10 behavior categories: Academic, Alcohol Use, Tobacco Use, Other Substance Use, Antisocial, Depression, Eating Disorders, Safety, Sexual Behavior, and Time Use. In addition to choosing one or more of these behaviors as intervention targets with the specified group, the user can enter and choose other behaviors under any of the categories. Other fields in the plan allow the user to enter the reasons for choosing the behavior, the estimated current prevalence, and the change in prevalence desired as a result of intervention.

Compare and Choose Programs Relevant to the Chosen Behaviors

This feature is the heart of the system and relies on a comprehensive database of detailed information about commercially available intervention and prevention programs (currently 90) that have been shown to influence the prevalence of healthy and harmful behaviors in youth. Included are programs that meet agency rating criteria and that have been demonstrated to be efficacious in randomized clinical trials. Some of the rating sources used are Substance Abuse and Mental Health Services Administration (SAMHSA), National Registry of Evidence-Based Programs and Practices; the Office of Juvenile Justice and Delinquency Program's (OJJDP) Model Programs Guide ratings for exemplary programs; the Helping America's Youth Program Tool for evidence-based programs that prevent and reduce delinquency or problem behaviors; and Blueprints for Violence Prevention programs. The inclusion process first identifies programs that have strong empirical support and meet the criteria for achieving a high rating by one or more agencies.

Programs selected for inclusion are entered into the database. Included in the program information is an overview of the program and the theoretical rationale upon which it is based; all agency ratings of the program; developer and vendor contact information; detailed costs of program training, materials, and administration; staffing requirements; and the behavior categories the program purports to influence. Additional information about the program includes languages in which it is available, geographical settings (urban, rural, suburban, tribal reservations), whether it is school or community based, ages and grade levels targeted, delivery media and activities, and references to studies that demonstrate program efficacy/effectiveness.

Users who have created an action plan will automatically be shown a list of those programs that address the behavior category of each of the chosen target behaviors in their plan. Alternatively, users who simply want to compare available programs without creating a plan may do so. In either case, the list of programs may be further restricted by setting requirements for specific geographic and institutional settings, grade level, and whether the program is intended as a universal, targeted, or indicated intervention. Users can then view side-by-side comparisons of any or all of the listed programs using the program information described above. This powerful feature saves users the time required to abstract information about programs from rating agency databases and establishing a common basis for comparison. On the basis of these comparisons, a user may select a specific program for a behavior and the choice will be entered automatically into the plan.

Assess Effects of the Selected Programs on the Target Behaviors and Make Necessary Changes

Using the same data sources that they employed to ascertain the prevalence of behaviors in conjunction with establishing their plan (e.g., local data, YBRSS, state assessment data), users assess the impact of the program they selected to influence those behaviors. Following this assessment, users may decide to change the program, change the target, or make no changes. The system does not force this assessment but provides a way to incorporate it into the plan as an entry into a notes field.

Record and Report Plans and Outcomes to Third Parties

Users can generate a report for any of the action plans they have created. The report lists the target behaviors in the plan, the reasons for their inclusion and the desired change in prevalence, programs selected, and plan notes. These reports are produced as pdf (portable document format) files and can be printed or e-mailed to third parties. Reports can be shared with others involved with the group for whom the plan was created, provide a rationale for program selection to funding agencies, or document what effects the program had on a specific behavior.

Secondary Features of the DSS

In addition to the foregoing, the system has several additional features to support user decision-making and plan management activities.

Program Updates

Program vendors are asked to verify annually the correctness of information about their program. This ensures that the program data provided to DSS users is current. This updating process allows vendors to inform DSS maintenance personnel about new articles on the use of their program and indicate any changes to cost or staffing information. Although the program vendors may subscribe to the system, they are restricted to using only the program comparison feature.

User Reviews

Users are invited to submit reviews to the DSS of their actual experiences with a program in real-world settings. Reviewers provide information about where they used the program, how long they used it, the pros and cons of using it, whether local modifications were needed, an overall user rating, and whether they would recommend the program to others. These reviews are available to other users as part of the program selection process. Program vendors subscribed to the system are prevented from writing reviews or contacting reviewers.

Transfer of Plans

This feature responds to the fact that there are often staffing changes among users who are responsible for a set of plans. Staffing changes in an organization require that new individuals be assigned to manage previously created plans. To address this problem, the system provides two roles—organizational administrator and user administrator—for each organization subscribing to the system. The organizational administrator is assigned at the time an organization subscribes. This person has an additional tab available that allows him or her to register and create users as user administrators. Both organizational and user administrators can transfer their organization's plans from one user to another.

Forums

The system provides a forum where all subscribers can interact. A second forum allows users to address questions to the system developers.

System Help

In addition to feature-specific online help files, the system users can click for more information on the elements on a given page. These are used to provide detailed information about agency rating schema, program inclusion criteria, details about the public cost of specific behaviors, and other items that may be of interest to the user but are not essential for using the system.

The Decision Support System for Youth Well-Being is an initial response to the problem of providing a simple management environment and tool for decision makers charged with using evidence-based practices. In its current form, the system appears to contain many of the elements of effective tools (e.g., http://www.preventioninstitute.org/

documents/GoodHealthCounts_Final.pdf, p. 45). These include establishing accountability, supporting actionable values-based decisions, being accessible and user-friendly, and being grounded in a plausible mechanism of change (feedback loop).

CONCLUSION

Nearly two decades ago, Geoffrey Moore published a now-classic book, called *Crossing the Chasm: Marketing and Selling High Technology Products to Mainstream Customers*, in which he traced the development pathways of high-tech companies within the Silicon Valley (see Moore, 1991). He documented the characteristics of successful and unsuccessful "dot-com" companies and provided interesting analyses of their history of development, their success or failure, and the reasons underlying same. He also identified the shared characteristics of successful and unsuccessful companies, described the factors leading to their rise and fall, and presented a technology-adoption life cycle that consisted of five phases, which include the following: *Innovators, Early Adopters, Early Majority, Late Majority, and Laggards*. The share of the target market audience for new technology products coming out of Silicon Valley in the 1980s for each of these groups was estimated by Moore to be 2.5%, 13.5%, 34%, 34%, and 16%. We believe this cycle has considerable relevance to the seismic shifting in educational practices to multitiered early-intervening services, using scientifically based practices, that has occurred in the field of education.

In Moore's book, the shape of this cycle is represented by a graphic that closely resembles the bell-shaped curve. As noted above, the technology life cycle is populated by five groups of target consumers arrayed under the graphic's curve from left to right. They are *innovators, early adopters, early majority, late majority, and laggards. Innovators* are described as any technology's enthusiasts who firmly believe in the benefits of technology, especially new technology, and its potential to enhance quality of life. They constantly scan the horizon for the latest innovations and are typically the first customers for new technology items. *Early adopters* tend to be the first to embrace, accept, and promote new innovations that can create a competitive advantage, make a break with the past, and lead to creation of a new organizational culture or a very different way of doing things. *Early majority* types make up the bulk of all technology infrastructure purchases and are not opposed to technological innovations. However, they do not see themselves as revolutionaries in terms of using the innovations to break with current practices. They do, however, generally view innovation as necessary to advance the organization's capabilities. They are described as highly pragmatic. *Late majority* types are generally pessimistic about their ability to gain any value from technological investments and are characterized as price-sensitive, highly skeptical, and very demanding. They are mostly conservative as a group. Finally, there are the *laggards*, who resist adoption of innovations and delight in criticizing and pointing out its flaws and defects. Typically, organizations work around the laggards in embracing new innovations and the changes that they produce.

Innovators represent the smallest group in Moore's bell-shaped, technology-adoption graphic. Early adopters and laggards share approximately equal proportions of the target consumer market, and early majority pragmatists and late majority conservatives occupy the largest and also perfectly equal areas under the curve. These two groups form the largest markets and are the ones that make the ultimate difference in terms of whether an innovation is broadly adopted and used. However, innovators are the ones who are perhaps most important in ultimately determining whether an innovation or product actually makes it to the mainstream market.

In our view, the parallels between Moore's technology life cycle and the patterns of innovation that are occurring in today's schools are striking. Professionals currently working in schools all know individuals who represent each of the categories of target consumers identified by Moore's analysis. In the large-scale school improvement process broadly referred to as RTI, some school psychologists have played the roles of innovators and early adopters (see Germann's foreword in this book). Some have worked for almost 30 years to improve school systems' capacity for implementing data-based decision making and evidence-based practices for *all* children to ensure positive outcomes and to prevent the need for special education referrals. Many of the contributors to this book have been innovators in their respective fields of expertise.

We also argue that the local, state, and even national accomplishments that have occurred in building more powerful interventions for *all* students using evidence-based approaches and programs have been influenced by the school psychologists who were early adopters. They saw the value of data-based decision making and of evidence-based interventions, aligned with students' needs, as providing their schools and their students with a competitive advantage. Their efforts certainly made a break with the past, especially with respect to a school culture preoccupied with wait-to-fail approaches to disability identification. Their continuing efforts have led to the creation of a new organizational culture and a very different way of doing things by enabling powerful, preventive practices and early intervention.

In 2010, we see most school psychologists as being early majority pragmatists, and we have attempted to devote this third edition to them in order to address their practical concerns. We also hope that this volume will have some impact on members of the late majority. Many school psychologists remain skeptical about whether the changes they are observing can be implemented successfully and ramped up to scale. The contributing authors recruited for this third edition have expertise in a broad range of experiences, innovations, trends, and critical issues relating to the education of the full range of students attending today's schools. As such, they have provided a valuable compendium of evidence-based approaches, programs, techniques, and tools that will make schools more effective organizations in fulfilling their societal mandate of developing all students academically and socially to their greatest capacity. We are deeply indebted to the authors for their seminal and timely contributions in this regard. We hope that in addition to providing pragmatic solutions for the early majority, we have also provided a set of interventions that meet the needs of some of those who currently are price-sensitive and very demanding. In the best of circumstances, perhaps we've even reached a few of the laggards.

REFERENCES

Batsche, G. M., Elliott, J., Graden, J., Grimes, J., Kovaleski, J. F., Prasse, D., et al. (2005). *Response to intervention: Policy considerations and implementation.* Alexandria, VA: National Association of State Directors of Special Education.

Boles, S., Biglan, A., & Smolkowski, K. (2006). Relationships among negative and positive behaviors in adolescence. *Journal of Adolescence, 29,* 33–52.

Brown-Chidsey, R., Bronaugh, L., & McGraw, K. (2009). *RTI in the classroom: Guidelines and recipes for success.* New York: Guilford Press.

Burdette, P. (2007). *Response to intervention as it relates to early intervention services.* Washington, DC: Project Forum at National Association of State Directors of Special Education (NASDSE).

Burns, B., & Hoagwood, K. (2002). *Community treatment for youth: Evidence-based interventions for severe emotional and behavioral disorders.* New York: Oxford University Press.

Crews, S. D., Bender, H., Cook, C. R., Gresham, F. M., Kern, L., & Vanderwood, M. (2007). Risk and protective factors of emotional and/or behavioral disorders in children and adolescents: A "mega"-analytic synthesis. *Behavioral Disorders, 32,* 64–77.

Deno, S. L. (1989). Curriculum-based measurement and alternative special education services: A fundamental and direct relationship. In M. R. Shinn (Ed.), *Curriculum-based measurement: Assessing special children* (pp. 1–17). New York: Guilford Press.

Detrich, R., Keyworth, R., & States, J. (2007). A Roadmap to evidence-based Education: Building an Evidence-Based Culture. *Journal of Evidence-Based Practices for Schools, 8*(1), p. 30.

Detrich, R., Keyworth, R., & States, J. (2008). *Advances in evidence-based education: A roadmap to evidence-based education.* Oakland, CA: Wing Institute.

Fantuzzo, J., Bulotsky-Shearer, R., McDermott, P. A., McWayne, C., Frye, D., & Perlman, S. (2007). Investigation of dimensions of social-emotional classroom behavior and school readiness for low-income urban preschool children. *School Psychology Review, 36,* 44–62.

Fixsen, D. L., Naoom, S. F., Blase, K. A., Friedman, R. M. & Wallace, F. (2005). *Implementation research: A synthesis of the literature* (FMHI Publication #231). Tampa, FL: University of South Florida, Louis de la Parte Florida Mental Health Institute, National Implementation Research Network.

Fletcher, J. M., & Vaughn, S. (2009). Response to intervention: Preventing and remediating academic difficulties. *Child Development Perspectives, 3*(1), 30–37.

Florida Center for Reading Research. (2007). *A principal's action plan outline for building a successful school-wide intervention system.* Tallahassee, FL: Author.

Glasgow, R. (2002). Evaluation of theory-based interventions: The RE-AIM model. In K. Glanz, F. M. Lewis, & B. K. Rimer (Eds.), *Health behavior and health education: Theory, research, and practice* (3rd ed., pp. 531–534). San Francisco: John Wiley & Sons.

Glasgow, R. E., Vogt, T. M., & Boles, S. M. (1999). Evaluating the public health impact of health promotion interventions: The RE-AIM framework. *American Journal of Public Health, 89,* 1322–1327.

Glover. T., Diperna, J., & Vaughn, S. (2007). Introduction to the special series on service delivery systems for response to intervention: Considerations for research and practice. *School Psychology Review, 36,* 523–526.

Gordon, R. S. (1983). An operational classification of disease prevention. *Public Health Reports, 98,* 107–109.

Graden, J., Christenson, S., & Casey, A. (1985). Implementing a prereferral intervention system: Part I: The model. *Exceptional Children, 51,* 377–387.

Hart, B., & Risley, T. R. (1995). *Meaningful differences in the everyday experience of young American children.* Baltimore: Brookes.

Hawkins, J. D., Catalano, R. F., Kosterman, R., Abbott, R., & Hill, K. G. (1999). Preventing adolescent health-risk behaviors by strengthening protection during childhood. *Archives of Pediatrics and Adolescent Medicine, 153,* 226–234.

Hawkins, J. D., Kosterman, R., Catalano, R., Hill, K. G., & Abbott, R. D. (2008). Effects of social development intervention in childhood 15 years later. *Archives of Pediatrics and Adolescent Medicine, 162,* 1133–1141.

Hirsch, E. (2003). Reading comprehension requires knowledge of words and the world: Scientific insights into the fourth-grade slump and nation's stagnant comprehension scores. *American Educator,* Spring, 10–19.

Lynch, R. G. (2004). *Exceptional returns: Economic, fiscal and social benefits of investment in early childhood development.* Washington, DC: Economic Policy Institute.

Merrell, K. W., & Buchanan, R. (2006). Intervention selection in school-based practice: Using public health models to enhance systems capacity of schools. *School Psychology Review, 35,* 167–180.

Moore, G. (1995). *Inside the tornado: Marketing strategies from Silicon Valley's cutting edge.* New York: Harper Collins.

National Center for Education Evaluation and Regional Assistance. (2008). *Reading First impact study: Interim report.* Washington, DC: U.S. Department of Education, Institute of Education Sciences.

Pericola Case, L., Speece, D. L., & Eddy Molloy, D. (2003). The validity of response-to-instruction paradigm to identify reading disabilities: A longitudinal analysis of individual differences and context factors. *School Psychology Review, 32,* 557–582.

Reschly, D. J., & Grimes, J. P. (1991). State department and university cooperation: Evaluation of continuing education and consultation and curriculum-based assessment. *School Psychology Review, 20,* 522–529.

Schoenwald, S. K., & Hoagwood, K. (2001). Effectiveness, transportability, and dissemination of interventions: What matters when? *Psychiatric Services, 52,* 1190–1197.

Shinn, M. R. (2007). Identifying students at risk, monitoring performance, and determining eligibility within response to intervention: Research on educational need and benefit from academic intervention. *School Psychology Review, 36,* 601–618.

Shinn, M. R., Walker, H. M., & Stoner, G. (2002). *Interventions for academic and behavior problems II: Preventive and remedial approaches.* Bethesda, MD: National Association of School Psychologists.

Stanovich, K. E. (1986). Matthew effects in reading: Some consequences of individual differences in the acquisition of literacy. *Reading Research Quarterly, 21,* 360–406.

Stanovich, K. E. (2000). Reading disability: Are reforms based on evidence possible? In K. E. Stanovich (Ed.), *Progress in understanding reading: Scientific foundations and new frontiers* (pp. 323–337). New York: Guilford Press.

Strain, P. S., & Timm, M. A. (2001). Remediation and prevention of aggression: An evaluation of the RIP program over a quarter century. *Behavioral Disorders, 26,* 297–313.

Sugai, G., Horner, R. H., & Gresham, F. (2002). Behaviorally effective school environments. In M. R. Shinn, H. M. Walker, & G. Stoner (Eds.), *Interventions for academic and behavior problems II: Preventive and remedial approaches,* (pp. 315–350). Bethesda, MD: National Association of School Psychologists.

Torgesen, J. K. (2001). The theory and practice of intervention: Comparing outcomes from prevention and remediation studies. In A. J. Fawcett & R. I. Nicolson (Eds.), *Dyslexia: Theory and good practice* (pp. 185–201). London: David Fulton Publishers.

Torgesen, J. K. (2002). Lessons learned from intervention research in reading: A way to go before we rest. In R. Stainthorpe (Ed.), *Literacy: Learning and teaching* [Monograph]. London: British Psychological Association.

Torgesen, J. K. (2005). *A principal's guide to intensive reading interventions for struggling readers in Reading First schools.* Washington, DC: U.S. Department of Education.

Torgesen, J. (2006). *A comprehensive K-3 reading assessment plan: Guidance for school leaders.* Portsmouth, NH: RMC Research Corporation, Center on Instruction.

Torgesen, J., Houston, D., & Rissman, L. (2007). *Improving literacy instruction in middle and high schools: A guide for principals.* Portsmouth, NH: RMC Research Corporation, Center on Instruction.

Torgesen, J., Houston, D., Rissman, L., & Kosanovich, M. (2007). *Teaching all students to read in elementary school.* Portsmouth, NH: RMC Research Corporation, Center on Instruction.

Vaughn, S., & Fuchs, L. S. (2003). Redefining learning disabilities as inadequate response to instruction: The promise and potential problems. *Learning Disabilities Research and Practice, 18,* 137–146.

Vaughn, S., & Linan-Thompson, S. (2004). *Research-based methods of reading instruction Grades K-3.* Alexandria, VA: Association for Supervision and Curriculum Development.

Walker, H. M., Horner, R. H., Sugai, G., Bullis, M., Sprague, J. R., Bricker, D., et al. (1996). Integrated approaches to preventing antisocial behavior patterns among school-age children and youth. *Journal of Emotional and Behavioral Disorders, 4,* 193–256.

Walker, H. M., Ramsey, E., & Gresham, F. M. (2004). *Antisocial behavior in school: Evidence-based practices* (2nd ed.). Belmont, CA: Wadsworth/Thomson Learning.

Walker, H. & Shinn, M. (2002). Structuring school-based interventions to achieve integrated primary, secondary, and tertiary prevention goals for safe and effective schools. In M. Shinn, H. Walker, & G. Stoner (Eds.), *Interventions for academic and behavior problems II: Preventive and remedial approaches.* Bethesda, MD: National Association of School Psychologists.

Wanzek, J., & Vaughn, S. (2007). Research-based implications from extensive early reading interventions. *School Psychology Review, 36,* 541–561.

Zigler, E., Taussig, C., & Black, K. (1992). Early childhood intervention: A promising preventative for juvenile delinquency. *American Psychologist, 47,* 997–1006.

CHAPTER 2

Supporting Response to Intervention (RTI) at School, District,
and State Levels

Martin J. Ikeda
Iowa Department of Education

Stan C. Paine
University of Oregon

Judy L. Elliott
Los Angeles Unified School District

INTRODUCTION

Response to intervention (RTI) combines universal screening of academic behavior problems with supplemental and intensive instructional support, to increase student performance (Gersten et al., 2008). RTI has proliferated in the professional literature and in school communities as a solution to (a) help school personnel design and implement scientifically based academic and behavioral programs, and (b) align or coordinate instructional resources to better affect student academic and behavioral well-being (Gersten et al., 2008; Gersten & Edomono, 2006; Kovaleski, 2007). The explosion of interest in RTI can be attributed in part to the use of RTI language in recent special education legislation.

RTI was seen as a better alternative for identifying students with disabilities because practices from 1975 through 2004 focused on finding students with disabilities and getting students into school buildings. In the 2000s, when academic performance of students with IEPs was examined, it became clear that, while students with disabilities were now accessing school buildings from which they were once excluded, students with disabilities were not accessing the general curriculum the same way as nondisabled peers. RTI, as defined in the Individuals with Disabilities Education Improvement Act (IDEA 2004), was a defensible way to identify students with

---

Address all correspondence and feedback on this chapter to Martin Ikeda at Marty.Ikeda@iowa.gov.

disabilities. IDEA also clarified that states had the option to prohibit commonly accepted practices for SLD identification, such as an IQ test. With the flexibility afforded in IDEA, states began working ardently to align state rules to IDEA. Contributors to the professional literature responded with descriptive articles to meet the need for information on how to (and how not to) craft policies and procedures for using RTI as a mechanism for special education identification.

Beyond special education entitlement lies another explanation for the proliferation of interest in RTI. Professionals who were implementing RTI even prior to the IDEA legislation have found that RTI is ultimately an initiative for all students (Grimes & Tilly, 1996; Ikeda, Tilly, Stumme, Volmer, & Allison, 1996). In lessons learned through implementing RTI, a highlight has been the integration of historically separate general and special education service delivery systems (Bollman, Silberglitt, & Gibbons, 2007; Graden, Stollar, & Poth, 2007; Ikeda et al., 2007; Marston, Lau, & Muyskens, 2007; Reschly, 2002).

The core of RTI is a decision-making framework for adopting, implementing, sustaining, and scaling up practices to promote the alignment of general and special education at the systems level (Graden et al., 2007; Ikeda et al., 2007). The decision-making framework involves understanding the performance of *all* students, adopting reasonable core programs to support learning for all students, providing more intensive and systematic support to students not meeting state performance standards, evaluating effects of support to students, and continually aligning instructional resources so that all students achieve at high levels (Batsche et al., 2006; Reschly, 2002). Although special education identification is an important decision in an RTI system, other decisions that precede special education are equally important.

In education, a referral-driven entitlement paradigm has long been the accepted practice. In a referral-driven paradigm, problems are thought to reflect something wrong or defective about the child, and the solution has long been to provide the child with services "at their level," oftentimes in isolation from their peers. RTI represents a step in a different direction than that found in a referral-driven entitlement paradigm. As Germann summarized in the foreword to this book, the efforts to entitle students to a special education program that matches a disability category have not necessarily met the original intent of IDEA. In RTI, the important decision is not whether the child fits into a disability category, nor is the important decision intended to ensure that the disability category leads to a predefined set of services that is the same for every child identified in that category. Instead, the primary decisions in RTI are about understanding the constellation of services that provide most, some, or few of the students access to the general curriculum. Secondary are the decisions that define when services need special education funding to be maintained. Tertiary are decisions about giving children suspected of having disabilities protections through identification, evaluation, and placement.

What is different with RTI than would be found in a non–RTI system is a mind-set that teaching matters and that, given appropriate instructional opportunity, all students can eventually access and perform in the general curriculum. In an RTI system, the old adage of "all students can learn" has become "teachers can adapt and teach to meet diverse learning needs." Systems engaged in RTI use a continuum of less-structured to more-structured accommodative and instructional practices, with evidence that practices have been attempted and validated before applying even more structured practices.

Prior to the systemic implementation of RTI, schools were often islands unto themselves. For example, if an examination of student data showed the core reading program to be weak, the school's principal often lacked the authority and/or funds to make a change. Most often a change of this magnitude (and importance) would be made at the level of a central office administrator. Likewise, if a core reading program resulted in large numbers of students failing to achieve satisfactorily, some school psychologists might prefer not to administer cognitive ability tests to individual students being referred by their teacher one-by-one. Instead school psychologists might want to provide consultative support to teachers to enhance core instruction so that all students perform better prior to the teacher nominating large numbers of students for special education evaluation. However, the procedures dictated from the state or central office—that students must be tested within the state-approved timeline once they are nominated by teachers—interferes with time to engage in instructional consultation.

Experience has taught early implementers of RTI that the first area in which RTI is discussed is as part of special education entitlement. RTI in its initial stage of implementation is viewed as "a way to find kids needing IEPs [individual education plans]" (Ikeda et al., 1996; Ikeda et al., 2007). As schools implement RTI as a mechanism to identify those children, school staff find that the state curriculum, district- or building-level instructional practices, and building-level assessments are not in alignment. This lack of alignment makes it difficult to evaluate whether student achievement is a function of a disability or a function of how the curriculum is being taught. The RTI effort shifts from a focus on low performance being a within-child deficit that is solved through special education identification, to low performance being a mismatch between the learner and the instruction, solved by analyzing student needs and providing more structured instruction.

However, experience with RTI implementation has taught that more than site-based change is needed. When RTI is implemented at the school building level, only students in that school benefit from RTI. Other students in the district are disadvantaged because decision making at their site is still focused on remediating problems with the individual child rather than on improving instructional access to the general education curriculum for all students.

Successful implementation of RTI, we have learned, is predicated on intentional staging at the school building, district, and state levels. That plan should begin with consensus building, in which RTI concepts are communicated broadly to implementers, and the foundations are taught, discussed, and embraced. Infrastructure building is another component for promoting and sustaining the intentional change to RTI. To build infrastructure, sites and districts examine their implementation process against the critical components of RTI to identify the structures and supports they need to put in place to support, stabilize, and institutionalize RTI practices.

In this chapter, we discuss how change can be managed at all levels of the educational system, from an experiential, "lessons learned" perspective. We summarize aspects of adopting, implementing, sustaining, and scaling up new practices, and we explore the benefits and pitfalls of adopting practices associated with RTI, based on our knowledge of schools, school districts, and political and practical influences of state education agencies.

MANAGING CHANGE IN SCHOOLS AT THE BUILDING LEVEL

Until RTI is solidly in place, school leaders should view it as an innovation. That is, the change will require thoughtful planning, training, support, and supervision to ensure that the implementation is done well and that it has the intended effects (Graden et al., 2007; Peterson, Prasse, Shinn, & Swerdlik, 2007). When the school or district has made a firm commitment to implement an RTI model, implementation should be given a high priority and a sustained focus, as it is an instructional initiative that is at the heart of the school's mission. The change process starts with a systematic self-study to evaluate which RTI features (e.g., teams, assessment tools, multitiered interventions) are in place in the school and which need to be built.

One of the guiding principles of RTI is the use of scientifically based interventions; therefore one of the challenges is to build a framework that supports the bridge between research (science) and practice. The gap between *what we know* (research knowledge) and *what we do* (use of research-based practices) in education is well documented (Carnine, 1999; Gersten & Smith-Jones, 2001; Greenwood & Abbott, 2001). For nearly 30 years, researchers have been addressing this gap by studying the adoption and implementation of research-based practices (Berman & McLaughlin, 1978; Hall & Hord, 1987; Hall & Loucks, 1977) and, more recently, by exploring the implementation and sustainability of practices and programs (Datnow, 2005; Fixsen, Naoom, Blase, Friedman, & Wallace, 2005).

Researchers have long been interested in a series of questions related to the use of scientifically supported knowledge and the process by which new procedures are incorporated into ongoing service delivery: What is the process by which practitioners apply knowledge derived from research? How do adults change the professional practices to which they are accustomed? How do groups make decisions to adopt and implement a new practice? What is required for the implementation of a new set of practices to have the desired effect? How can newly implemented practices and improved outcomes be sustained over time? Researchers have been interested in these questions because, given the results of studies of educational intervention, schools' failure to adopt practices that have been proved through research has limited the success of many school improvement initiatives.

Establishing new practices in education is often thought of as consisting of several stages: (a) *adoption*, that is, recognizing the need for more effective practices, making the decision to begin using the new procedures, and conducting the planning and training necessary to implement the procedures successfully; (b) *implementation*, ranging from the earliest days and the most fundamental use of the procedures to experienced implementation and polished use, including adapting practices as needed; (c) *sustainability*, that is, the ongoing use of the procedure or program over time and its incorporation into the culture of the organization, even as personnel change and initial seed money expires; and (d) *scaling*, the extension of practices across classrooms, grades, and schools. School personnel trained to recognize and support effective practices have much to offer at each stage of the change process.

Adopting Effective Practices at the Building Level

In the RTI adoption stage, schools implement structures to support the use of data in a new or more effective practice, the options available for scientifically based intervention, how the identified practice or program works, and evidence to support its effectiveness.

The No Child Left Behind (NCLB) Act of 2001 has been helpful at the school building level because the academic performance of all students in a school, including subgroups, has been judged against state performance standards. A school with high levels of achievement infers that, for their student population, instructional practices are effective. Schools with lower achievement levels infer that a gap exists between what is being taught, how the content is being taught, and what is being assessed.

RTI provides a structure schools can use when determining the need to adopt different practices. Many books on RTI have checklists or self-studies for schools to determine where the problems are and why the problems are happening. Schools can choose whether to use a self-study or select a checklist that best fits their school climate. Nevertheless, the important concept for individual schools is that data for *all* students are examined by all faculty members, and that the conversations around the need for change and subsequent commitment to change are managed at the school building level. These conversations give all teachers a chance to buy into the proposed changes and to give input on what the faculty needs to do differently to improve learning for all students.

RTI also emphasizes that student achievement is a function of alterable factors, such as the breadth and depth of the curriculum presented and the instructional methods used. Within-student factors like socioeconomic status or disability cannot be altered and, as such, should not be used to analyze where change needs to occur. Schools that focus on unalterable factors are merely delaying efforts to better understand how their curriculum is structured, where instruction needs to be more direct, and whether students have sufficient opportunity to demonstrate that what was taught was actually learned.

Implementing Effective Practices at the Building Level

In the implementation stage, teachers and administrators (a) participate in or lead the planning that will result in the rest of the faculty implementing RTI, (b) conduct or support the training needed to implement RTI, such as coaching teachers on the use of the procedure in the classroom, and (c) organize the data that will guide staff in their use of the new method. In mid- or later-stage implementation, the supports provided to teachers and others refine the implementation, identify system-level variables to support the practice, and help staff adapt to the inevitable changes in the school context, such as having a new principal or new key teachers), that could derail the sustainability of RTI.

Implementation occurs after teachers and administrators have analyzed student performance data and reviewed the literature on effective practices to find practices or programs with a high probability being effective in their school, No practice or program will work for all of the students all of the time. In determining what to implement, the faculty are committing to altering their curricula or instruction in ways that are observable and that are most likely to change student performance. The test of whether or not these changes were sufficiently robust occurs in the next assessment of student performance: did students actually improve in areas that should have been affected by changes in practices?

Sustaining Effective Practices at the Building Level

Once the school has achievement data that suggest that new instructional practices are having a positive impact on student performance, systems must be put in place so that effective practices continue (known as a feedback loop of system success). Student achievement, teacher commitment, teacher implementation, and efficiency (the ratio of implementation cost to effect obtained) are all areas in which a school's faculty evaluate data and discuss effect. Other factors that sustain effect include support for planning by the principal and the teachers leading the implementation effort, and support for those parts of the school culture that keep the implementation going. Supporting actions do not need to be formal and can include notes of thanks and celebrations of success.

Once RTI practices are known to work, safeguards must be in place to prevent implementation drift, which occurs when RTI practices become routine and shortcuts are used. Shortcuts can easily diminish the effectiveness of a program component. To safeguard against drift, the team can use the implementation checklists and walk-throughs to determine how well the actual implementation matches the implementation plan. In the walk-through, colleagues or administrators observe program components and talk with teachers about how to most responsively match the actual implementation to the plan.

Promoting and Managing the Scale-Up to New Sites

Once a school is seen to be successful with RTI, other schools in the district will want to replicate the effort. Success is usually difficult to quantify, but it involves demonstrated improvements in instructional alignment as a result of RTI, improvements in teacher attitudes, and better use of instructional resources. Changes in referral rates and general student achievement can be detected if evaluation structures are included as part of the implementation process, although most schools do not initially include such structures. School leaders wanting to implement RTI should (a) look to the district for policy, procedural, and resource support for RTI startup; (b) incorporate RTI planning into other standard planning processes at the school level, such as school improvement plans or Title I plans; (c) plan the necessary training for all those who will play a role in implementation, including certified teachers as well as paraprofessional staff who might be given assessment or instructional duties; and (d) communicate about the initiative with all interested stakeholders, including the school board, to provide pertinent information and to seek stakeholder support.

School leaders should be aware of where the school as a system and staff members as individuals are with respect to the stages of RTI program implementation (e.g., readiness, exploration, early implementation, established implementation, sustainability, and scale-up), as each stage has different training and support needs. *Innovation configurations* are checklists used throughout implementation of an innovation. These checklists describe initiatives to stakeholders, who then rate their individual perspective on their place in the change process (unsure of change, have knowledge of change but discomfort, are fully ready to adopt the change, are implementing the innovation). The checklists provide a systematic method for leaders to determine the clarity of the change process over time (Champion, 2003). The checklists also provide school leaders and teachers with a method for determining and evaluating professional development needs.

Incorporating Sustainability Into Change

School leaders will be more successful in implementing RTI if they attend to the *implementation drivers* at the school level (Fixsen et al., 2005). Implementation drivers are variables that can either *drive* or *derail* the success of the implementation. Several factors can function as implementation drivers at the school level, such as leadership, training and supervision, schedules, resource allocation, personnel practices, and data utilization. The principal of a school has the main leadership role, but specific roles and responsibilities are distributed through a school-level leadership team (implementation team, literacy team, and others), instructional coaches (if present), instructional specialists (Title 1, resource, English language learners), grade-level team leaders, and district support specialists (e.g., school psychologist, data specialist). It is up to these individuals and teams to ensure that all elements of the planned change are implemented and managed to result in a strong implementation and strong results.

Meeting Challenges to Scaling Up RTI at the Building Level

There are always challenges to address when implementing a change initiative such as RTI in an organization. Two predictable challenges schools might face include changes in personnel and changes in building or district priorities. Both can affect a school's fiscal and human resource allocation. Changes in personnel are a challenge, because typically a change initiative has a champion. Often the change champion has leadership status among peers in the building, such as a principal, school psychologist, literacy specialist, grade-level team leader, or district supervisor. However, when the personnel turnover involves the champion of the initiative, even if the changes are a legal requirement, the initiative can be vulnerable. To help sustain the initiative should a key proponent of the program leave the school, the principal or team should distribute leadership roles for the initiative among other administrators, supervisors, specialists, teacher leaders, and leadership teams to ensure their involvement in implementing and supporting the change initiative.

A change in priorities can also derail a program. A new leader who comes to the school or the district might have priorities other than the change initiative. Leaders of RTI initiatives working at the school level can counter this possibility by consistently participating in the district's RTI leadership team or by recruiting support for RTI from district leaders. Even more stabilizing is the strategy of incorporating language governing certain practices and procedures (e.g., RTI) into district policy or administrative procedures. When procedures become anchored in formal documents of the district, the corresponding practices are much less likely to drift away from what has been implemented and found to be effective.

MANAGING CHANGE IN SCHOOL DISTRICTS

One of the biggest challenges in improving student outcomes involves providing access to the tools and support students need to succeed—that is, moving away from a one-size-fits-all approach and moving toward differentiation based on talent and need. However, the historical silo structure of schools has gotten in the way of making the necessary changes in all of a district's schools.

Adopting Effective Practices at the District Level

Seldom does an evaluation of a student's classroom learning environment take place to examine what factors may be related to the student's reported lack of progress. Without a comprehensive evaluation of students within the context of the instructional environment, it is often difficult to reliably and validly indicate the true cause of poor student progress. It is imperative that practices include an analysis of variables directly related to academic success, such as academic engaged time, opportunities to respond, teacher presentation style, teacher–student monitoring procedures, academic learning time, and teacher expectations, to name just a few. To achieve the effective instruction that is at the heart of RTI, schools and districts must lead the culture change by shifting their practices.

A good place to start culture change is a self-evaluation at the school and district levels (http://www.NASDSE.org and http://www.floridarti.usf.edu provide some examples). Because any district will have schools that are well into implementing RTI practices, others that have pieces of the RTI framework, and still others that have no knowledge of RTI, self-evaluation helps schools identify where to begin with RTI implementation. District-level decisions must start with the assumption that the general curriculum is effective. If a district targets 80–90% of students to be proficient in the general curriculum, but data show it is only 45%, students are not provided with supplemental strategies outside of the general curriculum. Rather, pedagogy of the general curriculum must be addressed prior to any discussions about supplemental or targeted support to small groups or to individual students. This district decision is evidenced in the type and intensity of professional development as well as allocation of resources to allow deep analysis of data, instruction, and collaboration to take place.

Among the district's responsibilities is specifying what tools are to be used to measure and monitor student performance, and what evidence-based supplemental instruction will be provided. In addition to providing the tools needed to begin RTI implementation, the district has responsibility for collaborating with building principals and teacher-leaders to define the skills in data analysis and instruction that teachers will need to implement RTI.

Given the value of the data being gathered, some mechanism for analyzing data at classroom, building, and district levels is needed. Many districts have invested in a data management system for summarizing data at the student, teacher, and grade levels within the school, data for grade level across schools, and data for grade level within the district.

Implementing Effective Practices at the District Level

RTI is a decision-making framework that first examines how well all students are performing academically or socially, and then examines how supplemental supports in general education are affecting performance. RTI assumes that curriculum and instruction are pivotal in affecting performance, and assumes that academic failure is a result of students' not being taught important concepts, rather than blaming poor achievement on factors like language, culture, race, poverty, or disability. It is hard, if not impossible, to demonstrate that a student has a disability when that student is struggling in a class in which half of the students are not achieving grade-level benchmarks.

Generally, individual schools do not have the resources to provide supplemental and intensive instruction to more than 20% of their student population. Therefore, the district must work with schools to ensure that core instruction is effective for 80–90% of students. Core instruction must be responsive to the needs of all students. When large numbers of students are not meeting basic proficiency in the core curriculum, the district has the responsibility of working with individual schools that are struggling, or by taking a systemic look at programs and supports.

The first step that occurs both at the building and district levels of RTI implementation is to evaluate the effectiveness of core instruction. The second step involves engaging in root-cause or similar analysis to understand why the core instruction may not be having the desired effect (Preuss, 2003). In the third step, the district team determines how to supplement core instruction and where those supplements should occur. In some cases, the district will provide general education teachers with professional development on enhancing instruction, while in other cases the district may decide to purchase a packaged instructional program with known effect on the problem as analyzed.

An example of effective RTI implementation and coordination between the schools and district is where core instruction in math is actively being targeted. District and school site personnel must evaluate how well students are progressing and meeting benchmarks and identify what is missing in math instruction. Screening measures or benchmark assessments in math are administered to all students. Scores are analyzed at the group level to determine if large numbers of students are achieving the benchmark levels of performance in math.

The district staff determine if problems in math are occurring at all sites in the district or at only some sites. The district staff work with school teams to analyze the performance of students not achieving benchmark levels and to analyze what supplements to core programming can be provided, with what materials, and by whom. Data generated through RTI may in fact lead to replacing existing programs or instructional methodology with practices that have more effect. The enhancements to instruction are not simply the addition of content or time to programs that are not working in the first place.

Schools and districts that are successfully adopting and implementing the RTI framework have engaged in the process of resource mapping, which is a method that allows teachers to identify all of the academic and behavioral instruction and interventions that are available to students at the core, supplemental, and intensive levels. The map shows the range of resources available to supplement the general curriculum, as part of general education. Resource maps also identify the intensive supports provided when students have disabilities, so that all students make progress in the general curriculum. In the early stages of RTI implementation, when instructional resources are often applied without a systematic framework, it is common for schools and districts to find large gaps in resources when engaging in resource mapping. Over time, as more resources are identified and applied systematically, the resource maps show more comprehensive supports. District decision making plays a key role in supporting the implementation of system-wide RTI by identifying instructional programs and resources that schools will be supported with to address a wide range of learning and teaching needs.

One key component of this resource map is the degree to which supplemental and intensive interventions are integrated into the general curriculum. Supplemental or intensive may mean neither "separate place" nor "off-the-shelf purchased program." Students receiving instructional resources that are supplemental or intensive in nature have not been given a life sentence of exclusion from the general curriculum. In RTI, students must move fluidly between no supports, to supplemental and intensive instructional supports, depending on the needs of the class as well as the needs of the individual. Decisions about resources do not stop even when the child has a disability and an IEP. District leadership must be intentional and purposeful in articulating that special education is a resource designed to promote achievement toward grade-level standards and to downplay the notion of special education as having reduced expectations and as a "place to go" when all other interventions have failed.

Sustaining Practices at the District Level

In most cases districts have organized resources by categorical programs or by funding stream, such as Title 1, English language learners, talented and gifted, or special education. Unfortunately, the fact that a student qualifies for Title 1 or IDEA funding says nothing about that student's specific learning needs. In most cases, when a student does not progress in the general curriculum at the expected rate, she or he is placed under the microscope. The psychopathology is within the student, and often the student is referred for special education testing. In any system, traditional or RTI, the single best predictor of special education eligibility is the presence of a signed consent for full and individual evaluation.

To sustain new practices, funding must support enhancing core programming, providing supplemental support for at-risk learners, and evaluating effects of instructional changes. Professional development for teachers and administrators, on concepts such as ensuring that the curriculum is written in ways that all students can access the content (universal design), infusing effective instructional practices into daily classroom routines, implementing supplemental programs with integrity, and using data-based decision-making. Promoting a culture of data use, high expectations, and understanding of research-based practices is critical in sustaining change. Efforts to promote belief systems, while important, do not lead to sustainability. As Friend (2008) has found, "behavior precedes belief." By helping teachers change their practices, attitudes and beliefs will follow. Our experience confirms the idea that focusing on changing how practices are adopted and implemented results in changes in belief systems that support RTI.

Scaling Up District-Level Implementation

Scaling up RTI at the district level involves communicating with stakeholders, evaluating effects, and using data to determine resources needed by teachers.

As practices change, districts must carefully communicate to stakeholders the need for those changes, the desired effect, and the status of implementation. Crafting a shared vision with stakeholders is important to circumvent areas in which conflict or disagreement might occur (for example, should the district spend resources on strategies to increase citizenship?) or to work on a compromise (Senge, 1990).

It is crucial that ongoing program evaluation takes place when working toward systemic RTI implementation. There are three areas to consider when evaluating RTI effectiveness. First, if data indicated areas of concern with core programming, did the district address those concerns? Evaluating whether or not the general instructional program was enhanced is important, because if the general curriculum is flawed, any examination of movement between tiers or of effect on the special education identification rate also is flawed. Until general instruction is effective for 80% of students, any other evaluation index is contaminated.

Second, the district should address whether the supplemental practices are rigorous enough to effect change. There is controversy in both reading and math as to how explicit instruction needs to be to change achievement. Our experience is that supplemental programs need not be the Cadillac of all instructional programs. Programs that can reasonably articulate the population for whom the program is intended, the steps required to implement the program with fidelity, and a reasonable means to evaluate effects are likely sufficient as a supplemental program. After all, if the most rigorous program is implemented as part of the general education program expected for all children, and children fail to respond, what is left for implementation within an IEP?

The third area on which evaluation should focus is not the numbers of children with IEPs. Our data have been consistent over 15 years of implementation: the numbers of students identified for IEPs will stay the same or go down about 3%. We have no reason to believe that the wrong students are being identified as needing IEPs or that different students are being identified. Hence, RTI evaluation should focus on the quality of instruction being delivered in IEPs. Integrating what historically were separate special and general education systems is one of the systematic effects of RTI. When students need IEPs and are identified as part of an RTI system, there should be evidence that instructional programs have more rigor, and that special education teachers use data to effect instructional change. In the absence of this evidence, RTI is nothing more than new tests for old problems.

MANAGING CHANGE IN STATES

RTI by necessity is implemented "from the ground floor up." In other words, practices change at the school level, trickle up to the district level, then ultimately are scaled up to the state level. As Fullan (1999) wrote, "You can't mandate what matters." RTI is an example of how holding student achievement near and dear to our hearts results in policy changes to help sustain and facilitate continued school improvement.

Adopting Effective Practices at the State Level

States support adoption of practices by schools. Information clearinghouses that describe effective implementation and the factors that led to effective implementation can be maintained at state levels so that school- and district-level staff interested in adopting new ideas have contacts in-state to talk to about cost, effort, similarity of student needs, and effect.

In addition, states promote adoption of effective practices in instruction and assessment. Providing districts with tools against which core and supplemental programs—and corresponding data tools—can be judged is one support for statewide adoption of RTI. States also work with advocacy groups (teachers unions) and interest groups (learning disability associations) to answer questions, provide information, and create shared understanding. RTI belongs in general education to increase performance of all students. RTI is not a special education idea that is needed so that students can be identified as having a specific learning disability or other disability.

Implementing Effective Practices at the State Level

Implementation of RTI at the state level involves defining a process for promoting general school improvement. The process must be specific enough to articulate effective practices but generic enough to allow for variance in implementation at the local levels. States describe how to evaluate core programming, for example, ensuring that phonemic awareness, phonics, fluency, vocabulary, and comprehension are adequately addressed in any elementary-age reading program (National Institute of Child Health and Human Development, 2000). In addition, states promote effective instructional practices such as cooperative learning or peer-assisted learning. States also define the characteristics of ongoing assessment of student progress at core, supplemental, and intensive levels.

As instruction becomes more supplemental or intensive, so should assessment become more frequent and the skills assessed more discrete. An emphasis on flexibility depending on students' needs helps avoid the confrontations between constructivism and behaviorism that often surface in RTI implementation. Our experience is that both pedagogical approaches are appropriate if matched to students' needs, with higher-achieving students perhaps more appropriately served with more discovery learning approaches and less frequent, more student-centered assessment, and lower-achieving students perhaps more appropriately served with more direct instructional methods and more frequent assessment of more discrete skills.

In addition to general practice guidelines, state education agencies must also safeguard and promote policies to ensure compliance with NCLB and IDEA.

Policies to Ensure Compliance With NCLB

A discussion of state policies to ensure 100% compliance with NCLB is not the intent of this chapter. Nevertheless, the assessment component required under NCLB is part of the policy at state level that has an impact on RTI. States must have articulated grade-level content standards, tests that align with these standards, and performance levels considered, at a minimum, proficient and below proficient.

These state-level decisions are important because of the impact on how districts select and use assessment data, and on the funding streams used to support RTI implementation. One policy that must be made at the state level is that of defining scope and performance representative of the general curriculum. The state must provide schools with policies about the constellation of skills expected at each grade and content area, as well as the level of performance considered sufficient for accessing the general curriculum.

Policies to Ensure Compliance With IDEA

States have the responsibility to ensure that students suspected of having disabilities are identified, evaluated, and placed. Protections around identification, evaluation, and placement must be defined through state policy. For RTI, state policy must address when parental consent for evaluation must be obtained and the sufficiency of data needed for making decisions about (a) presence of disability and (b) need for specialized instruction. In addition, state policy around evaluation for special education entitlement must define and promote evaluation practices that are comprehensive, timely, and nondiscriminatory.

Within the context of changing models of service delivery including RTI, state education agencies must ensure that parental consent for evaluation for identification is obtained when data suggest the child may have a disability. Because special education evaluations look different when RTI is implemented, each state must craft its own procedures that local education agencies must follow in obtaining consent and completing the evaluation. In addition, the state must have standards for decision making around special education eligibility. An important consideration for states is that once consent for evaluation is obtained, the evaluation must be completed within 60 calendar days or other state-defined timeline.

In addition, the state must ensure that special education evaluation procedures include methods to assess the impact of factors such as the following on the performance of the student being evaluated: (a) lack of opportunity to receive scientifically based instruction in reading and math, (b) cultural factors, (c) second language effect on performance, and (d) poverty or mobility. These exclusionary factors preclude IEP teams from determining that a student has a disability, and IEP services would not be appropriate for students for whom the exclusionary factors could not be ruled out as contributing causes to their low performance.

Another important policy that states should consider involves aligning IEP resources with data generated during the RTI process. If RTI is designed to promote an integrated system in which special education is not a place but is a service to students who are disabled and need specialized instruction, then data from the RTI process should be used to develop IEPs. RTI cannot be judged successful if the numbers of children needing IEPs are reduced. Reducing special education numbers is something that could happen within a district but is not evidence of effective RTI. RTI must result in improved performance for all students, including students with IEPs. In an RTI system, students who are identified as having disabilities and needing IEPs have proved resistant to supplemental and intensive instruction provided in general education. Once identified as eligible for an IEP, the decision-making framework of RTI must still be used to ensure that all students are receiving instruction and are making progress toward grade-level performance expectations. States could consider a policy that IEP services need to meet or exceed supplemental and intensive services implemented during the RTI process. A policy requiring even more supports in special education ensures that even when on an IEP, students' instructional goals are aligned with grade-appropriate general curriculum, and services on an IEP are at least as rigorous as those services provided to students prior to IEP identification.

Sustainability at the State Level

Sustainability for RTI comes not from the state, but from the field. Two important ideas were raised earlier. First, change happens at the school level (you can't mandate what matters; Fullan, 1999). Second, behavior precedes belief (Friend, 2008). When schools implement RTI and begin demanding support from the state, including flexibility on state rules that may constrain RTI implementation, the state must respond. Taking their cue from schools and districts, state personnel still provide leadership to the field, but the leadership is in areas defined by the field as needing support. In RTI, the areas needing support will be many: implementing universal screening; managing data; setting performance criteria; evaluating core programming; evaluating supplemental programs; designing instructional strategies; monitoring progress; and adopting, implementing, and sustaining change. The state education agency provides seed grants, gives schools and districts access to experts, and crafts state practices and policies in school improvement and special education to support RTI.

CONCLUSION

As we have experienced special education through the years, the promise of special education in the 1970s was to give students with physical disabilities and significant cognitive disabilities access to public school and a free education appropriate for their needs. The promise of special education in the 1980s was to provide students with disabilities access to education in the least restrictive environment. The promise of special education in the 1990s was to provide students with disabilities an education based on more careful analysis of their educational needs, including functional behavior assessment. The promise of special education in the 2000s is access to the general curriculum and achievement toward grade-level content standards. Assessing the kinds of jobs and the living arrangements of students with disabilities after leaving high school must be done as part of states' Performance Plans in Special Education. Affecting the achievement gap for students with disabilities is required under NCLB.

RTI offers students the following:

- Viable and rigorous core curriculum in which *most* (e.g., 80%) students succeed. Reasonable differentiated instruction designed to promote learning is part of the general education continuum.

- For a smaller percentage of students, intensive instruction that is aligned with the general curriculum.
- For some students, IEP protections around fair evaluation practices and assurances that IEP goals represent grade-level standards and high performance expectations.
- For students with IEPs, assurances that IEP services are research based and sufficient for getting students with IEPs "caught up" to grade-level expectations.

For too long, special education has been seen as the solution for nearly all school problems. The irony of special education has been that it has been too focused on gatekeeping practices and special education entitlement rather than on the quality of programs and the outcomes produced (Brown, 1994; President's Commission on Excellence in Special Education, 2002). The promise of creating more powerful supports for positively affecting education for all children has long existed and forms the basis for RTI (Bijou, 1970). The increased emphasis on accountability for all students is forcing schools, districts, and state agencies to rethink how they practice.

In schools with high rates of failure, or large numbers of students at risk of failure, schools and districts cannot afford to solve problems one referral at a time. Instead, policies and practices are needed to support the use of assessment, data management, instructional principles, consultation, and evaluation. In turn, assessment data support decisions about instructional principles for individual children or small groups of students, and also provide some information needed to evaluate effects of RTI on school-, district-, and state-level changes in performance.

School systems now appear to accept that the data-based decision-making and accountability embedded in RTI are not short-lived, but will remain a challenge for schools. This is a challenge for which many systems seek solutions for improved school-based leadership and decision making.

An additional step states could use to promote systems change is to align accreditation standards with state licensing requirements so that all educators have similar training and are certified to implement skills in which their competence has been evaluated. All educators should have basic skills in evaluating achievement at the systems level. Educators should be knowledgeable about what skills need to be taught, and about different ways to both teach and assess content mastery. Universal design is one example of using media and instructional design so that the general curriculum is accessible to all learners (Center for Applied Special Technology, 2007).

All educators do not need to know how to provide supplemental supports, but all educators should know that special education is a resource to expand access to general education and not a separate curricular framework. School administrators and teachers need to understand that student performance can be affected through instruction, and that assessment data can be used to judge improvements in student performance at all levels of instruction. At the district level, evaluating the system's progress against the state-level achievement targets allows districts to change the level of resources so that by 2014 the reality at the state level will be that few children are left behind. RTI at present is emerging as a viable mechanism to increase the likelihood that all children will have the opportunity to benefit from education.

AUTHOR NOTE

The content of this paper reflects the opinions of the authors and are neither policies nor positions of their respective institutional affiliations. Special thanks to Mark R. Shinn for his copious editing and ongoing support for completion of this manuscript.

REFERENCES

Batsche, G., Elliott, J., Graden, J. L., Grimes, J., Kovaleski, J. F., Prasse, D., et al. (2006). *Response to intervention: Policy considerations and implementation*. Alexandria, VA: National Association of State Directors of Special Education.

Berman, P., & McLaughlin, M. W. (1978). *Federal programs supporting educational change. Vol. 8: Implementing and sustaining innovations*. Santa Monica, CA: RAND.

Bijou, S. W. (1970). What psychology has to offer education now. *Journal of Applied Behavior Analysis, 3,* 65–71.

Bollman, K. A., Silberglitt, B., & Gibbons, K. A. (2007). The St. Croix River Education District model: Incorporating systems-level organization and a multi-tiered problem-solving process for intervention delivery. In S. R. Jimerson, M. K. Burns, & A. M. VanDerHeyden (Eds.), *Handbook of response to intervention: The science and practice of assessment and intervention* (pp. 319–330). New York: Springer.

Brown, D. T. (1994). Will the real school psychologist please stand up: Is the past a prologue for the future of school psychology? The consolidation of the profession. *School Psychology Review, 23,* 589–600.

Carnine, D. (1999). Perspective: Campaigns for moving research into practice. *Remedial and Special Education, 20,* 2–6.

Center for Applied Special Technology. (2007, November). *Summary of 2007 national summit on universal design for learning working groups*. Report prepared for summit participants. Wakefield, MA: Author.

Champion, R. (2003). Taking measure: The innovation configuration. *Journal of Staff Development, 24,* 69–71.

Datnow, A. (2005). The sustainability of comprehensive school reform models in changing district and state contexts. *Educational Administration Quarterly, 41,* 121–153.

Fixsen, D., Naoom, S., Blase, K., Friedman, R., & Wallace, F. (2005). *Implementation research: A synthesis of the literature*. Tampa: University of South Florida, Louis de la Parte Florida Mental Health Institute.

Friend, M. (2008, July 22). *Turbulence, tribulation, and transformation: A look at the status of special education teacher presentation*. Plenary Session at the 2008 United States Department of Education, Office of Special Education Programs Project Director's Conference, Washington, DC.

Fullan, M. (1999). *Change forces: The sequel.* Philadelphia: Falmer Press.

Gersten, R., Compton, D., Connor, C. M., Dimino, J., Santoro, L., Linan-Thompson, S., et al. (2008). *Assisting students struggling with reading: Response to intervention and multi-tier intervention for reading in the primary grades. A practice guide* (NCEE 2009-4045). Washington, DC: U.S. Department of Education, National Center for Education Evaluation and Regional Assistance, Institute of Education Sciences. Retrieved from http://ies.ed.gov/ncee/wwc/publications/practice guides/

Gersten, R., & Edomono, J. (2006, January). RTI (Response to Intervention): Rethinking special education for students with reading difficulties (yet again). *Reading Research Quarterly, 41,* 99–108. doi:10.1598/RRQ.41.1.5

Gersten, R., & Smith-Jones, J. (2001). Reflections on the research to practice gap. *Teacher Education and Special Education, 24,* 356–361.

Graden, J. L., Stollar, S. A., & Poth, R. L. (2007). The Ohio integrated systems model: Overview and lessons learned. In S. R. Jimerson, M. K. Burns, & A. M. VanDerHeyden (Eds.), *Handbook of response to intervention: The science and practice of assessment and intervention* (pp. 288–299). New York: Springer.

Greenwood, C. R., & Abbott, M. (2001). The research to practice gap in special education. *Teacher Education and Special Education, 24,* 276–289.

Grimes, J. P., & Tilly, W. D. (1996). Policy and process: Means to lasting educational change. *School Psychology Review, 25,* 431–445.

Hall, G. E., & Hord, S. M. (1987). *Change in schools: Facilitating the process.* Albany: State University of New York Press.

Hall, G. E., & Loucks, S. F. (1977). A developmental model for determining whether the treatment is actually implemented. *American Educational Research Journal, 14,* 263–276.

Ikeda, M. J., Rahn-Blakeslee, A. R., Niebling, B. C., Gustafson, J. K., Allison, R., & Stumme, J. (2007). The Heartland Area Education Agency 11 problem-solving approach: An overview and lessons learned. In S. R. Jimerson, M. K. Burns, & A. M. VanDerHeyden (Eds.), *Handbook of response to intervention: The science and practice of assessment and intervention* (pp. 255–264). New York: Springer.

Ikeda, M. J., Tilly, W. D., III, Stumme, J., Volmer, L., & Allison, R. (1996). Agency-wide implementation of problem solving consultation: Foundations, current implementation, and future directions. *School Psychology Quarterly, 11,* 228–243.

Individuals with Disabilities Education Improvement Act of 2004, 20 U.S.C. § 1400 *et seq.*

Kovaleski, J. F. (2007). Response to intervention: Considerations for research and systems change. *School Psychology Review, 36,* 638–646.

Marston, D., Lau, M., & Muyskens, P. (2007). Implementation of the problem-solving model in the Minneapolis public schools. In S. R. Jimerson, M. K. Burns, & A. M. VanDerHeyden (Eds.), *Handbook of response to intervention: The science and practice of assessment and intervention* (pp. 279–287). New York: Springer.

National Institute of Child Health and Human Development. (2000). Teaching children to read: An evidence-based assessment of the scientific research literature on reading and its implications for reading instruction (NIH Publication No. 00-4769). Washington, DC: U.S. Government Printing Office.

No Child Left Behind Act of 2001, Pub. L. No. 107-110, 115 Stat. 1425 (2002).

Peterson, D. W., Prasse, D. P., Shinn, M. R., & Swerdlik, M. E. (2007). The Illinois flexible service delivery model: A problem-solving model initiative. In S. R. Jimerson, M. K. Burns, & A. M. VanDerHeyden (Eds.), *Handbook of response to intervention: The science and practice of assessment and intervention* (pp. 300–318). New York: Springer.

President's Commission on Excellence in Special Education. (2002). *A new era: Revitalizing Special Education for children and their families.* Washington, DC: U.S. Department of Education.

Preuss, P. G. (2003). *School leader's guide to root cause analysis: Using data to dissolve problems.* Larchmont, NY: Eye on Education.

Reschly, D. (2002, April). Change dynamics in special education assessment: Historical and contemporary patterns. *Peabody Journal of Education, 77*(2), 117–136. Retrieved September 12, 2008, from Academic Search Elite database.

Senge, P. (1990). *The fifth discipline: The art and practice of the learning organization.* New York: Doubleday.

CHAPTER 3

RTI as a Driving Force in Educational Improvement: Research, Legal, and Practice Perspectives

Frank Gresham
Louisiana State University

Daniel Reschly
Vanderbilt University

Mark R. Shinn
National-Louis University

INTRODUCTION

This chapter provides an in-depth review and analysis of the role of response to intervention (RTI) as a driving influence in educational improvement and describes how RTI became an entitlement process as well as a general referent for the development of multitiered early-intervening service delivery models. We argue that the foundations and early beginnings of the RTI movement were laid in the 1970s as reflected in the visionary thinking and empirical research of professionals such as W. C. Becker, S. Engelmann, S. L. Deno, J. E. Ysseldyke, B. Algozzine, M. C. Reynolds, and their contemporaries. The sets of educational assessment and intervention practices, known collectively as response to intervention, have had a profound impact on how educational services are currently delivered to children in Grades K–12 across the country. This effect is expected to grow in the coming years.

RTI is a multitiered framework or heuristic that represents a conceptual roadmap for providing graduated assistance and support services to students who are struggling academically and/or behaviorally in general education. RTI is based on the assumption that universal screening, early identification, and early intervening services, combined with evidence-based practices, can reduce and prevent subsequent school failure (Detrich, Keyworth, & States, 2008). Within an RTI educational context, students are

Address all correspondence and feedback on this chapter to Mark R. Shinn at markshinn@me.com.

assigned to increasingly intensive intervention levels (e.g., Tier 1, Tier 2, and Tier 3) based on their lack of responsiveness to quality curricular offerings at a prior level (Jenkins, Hudson, & Johnson, 2007; Shinn, 2007).

RTI is broadly considered to be one of the most innovative advances ever introduced into the field of education (Merrell & Buchanan, 2006). Its impact has been felt at all levels of the educational enterprise and has spilled over into the operations of educational agencies and systems at state as well as federal levels. RTI provides a valuable organizing platform for achieving some important educational outcomes, including (a) accurate, early identification of at-risk students through systematic universal screening; (b) early and individualized intervention for at-risk students matched to the severity and nature of their deficits; and (c) use of increasingly more intensive tiers of research-based instruction (Wanzek & Vaughn, 2007). The driving philosophy of RTI, and the practices that are organized and delivered based on RTI, continue to transform educational systems through improvement of their responsiveness to students' needs and a far more cost-efficient use of available schooling resources.

The chapter distinguishes between two basic interpretations of RTI. One interpretation is based in its use in the special education eligibility process for specific learning disabilities (SLD). The other interpretation represents a variety of approaches to the implementation of the multitiered early-intervening services model. In the latter case, RTI forms the basis for large-scale school improvement, ranging from ensuring that students receive evidence-based interventions in their general education classrooms, to improving special education services so they produce better outcomes. This chapter focuses on the research and legal underpinnings of the use of RTI in SLD identification. It also describes the history of RTI implementation in schools, in particular how these SLD identification practices were embedded in larger issues of school improvement for all students.

This chapter is divided into three major sections. The first section briefly reviews the trajectory of the field's attempts to cope more effectively with the problems of students who have the label of SLD and traces the role of research and resulting empirical evidence that has transformed our thinking about this schooling challenge. The second section provides an in-depth analysis of the impact of key federal legislation on the development, promotion, and adoption of improved practices in dealing with this school subpopulation. The third section describes some perspectives on professional practices that can result in quality enhancements of the instruction, supports, and services designed for all students. The descriptions in these three sections are based on three interdependent domains: (a) the gains in the research knowledge base with regard to what does and doesn't work, especially with respect to SLD identification; (b) how this knowledge was translated into core legal principles that stimulated policies and action research; and (c) how schools have embedded many of the RTI concepts and tools in school service delivery systems over the past three decades. Before these issues are dealt with, however, we provide a brief discussion of the origins of RTI and its emergence as a dominant heuristic and organizing principle in the delivery of more effective educational practices.

RTI IN CONTEXT: EARLY DEVELOPMENTS AND SEMINAL INFLUENCES

Changes in educational services for *all* students were stimulated by the No Child Left Behind Act (2001) and were "supercharged" through explicit changes in special education eligibility in the Individuals with Disabilities Education Act of 2004 (IDEA). In a radical move, with IDEA 2004, Congress granted local education agencies (LEAs) choice in how they preferred to identify students with specific learning disabilities. LEAs were no longer required to identify the condition of SLD based on an ability–achievement discrepancy. Instead, they were given the option of identifying SLD students based on their response to high-quality, scientifically based instruction (i.e., response to intervention). Historically, Congress granted state education agencies (SEAs) the responsibility to provide specific criteria for special education eligibility within fairly broad federal legal and regulatory guidelines. Congress also followed up with federal regulations in 2006 that (a) prevented SEAs from requiring the ability–achievement discrepancy method, and (b) ensured that an RTI process would be allowed.

Another change made by IDEA 2004 radically departed from previous legislation. That is, LEAs were given authority to use a portion of their federal special education dollars, up to 15%, to develop and implement coordinated early intervening services (CEIS). These services could be provided to students who were not currently identified as having special education needs but who required additional resources to benefit from their general education programs. In instances of disproportional placement rates for minority students within a school district, LEAs were *required* to spend this 15% for general education improvement. The law was clearly and explicitly giving LEAs permission not only to determine how they would identify SLD students but also to determine how they would *serve* students at risk or those with severe needs. LEAs could now spend federal special education dollars that previously had been highly restricted for purposes of prevention and early intervention.

For many practitioners, RTI came out of the blue. But for others, the changes were regarded as a logical result of refinements in the original *legal intentions* in disability rights begun in the early 1970s. This latter view was strengthened by research gains in the understanding of prevailing SLD identification practices—of what did and didn't work—as well as by more than 20-plus years of experience with implementing service delivery models that were targeted toward improved outcomes for all students—including those with disabilities. Knowledge of research outcomes affected successful service delivery systems, and evidence from successful service delivery systems affected law, and so on.

By 2004, a rich research base compelled changes in federal and state legal provisions regarding SLD (Reschly, 2008). Critical influences were the failure of the SLD identification process and the unabated growth in the number of students served under that category, as well as the accumulation of evidence that neither general nor special education applied what was known about scientifically based academic and behavioral interventions. This accumulated research evidence provided a hope that better results were possible for all students, but particularly for special education students, through application of these principles (Donovan & Cross, 2002; Lyon et al., 2001; National Reading Panel, 2000; President's Commission on Excellence in Special Education, 2002; Snow, Burns, & Griffin, 1998). A consensus emerged from research and policy that focused on building more cohesive systems of service delivery for all students by employing the following practices:

1. Scientifically based instruction to replace often weak and philosophy-driven intervention practices.
2. Universal screening to reduce reliance on a flawed referral-based model.
3. Promotion of early identification and early intervention approaches to avoid the pervasive "wait to fail" approach.
4. Progress monitoring with formative evaluation to ensure a commitment to improved outcomes with individual students.
5. An integrated accountability model acknowledging the interdependence of effective general, remedial, and special education programs rather than stand-alone and isolated services.

SECTION ONE: RTI AS A RESULT OF INCREASED KNOWLEDGE OF WHAT DOES AND DOES NOT WORK IN SLD IDENTIFICATION AND INTERVENTION

This section traces the history of research as it gradually pointed the way toward RTI practices that documented the cost inefficiency and lack of efficacy of what were once considered standard practices (i.e., ability–achievement discrepancy, special education services). Research simultaneously demonstrated the cost-effectiveness and consumer acceptability of a different SLD entitlement approach that decreased sole emphasis on child characteristics, and increased emphasis on instructional practices. The following topics are discussed in this section: (a) the failure of the ability–achievement discrepancy model, (b) the role of comparative research, (c) research on school-identified SLD (SI-SLD), (d) prediction of treatment outcomes, (e) processing approaches as a failed alternative, (f) the dual-discrepancy criterion in SLD identification, and (g) RTI and treatment validity.

The Failure of the Ability–Achievement Discrepancy Model

For nearly 30 years, the significant ability–achievement discrepancy was the cornerstone of SLD identification criterion. In 2004, 48 states used some variation of this discrepancy approach as their state's SLD criterion (Reschly & Hosp, 2004). However, in 2005, just 1 year later, the ability–achievement discrepancy was no longer required in IDEA 2004 because (a) comparative research failed to validate it as a distinguishing feature of SLD status, (b) school identification research demonstrated that schools were quite inconsistent in applying it to the classification process for students with and without the discrepancy, and, most important, (c) it failed to predict which students would benefit from intervention.

That the use of the ability–achievement discrepancy was and remains popular is understandable. For years, it was the major component of the federal SLD definition. Its use was commonplace and considered a best practice by many, and the logic of the ability–achievement discrepancy was intuitively appealing; that is, some students who seemed capable nevertheless had great difficulty with reading. For these students, learning problems were both unexpected and severe (i.e., discrepant underachievement) relative to their ability. Furthermore, it was natural to believe that those students with a severe, unexplained achievement discrepancy were different in some distinguishing way(s) from students showing no such discrepancies (i.e., nondiscrepant underachievement). Members of the latter group were considered to be working up to their ability and were typically referred to as "slow learners" in practice.

The Role of Comparative Research

Initial SLD research, such as the Isle of Wight studies conducted in the early to mid-1970s (Rutter & Yule, 1975), appeared to support this appealing theory and influenced inclusion of the ability–achievement discrepancy in the first federal SLD definition of the Education for All Handicapped Children Act (EAHCA, 1975). From these beginnings, though, arose scientific concerns about the method. Beginning with the federally funded research initiated on SLD identification practices at the University of Minnesota Institute for Research on Learning Disabilities in 1978 (e.g., Algozzine, Ysseldyke, & Shinn, 1982; Ysseldyke, Shinn, & Thurlow, 1978; Ysseldyke et al., 1983; Ysseldyke, Algozzine, Shinn, & McGue, 1982), researchers have collected more than a quarter century of results on the use of ability–achievement discrepancy and other SLD approaches. In the intervening years, several lines of converging evidence strongly suggested that the ability–achievement discrepancy was *not* a valid marker for the presence of SLD (Share, McGee, & Silva, 1989; Shaywitz, Escobar, Shaywitz, Fletcher, & Makuch, 1992; Stanovich & Siegel, 1994; Vellutino, Scanlon, & Lyon, 2000; Vellutino et al., 1996). These lines of research directly refuted the early Isle of Wight theory that discrepant low achievers (SLD) were different from nondiscrepant low achievers ("garden variety" low achievers). Overall, these studies clearly showed that discrepant and nondiscrepant low-achieving children did not differ on measures of reading achievement, response to instruction, cognitive abilities, phoneme awareness, short-term memory, visual processing, or word retrieval.

Because of the volume of studies, it is now possible to contrast low achievers (LA) with SLD groups on a variety of measures to examine results through meta-analyses (e.g., Fuchs, Fuchs, Mathes, Lipsey, & Roberts, 2002; Hoskyn & Swanson, 2000; Steubing et al., 2002). For example, Hoskyn and Swanson reviewed 19 studies that contrasted LA and SLD groups. Based on 274 weighted effect sizes, these authors found small and few statistically significant differences between the two groups on measures of cognitive skills related to reading (e.g., pseudoword reading, real-word phonetic analysis, speech-related phonological processing, automaticity, and spelling). Based on a regression model analysis, these authors concluded that both LA and SLD groups *share* a general phonological deficit, but not ability–achievement discrepancies—a conclusion consistent with other findings in reading disability research (Perfetti, Beck, Bell, & Hughes, 1987; Stanovich & Siegel, 1994; Torgesen, 1999; Torgesen & Burgess, 1998; Torgesen, Burgess, & Rashotte, 1996).

Shortly after the Hoskyn and Swanson study (2000), Steubing et al. (2002) conducted another meta-analysis using 46 studies that investigated the validity of the ability–achievement discrepancy for children with SLD in the domains of achievement, behavior, and cognitive skills. These studies included most of the 19 studies reviewed by Hoskyn and Swanson and identified many others of suitable quality. Steubing et al. reported statistically insignificant effect size differences between LA and SLD groups in the domains of achievement and behavior and small differences in the cognitive domain. They concluded that defining SLD on the basis of an ability–achievement discrepancy has very little validity.

Research on School-Identified SLD (SI-SLD)

In addition to nearly 30 years of comparative research findings—ranging from single studies to meta-analyses detailing the failure of ability–achievement discrepancy models (among others)—several programs of research have investigated the classification accuracy of students whom schools identified as SLD, or school-identified SLD (SI-SLD). One series of SI-SLD studies conducted in California demonstrated that schools often do not follow their state's SLD eligibility criteria (Bocian, Beebe, MacMillan, & Gresham, 1999; Gresham, MacMillan, & Bocian, 1996; MacMillan, Gresham, & Bocian, 1998; MacMillan, Gresham, Siperstein, & Bocian, 1996). In one study, Gresham et al. (1996) showed that school eligibility decisions resulted in *surprisingly low* rates of agreement with state criteria definitions of mild disability groups (SLD and mild mental retardation). Eligibility decision agreement was only 59.6% (true positives), which resulted in a 40.4% false negative error rate. A total of 19 students in the mild mental retardation group were identified as having a specific learning disability, creating a 44.0% false positive rate for SLD.

A similar line of SI-SLD research was also carried out in Minnesota. Ability–achievement discrepancies did not explain school SLD identification practices (Algozzine et al., 1982; Algozzine & Ysseldyke, 1987; Ysseldyke et al., 1982). For example, in a study by Peterson and Shinn (2002), Grade 3 SLD students from high- and low-performing communities were compared with the state's regression criterion. At best, classification accuracy was 67% in one district; it was 56% in the other district.

Prediction of Treatment Outcomes

The third influential body of knowledge that affected changes in use of the ability–achievement discrepancy consisted of studies that examined discrepant and nondiscrepant students' responses to reading instruction. *If* the ability–achievement discrepancy were a valid factor in SLD identification, the predicted outcomes would be that those students *with* ability–achievement discrepancies would benefit from reading instruction while those students who were *nondiscrepant* would not. No such results have been reported and, in fact, have been contraindicated. In multiple studies, discrepant and nondiscrepant low achievers did *not* differ in their response to instruction nor did the discrepancy approach inform instructional decisions (Fletcher, Lyon, Fuchs, & Barnes, 2007; L. Fuchs & D. Fuchs, 1998; Gresham, 2002; Gresham & Witt, 1997; Vaughn & Fuchs, 2003; Vellutino et al., 2000).

One of the principal reasons why the ability–achievement discrepancy approach to determining SLD was dropped in IDEA 2004 was its documented failure to work as shown in comparative research, school-based practice research, and predictive treatment research. The first body of research showed no reliable differences in ability–achievement discrepancies between SLD and low-achieving students. The second body showed that schools did not consistently use the ability–achievement discrepancy in their decision-making process. The third body showed that the discrepancy was irrelevant in terms of its benefit to intervention. Compounded with problematic psychometric issues (i.e., reliability of difference scores, regression) and social values issues (i.e., challenges in assessing ability with many student groups), a critical decision was made to no longer require the ability–achievement discrepancy as part of SLD identification.

Processing Approaches as a Failed Alternative

The IDEA 2004 definition of SLD states that it is "a disorder in one or more of the basic psychological processes involving understanding or using language, spoken or written, that may manifest itself in an imperfect ability to listen, think, speak, read, write, spell, or do mathematical calculations." Like the ability–achievement discrepancy approach, the theory that students with SLD have processing deficits is intuitively appealing. There must be some *reason* a student who seems capable is not learning to read. However, an appealing theory that attracts the interest of lawmakers does not necessarily make good practice or good science.

Some professionals take the SLD definition to mean that identifying processes and/or cognitive ability deficits is necessary to determine special education eligibility under the category of SLD and, in fact, that they are required by the law (Hale, Naglieri, Kaufman, & Kavale, 2004; Hale, Kaufman, Naglieri, & Kavale, 2006; Kavale, Kauffman, Bachmeier, & LeFever, 2008). However, there is nothing written in the law that necessarily requires the assessment and documentation of a processing disorder for eligibility determination. This discrepancy between legal definition and eligibility regulations is long-standing. In 2003, only 13 states required demonstration of a severe processing deficit (Reschly & Hosp, 2004). The vast majority of states (37, including federal regulations) ignored the processing definitions in their SLD entitlement regulations. For the 13 states that did include processing in their regulations, none were specific in how it was to be assessed, nor did they provide a criterion for defining *severity*. A state's inability to provide both a process for assessing a severe processing deficit and a criterion for defining severity is understandable, given the variety of measurement-related factors.

Nothing has changed in the statutory definition of SLD over the past 32 years. The statute has always used the language of processing as a *conceptual* or *theoretical* (i.e., *definitional*) explanation of learning difficulties. There has never been a requirement in either the statute or federal regulations that a so-called "processing disorder" be assessed and documented. In fact, federal regulations for IDEA 2004 state:

> The Department does not believe that an assessment of psychological or cognitive processing should be required in determining whether a child has an SLD. There is no current evidence that such assessments are necessary or sufficient for identifying SLD. Further, in many cases, these assessments have not been used to make appropriate intervention decisions. (p. 46651)

States' failure to include the definitional processing component in their regulations is based on empirical studies showing that, other than for phonological processing, reliable and valid measures of processing were not and currently are not available. A more serious problem, however, is that there is not a single *randomized clinical trial* using the Institute for Educational Sciences (IES) evidence-based standards that has related processing strengths to effective intervention outcomes. There are no experimental research studies showing a *causal* relationship between processing and academic performance. At best, any relations between processing and outcomes are correlational. Some processing measures may *moderate* (affect) academic performance, but they have not been demonstrated to *mediate* (cause) academic performance.

Because there is a correlation between scores on certain processing measures and achievement scores, it does not mean that the low processing score *causes* low achievement. Causality is demonstrated only through manipulation of the suspected causal variable. Without such manipulation (i.e., use of controlled experiments), results can be confounded by *moderator variables.*

A moderator variable (B) affects the direction or strength of the relation between a predictor variable (A) and a criterion variable (C). Thus, the impact of A on C varies with the level or value of B. A *mediator variable* specifies the manner or the mechanism by which a given effect occurs. In other words, the predictor causes the mediator, which, in turn, causes the criterion or outcome (see Baron & Kenny, 1986; Holmberg, 1997). For example, consider the potential interpretations of the processes Verbal Conceptualization (VC) and Working Memory (WM) and their relation to reading skill deficits (RD). VC correlates with RD. WM correlates with RD. VC correlates with WM. We thus have three correlations (VC:RD; WM:RD; VC:WM). Poor readers have lower VC than average or good readers. Poor readers have lower WM scores than average or good readers. However, it would be faulty logic, and poor science, to presume that VC and WM deficits necessarily *cause* poor reading skills (RD). Numerous studies have shown that groups of at-risk and SLD learners score lower on some processing measures. It does not necessarily follow that these processing deficits *cause* SLD. Again, this causal relation must be demonstrated by controlled experimentation.

Group mean differences on processing measures also do not necessarily imply that these measures are *diagnostically accurate* in SLD identification. This is an example of faulty reasoning based on the notion of inverse probabilities (Meehl & Rosen, 1955; Watkins, 2000). For example, the so-called ACID profile (low scores on Arithmetic, Coding, Information, and Digit Span) of the Wechsler scales is often considered a processing indicator of SLD. Conclusions such as these are derived by showing that a sample of students identified as SLD is found to have low scores on ACID subtests. Thus, the probability of any member of the SLD sample showing the ACID profile is high, given that the child is SLD. This method, however, is not how a referral in schools takes place. What we want to know is the probability that the student is SLD given an ACID profile. Inverse probabilities of this nature systematically overestimate diagnostic accuracy (Meehl & Rosen, 1955).

Another problem with the above practice is the misunderstanding of base rates. The practical value of a diagnostic indicator depends on intrinsic validity (i.e., discriminating power) and the base rates for the disorder one is trying to predict (Meehl & Rosen, 1955; Watkins, Glutting, & Youngstrom, 2005). When base rates deviate greatly from 50%, the use of diagnostic indicators having moderate validity will *increase* the number of erroneous decisions. Additionally, when the base rate of a disorder is extremely rare, the probability of false positive identification for the disability increases.

One cannot know the value of a test without knowing the base rate of the problem that is being detected. For example, consider a situation where a reading test detects 90% of students as having a reading disability. However, if the base rate of reading disability in a given school is 95%, the test would be worthless in predicting the presence of a reading disability. Some school psychologists fall into the trap of belief in associations between so-called diagnostic indicators (e.g., ACID profiles) and the presence of a disorder (e.g., SLD). These correlations are illusory, yet continue to dominate the thinking of many proponents of processing explanations of SLD.

Other than phonological processing, no data based on randomized clinical trials have shown a clear, consistent causal relation among measures of processing and effective instructional treatments or aptitude–treatment interactions (ATI). Although intuitively appealing, empirical evidence supporting the existence of ATIs remains inconsistent, questionable, and, mainly, nonexistent (Cronbach, 1975). The use of cognitive processing measures to identify cognitive strengths and weaknesses and to match instructional treatments to them has, for the most part, been uniformly unsuccessful.

The Dual-Discrepancy Criterion in SLD Identification

Response to intervention as an SLD identification process is most commonly operationalized as a *dual discrepancy* (L. Fuchs & Vaughn, 2005; Pericola Case, Speece, & Eddy Molloy, 2003; Shinn, 2007; Speece, Pericola Case, & Eddy Molloy, 2003; Vaughn & Fuchs, 2003). The first discrepancy is one of severe underachievement or *severe educational need*. The second discrepancy is the lack of response to high-quality intervention or lack of *educational benefit*. We suggest one thing that is "right" about RTI as an SLD identification process is that it provides special education to students with severe educational needs who have been demonstrated to *not* benefit from high-quality instruction or more intensive, evidence-based intervention. This is consistent with the concept of treatment validity.

In contrast to the lack of findings regarding the accuracy of either the ability–achievement discrepancy or processing to identify students with SLD accurately, almost 30 years of research has shown that the defining feature of SI-SLD has been *severe* low reading achievement compared with other low-performing students (Shinn, Tindal, & Spira, 1987; Shinn, Tindal, Spira, & Marston, 1987; Shinn, Tindal, & Stein, 1988; Shinn, Ysseldyke, Deno, & Tindal, 1986). Across these studies, SI-SLD students performed about one standard deviation lower than their low-achieving counterparts, and almost two standard deviations lower than typically achieving peers. These findings were confirmed in the meta-analyses by Fuchs, Fuchs, Mathes, Lipsey, and Eaton (2000), and Fuchs et al. (2002).

The second discrepancy is a lack of sufficient academic progress, given high-quality instruction. Its history can be traced to the National Research Council (NRC) report in which the validity of a special education classification system was evaluated on the basis of three criteria: (a) the quality of the general education program, (b) the value of the special education program in producing important outcomes for students, and (c) the accuracy and meaningfulness of the assessment process in the identification of disability (Heller, Holtzman, & Messick, 1982). Vaughn and Fuchs (2003) suggested that the first two criteria emphasized the *quality of instruction*, whereas the third criterion involved judgments of the quality of instructional environments and the student's response to instruction delivered in those environments. The third criterion described in the NRC report also is consistent with Messick's (1995) notion of evidential and consequential bases of test *use* and *interpretation*. That is, there must be an evidential basis and a consequential basis for using and interpreting tests in a certain way. If they do not exist, then one may conclude that there is insufficient evidence for the validity of a given assessment procedure.

RTI and Treatment Validity

It is clear that in RTI, the major goal of SLD identification is to identify effective interventions that will result in less severe educational need (i.e., reduce the gap) and greater educational benefit. Therefore, RTI as SLD entitlement is tied to the construct of *treatment validity*, sometimes called treatment utility of assessment. Treatment validity can be defined as the extent to which the assessment procedure contributes to beneficial outcomes for individuals (Cone, 1989; L. Fuchs & D. Fuchs, 1998; Hayes, Nelson, & Jarrett, 1987).

For any assessment procedure to have treatment validity, it must lead to the identification of relevant areas of concern (academic or behavioral), inform treatment planning, and be useful in evaluating treatment outcomes. The central feature is that there must be a clear and unambiguous relationship between the assessment data collected and the recommended intervention. Traditionally, many assessment procedures in school psychology have failed to demonstrate treatment validity because they do not inform instructional or behavioral intervention practices (Cronbach, 1975; Gresham, 2002; Gresham & Witt, 1997; Reschly, 2008). The concept of RTI depends largely on the treatment validity of measures used to determine adequate or inadequate treatment response. In short, assessment procedures having treatment validity not only inform the selection of intervention procedures but also are used to evaluate treatment outcomes.

The body of research reviewed in this section shows two important conclusions. First, the ability–achievement discrepancy, which was the core component of SLD identification for so long, proved to be untenable based on overwhelming empirical evidence. Second, the emerging literature on RTI as a replacement entitlement process—to improve outcomes for students with documented failure by providing high-quality instruction—appears to have substantial social validity.

SECTION TWO: ANALYSIS OF KEY FEDERAL LEGISLATION AND ITS IMPACT ON EFFECTIVE RTI-DRIVEN PRACTICES IN SERVING THE SLD SCHOOL POPULATION

The following topics are discussed in this section: (a) the legal foundations underlying response to intervention (RTI), (b) the No Child Left Behind Act, (c) the Individuals with Disabilities Education Act (IDEA 2004), (d) choices in SLD identification, (e) general education intervention and progress monitoring, (f) comprehensive evaluation, and (g) the role of cognitive testing in special education identification.

Legal Foundations Underlying Response to Intervention (RTI)

A number of legal provisions were established prior to 2000 in federal and state statutes and their accompanying regulations/rules that *could* have been and sometimes were interpreted as supporting RTI (e.g., ruling out lack of appropriate reading instruction as part of SLD entitlement). However, the most important developments have occurred since 2000, in part because of the convergence of research and its compelling evidence described earlier, dissatisfaction with some current service delivery items

(President's Commission on Excellence in Special Education, 2002), and evidence of successful practices in states such as Iowa and Pennsylvania. In this section, we discuss the resulting legal changes on educational systems and their impact on implementation of RTI both as an entitlement process for SLD and as a cornerstone for building scientifically based, multitiered early-intervening services over the next decade.

The No Child Left Behind Act

The No Child Left Behind Act of 2001 (NCLB), reauthorizing the Elementary and Secondary Education Act of 1965, arguably was the single most influential legal change that established the context for RTI as a broad label for the development of multitiered early-intervening services in educational programs in state and local education agencies. It also served as a critical component of the improvement actions in IDEA 2004. At its core, NCLB set forth three key provisions:

1. Annual yearly progress (AYP) requirements accompanied by sanctions for failure to meet goals.
2. Scientifically based research as the foundation for academic instruction and behavioral interventions.
3. Scientifically based reading instruction, including essential content and methods.

NCLB imposed greater accountability requirements for improved results on SEAs and LEAs through the AYP mechanism that was connected to markedly improved outcome goals or benchmarks to be achieved by 2013–2014. The exact AYP standards and assessments of progress are beyond the scope of this chapter; however, the emphasis on accountability and improved outcomes established an essential context within which RTI became highly relevant. Under these provisions, nearly all SEAs and LEAs were challenged to improve results for *all* students and for students in categories defined by race/ethnicity, language status, socioeconomic status, and disability status.

With NCLB, all students were included in the accountability provisions, including students with disabilities who had been previously excluded. In our experience, strong motivation to improve results is an essential component of the effective implementation of RTI principles. Absent the motivation to improve outcomes for all students, RTI as something more than SLD entitlement (i.e., multitiered early-intervening services) would be difficult to implement. The second major influence of the act on RTI was the commitment of Congress to *scientifically based instruction*, a phrase that appeared more than 180 times in the statute. To avoid any ambiguity, a definition of scientifically based was included in section 9101(37).

Recent documents from the U.S. Department of Education's Institute for Educational Sciences (IES) continue to emphasize randomized control trials as the method that yields results with the strongest scientific evidence to guide instruction. However, other research methodologies are recognized as useful when results are interpreted consistent with the limitations of the methodologies. Significantly for RTI, findings from single subject designs that apply rigorous methods and are replicated across subjects and investigators are recognized as establishing *experimental* evidence concerning effective interventions. There can be no doubt, however, about the commitment of Congress to prompting educators to implement the best scientific evidence as a cornerstone for service delivery for all students.

The endorsement of scientifically based reading instruction principles was the third major influence of NCLB on RTI. The act emphasizes teaching the essential components of reading derived from scientifically based research on instruction including *explicit and systematic instruction* (emphasis added) in phonemic awareness, phonics, vocabulary development, reading fluency including oral reading skills, and reading comprehension strategies as well as universal screening (NCLB section 1208). The emphasis on explicit and systematic instruction is added because many SEAs, institutions of higher education teacher preparation programs, and LEAs mention the five content components of reading without recognizing the critical feature of explicit and systematic instruction.

The importance of NCLB's emphasis on scientifically based reading (SBR) instruction is important to RTI for two reasons. First, SBR was later reinforced with clear and explicit language in IDEA 2004 such that a student could not be classified as having a disability if the determinant factor was lack of appropriate instruction in reading (i.e., SBR). Second, it established the need for SBR with all children and not just as a question first asked at the point of special education consideration for individual students. SBR would form the basis for the first tier of multitiered systems.

Systematic interventions to prevent behavior problems along with early identification treatment for problems that emerge later were not discussed extensively in NCLB. However, classroom behavior is mentioned in the requirements for applications from SEAs as states must provide:

> a description of how the local educational agency (LEA) will provide training to enable teachers to (A) teach and address the needs of students with different learning styles, particularly students with disabilities, students with special learning needs (including students who are gifted and talented), and students with limited English proficiency; and (B) improve student behavior in the classroom and identify early and appropriate interventions to help students described in subparagraph (A). (section 2122)

NCLB was a complex statute providing financial resources to SEAs and LEAs contingent on meeting several challenging requirements, including significantly improved results, implementation of scientifically based interventions, and implementing scientifically based reading instruction. These provisions fostered and established a positive context for RTI given the pervasive emphasis on evidence-based practices, progress monitoring with formative evaluation, and increasing intervention intensity based on children's needs.

Individuals with Disabilities Education Act (IDEA) of 2004

Congressional reauthorization of the Individuals with Disabilities Education Act (IDEA), signed into law on December 4, 2004, was designed *explicitly* to infuse the major NCLB principles into the education of students with disabilities. Explicit language integrates the two laws in the areas of (a) assessment, (b) AYP requirements, (c) highly qualified teachers, and, most important for RTI, (d) scientifically based instruction (34 C.F.R. 300.35) and especially so in reading (34 C.F.R. 300.306). Moreover, the requirements for eligibility, and not solely for SLD, either explicitly require or imply the use of RTI principles. Although IDEA's major RTI provisions are focused on the context of SLD eligibility determination, several have significant and broad implications for general education and for the services generally described as occurring at Tiers 1 and 2 in a multitiered early-intervening services system.

A critical congressional finding that appeared in an early section of IDEA 2004 endorsed school-wide literacy, positive behavior support (PBS), and prevention of disabilities (20 U.S.C. 1400.602(c)) and thereby implicitly endorsed RTI principles. The statute reads as follows:

> (5) Almost 30 years of research and experience has demonstrated that the education of children with disabilities can be made more effective by—

> (F) providing incentives for whole-school approaches, scientifically based early reading programs, positive behavioral interventions and supports, and early intervening services to reduce the need to label children as disabled in order to address the learning and behavioral needs of such children.

What drove RTI as a general label for multitiered, early intervening services appeared in the IDEA statute at section 614 b(6) in the context of SLD identification, as follows:

> a local educational agency shall not be required to take into consideration whether a child has a severe discrepancy between achievement and intellectual ability" (achievement areas listed), and "In determining whether a child has a specific learning disability, a local educational agency may use a process that determines if the child responds to scientific, research-based intervention.

In most discussions among professionals, the following phrase in the federal statute, "scientific, research-based intervention" is synonymous with response to intervention, although multiple meanings have been derived from it that sometimes confuse researchers and practitioners. The connection between RTI as a synonym for multitiered early-intervening services and the SLD eligibility process may not be obvious at first glance, but several factors lead to the connection.

First, research indicates that the most frequent reason for identification of SLD is poor reading skills (Donovan & Cross, 2002) and that many elementary classrooms do not provide the scientifically based reading instruction that can prevent reading difficulties (Lyon et al., 2001; Walsh, Glaser, & Wilcox, 2006).

Second, the *intent* of changing the SLD identification method was to foster a service delivery system that emphasizes prevention and both early identification and early intervention in general education through (a) universal screening beginning in kindergarten, (b) provision of scientifically based instruction, (c) increased instructional intensity, (d) measurement precision depending on children's needs and responses to instruction, and (e) decision making based on results. Although SLD identification is not specifically related to RTI implementation in general education, it does significantly promote RTI at these levels.

Further support for RTI as a multitiered early-intervening service delivery system versus use of RTI for the sole purpose of SLD entitlement comes from the IDEA statute and regulations regarding instruction in general education. Students cannot be identified as having a disability if there is a "lack of appropriate instruction in reading, including the essential components of reading instruction, or lack of appropriate instruction in math, or limited English proficiency" (34 C.F.R. 306). One obvious approach to answering the appropriate instruction question is whether 80–85% of students are on positive trajectories toward meeting state achievement standards, a criterion that is widely used in multitiered systems to determine the adequacy of the general education program.

Choices in SLD Identification

IDEA 2004 provides LEAs with a choice in how SLD is identified but also imposes some constraints according to the following IDEA regulation. The SEA:

> Must not require the use of a severe discrepancy between intellectual ability and achievement for determining whether a child has a specific learning disability; … must permit the use of a process based on the child's response to scientific, research-based intervention; and may permit the use of other alternative research-based procedures for determining whether a child has a specific learning disability. (34 C.F.R. 300.307)

The question at this point in the formulation of the regulations was whether SLD identification would be based only on RTI *plus* the other provisions about evaluations, or whether one or more alternative methods would be allowed. After intense lobbying from the testing industry, the final IDEA regulations permitted RTI plus a second option for SLD identification.

> The child does not make sufficient progress to meet age or State-approved grade-level standards in one or more of the areas identified in paragraph (a)(1) of this section when using a process based on the child's response to scientific, research-based intervention; or The child exhibits a pattern of strengths and

weaknesses in performance, achievement, or both, relative to age, State-approved grade-level standards, or intellectual development, that is determined by the group to be relevant to the identification of a specific learning disability, using appropriate assessments. (34 C.F.R. 300.309)

Two choices with many possible variations for SEA and LEA identification of SLD were established in the IDEA regulations and are being developed and implemented by the states. Consistent with trends over the last 30 years, a wide range of SEA SLD identification criteria are emerging (Reschly & Holdheide, 2009; Reschly & Hosp, 2004). To date, 40 of 50 states have completed SLD guidelines. A few states have prohibited use of the IQ–achievement discrepancy and have implemented RTI as the only approved method of SLD identification. Many other states permit RTI *or* a method of determining strengths and weaknesses, often quoting verbatim the regulation just cited. Some states require *both* for SLD eligibility; that is, RTI is required first, followed by an assessment of strengths and weaknesses over various and differing domains, such as intellectual ability, cognitive processes, psychological processes, and/or achievement areas. There is a clear trend since IDEA (2004, 2006) toward elimination of the ability–achievement severe discrepancy in SLD identification and toward using RTI as the principal method of SLD identification, but the magnitude of that trend is uncertain.

General Education Intervention and Progress Monitoring

The single most important IDEA 2004 provision regarding RTI as a coordinated early-intervening services approach is, in our opinion, the requirement that prior to or during referral to determine SLD eligibility, LEAs must provide the following:

> Data that demonstrate that prior to, or as a part of, the referral process, the child was provided appropriate instruction in regular education settings, delivered by qualified personnel; and (2) Data-based documentation of repeated assessments of achievement at reasonable intervals, reflecting formal assessment of student progress during instruction, which was provided to the child's parents. (34 C.F.R. 300.304–300.306)

These legal requirements mandate that appropriate instruction be provided to *all* students and, most important, that monitoring the progress of general education instruction be implemented as a standard practice. The latter provision is crucial to improved outcomes for all students and to implementation of progress monitoring for them and is a critical component of RTI in general education. All states that have revised their SLD identification criteria since 2004 have incorporated these criteria, and some have established guidelines regarding the number of progress monitoring assessments, the minimum time period, and the frequency of reports to parents (Reschly & Holdheide, 2009).

Although the general education progress reporting and parent reporting language applies only to SLD identification, we believe it will (and should) apply to all students in general education classrooms, particularly should they be referred for learning and behavior problems. The reasoning is twofold. First, formative evaluation (i.e., progress monitoring *during* instruction) is a component of effective instruction and should not occur only after a student is considered to be failing—no more than monitoring of blood pressure would occur only after a heart attack. Progress monitoring should be a component of positive and preventive practices. Second, *prior to or during a referral* it is impossible to know which disability category, if any, is appropriate for the student. It is only *after* the comprehensive evaluation is conducted and the multidisciplinary team meets with the parents to discuss results and educational needs that the category of disability can be determined. Hence, this requirement applies to all students referred from general education classrooms *regardless* of eligibility.

Comprehensive Evaluation

One of the most controversial issues in school psychology is whether the types of data collected during the RTI SLD entitlement process (e.g., documentation that the intervention has been implemented with fidelity, is scientifically based, and is evaluated using scientifically based progress monitoring methods) by themselves meet the legal requirements for the "full and individual evaluation" required for all students prior to the determination of special education eligibility and placements (34 C.F.R. 300.301). In our view, these types of RTI data alone clearly do not meet the "full and individual evaluation" requirement. The question remains as to what is required beyond these RTI data. The answer depends, in part, on whether the SEA uses a categorical system of eligibility, as most do, or a noncategorical system (e.g., Iowa). A critical IDEA regulation, unchanged since 1977, specifies:

> The child is assessed in all areas related to the suspected disability including, if appropriate, health, vision, hearing, social and emotional status, general intelligence, academic performance, communication status, and motor abilities. (34 C. F. R. 300.304)

This and other regulations suggest that extensive information, collected across multiple domains, should be gathered and considered in determining disability eligibility, educational needs, and special education placement. Significantly, this legal requirement allows *professional judgment* about the domains to be assessed. The regulation does not say to assess in *all* the areas listed; rather, it contains the qualification "if appropriate." The regulation should be interpreted as requiring consideration of many domains (perhaps 12 or more) through screening, followed by, when appropriate, in-depth assessment within specific domains (Reschly, 2008; Reschly & Bergstrom, 2009). The sequence of events should be *screening* for possible educationally related deficits in all domains, followed by (if a possible deficit is suspected) in-depth assessment and determination of its possible relationship to educational performance. Obviously, if screening indicates a low probability of an educationally related deficit, then in-depth assessment is wasteful and irrelevant to the goals of the evaluation.

The 12 domains in which screening should occur for all children and youth are health, vision, hearing, general intellectual functioning, reading, math, written language, adaptive behavior, communication, behavior, emotional regulation, and motor. To reiterate, in-depth assessment is needed *only* in those domains in which screening indicates possible educationally related deficits. This approach is illustrated in Table 1 for 4 of the 12 domains (Reschly, 2008).

The four domains of health status, reading, adaptive behavior, and intelligence are listed in Table 1 from the possible 12 or more domains in which screening should occur, followed by, if appropriate, in-depth assessment. For example, the school entrance physical examination, teacher observations, and nurse records and notes are sufficient for nearly all students to be screened for an educationally related health

Table 1. **Comprehensive Evaluation From Screening to In-Depth Assessment**

Domain	Screening Information: Is there a potential deficit?	In-Depth Assessment: Does an educationally related deficit exist?	Outcome
Health Status	Physical exam records. Teacher and nurse observations. Possible deficit? If no, stop. If yes, proceed to in-depth assessment.	Medical evaluation. If deficit(s) identified, consider medical treatment and educational implications.	Special education eligibility and placement if needed.
Reading	Group achievement tests, daily work, teacher records. If no, stop. If yes, proceed to in-depth assessment	Formal and informal diagnostic reading assessments, CBM in reading to determine progress.	Tier 2 interventions and possible special education and placement.
Adaptive Behavior	Teacher and parent observations and interview with brief screening measures. If no, stop. If yes, proceed to in-depth assessment.	Formal adaptive behavior measures supplemented by systematic observations and skills/competencies analysis.	Adaptive behavior interventions. Consideration of mental retardation eligibility and special education eligibility.
Intelligence	Achievement test results, teacher observations, and adaptive behavior screening results. If no evidence of mental retardation, stop. If mental retardation possible, proceed to in-depth assessment.	Administration of a comprehensive test of general intellectual functioning, interpreted appropriately.	Determination of mental retardation eligibility on the intelligence dimension. Consideration of special education eligibility and placement.

Note. From "School Psychology RTI Paradigm Shift and Beyond," by D. Reschly, 2008, in A. Thomas & J. Grimes (Eds.), *Best Practices in School Psychology V* (p. 12). Bethesda, MD: National Association of School Psychologists. Copyright 2008 by the National Association of School Psychologists. Reprinted with permission.

deficit. However, consider the situation of a student observed by the teacher to have higher rates than most students of needing to go to the restroom, being thirsty, and/or having variations in energy level. These are signs of a possible diabetic condition that, if untreated, could negatively affect educational performance. The screening information just described is not, of course, sufficient for a diagnosis. Given this screening information, the situation requires an in-depth assessment using a specialized medical evaluation. Similar reasoning applies to all other areas. For example, consider a student referred because of behavioral issues; school records and teacher classroom ratings indicate that the student reads at or above national age norms. This student does not, of course, need an in-depth, diagnostic reading assessment. A first-step screening process, followed by a more in-depth assessment when screening cannot answer the assessment question, is the basis for good educational decisions and is consistent with federal legal requirements under IDEA.

The Role of Cognitive Testing

The practice of routinely administering an individual general cognitive ability measure to children referred for special education should be reconsidered (Fletcher, Coulter, Reschly, & Vaughn, 2004; Fletcher et al., 2007; Fletcher & Reschly, 2005; Reschly, 2004). First, the ability–achievement discrepancy that required a cognitive ability test for SLD identification is no longer required. RTI is allowed by states as a means to determine SLD eligibility. If IQ–achievement discrepancy scores, and thus cognitive ability or processing scores, are no longer required because of a preference for SLD identification based on RTI, the next issue is the need for general cognitive ability assessment in any disability determination. If RTI is used in a categorical disability system, all students should be screened for significant, educationally related cognitive deficits through examination of group achievement test results, samples of academic work, and teacher ratings. If the information from these sources suggests cognitive performance is at a significantly below-average level, then, and only then, are cognitive ability measures relevant to educational decision making in the category of mental retardation. Cognitive ability tests and the largely parallel tests of hypothetical cognitive processes are useful in these circumstances to rule out mild mental retardation as a disability and as an exclusion factor in the diagnosis of specific learning disability (SLD). It is estimated that adoption of RTI in the identification of disabilities, especially SLD, would reduce IQ testing in schools by approximately 90% (Marston, 2002; Reschly, 2005).

Although RTI appears in IDEA primarily in the context of SLD identification, several specific provisions have significant implications for general education and the development and implementation of a multitiered early-intervening services system. The requirements concerning implementation of scientifically based instruction and progress monitoring are particularly important in establishing RTI in general education contexts. Decisions by SEAs and LEA practitioners about SLD identification and the necessary components of the full and individual evaluation requirement will further influence RTI expansion in general and special education. Clearly the legal context exists to markedly increase RTI in general and special education.

SECTION THREE: RTI PRACTICE PERSPECTIVES RESULTING FROM SUCCESSFUL IMPLEMENTATION OF A MULTITIERED EARLY-INTERVENING SERVICES MODEL

This chapter has made the case that the shift to a multitiered, early intervening services model that focuses on prevention and employs scientifically based practices is not a new concept, either from a research or legal perspective. What is also worth noting is that practices consistent with this concept have been implemented in schools and school districts since the late 1970s. As noted in the foreword to this book, current school improvement and service delivery efforts were a logical extension of a number of convergent societal efforts to improve schools through educational and psychological research. One such societal effort was the civil rights movement as reflected in federal legislation. Another civil rights effort was driven by a research perspective to investigate what worked to improve educational outcomes with poor children through Project Follow Through. The project, which ran from 1968 to 1977, is the largest educational research initiative ever conducted in American history. It compared a variety of programs designed to increase achievement for students from very low-income backgrounds. Results showed that only 2 of the 22 models evaluated, direct instruction (DI) and applied behavior analysis (ABA), produced consistent and positive results, with the DI model generating the most powerful effect sizes (Becker, 1977). This research showed that schools with large numbers of students at high risk for school failure could be improved using scientifically based practices.

The remainder of this section discusses the critical role of translating research into effective practices in the effort to improve schooling for all students. The following topics are discussed in this regard: (a) tracking the evolution of evidence-based practices applied in school contexts, (b) putting it together—first efforts, and (c) expanding efforts to statewide implementation.

Tracking the Evolution of Evidence-Based Practices Applied in School Contexts

Beginning in the late 1960s and early 1970s, there was a major national effort in the field of applied psychology and the experimental analysis of behavior to translate basic psychological science into effective techniques that could positively affect children, youth, and adults having a variety of societal problems, including mental retardation (Lindsley, 1964). Promising empirical work in the 1960s led to the promotion of a specific discipline to translate science into practice. Applied behavior analysis (ABA; Baer, Wolf, & Risley, 1968) offered the following vision: "A society willing to consider a technology of its own behavior apparently is likely to support that application when it deals with socially important behaviors, such as retardation, crime, mental illness, and education" (p. 91).

By the early 1970s, these applications—having the critical features of *careful environmental analysis* (at the level of individuals rather than groups) and *use of graphed time-series data*—had proliferated, especially around applications to social behavior and families (Becker, 1971b, 1971c; Becker & Thomas, 1971; Bijou, 1970). In education, the field of "precision teaching" evolved from this same set of principles (Branfield, 1970), with an emphasis on a learning hierarchy having a cornerstone of behavioral fluency and use of semi-logarithmic standard six-cycle or "celeration" charts (White & Haring, 1980). Pursuing a similar tact, but with an emphasis on more global or general outcome measures than discrete behaviors, and using equal interval charts versus celeration charts, Stanley Deno began working with special education teachers in 1971 at Seward School in Minneapolis to assess student academic progress or response to instruction.

As a result of these early efforts to translate science into practice and infuse them into service delivery systems, a set of philosophical commonalities emerged. First and foremost was an overarching sense of optimism that applications of science to educational practice, especially early in students' education, could not only remediate but potentially *prevent* problems. Another important philosophical principle was a sense that seeing the "problem" as *solely* within the student was not productive and more likely was counterproductive. In a paper first presented to school psychologists in 1971, and reproduced in the preface to the first and second editions of this book, Wesley C. Becker (1971a, 1991) put forth the following premise:

> Many current problems in education can be traced to practices, presumably derived from psychological research, which have had the effect of encouraging teachers to get rid of their teaching failures rather than learning to deal with them. Many of these doubtful practices center around the use of tests to "diagnose problems" and make recommendations on placement in special classes, treatment programs, the grouping of slow and fast learners, or grouping on the basis of readiness tests. Historically, many of these practices were generated from the application of a medical model to problems in clinical psychology which was subsequently transferred to educational problems. The basic idea was that if a child is failing to learn or behave appropriately in school, there is something wrong with the child. (1991, p. xxix)

The foundational principle derived from this reformulation was that it was *not* the underlying diagnosis that needed to be the focus of school action. Rather, it was the problem behavior and its intended *intervention* that were to be the focus. Potentially deep-seated causes (e.g., disabilities) of the problem were not viewed as the first and only assessment effort initiated (Reynolds & Birch, 1977); instead, efforts should be directed toward "diagnosing" the instruction or intervention being provided (Engelmann, Granzin, & Severson, 1979).

Putting It Together—First Efforts

In 1977, a comprehensive model for implementing a service delivery system based on many of the aforementioned methodological and philosophical principles was presented in a manual written by Stanley Deno and Phyllis Mirkin and published by the Council for Exceptional Children (Deno & Mirkin, 1977). *Data-Based Program Modification (DBPM): A Manual* described how schools can identify, intervene, and evaluate problems in school-age youth. At the core of the DBPM manual was a scientifically based data system that ultimately became known as curriculum-based measurement (CBM), in which each student's educational need was measured using a performance discrepancy compared with a norm of data-based expectations; progress was monitored frequently over time and was graphed relative to an a priori baseline of expected progress.

Shortly after, Gary Germann, working with Deno and Mirkin, began putting into practice his vision of DBPM in the Pine County Special Education Cooperative, in central Minnesota. By 1979, in the Pine County model, school psychologists no longer routinely administered ability tests as part of special education entitlement. It was the *performance discrepancy* that determined the need for special education. It was the *reduction* of the performance discrepancy that determined whether any intervention, including special education, was to be judged effective. In the Pine County model, the emphasis shifted from identifying disabilities to identifying effective interventions. For school psychologists, their primary role changed to that of consultants working with teachers and parents to reduce the discrepancy, not just identify it. Frequent monitoring of basic skills progress with particular attention to students' Individualized Education Program plan objectives became routine, rather than unusual. The Pine County model became *the* model of practice, and within a relatively few years, was described in a number of professional research reports (Tindal, Germann, & Deno, 1983; Tindal, Germann, Marston, & Deno, 1983), book chapters (Tindal, Wesson, Deno, Germann, & Mirkin, 1985), and journal articles (Germann & Tindal, 1985; Tindal & Germann, 1985).

In 1980, St. Paul Public Schools began their own implementation of DBPM and the Pine County model. A "discrepancy ratio" was used to screen referred students with limited English proficiency who were believed by teachers to need more intensive intervention. Progress for those students who received additional intervention was monitored frequently (i.e., once per week). In 1982, Minneapolis Public Schools moved toward large-scale implementation of the Pine County model, with 40 large elementary and middle schools in a diverse, urban school district. Efforts began with the adoption of the priority for CBM-based IEP goals and frequent progress monitoring. Complementing the progress monitoring process was the implementation of a cohesive and focused database for decision making, which involved the development of local norms for use in the contexts of special education referral screening, entitlement, and annual review decisions. Much of this work was summarized in the professional literature of the 1980s (see, e.g., Deno, Marston,

Shinn, & Tindal, 1983; Marston & Magnusson, 1985, 1988; and Shinn & Marston, 1985).

Expansion of Efforts to Statewide Implementation

Interest in how the DBPM manual was implemented through the Pine County model, and in school districts such as Minneapolis Public Schools, quickly attracted the attention of others schools and states across the nation. Most notably, a team of state leaders from Iowa, including Jeff Grimes and Dan Reschly, immediately tied in elements of its implementation into their state staff development project, Re-AIMs, which was designed to support and enhance behavioral consultation efforts in Iowa schools. Some of these early efforts are described in Ikeda, Tilly, Stumme, Volmer, and Allison (1996) and Reschly and Grimes (1991). Within a decade, Iowa's interest led to the Renewed Service Delivery System (RSDS), which culminated in statewide adoption of an early intervening, problem-solving service delivery system that was needs-based, data-driven, and noncategorical. Reschly, Tilly, and Grimes (1999) and Tilly, Reschly, and Grimes (1999) give excellent examples of how schools transitioned to the types of service delivery systems described in this book.

During the same period, a number of other important state initiatives, based on these promising practices, began in a number of communities and states. Among the most visible efforts were those of the Instructional Support Teams (ISTs) in Pennsylvania (Kovaleski, Gickling, Morrow, & Swank, 1999; Kovaleski, Tucker, & Stevens, 1996) and the Flexible Service Delivery System (FSDS) in Illinois (Peterson, Swerdlik, Prasse, & Shinn, 2007). However, these states and communities were not the only sites implementing services to all students within a preventive and data-driven approach. It was the widespread number of sites and the outcomes produced that enabled groups like the President's Commission on Excellence in Special Education (2002) to list successful practice and demonstration sites in their recommendations.

SUMMARY

In this chapter, we have tried to communicate that generically labeled RTI is not simply an SLD entitlement process. Rather, in a broader sense, RTI builds multitiered educational systems based on some very important foundational principles such as (a) early intervening services, (b) use of scientifically based practices, (c) a focus on use of data for identifying problems and evaluating their solutions, and (d) employing a more ecological approach in which environmental variables are targeted as agents of effecting change. We have tried to present an overarching historical perspective from the respective vantage points of research, law, and practice that have brought America to the point at which our nation is embarking on the most organized and proactive school improvement planning in decades.

Early in this chapter, we attempted to make a distinction between two interpretations of the term RTI, that is, first as an SLD eligibility process, and second, as a generic label for a variety of approaches to the implementation of multitiered early-intervening services. The core content of this chapter rests upon a brief recounting of the research history and legal perspectives around SLD identification. However, we would be remiss if we didn't also address the broader use of the RTI rubric as a school improvement process. The elements embedded within RTI, as a broad label for multi-tiered, early intervening services (e.g., routine universal screening, progress monitoring of key performance indicators), do not necessarily constitute a new framework or innovation in other fields of practice.

The field of medicine provides a useful example of how physicians utilize RTI concepts in their everyday practice to treat health problems. Physicians assess weight, blood pressure, and heart rate (i.e., performance indicators) each time they see a patient (screening), because measurement of these three indicators provide important "signs" of one's general physical health. These performance indicators have scientifically established benchmarks for both typical and atypical functioning and can determine whether changes in these status indicators are important for intervention. If weight and blood pressure indicators, for instance, exceed benchmark criteria, then a physician may recommend that the patient diet, exercise, and quit smoking. The next time the patient sees the physician, these same indicators are again measured; if the indicators still show no change (improvement), the physician may place the patient on a special diet and exercise regimen and tell him or her to stop smoking. The next time the patient sees the physician, these indicators are measured yet again, and if they still show no change, the physician may put the patient on medication, refer the patient to a dietician, and/or send the patient to a smoking cessation clinic. Finally, the next time the physician sees the patient, if the same indicator data are in the atypical range, then upon further assessment, the patient may need a more intensive intervention (e.g., surgery) to prevent death.

Several important points should be considered in this example. First, interventions received by any person are developed based on a discrepancy of some sort in the performance indicators being monitored. Second, the intervention intensity is increased only after the indicator data suggest that the patient shows an inadequate response to intervention. Third, treatment decisions are based on objective data collected continuously over time (data-based decision making). Fourth, the data that are collected are well-established indicators of general physical health. Finally, decisions about treatment intensity are based on the collection of more and more data as the patient is moved through each stage of treatment intensification. RTI can and should be used in schools in a parallel manner to make important educational decisions for children and youth.

REFERENCES

Algozzine, B., & Ysseldyke, J. E. (1987). Questioning discrepancies: Retaking the first step 20 years later. *Learning Disability Quarterly, 11,* 307–318.

Algozzine, B., Ysseldyke, J., & Shinn, M. R. (1982). Identifying children with learning disabilities: When is a discrepancy severe? *Journal of School Psychology, 20,* 299–305.

Baer, D. M., Wolf, M., & Risley, T. R. (1968). Some current dimensions of applied behavior analysis. *Journal of Applied Behavior Analysis, 1,* 91–97.

Becker, W. C. (1971a). *New roles for school psychologists.* Paper presented at the Role of the School Psychologist Conference, Florida State University, Tallahassee.

Becker, W. C. (1971b). *Parents are teachers.* Champaign, IL: Research Press.

Becker, W. C. (Ed.). (1971c). *An empirical basis for change in education.* Chicago: SRA.

Becker, W. C. (1977). Teaching reading and language to the disadvantaged: What we have learned from field research. *Harvard Educational Review, 47,* 518–543.

Becker, W. C. (1991). Foreword. In G. Stoner, M. R. Shinn, & H. M. Walker (Eds.), *Interventions for achievement and behavior problems* (pp. xix–xx). Bethesda, MD: National Association of School Psychologists.

Becker, W. C., & Thomas, D. R. (1971). *Teaching 1: A course in applied psychology.* Chicago: SRA.

Bijou, S. W. (1970). What psychology has to offer education—Now. *Journal of Applied Behavior Analysis, 3,* 65–71.

Bocian, K., Beebe, M., MacMillan, D., & Gresham, F. M. (1999). Competing paradigms in learning disabilities classification by schools and variations in the meaning of discrepant achievement. *Learning Disabilities Research and Practice, 14,* 1–14.

Branfield, R. H. (1970). Precision teaching: A useful technology for special education teachers. *Educational Technology, 10*(8), 22–26.

Cone, J. (1989). Is there utility for treatment utility? *American Psychologist, 44,* 1241–1242.

Cronbach, L. (1975). Beyond two disciplines of scientific psychology. *American Psychologist, 30,* 116–127.

Deno, S. L., & Mirkin, P. (1977). *Data-based program modification: A manual.* Reston, VA: Council for Exceptional Children.

Deno, S. L., Marston, D., Shinn, M. R., & Tindal, G. (1983). Oral reading fluency: A simple datum for scaling reading disability. *Topics in Learning and Learning Disability, 2,* 53–59.

Detrich, R., Keyworth, R., & States, J. (2008). *Advances in evidence-based education: A roadmap to evidence-based education.* Oakland, CA: Wing Institute.

Donovan, M. S., & Cross, C. T. (2002). *Minority students in special and gifted education.* Washington, DC: National Academy Press.

Education for All Handicapped Children Act of 1975. Pub. L. 94–142 (1975).

Elementary and Secondary Education Act (No Child Left Behind). Pub. L. 107–110 (Jan. 8, 2002).

Engelmann, S., Granzin, A., & Severson, H. (1979). Diagnosing instruction. *Journal of Special Education, 13,* 355–363.

Fletcher, J. M., Coulter, W. A., Reschly, D. J., & Vaughn, S. (2004). Alternative approaches to the definition and identification of learning disabilities: Some questions and answers. *Annals of Dyslexia, 54,* 304–331.

Fletcher, J. M., Lyon, G. R., Fuchs, L. S., & Barnes, M. A. (2007). *Learning disabilities: From identification to intervention.* New York: Guilford Press.

Fletcher, J. M., & Reschly, D. J. (2005). Changing procedures for identifying learning disabilities: The danger of perpetuating old ideas. *School Psychologist, 59,* 10–15.

Fuchs, D., Fuchs, L. S., Mathes, P. G., Lipsey, M. E., & Eaton, S. (2000). A meta-analysis of reading differences between underachievers with and without the learning disabilities label: A brief report. *Learning Disabilities: A Multidisciplinary Journal, 10*(1), 1–3.

Fuchs, D., Fuchs, L., Mathes, P., Lipsey, M., & Roberts, H. (2002). Is "learning disabilities" just a fancy term for low achievement? A meta-analysis of reading differences between low achievers with and without the label. In R. Bradley, L. Danielson, & D. Hallahan (Eds.), *Identification of learning disabilities: Research to practice* (pp. 737–762). Mahwah, NJ: Erlbaum.

Fuchs, L., & Fuchs, D. (1998). Treatment validity: A unifying concept for reconceptualizing the identification of learning disabilities. *Learning Disabilities Research and Practice, 13,* 204–219.

Fuchs, L. S., & Vaughn, S. R. (2005). Response to intervention as a framework for the identification of learning disabilities. *Forum for Trainers of School Psychologists*, Spring, 12–19.

Germann, G., & Tindal, G. (1985). Applications of direct and repeated measurement using curriculum-based assessment. *Exceptional Children, 51,* 110–121.

Gresham, F. M. (2002). Responsiveness to intervention: An alternative approach to the identification of learning disabilities. In R. Bradley, L. Danielson, & D. Hallahan (Eds.), *Identification of learning disabilities: Research to practice* (pp. 467–519). Mahwah, NJ: Erlbaum.

Gresham, F. M., MacMillan, D. L., & Bocian, B. (1996). Learning disabilities, low achievement, and mild mental retardation: More alike than different? *Journal of Learning Disabilities, 29,* 570–581.

Gresham, F. M., & Witt, J. C. (1997). Utility of intelligence tests for treatment planning, classification, and placement decisions: Recent empirical findings and future directions. *School Psychology Quarterly, 12,* 249–267.

Grimes, J. (1981). Shaping the future of school psychology. *School Psychology Review, 10,* 206–231.

Hale, J. B., Kaufman, A., Naglieri, J., & Kavale, K. (2006). Implementation of IDEA: Integrating response to intervention and cognitive assessment methods. *Psychology in the Schools, 43,* 753–770.

Hale, J. B., Naglieri, J. A., Kaufman, A. S., & Kavale, K. A. (2004). Specific learning disability classification in the new Individuals with Disabilities Education Act: The danger of good ideas. *School Psychologist, 58,* 6–13.

Hayes, S., Nelson, R., & Jarrett, R. (1987). The treatment utility of assessment: A functional approach to evaluating assessment quality. *American Psychologist, 42,* 963–974.

Hoskyn, M., & Swanson, H. L. (2000). Cognitive processing of low achievers and children with reading disabilities: A selective meta-analytic review of the published literature. *School Psychology Review, 29,* 102–119.

Jenkins, J., Hudson, R., & Johnson, E. (2007). Screening for at-risk readers in a response to intervention framework. *School Psychology Review, 36,* 582–600.

Ikeda, M. J., Tilly, W. D., III, Stumme, D., Volmer, L., & Allison, R. (1996). Agency-wide implementation of problem solving consultation: Foundations, current implementation, and future directions. *School Psychology Quarterly, 11,* 228–243.

Individuals with Disabilities Education Act of 2004, 20 U.S.C. §1400 *et seq,* and Assistance to States for the Education of Children with Disabilities and Preschool Grants for Children with Disabilities; Final Rule, 71 Fed. Reg. 46540 (Aug. 14, 2006).

Kavale, K. A., Kauffman, J. M., Bachmeier, R. J., & LeFever, G. B. (2008). Response to intervention: Separating the rhetoric of self-congratulation from the reality of specific learning disability identification. *Learning Disability Quarterly, 31,* 135–150.

Kovaleski, J. F., Gickling, E. E., Morrow, H., & Swank, H. (1999). High versus low implementation of instructional support teams: A case for maintaining program fidelity. *Remedial and Special Education, 20,* 170–183.

Kovaleski, J. F., Tucker, J. A., & Stevens, L. J. (1996). Bridging special and regular education: The Pennsylvania Initiative. *Educational Leadership, 53,* 44–47.

Lindsley, O. R. (1964). Direct measurement and prosthesis of retarded behavior. *Journal of Education, 147,* 47–49.

Lyon, G. R., Fletcher, J. M., Shaywitz, S. E., Shaywitz, B. A., Wood, F. B., Schulte, A., et al. (2001). Rethinking learning disabilities. In C. E. Finn Jr., A. J. Rotherham, & C. R. Hokanson Jr. (Eds.), *Rethinking special education for a new century* (pp. 259–287). Washington, DC: Thomas B. Fordham Foundation and Progressive Policy Institute.

MacMillan, D., Gresham, F. M., & Bocian, K. (1998). Discrepancy between definitions of learning disabilities and school practices: An empirical investigation. *Journal of Learning Disabilities, 31,* 314–326.

MacMillan, D., Gresham, F. M., Siperstein, G., & Bocian, K. (1996). The labyrinth of IDEA: School decisions on referred students with subaverage general intelligence. *American Journal on Mental Retardation, 101,* 161–174.

Marston, D. (2002). A functional and intervention-based assessment approach to establishing discrepancy for students with learning disabilities. In R. Bradley, L. Danielson, & D. P. Hallahan (Eds.), *Identification of learning disabilities: Research to practice* (pp. 437–447). Mahwah, NJ: Erlbaum.

Marston, D., & Magnusson, D. (1985). Implementing curriculum-based measurement in special and regular education settings. *Exceptional Children, 52,* 266–276.

Marston, D., & Magnusson, D. (1988). Curriculum-based assessment: District-level implementation. In J. Graden, J. Zins, & M. Curtis (Eds.), *Alternative educational delivery systems: Enhancing instructional options for all students* (pp. 137–172). Washington, DC: National Association of School Psychologists.

Meehl, P., & Rosen, A. (1955). Antecedent probability and the efficiency of psychometric signs, patterns, or cutting scores. *Psychological Bulletin, 55,* 194–216.

Merrell, K. & Buchanan, R. (2006). Intervention selection in school-based practice: Using public health models to enhance systems capacity of schools. *School Psychology Review, 35,* 167–180.

Messick, S. (1995). Validity of psychological assessment: Validation of inferences from person's responses and performances as scientific inquiry into score meaning. *American Psychologist, 50,* 741–749.

National Reading Panel. (2000). *Report of the National Reading Panel: Teaching children to read: An evidence-based assessment of the scientific research literature on reading and its implications for reading instruction.* Washington, DC: National Institute of Child Health and Human Development. http://www.nichd.nih.gov/publications/nrp/smallbook.pdf

No Child Left Behind Act of 2001. Pub. L. 107-110, 115 Stat. 1425 (2002).

Perfetti, C., Beck, I., Bell, L., & Hughes, C. (1987). Phonemic knowledge and learning to read are reciprocal: A longitudinal study of first grade children. *Merrill-Palmer Quarterly, 33,* 283–319.

Pericola Case, L., Speece, D. L., & Eddy Molloy, D. (2003). The validity of response-to-instruction paradigm to identify reading disabilities: A longitudinal analysis of individual differences and context factors. *School Psychology Review, 32,* 557–582.

Peterson, D. L., Swerdlik, M., Prasse, D., & Shinn, M. R. (2007). Flexible service delivery systems: A history of problem-solving in Illinois. In S. Jimerson (Ed.), *Handbook of response to intervention.* New York: Guilford Press.

Peterson, K. M., & Shinn, M. R. (2002). Severe discrepancy models: Which best explains school identification practices for learning disabilities? *School Psychology Review, 31,* 459–476.

President's Commission on Excellence in Special Education. (2002). *A new era: Revitalizing special education for children and their families.* Washington, DC: Author.

Reschly, D. J. (2004). Paradigm shift, outcomes criteria, and behavioral interventions: Foundations for the future of school psychology. *School Psychology Review, 33,* 408–416.

Reschly, D. J. (2005). LD identification: Primary intervention, secondary intervention, then what? *Journal of Learning Disabilities, 38,* 510–515.

Reschly, D. J. (2008). School psychology RTI paradigm shift and beyond. In A. Thomas & J. Grimes (Eds.), *Best practices in school psychology V* (pp. 3–15). Bethesda, MD: National Association of School Psychologists.

Reschly, D. J., & Bergstrom, M. K. (2009). Response to intervention. In T. B. Gutkin, & C. R. Reynolds (Eds.), *The handbook of school psychology* (4th ed., pp. 434–460). New York: Wiley.

Reschly, D. J., & Grimes, J. P. (1991). State department and university cooperation: Evaluation of continuing education and consultation and curriculum-based assessment. *School Psychology Review, 20,* 522–529.

Reschly, D. J., & Holdheide, L. R. (2009). Post-IDEA (2004) state SLD identification: Response to interventions effects. Nashville, TN: Vanderbilt University. Manuscript in preparation.

Reschly, D. J., & Hosp, J. L. (2004). State SLD policies and practices. *Learning Disability Quarterly, 27,* 197–213.

Reschly, D., Tilly, W. D., III, & Grimes, J. (Eds.). (1999). *Special education in transition.* Longwood, CO: Sopris West.

Reynolds, M. C., & Birch, J. W. (1977). *Teaching exceptional children in all America's schools.* Reston, VA: Council for Exceptional Children.

Share, D., McGee, R., & Silva, P. (1989). IQ and reading progress: A test of the capacity notion of IQ. *Journal of the American Academy of Child and Adolescent Psychiatry, 28,* 97–100.

Shaywitz, S., Escobar, M., Shaywitz, B., Fletcher, J., & Makuch, R. (1992). Distribution and temporal stability of dyslexia in an epidemiological sample of 414 children followed longitudinally. *New England Journal of Medicine, 326,* 145–150.

Shinn, M. R. (2007). Identifying students at risk, monitoring performance, and determining eligibility within response to intervention: Research on educational need and benefit from academic intervention. *School Psychology Review, 36,* 601–617.

Shinn, M. R., & Marston, D. (1985). Differentiating mildly handicapped, low-achieving and regular education students: A curriculum-based approach. *Remedial and Special Education, 6,* 31–45.

Shinn, M. R., Tindal, G., & Spira, D. (1987). Special education referrals as an index of teacher tolerance: Are teachers imperfect tests. *Exceptional Children, 54,* 32–40.

Shinn, M. R., Tindal, G., Spira, D., & Marston, D. (1987). Practice of learning disabilities as social policy. *Learning Disability Quarterly, 10,* 17–28.

Shinn, M. R., Tindal, G., & Stein, S. (1988). Curriculum-based assessment and the identification of mildly handicapped students: A research review. *Professional School Psychology, 3,* 69–85.

Shinn, M. R., Ysseldyke, J., Deno, S. L., & Tindal, G. (1986). A comparison of differences between students labeled learning disabled and low achieving on measures of classroom performance. *Journal of Learning Disabilities, 19,* 545–552.

Snow, C. E., Burns, M. S., & Griffin, P. (Eds.). (1998). *Preventing reading difficulties in young children.* Washington, DC: National Academy Press.

Speece, D. L., Pericola Case, L., & Eddy Molloy, D. (2003). Responsiveness to general education instruction as the first gate to learning disabilities identification. *Learning Disabilities Research and Practice, 18,* 147–156.

Stanovich, K., & Siegel, L. (1994). Phenotypic performance profiles of children with reading disabilities: A regression-based test of the phonological-core variable differences model. *Journal of Educational Psychology, 86,* 24–53.

Steubing, K., Fletcher, J., LeDoux, J., Lyon, G. R., Shaywitz, S., & Shaywitz, B. (2002). Validity of IQ-achievement discrepancy classification in reading disabilities: A meta-analysis. *American Educational Research Journal, 39,* 469–518.

Tilly, W. D., III, Reschly, D. J., & Grimes, J. (1999). Disability determination in problem-solving systems: Conceptual foundations and critical components. In D. J. Reschly, W. D. Tilly, III, & J. P. Grimes (Eds.), *Special education in transition: Functional assessment and noncategorical programming* (pp. 221–254). Longmont, CO: Sopris West.

Tindal, G., & Germann, G. (1985). Models of direct measurement in the determination of eligibility, monitoring of student progress, and the evaluation of program effects. *British Columbia Journal of Special Education, 9,* 365–382.

Tindal, G. A., Germann, G., & Deno, S. L. (1983). *Descriptive research on the Pine County norms: A compilation of findings* (No. 132). Minneapolis, MN: University of Minnesota, Institute for Research on Learning Disabilities.

Tindal, G. A., Germann, G., Marston, D., & Deno, S. L. (1983). *The effectiveness of special education: A direct measurement approach* (No. 123). Minneapolis, MN: University of Minnesota, Institute for Research on Learning Disabilities.

Tindal, G. A., Wesson, C., Deno, S. L., Germann, G., & Mirkin, P. (1985). The Pine County model for special education delivery: A data-based system. In T. Kratochwill (Ed.), *Advances in school psychology* (Vol. IV, pp. 223–250). Hillsdale, NJ: Erlbaum.

Torgesen, J. (1999). Phonologically based reading disabilities: Toward a coherent theory of one kind of learning disability. In R. Sternberg & L. Spear-Swerling (Eds.), *Perspectives on learning disabilities* (pp. 231–262). New Haven, CT: Westview Press.

Torgesen, J., & Burgess, S. (1998). Consistency of reading-related phonological processes throughout early childhood: Evidence from longitudinal-correlational and instructional studies. In J. Metsala & L. Ehri (Eds.), *Word recognition in beginning reading* (pp. 161–188). Hillsdale, NJ: Erlbaum.

Torgesen, J., Burgess, S., & Rashotte, C. (1996, April). *Predicting phonologically based reading disabilities: What is gained by waiting a year?* Paper presented at the annual meeting of the Society for the Scientific Study of Reading, New York.

Vaughn, S., & Fuchs, L. (2003). Redefining learning disabilities as inadequate response to instruction: The promise and potential problems. *Learning Disabilities Research and Practice, 18,* 137–146.

Vellutino, F., Scanlon, D., & Lyon, G. R. (2000). Differentiating between difficult-to-remediate and readily remediated poor readers: More evidence against the IQ-achievement discrepancy definition of reading disability. *Journal of Learning Disabilities, 33,* 223–238.

Vellutino, F., Scanlon, D., Sipay, E., Small, S., Pratt, A., Chen, R., et al. (1996). Cognitive profiles of difficult-to-remediate and readily remediated poor readers: Early intervention as a vehicle for distinguishing between cognitive and experiential deficits as basic causes of special reading disabilities. *Journal of Educational Psychology, 88,* 601–638.

Walsh, K., Glaser, D., & Wilcox, D. D. (2006). *What education schools aren't teaching about reading and what elementary teachers aren't learning.* Washington, DC: National Center on Teacher Quality. http://www.nctq.org

Wanzek, J., & Vaughn, S. (2007). Service delivery for response to intervention: Core components and directions for future research. *School Psychology Review, 36,* 526–540.

Watkins, M. (2000). Cognitive profile analysis: A shared professional myth. *School Psychology Quarterly, 15,* 465–479.

Watkins, M. W., Glutting, J. J., & Youngstrom, E. A. (2005). Issues in subtest profile analysis. In D. P. Flanagan & P. L. Harrison (Eds.), *Contemporary intellectual assessment: Theories, tests, and issues* (2nd ed., pp. 251–268). New York: Guilford Press.

White, O. R., & Haring, N. G. (1980). *Exceptional teaching* (2nd ed.). Columbus, OH: Merrill.

Ysseldyke, J. E., & Weinberg, R. A. (1981). Editorial comment: An introduction. *School Psychology Review, 10,* 116–120.

Ysseldyke, J. E., Algozzine, B., Shinn, M. R., & McGue, M. (1982). Similarities and differences between low achievers and students labeled learning disabled. *Journal of Special Education, 16,* 73–85.

Ysseldyke, J., Shinn, M. R., & Thurlow, M. (1978). University of Minnesota Institute for Research on Learning Disabilities. *Learning Disabilities Quarterly, 1,* 75–77.

Ysseldyke, J., Thurlow, M., Graden, J., Wesson, C., Algozzine, B., & Deno, S. L. (1983). Generalizations from five years of research on assessment and decision-making: The University of Minnesota Institute. *Exceptional Education Quarterly, 4,* 75–93.

CHAPTER 4

Building Healthy Communities to Promote Successful Development

Anthony Biglan
Oregon Research Institute

Erika Hinds
University of Oregon

Christine Cody
Oregon Research Institute

INTRODUCTION

Thanks to 50 years of behavioral science research, communities have the potential to reduce the entire range of problems of childhood and adolescence. Effective use of accumulated knowledge about the development and prevention of social, psychological, behavioral, and academic problems of children and adolescents has the potential to ensure that nearly every young person develops the skills, interest, and motivation to become a productive, caring, and psychologically flexible adult. This chapter provides a brief overview of the accumulated knowledge from the perspective of what communities can do to ensure successful development.

Major Problems of Adolescence

Over the past half century, behavioral scientists have delineated the most significant developmental problems of youth; pinpointed the major risk factors for those problems; and identified protective factors, programs, policies, and practices that can prevent most problem development. They also have found that diverse psychological, behavioral, and academic problems tend to be interrelated and largely result from the same risk factors.

Young people with any given problem are highly likely to have others (Biglan et al., 2004). For example, Boles, Biglan, and Smolkowski (2006) found that, in a representative sample of eighth-grade students in Oregon, those who reported antisocial behavior were five times as likely to report substance use as those not reporting any antisocial behavior. They were seven times as likely to report risky sexual behavior, nearly four times as likely to be depressed, and nearly three times as likely to report an eating disorder. Additionally, they were three times as likely not to use seat belts and bike helmets, and more than twice as likely to make poor use of their time (e.g., by skipping school and watching a great deal of television). Each of these behaviors co-occurred significantly with every other one.

Boles et al. (2006) also looked at these problems in relation to a set of positive behaviors that included exercising, volunteering, playing sports, being involved with a church or church group, doing chores, completing homework, and earning good grades. Students engaging in any of the negative behaviors were significantly less likely to report these positive behaviors.

Educators and others working on human development understand fully that problem behaviors come in bunches and result from the same set of risk factors. Nonetheless, acting on this knowledge has proved difficult. In particular, most communities and states have not integrated school and family support practices in ways that efficiently modify the entire range of risk factors that lead to diverse problems. Instead, they choose programs that tend to deal with a single problem, such as a mental disorder, drug abuse, delinquency, risky sexual behavior, or family dysfunction. They pay insufficient attention to the fact that any one problem is likely to have a connection to others and that, as a result, the youth and family likely need additional services they can get only from a different agency.

The Cost of Problem Behaviors

In 2004, economist Ted Miller outlined the complexities in determining the costs of problem behaviors (Biglan et al., 2004). He estimated the cost of the following adolescent behaviors: violent crime, property crime related to violence or substance abuse, binge drinking, heroin/cocaine abuse, high-risk sexual behavior, smoking, dropping out of school, and suicide attempts. He included the medical care costs, crime victim costs, lost productivity, and criminal justice and other governmental costs, such as family assistance and drug abuse treatment. He concluded that these adolescent problem behaviors cost the United States about $435 billion, about $340 billion of which is due to youth with multiple problems.

PRESCRIPTIONS FOR EFFECTIVE COMMUNITIES

With the large number of preventive interventions shown to reduce problems from infancy through adolescence, it should be possible to bring about a significant reduction in the prevalence of all major problems of childhood and adolescence. That is a bold claim, but evidence reviewed in this book shows that programs, policies, and practices exist that can prevent or ameliorate every common and costly youth problem. It is logical to conclude that, were these interventions combined and delivered in communities, they could have a very substantial impact.

In our view as researchers, the natural next step in prevention is to create comprehensive community interventions that combine the various prevention programs across the life span of children—from conception through adolescence—and reduce the prevalence of diverse problems. However, empirical evidence to support such a claim is generally lacking.

We recommend a systematic evaluation to determine whether putting a set of evidence-based programs, policies, and practices together can significantly reduce the prevalence of youth with multiple problems. However, even in the absence of such research, there is clear justification for schools and communities to implement evidence-based programs, policies, and practices, because evidence has already shown that each has value individually.

The key features of such a comprehensive community intervention should include (a) a system for monitoring child and adolescent well-being and the risk and protective factors that influence well-being; and (b) evidence-based programs, practices, and policies relevant to each developmental period. This chapter describes each of these components plus existing research that has evaluated community interventions for children or adolescents. The reader might think of this review as a prescription for what communities need to do to improve youth well-being.

A Monitoring System

The foundation for community efforts to improve well-being is an accurate system for monitoring well-being and a method of feeding that information back to the community to motivate and guide effective action. Such systems are increasingly in place (Mrazek, Biglan, & Hawkins, 2005). They ideally would combine survey and archival data to estimate (a) the proportion of young people achieving academic proficiency; (b) the prevalence of the most common problems of youth, including antisocial behavior, substance use, and risky sexual behavior; and (c) the rates of common problematic outcomes such as school dropouts, juvenile arrests, and teen pregnancy. The system should also provide estimates of key risk and protective factors. For example, communities need to know what proportion of families engage in effective child-rearing practices; the degree to which parents, schools, and communities provide adequate supervision of young people; and the degree to which norms in the community support the development of responsible, caring, and conscientious young people.

Communities with such monitoring systems could better develop them. Survey systems, such as the Communities That Care survey and the Oregon Healthy Teens survey, provide data about behavior and about risk and protective factors among adolescents (Boles et al., 2006; Kann et al., 2000). Additionally, most communities have archival data on key indicators of adolescent well-being. However, the data are generally not organized in a single place and readily available to community members.

Creating a website to present such data in a format would allow community members to aggregate the data at the school or community level, to look at trends across time, and to pinpoint key problems and risk factors that need targeting. It is well within the capacity of any state or large community to put this information together.

Such a system would be valuable over time. Accurate data on youth well-being could become part of the governance rituals of the community. School boards, city and county governments, and civic organizations concerned with youth well-being could routinely review the data and allocate their resources in light of progress and problems. The data could be available for any citizen to advocate for allocation of resources to specific problems.

Most important, the data would be available to gauge whether a specific program or policy already in place is having its desired effect. Over time, the evolution of the use of the system would influence the selection of additional and more effective child-rearing practices.

In the absence of such a system, many schools and communities may adopt evidence-based interventions but will not be able to track the impact of the interventions. That is, they will not know whether an intervention is having the same impact in their community as it did in the communities included in the original intervention study. Thus, monitoring systems are vital to ensuring that disseminated evidence-based practices, in fact, do achieve their potential.

Efficacious Interventions Throughout Development

At each stage of development, risk factors contribute to the development of youth problems. However, behavioral science research has advanced to the point that it is possible to ameliorate each risk factor and nurture successful development. To illustrate what communities can do, we provide a brief overview of some empirically supported interventions for each development stage.

Prenatal Period and Infancy

Problem development can begin during the prenatal period. Mothers who smoke, drink alcohol, or have poor nutrition are significantly more likely to have infants who are difficult to comfort (Biglan et al., 2004; Shonkoff & Phillips, 2000). For mothers without the patience and skills to comfort their infant, the result can be an irritable and uncooperative baby. If this pattern continues into early childhood, it is likely the child will become aggressive, which is a risk factor for continuing problems as he or she grows up (Patterson, Reid, & Dishion, 1992).

It is not surprising, therefore, that nurse visitation that provides support and guidance to mothers at risk for these problems has long-term benefits in preventing problem development. In a series of randomized experimental studies, Olds et al. (1998) found that nurses who helped economically and socially disadvantaged mothers during pregnancy and the first 2 years of their babies' lives were able to reduce mothers' abuse and neglect. The nurses were also able to prevent further pregnancies and help the mothers get off welfare, start work, and further their education. The results for the children were very encouraging. Children whose mothers received the nurse visitation demonstrated lower rates of healthcare encounters involving injuries and ingestions, performed better in school, and exhibited less delinquency in adolescence.

Such nurse home visitation should be available for poor mothers or mothers at risk for any other reason, such as developmental disabilities. It would ensure access to prenatal care and would encourage mothers not to drink or take drugs and to quit smoking. It would provide social support for mothers' efforts to gain further education and employment and to build their personal system of social support.

Early Childhood

Major risk factors in early childhood include parental poverty, abuse, or neglect; lack of parental stimulation; and parent–child conflict. Patterson et al. (1992) have identified a pattern of coercive interactions in which children and parents attempt to cope with each other's aversive behavior through their own aggressive acts. Through such acts, both parents and children achieve brief respites from the other's aversive behavior. In the process, the child develops a repertoire of aggressive behaviors and fails to develop social skills that elicit nurturing and warmth from parents, siblings, peers, and other caregivers. Such early aggressive behavior is a major risk factor for the development of delinquency, drug abuse, and other risky behaviors in later childhood and adolescence (Biglan et al., 2004).

Early childhood interventions focusing on parenting and behavior management strategies can prevent the development of deviant behavior. Many parenting interventions span early childhood through adolescence, but there are programs and interventions aimed specifically at early childhood. Webster-Stratton's *The Incredible Years* (Webster-Stratton, 1984) is designed to assist parents in understanding and coping with behavioral problems in children ages 3 to 8 years. It focuses on strengthening parenting competencies in areas such as monitoring, positive discipline, and limit setting. It also fosters parental involvement in children's school experiences, which promotes academic and social competencies and reduces conduct problems.

There is also strong evidence of the benefits of affordable, evidence-based preschool education available to families (Nelson, Westhues, & MacLeod, 2003). Such programs would provide high-quality instruction and support for social and physical development. Temple and Reynolds (2007) reviewed evidence from the Chicago Child–Parent Centers and related programs to determine the benefits and costs of investing in preschool education. They looked at results from two other well-known preschool programs, the High/Scope Perry Preschool Program and the Carolina Abecedarian Project, and other programs for both younger and older children. However, they focused on the Chicago program because it is still going and because other researchers had just completed a cost–benefit analysis on the program (Reynolds, Temple, Robertson, & Mann, 2002). They found statistically significant differences favoring those children who had been in the program. Across all the studies reviewed, attending preschool led to a 31% reduction in grade retention, a 50% reduction in special education placement, and a 32% reduction in dropping out of high school. The authors found "strong evidence that the consistently positive economic returns of high-quality preschool programs exceed most other educational interventions" (Temple & Reynolds, p. 126).

Lynch (2007) reviewed several studies of the best-known preschool programs to determine the cost-effectiveness of public spending on high-quality prekindergarten care. Compared with less expensive, but also less effective, private programs, the high-quality programs achieved significant results, making them worth their cost in terms of the benefits to the communities in which the children reside. Across states and programs, for example, Lynch found that pre-K programs increase the future earnings of their participants, lower the criminal activity of 25% of children who attend high-quality pre-K, and raise academic performance at a similar rate. Lynch argues for a nationwide commitment to high-quality early childhood education, "which would cost a significant amount of money upfront but would have a substantial payoff in the future" (p. 30). Lynch expects such a program to reduce costs for special education, criminal justice, and child welfare while increasing income earned and taxes paid by recipients of such programs.

Reynolds et al. (2007) conducted a long-term follow-up assessment with adults who had participated in a low-income kindergarten program 19 years earlier with the Chicago Child–Parent Center. They interviewed 1,539 adults who had attended the program at one of 20 sites or who had attended usual-care kindergarten during the same period in the Chicago area. Those who had attended the Chicago center went further in school and were less likely to be arrested.

Middle Childhood

Similar to early childhood, the key risk factors during this phase include abuse, neglect, family poverty, parent–child conflict, and aggressive social behavior. Parent–child conflict and subsequent learned aggression appear influential in the development of additional risk factors during middle childhood. Walker, Colvin, and Ramsey (1995) found that children who arrive at school with highly practiced sets of aggressive behavior have an increased chance of academic failure and peer rejection. Additionally, parental neglect may lead to intellectual deficits in children. Children who experience fewer opportunities to interact with their parents through reading and games fail to benefit from practicing language and social skills early in their development, subsequently placing them at a disadvantage academically.

Fortunately, school and family interventions are available to improve outcomes for children. The Good Behavior Game (GBG; Barrish, Saunders, & Wolf, 1969), for example, was designed to address early aggression and noncompliant behaviors in elementary school classrooms. The short game involves dividing the class into two groups and rewarding groups with less than a specified number of disruptive behaviors. Studies have demonstrated positive short- and long-term effects for children in preschool through sixth grade, students in special education, and adolescents labeled emotionally disturbed (Embry, 2002). In a randomized controlled trial, children in the GBG group showed a reduction of aggressive behavior in first grade and better outcomes with regard to delinquency, smoking, and substance use in sixth grade (Kellam & Anthony, 1998). Males ages 19–21 who had participated in the GBG as children showed reduced rates of conduct disorder and substance abuse (Kellam et al., 2008; Petras et al., 2008).

Some programs incorporate both school and parent interventions. For example, Linking the Interests of Families and Teachers (LIFT; Eddy, Reid, & Fetrow, 2000) addresses parent–child management and communication skills and children's peer interaction skills. It also includes a playground component that employs the Good Behavior Game to provide positive consequences for appropriate peer interactions. A 3-year randomized controlled trial evaluated the program's effectiveness for first and fifth graders. Researchers found that intervention children were less aggressive on the playground than control children were, and their teachers perceived them more positively than did teachers of control students. Additionally, their parents were less hostile toward them during problem-solving discussions. At 3-year follow-up, fifth graders who received LIFT had less association with deviant peers, lower likelihood of a first arrest, and fewer initiations of alcohol and marijuana use. The intervention appeared to work equally well for children who initially demonstrated higher levels of problem behavior.

Early Adolescence

At this stage, risk factors include poor parental monitoring, family conflict, movement into middle or junior high school, aggressive social behavior, and association with deviant peers (Biglan et al., 2004). Youth in early adolescence engage in more activities with peers away from home. Adolescent association with aggressive, disruptive, or drug-using peers promotes similar behavior. Rusby, Forrester, Biglan, and Metzler (2005) found an association between a lack of parental monitoring and development of various problem behaviors. Additionally, victimization (i.e., harassment or bullying) is common in middle and junior high school and is associated with deviant peer association, aggressive behavior, and delinquency. Rusby et al. also found victimization to predict greater substance use in girls.

School and family interventions can also prevent or alleviate problem behavior during early adolescence. Life Skills Training (LST; Botvin, 1985) is an example of a school-based intervention designed to prevent youth tobacco, alcohol, and drug use. Seventh graders learn social and problem-solving skills related to making decisions, becoming media literate (that is, they learn how advertisers try to influence them, knowledge that helps to "inoculate" them against the influence of ads for products like tobacco and alcohol), coping with negative emotions, managing personal behavior, communicating effectively, being assertive, and resisting peer pressure. Multiple studies have shown that LST had a significant impact on reducing cigarette, marijuana, and alcohol use after 3 years for those middle school students whose teachers taught at least 60% of the curriculum. A 6-year follow-up study indicated that LST effects lasted until the end of 12th grade (Botvin, Baker, Dusenbury, Botvin, & Diaz, 1995; Botvin et al., 2000).

The Adolescent Transitions Program (ATP; Dishion, Kavanagh, Schneiger, Nelson, & Kaufman, 2002) is a multilevel, family-centered intervention delivered in middle school. It targets teens at risk for experimenting with drugs and developing antisocial behaviors. The program works with parents on incorporating consequences for problem behavior, limiting access to potentially problematic situations, developing communication skills, and monitoring. Data from a randomized control study of 220 parents found the program effective in reducing observed negative parent–child interactions and youth smoking behaviors at 1-year follow-up (Dishion & Andrews, 1995). Additionally, teacher reports showed a decline in antisocial behaviors at school. Irvine, Biglan, Smolkowski, Metzler, and Ary (1999) replicated these results in a study of more than 300 families in eight Oregon communities.

Adolescence

The risk factors demonstrated during early adolescence may continue to develop and intensify as adolescents begin navigating high school. The peer group becomes an even more central focus; inadequate parental monitoring and communication can result in adolescent engagement in more extreme problem behavior. Patterson, DeBaryshe, and Ramsey (1989) held that deviant peer groups are responsible for development of various problem behaviors, including substance use and delinquency. Furthermore, engagement in deviant behavior at this stage of development is a risk factor for development of additional, more severe difficulties.

Comprehensive interventions addressing both school and family influences have shown benefits for adolescents. Chamberlain and colleagues designed Multidimensional Treatment Foster Care (MTFC; Chamberlain & Mihalic, 1998) for adolescents with severe behavioral and emotional problems. They based MTFC on the traditional foster care model, with an important distinction: foster parents receive extensive training in behavior management and become active members of the treatment team. The main features of the program include daily monitoring and consistent consequences for even minor rule infractions. When possible, adolescents return to their homes and the parents receive training and support. Studies of the effectiveness of MTFC indicated at follow-up that adolescents in foster care treatment spent significantly fewer days in lockup, were less likely to become incarcerated, and were more likely to return to family settings than those in the usual services control group (Chamberlain & Mihalic, 1998).

Multisystemic Therapy (MST) is an intensive family- and community-based program that uses evidence-based treatment approaches and has been shown to produce long-term positive outcomes for adolescents and their families (Henggeler, 1999). Eight randomized clinical trials of MST found that the intervention consistently produced decreases in substance use, rates of rearrest in the long term, self-reported criminal offending, and number of days of out-of-home placements compared with the usual services control groups (Thornton, Craft, Dahlberg, Lynch, & Baer, 2000).

Several community-level policies also have shown that they can prevent or ameliorate youth problems. Increasing the tax on cigarettes and/or beer has a well-documented effect in reducing youth use of these substances. Taxes on beer have helped to reduce alcohol-related car crashes. Jason et al. (2000) showed that, when access to tobacco decreased and the youth received fines for possession of tobacco, adolescent smoking also diminished.

Kernels: Simple, Readily Available Intervention

Another type of preventive intervention includes the many simple behavior-influencing procedures (termed *kernels*) that support child and adolescent development (Embry, 2004). Examples include numerous simple techniques for reinforcing young people's prosocial behavior, such as praise notes, posting of students' work, and prize bowls that provide random reinforcement in classrooms and after-school settings. Other kernels involve antecedents to behavior, such as signs and symbols in schools that guide transitions from one activity to another. Still others involve creating "relational networks" that enhance the reinforcing value of certain behaviors (Hayes, Barnes-Holmes, & Roche, 2001). For example, the PeaceBuilders program elaborates what it means to be a PeaceBuilder through stories and activities so that young people become more motivated to become PeaceBuilders (Embry, Flannery, Vazsonyi, Powell, & Atha, 1996). Finally, there are physiological kernels that affect behavior. For example, growing evidence indicates that omega-3 fatty acid supplementation reduces depressive and aggressive behaviors (Hibbeln, 2001).

Kernels are important supplements to programs and policies. Although programs and policies have great potential for improving child and adolescent development, most of them (implemented alone or jointly) still leave room for other practices that can support youth development, because there are so many situations for which no programs exist. Moreover, as people become facile with the use of kernels, they will find many new situations in which to use them.

PRINCIPLES FOR SUPPORTING SUCCESSFUL DEVELOPMENT

Effective preventive interventions share several general principles. A recent document published by the Center on Early Adolescence summarized those principles (Metzler et al., 2007).

Reinforce desirable behavior. Young people need much positive reinforcement. Virtually every effective prevention or treatment program for youth has, at its core, a set of procedures for reinforcing cooperative, prosocial behavior (Biglan, 2003). Unfortunately, the notion that reinforcement can be harmful has not completely died out. Community and school leaders should encourage parents, teachers, youth organizers, and community members to reinforce young people when they are cooperative, innovative, caring, or conscientious. Many of the kernels that Embry identified involve ways of increasing reinforcement (Embry, 2004). For example, communities can recognize the good work of young people by displaying their schoolwork in public places. They can provide schools with goods to use as part of their reward systems. They can ensure that every organization seeks ways to recognize young people's good efforts.

Monitor and be involved. Young people require monitoring to guide them, gently, in positive directions. Information about the importance of parental monitoring should be a component of any family support intervention, especially for families with adolescents. Parental and other adult involvement with youth should be encouraged. Community organizations should be encouraged to create family-friendly activities, and a review of public policies should take place to see that the community supports family-friendly activities.

Increasing adult involvement with young people may be one way to prevent adolescent involvement with risky behaviors and deviant peers. One of the highest risk situations for adolescents involves their being with peers of the same age with no adult supervision (Dishion & Dodge, 2005). Communities must make such situations rare and provide opportunities for activities that will engage youth common.

Structure and guide. Communities can reduce deviant peer group formation by structuring engaging activities where adults are also present. Churches, civic organizations, and youth organizations can create more places and events where adolescents can interact while adults are nearby. Schools and other organizations can develop meaningful roles for young people in which they genuinely contribute to the operation of the community. Sports venues are fine for many youth, but other organizations can provide venues for those interested in the arts, reading, or volunteering. Each of these places can offer fun activities for the youth while requiring the involvement of adults who will be there to guide, reinforce, teach, and coach them. Giving students meaningful roles in schools reduces problem behavior and encourages skill development (Rutter, Maughan, Mortimore, & Ouston, 1982).

Families, schools, and community organizations must be encouraged to give clear, consistent expectations to youth. However, when the youth do not meet expectations, it should not result in harsh punishment. Research in schools and families shows that punishment is often too harsh and therefore counterproductive (e.g., Mayer, 1995; Patterson et al., 1992). Families, schools, and the juvenile authority need to be encouraged to use mild but consistent consequences for misbehavior.

COMMUNITY INTERVENTIONS TARGETING SUBSTANCE USE

Despite the evidence that there are multiple interventions that could be made available in communities to significantly reduce a wide range of problems, most research testing community-wide preventive interventions has focused on reducing tobacco, alcohol, and other substance use, as in the following studies.

Project SixTeen

Project SixTeen was a comprehensive community intervention targeting adolescent tobacco use. The intervention focused on social influences to use tobacco and included a classroom-based prevention curriculum, media advocacy, youth antitobacco activities, family communication activities, and a systematic campaign to reduce tobacco sales to underage youth. A randomized controlled trial examined whether Project SixTeen was more effective than a school-based prevention program alone, such as Project PATH (Biglan, James, LaChance, Zoref, & Joffe, 1988). Eight Oregon communities received the complete intervention while eight others received the classroom curriculum alone. Youth were seventh- and ninth-grade students assessed using five annual surveys for self-reported cigarette and smokeless tobacco use, antisocial behavior, and other substance use during the previous month. At years 1 and 5 postintervention, a significantly lower prevalence of cigarette use appeared in communities that received the community-based intervention compared with those that received the school-based intervention alone. At year 2, ninth-grade boys in the community intervention reported lower smokeless tobacco use compared with those in the school intervention. Significant effects were also found for alcohol and marijuana use in ninth graders. That is, over 4 years, alcohol and marijuana use did not increase as rapidly in the community intervention group compared with the school-based intervention group.

Project Northland

Project Northland was a multimodal community intervention aimed at delaying onset of underage drinking and reducing adolescent alcohol use (Perry et al., 1996, 2000, 2002). The randomized community trial took place in 24 school districts and communities in Minnesota and spanned multiple years. It had two phases, the first of which focused on 6th- through 8th-grade students, and the second of which centered on 11th- and 12th-grade students. The intervention incorporated social–environmental approaches with individual behavior-change strategies and used direct-action community organizing, youth action teams, print media regarding healthy norms about underage drinking, parent education and involvement, and classroom-based social–behavioral curricula. During the second phase, Project Northland attempted to establish local policies requiring Responsible Beverage Service (RBS) training for on- and off-premise alcohol-serving establishments. Additionally, the project invited local merchants to participate in a gold-card incentive system that offered discounts to students who pledged to remain alcohol and drug free (Veblen-Mortenson et al., 1999).

Assessments of alcohol use and other behaviors occurred during Grades 6 through 12, and substantial reductions in alcohol use emerged at the completion of the second phase. At the end of eighth grade, intervention students reported significantly less alcohol use in the past week and in the past month, reduced peer influence on behavior, and better attitudes and normative beliefs regarding alcohol use compared with students in control communities (Perry et al., 1996).

Furthermore, youth who were not using alcohol at the beginning of the project reported significantly less alcohol, marijuana, and cigarette use at the end of eighth grade than those students who already had been using. However, teens already involved in early substance use did not experience similar benefits. At 10th grade, intervention effects waned (Perry et al., 2000), but the second phase intervention efforts appeared to counteract the decay. At the end of 12th grade, the increase of alcohol use and binge drinking in intervention schools was significantly less than in control schools (Perry et al., 2002). In addition, commercial access to alcohol significantly decreased in the intervention communities.

Communities Mobilizing for Change on Alcohol

Rather than addressing individual behavior change to prevent adolescent alcohol use, Communities Mobilizing for Change on Alcohol (CMCA) developed a social–environmental intervention aimed at reducing underage youth access to alcoholic beverages by changing policies and practices of major community institutions (Wagenaar et al., 2000). The goal of the project was to decrease the number of alcohol outlets selling to youth, reduce access to alcohol from noncommercial sources (e.g., parents, siblings, and peers), and change cultural norms that tolerate underage access to and consumption of alcoholic beverages. Strategy teams formed in each intervention community, comprising groups and organizations with the ability to effect change at the community level (e.g., local public officials, enforcement agencies, alcohol merchants and merchant associations, the media, and schools). Specific intervention activities to reduce access varied across communities and included efforts such as increasing enforcement of laws regarding underage sales, providing information to parents, and changing community events to make alcohol less accessible to underage youth.

Fifteen communities in Minnesota and Wisconsin were randomized into intervention (n = 7) or control (n = 8) groups. Postintervention data revealed lower levels of alcohol sales to underage youth at outlets and marginally lower alcohol sales to underage youth at bars and restaurants in the intervention communities. Phone surveys indicated that 18- to 20-year-olds in the intervention communities were less likely to attempt to purchase alcohol and less likely to provide alcohol to others. These young adults also reported lower rates of alcohol consumption during the past 30 days than the young adults in the control communities did. Researchers found no effects on the prevalence of heavy drinking in this age group, nor any significant effects on the drinking behaviors of 12th graders. Finally, arrests for driving under the influence of alcohol declined significantly more for 18- to 20-year-olds in the intervention communities than for those in the control communities (Wagenaar et al., 2000).

Community Trials Project

This 5-year national community prevention trial attempted to reduce alcohol-related injuries and deaths among all ages through community-based environmental prevention activities and policy change (Holder et al., 1997). Based on the premise that alcohol problems occur through interactions between individual, interpersonal, and social factors, the project focused the intervention on five domains: (a) community mobilization, (b) RBS training, (c) increased enforcement of driving while intoxicated (DWI) and perceived risk of drunken driving detection, (d) reduction of underage access to alcohol, and (e) reduction of alcohol availability through the use of local zoning and other municipal controls.

The group evaluated program effects by comparing three intervention communities and three matched control communities in Northern and Southern California and South Carolina. Sites were matched based on population (over 100,000 each), industry (e.g., commercial, agricultural, or tourism), and ethnicity (40% or more minority group members). Comparing experimental and control communities, the intervention produced significant reductions in nighttime crashes with injuries (10% lower), crashes in which the drivers self-reported "Have been drinking" (6% lower), assault injuries observed in emergency medical facilities (43% lower), and assaults requiring hospitalization (2% lower). Driving after self-reports of "Had too much to drink" and of driving when "Over the legal limit" were both lower (49% and 51% lower, respectively). There was also a significant reduction in problematic alcohol use even though the drinking population increased slightly over the course of the study. Average drinks per occasion declined by 6%, and the variance in drinking patterns (indirect measure of heavy drinking) declined 21% (Holder et al., 2000). With regard to alcohol sales to underage youth, there was a significant reduction in alcohol sales in the intervention communities compared with the control communities. Off-premise alcohol outlets in intervention communities were half as likely to sell to minors as those outlets in control communities. The study did not evaluate alcohol use by underage youth.

Saving Lives Project

Reducing alcohol-impaired driving and related driving risks for all ages was the aim of the Saving Lives Project (Hingson, McGovern, Howland, & Hereen, 1996). Project implementation involved the development of a task force led by a full-time city employee in every project community. Each task force designed specific activities for its community, including media campaigns, business information programs, speeding and drunk driving awareness days, speed-watch telephone hotlines, police training, high school peer–led education, Students against Drunk Driving chapters, and college prevention programs.

Hingson et al. (1996) compared six Massachusetts intervention communities and five control communities using a quasi-experimental design. Intervention and comparison communities had similar demographic characteristics (the comparison community was slightly more affluent), traffic citations, and fatal crashes. Compared with the 5 years before implementation, the 5 years of program activity was associated with a 25% decline in fatal crashes and a 25% decline in fatal crashes involving alcohol. Additionally, visible injuries per 100 crashes declined 5%, and proportions of vehicles observed speeding and teenagers who drove after drinking decreased by 50%. The most prominent reductions in crashes with injuries and fatalities occurred among 15- to 25-year-olds.

Midwestern Prevention Program

The Midwestern Prevention Program (MPP) was a multimodal community-based drug prevention program that evaluated effects on high-risk youth and a general population of youth. The program components included (a) a classroom curriculum targeting students in sixth and seventh grade; (b) parent training addressing prevention policy and parent–child communication skills; (c) training of community leaders for development of a drug abuse prevention task force; and (d) media promotion of prevention policies and norms (Pentz, MacKinnon, Flay, et al., 1989).

Evaluation included a quasi-experimental trial in Kansas City and a subsequent experimental trial in Indianapolis. Youth in MPP schools and in delayed MPP intervention schools had exposure to the media campaigns and to the school and community policy initiatives. Only the MPP intervention schools received the classroom curriculum and parent training. At 1-year follow-up, students reported significantly lower increases in cigarette, alcohol, and marijuana use in the week prior. Effects on smoking persisted in the Kansas City sample at 2-year follow-up and affected the prevalence of heavy and light smoking equally (Pentz, MacKinnon, Dwyer, et al., 1989). Carbon monoxide measures of smokers were also lower for 9th- and 10th-grade students in the MPP groups compared with students in control groups (Pentz, Dwyer, et al., 1989). The Indianapolis study, which randomly assigned schools to conditions, showed significantly less tobacco and marijuana use (but not less alcohol use) in the MPP schools than in control schools. Post hoc analyses revealed that private and parochial schools were largely responsible for the positive intervention effects in the Indianapolis schools (Pentz, Trebow, Hansen, & MacKinnon, 1990).

Johnson et al. (1990) examined the effects of MPP in high-risk youth in the Kansas City sample and found the intervention equally effective for both high- and low-risk youth. The program was more effective for seventh than for sixth graders. Chou et al. (1998) analyzed the Indianapolis data collected from students who reported any drug or alcohol use during the month before baseline. Through 3½ years post-baseline, they examined percentages of students whose reports of substance abuse during the past month declined from one assessment to the next. They found that MPP produced significant declines in cigarette, alcohol, and marijuana use through all follow-ups. Additional analyses indicated limited effects for baseline marijuana users and diminishing effects for early alcohol and cigarette users over time. Pentz et al. (1990) found that curriculum adherence and amount of student exposure to the curriculum (as reported by teachers) was significantly associated with lower rates of nearly all alcohol, tobacco, and marijuana use 18 months post-baseline.

Evaluation of Community Coalitions Implementing Evidence-Based Programs in Vermont

Flewelling et al. (2005) reported on an effort in Vermont to get communities to implement evidence-based programs for substance abuse prevention. Although their study was not a randomized trial, it did involve 23 communities that received funding for 3 years to create a community coalition that selected and implemented a set of evidence-based prevention strategies. Over 6 years, youth problem behaviors underwent biennial assessment using the Youth Risk Behavior Survey developed by the Centers for Disease Control and Prevention. Students in Grades 8 through 12 completed the assessments. Compared with the rest of the state, the communities receiving funds to implement evidence-based practices showed greater reductions in the prevalence of substance abuse, for all nine substances that they measured.

COMPREHENSIVE COMMUNITY INTERVENTIONS

Not all community interventions focus on the prevention of substance use. A few studies have evaluated comprehensive efforts to implement evidence-based programs designed to prevent a broader range of youth problems.

Communities That Care

Communities That Care (CTC) helps communities identify risk and protective factors that influence child and adolescent problems and implement evidence-based programs to prevent problem development. Each community forms a board, which then learns about risk, protection, and prevention. The community uses surveys of adolescents and archival community data to pinpoint the most prevalent problems and most elevated risk factors in that community. The community team selects preventive interventions and implements them in the community. The Community Youth Development Study experimentally evaluated CTC. By random assignment, 24 communities received or did not receive CTC. Fifth-grade students completed assessments annually for 3 years. By the 3rd year, CTC communities were lower than control communities were on targeted risk factors and on a measure of the initiation of delinquency (Feinberg, Riggs, & Greenberg, 2005). However, there were no differences on substance use initiation.

Prosper

Spoth, Greenberg, Bierman, and Redmond (2004) evaluated Prosper, a comprehensive community intervention, in a randomized trial. They randomly assigned 28 small Iowa and Pennsylvania communities to receive assistance in selecting and implementing parenting and school-based preventive interventions or to receive "normal programming." Community teams in the intervention communities chose among three evidence-based parenting interventions and three evidence-based classroom curricula. The communities received training and consultation from the Pennsylvania State University or Iowa State extension services. All teams chose to implement the Strengthening Families Program (Kumpfer, Molgaard, & Spoth, 1996). For the school-based program, four chose to implement Life Skills Training (Botvin, 1985), four chose Project Alert (Ellickson, 1985), and six chose All Stars (Hansen, Graham, Wolkenstein, & Rohrbach, 1991). Sixth-grade students received the family intervention during the spring term; when they went into seventh grade, they received the school-based programs. At 18 months following the initial baseline assessment, the students who had received the intervention were doing significantly better on a variety of measures of substance use, including lifetime use; initiation of substance use among those who had reported none at baseline; past month use of cigarettes; and past year drunkenness, marijuana use, or inhalant use.

Triple P

The Positive Parenting Program (Triple P), developed by Sanders and colleagues, is a way to help entire communities improve the quality of parenting (Prinz, Sanders, Shapiro, Whitaker, & Lutzker, 2009; Sanders & Markie-Dadds, 1996). Although the evidence strongly supports the impact of behaviorally oriented parenting programs (e.g., Serketich & Dumas, 1996; Thomas & Zimmer-Gembeck, 2007), most such programs focus on individual families; they do not seek to affect the prevalence of good parenting in the population. However, given the evidence of parenting programs' effectiveness, it is time we as a society raised our sights to try to increase the prevalence of good parenting and, thereby, decrease the prevalence of problem behaviors among children and adolescents.

Triple P, used as an outreach of the community, provides as much or as little guidance on parenting as a family needs and wants. Its five levels range from information about effective parenting and solutions for common child-rearing problems to intensive, multisession treatment for families with marital discord and children who have severe difficulties. Triple P reaches many families in the community through contacts with pediatricians. A meta-analysis of Triple P effects found it had moderate to large effects on parent-reported child behaviors and parenting experiences. It also found that the enhanced Triple P, which is the highest level of involvement with families, produced significant benefits for directly observed child behavior (Thomas & Zimmer-Gembeck, 2007).

CONCLUSION

The evidence reviewed in this and other chapters of this book shows that programs, policies, and practices are now available to enable communities to make a significant reduction in the prevalence of all major psychological and behavioral problems of adolescence. A willing community can implement programs, policies, and practices that enhance development throughout the life span of children. The result can be that many fewer young people will have problems with academic failure, depression, antisocial behavior, substance abuse, unwanted pregnancy, or sexually transmitted diseases.

Two distinct circumstances must be in place before communities can evolve toward the kind of successful childrearing that the evidence shows is possible. The first is dissemination of the economic benefit of effective practices. Much of this has already occurred, and existing analyses of the benefit-to-cost ratio for investing in preventive interventions are very encouraging. For example, Aos, Lieb, Mayfield, Miller, and Pennucci (2004), of the Washington State Institute for Public Policy, identified 16 crime-prevention programs that paid dividends in terms of reduced costs for treatment of crime victims and criminal justice system costs. The amount returned per dollar invested ranged from $2.64 to $38.05.

Second, and even more important, communities need to know that society sincerely wants to improve the well-being of all of its members. We possess the evidence, the knowledge, and the ability to bring about significant changes to prevent crime, drug abuse, school failure, and psychological suffering; we know we can do this cost-effectively. All that remains is to make a promise to reduce human suffering and ensure the well-being of every person.

AUTHOR NOTE

The National Cancer Institute (Grant CA 38273), the National Institute on Drug Abuse (Grant P30 DA 018760), and the National Institute on Alcohol Abuse and Alcoholism (Grant R01-AA014958) provided financial support for the authors' work on this chapter. Address all correspondence and feedback on this chapter to Anthony Biglan, e-mail: tony@ori.org.

REFERENCES

Aos, S., Lieb, R., Mayfield, J., Miller, M., & Pennucci, A. (2004). *Benefits and costs of prevention and early intervention programs for youth.* Olympia: Washington State Institute for Public Policy.

Barrish, H. H., Saunders, M., & Wolf, M. M. (1969). Good behavior game: Effects of individual contingencies for group consequences on disruptive behavior in a classroom. *Journal of Applied Behavior Analysis, 2,* 119–124.

Biglan, A. (2003). Selection by consequences: One unifying principle for a transdisciplinary science of prevention. *Prevention Science, 4,* 213–232.

Biglan, A., Brennan, P. A., Foster, S. L., Holder, H. D., Miller, T. L., Cunningham, P. B., et al. (2004). *Helping adolescents at risk: Prevention of multiple problem behaviors.* New York: Guilford Press.

Biglan, A., James, L. E., LaChance, P., Zoref, L., & Joffe, J. (1988). Videotaped materials in a school-based smoking prevention program. *Preventive Medicine, 17,* 559–584.

Boles, S., Biglan, A., & Smolkowski, K. (2006). Relationships among negative and positive behaviours in adolescence. *Journal of Adolescence, 29,* 33–52.

Botvin, G. J. (1985). The Life Skills Training Program as a health promotion strategy: Theoretical issues and empirical findings. *Special Services in the Schools, 1,* 9–23.

Botvin, G. J., Baker, E., Dusenbury, L., Botvin, E. M., & Diaz, T. (1995). Long-term follow-up results of a randomized drug abuse prevention trial in a white middle-class population. *Journal of the American Medical Association, 273,* 1106–1112.

Botvin, G. J., Griffin, K. W., Diaz, T., Scheier, L. M., Williams, C., & Epstein, J. A. (2000). Preventing illicit drug use in adolescents: Long-term follow-up data from a randomized control trial of a school population. *Addictive Behaviors, 25,* 769–774.

Chamberlain, P., & Mihalic, S. F. (1998). *Multidimensional Treatment Foster Care. Book eight.* In D. S. Elliott (Series Ed.), *Blueprints for Violence Prevention.* Boulder, CO: University of Colorado at Boulder, Institute of Behavioral Science.

Chou, C. P., Montgomery, S., Pentz, M., Rohrbach, L. A., Johnson, C. A., Flay, B., et al. (1998). Effects of a community-based prevention program on decreasing drug use in high-risk adolescents. *American Journal of Public Health, 88,* 944–948.

Dishion, T. J., & Andrews, D. W. (1995). Preventing escalation in problem behaviors with high-risk young adolescents: Immediate and 1-year outcomes. *Journal of Consulting and Clinical Psychology, 63,* 538–548.

Dishion, T. J., & Dodge, K. A. (2005). Peer contagion in interventions for children and adolescents: Moving towards an understanding of the ecology and dynamics of change. *Journal of Abnormal Child Psychology, 33,* 395–400.

Dishion, T. J., Kavanagh, K., Schneiger, A., Nelson, S., & Kaufman, N. K. (2002). Preventing early adolescent substance use: A family-centered strategy for the public middle school. In R. L. Spoth, K. Kavanagh, & T. J. Dishion (Guest Eds.), Universal family-centered prevention strategies: Current findings and critical issues for public health impact [Special issue]. *Prevention Science, 3,* 191–201.

Eddy, J. M., Reid, J. B., & Fetrow, R. A. (2000). An elementary school-based prevention program targeting modifiable antecedents of youth delinquency and violence: Linking the Interests of Families and Teachers. *Journal of Emotional & Behavioral Disorders, 8,* 165–186.

Ellickson, P. L. (1985). *An overview of Project Alert: A smoking and drug prevention experiment.* Paper presented at the 113th Convention of the American Public Health Association, Washington, DC.

Embry, D. D. (2002). The Good Behavior Game: A best practice candidate as a universal behavioral vaccine. *Clinical Child and Family Psychology Review, 5*(4), 273–297.

Embry, D. D. (2004). Community-based prevention using simple, low-cost, evidence-based kernels and behavior vaccines. *Journal of Community Psychology, 32,* 575–591.

Embry, D. D., Flannery, D., Vazsonyi, A., Powell, K., & Atha, H. (1996). Peace-Builders: A theoretically driven, school-based model for early violence prevention. *American Journal of Preventive Medicine, 22,* 91–100.

Feinberg, M. E., Riggs, N. R., & Greenberg, M. T. (2005). Social networks and community prevention coalitions. *Journal of Primary Prevention, 26,* 279–298.

Flewelling, R. L., Austin, D., Hale, K., LaPlante, M., Liebig, M., Piasecki, L., et al. (2005). Implementing research-based substance abuse prevention in communities: Effects of a coalition-based prevention initiative in Vermont. *Journal of Community Psychology, 33,* 333–353.

Hansen, W. B., Graham, J. W., Wolkenstein, B. H., & Rohrbach, L. A. (1991). Program integrity as a moderator of prevention program effectiveness: Results for fifth-grade students in the adolescent alcohol prevention trial. *Journal of Studies on Alcohol, 52,* 568–579.

Hayes, S. C., Barnes-Holmes, D., & Roche, B. (2001). *Relational frame theory: A post-Skinnerian account of human language and cognition.* New York: Kluwer/Plenum.

Henggeler, S. W. (1999). Multisystemic therapy: An overview of clinical procedures, outcomes, and policy implications. *Child Psychology and Psychiatry Review, 4,* 2–10.

Hibbeln, J. R. (2001). Seafood consumption and homicide mortality. A cross-national ecological analysis. *World Review of Nutrition & Dietetics, 88,* 41–46.

Hingson, R., McGovern, T., Howland, J., & Hereen, T. (1996). Reducing alcohol-impaired driving in Massachusetts: The Saving Lives Program. *American Journal of Public Health, 86,* 791–797.

Holder, H. D., Gruenewald, P. J., Ponicki, W. R., Treno, A. J., Grube, J. W., Saltz, R. F., et al. (2000). Effect of community-based interventions on high-risk drinking and alcohol-related injuries. *Journal of the American Medical Association, 284,* 2341–2347.

Holder, H. D., Saltz, R. F., Grube, J. W., Voas, R. B., Gruenewald, P. J., & Treno, A. J. (1997). A community prevention trial to reduce alcohol-involved accidental injury and death: Overview. *Addiction, 92*(Suppl. 2), 155–171.

Irvine, A. B., Biglan, A., Smolkowski, K., Metzler, C. W., & Ary, D. V. (1999). The effectiveness of a parenting skills program for parents of middle school students in small communities. *Journal of Consulting and Clinical Psychology, 67,* 811–825.

Jason, L. A., Katz, R., Pokorny, S. B., Engstrom, M., Tegart, G., & Curie, C. (2000). The relationship between youth tobacco control enforcement and crime rates in a Midwestern county. *American Journal of Health Promotion, 14,* 229–231.

Johnson, C. A., Pentz, M. A., Weber, M. D., Dwyer, J. H., Baer, N., MacKinnon, D. P., et al. (1990). Relative effectiveness of comprehensive community programming for drug abuse prevention with high-risk and low-risk adolescents. *Journal of Consulting and Clinical Psychology, 58,* 447–456.

Kann, L., Kinchen, S. A., Williams, B. I., Ross, J. G., Lowry, R., Grunbaum, J. A., et al. (2000). Youth risk behavior surveillance—United States, 1999. *Morbidity and Mortality Weekly Report, 49,* 1–94.

Kellam, S. G. & Anthony, J. C. (1998). Targeting early antecedents to prevent tobacco smoking: Findings from an epidemiologically based randomized field trial. *American Journal of Public Health, 88,* 1490–1495.

Kellam, S. G., Brown, C. H., Poduska, J. M., Ialongo, N. S., Wang, W., Toyinbo, P., et al. (2008). Effects of a universal classroom behavior management program in first and second grades on young adult behavioral, psychiatric, and social outcomes. *Drug and Alcohol Dependence, 95,* S5–S28

Kumpfer, K. L., Molgaard, V., & Spoth, R. (1996). The Strengthening Families Program for prevention of delinquency and drug use in special populations. In R. Peters & R. J. McMahon (Eds.), *Childhood disorders, substance abuse, and delinquency: prevention and early intervention approaches.* Newbury Park, CA: SAGE.

Lynch, R. G. (2007). What science tells us about pre–K in the states. A presentation at the National Invitational Conference of the Early Childhood Research Collaboration, *The Cost-Effectiveness of Public Investment in High-Quality Prekindergarten: A State Level Synthesis.* Minneapolis, MN.

Mayer, G. R. (1995). Preventing antisocial behavior in the schools. *Journal of Applied Behavior Analysis, 28,* 467–478.

Metzler, C. W., Biglan, A., Embry, D. D., Sprague, J. R., Boles, S. M., & Kavanagh, K. A. (2007). *Improving the well-being of adolescents in Oregon.* Eugene, OR: Center on Early Adolescence, Oregon Research Institute.

Mrazek, P., Biglan, A., & Hawkins, J. D. (2005). *Community-monitoring systems: Tracking and improving the well-being of America's children and adolescents.* Falls Church, VA: Society for Prevention Research.

Nelson, G., Westhues, A., & MacLeod, J. (2003). A meta-analysis of longitudinal research on preschool prevention programs for children. *Prevention and Treatment. Volume 6,* Article 31, posted December 31, 2003. Retrieved August 5, 2009, from http://web.ebscohost.com/ehost/pdf?vid=3&hid=5&sid=c8861d40-05ad-4912-9184-bcc364995d47%40sessionmgr4

Olds, D., Henderson, C. R., Jr., Cole, R., Eckenrode, J., Kitzman, H., Luckey, D., et al. (1998). Long-term effects of nurse home visitation on children's criminal and antisocial behavior: 15-year follow-up of a randomized controlled trial. *Journal of the American Medical Association, 280,* 1238–1244.

Patterson, G. R., DeBaryshe, B. D., & Ramsey, E. (1989). A developmental perspective on antisocial behavior. *American Psychologist, 44,* 329–335.

Patterson, G. R., Reid, J. B., & Dishion, T. J. (1992). *Antisocial boys: A social interactional approach.* Eugene, OR: Castalia.

Pentz, M. A., Dwyer, J. H., MacKinnon, D. P., Flay, B. R., Hansen, W. B., Wang, E. Y. I., et al. (1989). A multicommunity trial of primary prevention of adolescent drug abuse. *Journal of the American Medical Association, 261,* 3259–3266.

Pentz, M. A., MacKinnon, D. P., Dwyer, J. H., Wang, E. Y. I., Hansen, W. B., Flay, B. R., et al. (1989). Longitudinal effects of the Midwestern Prevention Project on regular and experimental smoking in adolescents. *Preventive Medicine, 18,* 304–321.

Pentz, M. A., MacKinnon, D. P., Flay, B. R., Hansen, W. B., Johnson, C. A., & Dwyer, J. H. (1989). Primary prevention of chronic diseases in adolescence: Effects of the Midwestern Prevention Project on tobacco use. *American Journal of Epidemiology, 130,* 713–724.

Pentz, M. A., Trebow, E. A., Hansen, W. B., & MacKinnon, D. P. (1990). Effects of program implementation on adolescent drug use behavior: The Midwestern Prevention Project (MPP). *Evaluation Review, 14,* 264–289.

Perry, C., Williams, C. L., Komro, K. A., Veblen-Mortenson, S., Stigler, M. H., Munson, K. A., et al. (2002). Project Northland: Long-term outcomes of community action to reduce adolescent alcohol use. *Health Education Research, 17,* 117–132.

Perry, C. L., Williams, C. L., Komro, K. A., Veblen-Mortenson, S., Forster, J. L., Bernstein-Lachter, R., et al. (2000). Project Northland high school interventions: Community action to reduce adolescent alcohol use. *Health Education & Behavior, 27,* 29–49.

Perry, C. L., Williams, C. L., Veblen-Mortenson, S., Toomey, T. L., Komro, K. A., Anstine, P. S., et al. (1996). Project Northland: Outcomes of a communitywide alcohol use prevention program during early adolescence. *American Journal of Public Health,* 956–965.

Petras, H., Kellam, S. G., Brown, C. H., Muthén, B., Ialongo, N. S., & Poduska, J. M. (2008). Developmental epidemiological courses leading to antisocial personality disorder and violent and criminal behavior: Effects by young adulthood of a universal preventive intervention in first- and second-grade classrooms. *Drug and Alcohol Dependence, 95,* S45–S59.

Prinz, R. J., Sanders, M. R., Shapiro, C. J., Whitaker, D. J., & Lutzker, J. R. (2009). Population-based prevention of child maltreatment: The U.S. Triple P System Population Trial. *Prevention Science, 10*(1), 1–12.

Reynolds, A. J., Temple, J. A., Robertson, D. L., & Mann, E. A. (2002). Age 21 cost-benefit analysis of the Title I Chicago child-parent centers. *Educational Evaluation and Policy Analysis, 24,* 267–303.

Reynolds, A. J., Temple, J. A., Suh-Ruu, O., Robertson, D. L., Mersky, J. P., Topitzes, J. W., et al. (2007). Effects of a school-based, early childhood intervention on adult health and well-being. *Archives of Pediatrics and Adolescent Medicine, 161*(8), 730–739.

Rusby, J. C., Forrester, K. K., Biglan, A., & Metzler, C. W. (2005). Relationships between peer harassment and adolescent problem behaviors. *Journal of Early Adolescence, 25,* 453–477.

Rutter, M., Maughan, B., Mortimore, P., & Ouston, J. (1982). Fifteen thousand hours: Secondary schools and their effects on children. Boston: Harvard University Press.

Sanders, M. R. & Markie-Dadds, C. (1996). Triple P: A multilevel family intervention program for children with disruptive behaviour disorders. In *Early intervention and prevention in mental health* (12th ed., pp. 59–85). Carlton South VIC, VIC, Australia: Australian Psychological Society.

Serketich, W. J., & Dumas, J. E. (1996). The effectiveness of behavioral parent training to modify antisocial behavior in children: A meta-analysis. *Behavior Therapy, 27,* 171–186.

Shonkoff, J. P., & Phillips, D. A. (2000). *From neurons to neighborhoods: The science of early childhood development.* Washington, DC: National Academy Press.

Spoth, R., Greenberg, M., Bierman, K., & Redmond, C. (2004). PROSPER Community-University Partnership Model for Public Education Systems: Capacity-building for evidence-based, competence-building prevention. *Prevention Science, 5,* 31–39.

Temple, J. A., & Reynolds, A. J. (2007). Benefits and costs of investments in preschool education: Evidence from the Child-Parent Centers and related programs. *Economics of Education Review, 26,* 126–144.

Thomas, R., & Zimmer-Gembeck, M. J. (2007). Behavioral outcomes of Parent-Child Interaction Therapy and Triple P - Positive Parenting Program: A review and meta-analysis. *Journal of Abnormal Child Psychology, 35,* 475–495.

Thornton, T. N., Craft, C. A., Dahlberg, L. L., Lynch, B. S., & Baer, K. (2000). *Best practices of youth violence prevention. A sourcebook for community action.* Atlanta, GA: Division of Violence Prevention, Centers for Disease Control and Prevention.

Veblen-Mortenson, S., Rissel, C. E., Perry, C. L., Wolfson, M., Finnegan, J. R., & Forster, J. (1999). Lessons learned from Project Northland: Community organization in rural communities. In N. Bracht (Ed.), *Health promotion at the community level* (2nd ed., pp. 105–117). Thousand Oaks, CA: SAGE.

Wagenaar, A. C., Murray, D. M., Gehan, J. P., Wolfson, M., Forster, J. L., Toomey, T. L., et al. (2000). Communities mobilizing for change on alcohol: Outcomes from a randomized community trial. *Journal of Studies on Alcohol, 61,* 85–94.

Walker, H. M., Colvin, G., & Ramsey, E. (1995). *Antisocial behavior in school: Strategies and best practices.* Belmont, CA: Brooks/Cole.

Webster-Stratton, C. (1984). *The Incredible Years Parent Training Manual: BASIC Program.* Seattle, WA: The Incredible Years.

CHAPTER 5

An Ecological Approach to Interventions With High-Risk Students in Schools: Using the Family Check-Up to Motivate Parents' Positive Behavior Support

Thomas J. Dishion
Elizabeth Stormshak
Chelsea Siler
Child and Family Center, University of Oregon

INTRODUCTION

Students' disruptive behavior at school is one of the greatest problems facing teachers, parents, and society. Youth who show problem behavior at school often have a variety of related concerns, including low achievement, low attendance, depression, and substance use. A substantial proportion of student problem behaviors can be managed from within the school system through the use of carefully designed behavior management systems (driven by functional assessments), such as school-wide positive behavior support (SWPBS; Crone & Horner, 2003; Horner & Carr, 1997; Sugai, Horner, & Sprague, 1999). SWPBS is designed to organize school discipline systems to reduce problem behavior and support student achievement. However, a subset (5–10%) of school-age children require intensive intervention and treatment in the school context. These youth are best served with a multiple-focus intervention that targets behavior across contexts, at home and at school (Dishion & Kavanagh, 2003).

Research on intervention outcomes strongly suggests that it is advisable to design interventions for these children that target and motivate parents to engage in family management practices to effect long-term change (Forgatch, Bullock, & DeGarmo, 2003; Kazdin, 2002). The interventions, however, must be realistic with respect to professionals' available time and must be coordinated with the school's efforts to promote the students' success (Dishion & Stormshak, 2007).

This chapter provides an overview of an ecological approach to family intervention and treatment that can be implemented in schools: the Child and Family Center's EcoFIT model, which consists of six unique features or assumptions. Interventions are empirically based, family centered, and assessment driven. Through interventions, the model addresses the social interactions in which children's mental health problems are embedded, a family's motivation to change, and the role of intervention within a health maintenance framework.

First, the intervention is based on empirical models of child and adolescent psychopathology in general and behavior problems in particular (e.g., Dishion & Patterson, 2006; Patterson, Reid, & Dishion, 1992). Although the establishment of empirically supported interventions for children and families is relatively recent, general principles can guide intervention decisions. Studying the literature on empirically supported interventions and on ineffective or harmful interventions for children and adolescents results in the following conclusions: (a) research indicates that interventions that mobilize adult caregivers, support skillful behavior management practices, and promote youth self-regulation tend to reduce behavior problems and emotional distress, such as anxiety and depression (Kazdin & Weisz, 2003); (b) interventions that aggregate youth without an appropriate level of supervision and structure, or that attempt to frighten youth out of misbehavior are less effective, and in some conditions iatrogenic (Dishion & Dodge, 2005).

An important synergism has emerged from research on the causes of psychopathology and from the literature on intervention effectiveness (Cicchetti & Toth, 1992; Dishion & Patterson, 1999). As this chapter discusses, etiological models have a very practical function. For example, longitudinal studies on the etiology of problem behavior repeatedly indicate that parenting practices in general and family management in particular are highly correlated with the degree of child and adolescent problem behavior (e.g., Loeber & Dishion, 1983). Family management, therefore, is central to effective ecological intervention with children and families.

A second feature of the EcoFIT approach to child and family interventions is that it is family centered. Effective interventions with children and adolescents involve an attempt to engage caregivers to lead the change process. Although interventions may target multiple systems, such as schools and families, changes will be more enduring if caregivers choose to engage in a change process that is guided by an awareness of their own interactions with the child and of the child's behavioral and emotional needs. There is substantial empirical support for a family-centered approach to child and adolescent interventions. The premise that family-centered strategies are effective for reducing child and adolescent problem behavior is strongly supported by treatment outcome research and prevention science literatures. (Examples of treatment outcome research can be found in Borduin & Henggeler, 1990; Dishion & Patterson, 1992; Eddy & Chamberlain, 2000; Henggeler, Schoenwald, Borduin, Rowland, & Cunningham, 1998; Kazdin, 2003; Liddle, 1999; Patterson, 1974; Sanders, 1999; Szapocznik & Kurtines, 1993; and Webster-Stratton, 1990. Prevention science literature includes, for example, Brody et al., 2004; Bugental et al., 2002; Conduct Problems Prevention Research Group, 2002; Forgatch & DeGarmo, 1999; Hawkins, Catalano, & Miller, 1992; Kumpfer, Molgaard, & Spoth, 1996; O'Donnell, Hawkins, Catalano, Abbott, & Day, 1995; Olds et al., 1997; Spoth, Redmond, & Shin, 1998; and Staton et al., 2004.)

Family-centered interventions have undergone a critical shift in the past 20 years, having moved from a treatment model that is delivered to clients in clinic settings to an intervention model involving recruitment of parents to engage in interventions in community settings such as schools (Stormshak, Dishion, Light, & Yasui, 2005). The approach described in this chapter is designed especially for public school settings yet is equally applicable to service settings such as preschools and welfare program-based family services (Dishion & Kavanagh, 2003; Shaw, Dishion, Supplee, Gardner, & Arnds, 2006).

A third feature of the EcoFIT model is that it is assessment driven, in that the intervention is based on a comprehensive, objective, and psychological assessment of the child, his or her family, and other relevant environments. Direct observations are a critical component of this assessment process. An ecological assessment can complement clinical impressions and increase the reliability and validity of the case conceptualization that underlies clinical judgment, and therefore improve the design of an effective intervention.

A fourth feature of the EcoFIT approach to intervention is the emphasis on addressing social interactions in which children's mental health problems are embedded. Developmental science has made tremendous progress during the past 30 years by more precisely identifying and measuring the functional dynamics of family and peer relationships that lead to psychopathology in children and adolescents (Dishion & Patterson, 2006). In particular, coercive parent–child interactions are related to antisocial behavior (e.g., Patterson et al., 1992), and targeting these interactions reduces problem behavior (Dishion, Patterson, & Kavanagh, 1992; Forgatch, 1991; Forgatch & DeGarmo, 2002). Recent work examines the role of family interaction and adolescent depression, with the aim of targeting these family interactions during the course of interventions to reduce adolescent depression (Connell & Dishion, 2008). From an ecological perspective, an effective intervention is one that considers relationship dynamics, and by doing so must necessarily assess social interactions and motivate change in order to improve both problem behavior and emotional adjustment.

The EcoFIT model differs from interventions that rely exclusively on functional assessments of problem behavior in that it examines the function of behavior across contexts (e.g., home, school, and community) for both the caregiver and the child. It has long been clear that children with behavior problems at school also tend to be difficult for parents to manage at home (Loeber & Dishion, 1984), and interventions with parents in the home improve child behavior at school (e.g., Dishion, Andrews, & Crosby, 1995; Forgatch et al., 2003; Patterson, 1974). Although the rationale is that parents can work with both contexts in which children's behavior may pose problems, the truth is that a child may engage in behaviors at school that are positively reinforced by peers as early as at age 6 and certainly by adolescence (Snyder et al., 2005; Dishion, Spracklen, Andrews, & Patterson, 1996). Thus, for interventions to be effective, especially for children with more severe problem behaviors, the ecology of the child and family must be examined when considering the function of behavior across settings.

A fifth feature of the EcoFIT model is that it explicitly addresses a family's motivation to change. Research during the past 15 years indicates that this step is a critical ingredient of effective interventions (Prochaska & Norcross, 1999). Miller and colleagues developed systematic approaches to addressing motivation to change, referred to as *motivational interviewing* (Miller & Rollnick, 2002). Giving feedback to families about their assessments in a supportive, nonconfrontational fashion is a critical component of motivational interviewing. The Child and Family Center's EcoFIT model includes an adaptation of this strategy, the Family Check-Up (FCU), which is conducted at home and at school. The FCU is central to an ecological approach to child and family interventions.

Finally, the sixth feature of an ecological approach is that it is grounded in a health maintenance framework (Stormshak & Dishion, 2002). This feature of the EcoFIT model is a radical departure from conventional approaches to both child and adult clinical and counseling psychology, which focus on "treating" mental health disorders as if there were a permanent cure. However, if one assumes an interaction between biological and environmental factors in mental health (see Rutter et al., 1997), then one accepts that some individuals are more vulnerable to environmental stress than are others, in terms of initial manifestations of disorder and of recurrence (Monroe & Harkness, 2005). Given variation in vulnerability to environmental stress, periodic assessments and interventions are needed to prevent, treat, or reduce harm associated with problem behavior and emotional distress. Integrating family interventions in the public school environment fits well with the health maintenance framework in that there are naturally occurring, clear time points when it is desirable and feasible to evaluate a student's school adjustment (academic, behavioral, and emotional) and to make adjustments to the school or family environments.

ECOFIT IN PUBLIC SCHOOLS

In the United States, the majority of children attend school up to age 18, with dropout rates increasing dramatically as youth enter late adolescence. Many of the behavioral problems that define the risk trajectory for serious delinquency and early-onset substance use are apparent in the public school setting (Dishion & Patterson, 1993; Loeber & Dishion, 1983). In addition, schools are the key setting where youth aggregate into peer groups, some of which exacerbate risk for problem behavior (Dishion, Duncan, Eddy, Fagot, & Fetrow, 1994; Kellam, 1990; Rutter, 1985). For these reasons, schools can be considered "as potential sites for service delivery as well as potential objects of intervention activity" (Trickett & Birman, 1989, p. 361).

Previous research has shown that intervention effects can span home and school if the approach used coordinates parenting and school interventions (Dishion, Patterson, & Kavanagh, 1992; Patterson, 1974). With this body of research in mind, Child and Family Center researchers designed the EcoFIT model to exclusively focus on parents, address the family dynamics of adolescent problem behavior, link with school procedures, be cost-effectively delivered, and comprehensively address the wide range of risks typical in school settings.

Enhancing communication and cooperation between parents and school staff can drastically affect parents' potential for monitoring their child's behavior, setting rules and limits for their child, and supporting their child's academic progress (Gottfredson, Gottfredson, & Hybl, 1993; Reid, 1993). Simply increasing specific information that parents receive regarding their child's attendance, homework, and class behavior will result in improved monitoring and support for the academic and social success of children at risk (Blechman, Taylor, & Schrader, 1981; Heller & Fantuzzo, 1993).

Interventions for helping parents change their parenting practices should be comprehensive and responsive to the developmental history of the child and family. Two important ways of achieving this end are (a) matching the level of need (the risk status of the child) to the level of support provided to parents, and (b) integrating diverse intervention levels to maximize and support protective parenting practices in a community setting (Dishion & Kavanagh, 2003).

Establishment of a School–Based Intervention

To implement family-centered interventions in the public school setting, it is necessary to create a context within the host environment. Leaders in public schools can take a variety of steps to facilitate home–school collaboration. The first and most pragmatic step is to create a family resource center in the school, a physical space that is appropriate for meetings with families and parents. The second step is to use a parent consultant, that is, a staff person trained to work with parents as a family ally. Third, a less tangible step, but important nonetheless, is for the principal and vice-principal to acknowledge daily that collaborating with and supporting families is central to the education of students. It is important for staff at every school to ask themselves: What are three changes we could make to increase involvement of parents?

Family Resource Center

The first step in establishing family-based services in a school setting is to create a family resource center (FRC), a physical space in the school that is staffed with a parent consultant. The FRC's goals would be to (a) establish an infrastructure for collaboration between school staff and parents, (b) promote norms and strategies for empirically validated family management practices, and (c) provide a vehicle through which a program of specific family-centered interventions can be implemented and coordinated with educational services in the school. Some examples are the Family Check-Up (FCU), parent management training, and follow-up academic monitoring services for parents.

It is critical for the FRC to have a parent consultant who is trained and knowledgeable in working therapeutically with parents. Moreover, other school staff must view this person as an ally when they are responding to a student's problem behavior and emotional difficulties, so that parents can be recruited early to effectively remediate the problem. When parents change their parenting practices, they face a difficult and emotional journey that requires skilled professionals who know how to use effective interventions as well as work with resistance to change (e.g., Patterson & Forgatch, 1985). A variety of strategies can be used to engage caregivers at various points in the continuum of risk, all of which serve to establish rapport and collaboration in the best interest of the student (Henggeler et al., 1998; Szapocznik & Kurtines, 1989). The key strategies are discussed below.

Home Visits

To work effectively with parents, parent consultants must visit families in their home (Szapocznik & Kurtines, 1989). In the early years of delivering our family intervention through public schools, we found that getting parents engaged, either through parent groups or the FCU process, requires that the parent first meet the parent consultant. We found at first that about 20% of the parents who initially agreed to participate in groups actually attended the group meeting. Among a new group of parents, however, a brief home visit pushed the attendance rate to more than 75%. Similarly, when we initially offered the FCU in a public school environment, we had relatively low engagement. However, conducting a brief home visit at the end of the summer, before the school year began, substantially increased the use of the FRC and the FCU.

Family Engagement

An important component to consider when implementing school interventions is how to effectively identify the families needing support. Thus, we designed a cost-effective screening strategy for proactively identifying students most in need of additional support in the public school environment. The approach is called the *multiple gating strategy* (Dishion & Patterson, 1993; Loeber & Dishion, 1987; Loeber, Dishion, & Patterson, 1984). The key concept is that decisions regarding children's level of risk are based largely on systematically collected data and less on day-to-day reactions of school staff to students' behavior. This approach has been adopted and found to be quite feasible in public schools (Feil, Walker, & Severson, 1995).

In general, we found that comprehensive teacher ratings of behavioral risk can be an inexpensive way to identify families who need interventions and who are likely to engage. Paradoxically, when analyzing the long-term results of our intervention program, we found that the families at highest risk were the most likely to engage in the intervention, and also the most likely to benefit. That is, 6 years later, compared with their randomly assigned controls, children of families who had children at high risk who were proactively identified and who engaged in the intervention were least likely to increase drug use or be arrested by the police (Connell, Dishion, Yasui, & Kavanagh, 2007.

The Family Check-Up

Selected interventions are designed for those youth who are identified as at high risk for an emergent behavioral problem. The Family Check-Up (FCU) is a selected intervention offering family assessment, professional support, and motivation to change. As described by Dishion and Kavanagh (2003), the FCU's in-depth method supports parents' accurate appraisal of their child's risk status and leads to a range of empirically supported interventions. This brief family intervention has been effective for reducing risk factors and promoting adjustment, and it can be implemented in a public school setting. An overview of the EcoFIT model linking the FCU with a set of interventions is summarized in Figure 1.

The FCU's three-session intervention is a goal-directed process initially designed to help clients change behavior (Dishion & Stormshak, 2007). In all instances the FCU's intervention consists of (a) an initial interview; (b) a comprehensive multiagent, multimethod assessment; and (c) a family feedback session (Miller & Rollnick, 2002). The treatment uses motivational interviewing techniques to encourage maintenance of current positive parenting practices and change of disruptive parenting practices.

The strength of EcoFIT in general and of the FCU in particular is the formal integration of diverse perspectives in developing motivation to change. Often, outpatient clinics use unstructured interviews and questionnaires and rely almost exclusively on parent reporting to guide their judgment about diagnosis and treatment. In contrast, EcoFIT integrates multiple perspectives and assessment strategies. Specifically, structured reports are obtained from parents, teachers, and the child and then compared using normative standards. In addition, the parent consultant directly observes family interactions. These diverse data sources provide the parent consultant

Figure 1. The Family Check-Up.

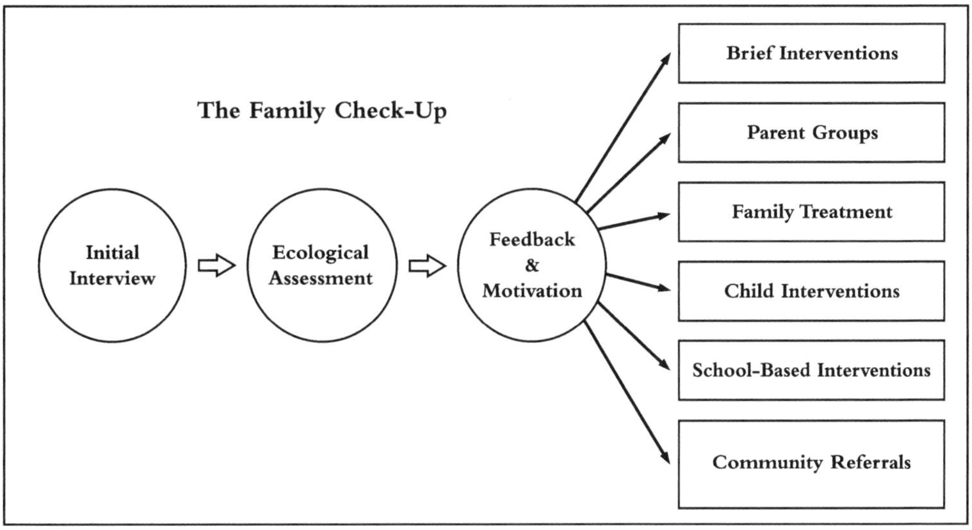

Note. From *Intervening in Children's Lives: An Ecological, Family-Centered Approach to Mental Health Care*, by T. J. Dishion and E. A. Stormshak, 2007, Washington, DC: American Psychological Association. Copyright 2007 by the American Psychological Association. Adapted with permission.

Figure 2. Merging and contrasting perspectives in case conceptualization.

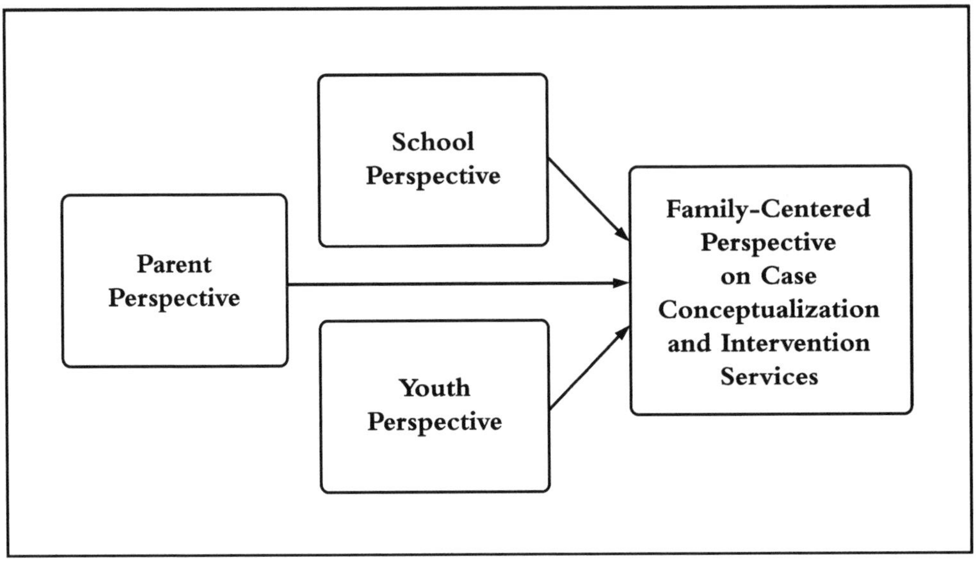

Note. From *Intervening in Children's Lives: An Ecological, Family-Centered Approach to Mental Health Care*, by T. J. Dishion and E. A. Stormshak, 2007, Washington, DC: American Psychological Association. Copyright 2007 by the American Psychological Association. Adapted with permission.

with a family-centered perspective, that is, one that is inclusive but not overly reliant on any one reporting agent (see Figure 2).

Feedback and Motivation

The motivational interviewing process and assessment results help parents choose appropriate services and reasonable change strategies. Not only are data useful for helping parents reconsider behaviors (e.g., aggressiveness) as serious problems that need attention and change, but data also guide the tailoring of the intervention to fit the school setting and individual family. Thus, a fundamental step in the feedback process is sharing data with the parent. Especially useful are data that come from other sources, such as the child, teachers, and caregivers, and from direct observation. Over the years, innovative family intervention researchers have suggested that providing feedback to parents from the findings of psychological assessments is conducive to change (Sanders & Lawton, 1993). The critical feature of such feedback is that it be presented in a way that supports and motivates the family to engage in the change process.

The FCU uses motivational interviewing and assessment information to help parents identify appropriate services and reasonable change strategies. Typically, this step occurs when parents come to the school's family resource center because of concerns about their adolescent's adjustment at home or at school or when they are notified of discipline problems in the school. FRC staff are trained to catch problems early and make recommendations for family intervention, in addition to implementing the typical child interventions that are common in schools.

Intervention Options

The EcoFIT approach is a tailored, adaptive intervention strategy; interventions that follow the FCU are tailored to the assessed and expressed needs of the family (Collins, Murphy, & Bierman, 2004). Unlike most parenting programs that have a set agenda (albeit a flexible delivery format), the final step of the EcoFIT approach includes a menu of choices that allows a focus on only one aspect of parenting. For example, a parent who is aware of his or her child's performance, and who knows only to criticize failures, would benefit tremendously from a tailored intervention about positive reinforcement. The FCU would have identified this need, as well as parenting strengths, and the feedback would be targeted to encourage the caregiver in the process of providing positive reinforcement.

The presumption underlying the menu of family intervention services is that a variety of family-centered interventions can be equally effective for reducing problem behavior (Webster-Stratton, 1984; Webster-Stratton, Kolpacoff, & Hollingsworth, 1988). The intervention menu typically includes three levels of intervention sessions (Dishion & Stormshak, 2007). The first level provides motivation, support, and problem solving of relatively minor problems and adjustment issues. The second level includes skill-building interventions. The third level includes a more intensive focus on multiple problems within the family. Following the FCU, many parents request only follow-up telephone calls from the parent consultant, often referred to as *check-ins*. A hierarchy of strategies is used for managing these brief intervention sessions.

Problem Solving

The first level of the EcoFIT intervention menu would be indicated in instances such as a recent and atypical drop in grades, a discipline problem at school, or recent problem behavior that is relatively isolated. On the basis of the strengths-and-weaknesses profile, the parent consultant may strategically collaborate with parents about how best to handle these difficulties. For example, in a family in which the parents have recently divorced, the adolescent daughter's grades have dropped. She reports normal class attendance, but a recent report card reveals many absences. The parent consultant may establish an e-mail connection with the parents regarding attendance so that one of the parents can monitor attendance on a daily basis and compare the daughter's report with that of the teachers. The monitoring system may itself alleviate the problem. It may also reveal more serious concerns, such as drug use, lying, and problems with peers, that require more intensive interventions, including limit setting and more pervasive monitoring in and out of school.

Skill Building

The second level of intervention includes *skill-building* interventions. These interventions involve actively working with parents to improve their family management skills and closely following the principles of parental management training (Forgatch, Patterson, & DeGarmo, 2005). The skills include positive reinforcement, limit setting, monitoring, problem solving, and communication. The sessions can be conducted either individually with parents, such as in behavioral family therapy, or in groups of parents. In either case, the Everyday Parenting curriculum, derived from more than 30 years of research at the Oregon Social Learning Center, serves as the manual for these interventions (see Figure 3; Dishion, Kavanagh, et al., 2003; Dishion, Stormshak, & Kavanagh, 2009).

Families at high risk are often contending with severe stressors that disrupt parents' emotional regulation and attention. On occasion, these stressors may be chronic and nascent and do not emerge until the parent consultant has established rapport and a working relationship with a family. For example, sexual abuse, an ongoing affair, or domestic violence may be kept quiet by a parent until he or she feels a connection to a professional with whom such an issue can be shared and addressed. Thus, the family goes into crisis not because of the stressor itself, but because it has been brought into the open once the parent has engaged in the intervention process.

Family Adaptation and Coping Interventions

Working with families with multiple problems, the third level of intervention, is often challenging with respect to addressing severe life stressors, potential abuse, and family disruption such as divorce and remarriage. Such family disruptions can create a volatile,

Figure 3. Everyday Parenting curriculum.

Incentives for Behavior Change
1. Positive behavior support/requests
2. Positive behavior support/praise
3. Behavior change plans/incentives
4. Behavior change plans/barriers

Limit Setting and Monitoring
6. Monitoring daily activities
7. Guidelines for limit setting
8. Proactive limit setting
9. Limit-setting challenges/regulation

Relationship Skills
10. Improving family relationships
11. Choosing solutions to family problem
12. Proactive parenting and plannings
13. Shared family routines

Family Check-Up (Tailor Sessions)

Feedback

Collaborate About Future Steps

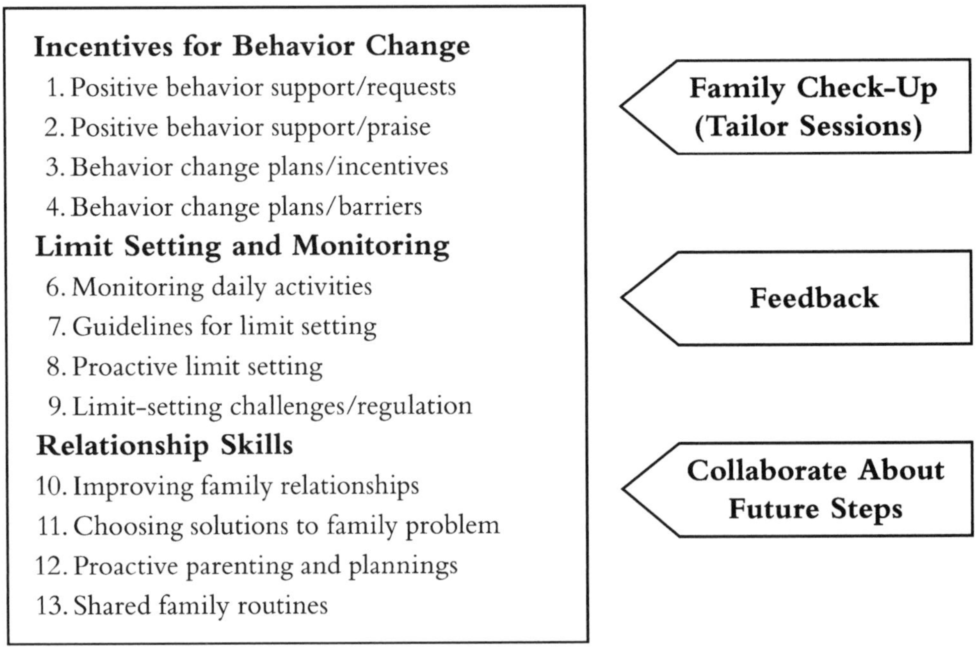

Note. From *Intervening in Children's Lives: An Ecological, Family-Centered Approach to Mental Health Care,* by T. J. Dishion and E. A. Stormshak, 2007, Washington, DC: American Psychological Association. Copyright 2007 by the American Psychological Association. Adapted with permission.

emotionally dysregulated atmosphere in which one or both parents cannot provide positive behavior support. Family adaptation and coping interventions are designed to reduce emotional dysregulation, support the parents' attention on family-centered issues, and provide support for positive, realistic coping that is within the parents' skill set and control.

As shown in Figure 4, these sessions address two interrelated client responses to severe stress and crises: the emotional response and parents' self-efficacy for coping with the stress.

Parents' own emotional response to stress can overwhelm them, and they may become distracted or engage in maladaptive coping and parenting. For example, a parent's response to learning about his or her partner's affair may have more severe implications for the children than the actual stressor does, as traumatic as it may seem. Acting out violently against the partner, suddenly moving to another location, and quitting work can have long-term disruptive effects on children and adolescents. Thus, one helpful service provided in the context of adaptive coping sessions would be timely intervention during crisis. In this case it would involve supporting the parent in coping with emotional reactions without acting them out, and refocus attention on issues of parenting and the long-term interests of the children in general.

The second helpful service is to provide the parent with improved self-efficacy, primarily by guiding parents to actions that are within their control, immediately beneficial, and minimally harmful to others. For example, interventions during an episode of domestic violence could involve (a) removal of the other parent and children to a safe shelter, (b) a court-ordered restraining order, and (c) structured

Figure 4. Family adaptation and coping interventions to reduce disruption during crises.

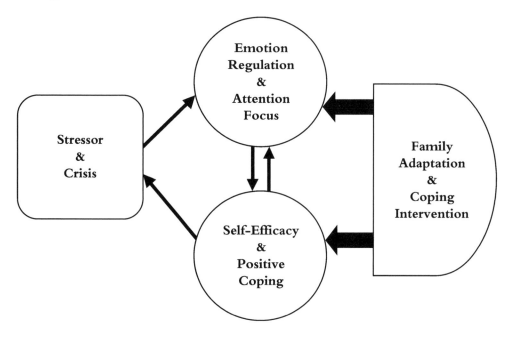

communication with the abusing partner regarding contact with the family during the next week. Thus, the safety of the caregiver and of the children would be ensured, and they would be placed in a supportive social context where problem solving could begin to address the immediate and long-term future of the family.

One of the EcoFIT goals is to help families become engaged with community resources that will best fit the family's long-term needs. Unlike many university-derived interventions, EcoFIT encourages collaborations with community agencies designed to support children and families. For example, if an intervention involves a mother in recovery from methamphetamine abuse, any response to a crisis should reinforce her involvement in services designed to keep her in recovery. When a breech in services occurs, the parent consultant can support the caregiver in taking steps to reengage in services.

There are a variety of barriers to effective parenting: some are historical (e.g., past abuse and trauma), some are contextual (poverty, low resources in communities), and others are chronic (e.g., long-term disabilities, health problems). In these circumstances a key role of the parent consultant is to support caregivers in the course of coping, problem solving, and making efforts to reduce harm to the youth. At times, this requires guiding the caregiver into services that are more appropriate to recovery or safety. Thus, one key function of the parent consultant during the FCU and beyond is to provide a parent with the insight and motivation to seek realistic levels of support to make family changes and to adapt to the stressor.

Structured Interventions

A school's family resource center can deliver a variety of specific interventions and address student and family needs relevant to the full range of the risk continuum, including the Family Check-Up. The FCU is the cornerstone of the service delivery system. This brief intervention ideally would be provided to families every year. A variety of structured interventions are offered subsequent to the FCU, and the following are the most common:

- Brief parenting interventions. This service focuses primarily on motivation but also includes problem-solving approaches to parenting challenges that may be transient (e.g., improving grades).
- School interventions. The parent consultant sets up a daily, weekly, or biweekly report to parents about their student's attendance, behavior in school, and completion of homework. This service is contingent on working with parents on positive reinforcement for meeting goals.
- Family management skill support. This set of services includes more intensive support for family management practices known to reduce the emergence and growth of problem behavior in children and adolescents.
- Support in crises and family disruption. This service focuses primarily on the parents' immediate response to acute crises and family disruption, in the context of sessions that emphasize adaptation and coping.

- Community referrals. A key concept of the EcoFIT model is that it is designed as a collaborative service that is adjusted from community to community. Therefore, referrals to services may vary depending on resources and cultural values.

OUTCOMES

Specific tests of the EcoFIT approach to engaging parents within the context of school are relatively rare. During the past 10 years, the Child and Family Center's researchers have been engaged in a randomized prevention trial in which half of the sixth-grade population of metropolitan middle schools were randomly assigned at the individual level to the FRC versus public middle school as usual. Parent consultants were each assigned to a school, where they attempted to engage parents of youth who were identified as at risk by teachers. Services were provided primarily in the seventh and eighth grades of middle school.

Engagement

We were able to engage 25% of the families in participating in the FCU during the 2 years of service across the three schools. Parent consultants conducted periodic telephone check-ins with an additional 25% of the families but did not conduct an FCU with them. Connell, Dishion, and Deater-Deckard (2006) found that single-parent families, those with students involved in a deviant peer group, and those rated by teachers as at high risk were the most likely to engage in the FCU.

During the course of the middle school years, the families at highest risk had an average of 6 hours of contact with the parent consultant. As one would expect, the contact time decreased as a function of the student's risk level. Students at moderate risk engaged in approximately 3.5 hours of contact. The families at low risk averaged less than 1 hour of contact. Contact included telephone calls as well as personal contact and was recorded by the parent consultants by the minute (Dishion, Kavanagh, Schneiger, Nelson, & Kaufman, 2002).

In an effectiveness trial of the EcoFIT model in another set of four public middle schools, parent consultants carefully counted the minutes of contact with parents of students. In many instances they used creative strategies to engage parents. In one middle school, the parent consultant established a coffee cart for parents and would meet parents as they dropped off their middle school child and picked up coffee. Findings from this study indicated that the number of parent contacts alone in Grades 6, 7, and 8 was associated with reductions in growth in teacher ratings of risk (Stormshak et al., 2005).

Randomized Intervention Effects

Several reports have been published about FRC intervention effects on substance use. The first report revealed that random assignment of students to the FCU in sixth grade was associated with reductions in substance use as well as in deviant peer involvement (Dishion, Kavanagh, et al., 2002; Dishion, Bullock, & Granic, 2002). In that study we found that for the youth at highest risk, reductions in drug use were mediated by changes in observed parental monitoring, such as establishing routines and setting limits (Dishion, Nelson, & Kavanagh, 2003).

Our recent analyses, reported in Connell et al. (2007), concur with these findings, suggesting that the most dramatic effects of EcoFIT are with sixth-grade students who are most severely problematic and whose families are most in need of services. Prevention trial statistical methods were used to incorporate the level of parents' engagement in the FCU into the evaluation of long-term outcomes. When an intention-to-treat design was used, outcomes for adolescents up to age 17 were modest. However, if one considers the level at which a family was engaged in the intervention, compared with that of control subjects who would also have likely engaged in the FCU intervention, the effects are quite dramatic.

This approach to analyzing engagement with an intervention is referred to as complier average causal effect (CACE) analysis (Jo, 2002). The challenge for many randomized prevention trials is that many of the participants do not actually engage in the intervention, especially when it is offered on a voluntary basis. For example, in a test of the EcoFIT model in our intervention trial in public middle schools, 25% of the families in the randomized intervention group engaged in a Family Check-Up when it was offered to all. Using CACE analyses, one can use the information collected prior to the intervention about those participants who engaged, and estimate an "engager" control group resembling those who eventually participated in the FCU. Similarly, those who are in the intervention group and declined the FCU can be used to identify those in the control group who would most likely decline intervention. CACE analysis revealed that single-parent families whose sixth-grade student reported deviant peer involvement and family conflict were the most likely to engage in the intervention condition.

Two outcome studies on these findings, which are summarized in Table 1, reveal the results for the intervention and control groups described earlier. In our analysis of problem behavior, we found a marked reduction in the percentage of youth in the intervention group who were arrested at least once (15% had been arrested) and who actually received the FCU, compared with the control (100% had been arrested). Thus, sixth-grade students at high risk were six times as likely to be arrested within the next 5 years if they were not offered the FCU. Similarly, they used marijuana five times more frequently during a 1-month period than did the intervention group. These findings were extended to marijuana and tobacco dependence by age 18 as well. These analyses revealed that random assignment to the EcoFIT intervention reliably reduced substance use, antisocial behavior, and the probability of arrest (Connell et al., 2006).

Table 1 also reveals that random assignment to the intervention resulted in a 50% reduction in days absent from high school during the 11th grade for those families who engaged in the FCU. Control students missed an average of 32 days during the school year, and intervention youth missed only 13 (Stormshak, Connell, & Dishion, in press).

Table 1. Outcomes of Applying EcoFIT in Public Schools

11th-grade outcomes	Intervention (received FCU)	Control (high-risk comparison)
Percentage arrested at least one time	15	100
Frequency of marijuana use in previous month	1	5
Days absent from school	13	32

Note. From "A school-based family-centered intervention to prevent substance use: The Family Check-Up," by T. J. Dishion, and E. A. Stormshak, 2009, in J. Bray & M. Stanton (Eds.), Blackwell handbook of family psychology (pp. 499–514). Malden, MA: Blackwell Publishing. Adapted with permission.

Another trend is particularly important to consider when inspecting Table 1. Although it is often said that family-based services offered in the school will be received only by families that are at low or no risk, this was not the case in our study. Our proactive approach to offering the FCU suggested that, in fact, the families who declined participation were those who were at the lowest risk of all. In other words, these parents accurately assessed their young adolescents' risk status and did not feel the need to receive information or support on behavior management strategies. This is an optimistic finding indeed, because it suggests that if schools have the appropriate outreach and engagement strategies in place for caregivers of the highest risk students, they are likely to reduce those students' long-term risk by supporting their use of positive behavior support strategies and coordinating with school staff in supporting student success.

CONCLUSION

This chapter provided an overview of the ecological approach to family intervention and treatment within the school setting. Nearly 20 years ago Dishion and colleagues set out to translate a developmental model of problem behavior into an effective intervention for reducing the emerging risks associated with childhood and adolescence (Dishion, Reid, & Patterson, 1988). The developmental model, then referred to as the Adolescent Transitions Program (ATP), contained constructs such as parental monitoring and deviant peer involvement that had not previously been explicitly addressed in behavioral family interventions. ATP was refined using positive findings (Dishion & Andrews, 1995; Dishion et al., 1992) and negative findings (e.g., Dishion, McCord, & Poulin, 1999) in our own work and that of others. Today ATP is a general set of principles for prevention and treatment of adjustment problems in children and families.

Until recently, family-based interventions have been difficult to integrate with a prevention model primarily because they were costly, but also because of the challenge of reaching families in need. Implementation of family intervention in a school setting, however, also addresses these cost issues. Our data show that in our intervention study, the families at highest risk are averaging 6 hours of contact over 2 years. Of course, their range of risk behavior is more extreme than that of families whose risk was found to be less, and some families require intensive support. However, this group is only a small subset of families within a public school environment, and intervention certainly could be accomplished by a full-time staff person with dedicated time and training for working with parents.

From our experience, the EcoFIT approach has promise, and effectiveness has been demonstrated for as much as 7 to 8 years. However, many improvements are needed, and work is in progress to advance knowledge about the following issues:

1. Proactive screening and identification. CFC researchers developed a brief teacher rating form that could apply to an entire class of middle school students. The measure has been helpful for identifying youth who could benefit from services. Unfortunately, teacher ratings are prone to bias in that the ratings are less valid for African American students, and minority students are much more likely to be identified as at risk (Yasui & Dishion, 2008).

2. Functional assessment. It would be useful to integrate recent advances in functional assessment into the FCU and EcoFIT process. The philosophy of functional assessment is consistent with our emphasis on social interactions. An informal functional assessment is included in CFC's videotaped family interactions; however, to date, functional assessments have not been formally incorporated in the design of our interventions. This seems an obvious omission in terms of the approach described in this chapter.

3. Cultural enhancements. In a family-centered model, it is critical to appreciate and be sensitive to the variety and strengths of different parenting patterns within cultures. Drs. Alison Boyd-Ball and Kate Kavanagh are currently implementing the EcoFIT model within three American Indian communities. Dr. Beth Stormshak is currently working on modifying the family-centered model to be culturally sensitive to African American and Latino families. Improvements in the EcoFIT approach during the next 5 years will likely lead to finely tuned guidelines to enhance cultural sensitivity and adaptability.

4. Infrastructure support. The interface between family and school is difficult to achieve without the use of recent technological advances such as the Internet. The Child and Family Center is currently working on a comprehensive Internet and intranet system that enhances student monitoring, incorporates the FCU, and provides resources for the menu of family-centered interventions.

5. Referral and integration into schools. When FRC personnel become part of a school system, the staff, teachers, counselors, or administrators start to proactively refer a child when they first identify concerns about behavior, peer associations, or emotional adjustment. Unfortunately, this outcome is often difficult to achieve, and schools can need as much as 3 years of experience with the FRC and its services before they actively use it in the referral process. It is clear that additional training is needed for school personnel such as teachers, principals, school

psychologists, counselors, and special educators to make effective use of the FRC, and to have an overall impact on student problem behavior and emotional adjustment.

6. Emotional adjustment of children. The vast majority of children do not come to the CFC in neat diagnostic packages. Many of the children and adolescents that therapists see are anxious and depressed, and their level of emotional distress actually feeds into the failure trajectory. Recently, CFC researchers found that the EcoFIT family-centered approach reduced adolescent reports of depression on the Children's Depression Inventory (CDI; Kovacs 1985), compared with the control group (Connell & Dishion, 2008). We are currently adjusting our family intervention to improve our potential to support child and adolescent emotional adjustment and reduce problem behavior.

There is no doubt that integrating family-centered interventions into the public school system would have public health benefits for children and adolescents. Such intervention services can now be cost-effectively delivered with respect to efficiently targeting families most in need and working to change parenting practices through motivation enhancement. Those of us who work to improve family cohesiveness and child and adolescent achievement now stand at a crossroads in promoting school-based interventions. We can continue to import programs such as EcoFIT into the school context, which requires intensive training, monitoring, accountability, and organization of change agents outside the system. Alternatively, we can change our graduate training of counselors and school psychologists, as well as of school principals, to provide these services as a key component of their professional role in the school context. The latter approach is a more promising long-term strategy for improving the education of children both in academic competencies and for meeting the social and emotional demands of living in the 21st century.

AUTHOR NOTE

This project was supported by grants DA16110 and DA07031 from the National Institutes of Health to the first author, and DA018374 from the National Institutes of Health to the second author. This work especially benefits from the contributions of the following colleagues at the Child and Family Center: Arin Connell, Kate Kavanagh, Peggy Veltman, and Charlotte Winter. Cheryl Mikkola is gratefully acknowledged for her help with this manuscript. The Portland Public Schools and the Project Alliance youth and families are appreciated for their participation in this research.

Correspondence regarding this research may be addressed to Thomas J. Dishion, PhD, Child and Family Center, 195 West 12th Avenue, Eugene, OR 97401-3408; phone (541) 346-4805; fax (541) 346-4858; e-mail dishion@uoregon.edu; http:// cfc.uoregon.edu.

REFERENCES

Blechman, E. A., Taylor, C. J., & Schrader, S. M. (1981). Family problem solving versus home notes as early intervention with high-risk children. *Journal of Consulting and Clinical Psychology, 49,* 919–926.

Borduin, C. M., & Henggeler, S. W. (1990). A multisystemic approach to the treatment of delinquent behavior. In R. J. McMahon & R. D. Peters (Eds.), *Behavior disorders of adolescence: Research, intervention and policy in clinical and school settings* (pp. 63–80). New York: Haworth.

Brody, G. H., Murry, V. M., Gerrard, M., Gibbons, F. X., Molgaard, V., McNair, L., et al. (2004). The Strong African American Families program: Translating research into prevention programming. *Child Development, 75*(3), 900–917.

Bugental, D. B., Ellerson, P. C., Rainey, B., Lin, E. K., Kokotovic, A., & O'Hara, N. (2002). A cognitive approach to child abuse prevention. *Journal of Family Psychology, 16,* 16–45.

Cicchetti, D., & Toth, S. L. (1992). The role of developmental theory in prevention and intervention. *Development & Psychopathology, 4*(4), 489–493.

Collins, L., Murphy, S., & Bierman, K. (2004). A conceptual framework for adaptive preventive interventions. *Prevention Science, 5,* 185–196.

Conduct Problems Prevention Research Group (2002). Evaluation of the first 3 years of the Fast Track Prevention Trial with children at high risk for adolescent conduct problems. *Journal of Abnormal Child Psychology, 30,* 19–35.

Connell, A., & Dishion, T. J. (2008). Reducing depression among at-risk early adolescents: Three-year effects of a family-centered intervention embedded within schools. *Journal of Family Psychology, 22*(4), 574–585

Connell, A., Dishion, T. J., & Deater-Deckard, K. (2006). Variable- and person-centered approaches to the analysis of early adolescent substance use: Linking peer, family, and intervention effects with developmental trajectories [Special issue]. *Merrill-Palmer Quarterly, 52*(3), 421–448.

Connell, A., Dishion, T. J., Yasui, M., & Kavanagh, K. (2007). An adaptive approach to family intervention: Linking engagement in family-centered intervention to reductions in adolescent problem behavior. *Journal of Consulting and Clinical Psychology, 75,* 568–579.

Crone, D. A., & Horner, R. H. (2003). *Building positive behavior support systems in schools: Functional behavioral assessment.* New York: Guilford Press.

Dishion, T. J., & Andrews, D. W. (1995). Preventing escalation in problem behaviors with high-risk young adolescents: Immediate and 1-year outcomes. *Journal of Consulting and Clinical Psychology, 63,* 538–548.

Dishion, T. J., & Andrews, D. W., & Crosby, L. (1995). Antisocial boys and their friends in early adolescence: Relationship characteristics, quality, and interactional process. *Child Development, 66,* 139–151.

Dishion, T. J., Bullock, B. M., & Granic, I. (2002). Pragmatism in modeling peer influence: Dynamics, outcomes, and change processes. In D. Cicchetti & S. Hinshaw (Eds.), How prevention intervention studies in the field of developmental psychopathology can inform developmental theories and models [Special issue]. *Development and Psychopathology, 14*(4), 995–1009.

Dishion, T. J., & Dodge, K. A. (2005). Peer contagion in interventions for children and adolescents: Moving toward an understanding of the ecology and dynamics of change. *Journal of Abnormal Child Psychology, 33*(3), 395–400.

Dishion, T. J., Duncan, T. E., Eddy, J. M., Fagot, B. I., & Fetrow, R. A. (1994). The world of parents and peers: Coercive exchanges and children's social adaption. *Social Development, 3,* 255–268.

Dishion, T. J., & Kavanagh, K. (2003). *Intervening in adolescent problem behavior: A family-centered approach.* New York: Guilford Press.

Dishion, T. J., Kavanagh, K., Schneiger, A., Nelson, S. E., & Kaufman, N. (2002). Preventing early adolescent substance use: A family-centered strategy for the public middle school ecology. In R. L. Spoth, K. Kavanagh, & T. J. Dishion (Eds.), Universal family-centered prevention strategies: Current findings and critical issues for public health impact [Special issue]. *Prevention Science, 3,* 191–201.

Dishion, T. J., Kavanagh, K., Veltman, M., McCartney, T., Soberman, L., & Stormshak, E. A. (2003). *Family Management Curriculum V.2.0: Leader's guide.* Eugene, OR: Child and Family Center Publications. http://cfc.uoregon.edu.

Dishion, T. J., McCord, J., & Poulin, F. (1999). When interventions harm: Peer groups and problem behavior. *American Psychologist, 54,* 755–764.

Dishion, T. J., Nelson, S. E., & Kavanagh, K. (2003). The Family Check-Up with high-risk young adolescents: Preventing early-onset substance use by parent monitoring [Special issue]. *Behavior Therapy, 34,* 553–571.

Dishion, T. J., & Patterson, G. R. (1992). Age effects in parent training outcome. *Behavior Therapy, 23,* 719–729.

Dishion, T. J., & Patterson, G. R. (1993). Childhood screening for early adolescent problem behavior: A multiple gating strategy. In M. Singer, L. Singer, & T. M. Anglin (Eds.), *Handbook for screening adolescents at psychosocial risk* (pp. 375–399). New York: Lexington.

Dishion, T. J., & Patterson, G. R. (1999). Model building in developmental psychopathology: A pragmatic approach to understanding and intervention. *Journal of Clinical Child Psychology, 28*(4), 502–512.

Dishion, T. J., & Patterson, G. R. (2006). The development and ecology of antisocial behavior in children and adolescents. In D. Cicchetti & D. J. Cohen (Eds.), *Developmental psychopathology. Vol. 3: Risk, disorder, and adaptation* (pp. 503–541). New York: Wiley.

Dishion, T. J., Patterson, G. R., & Kavanagh, K. (1992). An experimental test of the coercion model: Linking theory, measurement, and intervention. In J. McCord & R. E. Tremblay (Eds.), *The interaction of theory and practice: Experimental studies of interventions* (pp. 253–282). New York: Guilford Press.

Dishion, T. J., Reid, J. B., & Patterson, G. R. (1988). Empirical guidelines for the development of a treatment for early adolescent substance use. In R. E. Coombs (Ed.), *The family context of adolescent drug use* (pp. 189–224). New York: Haworth.

Dishion, T. J., Spracklen, K. M., Andrews, D. W., & Patterson, G. R. (1996). Deviancy training in male adolescent friendships. *Behavior Therapy, 27,* 373–390.

Dishion, T. J., & Stormshak, E. (2007). *Intervening in children's lives: An ecological, family-centered approach to mental health care.* Washington, DC: APA Books.

Dishion, T. J., Stormshak, E. A., & Kavanagh, K. (2009). *Everyday parenting: A therapist's guide for supporting family management practices.* Manual submitted for publication.

Eddy, J. M., & Chamberlain, P. (2000). Family management and deviant peer association as mediators of the impact of treatment condition on youth antisocial behavior. *Journal of Child Clinical Psychology, 5,* 857–863.

Feil, E. G., Walker, H. M., & Severson, H. H. (1995). The Early Screening Project for young children with behavior problems. *Journal of Emotional and Behavioral Disorders, 3*(4), 194–202.

Forgatch, M. (1991). The clinical science vortex: Developing a theory for antisocial behavior. In D. J. Pepler & K. H. Rubin (Eds.), *The development and treatment of childhood aggression* (pp. 291–315). Hillsdale, NJ: Erlbaum.

Forgatch, M. S., Bullock, B. M., & DeGarmo, D. S. (2003). *Parenting through change: An experimental test of the parent management training model for stepfamilies.* Manuscript in preparation.

Forgatch, M. S., & DeGarmo, D. S. (1999). Parenting through change: An effective prevention program for single mothers. *Journal of Consulting & Clinical Psychology, 67*(5), 711–724.

Forgatch, M. S., & DeGarmo, D. S. (2002). Extending and testing the social interaction learning model with divorce samples. In J. B. Reid & G. R. Patterson (Eds.), *Antisocial behavior in children and adolescents: A developmental analysis and model for intervention* (pp. 235–238). Washington, DC: American Psychological Association.

Forgatch, M. S., Patterson, G. R., & DeGarmo, D. S. (2005). Evaluating fidelity: Predictive validity for a measure of competent adherence to the Oregon Model of Parent Management Training. *Behavior Therapy, 36*(1), 3–13.

Gottfredson, D. C., Gottfredson, G. D., & Hybl, L. G. (1993). Managing adolescent behavior: A multiyear, multischool study. *American Educational Research Journal, 30,* 179–215.

Hawkins, J., Catalano, R., & Miller, J. (1992). Risk and protective factors for alcohol and other drug problems in adolescence and early adulthood. *Psychological Bulletin, 112,* 64–105.

Heller, L. R., & Fantuzzo, J. W. (1993). Reciprocal peer tutoring and parent partnership: Does parent involvement make a difference? *School Psychology Review, 22,* 517–534.

Henggeler, S. W., Schoenwald, S. K., Borduin, C. M., Rowland, M. D., & Cunningham., P. B. (1998). *Multisystemic treatment of antisocial behavior in children and adolescents.* New York: Guilford Press.

Horner, R. H., & Carr, E. G. (1997). Behavioral support for students with severe disabilities: Functional assessment intervention. *Journal of Special Education, 31,* 84–104.

Jo, B. (2002). Statistical power in randomized intervention studies with noncompliance. *Psychological Methods, 7,* 178–193.

Kazdin, A. E. (2002). Psychosocial treatments for conduct disorder in children and adolescents. In P. E. Nathan & J. M. Gorman (Eds.), *A guide to treatments that work* (2nd ed.; pp. 57–85). London: Oxford University Press.

Kazdin, A. E. (2003). Problem-solving skills training and parent management training for conduct disorder. In A. E. Kazdin & J. R. Weisz (Eds.), *Evidence-based psychotherapies for children and adolescents* (pp. 241–262). New York: Guilford Press.

Kazdin, A. E., & Weisz, J. R. (Eds.). (2003). *Evidence-based psychotherapies for children and adolescents.* New York: Guilford Press.

Kellam, S. G. (1990). Developmental epidemiological framework for family research on depression and aggression. In G. R. Patterson (Ed.), *Depression and aggression in family interaction* (pp. 11–48). Hillsdale, NJ: Erlbaum.

Kumpfer, K. L., Molgaard, V., & Spoth, R. (1996). The Strengthening Families Program for the prevention of delinquency and drug abuse. In R. D. Peters & R. J. McMahon (Eds.), *Preventing childhood disorders, substance abuse, and delinquency* (pp. 241–267). Newbury Park, CA: SAGE.

Liddle, H. A. (1999). Theory in a family-based therapy for adolescent drug abuse. *Journal of Clinical Child Psychology, 28,* 521–532.

Loeber, R., & Dishion, T. J. (1983). Early predictors of male delinquency: A review. *Psychological Bulletin, 94*(1), 68–99.

Loeber, R., & Dishion, T. J. (1984). Boys who fight at home and school: Family conditions influencing cross-setting consistency. *Journal of Consulting and Clinical Psychology, 52,* 759–768.

Loeber, R., & Dishion, T. J. (1987). Antisocial and delinquent youths: Methods for their early identification. In J. D. Burchard & S. N. Burchard (Eds.), *Prevention of delinquent behavior* (pp. 75–89). Newbury Park, CA: SAGE.

Loeber, R., Dishion, T. J., & Patterson, G. R. (1984). Multiple gating: A multistage assessment procedure for identifying youths at risk for delinquency. *Journal of Research in Crime and Delinquency, 21,* 7–32.

Miller, W. R., & Rollnick, S. (2002). *Motivational interviewing: Preparing people for change* (2nd ed.). New York: Guilford Press.

Monroe, S. M., & Harkness, K. L. (2005). Life stress, the "Kindling" hypothesis, and the recurrence of depression: Considerations from a life stress perspective. *Psychological Review, 112*(2), 417–445.

O'Donnell, J., Hawkins, J. D., Catalano, R., Abbott, R. D., & Day, L. E. (1995). Preventing school failure, drug use, and delinquency among low-income children: Long-term intervention in elementary schools. *American Journal of Orthopsychiatry, 65,* 87–100.

Olds, D., Eckenrode, L. J., Henderson, C. R., Kitzman, H., Powers, J., Cole, R., et al. (1997). Long-term effects of home visitation on maternal life course and child abuse and neglect. *Journal of the American Medical Association, 278,* 637–643.

Patterson, G. R. (1974). Interventions for boys with conduct problems: Multiple settings, treatments, and criteria. *Journal of Consulting and Clinical Psychology, 42,* 471–481.

Patterson, G. R., & Forgatch, M. S. (1985). Therapist behavior as a determinant for client resistance: A paradox for the behavior modifier. *Journal of Consulting and Clinical Psychology, 53,* 846–851.

Patterson, G. R., Reid, J. B., & Dishion, T. J. (1992). *Antisocial boys.* Eugene, OR: Castalia.

Prochaska, J. O., & Norcross, J. G. (1999). *Systems of psychotherapy.* Pacific Grove, CA: Brooks/Cole.

Reid, J. B. (1993). Prevention of conduct disorder before and after school entry: Relating interventions to development findings. *Journal of Development and Psychopathology, 5,* 243–262.

Rutter, M. (1985). Family and school influences on behavioral development. *Journal of Child Psychology & Psychiatry & Allied Disciplines, 26,* 349–368.

Rutter, M., Dunn, J., Simonoff, G., Pickles, A., Maughn, B., Ormel, J., et al. (1997). Integrating nature and nurture: Implications of person–environment correlations and interactions for developmental psychopathology. *Development and Psychopathology, 9,* 335–364.

Sanders, M. R. (1999). Triple P-Positive Parenting Program: Toward an empirically validated multilevel parenting and family support strategy for the prevention of behavior and emotional problems in children. *Clinical Child and Family Psychology Review, 2,* 71–90.

Sanders, N. R., & Lawton, J. M. (1993). Discussing assessment findings with families: A guided participation model of information transfer. *Child and Family Behavior Therapy, 15,* 5–33.

Shaw, D. S., Dishion, T. J., Supplee, L., Gardner, F., & Arnds, K. (2006). Randomized trial of a family-centered approach to the prevention of early conduct problems: Two-year effects of the FCU in early childhood. *Journal of Consulting and Clinical Psychology, 74*(1), 1–9.

Snyder, J., Schrepferman, L., Oeser, J., Patterson, G. R., Stoolmiller, M., Johnson, K., et al. (2005). Deviancy training and association with deviant peers in young children: Occurrence and contribution to early-onset conduct problems. *Development & Psychopathology, 17*(2), 397–413.

Spoth, R., Redmond, C., & Shin, C. (1998). Direct and indirect latent-variable parenting outcomes of two universal family-focused preventative interactions: Extending a public health oriented research base. *Journal of Consulting and Clinical Psychology, 66*(2), 385–399.

Staton, B., Cole, M., Galbraith, J., Li, X., Pendleton, S., Cottrel, L., et al. (2004). Randomized trial of a parent intervention. *Archives of Pediatrics and Adolescent Medicine, 158,* 947–955.

Stormshak, E. A., Connell, A., & Dishion, T. J. (in press). An adaptive approach to family-centered intervention in schools: Linking intervention engagement to academic outcomes in middle and high school. *Prevention Science.*

Stormshak, E. A., & Dishion, T. J. (2002). An ecological approach to child and family clinical and counseling psychology. *Clinical Child and Family Psychology Review, 5*(3), 197–215.

Stormshak, E. A., Dishion, T. J., Light, J., & Yasui, M. (2005). Implementing family-centered interventions within the public middle school: Linking service delivery change to change in problem behavior. *Journal of Abnormal Child Psychology, 33*(6), 723–733.

Sugai, G., Horner, R. H., & Sprague, J. R. (1999). Functional-assessment-based behavior support planning: Research to practice to research. *Behavior Disorders, 24,* 253–257.

Szapocznik, J., & Kurtines, W. M. (1989). *Breakthroughs in family therapy with drug-abusing and problem youth.* New York: Springer.

Szapocznik, J., & Kurtines, W. M. (1993). Family psychology and cultural diversity: Opportunities for theory, research, and application. *American Psychologist, 48,* 400–407.

Trickett, E. J., & Birman, D. (1989). Taking ecology seriously: A community development approach to individually based preventive interventions in schools. In L. A. Bond & B. E. Compas (Eds.), *Primary prevention and promotion in the schools: Primary prevention of psychopathology* (Vol. *12*; pp. 361–390). Newbury Park, CA: SAGE.

Webster-Stratton, C. (1984). Randomized trial of two parent-training programs for families with conduct-disordered children. *Journal of Consulting and Clinical Psychology, 52,* 666–678.

Webster-Stratton, C. (1990). Long-term follow-up of families with young conduct problem children: From preschool to grade school. *Journal of Clinical Child Psychology, 19,* 144–149.

Webster-Stratton, C., Kolpacoff, M., & Hollingsworth, T. (1988). Self-administered videotape therapy for families with conduct-problem children: Comparison with two cost-effective treatments and a control group. *Journal of Consulting and Clinical Psychology, 56,* 558–566.

Yasui, M., & Dishion, T. J. (2008). Direct observation of family management: Validity and reliability as a function of coder ethnicity and training. *Behavior Therapy, 39,* 336–347.

CHAPTER 6

Practice-Based Perspectives on Implementing a Three-Tier Reading Model

Christopher Parker
Jennifer Fleischmann
Judith E. Loughlin
Amanda Ryan
IDEAL Consulting Services

INTRODUCTION

With the implementation of the No Child Left Behind Act (NCLB) in 2001, and more specifically the Reading First initiative, America's public schools were encouraged to adopt and use a multitiered intervention model as a means for preventing and remediating Grades K–3 students' reading difficulties. The most popular multitiered model to emerge from Reading First schools is the three-tier reading model. Given the model's ties to other multitiered intervention models that have empirical evidence to suggest they improve academic outcomes for students (see Vaughn & Chard, 2006), the efficacy of the three-tier reading model has been thoroughly investigated. Findings published by researchers at the University of Texas, the University of Oregon, and Florida State University suggest that the assessment tools and intervention strategies employed within the three-tier reading model improve academic outcomes for students (see chapter 17).

Use of the model is not reserved for only districts and schools receiving Reading First funds. Another piece of federal legislature, the Individuals with Disabilities Education Improvement Act (IDEA 2004), encouraged schools outside the Reading First funding circle to use a multitiered intervention model to address students' basic skill deficits within the general education setting prior to considering special education entitlement. As such, more and more school personnel nationwide are seeking advice, guidance, and support related to implementing the three-tier reading model. This chapter provides a school-based perspective on how to develop, implement, and sustain a three-tier reading model at the elementary grade level.

Address all correspondence and feedback on this chapter to Christopher Parker at cparker@idealconsultingservices.com.

ORIGINS OF THE THREE-TIER READING MODEL

Although the specifics of a three-tier reading model have been conceptualized in different ways, three main ideas supporting the model remain consistent among publications and presentations:

1. They put into practice a system in which *all* students have an opportunity to become competent readers. The system would use multiple tiers of instruction, frequently 3, of increasing intensity tied to students' needs.
2. Identify which tier of instruction students should receive based on universal screening.
3. Monitor students' progress at the appropriate frequency to determine the effects of intervention.

As demonstrated throughout this book, the nomenclature for the tiers differs. The different labels are shown in Figure 1. Tier 1 is often referred to as universal instruction, core curriculum, or primary reading instruction. Tier 2 is labeled variously as strategic, secondary, or targeted group reading instruction. Tier 3 is referred to as intensive, tertiary, or targeted individualized reading instruction. The three tiers are differentiated by (a) duration of instruction, (b) the specificity and intensity of the curriculum and instruction, (c) the balance between whole-group versus small-group instruction, and (d) the frequency of progress monitoring (see chapter 11, this book).

Figure 1. **Three-tier reading model.**

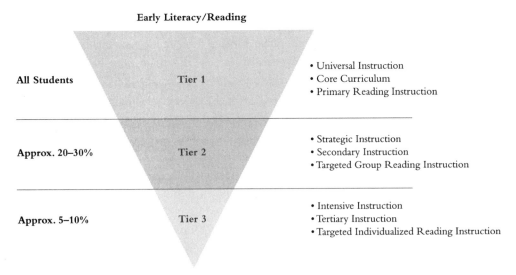

Note. From *Introduction to the 3-Tier Reading Model: Reducing Reading Disabilities for Kindergarten Through Third Grade Students* (4th ed.), by the Vaughn Gross Center for Reading and Language Arts at the University of Texas at Austin, 2005, Austin: Author. Copyright 2005 by the University of Texas. Adapted with permission.

Tier 1 Reading

Tier 1 promotes an instructional support framework for providing all students with quality reading instruction that addresses the five essential components of reading (i.e., phonemic awareness, phonics, fluency, vocabulary, and comprehension) as part of their general education program. NCLB suggests that instruction be delivered using scientifically based reading programs (e.g., Scott Foresman Reading Street, Harcourt Storytown, SRA Open Court, Houghton Mifflin Reading). However, for a number of reasons, such as philosophical or monetary, many schools do not use scientifically based general education reading programs for Tier 1 instruction.

Strong philosophical beliefs have led some school leaders and staff to adopt approaches linked to variations of whole language instruction, often masked as "balanced literacy" (Moats, 2007), including an overemphasis on guided reading procedures. In the case of fiscal constraints, schools often attempt to piece together a variety of smaller published scientifically based supplemental reading programs, each of which provides instructional methodology and materials to teach specific skills. For example, Wilson Fundations is a smaller program that focuses on the phonemic decoding of letter–sound correspondences, words, and connected text. However, such scientifically based supplemental reading programs were not intended by the programs' publishers to be used as a replacement for a core reading program. Therefore, layering supplemental programs to establish a universal-level core reading program may lead to an approach that is not comprehensive, direct, or systematic enough to meet the reading needs of most students. Whether a school is using one universal-level core program or a cluster of supplemental programs, the best way to think of Tier 1 instruction is as a general game plan developed by educators to teach the scope and sequence of reading skills expected to be mastered by the end of the school year for each grade level.

An underlying assumption critical to implementation of a three-tier reading model is that a school makes a commitment to spend a minimum of 90 minutes per day on Tier 1 reading instruction (see Vaughn Gross Center, 2005). This time frame is often referred to as the literacy block. Many schools have found a 120-minute literacy block to be more conducive to running the model effectively.

The length of the literacy block should be influenced by the pervasiveness and severity of the student population's reading needs. Thus, low-performing, low-income schools may need a 120-minute literacy block, whereas high-performing, high-income schools may need substantially less. Throughout the literacy block, the general education classroom teacher is responsible for implementing Tier 1 instructional strategies and activities. Delivery of the instructional strategies and activities is expected to occur through two main formats: whole-group instruction and small-group instruction. During whole-group instruction, the classroom teacher uses materials and lessons drawn from the core and/or supplemental programs to instruct all students, including those who may be receiving instruction through other tiers. The total amount of time devoted to whole-group instruction should not exceed one-third of the time scheduled for the entire literacy block (e.g., 30 minutes if implementing a 90-minute literacy block) with 20 minutes being the preferred time allotment.

To extend whole-group instruction beyond the recommended time frame may create a scenario in which the classroom teacher is covering content that is too basic for some students or too complicated for others. Some skills are more easily taught than others within a whole-group format, namely comprehension strategies (both listening and reading), vocabulary, and fluency. An overview of certain phonemic awareness and phonics skills may also be incorporated effectively within a whole-group format when teaching younger students.

General education teachers who are beginning implementation of a three-tier reading model often ask how they can effectively use the remaining time within the literacy block once whole-group instruction has finished. The simple answer is small-group instruction. A hallmark component of the three-tier reading model is to provide students with as many quality "doses" of teacher-led, small-group, skill-specific instruction as needed on a daily basis. Within Tier 1, small-group instructional time allows classroom teachers regular opportunities to work with flexible groups of 6–10 students to preteach, reteach, support, and/or extend skills and concepts initially covered within the whole-group instructional format (Foorman & Torgesen, 2001). It also will provide teachers with ongoing chances to incorporate three main features of best instructional practice: (a) specific examples, (b) timely corrective feedback, and (c) immediate reinforcement.

The small-group instructional component within Tier 1 typically lasts 20 minutes per group. The 20-minute time frame encourages classroom teachers to properly organize their materials before group time. It also helps teachers maintain a pace that increases students' academic engaged time and decreases students' behavioral disruptions during group time. Finally, a 20-minute time frame allows classroom teachers to meet with three small groups per day within the portion of the literacy block remaining beyond whole-group instructional time (i.e., 60 minutes if using a 90-minute block). As classroom teachers devise a plan for delivering quality, small-group instruction to their students, additional consideration must be given to the development of activities for students who are not participating in small groups. In real-world practice, classroom teachers have had much success properly engaging students who don't participate in groups with literacy centers and workstations, where small groups of students are encouraged to collaborate and complete a meaningful literacy activity related to the skills and concepts taught within teacher-led small groups.

Although Tier 1 instruction is put into place to meet the reading needs of all students, is it realistic to expect all students to master grade-level skills and concepts after being exposed only to the universal-level core reading program? Under the best of circumstances, most (about 80%) of the student population may be successful and become competent grade-level readers after being instructed only in a universal-level core program. In many communities, though, reading data suggest that only 50–60% of the student population are succeeding with an existing universal-level core reading program. When overall reading outcomes are so poor, school leaders need to consider whether modifications need to be made to the existing universal-level core reading program or whether an entirely new program needs to be adopted. In short, a safety net involving a research-based universal screening process, referred to as a benchmark assessment system, must be implemented to monitor the effectiveness of Tier 1 instruction for meeting the needs of most students.

A benchmark assessment system uses technically adequate measurement tools (i.e., tools with established reliability, validity, and utility) a minimum of three times per year to (a) conduct universal screening to identify early those students who are at risk, and (b) gauge students' responsiveness to the instructional practices and materials. When used in conjunction with the three-tier reading model, a benchmark assessment system will serve as the most basic level of ongoing progress monitoring. More specifically, it will give staff members an opportunity to conduct quarterly reading "well checks" to see whether students require more specific and intense instruction than what is being provided in their current tier of reading instruction. As such, a benchmark assessment approach helps create a dynamic process in which students may move among the three tiers based on response to instruction.

Tier 2 Reading

Universal screening, in Tier 1, is a cornerstone feature within three-tier models. Tier 2 is designed to provide more intensive instruction to students who are considered more at risk for reading failure. Once at-risk students have been identified through benchmark assessment, they may be considered for Tier 2. In most schools, 20–30% of the student population will demonstrate enough educational need to be considered for Tier 2 reading instruction. Tier 2 instruction can only be as effective as Tier 1 has been; that is, if appropriate Tier 1 instruction is lacking within a school, a higher percentage of students will appear to need Tier 2 assistance.

Effective implementation of Tier 2 instruction involves three important elements: instructional grouping format, instructional support personnel, and instructional tools. Upon being identified as needing Tier 2 support, students are taught as part of an instructional grouping format, within which they receive additional daily teacher-led, small-group instruction. Thus Tier 2 is supplemental instruction and typically lasts 20 minutes. This small-group instruction is often delivered to groups of three to five students. Although a number of mechanisms have been identified to determine who will serve as Tier 2 instructional support personnel, the preferred approach is to use other remedial program personnel as Tier 2 interventionists (Haager, Klingner, & Vaughn, 2007; King & Torgesen, 2006; Vaughn Gross Center, 2005). Examples of Tier 2 interventionists are reading coaches, reading specialists, speech and language therapists, paraprofessionals, and teachers supported through Title 1 funds. The instructional tools used within Tier 2 should also be scientifically based and specialized (i.e., provide instructional strategies and materials for teaching specific reading skills). Also, many scientifically based universal-level core reading programs include intervention components that work effectively as Tier 2 resources. For example, the Scott Foresman core reading program Reading Street includes My Sidewalks as a supplemental program. Given that Tier 2 interventionists will be responsible for using specialized programs, they must be provided with proper ongoing training and support on how to use the instructional tools with fidelity, or in a manner laid out by the developers of the programs.

Having identified Tier 2 students, selected Tier 2 interventions, and trained Tier 2 support personnel, schools must help practitioners with the logistical issues related to the delivery of Tier 2 instruction. School practitioners may ask the following questions:

1. Does Tier 2 instruction occur within the literacy block time frame?
2. Do students receive Tier 2 instruction in the classroom or within an alternative setting?
3. How long does Tier 2 instruction last before staff can determine its effectiveness?

Does Tier 2 Instruction Occur Within the Literacy Block Time Frame?

The main reason for having an established 90- to 120-minute literacy block is to allow enough time for Tiers 1 and 2 to take place during the segment of the school day devoted to language arts instruction. Whenever possible, utmost care is taken by school principals to avoid having Tier 2 instruction interfere with the teaching of other basic skill areas such as math. An example of an elementary school's literacy block schedule for a second-grade classroom is shown in Figure 2. In this classroom Tier 1 (both whole- and small-group instruction) and Tier 2 activities take place within the established literacy block. However, the classroom has two adults from 9:00 a.m. to 10:00 a.m. to meet with Tier 1 and Tier 2 small groups. Thus, Tier 2 students in this class would be engaged in the following reading activities during the 90-minute literacy block: 25 minutes of adult-led, whole-group instruction delivered by the classroom teacher (Tier 1), which includes an explanation of literacy centers; 5 minutes for transitioning to small-group activities; 20 minutes of adult-led, small-group instruction delivered by the classroom teacher (Tier 1); 20 minutes of adult-led, small-group instruction delivered by the Tier 2 interventionist (Tier 2); and 20 minutes of student-led, small-group literacy centers.

Do Students Receive Tier 2 Instruction in the Classroom or Within an Alternative Setting?

As shown in Figure 2, students' Tier 2 instruction often takes place within a general education classroom. However, in some instances, Tier 2 students will receive their instruction in an outside-the-classroom setting such as a Tier 2 interventionist's classroom or office. Furthermore, many classroom teachers and support personnel have found it productive to use cross-classroom grouping to meet the unique instructional needs of students. Cross-classroom grouping entails having students travel to an adjacent, same-grade classroom to join a small group of peers who have similar skill deficits (e.g., difficulty decoding words that contain an open syllable). Once grouped

Figure 2. Literacy block schedule for second-grade classroom (90 minutes).

8:30–8:40 Read-Aloud (WHOLE)	8:40–8:50 Discussion about Read-Aloud (WHOLE)	8:50–9:00 Discussion for Centers and Transition (WHOLE)	9:00–9:20 Small Reading Groups I (Tier 1/Group A – Teacher) (Tier 2/Group B – Interventionist) (Group C – Literacy Centers)
9:20–9:40 Small Reading Groups II (Tier 1/Group C – Teacher) (Tier 2/Group A – Interventionist) (Group B – Literacy Centers)	9:40–10:00 Small Reading Groups III (Tier 1/Group B – Teacher) (Tier 2/Group C – Interventionist) (Group A – Literacy Centers)		10:00–10:20 RECESS

according to their instructional needs, students are taught by an interventionist for approximately 20 minutes. Note that cross-classroom grouping procedures can work just as effectively with Tier 1 small groups.

How Long Does Tier 2 Instruction Last Before Staff Can Determine Its Effectiveness?
Most published three-tier reading model resources suggest that a round of Tier 2 instruction should last 10–12 weeks, or about 50 sessions (Vaughn Gross Center, 2005). This suggested time frame concurs with recent response-to-intervention (RTI) guidelines, which state that an intervention should be implemented for a minimum of 6–10 weeks before school personnel make an informed decision regarding its effectiveness (Fuchs, Fuchs, Hintze, & Lembke, 2007). Nonetheless, decisions related to the duration of Tier 2 instruction should be directly influenced by the severity of students' problems. As such, school personnel should either decrease or increase the number of intervention sessions within Tier 2 based on students' academic growth. If progress monitoring data suggest Tier 2 efforts are decreasing the achievement gap for struggling students, school personnel should consider transitioning these students back to Tier I instruction. If data reveal that Tier 2 efforts are not contributing to meaningful academic gains for low-performing students, school personnel should improve upon students' Tier 2 instruction and then increase the number of Tier 2 intervention sessions. Additional options include offering struggling students a 10- to 12-week round of Tier 3 instruction, and/or considering special education entitlement. We believe that the latter two options are less favorable than working to revise Tier 2 instruction, because implementation of Tier 3 typically requires a change in the interventionist involved and/or delivery of the intervention at a time outside of the scheduled literacy block. Regarding consideration of special education entitlement, the special education services provided could amount to less direct instruction than what was currently being offered as part of the Tier 2 instructional plan.

Critical to making timely and well-informed decisions about students' success within Tier 2 is a commitment to ongoing progress monitoring. Thus, school personnel must be willing to increase their data collection efforts for students receiving Tier 2 instruction. More specifically, they should conduct reading skills progress monitoring one to two times per month. This increase in formative evaluation, which entails assessing students' skills on a regular basis, is commonly referred to as strategic progress monitoring. Strategic progress monitoring will help classroom teachers and support personnel keep a finger on the literacy pulse of their students.

Tier 3 Reading

In many school districts, a small percentage of the student population will demonstrate reading difficulties so pervasive that they warrant Tier 3 instruction. Compared with Tier 2, Tier 3 consists of an even greater increase in the intensity of daily teacher-led, small-group, skill-specific instruction. Tier 3 instruction typically last 20 minutes, includes an adult–student ratio of 1:3, and is most commonly staffed by special education teachers. In many instances, Tier 3 service providers have expertise working with students with language-based learning issues, and they have been certified to use instructional programs developed for exceptional learners. Examples of programs that have established empirical evidence suggesting that the program improves reading outcomes for language-compromised students include the Orton Gillingham approach (http://www.orton-gillingham.com), Wilson Reading System (http://www.wilsonlanguage.com), Lindamood Phonemic Sequencing (LiPS) Program (http://www.lindamoodbell.com), Reading Mastery/Corrective Reading (http://www.sra.com), and Language! (http://www.sopriswest.com). As with Tier 2 instruction, instructional programs or strategies implemented as part of Tier 3 instruction must be delivered with fidelity.

In contrast to how well Tier 2 instruction fits within an established literacy block, Tier 3 instruction often takes place outside the block. The inclusion of Tier 3 outside the literacy block may create a scheduling issue. Specifically, if some students are going to receive their Tier 3 instruction outside of the literacy block, what will it take the place of: social studies, science, or enrichment? This scheduling concern is really a school-based concern, mainly because school leaders and staff members have strong opinions on whether it is acceptable for students to miss instructional time in one skill area versus another. Nonetheless, when considering how best to fit Tier 3 instruction into students' schedules, school personnel should keep in mind the comments of a 9-year-old struggling reader: "Reading affects everything you do" (Adams, 1990).

Students receiving Tier 3 instruction typically present with severe reading difficulties. In fact, this subgroup of the general student population has been referred to as the intensive care unit. Similar to how medical practitioners treat and examine the well-being of ICU patients, Tier 3 interventionists must work relentlessly when implementing and monitoring Tier 3 instructional strategies. As such, progress monitoring efforts will need to be augmented. Intensive progress monitoring requires the execution of weekly to biweekly reading "well checks." By increasing progress monitoring efforts for Tier 3 students, interventionists will increase the likelihood of finding a proper instructional fit for these students in a timely manner.

ASSESSMENT WITHIN THE THREE-TIER READING MODEL

Central to the implementation of the three-tier reading model is the need for a comprehensive, effective assessment plan. Such a plan should include a carefully selected assortment of tools that are designed to address four purposes of assessment: (a) screening, preferably at the universal level, (b) diagnostic assessment for instructional planning, (c) frequent progress monitoring, and (d) outcome evaluation for accountability and program evaluation. There is no shortage of assessment tools within the educational market. Thus, the selection process may appear to be an arduous undertaking. Nonetheless, the key to selecting appropriate assessment tools in the area of reading is to have school staff efficiently and systematically address each of the four assessment purposes.

During implementation of the three-tier reading model, the four purposes of assessment will need to be considered when examining students' early literacy and reading outcomes. This chapter mentions several examples of reading measures that lend themselves to screening, progress monitoring, diagnostics, and outcome evaluation; however, the tools selected for discussion purposes do not represent an exhaustive list. When considering how to restructure a school's assessment system, the first step is to examine what tools are already in place. Step 2 is to check whether existing measures allow staff to address the four purposes of assessment for all grades. Finally, if gaps exist within the assessment system, an action plan is developed for selecting tools with established reliability, validity, and utility.

Assessment Practices Used Within Tier 1

A benchmark assessment system allows staff members to use a universal screening tool to ensure that all students are on track to meet important literacy goals. Benchmark screening of all students is typically conducted three to four times across the school year. Given the large number of students involved during this screening process, the tools used must allow for quick and easy administration and scoring and give teachers timely feedback on students' performance levels.

Measures are available on the educational market to screen students' foundational reading skills. These measures, commonly referred to as general outcome measures or general outcome indicators, can be administered and scored quickly within a universal screening process, and are yoked to research-based standards of success (e.g., benchmarks, norms, and high-stakes test cut scores). The Curriculum-Based Measures of Reading task, which entails having a student read aloud for 1 minute from a standard grade-level passage and then scoring the number of words read correctly, is an example of a general outcome measure for reading competence (Deno, 1985, 1992; Deno, Marston, Shinn, & Tindal, 1983; Shinn, 1989; Shinn & Bamonto, 1998). The Dynamic Indicators of Basic Early Literacy Skills (DIBELS) includes subtests considered to be early literacy general outcome measures (Kaminski & Good, 1996, 1998). A selection of general outcome measures across several basic skill areas can be purchased from companies such as AIMSweb, Pro-Ed, Sopris West, and Voyager. Chapter 10 in this book describes the use of general outcome measures, including curriculum-based measures, in great detail.

Once screening data using general outcome measures have been collected, important questions will arise that will be answered through an outcome evaluation: How many students in a class, grade, or school have met research-based standards of success (such as the DIBELS benchmarks levels)? How many *more* students have met a benchmark from one assessment period to the next and from one year to the next? How do classrooms compare with one another? Do certain grade levels stand out as needing more support than others to achieve literacy goals? Evaluating data through such a lens can help schools gain useful insight related to whether students are developing mastery of grade-appropriate skills, concepts, and strategies. More specifically, staff will be better equipped to determine (a) the effectiveness of curricula and instruction, (b) the need for quality professional development, and (c) the allocation of resources. The use of grade-level data meetings and progress monitoring meetings, which is covered later within the chapter, provides a systematic process for addressing student outcomes as well as issues pertaining to curriculum, instruction, professional development, and resource allocation.

Assessment Practices Used Within Tier 2

Once a benchmark assessment system is established as part of Tier 1, students are identified either as being on track or as experiencing some level of risk relative to an identified standard of success, such as a benchmark or norm. If performance is below a predetermined standard of success, the student is identified as being in need of additional instructional support, or Tier 2 instruction (also called strategic, secondary, or targeted group reading instruction). At this juncture, two additional purposes of assessment are often discussed: diagnostic assessment and progress monitoring.

Diagnostic Assessment
The goal of diagnostic assessment is to pinpoint underlying skills that may be severely hindering students' reading progress. Diagnostic assessment entails examining students' relevant skills within a grade-level scope and sequence, identifying those that have been mastered, and targeting skill deficits for remediation within a logical, research-based sequence. To conclude that a targeted skill is underdeveloped, the examiner must assess the student on a sufficient sample of items. For example, an examiner would be discouraged from concluding that a student needs extra support with suffixes because

the student misread two words containing the suffix /-ed / during a 1-minute reading of connected text. However, the examiner may form a hypothesis from the screening and then attempt to test it by assessing the student further on the targeted skill. Unlike universal screening, diagnostic assessment is typically not timed and does take longer to conduct. However, this rigorous level of assessment should only be reserved for students who really need it.

Two additional assessment processes work well within a diagnostic framework: survey-level assessment (Fuchs & Shinn, 1989; Shinn, 1989, 1995; Shinn & Baker, 1996; Shinn, Collins, & Gallagher, 1998) and specific-level assessment (Howell, Fox, & Morehead, 1993; Howell & Nolet, 2000). Both contribute to instructional planning and diagnostic decision making for students in either Tier 2 or Tier 3. Survey-level assessment is a standardized variation of an informal reading inventory that uses curriculum-based measurement (CBM), and it involves examining a student's reading performance from successively lower levels of reading passages. The survey-level assessment typically begins with a student's grade placement to identify text levels that are appropriate for teacher-directed instruction and independent reading (i.e., instructional level and mastery level, respectively).

A specific-level assessment entails a qualitative analysis of a student's specific reading skills. The purpose of conducting a specific-level assessment with students is to identify what skills they do or do not perform correctly, to discover their patterns of performance, and to specify underlying skill deficits that may hinder their overall reading success (e.g., lacking mastery of short vowels). An initial step within the specific-level assessment process is to analyze a student's performance on specific items within already administered reading probes. During this phase, the examiner searches for patterns of word- and sentence-level errors. Such an analysis may also help the examiner develop hypotheses about "cracks" within the student's reading foundation.

Given that many diagnostic measures contain a limited sample of items that reportedly measure competence within a vast skill domain, an important next step in the specific-level assessment process is to confirm hypotheses with the use of narrow-band tests or skill inventories. Examples of such measures are the Word Attack Skills Test (Carnine, Silbert, Kame'enui, & Tarver, 2004), the Developmental Spelling Inventory (Bear, Invernizzi, Templeton, & Johnston, 2007), and the Quick Phonics Screener (Hasbrouck & Parker, 2001). Many scientifically based reading intervention programs also include assessment tools intended to indicate where best to place a student within the program's instructional scope and sequence. For example, the Wilson Assessment of Decoding and Encoding (WADE) is used in tandem with the Wilson Reading Program to make instructional placement decisions within the program. As part of the specific-level assessment process, classroom teachers are also encouraged to use any measures they have developed over the years, as long as the tools are perceived to have instructional utility. In summary, the use of diagnostic assessment involves much work. Yet the information gleaned fosters the development of high-quality, individualized interventions to be used within both Tiers 2 and 3.

Progress Monitoring

Best practice suggests that more frequent progress monitoring should be one of the cornerstone assessment techniques used in Tiers 2 and 3. Once students are identified as needing additional academic reading support, it is imperative that teachers and/or interventionists regularly monitor reading growth to ensure Tier 2 and/or Tier 3 strategies are helping students (a) meet predetermined individual goals and (b) catch up to typically performing, same-grade peers. When incorporated within a progress monitoring framework, tools such as CBM and DIBELS are used across time to guide instructional decision-making. Specifically, such measures allow school staff to take weekly to biweekly "snapshots" of students' growth across time. Once these data are collected, a series of decision rules should be considered to gauge whether struggling readers are catching up to typically performing, same-grade peers (see chapter 11 in this book for more about decision rules).

Assessment Practices Used Within Tier 3

In general, the assessment practices used in Tier 3 are very similar to those used in Tier 2. A noticeable difference between the two tiers is the number of students assessed. Far fewer students are expected to be assessed within Tier 3 than within the other two tiers (ideally, no more than 5% of the entire student population). Furthermore, the data collection process in Tier 3 may involve more time, resources, and specialized personnel (e.g., school psychologist). Student progress monitoring continues in Tier 3, but it is scheduled more frequently (i.e., weekly to biweekly), often involves tracking students' reading progress in lower-level materials, and may contribute to special education entitlement decisions.

THE ANALYSIS OF ASSESSMENT DATA

In the early stages of a three-tier reading model initiative, the most pressing consideration is to share benchmark assessment findings with staff so that reading instruction can be improved. As soon as benchmark assessment data are gathered and organized, all classroom teachers and support personnel meet during a general staff meeting to examine and discuss both school- and grade-level data (classroom data and individual student performance levels are discussed during grade-level data meetings, discussed later in this section). During these general staff meetings, data should be displayed graphically to review school- and grade-level goals for improving reading achievement; to analyze the percentage of students within each grade level who are scoring above, at, or below predetermined standards of success; and to monitor whether students are making gains from one benchmark assessment period to the next within the current school year or across multiple years. Upon displaying the data, principals are encouraged to walk school staff through a series of guiding questions:

- What percentage of classrooms has a high number of students attaining benchmark levels of achievement?
- What classrooms may need additional resource support to meet the needs of students?
- How are students doing over time?

Grade-level data meetings usually consist of all of the classroom teachers from a grade level plus the support staff who provide Tier 2 intervention to that grade level. The meetings may be led by the principal, the reading coach, a grade-level leader, or a combination of leaders. The data are distributed to team members in advance in a well-organized, user-friendly package. Presenting the data in a large three-ring binder, along with data interpretation materials, makes it easy for teachers to keep all of the materials necessary for data analysis meetings in one place from one benchmark period to the next. Teachers may be asked to look over the data in advance or to perform certain premeeting activities designed to prepare them for full participation at the meeting. To maximize efficiency and participation, the team can distribute handouts for everyone to follow while the team leader facilitates the meeting.

In the first year of a three-tier reading model initiative, analyzing student data will take much longer than it will once teachers have become accustomed to following various procedural aids, such as organizing worksheets, and to interpreting different charts and graphs. Ample time should be provided for these early meetings (up to 90 minutes) so that teachers can acclimate to the process. This is one area where time invested up front pays off in handsome dividends down the road. Given adequate time at the outset, teachers will more quickly overcome any anxiety about the mechanics of data interpretation and will resolve any questions they may not have asked about how the data analysis is going to be used. In short, teachers and support staff will be able to recognize more readily the instructional utility of the data.

The data discussed at the meetings focus on three levels: grade, classroom, and student. Analysis conducted during these meetings is directed toward finding answers to the guided questions printed at the beginning of this section. While each data analysis meeting focuses on student progress, the focal point shifts from one benchmark data collection period to the next (e.g., fall to winter). Moreover, progress monitoring meetings must be scheduled regularly to discuss whether Tiers 2 and 3 instructional efforts are effective in helping individual students make meaningful reading progress over time.

Fall Grade-Level Data Meetings

During the fall data analysis meeting, teachers examine students' baseline reading scores, group students for targeted Tier 1 instruction, and set achievement goals for individuals and groups. Students identified as moderately or severely behind in reading skills are further assessed using diagnostic measures and, based on the findings, identified for additional Tier 2 or Tier 3 instruction. Principals and reading coaches survey the level of educational need in each classroom to decide how best to assist classroom teachers with additional materials, training, and/or personnel.

Winter Grade-Level Data Meetings

At the winter meeting, changes in students' early literacy and/or reading progress are examined closely so that staff can identify students who need additional assistance through Tier 2 or Tier 3. Achievement goals for individuals and groups are analyzed and adjusted accordingly. Students not making adequate progress may be selected for further assessment to identify their specific skill deficits. If there is a concern about the reading performance level of an entire class or grade, additional support from the reading coach may be offered.

Spring Grade-Level Data Meetings

As the end of the school year draws near, spring data analysis meetings further examine individual student growth so that last-minute opportunities for quality instruction can be capitalized upon. Grade-level achievement data are used to group students into instructional cohorts for the upcoming school year, allowing the timely implementation of intervention services in the fall. Furthermore, prior to the end of the school year, all professionals teaching within a grade level conduct a self-examination of year-long (and possibly cross-year) literacy results to plan future professional development, acquire new materials, and target new areas of support.

Progress Monitoring Meetings

Implementing an effective system for collecting and using progress monitoring data is a critical task for schools attempting to implement a three-tier reading model. Once a benchmark assessment system is established, students who score below predetermined standards of success typically receive additional intervention services. These students should be monitored on a more frequent basis to determine if the intervention is working. Implementing a successful progress monitoring system requires planning and collaboration at the school level. Staff members need to be trained in a systematic process for analyzing student performance data, and they must be allowed to have regular, collegial conversations about how the information affects their instructional efforts. Administrators should plan for monthly meetings to discuss progress monitoring data.

HOW TO STRUCTURE SCHOOLS FOR EFFECTIVE THREE-TIER IMPLEMENTATION

The implementation of a three-tier reading model within a school is a complex project that takes planning, collaboration, and continuous refinement. A key aspect of implementation for a successful start-up is for the district- and school-level administrators to be well informed and to have a vision of what needs to be achieved. Administrators are critical in setting the stage for implementation by participating in and facilitating tasks, such as making thoughtful scheduling and staffing decisions.

Scheduling

One of the most critical aspects for ensuring school-wide reading success is to carefully plan the daily master schedule for the school. Ideally, the master schedule for the following year is developed during the spring, prior to the next fall's implementation. The school administrators may assemble a team to assist with schedule planning. Other team members typically include staff such as the reading specialist or coach, special education teacher, one classroom teacher for each grade level, and any special subject teachers who can participate. The development of a school schedule typically takes a minimum of one full school day. The process can be expedited if there is some preparation work done prior to the schedule planning meeting. For example, many smaller schools share itinerants (teachers of special subjects) with another school. Administrators need to find out which itinerants will be working in their schools and when. Additional information that will be helpful when planning the school schedule are the contractual start and end times for the school day and the breaks in schedule needed to accommodate teachers' required lunch and preparation periods.

The schedule planning meeting should begin by asking each staff member what his or her priorities are for next year's schedule. These priorities should be written up on a board or chart paper. The priorities of individual staff members may include an uninterrupted literacy block, 90 minutes for math, Grades K–2 lunch at the same time, and no specials—that is, no special subjects such as art, music, or physical education—for kindergartners at the beginning of the day. As the team develops the schedule, they will need to make compromises. However, by allowing team members to begin the meeting by sharing their priorities, they in turn will demonstrate flexibility when accepting direct changes to their routines.

Most schools begin with a blank master itinerant schedule with relevant daily time blocks clearly delineated (e.g., start time, recess time, lunch, itinerant periods throughout the day, and end time). Given that itinerants often have limited flexibility with their schedules, it is often helpful to begin with their assignments. When multiple itinerants are available for special subject classes during the same time slot, many schools opt to have these "specials" scheduled at the same time for several classes within a grade, thus creating a common planning time for the classroom teachers involved. Once the itinerants are assigned and specials are scheduled, the focus turns to instructional time.

One of the most critical, instructionally relevant scheduling tasks involves considering when the literacy block of 90–120 minutes will begin and end for each classroom. This block should be protected from interruptions such as recess, lunch, or specials to ensure that transitions do not negatively affect time devoted to reading instruction. Some administrators have implemented an even stricter version of the protected block concept by restricting announcements and assemblies during the literacy block. A few administrators have even sent letters home to parents asking them to refrain from removing their children from school for appointments while literacy time is scheduled. When administrators take steps such as these to protect the literacy block, they are sending an essential message to school staff and to the community that literacy instruction is a school priority.

In the primary grades, it is preferable to have the literacy block scheduled in the morning, when young children are typically less fatigued. Schools that decide to do so often assign itinerants to the lower grades after lunch. Some scheduling teams designate a suggested time for teaching each subject for each grade level. If dictation of instructional time is a new concept for a school, the revised schedule must be shared with staff members before a new school year begins. A scheduling team spokesperson, typically an administrator, must explain to staff that predetermined, subject-specific instructional blocks will allow all staff members ample time to fulfill curriculum requirements across all basic skill areas (i.e., early literacy, reading, language, writing, and math). Once such a schedule is implemented, many teachers are relieved that they no longer have to teach content in "spurts" and are thankful for schedule continuity.

Delivery of support services for students who are below research-based standards of success in reading is another critical factor to consider when setting up a school's schedule. Given the uncertainty surrounding the number of students in need of support services from year to year, many schools choose to use their spring benchmark data to get a preview of the services needed for the following fall, and adjust their schedules accordingly. Nonetheless, specific intervention schedules for each interventionist are often best finalized during the fall. This is particularly important for schools that deal with highly transient student populations. Naturally, having student enrollment in constant flux makes it difficult for interventionists to get a handle on their caseloads. Given that all instructional groups in the three-tier reading model are based on students' needs and therefore flexible (i.e., students move in and out of groups depending on their reading needs), most interventionists get used to the idea that students will come and go, whether because of a move to another school or because of a transition to a different instructional group.

The development of a school schedule is a challenging task. Moreover, the resulting schedule is never ideal for each teacher or specialist; however, with careful planning and the right team, the results can be highly considerate of children's needs. Many schools survey staff each year about their thoughts regarding the previous year's schedule and attempt to use the feedback to improve subsequent schedules.

Staffing

A school that sets out to implement a three-tier reading model must consider its resources and create a plan that best uses the personnel available within the school. If available, Title 1 teachers, reading coaches, reading specialists, and speech and language therapists can be used as Tier 2 and Tier 3 interventionists. However, problems arise when schools are not staffed with any or enough of these specialists to meet the needs of at-risk readers. For implementation of the three-tier reading model to work, all personnel within a school must be considered potential intervention providers. In schools that have successfully implemented the three-tier reading model, a variety of personnel have been used as interventionists, including special education teachers, teaching assistants, librarians, parent volunteers, and even teachers of special subject classes (e.g., a physical education teacher). By using a variety of staff members not historically considered to be direct service providers, schools find they are intervening with an extra 8 to 25 students per grade.

Use of Noncertified Teachers and Volunteers as Support Personnel

School leaders often are skeptical about using noncertified personnel, such as teaching assistants, and parent volunteers to deliver instruction to struggling students. However, when teaching assistants and parent volunteers are provided with high-quality, scientifically based reading programs, exceptional professional development, and ongoing support, they can dramatically improve student outcomes. For instance, as part of a program evaluation in a large urban school district, one of the authors of this chapter examined the effects of paraprofessional-led, small-group instruction on kindergartners' phonemic awareness and phonemic decoding skills and first-, second-, and third-grade students' oral reading fluency skills. To analyze the efficacy of the instructional practices on students' skill development, a statistical measure of practical significance called an effect size was calculated for each outcome. The findings yielded effect sizes ranging from 1.1 to 3.5 (Parker, 2006), with effect sizes beyond 0.8 considered to be statistically meaningful (Cohen, 1988).

To optimize the success of support personnel who are noncertified teachers or volunteers, it is important to assign them to an intervention program that is scripted and does not require the development of lessons or the creation of materials. Most scientifically based reading programs contain scripted lessons. Support personnel also should have a chance to gain expertise in one intervention program before being asked to learn additional programs. When support personnel are to be trained to implement new intervention programs, training sessions should be conducted across multiple days scheduled 10–12 weeks apart so they can learn how to implement smaller parts of the programs with fidelity. Monthly support sessions are also recommended, especially for intervention providers who are not trained as teachers. A school reading coach typically coordinates and runs initial trainings as well as support sessions. The support sessions, which may last 30 to 45 minutes, address the following issues: Where are you in the program? What questions do you have about the lessons? What questions or concerns do you have about the students in your intervention groups? The support sessions conclude with a preview of upcoming lessons.

A final consideration when supporting noncertified teachers as interventionists is to account for and schedule preparation time. Teaching assistants often do not have a contractual preparation period. This is a potential barrier to successful implementation of an intervention because, even with a highly scripted program, the interventionist must prepare the materials and read through the lessons in advance to deliver the strategies effectively. As such, school principals must give careful consideration as to how preparation time will be allotted to paraprofessionals prior to considering their use as interventionists.

Coordination of Educational Services

A critical issue related to staffing is the coordination of general education and special education services. In many schools, special education personnel only work with students who have individualized education plans. Reading teachers and Title 1 tutors typically work with struggling students who have not been identified with disabilities and who thus do not have education plans. In theory, this service delivery arrangement sounds reasonable. In practice, it can prevent struggling learners from receiving adequate support. For example, one of this chapter's authors encountered a school situation in which a full-time special education teacher had an intervention caseload of 9 students, yet the reading teacher carried an intervention caseload of 40 students. Moreover, there were 15 additional students who qualified for Tier 2 intervention based on their poor reading skills, but they could not receive extra support. Their reading skills were not low enough to warrant services delivered by the special education teacher, and the reading teacher no longer had any available intervention slots.

This school-based staffing problem became even more troublesome when the students' reading performance levels were closely examined. Students' reading data showed that many of the students in the two groups had similar reading abilities and instructional needs. For instance, the special education teacher was providing a phonemic decoding intervention to one student and the reading teacher was providing the same phonemic decoding intervention to a group of four students. There were also instances in which the students with education plans were receiving *fewer* intervention sessions than those being supported by the reading teacher (3 days per week versus 5 days per week). To precorrect for inequitable intervention caseloads and, more important, the unwillingness of certain interventionists to work with students who do not fit within preexisting service delivery groups (e.g., special education, Title 1, and English language learners), district leaders and school principals must make it clear to staff that all support personnel are considered general interventionists. As such, they will be required to devote unused intervention time to supporting students who demonstrate academic need.

Leadership

The literature on effective schools consistently underscores the significance of school leadership, particularly the role of the principal, in improving the school environment. Vibrant, productive schools—with highly motivated staff members and students who feel valued and committed to their own success—are often found to have an energetic, visionary principal who is involved at every level of school functioning. These findings are no less true for a school adopting an initiative to implement the three-tier reading model. In addition to the principal being a key supporter of the three-tier process, a designated reading coach will make many contributions to the success of the initiative. Ideally, the principal and the reading coach will design their roles and responsibilities to integrate their complementary sets of skills (see Torgesen, 2006; Torgesen, Houston, Rissman, & Kosanovich, 2007).

The Role of Principals

Being an effective instructional leader requires a wide range of skills and personal characteristics. Principals orchestrating the three-tier reading model within schools need to be visionary leaders. They must have a vivid image of what their schools should look like and be able identify the steps necessary to get there. They also must be able to communicate that vision to their staff and inspire others to join them in pursuing that vision. To do this, they must be able to convey both a clear description of the problems with the current situation and the potential value of structuring the school's efforts in a new way. This must be done while highlighting and honoring the enormous effort already made by the staff.

To initiate a conversation related to changes in literacy practices, many principals tell school personnel something like the following: "There is no doubt the entire staff has been working to the bone to improve literacy outcomes within the school. We have tried x, y, and z. But the fact of the matter is we have not yet gotten the results our students deserve. Research indicates that students like ours can be helped to achieve higher levels of literacy through the implementation of a multiyear initiative such as this." They then communicate the personal and professional benefits of participation—deepened professional learning, new instructional materials, higher student achievement, higher job satisfaction, opportunities for collaboration, and professional introspection—while acknowledging the significant challenges ahead. To give staff members a more concrete image of what the initiative may look like down the road, principals may arrange visits to successful schools that are one or two steps ahead in their implementation. Principals will make good use of outside trainers and consultants experienced in supporting staff through the stages of this change. Most important, when issues arise related to next steps, principals will help their staff explore possible solutions.

Although the initiative is for reading skills, it may be more important for principals to have strong school management skills than to know all about reading. Knowledge of reading acquisition can be acquired as the initiative progresses. Furthermore, principals may have knowledgeable reading coaches on site. For all students to become successful readers, however, schools need to be functioning well. Principals need to create a climate of orderliness and purposefulness. Schools need to be safe places for students to learn and for staff members to explore and implement new assessment and instructional practices. Schedules need to be conducive to the delivery of ongoing, direct support services for all students. Principals need to be excellent communicators. Most of all, principals need to demonstrate consistent follow-through so that staff can develop confidence that they will have the support they need to take a chance on a new three-tier reading model initiative.

As the initiative proceeds, effective principals function as schools' cheerleaders and the initiative's number one supporters. They take every opportunity to highlight both large and small successes. At the same time, they are not afraid to communicate clear expectations related to how each staff member will perform within the three-tier reading model. Principals remain goal oriented, keeping an eye on the big picture while being supportive of staff as they work through details. They make sure staff have the tools and training necessary to ensure their success. In fact, principals may be most capable of marshaling additional, unexpected resources when all else has failed to improve outcomes for struggling readers. For example, principals may be able to approve cross-class grouping, to set up "make and take" workshops to help teachers who need time to develop materials for centers, to find a paraprofessional with 15 minutes available in her schedule to provide additional support to a first grader struggling with basic phonics skills, to match a fifth-grade "reading buddy" with a third-grade student laboring with reading fluency, or to send a proposal to secure extra funds to purchase high-interest, low-level reading materials for struggling upper-grade students.

Some of the important actions principals can take to successfully implement the three-tier reading model in their schools revolve around their being highly visible during all steps of the initiative:

- Attend all professional development activities related to the initiative. Principals' active involvement serves a number of purposes. It is a powerful statement about their commitment to the initiative, gives them content knowledge they may lack, and allows them to participate with the entire staff to develop a common language and vision.
- Play a dynamic role in the analysis and use of data for making decisions about instructional groupings and intervention. For example, principals facilitate the interpretation and use of early literacy and reading data during grade-level data meetings.
- Conduct frequent classroom walk-throughs. These walk-throughs are quite different from contractual observations. They are brief, but occur frequently. They help principals to compile a series of mental snapshots of how the staff are implementing components of the model. Strong instructional leaders know what they are looking for, but a number of useful checklists are available for principals to use to enhance the effectiveness of the walk-through.

Principals function as a buffer against competing initiatives, which are common in schools looking for quick fixes to unacceptable student achievement. Although principals do not need to be experts in reading instruction at the onset of a three-tier reading model initiative, they do need to be deeply committed to the primacy of reading success for every student in their schools. They need to be vocal in their belief that the ability to read well will serve all children in every aspect of academics and life. As such, they need to protect their teachers' time and resources from becoming splintered by competing demands. Principals need to insist on protecting the uninterrupted reading block discussed in the section on scheduling. They need to protect the time set aside for professional analysis of the data, constantly reasserting their commitment to data-based instruction and ongoing program evaluation. Finally, principals need to build in time to celebrate success as often as possible.

The Role of Reading Coaches

Written resources exist that specify the special role reading coaches serve within any literacy initiative (see Hasbrouck and Denton, 2005; National Center for Reading First Technical Assistance, 2005). However, this section focuses on the particular tasks assumed by reading coaches to facilitate effective implementation of the three-tier reading model.

For starters, it is helpful to clarify three roles reading coaches are *not* responsible for fulfilling. First, they do not evaluate teachers. Second, they do not relay to principals any information gathered during their classroom observations. That would undermine any trust they had established with classroom teachers as they work together to bring about instructional changes. Third, they typically do not deliver direct reading services to students.

That being said, there is plenty for reading coaches to do. Primarily, reading coaches are committed to helping *all* students attain higher levels of reading success. They understand the goals of the initiative and help prioritize tasks to promote the attainment of both short- and long-term objectives. They also play a critical role in strengthening the connection between assessment and instruction. For example, reading coaches guide assessment teams in gathering and interpreting quality reading data, work with principals to review benchmark data, facilitate grade-level data meetings, and set up regular meetings for ongoing progress monitoring. In essence, reading coaches ensure that classroom teachers become experts at using their data.

Making sense of a wide array of materials and techniques that are part of scientifically based reading programs is a challenging undertaking for classroom teachers. As such, reading coaches must be available to support their classroom colleagues throughout the preparation and delivery of reading instruction. More specifically, reading coaches help teachers decide what instruction should take place in a whole group setting and what strategies should be employed within small reading groups. They help teachers become more explicit in their instructional delivery. Reading coaches also work with teachers to set up their classrooms for differentiated instruction, providing classroom management tips as well as content support for instructional centers. They observe instructional delivery within classrooms when invited. Their observations are guided by preobservation conversations with requesting teachers and are always followed up by postobservation meetings.

Perhaps the most important job of reading coaches is to understand the universal-level core program sufficiently. Developing expertise related to instructional objectives, timelines, and materials related to core instruction will allow reading coaches to guide staff in their attempts to differentiate instruction for all students. Similarly, reading coaches help classroom teachers and interventionists coordinate instruction for students struggling the most, and they arrange for intervention training and ongoing support to ensure implementation fidelity.

Finally, reading coaches are in a good position to evaluate the professional development needs of staff, to schedule new trainings when appropriate, and to provide follow-up support as needed. They also create a system of communication among administrators, classroom teachers, and reading intervention staff. As such, the role requires unique interpersonal qualities, a broad knowledge base, and a specialized skill set.

CONCLUSION

This chapter described the underlying principles and practices related to effective implementation of the three-tier reading model in elementary schools. At the core of the model are four fundamental elements:

1. Universal screening via benchmark assessment three times per year
2. Use of benchmark assessment data to ensure that students are receiving quality scientifically based reading instruction
3. Staff who are willing to adjust instructional efforts to maximize the effectiveness of daily doses of small-group, skill-specific instruction on students' reading outcomes
4. Use of progress monitoring data measured across all tiers at different frequencies to gauge intervention success

Details were also provided to help readers understand how differences in practice among Tiers 1, 2, and 3 will be realized by administrators, general education classroom teachers, reading coaches, special education teachers, and support personnel. To successfully implement all components of the three-tier reading model, schools must be ready for a 3- to 5-year commitment. Given that schools are often faced with numerous initiatives every year, questions will arise about whether such an arduous undertaking is worth the time and commitment. We believe, and the research suggests, that a three-tier reading model will allow school staff to better deliver reading instruction to all students.

REFERENCES

Adams, M. J. (1990). *Beginning to read: Thinking and learning about print*. Cambridge, MA: Massachusetts Institute of Technology.

Bear, D. R., Invernizzi, M., Templeton, S. R., & Johnston, F. (2007). *Words their way: Word study for phonics, vocabulary, and spelling instruction* (4th ed.). Upper Saddle River, NJ: Pearson Education.

Carnine, D. W., Silbert, J., Kame'enui, E. J., & Tarver, S. G. (2004). *Direct instruction reading* (4th ed.). Upper Saddle River, NJ: Pearson Education.

Cohen, J. (1988). *Statistical power analysis for the behavioral sciences* (2nd ed.). Hillsdale, NJ: Erlbaum.

Deno, S. L. (1985). Curriculum-based measurement: The emerging alternative. *Exceptional Children, 52,* 217–232.

Deno, S. L. (1992). The nature and development of curriculum-based measurement. *Preventing School Failure, 36*(2), 5–10.

Deno, S. L., Marston, D., Shinn, M. R., & Tindal, G. (1983). Oral reading fluency: A simple datum for scaling reading disability. *Topics in Learning and Learning Disability, 2,* 53–59.

Foorman, B., & Torgesen, J. K. (2001). Critical elements of classroom and small-group instruction to promote reading success in all children. *Learning Disabilities Research and Practice, 16,* 203–221.

Fuchs, L. S., Fuchs, D., Hintze, J., & Lembke, E. (2007). *Progress monitoring in the context of responsiveness-to-intervention.* Symposium conducted at the 2007 summer institute of the National Center on Student Progress Monitoring, Nashville, TN, July.

Fuchs, L. S., & Shinn, M. R. (1989). Writing CBM IEP objectives. In M. R. Shinn (Ed.), *Curriculum-based measurement: Assessing special children* (pp. 130–152). New York: Guilford Press.

Haager, D., Klingner, J. K., & Vaughn, S. (Eds.). (2007). *Validated reading practices for three tiers of intervention.* Baltimore, MD: Brookes.

Hasbrouck, J., & Denton, C. (2005). *The reading coach: A how-to manual for success.* Longmont, CO: Sopris West.

Hasbrouck, J., & Parker, R. (2001). *Quick Phonics Screener.* College Station: Texas A&M University.

Howell, K. W., Fox, S. L., & Morehead, M. K. (1993). *Curriculum-based evaluation: Teaching and decision-making* (2nd ed.). Pacific Grove, CA: Brooks/Cole.

Howell, K. W., & Nolet, V. (2000). Curriculum-based evaluation: Teaching and decision-making (3rd ed.). Belmont, CA: Wadsworth/Thompson Learning.

Individuals with Disabilities Education Improvement Act of 2004. 20 U.S.C. § 1400 et seq. (2004).

Kaminski, R. A., & Good, R. H. (1996). Assessment for instructional decisions: Toward a proactive/prevention model of decision-making for early literacy skills. *School Psychology Quarterly, 11,* 326–336.

Kaminski, R. A., & Good, R. H. (1998). Assessing early literacy skills in a problem-solving model: Dynamic indicators of basic early literacy skills. In. M. R. Shinn (Ed.), *Advanced applications of curriculum-based measurement.* New York: Guilford Press.

King, R., & Torgesen, J. K. (2006). Improving the effectiveness of reading instruction in one elementary school: A description of the process. In P. Blaunstein & R. Lyon (Eds.), *It doesn't have to be this way*. Lanham, MD: Scarecrow Press.

Moats, L. (2007). *Whole-language high jinx: How to tell when "scientifically based reading instruction" isn't*. Washington, DC: Fordham Foundation.

National Center for Reading First Technical Assistance. (2005). *Leading for reading success: An introductory guide for Reading First coaches*. Portsmouth, NH: RMC Research Corporation, Center on Instruction.

Parker, C. (2006). [Empirical evidence to support the use of early literacy and reading interventions with small groups of kindergarten, first-grade, second-grade, and third-grade students]. Unpublished raw data.

Shinn, M. R. (1989). Identifying and defining academic problems: CBM screening and eligibility procedures. In M. R. Shinn (Ed.), *Curriculum-based measurement: Assessing special children* (pp. 90–129). New York: Guilford Press.

Shinn, M. R. (1995). Best practices in curriculum-based measurement and its use in a problem-solving model. In A. Thomas & J. Grimes (Eds.), *Best practices in school psychology III* (pp. 547–567). Washington, DC: National Association of School Psychologists.

Shinn, M. R., & Baker, S. K. (1996). The use of curriculum-based measurement with diverse learners. In L. A. Suzuki, P. J. Meller, & J. G. Ponterro (Eds.), *Handbook of multicultural assessment: Clinical, psychological, and educational applications* (pp. 179–222). San Francisco: Jossey-Bass.

Shinn, M. R., & Bamonto, S. (1998). Advanced applications of curriculum-based measurement: "Big ideas" and avoiding confusion. In M. R. Shinn (Ed.), *Advanced applications of curriculum-based measurement* (pp. 1–31). New York: Guilford Press.

Shinn, M. R., Collins, V. L., & Gallagher, S. (1998). Curriculum-based measurement and its use in a problem-solving model with students from minority backgrounds. In M. R. Shinn (Ed.), *Advanced applications of curriculum-based measurement* (pp. 143–174). New York: Guilford Press.

Torgesen, J. K. (2006). *Intensive reading interventions for struggling learners in early elementary school: A principal's guide*. Portsmouth, NH: RMC Research Corporation, Center on Instruction.

Torgesen, J. K., Houston, D., Rissman, L., & Kosanovich, K. (2007). *Teaching all students to read in elementary school: A guide for principals*. Portsmouth, NH: RMC Research Corporation, Center on Instruction.

Vaughn, S., & Chard, D. (2006). Three-tier intervention research studies: Descriptions of two related projects. *Perspectives, 32*(1), 29–34.

Vaughn Gross Center for Reading and Language Arts at the University of Texas at Austin. (2005). *Introduction to the 3-tier reading model: Reducing reading disabilities for kindergarten through third grade students* (4th ed.). Austin: Author.

RESOURCES

For more information on quality literacy center activities for Grades K–5, see the *Instructional Materials for Teachers* link on the Florida Center for Reading Research website (http://www.fcrr.org)

For more information on effective Tier 2 instructional programs, see the *Teaching and Learning* link on the Florida Center for Reading Research website (http://www.fcrr.org), the *Materials* link on the Vaughn Gross Center for Reading and Language Arts website (http://www.meadowscenter.org/vgc/); and the *Supplemental and Intervention Programs* link on the Oregon Reading First website (http://oregonreadingfirst.uoregon.edu).

For more information on technically adequate early literacy and reading assessment tools, see the *Assessment* link on the Florida Center for Reading Research website (http://www.fcrr.org) and the *Assessment* link on the Oregon Reading First website (http://oregonreadingfirst.uoregon.edu).

For more information on instructional observation forms that can be used during classroom walk-throughs, see the *Teaching and Learning* link on the Florida Center for Reading Research website (http://www.fcrr.org), the *Leadership* link on the Oregon Reading First website, (http://oregonreadingfirst.uoregon.edu); and the *Reading* link on the RMC Research Corporation Center on Instruction website (http://www.centeroninstruction.org).

INTERVENTIONS

for Achievement and Behavior Problems in a Three-Tier Model Including RTI

CHAPTER 7

Training School Psychologists for Prevention and Intervention
in a Three-Tier Model

Thomas J. Power
University of Pennsylvania/The Children's Hospital of Philadelphia

Jennifer A. Mautone
The Children's Hospital of Philadelphia

Marika Ginsburg-Block
University of Delaware

INTRODUCTION

A paradigm shift has been unfolding gradually in the field of school psychology over the past 25 years, although clear evidence of change has not been apparent until just the past few years. The shift has moved the profession from focusing primarily on the use of assessment for special education determination to emphasizing data-based decision making for intervention planning and evaluation (Reschly & Ysseldyke, 1995).

Several developments within education and psychology have paved the way for a shift to a prevention and intervention focus for school psychology. First, a number of studies have demonstrated that placing students in special education typically does not accomplish meaningful change for those students (see U.S. Department of Education Office of Special Education and Rehabilitation Services, 2002). This line of research has led to an emphasis on developing special education interventions and programming to prevent placement into restricted educational settings.

Second, the evidence-based intervention (EBI) movement, which was emerging in medicine and psychology, began to have a major influence on research and practice in school psychology. This movement emphasized the need to shape practice using empirically based research and produced standards for evaluating the scientific rigor of practice-related research (Kratochwill & Stoiber, 2002).

Third, federal legislation (Individuals with Disabilities Education Improvement Act, 2004) has supported the use of an alternative to the ability–achievement discrepancy model on which the identification of specific learning disabilities (SLD) was based. That alternative, the response-to-intervention (RTI) model, emphasizes the use of progressively more intensive intervention approaches in response to data regarding the effectiveness of prevention and intervention strategies. At the core of the RTI movement is the use of a data-based decision-making approach to plan and evaluate instructional and behavioral interventions for students (Glover & DiPerna, 2007).

Fourth, a consensus of leaders in the field of school psychology has affirmed that change at a systems level (i.e., district, school, and classroom) is needed to promote successful outcomes for students (Dawson et al., 2004). Increasingly, the emphasis has been on identifying resources in the schools and building capacity for meaningful change (Schaughency & Ervin, 2006). Relatedly, there is recognition that success in school requires strong connections with families and community-based services dedicated to promoting the health and welfare of children (Power, DuPaul, Shapiro, & Kazak, 2003).

This paradigm shift has resulted in the need for significant changes in the preparation of school psychologists for effective practice. The purpose of this chapter is to outline critical components for school psychology training in prevention and intervention within the context of a three-tier model including RTI. Also, the chapter provides suggestions for how to organize coursework and practicum experiences to operationalize these components of training.

CRITICAL COMPONENTS OF TRAINING

Critical components of school psychology training in prevention and intervention in the context of a three-tier model include: (a) using data-based decision making; (b) selecting and implementing evidence-based, socially valid interventions; (c) selecting and implementing school-wide prevention programs; (d) building capacity for a three-tier model; (e) developing leaders in intervention and prevention programming; and (f) developing supervisory skills.

Using Data-Based Decision Making

Data-based decision making, one of a school psychologist's core functional competencies, provides a foundation for prevention and early intervention within a multitiered model (Ysseldyke et al., 2006). The main components of data-based decision making within this model are (a) screening (both individual and universal); (b) functional behavioral assessment (FBA); (c) progress monitoring; and (d) outcome evaluation. As experts in assessment (National Association of School Psychologists [NASP], 2003a) and evaluation, school psychologists should be prepared to play an important role in helping schools use data effectively for educational programming at both the individual and systems levels.

Universal screening is a primary prevention strategy that involves the collection and interpretation of performance measures for *all* students (Tier 1). The primary purpose of universal screening within a three-tier model is to identify students with potential learning and behavior needs so that they may be targeted for early intervention (Ikeda, Neessen, & Witt, 2008). Typically, students identified through this process receive Tier 2 instruction based on their individual needs. Screening data may also be used to evaluate whole-classroom or building-level performance, aiding school leadership in identifying teachers who may need support or evaluating the efficacy of the core curriculum (National Center on Response to Intervention, n.d.).

Data-based intervention planning is a process of analyzing instructional and behavioral information to plan interventions for students. For example, evaluations involving curriculum-based measurement (CBM) include a broad range of strategies for evaluating how students are responding to the curriculum. These methods offer a systematic approach to problem solving that can be highly useful in designing instructional strategies for struggling students (Howell, Hosp, & Kurns, 2008).

Functional behavioral assessment is a process by which the function of a behavior is determined through analysis of antecedents, consequences, and the frequency of the challenging behavior. Research has shown that interventions developed through FBA are significantly more effective in promoting desired behaviors than those developed in the absence of FBA (Cohn, 2004; Ingram, Lewis-Palmer, & Sugai, 2005). Strategies based on CBM and FBA may be used within all phases of a three-tier model to develop appropriate intervention strategies at the building, classroom, and student levels.

Progress monitoring is the application of data-based progress monitoring tools over time to evaluate the effects of intervention for individuals or groups. For basic skills (e.g., reading), CBM can be used to evaluate students' progress toward academic goals. The widespread use of different CBM progress monitoring tools, such as the Dynamic Indicators of Basic Early Literacy Skills (DIBELS; Good, Wallin, Simmons, Kame'enui & Kaminski, 2002), and AIMSweb (Shinn, 2005) is based on compelling research demonstrating the academic benefits of CBM (e.g., Fuchs, Deno, & Mirkin, 1984; Graney & Shinn, 2005).

Progress monitoring serves different functions within the three-tier problem-solving model (U.S. Department of Education, Office of Special Education Programs, n.d.). At Tier 1, universal screening data are typically obtained at several points over the course of the school year. These data may then be used to determine whether students are gaining, maintaining, or declining in their skill levels, as well as the extent to which students are on track to meet high-stakes tests or state standards (e.g., benchmarks). For students receiving Tier 2 or Tier 3 interventions, progress is monitored much more frequently (1–2 times per month or weekly), and this information is used to evaluate intervention effectiveness and modify instruction as needed. Progress monitoring also plays a role in special education eligibility decisions within this model, as these data are used summatively to determine student response to intervention. Finally, progress monitoring is used to measure the extent to which students with Individual Education

Plans (IEPs) are accomplishing their goals, to aid in instructional planning, and to determine continued eligibility for special education services.

Outcome evaluation involves the interpretation of data to answer the question of whether students have responded sufficiently to an intervention or inversely whether an intervention or curriculum has been effective in promoting student achievement. This process involves weighing not only student progress monitoring data, but also information about related factors, such as the nature (e.g., whether the intervention was evidence-based) and delivery (e.g., fidelity of implementation) of instruction. Objective strategies for evaluating student response to intervention within a three-tier model also may involve both rate of improvement and level of performance, although these strategies have been less well researched (Burns, Jacob, & Wagner, 2008; Fuchs, 2003).

Over the course of the past two decades, computerized technology has improved and become increasingly accessible to the general public. As these tools become more readily available, school psychologists have begun to integrate technology into their practice (McLeod & Ysseldyke, 2008). In fact, *School Psychology: A Blueprint for Training and Practice III* now includes technology as an area of competency for school psychologists (Ysseldyke et al., 2006). Frequently, school districts use computerized systems to manage progress monitoring data, and school psychologists must be aware of and able to use the various technologies that are available (McLeod & Ysseldyke).

Selecting and Implementing Evidence-Based, Socially Valid Interventions

In recent years there has been a push to more closely link educational research to educational practices. At the national level, expert panels, such as the National Reading Panel (National Institute of Child Health and Human Development, 2000) and now the National Mathematics Advisory Panel (2008), have been assembled to review the content-area literature and identify evidence-based instructional strategies. The Doing What Works (DWW) website (http://dww.ed.gov) was established by the U.S. Department of Education Office of Planning, Evaluation and Policy Development to guide educators in implementing evidence-based instructional practices. Current DWW topics include early childhood education, English language learners, and math and science education (U.S. Department of Education, Office of Planning, Evaluation and Policy Development, n.d.). National and international organizations in professional psychology, including the Campbell Collaboration in the social sciences, the Collaborative for Academic Social and Emotional Learning, and the American Psychological Association Divisions 16 and 53 (School Psychology and Child Clinical, respectively), and the Cochrane Collaboration in health care, have developed criteria for determining whether evidence of effectiveness exists for a particular intervention strategy. In some cases the groups have applied those criteria to the existing research literature. School psychologists must have a current understanding of evidence-based interventions and the tools to evaluate new and promising interventions that emerge from the ever-growing research literature.

Not only does effective implementation of an intervention involve the identification of empirically supported interventions; it also requires the use of factors that may support intervention effectiveness and anticipation of factors that may inhibit success. "Developmentally appropriate practices take into account what is known about child development and learning, what is known about the unique needs, strengths and interests of each child, and what is known about the cultural and social environments in which each child lives" (NASP, 2003b, p. 1). School psychologists must have a foundational understanding of child development to match interventions to student needs (Lavigne, Mattern, Pemberton, & Soslau, 2008). Bronfenbrenner's developmental ecological theory (1979) has had great influence on the practice of school psychology, providing a basis for developing interventions that address the child as a whole, recognizing and tapping into the multiple spheres of influence that contribute to a student's school success. Prevention and intervention programs that involve teachers, family, community members, and peers (e.g., Power, Karustis, & Habboushe, 2001; Power, Dowrick, Ginsburg-Block, & Manz, 2004; Rohrbeck, Ginsburg-Block, Fantuzzo, & Miller, 2003), as well as the interactions among these resources, have been shown to produce positive outcomes even for the most vulnerable youth served by school psychologists (Durlak, 1995; Fantuzzo, Davis, & Ginsburg, 1995; also see chapter 4).

Enhancing school psychology's responsiveness to diversity is one of NASP's six strategic goals (NASP, 2007). In recent years, *School Psychology Review* has published two special series devoted to advancing the practice of school psychology among diverse populations (Henning-Stout & James, 2000; Ingraham & Meyers, 2000), and another series on linking community systems and multidisciplinary professionals for prevention and intervention (e.g., Power, 2003). Given the proven value of engaging students through collaborative efforts between schools and communities, and given the increasingly diverse backgrounds of students in terms of socio-economic status, native language, and cultural background, cultural awareness and competence are foundational competencies for school psychologists (Ysseldyke et al., 2006).

Research and intervention strategies that are mindful of cultural and developmental contexts have a greater likelihood of success, as they inherently address issues such as program feasibility and acceptability, also known as *social validity* (e.g., Lyst, Gabriel, O'Shaughnessy, Meyers, & Meyers, 2005). Partnership approaches of this nature have been proposed in the literature, and mounting evidence of their effectiveness exists (e.g., Fantuzzo, Bulotsky-Shearer, & McWayne, 2006; Nastasi et al., 2007; Power et al., 2004). Thus, by focusing on shared goals, stakeholders are able to jointly construct durable prevention and intervention strategies that address challenges to intervention implementation. Strategies for increasing adherence to intervention protocols, such as standardizing intervention strategies, using integrity checklists, and providing technical assistance, including ongoing feedback, also contribute to intervention effectiveness by ensuring fidelity of implementation (Kratochwill & Stoiber, 2000; Yetter & Doll, 2007).

Selecting and Implementing School-Wide Prevention Programs

Traditionally, school psychologists have been trained to develop, implement, and evaluate interventions for individual children or small groups of children with identified needs. More recently, school psychology training and practice have increasingly focused on prevention of academic, behavioral, and health problems and promotion of *healthy behavior* (e.g., Power, Heathfield, McGoey, & Blum, 1999; Power, DuPaul, et al., 2003). School psychologists have shifted their practice from a sole focus on service provision to practice that includes a public health emphasis as well as an orientation toward service provision (Short & Talley, 1997). Additionally, with the recent shift from the discrepancy model of specific learning disability (SLD) identification to the RTI model has come an emphasis on implementation of universal or Tier 1 systems-wide interventions (Walker & Shinn, 2002). School-wide prevention programs fit within a public health orientation and maximize resources so services may be provided to large groups of children, whether or not they have identified needs (Power, 2000; Shapiro, 2000; Sugai & Horner, 2006; see chapter 16). Programs may be put in place to create a school climate that includes the necessary conditions to support the learning and development of all students, such as safety, high expectations for all students, support from adults and peers, and opportunities for social–emotional learning (Osher et al., 2008).

There has been an increased focus on the implementation of evidence-based interventions (EBIs) in schools, including interventions for individuals or small groups of students (Kratochwill & Stoiber, 2002; Schaughency & Ervin, 2006). Additionally, school-wide EBIs are designed to be delivered to the entire school population within the first tier of the three-tier model. For example, the Doing What Works website includes reviews of school-wide programs and practice guides related to school improvement (e.g., Herman et al., 2008).

When selecting and implementing programs for school-wide intervention, it is important to match the program to the needs and culture of the school. Partnership-based program development and evaluation (e.g., participatory action research) requires the active participation of key stakeholders in the school community in all aspects of the program, including program selection, planning and implementation, and progress monitoring or outcome evaluation (Nastasi et al., 2000; Power et al., 2005). Families should be encouraged to participate in school-wide programs as much as possible to ensure consistency between the home and school environment, which is critical for student success (Christenson & Sheridan, 2001). School psychologists may work with a team of stakeholders to conduct a universal screening and needs assessment to identify targets for school-wide programs and to ensure that screening data are closely linked to program selection (Ikeda et al., 2008).

The implementation of school-wide programming through a partnership process increases the likelihood that the programs will be accepted by members of the school community (Fantuzzo et al., 2006; Power et al., 2005). Challenges in implementation may still arise, even when a team of stakeholders is involved in program development and implementation. To address challenges to implementation, it is important that school-wide programs be monitored by a leadership team that includes representatives of all stakeholder groups, school administrators actively support the programs, and the majority of the school staff buy into program implementation (Horner, Sugai, Todd, & Lewis-Palmer, 2005; Lohrmann, Forman, Martin, & Palmieri, in press).

Building Capacity for a Three-Tier Model

The paradigm shift in school psychology from a refer–test–place model of special education assessment to an early intervention oriented model has resulted in the creation of a three-tier system of service delivery (Kratochwill, Volpiansky, Clements, & Ball, 2007; Reschly, 2008). Research strongly supports a variety of individual, classroom-based, and school-wide interventions to meet student needs at each level of the three-tier model—universal screening and intervention, selected interventions developed through a problem-solving process, and targeted intervention for individual students with specific needs. However, to sustain the implementation of these strategies and maximize their effectiveness, systems issues must be addressed (Ervin, Schaughency, Goodman, McGlinchey, & Matthews, 2006; Sugai & Horner, 2006).

In recent years, building the organizational resources of schools has been identified as a major component of school psychology practice (Ysseldyke et al., 2006). However, school psychologists often are not trained as systems change agents (Ervin & Schaughency, 2008). Researchers are increasingly examining methods that foster systems change (e.g., Fullan, Bertani, & Quinn, 2004; Hall & Hord, 2006). Therefore it is important that school psychologists have a working knowledge of the systems change literature (Ervin & Schaughency). For example, the Concerns-Based Adoption model (C-BAM; Hall & Hord) has been recommended for use by school psychologists as an approach to promote systems-wide change in schools (Ervin & Schaughency).

School psychologists are in a unique position to partner with school administrators to encourage systems-level change to support a three-tier model. For example, school-wide positive behavior support (SWPBS) is a three-tier service delivery model that focuses on prevention, implementation of evidence-based strategies, and change at the systems level (Sugai & Horner, 2006). Participatory action research strategies may be used to develop procedures that are tailored to the school's unique needs, demographics, and resources (Ervin et al., 2006; Nastasi et al., 2000).

As schools move toward the three-tier model of service delivery, a leadership team must be in place to develop, monitor, and evaluate systems-level changes (Horner et al., 2005). The team might also be involved with providing professional development opportunities for school staff. Additional training will be essential for school professionals as they undergo a major shift in their practice (Kratochwill et al., 2007). School psychologists, as leaders in their schools and districts, are well suited to take active roles in providing professional development for colleagues and directing the school leadership team. School psychologists also may be involved with coordinating systems of care, such as partnering with primary care providers or community mental health providers, to ensure that appropriate services are provided for students requiring Tier 3 intervention (Power, DuPaul, et al., 2003).

Developing Leaders in Intervention and Prevention Programming

The role of most school psychologists is to be a leader within the school. Historically, school psychologists have responded to the needs of individual students referred by teachers or parents as a result of learning and/or behavior problems. Within the context of a multitiered model, school psychologists are challenged to shift the unit of analysis from the individual child to the classroom context and whole-school setting (Shapiro, 2006).

School psychologists also have the opportunity to serve as leaders at a broader level—within their district and region, as well as at the state and national level. Gaps in knowledge and services within a school often reflect broader issues at a macrosystemic level that need to be addressed. For example, the challenge of developing literacy skills among young students is a problem that almost every school district in the nation faces. Further, preventing aggression and violence in schools is a universal concern.

Training in public health is highly beneficial for school psychologists who aspire to advocacy and leadership at a broad level (Power, DuPaul, et al., 2003). A public health orientation entails analyzing data available through large systems to detect trends, emerging problems, and gaps in services. An essential component of this model is the identification of factors that contribute to and protect against developmental risk (Strein, Hoagwood, & Cohn 2003). These methods of analysis are useful in designing policy initiatives that can have an impact on many school systems and the children they serve.

Training in program development is essential to school psychologists who are leaders at a regional and national level. A core component of program development is the delineation of a model of change that explains mechanisms of action, based upon existing theory and empirical research. A comprehensive review of research on the effectiveness of existing programs is needed to establish what works and to identify gaps in knowledge and services. Furthermore, including stakeholders in the process of program development is essential to design initiatives that are community responsive and successful in engaging students, families, school professionals, and key members of the community (Leff, Costigan, & Power, 2004).

School districts commonly develop and implement innovative programs, but strategies for program evaluation generally are substantially underdeveloped. School psychologists need training in program evaluation to serve as effective leaders and change agents. Program evaluation includes strategies to examine how effectively the program has been delivered (integrity evaluation), what effect the program is having on targeted behaviors (outcome evaluation), what value the program has in the school and community (social validity evaluation), and whether the program is changing factors that are significant for the community (impact evaluation). For more detail, see Power, DuPaul, et al. (2003).

Developing Supervisory Skills

A high percentage of school psychologists are placed in supervisory positions during their career, and some assume these roles early on, when they have very little experience in the field (Harvey & Struzziero, 2008). Supervision is a challenging professional role that requires considerable knowledge and competence. Furthermore, the stakes of supervision are high. Inadequate or poor supervision may lead to incompetent practice, unethical behavior, and culturally inappropriate actions.

Although many doctoral programs include coursework and training in supervision, relatively few specialist programs provide in-depth preparation in this area. Nonetheless, school psychologists at the doctoral and specialist levels generally report the need for substantially more preparation to assume supervisory functions (Hunley et al., 2000).

Some of the core domains of supervision include (a) developing and maintaining effective supervisory relationships, (b) promoting multicultural competence among trainees, (c) providing training in data-based decision making and the use of evidence-based practices, (d) preparing trainees to promote systems-level change, and (e) promoting ethical and legal practice (Harvey & Struzziero, 2008). To prepare school psychologists for effective practice in the context of a three-tier model, supervision in prevention and intervention program development, implementation, and evaluation are also core elements.

CROSS-CUTTING ISSUES IN TRAINING

Training programs intended to prepare school psychologists in the use of intervention and prevention in a three-tier model must address several issues beyond the critical components identified so far. These themes should apply throughout every semester and year of the training program.

Link coursework with practicum training. Integrating traditional graduate course instruction with practicum placements provides students with meaningful training experiences that enrich and accelerate the pace of learning. Practicum experiences offer students an opportunity to test and practice skills learned in their courses, and these experiences will lead to questions that will direct and focus course instruction.

Prepare students to integrate research and practice. In all aspects of their work, school psychologists are expected to use assessment and intervention strategies that are evidence-based (Ysseldyke et al., 2006). They need to know how to evaluate the current state of research on a particular topic and to determine the extent to which the current state of knowledge has been strongly substantiated. Furthermore, practitioners at the doctoral level learn to identify gaps in knowledge and conduct original research to inform future practice.

Prepare students to take a strategic approach to their career development. Throughout their schooling, students are taught to develop and refine their career goals, along with long-term and short-term objectives. Students are provided with mentoring to strategically select courses, field experiences, consultation, and directed readings that will enable them to achieve their goals and objectives.

Promote culturally competent practice. School psychologists must be effective in working with children and families from diverse backgrounds (Ysseldyke et al., 2006). Students need to be taught models and strategies of culturally competent practice, and they need practicum experiences in varied settings to learn how to work effectively with children and families from highly diverse backgrounds.

Promote ethical practice. Training in ethical practice cuts across all aspects of training, including didactic and practicum activities. Early in their training, students learn the ethical codes of the National Association of School Psychologists and the American Psychological Association (APA, 2002; NASP, 2000a). Throughout their training, students learn how to make decisions that reconcile competing ethical principles and standards that may be in conflict with laws and local policies. It is critical for coursework and practicum experiences to be well integrated so that students learn how to apply ethical standards in practice.

Prepare students for effective community collaboration. Effective practice in schools requires the ability to form strong collaborations in the community. Community systems that have an impact on how children develop in school and in the family are primary care practices and other health systems, after-school youth programs, human services and mental health agencies, and juvenile justice agencies (Power, DuPaul, et al., 2003).

Affirm the complementary nature of specialist-level and doctoral-level training. Although the APA has advanced a proposal under the Model Act for State Licensure of Psychologists (APA, 2007), which would restrict use of the term psychologist and potentially the practice of school psychology to doctoral-level providers, quality school psychology practitioners at both the specialist and doctoral levels are needed. Students at both the specialist and doctoral levels receive training in practice and systems change, which prepares them for leadership positions at district, regional, state, and national levels. Doctoral-level training places stronger emphasis on preparation to be trainers, supervisors, and independent researchers, and includes additional requirements to provide training in these areas.

INTEGRATED TRAINING EXPERIENCES

This section suggests courses that address critical components of training for intervention and prevention in a multitiered model. The focus is on coursework and practicum experiences directly related to training in intervention and prevention. Foundation courses in educational psychology, developmental psychology, psychometrics, cognitive and behavioral assessment, research methods, and statistics are not included. The following recommendations recognize that the curriculum and sequence of courses for programs differ greatly, depending on the unique mission of the program.

The courses described under years 1 and 2 are designed to be appropriate for students at both the specialist level and doctoral level. Courses included under years 3 and 4 are intended for individuals enrolled in doctoral programs, given the time constraints faced by specialist-level training programs. This content could, however, be reduced in scope and creatively included within specialist programs. Table 1 maps the suggested courses onto the functional and foundational competencies delineated in *School Psychology: A Blueprint for Training and Practice III* (Ysseldyke et al., 2006).

Year 1: Specialist and Doctoral Courses

The following courses are recommended in Year 1 of the specialist or doctoral-level program. Also included are suggestions for practicum experiences in Year 1.

Course 1: Data-Based Decision Making

This course provides trainees with a solid foundation for delivering school psychology services within a three-tier model. It addresses the mechanics of both data collection and data analysis to prepare school psychologists for making informed decisions about academic and behavioral interventions, primarily at the individual student level. The objectives of this course are for trainees to become knowledgeable about and competent in performing (a) universal (and individual) screening for academic performance and behavior to evaluate the adequacy of core instruction and identify students in need of Tier 2 or Tier 3 instruction (e.g., Ikeda et al., 2008); (b) progress monitoring and outcome assessment using CBM and treatment fidelity data to determine the appropriateness and effectiveness of instruction across the tiers (e.g., Hosp & Ardoin, 2008); and (c) functional behavioral assessment involving the evaluation of antecedents and consequences of behavior to determine the function of undesirable behaviors and develop appropriate strategies for prevention and remediation (Gresham, 2004).

This course includes a foundation in principles of measurement (e.g., reliability, validity, and norms) and various forms of assessment (e.g., norm-referenced versus criterion-based) and their use within a multitiered framework. The course emphasizes application of these strategies both within a multitiered intervention framework and through a developmental-ecological approach that considers the individual within his or her environmental context (e.g., Ysseldyke & Christenson, 2002). Therefore, training in data-based decision making is intended to produce school psychologists who know how to generate multiple hypotheses for explaining student performance, to evaluate those hypotheses using multiple data collection methods, and to use evaluation results to inform educational decisions.

Course 2: Development of Effective Instructional Intervention Strategies

This course prepares trainees to provide direct and indirect (i.e., consultative) instructional support services related to the development of reading, math, and writing

Table 1. Summary of Topics Covered in Core Courses and the Blueprint III Domains Addressed by Each Course

Course	Topics	Blueprint III Domain[a]
1. Data-based decision making	Assessment for intervention planning Universal and individual screening Scientifically based progress monitoring Outcome evaluation	1, 2, 3, 5, 6, 7
2. Development of effective instructional intervention strategies	Evidence-based academic interventions Collaborative consultation Social validity Intervention integrity Cultural competence Ethical practice	1, 4, 5, 7, 8
3. Development of effective strategies for emotional and behavioral problems	School-based mental health Evidence-based interventions Social validity Cultural competence Ethical practice	2, 4, 5, 7, 8
4. Creation of organizational contexts for change	Organizational consultation Educational leadership Prevention programming Program evaluation	3, 4, 7, 8
5. Doctoral seminar on organizational change	Organizational consultation Systems change Strategic planning Evaluation of systems change	4, 7, 8
6. Doctoral seminar on intervention development and evaluation	Evidence-based interventions Theories of change Grant writing Program evaluation	1, 2, 3, 4, 7, 8
7. Doctoral seminar on prevention program development and evaluation	Public health model Prevention programming Early career development Grant writing	1, 2, 3, 4, 7, 8
8. Doctoral seminar on supervision	Professional relationships Professional development Cultural competence Ethical practice	3, 4, 5, 6, 7, 8

Note. Issues related to cultural competence and ethical practice are integrated into each course.

The following is the key for identifying domains of training and practice as indicated in *School Psychology: A Blueprint for Training and Practice III* (Ysseldyke et al., 2006):

1 – Enhancing the development of cognitive and academic skills

2 – Enhancing the development of wellness, social skills, mental health, and life competencies

3 – Data-based decision making and accountability

4 – Systems-based service delivery

5 – Professional, legal, ethical, and social responsibility

6 – Technological applications

7 – Diversity awareness and sensitive service delivery

8 – Interpersonal and collaborative skills

skills. Course outcomes include enabling trainees to (a) identify, develop, and deliver evidence-based instructional strategies at Tiers 2 and 3; (b) work strategically to develop interventions sensitive to student development and culture; (c) anticipate and address barriers to implementation (e.g., feasibility); and (d) develop interventions through a collaborative process involving families, schools, and community resources. Emphasis on factors shown in the empirical literature to contribute to positive student outcomes are emphasized throughout this course (e.g., social and ecological validity, early intervention, engagement of multiple systems, and fidelity of implementation), as well as guidelines for critically evaluating strategies and the available evidence of their effectiveness (e.g., Collaborative for Academic, Social, and Emotional Learning [CASEL], 2003).

Year 1 Practicum Experiences

An essential component of preservice preparation for school psychologists is their field-based experiences, beginning with their first practicum (Tarquin & Truscott, 2006). During this experience, it is important that students receive supervision from both university-based and on-site supervisors who are knowledgeable about contemporary service delivery models such as a multitiered model, including RTI. In addition, planned field-based assignments should be well matched to students' skills and provide students with an opportunity to reinforce their didactic coursework through practice and timely feedback on their performance (NASP, 2000b). Field-based assignments within the first year should include both shadowing and observational activities to familiarize students with how schools and school psychologists function, as well as more active assignments that emphasize data-based decision making and instructional intervention, such as collecting and analyzing progress monitoring data for students receiving Tier 2 instruction in reading, or conducting a functional behavioral assessment for a student with poor conduct. A minimum of 2 days per week over the course of a 15-week semester, or 150 hours, is recommended for each practicum experience.

Year 2: Specialist and Doctoral Courses

The following courses are recommended in Year 2 of the specialist or doctoral-level program. Also included are suggestions for practicum experiences in Year 2.

Course 3: Development of Effective Strategies for Emotional and Behavioral Problems

This course provides an overview of systems of mental health service delivery for children and adolescents and highlights the need for school-based services. Students review the literature related to help seeking, barriers to care (e.g., Eiraldi, Mazzuca, Clarke, & Power, 2006), and school-based mental health services. The course prepares trainees to provide direct services to students as well as consult with school staff to develop individual and classroom-based behavioral interventions. Course objectives include (a) identifying the need for school-based behavioral health services; (b) developing and implementing evidence-based interventions for emotional and behavioral problems at Tiers 2 and 3; (c) ensuring that interventions are feasible, acceptable, developmentally appropriate, and sensitive to student culture; and (d) designing multimethod strategies for monitoring progress and evaluating outcomes.

Course 4: Creation of Organizational Contexts for Change

This course introduces students to the main concepts in systems-level change and organizational leadership. Students review the literature related to facilitators of and barriers to systems change. The main goal of the course is to prepare students to work effectively with school administrators and staff to develop, implement, and evaluate multitiered systems of service delivery (e.g., Ervin et al., 2006), with a particular emphasis on promoting the development of Tier 1 prevention and early intervention services. Students (a) discuss models of educational leadership, (b) learn methods for systems-level consultation, and (c) develop and present a professional development workshop to their peers related to course content.

Year 2 Practicum Experiences

During the second-year practicum experiences, it is critical that trainees are given opportunities to develop leadership skills related to prevention programming, school-based mental health services, and systems-level consultation. Students continue to receive supervision from both university-based and on-site supervisors, and practicum assignments are consistent with year 2 course objectives as much as possible. At this point in their training, students should be prepared to take an active role in the practicum experience. For example, students might (a) participate in student support team activities, (b) work with a school psychologist or guidance counselor to implement and evaluate an intervention for a student or small group of students with emotional or behavioral difficulties, or (c) consult with a classroom teacher to develop and monitor a behavioral intervention for a student with disruptive classroom behavior. Additionally, when possible, students should have opportunities to observe and participate in school leadership team activities related to implementation of a multitiered model of service delivery. A minimum of 2 days per week over the course of a 15-week semester, or 200 hours, is recommended for each practicum experience.

Years 3 and 4: Doctoral Courses

The following courses are suggested as a way of addressing the critical components of training within the context of doctoral-level programs. Each course is designed to be a seminar that involves students in active leadership roles within the class. Students are expected to give presentations, lead discussions, and provide feedback to each other about their work. The sequence of the courses is flexible and may vary across programs. It is strongly recommended that each course include experiential activities in schools to provide students opportunities to experiment and practice the skills they are learning.

Course 5: Doctoral Seminar on Organizational Change

This course provides advanced training in models for promoting change within large systems, such as schools and districts. An emphasis is placed on identifying organizational resources and building capacity for schools to support innovative prevention and intervention programming and the evaluation of outcomes. The course stresses the importance of connecting systems in the community to build capacity. Students are introduced to strategies to form partnerships within the school and community to promote school reform. Students are expected to work within a school on an organizational change project during the course.

Course 6: Doctoral Seminar on Intervention Development and Evaluation

This course focuses on intervention strategies for children and adolescents with identified instructional, behavioral, social, and health problems as they manifest in school. Students receive instruction in how to develop an intervention program based on existing theory and empirical research. The major project in the course is the preparation of a simulated application for an intervention development grant following the guidelines of the National Institute of Mental Health (NIMH). As part of this process, students are expected to conduct a thorough review of the literature that identifies gaps in knowledge, specify the aims and hypotheses for a study that will enable them to address gaps in the intervention science base, develop a cogent plan for developing an innovative intervention, and develop a research design for a pilot study of the effectiveness of the intervention.

Course 7: Doctoral Seminar on Prevention Program Development and Evaluation

This course emphasizes prevention strategies for all children as well as those at risk for problems in school. The major focus is on the development of innovative prevention programs in response to community-identified needs. Students are introduced to the public health model, including strategies for assessing need and identifying factors that contribute to and protect against risk. The major project in this course is to prepare a simulated application for an early-career mentored research award following NIMH guidelines. Students are expected to develop a cohesive career development plan and an innovative prevention research project that directly relates to their career plan.

Course 8: Doctoral Seminar on Supervision

This course prepares students to become supervisors in diverse settings, including schools, universities, hospitals, and community agencies. The course places strong emphasis on the development and maintenance of relationships that promote the optimal development of trainees. In addition, there is a major focus on promoting multicultural competence and ethical conduct in practice, as well as on promoting the use of technological innovations to enhance practice. With close supervision from university faculty and school psychologists in the field, students are given opportunities to provide supervision to 1st- and 2nd-year graduate students who are placed in practicum experiences in school settings.

Specialty Concentration Areas

Each training program has a unique mission, which is shaped in part by goals of the institution and priorities of the department and program faculty. Some programs have developed specialty areas of concentration that reflect this mission. For example, through the collaborative efforts of Lehigh University and The Children's Hospital of Philadelphia, students can receive specialized training in pediatric school psychology. The purpose of this program is to prepare school psychology leaders to link the school, family, and health systems of care to promote children's health and to intervene in cases of risk or disorder. Students in this program receive intensive practicum experiences in school and health settings. In addition, they receive a year-long sequence of seminars related to interventions for children with chronic illness and another year-long series focused on health promotion and prevention (Power, Shapiro, & DuPaul, 2003).

Other ideas for specialty concentration areas are early childhood intervention, program development, and multisystemic intervention. Table 2 presents suggested courses for several proposed areas of concentration.

Specialized Practicum Experiences and Internship

Although practicum experiences in school settings are especially important, trainees benefit greatly from placements in alternative contexts. For example, given that the major sites for the provision of mental health services in this country are schools and primary care, placement in training positions within the context of primary care pediatric practices are invaluable. Within these settings, trainees can learn strategies to promote collaboration between schools and primary care providers. In addition, practicum experiences in community-based and tertiary-care hospital settings, as well as mental health agencies, can offer valuable learning activities that serve the needs of children with health and mental health conditions.

Internships can be completed in a range of settings, including schools, health systems, and mental health clinics. Regardless of setting, it is imperative that students have opportunities to work with children in multiple systems. Furthermore, school psychology interns need in-depth training in intervention and prevention across a range of student and community needs and risk factors. Perhaps most importantly, interns need to work in a setting in which they have regular access to strong mentors who are committed to promoting their career development as school psychologists who have expertise in providing services within the context of a multitiered model.

Table 2. **Suggested Course Offerings for Proposed Specialty Concentration Areas**

Pediatric School Psychology
  Psychopharmacology
  Interventions for children with chronic illnesses
  Strategies for health promotion
Early Childhood Intervention
  Infant and preschool assessment linked to intervention
  Promotion of family involvement in education
  Multisystemic intervention
Program Development
  Advanced strategies in program development and evaluation
  Measurement development and adaptation
  Participatory action research methods
Multisystemic Intervention
  Conjoint behavioral consultation
  Intervention design and evaluation
  Evaluation of integrity, outcomes, acceptability, and impact

CONCLUSION

The paradigm and practice shift in school psychology that has been occurring over the past 25 years increasingly has emphasized the importance of prevention and intervention programming in the context of a three-tier model. This chapter proposed several core components of training to prepare school psychologists to function capably in the context of a three-tier model, including training in (a) data-based decision making, (b) selection and implementation of evidence-based intervention and prevention programs, (c) capacity building for schools in the use of a three-tier model, (d) leadership and organizational systems change, and (e) strategies for providing supervision and promoting career development.

To maximize effectiveness of training, several cross-cutting themes should permeate training programs: (a) linking didactic and practicum training, (b) integrating research with practice, (c) developing strategic career planning skills, (d) promoting culturally competent practice, (e) fostering ethical practice, and (f) developing community collaboration skills. This chapter outlined a series of courses that operationalize these critical components and cross-cutting themes for effective training. A two-year sequence for specialist-level and doctoral-level students was presented, and courses for doctoral trainees only were suggested. Additional recommendations for training in specialty concentration areas, such as pediatric school psychology, and internship training were offered.

AUTHOR NOTE

Address correspondence to Thomas Power, The Children's Hospital of Philadelphia, CHOP North – Room 1471, 34th St. and Civic Center Blvd., Philadelphia, PA 19104. E-mail: power@email.chop.edu.

Preparation of this chapter was supported by a leadership training grant from the U.S. Department of Education, Office of Special Education Programs (H325D060008).

REFERENCES

American Psychological Association. (2002). Ethical principles of psychologists and code of conduct. *American Psychologist, 57,* 1060–1073.

American Psychological Association. (2007). Model act for state licensure of psychologists. Retrieved July 2, 2008, from http://forms.apa.org/practice/modelactlicensure/ModelActforReview.pdf

Bronfenbrenner, E. (1979). *The ecology of human development: Experiments by nature and design.* Cambridge, MA: Harvard University Press.

Burns, M. K., Jacob, S., & Wagner, A. R. (2008). Ethical and legal issues associated with using response-to-intervention to assess learning disabilities. *Journal of School Psychology, 46,* 263–279.

Christenson, S. L., & Sheridan, S. M. (2001). *Schools and families: Creating essential connections for learning.* New York: Guilford Press.

Cohn, A. M. (2004). Positive behavioral supports: Information for educators. In A. S. Canter, L. Z. Paige, M. D. Roth, I. Romero, & S. A. Carroll (Eds.), *Helping children at home and school II: Handouts for families and educators* (pp. 71–74). Bethesda, MD: National Association of School Psychologists.

Collaborative for Academic, Social, and Emotional Learning. (2003). *Safe and sound: An educational leader's guide to evidence-based social and emotional learning (SEL) programs.* Chicago: Author.

Dawson, M., Cummings, J. A., Harrison, P. L., Short, R. J., Gorin, S., & Palomares, R. (2004). The 2002 multisite conference on the future of school psychology: Next steps. *School Psychology Review, 33,* 115–125.

Durlak, J. A. (1995). *School-based prevention programs for children and adolescents.* Thousand Oaks, CA: SAGE

Eiraldi, R. B., Mazzuca, L. B., Clarke, A. T., & Power, T. J. (2006). Service utilization among ethnic minority children with ADHD: A model of help-seeking behavior. *Administration and Policy in Mental Health and Mental Health Services Research, 33,* 607–622.

Ervin, R. A., & Schaughency, E. (2008). Best practices in accessing the systems change literature. In A. Thomas & J. Grimes (Eds.), *Best practices in school psychology V* (pp. 853–873). Bethesda, MD: National Association of School Psychologists.

Ervin, R. A., Schaughency, E., Goodman, S. D., McGlinchey, M. T., & Matthews, A. (2006). Merging research and practice agendas to address reading and behavior school-wide. *School Psychology Review, 35,* 198–223.

Fullan, M., Bertani, A., & Quinn, J. (2004). New lessons for district-wide reform. *Educational Leadership, 4,* 42–46.

Fantuzzo, J. W., Bulotsky-Shearer, R., & McWayne, C. M. (2006). The pursuit of wellness for victims of child maltreatment: A model for targeting relevant competencies, contexts, and contributors. In J. R. Lutzker (Ed.), *Preventing violence: Research and evidence-based intervention strategies* (pp. 69–91). Washington, DC: American Psychological Association.

Fantuzzo, J., Davis, G., & Ginsburg, M. (1995). Effects of collaborative learning and parent involvement on mathematics achievement and perceived competencies. *Journal of Educational Psychology, 87,* 272–281.

Fuchs, L. S. (2003). Assessing intervention responsiveness: Conceptual and technical issues. *Learning Disabilities Research and Practice, 18,* 172–186.

Fuchs, L. S., Deno, S. L., & Mirkin, P. K. (1984). The effects of frequent curriculum-based measurement and evaluation on pedagogy, student achievement, and student awareness of learning. *American Educational Research Journal, 21,* 449–460.

Glover, T. A., & DiPerna, J. C. (2007). Service delivery for response to intervention: Core components and directions for future research. *School Psychology Review, 36,* 526–540.

Good, R. H., Wallin, J. U., Simmons, D. C., Kame'enui, E. J., & Kaminski, R. A. (2002). *System-wide percentile ranks for DIBELS benchmark assessment* (Tech. Rep. No. 9). Eugene: University of Oregon.

Graney, S. B., & Shinn, M. R. (2005). Effects of reading curriculum-based measurement (R–CBM): Teacher feedback in general education classrooms. *School Psychology Review, 34,* 184–201.

Gresham, F. M. (2004). Current status and future directions of school-based behavioral interventions. *School Psychology Review, 33,* 326–343.

Hall, G. E., & Hord, S. M. (2006). *Implementing change: Patterns, principles, and potholes* (2nd ed.). Boston: Allyn & Bacon.

Harvey, V. S., & Struzziero, J. A. (2008). *Professional development and supervision of school psychologists: From intern to expert.* Thousand Oaks, CA: Corwin Press.

Henning-Stout, M., & James, S. (2000). Introduction to the mini-series on lesbian, gay, bisexual, transgender, and questioning youth: Their interests and concerns as learners in schools. *School Psychology Review, 29,* 155–157.

Herman, R., Dawson, P., Dee, T., Greene, J., Maynard, R., Redding, S., et al. (2008). *Turning around chronically low-performing schools: A practice guide* (NCEE #2008-4020). Washington, DC: U.S. Department of Education, Institute of Education Sciences, National Center for Education Evaluation and Regional Assistance. Retrieved July 2, 2008, from http://ies.ed.gov/ncee/wwc/practiceguides

Horner, R. H., Sugai, G., Todd, A. W., & Lewis-Palmer, T. (2005). Schoolwide positive behavior support. In L. M. Bambara & L. Kern (Eds.), *Individualized supports for students with problem behavior: Designing positive behavior plans* (pp. 359—390). New York: Guilford Press.

Hosp, J. L., & Ardoin, S. P. (2008). Assessment for instructional planning. *Assessment for Effective Intervention, 33*(2), 69–77.

Howell, K. W., Hosp, J. L., & Kurns, S. (2008). Best practices in curriculum-based evaluation. In A. Thomas & J. Grimes (Eds.), *Best practices in school psychology V* (pp. 349–362). Bethesda, MD: National Association of School Psychologists.

Hunley, S. A., Harvey, V. S., Curtis, M. J., Portnoy, L. A., Grier, J. E. C., & Hellffrich, D. (2000, June). School psychology supervisors: A national study of demographics and professional practices. *Communiqué, 28*(8), 32–33.

Ikeda, M. J., Neessen, E., & Witt, J. C. (2008). Best practices in universal screening. In A. Thomas & J. Grimes (Eds.), *Best practices in school psychology V* (pp. 103–114). Bethesda, MD: National Association of School Psychologists.

Individuals with Disabilities Education Improvement Act of 2004. 20 U.S.C. § 1400 *et seq.* (2004).

Ingraham, C. L., & Meyers, J. (2000). Introduction to multicultural and cross-cultural consultation in schools: Cultural diversity issues in school consultation. *School Psychology Review, 29,* 315–319.

Ingram, K., Lewis-Palmer, T., & Sugai, G. (2005). Function-based intervention planning: Comparing the effectiveness of FBA function-based and non-function-based intervention plans. *Journal of Positive Behavior Interventions, 7,* 224–236.

Kratochwill, T. R., & Stoiber, K. C. (2000). Empirically supported interventions and school psychology: Conceptual and practice issues—part II. *School Psychology Quarterly, 15,* 233–253.

Kratochwill, T. R., & Stoiber, K. C. (2002). Evidence-based interventions in school psychology: Conceptual foundations of the procedural and coding manual of Division 16 and the Society for the Study of School Psychology Task Force. *School Psychology Quarterly, 17,* 341–389.

Kratochwill, T. R., Volpiansky, P., Clements, M., & Ball, C. (2007). Professional development in implementing and sustaining multitier prevention models: Implications for response to intervention. *School Psychology Review, 36,* 618–631.

Lavigne, N. C., Mattern, R. A., Pemberton, E. F., & Soslau, E. (2008). Pre-service teachers' application of conceptual knowledge pertaining to developmentally appropriate practice. Manuscript submitted for publication.

Leff, S. S., Costigan, T. E., & Power, T. J. (2004). Using participatory-action research to develop a playground-based prevention program. *Journal of School Psychology, 42,* 3–21.

Lohrmann, S., Forman, S., Martin, S., & Palmieri, M. (in press). Understanding school personnel's resistance to adopting SWPBS at a universal level of intervention. *Journal of Positive Behavioral Interventions.*

Lyst, A. M., Gabriel, S., O'Shaughnessy, T. E., Meyers, J., & Meyers, B. (2005). Social validity: Perceptions of check and connect with early literacy support. *Journal of School Psychology, 43,* 197–218.

McLeod, S., & Ysseldyke, J. (2008). Best practices in digital technology usage by data-driven school psychologists. In A. Thomas & J. Grimes (Eds.), *Best practices in school psychology V* (pp. 1859–1867). Bethesda, MD: National Association of School Psychologists.

Nastasi, B. K., Hitchcock, J. H., Burkholder, G., Varjas, K., Sarkar, S., & Jayasena, A. (2007). Assessing adolescents' understanding of and reactions to stress in different cultures: Results of a mixed-methods approach. *School Psychology International, 28,* 163–178.

Nastasi, B. K., Varjas, K., Schensul, S. L., Silva, K. T., Schensul, J. J., & Ratnayake, P. (2000). The participatory intervention model: A framework for conceptualizing and promoting intervention acceptability. *School Psychology Quarterly, 15,* 207–232.

National Association of School Psychologists. (2000a). *Professional conduct manual* (3rd ed.). Bethesda, MD: Author.

National Association of School Psychologists. (2000b). *Standards for training and field placement programs in school psychology.* Bethesda, MD: Author.

National Association of School Psychologists. (2003a). *Position statement on school psychologists' involvement in the role of assessment.* Bethesda, MD: Author.

National Association of School Psychologists. (2003b). *Position statement on early intervention services.* Bethesda, MD: Author.

National Association of School Psychologists. (2007). *NASP strategic plan.* Retrieved July 4, 2008, from http://www.nasponline.org/about_nasp/strategicplan.pdf

National Center on Response to Intervention. (n.d.). *School based RTI practices: School-wide screening.* Retrieved July 4, 2008, from http://www.rti4success.org/index.php?option=com_content&task=view&id=613&Itemid=2

National Institute of Child Health and Human Development. (2000). *Report of the National Reading Panel: Teaching children to read: An evidence-based assessment of the scientific research literature on reading and its implications for reading instruction: Reports of the subgroups* (NIH Publication No. 00-4754). Washington, DC: U.S. Government Printing Office.

National Mathematics Advisory Panel. (2008). *Foundations for success: The final report of the National Mathematics Advisory Panel.* Washington, DC: U.S. Department of Education.

Osher, D., Sprague, J., Weissberg, R. P., Axelrod, J., Keenan, S., Kendziora, K., et al. (2008). A comprehensive approach to promoting social, emotional, and academic growth in contemporary schools. In A. Thomas & J. Grimes (Eds.), *Best practices in school psychology V* (pp. 1263–1278). Bethesda, MD: National Association of School Psychologists.

Power, T. J. (2000). Commentary: The school psychologist as a community-focused public health professional: Emerging challenges and implications for training. *School Psychology Review, 29,* 557–559.

Power, T. J. (2003). Promoting children's mental health: Reform through interdisciplinary and community partnerships. *School Psychology Review, 32,* 3–16.

Power, T. J., Blom Hoffman, J., Clarke, A. T., Riley-Tillman, T. C., Kelleher, C., & Manz, P. H. (2005). Reconceptualizing intervention integrity: A partnership-based framework for linking research with practice. *Psychology in the Schools, 42,* 495–507.

Power, T., Dowrick, P., Ginsburg-Block, M., & Manz, P. (2004). Partnership-based, community assisted early intervention for literacy: An application of the participatory intervention model. *Journal of Behavioral Education, 13,* 93–115.

Power, T. J., DuPaul, G. J., Shapiro, E. S., & Kazak, A. E. (2003). Promoting children's health: Integrating school, family, and community. New York: Guilford Press.

Power, T. J., Heathfield, L., McGoey, K., & Blum, N. J. (1999). Managing and preventing chronic health problems: School psychology's role. *School Psychology Review, 28,* 251–263.

Power, T. J., Karustis, J. L., & Habboushe, D. F. (2001). *Homework success for children with ADHD: A family-school intervention program.* New York: Guilford Press.

Power, T. J., Shapiro, E. S., & DuPaul, G. J. (2003). Preparing psychologists to link systems of care in managing and preventing children's health problems. *Journal of Pediatric Psychology, 28,* 147–155.

Reschly, D. J. (2008). School psychology paradigm shift and beyond. In A. Thomas & J. Grimes (Eds.), *Best practices in school psychology V* (pp. 3–15). Bethesda, MD: National Association of School Psychologists.

Reschly, D. J., & Ysseldyke, J. E. (1995). School psychology paradigm shift. In A. Thomas & J. Grimes (Eds.), *Best practices in school psychology III* (pp. 17–31). Washington, DC: National Association of School Psychologists.

Rohrbeck, C., Ginsburg-Block, M., Fantuzzo, J., & Miller, T. (2003). Peer assisted learning interventions with elementary school students: A Meta-analytic review. *Journal of Educational Psychology, 95,* 240–257.

Schaughency, E., & Ervin, R. (2006). Building capacity to implement and sustain effective practices to better serve children. *School Psychology Review, 35,* 155–166.

Shapiro, E. S. (2000). School psychology from an instructional perspective: Solving big, not little problems. *School Psychology Review, 29,* 560–572.

Shapiro, E. S. (2006). Are we solving the big problems? *School Psychology Review, 35,* 260–265.

Shinn, M. R. (2005). *AIMSweb response to intervention (RTI): A standard protocol-based system for managing and reporting problem-solving outcomes.* Eden Prairie, MN: Edformation, Inc.

Short, R. J., & Talley, R. C. (1997). Rethinking psychology in the schools: Implications of recent national policy. *American Psychologist, 52,* 234–240.

Strein, W., Hoagwood, K., & Cohn, A. (2003). School psychology: A public health perspective: I. Prevention, populations, and systems change. *Journal of School Psychology, 41,* 3–28.

Sugai, G., & Horner, R. R. (2006). A promising approach for expanding and sustaining school-wide positive behavior support. *School Psychology Review, 35,* 245–259.

Tarquin, K. M., & Truscott, S. D. (2006). School psychology students' perceptions of their practicum experiences. *Psychology in the Schools, 43,* 727–736.

U.S. Department of Education, Office of Planning Evaluation and Policy Development. (n.d.). Doing what works overview. Retrieved July 18, 2008, from http://dww.ed.gov/content.cfm?cGroup=Overview

U.S. Department of Education, Office of Special Education and Rehabilitative Services. (2002). *A new era: Revitalizing special education for children and their families.* Washington, DC: Author.

U.S. Department of Education, Office of Special Education Programs. (n.d.). National Center on Student Progress Monitoring. Retrieved July 15, 2008, from http://www.studentprogress.org

Walker, H. M., & Shinn, M. R. (2002). Structuring school-based interventions to achieve integrated primary, secondary, and tertiary prevention goals for safe and effective schools. In M. R. Shinn, H. M. Walker, & G. Stoner (Eds.), *Interventions for academic and behavior problems II: Preventive and remedial approaches* (pp. 1–26). Bethesda, MD: National Association of School Psychologists.

Yetter, G., & Doll, B. (2007). The impact of logistical resources on prereferral team acceptability. *School Psychology Quarterly, 22,* 340–357.

Ysseldyke, J. E., & Christenson, S. L. (2002). *Functional assessment of academic behavior: Creating successful learning environments.* Longmont, CO: Sopris West.

Ysseldyke, J., Burns, M., Dawson, P., Kelley, B., Morrison, D., Ortiz, S., et al. (2006). *School psychology: A blueprint for training and practice III.* Bethesda, MD: National Association of School Psychologists.

INTERVENTIONS

for Achievement and Behavior Problems in a Three-Tier Model Including RTI

CHAPTER 8

Implementing Proven Research in School-Based Practices: Progress Monitoring Within a Response-to-Intervention Model

Edward S. Shapiro
Center for Promoting Research to Practice, Lehigh University

Alexandra Hilt-Panahon
Minnesota State University

Karen L. Gischlar
Montclair State University

INTRODUCTION

Over the past decade, a significant effort has emerged in many fields to identify and define evidence-based practice. Arising from areas such as psychology, medicine, and prevention science, the effort is based on the idea that practitioners should have a set of empirically validated interventions that can be selected and matched to identified problems (Hoagwood, Burns, Kiser, Ringeisen, & Schoenwald, 2001; Kratochwill & Stoiber, 2002; Power, 2002). These interventions have sufficient research to support an anticipated successful outcome. Indeed, this approach has long been present in medicine, where major professional organizations such as the American Academy of Pediatrics provide recommendations on the implementation of practices to their physician members based on research findings.

In school psychology, the development of evidence-based intervention (EBI) has been led by the work of Tom Kratochwill and colleagues through the Task Force on Evidence-Based Interventions (e.g., Kratochwill, 2005; Kratochwill & Shernoff, 2004). The primary objective of the task force has been to develop a coding process for examining empirically based research and to publish the results of these reviews in many domains of intervention relevant for school psychologists (Kratochwill & Stoiber, 2002). Although the use of EBIs presents many challenges, the concept of providing practice guidelines for the field of school psychology remains a significant advance for the effective delivery of school psychology practice.

Among the many evidence-based practices that have emerged over the past decade is progress monitoring. Defined by the National Center on Student Progress Monitoring as repeated, systematic assessment of behavior, progress monitoring is a science-based practice that is used to assess student academic and behavioral performance and evaluate the effectiveness of intervention. Progress monitoring can be used to determine and set goals and to assess the rate of learning and outcomes over time (Deno, Fuchs, Marston, & Shin, 2001; Fuchs, 2002). It also is a critical variable for fully understanding the impact of evidence-based interventions (Foegen, Jiban, & Deno, 2007; McMaster & Espin, 2007; Wayman, Wallace, Wiley, Tichá, & Espin, 2007). In the domain of academic intervention, progress monitoring should be linked to and drive instructional change, which means the measures used need to be sensitive to outcomes of instruction (Deno, 2003).

With the passage of the No Child Left Behind (NCLB) Act in 2001 and the Individuals with Disabilities Education Improvement Act (IDEA) in 2004, the requirement for systematic, ongoing assessment of children's academic and behavioral progress has become a part of federal law. Although the laws do not use the term *progress monitoring*, they require that data-based documentation of repeated assessments of achievement be performed at reasonable intervals, reflecting formal assessment of student progress during instruction. The documentation is to be provided to children's parents. As such, the interpretation of many schools is that the requirement for ongoing assessment can best be met by the use of progress monitoring.

To make progress monitoring a part of the everyday experiences of teachers and students, system-wide change must occur in districts across the country. Shapiro (2009) described how one state brought progress monitoring to the level of statewide implementation. The project began with a small, 1-year pilot to demonstrate efficacy of implementation among general and special education teachers who received professional development provided by consultants across 14 sites statewide (Shapiro, Edwards, & Zigmond, 2005). Feedback from the statewide pilot was used to scale up the project and provide a cadre of trained technical advisers to support local districts and teachers statewide in conducting progress monitoring. Outcomes of the 2-year scaling-up process showed that 408 out of 501 school districts statewide participated in training. Across the 408 districts that had personnel who attended Level 1 training (introduction and basics of progress monitoring implementation), 135 districts (33%) indicated that they were implementing progress monitoring across all special education students, 188 districts (47%) indicated that they were implementing progress monitoring at the building or class level, and 48 districts (12%) indicated that they were not implementing progress monitoring.

Bringing progress monitoring to this level required knowledge of how large-scale processes can be brought to the scale of system-wide change. This chapter describes the implementation of progress monitoring at the system level in schools putting a response-to-intervention (RTI) model in place. The chapter describes the importance of system-wide change, the training needed by staff delivering the training, the implementation process, and outcomes of using the evidence-based practice of progress monitoring in these schools.

HOW SYSTEM CHANGE COMES ABOUT

Educational systems are increasingly being required, through federal mandates, to implement evidence-based practices and standards. The NCLB, in 2001, and the IDEA 2004 reauthorization require schools to produce evidence of improved performance and outcomes for all students, including those at risk for failure (Roach, Salisbury, & McGregor, 2002). Historically, educational policy in most states has been exclusionary, with services being provided to those students who demonstrated the greatest potential to learn. Schools were not required to alter programs to meet the needs of individual students until well into the 20th century (Hardman & Dawson, 2008). In 1983, with the publication of *A Nation at Risk* (National Commission on Excellence in Education, as cited in Hardman & Dawson), the federal government began to take an increasingly active role in ensuring that states and local education agencies were held accountable for the progress of all students. However, the federal push for a standards-driven educational system prompted an uneven response. Although some state educators and policy makers viewed the increasing call for standards as an intrusion, others have deemed it to be the leverage necessary to improve their school systems (Hardman & Dawson).

The school change, or reform, movement in the United States has been characterized metaphorically as a wave. The first wave was related to meeting national goals, and the second wave involved school restructuring (Valencia & Wixson, 1999). Currently the nation is in the third wave, *systemic reform*. Systemic reform involves comprehensive change designed to modify schools in a coordinated and integrated manner to achieve clearly stated educational goals. The priority is to establish ambitious curricular content and achievement standards and to produce evidence that standards have been met through valid assessment practices. Together, the alignment of curriculum and assessment produces an accountability system for monitoring the efficiency and effectiveness of schools. Reform of this magnitude calls for the augmentation and/or restructuring of teacher preparation programs, instructional materials, governance, and finance (Hoy & Miskel, 2001).

Research has identified several factors that are common across school systems that have successfully undergone change and met accountability standards (e.g., Green & Etheridge, 2001; Roach et al., 2002; Schaughency & Ervin, 2006; Shroyer, Yahnke, Bennett, & Dunn, 2007). Green and Etheridge, in conjunction with the National Education Association, identified eight school districts across the United States (six in year 1 of the study, with an additional two in year 2) where systemic changes had occurred, including the establishment of learning standards and accountability measures. As indicated in Figure 1, they identified six practices common to successful systemic reform: creative tension, leadership, participation, commitment and focus, collaborative relationships, and professional development.

Creative tension was identified as the driving force behind change across the school districts and was defined as "pervasive dissatisfaction with the current situation in conjunction with stakeholders envisioning better conditions" (Green & Etheridge,

Figure 1. Six critical dimensions of systemic change.

2001). Leadership, the second factor, was described as flexible, collaborative, and empowering in districts that were successful in implementing system-wide change. The third factor, participation, advocated open dialogue among the stakeholder groups. Through shared decision making, common beliefs and support for establishing standards and accountability measures emerged. The fourth factor, commitment and focus, was described as a strong set of core values that served as the basis for all decisions. The leaders worked to maintain those values and to ensure that all participants understood and worked from those values. The fifth factor, collaborative relationships, occurred across stakeholder groups, but the relationship between the district and the teachers' union was deemed especially important at each site. The unions expanded their roles beyond the traditional contract advocacy and negotiations to include facilitation of change. Finally, professional development was restructured to include a systemic focus, a school-level focus, and a human focus, which recognized the individual needs of district employees. Professional development became oriented around outcomes and was continuous across all levels of personnel, from the individual schools through the central offices (Green & Etheridge).

The largest barriers to successful reform included the way districts manage the process and the extent of teacher participation in the change process. Among the ways to address these barriers and bridge the research-to-practice gap is forming university–district relationships and restructuring teacher preparation programs (Shroyer et al., 2007). Goodlad (as cited in Shroyer et al.) asked, "What comes first, good schools or good teaching?" and, in response, suggested that both must occur simultaneously, with all stakeholders working as equal partners.

The following case example illustrates how a partnership between a university and a school district was forged to aid in the implementation of a progress monitoring model in three elementary schools. The district had made the decision to move toward a standards-based system in response to increased calls for best practices in educating all students. The district formed a partnership with a university that was able to provide training, personnel support, and financial resources. As demonstrated in the literature, key aspects of implementation were included, such as district commitment, vision, leadership, ongoing professional development, and, most important, the fostering of collaborative relationships among all stakeholders.

IMPLEMENTATION OF PROGRESS MONITORING: AN EXAMPLE OF SYSTEM CHANGE

A university–school partnership was formed to assist the implementation of school-wide progress monitoring by the staff at three elementary schools in one district within the context of a response-to-intervention model. Our team at the university assisted the schools in the process of planning, training, and implementing all aspects of RTI, including progress monitoring, high-quality instructional practices, and tiered interventions for reading. The process described in this chapter reflects only what relates to progress monitoring. (See Shapiro, Zigmond, Wallace, & Marston, in press; also see Jimerson, Burns, & VanDerHeyden, 2007.)

Planning

Change in schools can be difficult, especially when large-scale change is planned. In the case of implementing progress monitoring and data-based decision making, teachers, staff, and administrators were required to rethink how instructional decision making would occur. Although all teachers conduct assessments of student learning through both formal and informal processes (i.e., tests and observational judgments), progress monitoring involves a systematic and empirically based procedure for collecting data that is not commonly used by most teachers. Implementing progress monitoring at the three schools required school-wide change and was difficult for all staff involved. As a result, careful planning was necessary to ensure a smooth implementation and to ensure sustainability of the procedures after the project ended. Planning prior to implementing progress monitoring was crucial to the success of the model.

When planning began, consideration was given to the participating district's level of readiness for change. As described by Green and Etheridge (2001), creative tension is a key factor in bringing about effective school change. This readiness for change was evident in the studied district. District administrators realized the importance of student progress monitoring and data-based decision making. Neither was occurring sufficiently in the district, according to an evaluation of current practices. At the time the district agreed to participate in the project, all of its elementary schools were collecting benchmark reading data as a screening measure with the *Dynamic Indicators of Basic Early Literacy Skills* (DIBELS; Good & Kaminski, 2002). However, schools were not consistently using data obtained from the screening process for decision making, with the exception of one school that had been implementing an RTI model for the past several years. In addition, although data from DIBELS were being collected for benchmarking, systematic progress monitoring using the DIBELS measures had not been implemented anywhere in the district. The district administration was eager to begin using the benchmarking data already being collected as well as to introduce new data sources (i.e., progress monitoring) to improve instruction and student performance.

Preparation is the key to successfully implementing a change model, so planning began 8 months before progress monitoring was to start being implemented in the schools. We began with an initial planning meeting with all stakeholders, including key administrators at the district level, individuals from the state technical assistance and training center, and project staff. At the meeting we presented a general overview of the project, including a proposed time line for training and implementation, and addressed questions and concerns. Once the administration fully understood all aspects of the project, we led a discussion of which schools would participate. Schools were chosen for participation based on school-level needs, level of readiness for change, and leadership within the schools. The meeting also included planning for next steps, such as how to present the model to the principals of the participating schools.

Given the importance of leadership in implementing change, the principals of selected schools had to be strongly supportive of the project and understand their role in the change process. We held a meeting with all three principals to explain the project and answer any questions or concerns. After the principals had a full understanding of the project, participants discussed how to present the project to the staff and constructed an outline of the professional development needs of the participating teachers. It was important to solicit the input of the principals and district administration in this process.

Finally, we met with the staff of all three schools to inform them of the project and answer questions and concerns. In separate meetings at each of the three schools, our project staff presented a general overview of the project and helped participants develop a time line for training and implementation. Concerns of teachers and school staff were alleviated by providing them as much information as possible related to how progress monitoring would be implemented and how that would affect their instruction. During these meetings, teachers completed a staff development survey to help identify training needs at each school. The results of the survey were used to plan professional development sessions at each of the participating schools.

Professional Development

Professional development was an ongoing process conducted throughout the course of the project. Implementation of progress monitoring was staggered across the three schools, so that one school implemented the model in year 1 of the project while the other two schools served as lag comparison schools. The two comparison schools then implemented the model in the second year. Professional development sessions that were offered to the intervention school in year 1 were replicated in year 2 with the other two participating schools.

To maximize the potential for success, we provided training and ongoing support to teachers and staff before implementing the progress monitoring. For the first intervention school, this training consisted of four 45-minute sessions held in the spring of the year prior to implementation. The first session was the overview and question-and-answer meeting. The next three sessions were developed based on needs identified through the professional development surveys completed at the first meeting. From information gathered in the surveys, it was evident that the teachers wanted additional training in the use of data to make instructional decisions. Although the district had been collecting and entering benchmark reading data into the DIBELS database for several years before the start of the project, these data were not used to aid in instructional decision making. The professional development sessions focused on providing teachers with a rationale for data-based decision making, methods for using data to guide instruction, and opportunities to practice what was learned.

Unlike the initial overview training, the professional development sessions were met with a great deal of resistance from some of the teachers. In particular, teachers were concerned about the use of DIBELS Oral Reading Fluency (DORF) as a measure to monitor student reading progress. Some teachers felt that this measure would not provide an accurate assessment of students' ability in reading. To address these concerns, research related to DORF, the link between DORF and comprehension, the use of DORF for progress monitoring, and the predictive validity of DORF in the state assessment measure were discussed (Deno, Mirkin, & Chiang, 1982; Fuchs, Fuchs, & Maxwell, 1988; Keller-Margolis, Shapiro, & Hintze, 2008; Shapiro, Keller, Lutz, Santoro, & Hintze, 2006; Shinn, Good, Knutson, Tilly, & Collins, 1992; Wayman, Wallace, Wiley, Tichá, & Espin, 2007). In addition, teachers expressed concerns about the added responsibilities associated with progress monitoring, for example, about the time it would take to conduct assessments and how instructional time would be affected. In discussing these concerns, we focused on the benefits of implementing progress monitoring and how these data can improve instruction. In addition, we showed how teachers' input into the progress monitoring process would minimize the impact on their schedules and loss of instructional time.

Beyond the four sessions held in the spring, a week-long training in the summer for key members of the school staff was conducted. These key members would serve as the data-based decision-making team for the school. Team members were chosen to represent a variety of staff areas, including, but not limited to, the principal, general and special education teachers, reading specialist, instructional support teacher, school psychologist, and librarian. Among the team members' responsibilities was serving as facilitators for progress monitoring within the school by providing training and assistance to staff. As such, it was important to provide them with the necessary training to fulfill this role prior to the start of school. During the 1-week session training was provided in all aspects of progress monitoring, including administration and scoring of probes, use of a computer-based data management system, interpretation of data, and use of data to guide instructional decisions.

The school year began with a full day of training in progress monitoring for the entire staff of the school. This training included demonstration of the administering and scoring of progress monitoring probes, with time allowed for school staff to practice, plus discussion of how to read and interpret progress monitoring graphs and use the data to inform instruction. The skills learned at this professional development meeting were then applied in the school. Subsequent professional development sessions across the school year were planned so that each session built on previous sessions. In each session, information from the previous session was reviewed, practice was conducted with the skills learned, and new information was introduced. Professional development was viewed as an ongoing process in which teachers would continually learn and improve skills related to progress monitoring.

In addition to initial professional development sessions, project staff from the university provided feedback to teachers as needed through frequent and ongoing consultation and coaching. Project staff were on site 4 to 5 days a week during the initial stages of implementation at each school and served as coaches for school personnel. Spouse (2001) described the four main roles of a coach, including supervising, teaching in vivo, providing assessment and feedback, and offering emotional support. University project staff fulfilled all these roles throughout the course of the project. Initially, project staff supervised the implementation of progress monitoring and then regularly conducted observations and provided feedback and assistance as needed. Coaching in the classroom helped increase effectiveness. Finally, project staff listened to teachers' concerns and encouraged them through challenges.

Implementation

Implementation began with a preparation period at the beginning of year 1. During this time a data team made up of school personnel and project staff was responsible for planning and executing all tasks necessary to start progress monitoring. The team met to discuss the best way to conduct progress monitoring. Several suggestions were offered, including monitoring one student each day at the end of the designated time for small group instruction, having a "SWAT team" of teachers that would monitor all students in the building, or having classroom teachers monitor their own students. It was decided that having teachers monitor their own students would be best for this school. Other preparation activities conducted by the team included assessing students for instructional level and organizing materials for teachers. Before progress monitoring began, each teacher was provided with everything he or she would need, including the booklets containing the DIBELS materials for assessment, as well as a schedule for monitoring.

Progress monitoring was conducted at all grade levels (K–5) for all students in the schools at varying levels of intensity, depending on the student's needs. All students were tested three times during the school year using DIBELS to establish benchmark data (Good & Kaminski, 2002). Students who were identified through universal screening as performing below the cut score, or benchmark, were monitored more frequently, ranging from twice a week for students found to be in the "some risk" for reading difficulties category to once a week for those in the "at risk" category.

Given that many students in the district were reading well below grade level, teachers were concerned about using only grade-level material for monitoring. They believed this measure would not accurately reflect student growth and ability. As a result, the team decided that students would be monitored at their instructional level. Instructional level was determined by conducting a survey-level assessment for all students who would be monitored (Shapiro, 2004). Data from the survey-level assessment then served as baseline for goal setting. For students whose survey-level assessment identified that they were to be monitored at grade level, benchmarks for the next assessment period were used to set goals. For those whose survey-level assessment indicated that instructional level was below grade level, goals were set using the 50th percentile of the level at which the student was being monitored. When students reached their goal, a survey-level assessment was again conducted to determine if the student's reading rate was now at or above the 25th percentile of the next higher grade level. These decision rules for when to move students to the next higher level of monitoring are described by Shapiro (2008).

Teachers began monitoring students in the 2nd week of October. This followed the preparation period and started 1 week after the initiation of small group instruction that was being implemented as part of the schools' larger RTI project. Each teacher was responsible for monitoring all students in his or her classroom that were below benchmark and assigning them to either a strategic group or intensive skill group. Students in the strategic group were those scoring below benchmark levels but above the defined cut point for being at risk. Those put into the intensive group were below the cut point for at-risk students on the benchmark assessment. Students in the strategic group were considered at some risk for reading failure and were monitored once every 2 weeks. Students in the intensive group were considered deficient in reading. These children received more intensive intervention and were monitored weekly.

A weekly 30-minute period was designated for progress monitoring at each grade level. Teachers were expected to monitor students in the strategic and intensive groups in their classes during this time. To minimize the amount of instructional time lost, each teacher was assigned a support person, such as a special education teacher, reading specialist, or librarian, to help during this 30-minute period. The teacher and support person divided responsibilities in a way that worked best for the class. For example, one teacher may have chosen to monitor identified students while the reading specialist conducted a lesson with the class. Another teacher may have assigned a short independent activity for students to work on at their seats while both the teacher and support person assessed individual students.

Progress monitoring was conducted weekly throughout the school year. Teachers conducting the progress monitoring were responsible for entering student data into a Web-based data management system each week. Grade-level teams met monthly to review student progress and make instructional decisions based on data.

Sustainability

As the project moved from the 1st to the 2nd year of implementation, the focus shifted from training and professional development to the sustainability of progress monitoring procedures after the project ended. From the planning stages and throughout the initial implementation process, we had worked closely with the district to plan for the sustainability of procedures after the project ended. The support provided by project staff was designed to foster school staff independence in planning and organizing their school's progress monitoring and in evaluating the results. Support for the staff was *scaffolded*, meaning that the level of support provided was commensurate with that needed. As the staff's proficiency increased, support was systematically withdrawn and new responsibilities were added. For example, during the 1st year of implementation, most of the work necessary to prepare for progress monitoring was done by project staff. All materials were gathered and organized, schedules were developed, and training was conducted by project staff. This was done to minimize the workload and the amount of change experienced by teachers at any given time. As teachers became more skilled in progress monitoring, additional responsibilities were transferred from project to school staff.

Planning for the 2nd year of implementation began in the spring of year 1 and included discussion of the transfer of responsibilities. A meeting was held at each school to discuss all activities necessary to maintain progress monitoring, and how and when transfer of those responsibilities would take place. All participants agreed that the school staff members were ready to take on the majority of the responsibilities at the start of the new school year. For a few tasks, the school staff felt that some additional training and support were necessary to ensure a successful transition. A time line for training and transfer was developed for these tasks and executed by the middle of the 2nd year. The school was operating almost independently by winter of the second year. The project staff remained in a consultative role throughout the 2nd year.

Throughout the project's implementation, it was important for the university staff providing support to pay particular attention to the variables identified by the literature as maximizing the project's potential for success. The district was ripe for change, having already taken steps toward change by implementing benchmark testing. In addition, a project viewed as a precursor to RTI, involving a school-wide change model, had already been implemented at the district's lowest performing school with great success. This willingness to alter existing practices was important to initiating the change process as well as to maintaining it after the project ended. Another important variable for success, leadership, was evident at all levels, in the district, school, and grades. Leaders had been identified and worked collaboratively to ensure success. The commitment of the school staff also helped make the implementation successful.

Despite initial skepticism on the part of many, once teachers began to see positive results for their students, most were committed to the process. Throughout the planning, implementation, and maintenance phases, input from the teachers and staff was vital to ensure a sense of ownership of the project and commitment to success. Throughout the course of the project, fostering a sense of collaboration and open communication across the many stakeholders was critical. All factors working together—a willingness to embrace change, leadership, collaboration, and communication—led to the successful implementation of progress monitoring procedures at all three schools.

How Success Was Judged

Overall outcomes of progress monitoring are reflected by several indexes, which collectively examine the impact of the efforts to scale up the use of progress monitoring. During the 2007–2008 school year, across three K–5 schools, progress monitoring was conducted on 630 out of the total of 1,290 students combined across the three schools (some students were monitored on multiple measures) and involved 46 staff members across the three schools. Progress monitoring was used to drive instructional decisions for each of these students. Evidence of that relationship was found by examining the number of students who were at or near their target level of performance that had been set during the delivery of the supplemental intervention provided as part of the RTI model. Across the 569 students with sufficient data for determining target outcomes, 229, or about 40%, achieved outcomes by the end of the school year that were near or above the students' target levels, demonstrating that in a large percentage of cases progress monitoring reflected gains in reading.

Another measure of success in the use of progress monitoring is changes in the number of decisions related to intervention—changes in the type of intervention, in goals, or in the level of progress monitoring—by student across years of implementation (see Figure 2). The expectation is that with each subsequent year of implementation, staff would be using the data more often to make instructional changes as they received advanced training and acquired experience. The data showed that teams made more decisions related to instructional change during the 2nd year.

LESSONS LEARNED AND RECOMMENDATIONS

As described by Fixsen, Naoom, Blase, Friedman, and Wallace (2005) implementation of progress monitoring involves coordinated change at four levels: system, organization, program, and practice. Research has shown that for implementation of large-scale systemic change to be effective, several factors must first be in place. First, the practitioners who carry out the change must be carefully selected and undergo comprehensive training, coaching, and performance feedback. Second, the organization (e.g., a school or agency) must provide the means for training, coaching, and giving feedback. Third, practitioners

Figure 2. Average number of intervention-related changes per student across 2 years of RTI implementation.

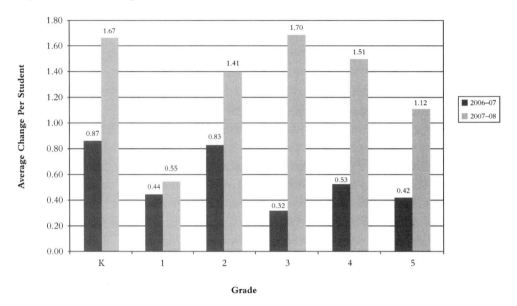

and consumers must be fully involved in the process of developing and implementing change. Fourth, implementation and sustainability of programs must be supported through policies, regulations, and funding at the state and federal levels.

As in previous research, these variables played an important role in the success of the implementation process. Using the context of the factors listed above, we could begin to evaluate the effectiveness of the district's implementation and areas for improvement. Throughout the implementation process, our project team learned valuable lessons related to effective implementation of system-wide change in schools.

For any change effort to be successful, the individuals who carry out interventions must be carefully selected and possess the qualities associated with effective implementation, such as knowledge of the intervention and experience (Fixsen et al., 2005). The district administration in which we worked was familiar with implementing progress monitoring and RTI and understood the value of systematic implementation. Although the individual teachers in the three schools did not have extensive knowledge about the specific interventions that would be introduced, they were well trained and knowledgeable about effective teaching practices. This level of expertise laid the foundation for professional development in the area of progress monitoring.

Professional development was an integral component of the implementation of progress monitoring in this district. Training for teachers was an ongoing process. As research has shown, the "train and hope" model of implementation is not effective for promoting lasting change (Stokes & Bear, 1977). Instead, training for school staff consisted of professional development sessions that contained those elements shown in the research to be necessary for success. These include presenting information, providing demonstration of the skills being taught, and allowing practice during the session (Joyce & Showers, 2002). Follow-up to professional development was also critical. During the weeks immediately after training, our staff worked individually with teachers within their classroom environment to model and assist with the teachers' implementation of progress monitoring. Professional development sessions occurred regularly and addressed topics that school staff identified as necessary for their success. The result was teachers who were much more responsive, which proved to be very important to the success of the professional development sessions.

Before beginning the implementation process, individuals must be well trained in all procedures and feel prepared, even if ensuring that sense of preparedness delays the start of an intervention. Providing adequate time for training and preparation can greatly improve morale and potentially improve sustainability. This was evident when examining the difference between 1st- and 2nd-year schools with respect to the teachers' sense of preparedness and willingness to begin implementation. Just before the start of the school year, the teachers at the year 1 school received training in progress monitoring and in providing the necessary interventions. Teachers were trained and their ability to conduct progress monitoring was assessed prior to the start of implementation. Despite having an assessment of the fidelity of their practice interventions, the teachers reported feeling rushed and requested that they have additional time before implementation began. In contrast, training for the 2nd-year schools began the school year before implementation was to begin. This delay was in response to the feedback provided by the year 1 teachers, and it gave year 2 teachers a few additional months to become familiar with procedures and to prepare for the change. Despite the fact that the training was identical and that levels of fidelity were high across all schools, those that had additional time reported feeling more prepared.

In addition to the initial professional development, the university staff provided ongoing coaching throughout the implementation process. Two valuable lessons related to coaching were learned. First, coaching time varies widely in the literature, so there is no prescribed amount of time to spend in this role (Fixsen et al., 2005). In this project, devoting a large amount of time initially was beneficial in the long run. Our university staff was on site at the schools 20 to 30 hours a week during the first few months of implementation. Although this was time-consuming, it gave our project team the opportunity to observe progress monitoring firsthand and to work with teachers to correct any problems. In addition, a continued presence showed teachers that both the university staff and teachers were accountable for implementation and that teachers had the support they needed to be successful. The value of devoting this time initially became more apparent as the year progressed, and the university staff presence faded significantly by midyear. Thus, the initial investment of time prepared school staff to become independent more quickly, saving time and effort over the course of the project. The use of coaching should be taken into consideration when planning for implementation, as it may potentially save time, resources, and manpower that are scarce in many districts.

The second lesson related to coaching was that *all aspects* of the role of coach are necessary for success. Specifically, we did not realize the vital role that providing emotional support would play until we experienced it. A good portion of our project team's time was spent talking with teachers, listening to concerns, and providing encouragement. Although these activities were not necessarily directly related to implementation, they allowed us to build trust and a sense of reciprocity with school staff that supported effective implementation.

Another factor in effective implementation is that the organization, in this case the school district, must provide a means for training, feedback, and coaching to occur (Fixsen et al., 2005). Although the coaching does not necessarily need to be from a source outside the school, the presence of coaches throughout the implementation process is critical. The organization's readiness for change and the climate of the organization as a whole are also crucial. It was fortunate that the district in this project was ripe for change. As such, the district-level administration was fully supportive of all implementation activities. The administration provided professional development time, hired substitutes so that teachers could attend trainings, and even hired a district employee to serve as a liaison between the district and the university project staff. This individual was able to help with training, coaching, and coordination of project activities. Without this level of support from the district, this project likely would not have achieved the level of success that it did. When attempting to implement change, the amount of support that can and will be provided should be carefully considered and planned for accordingly.

When implementing change, the initiating organization must fully involve all the school staff in the process (Fixsen et al., 2005). Likewise, as noted by Kurns and Tilly (2008) in the National Association of State Directors of Special Education's blueprints for RTI implementation, three key elements of successful change involve consensus building, infrastructure building, and implementation. The project addressed these factors in several ways. First, the value of planning was a part of the implementation process, and planning for implementation began several months before the start of the project. This allowed the researchers, administrators, and teachers involved to prepare for the changes ahead. By incorporating a systematic plan for building capacity within the school system and for transferring responsibilities from the project staff to all of the school staff, we were able to introduce changes to the existing instructional practices that had positive effects on student performance. This planning provided the means for all stakeholders to have input in the implementation process, to voice concerns, and to prepare for the changes ahead.

Beyond the initial planning, we also continually solicited the thoughts, opinions, and ideas of all stakeholders, building consensus for all components of implementation. Specifically, we frequently met with teachers as a group as well as individually to get their input. We attempted to address concerns that arose, if at all possible. For those concerns that could not be addressed (e.g., not enough instructional time in the day), we worked with teachers to come up with solutions that could work within the limitations of the situation. In addition, we conducted formal teacher focus groups once a year to solicit input about specific questions related to implementation. To gather information from other stakeholders, we also formed a Parent Advisory Board. This group met periodically throughout the course of the project to gather information from parents about the types and forms of information they believed would be valuable. These meetings were extremely helpful in providing information that we would not otherwise have collected.

Finally, for change to be truly successful, it must be supported at all levels—including at the level of the organization as well as state and national levels (Fixsen et al., 2005). The ultimate goal of any change effort is for that change to be adopted into common practice and to have lasting impact. For this to occur, planning for sustainability must occur at all levels throughout the process. The systematic plan for implementation that was developed for the project included all aspects of the development and introduction of the model, including design, training, implementation, and sustainability. Initially, when planning for the introduction of the model in the schools, we always considered how this model could be maintained by school personnel independent of additional supports. For example, progress monitoring was implemented using only existing staff and resources. In addition, teachers were given much say in how and when progress monitoring would be conducted to ensure that it worked for teachers and therefore would continue in the future. As a result, we recommend that before education professionals initiate any school change model, they should carefully consider the variables that may affect sustainability in their states and districts and how those may be addressed.

Throughout the implementation of this project, our project team took several steps to ensure that school personnel could continue the procedures after the project ended. Specifically, constant feedback from staff as well as direct observations provided us with knowledge related to those skills that teachers had acquired and those that needed additional training and support. By reducing support when it was no longer needed, we were able to gradually fade the presence of our university staff in the schools without loss of integrity of the model. This gradual fading of support was very effective in promoting independence. Had the university staff maintained a high level of involvement until the end of the project, school personnel would not have had the opportunity to manage the model on their own.

Ultimately, all individuals involved in the process of school change will need to understand that the process is slow and usually not smooth along the way. Change is difficult, whether it is welcomed or not. This difficulty is exacerbated when individuals need to change not only their actions but also their thoughts and attitudes. The introduction of progress monitoring into the three schools we worked with not only changed how teachers evaluated student progress, it also made many teachers reconsider how they thought about their students and student failure. This type of change can be extremely difficult and slow. For all involved, flexibility and a willingness to adapt and change is necessary for success.

AUTHOR NOTE

Preparation of this chapter was partially supported by Grant # H326M050001, Project MP3: Monitoring Progress in Pennsylvania Pupils from the U.S. Department of Education to the first author. The material presented is solely the viewpoint of the authors and does not represent the U.S. Department of Education. Address all correspondence and feedback on this article to Dr. Edward S. Shapiro, Center for Promoting Research to Practice, L-111 Iacocca Hall, Lehigh University, Bethlehem, PA, 18015, ed.shapiro@lehigh.edu.

REFERENCES

Deno, S. L. (2003). Developments in curriculum-based measurement. *Journal of Special Education, 37,* 184–192.

Deno, S. L., Fuchs, L. S., Marston, D., & Shin, J. (2001). Using curriculum-based measurement to establish growth standards for students with learning disabilities. *School Psychology Review, 30,* 507–524.

Deno, S. L., Mirkin, P. K., & Chiang, B. (1982). Identifying valid measures of reading. *Exceptional Children, 5,* 36–45.

Fixsen, D. L., Naoom, S. F., Blase, K. A., Friedman, R. M., & Wallace, F. (2005). *Implementation research: A synthesis of the literature* (FMHI Publication #231). Tampa, FL: University of South Florida, Louis de la Parte Florida Mental Health Institute, National Implementation Research Network.

Foegen, A., Jiban, C., & Deno, S. (2007). Progress monitoring in mathematics: A review of the literature. *Journal of Special Education, 41*(2), 121–139.

Fuchs, L. S. (2002). Best practices in defining student goals and outcomes. In A. Thomas & J. Grimes (Eds.), *Best practices in school psychology IV* (pp. 553–563). Bethesda, MD: National Association of School Psychologists.

Fuchs, L. S., Fuchs, D., & Maxwell, L. (1988). The validity of informal reading comprehension measures. *Remedial and Special Education, 9,* 20–28.

Good, R. H., III, & Kaminski, R. A. (2002). *Dynamic indicators of basic early literacy skills* (6th ed.). Eugene, OR: Institute for the Development of Educational Achievement.

Green, R. L., & Etheridge, C. P. (2001). Collaborating to establish standards and accountability: Lessons learned about systemic change. *Education, 121,* 821–829.

Hardman, M. L., & Dawson, S. (2008). The impact of federal public policy on curriculum and instruction for students with disabilities in the general classroom. *Preventing School Failure, 52,* 5–11.

Hoagwood, K., Burns, B. J., Kiser, L., Ringeisen, H., & Schoenwald, S. K. (2001). Evidence-based practice in child and adolescent mental health services. *Psychiatric Services, 52,* 1179–1189.

Hoy, W. K., & Miskel, C. G. (2001). *Educational administration: Theory, research, and practice.* New York: McGraw-Hill.

Individuals with Disabilities Education Improvement Act of 2004, 20 U.S.C. § 1400 *et seq.* (2004) (reauthorization of the Individuals with Disabilities Education Act of 1990).

Jimerson, S. R., Burns, M. K., & VanDerHeyden, A. M. (Eds.). (2007). *Handbook of response to intervention: The science and practice of assessment and intervention.* New York: Springer.

Joyce, B., & Showers, B. (2002). *Student achievement through staff development* (3rd ed.). Alexandria, VA: Association for Supervision and Curriculum Development.

Keller-Margolis, M. A., Shapiro, E. S., & Hintze, J. M. (2008). Long-term diagnostic accuracy of curriculum-based measures in reading and mathematics. *School Psychology Review, 37,* 374–390.

Kratochwill, T. R. (2005). Theories of change and adoption of innovations: The evolving evidence-based intervention and practice movement in school psychology. *Psychology in the Schools, 42,* 475–494.

Kratochwill, T. R., & Shernoff, E. S. (2004). Evidence-based practice: Promoting evidence-based interventions in school psychology. *School Psychology Review, 33,* 34–48.

Kratochwill, T. E., & Stoiber, K. C. (2002). Evidence-based interventions in school psychology: Conceptual foundations of the procedural and coding manual of Division 16 and the Society for the Study of School Psychology task force. *School Psychology Quarterly, 17,* 341–389.

Kurns, S., & Tilly, D. (2008). *Response to intervention blueprints: School building level edition.* Alexandria, VA: National Association of State Directors of Special Education.

McMaster, K., & Espin, C. (2007). Technical features of curriculum-based measurement in writing. *Journal of Special Education, 41,* 6–84.

National Center on Student Progress Monitoring. http://www.studentprogress.org

No Child Left Behind Act of 2001, 20 U.S.C. 70 § 6301 *et seq.* (2002).

Power, T. J. (2002). Preparing school psychologists as interventionists and preventionists. In M. R. Shinn, H. M. Walker, & G. Stoner (Eds.), *Interventions for academic and behavior problems II: Prevalence and remedial approaches* (pp. 1047–1065). Bethesda, MD: National Association of School Psychologists.

Roach, V., Salisbury, C., & McGregor, G. (2002). Applications of a policy framework to evaluate and promote large-scale change. *Exceptional Children, 68,* 451–464.

Schaughency, E., & Ervin, R. (2006). Building capacity to implement and sustain effective practices to better serve children. *School Psychology Review, 35,* 155–166.

Shapiro, E. S. (2004). *Academic skills problems: Direct assessment and intervention* (3rd ed.). New York: Guilford Press.

Shapiro, E. S. (2008). Best practices in setting progress monitoring goals for academic skill improvement. In A. Thomas & J. Grimes (Eds.), *Best practices in school psychology V* (pp.141–158). Bethesda, MD: National Association of School Psychologists.

Shapiro, E. S. (2009). Statewide scaling up of progress monitoring practices. In S. Rosenfield & V. Berninger (Eds.), *Implementing evidence-based academic interventions in school settings* (pp. 321–349). New York: Oxford University Press.

Shapiro, E. S., Edwards, L., & Zigmond, N. (2005). Progress monitoring of mathematics among students with learning disabilities. *Assessment for Effective Intervention, 30*, 15–32.

Shapiro, E. S., Keller, M., Lutz, J. G., Santoro, L. E., & Hintze, J. M. (2006). Curriculum-based measures and performance on state assessment and standardized tests: Reading and math performance in Pennsylvania. *Journal of Psychoeducational Assessment, 24*, 19–35.

Shapiro, E. S., Zigmond, N., Wallace, T., & Marston, D. (in press). *Models of response-to-intervention implementation: Tools, outcomes, and implications.* New York: Guilford Press.

Shinn, M. R., Good, R. H., Knutson, N., Tilly, W. D., & Collins, V. L. (1992). Curriculum-based measurement of oral reading fluency: A confirmatory analysis of its relation to reading. *School Psychology Review, 21*, 459–479.

Shroyer, G., Yahnke, S., Bennett, A., & Dunn, C. (2007). Simultaneous renewal through professional development school partnerships. *Journal of Educational Research, 100*, 211–223.

Spouse, J. (2001). Bridging theory and practice in the supervisory relationship: A sociocultural perspective. *Journal of Advanced Nursing, 33*(4), 512–522.

Stokes, T. F., & Baer, D. M. (1977). An implicit technology of generalization. *Journal of Applied Behavior Analysis, 10*, 349–367.

Valencia, S. W., & Wixson, K. K. (1999). *Policy oriented research on literacy standards and assessment* (CIERA Report No. 3-004). Ann Arbor, MI: University of Michigan, Center for the Improvement of Early Reading Achievement.

Wayman, M. M., Wallace, T., Wiley, H. I., Tichá, R., & Espin, C. A. (2007). Literature synthesis on curriculum-based measurement in reading. *Journal of Special Education, 41*, 85–120.

CHAPTER 9

Prevention and Early Interventions to Promote Healthy Children in Schools

Herbert H. Severson
Oregon Research Institute, Eugene

INTRODUCTION

Substance use by adolescents is a major public health problem in the United States. Substance use is associated with problematic consequences and creates difficulties, not only for individual children, but also for their families and communities. Substance use has been related to negative health outcomes and implicated in school-related problems of learning and behavior. Increased efforts to curb the use of tobacco, alcohol, and other drugs among teens have resulted in significant reductions in substance use over the past decade; however, both social and illicit drug use is still prevalent. The proportion of young people reporting use of any illicit drug in the last 12 months is 21%, 36%, and 48% in Grades 8, 10, and 12, respectively (Johnston, O'Malley, Bachman, & Schulenberg, 2007). Rates of tobacco and alcohol use among youth are also exceedingly high. According to the most recently published results of the Youth Risk Behavior Survey, nationwide, 70.4% of students have tried cigarette smoking (including those who took only one or two puffs), and 23% of high school students had smoked cigarettes during the past 30 days (Eaton et al., 2006).

Alcohol is the most common drug used by middle and high school students, with more than 50% reporting that they had drunk alcohol during the past 30 days (Centers for Disease Control and Prevention [CDC], 2000). Additionally, more than half of 12th graders and 20% of 8th graders in 2006 reported having been drunk at least once in their life. This shows clearly that teenagers' drug involvement is not merely a passing experimental phase; for many, drug use has become part of a daily lifestyle. These figures, already alarming, probably do not accurately reflect the scope of the problem, since they fail to assess alcohol, tobacco, and drug use among teenagers not attending school, a population in which these behaviors are significantly higher. High school dropouts are more likely to use substances than students who stay in school, and substance use has been strongly related to adolescents' poor mental health, engagement in risky social behaviors, and academic failure (Mensch & Kandel, 1988; Tolan, Szapocznik, & Sambrano, 2007).

Though the public interest tends to focus on curtailing the use of illicit drugs such as marijuana, cocaine, and methamphetamines, common popular drugs such as cigarettes and alcohol may pose a greater threat to public health. Use of tobacco products appears to be a very common habit, as evidenced by high use rates through the high school years. The percentage of students starting to use tobacco also appears to increase as teenagers enter high school. Female students in Grades 10, 11, and 12 were significantly more likely than female students in ninth grade to have tried cigarette smoking (75%, 72%, and 76%, respectively, compared with 60%). Male students in 12th grade were significantly more likely than male students in 9th and 11th grades (80%, compared with 63% and 68%, respectively) to report this behavior (CDC, 2000). Alcohol use is also very prevalent among youth nationwide, with 74% of students reporting that they had consumed more than one alcoholic drink (one beer, glass of wine, shot of liquor, or its equivalent) during their lifetime, and 43% saying they had consumed more than one drink of alcohol on more than one of the 30 days preceding the 2005 Youth Risk Behavior Survey (Eaton et al., 2006). Additionally, 26% of students had consumed more than five drinks of alcohol on more than one occasion during the 30 days preceding the survey, and this is viewed as an index of drinking to intoxication.

Given the use patterns of the past decade, reported above, and the fact that smoking has been linked to more deaths than all other lifestyle factors, including the use of "hard" drugs (e.g., opioids such as heroin, cocaine, and methamphetamines, which are all physically addictive, are severely psychologically addictive, and pose serious health and social risk), any efforts to prevent drug use must target tobacco use as well as use of illicit substances (Lynch & Bonnie, 1994). Prevention efforts should focus on the most prevalent drugs used by teens—tobacco (cigarettes and chew), alcohol, and marijuana—for two reasons. First, students and parents see the social substances as the most prevalent, and second, these substances are most often the drugs of initiation for young people.

Although many risk factors are beyond the scope of a school-based intervention, such as substance use by parents and substance accessibility, evidence increasingly points to the efficacy of early interventions to reduce tobacco, alcohol, and drug use and abuse. Teachers, school personnel, and communities at large have an obligation to establish prevention and treatment programs for children and adolescents in order to avoid negative health outcomes associated with substance use.

This chapter provides a review of primary and secondary prevention for addressing substance use in U.S. schools. The chapter focuses on early interventions and universally applied interventions that are largely school based. These approaches can be viewed as a public health model because they involve widely adopted and proactively implemented interventions to prevent youth from using and abusing controlled substances. The model assumes that the application of preventive interventions in schools can ameliorate many of the more serious problems that co-occur and are related to substance use. The prevention and early intervention model also is potentially more cost-effective, because intervention services for substance-using adolescents can be expensive and involve access to limited services from community resources. Tobacco use prevention is the primary example for illustrating this overall approach, although other forms of substance abuse would also be appropriate targets of this approach.

THE IMPORTANCE OF PREVENTION AND EARLY INTERVENTION

Substance use is especially problematic when it begins in childhood or early adolescence (Loeber, Stouthhamer-Loeber, & White, 1999). It can interfere with the development of cognitive, emotional, and social competencies in children and adolescents and can compromise later functioning as an adult in domains such as marriage, parenting, and employment. The earlier the use of substances occurs in a child's development, the more likely it is to progress to abuse (Grant, Stinson, & Harford, 2001). There is also increasing evidence that the early use of drugs may affect the brain's development, raising concerns about the initiation and use of drugs and alcohol at earlier ages (Brown, Tapert, Granholm, & Delis, 2000; Ehrenreich et al., 1999).

Early Initiation of Substance Use

It is possible to trace the leading causes of mortality and morbidity among youth to a relatively small number of preventable health-risk behaviors that begin during adolescence and may extend into adulthood (Kolbe, Kann, & Collins, 1993). Surveys of drug use among youth confirm not only that drugs are being used but also that the age of initial use for most drugs is at the elementary school level. Studies of cigarette, chewing tobacco, and marijuana use reported experimentation as early as the fourth and fifth grades. This early experience with drug use is positively related to subsequent regular use and abuse (Andrews, Tildesley, Hops, Duncan, & Severson, 2003; Severson, 1984). A number of researchers have shown repeatedly that initiation of alcohol and drug use at an early age is one of the strongest predictors of later substance abuse (Grant & Dawson, 1997; Robins & Przybeck, 1985; Zucker, 2003). Others have found that early drug use leads to a wide range of antisocial behaviors and subsequent school failure (Biglan, Wang, & Walberg, 2003; Donovan & Jessor, 1978). Substance use by adolescents often occurs in the context of other behaviors, such as delinquency, school failure, high-risk sexual behavior, and low self-esteem (Biglan et al., 1990; Bry, McKeon, & Padina, 1982; Hundleby, Carpenter, Ross, & Mercer, 1982). Indeed, the number of problems a youth experiences, such as poor relationships with parents or peers, psychopathology, and low grade point average, increases the risk of concurrent and later drug use (Newcomb, Maddahian, & Bentler, 1986).

Because risk behaviors vary by age, the interventions to address them must be sensitive to developmental changes, age appropriate, and appropriately timed to have maximum effect (Brener & Collins, 1998). Jessor and Jessor (1977) first established that youth who use tobacco, alcohol, and other drugs at an early age are also at risk for many other risk outcomes, such as social aggression, risky sexual behavior, and school failure. This finding has subsequently been confirmed by other researchers, who elaborated the developmental profile that youth experimenting with tobacco, alcohol, and other drugs (mainly marijuana) are much more likely to engage in multiple risk behaviors and be at much higher risk for serious adjustment problems. Youth who engage in two or more of these behaviors have been labeled as multiproblem youth, and research has documented the high-risk nature of these youth (Biglan et al., 2004). Because youth who engage in substance use at an early age are more likely to abuse other drugs, mainly marijuana, and to engage in other high-risk behaviors, school personnel must focus on early preventive interventions designed to have the broadest impact on young people. Such a focus can prevent both substance use and the development of other risk behaviors.

Although substance abuse has only recently achieved widespread public attention, illicit drug use has been of major concern to schools, communities, and health professionals for decades. Not only do the rates of substance use remain high, but the average age of initiation for most substances also has decreased (CDC, 2000). Young people typically experiment with a wide range of behaviors and lifestyles as they seek to define a personal identity and declare independence from their parents. Several factors contribute to an adolescent's choice to begin experimenting with drugs, including social pressures from peers and family, positive depictions of substance use (especially tobacco) in the popular media, perceptions of use as normative behavior, antisocial behavior patterns, and personality factors such as low self-esteem, low confidence, or low self-efficacy.

Two early measures of a student's being at risk for subsequent use of substances are (a) the student's interpretation of normative beliefs and subjective (that is, perceived) norms about substance use by others and (b) the student's intentions to use the substance. Perceived norms are the extent to which students believe that the use of alcohol and tobacco and other drugs are normative among their peers. Researchers have demonstrated, for example, that perceived norms are a strong predictor throughout development and that increases in measures of perceived norms during the elementary grades (fourth through seventh grades, but as early as the second grade) predicted increases in intentions to smoke and intentions to use both alcohol and tobacco as a teen (Andrews, Hampson, Barckley, Gerrard, & Gibbons, 2008). Once substance use begins, the physiological addictive process supports continued use despite the harmful effects. Adolescence is a time of great developmental change. Physical and psychological addiction can occur more quickly than many youth think it will, and cessation is often difficult. The results of tobacco cessation studies often show lower success rates among youth than among adults, even when the actual level of tobacco use is lower for youth, which presumably reflects a lower level of nicotine addiction in this population of users (Sussman, Sun, & Dent, 2006).

The Relationships Between Substance Use and Depression

Epidemiological studies have consistently found that substance abuse and depression co-occur among adolescents at a significantly higher rate than would be expected by chance. For example, adolescents with a history of substance abuse or dependence have approximately a fourfold increase in the rate of depression (Lewinsohn, Hops, Roberts, Seeley, & Andrews, 1993). Evidence suggests that the association between substance abuse and depression may be even stronger in adolescents than adults (Clark, Kirisci, & Tarter, 1998; Rohde, Lewinsohn, & Seeley, 1991). Substance abuse and dependence has been found to precede depression in approximately two thirds of adolescents with both conditions (Rohde et al., 1991). In addition, prospective research has consistently shown that substance abuse predicts future depression (e.g., Hallfors, Waller, Bauer, Ford, & Halpern, 2006; Rao, Daley, & Hammen, 2000; Swendsen & Merikangas, 2000). Brown, Lewinsohn, Seeley, and Wagner (1996) found that smokers were twice as likely to develop an episode of major depressive disorder (MDD) and seven times more likely to develop an episode of drug abuse and dependence in the ensuing 12 months as were nonsmokers. Hence, preventing substance abuse, including smoking, in adolescents may also reduce the incidence of both depression and other substance use problems (Kessler & Price, 1993).

Youth with substance use and abuse problems have high rates of comorbidity with conduct disorders and depression. For example, Clark et al. (1997) reported that, in a sample of alcohol-dependent adolescents seeking treatment, 89% also had conduct disorder, MDD, or both. Miller-Johnson and colleagues also reported that both depression and conduct disorders are linked to an increased risk for substance use and that co-occurrence of the two disorders elevates this overall risk (Miller-Johnson, Lochman, Cole, Terry, & Hyman, 1998). Compared with other groups, the comorbid group reported the most frequent use of tobacco at Grade 6, alcohol at Grade 8, and marijuana at Grades 6 and 8. Adolescents with high levels of conduct disorder in early adolescence were at increased risk for high rates of tobacco, alcohol, and marijuana use over time, with this effect more pronounced for males than for females. Both studies suggest that preventive efforts designed to increase resistance to substance use would be useful for youngsters exhibiting early conduct disorders.

School personnel have the responsibility, as well as the opportunity, to be the first line of defense against negative health outcomes and to intervene early to interrupt the cycle of initiation and addiction. For school-based prevention to be effective, however, the adopted intervention programs need to begin before the behavior has escalated into a regular use pattern. For example, in the case of smoking, over 90% of adult smokers reported that they were regular users before leaving high school; 62% reported that they had at least tried cigarettes by the ninth grade. Research shows that, among seventh graders, 10% reported having used cigarettes, 14% of the boys reported having used chewing tobacco, and 23% of boys and girls reported having used alcohol in the previous week (Forrester, Biglan, Severson, & Smolkowski, 2007). More serious than use of any alcohol in the past week is the fact that 11% of seventh graders reported that they had consumed five or more drinks on a single occasion in the previous week, which is a standard measure used by researchers to define alcohol-induced impairment.

The Relationships Between Smoking and Other Problem Behaviors

A large amount of research finds smoking behavior correlated with engagement in other problem behaviors, including all forms of substance use, antisocial behavior, high-risk sexual behavior, and academic failure (Arnett, 1992; Biglan et al., 2004; Biglan & Smolkowski, 1999; Jessor, 1991). However, most of these studies correlate rates of engagement among diverse risk behaviors, which makes it difficult to gauge the size of subgroups engaging in one, two, three, or more of them. Moreover, the correlational approach does not address the degree to which youth engage in the behaviors at problematic levels. For smoking, studies' failure to address that degree of engagement may not be a serious limitation, because any level of regular smoking puts a person at greater risk for harm or disease. However, in the case of alcohol use, which is normative among adolescents, it may be important to distinguish between levels of use (such as binge drinking) that are predictive of concurrent health risks or later alcoholism and levels that are unlikely to lead to such outcomes (Holder, 1998). A strong relationship is seen between the self-reported behavior of binge drinking and illicit drug use (Johnston, O'Malley, & Bachman, 2001).

In other correlational studies, the percentage of destructive outcomes such as suicide, homicide, depression, and health-related problems was much higher among adolescents who reported drinking alcohol than among those who did not (Hanna, Hsiao-ye, & Dufoour, 2000). Willard and Schoenborn (1995) present data on the co-occurrence of cigarette smoking and other risk behaviors from a large and representative sample of individuals ages 12–21. Respondents reported the proportion of current smokers (one or more cigarettes in the last month) who engaged in each of a range of problem behaviors. Table 1 presents the behaviors that significantly co-occurred with smoking.

Table 1. The Co-Occurrence of Smoking and Other Problem Behaviors

Problem Behavior	Percent Currently Smoking (SE)	Percent Never Smoked (SE)
Drank alcohol in past month	74.4 (1.11)	23.0 (1.02)
Drank five or more drinks in a row	50.3 (1.22)	9.5 (0.69)
Used marijuana in past month	26.5 (1.02)	1.5 (.025)
Used smokeless tobacco in past month (boys only)	28.1 (1.76)	4.1 (0.52)
Carried a weapon	25.6 (1.12)	9.5 (0.59)
Had a physical fight in past year	54.7 (1.09)	29.0 (0.86)
Ever had sexual intercourse	80.0 (0.99)	41.4 (1.40)

Note. From Health-Risk Behaviors Among Persons Aged 12–21 Years — United States, 1992, by the Centers for Disease Control and Prevention, 1994b, *MMWR 43*(13), 231–235.

The comorbidity of cigarette smoking and MDD among adolescents has received considerable attention in recent literature. Brown et al. (1996) reported that adolescent smokers were more than twice as likely to exhibit a major depressive disorder (odds ratio = 2.28). The finding that smoking is a risk for MDD in adolescents is consistent with adult findings by Breslau, Kilbey, and Andreski (1991), who found that nicotine dependence predicted episodes of MDD during their 14-month follow-up.

These studies possibly show that the onset of smoking makes engagement in other problem behaviors more likely, providing another justification for efforts to prevent adolescent smoking. However, the evidence on this point is equivocal. Perhaps smoking changes adolescents in ways that make them more susceptible to the reinforcing properties of other substances. It also could be that, for the young smoker, smoking is associated with a rule violation so that initiation of smoking desensitizes him or her to other forms of rule violation. In any case, even if preventing smoking does not help prevent other problem behaviors, there is ample justification for major efforts to prevent tobacco use as a health promotion strategy. The potential for such a positive "spread effect" phenomenon resulting from smoking prevention efforts is a question that urgently needs investigating.

PEER AND PARENTAL INFLUENCES ON YOUTH TOBACCO USE

The addictive nature of cigarettes and smokeless tobacco is now well established. The 1988 surgeon general's report documented the addictive quality of tobacco and identified nicotine as the drug in tobacco that leads to addiction (U.S. Department of Health and Human Services [USDHHS], 1988). However, nicotine addiction does not explain a person's choice to begin experimenting with tobacco; other factors motivate and support that choice. Though many factors may influence the onset of tobacco use in youth, two variables have emerged as most clearly influential: peer influences and parental influences.

Peer Influences on Tobacco Use

Peers are the single greatest influence on young people to begin using tobacco. The surgeon general's report described substantial evidence of peer influence on adolescent tobacco use (USDHHS, 1994). For most adolescents, tobacco use initiation is influenced by peers who use tobacco, and the majority of cigarette experimentation occurs in the presence of other adolescents who are smoking (Bauman, Foshee, & Haley, 1991; Friedman, Lichtenstein, & Biglan, 1985). Peer influence can be conceptualized as both passive and active (Read, Wood, & Capone, 2005). Passive influence indicates direct modeling peers' behavior, including the normative influence of the group; active influence involves receiving peers' direct offers or pressure to use tobacco or other drugs. Direct or active influence among peers can relate both to smoking and to other substance use. According to Wood, Read, Mitchell, and Brand

(2004), the frequency of direct offers, for example, has been related to more frequent and episodic drinking among college students, and the frequency of marijuana offers from peers predicts marijuana use in adolescents (Ellickson, Tucker, Klein, & Saner, 2004).

Longitudinal studies also point to the crucial influence of peer smoking as a passive peer influence. In one study, 60% of 11- to 17-year-olds reported that they had first smoked with close friends (Hahn et al., 1990). In a 1992 review of the recent prospective research in the field, Conrad, Flay, and Hill (1992) found that friends' smoking predicted some phase of adolescent smoking in 88% of the longitudinal studies reviewed.

Parental Influences on Tobacco Use

Researchers have extensively studied the influence of parents on an adolescent's tobacco use initiation, but most studies have focused on parental modeling of smoking behavior as a predictor of youth smoking. Though evidence shows that parents who smoke are more likely to have children who take up the habit, this relationship often is modest and sometimes has not emerged (Ary & Biglan, 1988; USDHHS, 1994). Bauman, Foshee, Linzer, and Koch's (1990) study showed that youth smoking is more strongly related to whether a parent has ever smoked than to a parent's current smoking status, suggesting that parental influences on youth smoking may be attributable to factors other than modeling. Positive or neutral parental attitudes toward tobacco use and easy youth access to cigarettes when parents are smokers are examples of such factors.

Even if parents' tobacco use has a powerful influence on an adolescent's decision to begin using tobacco, the modeling process is contingent on the nature of the parent–child relationship (Andrews, Hops, & Duncan, 1997). High levels of family conflict contribute to the development of diverse youth problem behaviors, including tobacco use (Ary et al., 1999; Ary, Duncan, Duncan, & Hops, 1997; Patterson, Reid, & Dishion, 1992). When parental attempts to influence children's behavior results in conflict, it threatens development of the necessary family systems to ensure positive growth. Some compelling prevention approaches include finding ways for parents to (a) set and enforce effective rules about their children's association with peers who engage in problem behavior, (b) express their desire that their children will decide to remain tobacco free, and (c) to communicate these concepts with minimal conflict (Biglan et al., 1996).

Other, more general parenting practices also influence whether children are likely to initiate tobacco use. A growing body of evidence consistently identifies two ways in which parents can effectively prevent their children from drifting toward problem behaviors: (a) by curtailing their children's association with deviant peers, and (b) by making and enforcing rules about where and with whom their children spend their free time (Ary et al., 1999; Ary et al., 1997; Irvine, Biglan, Smolkowski, Metzler, & Ary,

1999). Such limit-setting practices can contribute directly to preventing experimentation with tobacco and other problem behaviors.

To change substance use patterns, parents and educators must identify users at the early stages of use and apply effective prevention tactics to reduce the number of adolescents who go on to regular use. Researchers have strived to identify the most effective means of prevention over the past 30 years.

A RECENT HISTORY OF PREVENTION EFFORTS

There are two ways to view prevention efforts—as either primary or secondary. *Primary prevention* is designed to prevent a target person (or population) from engaging in a particular behavior and takes place before the onset of the behavior. *Secondary prevention* aims to inhibit the person (or population) from continuing a behavior they have already initiated. The distinction between these two types of prevention may blur when researchers attempt to study drug use. For example, if one were to intervene in the sixth grade and focus on smoking prevention, researchers would consider the intervention to be primary because most sixth-grade students are not smokers. However, because some students of that age reported having experimented with tobacco, and the age of onset is known to be decreasing over time, the intervention must include secondary prevention components as well.

Substance Use Prevention Strategies and Interventions

In the early 1970s, school-based prevention models traditionally focused on providing facts about the harmful effects of using drugs. Many programs attempted to deter the behavior by using scare tactics aimed at instilling fear of the physical and punitive consequences of using substances. Empirical evaluation of such programs, however, indicated that they were *not* effective in achieving reductions in youth drug use (Botvin, Baker, Filazzola, & Botvin, 1990); in fact, in some cases, evidence showed that these strategies actually led to increased use (e.g., Swisher, Crawford, Goldstein, & Yura, 1971). Although educating youth about the harmful effects of drug use may increase their knowledge about such consequences, and in some cases may change their attitudes toward drug use, education alone has little impact on subsequent drug use behavior (e.g., Kearney & Hines, 1980; Kim, 1988).

As described earlier, all empirically validated school-based tobacco prevention programs contain components that target peer influences. However, efforts to address those influences within the classroom setting have inherent limits. Students at highest risk to begin using tobacco may frequently be absent from school and may be less engaged in classroom activities than other students. Antitobacco messages will have more impact on high-risk youth when placed in the context of groups to which those youth already belong, and those groups are likely to exist outside the school environment (Glynn, Anderson, & Schwarz, 1991).

In recent efforts, youth antitobacco activities occurring outside the classroom have shown promise (Biglan, Ary, Smolkowski, Duncan, & Black, 2000; Pentz et al., 1992). For example, adolescents have been involved in creative activities (such as designing antitobacco posters or T-shirts), planning activities (such as sponsoring an antitobacco dance, sports tournament, or other event), and policy activities (such as advocating for clean indoor air policies in the community). Identifying youth at highest risk to begin use, and finding ways to involve them in such activities, is strategic to the success of those activities in targeting peer influences on adolescent tobacco use.

Effective Tobacco Prevention Strategies

Reviews and meta-analyses of school-based prevention for smoking and tobacco use have produced mixed results. They generally have found that programs that are interactive, teach about social influences, and provide opportunities to practice social skills have reduced smoking initiation by about 12% on average (Tobler et al., 2000). However, some programs that purport to use the same strategies have reported no significant effects of their interventions (Ennett, Tobler, Ringwalt, & Flewelling, 1994; Peterson, Kealey, Mann, Marek, & Sarason, 2000). Recent National Institutes of Health (NIH) reviews of the state of the science showed short-term effectiveness of school-based interventions but recommended that these programs extend into the high school setting to increase effectiveness and maintain long-term reductions in tobacco use. Wiehe, Garrison, Christakis, Ebel, and Rivara (2005) reported in their meta-analysis of eight studies, which focused on 12th grade (or 18 years old at follow-up), that only one program was effective. That program was the LifeSkills Training program (Botvin & Eng, 1982), which is described later. More encouraging was the report by Skara and Sussman (2003), which assessed 25 studies with long-term follow-up and noted that 15 of those had effects persisting 2 or more years after the intervention. The average effect size was a reduction in smoking of more than 11%. They also recommended booster sessions in high school to extend and maintain the effects of the school-based programs that were largely implemented in middle schools.

A recent Institute of Medicine report recommended three interventions with good empirical support for their efficacy (Bonnie, Stratton, Wallace, & Committee on Reducing Tobacco Use, 2007). Flay (2007) prepared an appendix to the report that reviewed the effectiveness of school-based smoking prevention programs; Flay used three interventions as excellent examples of efficacious programs with good outcome research to support their use. These programs, described in more detail below, largely use the social influence approach to guide the content. Hansen, Malotte, and Felding (1988) provided a good description of this model, and Sussman et al. (1995) provided an excellent description of this theoretical framework for preventive interventions. Two core elements of these approaches are (a) resistance skills training, which teaches students skills to resist general and specific social pressures to smoke, and (b) normative education, which corrects student misperceptions of prevalence and acceptability of use. Social influence strategies involve teaching young people not only the skills to resist pressures to use tobacco and other drugs, but also the general problem-solving, decision-making, and social and assertiveness skills that contribute to the child's overall life success.

In addition to the school-based interventions, researchers have advocated community interventions to support alternatives to the use of substances by youth, such as by enlisting the help of a wide cross-section of community representatives to work to alter community knowledge, attitudes, and practices related to drug use (Biglan et al., 2004; Flay, 2000, 2007). Some authors have also suggested that parent- or family-based interventions can enhance and strengthen school-based programs (Biglan, Ary, & Wagenaar, 2000). Although extensive research has documented the influence of parenting practices on an adolescent's drug and alcohol use, no one has yet shown that interventions targeting parents have had a preventive effect on smoking and tobacco use. Some interventions have been successful in increasing parent–child interactions and communications about the risks of tobacco use and demonstrated changes in attitudes, but few studies have examined whether these changes actually result in reductions in youth smoking (Bonnie et al., 2007). Though the Institute of Medicine report recommends intervention components that support parents in setting clear standards and expectation for tobacco and drug use, these components need to be viewed as adjuncts to the school-based interventions described below. Another recommendation is that schools adopt clear, fair, and consistently enforced policies, which can help adolescents in deciding not to use tobacco and other drugs.

Behavioral science researchers now realize that addressing problem behaviors that are highly prevalent, such as drug use, requires efforts that go beyond interventions targeted at the individual (Biglan, 1995). The value of such interventions is limited when the adolescent faces influences from factors specific to the individual that a one-on-one setting cannot address. For example, treating an adolescent's smoking addiction may be difficult when that adolescent's peer group includes many smokers, or when the young person repeatedly faces exposure to powerful tobacco marketing messages. In addition, even though school-based prevention curricula have proved effective, those effects are often modest and short term (NIH, 2006). There is a need to enhance school-based prevention with community-wide programs that target other elements in the social environment surrounding youth, such as peers, parents, community organizations, and the media.

Tobacco Prevention: A Model for Other Drug Use Prevention

For several reasons, currently recognized best practices for tobacco use prevention provide a satisfactory model for strategies to prevent the use of alcohol, marijuana, and other drugs. First, although public interest may place primary focus on the problem of illicit drug use, tobacco use kills more people in the United States each year than do alcohol, drug abuse, AIDS, car accidents, homicides, suicides, and fires *combined*. Every day nearly 4,000 adolescents in this country smoke their first cigarettes on the way to becoming regular smokers as adults (Substance Abuse and Mental Health Services Administration [SAMHSA], 2007). More than 5 million children living today will die prematurely because of a decision they will make in adolescence—the decision to smoke cigarettes (CDC, 2000). Clearly, efforts to prevent *any* drug use should target tobacco use as a central theme. In many states, school-level tobacco prevention education is mandated.

Second, a body of research evidence now points to the role of tobacco as a "gateway" drug; that is, it initiates a progression in which a young person's use of a legal, or more easily attainable, drug precedes the use of illicit substances (e.g., Baily, 1992; Henningfield, Clayton, & Pollin, 1990; Kandel, 2000; Kandel & Yamaguchi, 1993). Some researchers have argued that the effects of nicotine on the brain may predispose one to experimentation with other drugs; others have hypothesized that the behavioral patterns learned by youth who obtain tobacco products then translate into behaviors that facilitate experimentation with other drugs. Thus, preventive efforts targeting tobacco use can help decrease the likelihood that an adolescent will go on to illicit substance use.

Third, findings from some studies have indicated that programs aimed at preventing tobacco use may contribute to discouraging other substance use (e.g., Biglan, Ary, Smolkowski, Duncan, & Black, 2000; Flay, 1985; Johnson, Pentz, & Weber, 1992). Viewing tobacco use as one facet of a constellation of adolescent problem behaviors, combined with the evidence that smoking is frequently the first of these behaviors to emerge, strengthens the notion that effective tobacco use prevention programs can serve as models for preventing other substance use (Biglan et al., 2004; Duncan, Duncan, Biglan, & Ary, 1998; Kandel, 2000). Additionally, recent studies have shown that elementary school students' attitudes toward tobacco and other drugs are predictive of subsequent use of these substances, which supports the notion that schools can intervene early to prevent the onset and use of these substances (Andrews et al., 2003).

WHAT SCHOOL PSYCHOLOGISTS CAN DO

As discussed previously in this chapter, the social context within which young people decide whether to initiate tobacco use includes schools, parents, peers, and the community. Evidence clearly supports five strategies for preventing tobacco use that target these influences: (a) presenting a school-based prevention curriculum, (b) linking youth with cessation programs, (c) developing appropriate school policies, (d) involving parents in delivering prevention messages, and (e) implementing community-wide programs. The school psychologist need not be a prevention expert to make a difference but can serve as a resource for the school, an advocate for the importance of tobacco prevention and cessation, and a facilitator between the school and community to work on tobacco control.

School-Based Curricula

School-based prevention programs are crucial in substance abuse prevention; estimates indicate that over 90% of regular users of tobacco initiated use before they left high school (Flay, 1993). Schools offer unique access to adolescents, and the prevention of smoking and other addictive behaviors fits well within the mission of schools' current health curriculum and community values for health promotion. Several studies have shown that school-based tobacco prevention programs significantly reduce or delay adolescent smoking by identifying the social influences that promote tobacco use among youth and by teaching skills to resist such influences (CDC, 1994a; Bonnie et al., 2007; Lynch & Bonnie, 1994). Programs that vary in format, scope, delivery methods, and community setting have produced reductions in smoking prevalence rates of between 25% and 60% for intervention and nonintervention groups, respectively but most estimates of the impact of these programs are that they reduce smoking and tobacco use approximately 12% on average (Bruvold, 1990). However, the programs described below, which use more sessions and provide more opportunities to learn and practice social skills, can reduce smoking by 22–28% (see Bonnie et al., 2007). Because many students begin using tobacco before high school and form their impressions about tobacco use even earlier, tobacco-use prevention education must begin in elementary school and continue through middle and high school grades (USDHHS, 1994). However, in practical terms, most of the current programs focus on middle school students, as this is the period in which many students experiment with tobacco and other drugs. It is highly recommended that the health curricula be integrated into the educational program.

Although Murray, Pirie, Luepker, and Pallonen's (1989) long-term follow-up of early prevention programs indicated that the effect may dissipate over time, recent evidence indicates the significant strength and effectiveness of school-based tobacco prevention programs. A program can offer 15 or more sessions over a 2- to 4-year period starting in the upper elementary grades or middle school, preferably with some content delivered in high school. Additionally, having community-wide programs that involve parents and community organizations can enhance these results and increase their impact. The use of multiple modalities increases efficacy over results obtained in school-only programs (Flay, 2007). Other elements of a successful prevention program can include establishing school policies, using mass media, and enforcing age restrictions on youth's access to tobacco products. Booster sessions that reinforce the classroom intervention in subsequent years can enhance the impact of any school-based program. For example, if teaching peer refusal skills were an integral part of the seventh-grade intervention, booster sessions in the eighth and ninth grades would reinforce these skills and would provide additional opportunities for behavioral rehearsal and peer feedback. Similarly, the additional measure of involving parents and community organizations in tobacco prevention or getting students to become active in community antitobacco activities, such as working on tobacco-free workplace ordinances, can significantly enhance the modest effects of a classroom-only program (Biglan et al., 1996).

The school-based tobacco prevention program forms the essential core element to successful prevention of teen tobacco use. While school-based programs with as few as five lessons have been successful in delaying tobacco use onset, greater exposure to the program over a longer period of time appears to be more successful in preventing tobacco use. Glynn (1989) identified essential elements of successful school-based tobacco prevention programs, which included information about the social consequences and short-term health effects of tobacco use; information about social influences on tobacco use, especially peer, parent, and media influences; and training in refusal skills, including modeling and practice of skills.

In addition to the guidelines suggested by Glynn, the CDC Office on Smoking and Health published *Guidelines for School Health Policies and Programs for Tobacco Use Prevention* (Kann, Brener, & Wechsler, 2007; School Health Policies and Programs Study, 2007). The guidelines suggest specific tobacco-free policies for schools, cite specific evidence-based curricula, and describe recommended teacher training, procedures for parental involvement, and procedures for implementing cessation services. In addition, the American Cancer Society published the standards for school-based tobacco education (Joint Committee on National Health Education Standards, 2007).

Four Exemplary School-Based Prevention Programs

The school psychologist can support school-based tobacco prevention programs by identifying efficacious and empirically validated school-based prevention programs promoted by the National Cancer Institute and CDC Office on Smoking and Health. A number of publications provide information on what concepts and information to include in a school-based curriculum: *Best Practices for Comprehensive Tobacco Control Programs* (CDC, 1999), *School Health Guidelines to Prevent Tobacco Use, Addiction, and Exposure to Secondhand Smoke* (CDC, 2008), *National Health Education Standards: Achieving Excellence* (Joint Committee on National Health Education Standards, 2007), and *Guidelines for School Health Programs to Prevent Tobacco Use and Addiction* (CDC, 1994a). Each provides a good source of information on proven school-based intervention programs and the content that should be included in the programs. The 2007 Institute of Medicine report cited selected school-based programs for middle school students (Grades 6, 7, and 8) that produced an average short-term reduction in smoking onset of 22% to 28% (Bonnie et al., 2007). These are reviewed here as exemplary programs to consider for adoption.

LifeSkills Training (LST)

The first exemplary program that has demonstrated consistent impact is the LifeSkills Training (LST) program, developed by Botvin and colleagues (Botvin & Dusenbury, 1989; Botvin & Eng, 1982). LST consists of 30 sessions; students receive 15, 10, and 5 sessions in Grades 7, 8, and 9, respectively. The program has five specific objectives. The first two are to teach a wide array of personal and social skills that help students resist direct pressures to smoke and to enhance students' self-esteem, self-mastery, and self-confidence in order to decrease their susceptibility to indirect social pressures to smoke. Its other objectives are to prepare students to cope with anxiety induced by social situations, to enhance students' knowledge of the actual prevalence of smoking among adolescents and adults, and to promote attitudes and beliefs consistent with nonsmoking.

Multiple evaluations of this program over 25 years have demonstrated the effectiveness of the LST program, which has been successful with different providers and in different school settings (Botvin, 2000; Botvin & Griffin, 2002). In the most comprehensive evaluation of the LST program to date, 56 schools in three different geographic regions entered—by random assignment—one of three study conditions: LST plus 1-day teacher training, LST plus video training for teachers, and a control condition. The project reported significant positive effects for cigarette use and for smoking-related knowledge, attitudes, and normative expectations. In most cases, the two treatment conditions had similar results: students in both groups demonstrated more positive effects than did students in the control group (Botvin et al., 1990). The level of implementation for the program ranged from 27% to 97% by teacher reports, with about 75% of the students receiving 60% of the intervention. These results are very encouraging, since it is likely that most schools will not fully implement the program in the way the researchers designed it. This research demonstrates positive effects of the LST program, whether delivered by project staff, older peers, or regular classroom teachers (Botvin, Baker, Dusenbury, Botvin, & Diaz, 1995).

Project TNT (Toward No Tobacco)

Another program that has credible evidence of sustained impact on youth smoking rates, and that was identified by the CDC as a program that works, is Project Towards No Tobacco Use (Project TNT; Dent et al., 1995). Project TNT, which is described in detail in *Developing School-Based Tobacco Use Prevention and Cessation Programs* (Sussman et al., 1995), focuses on activities that attempt to alter the social influences thought to have an impact on adolescent smoking. They identify normative social influence (a group wants its members to act in ways consistent with the group's norms) and informational influence (social groups provide information to socialize others). One example of normative social influence is when children accept offers of cigarettes or chew to gain acceptance in a group. Teaching children to identify social pressure to smoke and giving them refusal skills would be important elements in reducing negative influences. Project TNT helps to translate informational influences into prevention activities by identifying social images to which students aspire—such as independence, maturity, and gregariousness—and then countering the advertising or media efforts that have been used to create these positive images of smokers.

Sussman and colleagues at the University of Southern California have conducted a number of longitudinal studies and have reported positive preventive effects for the TNT curriculum (Sussman et al., 1993; Sussman et al., 1995). The authors reported that, in a large randomized trial, students exposed to the TNT program reported a reduction in smoking of 34% relative to the control group at the end of the program

(Grade 8) and 30% at follow-up (Grade 9). These programs generally have targeted seventh-grade students and involved 10 class periods to present the intervention fully.

Project SHOUT (Students Helping Others Understand Tobacco)

Project SHOUT used trained college undergraduates to teach 18 sessions to seventh and eighth graders (Eckhardt, Woodruff, & Elder, 1997; Elder et al., 1993). These sessions provided information about health consequences of smoking, celebrity endorsements of nonsmoking, antecedents and consequences of smoking, decision-making skills, resistance skills, advocacy (letters to newspapers and tobacco companies, participation in community mobilization projects), and encouraged public commitment not to use tobacco. A unique aspect of Project SHOUT was the use of follow-up newsletters and phone calls in the ninth grade. When the participants were in the ninth grade, each student received four phone calls and five newsletters from trained undergraduate counselors. The program had tailored the calls and the newsletters to the tobacco use status of the students. The program underwent rigorous randomized trial evaluation that involved 22 schools with an ethnically diverse population in San Diego, California. Though effects were modest after 8th grade, the effects increased over time and were very significant by the 9th and 11th grades. For self-reported tobacco use in the past 30 days, the reduction at the 9th grade was 30%; by the 11th grade, it was 44%. The results of this evaluation study suggest that the use of college students as volunteers (which kept the cost low) can be a very effective adjunct to the school-based program. Considerable research shows that the use of same-age or older peers to assist in the program can enhance a program's effectiveness (Flay, 2000). The results also support the notion that providing brief follow-up interventions with students at the high school level can greatly enhance the effectiveness of the program offered in middle schools.

Tobacco and Alcohol Prevention Project (TAPP)

TAPP was a 15-session social influence-oriented program developed at the University of California at Los Angeles in the early 1980s (Hansen et al., 1988). The program has two core elements: (a) resistance skills training, to teach students to resist the specific and general social pressures to smoke, and (b) normative education, to correct students' misperceptions of prevalence and acceptability of use. The program used open discussions, peer leaders as instructors, and behavioral rehearsal to ensure that students learned the skills. TAPP also included media literacy activities to combat tobacco-marketing messages, information about parental influences, and information about consequences of using tobacco, and required that participants make a public commitment not to smoke. The use of peer leaders probably enhanced the effects of the intervention over what would have occurred with teacher-only delivery (Klepp, Halper, & Perry, 1986; Tobler, 1992). The teachers received 2 days of training to conduct the intervention; the result of the randomized controlled trial was a 26% reduction in smoking at 1-year follow-up.

School-Based Approaches to Reduce Tobacco Use Through Tobacco Cessation Programs

The school psychologist can become involved in setting up diversion or cessation programs for students already using tobacco on middle or high school campuses. School administrators and teachers are more likely to enforce tobacco-free policies or act in response to violations of rules when they believe the consequences for violating these rules are consistent and appropriate and that a reasonable diversion or treatment program is in place to assist users in quitting. Even if users do not quit smoking or chewing immediately, their attendance and participation in an after-school diversion program may move them toward quitting by educating them about the risks of using tobacco and the benefits of quitting.

Any comprehensive program to reduce tobacco use must include assistance in quitting, as many young people are already dependent on cigarettes or moist snuff when they contact the program. Unfortunately, there are far fewer school-based programs to help adolescent smokers and chewers quit, and the published studies have shown limited effectiveness. A growing number of studies have been conducted on adolescent cessation of tobacco use, but they vary considerably in scientific quality, with many being anecdotal. (See Sussman [2002], which reviewed 66 published studies in adolescent tobacco cessation and 17 studies of self-initiated cessation.) It has been encouraging that national probability samples indicate that adolescents express an interest in quitting and have attempted to quit (CDC, 1998). Researchers have tried a variety of channels for delivery of smoking cessation, including classroom-based programs, computer-based programs, special group treatments, and interventions through school-based clinics. Programs that try explicitly to recruit adolescent smokers and chewers into cessation programs report positive responses to the offer of a program in school (Eakin, Severson, & Glasgow, 1989; Sussman, 2001).

One model of a school-based cessation study recruited students to attend four sessions on the immediate physiological effects of smoking (e.g., high levels of carbon monoxide in their expired air after just a couple of puffs on a cigarette) and on social cues that influence adoption of the smoking habit. The program, which was implemented in 10th-grade health classes in three California high schools (n = 477), resulted in a significantly greater percentage of subjects reporting abstinence, compared with a control group (Perry, Killen, Telch, Slinkard, & Danaher, 1980).

Adolescents may be reluctant to participate in multisession stop-smoking programs for several reasons. Young smokers may worry that teachers or parents will learn that they smoke (since parental permission is required for participation), and long-term health consequences such as cancer may not be salient to young people who are healthy. As schools have gone "tobacco free," many students get referrals for disciplinary action when they are caught smoking on school property. Although cessation rates among students attending mandatory cessation meetings owing to rule infractions might be expected to be low, these programs can have some success in helping smokers quit if the programs are well organized and structured to promote cessation (Lynch & Bonnie, 1994).

One approach that shows promise is a diversion program in which students caught using tobacco on campus are required to attend an educational program that is designed to divert them from using tobacco. One example of this is a multiple-session educational program developed by the American Lung Association. Though a mandatory education program may result in low rates of cessation, such as the 14% success rate reported by USDHHS (1994) in the evaluation trial, a diversion program provides school administrators with a way to deal with violation of school tobacco use policies and promotes enforcement of those rules while supporting teen cessation. A structured curriculum for high-risk youth shows promise and could work well in conjunction with student referral to a diversion program (Sussman et al., 1995).

Project EX is a classroom-based program for smoking prevention and cessation that reported reductions in weekly and monthly smoking in alternative high schools in the Los Angeles area (Sussman, Miyano, Rohrbach, Dent, & Sun, 2007). The program is unique in that it focuses on cessation, since its participants had a high smoking rate at baseline and the program took place in high schools with high-risk youth.

The National Cancer Institute recently funded several randomized clinical trials to test innovative strategies to encourage cessation of tobacco use among teens, but the trial results are not yet known. Recent programs that use interactive computer-based cessation in a game-like format show promise in helping adolescent smokers and chewers quit (Fisher, Severson, Christiansen, & Williams, 2001). The Internet may also provide an avenue for supporting cessation among young people, as they often use the Web for other sources of health information and could access a quitting program anonymously at any time. The removal of some of the barriers to cessation assistance make the Web-delivered programs attractive; however, although most current online programs are not youth oriented, they might still be helpful to smokers and chewers seeking cessation assistance. A recent study is evaluating the efficacy of providing a Web-based cessation program for young chewers. The MyLastDip.com website and the study funded by the National Cancer Institute show great promise for providing a unique program targeting smokeless tobacco users between the ages of 15 and 26 (Severson et al., 2009).

Interactive Computer-Based Tobacco Prevention Programs

Teachers also can use interactive computer-based programs for tobacco education. One approach is an interactive program on CD-ROM that students can use to learn about the dangers and health risks of tobacco use. The game-like activities engage middle school students in learning key information about tobacco use, with each activity focused on mediating mechanisms previously shown to relate to the subsequent use of tobacco. Both teachers and students responded positively to the activities. Although no long-term evaluation of the program has been conducted, the results of a randomized clinical trial evaluating the efficacy of the Tobacco World program were very positive, with six of the nine program activities significantly affecting the targeted mediating mechanisms. The students had reduced intentions to smoke and more negative attitudes toward smoking than did control subjects using standard curriculum (Severson et al., 2007).

Another approach that used the Internet was Consider This, an interactive multimedia prevention program for youth that addresses the role of media, friends, and oneself in determining social and health behavior, making effective decisions, and resisting social influences, with messages tailored for adolescents experimenting with smoking or vulnerable to starting (Buller et al., 2001; Hall et al., 2001). Researchers tested the program in both the United States and Australia, using a pretest- and posttest-group randomized design (Buller et al., 2008). In the Australian trial, compared with children in the control group, a greater proportion of children who were exposed to Consider This, and who reported (at baseline) smoking a whole cigarette in the past 30 days, said at follow-up that they had not smoked one in the past 30 days. In addition, at posttest assessment there was also a change in perceived norms among children who had participated in the intervention, in that they were more likely to believe that fewer children had tried smoking or smoked at least once a week and that fewer adults smoked cigarettes (perceived norms). An intent-to-treat analysis on change in 30-day smoking showed confirmed treatment effects. The American trial showed that exposure to Consider This increased students' intentions not to smoke in the future.

Another innovative approach to substance and tobacco use prevention is a focus on using classroom-behavior management strategies, such as the Good Behavior Game. Its authors designed this intervention to reduce aggressive behavior in elementary-grade children. Studies have shown that the program is an effective intervention that can significantly reduce aggressive behavior in the first grade and maintain this change over several years (Kellam, Ling, Merisca, Brown, & Ialongo, 1998). Though researchers have not yet reported on whether this intervention was associated with reductions in illicit drug or alcohol use, they have reported that boys who received the intervention were significantly less likely to be smoking at age 14 (Kellam & Anthony, 1998). The intervention is a good demonstration of the potential effect of using behavior management strategies to reduce aggression in young children and of how this might be an effective prevention for smoking for boys who exhibit aggressive behavior at a young age.

School Policy as an Intervention

Outside the home, the school constitutes an adolescent's principal environment. The school environment prescribes social norms—directly or indirectly—through policy, teacher expectations and behavior, and peer group actions. Schools have the opportunity to promote tobacco-free norms, counter protobacco messages, and provide an environment that supports healthy choices.

Most schools now have written policies that ban smoking on school grounds, restrict students from leaving school grounds, and ban smoking near school. Schools with policies in all these areas have significantly lower rates of smoking than do schools with fewer policies (Pentz et al., 1989). Elder et al. (1993) reported that, in their evaluation of 96 schools in four states, implementation and enforcement of school policies appeared crucial to school-based interventions. Now that most schools and public places ban smoking, the nonsmoking policy is a necessary condition, but the critical variable is likely the enforcement of that policy, accompanied by strong commitment to protecting nonsmokers from harmful exposure to tobacco smoke.

Involvement of Parents

Research has shown that parental smoking and attitudes toward tobacco use affect a teen's use of tobacco (USDHHS, 1994). School psychologists could help motivate parents to become involved in school efforts to prevent use of tobacco by students. Interventions that promote connections between parents and teachers have proved to be more efficacious than didactically based interventions (Tobler, Lessard, Marshall, Ochshorn, & Roona, 1999). Lochman and van den Steenhoven (2002) found family-based approaches to be effective in decreasing risks of substance use among youth. There are many ways to involve parents: by having them help with tasks in which they interact with their child on health curriculum activities, by engaging them in structured approaches to family–school interface such as the Family Check-Up (Dishion, Kavanagh, Schneiger, Nelson, & Kaufman, 2002). The Family Check-Up engages the parents in a three-session intervention that uses motivational interviewing to assess the problems their child is experiencing in school and provides feedback in the final interview (Dishion & Kavanagh, 2003). Another popular and well-researched method for teaching parents more effective parenting is with proven programs such as the Incredible Years (Webster-Stratton & Reid, 2003).

Biglan et al. (1996) found that school-prompted parent–child interactions about tobacco use could influence adolescents' perceptions that their parents do not want them to use tobacco. Middle school students took home quizzes about tobacco use to do as homework assignments. The students were instructed to ask their parents the questions on the quiz and to give them immediate feedback by telling them the correct answers. Students then brought the quizzes back to school (signed by the parents to indicate they had completed the quiz) in exchange for a small incentive, such as a granola bar, candy, or a coupon. In some cases, students returning the assignments also entered a competition for a larger incentive (a party for the classroom with the highest return rate). This activity increased both students' and parents' knowledge about the harmful effects of tobacco use and induced more negative attitudes toward the use of tobacco. These findings suggest that parents can be encouraged to tell their children that they do not want them to use tobacco and to set limits on activities that would put their children at risk to experiment with tobacco.

The school psychologist can also help get parents involved in prevention. Most parents, even those who smoke, would say that they do not want their children to become addicted to tobacco. The school psychologist can make presentations showing parents how to talk to their children about tobacco and drug use. Student take-home assignments can encourage students to discuss with their parents the school's rules and consequences for tobacco use. In one project, videotapes are being developed as part of homework assignments for sixth graders. Students will be asked to watch the video with their parents, discuss and do problem solving for issues presented on the video, and complete brief homework assignments that will be signed by the parent (Gordon, Biglan, & Smolkowski, 2008). The prime objective is to promote parent–child communication around rules, expectations, and consequences related to the child's use of tobacco.

Community Programs

Community-based strategies to prevent youth tobacco use are now acceptable and important adjuncts to school-based and educational programs (USDHHS, 1994). A youth's social environment may contain strong prompts to initiate tobacco use, such as industry marketing ploys or the presence of adult role models who smoke. Thus, mobilizing facets of that social environment—that is, parents, the media, policy makers, the religious community, social services, and business leaders—can enhance the effects of concerted prevention efforts.

The Centers for Disease Control and Prevention has identified four best practices for community programs aimed at tobacco prevention. They are (a) building community coalitions to increase the number of organizations and individuals who plan and conduct community-level education programs, (b) creating counter-marketing campaigns to support local tobacco control initiatives and policies with prohealth messages, (c) promoting the adoption of public and private tobacco control policies, and (d) measuring outcomes using validated evaluative tools (CDC, 1999). These practices can work to change community norms, thus changing the perceived acceptability of tobacco use for a community's young people.

Efforts to reduce illegal sales of tobacco to minors are another example of practices aimed at changing community norms about youth tobacco use. Biglan et al. (1995, 1996) developed a program (Reward and Reminder) that rewarded clerks for not selling tobacco products to underage youth, and reminded them of the law when they were willing to sell. The authors found that the program significantly reduced the levels of illegal tobacco sales. In addition to clerk rewards and reminders, the program includes three other components: (a) obtaining endorsement and support from community leaders, (b) generating media coverage for the campaign, and (c) providing feedback to merchants about their rates of sales to minors. Other states and communities have successfully replicated this program.

School psychologists can aid a community-level program in several ways. First, they can become involved in a local tobacco-free coalition or provide a link between the school and a community coalition. Second, they can help parents form a local network that would support parenting skills education, community norms about monitoring and behavioral programs for parents and children, and social support for parents. Third, school psychologists can offer support to local initiatives for policy change—for example, helping to identify a student group willing to participate in advocating for smoke-free environments in the school and community.

TRAINING IMPLICATIONS

The current training of preservice school psychologists may be inadequate in promoting prevention of tobacco and drug use in the schools. A useful component of professional training would be a course covering preventive models and teaching students how to implement prevention programs, combined with the consultation and intervention skills that are already part of a school psychologist's repertoire.

Another clear training need for school psychologists to become effective proponents of prevention is to learn the public health perspective. This perspective is based on understanding and accepting the primary role of prevention in the amelioration of problems. Most psychologists have a great deal of practice in promoting and setting up interventions for students already identified as having a problem; however, a prevention approach couples a psychologist's experience and practical knowledge about early screening and problem identification with advocating for preventive programs in the schools. A course in prevention might cover the behavioral epidemiology of problems most likely to confront psychologists in the schools, preventive interventions that others have tried, and their relative levels of success. At the very minimum, the school psychologist can be a resource for finding and promoting the use of empirically evaluated prevention and intervention programs in the schools. Even if school psychologists are not directly responsible for health promotion or drug prevention in schools, they can provide strong voices for having the schools use proven, effective programs. The Office of Juvenile Justice and Delinquency Prevention and the Substance Abuse and Mental Health Services Administration have compiled lists of exemplary substance use programs (Mihalic, Irwin, Elliot, Fagan, & Hansen, 2001; SAMHSA, 2007). Additionally, the joint committee on National Health Education Standards has published guidelines for key content that should be included in school-based prevention and health education (CDC, 2008).

For school psychologists in practice, there are many accredited continuing education programs, public health workshops, and inservice training opportunities that are available to address tobacco and other substance use prevention. Examples of training opportunities include the annual meetings of the Society for Prevention Research, the American Public Health Association, National Association for School Psychologists, American Psychological Association, and conferences hosted by state-level alcohol, tobacco, and other drug prevention and treatment groups.

CONCLUSION

Prevention is not easy work. In many ways, it can be frustrating, because it involves coordinating more people and components than the "diagnose and remediate" model does. Screening, as well as intervention, must occur in the context of general education. Educating teachers about student behaviors to notice and developing cost-effective ways to screen for problem behaviors may put school psychologists in an uncomfortable or unfamiliar position. On the other hand, prevention helps put the school psychologist in the mainstream of education and promotes participation in the education process. Promoting health and drug prevention can be quite rewarding and can visibly broaden the impact of the psychologist's work. One key point to remember is that early drug use behaviors are strongly related to other problematic forms of behavior and may precede the behavior problems that lead to both referrals and outcomes that are even more serious, such as school failure and dropout. Prevention cannot replace essential approaches in working with intense problems that require assessment and treatment, but preventive interventions can provide a valuable adjunct to those efforts. Training in prevention, screening, early classroom intervention, and links to community programs can promote the school psychologist's participation in all levels of school programming and, in the end, ensure a broader context for this professional role.

REFERENCES

Andrews, J. A., Hampson, S. E., Barckley, M., Gerrard, M., & Gibbons, F. X. (2008). The effect of early cognitions on cigarette and alcohol use in adolescence. *Psychology of Addictive Behaviors, 22,* 96–106.

Andrews, J. A., Hops, H., & Duncan, S. C. (1997). Adolescent modeling of parent substance use: The moderating effect of the relationship with the parent. *Journal of Family Psychology, 11,* 259–270.

Andrews, J. A., Tildesley, H. H., Hops, H., Duncan, S. C., & Severson, H. H. (2003). Elementary school age children's future intentions and use of substances. *Journal of Clinical Child and Adolescent Psychology, 32,* 556–567.

Arnett, J. (1992). Reckless behavior in adolescence: A developmental perspective. *Developmental Review, 12,* 339–373.

Ary, D. V., & Biglan, A. (1988). Longitudinal changes in adolescent cigarette smoking behavior: Onset and cessation. *Journal of Behavioral Medicine, 11,* 361–382.

Ary, D. V., Duncan, T. E., Biglan, A., Metzler, C. W., Noell, J. W., & Smolkowski, K. (1999). Development of adolescent problem behavior. *Journal of Abnormal Child Psychology, 27*(2), 141–150.

Ary, D. V., Duncan, T. E., Duncan, S. C., & Hops, H. (1997). Adolescent problem behavior: The influence of parents and peers. *Behaviour Research and Therapy, 37,* 217–230.

Baily, S. L. (1992). Adolescents' multi-substance use patterns: The role of heavy alcohol and cigarette use. *American Journal of Public Health, 82,* 1220–1224.

Bauman, K. E., Foshee, V. A., & Haley, N. J. (1991). *The interaction of sociological and biological factors in the onset of cigarette smoking.* Chapel Hill: University of North Carolina Press.

Bauman, K. E., Foshee, V. A., Linzer, M. A., & Koch, G. G. (1990). Effect of parental smoking classification on the association between parental and adolescent smoking. *Addictive Behaviors, 15,* 413–422.

Biglan, A. (1995). *Changing cultural practices: A contextualist framework for intervention research.* Reno, NV: Context Press.

Biglan, A., Ary, D. V., Smolkowski, K., Duncan, T., & Black, C. (2000). A randomized controlled trial of a community intervention to prevent adolescent tobacco use. *Tobacco Control, 9,* 24–32.

Biglan, A., Ary, D. V., & Wagenaar, A. C. (2000). The value of interrupted time-series experiments for community intervention research. *Prevention Research, 1*(1), 31–49.

Biglan, A., Ary, D. V., Yudelson, H., Duncan, T. E., Hood, D., James, L., et al. (1996). Experimental evaluation of a modular approach to mobilizing antitobacco influences of peers and parents. *American Journal of Community Psychology, 24,* 311–339.

Biglan, A., Brennan, P. A., Foster, S. L., Holder, H. D., Miller, T. L., Cunningham, P. B., et al. (2004). *Helping adolescents at risk: Prevention of multiple problem behaviors.* New York: Guilford Press.

Biglan, A., Henderson, J., Humphreys, D., Yasui, M., Whisman, R., Black, C., et al. (1995). Mobilizing positive reinforcement to reduce youth access to tobacco. *Tobacco Control, 4,* 42–48.

Biglan, A., Metzler, C. A., Wirt, R., Ary, D., Noell, J., Ochs, L., et al. (1990). Social and behavioral factors associated with high-risk sexual behavior among adolescents. *Journal of Behavioral Medicine, 13,* 245–261.

Biglan, A., & Smolkowski, K. (1999). Critical influences on the development of adolescent problem behavior. In D. B. Kandel (Ed.), *Stages and pathways of drug involvement: Examining the gateway hypothesis.* Los Angeles: UCLA Youth Enhancement Service.

Biglan, A., Wang, M. C., & Walberg, H. J. (2003). *Preventing youth problems.* New York: Kluwer Academic/Plenum Press.

Bonnie, R. J., Stratton, K., Wallace, R. B., & Committee on Reducing Tobacco Use. (2007). *Ending the tobacco problem: A blueprint for the nation.* Washington, DC: Institute of Medicine.

Botvin, G. (2000). Preventing drug abuse in schools: Social and competence enhancement approaches targeting individual-level etiologic factors. *Addictive Behaviors, 25,* 887–897.

Botvin, G. J., Baker, E., Dusenbury, L., Botvin, E. M., & Diaz, T. (1995). Long-term follow-up results of a randomized drug abuse prevention trial in a white middleclass population. *Journal of the American Medical Association, 273,* 1106–1112.

Botvin, G. J., Baker, E., Filazzola, A. D., & Botvin, E. M. (1990). A cognitive-behavioral approach to substance abuse prevention: One-year follow-up. *Addictive Behaviors, 15,* 47–63.

Botvin, G. J., & Dusenbury, L. (1989). Primary prevention and promotion in the schools. In L. A. Bond & B. E. Compas (Eds.), *Primary prevention of psychopathology* (Vol. 12, pp. 146–178). Thousand Oaks, CA: SAGE.

Botvin, G. J., & Eng, A. (1982). The efficacy of a multicomponent approach to the prevention of cigarette smoking. *Preventive Medicine, 11,* 199–211.

Botvin, G. J., & Griffin, K. W. (2002). Life skills training as a primary prevention approach for adolescent drug abuse and other problems behaviors. *International Journal of Mental Health, 4*(1), 41–47.

Brener, N. D., & Collins, J. L. (1998). Co-occurrence of health-risk behaviors among adolescents in the United States. *Journal of Adolescent Health, 22,* 209–213.

Breslau, N., Kilbey, M., & Andreski, P. (1991). Nicotine dependence, major depression, and anxiety in young adults. *Archives of General Psychiatry, 48,* 1069–1074.

Brown, R. A., Lewinsohn, P. M., Seeley, J. R., & Wagner, E. F. (1996). Cigarette smoking, major depression, and other psychiatric disorders among adolescents. *Journal of the American Academy of Child and Adolescent Psychiatry, 35,* 1602–1610.

Brown, S. A., Tapert, S. F., Granholm, E., & Delis, D. C. (2000). Neurocognitive functioning of adolescents: Effects of protracted alcohol use. *Alcoholism: Clinical and Experimental Research, 24*(2), 164–171.

Bruvold, W. H. (1990). A meta-analysis of the California school-based risk reduction program. *Journal of Drug Education, 20*(2), 139–152.

Bry, B. H., McKeon, P., & Padina, R. J. (1982). Extent of drug use as a function of number of risk factors. *Journal of Abnormal Psychology, 91,* 237–279.

Buller, D. B., Woodall, W. G., Hall, J. R., Borland, R., Ax, B., Brown, M., et al. (2001). A Web-based smoking cessation and prevention program for children ages 12 to 15. In R. Rice & C. Atkin (Eds.), *Public communication campaigns* (3rd ed.; pp. 357–372). Thousand Oaks, CA: SAGE.

Buller, D. B., Borland, R., Woodall, W. G., Hall, J. R., Hines, J. M., Burris-Woodall, P., et al. (2008, April). Randomized trials on *Consider This,* a tailored Internet-delivered smoking prevention program for adolescents. *Health Education Behavior, 35*(2), 260–281.

Centers for Disease Control and Prevention. (1994a). Guidelines for school health programs to prevent tobacco use and addiction. *MMWR, 43*(RR-2), 1–18. http://www.cdc.gov/mmwr/preview/mmwrhtml/00026213.htm

Centers for Disease Control and Prevention (CDC). (1994b). Health-risk behaviors among persons aged 12–21 years — United States, 1992. *MMWR 43*(13), 231–235.

Centers for Disease Control and Prevention (CDC). (1998). Tobacco use continues to rise among U.S. high school students. *Public Health Reports, 113*(July/August), 300.

Centers for Disease Control and Prevention (CDC). (1999). *Best practices for comprehensive tobacco control programs, August 1999.* Atlanta, GA: U.S. Department of Health and Human Services, Centers for Disease Control and Prevention, National Center for Chronic Disease Prevention and Health Promotion, Office on Smoking and Health.

Centers for Disease Control and Prevention (CDC). (2000). *Quick stats on female adolescents. MMWR: CDC Surveillance Summaries, 49*(SS-5), 1–94.

Centers for Disease Control and Prevention (CDC). (2008). *Guidelines for school health programs to prevent tobacco use: Summary.* Atlanta, GA: U.S. Department of Health and Human Services, Centers for Disease Control and Prevention. http://www.cdc.gov/healthyYouth/tobacco/guidelines/summary.htm

Clark, D. B., Kirisci, L., & Tarter, R. E. (1998). Adolescent versus adult onset and the development of substance use disorders in males. *Drug and Alcohol Dependence, 49,* 115–121.

Clark, D. B., Pollock, N., Bromberger, J. T., Bukstein, O. G., Mezzick, A. C., Bromberger, J. T., et al. (1997). Gender and co-morbid psychopathology in adolescents with alcohol dependence. *Journal of the American Academy of Child and Adolescent Psychiatry, 36,* 1195–1203.

Conrad, K. M., Flay, B. R., & Hill, D. (1992). Why children start smoking cigarettes: Predictors of onset. *British Journal of Addiction, 87*(12), 1711–1724.

Dent, C. W., Sussman, S., Stacy, A. W., Craig, S., Burton, D., & Flay, B. R. (1995). Two-year behavior outcomes of Project Towards No Tobacco Use. *Journal of Consulting and Clinical Psychology, 63,* 676–677.

Dishion, T. J., Kavanagh, K. (2003). *Intervening in adolescent problem behavior: A family-centered approach.* New York: Guilford Press.

Dishion, T. J., Kavanagh, K., Schneiger, A., Nelson, S., & Kaufman, N. (2002). Preventing early adolescent substance use: A family-centered strategy for the public middle-school ecology. In R. L. Spoth, K. Kavanagh, & T. J. Dishion (Eds.), Universal family-centered prevention strategies: Current findings and critical issues for public health impact [Special issue]. *Prevention Science, 3,* 191–201.

Donovan, J. E., & Jessor, R. (1978). Adolescent problem drinking: Psychosocial correlates in a national sample study. *Journal of Studies on Alcohol, 39,* 1506–1524.

Duncan, S. C., Duncan, T. E., Biglan, A., & Ary, D. (1998). Contributions of the social context to the development of adolescent substance use: A multivariate latent growth modeling approach. *Drug and Alcohol Dependence, 50,* 57–71.

Eakin, E., Severson, H. H., & Glasgow, R. E. (1989). Development and evaluation of a smokeless tobacco cessation program. *Journal of the National Cancer Institute Monographs, 8,* 95–100.

Eaton, D. K., Kann, L., Kinchen, S., Ross, J., Hawkins, J., Harris, W. A., et al. (2006). Youth risk behavior surveillance – United States, 2005. *Journal of School Health, 76,* 353–372.

Eckhardt, L., Woodruff, S. I., & Elder, J. P. (1997). Related effectiveness of continued, lapsed, and delayed smoking prevention intervention in senior high school students. *American Journal of Health Promotion, 11*(6), 418–421.

Ehrenreich, H., Rinn, T., Kunert, H. J., Moeller, M. R., Poser W., Schilling L., et al. (1999). Specific attentional dysfunction in adults following early start of cannabis use. *Psychopharmacology (Berl), 142,* 295–301.

Elder, J. P., Wildey, M., deMoor, C., Sallis, J F., Eckhardt, L., Edwards, C., et al. (1993). The long-term prevention of tobacco use among junior high school students: Classroom and telephone interventions. *American Journal of Public Health, 83*(9), 1239–1244.

Ellickson, P. L., Tucker, J. S., Klein, D. J., & Saner, H. (2004). Antecedents and outcomes of marijuana use initiation during adolescence. *Preventive Medicine, 39*(5), 976–984.

Ennett, S. T., Tobler, N. S., Ringwalt, C. L., & Flewelling, R. L. (1994). How effective is drug abuse resistance education? A meta-analysis of Project DARE outcome evaluations. *American Journal of Public Health, 84*(9), 1394–1401.

Fisher, K. J., Severson, H. H., Christiansen, S. J., & Williams, C. (2001). Using interactive technology to aid smokeless tobacco cessation: A pilot study. *American Journal of Health Education, 32*(6), 332–340.

Flay, B. R. (1985). Psychosocial approaches to smoking prevention: A review of findings. *Health Psychology, 4,* 449–488.

Flay, B. R. (1993). Youth tobacco use: Risks, patterns, and control. In C. T. Orleans & J. Slade (Eds.), *Nicotine addiction: Principles and management.* New York: Oxford University Press.

Flay, B. R. (2000). Approaches to substance use prevention utilizing school curriculum plus social environment change. *Addictive Behaviors, 25,* 861–885.

Flay, B. R. (2007). The long-term promise of effective school-based smoking prevention programs. In R. Bonnie, K. Stratton, & R. B. Wallace (Eds.), *Ending the tobacco problem: A blueprint for the nation* (pp. 449–477). Washington, DC: Institute of Medicine.

Forester, K. A., Biglan, A., Severson, H. H., & Smolkowski, K. (2007). Predictors of smoking onset over two years. *Nicotine and Tobacco Research, 9,* 1259–1267.

Friedman, L. S., Lichtenstein, E., & Biglan, A. (1985). Smoking onset among teens: An empirical analysis of initial situations. *Addictive Behaviors, 10,* 1–13.

Glynn, T. J., (1989). Essential elements of school-based smoking prevention programs. *Journal of School Health, 59,* 181–188.

Glynn, T. J., Anderson, D. M., & Schwarz, L. (1991). Tobacco-use reduction among high-risk youth: Recommendations of a National Cancer Institute Expert Advisory Panel. *Preventive Medicine, 20,* 279–291.

Gordon, J. S., Biglan T. Smolkowski, K. (2008). The impact on tobacco use of branded youth antitobacco activities and family communications about tobacco. *Prevention Science, 9*(2), 73–87.

Grant, B. F., & Dawson, D. A. (1997). Age of onset of alcohol use and its association with DSM-IV alcohol abuse and dependence: Results from the National Longitudinal Alcohol Epidemiologic Survey. *Journal of Substance Abuse, 9,* 103–110.

Grant, B. F., Stinson, F. S., & Harford, T. (2001). The 5 year course of alcohol abuse among adults. *Journal of Substance Abuse, 13,* 229–238.

Hahn, G., Charlin, V. L., Sussman, S. Y., Dent, C. W., Manzi, J., Stacy, A. W., et al. (1990). Adolescents' first and most recent use situations of smokeless tobacco and cigarettes: Similarities and differences. *Addictive Behaviors, 15,* 439–448.

Hall, J. R., Ax, B., Brown, M., Buller, D. B., Woodall, W. G., & Borland, R. (2001). Challenges to producing and implementing the *Consider This* Web-based smoking prevention and cessation program. *Electronic Journal of Communication, 11*(3–4).

Hallfors, D. D., Waller, M. W., Bauer, D., Ford, C. A., & Halpern, C. T. (2006). Which comes first in adolescent – sex and drugs or depression? *American Journal of Preventive Medicine, 29,* 163–170.

Hanna, E. Z., Hsiao-ye, Y., & Dufoour, M. (2000, June). *The relationship of drinking alone and other substance use alone and in combination to health and behavior problems among youth aged 12–16: Findings from the Third National Health and Nutrition Examination Survey (NHANES III).* Paper presented at the 23rd Annual Scientific Meeting of the Research Society on Alcoholism, Denver, CO.

Hansen, W. B., Malotte, C. K., & Felding, J. E., (1988). Evaluation of a tobacco and alcohol abuse prevention curriculum for adolescents. *Health Education Quarterly, 1,* 93–114.

Henningfield, J. E., Clayton, R., & Pollin, W. (1990). Involvement of tobacco in alcoholism and illicit drug use. *British Journal of Addiction, 85,* 279–292.

Holder, H. (1998). *Alcohol and the community: A systems approach to prevention.* Cambridge, UK: Cambridge University Press.

Hundleby, J. D., Carpenter, R. A., Ross, R. A., & Mercer, G. W. (1982). Adolescent drug use and other behaviors. *Journal of Child Psychology and Psychiatry, 23,* 61–68.

Irvine, A. B., Biglan, A., Smolkowski, K., Metzler, C. W., & Ary, D. V. (1999). The effectiveness of a parenting skills program for parents of middle school students in small communities. *Journal of Consulting and Clinical Psychology, 67,* 811–825.

Jessor, R. (1991). Risk behavior in adolescence: A psychosocial framework for understanding and action. *Journal of Adolescent Health, 12*(8), 597–605.

Jessor, R., & Jessor, S. L. (1977). *Problem behavior and psychosocial development: A longitudinal study of youth.* New York: Academic Press.

Johnson, C. A., Pentz, M. A., & Weber, M. D. (1992). Relative effectiveness of comprehensive community programming for drug abuse prevention with high risk and low risk adolescents. *Journal of Consulting and Clinical Psychology, 58,* 447–456.

Johnston, L. D., O'Malley, P. M., & Bachman, J. G. (2001). *The Monitoring the Future national survey results on adolescent drug use: Overview of key findings, 2000* (NIH Publication No. 01-4923). Bethesda, MD: National Institute on Drug Abuse.

Johnston, L. D., O'Malley, P. M., Bachman, J. G., & Schulenberg, J. E. (2007). *Monitoring the Future national results on adolescent drug use: Overview of key findings, 2006* (NIH Publication No. 07-6202). Bethesda, MD: National Institute on Drug Abuse.

Joint Committee on National Health Education Standards. (2007). *National Health Education Standards: Achieving Excellence* (2nd ed.). Atlanta: American Cancer Society. Retrieved November 11, 2009, from http://www.cdc.gov/HealthyYouth/SHER/standards/index.htm

Kandel, D. B. (2000). Examining the gateway hypothesis: Stages and pathways of drug involvement. In D. B. Kandel (Ed.), *Examining the gateway hypothesis.* New York: Cambridge University Press.

Kandel, D. B., & Yamaguchi, R. (1993). From beer to crack: Developmental patterns of drug involvement. *American Journal of Public Health, 83,* 851–855.

Kann, L., Brener, N. D., & Wechsler, H. (2007). Overview and summary: School health policies and programs study 2006. *Journal of School Health, 77,* 385–397.

Kearney, A. L., & Hines, M. H. (1980). Evaluation of the effectiveness of a drug prevention education program. *Journal of Drug Education, 10,* 127–134.

Kellam, S. G., Anthony, J. C. (1998). Targeting early antecedents to prevent tobacco smoking: Findings from an epidemiologically based randomized trial. *American Journal of Public Health, 88,* 1490–1495.

Kellam, S. G., Ling, X., Merisca, R., Brown, C. H., & Ialongo, N. (1998), The effect of the level of aggression in the first-grade classroom on the course and malleability of aggressive behavior into middle school. *Developmental and Psychopathology, 10,* 165–185.

Kessler, R. C., & Price, R. H. (1993). Primary prevention of secondary disorders: A proposal and agenda. *American Journal of Community Psychology, 21,* 607–633.

Kim, S. (1988). A short- and long-term evaluation of "Here's Looking at You" alcohol education program. *Journal of Drug Education, 18*(3), 235–242.

Klepp, K. I., Halper, A., & Perry, C. L. (1986). The efficacy of peer leaders in drug abuse prevention. *Journal of School Health, 56,* 407–411.

Kolbe, L. J., Kann, L. & Collins, J. L. (1993). Overview of the Youth Risk Behavior Surveillance System. *Public Health Reports, 108* (Suppl.1), 2–10.

Lewinsohn, P. M., Hops, H., Roberts, R. E., Seeley, J. R., & Andrews, J. A. (1993). Adolescent psychopathology: I. Prevalence and incidence of depression and other DSM-III-R disorders in high school students. *Journal of Abnormal Psychology, 102,* 133–144.

Lochman, J. E., & van den Steenhoven, A. (2002). Family-based approaches to substance abuse prevention. *Journal of Primary Prevention, 23*(1), 49–114.

Loeber, R., Stouthhamer-Loeber, M., & White, H. R. (1999). Developmental aspects of delinquency and internalizing problems and their association with persistent juvenile substance use between the ages of 7 and 18. *Journal of Clinical Child Psychology, 28,* 322–332.

Lynch, B. S., & Bonnie, R. J. (Eds.). (1994). *Growing up tobacco free: Preventing nicotine addiction in children and youth.* Washington, DC: Institute of Medicine.

Mensch, B. S., & Kandel, D. B. (1988). Do job conditions influence the use of drugs? *Journal of Health and Social Behavior, 29*(2), 169–184.

Mihalic, S., Irwin, K., Elliott, D., Fagan, A., & Hansen, D. (2001). *Blueprints for violence prevention* (NCJ 187079). Washington, DC: U.S. Department of Justice, Office of Justice Programs, Office of Juvenile Justice and Delinquency Prevention.

Miller-Johnson, S., Lochman, J. E., Cole, J. D., Terry, R., & Hyman, C. (1998). Comorbidity of conduct and depressive problems at sixth grade: Substance use outcomes across adolescence. *Journal of Abnormal Child Psychology, 26,* 221–232.

Murray, D. M., Pirie, P., Luepker, R. V., & Pallonen, U. (1989). Five- and six-year follow-up results from four seventh-grade smoking prevention strategies. *Journal of Behavioral Medicine, 12,* 207–218.

Newcomb, M. D., Maddahian, E., & Bentler, P. M. (1986). Risk factors for drug use among adolescents: Concurrent and longitudinal analyses. *American Journal of Public Health, 76,* 525–531.

National Institutes of Health (NIH). (2006). *Final statement: National Institutes of Health state-of-the-science conference statement, tobacco use: Prevention, cessation, and control.* Retrieved January 18, 2007, from http://consensus.nih.gov/2006/ TobaccoStatementFinal090506.pdf

Patterson, G. R., Reid, J. B., & Dishion, T. J. (1992). *Antisocial boys: A social interactional approach* (Vol. 4). Eugene, OR: Castalia.

Pentz, M. A., Dwyer, J. H., MacKinnon, D. P., Flay, B. R., Hansen, W. B., Wang, E., et al. (1989). A multicommunity trial for primary prevention of adolescent drug abuse. *Journal of American Medical Association, 261,* 3259–3266.

Pentz, M. A., Johnson, C. A., Dwyer, J. H., MacKinnon, D. M., Hansen, W. B., & Flay, B. R. (1992). A comprehensive community approach to adolescent drug abuse prevention: Effects on cardiovascular disease risk behaviors. *Annals of Medicine, 21,* 219–222.

Perry, C. L., Killen, J. D., Telch, M. J., Slinkard, L. A., & Danaher, B. G. (1980). Modifying smoking behavior of teenagers: A school-based intervention. *American Journal of Public Health, 70,* 722–725.

Peterson, A. V., Jr., Kealey, K. A., Mann, S. L. Marek, P. M., & Sarason, I. G. (2000). Hutchinson smoking prevention project: Long-term randomized trial in school-based tobacco use prevention—Results on smoking. *Journal of the National Cancer Institute, 92*(24), 1979–1991.

Rao, U., Daley, S. E., & Hammen, C. (2000). Relationship between depression and substance use disorders in adolescent women during the transition to adulthood. *Journal of the American Academy of Child and Adolescent Psychiatry, 39,* 215–222.

Read, J. P., Wood, M. D., & Capone, C. (2005). A prospective investigation of relations between social influences and alcohol involvement during the transition into college. *Journal of Studies on Alcohol, 66,* 23–34.

Robins, L. N., & Przybeck, T. R. (1985). Age of onset of drug use as a factor in drug and other disorders. In C. I. Jones & R. J. Battjes (Eds.), *Etiology of drug abuse: Implications for prevention* (pp. 178–192). Rockville, MD: National Institute on Drug Abuse.

Rohde, P., Lewinsohn, P. M., & Seeley, J. R. (1991). Comorbidity of unipolar depression: II. Comorbidity with other mental disorders in adolescents and adults. *Journal of Abnormal Psychology, 54,* 653–660.

School Health Policies and Programs Study (SHPPS). (2007). Tobacco use prevention: Health education. *Journal of School Health, 77*(8). Retrieved February 4, 2008, from http://www.cdc.gov/HealthyYouth/shpps/2006/factsheets/pdf/FS_Tobacco_SHPPS2006.pdf

Severson, H. H. (1984). Adolescent social drug use: School prevention programs. *School Psychology Review, 13,* 150–160.

Severson, H. H., Arthun, C., Widdop, C., Shaw, T., Christiansen, S., Sarnoff-Wood, A., et al. (2007, October). Tobacco world: Interactive tobacco prevention for middle school students. Presented at the National Conference on Tobacco or Health, Minneapolis, MN.

Severson, H. H., Danaher, B. G., & Tyler, M. (2009, June). MyLastDip.com: Developmentand initial enrollment. Poster presented at the National Conference on Tobacco or Health, Phoenix, AZ.

Skara, S., & Sussman, S. (2003). A review of 25 long-term adolescent tobacco and other drug use prevention program evaluations. *Preventive Medicine: An International Journal Devoted to Practice and Theory, 37*(5), 451–474.

Substance Abuse and Mental Health Services Administration (SAMHSA). (2007). *Results from the 2006 National Survey on Drug Use and Health: Detailed tables. Table 4.3b.* Washington, DC: U.S. Department of Health and Human Services, Office of Applied Studies. Retrieved February 15, 2008, from http://oas.samhsa.gov/NSDUH/2k6nsduh/tabs/sect4petabs1to4.pdf

Sussman, S. (2001). School-based tobacco use prevention and cessation: Where are we going? *American Journal of Health Behavior, 25*(3), 191–199.

Sussman, S. (2002). Effects of sixty-six adolescent tobacco use cessation trials and seventeen prospective studies of self-initiated quitting. *Tobacco Induced Diseases, 1,* 35–81.

Sussman, S., Dent, C. W., Burton, D., Stacy, A. W., & Flay, B. R. (1995). *Developing school-based tobacco use prevention and cessation programs.* Thousand Oaks, CA: SAGE.

Sussman, S., Miyano, J., Rohrbach, L. A., Dent, C. W., & Sun, P. (2007). Six-month and one-year effects of Project EX-4: A classroom-based smoking prevention and cessation intervention program. *Addictive Behaviors, 32,* 3005–3014.

Sussman, S., Sun, P., & Dent, C. W. (2006). A meta-analysis of teen cigarette smoking cessation. *Health Psychology, 25,* 249–257.

Sussman, S. Y., Dent, C. W., Simon, T. R., Stacy, A. W., Burton, D., & Flay, B. R. (1993). Identification of which high-risk youth smoke cigarettes regularly. *Health Values, 17,* 42–53.

Swendsen, J. D., & Merikangas, K. R. (2000). The comorbidity of depression and substance use disorders. *Clinical Psychology Review, 20*(2), 173–189.

Swisher, J. D., Crawford, J. L., Goldstein, R., & Yura, M. (1971). Drug education: Pushing or preventing? *Peabody Journal of Education, 49,* 68–75.

Tobler, N. S. (1992). Drug prevention programs can work: Research findings. *Journal of Addictive Diseases, 11*(3), 1–28.

Tobler, N. S., Lessard, T., Marshall, D., Ochshorn, P, & Roona, M. (1999). Effectiveness of school based drug prevention programs for marijuana use. *School Psychology International 20,* 105–137.

Tobler, N. S., Roona, M. R., Ochshorn, P., Marshall, D. G., Streke, A. V., & Trackpole, K. M. (2000). School based adolescent drug prevention programs: 1998 meta-analysis. *Journal of Primary Prevention, 20*(4), 275–336.

Tolan, P., Szapocznik, J., & Sambrano, S. (2007). *Preventing youth substance abuse.* Washington, DC: American Psychological Association.

U.S. Department of Health and Human Services (USDHHS). (1988). *The health consequences of smoking: Nicotine addiction: A report of the surgeon general* (DHHS Publication No. CDC 88-8406). Washington, DC: U.S. Department of Health and Human Services, Public Health Service, Centers for Disease Control and Prevention, National Center for Chronic Disease Prevention and Health Promotion, Office on Smoking and Health.

U.S. Department of Health and Human Services (USDHHS). (1994). *Preventing tobacco use among young people: A report of the surgeon general.* Atlanta, GA: U.S. Department of Health and Human Services, Public Health Service, Centers for Disease Control and Prevention, National Center for Chronic Disease Prevention and Health Promotion, Office on Smoking and Health.

Webster-Stratton, C., & Reid, M. J. (2003). The incredible years parents, teachers, and children training series: A multifaceted treatment approach for young children with conduct problems. In A. E. Kazdin (Ed.), *Evidence based psychotherapy for children and adolescents* (pp. 224–240). New York: Guilford Press.

Wiehe, S. E., Garrison, M. M., Christakis, D. A., Ebel, B. E., & Rivara, F. P. (2005). A systematic review of school-based smoking prevention trials with long-term follow-up. *Journal of Adolescent Health, 36,* 162–169.

Willard, J. C., & Schoenborn, C. A. (1995). Relationship between cigarette smoking and other unhealthy behaviors among our nation's youth: United States, 1992. *Advance Data from Vital and Health Statistics, 263,* 1–12. Retrieved from the CDC, National Center for Health Statistics website: http://www.cdc.gov/nchs/data/ad/ad263.pdf

Wood, M. D., Read, J. P., Mitchell, R. E., & Brand, N. H. (2004). Do parents still matter? Parent and peer influences on alcohol involvement among recent high school graduates. *Psychology of Addictive Behaviors, 18,* 19–30.

Zucker, R. (2003). Causal structure of alcohol use and problems in early life: Multilevel etiology and implications for prevention. In A. Biglan, M. C. Wang, & H. J. Walberg (Eds.), *Preventing youth problems.* New York: Kluwer Academic/Plenum Press.

CHAPTER 10

Building Safe and Healthy Schools to Promote School Success: Critical Issues, Current Challenges, and Promising Approaches

Jeffrey R. Sprague
Hill M. Walker
Institute on Violence and Destructive Behavior, University of Oregon

INTRODUCTION

Creating and maintaining a safe and healthy school environment, one in which children and youth can be free of fear from all forms of violence and able to learn and develop freely, remains a major concern in the United States. Improving school safety is an important priority, even though the most serious forms of violent juvenile crime (i.e., rape, sexual assault, robbery, aggravated assault, and homicide) rarely occur in schools.

Every school in the United States has been affected by the changed landscape of school safety and security. Electronic and mechanical approaches that involve the use of sophisticated technology to solve school security problems are now standard fare in many school settings, especially those serving urban areas (Green, 1999). Crisis intervention planning and staff training for a potential school tragedy are now required elements in the operational procedures of many school districts and individual schools (Paine & Sprague, 2002). Schools serving deteriorating urban communities and neighborhoods routinely employ public safety and school resource officers as part of the regular school staff, and this practice is spreading rapidly to suburban communities as well (Atkinson & Kipper, 1999). Violence prevention curricula are used routinely to teach anger management and conflict-resolution skills to all students in thousands of schools. For example, the Second Step Violence Prevention Curriculum, developed by the Committee for Children (2002, 2008), is currently used in 25,000 U.S. schools.

Federal agencies, including the U.S. Office of Safe and Drug-Free Schools (now under the Office of Homeland Security), have created expert panels and technical

Address all correspondence and feedback on this chapter to Jeff Sprague at jeffs@uoregon.edu.

assistance documents to review and recommend intervention approaches that will enhance school safety and guide schools and communities when responding to a violent incident (Poland, 1994). School officials are now open to preventive approaches that were given scant attention just a few years ago. More ominously, enormous pressures are mounting among educators to profile potentially at-risk students and to identify those considered most likely to commit an act of school violence, even though acceptable and valid methods for accomplishing this goal remain obscure, and the risks to the individual student can be severe (Cornell, 2006). With the exception of attempts to profile potential school shooters, the *collective* impact of these changes is generally positive and has contributed to safer and more effective schools.

Although most schools in the United States remain relatively safe places for children, youth, and the adults who teach and support them (Dinkes, Cataldi, & Lin-Kelly, 2007), no school is immune from antisocial behaviors and the potential for violence, and some schools have serious problems with violence. The extent of the challenge will differ in intensity and frequency across schools, districts, and communities. It is well known that the onset and development of antisocial behavior are associated with a variety of school, community, and family risk factors (Sprague et al., 2002; Walker, Colvin, & Ramsey, 1995). The challenge is to reduce the number and intensity of these risk factors and to buffer their impact where possible.

School leaders and administrators face extreme challenges in this regard and seek access to the best, most reliable information available for making schools safer and free of violence. Federal reports now regularly provide a detailed picture of school safety and school climate. In general, the picture is clearer than it was 10 years ago, and, fortunately, some forms of violence are on the decline.

From 1992 to 1999, a consistent pattern was observed in the number of homicides at school (Dinkes et al., 2007). During this period, between 28 and 34 homicides of school-age youth occurred at school in each school year. The number of school-associated homicides declined from 33 to 13 between the 1998–1999 and 1999–2000 school years. Homicides at school increased from 11 to 21 between the 2000–2001 and 2004–2005 school years, and dropped to 14 in 2005–2006. The percentage of youth homicides occurring at school remained at less than 2% of the total number of youth homicides, even though the absolute number of homicides of school-age youth at school varied across the years. Between the 1992–1993 and 2004–2005 school years, from one to eight school-age youth committed suicide at school each year, with no consistent pattern of increase or decrease. Figure 1 illustrates this multiyear pattern.

TRENDS IN SCHOOL VIOLENCE AND PREVENTION

Traditionally, schools have been considered havens where our children and youth could learn, achieve, and develop in relative safety. Over the past two decades, however, our society has been galvanized and shocked by the growth in youth violence and crime. The spillover of youth violence and crime into school settings has changed

Figure 1. Number of homicides and suicides of youth ages 5–18 at school, 1992–2006.

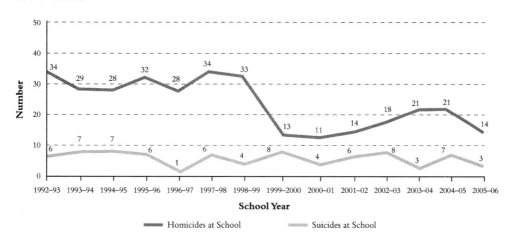

Note. From *Indicators of school crime and safety: 2007* (NCES 2008–021/NCJ 219553), by R. Dinkes, E. F. Cataldi, & W. Lin-Kelly, 2007, Washington, DC: National Center for Education Statistics, Institute of Education Sciences, U.S. Department of Education, and Bureau of Justice Statistics, Office of Justice Programs, U.S. Department of Justice. In the public domain. Data for the 2005–2006 school year are considered preliminary.

our collective perceptions of school safety and caused severe disruptions in the social ecology of schools. The following material provides an overview and analysis of these developments and offers some solutions as to how educators and the larger society should respond to them.

Factors Contributing to School Violence

A major variable influencing school violence is today's deviant peer culture (Dishion, Dodge, & Lansford, 2006). Increasingly, youth are immersed in a peer culture that is coarse, crude, cruel, uncaring, and often destructive to an individual's self-esteem. Bullying, sexual harassment, and mean-spirited teasing are common behaviors in many of today's school settings, and they poison the schools' social climates (Swearer & Cary, 2007). These destructive processes are often encouraged and supported by the presence and attention of peer bystanders. Bullying and harassment may lead students to perceive schools as unsafe places, and in trying to ensure their own safety, they may begin to skip school activities or avoid certain places within school (Schreck & Miller, 2003). In the School Crime Supplement to the National Crime Victimization Survey (U.S. Department of Commerce, 2005), students ages 12–18 were asked whether they had avoided school activities or one or more school places because they were fearful that someone might attack or harm them. In 2005, some 6% of students reported that they had avoided a school activity or one or more places in school in the previous 6 months because of fear of attack or harm (2% and 4%, respectively). Fully two thirds of school shooters interviewed by the U.S. Secret Service were teased and bullied in their school careers.

Students' experience of theft and violence at school and while going to and from school can lead to a disruptive and threatening environment, physical injury, and emotional stress, and can be an obstacle to student achievement (Walker & Epstein, 2001). Data from the National Crime Victimization Survey show that in 2005 students ages 12 to 18 were victims of about 1.5 million nonfatal crimes (i.e., theft plus violent crime) while they were at school and about 1.2 million nonfatal crimes while they were away from school. These figures represent total crime victimization rates of 57 crimes per 1,000 students at school, and 47 crimes per 1,000 students away from school (Dinkes et al., 2007).

Between 1992 and 2005, the total crime victimization rates for students ages 12 to 18 *declined* both at school and away from school. This pattern held for the total crime rate as well as for thefts, violent crimes, and serious violent crimes. However, theft was more likely to occur in school than outside of school (868,000 reported incidents, compared with 610,000). This translates into 33 thefts per 1,000 students at school, compared with 23 thefts per 1,000 students away from school. At the same time, the rates for serious violent crime were *lower* at school than away from school in each year from 1992 to 2005. Students in suburban areas had a lower rate of violent victimization at school and away from school than students in urban areas, while no difference was found between the rates of violent victimization in suburban and rural areas.

It is remarkable that so many of today's youth are, in some instances, willing to "write off" the rest of their lives to settle their grievances by using violence against their peers, teachers, and even parents. Many of these youth are very likely suicidal, extremely depressed, and in urgent need of mental health services and support (Cornell, 2006). At-risk students who hold these views and manifest these behavioral characteristics are at severe risk to themselves as well as to key social agents in their lives. In addition, they can represent a serious threat to the safety of the entire school population.

Children and youth in the United States are at increased risk for antisocial behavior and negative school and life outcomes. This increased risk is largely due to the changing social, economic, and cultural conditions of our society over the past several decades (Loeber & Farrington, 2001; Sprague & Walker, 2005). Growing numbers of children and youth are exposed to a host of risk factors such as poverty, abuse, neglect, criminal or substance use by parents, harsh and inconsistent parenting practices, and limited exposure to language and reading prior to the beginning of their school careers (Patterson, Reid, & Dishion, 1992; Reid & Patterson, 1989). As a result, the number of children and youth with aggressive, noncompliant, and acting-out behaviors in schools has been rising steadily. These students are entering the public school system unprepared for the experience of schooling and often bring emerging antisocial behavior patterns with them (Loeber & Farrington). Antisocial behavior and high levels of aggression evidenced early in a child's life are among the best predictors of academic failure and delinquency in later years (Patterson et al., 1992).

The statistics cited above leave little doubt that the declining social conditions in American society have spilled over into the process of schooling in very unfortunate ways. Thousands of students today enter school with a history of exposure to multiple and overlapping risks, such as the violence described above, in addition to poverty, divorce, and domestic violence. These risk factors negatively affect today's students in family, school, neighborhood, and community contexts. The cumulative effect of these risks is to place vulnerable children and youth on a pathway to destructive outcomes that are manifested in adolescence and young adulthood (e.g., drug and alcohol abuse, delinquency, violent acts, and criminal behavior). In the absence of off-setting protective factors or the ability to access key support services and structures, it is unlikely that these individuals will be able to get off this destructive path if it has not been accomplished by the end of the primary grades (Biglan, Wang, & Walberg, 2003; Kauffman, 1999). Rather, these individuals will likely require continued supports and services throughout their lives to reduce the ongoing harm they cause to themselves and others.

These noted problems compete directly with the instructional mission of schools. The result is decreased academic achievement and a lower quality of life for students and staff alike. These outcomes illustrate the clear link that exists between declining safety in the school, school violence, and academic achievement. It is not possible to achieve national educational goals and meaningful reform without addressing these disturbing conditions (Colvin, Kame'enui, & Sugai, 1993; Elias et al., 1997).

Major Trends in Youth Violence Prevention and School Safety

Efforts to improve school safety have been expressed in five major trends over the past two decades, each of which continues to shape and define the critical issues regarding school safety. These five major trends, which now overlap and blend together, include (a) responses to violent juvenile crime, (b) prevention of and responses to mass school shootings, (c) integration and implementation of universal prevention initiatives in schools, (d) interpretation of school violence as domestic terrorism, and (e) national efforts to address child and youth mental health issues, with schools as a center of intervention efforts.

Responses to Violent Juvenile Crime

The overall juvenile crime rate and the alarming rates of interpersonal violence in families and communities have been associated with a dramatic escalation in the number of children who bring antisocial behavior patterns to the schooling experience. In the past several decades, the number of children and families displaying antisocial behavior patterns has surged significantly and remains high (Patterson, Reid, & Dishion, 1992; Reid, Patterson, & Snyder, 2002). Although violent juvenile crime peaked in 1992 and has since declined, concerns about the proportion of antisocial and violent youth in schools and communities remain (Dinkes et al., 2007; Loeber &

Farrington, 2001). Rates of incarceration of adults and youth in the United States are among the highest in the world, and clearly represent an ineffective response to this growing problem (Lipsey, 1992).

Prevention of and Responses to Mass School Shootings

In the 1990s, the United States and its public schools were profoundly shaken by a series of school shootings that changed the landscape of school security and destroyed, perhaps forever, the sense of relative safety that students, families, and educators traditionally held about the schooling process. All concerned with the schooling of vulnerable children and youth were powerfully affected by these terrible events. Even though schools are one of the *safest* places for children and youth, compared with other social settings, Americans no longer regard school settings as safe havens, in which students are free to develop academically and socially, unburdened by concern for their personal safety (Kingery & Walker, 2002). In the wake of the school shootings in the mid- to late 1990s, students and parents were traumatized on a broad scale by fears of school tragedies and concerns about lack of school security.

The pattern of school shootings has continued into the 21st century, punctuated by the 2005 incident in Red Lake, Minnesota, where a 16-year-old killed his grandfather and a companion, then went to school, where he killed a teacher, a security guard, five students, and finally himself, leaving a total of 10 dead. In addition, school shootings occurred that involved adults as perpetrators, including the 2006 incident in Nickel Mines, Pennsylvania, where a man entered the one-room West Nickel Mines Amish School and shot 10 schoolgirls, ranging in age from 6 to 13 years, and then shot himself. Five of the girls and the criminal died. The phenomenon has also spread to college campuses, including the 2007 incident at Virginia Tech, where a student killed two other students in a dorm, then killed 30 more 2 hours later in a classroom building. His suicide brought the death toll to 33, making this shooting rampage the most deadly in U.S. history.

An early significant response to these shooting tragedies was the passage of the Gun-Free Schools Act of 1994, which almost 15 years ago required that any child or youth possessing a weapon in school be expelled for 1 calendar year. This act has resulted in a substantial increase in the number of suspensions and expulsions in schools, but little is known about the follow-up support or treatment of these youth (Cornell & Sheras, 2006).

Integration and Implementation of Universal Prevention Initiatives in Schools

Mass school shootings, while alarming, remain extremely low-frequency events (Centers for Disease Control and Prevention, 2008). However, schools and communities need to be prepared to prevent and respond to such incidents. The U.S. Department of Education's Readiness and Emergency Management for Schools Technical Assistance Center (http://rems.ed.gov/index.cfm) has been established to provide technical and grant assistance. School personnel also have recognized the power and positive impact of their daily interactions with students. This need has been expressed best in the national initiative to promote school-wide positive behavior supports (SWPBS; http://www.pbis.org; Sugai & Horner, 2002), funded by the U.S. Office of Special Education Program. (Chapter 16 in this book describes these practices in more detail.)

Evidence suggests that sustained use of SWPBS practices can alter the trajectory of at-risk children toward destructive outcomes and prevent the onset of high-risk behavior in typically developing children (O'Donnell, Hawkins, Catalano, Abbott, & Day, 1995). Effective and sustained implementation of SWPBS is expected to create a more responsive school climate that supports the twin goals of schooling for all children: academic achievement and social development (Sprague, Sugai, & Walker, 1998; Sugai, Horner, & Gresham, 2002).

As of 2008, more than 7,000 schools across the country have actively implemented SWPBS. These schools are reporting reductions in problem behavior, improved perceptions of school safety, and better academic outcomes (Horner et al., in press). Although no direct evidence links SWPBS implementation and reduced school violence, there is some evidence of an increased perception of safety in SWPBS schools (Horner et al., in press).

Interpretation of School Violence as Domestic Terrorism

Two series of events sparked an interpretation of school shootings as domestic terrorism. First, there were the famous planned mass school shootings that occurred in the United States in the mid- to late-1990s and those that still occur nearly annually. Second, events following the September 11, 2001, World Trade Center attacks spurred the federal government to move the Office of Safe and Drug Free Schools under the newly established Office of Homeland Security.

A watershed event in the history of school shootings occurred on March 24, 1998, when the safety of the Westside Middle School in Jonesboro, Arkansas, was shattered by an act of domestic terrorism planned and carried out by two young students who attended the school. Five people were killed—four students and a teacher—and 10 were injured, including one teacher. The perpetrators were two students, 13-year-old Mitchell Johnson and 11-year-old Andrew Golden, who were wearing camouflaged clothes and shooting ambush style from the woods. The youth arranged for a fire alarm to be set off; then they shot at teachers and students leaving the building. Many of the school shooting tragedies that followed Jonesboro were similar in type and scope, and their cumulative effect was to permanently alter approaches to school security and student safety. The total number of students killed and wounded on school grounds in the decade of the 1990s was close to the number of casualties in earlier decades; however, the magnitude and impact of the tragedies during the latter half of the decade tended to be *qualitatively* different in terms of the following factors:

- The number of people killed and wounded *per incident*
- The randomness by which victims were selected as targets

- The careful planning and conspiratorial nature of these school shootings
- The use of school shootings as an instrument in settling scores for grievances, real or imagined

Because these features also characterize acts of terror, the tragedies generated unprecedented levels of concern and outrage. In particular, the tragedy at Columbine High School in Columbine, Colorado, stands out. On April 20, 1999, two students, Eric Harris and Dylan Klebold, embarked on a planned massacre, killing 12 students and a teacher and injuring 24 others before committing suicide. It is the fourth-deadliest school massacre in United States history, after the 1927 Bath School disaster, the 2007 Virginia Tech massacre, and the 1966 University of Texas massacre, and the deadliest for an American high school.

The event reflected a dedicated commitment by two high school students to redress their grievances through revenge-seeking actions aimed at innocent students and school personnel. The shock, grief, and outrage that followed the tragedy of Columbine galvanized the federal government into taking a series of dramatic actions geared toward improving school safety. One of these actions was the creation of the *Early Warning/Timely Response* document to help schools enhance their overall safety (Dwyer, Osher, & Warger, 1998). The document, jointly sponsored by the U.S. Departments of Justice and Education, was produced by a 25-member panel of experts that included the authors of this chapter. All 125,000 public and private U.S. schools received a copy of *Early Warning/Timely Response* during the fall of 1998.

In a related action, the U.S. Departments of Education, Health and Human Services, and Justice developed the Safe Schools/Healthy Students Initiative in 1999. The initiative is a discretionary grant program that provides students, schools, and communities with federal funding to implement a coordinated set of activities, programs, and services that focus on promoting healthy childhood development and preventing violence and abuse of alcohol and other drugs. Grantees must demonstrate a partnership with their local public mental health authority, law enforcement agency, and juvenile justice program and be able to submit a single application for federal funds to support a variety of coordinated activities, curricula, programs, and services. Grants totaling approximately $50 million–$100 million have been awarded to communities annually since this program's inception in 1999. Although a local evaluation is required of grantees, little is known about the relative efficacy of these initiatives (Jimerson & Furlong, 2006).

Finally, analyses of the characteristics of school shooters by the U.S. Secret Service and a threat assessment protocol developed by the Federal Bureau of Investigation (FBI) provide valuable information aimed at helping school personnel assess the level of risk presented by student threats (Fein, Vossekuil, & Holden, 1995; Vossekuil, Fein, Reddy, Borum, & Modzeleski, 2002). These actions have raised awareness of the factors that contribute to a lack of school safety and have stimulated a broad range of protective activities by schools and communities.

Integration of Mental Health Interventions in Schools

Mental health conditions that directly interfere with students' ability to meet the academic expectations of schools certainly contribute to an increased risk of academic and social failure, including school violence. Students whose mental health needs are unidentified or inadequately addressed are at increased risk of juvenile delinquency and involvement in the criminal justice or mental health systems as young adults (See Mash & Dozois, 2003).

The surgeon general's report on mental health (U.S. Department of Health and Human Services, 2001) indicated that 3–5% of school-age children are diagnosed with attention deficit hyperactivity disorder in a 6-month period, 5% of youth ages 9–17 are diagnosed with major depression, and the combined prevalence of various anxiety disorders for children ages 9–17 is 13%. About one fifth of the children and adolescents in the United States experience the signs and symptoms of a mental health adjustment problem in the course of a year.

In a recent survey of 83,000 representative elementary, middle, and high schools across the United States, Foster et al. (2005) found that 73% of the schools reported that "social, interpersonal, or family problems" were the most frequent mental health problems for males and females. For males, aggression or disruptive behavior and behavior problems associated with neurological disorders were the second and third most frequent problems. For females, anxiety and adjustment issues were the second and third most frequent problems.

Although these data suggest that a substantial percentage of students manifest conditions that negatively affect their mental health, many who have such needs are not identified (Hoagwood et al., 2007). The failure to adequately address students' mental health adjustment as dynamic, or changing, may be related to a lack of proper screening and identification practices; that is, much of the knowledge is based on discrete points in time for a child or a context for behavior, rather than taking into account the changes that occur in children's mental health status over time (Mash & Dozois, 2003).

CONCEPTUAL MODELS OF SCHOOL SAFETY

The *absence* of violence is only one element among a larger constellation of positive factors that characterize safe and effective schools. Researchers have reframed the issue of school violence within a conceptual model of school safety that (a) includes both developmental and educational concepts, and (b) emphasizes prevention and schooling effectiveness (Jimerson & Furlong, 2006). Effectively coping with school violence requires careful attention to a broad range of considerations; for example, schools that are free of violence are also effective at teaching and evince a caring, nurturing, inclusive, and accepting environment.

Recognizing that no school can ever be made 100% safe, we wrote in 2005 that school safety is best conceptualized along a *bipolar* dimension (Sprague & Walker,

Figure 2. Bipolar dimensions of school safety.

Bipolar Dimensions and Attributes of Unsafe and Safe Schools With Associated Risk and Protective Factors

Unsafe Schools
(Lack of cohesion, chaotic, stressful, disorganized, poorly structured, ineffective, high risk, gang activity, violent incidents, unclear behavioral and academic expectations)

Safe Schools
(Effective, accepting, freedom from potential physical and psychological harm, absence of violence, nurturing, caring, and protective)

School-Based Risk Factors
- Poor design and use of school space
- Overcrowding
- Lack of caring but firm disciplinary procedures
- Insensitivity and poor accommodation to multicultural factors
- Student alienation
- Rejection of at-risk students by teachers and peers
- Anger and resentment at school routines and demands for conformity
- Poor supervision

School-Based Protective Factors
- Positive school climate and atmosphere
- Clear and high performance expectations for all students
- Inclusionary values and practices throughout the school
- Strong student bonding to the school environment and the schooling process
- High levels of student participation and parent involvement in schooling
- Provision of opportunities for skill acquisition and social development
- School-wide conflict resolution strategies

Note. From *Safe and Healthy Schools: Practical Prevention Strategies*, by J. R. Sprague & H. M. Walker, 2005, New York: Guilford Press. Reprinted with permission.

2005). This conception is illustrated along a continuum from unsafe to safe (see Figure 2). The relative safety of schools is represented in terms of the number and nature of the *risk* factors and *protective* factors that are present. As with individuals, risk factors and conditions move the school in the direction of *less safety*. The greater the number of risk factors or conditions, the greater the risk, and the longer they are in evidence, the greater is their destructive impact on the school's safety.

The protective factors listed in Figure 2 have the potential to buffer, offset, and reduce the destructive impact of risk conditions on the school's status and operation. Schools can be distributed along this dimension in terms of performance indicators that document how relatively safe or unsafe they are—for example, the number of victimization incidents in school; school and neighborhood crime; the number of disciplinary referrals, suspensions, and expulsions per student and for the whole school; academic achievement levels; attendance; the quality of the school's disciplinary practices; the school's social climate; the presence or absence of gang activity, and so on. Although there is no reliable composite index of these measures, one could be developed and used to locate an individual school along this continuum.

The continuum of school safety should not be thought of in absolute terms such as safe or unsafe, but rather in comparative terms such as *safer* versus *less safe*. It is the responsibility of school and community leaders to do everything in their power to maximize the safety and security of their schools. As the social conditions (e.g., family and community environments) in neighborhoods continue to deteriorate, the challenge for educators—of maintaining acceptable school safety levels—grows more difficult. A focus on school safety requires a greater investment of resources that would otherwise be allocated to the positive social and academic development of students.

More than 15 years ago, the American Psychological Association produced a superb synthesis of the knowledge base related to the prevalence of violence among youth and associated causal factors (APA, 1993). The Commission on Violence and Youth's report recommended approaches for addressing this problem that are still highly germane to the safety of today's schools and can be used to move a school toward greater security (Table 1).

Within the context of schooling, McEvoy and Welker (2000) analyzed the evidence base relating to academic underachievement, learning problems, and antisocial behavior. They make a persuasive case that the majority of failed attempts to make schools safer tend to have three negative characteristics in common:

Table 1. Youth Violence: Observations of the APA Commission on Violence and Youth

- Violence is not the human condition; it is learned behavior that is preventable.
- Violence cuts across all lines of culture and ethnicity; it is not exclusive to any single group or class.
- Prevention of violence requires education of and by all segments of society; it also requires a reassessment of how conflict is viewed and resolved.
- There are four individual social experiences that contribute powerfully to the increase in violence among children and youth: easy access to firearms (especially handguns), early involvement with drugs and alcohol, association with antisocial groups, and pervasive exposure to violent acts portrayed in the media.
- Schools must be a hub or key center of activity in the development of comprehensive, interagency interventions for the prevention and remediation of violent behavior.

Note. From *Violence and Youth: Psychology's Response. Volume 1: Summary Report of the American Psychological Association Commission on Violence and Youth*, by the American Psychological Association, 1993, Washington, DC: Author. Reprinted with permission.

1. The efforts have failed to take into account the *interrelationship* that exists among these three dimensions (i.e., academic underachievement, learning problems, and antisocial behavior).
2. They have tended to focus on characteristics and attributes of *individual* students, to the exclusion of the known risk factors and conditions that are predictive of antisocial behavior and underachievement.
3. They overlook the fact that school climate is a powerful variable in the *mix of causal factors* and needs to be addressed in the school safety agenda.

There is strong support for these school-wide interventions because they clearly communicate and enforce consistent behavioral expectations for all students and create a climate of competence and mutual respect within the school setting (Hahn et al., 2007). Examples of such programs include the Second Step Violence Prevention Curriculum (Frey, Hirschstein, & Guzzo, 2000), the school-wide positive behavior support (SWPBS) model (Horner, Sugai, Lewis-Palmer, & Todd, 2001), the Best Behavior staff development program (Sprague & Golly, 2004), and the school-wide ecological intervention approach (Nelson, Martella, & Marchand-Martella, 2002). All of these intervention models are empirically based; when assessed using both school-wide measures and measures of individual student behavior, they are shown to be effective if implemented with fidelity.

Although much remains to be discovered regarding the general and specific effects of the school-wide interventions listed above, there is encouraging evidence of their effectiveness. These programs typically are designed to be delivered to all students in a school, regardless of students' risk status. Hahn and colleagues (2007) conducted a comprehensive meta-analysis of school-wide programs, including those using cognitive and affective instruction, social skills instruction, environmental change strategies at the classroom or school level, peer mediation, and behavior modification programs. The results provide evidence that universal, school-based programs can decrease rates of violence among school-age children and youth. Program effects were consistent across all grade levels.

The knowledge base outlined above in Table 1 documents the broad range of progress that has been made in understanding the origins of antisocial behavior patterns, how they develop over the long term, and the risk and protective factors that account for them. However, the gap between what is known about effective intervention with these problems and actual practice in schools is far too wide and needs to be systematically addressed as part of larger community efforts (see Biglan et al., 2003). This gap is especially true in the context of school safety.

SOURCES OF VULNERABILITY OF SCHOOL SAFETY

Major areas of vulnerability with regard to school safety and security have been described and analyzed by Sprague and his colleagues (Sprague et al., 2002; Sprague & Walker, 2005). These authors designate the following areas as vulnerable to significant threats:

1. The design, use, and supervision of school space.
2. The administrative and management practices of the school.
3. The nature of the neighborhood and community served by the school.
4. The characteristics of the students enrolled.

These four factors are illustrated in Figure 3, which provides indicators of each type of school safety vulnerability. If an individual school registers a *positive* profile across these dimensions, it is much more likely to experience acceptable levels of safety and security than if it registers a *negative* profile, where many sources of vulnerability are in evidence. Any comprehensive approach to ensuring a school's safety should evaluate and address these dimensions of risk.

Design, Use, and Supervision of School Space

The architectural design and operation of school space can be an important source of vulnerability with regard to a school's overall safety, making the prevention and response to incidents of school violence more difficult. For example, the number of unlocked and unmonitored entrances to the school, the nature and amount of

Figure 3. Sources of vulnerability in school settings.

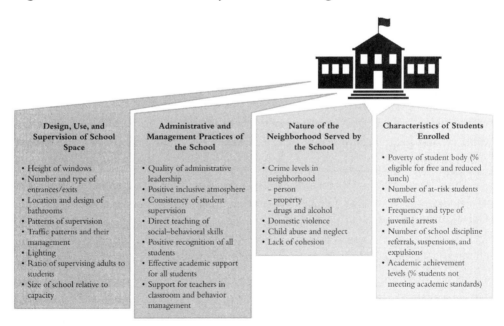

Note. From "Sources of Vulnerability to School Violence: Systems-Level Assessment and Strategies to Improve Safety and Climate," by J. Sprague, H. Walker, S. Sowards, C. Van Bloem, P. Ebethardt, and B. Marshall, 2002, in M. R. Shinn, H. M. Walker, and G. Stoner (Eds.), *Interventions for Academic and Behavior Problems II: Preventive and Remedial Approaches*, p. 298, Bethesda, MD: National Association of School Psychologists. Copyright 2002 by National Association of School Psychologists. Reprinted with permission.

supervision available for common areas (e.g., hallways, playgrounds, cafeterias), the location of bathrooms, the ability of school personnel to conduct surveillance of school grounds, and the size of hallways that are typically crowded with students during certain periods of the day are all areas that could be vulnerable. Areas that are found to be vulnerable require architectural retrofitting or allocation of staff resources, such as security personnel or additional supervisory staff members. School design and retrofitting to enhance school safety comes from the work of experts in crime prevention through environmental design (CPTED; Crowe, 2000). Schneider, Walker, and Sprague (2000) provide a thorough treatment of this topic specific to schools. The Schneider et al. book includes a description of key CPTED concepts and principles, the relevance of CPTED as a strategy for improving school safety and security, school-site CPTED evaluation procedures, case-study applications of CPTED principles, the role of architects in school design, and CPTED-based policy recommendations for consideration by school districts.

Administrative and Management Practices of the School

Research indicates that safer schools tend to be more effective schools and vice versa (Sprague et al., 2002). As such, the administrative and management practices of the school's leadership and staff have a tremendous influence on the social climate and overall safety of the school. All students should perceive themselves as accepted and valued members of the school's population; as fully able to participate in the extracurricular activities of the school; and as free from bullying, mean-spirited teasing, discrimination, or harassment. It is of critical importance that at-risk students who are socially marginalized and/or show signs of depression or other serious mental health problems receive the appropriate services and types of support (Stormshak, Connell, & Dishion, 2007). Effective administrative practices include using alternatives to traditional out-of-school suspension, systematic use of an objective threat assessment protocol, and frequent monitoring of disproportionate application of these procedures to minority children and youth (Cornell, 2006; Cornell & Sheras, 2006; Johns, Carr, & Hoots, 1997; Skiba & Knesting, 2001).

The Nature of the Neighborhood

The neighborhoods and communities served by schools have a direct influence on the school and its overall safety. Schools that serve neighborhoods with high frequencies of police calls, street crime, poverty, unsupervised youth, and deteriorating infrastructure and buildings are much more likely to be unsafe than those whose attendance areas do not have these characteristics (Crowe, 2000). It has been said that an individual school can be no safer than the neighborhoods and communities it serves. This statement may or may not hold true, depending on the social and environmental conditions under which the school operates. For example, some schools located in chaotic and dangerous urban environs are fortress-like structures that *appear* to be safer than their surrounding neighborhoods. Whenever possible, schools should be integrated into the communities they serve and be viewed as partners with the other local agencies that serve children, youth, and families. However, when violence and serious crime are common occurrences in proximal neighborhoods, realizing this goal may be difficult. In such situations, schools have very few options for improving the safety of the neighborhoods and communities they serve.

Characteristics of the Students Enrolled

The fourth source of vulnerability in Figure 3 is the overall school profile in terms of poverty level; number of students at risk for antisocial behavior and mental health problems; frequency and types of juvenile arrests; number of school referrals, suspensions, and expulsions; and academic achievement levels. These dimensions are related, to a very large extent, to how students behave in school and whether they display rule-governed forms of behavior. This vulnerability source provides the most direct avenue whereby the toxic conditions of society infiltrate and disrupt the process of schooling. Students who come from highly at-risk backgrounds and experience chaos and family and neighborhood stressors on a daily basis typically reflect these influences in how they behave in the school context. Too often, the consequences of these stressors are negative for the individual as well as the school environment.

The majority of attempts to make schools safe have focused on the student population and its behavioral characteristics, and a comprehensive school safety plan should include universal screening procedures (Sprague, Cook, Wright, & Sadler, 2008; Walker et al., 1990; Walker, Severson, & Feil, 1995). Universal screening procedures are designed to detect teacher-related adjustment problems (such as compliance with requests), peer-related adjustment problems (such as bully victimization or perpetration, affiliation with deviant peers), and school adjustment (such as attendance and work completion; Sprague et al., 2008). However, any comprehensive and successful school safety effort also must address the other three sources of vulnerability. The following section provides information and guidelines about how to assess a school's relative safety and to recognize the danger signs early in the risk-escalation process.

SCHOOL SAFETY STRATEGIES IN A THREE-TIERED MODEL: MOVING FROM ASSESSMENT TO INTERVENTION

Educators are inundated with advice regarding effective school safety interventions but receive scant help in integrating and sustaining effective practices. Any selection of interventions must be based on a thorough assessment of the school's overall functioning, with special attention to disciplinary referral patterns, suspensions and expulsions, self-reported violence perpetration and victimization, and the security of the school building and grounds (Boles, Biglan, & Smolkowski, in press; Irvin, Tobin, Sprague, Sugai, & Vincent, 2004; Schneider et al., 2000; Sprague et al., 2002; Sugai, Lewis-Palmer, Todd, & Horner, 2000). Thorough needs assessments in these areas (and others) can guide planning, avoid overlapping or conflicting services, and serve as the basis for evaluating change over time.

Recommendations from the surgeon general's report on school violence (2001) provide a compelling rationale for adopting a prevention approach in which the school is organized as a hub of intervention activities that focus on preventing the development of destructive antisocial peer networks and the reinforcement of deviancy. This report recommends, first, that "an intolerant attitude toward deviance" be established by focusing on breaking up antisocial peer networks and changing the social climate of the school. Second, it recommends that the public increase its commitment to school, so that academic success is accessible to all children and positive school climates are established. Third, the report recommends that students be taught and encouraged to display the skills and forms of behavior that enable them to respond adaptively to events that occasion and promote antisocial behavior, such as bullying and harassment or drug use.

This landmark report is buttressed by parallel recommendations from at least two other reports that address the challenges of bringing effective interventions to scale. Greenberg and his colleagues have outlined the research on effective, school-based interventions for antisocial behavior at the primary, secondary, and tertiary levels of prevention (Greenberg, Domitrovich, & Bumbarger, 1999). The authors and others have recommended that schools offer coordinated, integrated interventions at all three levels (Gottfredson, 2001; Walker & Epstein, 2001).

The challenge then becomes how to give schools the capacity to adopt and sustain the processes, organizational structures, and systems that will enable them to carry out promising and proven interventions (Fixsen, Naoom, Blase, Friedman, & Wallace, 2005). Gottfredson and Gottfredson conducted the National Study of Delinquency Prevention in Schools, the first of its kind. They argue convincingly that the problem is not the availability of *effective* programs (i.e., those that work), but rather that the problem is one of *efficacy* (i.e., helping typical schools adopt and carry out the interventions and approaches in a manner that demonstrates their effectiveness). It is likely, therefore, that the problem of overlapping or poorly implemented intervention approaches is affected by a lack of useful needs assessment information to guide the implementation process (Gottfredson & Gottfredson, 2001; Gottfredson, Gottfredson, & Czeh, 2000).

Schools have always been judged by how well their students perform academically. Although destructive or violent behavior is a top concern and a direct influence on academic performance, systematic approaches to assessing schools on the basis of *behavioral* success or failure are not currently well developed. However, U.S. schools are experiencing a strong push toward accountability on just that front (Sprague et al., 2008). We recommend the following broad strategies for integrating school safety and prevention initiatives that are based on empirical evidence as well as on practical experience:

1. Conduct a school safety needs assessment.

   a. Begin with the Oregon School Safety Survey (Sprague, Colvin, & Irvin, 1995).
   b. Conduct a CPTED analysis and make needed changes in school architecture and supervision.
   c. Use a standardized threat assessment and follow-up protocol.

2. Develop a comprehensive school safety and crisis-response plan.
3. Conduct universal screening for antisocial behavior.
4. Develop and implement a three-tier intervention plan.

   a. Create a positive, inclusive school climate and culture.
   b. Address the peer culture and its challenges of deviant peer group formation, bullying, and harassment.
   c. Collaborate with parents to make the school safer.
   d. Support at-risk youth throughout their school careers.

Conduct a School Safety Needs Assessment

Parents, schools, and community leaders need to make informed judgments about which systems are in place to prevent school violence and antisocial behavior. Title IV of the No Child Left Behind (NCLB) Act requires public schools to focus on information from a comprehensive needs assessment in building and maintaining a school environment that is safe and conducive to learning.

To receive funds under Title IV, Part A, schools must adhere to the NCLB Principles of Effectiveness, as follows:

1. Assess the school safety, risk, and protective influences on the school.
2. Establish measurable goals and objectives for improvement that are based on those identified needs.
3. Base projected changes on appropriate measurements.
4. Use evidence-based interventions for effecting improvement.

School safety plans must target what is required for the school to become safer and describe the activities or programs to be adopted that will address those targets. These activities and programs must show research evidence of effectiveness in improving school safety, involve parents in the assessment process, and include performance measures to gauge effectiveness. In addition, each school district must have a comprehensive plan for school safety that includes policies, security procedures, prevention activities, crisis response procedures, and a code of conduct for students that incorporates a "wrong and harmful" message about illegal drug use and violence. The plan needs to be made available to the public for review and comment.

Because of the importance of gathering and maintaining consistent data that provide a picture of how a school is performing, Title IV requires school districts to monitor and report truancy rates; suspensions and expulsions related to drugs and violence; the incidence, prevalence, and age of onset of alcohol use, drug use, and violence by youths; and incidents of criminal activity on school property. As part of this process, youth are also asked about their perceptions of health risks.

School safety assessment procedures can be relatively straightforward. The assessment process should begin with tools such as the Oregon School Safety Survey (Sprague et al., 1995). A tool such as this allows stakeholders to provide input on particular areas of concern to them. This free survey should be completed annually by all key school stakeholders (e.g., parents, teachers, administrators, classified staff, and students). The survey asks respondents to rate the presence and extent of 17 risk and 16 protective factors associated with increases or decreases in school violence and discipline problems. Risk factors include poverty, child abuse, graffiti, bullying, and deteriorating physical facilities. Protective factors include positive teacher–student relationships, parent involvement, student supervision, and high academic expectations. A Likert rating scale of 1 to 4 ("Not at all" to "Extensive") is used to produce average ratings for each item. The survey has been shown to be sensitive to intervention effects (Horner et al., in press).

Conduct a CPTED Analysis and Make Changes in School Architecture and Supervision

Every school can benefit from an assessment of its environmental design to evaluate whether the school is a safe and secure place to learn and work. A school site riddled with criminal activity has an obvious need for such an assessment, but even campuses that seem at first glance to be orderly and secure may, when inspected, be found to present a multitude of risks.

It takes only one tragedy to make the benefits of preventive assessment crystal clear in hindsight for any school. Even relatively minor environmental flaws are worthy of attention and action. For example, if someone trips over broken steps and is injured because of deferred maintenance, serious litigation may result. If nothing is done to actively discourage drug dealers or other criminals from entering school campuses, the district incurs a risk of liability that may threaten its insurability. Whenever there is a history of trouble, or if future problems can be anticipated, one can reasonably anticipate eventual personal injuries, as well as subsequent legal actions.

CPTED assessment procedures can be relatively straightforward to apply in schools (Crowe, 2000; Schneider et al., 2000). The CPTED assessment process begins with a close look at the neighborhood. Typically, neighborhood and community problems spill over into the school setting. Conditions noted during evaluation of the community or neighborhood will give school officials clues as they devise remedies geared toward making both the school and the neighborhood safer for their students. An evaluation team begins by working slowly around the outside of the school while taking notes, starting away from the school building and circling back in. A team may include an administrator, a teacher, a student, a custodian, and a school resource officer. A diverse team can provide a broad perspective and valuable information to this process. Once the walk-through is completed, more extensive planning and recommendations are completed by a CPTED expert, such as a local architect, or by a police expert in school safety.

Use a Standardized Threat Assessment and Follow-Up Protocol

A child who threatens violent behavior obviously cannot be ignored, and a threat assessment protocol must be in place (Cornell & Sheras, 2006). The work of Cornell and his colleagues at the University of Virginia is exemplary and represents the best empirical knowledge of threat assessment protocols for schools. They recommend the establishment of a threat assessment team that includes school administrators, school resource officers, a school psychologist and/or counselor, and teachers. A clear set of steps are specified in conducting a student threat assessment, including a follow-up school safety plan, and are based on the standards put forth by the U.S. Secret Service and the FBI (Fein et al., 1995).

The investment of effort and resources needed to create and enact these components will vary by school site and neighborhood. The higher the crime-risk status of the neighborhoods served by a particular school, the less safe that school is likely to be and the greater the effort and resources that will be required. Regardless of the degree of risk that exists, individual schools can systematically assess and address a number of risk and protective factors as part of an overall school safety enhancement plan.

Develop a Comprehensive School Safety and Crisis-Response Plan

The four primary approaches to consider when securing a school to address identified safety concerns are (a) the appropriate use of school security technology, (b) employment of school resource officers, (c) use of CPTED principles and techniques, and (d) use of a standardized threat assessment protocol (Cornell & Sheras, 2006). Applied in combination, these approaches can be effective in reducing the probability of a school shooting tragedy. Currently, the first, second, and third approaches are built into the federally funded Safe Schools/Healthy Students initiative being implemented in many school districts across the country. Considerable progress has been made in the development and appropriate use of security technology to make schools safer without turning them into fortresses (Green, 1999).

The key elements that should be addressed in a comprehensive school safety plan are as follows:

1. School safety audits that evaluate vulnerabilities due to structural characteristics of the building and patterns of building usage.
2. A crisis intervention plan that allows school personnel to respond to and control crises that have potential for violence or reduced school safety (Paine & Sprague, 2002).

3. A well-established communication plan that provides interactive linkages between school personnel, public safety, and parents.

These three elements would be essential to improving the safety and security of any school building and grounds. Well-developed procedures exist for assessing a school's degree of risk and for implementing each of the components listed above. These elements are also being used increasingly in schools across the country. School administrators should be aware of the status, advantages, and limitations of these elements when considering implementation of school safety options and strategies.

Conduct Universal Screening for Antisocial Behavior

In the past decade, the use of universal screening procedures to identify students who are struggling academically and behaviorally has been expanded considerably. For example, the emergence of comprehensive progress monitoring procedures to detect early reading failure and to monitor strategies to address reading problems has now expanded into broad-based applications by educational specialists (Good & Kaminski, 2002; also see chapters 1 and 9 of this book). As a result, educators are currently in a far stronger position to prevent reading problems and failure because all primary-grade students can now be screened for these problems in an accurate, cost-efficient manner. Universal screening methods can also help school personnel understand the distribution and types of risk factors for violence and antisocial behavior among their students.

Similarly, schools now have the ability to detect, early in their school careers, those at-risk students who may develop serious antisocial and externalizing behavior problems. It is well recognized that comprehensive early intervention—involving parents, teachers, and peers—can result in the prevention of later negative outcomes for this subpopulation (Reid et al., 2002). Albers, Glover, and Kratochwill (2007) recently published a review of the current knowledge base in this area, which shows considerable progress in schools' capacity to achieve this important goal. As with academic problems, cost-efficient procedures are now available that allow professionals to identify students with antisocial or externalizing behavioral challenges. Schools provide an ideal setting for the universal screening and early detection of students who are at risk for such behavior patterns. Early screening that is brief, accurate, research based, and simple to implement, when combined with exposure of identified students to evidence-based interventions, can produce valuable outcomes for at-risk student populations.

Walker and his colleagues identified and described three recommended approaches to conducting such screening, as summarized here (see Walker, Colvin, & Ramsey, 1995; Walker, Ramsey, & Gresham, 2004). The following sections summarize Drummond's Student Risk Screening Scale (1994), Achenbach's Child Behavior Checklist (1991), and Walker and Severson's Systematic Screening for Behavior Disorders (1990). (Also see chapter 25 in this book.)

Drummond Approach

Drummond (1994) developed and investigated the efficacy, as well as the psychometric properties, of the Student Risk Screening Scale (SRSS), which asks teachers to provide assessments of recognized indicators and precursors of emerging antisocial behavior patterns among elementary-age students. The SRSS consists of seven items that teachers rate along a frequency dimension, as follows: 0 = never; 1= occasionally; 2 = sometimes; and 3 = frequently. The SRSS items are:

1. Stealing
2. Lying, cheating, and sneaking
3. Behavior problems
4. Peer rejection
5. Low academic achievement
6. Negative attitude
7. Aggressive behavior

The teacher rates each student in the classroom on the SRSS items using a matrix rating form on which student names are listed down the left side of the form and the SRSS items are arrayed across the top. The teacher enters a single rating per item opposite each listed student's name. SRSS scores can range from 0 to 21. Drummond has established three levels of risk based on total SRSS score: high risk = 9–21, moderate risk = 4–8, and low risk = 0–3. It is recommended that each high-risk student be further evaluated for possible referral to receive specialized mental health or behavioral support services.

Drummond has demonstrated that the SRSS discriminates between high-, moderate-, and low-risk students on a range of academic and behavioral measures, including grade point average, number of classes failed, achievement test scores, number of students receiving academic remediation services, and both minor and major disciplinary offenses. Lane, Kalberg, Parks, & Carter (2008) recently published a study to investigate the score reliability and validity of the SRSSs used at the high school level. Their study involved 674 high school students, and they found high levels of internal consistency, inter-rater reliability, and test–retest reliability for the SRSS, with moderate convergent validity coefficients obtained with Goodman's Strengths and Difficulties Questionnaire. The SRSS is a highly recommended tool for conducting universal, school-wide screening for antisocial behavior and has been well received by educational practitioners and researchers alike.

Achenbach Approach

In this approach, the classroom teacher uses teacher nominations of students and Likert ratings on the aggression subscale of the Achenbach Child Behavior Checklist to identify and evaluate the behavioral status of students with challenging behavior (1991). The Achenbach approach has emerged as the gold standard for assessing psychopathology among children and youth. The aggression subscale of this instrument has a relatively small number of items that define an antisocial, aggressive behavior pattern, such as explosive, defiant, cruel, bullying, and fighting. The psychometric properties of this instrument are superb and have been well established through a broad array of studies.

Parent ratings of teacher-nominated students can also be used to supplement the screening process and may or may not confirm concerns regarding the student's school behavior. Those students who show elevated profiles on the aggression subscale (i.e., two or more standard deviations above normative levels), in both home and school settings, very likely have serious behavior problems that warrant systematic attention from educational specialists and mental health professionals.

This screening approach is relatively simple to implement. Teachers should be provided with a clear definition of an antisocial, externalizing behavior pattern characterized by both examples and nonexamples. Then, using the definition, teachers would simply nominate those students in the class whose typical or characteristic behavior most closely matches the definition. The final step would be to have the teacher and/or parents of the nominated students rate the student's behavior on the aggression subscale of the Achenbach checklist.

Walker and Severson Approach

Walker and Severson (1990) developed the Systematic Screening for Behavior Disorders (SSBD) multiple-gating procedure for use in providing universal screening for all students in elementary classrooms to detect students who may be at risk for either externalizing or internalizing behavior problems. The SSBD uses a combination of teacher nominations in screening stage 1 and Likert ratings on measures of adaptive, maladaptive, and critical events forms of behavior in screening stage 2. An optional third screening stage can be used to record behavioral observations in classroom and playground settings (see chapter 25). All the measures used in stages 2 and 3 of the SSBD are based on national norms and provide the basis for deriving cutoff points to determine which students move on to additional screening and evaluation.

The three screening stages of the SSBD are linked or interconnected so that only those students with the most serious behavior profiles move on to additional screening stages. Stage 1 provides each student in a classroom with an equal chance to be nominated by the general education teacher for either an externalizing or an internalizing behavior pattern based upon thoroughly test definitions of both. The teacher then rank orders all nominated students on each dimension (i.e., externalizing, internalizing) as to which students' typical behavior matches the definition most closely. The top three ranked students on each dimension then move to screening stage 2, where they are rated on frequency-of-occurrence measures using the stage 2 rating instruments. Only those students exceeding stage 2 normative cutoff points are recommended for further screening in stage 3 using the classroom and playground codes. In stage 3, a stopwatch recording of academic engaged time is used in the classroom; the playground code records the target student's social behavior with peers in terms of its frequency, quality, and distribution across playground activities. Those students exceeding stage 3 cutoff points are recommended for referral to school-based specialists (e.g., mental health, special education, or school-wide assistance teams) for further evaluation and decision-making.

The SSBD has been used extensively by educational practitioners and researchers alike. It has excellent psychometric characteristics and has been recommended as a best practice in a number of reviews of school-based screening. A comprehensive update of the screening system and recent research conducted on the SSBD was included in a recent special issue of the *Journal of School Psychology*, which was devoted to universal screening procedures and critical issues (Albers, Glover, & Kratochwill, 2007; Severson, Walker, Hope-Doolittle, Kratochwill, & Gresham, 2007). In addition, Caldarella, Young, Richardson, Young, and Young (2008) successfully validated the SSBD for use with middle and junior high school students. Finally, Walker and his colleagues extended the SSBD downward into a preschool version that is appropriate for use with 3- to 5-year-olds (see Walker, Severson, & Feil, 1995). Research on the SSBD and Early Screening Project has continued over the past two decades, supported by a series of competitively awarded federal grants, expanding the knowledge base and broadening the applications of these screening systems.

Regardless of which universal screening procedure a school team selects, it is important that such screenings occur proactively and on a regular basis, in accordance with the school safety plan. Ideally, systematic screening efforts should be initiated after the beginning of the school year and again following the start of the new calendar year. At least 1 month should be allowed at the beginning of the school year for teachers to become familiar with their students' behavioral characteristics.

Develop and Implement a Three-Tier Intervention Plan

This section contains recommended strategies for building a three-tier intervention plan for the school. These recommendations are based on best practices, and the available evidence supports their application in today's schools (Jimerson & Furlong, 2006).

Five strategic approaches have the potential to move schools in the direction of greater safety and reduce the likelihood, over time, of a school tragedy erupting. The more at risk a school is perceived to be, the more important and relevant these strategies become and the greater the investment required. Furthermore, their relevance and importance increase from elementary to middle to high school settings.

Create a Positive, Inclusive School Climate and Culture

Research shows that a school climate that is positive, inclusive, and accepting is a key component of an effective school (Gottfredson et al., 2000). School-wide approaches are the best for dealing with the challenges of youth violence prevention and school safety and security (Hahn et al., 2007). Too often, there is a singular focus on the most serious student offenders without a concomitant plan for addressing the potential needs and problems of the full population of students in the school. A comprehensive, school-wide plan ultimately prevents or reduces serious offenses. School-wide approaches can change the climate of a school and reduce the likelihood that the problems characteristically presented by at-risk students will escalate out of control.

To prevent minor, as well as serious, antisocial behavior, educators are turning to a comprehensive and proactive approach to discipline commonly referred to as school-wide positive behavior support (Gresham, Sugai, Horner, Quinn, & McInerny, 2000; Sprague & Golly, 2004; Sugai et al., 2002). SWPBS is based on the assumption that when faculty and staff in a school actively teach and acknowledge expected behavior (such as be safe, respectful, responsible), the proportion of students with serious behavior problems will be reduced, along with a reduced risk for violence, and the school's overall climate will improve (see chapter 16 in this book).

Address the Peer Culture and Its Challenges

A primary target for prevention and safer-schools efforts should be the peer culture (Dishion et al., 2006). The norms, actions, beliefs, and values within broad sectors of today's peer culture are socially destructive and demeaning. Many youth experience a "trial by fire" process in negotiating the complex and difficult social tasks involved in finding their place in this peer culture. Far too many fail this critical test, become lost within it, and wander aimlessly while seeking an acceptance that is generally not forthcoming. They become homeless persons within the larger peer group and their lack of fit is well known to their peers and teachers (see chapter 28 in this book). This painful reality forces many marginalized youth to affiliate with atypical or deviant peer groups, which can prove highly destructive for them.

Transforming this destructive peer culture is perhaps the most formidable task in the area of school safety. This culture is not of the school's making, but schools, collectively, make up perhaps the only social institution, excluding the family, that is capable of addressing it effectively. The following strategies are recommended for consideration in this regard.

*1. **Involve students as key partners in making schools safe and free of violence.*** Encouraging students' school engagement and commitment to conventional pursuits is increasingly recognized as essential to promoting academic achievement and preventing antisocial and violent behavior (Blum, 2005; Gottfredson, 2001). One example of such a program is Students Against Violence Everywhere (SAVE; Riley & Segal, 2002). SAVE is a student-initiated program that promotes nonviolence within schools and communities. The program teaches about the effects and consequences of violence and helps provide safe activities for students, parents, and communities. As reported by students and advisers, SAVE improves school environments by teaching students how to manage and resolve conflict, reduces violence, and helps more students get involved. Students report that they joined SAVE to improve the school environment by making the school a safer place, and students who participate in SAVE demonstrate increased self-esteem and confidence, conflict resolution skills, presentation and public speaking skills, and knowledge about different violence-prevention strategies.

Programs like SAVE are designed to transform peer attitudes and beliefs about the risks to school safety that emerge from their culture. The programs promote peer ownership of the tasks involved in preventing school tragedies and are highly recommended as a first strategy for enlisting a school's peer culture in this effort.

2. Bully-proof the school setting by adopting effective antibullying and antiharassment programs. In addition to the common elements of SWPBS, other evidence-based bully prevention programs are available, such as Bully Proofing Your School (Garrity, Jens, Porter, Sager, & Short-Camilli, 2000) and Steps to Respect (Frey, Hirschtein, Edstrom, & Snell, 2009).

The best disinfectant for bullying, mean-spirited teasing, and harassment is sunlight—that is, exposure. These events need to be defined as clearly unacceptable by everyone involved in the school—administrators, teachers, other school staff, students, and parents—and made public when they do occur. Students should be given strategies for reporting and for adaptively coping with these events. Furthermore, the reporting of those who commit these acts should be made acceptable. The programs cited above incorporate these basic principles and strategies.

A new challenge for educators and parents is the practice of cyberbullying, which is the use of social aggression, threats, and harassment via the Internet and mobile technologies (Willard, 2007). Students post harmful or fraudulent material or engage in other forms of threatening behavior through these media. Very little is known about the patterns and outcomes of cyberbullying, and much research is needed on both school policy and methods to deter this damaging and potentially wide-ranging form of bullying and harassment.

3. Teach anger-management and conflict-resolution techniques as part of regular curricula. Universal school-based programs that are intended to prevent violent behavior have been developed and tested at all grade levels, from prekindergarten through high school. These programs can be targeted to high-risk schools and to selected grades. All students in targeted grades receive the programs in their own classrooms, not in special pullout sessions. There is strong evidence that these universal programs decrease rates of violence among school-age children and youth, although the effect sizes vary greatly across programs and age groups (Gottfredson, 2001; Hahn et al., 2007).

These programs are designed to teach all students in a given school or grade about the problem of violence and its prevention or about one or more of the following topics or skills intended to reduce aggressive or violent behavior: emotional self-awareness, emotional control, self-esteem, positive social skills, social problem solving, conflict resolution, and teamwork. The Collaborative for Academic, Social and Emotional Learning (CASEL; http://www.casel.org/about/overview.php) is a not-for-profit organization that works to advance the science and evidence-based practices of the field of social and emotional learning (SEL). CASEL synthesizes and integrates scientific findings regarding the teaching and management of social–emotional strategies for students. It is a widely used and highly recommended resource by educators in the teaching and development of socially effective behavior in children and youth.

Collaborate With Parents in Making the School Safer

With each new school shooting tragedy, parents of school-age children and youth seek greater assurances that their child's school is safe, and increasingly they are asking for a voice and role in helping the school attain this goal. Parents have much to offer in this regard and can be a powerful force in bringing greater safety and a sense of security to the school setting. Four strategies are recommended for involving parents in making a school safer:

1. Create a parent advisory group devoted to school safety issues for that school, and ensure that parents are involved in all aspects of school planning. Such an advisory group would bring valuable knowledge, experience, and advocacy to the process of dealing with school-related safety challenges. The group could also serve as a forum for reacting to district-and state-level policy directives in this area.

2. Encourage parents to teach their children adaptive, nonviolent methods of responding to bullying, teasing, and harassment at school and to teach children not to fight back. In the majority of cases, fighting back is not effective and may escalate the situation to dangerous levels. Furthermore, it is more likely to increase the probability of the offensive behavior recurring, rather than reduce it. A school-based, antibullying program that has parental support and involvement is likely to be much more effective.

3. Make information on effective parenting practices available to parents, and provide access to parent training classes and supports to those parents who seek additional guidance. Five generic parenting practices are instrumental in determining how children develop: (a) discipline, (b) monitoring and supervision, (c) parent involvement in children's lives, (d) positive family-management techniques, and (e) effective crisis-intervention and problem-solving methods. A large number of available parent training programs address these parenting practices (Dishion & Kavanagh, 2003; Patterson, 1982; Patterson et al., 1992; also see chapter 5 in this book).

4. Support at-risk and antisocial youth throughout their school careers using indicated or tertiary interventions. Youth with serious mental health problems and disorders who are alienated, socially rejected, and taunted by peers can be dangerous to themselves and others. These students are often well known to peers and staff in the school and should be given appropriate professional and parental attention, access to services, and social support (Dishion & Stormshak, 2007; Patterson et al., 1992).

CONCLUSION

As a general rule, policy lags well behind the research that validates the evidence-based approaches on which practices are based. This is especially true in the areas of school safety and violence prevention. The pressures and demands of the moment force school administrators into making decisions about school safety strategies and tactics that may appear promising but might not prove effective through the research process (for example, zero tolerance, which is appealing to some schools but is not effective). Thus, schools are left to choose among practices that appear promising, relying on experience and using best judgment, until the knowledge base on school safety becomes more solid, cohesive, evidence based, and widely used. The strategic actions described briefly above represent what is currently known about these complex issues.

Historically, schools and school systems have remained comparatively detached players in the prevention of youth violence. Unfortunately, society's problems have now spilled over into the process of schooling, so that ensuring school safety has emerged as a very high priority among parents of school-age children and youth. Bullying, mean-spirited teasing, sexual harassment, and victimization are relatively commonplace occurrences on school campuses. Schools will continue to respond reactively to these crisis events as they occur. However, they also must begin investing in proactive, preventive approaches that will reduce the likelihood of future occurrences.

An enormous amount of federal and state resources has been and continues to be invested in school safety and violence prevention following the school shooting tragedies of the past three decades. It is extremely important that these resources be used to promote the adoption of best professional practices and that proven, evidence-based interventions be implemented. These developments also create significant opportunities for school professionals, including counselors, general educators, school psychologists, special educators, and social workers, to collaborate more effectively and to forge new working relationships with families and community agencies.

If schools can implement with integrity the practices that are currently known regarding these problems, the effort will achieve a major positive impact. The stakes are high for U.S. society and its public and private school systems. Yet the potential gains are well worth the investment and effort. Careful assessment and planning for school safety provides the cornerstone for any school's success.

REFERENCES

Achenbach, T. (1991). *The child behavior checklist: Manual for the teacher's report form.*

Albers, C. A., Glover, T. A., & Kratochwill, T. R. (2007). Introduction to the special issue: How can universal screening enhance educational and mental health outcomes? *Journal of School Psychology, 45,* 113–116.

American Psychological Association (APA). (1993). *Violence and youth: Psychology's response. Volume 1: Summary report of the American Psychological Association Commission on Violence and Youth.* Washington, DC: Author.

Atkinson, A. J., & Kipper, R. J. (Eds.). (1999). The Virginia school resource officer program guide. Retrieved from http://www.dcjs.virginia.gov/forms/cple/sroguide.pdf

Biglan, T., Wang, M., & Walberg, H. (2003). *Preventing youth problems.* New York: Kluwer Academic/Plenum Press.

Blum, R. (2005). *School connectedness: Improving the lives of students.* Baltimore: Johns Hopkins Bloomberg School of Public Health.

Boles, S., Biglan, A., & Smolkowski, K. (in press). Relationships among negative and positive behaviors in adolescence. *Journal of Adolescence.*

Caldarella, P., Young, E. L., Richardson, M. J., Young, B. J., & Young, K. R. (2008). Validation of the systematic screening for behavior disorders in middle and junior high school. *Journal of Emotional and Behavioral Disorders, 16,* 105–117.

Centers for Disease Control and Prevention (CDC). (2008). School-associated student homicides—United States, 1992–2006. *Morbidity and Mortality Weekly Report, 57,* 33–36.

Colvin, G., Kame'enui, E. J., & Sugai, G. (1993). School-wide and classroom management: Reconceptualizing the integration and management of students with behavior problems in general education. *Education and Treatment of Children, 16,* 361–381.

Committee for Children. (2002, 2008). *Second Step Violence Prevention Curriculum.* Seattle, WA: Author. Available from http://www.cfchildren.org

Cornell, D. (2006). *School violence: Fears versus facts.* Mahwah, NJ: Erlbaum.

Cornell, D., & Sheras, P. (2006). *Guidelines for responding to student threats of violence.* Longmont, CO: Sopris West.

Crowe, T. (2000). *Crime prevention through environmental design* (2nd ed.). Boston: Butterworth-Heinman.

Dinkes, R., Cataldi, E. F., & Lin-Kelly, W. (2007). *Indicators of school crime and safety: 2007* (NCES 2008-021/NCJ 219553). Retrieved August 7, 2008, from http://nces.ed.gov/programs/crimeindicators/crimeindicators2007

Dishion, T. J., Dodge, K. A., & Lansford, J. E. (2006). Findings and recommendations: A blueprint to minimize deviant peer influence in youth interventions and programs. In *Deviant peer influences in programs for youth: Problems and solutions* (pp. 366–394). New York: Guilford Press.

Dishion, T. J., & Kavanagh, K. (2003). *Intervening in adolescent problem behavior: A family-centered approach.* New York: Guilford Press.

Dishion, T. J., & Stormshak, E. (2007). *Intervening in children's lives: An ecological, family-centered approach to mental health care.* Washington, DC: APA Books.

Drummond, T. (1994). The Student Risk Screening Scale (SRSS). Grants Pass, OR: Josephine County Mental Health Program.

Dwyer, K., Osher, D., & Warger, C. (1998). *Early warning, timely response: A guide to safe schools.* Washington, DC: U.S. Department of Education. Retrieved July 29, 2008, from http://cecp.air.org/guide/default.asp

Elias, M., Zins, J., Weissbert, R., Frey, K., Greenberg, M., Haynes, N., et al. (1997). *Promoting social and emotional learning: Guidelines for educators.* Alexandria, VA: Association for Supervision and Curriculum Development.

Fein, R., Vossekuil, B., & Holden, G. (1995). Threat assessment: An approach to prevent targeted violence. *National Institute of Justice: Research in Action,* June, 1–7.

Fixsen, D. L., Naoom, S. F., Blase, K. A., Friedman, R. M., & Wallace, F. (2005). *Implementation research: A synthesis of the literature* (FMHI Publication No. 231). Tampa, FL: University of South Florida, Louis de la Parte Florida Mental Health Institute, National Implementation Research Network.

Foster, S., Rollefson, M., Doksum, T., Noonan, D., Robinson, G., & Teich, J. (2005). *School mental health services in the United States 2002–2003* (DHHS Publication No. SMA 05-4068. Rockville, MD: Center for Mental Health Services, Substance Abuse and Mental Health Services Administration. Retrieved January 20, 2006, from http://www.samhsa.gov/publications/allpubs/sma05-4068

Frey, K. S., Hirschstein, M. K., & Guzzo, B. A. (2000). Second step. Preventing aggression by promoting social competence. In M. H. Epstein & H. Walker (Eds.), *Making schools safer and violence free. Critical issues, solutions, and recommended practices.* Austin, TX: PRO-ED.

Frey, K. S., Hirschstein, M., Edstrom, L., & Snell, J. (2009). Observed reductions in school bullying, nonbullying aggression, and destructive bystander behavior: A longitudinal evaluation. *Journal of Educational Psychology, 101,* 466–481.

Garrity, C., Jens, K., Porter, W., Sager, N., & Short-Camilli, C. (2000). *Bully-proofing your school: A comprehensive approach for elementary schools* (2nd ed.). Longmont, CO: Sopris West.

Good, R., & Kaminski, R. (2002). *Dynamic indicators of basic early literacy skills* (6th ed.). Eugene, OR: Institute for the Development of Educational Achievement.

Gottfredson, D. C. (2001). *Schools and delinquency.* New York: Cambridge University Press.

Gottfredson, D. C., & Gottfredson, G. D. (2001). Quality of school-based prevention programs: Results from a national survey. *Journal of Research in Crime and Delinquency, 39,* 3–35.

Gottfredson, G., Gottfredson, D., & Czeh, E. (2000). *National study of delinquency prevention in schools.* Ellicott City, MD: Gottfredson Associates.

Green, M. (1999). *The appropriate and effective use of security technologies in U.S. schools. A guide for schools and law enforcement agencies.* Washington, DC: U.S. Department of Justice.

Greenberg, M. T., Domitrovich, C., & Bumbarger, B. (1999). *Preventing mental disorders in school-age children: A review of the effectiveness of prevention programs.* Rockville, MD: U.S. Department of Health and Human Services, Center for Mental Health Services, Substance Abuse Mental Health Services Administration.

Gresham, F. M., Sugai, G., Horner, R. H., Quinn, M. M., & McInerney, M. (2000). *School-wide values, discipline, and social skills.* Washington, DC: American Institutes for Research and the U.S. Department of Education Office of Special Education Programs.

Gun-Free Schools Act of 1994. 20 U.S.C. Chapter 70, Strengthening and Improvement of Elementary and Secondary Schools (1994).

Hahn, R., Fuqua-Whitley, D., Wethington, H., Lowy, J., Crosby, A., Fullilove, M., et al. (2007). Effectiveness of universal school-based programs to prevent violent and aggressive behavior: A systematic review. *American Journal of Preventive Medicine, 33*(2S), S114–S129.

Hoagwood, K., Olin, S. S., Kerker, B., Kratochwill, T., Crowe, M., & Saka, N. (2007). Empirically based school interventions targeted at academic and mental health functioning. *Journal of Emotional and Behavioral Disorders, 15,* 66–92.

Horner, R., Sugai, G., Lewis-Palmer, T., & Todd, A. (2001). Teaching school-wide behavioral expectations. *The Report on Emotional and Behavioral Disorders in Youth, 1,* 77–79; 93–96.

Horner, R., Sugai, G., Smolkowski, K., Todd, A., Nakasato, J., & Esperanza, J. (in press). A randomized control trial of school-wide positive behavior support in elementary schools. *Journal of Positive Behavioral Interventions.*

Irvin, L. K., Tobin, T. J., Sprague, J. R., Sugai, G., & Vincent, C. G. (2004). Validity of office discipline referral measures as indices of school-wide behavioral status and effects of school-wide behavioral interventions. *Journal of Positive Behavioral Interventions, 6,* 131–147.

Jimerson, S. R., & Furlong, M. J. (2006). *The handbook of school violence and safety.* Mahwah, NJ: Erlbaum.

Johns, B. H., Carr, V. G., & Hoots, C. W. (1997). *Reduction of school violence: Alternatives to suspension* (2nd ed.). Horsham, PA: LRP Publications.

Kauffman, J. M. (1999). How we prevent the prevention of emotional and behavioral disorders. *Exceptional Children, 65,* 448–469.

Kingery, P. M., & Walker, H. M. (2002). What we know about school safety. In M. Shinn, H. Walker, & G. Stoner (Eds.), *Interventions for academic and behavior problems. II: Preventive and remedial approaches* (pp. 71–88). Bethesda, MD: National Association of School Psychologists.

Lane, K. L., Kalberg, J. R., Parks, R. J., & Carter, E. W. (2008). Student Risk Screening Scale: Initial evidence for score reliability and validity at the high school level. *Journal of Emotional and Behavioral Disorders, 16,* 178–190.

Lipsey, M. W. (1992). Juvenile Delinquency Treatment. In T. D. Cook (Ed.), *Meta-Analysis for Explanation* (pp. 83–127). New York: Russell Sage Foundation.

Loeber, R., & Farrington, D. (2001). *Child delinquents.* Thousand Oaks, CA: SAGE.

Mash, E. J., & Dozois, D. J. (2003). Child psychopathology: A developmental-systems perspective. In E. J. Mash & R. A. Barkley (Eds.), *Child psychopathology* (2nd ed., pp. 3–74). New York: Guilford Press.

McEvoy, A., & Welker, R. (2000). Antisocial behavior, academic failure, and school climate: A critical review. *Journal of Emotional and Behavioral Disorders, 8,* 130–140.

Nelson, J. R., Martella, R., & Marchand-Martella, N. (2002). Maximizing student learning: The effects of a comprehensive school-based program for preventing problem behaviors. *Journal of Emotional and Behavioral Disorders, 10,* 136–148.

O'Donnell, J., Hawkins, J., Catalano, R., Abbott, R., & Day, L. (1995). Preventing school failure, drug use, and delinquency among low-income children: Long-term intervention in elementary schools. *American Journal of Orthopsychiatry, 65,* 87–100.

Paine, C. K., & Sprague, J. R. (2002). Dealing with a school shooting disaster: Lessons learned from Springfield, Oregon. *Emotional and behavioral disorders in youth, 2*(2), 35–40.

Patterson, G. R. (1982). *Coercive family process (Vol. 3): A social learning approach.* Eugene, OR: Castalia Press.

Patterson, G. R., Reid, J. B., & Dishion, T. J. (1992). *Antisocial boys.* Eugene, OR: Castalia Press.

Poland, S. (1994). The role of school crisis intervention teams to prevent and reduce school violence and trauma. *School Psychology Review, 23,* 175–189.

Reid, J. B., & Patterson, G. R. (1989). The development of antisocial behaviour patterns in childhood and adolescence. *European Journal of Personality, 3,* 107–119.

Reid, J., Patterson, G., & Snyder, J. (2002). *Antisocial behavior in children and adolescents: A developmental analysis and model for intervention.* Washington, DC: American Psychological Association.

Riley, P. L., & Segal, E. C. (2002). Preparing to evaluate a school violence prevention program: Students Against Violence Everywhere. *Journal of School Violence, 1*(2), 73–87.

Schneider, T., Walker, H., & Sprague, J. (2000). *Safe school design: A handbook for educational leaders.* Eugene, OR: ERIC Clearinghouse on Educational Management, University of Oregon, College of Education.

Schreck, C. J., & Miller, J. M. (2003). Sources of fear of crime at school: What is the relative contribution of disorder, individual characteristics, and school security? *Journal of School Violence, 2,* 57–77.

Severson, H. H., Walker, H. M., Hope-Doolittle, J., Kratochwill, T. R., & Gresham, F. M. (2007). Proactive, early screening to detect behaviorally at-risk students: Issues, approaches, emerging innovations, and professional practices. *Journal of School Psychology* [Special issue], *45,* 193–223.

Skiba, R. J., & Knesting, K. (2001). Zero tolerance, zero evidence: An analysis of school disciplinary practice. In R. J. Skiba & G. G. Noam (Eds.), *New directions for youth development (no. 92): Zero tolerance: Can suspension and expulsion keep schools safe?* (pp. 17–43). San Francisco: Jossey-Bass.

Sprague, J., Colvin, G., & Irvin, L. (1995). *The Oregon School Safety Survey.* Eugene, OR: University of Oregon, Institute on Violence and Destructive Behavior. http://www.uoregon.edu/~ivdb

Sprague, J. R., Cook, C. R., Wright, D. B., & Sadler, C. (2008). *RTI and behavior: A guide to integrating behavioral and academic supports.* Horsham, PA: LRP Publications.

Sprague, J., & Golly, A. (2004). *Best behavior: Building positive behavior support in schools.* Longmont, CO: Sopris West.

Sprague, J. R., Sugai, G., & Walker, H. (1998). Antisocial behavior in schools. In T. S. Watson & F. M. Gresham (Eds.), *Handbook of child behavior therapy* (pp. 451–474). New York: Plenum Press.

Sprague, J. R., & Walker, H. M. (2005). *Safe and healthy schools: Practical prevention strategies.* New York: Guilford Press.

Sprague, J., Walker, H., Sowards, S., Van Bloem, C., Eberhardt, P., & Marshall, B. (2002). Sources of vulnerability to school violence: Systems-level assessment and strategies to improve safety and climate. In M. R. Shinn, H. M. Walker, & G. Stoner (Eds.), *Interventions for academic and behavior problems II: Preventive and remedial approaches* (pp. 295–314). Bethesda, MD: National Association of School Psychologists.

Stormshak, E. A., Connell, A., & Dishion, T. J. (2007, April). *Results from a family-centered intervention predicting changes in school engagement from middle to high school.* Presented at the Society for Research in Child Development, Annual Convention, Boston, MA.

Sugai, G., & Horner, R. (2002). The evolution of discipline practices: School-wide positive behavior support. *Child and Family Behavior Therapy, 24,* 23–50.

Sugai, G., Horner, R. H., & Gresham, F. (2002). Behaviorally effective environments. In M. R. Shinn, H. M. Walker, & G. Stoner (Eds.), *Interventions for academic and behavior problems II: Preventive and remedial approaches.* Bethesda, MD: National Association for School Psychologists.

Sugai, G., Lewis-Palmer, T., Todd, A. W., & Horner, R. (2000). *Effective Behavior Support (EBS) survey: Assessing and planning behavior support in schools.* Eugene, OR: University of Oregon.

Swearer, S. M., & Cary, P. T. (2007). *Perceptions and Attitudes Toward Bullying in Middle School Youth: A Developmental Examination Across the Bully/Victim Continuum.* New York: Haworth Press.

U.S. Department of Commerce. (2005). *School crime supplement to the National Crime Victimization Survey.* Washington, DC: U.S. Census Bureau.

U.S. Department of Health and Human Services. (2001). *Youth violence: A report of the surgeon general.* Washington, DC: Author.

Vossekuil, B., Fein, R. A., Reddy, M., Borum, R., & Modzeleski, B. (2002). *The final report and findings of the Safe School Initiative: Implications for the prevention of school attacks in the United States.* Washington, DC: U.S. Secret Service and U.S. Department of Education.

Walker, H. M., Colvin, G., & Ramsey, E. (1995). *Antisocial behavior in school: Strategies and best practices.* Pacific Grove, CA: Brooks/Cole.

Walker, H. M., & Epstein, M. H. (2001). *Making schools safer and violence free: Critical issues, solutions, and recommended practices.* Austin, TX: PRO-ED.

Walker, H. M., Ramsey, E., & Gresham, F. M. (2004). *Antisocial behavior in school: Evidence-based practices* (2nd ed.). Belmont, CA: Wadsworth/Thomson Learning.

Walker, H. M., & Severson, H. H. (1990). *Systematic Screening for Behavior Disorders (SSBD): User's guide and technical manual.* Longmont, CO: Sopris West.

Walker, H. M., Severson, H. H., & Feil, E. G. (1995). *The Early Screening Project: A proven child-find process.* Longmont, CO: Sopris West.

Walker, H. M., Severson, H. H., Todis, B. J., Block-Pedego, A. E., Williams, G. J., Haring, N. G., et al. (1990). Systematic Screening for Behavior Disorders (SSBD): Further validation, replication and normative data. *Remedial and Special Education, 11,* 32–46.

Willard, N. E. (2007). *Cyber bullying and cyber threats: Responding to the challenge of online social aggression, threats, and distress.* Champaign, IL: Research Press.

INTERVENTIONS

for Achievement and Behavior Problems in a Three-Tier Model Including RTI

CHAPTER 11

Building a Scientifically Based Data System for Progress Monitoring and Universal Screening Across Three Tiers, Including RTI Using Curriculum-Based Measurement

Mark R. Shinn
National-Louis University

INTRODUCTION

In the past decade, educational science and quality school-based practices have come together to develop more unified, positive, and preventive service delivery systems for academic performance and behavioral support in America's schools. Among the numerous labels for these service delivery systems are early-intervening services, coordinated early-intervening services (CEIS), multitiered early-intervening services, and a three-tier problem-solving model. However, the most common term for these types of service delivery systems is *response to intervention* (RTI).

The term RTI has generated considerable controversy and confusion. To some in the field, the term describes an allowable, if not encouraged, entitlement process to determine special education eligibility for specific learning disabilities (SLD). For many others, RTI is a generic term for a much broader service delivery system that has among its components (a) multitiered interventions (e.g., three tiers) of increasing intensity to address academic performance and behavior, and (b) data-based decision making, including universal screening and progress monitoring. This latter use of RTI constitutes the context for this chapter. The chapter also illustrates how curriculum-based measurement (CBM), a set of simple, time-efficient, and scientifically based basic skills tests, can be used across multiple tiers for universal screening and progress monitoring. The academic area of reading is used as primary example.

OVERVIEW OF UNIVERSAL SCREENING AND PROGRESS MONITORING

Over the past 30 years, a large body of knowledge has been generated that demonstrates what methods enable students to become competent readers. Adams (1990) noted that to be able to read well, children must read widely, and in order for them to read widely, they must be able to read well. Furthermore, good and wide reading must be accomplished early. Torgesen (1998, 2004) has reported that in order to ensure this healthy start, schools must (a) increase the quality, consistency, and "reach" of instruction in every kindergarten–Grade 3 classroom; (b) engage in *universal screening* and timely and valid assessments of reading growth (i.e., *frequent progress monitoring*); and (c) provide more intensive interventions to "catch up" struggling readers.

This chapter focuses on the second requirement, while chapters 18 and 6 in this book devote considerable attention to the first and third. Not only are universal screening and progress monitoring important for getting all students off to a healthy start in reading in Grades K–3, they also are foundational components in multitiered coordinated early-intervening services. In addition, progress monitoring is both a legal requirement and "best practice" in RTI as a special education entitlement process for specific learning disabilities (Burdette, 2007; Fuchs & Vaughn, 2005).

Common Universal Screening Practices in a Multitiered CEIS Model

In universal screening, *all* students are tested using a standard measure for determining which learners may be sufficiently different from expectations to warrant more intensive interventions. Universal screening differs from individual screening, which involves testing a subset of students, usually one at a time, in a process that typically is initiated by teacher referral. Although teacher referral is generally accurate for identifying academic problems (Algozzine, Christenson, & Ysseldyke, 1982; Gerber & Semmel, 1984) and behavior problems (Walker & Severson, 1994), it has been shown that this process has bias for both gender and ethnicity (Shinn, Tindal, & Spira, 1987). By testing all students and eliminating identification by referral, individual teacher bias can be minimized.

Schools, of course, have considerable experience with universal screening in areas other than academics. For example, universal hearing and vision screening have been common educational practice for more than 50 years. When schools engage in the process of implementing multitier service delivery systems, they go beyond hearing and vision screening and expand universal screening to reading. When they do so, two universal screening approaches for reading might be employed that can be likened to the medical treatment approaches (a) *titration* and (b) *triage*. In both approaches, decisions to provide more intensive interventions are based on set criteria, or "cut scores." Most often, these cut scores are *normative*, and students performing below a certain percentile (e.g., the 25th percentile) receive more intensive intervention. In other instances, the cut score is based on level of performance tied to a *standard*. For example, a standards-based cut score is often used with Dynamic Indicators of Basic Early Literacy (DIBELS; Kaminski & Good, 1998), where on a measure such as phonemic segmentation fluency (PSF), performance below a specified value (e.g., 35) would suggest the need for Tier 2 intervention.

Universal Screening as Titration

According to Wikipedia, *titration* is a medical term describing the process of "gradually adjusting the dose of a medication until the desired effect is achieved." In this most frequently occurring universal screening approach, all students are tested, and those below the cut score are identified as potential candidates for more intensive Tier 2 reading intervention. This approach is called titration because Tier 3 interventions are not provided until students have been shown not to respond to Tier 2 interventions (Fletcher, Coulter, Reschly, & Vaughn, 2004; Fuchs & Fuchs, 2005; Vaughn & Fuchs, 2003). In other words, the *dosage*—the intensity of treatment—is based on a judgment regarding whether the Tier 2 intervention had its desired effect. Furthermore, the decision to change tiered interventions is not based on the universal screening data, but on progress monitoring data. In an extension of the titration metaphor, those students who do not respond to Tier 3 may be considered for an even more intensive dosage, that is, special education entitlement, as part of RTI. Although this titration model is defensible and quite common, it can be viewed as another "wait-to-fail" approach, albeit based on student achievement data rather than on an ability–achievement discrepancy.

Universal Screening as Triage

The second, less common approach to universal screening is referred to as *triage*. According to Wikipedia, triage is a process used in a "scene of mass casualty, in order to sort patients into those who need critical attention and immediate transport to the hospital and those with less serious injuries." When universal screening data in reading are used in triage, students' scores allow for immediate alignment with *any* of the tiers appropriate to the severity of their needs. In a three-tier model, students whose scores are average or above receive the core reading instructional program (i.e., Tier 1). Students whose scores are below average (e.g., 25th percentile) may receive Tier 2 reading intervention in addition to their Tier 1 program. Students with the greatest reading needs (e.g., below the 10th percentile) may receive the most powerful, intense intervention, Tier 3. In a triage approach, there is no need to fail at a particular tier before receiving a more intensive intervention. Instead, students are provided services at an appropriate level as soon as the need is identified.

Common and Preferred Universal Screening Tools

Within certain parameters (e.g., sensitivity, specificity), nearly any reliable and valid achievement test *may* be suitable for use in universal screening. Typically, schools select a reading screening tool that is (a) already in use in general education classrooms, and (b) consistent with a district's reading philosophy. Examples of measures that are employed include high-stakes state tests, extant group-administered achievement tests, individually administered achievement tests (both lengthy and short), computerized tests, and a variety of informal assessment strategies such as running records. Unfortunately, schools too rarely consider time efficiency and cost-effectiveness when selecting their screening tools.

For best practices, schools instead should first consider the potential screener's technical adequacy, and then include time and cost-efficient considerations. Ideally, students with more intensive reading needs would be identified accurately with minimal loss of instructional time and financial expense. Significant value to the screener can be added if the tool is also validated for progress monitoring.

Common Progress Monitoring Practices in a Multitiered Model

In practice, less attention has been directed toward schools' systems of progress monitoring in reading, despite what one would expect. One would assume that schools are adept at monitoring academic progress, given that the purpose of schools is learning. However, it has been well established that monitoring the progress of learners has been, and remains, an area of weakness in instructional practice (Baker, O'Neil, & Linn, 1993; Deno, 1986, 2005; Fuchs & Fuchs, 1984, 2008).

When schools begin to employ progress monitoring systems across multiple tiers, three broad approaches have been identified, referred to here as (a) unspecified and discontinuous progress monitoring, or "independent contracting"; (b) specified, continuous, but inadequate progress monitoring; and (c) specified, continuous, and adequate progress monitoring.

Independent Contracting Progress Monitoring

In spite of the emphasis given by the No Child Left Behind Act of 2001 (NCLB) and the Individuals with Disabilities Education Act (IDEA 2004) to assessing student achievement over time, some schools continue to pay little attention to progress monitoring. These progress monitoring practices can be described as unspecified because they lack an overall plan for implementation. In these schools, any progress monitoring practices that may exist are ones that have been in use for years. Progress monitoring also is discontinuous, because each intervention program or tier uses different progress monitoring tools. It may seem as though every program is conducting monitoring its own way, or what could be called "independent contracting."

For example, general education (Tier 1) may use group achievement tests, curriculum-embedded assessments, informal tests, or repeated administrations (e.g., three to four) of the universal screening test. In Tier 2, different progress monitoring approaches may be used, such as curriculum-embedded assessments from a different curriculum or informal teacher-made tests. In Tier 3, progress monitoring approaches most commonly include lengthy and infrequent (e.g., once per year) individualized achievement tests and/or yet another type of curriculum-embedded assessments.

In this independent contracting approach, there is little effort to build a *comprehensive*, systematic service delivery system with the features of coordinated early-intervening services (Burdette, 2007). There is little emphasis on processes to evaluate systematically if the solution was effective or needed modification. Furthermore, many of the traditional progress monitoring methods that are employed are not scientifically based (Fuchs & Fuchs, 2008); as a result, decisions about when or if a student has responded to an intervention (i.e., made adequate progress) may be contentious and driven by opinion.

Specified, Continuous, but Inadequate Progress Monitoring

In settings where there has been an effort to specify progress monitoring tools and to use the same tests and data base across intervention tiers or programs (i.e., building *continuous* progress monitoring practices), it is common for schools to build their progress monitoring process for reading using their universal screening tests. The presumption is that if the universal screening reading test is administered over time, it is valid for making progress decisions in general education and at different tiers. This approach is more prescriptive and has more continuity than the independent contracting approach, because all programs or tiers use the same data to evaluate progress. However, too often, the tests used may not be technically adequate (e.g., reliable, valid) for progress monitoring purposes. Because IDEA 2004 requires that assessments be technically adequate, legal and practice problems may arise when measures that lack these features are used to determine (a) progress toward individual education plan (IEP) goals (Fuchs, Fuchs, & Deno, 1985; Shinn & Shinn, 2000) and (b) response to intervention as part of SLD eligibility determination (Fuchs & Vaughn, 2005; Pericola Case, Speece, & Eddy Molloy, 2003; Vaughn & Fuchs, 2003).

The primary difficulty in creating a progress monitoring system based on universal screening reading tests, such as high-stakes state tests or group achievement tests, is that these measures are *summative* tests. That is, they were designed to assess the effects of instruction *after* instruction has occurred. Summative tests are constructed to be sensitive to *between*-person differences (Howell, Kurns, & Antil, 2002; Howell & Nolet, 1999). In other words, a valid summative reading test that is useful for universal screening should distinguish between poor readers and good readers. Summative evaluation, when conducted properly with valid measures and when used to improve motivation and systemic instructional practices (e.g., curriculum choices), has the potential to improve student achievement through accountability. However, summative measures generally are not useful for progress monitoring (Fuchs, 1994; Fuchs & Fuchs, 1999, 2002; D. Fuchs, L. S. Fuchs, Benowitz, & Berringer, 1987). In addition, these summative tests lack sufficient alternate forms and frequently are expensive in terms of cost and lost instructional time.

Specified, Continuous, and Adequate Progress Monitoring

The preferred progress monitoring system within a multitiered CEIS such as RTI is *specified* explicitly, is *continuous* (i.e., the same assessment tools are used across tiers), and is *adequate*, or scientifically based. Fortunately, considerable guidance in the selection of scientifically based progress monitoring tools is available (Fuchs & Fuchs, 2004). The U.S. Department of Education Office of Special Education Programs (OSEP) funded the National Center for Student Progress Monitoring (NCSPM) for a 5-year period beginning in 2003 to support the identification and dissemination of scientifically based progress monitoring tools. Given the importance of scientifically based progress monitoring within an RTI paradigm, the NCSPM was incorporated into the OSEP's National Center on Response to Intervention (NCRTI) in 2008.

As part of their mission, the NCSPM published a set of standards for frequent progress monitoring tools based on the Standards for Educational and Psychological Testing developed by the joint committee appointed by the American Educational Research Association (AERA), the American Psychological Association (APA), and the National Council on Measurement Used in Education (NCMUE), and the Individuals with Disabilities Education Act (IDEA). According to these standards, scientifically based progress monitoring tools must (a) be reliable, generating accurate data through evidence of high parallel form and test reliability; (b) be valid, in that they measure the achievement construct of interest, including concurrent and predictive validity; (c) provide evidence of at least nine alternate forms of equivalent difficulty; (d) be sensitive to student improvement after short periods of time; (e) be linked to benchmarks specifying adequate yearly progress; (f) specify rates of improvement for typically developing students and NCLB subgroups; and (g) show evidence that the use of the progress monitoring tool results in changes in teacher instructional planning and improves student achievement. Schools that use progress monitoring tools that meet these standards are able to build decision-making practices that are explicit and specific, are continuous across tiers, and are scientifically based.

OVERVIEW OF CURRICULUM-BASED MEASUREMENT: A SET OF SCIENTIFICALLY BASED PROGRESS MONITORING TOOLS

There is widespread support for curriculum-based measurement (CBM) as a scientifically based progress monitoring tool. For example, the Review of Progress Monitoring Tools chart, now available at the National Center on Response to Intervention website, indicates that most of the tools meeting standards are types of CBM (Deno, 1985, 1995, 2002, 2003; Deno, Mirkin, & Chiang, 1982; Fuchs & Deno, 1991, 1994; Fuchs, Fuchs, Hamlett, Walz, & Germann, 1993; Fuchs & Fuchs, 1986a, 1992, 1999, 2008; Fuchs, Fuchs, Hosp, & Jenkins, 2001; Shinn, 1989, 1998, 2008). CBM also was reviewed favorably for use in progress monitoring as part of the Reading First assessment evaluation process (Kame'enui, 2002).

CBM has been in use for almost three decades in public schools. Its initial use was as a tool to assess the progress of students with disabilities toward their IEP basic skills goals and to judge the effectiveness of their special education instructional programs (Germann & Tindal, 1985; Marston & Magnusson, 1985). Beginning in the early 1980s, the use of CBM quickly expanded to individual screening and entitlement decisions for students referred for special education (Marston, Mirkin, & Deno, 1984; Tindal & Germann, 1985).

Features and History of CBM

CBM is a family of assessment instruments that are designed to assess basic skills progress using tests with several common features. CBM tests are (a) standardized, (b) brief (i.e., usually less than 5 minutes), (c) easy to administer and score over time, (d) technically adequate, and (e) sensitive to improvement. Originally developed by Stanley Deno and a pool of graduate students, CBM was the product of directed research to address the need for scientifically based and pragmatic ways to write IEP goals and monitor progress. For early outcomes of this research program, see Deno, Marston, and Mirkin (1982) or Deno, Mirkin, and Chiang (1982); for a historical context, see the foreword in this book.

Originally, CBM assessment probes were developed from the specific curriculum used in a school's general education classrooms. However, this curriculum-specific approach, although defensible, was pragmatically challenging given curriculum differences within and between schools and over time. More importantly, this curriculum-specific approach generated test probes that ranged in difficulty level because of the inherent variability in the source curricula. Subsequent research found that alternate form reliability could be increased through use of standard probes, with further gains in logistics and without a loss in validity of progress decisions (Fuchs & Deno, 1992; Hintze & Shapiro, 1997; Hintze, Shapiro, & Lutz, 1994).

As a result, *standardized* CBM test materials that assessed basic skills in *general* rather than specific curriculum became the model of practice with different publishers of CBM materials, like any achievement test. For example, DIBELS (Kaminski & Good, 1996, 1998) is a publisher of CBM materials with an emphasis on early reading skills. Similarly, AIMSweb is a publisher of CBM materials in a variety of basic skills areas, and Monitoring Basic Skills Progress (MBSP) and Yearly Progress Pro (Fuchs, Fuchs, & Hamlett, 1995) are publishers of CBM reading and math test materials.

CBM Reading and Other Basic Skill Measures

In the area of reading, two CBM measures are the most common: (a) a 1-minute oral reading test (reading curriculum-based measurement; R-CBM) and (b) a 3- to 5-minute silent reading test (Maze). Additionally, there are a variety of early reading CBM measures, including Letter Naming Fluency (LNF), Letter Sound Fluency (LSF),

Phonemic Segmentation Fluency (PSF), and Nonsense Word Fluency (NWF). They are similar to other CBM measures in terms of their test construction and administration features (e.g., short tests, reliability, and validity). However, they differ from the other CBM measures in that these early literacy measures are used in a mastery monitoring approach. See Fuchs and Deno (1991) for more detail on the differences between mastery monitoring and general outcome measurement.

In R–CBM, a student reads standard passages aloud, and the number of words read correctly (WRC) is counted. In contrast to popular interpretation, it would not be accurate to characterize R–CBM only as a measure of oral reading fluency (Samuels, 2007). The construct measured when students read aloud is *general reading ability* or word-level reading ability (Fuchs et al., 2001; Shinn, Good, Knutson, Tilly, & Collins, 1992). Extensive reviews of the technical adequacy of R–CBM have been published over the previous two decades (Good & Jefferson, 1998; Marston, 1989; Miura Wayman, Wallace, Ives Wiley, Ticha, & Espin, 2007).

Maze is another measure of general reading ability within the family of curriculum-based measurement (Fuchs & Fuchs, 1992; Fuchs, Fuchs, Hamlett, & Ferguson, 1992; Shin, Deno, & Espin, 2000; Shinn & Shinn, 2003). In maze, students read a passage silently and select from three choices one word that correctly preserves the meaning of the passage. The number of correct choices is counted. Although maze measures the same construct as R–CBM, it has the advantage of being administered in small or large group settings, so that economies of time can be obtained with older students (i.e., higher than Grade 3).

Although there is less published research on them, there are mature CBM tools in other basic skill areas with a history of use by schools for progress monitoring and universal screening since the late 1970s. Their use as scientifically based progress monitoring tools is evaluated annually by the NCRTI's Progress Monitoring Technical Review Committee. These CBM tests include spelling, written expression, mathematics, and early numeracy. (For spelling, see Deno, Mirkin, Lowry, & Kuehnle, 1980; Fuchs, Fuchs, Hamlett, & Allinder, 1991; for written expression, see Espin et al., 2000; McMaster & Espin, 2007; for mathematics computation and mathematics application and problem solving see Foegen, Jiban, & Deno, 2007; Fuchs, Fuchs, et al., 1994; Fuchs, Fuchs, Karns, Hamlett, & Katzaroff, 1999; Thurber & Shinn, 2002; for early numeracy see Clarke & Shinn, 2004.)

DEVELOPMENT OF PROGRESS MONITORING SYSTEMS ACROSS TIERS: WORKING BACKWARD

To develop a high-quality data system for multitiered early-intervening services, including RTI, it is recommended that schools proceed "backward," beginning with progress monitoring in Tier 3, then in Tier 2, and after doing this, only then identify their universal screener. This backward approach contrasts with conventional practice, in which universal screening tools are selected first, and only then are progress monitoring tools identified for use at Tier 1, then Tier 2, then Tier 3. A comparison of two different approaches for creating a scientifically based progress monitoring and universal screening data system is shown in Figure 1. The left column illustrates the conventional sequence, in which reading achievement tools commonly employed in general education classrooms are used first as universal screeners, then as general education progress monitoring tools, with the presumption that these tools can be used for progress monitoring at other tiers.

Steps 1 and 2. Ensure Quality Progress Monitoring for Students Who Need It and Are Entitled to It

The right column in Figure 1 illustrates the preferred "backward" or reverse sequence in which schools develop their data system, beginning with progress monitoring for students who have a reading IEP goal (Fuchs & Fuchs, 2008; Shinn & Shinn, 2000). This sequence is recommended because CBM meets standards for scientifically based progress monitoring tools, including a demonstrated impact on student achievement. Published studies report effect sizes of .5 and greater when CBM is used to identify individualized goals and to monitor progress for students with disabilities (Fuchs & Fuchs, 1986b, 2004).

Figure 2 shows an example of two special education students whose progress on reading IEP goals was monitored using CBM. Each dot on these two graphs represents one R–CBM score on a given day. The first graph (Grade 2) demonstrates that the student's rate of improvement (trend line) exceeds the target goal (shown by the aim line), indicating that the IEP goal has been met and intervention should continue. In contrast,

Figure 1. A comparison of common and recommended sequences for developing a scientifically based progress monitoring and universal screening data system.

Most Common Sequence of Building RTI Data Systems Across Tiers	Recommended Sequence of Building RTI Data Systems Across Tiers
Identify Universal Screener	Step 1. Tier 3 Progress Monitoring Tool
⬇	⬇
Tier 1 Progress Monitoring Tool	Step 2. RTI Entitlement Progress Monitoring Tool
⬇	⬇
Tier 2 Progress Monitoring Tool	Step 3. Identify Universal Screener
⬇	⬇
Tier 3 Progress Monitoring Tool	Step 4. Tier 1 Progress Monitoring Tool
⬇	⬇
RTI Entitlement Progress Monitoring Tool	Step 5. Tier 2 Progress Monitoring Tool

Figure 2. An illustration of progress monitoring toward two students' IEP goals, using CBM.

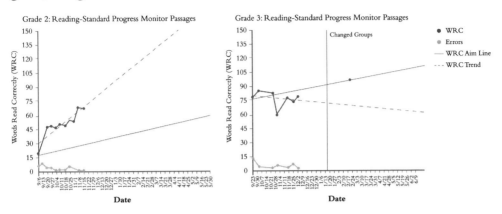

the graph on the right (Grade 3) illustrates the opposite pattern (i.e., the student's rate of progress is below the aim line, indicating that the intervention should be revised in line with the 1997 IDEA reauthorization's IEP requirements [Shinn & Shinn, 2000]).

In the backward-design approach, CBM provides symmetry to progress monitoring practices. The same progress monitoring tool that is used to identify IEP goals and to monitor progress *after* special education eligibility (i.e., CBM; Step 1 in the recommended sequence shown in Figure 1) also guides goal setting and progress monitoring *prior to* entitlement (Step 2 in Figure 1). Both before and after the special education entitlement process, the steps are the same: (a) valid progress monitoring measures are used, (b) individualized goals are written and represented on a graph, (c) data are collected over time, (d) the rate of progress is calculated and compared with an expected rate of progress, and (e) a judgment is made about progress and response to the intervention. The only major difference between Steps 1 and 2 is the period over which progress monitoring occurs. For an IEP, the time frame is for an annual goal, whereas for an entitlement decision within RTI, the goal may be written for a much shorter period (e.g., 6–10 weeks). Figure 3 illustrates a student whose progress is monitored twice per week over a 6-week period using an R-CBM probe to determine response to a high-quality reading intervention compared with a prescribed standard of adequate progress.

Step 3. Adopt the Quality Progress Monitoring Tool as a Universal Screener

As shown in Step 3 of Figure 1, the tool (i.e., CBM) used for progress monitoring toward IEP goals and as part of the RTI entitlement decision is identified as the general education universal screener. All students are screened using R-CBM; for older

Figure 3. An illustration of progress monitoring using R-CBM as part of an RTI entitlement decision.

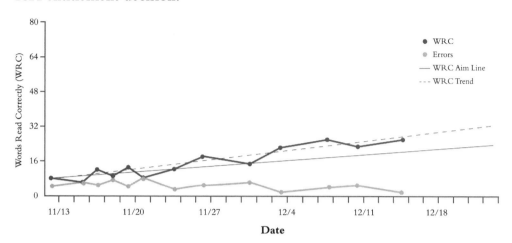

students, maze may be substituted. Each student's score is compared with the cut score or criterion. An illustration of how R–CBM and Maze is used with a student as part of a triage universal screening model is shown in Figure 4.

In this example, the dot represents an individual student's R–CBM score from the fall universal screening. In multitiered early-intervening services, it is recommended that a grade-level team review the screening data to match the intervention intensity with the severity of the reading problem. For example, using a normative approach, students who score below average (e.g., 10th–25th percentile) may be recommended for a Tier 2 intervention, and those who score well below average (e.g., below the 10th percentile) may be recommended for a Tier 3 intervention, as in this figure.

Step 4. Expand Universal Screening to a Benchmark Approach for Progress Monitoring

Proceeding with the recommended sequence for developing a data system (illustrated in Figure 1), the universal screening process using R–CBM then is expanded into a *benchmark* approach to provide a feasible general education progress monitoring system (Shinn, 2008). In a benchmark assessment approach, the universal screening method is repeated three to four times per year, as shown in Figure 5.

Following the school's universal screening process (shown as the fall benchmark period), the student, Arianna, was provided a Tier 2 intervention, in addition to

Figure 4. An example of R-CBM and Maze used in universal screening in a triage approach.

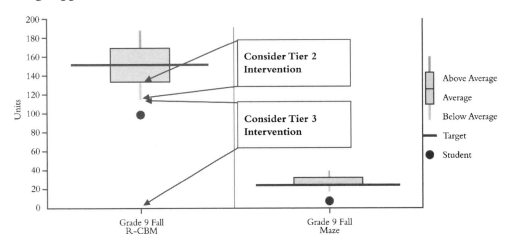

Grade, Benchmark Period, and Outcome Measure

Figure 5. Progress monitoring using R-CBM for a student in Tier 1 using a benchmark approach.

Arianna (Grade 2)

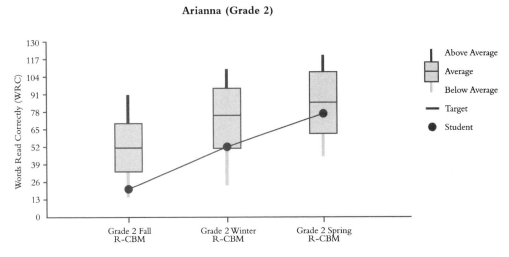

Grade, Benchmark Period, and Outcome Measure

core Tier 1 instruction, because her R-CBM score was below average. By the winter benchmark period, the gap had been reduced, and she no longer required the Tier 2 intervention. Spring benchmark results illustrated that Arianna maintained an adequate rate of progress. When CBM is used in a benchmark report and the information is provided to parents, it meets the IDEA 2004 requirements for "data-based documentation of repeated assessments of achievement at reasonable intervals, reflecting formal assessment of student progress during instruction, which was provided to the child's parents" (34 C.F.R. 300.304–300.306).

Step 5. Ensure Continuous Progress Monitoring by Specifying Frequency for Tier 2

The final step in the recommended sequence for developing a multitiered progress monitoring system using CBM is to identify the progress monitoring strategies for students who receive a Tier 2 intervention. An example of one approach is illustrated in Figure 6.

Emma, a fifth grader, received a Tier 2 intervention in addition to her core program after the universal screening was completed using the fall benchmark assessment. In this instance, an approach called *strategic monitoring* was used to monitor her progress more frequently (i.e., once per month) than students who

Figure 6. Progress monitoring using R-CBM more frequently for a student receiving a Tier 2 intervention using a strategic monitoring approach.

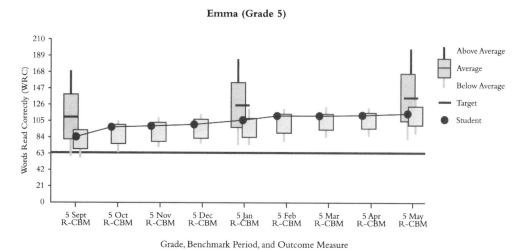

Emma (Grade 5)

Grade, Benchmark Period, and Outcome Measure

received Tier 1 instruction only (three times per year). However, her progress was monitored *less frequently* than students who received Tier 3 intervention (i.e., one to two times per week), because her reading problem was less severe than theirs. The frequency of Tier 2 progress monitoring varies from once per month to once per week, depending on the resources available.

How to Put It All Together

When a data system is designed in this way using CBM, it provides a clearly specified, continuous, and adequate (i.e., scientifically based) process for making efficient and effective decisions within a multitiered CEIS model including RTI. A graphic organizer of this data system, which illustrates when universal screening and increasingly intense progress monitoring practices are used and for which students, is depicted in Figure 7. In contrast to many current practices, a progress monitoring database is generated within and across years, minimizing the need to collect new data should there be a concern about an individual student's progress.

Figure 7. A three-tier model for universal screening and progress monitoring for R-CBM.

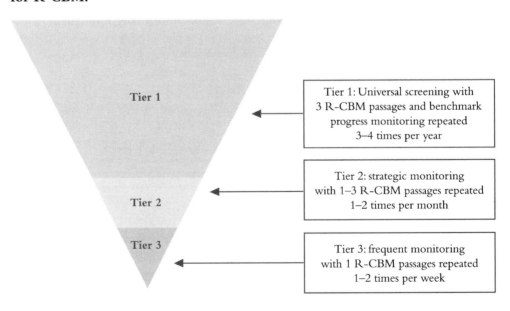

Note. From "Best Practices in Curriculum-Based Measurement and Its Use in a Problem-Solving Model," by M. R. Shinn, 2008, in A. Thomas & J. Grimes (Eds.), *Best Practices in School Psychology V* (p. 247), Bethesda, MD: National Association of School Psychologists. Copyright 2008 by the National Association of School Psychologists. Adapted with permission.

SPECIFIC UNIVERSAL SCREENING AND PROGRESS MONITORING PRACTICES AND ISSUES IN USING CBM IN A MULTITIERED MODEL

In this section, the use of CBM for universal screening and progress monitoring at each tier is described, and common issues of controversy are identified.

Tier 3 Goals and Frequent Progress Monitoring

When intensive reading needs are identified through a *triage* approach to universal screening (e.g., a student reads below the 10th percentile), a student may immediately receive a Tier 3 intervention. In addition, when students do not respond to a Tier 2 intervention in a *titration* model, they may receive a Tier 3 intervention. When students have severe reading needs and do not respond to a high-quality Tier 3 intervention, they may be entitled to special education, provided eligibility criteria have been met. In each of these instances, students should be entitled to frequent progress monitoring of their response to the reading intervention using CBM with individualized goals. The process for identifying individualized goals and conducting progress monitoring using CBM is described in this section.

Practices

Annual goals are written based on a student's performance on graded R-CBM probes using a process called survey-level assessment (SLA). In an SLA, a student reads three passages at consecutive levels of the curriculum until he or she reads successfully, as defined by a normative score comparing performance with that of other students on those same passages. For example, as illustrated in Figure 8, Carlos, a sixth grader, read passages successively beginning at Grade 6, to Grades 5, 4, 3, and 2, the last of which he read normatively as well as other Grade 2 students. An annual goal for this student might read, "In 1 year, when given a randomly sampled passage from the Grade 4 reading passages, Carlos will read 125 words correctly with 4 or fewer errors."

When writing an individualized goal, the team must consider whether it is plausible for the student to eliminate the gap (i.e., be successful in Grade 6 material) in 1 year. If it is determined that this is not plausible, a lower goal would be written, but one that would be expected to reduce the gap (e.g., to read Grade 4 material successfully). For example, whereas Carlos was expected to be reading at 125 WRC in 1 year, another Grade 6 student with a more severe reading performance discrepancy may be expected to read 100 WRC from Grade 3 passages in 1 year. For more detail regarding the use of CBM to write IEP goals, the reader is referred to Fuchs and Shinn (1989); Deno, Mirkin, and Wesson (1984); Shinn (2003a); and Shinn and Shinn (2000).

CBM progress monitoring uses a general outcome measurement approach, which samples student performance on a standardized task of consistent difficulty, over time,

Figure 8. A survey-level assessment for a Grade 6 student with severe reading needs.

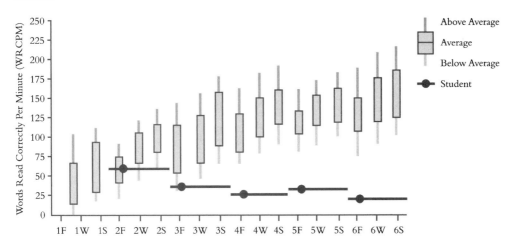

Benchmark Period (Fall, Winter, and Spring)

to determine if adequate growth is occurring (Fuchs & Deno, 1991; Fuchs & Shinn, 1989; Shinn, 2003a; Shinn & Shinn, 2000). For progress monitoring purposes, a student reads a single randomly sampled R-CBM passage from the goal material once or twice per week. For Carlos, this would be one or two passages per week from Grade 4 passages. As illustrated in Figure 9, a line drawn from a student's first R-CBM score (i.e., the current level of performance) to the criterion score at the goal date (i.e., the aim line) reflects adequate progress.

For students who are receiving Tier 3 interventions but who are not eligible for special education, it is highly desirable to monitor their progress in their grade-level material. That is, a Grade 3 student receiving a Tier 3 intervention would have a goal to be successful in Grade 3 materials. However, this decision would be made following the completion of an SLA. Figure 10 presents SLA results from a student identified as a candidate for Tier 3 intervention based on R-CBM scores below the 10th percentile. Results show that although the student is below the 10th percentile compared with other students at the same grade (i.e., that the scores are below the line representing below average), the student reads Grade 2 material successfully. Thus, the goal is Grade 3 successful reading, and progress is monitored one to two times per week using Grade 3 passages.

Controversies

Two major controversies are associated with the use of CBM for goal setting and progress monitoring at Tier 3. The first controversy is a distinct gap between the knowledge base

Figure 9. An illustration of progress monitoring toward two students' IEP goals, using CBM.

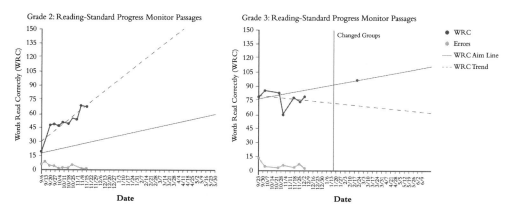

Figure 10. A survey-level assessment for a student identified for potential Tier 3 services using R-CBM.

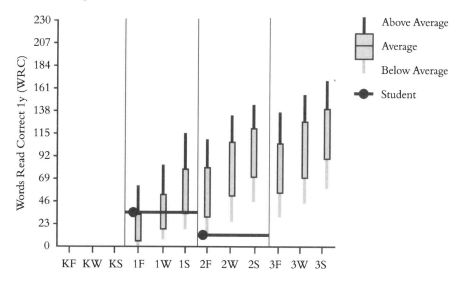

and standard practice. That is, despite long-standing concerns over the quality of IEP goals and progress monitoring practices (Fuchs, Deno, & Mirkin, 1982; Smith, 1990), these have remained largely unchanged since 1975 (Bateman & Linden, 1998; Giangreco, Dennis, Edelman, & Chigee, 1994; Shinn & Shinn, 2000). This gap between scientifically based IEP progress monitoring practices and what typically occurs in schools remains wide, despite professionals' familiarity with CBM (Shapiro, Angello, & Eckert, 2004) and the wide availability of excellent resources (e.g., NCRTI).

A second controversy concerns the goal-setting process. For example, although at least four possible methods for setting a criterion for success have been identified, not a single comparative study of these approaches has been conducted. More guidance about goal setting is needed (Fuchs, Fuchs, & Deno, 1985).

Progress Monitoring and RTI as an Entitlement Process

In assessing RTI as an SLD entitlement process, a *dual-discrepancy* approach has been recommended (Fuchs, Fuchs, & Speece, 2002; Pericola Case et al., 2003). A student who exhibits a dual discrepancy has (a) severe low achievement relative to peers (i.e., discrepancy in educational need), which can be assessed economically and accurately using R-CBM data from universal screening; and (b) a low rate of improvement, which can be determined from progress monitoring data showing a lack of response to appropriate instruction (i.e., discrepancy of educational benefit; Shinn, 2007).

Practices

Two progress monitoring approaches can be used in an RTI entitlement process: (a) using extant CBM data from frequent progress monitoring, and (b) developing a new progress monitoring plan. For a student who has been receiving an appropriate (i.e., high quality, high intensity) Tier 3 intervention along with CBM progress monitoring, these data provide the basis for the judgment of appropriate response to intervention. In the second instance, if a student has not received a Tier 3 intervention and is considered for special education entitlement, then a short-term goal (e.g., 6 weeks) would need to be written and progress would be monitored during the intervention period.

An example of progress monitoring as part of RTI entitlement for a Grade 2 student is shown in Figure 3. The goal is written so that if the goal were attained, the gap in reading Grade 2 material, compared with peers, would be reduced. It is preferable that a sample of at least 10 data points be obtained. If the goal was written for a 6-week time frame and student progress was monitored twice per week, a judgment of adequate progress would be based on 12 data points. If the goal were written for an 8-week time frame, a judgment of adequate progress would be based on 16 data points.

Controversies

If schools use CBM to write quality IEP goals and monitor progress for students with disabilities, extending these practices as described in this section for RTI entitlement is reasonably simple. However, if scientifically based progress monitoring using CBM is not standard practice within a district's special education program, schools will need to add this capacity in addition to the numerous challenges associated with developing intensive multitiered coordinated early-intervening services.

In addition, there is not a consensus regarding appropriate goal-setting practices within the RTI entitlement process. While some would assert that adequate progress is defined as a rate of improvement equivalent to typically developing peers, others argue that adequate progress must reduce the achievement gap. Further research to address this question would assist practitioners in using CBM for RTI entitlement.

CBM and Universal Screening

Since the early 1980s, CBM has been used to screen individual students for potential reading difficulties (Marston, Deno, & Tindal, 1984; Marston, Mirkin, & Deno, 1984). However, this screening typically began with special education referral one student at a time. Getting *all* students off to a good reading start begins by implementing a universal screening process in which *all* students are tested to identify potentially at-risk students. CBM is a time-efficient tool for this process. More important, there is an accumulating body of knowledge supporting the validity of using CBM in universal screening (Stage & Jacobsen, 2001). In universal screening, two measures of predictive efficiency are most important: (a) *sensitivity*, or true positives (i.e., those students predicted to not pass the criterion test who in fact do not pass), and (b) *specificity*, or true negatives (i.e., those students predicted to pass the criterion test who do pass). Two recent studies that compared the diagnostic accuracy and predictive validity of R-CBM with high-stakes state reading tests reported ranges of predictive efficiency of .65 to .76 for sensitivity and .78 to .82 for specificity, with predictions from the winter Grade 1 R-CBM and the end of Grade 3 state reading test (Hintze & Silberglitt, 2005; Silberglitt & Hintze, 2005).

Practices

When R-CBM is used in universal screening, students typically read three graded passages, and the median WRC is counted. This process is completed in approximately 5 minutes per student when the examiners are well trained. Many CBM publishers also offer options for collecting, scoring, and reporting options using hand-held electronic devices that can increase efficiency further. With older students (e.g., Grade 5 and above), some economies of time can be achieved by substituting maze—a 3- to 5-minute silent reading test that can be administered to students in groups through pencil-and-paper testing or through use of a computer—instead of R-CBM (Stage & Jacobsen, 2001).

As discussed earlier in the chapter, universal screening practices most often are based on the titration approach, in which at-risk students are identified for consideration for Tier 2 interventions. Progress through the remaining tiers and potential special education entitlement is based on CBM progress monitoring data. In the titration approach, the first student on the left in Figure 11 would receive the core reading program through Tier 1 instruction, while both students to the right would be considered for Tier 2 intervention.

Increasingly, however, schools are using the triage approach, in which interventions other than Tier 2 are considered, based on the severity of the reading problem identified through universal screening. Students performing below average (e.g., 10th to the 25th percentile) may be recommended for Tier 2 intervention. Students well below average (e.g., below the 10th percentile) may be recommended for intensive Tier 3 interventions. In Figure 11, the first student on the left would receive the core reading program through Tier 1 instruction. However, within a triage approach, the middle student likely would be recommended to receive a Tier 2 intervention, while the student to the right may be considered for Tier 3 intervention.

Controversies

To date, there are no studies comparing the titration and triage approaches to universal screening with respect to effects on achievement. It is plausible that the sooner a student with a severe reading problem receives the most intensive intervention, the greater the likelihood of reducing the reading achievement gap. From a social validity perspective, it is plausible that the triage approach may be judged more favorably by teachers and parents because there is no need for a student to first fail in less-intensive interventions.

Considerable controversy exists regarding how the criteria for defining students as potentially at risk are specified. There are no empirically validated standards for using

Figure 11. Results of universal screening using R–CBM in a benchmark approach for three students.

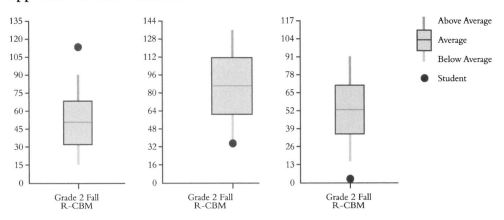

R–CBM or any other test for this purpose. Instead, some researchers propose that such criteria are derived from the value judgments of the school personnel, based in part on the availability of intervention resources (Deno, 1989; Shinn, Good, & Parker, 1999). For example, in a district with significant resources for outside-the-classroom support, 25% of students may be served in Tier 2 interventions. The normative cut score for this setting would be those scores below the 35th percentile for Tier 2 interventions and below the 10th percentile for Tier 3. In districts with fewer outside-the-classroom support resources, it may be possible to provide Tier 2 interventions to only 15% of students. In that case, the criterion for potential Tier 2 intervention would be scores below the 25th percentile.

In part, to offset the challenges introduced by setting cut scores based on normative data (e.g., intervening with X percent of students), some schools have chosen to link their cut scores to *standards*. These standards are indeed more objective than normative cut scores based on social values and available resources, because they are derived by examining correlations of R–CBM with state high-stakes reading tests and predictive validity. Through the use of statistical methods (e.g., receiver operator characteristic [ROC] curves, logistic regression), critical values associated with high and low probabilities of passing the high-stakes test can be computed. An excellent example is shown in Figure 12, which displays critical R–CBM scores for Grades 1 to 8 fall, winter, and spring benchmarks as they relate to state standards. As illustrated in this figure, a score of 80 WRC or greater at the beginning of Grade 3 is associated with a high probability of exceeding state standards. A score of 60 WRC or lower is associated with a low likelihood of passing the state test.

When this *standards-based* approach to universal screening is used, those students who are less likely to meet or exceed state standards may be considered for a Tier 2 "strategic" intervention (Simmons et al., 2002). The standards-based universal

Figure 12. Standards-based cut scores across Grades 1 to 8 based on R-CBM scores and the Illinois Standards Achievement Test (ISAT).

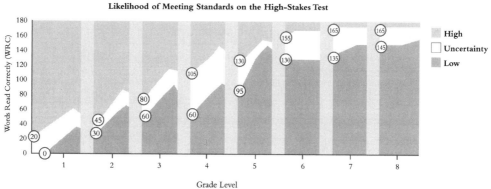

Note. This figure was developed by Ben Ditkowsky, PhD from http://measuredeffects.com. Reprinted with permission.

screening approach is discussed in the section on controversy rather than practices because of the unintended consequences of this approach. For example, in a low-performing school, more than 60% of the students were identified as needing Tier 2 interventions because they performed below the R–CBM standards-based cut score. Of course, the school did not have sufficient resources to deliver this magnitude of Tier 2 intervention *in addition* to their core Tier 1 program.

Although intuitively appealing, a standards-based approach is best used for *program evaluation* purposes instead of universal screening. That is, a school that has more than 60% of students being unlikely to pass the state test suggests the need to *improve the core* (i.e., Tier 1) program rather than target individual students for intervention.

IMPLEMENTATION OF PROGRESS MONITORING IN THREE TIERS USING A BENCHMARK AND STRATEGIC MONITORING APPROACH

Monitoring progress toward IEP goals to evaluate the effects of special education intervention or to evaluate RTI as part of special education entitlement requires *frequent* (e.g., at least once per week) progress monitoring. However, progress monitoring is an important component of school success for *all* students. If all students benefit from progress monitoring, the question becomes one of how to do it in a manner that is *feasible,* one of a number of important criteria in a school-based progress monitoring model (Fuchs & Fuchs, 1999). Schools have been successful in making progress monitoring feasible by using benchmark assessment for all students and by using strategic monitoring for students at risk.

Tier 1 Benchmark Assessment

Benchmark assessment, benchmark testing, or "benchmarking" are synonymous terms used to describe the process of using CBM for universal screening *and* progress monitoring. When R–CBM is used in benchmarking, the initial universal screening process is repeated two to three more times during the academic year (e.g., winter and spring). Following this practice, benchmarking consists of a fall universal screening and two subsequent progress monitoring assessments, requiring approximately 15 minutes per student per year using R–CBM, and less than 20 minutes per year for an entire grade using maze materials.

Practices

Two common approaches are used in the benchmark reading assessments. In the first approach, the same test materials (i.e., passages or maze) are used each time. Although this approach ensures that the test probes are of equal difficulty, there are potential costs involved. The first relates to possible loss of test security; since the specific passages are known in advance, it is possible that students will practice them, invalidating their usefulness as a progress monitoring tool. Additionally, given that the same passages are used repeatedly, there is the small likelihood of a practice effect, although no study has validated this effect during benchmarking. Finally, there is the potential problem of examiner fatigue. When examiners are routinely and frequently engaging in the same testing practices, error can be increased by this repetition over time.

The second approach for benchmarking uses alternate forms, in which different R-CBM or maze probes are used each time. This approach eliminates the effects of loss of test security, practice, and potential examiner fatigue. However, it introduces the potential disadvantage of each set of probes differing in difficulty. As a consequence, when this benchmark approach is used, it is important that the pool of potential assessment materials be studied with respect to their alternate form reliability and evidence of equal difficulty be provided.

Following the administration of R-CBM or maze probes during a benchmark period, each student's scores are graphed on a normative chart and a decision is made regarding the student's rate of improvement and current performance level. An example of benchmark assessment for a Grade 2 student over three testing periods is shown in Figure 5. The fall benchmark score for Arianna was used for purposes of universal screening. Because these data indicated her performance was below average, the grade-level team recommended a Tier 2 intervention. By the winter benchmark, Arianna's rate of improvement was above that of typical students and the achievement gap was reduced. By the spring benchmark, she read as well as other students.

By compiling benchmark scores across years, a graphic display of reading progress from one grade to another can be created. Such a display may be particularly useful for tracking progress and reporting to parents of students receiving special education or other remedial services.

The R-CBM benchmark scores for a student from mid-Grade 1 to the beginning of Grade 4 are shown in Figure 13. Although Peter demonstrates very low reading scores, his reading improved each year and at about the same rate as typically developing peers who received the same instruction. However, if the goal was to reduce the reading skill gap, the reading program was not accomplishing its intended outcome. In Grade 4, the school moved to building a multitiered early-intervening service model.

Controversies

The principal controversies regarding benchmarking are related to ownership and logistics. With respect to the former, in a number of districts, benchmarking evolved from developing local norms. In local norming, a *subset* of students is tested to assist in screening individual students referred for special education (Stewart & Silberglitt, 2008). This subset of students often is tested by a group of special educators, and general education teachers typically are not involved. When the local norming process expands to benchmarking all students, and general education teachers are expected to participate in testing, some perceive this as more work. The second issue concerns making the benchmarking process as efficient as possible. Even an individual student 5-

Figure 13. A fourth-grade student's benchmark scores from mid-first grade to early fourth grade.

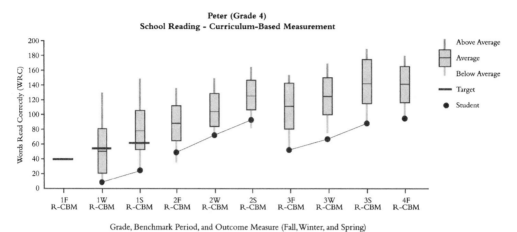

Note. From *AIMSweb*. Copyright © 2008 NCS Pearson, Inc. Reproduced with permission. All rights reserved. "*AIMSweb*" is a trademark, in the US and/or other countries, of Pearson Education, Inc. or its affiliates(s).

minute benchmark assessment compounds into hours when multiplied by the number of students tested. Every effort should be made to ensure that data are collected in an efficient manner, and specific training materials have been developed to facilitate this goal (Shinn, 2003b).

Tier 2 Progress Monitoring Using a Strategic Approach

In a multitiered model, students who receive Tier 2 interventions are provided more intensive interventions because they are at greater risk for reading failure. Because of this risk, schools also monitor their progress more frequently than that of the students who receive Tier 1 intervention alone, but typically not with the regularity of progress monitoring for students who receive Tier 3 interventions. The type of progress monitoring practices used with students at risk but without severe educational need is called *strategic monitoring*, to distinguish it from benchmarking or frequent progress monitoring.

Practices

The strategic monitoring process is similar to that of benchmarking. Students' progress is monitored using grade-level reading probes (i.e., a Grade 3 student receiving a Tier 2 intervention would be assessed using Grade 3 passages), and the individual student's goal is to achieve at the same rate as typically developing students. Strategic monitoring differs from benchmarking in the frequency of progress monitoring.

Most commonly, strategic monitoring involves monthly testing, using the three benchmark scores and repeating the benchmark assessment in the months when there is no benchmarking. To illustrate, in a school where benchmarking occurs in the fall for purposes of universal screening and is repeated in January and late April for progress monitoring, students receiving Tier 2 intervention would read three passages from grade-level material for strategic monitoring during months without benchmarking (e.g., October, November, December, etc.). This strategic monitoring approach requires a commitment of approximately 5 minutes per month per student. An example of a student whose progress is monitored strategically is shown in Figure 6.

In this figure, Emma's score is represented by the dot and is compared with the box and whisker plot of all the students in the school or district and with the disaggregated subset of other students who receive Tier 2 interventions. Each month that strategic monitoring takes place, the scores are plotted against other students who receive Tier 2, until the next benchmark, when the scores are compared with all students, as well as with the disaggregated subgroup of students in Tier 2. Figure 6 illustrates that Emma is making the same rate of progress as other students overall, as well as other students receiving the Tier 2 interventions.

A second, but less common approach to strategic monitoring is to use the type of progress monitoring practices in Tier 3 or for IEP progress monitoring. When this approach is used, the process is different in two regards. First, the student is tested in grade-level materials with standard goals rather than through an individualized goal-setting process. Second, progress is monitored more frequently, usually every other week or once per week.

Controversies

The primary controversies in Tier 2 progress monitoring are twofold. First, as noted in chapters 6 and 18 in this book, the real challenge in developing multitiered early-intervening services is ensuring coordinated and powerful Tier 2 interventions. Establishing a common, scientifically based progress monitoring system is part of that challenge. The second controversy concerns identifying which progress monitoring practices are most effective in increasing student achievement. To date, there have been no comparative studies examining which CBM progress monitoring practices (e.g., frequency, goal-setting practices) produce the best outcomes with at-risk students.

UNIVERSAL SCREENING AND PROGRESS MONITORING IN THREE TIERS IN EARLY LITERACY

Although some students are reading when they enter first grade, typically achieving early first graders earn very low scores on R-CBM first-grade passages. With the exception of some high-achieving communities, the distribution of R-CBM scores is positively skewed, with many students earning scores of less than 5 WRC (Rodden-Nord & Shinn, 1991). About the middle of first grade, R-CBM begins to be more useful for identifying at-risk students and for progress monitoring.

Because a major goal of reading success is early detection of students at risk for reading difficulties, waiting until most students can read R–CBM Grade 1 passages is not acceptable. This is a well-known shortcoming of R–CBM Grade 1 passages, and educators have long sought to develop other assessment tools for identifying at-risk students and for progress monitoring in kindergarten and early Grade 1.

A synthesis of the scientific research on reading by the National Reading Panel (2000) provided some critical reading skills that could (and should) be assessed in kindergarten and early Grade 1, including phonemic awareness and elements of phonics, including letter names and sounds, and the ability to read nonsense words or lists of phonetically regular words. Unfortunately, no *single* measure that can be used continuously across these early literacy skills has been validated as an early literacy progress monitoring tool. As a result, different early reading skills must be assessed at different periods.

DIBELS (Kaminski & Good, 1996, 1998) was developed as a downward extension of CBM to early literacy to help solve the problem of waiting for R–CBM to be sensitive to between- and within-student reading differences. DIBELS initially consisted of these early literacy tests: Initial Sound Fluency (ISF), Phonemic Segmentation Fluency (PSF), and Nonsense Word Fluency (NWF). It was later expanded to include Letter Naming Fluency (LNF), an R–CBM task, and other measures of vocabulary and comprehension.

Although DIBELS has been referred to as a progress monitoring tool for general outcome measurement, in which a single skill can be used to monitor progress over an extended period of time, most DIBELS measures fit more closely with a mastery monitoring approach. In mastery monitoring, specific subskills are assessed at specific times in line with a logical or empirical sequence (Fuchs & Deno, 1991). With DIBELS, the measures represent a developmental hierarchy, with ISF viewed as a precursor to PSF, PSF as a precursor to NWF, and NWF as a precursor to R–CBM.

When using DIBELS, multiple measures are administered to all students at each benchmark period in kindergarten through Grade 2, both for universal screening and progress monitoring, as described in this chapter for R–CBM (see Kaminski, Cummings, Powell-Smith, & Good, 2008, for more detail on specific DIBELS practices). DIBELS differs from R–CBM in two ways. First, in universal screening, DIBELS almost always uses a standards–based approach. Reports target students whose scores fall below a criterion linked to a state test for additional intervention. Second, because implicitly it is a mastery monitoring approach, different early literacy skills must be targeted for progress monitoring at Tiers 2 and 3 at different times. For example, in early kindergarten a student receiving a Tier 2 reading intervention may first be progress monitored using PSF and then be progress monitored with NWF when the PSF criterion is attained.

In kindergarten, up to four DIBELS measures may be given to all students. In the fall of Grade 2, according to DIBELS benchmark specifications (Kaminski et al., 2008), students still are tested on NWF. As a consequence of administering multiple subskill tests to all students over time, DIBELS has been criticized for overtesting students

(Pearson, 2006) and for being logistically challenging (Fuchs, Fuchs, & Compton, 2004).

To improve feasibility, it is suggested that three alternative approaches to early literacy universal screening and progress monitoring be considered. First, LNF might be used *only* as a fall kindergarten screener. This type of measure has a long-standing empirically demonstrated predictive relation to reading failure (Bond & Dykstra, 1967) that has been replicated in recent years (Elliott, Lee, & Tollefson, 2001; Hintze, Ryan, & Stoner, 2003). Its efficiency and accuracy make it an excellent universal screening tool. However, there is no evidence that LNF is useful as a progress monitoring tool.

Second, it is suggested that these literacy tools be used in a *multiple-gating* approach. In a multiple-gating approach, all students are tested on the *highest skill* in a hierarchical skill set. For example, if a Grade 1 student performs satisfactorily on R-CBM, a measure of general reading ability, then that student would not be tested on any of the DIBELS subskills (e.g., NWF, PSF). Similarly, a kindergarten student who performs satisfactorily on NWF would not be tested on PSF. This multiple gating approach reduces the amount of testing for all students and enables schools to collect the most information on the students who are at greatest risk.

Third, it is suggested that schools use Letter Sound Fluency (LSF) as the primary measure for universal screening *and* progress monitoring after the fall kindergarten benchmarking. LSF is another measure of the alphabetic principle, it is very easy to administer, and it works well as a universal screener. In a predictive validity study with over 2,000 students, kindergarten LSF was shown to be superior to PSF as a predictor of spring Grade 1 reading (.66 vs. .35; Silberglitt, 2007). In this same longitudinal study, LSF also demonstrated considerable sensitivity to improvement, with changes in means from 10.1 to 21.5 to 40.3 letter sounds at each benchmark. As a progress monitoring tool, LSF is highly correlated with PSF and NWF and can simplify mastery monitoring by providing a single progress monitoring test. Additionally, letter sounds are a more suitable and authentic instructional target than either PSF or NWF.

CONCLUSION

This chapter illustrated how curriculum-based measurement—a set of simple, inexpensive, time-efficient, and scientifically based basic skills tests—can be used across multiple tiers for progress monitoring and universal screening. Although CBM for reading was used as the primary exemplar, CBM applications for older students and younger students were included (e.g., maze, and modifications or additions to DIBELS).

With more than 250 published journal articles and book chapters on R-CBM alone, curriculum-based measurement is highly endorsed as an evidence-based practice for universal screening and progress monitoring. Certainly, CBM is a cornerstone of RTI, especially when RTI is conceived as multitiered early-intervening services.

Despite more than 30 years of research and applied practice, CBM remains underutilized within educational settings, which too frequently retain traditional, albeit questionable measures for screening and progress monitoring. It is hoped that this chapter, and other relevant contributions within this volume, will provide practitioners with the necessary information, skills, and resources for translating what works to widespread school practice.

REFERENCES

Adams, M. J. (1990). *Beginning to read: Thinking and learning about print*. Cambridge, MA: MIT Press.

Algozzine, B., Christenson, S., & Ysseldyke, J. (1982). Probabilities associated with the referral to placement process. *Teacher Education and Special Education, 5,* 19–23.

Baker, E. L., O'Neil, H. F., & Linn, R. L. (1993). Policy and validity prospects for performance-based assessment. *American Psychologist, 48,* 1210–1218.

Bateman, B. D., & Linden, M. A. (1998). *Better IEPs*. Longmont, CO: Sopris West.

Bond, G. L., & Dykstra, R. (1967). The cooperative research program in first-grade reading instruction. *Reading Research Quarterly, 2,* 5–14.

Burdette, P. (2007). *Response to intervention as it relates to early intervention services*. Washington, DC: Project Forum at National Association of State Directors of Special Education.

Deno, S. L. (1985). Curriculum-based measurement: The emerging alternative. *Exceptional Children, 52,* 219–232.

Deno, S. L. (1986). Formative evaluation of individual student programs: A new role for school psychologists. *School Psychology Review, 15,* 358–374.

Deno, S. L. (1989). Curriculum-based measurement and alternative special education services, A fundamental and direct relationship. In M. R. Shinn (Ed.), *Curriculum-based measurement: Assessing special children* (pp. 1–17). New York: Guilford Press.

Deno, S. L. (1995). School psychologist as problem solver. In A. Thomas & J. Grimes (Eds.), *Best practices in school psychology III* (pp. 471–484). Washington, DC: National Association of School Psychologists.

Deno, S. L. (2002). Problem-solving as best practice. In A. Thomas & J. Grimes (Eds.), *Best practices in school psychology IV* (pp. 37–55). Bethesda, MD: National Association of School Psychologists.

Deno, S. L. (2003). Developments in curriculum-based measurement. *Journal of Special Education, 37,* 184–192.

Deno, S. L. (2005). Problem-solving assessment. In R. Brown-Chidsey (Ed.), *Assessment for intervention: A problem-solving approach* (pp. 10–40). New York: Guilford Press.

Deno, S. L., Marston, D., & Mirkin, P. (1982). Valid measurement procedures for continuous evaluation of written expression. *Exceptional Children, 48,* 68–71.

Deno, S. L., Mirkin, P., & Chiang, B. (1982). Identifying valid measures of reading. *Exceptional Children, 49,* 36–45.

Deno, S. L., Mirkin, P. K., Lowry, L., & Kuehnle, K. (1980). *Relationships among simple measures of spelling and performance on standardized achievement tests.* Minneapolis, MN: University of Minnesota, Institute for Research on Learning Disabilities.

Deno, S. L., Mirkin, P., & Wesson, C. (1984). How to write effective data-based IEPs. *Teaching Exceptional Children, 16,* 99–104.

Elliott, J., Lee, S. W., & Tollefson, N. (2001). A reliability and validity study of the Dynamic Indicators of Basic Early Literacy Skills–Modified. *School Psychology Review, 30,* 33–49.

Espin, C., Shin, J., Deno, S. L., Skare, S., Robinson, S., & Benner, B. (2000). Identifying indicators of written expression proficiency for middle school students. *Journal of Special Education, 34,* 140–153.

Fletcher, J. M., Coulter, W. A., Reschly, D. J., & Vaughn, S. (2004). Alternative approaches to the definition of learning disabilities: Some questions and answers. *Annals of Dyslexia, 54,* 304–331.

Foegen, A., Jiban, C., & Deno, S. L. (2007). Progress monitoring measures in mathematics: A review of the literature. *Journal of Special Education, 41,* 121–139.

Fuchs, D., Fuchs, L. S., Benowitz, S., & Berringer, K. (1987). Norm-referenced tests: Are they valid for use with handicapped students? *Exceptional Children, 54,* 263–271.

Fuchs, L. S. (1994). *Connecting performance assessment to instruction.* Reston, VA: Council for Exceptional Children.

Fuchs, L. S., & Deno, S. L. (1991). Paradigmatic distinctions between instructionally relevant measurement models. *Exceptional Children, 57,* 488–500.

Fuchs, L. S., & Deno, S. L. (1992). Effects of curriculum within curriculum-based measurement. *Exceptional Children, 58,* 232–243.

Fuchs, L. S., & Deno, S. L. (1994). Must instructionally useful performance assessment be based in the curriculum? *Exceptional Children, 61,* 15–24.

Fuchs, L. S., Deno, S. L., & Mirkin, P. K. (1982). *Special education practice in evaluating student progress toward goals* (No. IRLD-RR-81). Minneapolis, MN: University of Minnesota, Institute for Research on Learning Disabilities.

Fuchs, L. S., & Fuchs, D. (1984). Criterion-referenced assessment without measurement: How accurate for special education. *Remedial and Special Education, 5,* 29–32.

Fuchs, L. S., & Fuchs, D. (1986a). Curriculum-based assessment of progress towards long- and short-term goals. *Journal of Special Education, 20,* 69–82.

Fuchs, L. S., & Fuchs, D. (1986b). Effects of systematic formative evaluation on student achievement, A meta-analysis. *Exceptional Children 53,* 199–208.

Fuchs, L. S., & Fuchs, D. (1992). Identifying a measure for monitoring student reading progress. *School Psychology Review, 21,* 45–58.

Fuchs, L. S., & Fuchs, D. (1999). Monitoring student progress toward the development of reading competence: A review of three forms of classroom-based assessment. *School Psychology Review, 28,* 659–671.

Fuchs, L. S., & Fuchs, D. (2004). *What is scientifically based research on progress monitoring?* Washington, DC: National Center on Progress Monitoring, American Institute for Research, Office of Special Education Programs.

Fuchs, L. S., & Fuchs, D. (2005). Responsiveness-to-intervention: A blueprint for practitioners, policymakers, and parents. *Teaching Exceptional Children*, Sept./Oct., 57–61.

Fuchs, L. S., & Fuchs, D. (2008). Best practices in progress monitoring reading and mathematics at the elementary level. In A. Thomas & J. Grimes (Eds.), *Best practices in school psychology V* (pp. 2147–2164). Bethesda, MD: National Association of School Psychologists.

Fuchs, L. S., Fuchs, D., & Compton, D. L. (2004). Monitoring early reading development in first grade: Word identification fluency versus nonsense word fluency. *Exceptional Children, 71,* 7–21.

Fuchs, L. S., Fuchs, D., & Deno, S. L. (1985). The importance of goal ambitiousness and goal mastery to student achievement. *Exceptional Children, 52,* 63–71.

Fuchs, L. S., Fuchs, D., & Hamlett, C. (1995). *Monitoring basic skills progress (MBSP): Basic math computation and basic math concepts and applications.* Austin, TX: Pro-Ed.

Fuchs, L. S., Fuchs, D., Hamlett, C. L., & Allinder, R. M. (1991). The contribution of skills analysis to curriculum-based measurement in spelling. *Exceptional Children, 57,* 443–452.

Fuchs, L. S., Fuchs, D., Hamlett, C. L., & Ferguson, C. (1992). Effects of expert system consultation within curriculum-based measurement using a reading maze task. *Exceptional Children, 58,* 436–450.

Fuchs, L. S., Fuchs, D., Hamlett, C. L., Thompson, A., Roberts, P. H., & Kupek, P. (1994). Technical features of a mathematics concepts and applications curriculum-based measurement system. *Diagnostique, 19,* 23–49.

Fuchs, L. S., Fuchs, D., Hamlett, C. L., Walz, L., & Germann, G. (1993). Formulative evaluation of academic progress: How much growth can we expect? *School Psychology Review, 22,* 27–48.

Fuchs, L. S., Fuchs, D., Hosp, M. K., & Jenkins, J. R. (2001). Oral reading fluency as an indicator of reading competence: A theoretical, empirical, and historical analysis. *Scientific Studies of Reading, 5,* 239–256.

Fuchs, L. S., Fuchs, D., Karns, K., Hamlett, C. L., & Katzaroff, M. (1999). Mathematics performance assessment in the classroom: effects on teacher planning and student problem solving. *American Educational Research Journal, 36,* 609–646.

Fuchs, L. S., Fuchs, D., & Speece, D. L. (2002). Treatment validity as a unifying construct for identifying learning disabilities. *Learning Disability Quarterly, 25,* 33–45.

Fuchs, L. S., & Shinn, M. R. (1989). Writing CBM IEP objectives. In M. R. Shinn (Ed.), *Curriculum-based measurement: Assessing special children* (pp. 132–154). New York: Guilford Press.

Fuchs, L. S., & Vaughn, S. R. (2005). Response to Intervention as a framework for the identification of learning disabilities. *Forum for Trainers of School Psychologists,* Spring, 12–19.

Gerber, M., & Semmel, M. (1984). Teachers as imperfect tests: Reconceptualizing the referral process. *Educational Psychologist, 19,* 137–148.

Germann, G., & Tindal, G. (1985). Applications of direct and repeated measurement using curriculum based assessment. *Exceptional Children, 51,* 110–121.

Giangreco, M. F., Dennis, R. E., Edelman, S. W., & Chigee, J. C. (1994). Dressing your IEP for the general education climate: Analysis of IEP goals and objectives for students with multiple disabilities. *Remedial and Special Education, 15,* 288–296.

Good, R. H., & Jefferson, G. (1998). Contemporary perspectives on curriculum-based measurement validity. In M. R. Shinn (Ed.), *Advanced Applications of Curriculum-Based Measurement* (pp. 61–88). New York: Guilford Press.

Hintze, J. M., Ryan, A. L., & Stoner, G. (2003). Concurrent validity and diagnostic accuracy of the Dynamic Indicators of Basic Early Literacy Skills and the Comprehensive Test of Phonological Processing. *School Psychology Review, 32,* 541–556.

Hintze, J. M., & Shapiro, E. S. (1997). Curriculum-based measurement and literature-based reading: Is curriculum-based measurement meeting the needs of changing reading curricula. *Journal of School Psychology, 35,* 351–375.

Hintze, J. M., Shapiro, E. S., & Lutz, J. G. (1994). The effects of curriculum on the sensitivity of curriculum-based measurement of reading. *The Journal of Special Education, 28,* 188–202.

Hintze, J. M., & Silberglitt, B. (2005). A longitudinal examination of the diagnostic accuracy and predictive validity of R-CBM and high stakes testing. *School Psychology Review, 34,* 372–386.

Howell, K. W., Kurns, S., & Antil, L. (2002). Best practices in curriculum-based evaluation. In A. Thomas & J. Grimes (Eds.), *Best practices in school psychology IV* (pp. 671–698). Bethesda, MD: National Association of School Psychologists.

Howell, K. W., & Nolet, V. (1999). *Curriculum-based evaluation: Teaching and decision making* (3rd ed.). Atlanta, GA: Wadsworth.

Individuals with Disabilities Education Improvement Act of 2004. 34 C.F.R. 2004.

Kame'enui, E. J. (2002). *Final report on analysis of reading assessment instruments for K-3.* Eugene, OR: Institute for Educational Achievement.

Kaminski, R. A., Cummings, K. D., Powell-Smith, K. A., & Good, R. H. (2008). Best practices in using Dynamic Indicators of Basic Early Literacy Skills (DIBELS) for formative assessment and evaluation. In A. Thomas & J. Grimes (Eds.), *Best practices in school psychology V* (pp. 1181–1204). Bethesda, MD: National Association of School Psychologists.

Kaminski, R. A., & Good, R. H. (1996). Toward a technology of assessing basic early literacy skills. *School Psychology Review, 25,* 215–227.

Kaminski, R. A., & Good, R. H. (1998). Assessing early literacy skills in a problem-solving model: Dynamic indicators of basic skills. In M. R. Shinn (Ed.), *Advanced applications of curriculum-based measurement* (pp. 113–142). New York: Guilford.

Marston, D. (1989). Curriculum-based measurement, What is it and why do it? In M. R. Shinn (Ed.), *Curriculum-based measurement: Assessing special children* (pp. 18–78). New York: Guilford Press.

Marston, D., Deno, S. L., & Tindal, G. (1984). Eligibility for learning disabilities services: A direct and repeated measurement approach. *Exceptional Children, 50,* 554–555.

Marston, D., & Magnusson, D. (1985). Implementing curriculum-based measurement in special and regular education settings. *Exceptional Children, 52,* 266–276.

Marston, D., Mirkin, P. K., & Deno, S. L. (1984). Curriculum-based measurement: An alternative to traditional screening, referral and identification of learning disabled students. *Journal of Special Education, 18,* 109–118.

McMaster, K., & Espin, C. (2007). Technical features of curriculum-based measurement in writing. *Journal of Special Education, 41,* 68–84.

Miura Wayman, M., Wallace, T., Ives Wiley, H., Ticha, R., & Espin, C. (2007). Literature synthesis on curriculum-based measurement in reading. *Journal of Special Education, 41,* 85–120.

National Center on Response to Intervention (NCRTI). (2009). Review of Progress Monitoring Tools. Website of the U.S. Office of Special Education Programs, Progress Monitoring Technical Review Committee: http://www.rti4success.org/chart/progressMonitoring/progressmonitoringtoolschart.htm

Pearson, P. D. (2006). Foreword. In K. S. Goodman (Ed.), *The truth about DIBELS: What it is. What it does* (pp. v–xix). Portsmouth, NH: Heinemann.

Pericola Case, L., Speece, D. L., & Eddy Molloy, D. (2003). The validity of response-to-instruction paradigm to identify reading disabilities: A longitudinal analysis of individual differences and context factors. *School Psychology Review, 32,* 557–582.

Rodden-Nord, K., & Shinn, M. R. (1991). The range of reading skills within regular education classrooms and understanding of special education services for the mildly handicapped. *Journal of Special Education, 24,* 441–453.

Samuels, S. J. (2007). The DIBELS tests: Is speed of barking at print what we mean by reading fluency? *Reading Research Quarterly, 42,* 563–566.

Shapiro, E. S., Angello, L. M., & Eckert, T. L. (2004). Has curriculum-based assessment become a staple of school psychology practice? An update and extension of knowledge, use, and attitudes from 1990 to 2000. *School Psychology Review, 33,* 249–257.

Shin, J., Deno, S. L., & Espin, C. (2000). Technical adequacy of the maze task for curriculum-based measurement of reading growth. *Journal of Special Education, 34,* 164–172.

Shinn, M. R. (Ed.). (1989). *Curriculum-based measurement: Assessing special children.* New York: Guilford Press.

Shinn, M. R. (Ed.). (1998). *Advanced applications of curriculum-based measurement.* New York: Guilford Press.

Shinn, M. R. (2003a). *AIMSweb training workbook: Progress monitoring strategies for writing individualized goals in general curriculum and more frequent formative evaluation.* Eden Prairie, MN: Edformation, Inc.

Shinn, M. R. (2003b). *AIMSweb training workbook: Organizing and implementing a benchmark assessment program.* Eden Prairie, MN: Edformation, Inc.

Shinn, M. R. (2007). Identifying students at risk, monitoring performance, and determining eligibility within RTI: Research on educational need and benefit from academic intervention. *School Psychology Review, 36,* 601–617.

Shinn, M. R. (2008). Best practices in curriculum-based measurement and its use in a problem-solving model. In A. Thomas & J. Grimes (Eds.), *Best practices in school psychology V* (pp. 243–262). Bethesda, MD: National Association of School Psychologists.

Shinn, M. R., Good, R. H., Knutson, N., Tilly, W. D., & Collins, V. (1992). Curriculum-based reading fluency: A confirmatory analysis of its relation to reading. *School Psychology Review, 21,* 458–478.

Shinn, M. R., Good, R. H. I., & Parker, C. (1999). Non-categorical special education services with students with severe achievement deficits. In D. J. Reschly, W. D. I. Tilly, & J. P. Grimes (Eds.), *Special education in transition: Functional assessment and noncategorical programming* (pp. 81–106). Longmont, CO: Sopris West.

Shinn, M. R., & Shinn, M. M. (2000). Writing and evaluating IEP goals and making appropriate revisions to ensure participation and progress in general curriculum. In C. F. Telzrow & M. Tankersley (Eds.), *IDEA amendments of 1997: Practice guidelines for school-based teams* (pp. 351–381). Bethesda, MD: National Association of School Psychologists.

Shinn, M. R., & Shinn, M. M. (2003). *AIMSweb training workbook: Administration and scoring of reading maze for use in general outcome measurement.* Eden Prairie, MN: Edformation, Inc.

Shinn, M. R., Tindal, G., & Spira, D. (1987). Special education referrals as an index of teacher tolerance: Are teachers imperfect tests. *Exceptional Children, 54,* 32–40.

Silberglitt, B. (2007). *Using AIMSweb early literacy measures to predict successful first-grade readers.* Eden Prairie, MN: Edformation, Inc.

Silberglitt, B., & Hintze, J. M. (2005). Formative assessment using CBM-R cut score to track progress toward success on state-mandated achievement tests: A comparison of methods. *Journal of Psychoeducational Assessment, 23,* 304–325.

Simmons, D. C., Kame'enui, E. J., Good, R. H., Harn, B., Cole, C., & Braun, D. (2002). Building, implementing, and sustaining a beginning reading improvement model: Lessons learned school by school. In M. R. Shinn, H. M. Walker, & G. Stoner (Eds.), *Interventions for academic and behavior problems II: Preventive and remedial approaches.* Bethesda, MD: National Association of School Psychologists.

Smith, S. W. (1990). Individualized educational programs (IEPs) in special education: From intent to acquiescence. *Exceptional Children, 57,* 6–14.

Stage, S. A., & Jacobsen, M. D. (2001). Predicting student success on a state-mandated performance-based assessment using oral reading fluency. *School Psychology Review, 30,* 407–419.

Stewart, L. H., & Silberglitt, B. (2008). Best practices in developing academic local norms. In A. Thomas & J. Grimes (Eds.), *Best practices in school psychology V* (pp. 225–242). Bethesda, MD: National Association of School Psychologists.

Thurber, R. S., & Shinn, M. R. (2002). What is measured in mathematics tests? Construct validity of curriculum-based mathematics measures. *School Psychology Review, 31,* 498–513.

Tindal, G., & Germann, G. (1985). Models of direct measurement in the determination of eligibility, monitoring of student progress, and the evaluation of program effects. *British Columbia Journal of Special Education, 9,* 365–382.

Torgesen, J. K. (1998). Catch them before they fall: Identification and assessment to prevent reading failure in young children. *American Educator*, Spring, 32–39.

Torgesen, J. (2004). Lessons learned from the last 20 years of research in the interventions for students who experience difficulty learning to read. In P. McCardle & V. Chhabra (Eds.), *The voice of evidence in reading research* (pp. 225–229). Baltimore: Brookes.

Vaughn, S., & Fuchs, L. S. (2003). Redefining learning disabilities as inadequate response to instruction: The promise and potential problems. *Learning Disabilities Research and Practice, 18,* 137–146.

Walker, H. M., & Severson, H. (1994). Replication of the Systematic Screening for Behavior Disorders (SSBD) procedure for the identification of at risk children. *Journal of Emotional and Behavioral Disorders, 2,* 66–74.

Wikipedia. (n.d.). http://en.wikipedia.org/wiki/

CHAPTER 12

Designing and Implementing Effective Preschool Programs: A Linked Systems Approach for Social–Emotional Early Learning

Jane Squires
University of Oregon

INTRODUCTION

Problems in social, emotional, and behavioral domains are a common part of growing up for most preschool children and their families—tantrums at the grocery store, refusal to eat a certain color of food, extreme fears surrounding bedtime. Reports by parents and teachers regarding young children's common behavior problems usually follow children's stages of developmental maturation (Campbell, 2002). In infancy, the most frequent concerns focus on eating, sleeping, and crying. Feeding and sleeping difficulties continue to be reported up to age 2, when toileting becomes the main focus. The greatest number of parental concerns are reported around age 3, when difficulties with discipline and peer interactions are at the forefront. Problems with peers, self-regulation, tantrums, and overactivity appear to decrease after age 3 in most children (Campbell). Problem behaviors in preschool children, therefore, must be examined with a developmental lens and a focus on the children's interactions with the environment, both in the home and in the community (Sameroff & Fiese, 2000).

Prevalence studies and associated estimates of behavior problems in young children vary widely, with problem behaviors noted in 5% to 30% of young children (Conroy & Brown, 2004). Young children who live in impoverished environments are more likely to have behavioral and learning problems than their economically advantaged peers (Hart & Risley, 1995). Of children in Head Start, 16% to 30% are estimated to have externalizing problems and 7% to 31% are estimated to have internalizing problems (Mowder, Unterspan, Knuter, Goode, & Pedro, 1993; Qi & Kaiser, 2003; Webster-Stratton, 1999). For young children with disabilities and children living in foster care, these numbers are even higher, ranging from 40% to 50% (Hebbeler et al., 2005). Children in preschool (up to age 5) are expelled from classrooms at a rate 3.2 times that of children in grades K–12 (Gilliam, Meisels, & Mayes, 2005; Gilliam & Shabar, 2006).

Early problems in social–emotional competence may diminish the development of children's healthy relationships with peers and adults. Furthermore, these problems may hinder or compromise the acquisition of important adaptive, cognitive, and communication skills (Dunlap et al., 2006; Squires & Bricker, 2007). Research indicates that severe disturbances in social–emotional competence do not fade and, without intervention, tend to intensify over time (LaVigne et al., 1996; Severson & Walker, 2002; Walker, Zeller, Close, Webber, & Gresham, 1999). LaVigne and colleagues found that 50% of 2- to 3-year-olds and 65% of 4- to 5-year-olds diagnosed with a behavior disorder had the same disorder a year later; 76% had the same disorder 3 years later.

Recent findings from brain imaging research, using techniques such as magnetic resonance imaging (MRI) and positron emission tomography (PET), have illustrated the serious effects of emotions on the developing brain. These technologies reveal the consequent neurological impact on delays or problems in social, emotional, and behavioral domains (Cicchetti & Cohen, 2006; Shore, 1997). Evidence of the stability of serious behavior problems, coupled with the plasticity of the human brain in the early childhood years, supports the need for well-organized and effective systems for early identification and intervention to enhance social–emotional competence in the early years and beyond (Dunlap et al., 2006; Severson & Walker, 2002).

EARLY IDENTIFICATION AND PREVENTION

Nurturing, constructive, and developmentally appropriate early experiences are the essential foundation for infants and young children, enabling them to (a) acquire important early processes such as self-regulation, (b) shape positive views and expectations about their social world, and (c) permit necessary neural growth and organization (Shonkoff & Phillips, 2000; Squires & Bricker, 2007). The longer children experience environments that do not foster the development of positive and constructive self-image, regulation of emotion, and social perceptions, the greater the potential harm. Communities need to put in place strategies for prevention, early identification, and early intervention to maximize children's potential to be contributing members of society.

The key to young children's social–emotional well-being is to offer families and caregivers, including preschool teachers and child-care providers, a range of services corresponding to the seriousness of specific needs. This hierarchy of service options and stages has been represented as a pyramid in this book and elsewhere (e.g., Fox, Dunlap, Hemmeter, Joseph, & Strain, 2003; Horner, Sugai, Todd, & Lewis-Palmer, 2005). The hierarchy begins with a broad base of prevention activities and moves to progressively more specialized and targeted interventions.

A Three-Tier Prevention Approach

The three-tier prevention approach is a pyramid of service options focused on both prevention and intervention to alleviate social–emotional problems (Figure 1). Tier 1

Figure 1. Three-tier pyramid for improving social–emotional competence.

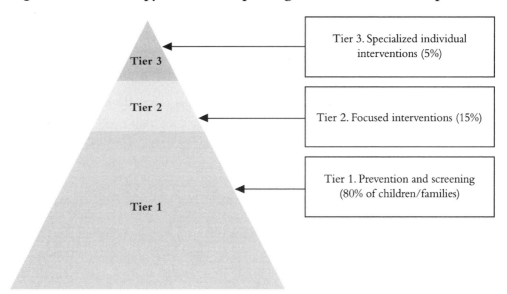

Tier 3. Specialized individual interventions (5%)

Tier 2. Focused interventions (15%)

Tier 1. Prevention and screening (80% of children/families)

Note. From *An Activity-Based Approach to Developing Young Children's Social and Emotional Competence* (p. 19), by J. Squires and D. Bricker, 2007, Baltimore: Brookes. Adapted with permission.

represents low-cost community systems for universal prevention strategies that can be used with large groups of children and families. Examples of Tier 1 activities include quality child-care and well-baby clinics for families, and universal screening focused on early identification of social–emotional problems for young children. In the classroom, pairing of universal screening with evidence-based social–emotional teaching strategies is recommended to promote children's social–emotional competence (Dunlap et al., 2006; Fox et al., 2003). These prevention and promotion strategies enhance children's skills, including peer interaction, friendship skills, recognition and communication of emotions, problem solving, and anger and impulse control (Hemmeter & Ostrosky, 2007).

Universal classroom strategies also include attention given to the physical classroom design (such as well-defined learning centers), organization (a schedule that is regularly followed), and verbal interactions with children, families, and other teachers (Fox et al., 2003). Additionally, children are exposed to clearly defined behavioral expectations (such as use quiet voices inside, use listening ears) that are explicitly taught during large-group instruction such as circle time (Benedict, Horner, & Squires, 2007; Stormont, Lewis, & Buckner, 2005; Sugai et al., 2000). Often these expectations are translated into classroom rules and appear in a poster with pictures for children and others to refer to in the classroom. Benedict and colleagues (2007) recommend putting three to five simple expectations and pictures on rules posters, such as "keep hands and feet to yourself" and "walk in the classroom and halls." Explicit teaching of the expectations should occur frequently with examples and nonexamples of rule-following behaviors given daily. At the primary, or universal, prevention level, children also should receive feedback, such as descriptive praise, about their use of socially appropriate behaviors throughout the day, using positive, supportive strategies (Stormont et al., 2005).

Tier 2 represents more focused intervention strategies for groups of children and families who have significant environmental risk factors and/or show early signs of problematic behaviors (Hawken & Horner, 2003). Examples of Tier 2 activities include specialized parenting classes, therapeutic preschool and child-care settings, and playgroups focused on relationship building. In the classroom, Tier 2 activities may involve small-group activities using commercially available curricula such as the Creative Curriculum and the Dinosaur Program, peer or "buddy" programs, and teacher-implemented strategies that are used throughout the day, such as using picture schedules and verbal cues to support children's use of self-regulation strategies during transitions (Dombro, Colker, & Dodge, 2002; Fox et al., 2003; Webster-Stratton, 1997).

Tier 3 represents the most intensive and costly service options, those designed to target a limited number of children and families who show clear and persistent signs of social–emotional and behavioral problems. For families, individualized counseling and one-on-one behavior consultation in the home are examples of Tier 3 activities. In the classroom, individualized Tier 3 approaches include function-based behavioral support planning and special education services (O'Neil et al., 1997). Through function-based support planning, effective interventions for decreasing problem behavior and supports for increasing prosocial behaviors in young children can be successfully undertaken. For specific steps and worksheets for conducting functional behavioral assessments and writing behavioral support plans for young children, see Russell and Horner in Squires and Bricker (2007); March et al. (2000); and Carr et al. (2002). Recommended practices and evidence-based strategies for social–emotional interventions for young children, as well as early childhood personnel training strategies using a three-tier model, can be found at the Center for Social and Emotional Foundations of Early Learning (http://www.vanderbilt.edu/csefel) and the Technical Assistance Center on Social Emotional Intervention (http://www.challengingbehavior.org).

A Linked Systems Model for Improving Developmental/Behavioral Outcomes

This three-tiered prevention model is situated in a larger linked system framework appropriate for preschool and early intervention settings (Bricker, 1989; Pretti-Frontczak & Bricker, 2004). The linked system is presented in Figure 2 and is composed of five distinct processes: screening, assessment, goal development, intervention, and ongoing evaluation. Although these processes are distinct, the information generated by each process is directly related or relevant to the subsequent process. That is, screening outcomes are relevant to assessment, and outcomes for assessment are directly relevant to goal development. In turn, goal development drives intervention efforts, and finally, the evaluation process is critical to determining the effectiveness of the previous assessment, goal development, and intervention processes.

Figure 2. Five processes of the linked system framework and their relationship to each other.

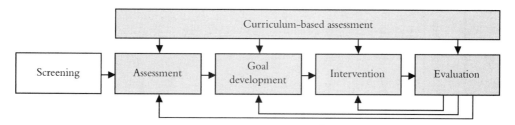

Note. From *An Activity-Based Approach to Developing Young Children's Social and Emotional Competence* (p. 43), by J. Squires and D. Bricker, 2007, Baltimore: Brookes. Adapted with permission.

This framework is appropriate for targeting social–emotional competence in young children in home and center-based settings (Squires & Bricker, 2007).

Universal Screening

Screening is a brief, formal evaluation of developmental skills intended to identify those children with potential problems who should be referred for a more in-depth assessment (Squires, Bricker, & Twombly, 2002). Screening instruments are usually quick, are easy to administer, and should yield valid and reliable results. Empirical evidence supports the need for ongoing developmental and behavioral screening conducted at repeated intervals in order to identify problems as soon as they are apparent and to implement interventions at the earliest time possible (American Academy of Pediatrics, 2002, 2006; Squires, Nickel, & Eisert, 1996). Through universal screening and identification, many problems are prevented before they become ingrained in young children's behavioral patterns (Severson, Walker, Hope-Doolittle, Kratochwill, & Gresham, 2007). Selected social–emotional screening instruments for preschool children are listed in Table 1; a summary with additional measures can be found in Ringwalt (2008). Screening is suggested in environments such as child care, preschool classes, home day-care programs, and home visiting programs. Simple screening tools, often completed by parents, can be administered at minimal cost and with the valuable input of parents or caregivers.

As the first step or process of the linked system, screening yields one of three outcomes: (a) developmental and behavioral status is typical, (b) developmental status is at risk, and (c) developmental status is questionable. As presented by Squires and Bricker (2007), Figure 3 shows those children needing further assessment can be referred to a developmental, behavioral, or mental health specialist for an in-depth assessment to determine eligibility for early intervention, early childhood special education, or mental health services. Children whose developmental status is near the cutoff scores, indicating potential delays, can be referred for further assessment if parents and teachers think more assistance and supports are needed, or monitored at frequent intervals to make sure their development is proceeding on track. Prevention

Table 1. Screening Tools

Name	Author and Copyright Year	Age Range	Administration	Psychometric Data
Ages & Stages Questionnaires: Social–Emotional (ASQ: SE)	J. Squires, D. Bricker, & E. Twombly (2002)	3–66 months	10–15 minutes Parent	Normative sample of 3,000 Test–retest validity data Sensitivity .78 Specificity .95
Behavioral Assessment of Baby's Emotional and Social Style (BABES)	K. M. Finello & M. K. Poulsen (1996)	Birth–36 months	10 minutes Parent	Limited; under development
Brief Infant/Toddler Social Emotional Assessment (BITSEA)	A. Carter & M. Briggs-Gowan (2006)	12–36 months	Parent, child-care provider	Normative sample of 600, not geographically distributed Test–retest = .80–.92 Inter-rater:.64–.78
Conners' Rating Scale–Revised	C. K. Conners (1997)	3–17 years	10 minutes Parent, teacher	Sample size = 8,000, multicultural
Devereux Early Childhood Assessment for Infants and Toddlers (DECA-I/T)	Devereux Foundation (2007)	Birth–3 years	10 minutes Trained testers	Normative sample of 2,143, geographically distributed Inter-rater = .47–.64 Test–retest = .83–.98 Internal consistency= .79–.94 Small validity sample
Devereux Early Childhood Assessment Program (DECA)	Devereux Foundation (1998)	2–5 years	10 minutes Trained testers	Normative sample of 2,000 Inter-rater = .59–.77 Test–retest = .55–.94 Sensitivity = .69
Early Screening Project (ESP)	H. M. Walker, H. H. Severson, & E. Feil (1995)	3–5 years	Stage 1: 1 hour Stage 2: 1 hour Stage 3: 40 minutes Teacher, counselor, parent	Normative sample of 2,853 Test–retest = .77 Inter-rater = .87 Sensitivity = .80 Specificity = .94 Concurrent validity = .72

Table 1. *(continued)*

Name	Author and Copyright Year	Age Range	Administration	Psychometric Data
Eyberg Child Behavior Inventory (ECBI)	S. Eyberg (n.d.)	2–16 years	10 minutes Parent	Test–retest = .75–.86 Inter–rater = .79–.86 Sensitivity = .80 Specificity = .86
Functional Emotional Assessment Scale (FEAS)	G. DeGangi & S. Greenspan (2000)	7 months –4 years	15–20 minutes Professional	Norms not nationally representative Inter–rater reliability > .80
Greenspan Social–Emotional Growth Chart	S. Greenspan (2004)	0–42 months	10 minutes Family or caregiver	Reliability = 0.83 –0.94, depending on age band
Infant/Toddler Symptom Checklist	G. DeGangi, S. Poisson, R. Sickel, & A. S. Santman Wiener (1999)	7–30 months	10 minutes Parent	Normative sample of 94% white Limited validity studies Sensitivity = .78 Specificity = .84
Parenting Stress Index (PSI), 3rd ed. – Short Form	R. R. Abidin (1995)	Birth–12 years	20–30 minutes Parent	Small sample Test–retest = .84
Preschool and Kindergarten Behavior Scale (PKBS), 2nd ed.	K. Merrell (2002)	3–6 years	8–12 minutes Parent and teacher	Test–retest = .62–.87 Inter–rater = .36–.63
Social Skills Rating System (SSRS)	F. M. Gresham & S. N. Elliot (n.d.)	3–18 years	15–25 minutes Parent and teacher	Normative sample of 4,000, stratified Test–retest = .65–.93
Temperament and Atypical Behavior Scale (TABS) Screener	S. J. Bagnato, J. T. Neisworth, J. Salvia, & F. M. Hunt (1999)	11– 71 months	5 minutes Parent, professional	Validity R = .42–.64 Sensitivity = .60
Vineland Social–Emotional Early Childhood Scale (SEEC)	S. Sparrow, D. Balla, & D. Cicchetti (1998)	Birth–5 years and 11 months	15–20 minutes Professional	Based on 1984 data

Note. From *User's Guide, Ages and Stages Questionnaires: Social–Emotional: A Parent-Completed Child-Monitoring System* (pp. 10–11), by J. Squires, D. Bricker, & E. Twombly, 2002, Baltimore: Brookes. Adapted with permission.

Figure 3. Universal screening in linked systems model for social–emotional intervention.

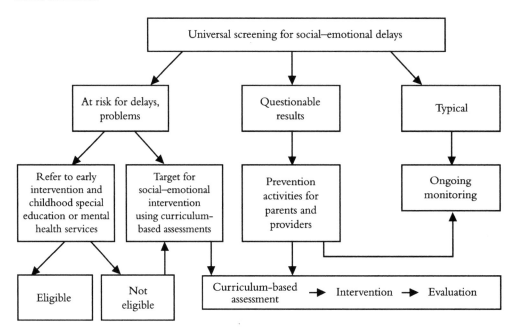

activities targeting behavioral needs can be given to parents and to classroom teachers. Examples are environmental arrangement, guidelines for positive behavioral support, use of natural consequences, and activities to promote social skills and emotional regulation (e.g., breathing deeply and counting to 10 before responding, or using puppets for role playing and problem solving).

Assessment

The assessment process in this linked system model is not designed to determine eligibility for services for young children; rather, the purpose is to produce outcomes that are directly applicable to the development of social–emotional intervention goals and content for children and caregivers to prevent social–emotional problems. A specific type of criterion-referenced assessment, a curriculum-based or curriculum-embedded assessment, is suggested for this process, and should be one with established validity and reliability. Examples include the Creative Curriculum (Dodge & Colker, 1992), High/Scope (High/Scope Press); Assessment, Evaluation, and Programming System (AEPS; Bricker, 2002); and the Carolina Curriculum for Infants and Toddlers with Special Needs (Johnson-Martin, Attermeier, & Hacker, 2004a) and Carolina Curriculum for Preschoolers with Special Needs (Johnson-Martin et al., 2004b). These curriculum-based assessments (CBAs) are composed of items that have associated criteria or examples, and curriculum activities.

Most curriculum-based measures contain items that are functional, targeting behaviors that enhance children's daily living skills and independence. For example, on the AEPS, items in the social domain include the following: "Responds to communication with familiar adult" (0 to year 3 level); "Joins in cooperative activity" and "Negotiates to solve conflict" (year 3–6 level). By using published CBAs with established validity and reliability, a more effective and targeted teaching approach often results, with children's developmental needs identified through an assessment process, followed by targeting of curricular activities focused on these specific needs. As shown in Figure 2, the assessment, goal development, intervention, and evaluation processes are all generated and linked through the use of a CBA. That is, by assessing a child with a CBA, the tester can identify the skills a child can do as well as goals and objectives that target skills the child hasn't yet mastered. The curriculum component of the CBA will provide steps for teaching these goals, and ongoing evaluation can occur through probes and ongoing data collection on these goals. Selected recommended curriculum-based measures with social–emotional or behavioral components can be found in Table 2.

Goal Development

Following screening and assessment, goal development is the next process in this linked system model. Results from the CBA should be used to develop social–emotional goals for the child. With the assistance of caregivers or family, the CBA results can be reviewed, and the child's strengths and needs, as well as caregiver concerns, can be identified. By reviewing the CBA and soliciting caregiver input, intervention goals can be identified that are functional and useful for the child across settings. These goals can also be rank ordered, with the caregiver identifying which goals are most important as intervention priorities (usually no more than two or three). After goals have been selected, daily routines and activities can be identified that may provide opportunities for practicing the targeted goals throughout the child's day. Finally, a time line should be established for the child to attain these priority goals. This time line will vary, depending on the type of goal, opportunities for practice, and the child's current behavioral repertoire. The curriculum portion of the CBA will assist in identifying intervention steps to follow to reach these goals and will provide suggestions for materials and activities for the intervention phase.

Activity-Based Intervention

Once a curriculum-based assessment has been administered and goals have been prioritized and selected with help of the parents or caregivers, intervention on these goals can occur. Activity-based intervention consists primarily of embedding learning or practice opportunities into the everyday authentic (that is, meaningful) activities of children and families, as defined in Table 3, and can be used with any curriculum-based measure (Bricker, 2002). *Embedding* refers to addressing the targeted social-emotional/behavioral goals during daily activities, routines, and events in a manner that provides varied and multiple learning opportunities for children (Pretti-Frontczak & Bricker, 2004).

Embedding of goals can occur in the home and classroom during *routine activities* such as dressing, eating or snack times, and story time. Embedding can also occur

Table 2. Selected General Early Childhood Social–Emotional Curricula and Assessments

Curriculum/Assessment Name	Description
Active Learning Series D. Cryer, T. Harms, & B. Bourland (1988–1996) Ordering information: Dale Seymour Publications Kaplan (http://www.kaplanco.com) (800) 334–2014	• Based on the Early Childhood Environment Rating Scales (ECERS-R) • Series of seven curriculum guides • More than 300 age-appropriate activities for listening and talking, activities for social growth, and suggestions for physical development and creative learning • Activities designed to help children "develop their minds and bodies in a safe and healthy environment" • Written for teachers of infants, toddlers, and children ages 2–5 years and separate guide for children with disabilities • Materials, required time, number of children, indoor/outdoor location specified for each activity
Al's Pals: Kids Making Healthy Choices J. Dubas (1998) Ordering information: Wingspan, LLC http://www.wingspanworks.com (804) 967-9002	• Includes 46 lesson manuals, puppets, audiotapes or CD-ROMs, parent letters, songbooks, school-to-home message pads, and a puppet house • Teacher training component as well as resiliency-based curriculum • Psychometric data supporting decreasing problem behavior using trained teachers • For preschool children ages 4–5 years
Assessment, Evaluation, and Programming System (AEPS), 2nd Edition D. Bricker (Ed.) (2002) Curriculum for birth–3 years Curriculum for 3–6 years Ordering information: Paul H. Brookes Publishing Co. http://www.brookespublishing.com (800) 638-3775	• Curriculum component of comprehensive curriculum-based assessment • Psychometric data supporting the system • Designed for children with disabilities but also appropriate for at-risk populations • Directly linked to assessment/evaluation and family participation components • Developmentally sequenced activities that move from simple to more advanced skills • Based on ecological and transactional theory
Beautiful Beginnings: A Developmental Curriculum for Infants and Toddlers H. Raikes & J. Whitmer (2006) Ordering information: Paul H. Brookes Publishing Co. http://www.brookespublishing.com (800) 638-3775	• Curriculum divided into six age ranges between birth and age 3 • Includes more than 350 activities and forms for photocopying • Builds on children's natural strengths and interests • Fosters development in eight key areas, including communication, gross motor, fine motor, intellectual, discovery, social, self-help, and pretend • Low-cost activities that are easily implemented in Head Start and child-care centers and homes • Includes forms for tracking progress and stickers to celebrate accomplished goals • Includes CD-ROM with all forms and activities

Table 2. (*continued*)

Curriculum/Assessment Name	Description

The Carolina Curriculum for Infants and Toddlers with Special Needs, 3rd Edition
The Carolina Curriculum for Preschoolers with Special Needs, 2nd Edition
N. Johnson-Martin, S. Attermeier, & B. Hacker (2004)
Ordering information:
Paul H. Brookes Publishing Co.
http://www.brookespublishing.com
(800) 638-3775
	• Curriculum component of comprehensive curriculum-based assessment
	• Curricula items that follow the same format:
	  – Title
	  – Objective
	  – Materials needed
	• Teaching procedures
	• Integration strategies
	• Sensorimotor adaptations
	• Functional activities targeted
	• Specific information on disabilities
	• Adaptations for hearing, motor, and visual impairments
	• Designed for children with disabilities
	• Directly linked to assessment/evaluation component
	• Divided into 22 logical teaching sequences covering five developmental domains, including social adaptation
	• Reliability, validity, and program efficacy data
	• Classroom tips for effective teaching

Center on the Social and Emotional Foundations of Early Learning Vanderbilt University, Department of Special Education Available for download: http://www.vanderbilt.edu/csefel/training.html	• Training materials and "What Works" briefs for promoting social and emotional competence in infants, toddlers, and preschool children • Training modules that include video clips, PowerPoint slides, and participant handouts • Practical strategies that include tools and resources for preschool teachers and caregivers • Parent training modules and family tools
Creating Teaching Tools for Young Children with Challenging Behavior (TTYL) R. Lentini, B. J. Vaughn, & L. Fox (2005)	• Materials designed to be used by educators of young children, higher education personnel, and inservice training personnel who support programs for young children
Early Intervention Positive Behavior Support Ordering information: Division of Applied Research and Educational Support Available for download: http://challengingbehavior.fmhi.usf.edu/tools.html	• Reproducible CD-ROM that includes user's manual, tips sheets, and reproducible forms necessary to gather information prior to strategy selection and implementation of supports
Creative Curriculum for Infants and Toddlers A. Dombro, L. Colker, & D. Dodge (2002) Teaching Strategies Ordering information: Delmar Thomson Learning http://www.teachingstrategies.com (800) 637-3652	• Research-based preschool curriculum model based on Piaget's theories of child development • Focus on 10 interest areas or activities in the environment (i.e., blocks, house corner, table toys, art, sand, water, library corner, music, movement, cooking, computers, and the outdoors)

Table 2. (*continued*)

Curriculum/Assessment Name	Description

Creative Curriculum for Early Childhood
D. Dodge & L. Colker (1992)
Teaching Strategies
Ordering information:
Delmar Thomson Learning
http://www.teachingstrategies.com
(800) 637-3652
	• Helps teachers understand how to work with children at different developmental levels to promote learning
	• Guides teachers in adapting the environment to make it more challenging
	• Includes a parent component
	• Infant curriculum, including:
	  – Comprehensive framework for planning and implementing quality activities
	  – Focus on building social relationships
	  – Emphasis on what children learn during the first 3 years
	  – Experiences to achieve learning goals
	  – Staff and parents' guidelines for reaching goals
	• Preschool (4th ed.) curriculum components:
	  – How Children Develop and Learn
	  – The Learning Environment
	  – What Children Learn
	  – The Teacher's Role
	  – The Family's Role

Devereux Early Childhood Assessment (DECA) Devereux Foundation (1998) Ordering information: http://www.devereuxearly childhood.org (866) TRAIN-US	• Strengths-based system designed to promote resilience in children ages 2–5 • Includes assessment, family partnerships, and follow-up efforts that respond to children's individual characteristics and acknowledge the role of families • Classroom focus • Emphasis on social and emotional well-being • Encourages partnerships between teachers and families • Recommends classroom strategies that fit within an early childhood program's current • Supports effective collaboration between home and school • Stresses the importance of being a data-driven early care and education professional

Hawaii Early Learning Profile (HELP)
  for Infants and Toddlers Assessment
  and Curriculum Guide
Vort Corporation (1995)
Ordering information:
http://www.vort.com
(650) 322-8282
	• Curriculum component of comprehensive curriculum-based assessment
	• Focuses on children's strengths as well as needs
	• Provides adaptations for assessing and teaching each skill
	• Provides clearly written intervention plans, activities
	• Offers an easy-to-follow developmental sequence

Hawaii Early Learning Profile (HELP)
  for Preschoolers Assessment and
  Curriculum Guide
Vort Corporation (1995)
Ordering information:
http://www.vort.com
(650) 322-8282
	• HELP at Home (birth–3): Includes parent handouts, curriculum resources
	• HELP for Preschoolers: Activities at Home, including parent handouts and curriculum resources

Table 2. (*continued*)

Curriculum/Assessment Name	Description
High Reach Learning S. Mayberry & K. Kelley (n.d.) Ordering information: http://www.highreach.com (800) 729-9988	• Learning materials for 3–12 months, 12–24 months, 2+ years, 3+ years, older 3s/4+ years, and pre-K/4+ • Theme-based curriculum with child-initiated plus teacher-initiated and teacher-facilitated learning opportunities • Activities designed to promote development of the whole child • All support teaching tools and activities built in • Materials included for children and families to strengthen the school-to-home connection • Addresses social, emotional, cognitive, and physical domains
HighScope HighScope Educational Research Foundation Ordering information: http://www.highscope.org (734) 485-2000	• Curriculum component of comprehensive curriculum-based assessment • Curricula focus on constructionist Piagetian activities for early childhood settings • Small- and large-group instructional activities • Children seen as active learners in classroom settings with rich materials • Adult role: challenge, support, and extend children's learning in social/academic development

The Ounce Scale
S. Meisels (2003)
Ordering information:
Pearson Early Learning
http://www.pearsonearlylearning.com
(800) 552-2259
	• For infants/toddlers ages birth–42 months
	• Observational assessment tool that transforms developmental information into guidelines for intervention
	• Focus on observation of children's functional behaviors by both parents and service providers
	• Children's performance measured within everyday routines and activities
	• Three components:
	  – Observation Record: For observing and documenting behaviors
	  – Family Album: For parents to record developmental observations
	  – Developmental Profile: To evaluate developmental progress over time

Table 2. (*continued*)

Curriculum/Assessment Name	Description
Pathways to Competence for Young Children: A Parenting Program S. Landy & E. Thompson (2006) Ordering information: Paul H. Brookes Publishing Co. http://www.brookespublishing.com (800) 638-3775	• Ten-step program to teach parents how to foster children's social–emotional development in nine key areas • Demonstrates strategies on helping parents manage children's difficult behaviors • Provides information on attachment, emotion regulation, and temperament • Includes group discussions, lessons, activities and exercises, and role-play scenarios • Looks at how a parent or caregiver's upbringing influences how they parent today • Includes flexible program for various group sizes and types • Includes CD-ROM with more than 140 handouts • Contains numerous components for preschool classroom teachers for improving social–emotional competence and providing positive behavior supports • Provides a user's manual and teaching toolkit, including forms for developing PBS classroom, such as tips for establishing Buddy System, Teacher Tools, Turtle Technique, Scripted Story Tips, Feeling Vocabulary Tips, Home Kit, supporting articles • Includes downloadable CD-ROM with complete materials, manual
Social–emotional intervention for at-risk 4-year-olds S. Denham & R. Burton (1996) Journal of School Psychology, *34*(3) 225–245 Also see: Denham, S. & Burton, R. (2003). *Social Emotional Prevention and Intervention Programming for Preschoolers.* NY: Springer Publishing (http://www.springer.com)	• Relationship building through floor time • Didactic lessons in regulating emotions • 32-week intervention, 4 days per week • Empirical evidence to support increased peer and social skills and reduced negative emotion

Note. From *An Activity-Based Approach to Developing Young Children's Social and Emotional Competence* (pp. 247–250), by J. Squires & D. Bricker, 2007, Baltimore: Brookes. Adapted with permission

during *planned activities* that caregivers arrange, such as water play with specific materials that encourage cooperation (for example, funnels and drops of soap in a water tub). Finally, embedding of goals can occur through *environmental arrangement*. For example, toys that encourage interaction are included in classroom activity centers, such as blocks and dress-up clothes. Environmental arrangement can involve manipulation of the environment so that certain interactions occur, such as putting favorite toys out of reach so that some communication with adults is required to obtain the objects. Also, too few eating utensils can be given during snack time, requiring children to negotiate sharing or dividing of available utensils.

Table 3. Elements of Activity-Based Intervention

Element	Definition

1. Goals are embedded in
  a. child-direct activities
  b. routine activities
  c. planned activities
	Learning or practice opportunities are included in everyday, natural activities.

2. Children are provided multiple and varied learning opportunities.	High-frequency and varied learning opportunities are offered to children. Children practice new skills across a range of people, settings, and conditions.
3. Child goals are functional and generative (useful across settings).	Transactions and embedded learning opportunities focus on behaviors that expand communicative, adaptive, motor, social, and problem-solving skills.
4. Children are provided timely and integral feedback or consequences.	Naturally occurring consequences are associated with desired child behaviors (e.g., child asks for and receives favorite toy; child puts on coat and is allowed to go outside to play).

In addition to embedding goals in routine and planned activities and using environmental arrangement, activity-based intervention should provide children with multiple and varied learning opportunities. These learning opportunities need to be relevant and meaningful, match the child's current developmental level, and be tailored to the child's interests and motivation. Finally, children should be provided with timely and appropriate feedback and consequences. This feedback or consequences must be immediate so that children can discern the relationship between their responses and subsequent consequences. Positive and logical consequences are most effective for children, such as when a child receives a favorite toy or food when he or she requests it, and games or other positive attention when a child responds to an adult initiation.

Evaluation

The fifth and final process in the linked system approach is evaluation. Two types of evaluation are necessary for effective intervention: (a) ongoing monitoring of progress toward individual child goals (usually selected from the CBA), and (b) assessment of the overall program impact on participating children and families. Progress may be monitored daily, weekly, or monthly to determine if intervention strategies are providing appropriate and sufficient learning opportunities to attain the targeted skills. Assessing overall program impact requires data gathering for quarterly and annual evaluation, which is often more global than when monitoring individual child progress.

Two types of evaluation measures can be used for monitoring progress toward social–emotional goals. These two types include critical skills mastery using CBAs and general outcome measures, as shown in Table 4 (Hemmeter, Joseph, Smith, & Sandall, 2001).

Critical skills monitoring based on curriculum-based assessments has been in use in early intervention and early childhood special education and in some early childhood programs as a means of effective progress monitoring. Home visitors and teachers, with the assistance of family members and caregivers, provide ongoing progress monitoring

Table 4. **Types of Progress Monitoring**

Type	Definition	Examples
Critical Skills	Critical skills for developmental progress are identified through CBA; curriculum from CBA used for curriculum activities or steps and CBA administered repeatedly for progress monitoring and program evaluation.	Initiating communication with familiar adults and peers, using words to make needs known; playing cooperatively with peers. Test items from CBAs such as AEPS, Hawaii, High/Scope, and the Carolina Curriculum for Infant and Toddlers and for Preschoolers
General Outcome Measures	Selected key skills are identified and probed over time, most often used with academic skills.	Picture naming, rhyming, alliteration, letter–sound correspondence. Indicators from IGDIs, DIBELS.

based on a child's progress toward goals and objectives specified through the administration of the CBA. Ongoing progress monitoring first requires that goals to be monitored are identified and the criteria for success defined. For example, to monitor the goal of social participation, success will need to be defined. For 3-year-old Lily, joining two different games during 1 week might be the criteria for success. For infant Jamud, whose goal is participation in social games with an adult, one time daily playing peek-a-boo or tickle might be the target. Data collection strategies need to be developed that are easy to do and sustainable over time, such as marking the frequency of target behaviors on a sticky note by a diapering table or on a clipboard near the snack table. Who will do the monitoring, the frequency, and the criteria for success will all need to be identified before data collection begins. Often programs have goals and guidelines that will help to determine what "success" is, such as progress toward goals identified on a child's Individualized Family Service Plan (IFSP) or Individualized Education Program (IEP), and family and staff satisfaction with the program.

General outcome measures (GOMs) have been borrowed from school-age academic reading and math programs and chart critical skills mastered toward specified goals. GOM models developed specifically for young children, such as Recognition and Response and Individual Growth and Development Indicators (IGDIs) may assist in charting children's progress toward specific goals in domains including language and motor behaviors (Carta et al., 2005; Coleman, Buysee, & Neitzel, 2006; Missall, Carta, McConnell, Walker, & Greenwood, 2008). GOMs and IGDIs are quick and easy to administer and applicable to monitoring early academic skills and some additional developmental behaviors over time. GOMs are frequently used in settings with children who are at risk for academic failure, such as those in Head Start classrooms, whose ongoing progress is not monitored regularly with CBAs. Critical skills monitoring with CBAs may be more time consuming to use; however, CBAs are more comprehensive and provide interventionists with concrete, functional suggestions for ways to modify daily intervention activities with young children and families to promote acquisition of social–emotional competence skills.

Ongoing data collection allows data-based decisions to be made regarding the intervention strategies and the child's growth. Without the gathering of data on child progress and the evaluation of the success of the program, the effectiveness of efforts to improve behavioral outcomes of children cannot be determined.

CONCLUSION

This chapter has proposed a linked-system framework that is embedded in a three-tier prevention approach for improving young children's social–emotional competence. In the first process, standardized screening assessments are administered to children and families to identify children who may need more intensive intervention approaches. Assessment is the second process, in which those children found by the screening test to be at increased risk for social–emotional or behavioral problems are referred for a more in-depth evaluation and/or administered a curriculum-based assessment focused on social–emotional competence. Intervention—specifically activity-based intervention—is the third process in the linked system framework; in that process children's goals are selected based on results from a CBA. Intervention activities involve embedding these children's goals in ongoing planned and routine activities using environmental arrangement. Finally, evaluation is the last process in which children's progress toward their individual goals and overall program effectiveness are continually monitored and modified based on collected data.

With potentially harmful risk factors increasing in young children's environments, such as prenatal drug exposure, extreme poverty, and witnessing of violence in the neighborhood, it is critical that social, emotional, and behavioral domains be addressed in early childhood programs (Perry, Kaufmann, & Knitzer, 2007). In order to identify universal screening for social–emotional and behavioral competence, it is necessary to identify, at least annually, those children needing more intensive interventions. In addition, systematic, ongoing intervention and evaluation are necessary to determine the effectiveness of intervention efforts. Increasingly structured and targeted approaches may be necessary when universal prevention efforts, such as providing rich and responsive environments, are not successful.

The development of behavioral and social–emotional competence is of critical importance for promoting early and optimal learning experiences for young children. Prevention and early intervention efforts can assist in the acquisition of necessary skills for successful functioning in preschool and community environments–and ultimately for successful functioning in the school years and beyond.

REFERENCES

American Academy of Pediatrics. (2002). *Bright futures in practice*. Retrieved August 4, 2008, from http://www.brightfutures.aap.org/

American Academy of Pediatrics. (2006). Identifying infants and young children with developmental disorders in the medical home: An algorithm for developmental surveillance and screening. *Pediatrics, 188*(1), 405–420.

Benedict, E., Horner, R., & Squires, J. (2007). Assessment and implementation of positive behavior support in preschools. *Topics in Early Childhood Special Childhood Education, 27,* 174–192.

Bricker, D. (1989). *Early intervention for at-risk and handicapped infants, toddlers, and preschool children.* Palo Alto, CA: VORT Corp.

Bricker, D. (2002). *Assessment, evaluation, and programming system for infants and children* (Vols. 1–4). Baltimore: Brookes.

Campbell, S. B. (2002). *Behavior problems in preschool children: Clinical and developmental issues* (2nd ed.). New York: Guilford Press.

Carr, E. G., Dunlap, G., Horner, R. H., Koegel, R. L., Turnbull, A. P., Sailor, W., et al. (2002). Positive behavior support: Evolution of an applied science. *Journal of Positive Behavior Interventions, 4,* 4–16, 20.

Carta, J. J., Greenwood, C. R., Walker, D., Kaminski, R., Good, R., McConnell, S., et al. (2005). Individual growth and development indicators (IGDIs): Assessment that guides intervention for young children. *Young Exceptional Children Monograph Series, 4,* 15–27.

Cicchetti, D., & Cohen, D. (2006). *Developmental psychopathology: Vol. 2, Developmental neuroscience* (2nd ed.). New York: John Wiley & Sons.

Coleman, M., Buysee, V., & Neitzel, J. (2006). *Recognition and response: An early intervening system for young children at risk for learning disabilities. Full report.* Chapel Hill: University of North Carolina at Chapel Hill, FPG Child Development Institute.

Conroy, M., & Brown, W. (2004). Early identification, prevention, and early intervention with young children at risk for emotional or behavioral disorders: Issues, trends, and a call for action. *Behavioral Disorders, 29,* 224–236.

Dodge, D., & Colker L. (1992). *The Creative Curriculum for Early Childhood.* Washington, DC: Teaching Strategies.

Dombro, A., Colker, L., & Dodge, D. (2002). *The Creative Curriculum for Infants and Toddlers.* Washington, DC: Teaching Strategies.

Dunlap, G., Strain, P., Fox, L., Carta, J., Conroy, J., Smith, B., et al. (2006). Prevention and intervention with young children's challenging behavior: A summary of current knowledge. *Behavioral Disorders 32,* 29–45.

Fox, L., Dunlap, G., Hemmeter, M., Joseph, G. E., & Strain, P. (2003). The teaching pyramid: A model for supporting social competence and preventing challenging behavior in young children. *Young Children, 58,* 48–52.

Gilliam, W., Meisels, S., & Mayes, L. (2005). *Screening and surveillance in early intervention systems. The Developmental Systems Approach to Early Intervention.* Baltimore: Brookes.

Gilliam, W., & Shabar, G. (2006). Preschool and child care expulsion and suspension rates and predictors in one state. *Infants and Young Children 19,* 228–245.

Hart, B., & Risley, T. (1995). *Meaningful differences in the everyday experience of young American children.* Baltimore: Brookes.

Hawken, L. H., & Horner, R. H. (2003). Evaluation of a targeted intervention within a schoolwide system of behavior support. *Journal of Behavioral Education, 12,* 225–240.

Hebbeler, K., Spiker, D., Baily, D., Scarborough, A., Mallik, S., Simeonsson, R., et al. (January, 2007). *Early intervention for infants and toddlers with disabilities and their families: Participants, services, and outcomes.* Retrieved from the National Early Intervention Longitudinal Study website: http://www.sri.com/neils

Hemmeter, M., Joseph, G., Smith, B., & Sandall, S. (2001). *DEC recommended practices program assessment: Improving practices for young children with special needs and their families.* Longmont, CO: Sopris West.

Hemmeter, M., & Ostrosky, M. (2007). *Recommended practices: Identifying and monitoring outcomes related to children's social-emotional development.* Retrieved July 31, 2008, from http://www.lookatmegrow.org/downloads/Outcomes.pdf

Horner, R. H., Sugai, G., Todd, A. W., & Lewis-Palmer, T. (2005). School-wide positive behavior support: An alternative approach to discipline in schools. In L. Bambara & L. Kern (Eds.), *Individualized supports for students with problem behavior: Designing positive behavior plans* (pp. 359–390). New York: Guilford Press.

Johnson-Martin, N., Attermeier, S., & Hacker, B. (2004a). *The Carolina Curriculum for Infants and Toddlers with Special Needs* (3rd ed.). Baltimore: Brookes.

Johnson-Martin, N., Attermeier, S., & Hacker, B. (2004b). *The Carolina Curriculum for Preschoolers with Special Needs* (2nd ed.). Baltimore: Brookes.

LaVigne, J., Gibbons, R., Christoffel, K., Arend, R., Rosenbaum, D., Binns, H., et al. (1996). Prevalence rates and correlates of psychiatric disorders among preschool children. *Journal of the American Academy of Child and Adolescent Psychiatry, 35,* 204–214.

March, R., Horner, R., Lewis-Palmer, T., Brown, D., Crone, D., Todd, A., et al. (2000). *Functional Assessment Checklist: Teachers and Staff (FACTS).* Eugene, OR: Educational and Community Supports.

Missall, K. N., Carta, J. J., McConnell, S. R., Walker, D., & Greenwood, C. R. (2008). Using individual growth and development indicators to measure early language and literacy. *Infants & Young Children, 21,* 241–253.

Mowder, B., Unterspan, D., Knuter, L., Goode, C., & Pedro, M. (1993). Psychological consultation and Head Start. *Journal of Early Intervention, 17,* 1–7.

O'Neil, R., Horner, R., Albin, R., Sprague, J., Storey, K., & Newton, J. (1997). *Functional behavioral assessment and program development for problem behaviors.* Belmont, CA: Wadsworth.

Perry, D., Kaufmann, R., & Knitzer, J. (Eds.). (2007). *Early childhood social and emotional health: Building bridges between services and systems.* Baltimore: Brookes.

Pretti-Frontczak, K., & Bricker, D. (2004). *An Activity-based approach to early intervention* (3rd ed.). Baltimore: Brookes.

Qi, C. Huaqing, & Kaiser, A. P. (2003). Behavior problems of preschool children from low-income families: Review of the literature. *Topics in Early Childhood Special Education, 23,* 188–216.

Ringwalt, S. (2008). *Developmental screening and assessment instruments with an emphasis on social and emotional development for young children ages birth through five.* Chapel Hill: University of North Carolina, FPG Child Development Institute, National Early Childhood Technical Assistance Center. http://www.netac.org

Sameroff, A., & Fiese, B. (2000). Models of development and developmental risk. In C. Zeanah (Ed.), *Handbook of infant mental health* (2nd ed., pp. 3–19). New York: Guilford Press.

Severson, H., & Walker, H. (2002). Pro-active approaches for identifying children at-risk for socio-behavioral problems. In F. Gresham (Ed.), *Interventions for students with or at-risk for emotional and behavioral disorders.* Boston: Allyn & Bacon.

Severson, H., Walker, H., Hope-Doolittle, J., Kratochwill, T., & Gresham, F. (2007). Proactive, early screening to detect behaviorally at-risk students: Issues, approaches, emerging innovations, and professional practices. *Journal of School Psychology, 45,* 193–223.

Shonkoff, J., & Phillips, D. (2000). *From neurons to neighborhoods: The science of early childhood development.* Washington, DC: National Academy Press.

Shore, R. (1997). *Rethinking the brain: New insights into early development.* New York: Families and Work Institute.

Squires, J., & Bricker, D. (2007). *An activity-based approach to developing young children's social and emotional competence.* Baltimore: Brookes.

Squires, J., Bricker, D., & Twombly, E. (2002). *User's guide, Ages and stages questionnaires: Social-emotional: A parent-completed child-monitoring system.* Baltimore: Brookes.

Squires, J., Nickel, R. E., & Eisert, D. (1996). Early detection of developmental problems: Strategies for monitoring young children in the practice setting. *Journal of Developmental and Behavioral Pediatrics, 17,* 410–427.

Stormont, M., Lewis, T., & Buckner, R. (2005). Positive behavior support systems: Applying key features in preschool settings. *Teaching Exceptional Children, 37*(6), 42–49.

Sugai, G., Horner, R., Dunlap, G., Hieneman, M., Lewis, T., Nelson, C., et al. (2000). Applying positive behavior support and functional behavioral assessment in schools. *Journal of Positive Behavior Interventions, 2,* 131–143.

Walker, H., Severson, H., & Feil, E., (1995). Early screening project: A proven child-find process. Longmont, CO: Sopris West.

Walker, H., Zeller, R., Close, D., Webber, J. & Gresham, F. (1999). The present unwrapped: Change and challenge in the field of behavioral disorders. *Behavioral Disorders, 24,* 293–304.

Webster-Stratton, C. (1997). Early intervention for families of preschool children with conduct problems. In M. Guralnick (Ed.), *The effectiveness of early intervention.* Baltimore: Brookes.

Webster-Stratton, C. (1999). *How to promote children's social and emotional competence.* London: Paul Chapman.

CHAPTER 13

Think Smart, Stay Safe: Aligning Elements Within a Multilevel Approach to School Violence Prevention

Michael J. Furlong
Camille Jones
Elena Lilles
University of California–Santa Barbara

James Derzon
Center for Public Health Research and Evaluation, Battelle

One of the first comprehensive school safety planning guides was created for the California Department of Education in 1989, before much of the widespread media, public policy, and professional research interest in the topic developed (Furlong, Morrison, & Clontz, 1991). The guide was created with broad input from educators, parents, students, and law enforcement and other community representatives. Even during those early days, discussions about how to prevent school violence focused primarily on ways to promote safe, caring, and supportive learning contexts. Safe schools were envisioned as being welcoming and open environments. Concerns about school violence increased during the 1990s following several school shooting events. The response in many states was zero-tolerance disciplinary policies, which have since been shown to be not only ineffective, but also associated with an increase in the incidence of school violence (Mayer & Leone, 1999; Morrison & D'Incau, 1997; Reynolds et al., 2006; Skiba & Petersen, 1999).

Since the 1990s, approaches to address school violence as a research topic and an applied educational practice have matured, but they have retained the core focus on preventing violence through comprehensive strategies that balance the security needs of campuses with efforts to promote students' development through safe, caring, and responsive school contexts (Greenberg et al., 2003; Skiba et al., 2000). Of course, the perennial challenge for schools remains—how to implement comprehensive, effective programs that address local needs using available resources.

Address all correspondence and feedback on this chapter to Michael Furlong at mfurlong@education.ucsb.edu.

The aim of this chapter is to look at the status of efforts to prevent school violence using multilevel intervention methods discussed throughout this book. The first section examines how schools and communities define school violence, because that viewpoint influences the selection of universal, targeted, and indicated intervention strategies within the multitier model. Using national school violence indicators, we address the question of whether school violence is increasing or decreasing at the national level, and relate this to the need to collect local school and community incidence information.

The second section of the chapter presents current information about prevention and intervention practices that broadly assume a multilevel strategy. Given other excellent resources available on this subject, we do not review specific violence prevention programs or programs that have already been reviewed extensively by the National Association of School Psychologists (see the appendix for essential online resources that list research-supported interventions; also see Cornell, 2006; Gerler, 2004; Jimerson & Furlong, 2006; Larson & Busse, 2006; Smith & Sandu, 2004; Sprague & Walker, 2004). Instead, we examine school violence program strategies that are supported through meta-analytic studies in order to examine which general strategies currently have the best empirical support. In addition, we present a framework with which to organize multilevel school violence prevention strategies that are aligned across students' developmental levels, policy, measurement and evaluation, specific intervention strategies, and outcome accountability levels.

The third section of this chapter argues that multitier school safety efforts must be implemented within a district's larger purpose and vision through a coordinated safe school plan. Such an approach considers several contemporary topics on school violence prevention and intervention that are essential elements of any comprehensive approach to preventing, and responding to, school violence. We explore the relation between school violence prevention efforts, threat assessment, and crisis preparation and response.

In the fourth section of this chapter, we summarize research findings on the effectiveness of school violence prevention and intervention efforts. The focus of this section is on a comprehensive meta-analysis of school-based intervention that provides an overview of promising practices, but also on the limits of what is known about the effectiveness of school violence prevention and intervention strategies.

Finally, bullying and harassment, aggression, vandalism, and gangs, along with social skills and positive disciplinary approaches, are clearly related, and any comprehensive school safety initiative using a multilevel strategy should integrate all of these topics. However, given space limits and the topics of other chapters in the book, this chapter focuses more generally on school violence.

DEFINITION AND SCOPE OF SCHOOL VIOLENCE

Since school violence emerged as a problem in U.S. schools, researchers, policy makers, and educators have yet to agree on the definition and the elements and scope of that problem. Henry (2000), writing from a sociological perspective, argued that early definitions of school violence were too myopic and that a viable definition would be expansive and include various uses of power, from any source, that results in harm—physical, psychological, and social. This view was also offered by Furlong et al. (1991), who stated that school violence encompasses not just the behaviors of individual students, staff, and intruders, but also the broader impact upon the social setting in which these behaviors occur, a perspective supported by the research of Mayer and Leonne (1999).

Despite the lack of a universal definition of school violence, there is broad agreement that it includes specific types of overt aggressive behaviors (e.g., physical fights on campus, bullying, and physical assault) and covert behaviors (e.g., threats or injury at school, weapons possession, or sexual or other harassment). This perspective was articulated by the California Commission on Teacher Credentialing when it developed school violence and safety training standards for teachers and other personnel:

> Government officials, researchers, and especially educators must consider the *big picture* as they develop strategies to address violence in schools (and in the home, the community, and society as a whole). Any act that causes harm must be incorporated into the definition of violence. Otherwise, we will never get at the root causes of the more serious violent acts. (Dear, 1995, p. 12)

Efforts to monitor and track school violence have largely focused on very specific types of victimization, as measured by reported exposure to aggressive acts or gestures and reports of feeling safe at school. Two national surveys that have been conducted since the early 1990s are the Youth Risk Behavior Survey (YRBS; Centers for Disease Control and Prevention, 2007) and the National Crime Victimization Survey (U.S. Department of Justice, 2007). These surveys include school violence victimization questions and are the primary sources of data for school safety reports issued by the federal government.

The YRBS is completed biennially by approximately 15,000 students in Grades 9–12 and is used to estimate the incidence of community and school violence risk behaviors. Figure 1 shows the 14-year trend (1993–2007) of four experiences reported by students in the YRBS using weighted samples representative of the participating states. Although concerns about school violence are periodically and strongly reinforced whenever a school shooting involving a youth occurs, the general trend is a decrease in physical fights and weapon carrying at school. Table 1 also shows that the percentage of students reporting violence-related experiences in the community or on school property generally decreased between 1993 and 2007. Being in a fight, carrying a weapon, being threatened, and having personal property stolen or vandalized were all reported to occur significantly less often. Ironically, over the same time, there was a significant increase in the percentage of students reporting that they stayed away from school one or more times during the 30 days preceding the survey because they felt unsafe. Consistent with this trend, one study reported that global perceptions of school safety as measured by this item are not correlated with actual violence victimization (Rosenblatt & Furlong, 1997).

Figure 1. National school violence and safety trends, 1993–2007, for students in Grades 9–12 in 37–44 participating states.

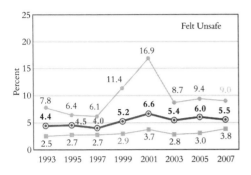

Panel A: Felt unsafe at or going to school, at least once in past 30 days

Panel B: Was in a physical fight at school, at least one in past 12 months

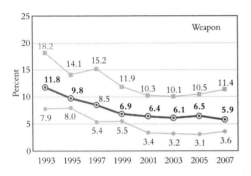

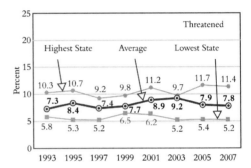

Panel C: Carried weapon (gun, knife, or club) at school, at least once in past 30 days

Panel D: Was threatened or injured with weapon at school, at least once in past 30 days

Note. Adapted from 2007 Youth Risk Behavior Survey report table. http://www.cdc.gov/HealthyYouth/yrbs/pdf/yrbs07_us_violence_school_trend.pdf

As shown by the survey, the most common forms of victimization at school are physical fights and theft. Behaviors linked with more serious concerns about school safety, such as weapon possession, occur much less often and have decreased significantly. Although national trends may be useful for establishing federal policy, school districts might focus their attention on monitoring that is related to local incidence of school violence and locally established priorities, such as a school with higher than desired levels of harassment, physical fights, or weapon possession. In our view, using local monitoring data for decision making and to evaluate program effectiveness is a necessary element of a multilevel school violence strategy.

SCHOOL VIOLENCE PREVENTION AND INTERVENTION

Recently, the custom has been to organize school violence prevention programs using a multitier model that has as its foundation the implementation of evidence-supported

Table 1. Unintentional Injuries and Violence, for States and Communities, 1993 and 2007 for Students in Grades 9–12 (Weighted Results)

YRBS Items	1993 Percentage once or more times	2007 Percentage once or more times	Trend
Community context items			
Students who carried a gun on one or more of past 30 days	7.9	5.2	1993–1999 Decrease★ 1999–2007 No change
Students who were in a physical fight one or more times during past 12 months	41.8	35.5	1993–2003 Decrease★ 2003–2007 Increased★
Students who were injured in a physical fight and had to be treated by a doctor or nurse one or more times during past 12 months	4.0	4.2	1993–1997 No change
School context items			
Students who carried a weapon such as a gun, knife, or club on school property on one or more of the past 30 days	11.8	5.9	1993–2003 Decrease★ 2003–2007 No change
Students who did not go to school because they felt unsafe at school or on their way to or from school on one or more of the past 30 days	4.4	5.5	1993–2007 Increase★
Students who had been threatened or injured with a weapon such as a gun, knife, or club on school property one or more times during past 12 months	7.3	7.8	1993–2007 No change
Students who were in a physical fight on school property one or more times during past 12 months	16.2	12.4	1993–2003 Decrease★ 2001–2007 No change

Note. Adapted from Centers for Disease Control and Prevention, Youth Risk Behavior Survey, *Youth Online: Comprehensive Results.* Retrieved September 11, 2009, from http://www.cdc.gov/HealthyYouth/yrbs/pdf/yrbs07_us_violence_trend.pdf and http://www.cdc.gov/HealthyYouth/yrbs/pdf/yrbs07_us_violence_school_trend.pdf
★$p < .05$.

programs to address the *universal* needs of all students (Tier 1). More intensive interventions and related strategies are then *targeted* in Tier 2 to only those students who become involved in school violence as perpetrator or victim. Finally, at Tier 3, *indicated* interventions are used with youth in need of intensive services (Consortium to Prevent School Violence, 2006; Walker et al., 1996; Walker & Shinn, 2002). This approach uses a public health, behavioral intervention, and educational model (Doll & Cummings, in press) with specific psychologically based clinical interventions for targeted students with intensive needs. This approach has served schools and communities well during the early era of research and practice for preventing school violence. Using a multilevel approach may be well suited to helping communities and decision makers sort out and think clearly about local aspects of school violence, because it requires building shared definitions and basing decisions on evidence. It offers a framework for making choices and responding to different levels of observed behavior and assessing the possibility (risk) of future violence.

The University of Oregon Three-Tier Model

Preventing or reacting to school violence should be a well thought out process. Reflecting the need for careful school safety planning, Walker et al. (1996) were the first to promote and apply the multitier approach for preventing school violence. They argued that selected interventions should be designed so that they not only target the individual student but also target a school in its entirety. Sprague et al. (2003) stated that a thorough intervention plan should include a preventive school-wide discipline plan, social skills instruction, restructuring of curriculum, behaviorally based positive interventions, and early screening and identification of antisocial behavior patterns. The interventions should also be based on a three-tier model to target all levels of need, including those students at high risk who are already exhibiting violent behaviors (Sprague et al., 2003; Walker at al., 1996).

The appropriate intervention for a specific school can best be determined by assessing the associated risk factors within the school and its surrounding community. In one study using this strategy, Sprague et al. (2003) propose a model that assesses risk factors within schools, neighborhoods, and families, which act as predictors of violence probability at school. The researchers evaluated archival data of risk factors at middle schools, including the following: (a) percentage of students eligible for free or reduced lunch, (b) percentage of students not meeting state academic standards, (c) family mobility in and out of district, (d) documented family violence per zip code, (e) documented reports of child abuse per zip code, (f) alcohol and drug crimes in neighborhood, (g) antisocial behavior in neighborhood, and (h) the principal's self-report of the school's disciplinary system. Results indicated that, with the exception of the principal's self-report, schools high in one risk factor of school violence were often high in other risk factors. These findings compare to previous research showing that low income and poverty are generalized indicators of the risk of violence both on and off school campuses (Sprague et al., 2003).

Implementation of the Three-Tier Model in the Safe Schools/Healthy Students Initiative

The Safe Schools/Healthy Students (SS/HS) Initiative is the primary program through which the federal government has supported community efforts to reduce school violence, promote healthy child development, and build school environments that are safe, disciplined, and drug free. Launched in 1999 by an unprecedented blending of funds from the departments of Education, Health and Human Services, and Justice, the SS/HS Initiative's mission is to promote evidence-based practice that addresses school safety and the reduction of substance abuse among the nation's youth, schools, and communities. SS/HS was developed to spur fundamental changes in how schools and communities work together, to improve services, and to provide students, families, and schools with appropriate support to reduce school violence (Felix, Furlong, Sharkey, & Osher, 2007).

The SS/HS Initiative is the single most expansive effort to implement multilevel, comprehensive school and community violence prevention in the United States. This multiagency federal program provides the best practical examples of how schools are cooperating with their communities to reduce school violence and enhance positive student development. A review of the SS/HS programs provides a starting point for ideas and inspiration about how to implement comprehensive school safety planning. As a result of this grant initiative, hundreds of communities now can provide practical advice about implementing comprehensive strategies for school and community violence prevention and intervention.

How SS/HS works. Funding through the SS/HS Initiative is provided to local education agencies (LEAs) throughout the United States. To ensure that schools and community agencies will work together to provide evidence-based services, grant applications must outline how LEAs collaborate with community agencies, including the public mental health system, juvenile justice agencies, local law enforcement, and other community-based organizations. Requirements to combine LEAs and outside resources aim to bring about structural change within schools and communities to implement best practices for providing students, families, and communities with services.

LEAs can choose interventions to implement with community support as long as they address each of the following elements: (a) provide a safe school environment; (b) offer alcohol, drug, and violence prevention activities and early intervention for troubled students; (c) offer school and community mental health intervention programs (preventive and treatment); (d) offer early childhood psychosocial and emotional developmental programs; (e) support and connect schools and communities; and (f) support safe-school policies (SS/HS Initiative, 2007). In addition to these areas, programs address other elements based on the needs of the community being served (Felix et al., 2007). Services provided include various age groups, locations of service (e.g., at schools or in homes), and methods of intervention. Overall, grants are designed to support LEAs in the development of community-wide approaches to creating safe and drug-free schools and promoting healthy childhood development (Furlong, Paige, & Osher, 2003).

SS/HS outcomes and findings. By 2009, 365 LEAs had received SS/HS funding. Hence, the evaluation of these programs was important to understand the effectiveness of large initiatives that used a multilevel organizational strategy (Felix et al., 2007). Part of the SS/HS Initiative's grant application requires the applicant to outline how the selected interventions will be evaluated, and how each program uses the findings in planning the interventions, making adjustments to services, and evaluating the progress of initial objectives and outcomes. The SS/HS Initiative draws on the best practices of education, justice, social services, and mental health systems to provide integrated and comprehensive resources for prevention programs and prosocial services for youth. The initiative partners implement comprehensive, community-specific services aiming to reduce school violence, alcohol, and other drug abuse, and to promote student mental health (SS/HS Evaluation Toolkit, 2008).

Although the SS/HS Initiative sites are responsible for their individual program evaluation, the Research Triangle Institute (RTI) and the RMC Research Corporation also conduct a national evaluation of the SS/HS Initiative. Their initial evaluation included gathering information from 97 communities between 2000 and 2003 and performing a more in-depth evaluation among 17 sentinel sites selected throughout the country to gain a thorough understanding of process and outcome information (Safe Schools/Healthy Students, n.d.). The SS/HS national evaluation examines selected sentinel site surveys of key members of all individual sites, evaluates archival data from school districts, and collects information through a variety of other survey instruments. Information about the evaluation process, including methodologies and the surveys used, can be found at the SS/HS website (see appendix). The findings of these various research efforts have not yet been released to the general public, but school districts seeking additional information can contact individual programs (Felix et al., 2007).

Felix et al. (2007) provide a comprehensive overview of the SS/HS Initiative. They sent surveys about program evaluation practices to each of the 230 SS/HS sites in February 2006, with a follow-up in April 2006. Of the 230 sites that received surveys, 49 responded. Although a limited sample, it provides useful information on the evaluation process and strategies, the implementation of various evaluation-research designs, and methods for measuring outcomes related to selected SS/HS objectives. In addition to compiling survey responses, Felix et al. reviewed published articles, book chapters, conference presentations, and literature searches.

Despite limited published information on the SS/HS program outcomes, examples of the benefits are being seen in participating students, schools, and communities. At the end of one SS/HS project, outcomes included a decrease in student risk factors, an increase in student protective factors, and students feeling safer at school (Cross, Mohajeri-Nelson, & Newman-Gonchar, 2007). Additionally, students in one county area had a reduction in the number of students vulnerable for dropping out when exposed to the Think First anger management program (Massey, Boroughs, & Armstrong, 2007). One school district that used the Second Step program in elementary schools and the Life Skills program at middle schools saw a reduction of behavior problems at all grade levels (Harris, McFarland, Siebold, Aguilar, & Sarmiento, 2007). Information pertaining to the SS/HS evaluation is also providing valuable guidance on which evaluation strategies are compiling the most useful information for future implementation of SS/HS projects.

SCHOOL SAFETY PLANNING

Furlong et al. (2005) and many others have suggested that prevention programs should not be taken off the shelf and implemented without prior planning that identifies school-site needs and matches program content with the school's violence prevention objectives. Real-world evidence for this can be taken from the SS/HS Initiative (see Felix et al., 2007). Although all 40 grantees in 2005 were required to use interventions with empirical research backing their effectiveness, no single intervention was used by a majority of the sites. The packaged intervention programs that were used most often were Parents as Teachers, Life Skills Training, Too Good for Drugs, Too Good for Violence, Second Step: A Violence Prevention Curriculum, Strengthening Families Program, Project Alert, Positive Behavioral Interventions and Supports, Reconnecting Youth, Olweus Bullying Prevention Program, the Incredible Years, and various peer mediation curricula. Even in these well-funded school–community projects, no single intervention was widely adopted, even at the universal level of the three-tier model.

The array of interventions used by SS/HS grantees shows that there is limited consensus about which specific interventions should be included in school safety plans. From our experience, it appears that school districts select intervention strategies to match their specific school safety mission, goals, and values. Given the need for each school to thoughtfully develop its own school safety plan, principals, teachers, support staff, and parents will want to integrate the process of school safety planning with other school improvement efforts. Schools can consider their unique school safety needs by addressing these fundamental questions: Which problems are we likely to face at *our* school? What are the primary short-term and long-term objectives of *our* school violence prevention efforts? Who are the targets of the violence of *our* prevention efforts? How is *our* prevention effort tied to broader community-level violence prevention efforts? Five years from now, how will *our* school know if the violence prevention programs worked?

Although using the three-tier model has clear advantages for comprehensive planning to prevent school violence and to promote school safety, it does not substitute for the hard work needed at each school site to understand campus conditions and to implement strategies that are best matched to local objectives. The task of developing a multitier program at a specific school is more complex than merely looking for the best and most cost-effective interventions that would fit at the universal, targeted, and indicated levels. If applied, such a strategy might lead one elementary school to obtain and receive training to implement the Second Step program as a universal intervention. The same school could also adopt the First Step program for targeting interventions for specific students who show early signs of behavioral difficulties. Finally, the school could also develop a memorandum of understanding with the regional mental health authority to support cross-agency services for students identified with severe mental health needs. Of course, other combinations of programs could make sense in different schools. It is reasonable to expect that if a specific school implemented a multilevel strategy with fidelity, they would realize positive outcomes for the students served and for the general campus climate. However, schools that design and implement violence prevention and safety enhancement interventions across their three levels without attending to how the interventions are coordinated will not attain the most desired outcomes.

One way to coordinate a multilevel school safety plan is for local school safety planning teams to devise a strategy that aligns the following elements: policy and mission (Why is this important?), assessment of campus conditions (What are the school's needs?), programs and services (What will we do?), and progress monitoring (How are we doing?). In addition, the plan should outline essential components. These elements are shown in Figure 2, with key reference documents and resources.

Policy and Mission

Before selecting which programs and services should be included in a multilevel safety plan, school safety planning teams should explore, discuss, and establish a shared purpose and mission. This process includes the exploration of staff, parent, and community values and expectations about student behavior; staff supportive behavior; and beliefs about children and their developmental process. Without a shared vision for the mission and purpose of the school safety plan, implementation efforts could fail because of inconsistent resolve to implement the programs it includes. An excellent example of this is the requirement that, in schools implementing positive behavior support (PBS) strategies, at least 80% of the teachers agree to participate in its specific

Figure 2. Aligning components for multitier school safety planning.

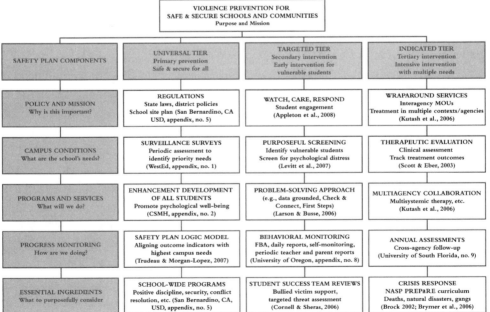

components (U.S. Department of Education, OSEP, n.d.). In addition to establishing the school-level mission, the planning team should examine local and state school board policies, particularly as they relate to student disciplinary practices, and reconcile any conflicting policies and practices. As an obvious example, a school seeking to implement a PBS strategy would require clarification in a district or state that had very strict and inflexible disciplinary actions mandated for specific student infractions.

Assessment of Campus Conditions

Of course, planning to solve the wrong problem or a nonexistent problem is a waste of everyone's time and effort. For this reason, any multitier safety plan should include some mechanism to monitor the safety experiences of students and staff. One approach used by many jurisdictions to collect information on school safety is the administration of periodic surveys, at the universal or school-wide level, to students and staff. Examples are the Youth Risk Behavior Survey, the California Healthy Kids Survey, and the Oregon School Safety Survey (Sprague, Colvin, & Irvin, 1995). These surveys inquire about school violence victimization (including perpetration), and schools can administer them anonymously, either annually or biennially. The resulting survey reports are an efficient way for schools to assess campus conditions.

In one study, Furlong, Morrison, Bates, and Chung (1998) found that across more than 60 California schools, no single school had the highest reported incidence on more than 4 of 21 school violence victimization experiences. Most schools had one or two types of victimization that were commonly reported, indicating that all schools could identify a school safety issue of primary importance. Specifically, different schools tended to identify different types of victimization. Each school could identify its own school safety issues and see how those safety issues related across schools. Finally, another approach to understanding a school's safety experiences is to assess campus hot spots, locations where students report the highest frequency of victimization (see Astor, Meyer, & Behre, 1999).

In addition to the general assessment of campus conditions, a multilevel safety plan also should assess the needs of students involved in specific targeted interventions. At the targeted level, Sugai, Sprague, Horner, and Walker (2000) suggested using behavioral data from office referrals. Others have suggested using more general mental health screening (see also Severson, Walker, Hope-Doolittle, Kratochwill, & Gresham, 2007). Finally, district and community mental health staff can evaluate information from more intensive clinical assessments to identify needs among those youths with intensive needs (see Levitt, Saka, Romanelli, & Hoagwood, 2007).

Programs and Services

The specific programs implemented by school staff and collaborating community agencies are the heart of any comprehensive school safety plan. All programs, regardless of level, should be selected from among those that have a reputable foundation in high-quality research (see the appendix for resources with information on evidence-supported programs). However, selected programs also should be aligned with the mission and purpose of the school safety plan and address high-priority campus needs. For example, if school bullying is a predominant concern on campus, then a school might elect to implement the Olweus Bullying Prevention Program as a universal strategy. Another way school planning teams can align safety program components within and across schools is by considering how a selected program can be articulated across grade levels or student developmental levels. For example, the Second Step program is developmentally sequenced across grade levels.

Progress Monitoring

Before the school safety planning team considers implementing the components of a safety plan, its members must identify key outcome indicators for assessing progress toward desired objectives. These indicators should be clearly aligned with the safety plan's purpose and campus needs and with selected programs at and across all three tiers. Progress monitoring can be formally arranged in a program logic model format, a general framework for describing desired goals, the activities to be implemented to reach the goals, and which indicators will be used to assess progress toward reaching the desired goals (see SS/HS Evaluation Toolkit, 2008, for a logic model template for school safety planning).

Whether a logic model or another planning method is used, the safety plan must specify how outcomes will be assessed across all three levels. At the universal level, it is highly desirable to be able to document long-term reduction in behaviors such as fighting and bullying, but these indicators would not show enough to be useful for every campus. At the secondary targeted level, individualized behavioral monitoring or specialized surveys may be needed to determine if students who have engaged in high-risk behavior have made progress in reducing the risk of violence. For example, although at the universal level it may be sufficient to ask all students about their weapon possession at school in the past 30 days, this outcome indicator may be insufficient to assess whether students receiving targeted interventions have improved. The assessment must also measure an actual reduction in the incidence of students who reported bringing a weapon to school multiple times (Furlong, Morrison, Austin, Huh-Kim, & Skager, 2001). The chronic weapon carrier may be a matter of specific concern on certain campuses, so outcome indicators should be designed to measure the success of targeted interventions to reduce risk. Finally, assessing the effectiveness of a school's multitier effort should include regular cross-agency communication, particularly about students who may have been significantly involved with the juvenile justice system.

Essential Components of School Violence Prevention Strategies

In addition to the elements of a school violence prevention strategy described above, schools must consider other essential components if their efforts are to be truly comprehensive.

Threat Assessments and Predicting the Likelihood of School Violence

Any multilevel program for school violence must address the potential risk of a few students committing acts of extreme violence. The occurrence of rare, but tragic, school shootings punctuates the need for schools to consider and plan for the unthinkable. For this small group of high-risk students, schools must have a system in place to evaluate the level of danger such students pose to the school community and to themselves when they make a targeted threat to a staff member or student. The appropriate response to students who make a threat to an identifiable target, such as a person or a place, is to conduct a threat assessment. Threat assessment allows educators to become aware of the motivation and context associated with students' threats of violent behavior. For instance, students' products, such as written reports and Web postings, may show them to be potential threats to themselves or others in the school environment. In such cases, a teacher, administrator, school psychologist, or other school personnel may deem it necessary to conduct a formal threat assessment to ensure the safety of the intended target and others in the school setting. A threat assessment is different from criminal profiling, which would identify common characteristics of students who engage in violent acts (specific style of dress, gang affiliation) as a means to look for possible future perpetrators. Overall, threat assessment aims to prevent violent acts from occurring, rather than stigmatize a student who may pose an unspecified threat.

Threat assessment originated in the Secret Service as a means to observe people who attack public officials. It evolved into an analysis of various potentially violent situations, such as threats in the workplace and threats in the school environment. Typically, a threat assessment is conducted when a person is a threat to self or others, participates in violent acts, or exhibits behaviors that threaten targeted violence. With regard to school violence, threat assessment is an important intervention tool, as it intends to stop violence on the school campus before it starts (Griffiths, Sharkey, & Furlong, 2008).

When educators have reason to believe the circumstances surrounding a threat made by a student pose a threat to a specific student or teacher within the school system, a threat assessment is conducted to determine the severity of the threat. Two threat assessment procedures have been used extensively in schools and are the only ones to provide written documentations of procedures and the consequences of their use—the Dallas Threat of Violence Risk Assessment (Ryan-Arredondo et al., 2001) and the Virginia Model for Student Threat Assessment (Cornell, 2006; Cornell & Sheras, 2006). The Virginia model offers an implementation guide and suggests that the following steps be used:

Step 1—The principal should evaluate the threat by obtaining information regarding the threat through interviews, written statements, and an evaluation of the circumstances of the threat.

Step 2—Educators should identify potential problems surrounding the assessment, such as regarding competence, validity of assessment, informed consent, confidentiality, and possible harm to self and the potential victim.

Step 3—Administrators, teachers, and other school personnel should adhere to their respective ethics code of conduct.

Step 4—The official should determine whether the threat is serious or very serious.

Step 5—When the threat is "serious and substantive," school personnel should consult with the potential victim, the perpetrator, and parents or guardians.

Step 6—When threat is "very serious," school personnel should consider possible and probable courses of action (notifying the police, immediately informing the potential victim, and/or intervening in the threat).

Step 7—For all courses of action taken in the threat assessment process, a school team should consider and discuss possible consequences of the actions.

When implementing threat assessments such as the Virginia model, Griffiths et al. (2008) provide a guide with which to consider relevant legal and moral principles, which support ethical decision making.

Ready or Not: Preparing for School Crisis

No matter what efforts are taken to prevent violence, crises may occur, and how schools manage them can have an effect on future school security and safety; hence, schools must be prepared to prevent crises if possible and to respond purposefully if they are unavoidable. Nickerson and Zhe (2004) conducted a survey of 197 practicing school psychologists, all members of the National Association of School Psychologists. The survey asked about which crisis interventions were being used in the school and which interventions were thought to be most effective. This study added to previous studies and contained information on the types of crisis situations experienced in school settings, the crisis prevention and intervention activities taking place in schools, and the perceived effectiveness of these strategies (Allen et al., 2002; Wise, Smead, & Huebner, 1987). It also asked about the perceived role of the school psychologist in school crisis prevention and intervention, the information sources used to select crisis interventions, the barriers to additional services, and what is needed to improve crisis prevention and intervention efforts.

Results of the Nickerson and Zhe (2004) study indicated that the most common events reported as requiring crisis intervention responses were physical assaults between students, serious illness or death of students, unexpected student deaths, suicide attempts, and guns or weapons at schools. More than half of the respondents reported having firsthand experience with these types of crises at least four times within their careers. This level of experience brings attention to the serious need for training in effective crisis intervention response methods and for including those responses in all safety plans. Nickerson and Zhe also found that the crisis response team was the method used most often, as well as the single intervention perceived by school psychologists to be the most effective, with 93% of schools using crisis response teams. This finding matches other research on the effectiveness of crisis response teams (Brock, 2002). Prevention education programs, including anger management programs and social skills training, were also reported as being used in 89% of the schools.

According to their study, other crisis prevention programs and interventions used in schools included peer mediation, police resource officers, crisis drills and plans, and violence prevention programs. It was also very common (90% of responses) for school psychologists to provide teachers with information about school and community services available for students. The most common method of crisis intervention for families was referral to available services.

The results from Nickerson and Zhe's study show that many of the interventions reportedly being used in schools and by school psychologists are those backed up with empirical evidence. More controversial methods were not reported to be used as frequently or thought to be as effective; for example, metal detectors were used at only 9% of the schools. Recognizing the need for comprehensive school crisis training, NASP (2007) developed the PREPaRE curriculum:

P—Prevent and prepare for psychological trauma
R—Reaffirm physical health and perceptions of security and safety
E—Evaluate psychological trauma risk
P—Provide interventions
a—and
R—Respond to psychological needs
E—Examine the effectiveness of crisis prevention and intervention.

PREPaRE is the most structured and accessible school crisis training program available. It was developed by school psychologists who have extensive experience assisting schools in their response to the most critical school crisis needs of the past decade. Information about other school crisis response planning procedures is available from the U.S. Department of Education (n.d.).

EFFECTIVENESS OF SCHOOL VIOLENCE PREVENTION AND INTERVENTION PROGRAMS

Despite promising initiatives such as SS/HS, local school districts still must shoulder the responsibility of assessing their local school safety needs and selecting programs that they deem most appropriate for their campuses. There is no authoritative source of information about which prevention or intervention programs are efficacious and effective, because of the recency of research on school violence prevention programs and the diversity of U.S. school settings. Furthermore, although some specific universal programs, such as positive behavioral supports (U.S. Department of Education, OSEP, n.d.) and Second Step (Center for Children, n.d.) have strong research support, no single study has examined the comparative effectiveness of implementing such programs within a multitier strategy. Some uncontrolled research has come from the SS/HS Initiative projects.

To date, the most detailed and independent analysis of school violence prevention programs was completed by Derzon (2006). He completed a meta-analysis that reviewed literature on school-based violence prevention programs and whether such programs were effective in reducing violent and aggressive behaviors. The investigation included studies of intervention programs in which at least part of the procedure was delivered in the school setting. In order to be included in the analysis, studies also had to include prevention, reduction, treatment, or remediation of violent or antisocial behavior as a primary outcome measure. Studies had to follow either an experimental or quasi-experimental design, produce quantitative data sufficient for calculating or approximating effect size, and include at least one outcome measure. Eligible studies included student participants who were between the ages of 5 and 18. All studies were published in 1950 or later. The identified studies included 83 research cohorts involving 74 school-based violence prevention programs.

To perform analyses, studies were sorted into 10 groups based on types of outcome variables, including verbal aggression, disruptive aggression, aggressively inclined, carried a weapon at school, mixed crimes, fights, problem behavior, suspensions, mixed violence, and physical violence. This meta-analysis showed that there is strikingly little information available on the effectiveness of school-based programs aimed at preventing or reducing violent behavior. Of 261 articles found with the term *violence* in the title, only five independent samples presented data on the effectiveness of a program for reducing or preventing interpersonal violence, and eight reported estimates of effectiveness on the prevention of fighting. This shows that remarkably little is known about the effectiveness of school-based prevention programs for reducing violence.

Of the results gathered from the studies included in the meta-analysis, the most commonly reported outcome variable was the effectiveness of the prevention programs in reducing aggressive and disruptive behaviors. Only one third of the school-based violence prevention programs reported effective outcomes, reducing aggressive and disruptive behaviors by about 6% and criminal behavior by about 20%, which are very modest findings.

Another commonly reported outcome variable was school suspensions, which were reduced 12% on average. Derzon (2006) notes, however, that suspensions indicate administrators' responses to student behavior, not the actual behavior itself. With the implementation of prevention programs at a school, administrators may change their policy on suspensions and see it as more profitable to keep students in school receiving intervention than suspending them. This makes suspensions a weak indicator for outcome information.

In studies that reported violence mixed with some other antisocial outcomes and studies reporting problem behaviors, students in intervention conditions reported significantly more negative behaviors than students in the comparison conditions. Derzon (2006) provides hypotheses for this, noting that program outcomes were based on student recall. If a program brings attention to outcome variables, the recall of self and peer behaviors may be altered throughout the course of intervention. Therefore, problem behaviors could have been rated more frequently as the intervention continued, whereas no real change was occurring, which raises questions about the use of self-reported school violence data for outcome indicators.

Overall, the school-based violence prevention programs reviewed by Derzon (2006) were generally effective in reducing or preventing violence and other antisocial behaviors. In addition, several other studies that did not meet the criteria for this meta-analysis reported effective violence prevention methods. Though too late to be included in Derzon's meta-analysis, the number of high-quality school violence research studies has increased in the past few years. The knowledge base about the effectiveness of school violence prevention programs is growing.

CONCLUSION

One of the values of the three-tier framework as applied to school violence prevention and school safety planning is its emphasis on linking objectives to practices that potentially benefit all students. The framework emphasizes early identification and prevention and provides a purpose and rationale that avoids limiting school violence prevention activities to reactionary practices that are associated only with students who commit aggressive acts on campus or who otherwise become involved in campus disciplinary procedures. The implementation of the three-tier strategy, however, is influenced by the commitment and flow of resources at each school site. As implemented by the SS/HS Initiative, the approach requires a substantial commitment of personnel and financial resources to address and reduce school violence. The process should not be entered into lightly. A lot of time and effort is needed to create buy-in to common definitions of violence, document the problem, adopt interventions to fit the problem, implement the interventions, and evaluate the results. This commitment could overwhelm or displace other valuable programs or school products, and the first half of the exercise may drain resources from actually doing something.

The three-tier approach also offers a way of defining school safety problems and deciding how resources will be spread across needs before jumping into a solution. Once a school does commit to a solution, the three-tier approach offers a way to monitor implementation, use milestones or benchmarks, and make sure something of value is actually being done and accomplished. The more complicated the intervention, the more critical (and difficult) it becomes to do it well. If a solution is adopted fully, a school needs to be prepared to commit the necessary resources. For example, multisystemic therapy, mentioned in Figure 2 at the indicated tier, is estimated by Miller and Levy (2000) to cost $4,500 per student, or a total of $90,000 if just 1% of the 2,000 students at a high school are served. Add to this the costs associated with a classroom-based universal program such as Second Step, ongoing staff training for special targeted interventions, and annual school safety survey assessments and interpretation, and it is easy to see that a three-tier strategy cannot be fully implemented without broad school and community investment.

The three-tier framework may appear to be deceptively simple if school administrators and educators conclude that all it requires is to select and implement an evidence-based program at each of the three levels. To help schools plan and implement school safety interventions and practices, we offered the framework in Figure 2 and this chapter as a way to meaningfully integrate policies, practices, assessment, and evaluation. Such integration of purposes and practices may be essential to the long-term stability and success of efforts to promote safe, secure, and peaceful schools using a multitier strategy.

REFERENCES

Allen, M., Burt, K., Bryan, E., Carter, D., Orsi, R., & Durkan, L. (2002). School counselors' preparation for and participation in crisis intervention. *Professional School Counseling, 6*, 96–102.

Appleton, J., Christenson, S., & Furlong, M. J. (2008). Student engagement with school: Critical conceptual and methodological issues of the construct. *Psychology in the Schools, 45*, 365–465.

Astor, R. A., Meyer, H., & Behre, W. J. (1999). Unowned places and times: Maps and interviews about violence in high schools. *American Educational Research Journal, 36*, 3–42.

Brock, S. E. (2002). Crisis theory: A foundation for the comprehensive crisis prevention and intervention team. In S. E. Brock, P. J. Lazarus, & S. R. Jimerson (Eds.), *Best practices in school crisis prevention and intervention* (pp. 5–17). Bethesda, MD: National Association of School Psychologists.

Brymer, M., Jacobs, A., Layne, C., Pynoos, R., Ruzek, J., Steinberg, A., et al. (2006). *Psychological first aid: Field operations guide* (2nd ed.). National Child Trauma Stress Network and National Center for PTSD. Retrieved November 12, 2007, from http://www.nctsn.org

Center for Children. (n.d.). *Second Step: A violence prevention curriculum.* http://www.cfchildren.org/programs/ssp/research/

Centers for Disease Control and Prevention (CDC). (n.d.). *Youth Risk Behavior Surveillance System, Youth Online: Comprehensive results.* Retrieved October 18, 2007, from http://apps.nccd.cdc.gov/yrbss/

Consortium to Prevent School Violence. (2006). *Fall 2006 school shootings position statement.* Retrieved September 6, 2009 from http://www.preventschoolviolence.org/

Cornell, D. (2006). *School violence: Fears versus facts.* Mahwah, NJ: Lawrence Erlbaum.

Cornell, D., & Sheras, P. (2006). *Guidelines for responding to student threats of violence.* Longmont, CO: Sopris West.

Cross, J. E., Mohajeri-Nelson, N., & Newman-Gonchar, R. (2007). Project LINK: Improving risk and protective factors through comprehensive services. *Journal of School Violence, 6,* 23–55.

Dear, J. (1995). *Creating caring relationships to foster academic excellence: Recommendations for reducing violence in California schools. Final report.* (ERIC Education Resources No. ED391217). Retrieved September 6, 2009, from http://www.eric.ed.gov/ ERICWebPortal/custom/portlets/recordDetails/detailmini.jsp?_nfpb=true&_ &ERICExtSearch_SearchValue_0=ED391217&ERICExtSearch_SearchType_ 0=eric_accno&accno=ED391217

Derzon, J. (2006). How effective are school-based violence prevention programs in preventing and reducing violence and other antisocial behaviors? A meta-analysis. In S. R. Jimerson & M. J. Furlong (Eds.), *Handbook of school violence and school safety* (pp. 429–441). Mahwah, NJ: Lawrence Erlbaum.

Doll, B., & Cummings, J. (2008). Best practices in population-based school mental health services. In A. Thomas & J. Grimes (Eds.), *Best practices in school psychology V* (pp. 1333–1348). Bethesda, MD: National Association of School Psychologists.

Felix, E. D., Furlong, M. J., Sharkey, J. D., & Osher, D. (2007). Implication for evaluating multi-component, complex prevention initiatives: Taking guidance from the Safe Schools/Healthy Students Initiative. *Journal of School Violence, 6,* 3–22.

Furlong, M. J., Felix, E. D., Sharkey, J. D., & Larson, J. (2005). Preventing school violence: A plan for safe and engaging schools. *Principal Leadership, 6*(1), 11–15.

Furlong, M. J., Morrison, G. M., Austin, G., Huh-Kim, J., & Skager, R. (2001). Using student risk factors in school violence surveillance reports: Illustrative examples for enhanced policy formation and implementation. *Journal of Law and Policy, 23,* 271–295.

Furlong, M. J., Morrison, R., Bates, M., & Chung, A. (1998). School violence victimization among secondary students in California: Grade, gender, and racial-ethnic incidence patterns. *California School Psychologist, 3,* 71–87.

Furlong, M. J., Morrison, R. L., & Clontz, D. (1991). Broadening the scope of school safety. *School Safety* (Winter), 23–27.

Furlong, M., Paige, L. Z., & Osher, D. (2003). The Safe Schools/Healthy Students (SS/HS) Initiative: Lessons learned from implementing comprehensive youth development programs. *Psychology in the Schools, 40,* 447–456.

Furlong, M. J., Pavelski, R., & Saxton, J. (2002). The prevention of school violence. In S. Brock, P. Lazarus, & S. Jimerson (Eds.), *Best practices in school crisis prevention and intervention* (pp. 131–149). Bethesda, MD: National Association of School Psychologists.

Gerler, E. R. (2004). *Handbook of school violence.* Binghamton, NY: Haworth.

Greenberg, M. T., Weissberg, R. P., Utne O'Brien, M., Zins, J. E., Fredericks, L., Resnik, H., et al. (2003). Enhancing school-based prevention and youth development through coordinated social, emotional, and academic learning. *American Psychologist, 58,* 466–474.

Griffiths, A., Sharkey, J. D., & Furlong, M. J. (2008). Targeted threat assessment: Ethical considerations for school psychologists. *School Psychology Forum: Research in Practice. 2*(2), 30–48.

Harris, E., McFarland, J., Siebold, W., Aguilar, R., & Sarmiento, A. (2007). Universal prevention program outcomes: Safe Schools/Healthy Students in a rural, multicultural setting, *Journal of School Violence, 6,* 75–91.

Henry, S. (2000). What is school violence? An integrated definition. *Annals of the American Academy of Political and Social Science, 567,* 16–29.

Jimerson, S. R., & Furlong, M. J. (Eds.). (2006). *Handbook of school violence and school safety: From research to practice.* Mahwah, NJ: Lawrence Erlbaum.

Kutash, K., Duchnowski, A. J., & Lynn, N, (2006). *School-based mental health: An empirical guide for decision-makers.* Tampa, FL: University of South Florida, Louis de la Parte Florida Mental Health Institute, Department of Child & Family Studies. Research and Training Center for Children's Mental Health. Retrieved September 6, 2009, from http://rtckids.fmhi.usf.edu/rtcpubs/study04/

Larsen, T., & Samdal, O. (2007). Implementing Second Step: Balancing fidelity and program adaptation. *Journal of Educational and Psychological Consultation, 17,* 1–29.

Larson, J. (2008). Best practices in school violence prevention. In A. Thomas & J. Grimes (Eds.), *Best practices in school psychology V* (pp. 1291–1308). Bethesda, MD: National Association of School Psychologists.

Larson, J., & Busse, R. T. (2006). A problem-solving approach to school violence prevention. In S. R. Jimerson & M. J. Furlong (Eds.), *Handbook of school violence and safety* (pp. 73–88). Mahwah, NJ: Lawrence Erlbaum.

Larson, J., Smith, D. C., & Furlong, M. J. (2002). Best practices in school violence prevention. In A. Thomas & J. Grimes (Eds.), *Best practices in school psychology IV* (pp. 1081–1097). Bethesda, MD: National Association of School Psychologists.

Levitt, J. M., Saka, N., Romanelli, L. H., & Hoagwood, K. (2007). Early identification of mental health problems in schools: The status of instrumentation. *Journal of School Psychology, 45,* 163–191.

Massey, O. T., Boroughs, M., & Armstrong, K. H. (2007). School violence interventions in the Safe Schools/Healthy Students Initiative: Evaluation of two early intervention programs. *Journal of School Violence, 6,* 57–74.

Mayer, M. J., & Leone, P. E. (1999). A structural analysis of school violence and disruption: Implications for creating safer schools. *Education and Treatment of Children, 22,* 333–356.

Miller, T. R., & Levy, D. T. (2000). Cost-outcome analysis in injury prevention and control: Eighty-four recent estimates for the United States. *Medical Care, 38,* 562–582.

Morrison, G. M., & D'Incau, B. (1997). The web of zero-tolerance: Characteristics of students who are recommended for expulsion from school. *Education and Treatment of Children, 20,* 316–335.

National Association of School Psychologists. (n.d.). *Position Statement: School Violence.* Retrieved September 6, 2009, from http://www.nasponline.org/about_nasp/position_paper.aspx

National Association of School Psychologists. (2007). *PREPaRE: School crisis prevention and intervention training curriculum.* Available from http://www.nasponline.org/prepare/index.aspx

Nickerson, A. B., & Zhe, E. J. (2004). Crisis prevention and intervention: A survey of school psychologists. *Psychology in the Schools, 41,* 777–788.

Reynolds, C. R., Conoley, J., Garcia-Vazquez, E., Graham, S., Sheras, P., Skiba, R., et al. (2006). *Are Zero Tolerance Policies Effective in the Schools? An Evidentiary Review and Recommendations A report by the American Psychological Association Zero Tolerance Task Force.* Washington, DC: American Psychological Association. Retrieved November 1, 2007, from http://www.apa.org/releases/zerotolerance.html

Rosenblatt, J. A., & Furlong, M. J. (1997). Assessing the reliability and validity of student self-reports of campus violence. *Journal of Youth and Adolescence, 26,* 187–202.

Ryan-Arredondo, K., Renouf, K., Egyed, C., Doxey, M., Dobbins, M., Sanchez, S., et al. (2001). Threats of violence in schools: The Dallas Independent School District's response. *Psychology in the Schools, 38,* 185–196.

Safe Schools/Healthy Students. (n.d.). *SS/HS National Evaluation.* Retrieved October 2, 2009, from http://www.sshs.samhsa.gov/community/evaluation.aspx

Safe Schools/Healthy Students Evaluation Toolkit. (2008). *Safe Schools/Healthy Students Final Logic Model WorkSheet.* Retrieved September 6, 2009, from the National Center for Mental Health Promotion and Youth Violence Prevention website: http://www.promoteprevent.org/Resources/evaluation_toolkit/Logic%20Model%20Instructions%2008.pdf

Scott, T. M., & Eber, L. (2003). Functional assessment and wraparound as systemic school processes: Primary, secondary, and tertiary systems examples. *Journal of Positive Behavior Interventions, 5,* 131–143.

Severson, H. H., Walker, H. M., Hope-Doolittle, J., Kratochwill, T. R., & Gresham, F. M. (2007). Proactive, early screening to detect behaviorally at-risk students: Issues, approaches, emerging innovations, and professional practices. *Journal of School Psychology, 45,* 193–223.

Skiba, R., Boone, K., Fontanini, A., Wu, T., Strassell, A., & Peterson, R. (2000). *Preventing school violence: A practical guide to comprehensive planning.* Bloomington, IN: The Safe and Responsive Schools Project, Indiana Policy Center, Indiana University.

Skiba, R. J., & Peterson, R. L. (1999). The dark side of zero tolerance: Can punishment lead to safe schools? *Phi Delta Kappan, 80,* 372–376, 381–382.

Smith, D. C., & Sandu, D. S. (2004). Toward a positive perspective on violence prevention in schools: Building connections *Journal of Counseling and Development, 82,* 287–293.

Sprague, J., & Walker, H. M. (2004). *Safe and healthy schools: Practical prevention strategies.* New York: Guilford.

Sprague, J., Walker, H. M., Sowards, S., Van Bloem, C., Eberhardt, P., & Marshall, B. (2002). Sources of vulnerability to school violence: Systems-level assessment and strategies to improve safety and climate. In M. R. Shinn, H. M. Walker, & G. Stoner (Eds.), *Interventions for academic and behavior problems II: Preventive and remedial approaches* (pp. 295–314). Bethesda, MD: National Association of School Psychologists.

Sugai, G., Sprague, J. R., Horner, R. H., & Walker, H. M. (2000). Preventing school violence: The use of office discipline referrals to assess and monitor school-wide discipline interventions. *Journal of Emotional and Behavioral Disorders, 8,* 94–101.

Trudeau, J., & Morgan-Lopez, A. (2007, November). *School violence and safety in the Safe Schools/Healthy Students Initiative.* Paper presented at the annual meeting of the American Society of Criminology, Royal York, Toronto.

U.S. Department of Education. (n.d.). *Crisis response: Creating safe schools.* Retrieved September 6, 2009, from http://www.ed.gov/admins/lead/safety/training/responding/crisis_pg34.html

U.S. Department of Education. Office of Safe and Drug-Free Schools. (2008). *2008 Safe Schools/Healthy Students Initiative Grants.* Retrieved September 6, 2009, from the Safe Schools/Healthy Students website: http://www.sshs.samhsa.gov/Announcements/2008Announcement.aspx

U.S. Department of Education. Office of Special Education Programs (OSEP). (n.d.). Technical Assistance Center on Positive Behavioral Interventions and Supports. Effective Schoolwide Interventions. Retrieved September 6, 2009, from http://www.pbis.org/default.aspx

U.S. Department of Justice. (2007). *National Crime Victimization Survey* (2007). Bureau of Justice Statistics. Retrieved October 20, 2007, from http://www.ojp.usdoj.gov/bjs/cvict.htm

Walker, H. M., Horner, R. H., Sugai, G., Bullis, M., Sprague, J., Bricker, D., et al. (1996). Integrated approaches to preventing antisocial behavior patterns among school-age children and youth. *Journal of Emotional and Behavioral Disorders, 4,* 194–209.

Walker, H. M., & Shinn, M. R. (2002). Structuring school-based interventions to achieve integrated primary, secondary, and tertiary prevention goals for safe and effective schools. In M. R. Shinn, H. M. Walker, & G. Stoner (Eds.), *Interventions for academic and behavior problems: Preventive and remedial approaches* (pp. 1–27). Bethesda, MD: National Association of School Psychologists.

Wise, P. S., Smead, V. S., & Huebner, E. S. (1987). Crisis intervention: Involvement and training needs of school psychology personnel. *Journal of School Psychology, 25,* 185–187.

APPENDIX. KEEPING AN EYE ON ESSENTIAL SCHOOL VIOLENCE RESOURCES

Many online resources address school violence and safety-related matters—so many, in fact, that it is impossible to track and manage them all. Listed below are some of the most stable and central sources of high-quality general information about best practices and recent innovations in school violence prevention and intervention.

1. California Healthy Kids Survey (CHKS), WestEd
   http://www.wested.org/hks
   Description: The CHKS assesses general risk factors associated with safe and drug-free school objectives. It has a core module and additional modules that assess resilience, tobacco use, alcohol and other drug use, physical health, sexual behavior, after-school programming, and staff perceptions of campus climate.

2. Center for School Mental Health (CSMH), University of Maryland School of Medicine
   http://csmh.umaryland.edu/
   Description: This national technical assistance center emphasizes theory, research, practice, and training related to mental health and psychosocial concerns, using school-based interventions.

3. Office of Juvenile Justice and Delinquency Prevention, Hamilton Fish Institute
   http://www.hamfish.org/
   Description: The Hamilton Fish Institute on School and Community Violence, at George Washington University, provides information, research, and support to make schools safer for high achievement. It holds an annual school violence and safety conference that presents an array of practical, data-supported school violence prevention strategies.

4. Safe Schools/Healthy Students (SS/HS) Initiative
   http://www.sshs.samhsa.gov/
   Description: The Safe Schools/Healthy Students Initiative, of the U.S. Departments of Education, Health and Human Services, and Justice, is the single largest federal grant-making effort to support school–community collaboration to implement model strategies aimed to reduce school violence.

5. San Bernardino City Unified School District, Managing On-Site Discipline for Effective Learning (MODEL)
   http://www.modelprogram.com/district-wide-pbs-.html
   Description: This website provides an in-depth look at the three-tier positive behavior support (PBS) program, MODEL, used in the San Bernardino City, California, Unified School District.

6. TeachSafeSchools.org
   http://www.teachsafeschools.org/index.html
   Description: This nonprofit website is supported by the Melissa Foundation (Melissa Institute for Violence Prevention & Treatment) and provides evidence-based information and techniques to assist the school community in the prevention of school violence. It provides practical information on all aspects of school safety planning and is specifically organized using the three-tier prevention strategy.

7. UCLA School Mental Health Project (SMHP), Center for Mental Health in Schools
   http://www.smhp.psych.ucla.edu/
   Description: This national technical assistance center seeks to enhance policies and programs in school mental health to improve learning and success for students.

8. University of Oregon, Institute on Violence and Destructive Behavior
   http://www.uoregon.edu/~ivdb/
   Description: This center is the originator of the three-tier approach to school violence prevention and, more generally, of the positive behavior intervention support model. This site has numerous research-derived resources.

9. University of South Florida Research & Training Center for Children's Mental Health: School-Based Mental Health Services
   http://rtckids.fmhi.usf.edu/sbmh/default.cfm
   Description: The USF research center is the premier site nationally for research involving children's mental health services related to both policy and cross-agency service delivery to students who need intensive mental health services.

APPENDIX. (continued)

10. U.S. Department of Education, Institute of Education Sciences, National Center for Education Statistics
http://nces.ed.gov/programs/crime/
Description: Currently, two surveys are being conducted on a regular basis by NCES: the School Survey on Crime and Safety (SSOCS), a survey of public schools and principals; and the School Crime Supplement (SCS) to the National Crime Victimization Survey (NCVS), a survey of students ages 12–18.

CHAPTER 14

Evidence-Based Social Skills Interventions: Empirical Foundations for Instructional Approaches

Frank M. Gresham
Louisiana State University

INTRODUCTION

Children and youth with serious emotional, behavioral, and social difficulties present substantial challenges for schools, teachers, parents, and peers. These challenges cut across disciplinary, instructional, and interpersonal domains and frequently create chaotic home, school, and classroom environments. Children at risk for emotional and behavioral disorders (EBD) often overwhelm the capacity of schools to effectively accommodate their instructional and disciplinary needs. Schools are charged with teaching an increasingly diverse student population in terms of prevailing attitudes and beliefs, behavioral styles, racial–ethnic and language backgrounds, socioeconomic levels, and risk status (Walker, Ramsay, & Gresham, 2004). Also, pressures for higher academic standards and outcomes for all students currently are approaching nearly unattainable levels, particularly for students with severe behavioral challenges. Students bringing these behavioral challenges to the school context often create turbulent classroom and school environments thereby disrupting the learning and achievement of other students.

Children with or at risk for EBD experience significant difficulties in developing and maintaining satisfactory interpersonal relationships, displaying prosocial behavior patterns, and achieving social acceptance of peers and teachers (Gresham, 1997, 1998; Maag, 2005, 2006; Walker et al., 2004). These social competence deficits lead to short-term, intermediate, and long-term difficulties in educational, psychosocial, and vocational domains of functioning (Kupersmidt, Coie, & Dodge, 1990; Newcomb, Bukowski, & Pattee, 1993; Parker & Asher, 1987). The fact that most children at risk for EBD exhibit severe social competence deficits dictates that school professionals design and implement effective intervention strategies to remediate these children's interpersonal difficulties.

In the definition of *emotional disturbance* specified in the Individuals with Disabilities Education Improvement Act (IDEIA, known as IDEA 2004), social competence difficulties are part of the eligibility standards in two of the five defining criteria: (a) "an inability to build or maintain satisfactory interpersonal relationships with peers and teachers" and (b) "the expression of inappropriate behavior or feelings under normal circumstances." Moreover, many students at risk for mental health difficulties demonstrate substantial social skills deficits. Social competence or interpersonal difficulties are part of the diagnostic criteria for many disorders of childhood and adolescence, as specified in the *Diagnostic and Statistical Manual of Mental Disorders* (*DSM-IV*; American Psychiatric Association, 1994). Given the nature of these deficits among children and youth at risk for EBD, social skills represent a vitally important focus of intervention efforts.

Substantial empirical evidence suggests that more than 20% of the school-age population could qualify for mental health services and diagnoses (Angold, 2000; Hoagwood & Erwin, 1997). However, given that only about 1% of school-age children are served under the IDEA 2004 category of emotionally disturbed, many students in public school classrooms clearly are not receiving appropriate intervention services for their psychosocial adjustment problems (Walker, Nishioka, Zeller, Severson, & Feil, 2000).

Over the past two decades, children and youth experiencing emotional and behavioral disorders in school settings have been one of the key target subpopulations for the application of social skills training procedures, although they remain greatly underserved in this regard. The purpose of this chapter is to describe and classify the types of deficits to which these procedures have been applied, to review the scope and success of these efforts, and to suggest recommended intervention and evaluation strategies that, if implemented with integrity, can lead to better outcomes and greater social effectiveness for EBD students. The chapter addresses the following major topics: (a) social skills and social competence, (b) social skills versus problem behaviors, (c) classification of social skills deficits, (d) social skills and competing problem behaviors, (e) social skills deficits and risk and protective factors in EBD, (f) review of evidence-based social skills interventions, (g) methodological and conceptual issues in social skills training (SST), and (h) generalization and maintenance issues, followed by concluding comments.

SOCIAL SKILLS AND SOCIAL COMPETENCE

In the past two decades, there has been an explosion of professional interest and investment in the development of children's social effectiveness in general and in the social effectiveness of at-risk students in particular (Elksnin & Elksnin, 2006; Gresham & Elliott, 1990; Maag, 2006; Merrell & Gimpel, 1998). A number of professional developments stimulated and maintained interest in this topic. These developments included (a) the work of behavior therapists and applied behavior analysts in isolating and teaching discrete forms of prosocial behavior, (b) the assertion-training and affective education movements, (c) the deinstitutionalization and mainstreaming movements, and (d) the regular education and full-inclusion initiatives. These rather diverse developments each independently highlighted the importance of social behavior for school and postschool success.

Definitions of Social Skills

Numerous definitions of social skills have been developed over the past 30 years. Merrell and Gimpel (1998) identified at least 15 definitions of the term *social skills* that have appeared in the professional literature. Despite these variations, social skills are perhaps best described as a *behavioral response class*, because specific social behaviors are grouped under the generic category of social skills. Conceptually, social skills are a set of competencies that (a) help initiate and maintain positive social relationships, (b) contribute to peer acceptance and friendship development, (c) result in satisfactory school adjustment, and (d) allow individuals to cope with and adapt to the demands of the social environment (Gresham, 1998, 2002). Social skills also can be defined as socially acceptable and learned forms of behavior that enable an individual to interact effectively with others and to avoid or escape unacceptable behavior that results in negative social interactions with others (Elliott & Gresham, 2008; Gresham & Elliott, 1990, 2008).

A useful way of thinking about social skills is based on the concept of *social validity* (Kazdin, 1977; Wolf, 1978). In this approach, social skills can be defined as social behaviors occurring in specific situations that result in important social outcomes for children and youth (Gresham, 1986). Socially important outcomes are those outcomes that social agents in the child's environment (e.g., peers, teachers, parents) consider important, adaptive, and functional within specific settings. Put differently, socially important outcomes are those that help individuals adapt both to societal expectations and to the behavioral demands of specific environments (Walker et al., 1998).

Research has shown that some of the most socially important outcomes for children and youth include peer acceptance, academic achievement and school adjustment, and teacher and parent acceptance (DiPerma & Elliott, 2002; Gresham, 2002; Gresham & Elliott, 1990; Hersh & Walker, 1983; Newcomb et al., 1993; Parker & Asher, 1987; Walker, Irvin, Noell, & Singer, 1992). It is well established that children who are poorly accepted or rejected by peers, who have few friendships, and who adjust poorly to schooling are at much greater risk for lifelong maladaptive outcomes. Parker and Asher showed that children having difficulties in peer relationships often demonstrate a behavior pattern that can be described as antisocial, aggressive, and characterized by repeated school norm violations. This behavior pattern is characteristic of many children with or at risk for EBD. In the absence of effective interventions, this behavior pattern is likely to continue and to develop into more virulent and resistant forms of maladaptive behavior (Patterson, DeBaryshe, & Ramsay, 1989; Reid, 1993; Walker et al., 2004).

Social Skills Versus Social Competence

In the theoretical conceptualization of social behavior, social skills and social competence are two distinct elements of social behavior. *Social skills* are a specific class of behaviors that an individual exhibits in order to complete a social task. Social tasks might include approaching a peer group, having a conversation, making friends, playing a game with peers, and so forth. *Social competence*, in contrast, is an evaluative term based on judgments (given certain criteria) that an individual has performed a social task adequately. As noted above, these judgments are made by influential social agents with whom the individual interacts frequently within natural environments (e.g., school, home, community). Thus, social skills are specific behaviors exhibited in specific situations that lead to judgments by others that these behaviors were competently displayed (or not competently displayed) in accomplishing social tasks.

Competence does not necessarily imply exceptional performance; it only indicates that a given social performance was considered adequate (McFall, 1982). Gresham (1986) suggested that evaluations of social competence might be based on three criteria: (a) relevant judgments of an individual's social behavior (e.g., by peers, teachers, and parents), (b) evaluations of social behavior relative to explicit, pre-established criteria (e.g., number of steps successfully performed or completed in the performance of a social task), and (c) behavioral performances relative to a normative standard (e.g., scores on social skills rating scales).

SOCIAL SKILLS VERSUS PROBLEM BEHAVIORS

Acceptable levels of mastery on selected social skills have the potential to positively affect both academic performance and social status. However, a range of problem behaviors can disrupt school adjustment and negate the positive impact of social skills. Both are discussed briefly below.

Social Skills as Academic Enablers

Researchers have documented meaningful and predictive relationships between children's social behaviors and their long-term academic achievement (DiPerma & Elliott, 2002; Malecki & Elliott, 2002; Wentzel, 1993; Wentzel & Watkins, 2002). The notion of *academic enablers* evolved from the work of researchers who explored the relationship between students' nonacademic behaviors (e.g., social skills and motivation) and their academic achievement (Gresham & Elliott, 1990; Malecki, 1998; Wentzel, 1993; Wigfield & Karpathian, 1991). DiPerma and Elliott (2000) distinguished between academic skills and academic enablers. Academic skills are viewed as the basic and complex skills that are the primary focus of academic instruction. In contrast, academic enablers are attitudes and behaviors that allow a student to participate in and ultimately benefit from academic instruction in the classroom. Research using the Academic Competence Evaluation Scales (ACES) showed that academic enablers were moderately related to students' academic achievement as measured by standardized tests (*Mdn r* = .50; DiPerma & Elliott, 2000). In a major longitudinal study, Caprara and colleagues found that social skills of third graders, as assessed by teachers, were better predictors of eighth-grade academic achievement than achievement test results in third grade (Caprara, Barbaranelli, Pastorelli, Bandura, & Zimbardo, 2000). Even stronger findings were reported by Malecki and Elliott (2002), who showed that social skills correlated approximately .70 with end-of-year academic achievement as measured by high-stakes tests. It thus appears that social skills are vitally important academic enablers for children in schools.

Problem Behaviors as Academic Disablers

Whereas social skills or prosocial behaviors function as academic enablers, it has been documented that problem behaviors, particularly externalizing behavior patterns, interfere or compete with the acquisition and performance of both social and academic skills (Gresham, 2005a; Gresham & Elliott, 2008). In other words, these competing problem behaviors have been known to function as *academic disablers* in that they often cause decreases in academic achievement. Children with externalizing behaviors, such as aggression, noncompliance, or teacher defiance, often have moderate to severe academic skill deficits that are reflected in below-average academic achievement (Coie & Jacobs, 1993; Hinshaw, 1992; Offord, Boyle, & Racine, 1989; Reid, 1993). It is unclear whether these academic problems are primarily the causes or consequences of problem behaviors; however, there is little doubt that they greatly exacerbate them. As these children progress through their school careers, their academic deficits and achievement problems become even more severe (Walker, Shinn, O'Neill, & Ramsay, 1987).

Classification of Social Skills Deficits

Another important distinction that has direct implications for the design and delivery of social skills intervention programs is that between social skill *acquisition deficits* and social skill *performance deficits* (Gresham, 1981). These two types of deficits require different intervention approaches and different settings, such as the general education classroom versus pullout situations that are indicated for different tiers of intervention.

Acquisition deficits result from a lack of knowledge about how to perform a given social skill, an inability to fluently enact a sequence of social behaviors, or difficulty in knowing which social skill is appropriate in specific situations (Gresham, 1981, 2002). Thus, acquisition deficits can result from lack of social–cognitive abilities, difficulties in integrating fluent response patterns, or deficits in appropriate discrimination of social situations. Acquisition deficits can be characterized as "can't do" problems because the child cannot perform a given social skill under the most optimal conditions of motivation. Remediation of acquisition deficits requires directly teaching the social skill using established principles of social skills instruction. These procedures are listed under I in Table 1.

Table 1. Evidence-Based Strategies for Social Skills Intervention

I. Promoting skill acquisition
    A. Modeling
    B. Coaching
    C. Behavioral rehearsal
    D. Social problem solving
II. Enhancing skill performance
    A. Manipulation of antecedents
        1. Peer-mediated interventions
        2. Cuing or prompting
        3. Precorrection
        4. Choice
    B. Manipulation of consequences
        1. Social praise
        2. Error correction
        3. Performance feedback
        4. Behavioral contracts
        5. School-to-home notes
        6. Activity reinforcement
        7. Token or point systems
    C. Removal of competing problem behaviors
        1. Differential reinforcement of other behavior (DRO)
        2. Differential reinforcement of incompatible behavior (DRI)
        3. Differential reinforcement of low rates of behavior (DRL)
        4. Differential reinforcement of alternative behavior (DRA)
        5. Differential negative reinforcement for alternative behaviors (DNRA–Escape Extinction)
        6. Cognitive coping skills training
        7. Anger control training
        8. Self-instructional training
        9. Self-monitoring
       10. Social problem solving
    D. Generalization and maintenance
        1. Topographical generalization
           a. Training diversely
           b. Exploiting functional contingencies
           c. Incorporating functional mediators
        2. Functional generalization
           a. Identifying strong competing stimuli
           b. Identifying strong competing problem behaviors
           c. Identifying functionally equivalent behaviors
           d. Increasing the reliability and efficiency of functionally equivalent behaviors
           e. Decreasing the reliability and efficiency of competing problem behaviors

Note. From "Teaching Social Skills to High-Risk Children and Youth: Preventive and Remedial Strategies," p. 417, by F. M. Gresham, in *Interventions for Academic and Behavior Problems II: Preventive and Remedial Approaches*, edited by M. R. Shinn, H. M. Walker, & G. Stoner, 2002, Bethesda, MD. Copyright 2002 by the National Association of School Psychologists. Adapted with permission.

Performance deficits are the failure to perform a given social skill at acceptable levels even though the child knows how to perform the social skill. These types of social skills deficits can be thought of as "won't do" problems in that the child knows what to do but does not perform a particular social skill at an acceptable frequency. These types of social skill deficits can best be thought of as motivational or performance problems rather than learning or acquisition problems. Remediation of performance deficits *does not require* direct instruction in teaching social skills; rather, it requires manipulation of the antecedents and consequences of the social skill to make its occurrence more likely. Recommended procedures for addressing performance deficits are listed under II in Table 1.

Social Skills and Competing Problem Behaviors

Another important component of social skills deficits involves *competing problem behaviors*; that is, behaviors that interfere with, or block, the acquisition of a given social skill (Elliott & Gresham, 2008; Gresham & Elliott, 1990). Competing problem behaviors can be broadly classified as either *externalizing* behavior patterns, such as noncompliance, aggression, or coercive behaviors, or *internalizing* behavior patterns, such as social withdrawal, anxiety, or depression. For example, a child with a history of noncompliant, oppositional, and coercive behavior may never learn prosocial behavioral alternatives such as sharing, cooperation, and self-control because of the absence of opportunities to learn these skills caused by the competing aversive behaviors (Eddy, Reid, & Curry, 2002). Similarly, a child with a history of social anxiety, social withdrawal, and shyness may never learn appropriate social skills and behaviors because of withdrawal from the peer group, thereby creating an absence of the opportunities to learn and master peer-related competencies (Gresham, Van, & Cook, 2006).

Social skill performance deficits, as previously described, are primarily due to motivational factors rather than a lack of knowledge of how to enact a given social skill. One of the most conceptually powerful principles of learning used to explain the relationship between social skill performance deficits and competing problem behaviors is the "matching law" (Herrnstein, 1961, 1970). The matching law states that the relative rate of any given behavior matches the relative rate of reinforcement for that behavior. In other words, response rate matches reinforcement rate. Matching is studied in what are known as concurrent schedules of reinforcement, which are an experimental arrangement in which two or more behaviors are reinforced according to two or more simultaneous, but quantitatively different, schedules of reinforcement (i.e., concurrently).

Matching deals with the issue of "choice behavior"; that is, behaviors having a higher rate of reinforcement will be chosen (i.e., performed) by individuals more frequently than behaviors reinforced at lower rates. For example, if disruptive classroom behavior is reinforced every 4 times it occurs and prosocial behavior is reinforced every 20 times it occurs (concurrent reinforcement), then the matching law would predict that, on average, classroom disruptive behavior will be performed by a student five times more frequently than prosocial behavior, based on the ratio between the two concurrent schedules of reinforcement. Research in naturalistic environments has consistently shown that behavior observed under concurrent schedules of reinforcement closely follows the matching law (Martens, 1992; Martens & Houk, 1989; Martens, Lochner, & Kelly, 1992; Snyder & Stoolmiller, 2002).

Maag (2005) suggested that one way to decrease competing problem behaviors is to teach *positive replacement behaviors*, or what he called replacement behavior training (RBT). Use of RBT may help solve many of the problems described in the social skills training literature, such as poor generalization and maintenance, modest effect sizes, and a lack of social validity in target behavior selection. RBT is based on the premise of functional analysis of behavior. The goal of RBT is to identify a prosocial behavior that serves the same function as the competing or inappropriate problem behavior (that is, a functionally equivalent behavior). Two or more behaviors are functionally equivalent if they produce similar amounts of reinforcement from the social environment (Horner & Billingsley, 1988).

For example, a child engages in disruptive behavior in the classroom and a functional behavioral assessment suggests that the behavior is being maintained by social attention from peers and the teacher. An RBT approach would identify a prosocial behavioral alternative such as work completion that would likely result in peer and teacher attention (i.e., it would serve the same function). RBT depends largely on principles derived from the matching law, in which the rates of reinforcement for prosocial behavior are increased and rates of reinforcement for competing problem behaviors are decreased, thereby encouraging children to choose appropriate behaviors over inappropriate behaviors. Elliott and Gresham (1991) recommended similar strategies based on differential reinforcement techniques to decrease occurrences of competing problem behaviors and to increase occurrences of prosocial behaviors. These procedures are listed in Table 1.

Social Skills and Risk and Protective Factors in EBD

Walker and Severson (2002) suggested that children having characteristics of emotional and behavioral disorders are at risk for a host of negative developmental outcomes, many of which place children on destructive paths that often lead to unfortunate consequences, such as school failure and dropout, alcohol and substance abuse, delinquency, social rejection, and violent and destructive behavior patterns. These risk factors interact in complex ways, and it is unlikely that a single risk factor is responsible for the development of EBD for a particular child. Given that single risk factors may have multiple outcomes and that a great deal of overlap occurs between behavioral markers, interventions that focus on reducing risk in interacting risk factors may directly affect multiple outcomes (Coie et al., 1993; Dryfoos, 1990). Researchers typically find a nonlinear relationship between risk factors and outcomes, suggesting that a single risk factor may have a small effect on an individual, but they also find that rates of EBD increase rapidly and exponentially with the accumulation of additional risk factors (Rutter, 1979; Sameroff, Seifer, Barocas, Zax, & Greenspan, 1987).

Walker and Severson (2002) identified a number of risk and protective factors specifically within the realm of social competence that could be targeted for intervention efforts. For example, poor problem solving, poor social skills, lack of empathy, bullying, and peer rejection represent important risk factors for children who may develop EBD. A recent synthesis of meta-analyses of the risk and protective factors literature also found that a sociometric status of *controversial*, *rejected*, or *neglected*, as well as poor social skills, were significant risk factors for children with externalizing and internalizing EBD (Crews et al., 2007).

Although children with EBD have a number of social competence risk factors, there are also a number of factors that buffer the maladaptive outcomes created by these same risk factors. *Protective factors* are variables that reduce the likelihood of maladaptive outcomes, given prevailing conditions of risk. Protective factors in the realm of social competence include social–cognitive skills, prosocial behavior patterns, and peer acceptance. Meta-analytic synthesis by Crews et al. (2007) found that positive play activities, a sociometric status of *popular*, and prosocial behavior patterns served as significant protective factors for children with both externalizing and internalizing EBD.

This brief review of the meta-analytical literature of risk and protective factors indicates that children with characteristics of EBD experience a number of risk factors that interact in complex ways to produce negative developmental trajectories. Unfortunately, many of these risk factors are immutable and are not amenable to change by schools. However, there are risk factors that can be targeted for intervention by schools, particularly within the realm of social competence. Moreover, it has been demonstrated in the literature that many behaviors within the construct of social competence serve as important protective factors that buffer the pernicious effects of the risk factors associated with EBD.

REVIEW OF EVIDENCE-BASED SOCIAL SKILLS INTERVENTIONS

Various service delivery and instructional approaches have been designed to remediate deficits in children's social competence functioning. Of these approaches, this chapter examines social skills training (SST), one of the most popular intervention approaches for this population. SST is designed to remediate children's social skills acquisition and performance deficits and to reduce or eliminate competing problem behaviors (Gresham, Sugai, & Horner, 2001). An important question to be answered in this regard is whether or not SST is efficacious in promoting the acquisition, performance, generalization, and maintenance of prosocial behavior patterns; reducing competing problem behaviors; and enhancing interpersonal relationships with peers and adults. Several meta-analytical reviews have addressed this question, with some reviews yielding conflicting conclusions, as indicated below.

Meta-Analytical Findings for Social Skills Training

Seven meta-analyses of the social skills training literature have been conducted since 1985 (Ang & Hughes, 2001; Beelmann, Pfingsten, & Losel, 1994; Cook et al., 2008; Losel & Beelman, 2003; Quinn, Kavale, Mathur, Rutherford, & Forness, 1999; Schneider, 1992; Schneider & Byrne, 1985). These meta-analyses have focused on children and youth with behavioral difficulties; they involved approximately 338 studies and included over 25,000 students 3–18 years of age. Reviews of these meta-analyses show that the construct of social skills has been consistently defined for research synthesis purposes. These meta-analyses suggest that the social skills construct can be divided into three major categories: social interaction, prosocial behavior, and social–cognitive skills. Correlates of social skills fall into two categories: problem behavior (externalizing and internalizing), and academic achievement and performance. These social skill categories and behavioral correlates are consistent with a number of other researchers' work in the area of social skills (Caldarella & Merrell, 1997; Coie, Dodge, & Coppotelli, 1982; Dodge, 1986; Elliott & Gresham, 2007; Gresham, 2002; Gresham & Elliott, 1990, 2008; Walker & McConnell, 1995; Walker et al., 1992).

Six of the seven meta-analyses used group experimental designs and showed a grand mean effect size $r = .29$ (range $= .19–.40$), suggesting that overall, approximately 65% of the participants in the SST groups improved compared with 35% of those in the control groups, based on the binomial effect size display (Rosenthal & Rosnow, 1991). If Cohen's (1977) conventional standards are used, an effect size of this magnitude would be considered moderate. In the six meta-analyses considered, it is clear that SST produced practically significant changes in social behavior based on percentages of participants in the SST groups who showed improvement. The meta-analysis of SST conducted by Quinn et al. (1999), ostensibly with children and youth who had emotional and behavioral disorders, were inconsistent with these findings. A critique of the Quinn et al. meta-analysis raises questions about the internal validity of the studies reviewed.

Only 2 of the 35 studies in the Quinn et al. (1999) meta-analysis included children who were receiving special education services under the category of emotionally disturbed. The 35 studies included in the Quinn et al. meta-analysis did not have to meet the more stringent inclusion criteria of the six meta-analyses described earlier. Whereas the six meta-analyses required a control group and either an experimental or quasi-experimental design, these were not mentioned as inclusion criteria in the Quinn et al. meta-analysis. Instead, Quinn et al. used a three-point rating scale to estimate the internal validity of the 35 studies they included in their review. Thus, this meta-analysis was dominated by studies of low or moderate internal validity.

An overall effect size of $r = .10$ across the 35 studies was reported. A binomial effect size display suggests that 55% of the participants in the SST groups improved and 45% of the controls improved. The effect size of $r = .10$ is small and is significantly lower than the average effect size of $r = .29$ reported in the other meta-analyses.

Because of several important methodological flaws in the Quinn et al. (1999) meta-analysis, it should not be interpreted as reflecting the status of SST for children and youth with or at risk for EBD in terms of construct validity, internal validity, external validity, and social validity (see Gresham, Cook, Crews, & Kern, 2004, for a more detailed discussion of these issues).

The meta-analytic reviews of the SST literature referenced above suggest that SST is an efficacious intervention for children with or at risk for EBD. However, all of the SST studies included in the above meta-analyses must be considered Tier 2, or selected interventions, because these interventions typically are delivered on an individual or small group basis, reflecting an obvious gap in the SST literature. However, evidence-based Tier 1 and Tier 3 social skills interventions do exist. Figure 1 presents a number of evidence-based interventions across all three tiers of intervention intensity.

Figure 1. Multitier evidence-based social skills interventions.

Intensive Interventions
• Function-Based Assessment
• Replacement Behavior Training

Selected Interventions
• School–Home Note
• Behavioral Contracts
• Self-Management Strategies
• Peer-Mediated Interventions
• Differential Reinforcement Strategies

Universal Interventions
• Good Behavior Game
• Check-Connect-Expect
• Positive Behavior Support
• Class-Wide Intervention Program

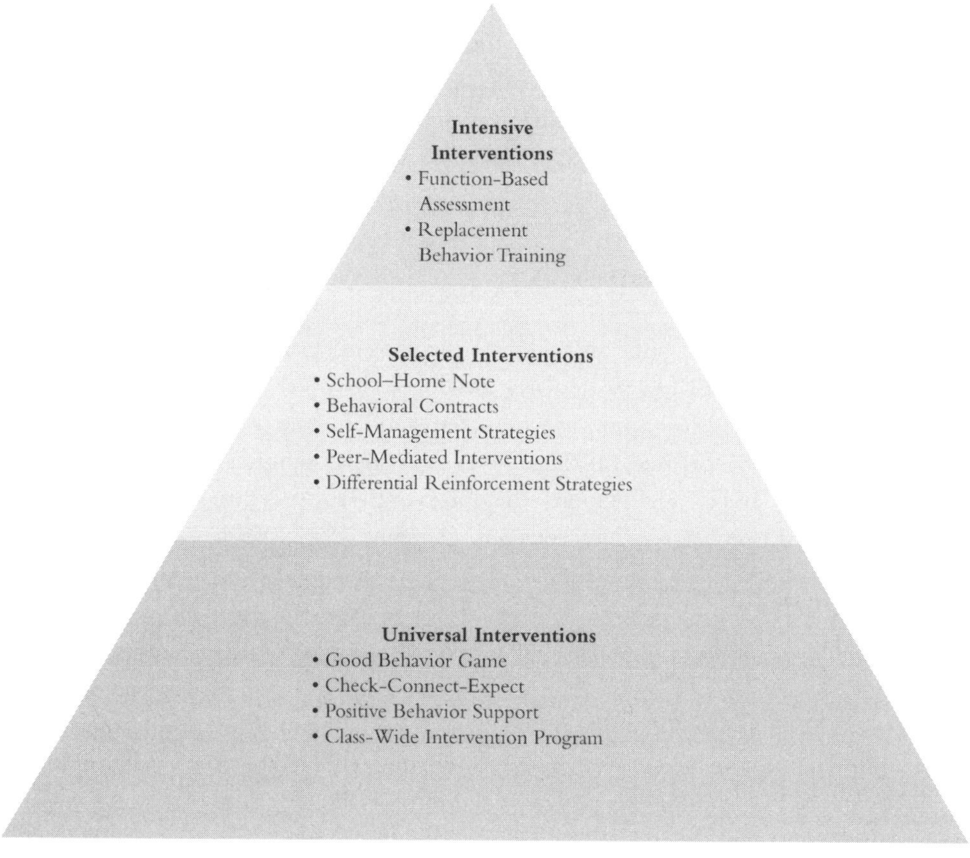

Note. From "Source of Vulnerability to School Violence: Systems-Level Assessment and Strategies to Improve Safety and Climate," p. 303, by J. Sprague, H. Walker, S. Sowards, C. Van Bloem, P. Eberhardt, & B. Marshall, in *Interventions for Academic and Behavior Problems II: Preventive and Remedial Approaches*, edited by M. R. Shinn, H. M. Walker, & G. Stoner, 2002, Bethesda, MD. Copyright 2002 by the National Association of School Psychologists. Adapted with permission.

Quantitative reviews of this literature suggest that almost two-thirds of children receiving SST will show some degree of measureable improvement, compared with only one third of children in control or usual-care groups. SST produces moderate effect size estimates using conventional standards for the calculation of effect sizes. Despite these positive findings, several important methodological and conceptual issues have yet to be addressed in the SST literature, as described in the following sections.

METHODOLOGICAL AND CONCEPTUAL ISSUES IN SST

As noted, social skills training has been shown to produce, on average, moderate effect sizes based on meta-analytic reviews of the SST literature. However, other syntheses of meta-analyses have indicated that SST produces only negligible effects on children's social behavior (Quinn et al., 1999). Although there are potentially many explanations for these inconsistent findings, four major explanations have been proffered repeatedly in the literature to account for SST outcomes: (a) social validity of assessments, (b) matching of treatments to types of deficits, (c) treatment integrity issues, and (d) generalization and maintenance (Beelmann et al., 1994; Gresham, 1997, 1998; Gresham, Sugai & Horner, 2001; Maag, 2005, 2006; Schneider, 1992). These SST issues are discussed briefly in the following sections.

Social Validity of SST Assessments

Social validity is a critical concept when considering SST interventions for children with or at risk for EBD, particularly when it involves interpreting the SST literature, because there is a wide gap between standard practices and best practices. Social validity can be defined on three levels: (a) social significance of the goals of intervention, (b) social acceptability of intervention procedures, and (c) social importance of the effects of interventions (Kazdin, 1977; Wolf, 1978). In short, social validation addresses three fundamental questions with respect to social skills interventions (Gresham & Lopez, 1996): (a) What behavior should we change? (b) How should we change it? and (c) How will we know the intervention is effective?

Maag (2006) suggested that one of the most important issues in teaching social skills is deciding whether the behaviors targeted for change will enhance the quality of life of the participants. Hawkins (1991) preferred the term *habilitative validity* to social validity because he maintained that the goals of all interventions are to enhance an individual's adaptation or "habilitation" to whatever social environments in which they might find themselves. Gresham and Elliott (1990, 2008) have built social validation into their assessment instruments by having key informants (teachers and parents) rate the *importance* as well as the *frequency* of each social skill.

Social Significance Measures

Many social skills studies have been conducted without a clear idea of the *social significance* of the skills to be taught in the intervention. A major methodological flaw in much of the SST research is the lack of correspondence between behaviors that are assessed and behaviors that are taught in the intervention. For example, 13 studies included in the Quinn et al. (1999) meta-analysis were based on "commercially available social skills programs"; however, the specific behaviors taught in these programs were not based on an assessment of the participants' skill deficits, nor did practitioners consider how important consumers of the treatments (i.e., teachers) viewed these target behaviors. It appears that in many SST studies, little thought is given to the social significance of the behaviors being taught. A prototypical social skill intervention involves "rounding up the usual suspects," giving them social skills training (typically in a small pullout group format), teaching them social behaviors that the researchers thought were important to teach, and not planning or programming for generalization and maintenance (Gresham, 1997, 1998).

Social Acceptability Measures

The *social acceptability* of SST to treatment consumers is an important aspect of teaching prosocial behaviors to children with EBD. Treatment acceptability can be defined as judgments regarding whether a given treatment is (a) fair in relation to a given problem, (b) reasonable, and (c) consistent with what a treatment should be (Kazdin, 1981). Witt and Elliott (1985) specified reciprocal relationships among the four characteristics of treatment: *acceptability*, *use*, *integrity*, and *effectiveness*. According to Witt and Elliott, treatment acceptability is the most important initial criterion for selection and use of an intervention. In their model, more acceptable treatments have a higher probability of being adopted and implemented relative to less acceptable treatments. The use and effectiveness of treatments are moderated by the integrity with which treatments are implemented (Gresham, 1989; Gresham, Gansle, & Noell, 1993; Gresham & Lopez, 1996).

Very little is known about the acceptability of SST interventions because researchers typically have not included acceptability assessments in their research (Gresham et al., 2004). Research in other areas seems to relate treatment acceptability to the complexity of treatment, time required to implement treatments, and treatment implementers' knowledge and expertise (Elliott, 1988; Witt & Elliott, 1985).

Socially Important Outcome Measures

Socially valid outcome measures are those that detect *socially important*, rather than trivial, effects for individuals. Outcome measures in SST can be classified based on a social validity criterion (Gresham, 1983, 1998; Gresham, Sugai, & Horner, 2001). In this classification system, Type I measures represent a socially valid treatment goal, because social systems (e.g., schools, mental health agencies) and significant others (teachers, parents) refer children based on these treatment goals. Type I measures are socially valid in the sense that they predict long-term outcomes that are important to society, such as school dropout, delinquency, adult mental health difficulties, and arrest rates (Kupersmidt et al., 1990; Parker & Asher, 1987; Walker et al., 2004). Type I measures include sociometric status, friendship status, teacher and parent judgments of social behavior, and certain types of archival data (e.g., disciplinary referrals, school suspensions, and arrest rates).

Type I measures are inherently socially valid, but they may not be sensitive to detecting relatively short-term treatment effects. Although many treatment consumers may consider these measures the bottom line in indicating significant treatment outcomes, overreliance on these types of measures may ignore a great deal of behavior change (Kazdin, 2001). Exclusive use of these measures to evaluate SST outcomes may lead to Type II errors in hypothesis testing (i.e., retaining a false null hypothesis). It may be that quite large and sustained changes in social behavior are required before these behavior changes affect Type I measures of social functioning. Sechrest, McKnight, and McKnight (1996) suggested using the method of *just noticeable differences* (JND) in measuring treatment outcomes. In the JND approach, the question becomes: How much of a difference in social behavior is required before it is noticed by significant others in the child's environment? Large, positive, and consistent changes in social interactions between a target child and peers is required before these behavior changes are reflected in sociometric status, friendship status, and parent and teacher ratings of social behavior (Gresham, 1998; Gresham et al., 2004).

Type II measures are indicators or correlates of individuals' standings on Type I measures. Based on demonstrated empirical relationships with Type I measures, Type II measures predict important social outcomes for children and youth (Gresham, 1983, 1998). The most frequently used Type II measures are direct observations of social behavior in naturalistic settings such as the classroom, playground, home, and community settings. These measures are used frequently in SST research and are involved exclusively in investigations that use single case experimental designs.

A major advantage of direct observation measures in SST programs is that they are highly sensitive in detecting treatment effects. One weakness in the SST literature is that Type II measures of social behavior are often not based on a sound theoretical framework or taxonomy. Also, exclusive reliance on Type II measures may lead to greater Type I errors in hypothesis testing (i.e., rejecting a true null hypothesis). The taxonomy mentioned earlier by Caldarella and Merrell (1997) provides a sound basis for behavioral definitions of social behavior (peer relation skills, self-management skills, assertion skills, and compliance skills). Additionally, the social skills domains in the Social Skills Rating System (Gresham & Elliott, 1990) provide a strong theoretical basis for deriving Type II direct observation measures (cooperation, assertion, responsibility, empathy, and self-control). More recent work using direct behavior ratings—a hybrid scale with characteristics of both direct observation and behavior rating scales—holds promise as a Type II measure. Despite the advantages of direct behavior ratings, recent work suggests that these measures may not be generalizable across raters, target behaviors, or time (Chafouleas, Christ, Riley-Tillman, Briesch, & Chanese, 2007).

One approach to using behavior ratings to monitor progress is to develop change-sensitive behavior rating scales. Change-sensitive rating scales have been developed and used as progress monitoring tools to assess stimulant medication in classroom settings for children with attention deficit hyperactivity disorder (ADHD). DuPaul and Stoner (2003) suggested that ratings of ADHD core symptoms (inattention, impulsivity, and hyperactivity) can be collected across dosage conditions to assist physicians in evaluating and titrating stimulant medication. Fabiano et al. (2007) used brief versions (five-item Inattention–Overactivity scale and five-item Oppositional Defiant scale) of the Conners Teacher Rating Scales completed daily by teachers to evaluate medication dosage effects for children with ADHD (Inattention/Overactivity with Aggression, or IOWA; Conners, 1997; Milich & Loney, 1982). Various other focused and change-sensitive rating scales have been developed and used in this manner, including the ADD-H Comprehensive Teacher Rating Scale (Ullman, Sleator, & Sprague, 1985) and the ADHD Rating Scale-IV (DuPaul, Erwin, Hook, & McGoey, 1998). These brief behavior rating scales are preferred to more comprehensive, broadband measures because brief ratings provide more focused information about behavior change and are more practical and efficient for teachers and parents to complete.

Similar logic could be applied to developing change-sensitive social skills measures using extant behavior rating scales such as the Social Skills Rating System, the Social Skills Improvement System: Rating Scales, and the Walker-McConnell Scales of Social Competence and School Adjustment (Gresham & Elliott, 1990, 2008; Walker & McConnell, 1995). In fact, work is under way to develop brief behavior rating scales for both social skills and competing problem behaviors (Gresham & Cook, 2008).

Type III measures are the least socially valid in measuring social competence of children because they show weak or nonexistent relationships with Type I or Type II measures; however, Type III measures may have some face validity, because they appear to be measuring important aspects of social skills (Gresham, 1986, 1998). For example, behavioral role-play measures (conducted in analog settings), social problem-solving measures, and various indexes of social cognition all can be classified as Type III measures. There is little evidence to suggest that these measures are related to naturally occurring social behaviors observed in authentic educational settings, sociometric status, or teacher and parent judgments of social behavior. A number of studies in the meta-analyses reviewed used Type III measures of social skills. What is typically found is that social problem–solving interventions produce significant changes on social problem-solving measures, but almost no effects on either social interaction skills or sociometric status (see Ang & Hughes, 2001; Beelmann et al., 1994; Schneider, 1992).

Matching of Interventions to Types of Deficits

Studies in the meta-analyses described earlier failed to match specific types of social skills deficits to specific intervention strategies. Most social skills studies deliver a treatment to children with an almost complete disregard for the types of social skills deficits children may have (Gresham, 1998). In fact, most research suggests that little systematic effort is devoted to assessing whether children should be taught the specific target behaviors in SST programs.

Because acquisition deficits and performance deficits differ (i.e., *can't do* versus *won't do*), instructional strategies for remediating the deficits are fundamentally different. Instructional procedures used for acquisition deficits assume that the child does not have the skill in his or her repertoire or does not know a critical step in performing a social skill sequence. Specific intervention strategies for acquisition deficits typically involve both live and symbolic modeling, coaching, behavioral rehearsal, and performance feedback (see Table 1; Elksnin & Elksnin, 2006; Elliott, & Gresham, 2008; Gresham, 2002; Maag, 2006).

Procedures for enhancing the performance of previously acquired social skills are based on manipulation of antecedents and consequences of desired social behaviors. These interventions typically occur in naturalistic settings, such as classrooms and playgrounds, using antecedent-based (e.g., peer initiation, peer tutoring, and incidental teaching) or consequent-based (e.g., differential reinforcement, group contingencies, and prompting and shaping) intervention procedures.

Recent developments in the use of functional behavioral assessment procedures and positive behavior support planning increase the "fit" between social skills interventions and reductions in competing problem behaviors (Horner, 1994; Horner & Carr, 1997; Lewis & Sugai, 1996). In these approaches, interventionists develop testable hypotheses about predictable occasioning and maintaining functions. Using these hypotheses, interventionists identify competing replacement behaviors (i.e., social skills) and develop, implement, and monitor specifically designed behavior support plans (Gresham, Watson, & Skinner, 2001). These types of interventions can be thought of as Tier 3, or targeted and intensive interventions.

Treatment Integrity

There is little evidence in the meta-analyses of the SST literature that these interventions were implemented as planned or intended. A fundamental goal of all intervention research is the unequivocal demonstration that changes in a dependent variable are due to systematic and manipulated changes in an independent (treatment) variable and not due to extraneous variables. Treatment integrity (sometimes called treatment fidelity or procedural reliability) refers to the degree to which a treatment is implemented as planned or intended (Gresham, 1989, 1997, 2005b; Gresham, Gansle, Noell, Cohen, & Rosenblum, 1993; McIntyre, Gresham, DiGennaro, & Reed, 2007). Treatment integrity is concerned with the *accuracy* and *consistency* with which treatments are implemented.

Given the paucity of treatment integrity data in the SST literature, a review of SST meta-analyses cannot conclusively determine whether an SST program is ineffective because it is a poor treatment or if it would be more effective if it were implemented with greater integrity. Failure to ensure the integrity with which SST treatments are implemented poses several threats to the ability to draw valid inferences in treatment outcome research, especially regarding the effects of SST interventions on children's social competence. Monitoring of treatment integrity should be a high priority in the conduct of future SST research.

Generalization and Maintenance Issues

One of the most persistent weaknesses of the SST literature is its failure to demonstrate sufficient generalization and maintenance effects for the social skills taught. Three reasons have been noted in the literature accounting for this outcome: (a) failure to adequately program for generalization and maintenance, (b) failure to match instructional procedures to specific types of deficits, and (c) failure to target socially valid behaviors (Gresham, Sugai, & Horner, 2001; Maag, 2006). Generalization errors result from inadequate stimulus control over social skills relative to competing problem behaviors. Horner and Billingsley (1988) have suggested that a *functional approach* is needed to program for generalization and maintenance. One example of generalization errors is shown here within the context of competing problem behaviors: A child has acquired a new, adaptive social skill and demonstrates excellent generalization across new situations. When the child encounters a new situation that contains a strong competing stimulus, such as a highly disliked peer, this competing stimulus is likely to elicit old, undesirable behaviors (e.g., verbal and physical aggression). The practical effect is that the new adaptive social skill does not generalize to situations containing the strong competing stimulus.

One reason, among many, that socially skilled behaviors may fail to generalize is because the newly taught skill is masked or overpowered by older and stronger competing behaviors. This concept is important for understanding why some behaviors generalize to new situations, but others do not, and why a behavior that has been maintained for a long time might begin to deteriorate.

Competing behaviors are often performed instead of socially skilled behaviors because the competing behavior is more efficient and reliable than the socially skilled behavior. *Efficient* in this instance means that the behavior produces immediate reinforcement with less response effort than an inefficient behavior (i.e., it is easier to do). For example, pushing into line may be more efficient for some children than waiting and asking politely to get into line. In this case, the behaviors of pushing and asking politely are said to be *functionally equivalent* behaviors in that they produce the same consequences with less response effort for the former than for the latter. *Reliable* means that a given behavior produces more consistent reinforcement than a less reliable behavior. Using the prior example, pushing may be a more reliable behavior than asking politely. SST interventions must program for generalization and maintenance for long-term effectiveness by taking this into account.

CONCLUSION

Children and youth with severe social, emotional, and behavioral excesses and deficits are at risk for numerous short-term and long-term negative outcomes. The etiology of specific social–behavioral patterns for individuals at risk for EBD is complex. A single risk factor is not likely to be responsible for any given behavior pattern, nor is any single protective factor likely to be sufficient to prevent the development of challenging behavior patterns. This chapter described how the facilitation of prosocial behavior patterns—that is, social skills—coupled with the reduction of competing problem behaviors may produce positive outcomes and reduce negative outcomes for children who are at risk for EBD.

In this chapter, social skills were viewed as *protective factors* that reduce the negative effects of externalizing and internalizing problem behaviors. Protective factors may achieve their effects in one or more of the following ways: (a) they directly decrease the effects of problem behaviors, (b) they interact with risk factors to buffer their effects, (c) they disrupt the mediational chain by which risk factors lead to EBD, and (d) they prevent the initial occurrence of risk factors (see Coie et al., 1993). In the same way that reinforcers and punishers are distinguished by their effects on the probability of a particular behavior occurring in the future, risk and protective factors can be distinguished only by the effect exerted on the probability of positive and negative outcomes.

Social skills were defined as a specific class of behaviors that allow an individual to successfully accomplish a social task. Social tasks include things such as making a friend, playing a game with peers, or having a conversation. Social competence, on the other hand, was defined as an evaluation based on judgments by others that an individual has performed a social task adequately. These judgments are made by social agents (parents, teachers, or peers) with whom an individual interacts in natural environments (school, home, community). Social skills cannot be defined independently of the social judgments and the social contexts in which behavior occurs.

The literature is quite clear that various social "judges" use different criteria to determine social competence. For example, peers judge the behavior of a particular child to be socially competent if it is characterized by behaviors such as cooperation, supporting peers, leading peers, and affiliating with peers (Walker et al., 1992). In contrast, teachers judge the behavior of a child to be socially competent if it is characterized by behaviors such as complying with teacher directives, following classroom rules, working independently, and listening carefully to the teacher (Elliott & Gresham, 2007; Walker et al., 1992).

This chapter also described how social skills can function as *academic enablers* and how problem behaviors can function as *academic disablers*. Social skills moderate the acquisition of academic skills, according to research showing that teacher ratings of social skills are often better long-term predictors of academic performance than are measures of academic achievement (Caprara et al., 2000). These findings suggest that universal or Tier 1 social skills interventions should improve the academic performance of entire classrooms by making them less chaotic and thus more conducive to learning.

Problem behaviors by students create chaotic, disruptive classroom environments that are not conducive to learning. This chapter presented a way of thinking about academic disablers in terms of competing problem behaviors. In this view, competing problem behaviors effectively interfere with the acquisition or performance of particular social skills. The *matching law* was discussed as a useful way of understanding how competing problem behaviors interfere with the performance of socially skilled behaviors. The law states that the relative rate of any behavior is based on the relative rate of reinforcement for that behavior (i.e., response rate matches reinforcement rate). It was recommended that concepts derived from the matching law could be used to identify functionally equivalent behaviors in replacement behavior training, that is, identifying and reinforcing a functionally equivalent socially skilled behavior to replace a competing problem behavior that serves the same function.

This chapter also discussed the evidence base for social skills training with children and adolescents. Based on seven meta-analyses involving 338 studies and including over 25,000 children and youth (ages 3–18 years), a moderate overall effect size was found to average $r = .29$ ($d = .60$). This effect size suggests that 65% of children undergoing social skills training will improve. It was noted that virtually all of the studies in these meta-analyses could be considered Tier 2 (targeted) interventions. The 35% of students who were weak responders to these interventions may be considered eligible for Tier 3 (intensive) interventions.

Several methodological and conceptual issues were discussed that relate to the outcomes produced by social skills intervention efforts. One issue in the social skills intervention literature is the choice of outcome measure used to document the effects of intervention. Outcome assessments were classified as Type I, II, and III measures based on a social validity criterion. Type I measures might be considered *social impact* measures because social systems and significant others often refer children based on these types of measures. Social impact measures include judgments by others (e.g., teachers, parents, or peers), disciplinary referrals, school suspensions, and truancy rates.

Type II measures were described as indicators or correlates of Type I measures that are typically more sensitive to change. Systematic direct observations of social behavior are the most frequently used Type II measures. Type III measures were not recommended because of their weak relationships with Type I and Type II measures.

Another methodological issue noted was the matching of specific intervention strategies to the type of social skill deficit (acquisition or performance deficits). Acquisition deficits reflect an absence of a skill and thus require direct instructional strategies to teach the skill. Performance deficits reflect motivational deficits and require procedures to increase the frequency of prosocial behavior and to decrease the frequency of competing problem behaviors.

Treatment integrity of social skills interventions was identified as a key area of concern in interpreting the social skills literature. There was little evidence found in the meta-analytic literature that the interventions were implemented as planned or intended. This is not only an important research issue, but also a critically important practical issue when delivering social skills interventions in the schools.

Finally, the issues of generalization and maintenance of social skills continue to be a bothersome aspect of the field. Failure to achieve sufficient generalization and maintenance effects stems from researchers and practitioners not adequately programming for generalization and maintenance and not selecting socially valid target behaviors (i.e., ones that should produce a higher rate of reinforcement from the environment). Procedures were recommended to enhance generalization and maintenance outcomes by making socially skilled behaviors more efficient and reliable and making competing problem behaviors less efficient and reliable.

REFERENCES

American Psychiatric Association. (1994). *Diagnostic and statistical manual of mental disorders* (4th ed.). Washington, DC: Author.

Ang, R., & Hughes, J. (2001). Differential benefits of skills training with antisocial youth based on group composition: A meta-analytic investigation. *School Psychology Review, 31,* 164–185.

Angold, A. (2000, December). *Preadolescent screening and data analysis.* Paper presented at the 2nd Annual Expert Panel Meeting on Preadolescent Screening Procedures. Sponsored by the Substance Abuse and Mental Health Services Administration. National Institutes of Health, Washington, DC.

Beelmann, A., Pfingsten, U., & Losel, F. (1994). Effects of training social competence in children: A meta-analysis of recent evaluation studies. *Journal of Clinical Child Psychology, 23,* 260–271.

Caldarella, P., & Merrell, K. (1997). Common dimensions of social skills in children and adolescents: Taxonomy of positive social behaviors. *School Psychology Review, 26,* 265–279.

Caprara, G., Barbaranelli, C., Pastorelli, C., Bandura, A., & Zimbardo, P. (2000). Prosocial foundations of children's academic achievement. *Psychological Science, 11,* 302–305.

Chafouleas, S. M., Christ, T., Riley-Tillman, T. C., Briesch, A., & Chanese, J. (2007). Generalizability and dependability of direct behavior ratings to assess social behavior of preschoolers. *School Psychology Review, 36,* 63–79.

Cohen, J. (1977). *Statistical power analysis for the behavioral sciences* (Rev. ed.). New York: Academic Press.

Coie, J., Dodge, K., & Coppotelli, H. (1982). Dimensions and types of social status: A cross-age perspective. *Developmental Psychology, 18,* 557–570.

Coie, J., & Jacobs, M. (1993). The role of social context in the prevention of conduct disorder [Special issue]. *Development and Psychopathology, 5,* 26–27.

Coie, J., Watt, N., West, S., Hawkins, J., Asarnow, J., Markman, H., et al. (1993). The science of prevention: A conceptual framework and some directions for a national research program. *American Psychologist, 48,* 1013–1022.

Conners, K. (1997). *Conners Rating Scales–Revised technical manual.* North Tonawanda, NY: Multi-Health Systems.

Cook, C. R., Gresham, F. M., Kern, L., Barreras, R. B., Thornton, S., & Crews, S. D. (2008). Social skills training for secondary students with emotional and/or behavioral disorders: A review and analysis of the meta-analytic literature. *Journal of Emotional and Behavioral Disorders, 16,* 131–144.

Crews, S. D., Bender, H., Gresham, F. M., Kern, L., Vanderwood, M., & Cook, C. R. (2007). Risk and protective factors of emotional and/or behavioral disorders in children and adolescents: A "mega"-analytic synthesis. *Behavioral Disorders, 32,* 64–77.

DiPerma, J., & Elliott, S. N. (2000). Academic Competence Evaluation Scales. San Antonio, TX: The Psychological Corporation.

DiPerma, J., & Elliott, S. N. (2002). Promoting academic enablers to improve student achievement: An introduction to the mini-series. *School Psychology Review, 31,* 293–297.

Dodge, K. (1986). A social information processing model of social competence in children. In M. Perlmutter (Ed.), *Minnesota symposium on child psychology* (Vol. 18, pp. 77–125). Hillsdale, NJ: Erlbaum.

Dryfoos, J. (1990). *Adolescents at risk: Prevalence and prevention.* New York: Oxford University Press.

DuPaul, G., Erwin, R., Hook, C., & McGoey, K. (1998). Peer tutoring for children with attention deficit hyperactivity disorder: Effects on classroom behavior and academic performance. *Journal of Applied Behavior Analysis, 31,* 579–592.

DuPaul, G., & Stoner, G. (2003). *ADHD in schools: Assessment and intervention strategies* (2nd ed.). New York: Guilford Press.

Eddy, J., Reid, J., & Curry, V. 2002. The etiology of youth antisocial behaviour, delinquency, and violence in a public health approach to prevention. In M. Shinn, H. Walker, & G. Stoner (Eds.), *Interventions for academic and behaviour problems II: Preventive and remedial approaches* (pp. 27–51). Bethesda, MD: National Association of School Psychologists.

Elksnin, L., & Elksnin, N. (2006). *Teaching social-emotional skills at school and home.* Denver: Love.

Elliott, S. N. (1988). Acceptability of behavioral treatments in educational settings. In J. Witt, S. Elliott, & F. M. Gresham (Eds.), *Handbook of behavior therapy in education* (pp. 121–150). New York: Plenum Press.

Elliott, S.N., & Gresham, F. M. (1991). *Social skills intervention guide.* Minneapolis, MN: Pearson Assessments.

Elliott, S. N., & Gresham, F. M. (2007). *Social skills improvement system: Classroom intervention guide.* Bloomington, MN: Pearson Assessments.

Elliott, S. N., & Gresham, F. M. (2008). *Social skills improvement system: Intervention guide.* Bloomington, MN: Pearson Assessments.

Fabiano, G., Pelham, W., Gnaby, E., Burrows-MacLean, L., Coles, E., Chacko, A., et al. (2007). The single and combined effects of multiple intensities of behavior modification and methylphenidate for children with attention-deficit hyperactivity disorder in a classroom setting. *School Psychology Review, 36,* 195–216.

Gresham, F. M. (1981). Social skills training with handicapped children: A review. *Review of Educational Research, 51,* 139–176.

Gresham, F. M. (1983). Social validity in the assessment of children's social skills: Establishing standards for social competency. *Journal of Psychoeducational Assessment, 1,* 299–307.

Gresham, F. M. (1986). Conceptual issues in the assessment of social competence in children. In P. Strain, M. Guralnick, & H. Walker (Eds.), *Children's social behavior: Development, assessment, and modification* (pp. 143–180). New York: Academic Press.

Gresham, F. M. (1989). Assessment of treatment integrity in school consultation and prereferral intervention. *School Psychology Review, 18,* 37–50.

Gresham, F. M. (1996). Treatment integrity in single-subject research. In R. Franklin, D. Allison, & B. Gorman (Eds.), *Design and analysis of single-case research* (pp. 93–118). Mahwah, NJ: Erlbaum.

Gresham, F. M. (1997). Social competence and students with behavior disorders: Where we've been, where we are, and where should we go. *Education and Treatment of Children, 20,* 233–250.

Gresham, F. M., (1998). Social skills training: Should we raze, remodel, or rebuild? *Behavioral Disorders, 24,* 19–25.

Gresham, F. M. (2002). Teaching social skills to high-risk children and youth: Preventive and remedial strategies. In M. Shinn, H. Walker, & G. Stoner (Eds.), *Interventions for academic and behavior problems II: Preventive and remedial approaches* (2nd ed., pp. 403–432). Bethesda, MD: National Association of School Psychologists.

Gresham, F. M. (2005a). Response to intervention (RTI): An alternative means of identifying students as emotionally disturbed. *Education and Treatment of Children, 28,* 328–344.

Gresham, F. M. (2005b). Treatment integrity and therapeutic change: Commentary on Perepletchikova and Kazdin. *Clinical Psychology: Science and Practice, 12,* 391–394.

Gresham, F. M., & Cook, C. R. (2008). *Development and validation of progress monitoring tools for social behavior* (Grant No. R324A090098, 2009–2013). Washington, DC: U.S. Department of Education, Institute for Educational Sciences, U.S. Department of Education.

Gresham, F. M., Cook, C. R., Crews, S. D., & Kern, L. (2006). Social skills training for children and youth with emotional and behavioral disorders: Validity considerations and future directions. *Behavioral Disorders, 30,* 32–46.

Gresham, F. M., & Elliott, S. N. (1990). *Social Skills Rating System.* Bloomington, MN: Pearson Assessments.

Gresham, F. M., & Elliott, S. N. (2008). *Social skills improvement system: Rating scales.* Bloomington, MN: Pearson Assessments.

Gresham, F. M., Gansle, K., & Noell, G. (1993). Treatment integrity in applied behavior analysis with children. *Journal of Applied Behavior Analysis, 26,* 257–263.

Gresham, F. M., Gansle, K., Noell, G., Cohen, S., & Rosenblum, S. (1993). Treatment integrity of school-based behavioral intervention studies: 1980–1990. *School Psychology Review, 22,* 254–272.

Gresham, F. M., & Lopez, M. F. (1996). Social validation: A unifying concept for school-based consultation research and practice. *School Psychology Quarterly, 11,* 204–227.

Gresham, F. M., Sugai, G., & Horner, R. (2001). Interpreting outcomes of social skills training for students with high-risk disabilities. *Exceptional Children, 67,* 331–344.

Gresham, F. M., Van, M. B., & Cook, C. R. (2006). Social skills training for teaching replacement behaviors: Remediation of acquisition deficits for at-risk children. *Behavioral Disorders, 30,* 32–46.

Gresham, F. M., Watson, T. S., & Skinner, C. H. (2001). Functional behavioral assessment: Principles, procedures, and future directions. *School Psychology Review, 30,* 156–172.

Hawkins, R. (1991). Is social validity what we are interested in? Argument for a functional approach. *Journal of Applied Behavior Analysis, 24,* 205–213.

Hersh, R., & Walker, H. M. (1983). Great expectations: Making schools effective for all students. *Policy Studies Review, 2,* 147–188.

Herrnstein, R. J. (1961). Relative and absolute strength of response as a function of frequency of reinforcement. *Journal of the Experimental Analysis of Behavior, 4,* 267–272.

Herrnstein, R. J. (1970). On the law of effect. *Journal of the Experimental Analysis of Behavior, 13,* 243–266.

Hinshaw, S. (1992). Externalizing behavior problems and academic underachievement in childhood and adolescence: Causal relationships and underlying mechanisms. *Psychological Bulletin, 111,* 127–155.

Hoagwood, K., & Erwin, H. (1997). Effectiveness of school-based mental health services for children: A 10-year research review. *Journal of Child and Family Studies, 6,* 435–451.

Horner, R. (1994). Functional assessment: Contributions and future directions. *Journal of Applied Behavior Analysis, 27,* 401–404.

Horner, R., & Billingsley, F. (1988). The effects of competing behavior on the generalization and maintenance of adaptive behavior in applied settings. In R. Horner, G. Dunlap, & R. Koegel (Eds.), *Generalization and maintenance: Lifestyle changes in applied settings* (pp. 197–220). Baltimore: Brookes.

Horner, R., & Carr, E. (1997). Behavioral support for students with severe disabilities: Functional assessment and comprehensive intervention. *Journal of Special Education, 31,* 84–104.

Kazdin, A. (1977). Assessing the clinical or applied significance of behavior change through social validation. *Behavior Modification, 1,* 427–452.

Kazdin, A. (1981). Acceptability of child treatment techniques: The influence of treatment efficacy and adverse side effects. *Behavior Therapy, 12,* 493–506.

Kazdin, A. (2001). Almost clinically significant ($p < .10$): Current measures may be only one approach to clinical significance. *Clinical Psychology: Science and Practice, 8,* 455–462.

Kupersmidt, J., Coie, J., & Dodge, K. (1990). The role of peer relationships in the development of disorder. In S. Asher & J. Coie (Eds.), *Peer rejection in childhood* (pp. 274–308). New York: Cambridge University Press.

Lewis, T., & Sugai, G. (1996). Functional assessment of problem behavior: A pilot investigation of comparative and interactive effects of teacher and peer social attention on students in general education settings. *School Psychology Quarterly, 11,* 1–19.

Losel, F., & Beelmann, A. (2003). Effects of child skills training in preventing antisocial behavior: A systematic review of randomized evaluations. *Annals of the American Academy of Political and Social Science, 857,* 84–109.

Maag, J. W. (2005). Social skills training for youth with emotional and behavioral disorders and learning disabilities: Problems, conclusions, and suggestions. *Exceptionality, 13,* 155–172.

Maag, J. W. (2006). Social skills training for students with emotional and behavioral disorders; A review of reviews. *Behavioral Disorders, 32,* 5–17.

Malecki, C. M. (1998). *The influence of elementary students' social behaviors on academic achievement.* Unpublished doctoral dissertation, University of Wisconsin–Madison.

Malecki, C. M., & Elliott, S. N. (2002). Children's social behaviors as predictors of academic achievement: A longitudinal analysis. *School Psychology Quarterly, 17,* 1–23.

Martens, B. K. (1992). Contingency and choice: The implications of matching theory for classroom instruction. *Journal of Behavioral Education, 2,* 121–137.

Martens, B. K., & Houk, J. L. (1989). The application of Herrnstein's law of effect to disruptive and on-task behavior of a retarded adolescent girl. *Journal of the Experimental Analysis of Behavior, 51,* 17–27.

Martens, B. K., Lochner, D. G., & Kelly, S. Q. (1992). The effects of variable-interval reinforcement on academic engagement: A demonstration of matching theory. *Journal of Applied Behavior Analysis, 25,* 143–151.

McIntyre, L. L., Gresham, F. M., DiGennaro, F. D., & Reed, D. D. (2007). Treatment integrity of school-based interventions with children in *Journal of Applied Behavior Analysis* from 1991–2005. *Journal of Applied Behavior Analysis, 40,* 659–672.

Merrell, K., & Gimpel, G. (1998). *Social skills of children and adolescents: Conceptualization, assessment, and treatment.* Mahwah, NJ: Erlbaum.

Newcomb, A., Bukowski, W., & Pattee, L. (1993). Children's peer relations: A meta-analytic review of popular, rejected, neglected, controversial, and average sociometric status. *Psychological Bulletin, 113,* 306–347.

Offord, D., Boyle, M., & Racine, Y. (1989). Ontario Child Health Study: Correlates of disorder. *Journal of the American Academy of Child and Adolescent Psychiatry, 28,* 856–860.

Parker, J., & Asher, S. (1987). Peer relations and later personal adjustment: Are low-accepted children at risk? *Psychological Bulletin, 102,* 357–389.

Patterson, G., DeBaryshe, B., & Ramsay, E. (1989). A developmental perspective on antisocial behavior. *American Psychologist, 44,* 329–335.

Quinn, M., Kavale, K., Mathur, S., Rutherford, R., & Forness, S. (1999). A meta-analysis of social skill interventions for students with emotional and behavioral disorders. *Journal of Emotional and Behavioral Disorders, 7,* 54–64.

Reid, J. (1993). Prevention of conduct disorder before and after school entry: Relating interventions to developmental findings. *Development & Psychopathology, 5,* 311–319.

Rosenthal, R., & Rosnow, R. (1991). *Essentials of behavioral research: Methods and data analysis* (2nd ed.). New York: McGraw-Hill.

Rutter, M. (1979). Protective factors in children's responses to stress and disadvantage. In J. Rolf (Ed.), *Primary prevention of psychopathology: Vol. 3. Social competence in children* (pp. 49–74). Hanover, NJ: University Press of New England.

Sameroff, A., Seifer, R., Barocas, R., Zax, M., & Greenspan, S. (1987). Intelligence quotient scores of 4-year-old children: Social-environmental risk factors. *Pediatrics, 79,* 343–350.

Schneider, B. (1992). Didactic methods for enhancing children's peer relationships. *Clinical Psychology Review, 12,* 363–382.

Schneider, B., & Byrne, B. (1985). Children's social skills training: A meta-analysis. In B. Schneider, K. Rubin, & J. Ledingham (Eds.), *Children's peer relations: Issues in assessment and intervention* (pp. 175–190). New York: Springer-Verlag.

Sechrest, L., McKnight, P., & McKnight, K. (1996). Calibration of measures for psychotherapy outcome studies. *American Psychologist, 51,* 1065–1071.

Sprague, J., Walker, H., Sowards, S., Van Bloem, C., Hberhardt, P., Marshall, B. 2002. Source of vulnerability to school violence: Systems-level assessment and strategies to improve safety and climate. In M. R. Shinn, H. M. Walker, & G. Stoner (Eds.), *Interventions for academic and behavior problems II: Preventive and remedial approaches.* Bethesda, MD: National Association of School Psychologists.

Ullman, R., Sleator, E., & Sprague, R. (1985). Introduction to the use of the ACTeRS. *Psychopharmacology Bulletin, 21,* 915–920.

Walker, H. M., Forness, S., Kauffman, J., Epstein, M., Gresham, F. M., Nelson, C. M.,et al. (1998). Macro-social validation: Referencing outcomes in behavioral disorders to societal issues and problems. *Behavioral Disorders, 24,* 130–140.

Walker, H. M., Hope-Doolittle, J., Kratochwill, T., Severson, H., & Gresham, F. M. (2007). Proactive early screening to detect behaviorally at-risk students: Issues, approaches, emerging innovations, and professional practice. *Journal of School Psychology, 45,* 193–223.

Walker, H. M., Irvin, L., Noell, J., & Singer, G. (1992). A construct score approach to the assessment of social competence: Rationale, technological considerations, and anticipated outcomes. *Behavior Modification, 16,* 448–474.

Walker, H. M., & McConnell, S. (1995). *Walker-McConnell Scale of Social Competence and School Adjustment.* Florence, KY: Thomson Learning.

Walker, H. M., Nishioka, V., Zeller, R., Severson, H., & Feil, E. (2000). Causal factors and potential solutions for the persistent under-identification of students having emotional and behavioral disorders in the context of schooling. *Assessment for Effective Intervention, 26,* 29–40.

Walker, H. M., Ramsay, E., & Gresham, F. M. (2004). *Antisocial behavior at school: Evidence-based practices.* Belmont, CA: Wadsworth/Thomson Learning.

Walker, H. M., & Severson, H. (2002). Developmental prevention of at-risk outcomes for vulnerable antisocial children and youth. In K. Lane, F. M. Gresham, & T. O'Shaughnessy (Eds.), *Interventions for children with or at risk for emotional and behavioral disorders* (pp. 177–194). Boston: Allyn & Bacon.

Walker, H. M., Shinn, M., O'Neill, R., & Ramsay, E. (1987). A longitudinal assessment of the development of antisocial behavior in boys: Rationale, methodology and first year results. *Remedial and Special Education, 8*(4), 7–16, 27.

Wentzel, K. R. (1993). Does being good make the grade? Social behavior and academic competence in middle school. *Journal of Educational Psychology, 85,* 357–364.

Wentzel, K. R., & Watkins, D. E. (2002). Peer relationships and collaborative learning as contexts for academic enablers. *School Psychology Review, 31,* 366–377.

Wigfield, A., & Karpathian, M. (1991). Who am I and what can I do? Children's self-concepts and motivation in achievement situations. *Educational Psychologist, 26,* 233–261.

Witt, J. C., & Elliott, S. N. (1985). Acceptability of classroom management strategies. In T. R. Kratochwill (Ed.), *Advances in school psychology* (Vol. 4, pp. 251–288). Hillsdale, NJ: Erlbaum.

Wolf, M. M. (1978). Social validity: The case for subjective measurement, or how applied behavior analysis is finding its heart. *Journal of Applied Behavior Analysis, 11,* 211–226.

CHAPTER 15

School-Based Prevention and Intervention for Depression and Suicidal Behavior

John R. Seeley
Paul Rohde
Laura Backen Jones
Oregon Research Institute

INTRODUCTION

Prior to the 1970s, depression among children and adolescents received relatively little empirical or theoretical attention. Indeed, some researchers maintained that depression did not exist in youth and that the criteria listed in the *Diagnostic and Statistical Manual of Mental Disorders* (*DSM*; American Psychiatric Association, 1952) needed to be modified for use with children and adolescents (Glaser, 1967; Toolan, 1962). Beginning in the 1970s, a number of researchers began to focus on mood disorders in children and adolescents, concluding that depressive disorders clearly occur during this developmental period, are clinically debilitating, and are associated with numerous negative sequelae, including future psychopathology (e.g., Albert & Beck, 1975; Carlson & Cantwell, 1979; Cytryn & McKnew, 1972; Kashani, & Simonds, 1979; Kovacs, Feinberg, Crouse-Novak, Paulauskas, & Finkelstein, 1984; Orvaschel, Walsh-Allis, & Ye, 1988; Rutter, 1986). As a result of these early investigations, epidemiologic and intervention research on depression within school-age youth has increased dramatically over the past two decades.

Depression is now considered to be one of the most prevalent mental disorders among adolescents, with approximately 20% experiencing an episode of depression during the teenage years (Lewinsohn, Hops, Roberts, Seeley, & Andrews, 1993; Newman et al., 1996). During the past century, successive birth cohorts appear to have experienced increasingly higher lifetime prevalence rates of depression (Kessler et al., 2003; Lewinsohn, Rohde, Seeley, & Fischer, 1993). Epidemiologic data on the lifetime

Address all correspondence and feedback on this chapter to John R. Seeley, Oregon Research Institute, 1715 Franklin Boulevard, Eugene, Oregon, 97403-1983.

prevalence of depression have indicated a 10-fold increase in the risk in youth over the past century, suggesting that U.S. schools are in an epidemic of depression (Klerman & Weissman, 1989; Seligman, 2000). Adolescent depression predicts future suicide attempts, substance abuse, antisocial behavior, academic problems, interpersonal problems, and unemployment (Gotlib, Lewinsohn, & Seeley, 1998; Lewinsohn, Rohde, Klein, & Seeley, 1999; Lewinsohn, Rohde, Seeley, Klein, & Gotlib, 2003; Newman et al., 1996; Reinherz, Giaconia, Hauf, Wasserman, & Silverman, 1999). Unfortunately, most adolescents who suffer from depression do not receive treatment (Lewinsohn, Rohde, & Seeley, 1998b; Newman et al., 1996). The World Health Organization (2007) projects that depression will become the second leading contributor to the global burden of disease by 2020.

Commensurate with the increasing rates of depression has been an increase in suicide among the nation's youth. The suicide rate among youth ages 15–19 is 300% higher than in the 1960s, making it the third leading cause of death in this age group, exceeded only by unintentional injury and homicide (National Center for Injury Prevention and Control, 2002). Many more youth attempt than successfully complete suicide. For every one adolescent suicide death, approximately 32 adolescents are treated for self-inflicted injuries, and even more adolescents make a suicide attempt that does not require medical attention (Lubell & Vetter, 2006). In a recent study, 1 in 6 U.S. high school students disclosed seriously considering suicide in the past year, and 1 student in 12 reported engaging in at least one attempt (Grunbaum, 2003). Youth who attempt suicide are much more likely to make future attempts, and those who make multiple attempts have a heightened risk for committing suicide during adolescence and adulthood (Brent, Baugher, Bridge, Chen, & Chiappetta, 1999; Fombonne, Wostear, Cooper, Harrington, & Rutter, 2001; Shaffer et al., 1996).

Clearly, public health campaigns to effectively prevent and treat depression and suicidal behavior in youth are imperative in order to curtail this insidious epidemic. Given the central role of schools in providing access to mental health services for youth, school settings and staff are essential for mounting large-scale depression and suicide prevention campaigns (Burns et al., 1995). Indeed, there has been a recent call for school psychologists to be catalysts in this regard (Herman, Merrell, Reinke, & Tucker, 2004; Reinke, Herman, & Tucker, 2006).

The purpose of this chapter is to review the current state of the field with respect to implications for school-based intervention efforts for depression and suicidal behavior. In doing so, we describe (a) the public health system's prevention paradigm and alignment with the three-tier intervention model, (b) the scope and nature of the problem of adolescent depression and suicidal behavior, (c) assessment and screening instruments and procedures, and (d) evidence-based universal and targeted prevention approaches and tertiary-level interventions. As it is beyond the scope of this chapter to conduct an exhaustive review of the available intervention programs, we draw upon examples from the research literature to illustrate these various approaches. We conclude by identifying important directions for future school-based intervention research and practice.

PUBLIC HEALTH PREVENTION MODEL

The three-tier intervention model presented in chapter 1 is based on the original public health classification system developed by the Commission on Chronic Illness (1957). The three levels of the model correspond to the three types of prevention: primary, secondary, and tertiary. In 1994, the Institute of Medicine (IOM) proposed an alternative mental health spectrum for psychiatric disorders that ranges from prevention to treatment to maintenance (Mrazek & Haggerty, 1994). In the IOM paradigm, the term *prevention* is reserved for interventions that occur before the initial onset of the mental disorder. Following Gordon's (1983, 1987) classification system for biological disease prevention, the IOM paradigm includes three levels of preventive interventions: *universal, selective,* and *indicated.* Universal prevention programs are administered to the entire population regardless of risk status. Selective preventive interventions target subgroups of the population whose risk for developing a disorder is significantly elevated on the basis of known risk factors for the disorder. Indicated prevention programs target individuals who have prodromal or subthreshold symptoms of the disorder but are below the clinical criteria for a diagnosis. Thus, selective and indicated prevention programs can be considered targeted prevention approaches. For the purposes of this review, we align the IOM prevention paradigm with the three-tier model as follows: universal interventions are included in the first tier, targeted interventions (i.e., selective and indicated) are included in the second tier, and treatment interventions are included in the third tier.

The IOM paradigm also proposes the following five stages of preventive intervention research: (a) identify the problem or disorder and review information to determine its extent, (b) determine the risk and protective factors that may be amenable to intervention, (c) conduct pilot studies and efficacy trials aimed at reducing the risk factors and promoting the protective factors, (d) conduct effectiveness trials of the intervention in real-world conditions, and (e) implement the preventive intervention in large-scale community campaigns. As described subsequently in this chapter, considerable progress has been made in the first three stages with respect to extant research on depression and suicide prevention. However, much still remains to be accomplished in the latter two stages in order to reduce the incidence of depression and suicidal behavior.

SCOPE OF THE PROBLEM

During the past 30 years, extensive research has been conducted with respect to the epidemiology and etiology of adolescent depression and suicidal behaviors. The following sections provide a brief review of this research.

Epidemiology

Depression

According to the *DSM-IV* classification system for mental disorders, depressive disorders include major depressive disorder (MDD) and dysthymia (American Psychiatric Association, 1994). MDD among children and adolescents has the same set of symptoms and criteria for diagnosis as with adults. To meet criteria for MDD, an individual must have experienced five or more symptoms during the same 2-week period. At least one of the symptoms must be either a depressed mood (or irritable mood for children and adolescents) or loss of interest or pleasure. The other symptoms include changes in weight or failure to make necessary weight gains during childhood, sleep problems, psychomotor agitation or retardation, fatigue or loss of energy, feelings of worthlessness or excessive guilt, difficulty concentrating or indecisiveness, and repeated suicidal ideation or plans for suicide, as well as attempts. The essential feature of dysthymia in children and adolescents is a chronically depressed mood that occurs for most of the day, for more days than not, and for at least 1 year (2 years for adults). In addition, two or more of the following six symptoms must be present to meet criteria for dysthymia: poor appetite or overeating, insomnia or hypersomnia, low energy or fatigue, low self-esteem, poor concentration or difficulty making decisions, and feelings of hopelessness.

The basic epidemiologic parameters include *point prevalence* (percentage of the sample who are in an episode of disorder at the time of the assessment), *lifetime prevalence* (percentage who have experienced an episode during their lifetime), and *incidence* (percentage who are not depressed at the beginning of an observation period but who develop an episode during a specified period of time). Incidence rates are customarily divided into *first incidence* (percentage that develop an episode for the first time during the observation interval) and *recurrence* (percentage of individuals with a previous episode that develop another episode during the interval). From a public health perspective, the total incidence rate (percentage of first incident and recurrent cases combined) is important for planning the delivery of mental health services because it indicates how many individuals in the population will become depressed during a certain time period.

Data from the Oregon Adolescent Depression Project (OADP) provide estimates for the prevalence and incidence of depression and suicidal behavior during childhood and adolescence (Lewinsohn, Hops, et al., 1993). OADP participants were randomly selected in three cohorts from nine senior high schools representative of urban and rural districts in western Oregon. A total of 1,709 adolescents completed the initial assessment (T1), which included a diagnostic interview and questionnaire assessment. Approximately 1 year later (T2), 1,507 (88%) of the participants completed a second diagnostic interview and questionnaire assessment. Average age of the OADP sample at T1 was 16.6 years (*SD* = 1.2, range = 14–18). Slightly over half of the participants (53%) were female; 91% were White; 12% had repeated a grade in school; 53% were living with both biological parents at the time of the T1 interview, and an additional

18% were living with a biological parent and stepparent. Most participants resided in households in which one or both parents worked as a minor professional or professional (for more detail, see Lewinsohn, Hops, et al., 1993).

Prevalence and incidence rates of MDD and dysthymia based on the OADP are presented in Table 1. As can be seen, depression is quite common during adolescence. The lifetime prevalence rate of MDD for participants at T1 was especially high (19%). Conversely, the lifetime prevalence of dysthymia was only 3% during adolescence. The 1-year first incidence rate for MDD was 7% for girls and 4% for boys; the rate of MDD recurrence for the T1–T2 interval of 1 year was 21% for girls and 9% for boys.

OADP prevalence rates for adolescent MDD are comparable to the rates that have been reported for adults in more recent studies, such as the National Comorbidity Survey Replication (Kessler et al., 2003). Our tentative conclusion is that the prevalence of depression in older adolescents is at adult levels. Previous research reporting much lower rates of depression in younger children suggests a substantial increase in the prevalence of depression from childhood to adolescence (e.g., Costello et al., 1996; Fleming, Offord, & Boyle, 1989). Although the OADP rates of depression onset in childhood are low, the annual incidence rate increases from 1–2% at age 13 to 3–7% at age 15 (see Figure 1).

Gender differences in the rate of depression among adults have consistently reported a ratio of 2:1 (Nolen-Hoeksema, 2002). Conversely, most studies of preadolescent children (i.e., 12 years of age or younger) find no gender difference in rates of depression, or find a slight elevation in boys compared with girls (e.g., Brooks-Gunn & Petersen, 1991; Garrison, Schluchter, Schoenbach, & Kaplan, 1989; Nolen-Hoeksema, Girgus, & Seligman, 1991; Petersen, Sarigiani, & Kennedy, 1991; Rutter, 1986). A significant gender difference was found in the OADP, with females being twice as likely as males to be depressed. Comparing the OADP results with other

Table 1. Prevalence and Incidence of Major Depressive Disorder (MDD) and Dysthymia (percentage of sample)

	Total Sample		Female Sample		Male Sample	
	MDD	**Dysthymia**	**MDD**	**Dysthymia**	**MDD**	**Dysthymia**
Point Prevalence						
T1	2.9	0.5	3.4	0.6	2.0	0.5
T2	3.1	0.1	3.6	0.3	2.6	0.0
Lifetime Prevalence						
T1	18.5	3.2	24.8	4.0	11.6	2.3
T2	24.0	3.0	31.6	4.1	15.2	1.7
1-Year Incidence						
Total incidence	7.8	0.1	10.4	0.1	4.8	0.0
First incidence	5.7	0.1	7.1	0.1	4.4	0.0
Recurrence	17.9	0.0	21.1	0.0	9.1	0.0

Figure 1. Cumulative proportion experiencing onset of major depressive disorder, as a function of age and gender.

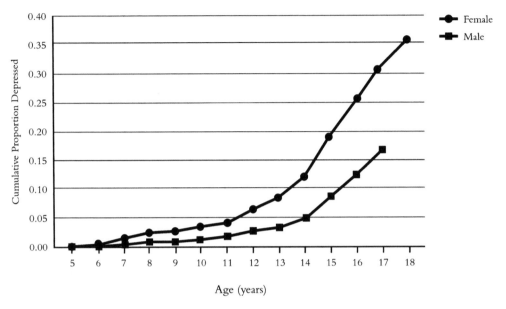

Note. From "Major Depressive Disorder in Older Adolescents: Prevalence, Risk Factors, and Clinical Implications," by P. M. Lewinsohn, P. Rohde, and J. R. Seeley, 1998, *Clinical Psychology Review, 18*(7), pp. 765–794. Reprinted with permission.

studies (Nolen-Hoeksema & Girgus, 1994; Petersen et al., 1991) suggests that the gender difference in MDD rates probably emerges in the relatively small window between the ages of 11 and 14, as depicted in Figure 1.

Suicidal Behavior

Although the prevalence rate of suicide in adolescents has increased over 300% since the 1960s, the overall base rate for completed suicide in 2002 was 7.4 per 100,000 for youth age 15–19 (Commission on Adolescent Suicide Prevention, 2005); suicide before the age of 12 is very rare. Because the rate of suicide completion is so low, epidemiologic research has focused more broadly on suicidal behavior such as suicide attempts and ideation. According to the 2003 Youth Risk Behavior Survey data (Grunbaum et al., 2003), 9% (male = 5%, female = 12%) of U.S. high school students surveyed made one or more attempts during the previous 1-year period. With respect to suicide ideation, 17% (male = 12%, female = 22%) of students reported that they had seriously considered attempting suicide in the past year. The onset-age curves for suicide attempts based on the OADP data are presented in Figure 2. As can been seen, the onset-age curves for suicide attempts are similar to those for MDD presented in Figure 1, in which the incidence rate dramatically increases at about the age of 12.

Etiology: Risk and Protective Factors

Depression

Lewinsohn and Essau (2002) provide a review of the epidemiologic evidence that has identified the psychosocial risk and protective factors for adolescent depression. These factors include both individual (person-related) and environmental risks. Individual factors include female gender, pubertal timing, elevated depressive symptomatology, depressotypic cognitive style, poor physical health, poor academic functioning, poor coping skills, low self-esteem, low self-rated social competence, excessive emotional reliance on others, externalizing behavior problems, internalizing behavior problems, and a previous history of psychopathology. Contextual factors include family conflict, marital discord, low level of family support, parental history of depression, social adversity, low peer support, major life events, and daily hassles. Although some of these risk and protective factors are not directly modifiable (e.g., female gender, family history of depression, social adversity), interventions for depression have been developed to ameliorate individual risk factors (e.g., depressotypic cognitions) and build or enhance protective factors (e.g., coping skills, increasing pleasant activities, problem-solving skills).

Garber (2006) advocates that, in addition to the identification of risk factors, it is important to examine the risk mechanisms that may illuminate the intervening paths that link risk factors to depression onset. A particularly significant lacuna in the literature is the absence of research regarding how risk and protective factors work

Figure 2. Cumulative proportion experiencing first suicide attempt as a function of age and gender.

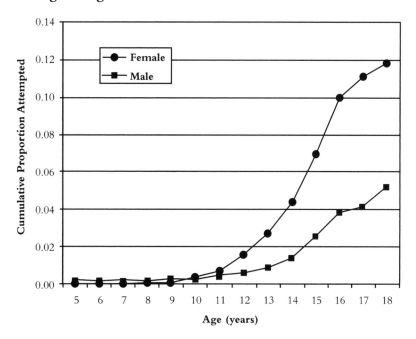

interactively to increase the risk for depression. Two psychosocial mechanistic models that have received considerable research attention include the cognitive vulnerability model (Abramson, Metalsky, & Alloy, 1989; Beck, 1967) and the stress-buffering model (Brown & Harris, 1978; Cohen & Wills, 1985). The cognitive vulnerability model posits that negative cognitions represent a diathesis that, in combination with stressful events, leads to negative thoughts, which in turn increase the risk for depression. Regarding a protective mechanism, the stress-buffering model proposes that social support or coping skills mitigate the relation between stressful life events and the onset of depression. Such risk mechanisms have been the target of preventive interventions described later in this chapter.

Suicidal Behavior

Although research studies have revealed some common factors, there are no simple answers as to the cause of youth suicide. Expert consensus is that an individual's biological characteristics interact with environmental forces to influence the development of suicidal behavior (Evans, Hawton, & Rodham, 2004). Individual characteristics such as substance abuse (Shaffer et al., 1996), poor interpersonal problem solving (Rotheram-Borus, 1990), and aggressive–impulsive tendencies (Sourander, Helstelä, Haavisto, & Bergroth, 2001) are related to suicidal behavior, as is academic failure (Lubell & Vetter, 2006). The period preceding the suicide is often marked by stressful events, such as the loss of a loved one (Cole & Siegel, 2003) or physical abuse (Johnson et al., 2002). Over 90% of youth who commit suicide experience at least one major psychiatric disorder (Gould, Greenberg, Velting, & Shaffer, 2003). Of these disorders, depression is by far the most common (American Association of Suicidology, 2007). Furthermore, comorbidity between depression and conduct disorder or substance abuse has been linked to a twofold increase in the risk for suicidal behavior compared with non-comorbid depression (Lewinsohn, Rohde, & Seeley, 1995; Seeley, 2002). Contextual risk factors include firearm availability (Shah, Hoffman, Wake, & Marine, 2000), suicide contagion (Gould, 2001), and poor family environment (Wagner, Silverman, & Martin, 2003). On the other hand, student connectedness with school was the primary protective factor identified by the National Longitudinal Study of Adolescent Health (Resnick et al., 1997).

ASSESSMENT AND SCREENING

Semistructured diagnostic interviews are considered to be the gold standard for assessing mental disorders. However, because diagnostic interviews can be resource intensive (e.g., requires training and administration time), self-report questionnaires are often used to identify at-risk youth. Although self-report questionnaires require fewer resources to administer compared with diagnostic interviews, they are typically more limited with respect to classification accuracy (e.g., higher false-positive rates). Given such a trade-off between convenience and accuracy, multistage screening strategies have been developed in which self-report questionnaires are administered in the first screening stage, followed by diagnostic interviews among those who screen positive.

Diagnostic Interviews

Standardized and comprehensive interviews for children and adolescents include the Schedule for Affective Disorders and Schizophrenia for School-Age Children (K-SADS; Orvaschel, Puig-Antich, Chambers, Tabrizi, & Johnson, 1982); the Diagnostic Interview Schedule for Children (DISC; Costello, Edelbrock, & Costello, 1985); the Diagnostic Interview for Children and Adolescents (DICA; Herjanic & Reich, 1982); and the Child and Adolescent Psychiatric Assessment (CAPA; Angold et al., 1995). A review of these interviews is provided by Essau, Hakim-Larson, Crocker, and Petermann (1999). We encourage a comprehensive assessment of all *DSM-IV* criteria for major depression and dysthymia as a way of gauging the presence of depressive disorders and suicidal ideation. In addition, given the frequent occurrence of comorbid psychopathology in depressed adolescents, we strongly advise the use of semistructured interviews to consistently and systematically assess a broad range of mental disorders, including alcohol or drug abuse and dependence, posttraumatic stress disorder and other anxiety disorders, conduct and oppositional defiant disorders, and attention deficit hyperactivity disorder (ADHD).

Self-Report Depression Questionnaires

In addition to semistructured interviews, several questionnaires are available to assess for the presence of depressive symptoms. These instruments focus on current depressive symptomatology and may be particularly valuable for tracking change over time. In addition to monitoring change, self-report questionnaires are useful for both screening and therapeutic purposes, as they identify specific problem areas that need attention. Screening for depression is especially important because adolescents may not readily volunteer that they are severely depressed or suicidal, although they do appear willing to admit these difficulties if asked directly (Reynolds, 1986).

For adolescents, we recommend the Center for Epidemiologic Studies–Depression Scale (CES-D; Radloff, 1977), which is in the public domain, and the Beck Depression Inventory (BDI; Beck, Ward, Mendelson, Mock, & Erbaugh, 1961). The original BDI was revised to correspond to *DSM-IV* symptom criteria (BDI-II; Beck, Steer, & Brown, 1996) and is appropriate for adolescents aged 13 years or older. Although the CES-D and BDI were developed for use with adults, they are easy to administer and have been shown to be reliable and valid screeners for depression in adolescent samples (Roberts, Lewinsohn, & Seeley, 1991). Other youth self-report measures that are commonly used include the Reynolds Adolescent Depression Scale (RADS; Reynolds, 1987a); the Children's Depression Inventory (CDI; Kovacs, 1985); and the Mood and Feelings Questionnaire (MFQ; Angold et al., 1987). Detailed descriptions and summaries of the psychometric properties of these instruments have been presented by Reynolds (1994) and Essau et al. (1999).

Multistage Identification

Depression screening tests are usually employed as the first stage of a multistage process in which those who score above a specified cutoff are identified as putative cases (Reynolds, 1991). Universal screening can serve as an efficient and effective first step in large settings, such as schools. The identified youth may be given another screening at a later date using a serial screening strategy. In the final stage, a semistructured diagnostic interview such as the K-SADS is administered, from which a definitive diagnosis is established. The screening is a fast, economical, accurate, and valid way of identifying as many cases in the population as possible, without diagnostically interviewing everyone. Large-scale screening procedures that have been developed for adults, such as the National Depression Screening Day, should be expanded to include school-age children, beginning with youth about age 11, as indicated by Figures 1 and 2.

Assessment of Suicidal Behavior

The rates of suicide-related behaviors among adolescents underscore the need for proactive methods of identifying at-risk youth before they escalate to more self-destructive behavior. Even if the youth does not ultimately engage in suicidal behavior, it is important to identify a youth experiencing distress that results in suicidal ideation, and to refer him or her to mental health services. All screening measures to date produce false positives, but the cost of this error is minimal compared with the cost of false negatives. It is better to raise a concern than to miss an at-risk youth. When programs provide a systematic and sensitive follow-up to the screening, distressed youth can get the help and follow-up care they need. This care will generally need to be initiated by the school, although back-up support from mental health providers with more experience in dealing with suicidal adolescents may be available.

   We strongly recommend that the assessment of current and past suicidal behavior (ideation and attempts) be a routine component of assessment procedures with distressed adolescents. Several psychometrically sound suicide behavior assessment instruments have been developed and evaluated. The National Institute of Mental Health commissioned a review of the suicide assessment measures for adolescents (Goldston, 2000, 2003). Recommended self-report measures of suicidal ideation include the Columbia Suicide Screen (Shaffer et al., 2004), the Suicidal Ideation Questionnaire (Reynolds, 1987b), which has two forms specifically developed for adolescents (Grades 7–9 and 10–12), and the Beck Scale for Suicide Ideation (Beck & Steer, 1991).

One of the most widely used high school suicide screening programs is the Columbia TeenScreen Program (Shaffer et al., 2004). Using a multistage strategy, students complete the brief Columbia Suicide Screen self-report questionnaire in the first stage. Those who screen positive are administered a diagnostic interview (i.e., the DISC) during the second stage to assess a comprehensive range of psychiatric symptoms and disorders. During the third stage, youth who have been identified as meeting *DSM-IV* criteria for a psychiatric disorder are evaluated by a mental health clinician, who determines whether the student needs to be referred for further evaluation or tertiary-level treatment. Evaluation of the Columbia TeenScreen Program indicates that most of the students who have been identified as high risk for suicide were not previously recognized as such, and very few had received prior treatment.

Stigmatization

Stigmatization of students is a key issue for school-based mental health screening and assessment. Stigmatization occurs when students are pejoratively categorized in a way that sets them apart from their peers as socially unacceptable (Penn et al., 2005). In a review of the literature, Wahl (2002) concluded that negative attitudes toward persons with mental illness are evident as early as the third grade. Furthermore, a 2002 survey of adolescents ages 14–22 found that peers with major depression were perceived as more likely to be violent and as less likely to do well in school than those without major depression (Penn et al.).

Stigmatization has been found to be associated with reduced self-esteem (Link, Struening, Neese-Todd, Asmussen, & Phelan, 2001), increased symptoms and stress (Markowitz, 1998), and reduced help-seeking on the part of adolescents (Penn et al., 2005). One of the most effective means to reduce stigma is to educate staff and professionals who work with adolescents (Penn et al.). In addition, adolescents who are informed about mental illness, both in terms of facts and myths, are less likely to stigmatize others and more likely to seek help and adhere to treatment (Penn et al.). Thus, it is recommended that schools provide both school staff and students with education about destigmatizing mental illness using universal prevention programs prior to implementing screening programs.

UNIVERSAL APPROACHES TO DEPRESSION AND SUICIDE PREVENTION

Research on universal interventions for the prevention of depression and suicidal behavior in adolescence has burgeoned in the past three decades. As summarized in the following sections, the universal approaches have typically focused on preventing depression or suicidal behavior rather than taking a more integrated approach for these highly related problems. However, recent efforts that focus on improving environmental contexts such as school climate provide a foundation for a more integrated approach toward the prevention of depression and suicidal behavior as discussed below.

Preventing Depression

Over the past 20 years, several efficacy and effectiveness trials have been conducted to evaluate school-based universal interventions for preventing youth depression. Because the intervention formats typically include large-group presentations or classroom curriculum modifications, one of the strengths of the universal prevention approach is that it minimizes stigmatization associated with mental health treatment (Spence, Sheffield, & Donovan, 2003). Most universal programs are manualized and include a variety of instructional methods (e.g., didactic sessions; cartoons; individual, small-group, and whole-class interactive exercises and activities; homework and skill practice; mood monitoring and diary keeping). Universal prevention approaches for adolescents typically employ principles based on cognitive–behavioral therapy, interpersonal therapy, problem-solving skills training, and social skills training. (For cognitive–behavioral therapy, see Clarke, Hawkins, Murphy, & Sheeber, 1993; Hains & Ellman, 1994; Merry, McDowell, Wild, Bir, & Cunliffe, 2004; Lowry-Webster, Barrett, & Dadds, 2001; Pössel, Horn, Groen, & Hautzinger, 2004; Sheffield et al., 2006; Shochet et al., 2001; Spence et al., 2003. For interpersonal therapy, see Merry et al., 2004; Shochet et al., 2001. For problem-solving skills training, see Hains & Ellmann, 1994; Sheffield et al., 2006; Spence et al., 2003. For social skills training, see Pattison & Lynd-Stevenson, 2001; Pössel et al., 2004.)

Although several efficacy trials of universal prevention programs have found significant reductions in depressive symptoms from baseline to postintervention, most have not found effects that persisted into long-term follow-up. In addition to efficacy research, several effectiveness trials have evaluated universal prevention programs for adolescents that were delivered by endogenous providers (e.g., school teachers) rather than research staff, which is a key feature of effectiveness research (e.g., Clarke et al., 1993; Lowry-Webster et al., 2001; Roberts, Kane, Thomson, Bishop, & Hart, 2003; Sheffield et al., 2006; Spence et al., 2003, 2005). One rigorous trial found that an eight-session universal cognitive–behavioral depression prevention program, delivered by school teachers, produced significantly greater reductions in depressive symptoms from baseline to postintervention relative to assessment-only controls. However, these effects were no longer significant at 1-year or 4-year follow-up (Spence et al., 2003, 2005). Most universal prevention effectiveness trials have not produced significant effects from baseline to postintervention, and none have been shown to decrease the incidence of future depressive episodes.

Given the limited available evidence for the efficacy and effectiveness of universal interventions described above, depression prevention experts have recently called into question whether widespread dissemination of universal school-based interventions can be justified at this juncture (Spence & Shortt, 2007). This limited evidence may be due, in part, to the weak methodological rigor that has been employed in most evaluations conducted to date. Spence and Shortt further conclude that current, brief interventions may not provide enough dosage to produce lasting effects. In addition, they propose that universal interventions need to move beyond an exclusive focus on the individual-related factors and include broader ecological approaches that emphasize the family and school contexts. To this end, *beyondblue*, an Australian depression prevention initiative, is currently evaluating the impact of an extensive universal school-based preventive intervention that combines (a) a 3-year psychosocial skills curriculum, (b) a school-wide approach to building a supportive school climate, and (c) effective links to appropriate services for youth experiencing emotional difficulties (Spence et al., 2005).

Preventing Suicidal Behavior

Schools can play a key role in preventing youth suicide and in identifying youth who need referral to mental health services (Potter & Stone, 2003). School education codes include the mandate not only to educate but also to protect students (Lazear, Roggenbaum, & Blase, 2003). In the United States, high schools are mandated to provide suicide prevention education. This education is mandated because experts agree that schools have a powerful influence on youth well-being. Many adolescents' lives revolve around the school setting (Gould et al., 2003); their social development is more influenced by school-related factors than factors from almost any other setting (Kalafat & Elias, 1995).

Schools can involve staff in suicide prevention in a variety of ways, including developing district-wide school policies concerning student suicide (King, 2001), creating linkages between schools and community mental health resources (Poland, 1995), and involving school staff in gatekeeper training programs. Gatekeeper programs train adults who interact with or observe students on a daily basis to recognize youth who may be at risk for suicide and to respond appropriately (Lazear et al, 2003; Cole & Siegel, 2003). Gatekeeper training is the most widely used youth suicide prevention method in high schools (Kalafat, 2003).

Since 1980, a multitude of school-based gatekeeper programs have been initiated (Kalafat & Elias, 1995). The four most common training programs for staff gatekeepers include Suicide Options, Awareness and Relief (SOAR); the Applied Suicide Intervention Skills Training (ASIST); Question, Persuade, Refer (QPR); and SAFE:TEEN. SOAR consists of an 8-hour training course for school counselors. Although no randomized controlled trials have been published to date for this program, evaluations of pre–post results show that immediately after training, counselor knowledge and sense of comfort with intervening increased. However, the results were most prominent with newly trained members, suggesting a need for ongoing training (King & Smith, 2000). ASIST is a 2-day workshop for adults working with youth that focuses on increasing awareness and understanding of suicide and developing readiness to prevent adolescent suicidal behavior. Pre–post evaluations of participants suggest increased knowledge and willingness to intervene, but data have not yet been reported to support the long-term effectiveness of the program (Commission on Adolescent

Suicide Prevention, 2005). QPR Gatekeeper Training for Suicide Prevention includes a CD-ROM program that covers key topics of suicide prevention. A recent randomized controlled trial of a high school adaptation of QPR showed that training increased self-reported knowledge, gatekeeper self-efficacy, and services accessed by students (Wyman et al., 2008). SAFE:TEEN is a comprehensive gatekeeper approach that includes staff, parents, and peers, with a 2-day staff training component. Evaluations of SAFE:TEEN show increased knowledge and willingness to intervene, and a county-wide follow-up demonstrated reduced county suicide rates over a 5-year period after implementation (Kalafat & Ryerson, 1999).

It would be optimal if *all* secondary school staff working with students had access to tools that support the long-term maintenance of their knowledge and skills in youth suicide prevention. Kalafat & Elias (1995) argue that such an approach is particularly appropriate in targeting a student's sense of social alienation, withdrawal, and weak social supports, all serious risk factors. Surrounding a student with caring individuals not only reduces an adolescent's sense of isolation, it also increases the number of people who can be alert for signs of distress.

Connecting With At-Risk Youth

It can be difficult for school staff to cultivate and maintain positive relationships with youth who exhibit behavioral patterns of withdrawal and irritability commonly associated with depression. Research has shown that school personnel tend to either avoid students with depressive characteristics (Morris, 1980) or engage in conflicted interactions with them (Martin, 1989). School personnel have preconceived notions about the qualities of a model student. Students are viewed as more teachable when they show high attentional focus and adaptability, amiability, and low reactivity. Adolescents with symptoms of depression tend to appear on the "less teachable" end of the continuum: distractible, inflexible, withdrawn, and reactive, thus eliciting more aversive reactions from school staff (Pullis, 1985). When teachers think students are capable of, but not practicing, self-control, they are more likely to respond with increased punitive and coercive strategies. Students, in turn, may come to avoid achievement situations and disengage further from classroom activities (Rothbart & Jones, 1998). Such a pattern is undoubtedly detrimental to student academic and psychosocial outcomes.

Though much attention has been given to equipping staff to effectively handle externalizing student behavior such as arguing and fighting, training in addressing internalizing behaviors is seriously lacking. Increasing staff understanding of issues related to depression and other unique developmental challenges faced by adolescents can be extremely helpful in shifting the focus in school personnel from negative attributions of purposeful misbehavior to active problem solving, which can lead to reduced conflict. When adolescents feel accepted and respected as individuals, the focus can move from one of accusation to one of support (Rothbart & Jones, 1998).

The importance of staff accessibility and support cannot be overstated. Quality relationships with other adults can buffer the impact of risk factors on outcomes for vulnerable adolescents. Adult accessibility, including empathy, warmth, and respect toward adolescents, is one of the most significant factors in preventing adolescent suicide (Toumbourou & Gregg, 2002). In schools where students feel connected (e.g., feel staff are responsive, feel they are a contributing part of their school), rates of suicidal ideation and emotional distress are lower (King, 2001). Youth who have positive relationships with school personnel have a reduced risk of suicide attempts and completions, and better mental health outcomes (Lubell & Vetter, 2006).

Having an accessible staff not only reduces the risk of adolescent suicide, it also increases the likelihood that signs of risk are detected as early as possible. Only a very small percentage of youth suffering from mental illness are identified in school settings (Horwitz, Leaf, Leventhal, Forsyth, & Speechley, 1992; Levitt, Saka, Romanelli, & Hoagwood, 2007). To be better equipped to recognize youth at risk for suicide, staff need training in how to be approachable and build positive relationships with youth. Training for staff must address the importance of behaving in a respectful, caring, and nurturing way with adolescents, and in being attentive to their needs. Adolescent youth are much more likely to approach an adult with whom they have a relationship (Kalafat & Elias, 1995), and it is within the context of a relationship that adults can recognize warning signs in youth, and get them the help they need. Supportive teacher behaviors and skills can be taught as part of a school-wide effort to foster a positive school climate. School climate has a direct effect on the health, safety, performance, and feelings of connectedness that staff and students have for schooling.

Using Universal Evidence-Based Programs to Create a Positive School Climate

Evidence is accumulating that indicates which aspects of the school environment can create or aggravate risk factors for adolescent internalizing disorders, such as depression and suicidal behavior, and which of these factors could be modified to reduce risk (Reinke & Herman, 2002). One element of effective prevention programs is to include protective elements to counter the development of risk (UCLA School Mental Health Project, 2003; White & Jodoin, 1998). Programs targeting a more supportive, interdependent school climate, where help-seeking is viewed as normative, serve a protective role in suicide prevention (Hazell & King, 1996).

As described in previous chapters, schools are increasingly implementing multilevel school-wide initiatives to improve school climate such as those based on school-wide positive behavior supports (SWPBS; Sugai, Horner, & Gresham, 2002). SWPBS prescribes proactive strategies for defining, teaching, and supporting appropriate student behaviors. At the universal level of intervention, SWPBS includes a system of training marked by consistent rules and consequences, encouragement, and clear expectations across all school settings. The expected outcome of SWPBS training is to create the type of nurturing environment that is critical to fostering adolescents' healthy social and emotional development. Extensive research supports the success of SWPBS systems in reducing discipline problems and promoting positive school climate with existing school resources (Sugai et al., 2002; Taylor-Greene et al., 1997; Todd, Horner, Sugai, & Sprague, 1999). SWPBS interventions have effectively decreased the number of office referrals due to problem behavior, improved academic and social climates of the school, and created a more positive learning environment for both students and teachers (Metzler, Biglan, Rusby, & Sprague, 2001; Sprague et al., 2001).

Although SWPBS is intended to influence a wide range of student behavior, studies of its implementation have typically focused on outcomes related to student externalizing behavior (Herman et al., 2004; Lane, Wehby, Robertson, & Rogers, 2007). An improved school climate would also likely promote protective factors and reduce risk factors for depression and suicidal behavior (Herman et al.). For example, staff training in creating a warm and nurturing environment, by engaging in simple behaviors such as making eye contact and referring to the student by name, can increase students' feelings of connectedness to the school. Given what we know about positive school climate and reduced risk for adolescent suicide, it is likely that youth vulnerable to developing depression or suicidal behavior would benefit from the SWPBS approach. Indeed, Lane et al. (2007) recently found that students with internalizing behavior problems were the most responsive to SWPBS compared with youth having externalizing and comorbid problem behaviors.

TARGETED YOUTH PREVENTION PROGRAMS

Similar to the research on universal prevention described above, targeted interventions to date have been developed and evaluated in separate research silos of depression or suicidal behavior prevention. The following sections provide a brief review of the efficacy and effectiveness research on targeted prevention efforts.

Targeted Depression Prevention

Several efficacy trials have evaluated selective and indicated depression prevention programs that are targeted to at-risk adolescents (e.g., Clarke et al., 1995; Jaycox, Reivich, Gillham, & Seligman, 1994; Peden, Rayens, Hall, & Beebe, 2001; Seligman, Schulman, DeRubeis, & Hollon, 1999). Previous studies have targeted youth with various risk factors, including poverty (Cardemil, Reivich, & Seligman, 2002), recent death of a parent (Sandler et al., 1992), recent parental divorce (Wolchik et al., 2002), parental depression (Beardslee et al., 1997), female gender (Quayle, Dzuirawiec, Roberts, Kane, & Ebsworthy, 2001), negative cognition style (Seligman et al., 1999), and family conflict (Jaycox et al.). Several indicated depression prevention trials have targeted adolescents with elevated depressive symptoms but below threshold for a clinical diagnosis (e.g., Clarke et al., 1995, 2001; Stice, Burton, Bearman, & Rohde,

2006; Stice, Rohde, Seeley, & Gau, 2008). Research findings to date indicate that such secondary prevention efforts have been more successful than the universal depression programs. Indeed, a recent meta-analysis of 30 depression prevention trials found the postintervention effect size was .30 for selective interventions, .23 for indicated interventions, and .12 for universal interventions (Horowitz & Garber, 2006). At follow-up, the mean effect sizes were .34, .31, and .02, for selective, indicated, and universal interventions, respectively. Whereas the utility of disseminating current universal interventions for preventing depression has been recently questioned, as described in the earlier section on preventing depression (e.g., Spence & Shortt, 2007), the evidence for the efficacy of targeted interventions is more compelling. Two exemplars for targeted depression programs are described next.

Clarke et al. (1995) conducted a randomized controlled trial to examine whether a school-based program using group cognitive therapy for preventing depression would significantly reduce the incidence of unipolar affective disorders in youth at risk for future depression. Ninth-grade adolescents in three high schools were identified as potentially at risk for depression through school-wide administration of the CES-D scale, followed by a structured diagnostic interview (the K-SADS) for the adolescents with elevated depressive symptoms. The adolescents identified as not currently depressed but with elevated CES-D scores were invited to participate in the prevention study; 150 accepted and were randomly assigned to either (a) a 15-session, after-school, cognitive–behavioral preventive intervention ($n = 76$); or (b) a "usual care" control condition ($n = 74$). The intervention, titled the Adolescent Coping with Stress Class (Clarke & Lewinsohn, 1995), consisted of fifteen 45-minute sessions in which participants are taught cognitive-behavioral therapy (CBT) techniques to identify and challenge negative or irrational thoughts that may contribute to the development of future affective disorder. Survival analysis results indicated significantly fewer of the at-risk youth in the intervention group developed either MDD or dysthymia during the 12-month follow-up period compared with the control group (14% vs. 26%, respectively).

The Penn Optimism Program (Gillham & Reivich, 1999; Gillham, Reivich, Jaycox, & Seligman, 1995; Jaycox et al., 1994) is another targeted depression prevention program that has been extensively evaluated. This prevention program contains two major components: a cognitive component and a social problem-solving component. The cognitive component was based on the cognitive vulnerability model of depression (Beck, 1967, 1976; Ellis, 1962; Seligman, 1991), including negative self-evaluation, dysfunctional attitudes, and low expectations for self-performance. The intervention was delivered to small groups of 10- to 13-year-old youth during twelve 1½-hour weekly sessions. Students were taught to identify negative beliefs, evaluate these beliefs, and generate more realistic alternatives. The social-problem-solving component focused on conduct and interpersonal problems that are often associated with depression in youth. Students were taught to think about their goals before acting, generate possible solutions for problems, and make decisions by weighing the pros and cons of each option. Students were also taught techniques for coping with parental conflict as well as behavioral techniques to enhance assertiveness, negotiation, and relaxation. Screening criteria included both selective and indicated approaches by identifying at-risk youth based on either self-reported parental conflict or self-reported elevated depressive symptoms. Compared with a matched comparison group, program participants reported significantly fewer depressive symptoms immediately following the program and at 6-month and 2-year follow-ups. Moreover, teachers also reported better classroom behavior in intervention participants compared with control participants.

Although several effectiveness trials have been conducted for universal preventive interventions for depression, as described earlier, we could locate only one targeted depression prevention effectiveness trial where endogenous providers delivered the intervention. Using an adaptation of the Penn Optimism Program for mainland Chinese youth, Yu and Seligman (2002) found that a 10-session teacher-delivered CBT program for students with elevated depressive symptoms or family conflict produced greater reductions in depressive symptoms than assessment-only controls, from baseline to postintervention, baseline to 3-month follow-up, and baseline to 6-month follow-up. Given the mounting evidence for the efficacy of school-based targeted depression prevention programs, more effectiveness research is clearly warranted.

Targeted Suicide Prevention

Few school-based targeted suicide prevention programs have been developed and rigorously evaluated to date. The most comprehensive targeted school-based interventions have been developed and evaluated by Eggert, Thompson, and their colleagues (Eggert, Karovsky, & Pike, 1999; Eggert, Thompson, Herting, & Nicholas, 1994, 1995; Thompson, Eggert, & Herting, 2000; Thompson, Eggert, Randell, & Pike, 2001). The interventions are targeted to youth who are deemed to be at risk of dropping out of high school. Based on both selective and indicated approaches, a multiple gating procedure is used to first identify students who are at risk of dropping out based on school attendance and academic performance data as well as on referrals from teachers, counselors, or other gatekeepers. The second gate includes an assessment of suicide risk; youth identified as not at risk for suicide are screened out. The interventions are aimed at reducing suicidal behavior by improving the students' personal resources that enhance self-esteem and sense of control, decision making, and social support resources.

Eggert, Thompson, and colleagues evaluated three preventive interventions, including a small-group intervention titled Personal Growth Class (PGC; Eggert et al., 1994, 1995; Thompson et al., 2000), a brief individually delivered intervention called Counselors Care (C-CARE), and the Coping and Support Training (CAST) program, which combines the PGC and C-CARE intervention approaches (Thompson et al., 2001). PGC is a semester-long class that includes life skills training using strategies of group process; peer and teacher support; goal setting; and weekly monitoring of mood management, substance use, and school performance. C-CARE is a standardized individual intervention approach delivered by trained research staff consisting of (a) a 2-hour computer-assisted suicide assessment; (b) a brief motivational counseling session to enhance empathy and reinforce positive coping skills and help-seeking behaviors, and increase access to services; and (c) a social network connections component to link youth with a school-based case manager or a favorite teacher, and to contact the youth's parent or guardian to enhance immediate support and communication. CAST is a small-group intervention delivered in twelve 1-hour sessions over 6 weeks, targeting mood management, improved school performance, and reduced substance use. Each session includes helping students apply newly acquired skills and gain support from family and other trusted adults.

In a randomized efficacy trial with 100 at-risk students, compared with an assessment-only control group, PGC participants reported significant improvement in self-perceived ability to manage problem circumstances. A subsequent large, three-group randomized control trial compared CAST, C-CARE, and usual care conditions with 460 high school students. Compared with usual care, CAST and C-CARE showed significant reductions in positive attitudes toward suicide, suicidal ideation, depression, and hopelessness. CAST was found to be the most effective approach toward enhancing and sustaining personal control and problem-solving coping skills. Given these promising findings, further development and evaluation of school-based targeted approaches to suicide prevention are warranted.

TERTIARY-LEVEL INTERVENTION AND COMMUNITY RESOURCES

With a few exceptions, tertiary-level treatment for youth who are clinically depressed or suicidal seldom occurs within the schooling context (e.g., Mufson, Dorta, Moreau, & Weissman, 2005; Stark, 1990; Stark, Hargrave, Schnoebelen, Simpson, & Molnar, 2005). Brener, Martindale, and Weist (2001) indicate that school-based mental health programs have been implemented in less than 10% of U.S. schools. However, school-based mental health programs are being increasingly adopted by school districts across the country (Adelman & Taylor, 1999). For example, there is a national movement to establish expanded school mental health (ESMH) programs that provide comprehensive mental health services, including assessment, case management, therapy, and prevention through partnerships between schools and community mental health agencies (Weist, 1997; Weist & Albus, 2004). ESMH programs have been shown to improve school climate regarding mental health and reduce student referral for special education services (Bruns, Walrath, Glass-Siegel, & Weist, 2004). By partnering with community agencies, schools can link students to evidence-based tertiary-level services such as psychotherapy and pharmacotherapy.

Psychotherapy

Available research supports the use of certain forms of psychotherapy in treatment for youth depression (Birmaher et al., 1996; Curry, 2001). CBT has been found to be superior to wait-list conditions and generally more efficacious than alternative treatments (Kahn, Kehle, Jenson, & Clark, 1990; Kroll, Harrington, Jayson, Fraser, & Gowers, 1996; Lerner & Clum 1990; Reynolds & Coats, 1986; Rosselló & Bernal, 1999). Brent et al. (1997) contrasted CBT, systemic behavior family therapy, and nondirective supportive therapy for adolescent depression and found that CBT resulted in higher remission rates compared with the other two treatments, although differences faded during 2-year follow-up (Birmaher et al., 2000). With respect to delivering CBT within the school setting, Stark and colleagues (Stark & Kendall, 1996; Stark et al., 2004) have developed a school-based program for preadolescent girls that can be administered individually or in small groups and includes a parent training component and a teacher consultation component; however, outcome data are not yet available. The Adolescent Coping with Depression course (Clarke, Lewinsohn, & Hops, 1990; Rohde, Lewinsohn, Clarke, Hops, & Seeley, 2005), an efficacious CBT psychoeducational program for adolescents 14 and older, also has the potential to be delivered within schools by trained staff (e.g., counselors, school psychologists, social workers, or behavior specialists). However, effectiveness research is clearly needed to evaluate whether CBT can be delivered with adequate fidelity and competence by trained staff within the school setting.

In addition to CBT, interpersonal psychotherapy for adolescents (IPT-A) has also proved to be efficacious in treating adolescent depression (Mufson et al., 1994; Mufson, Weissman, Moreau, & Garfinkel, 1999; Mufson et al., 2005). IPT-A addresses common adolescent developmental issues that are associated with depression, including separation from parents, authority and autonomy in the parent–teen relationship, development of dyadic interpersonal relationships, peer pressure, loss, and issues related to single-parent families. Mufson and colleagues (2005) recently evaluated the effectiveness of IPT-A delivered by trained staff in school-based mental health clinics in New York City. Compared with a treatment-as-usual control group, the IPT-A group showed significantly greater reductions in depressive symptomatology, faster recovery time, and improved levels of social functioning. Thus, IPT-A represents a promising treatment approach that has been effectively implemented within school-based mental health clinics.

Pharmacotherapy

Pharmacological treatment of adolescent depression remains controversial. Although earlier research found no support for tricyclics (American Academy of Child and Adolescent Psychiatry, 1998), recent findings for the selective serotonin reuptake inhibitors (SSRIs) have been more promising (e.g., Ambrosini, 2000; Emslie et al., 1997). The Treatment for Adolescents with Depression Study (TADS) recently provided strong support for fluoxetine (TADS Team, 2004). However, as with other trials, TADS found a small but significant increase in SSRI-associated suicidality, which led the Food and Drug Administration to recently issue a "black box" warning to the entire category of antidepressants. Given the safety questions regarding antidepressants for depressed adolescents, the fact that comorbid depression and substance abuse are associated with an increased suicidality, and that some degree of substance use reduction is necessary before initiating SSRIs with depressed substance-abusing adolescents (e.g., Riggs & Davies, 2002), evaluating psychosocial treatments for adolescent depression continues to be an important priority.

CONCLUSION AND FUTURE DIRECTIONS

The overarching goal of this chapter was to review school-based approaches to the prevention and treatment of youth depression and suicidal behavior within the context of the three-tier intervention model. Although considerable progress has been made in this regard, the efforts to date have been rather fragmented and piecemeal. In order to move toward a response-to-intervention (RTI) framework, the three-tier intervention approaches studied need to be conducted in more carefully coordinated and concerted efforts. Furthermore, given the close ties between youth depression and suicidal behavior, the use of universal, targeted, and tertiary-level interventions should be integrated and complementary, rather than treating the behaviors as independent problems.

A number of future research directions have already been discussed throughout this chapter. We conclude with a few additional topics that warrant future research attention. Methods of effectively engaging and working with the parents of depressed and/or suicidal adolescents for either prevention or treatment interventions have yet to be developed. Connecting with families when interventions are provided in the school is even more challenging. However, given the generally small or nonsignificant effects for many prevention interventions, including parents has the potential to boost effectiveness.

Another important direction for future research involves the optimal timing of prevention interventions. Risk for depression and suicidal behaviors waxes and wanes among adolescents, as does the motivation to engage in and benefit from prevention programs. Information regarding the optimal methods of conducting periodic screening or "catching" adolescents when they become at risk is not currently available. Universal prevention efforts presumably are not affected by the timing of their delivery, but selective and indicated prevention interventions are strongly influenced by the timing of risk or elevated symptom status. Data on basic factors such as the duration of elevated risk or subthreshold symptom status in relation to the timing of prevention are unknown and warrant further research.

The impact of cultural, racial, and ethnic differences on engaging in and benefiting from both prevention and treatment efforts is another very understudied topic. Potential ways of tailoring programs to enhance effectiveness and the impact of client–therapist matching on race and ethnicity are additional areas for future research.

Lastly, as efficacy data continue to emerge, efforts at training school personnel in providing evidence-based approaches will be needed, along with research on promoting the widespread adoption of these programs by the schools. Schools are an ideal setting for mounting large-scale campaigns to effectively prevent and treat youth depression and suicidal behavior. The involvement of school psychologists and staff are essential for mounting such prevention efforts. It is our hope that by promoting protective factors and ameliorating modifiable risk factors through school-based interventions, the long-standing difficulties associated with youth depression and suicidal behavior may be averted.

REFERENCES

Abramson, L. Y., Metalsky, G. I., & Alloy, L. B. (1989). Hopelessness depression: A theory-based subtype of depression. *Psychological Review, 96,* 358–372.

Adelman, H. S., & Taylor, L. (1999). Mental health in schools and system restructuring. *Clinical Psychology Review, 19,* 137–163.

Albert, N., & Beck, A. T. (1975). Incidence of depression in early adolescence: A preliminary study. *Journal of Youth and Adolescence, 4,* 301–306.

Ambrosini, P. J. (2000). Historical development and present status of the Schedule for Affective Disorders and Schizophrenia for School-Age Children (K-SADS). *Journal of the American Academy of Child and Adolescent Psychiatry, 39,* 49–58.

American Academy of Child and Adolescent Psychiatry. (1998). Practice parameters for the assessment and treatment of children and adolescents with depressive disorders. *Journal of the American Academy of Child and Adolescent Psychiatry, 37*(10 Suppl.), 63S–83S.

American Association of Suicidology. (2007). *Facts about suicide and depression.* [Online]. Available: http://www.suicidology.org/associations/1045/files/Depression.pdf [March 2008].

American Psychiatric Association. (1952). *Diagnostic and statistical manual of mental disorders* (1st ed.). Washington, DC: American Psychiatric Association.

Angold, A., Prendergast, M., Cox, A., Rutter, M., Harrington, R., & Simonoff, E. (1995). The Child and Adolescent Psychiatric Assessment: CAPA. *Psychological Medicine, 25,* 739–754.

Angold, A., Weissman, M. M., John, K., Merikangas, K. R., Prusoff, B. A., Wickramaratne, P., et al. (1987). Parent and child reports of depressive symptoms in children at low and high risk of depression. *Journal of Child Psychology and Psychiatry, 28,* 901–915.

Beardslee, W. R., Wright, E. J., Salt, P., Drezner, K., Gladstone, T. R., Versage, E. M., et al. (1997). Examination of children's responses to two preventive intervention strategies over time. *Journal of the American Academy of Child and Adolescent Psychiatry, 36,* 196–204.

Beck, A. T. (1967). *Depression: Clinical, experimental, and theoretical aspects.* New York: Harper & Row.

Beck, A. T. (1976). *Cognitive therapy and the emotional disorders.* New York: International Universities Press.

Beck, A. T., & Steer, R. A. (1991). *Beck Scale for Suicide Ideation.* San Antonio, TX: Harcourt Brace Educational Measurement.

Beck, A. T., Steer, R. A., & Brown, G. K. (1996). *Beck Depression Inventory* (2nd ed.). San Antonio, TX: Harcourt Brace Educational Measurement.

Beck, A. T., Ward, C. H., Mendelson, M., Mock, J., & Erbaugh, J. (1961). An inventory for measuring depression. *Archives of General Psychiatry, 4,* 561–571.

Birmaher, B., Brent, D. A., Kolko, D., Baugher, M., Bridge, J., Holder, D., et al. (2000). Clinical outcome after short-term psychotherapy for adolescents with major depressive disorder. *Archives of General Psychiatry, 57,* 29–36.

Birmaher, B., Ryan, N. D., Williamson, D. E., Brent, D. A., Kaufman, J., Dahl, R. E., et al. (1996). Childhood and adolescent depression: A review of the past 10 years. Part 1. *Journal of the American Academy of Child and Adolescent Psychiatry, 35,* 1427–1439.

Brener, N. D., Martindale, J., & Weist, M. D. (2001). Mental health and social services: Results from the School Health Policies and Programs Study 2000. *Journal of School Health, 71,* 305–312.

Brent, D. A., Baugher, M., Bridge, J., Chen, T., & Chiappetta, L. (1999). Age- and sex-related risk factors for adolescent suicide. *Journal of the American Academy of Child and Adolescent Psychiatry, 38,* 1497–1505.

Brent, D. A., Holder, D., Kolko, D., Birmaher, B., Baugher, M., Roth, C., et al. (1997). A clinical psychotherapy trial for adolescent depression comparing cognitive, family, and supportive therapy. *Archives of General Psychiatry, 54,* 877–885.

Brooks-Gunn, J., & Petersen, A. (1991). Studying the emergence of depression and depressive symptoms during adolescence. *Journal of Youth and Adolescence, 20,* 115–119.

Brown, G. W., & Harris, T. (1978). *Social origins of depression: A study of psychiatric disorder in women.* New York: Free Press.

Bruns, E. J., Walrath, C., Glass-Siegel, M. G., & Weist, M. D. (2004). School-based mental health services in Baltimore: Association with school climate and special education referrals. *Behavior Modification, 28,* 491–512.

Burns, B. J., Costello, E. J., Angold, A., Tweed, D., Stangl, D., Farmer, E. M. Z., et al. (1995). Children's mental health service use across service sectors. *Health Affairs, 14*(3), 147–159.

Cardemil, E. V., Reivich, K. J., & Seligman, M. E. P. (2002). The prevention of depressive symptoms in low-income minority middle school students. *Prevention and Treatment, 5,* (article 8). Retrieved from http://journals.apa.org/prevention/volume5/pre0050008a.html

Carlson, G. A., & Cantwell, D. P. (1979). A survey of depressive symptoms in a child and adolescent psychiatric population. *Journal of the American Academy of Child and Adolescent Psychiatry, 18,* 587–599.

Clarke, G. N., Hawkins, W., Murphy, M., & Sheeber, L. (1993). School-based primary prevention of depressive symptomatology in adolescents: Findings from two studies. *Journal of Adolescent Research, 8,* 183–204.

Clarke, G. N., Hawkins, W., Murphy, M., Sheeber, L. B., Lewinsohn, P. M., & Seeley, J. R. (1995). Targeted prevention of unipolar depressive disorder in an at-risk sample of high school adolescents: A randomized trial of a group cognitive intervention. *Journal of the American Academy of Child and Adolescent Psychiatry, 34,* 312–321.

Clarke, G. N., Hornbrook, M., Lynch, F., Polen, M., Gale, J., Beardslee, W., et al. (2001). A randomized trial of a group cognitive intervention for preventing depression in adolescent offspring of depressed parents. *Archives of General Psychiatry, 58,* 1127–1134.

Clarke, G. N., & Lewinsohn, P. M. (1995). *The Adolescent Coping with Stress Class: Leader manual.* Retrieved July 2, 2008, from http://www.kpchr.org/public/acwd/acwd.html.

Clarke, G. N., Lewinsohn, P. M., & Hops, H. (1990). *Leader's manual for adolescent groups: Adolescent Coping with Depression Course.* Kaiser Permanente Center for Health Research. Retrieved July 2, 2008, from http://www.kpchr.org/public/acwd/acwd.html

Cohen, S., & Wills, T. A. (1985). Stress, social support, and the buffering hypothesis. *Psychological Bulletin, 98,* 310–357.

Cole, E., & Siegel, J. A. (2003). Suicide prevention in schools: Facing the challenge. In E. Cole & J. A. Siegel (Eds.), *Effective consultation in school psychology* (Rev. ed.; pp. 415–461). Ashland, OH: Hogrefe & Huber.

Commission on Adolescent Suicide Prevention. (2005). In D. I. Evans et al. (Eds.), *Treating and preventing adolescent mental health disorders: What we know and what we don't know* (pp. 434–493). New York: Oxford University Press.

Commission on Chronic Illness. (1957). *Chronic illness in the United States. Volume 1.* Cambridge, MA: Harvard University Press.

Costello, E. J., Angold, A., Burns, B. J., Strangl, D. K., Tweed, D. L., Erkanli, A., et al. (1996). The Great Smoky Mountains Study of Youth: Goals, design, methods, and the prevalence of *DSM-III-R* disorders. *Archives of General Psychiatry, 53,* 1129–1136.

Costello, E. J., Edelbrock, C. S., & Costello, A. J. (1985). Validity of the NIMH Diagnostic Interview Schedule for Children: A comparison between psychiatric and pediatric referrals. *Journal of Abnormal Child Psychology, 13,* 579–595.

Curry, J. (2001). Specific psychotherapies for childhood and adolescent depression. *Biological Psychiatry, 49,* 1091–1100.

Cytryn, L., & McKnew, D. H., Jr. (1972). Proposed classification of childhood depression. *American Journal of Psychiatry, 129,* 149–155.

Eggert, L. L., Karovsky, P. P., & Pike, K. C. (1999). *Washington state youth suicide prevention program: Pathways to enhancing community capacity in preventing youth suicidal behaviors. Final report.* Seattle, WA: University of Washington School of Nursing.

Eggert, L. L., Thompson, E. A., Herting, J. R., & Nicholas, L. J. (1994). A prevention research program: Reconnecting at-risk youth. *Issues in Mental Health Nursing, 15,* 107–135.

Eggert, L. L., Thompson, E. A., Herting, J. R., & Nicholas, L. J. (1995). Reducing suicide potential among high-risk youth: Tests of a school-based prevention program. *Suicide and Life-Threatening Behavior, 25*(2), 276–296.

Ellis, A. (1962). *Reason and emotion in psychotherapy,* New York: Lyle Stuart.

Emslie, G. J., Rush, A. J., Weinberg, W. A., Kowatch, R. A., Hughes, C. W., Carmody, T., et al. (1997). A double-blind randomized placebo-controlled trial of fluoxetine in children and adolescents with depression. *Archives of General Psychiatry, 54,* 1031–1037.

Essau, C. A., Hakim-Larson, J., Crocker, A., & Petermann, F. (1999). Assessment of depressive disorders in children and adolescents. In C. A. Essau & F. Petermann (Eds.), *Depressive disorders in children and adolescents: Epidemiology, risk factors, and treatment* (pp. 27–67). Northvale, NJ: Jason Aronson.

Evans, E., Hawton, K., & Rodham, K. (2004). Factors associated with suicidal phenomena in adolescents: A systematic review of population-based studies. *Clinical Psychology Review, 24,* 957–979.

Fleming, J. E., Offord, D. R., & Boyle, M. H. (1989). Prevalence of childhood and adolescent depression in the community: Ontario child health study. *British Journal of Psychiatry, 155,* 647–654.

Fombonne, E., Wostear, G., Cooper, V., Harrington, R., & Rutter, M. (2001). Maudsley long-term follow-up of child and adolescent depression. 2. Suicidality, criminality and social dysfunction in adulthood. *British Journal of Psychiatry, 179,* 218–223.

Garber, J. (2006). Depression in children and adolescents: Linking risk research and prevention. *American Journal of Preventive Medicine, 31*(6, Suppl.), 104–125.

Garrison, C. Z., Schluchter, M. D., Schoenbach, V. J., & Kaplan, B. K. (1989). Epidemiology of depressive symptoms in young adolescents. *Journal of the American Academy of Child and Adolescent Psychiatry, 28,* 343–351.

Gillham, J., & Reivich, K. J. (1999). Prevention of depressive symptoms in school children: A research update. *Psychological Science, 10,* 461–462.

Gillham, J. E., Reivich, K. J., Jaycox, L. H., & Seligman, M. E. P. (1995). Prevention of depressive symptoms in school children: Two-year follow-up. *Psychological Science, 6*(6), 343–351.

Glaser, K. (1967). Masked depression in children and adolescents. *American Journal of Psychotherapy, 21,* 565–574.

Goldston, D. B. (2000). *Assessment of suicidal behaviors and risk among children and adolescents* (Technical report submitted to NIMH under Contract No. 263-MD-909995). Washington, DC: National Institute of Mental Health.

Goldston, D. B. (2003). *Measuring suicidal behaviors and risk among children and adolescents.* Washington, DC: American Psychological Association.

Gordon, R. (1983). An operational classification of disease prevention. *Public Health Reports, 98,* 107–109.

Gordon, R. (1987). An operational classification of disease prevention. In H. Steinberg & M. Silverman (Eds.), *Preventing mental disorders: A research perspective* (pp. 20–26). Rockville, MD: U.S. Department of Health and Human Services.

Gotlib, I. H., Lewinsohn, P. M., & Seeley, J. R. (1998). Consequences of depression during adolescence: Marital status and marital functioning in early adulthood. *Journal of Abnormal Psychology, 107,* 686–690.

Gould, M. S. (2001). Suicide and the media. In H. Hendin, & J. J. Mann (Eds.), *The clinical science of suicide prevention* (Vol. 932, pp. 200–224). New York: Annals of the New York Academy of Sciences.

Gould, M. S., Greenberg, T., Velting, D. M., & Shaffer, D. (2003). Youth suicide risk and preventive interventions: A review of the past 10 years. *Journal of the American Academy of Child and Adolescent Psychiatry, 42,* 386–405.

Grunbaum, J. A., Kann, L., Kinchen, S., Ross, J., Hawkins, J., Lowry, R., et al. (2003). Youth risk behavior surveillance—United States, 2003. *Morbidity and Mortality Weekly Report, 53,* 1–96.

Hains, A., & Ellman, S. (1994). Stress inoculation training as a preventative intervention for high school youths. *Journal of Cognitive Psychotherapy, 8,* 219–232.

Hazell, P., King, R. (1996). Arguments for and against teaching suicide prevention in schools. *Australian and New Zealand Journal of Psychiatry, 30,* 633–642.

Herjanic, B., & Reich, W. (1982). Development of a structured psychiatric interview for children: Agreement between child and parent on individual symptoms. *Journal of Abnormal Child Psychology, 10,* 307–324.

Herman, K., Merrell, K., Reinke, W., & Tucker, C. M. (2004). The role of school psychology in preventing depression. *Psychology in Schools, 41,* 763–775.

Horowitz, J. L., & Garber, J. (2006). The prevention of depressive symptoms in children and adolescents: A meta-analytic review. *Journal of Consulting and Clinical Psychology, 74,* 401–415.

Horwitz, S. M., Leaf, P. J., Leventhal, J. M., Forsyth, D. R., & Speechley, K. N. (1992). Identification and management of psychosocial and developmental problems in community-based, primary care practices. *Pediatrics, 89,* 480–485.

Jaycox, L. H., Reivich, K. J., Gillham, J., & Seligman, M. E. P. (1994). Prevention of depressive symptoms in school children. *Behavior Research Therapy, 32,* 801–816.

Johnson, J. G., Cohen, P., Gould, M. S., Kasen, S., Brown, J., & Brook, J. S. (2002). Childhood adversities, interpersonal difficulties, and risk for suicide attempts during late adolescence and early adulthood. *Archives of General Psychiatry, 59,* 741–749.

Kahn, J. S., Kehle, T. J., Jenson, W. R., & Clark, E. (1990). Comparison of cognitive-behavioral, relaxation, and self-modeling interventions for depression among middle-school students. *School Psychology Review, 19,* 196–210.

Kalafat, J. (2003). School approaches to youth suicide prevention. *American Behavioral Scientist, 46,* 1211–1223.

Kalafat, J., & Elias, M. J. (1995). Suicide prevention in an educational context: Broad and narrow foci. *Suicide and Life-Threatening Behavior, 25*(1), 123–133.

Kalafat, J., & Ryerson, D. M. (1999). The implementation and institutionalization of a school-based youth suicide prevention program. *Journal of Primary Prevention, 19,* 157–175.

Kashani, J., & Simonds, J. F. (1979). The incidence of depression in children. *American Journal of Psychiatry, 136,* 1203–1205.

Kessler, R. C., Berglund, P., Demler, O., Jin, R., Koretz, D., Merikangas, K. R., et al. (2003). The epidemiology of major depressive disorder: Results from the National Comorbidity Survey Replication (NCS-R). *Journal of the American Medical Association, 289,* 3095–3105.

King, K. A. (2001). Developing a comprehensive school suicide prevention program. *Journal of School Health, 71,* 132–137.

King, K. A., & Smith, J. (2000). Project SOAR: A training program to increase school counselor's knowledge and confidence regarding suicide prevention intervention. *Journal of School Health, 70,* 402–407.

Klerman, G. L., & Weissman, M. M. (1989). Increasing rates of depression. *Journal of the American Medical Association, 261,* 2229–2235.

Kovacs, M. (1985). The Children's Depression Inventory. *Psychopharmacology Bulletin, 21,* 995–998.

Kovacs, M., Feinberg, T. L., Crouse-Novak, M. A., Paulauskas, S. L., & Finkelstein, R. (1984). Depressive disorders in childhood. I. A longitudinal prospective study of characteristics and recovery. *Archives of General Psychiatry, 41,* 229–237.

Kroll, L., Harrington, R., Jayson, D., Fraser, J., & Gowers, S. (1996). Pilot study of continuation cognitive-behavioral therapy for major depression in adolescent psychiatric patients. *Journal of the American Academy of Child and Adolescent Psychiatry, 35,* 1156–1161.

Lane, K. L., Wehby, J. H., Robertson, E. J., & Rogers, L. A. (2007). How do different types of high school students respond to schoolwide positive behavior support programs? Characteristics and responsiveness of teacher-identified students. *Journal of Emotional and Behavioral Disorders, 15,* 3–20.

Lazear, K., Roggenbaum, S., & Blase, K. (2003). *Youth suicide prevention school-based guide* (FMHI Series Publication #218-0). Tampa, FL: Department of Child and Family Studies, Division of State and Local Support, Louis de la Parte Florida Mental Health Institute, University of South Florida.

Lerner, M. S., & Clum, G. A. (1990). Treatment of suicide ideators: A problem-solving approach. *Behavior Therapy, 21,* 403–411.

Levitt, J. M., Saka, N., Romanelli, L. H., & Hoagwood, K. (2007). Early identification of mental health problems in schools: The status of instrumentation. *Journal of School Psychology, 45,* 163–191.

Lewinsohn, P. M., & Essau, C. (2002). Depression in adolescents. In I. H. Gotlib & C. Hammen (Eds.), *Handbook of depression* (pp. 541–559). New York: Guilford Press.

Lewinsohn, P. M., Hops, H., Roberts, R. E., Seeley, J. R., & Andrews, J. A. (1993). Adolescent psychopathology: I. Prevalence and incidence of depression and other DSM-III-R disorders in high school students. *Journal of Abnormal Psychology, 102,* 133–144.

Lewinsohn, P. M., Rohde, P., Klein, D. N., & Seeley, J. R. (1999). Natural course of adolescent major depressive disorder: I. Continuity into young adulthood. *Journal of the American Academy of Child and Adolescent Psychiatry, 38,* 56–63.

Lewinsohn, P. M., Rohde, P., & Seeley, J. R. (1995). Adolescent psychopathology: III. The clinical consequences of comorbidity. *Journal of the American Academy of Child and Adolescent Psychiatry, 34,* 510–519.

Lewinsohn, P. M., Rohde, P. Seeley, J. R. (1998a). Major depressive disorder in older adolescents: Prevalence, risk factors, and clinical implications. *Clinical Psychology Review* 765–794.

Lewinsohn, P. M., Rohde, P., & Seeley, J. R. (1998b). Treatment of adolescent depression: Frequency of services and impact on functioning in young adulthood. *Depression and Anxiety, 7,* 47–52.

Lewinsohn, P. M., Rohde, P., Seeley, J. R., & Fischer, S. (1993). Age-cohort changes in the lifetime occurrence of depression and other mental disorders. *Journal of Abnormal Psychology, 102,* 110–120.

Lewinsohn, P. M., Rohde, P., Seeley, J. R., Klein, D. N., & Gotlib, I. H. (2003). Psychosocial functioning of young adults who have experienced and recovered from major depressive disorder during adolescence. *Journal of Abnormal Psychology, 112,* 353–363.

Link, B. G., Struening, E. L., Neese-Todd, S., Asmussen, S., & Phelan, J. C. (2001). Stigma as a barrier to recovery: The consequences of stigma for the self-esteem of people with mental illness. *Psychiatric Services, 52,* 1621–1626.

Lowry-Webster, H., Barrett, P., & Dadds, M. (2001). A universal prevention trial of anxiety and depressive symptomatology in childhood: Preliminary data from an Australian study. *Behaviour Change, 18,* 36–50.

Lubell, K. M., & Vetter, J. B. (2006). Suicide and youth violence prevention: The promise of an integrated approach. *Aggression and Violent Behavior, 11,* 167–175.

Markowitz, F. E. (1998). The effects of stigma on the psychological well-being and life satisfaction of persons with mental illness. *Journal of Health and Social Behavior, 39,* 335–347.

Martin, R. P. (1989). Activity level, distractibility, and persistence: Critical characteristics in early schooling. In G. A. Kohnstamm, J. E. Bates, and M. K. Rothbart (Eds.), *Temperament in childhood* (pp. 451–462). Chichester, U.K.: Wiley.

Merry, S., McDowell, H., Wild, C. J., Bir, J., & Cunliffe, R. (2004). A randomized placebo-controlled trial of a school-based depression prevention program. *Journal of the American Academy of Child and Adolescent Psychiatry, 43,* 538–547.

Metzler, C. W., Biglan, A., Rusby, J. C., & Sprague, J. R. (2001). Evaluation of a comprehensive behavior management program to improve school-wide positive behavior support. *Education & Treatment of Children, 24,* 448–479.

Morris, M. (1980). Childhood depression in the primary grades: Early identification, a teacher consultation remedial model, and classroom correlates of change. *Interchange, 11,* 61–75.

Mrazek, P. J., & Haggerty, R. J. (1994). *Reducing risks for mental disorders: Frontiers for preventive intervention research.* Washington, DC: National Academy Press.

Mufson, L., Dorta, K. P., Moreau, D., & Weissman, M. M. (2005). Efficacy to effectiveness: Adaptations of interpersonal psychotherapy for adolescent depression. In P. S. Jensen & E. D. Hibbs (Eds.), *Psychosocial treatments for child and adolescent disorders: Empirically based strategies for clinical practice* (2nd ed., pp. 165–186). Washington, DC: American Psychological Association.

Mufson, L., Moreau, D., Weissman, M. M., Wickramaratne, P., Martin, J., & Samoilov, A. (1994). Modification of interpersonal psychotherapy with depressed adolescents (IPT-A): Phase I and II studies. *Journal of the American Academy of Child and Adolescent Psychiatry, 33,* 695–705.

Mufson, L., Weissman, M. M., Moreau, D., & Garfinkel, R. (1999). Efficacy of interpersonal psychotherapy for depressed adolescents. *Archives of General Psychiatry, 56,* 573–579.

National Center for Injury Prevention and Control. (2002). *CDC Injury Research Agenda.* Atlanta, GA: Centers for Disease Control and Prevention.

Newman, D. L., Moffitt, T. E., Caspi, A., Magdol, L., Silva, P. A., & Stanton, W. R. (1996). Psychiatric disorder in a birth cohort of young adults: Prevalence, comorbidity, clinical significance, and new case incidence from ages 11–21. *Journal of Consulting and Clinical Psychology, 64,* 552–562.

Nolen-Hoeksema, S. (2002). Gender differences in depression. In I. H. Gotlib & C. L. Hammen (Eds.), *Handbook of depression* (pp. 492–509). New York: Guilford Press.

Nolen-Hoeksema, S., & Girgus, J. S. (1994). The emergence of gender differences in depression during adolescence. *Psychological Bulletin, 115,* 424–443.

Nolen-Hoeksema, S., Girgus, J. S., & Seligman, M. E. P. (1991). Sex differences in depression and explanatory style in children. *Journal of Youth and Adolescence, 20,* 233–245.

Orvaschel, H., Puig-Antich, J., Chambers, W. J., Tabrizi, M. A., & Johnson, R. (1982). Retrospective assessment of prepubertal major depression with the Kiddie-SADS-E. *Journal of the American Academy of Child and Adolescent Psychiatry, 21,* 392–397.

Orvaschel, H., Walsh-Allis, G., & Ye, W. (1988). Psychopathology in children of parents with recurrent depression. *Journal of Abnormal Child Psychology, 16,* 17–28.

Pattison, C., & Lynd-Stevenson, R. M. (2001). The prevention of depressive symptoms in children: Immediate and long-term outcomes of school-based program. *Behaviour Change, 18,* 92–102.

Peden, A. R., Rayens, M. K., Hall, L. A., & Beebe, L. H. (2001). Preventing depression in high-risk college women: A report of an 18-month follow-up. *Journal of American College Health, 49,* 299–306.

Penn, D. L., Judge, A., Jamieson, P., Garczynski, J., Hennessy, M., & Romer, D. (2005). Stigma. In D. I. Evans et al. (Eds.), *Treating and preventing adolescent mental health disorders: What we know and what we don't know* (pp. 531–543). New York: Oxford University Press.

Petersen, A. C., Sarigiani, P. A., & Kennedy, R. E. (1991). Adolescent depression: Why more girls? *Journal of Youth and Adolescence, 20,* 247–271.

Poland, S. (1995). Suicide intervention. In A. Thomas & J. Grimes (Eds.), *Best practices in school psychology III* (pp. 459–468). Bethesda, MD: National Association of School Psychologists.

Pössel, P., Horn, A. B., Groen, G., & Hautzinger, M. (2004). School-based prevention of depressive symptoms in adolescents: A 6-month follow-up. *Journal of the American Academy of Child and Adolescent Psychiatry, 43,* 1003–1010.

Potter, L. B., & Stone, D. (2003). Suicide prevention in schools: What can and should be done? *American Journal of Health Education, 34,* S35–S41.

Pullis, M. E. (1985). LD students' temperament characteristics and their impact on decisions by resource and mainstream teachers. *Learning Disability Quarterly, 8,* 109–122.

Quayle, D., Dzuirawiec, S., Roberts, C., Kane, R., & Ebsworthy, G. (2001). The effect of an optimism and life skills program on depressive symptoms in preadolescence. *Behaviour Change, 18,* 194–203.

Radloff, L. S. (1977). The CES-D Scale: A self-report depression scale for research in the general population. *Applied Psychological Measurement, 1,* 385–401.

Reinherz, H. Z., Giaconia, R. M., Hauf, A. M. C., Wasserman, M. S., & Silverman, A. B. (1999). Major depression in the transition to adulthood: Risks and impairments. *Journal of Abnormal Psychology, 108,* 500–510.

Reinke, W. M., & Herman, K. C. (2002). Creating school environments that deter antisocial behaviors in youth. *Psychology in the Schools, 39,* 549–560.

Reinke, W. M., Herman, K. C., & Tucker, C. M. (2006). Building and sustaining communities that prevent mental disorders: Lessons from the field of special education. *Psychology in the Schools, 43,* 313–329.

Resnick, M. D., Bearman, P. S., Blum, R. W., Bauman, K. E., Harris, K. M., Jones, J., et al. (1997). Protecting adolescents from harm: Findings from the National Longitudinal Study on adolescent health. *Journal of the American Medical Association, 278,* 823–832.

Reynolds, W. M. (1986). A model for the screening and identification of depressed children and adolescents in school settings. *Professional School Psychology, 1,* 117–129.

Reynolds, W. M. (1987a). *Reynolds Adolescent Depression Scale.* Odessa, FL: Psychological Assessment Resources.

Reynolds, W. M. (1987b). *Suicidal Ideation Questionnaire: Professional manual.* Odessa, FL: Psychological Assessment Resources.

Reynolds, W. M. (1991). Psychological intervention for depression in children and adolescents. In G. Stoner, M. R. Shinn, & H. M. Walker (Eds.), *Interventions for achievement and behavior problems* (pp. 649–683). Silver Spring, MD: National Association of School Psychologists.

Reynolds, W. M. (1994). Assessment of depression in children and adolescents by self-report questionnaires. In W. M. Reynolds & H. F. Johnston (Eds.), *Handbook of depression in children and adolescents* (pp. 209–234). New York: Plenum Press.

Reynolds, W. M., & Coats, K. I. (1986). A comparison of cognitive-behavioral therapy and relaxation training for the treatment of depression in adolescents. *Journal of Consulting and Clinical Psychology, 54,* 653–660.

Riggs, P. D., & Davies, R. D. (2002). A clinical approach to integrating treatment for adolescent depression and substance abuse. *Journal of the American Academy of Child and Adolescent Psychiatry, 41,* 1253–1255.

Roberts, C., Kane, R., Thomson, H., Bishop, B., & Hart, B. (2003). The prevention of depressive symptoms in rural school children: A randomized controlled trial. *Journal of Consulting and Clinical Psychology, 71,* 622–628.

Roberts, R. E., Lewinsohn, P. M., & Seeley, J. R. (1991). Screening for adolescent depression: A comparison of depression scales. *Journal of the American Academy of Child and Adolescent Psychiatry, 30,* 58–66.

Rohde, P., Lewinsohn, P. M., Clarke, G. N., Hops, H., & Seeley, J. R. (2005). The Adolescent Coping With Depression Course: A cognitive-behavioral approach to the treatment of adolescent depression. In E. D. Hibbs & P. S. Jensen (Eds.), *Psychosocial treatments for child and adolescent disorders: Empirically based strategies for clinical practice* (pp. 219–237). Washington, DC: American Psychological Association.

Rosselló, J., & Bernal, G. (1999). The efficacy of cognitive-behavioral and interpersonal treatments for depression in Puerto Rican adolescents. *Journal of Consulting and Clinical Psychology, 67,* 734–745.

Rothbart, M. K., & Jones, L. B. (1998). Temperament, self-regulation and education. *School Psychology Review, 27,* 479–491.

Rotheram-Borus, M. J. (1990). Adolescents' reference-group choices, self-esteem, and adjustment. *Journal of Personality and Social Psychology, 59,* 1075–1081.

Rutter, M. (1986). The developmental psychopathology of depression: Issues and perspectives. In M. Rutter, C. Izard, & P. Read (Eds.), *Depression in young people: Developmental and clinical perspectives* (pp. 3–30). New York: Guilford Press.

Sandler, I., West, S., Baca, L, Pillow, D., Gersten, J., Rogosch, F., et al. (1992). Linking empirically based theory and evaluation: The Family Bereavement Program. American *Journal of Community Psychology,20,* 491–521.

Seeley, J. R. (2002). Comorbidity between conduct disorder and major depression: Phenomenology, correlates, course, and familial aggregation. *Dissertation-Abstracts-International-Section-A:-Humanities-and-Social-Sciences, Vol. 62,* 12-A.

Seligman, M. E. P. (1991). *Learned optimism.* New York: Knopf.

Seligman, M. E. P. (2000). Positive psychology: An introduction. *American Psychologist, 55,* 5–14.

Seligman, M., Schulman, P., DeRubeis, R., & Hollon, S. (1999). The prevention of depression and anxiety. *Prevention and Treatment, 2* (article 8). Retrieved from http://journals.apa.org/prevention/volume2/pre0020008a.html

Shaffer, D., Gould, M. S., Fisher, P., Trautman, P., Moreau, D., Kleinman, M., et al. (1996). Psychiatric diagnosis in child and adolescent suicide. *Archives of General Psychiatry, 53,* 339–348.

Shaffer, D., Scott, M., Wilcox, H., Maslow, C., Hicks, R., Lucas, C. P., et al. (2004). The Columbia Suicide Screen: Validity and reliability of a screen for youth suicide and depression. *Journal of the American Academy of Child and Adolescent Psychiatry, 43,* 71–79.

Shah, S., Hoffman, R. E., Wake, L., & Marine, W. M. (2000). Adolescent suicide and household access to firearms in Colorado: Results of a case-control study. *Journal of Adolescent Health, 26,* 157–163.

Sheffield, J. K., Spence, S. H., Rapee, R. M., Kowalenko, N., Wignall, A., Davis, A., et al. (2006). Evaluation of universal, indicated, and combined cognitive-behavioral approaches to the prevention of depression among adolescents. *Journal of Consulting and Clinical Psychology, 74,* 66–79.

Shochet, I. A., Dadds, M. R., Holland, D., Whitefield, K., Harnett, P. H., & Osgarby, S. M. (2001). The efficacy of a universal school-based program to prevent adolescent depression. *Journal of Clinical Child Psychology, 30,* 303–315.

Sourander, A., Helstelä, L., Haavisto, A., & Bergroth, L. (2001). Suicidal thoughts and attempts among adolescents: A longitudinal 8-year follow-up study. *Journal of Affective Disorders, 63,* 59–66.

Spence, S. H., Sheffield, J. K., & Donovan, C. L. (2003). Preventing adolescent depression: An evaluation of the problem solving for life program. *Journal of Consulting and Clinical Psychology, 71,* 3–13.

Spence, S. H., Sheffield, J. K., & Donovan, C. L. (2005). Long-term outcome of a schoolbased, universal approach to prevention of depression in adolescents. *Journal of Consulting and Clinical Psychology, 73,* 160–167.

Spence, S. H., & Shortt, A. L. (2007). Can we justify the widespread dissemination of universal, school-based interventions for the prevention of depression among children and adolescents? *Journal of Child Psychology and Psychiatry, 48,* 526–542.

Sprague, J., Walker, H., Golly, A., White, K., Myers, D. R., & Shannon, T. (2001). Translating research into effective practice: The effects of a universal staff and student intervention on indicators of discipline and school safety. *Education and Treatment of Children, 24,* 495–511.

Stark, K. D. (1990). *Childhood depression: School-based intervention.* New York: Guilford Press.

Stark, K. D., Hargrave, J. L., Schnoebelen, S., Simpson, J. P., & Molnar, J. (2005). Treatment of childhood depression. In P. C. Kendall (Ed.), *Child and adolescent therapy: Cognitive behavioral procedures* (3rd ed.). New York: Guilford Press.

Stark, K., & Kendall, P. C. (1996). *Treating depressed children: Therapist manual for "Taking Action."* Ardmore, PA: Workbook Publishing.

Stark, K. D., Schnoebelen, S., Simpson, J., Hargrave, J., Glenn, R., & Molnar, J. (2004). Treating depressed children: Therapist manual for ACTION. Ardmore, PA: Workbook Publishing.

Stice, E., Burton, E., Bearman, S. K., & Rohde, P. (2006). Randomized trial of a brief depression prevention program: An elusive search for a psychosocial placebo control condition. *Behavior Research Therapy, 45,* 863–876.

Stice, E., Rohde, P., Seeley, J. R., & Gau, J. M. (2008). Brief cognitive-behavioral depression prevention program for high-risk adolescents. *Journal of Consulting and Clinical Psychology, 76,* 595–606.

Sugai, G., Horner, R. H., & Gresham, F. M. (2002). Behaviorally effective school environments. In M. R. Shinn, H. M. Walker, & G. Stoner (Eds.), *Interventions for academic and behavior problems II: Preventive and remedial approaches.* Bethesda, MD: National Association of School Psychologists.

TADS Team. (2004). Fluoxetine, cognitive-behavioral therapy, and their combination for adolescents with depression: Treatment for Adolescents with Depression Study (TADS) randomized controlled trial. *Journal of the American Medical Association, 292,* 807–820.

Taylor-Greene, S., Brown, D., Nelson, L., Longton, J., Gassman, T., Cohen, J., et al. (1997). School-wide behavioral support: Starting the year off right. *Journal of Behavioral Education, 7,* 99–112.

Thompson, E. A., Eggert, L. L, & Herting, J. R. (2000). Mediating effects of an indicated prevention program for reducing youth depression and suicide risk behaviors. *Suicide and Life-Threatening Behavior, 30,* 252–271.

Thompson, E. A., Eggert, L. L., Randell, B. P., & Pike, K. C. (2001). Evaluation of indicated suicide risk prevention approaches for potential high school dropouts. *American Journal of Public Health, 91,* 742–752.

Todd, A. W., Horner, R. H., Sugai, G., & Sprague, J. R. (1999). Effective behavior support: Strengthening school-wide systems through a team-based approach. *Effective School Practices, 17,* 23–37.

Toolan, J. M. (1962). Depression in children and adolescents. American Journal of *Orthopsychiatry, 32,* 404.

Toumbourou, J. W., & Gregg, E. (2002). Impact of an empowerment-based parent education program on the reduction of youth suicide factors. *Journal of Adolescent Health, 31,* 227–285.

UCLA School Mental Health Project. (2003). *Mental health in schools: An overview.* UCLA School Mental Health Project Center for Mental Health in Schools. Available at http://smhp.psych.ucla.edu/aboutmhinschools.htm

Wagner, B. M., Silverman, M. A., & Martin, C. E. (2003). Family factors in youth suicidal behaviors. *American Behavioral Scientist, 46,* 1171–1191.

Wahl, O. F. (2002). Children's view of mental illness: A review of the literature. *Psychiatric Rehabilitation Skills, 6,* 134–158.

Weist, M. D. (1997). Expanded school mental health services: A national movement in progress. In T. H. Ollendick & R. Prinz (Eds.), *Advances in clinical child psychology* (Vol. 19, pp. 321–352). New York: Plenum Press.

Weist, M. D., & Albus, K. E. (2004). Expanded school mental health: Exploring program details and developing the research base. *Behavior Modification, 28,* 463–471.

White, J., & Jodoin, N. (1998). *Before the Fact Interventions: A manual of best practices in youth suicide prevention.* Vancouver: Suicide Prevention Information & Resource Centre of British Columbia, Co-Operative University-Provincial Psychiatric Liaison (CUPPL).

Wolchik, S. A., Sandler, I. N., Millsap, R. E., Plummer, B. A., Greene, S. M., Anderson, E. R., et al. (2002). Six-year follow-up of preventive interventions for children of divorce. A randomized controlled trial. *Journal of the American Medical Association, 288,* 1874–1881.

World Health Organization (2007). *What is depression?* Retrieved November 28, 2007, from http://www.who.int/mental_health/management/depression/definition/en/

Wyman, P. A., Brown, C. H., Inman, J., Cross, W., Schmeelk-Cone, K., Guo, J., et al. (2008). Randomized trial of a gatekeeper program for suicide prevention: 1-year impact on secondary school staff. *Journal of Consulting and Clinical Psychology, 76,* 104–115.

Yu, D. L., & Seligman, M. (2002). Preventing depressive symptoms in Chinese children. *Prevention & Treatment, 5* (article 9). http://journals.apa.org/prevention/volume5/pre0050009a.html

CHAPTER 16

Implementing Positive Behavior Support in Elementary Schools

Andy J. Frey
Amy Lingo
University of Louisville

C. Michael Nelson
University of Kentucky

INTRODUCTION

Positive behavior interventions and support (PBIS) is the systematic application of effective instructional and behavioral practices that are designed to achieve desired social and learning outcomes as they prevent problem behaviors (Sugai & Horner, 2008). It embraces three fundamental principles that enhance student success: (a) promoting evidence-based practices, (b) supporting change in discipline practices, and (c) building local capacity to sustain effective practices over time (Coyne, Simonsen, & Faggella-Luby, 2008; Sugai & Horner, 2006). When PBIS is adopted and used across the entire school, it is referred to as school-wide positive behavior support (SWPBS). Horner and Sugai (2009) define SWPBS as "a systems approach to establishing the social culture and behavioral supports needed for all children in a school to achieve both social and academic success. School-wide PBIS is not a packaged curriculum, but an approach that defines core elements that can be achieved through a variety of strategies" (p. 1).

Currently, SWPBS is being implemented in more than 9,000 schools across the United States and is demonstrating positive effects on student behavior and school climate (Bradley, Doolittle, Lopez, Smith, & Sugai, 2007; Horner et al., 2009; Sugai & Horner, 2008). The majority of states have developed leadership teams to implement the approach statewide, and, supported by resources developed by the National Center on Positive Behavioral Interventions and Supports, many districts and states are using blueprints to facilitate large-scale implementation. This chapter presents an overview of SWPBS, pointing out its relationship to response to intervention (RTI), an approach that is becoming familiar to school support staff responsible for identifying students with a specific learning disability. Referring to RTI, the Individuals with Disabilities Education Improvement Act of 2004 permits school districts to "use a process that determines if the child responds to scientific, research-based intervention as a part of the evaluation procedures" (IDEA 2004). The method can replace identification that uses the discrepancy between ability and achievement to identify students with learning difficulties. The potential roles of school psychologists, school social workers, and other student support personnel in the implementation of SWPBS in elementary schools also are described in this chapter.

School-wide PBIS includes four key elements: (a) student outcomes relative to desired changes in student academic and social behavior, (b) research-validated practices to support student behavior, (c) systems to support staff behavior, and (d) collection and use of data for decision-making (see Figure 1; Sugai & Horner, 2002). Although SWPBS addresses both academic and behavioral dimensions of educational performance (Darch & Kame'enui, 2004; Lane, 2004; McIntosh, Chard, Boland, & Horner, 2006; Scott, Nelson, & Liaupsin, 2001; Scott & Shearer-Lingo, 2002), the focus of this chapter is on SWPBS as a behavioral system.

Several features distinguish SWPBS relative to traditional approaches to student discipline in schools:

Figure 1. The four key elements of positive behavior support.

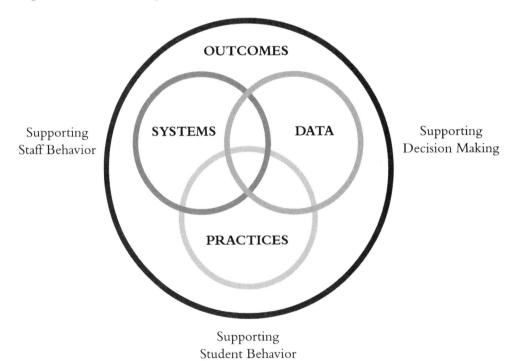

Note. Reprinted from "The Evolution of Discipline Practices: School-Wide Positive Behavior Supports," by G. Sugai and R. H. Horner, 2002, *Child and Family Behavior Therapy, 24,* pp. 23–50. In the public domain.

- An emphasis on prevention of problem behavior
- Active instruction of behavioral skills
- A continuum of consequences for problem behavior
- Function-based interventions for children with the most challenging problem behaviors
- A systematic approach to supporting effective behavioral interventions within the school
- Use of data to guide decisions regarding the fidelity and effectiveness of the interventions being implemented (Horner, Sugai, Todd, & Lewis-Palmer, 2005; Simonsen & Sugai, 2007)

Both SWPBS and RTI are based on a multitiered model of prevention and intervention (see Figure 2). At Tier 1, primary prevention practices focus on supporting academic success and desirable behavior and preventing initial occurrences of academic failure or problem behavior. Tier 1 practices apply to all students and are used by all adults in the school setting. Examples of Tier 1 practices include using effective, evidence-based instructional practices; establishing and teaching behavioral expectations to all students; modifying environmental arrangements (i.e., altering the physical or interactional aspects of those locations where problem behavior frequently occurs and providing active supervision); and applying positive consequences to

Figure 2. Academic and behavioral dimensions of school-wide positive behavior support.

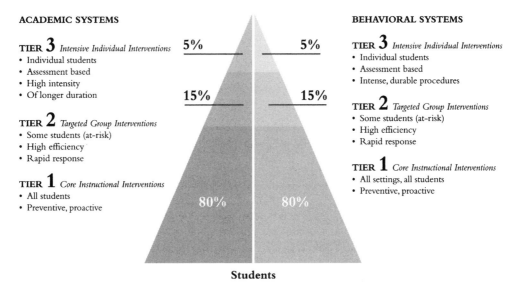

ACADEMIC SYSTEMS

TIER 3 *Intensive Individual Interventions* 5%
- Individual students
- Assessment based
- High intensity
- Of longer duration

15%

TIER 2 *Targeted Group Interventions*
- Some students (at-risk)
- High efficiency
- Rapid response

TIER 1 *Core Instructional Interventions*
- All students
- Preventive, proactive

80%

BEHAVIORAL SYSTEMS

TIER 3 *Intensive Individual Interventions* 5%
- Individual students
- Assessment based
- Intense, durable procedures

15%

TIER 2 *Targeted Group Interventions*
- Some students (at-risk)
- High efficiency
- Rapid response

TIER 1 *Core Instructional Interventions*
- All settings, all students
- Preventive, proactive

Students

Note. From "Behaviorally Effective School Environments," by G. Sugai, R. H. Horner, and F. Gresham, 2002, in *Interventions for Academic and Behavior Problems II: Preventive and Remedial Approaches,* 2nd ed., p. 320, by M. R. Shinn, H. M. Walker, and G. Stoner (Eds.), Bethesda, MD: National Association of School Psychologists. Copyright 2002 by the National Association of School Psychologists. Adapted with permission.

encourage desired behavior and negative consequences to discourage undesirable behavior. Other examples of Tier 1 practices are developing linkages between the school and the community and between the school and students' homes.

Tier 2 interventions seek to prevent repeated academic failure and the reoccurrence of problem behavior, and they focus on those students who need more support than is offered through Tier 1. These strategies should be *efficient* to apply and *effective* in terms of producing rapid improvement in students' behavior. Examples include school-wide peer tutoring, social skill groups, mentoring programs, and homework clubs. Specialized, Tier 2 intervention procedures, such as check-in/check-out (CICO) and the First Step to Success intervention, are described later in this chapter (Sandomierski, Kincaid, & Algozzine, 2007; Walker et. al 1997).

Finally, Tier 3 interventions focus on students who have serious academic or behavioral problems that constitute a chronic condition that has not responded to Tier 1 or Tier 2 interventions. The goal is to reduce the negative impact of the condition on the student's functioning. Tier 3 interventions consist of intensive individualized strategies that are implemented for extended periods of time (referred to as *durable*) and frequently involve community agencies (Eber, Breen, Rose, Unizycki, & London, 2008; Eber, Sugai, Smith, & Scott, 2002). Students who exhibit chronic academic failure may be referred for intensive remedial instruction or special education evaluation. An individual education plan (IEP), behavior intervention plan (BIP), or wraparound plan may be developed for students who require Tier 3 support.

Most public schools have access to a variety of support service providers whose primary role is to eliminate barriers to student learning. However, in applying SWPBS, these personnel—among them, school psychologists, school social workers, school counselors, and behavior specialists—may need to rethink their current approaches to addressing student needs. Specifically, to lead SWPBS initiatives, practitioners must be well grounded in an ecological approach. An ecological perspective emphasizes the importance of interventions that target multiple systems, that is, the child, family, school organization, and community. The effective implementation of all three tiers of SWPBS and RTI involves developing linkages between schools, families, and communities. Therefore, providers of support services must be skilled not only in providing direct services to children who exhibit challenging behavior, but also in leading prevention efforts that support children indirectly through building the capacity of family members, other school staff, and community agencies to improve student outcomes.

THE INTEGRATION OF SCHOOL-WIDE PBIS AND RTI APPROACHES

Multitiered positive behavior interventions are used to identify students whose behavioral and emotional needs require more individualized services so they can benefit from their school experience. Use of the multitiered model of positive behavior support can help schools identify students who fail to respond to interventions at each level, that is, students whose behavioral and emotional needs dictate increasingly more individualized and powerful services. Thus, SWPBS involves the same decision-making framework as response to intervention. Batshe et al. (2005) defined RTI as the practice of (a) providing effective instruction and interventions based on students' needs and (b) regularly monitoring students' progress to guide decisions about changes in instruction or goals. The multitiered model suggests that more intensive interventions should be considered for individual students based on their response (or lack thereof) to interventions at prior levels of prevention. Figure 3 depicts how SWPBS and the RTI process can work together in making decisions about which students should receive interventions at each level.

As illustrated in Figure 3, when Tier 1 strategies are in place and are effective, it may be anticipated that approximately 80% of students will be successful. However, another 20% can be expected to need greater levels of support to be successful. Tier 2 strategies, if properly implemented, will allow many of these students (perhaps another 15%) to be successful. Yet, even with primary and secondary prevention supports in

Figure 3. Use of RTI in a positive behavior support framework as a basis for making intervention decisions.

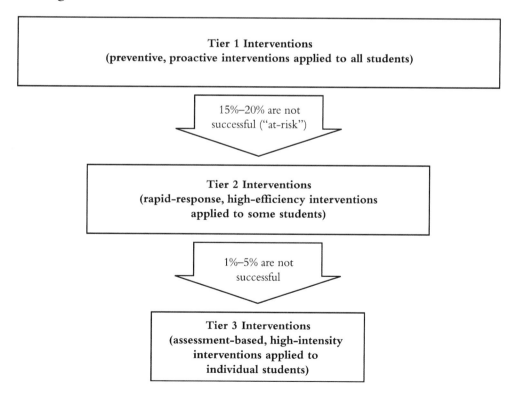

Note. From *Strategies for Addressing Behavior Problems in the Classroom*, by M. M. Kerr and C. M. Nelson, 2010, Upper Saddle River, NJ: Pearson Education. Copyright 2010 by Pearson Education, Inc. Reprinted with permission.

place, as many as 5% of students will demonstrate a need for Tier 3 interventions, the most intensive level of support. Although these proportions originally were extrapolated from a public health model of prevention, they are beginning to be validated empirically in the educational context (Horner et al., 2005; Spaulding et al., in press; Walker et al., 1996). Thus, both SWPBS and RTI frameworks direct school personnel to monitor student success across all three tiers and to make data-based decisions regarding which students require more intensive levels of intervention. By employing data-based decision making, schools can more effectively direct resources to where they are needed.

IMPLEMENTATION OF SCHOOL-WIDE POSITIVE BEHAVIOR SUPPORT

Public concerns regarding school safety, particularly with regard to student behavior, have prompted researchers and practitioners to think in terms of preventive practices. In response, a number of school-wide efforts have been designed to address school climate, such as initiatives for safe and drug-free schools, and to address specific issues, such as character education and bullying. Within the SWPBS model, schools are considered to be host environments, that is, settings which embrace and support the use of effective practices (Horner & Sugai, 2009). As illustrated in Figure 1, the four key elements of SWPBS implementation are (a) identifying meaningful student outcomes; (b) establishing and investing in school-wide systems, including creating a school-wide PBIS leadership team; (c) selecting and implementing contextually appropriate evidence-based practices organized within the multitiered framework; and (d) collecting and using data to make decisions (Simonsen, Sugai, & Negron, 2008). Outcomes can be measured by examining data such as office discipline referral (ODR) rates, suspensions and expulsions, behavior rating scales, or state- or district-wide test scores.

Creating a team to oversee the SWPBS implementation for the school involves selecting representatives from all stakeholders in the school (teachers, noninstructional and noncertified personnel, parents, students, and a school administrator). One or two of the team members are selected to serve as a team coach, responsible for facilitating team meetings and serving as a liaison between the leadership team and SWPBS trainers (Simonsen, 2010). Procedures should be in place that help decision makers use data as frequently as necessary. Finally, arrangements should be made for the school staff to receive training in SWPBS, which may be accessed by contacting a statewide SWPBS leadership team, or by visiting the U.S. Department of Education's PBIS website (http://www.pbis.org). Examples in the following sections show a range of practices in educational settings and describe the roles support service personnel can take in implementing the SWPBS process at each level of intervention. Table 1 highlights the major characteristics of SWPBS Tier 1, 2, and 3 interventions.

Table 1. Characteristics of SWPBS Tier 1, 2, and 3 Interventions

Prevention Tier	Goal	Core Elements	Features
Tier 1 Primary Prevention	Prevent initial occurrences of problem behavior	• Definition of behavioral expectations • Teaching of behavioral expectations • Reward system for appropriate behavior • Continuum of consequences for problem behavior • Continuous collection and use of data for decision making • Development of school and community/home linkages	• Apply to all students • Apply to all settings • Consist of rules, routines, arrangements • Implemented by all staff
Tier 2 Secondary Prevention	Prevent reoccurrences of problem behavior	• Universal screening • Progress monitoring for at-risk students • System for increasing structure and predictability • System for increasing contingent adult feedback • System for linking academic and behavioral performance • System for increasing home–school communication • Collection and use of data for decision making	• Minimal time needed to implement • Procedures that are similar for groups of students • Typically provide extra doses of primary interventions • Implementation coordinated by a school-wide team
Tier 3 Tertiary Prevention	Reduce impact of a condition on functioning	• Functional behavioral assessment • Team-based comprehensive assessment • Linking of academic and behavior supports • Individualized intervention • Collection and use of data for decision making	• Individualized planning and implementation • Function-based intervention plans • Wraparound planning • Implementation by teams established for individual students

Note. Adapted from *Is School-Wide Positive Behavior Support an Evidence-Based Practice?* (p. 2), by OSEP Center on Positive Behavioral Interventions and Supports, 2009, March. Retrieved from http://www.pbis.org/common/pbisresources/publications/EvidenceBaseSWPBS08_04_08.doc. In the public domain.

The SWPBS Leadership Team

An important component of SWPBS implementation is the creation of a leadership team to guide and sustain implementation efforts. The team serves as an organizational structure that represents various stakeholder groups within the school and community. Leadership team members should have collective competence in behavioral intervention, establish a regular and efficient way to communicate with the school staff as a whole, and be actively endorsed by the school administration (Sugai & Horner, 2002). Principals must be on the team because of their decision-making authority, and parents also should be included as team members. Whenever possible, this leadership team should govern all behavior-related initiatives, actions, and decisions. The team must meet at least monthly, and meetings should be guided by a proactive approach to problem solving.

The SWPBS leadership team is responsible for securing agreements and supports (e.g., readiness requirements), developing a data-based implementation plan for SWPBS, arranging for high fidelity of implementation, and conducting formative data-based monitoring (Sugai & Horner, 2002). Leadership teams must secure staff agreements regarding the nature and priority of staff development efforts and needs, a long-term staff commitment to the effort (at least 3 years), and consensus regarding the importance of taking a preventive and instructional approach to behavior management. Implementation plans are maximized when 80% or more of staff have provided assurance of their commitment, typically obtained by an active vote.

The leadership team also coordinates the collection and review of school-wide data to determine which school policies and practices within each of four school-wide systems—school-wide, classroom, non-classroom, and individual student—need to be maintained or improved, or whether new policies and procedures should be adopted. Data may be in the form of behavior incidence reports, ODRs, self-assessment inventories, surveys, or checklists.

Leadership teams must plan the application of SWPBS across the school setting, represented by the four overlapping systems that support school-wide, classroom, non-classroom, and individual student implementation (see Figure 4). These school-wide systems consist of the rules, routines, and arrangements of physical space and supervision that apply across the entire school environment—in classroom and non-classroom settings—as well as the systems (individualized supports) that are developed for individual students.

Planning and Implementation Resources

The majority of states have state leadership teams that coordinate training and provide information and support services for SWPBS implementation. Many states also host PBIS websites. The National Technical Assistance Center for Positive Behavior Interventions and Supports maintains a comprehensive website (http://www.pbis.org) that contains a wealth of resources, including tools for training and implementation, research and evaluation reports, PowerPoint presentations, videos, newsletters, and links to related resources. The National Association for Positive Behavior Support (http://www.apbs.org) publishes a quarterly research journal and hosts an annual conference. The reference list at the end of this chapter includes citations for the curricula and programs mentioned in this chapter.

Figure 4. School-wide positive behavior support systems.

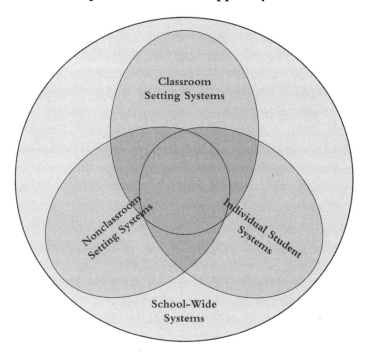

Note. Adapted from "Discipline and Behavioral Support: Practices, Pitfalls, and Promises," by G. Sugai and R. Horner, 1999, *Effective School Practices 17*(4), p. 14. In the public domain.

Tier 1 Primary Prevention

The overarching goal of SWPBS at Tier 1, the primary prevention level, is to support appropriate behaviors for all students by creating safe and nurturing school environments and to prevent initial instances of academic or social failure among all students. The principal criteria for Tier 1 practices are that they are evidence based, of high quality, and able to be universally applied, that is, by all school personnel, using available resources. Corollary outcomes of this goal are greater academic achievement for all students and fewer students requiring support at the secondary and tertiary levels.

The SWPBS Plan and Tier 1 Strategies

The SWPBS implementation plan generally focuses on efforts to improve one system-related objective at a time. Implementation plans should include measurable objectives, a 1- to 3-year timeline of events, specific activities that lead to these outcomes, staff development and training activities, and resource and support needs. The objective of staff development and training is to give staff members adequate training opportunities to gain necessary skills and to use positive reinforcement for staff members who execute practices as designed. Valid and reliable data systems should be established and in place before the plan is implemented and should include mechanisms for storing, manipulating, and summarizing data efficiently to permit data-based decision making.

Tier 1 strategies are applied school-wide, in both classroom and non-classroom settings, such as hallways, the cafeteria, and other common areas. Specific practices associated with Tier 1 prevention typically are incorporated into the following strategies:

- Establishing and teaching behavioral expectations to all students
- Making environmental arrangements and providing active supervision
- Applying consequences to encourage desired behavior and discourage undesirable behavior
- Developing school and community linkages
- Developing school and home linkages

Establishing and teaching behavioral expectations. A central SWPBS strategy at Tier 1 is to establish and define behavioral expectations for all students throughout the school. These expectations should be written by the entire staff and reflect the important social values of the school (Horner et al., 2005). Staff members identify a limited number of positively stated expectations (three to five). Next, the SWPBS leadership team defines these expectations in the context of all settings and routines in the school, often using a matrix format in which expectations are entered as row headings, and routines and settings are written as column headings. The team then describes what it looks like to follow each expectation within each setting or routine (Simonsen, Sugai, et al., 2008). These descriptions constitute a set of rules for each setting and routine. An example of an expectation that is established in many schools is "show respect." Figure 5 illustrates how this expectation is expressed in the expectations–routines matrix. In the classroom, to show respect means that students stay on task and complete assignments (respect self), get permission before speaking

Figure 5. Sample matrix of "show respect" expectations within routines and settings.

Setting, Routines	CLASSROOM	HALLWAY	CAFETERIA	RESTROOM
Expectations RESPECT SELF	• Stay on task • Complete assignments	• Walk on right	• Use good table manners	• Wash hands
RESPECT OTHERS	• Get permission before speaking • Line up by rows for dismissal	• Stay in line	• Keep hands and feet to self	• Use inside voice
RESPECT PROPERTY	• Return books and magazines	• Put trash in cans	• Pick up trash	• Flush

(respect others), and return books and magazines to the appropriate locations after using them (respect property). In nonclassroom environments such as the cafeteria, to show respect means to use good table manners (respect self), keep hands and feet to oneself (respect others), and pick up the trash at the lunch table (respect property).

The SWPBS leadership team often develops lesson plans for teaching each expectation within each routine or setting. Teachers and other staff use these lesson plans to actively teach the expectations to students, including concrete examples of positive behaviors in the contexts to which they apply. For example, staff would teach students the meaning of showing respect using concrete examples of how to show respect and how not to show respect in both the classroom and the cafeteria. Other practices used with this strategy include providing students with repeated opportunities to practice positive instances of showing respect, and giving them frequent acknowledgment for displaying respectful behavior in these contexts. When a student violates a rule, the initial response is for the staff member to provide an error correction, just as she would do if the student made an academic error. For example, if a student disrupts a class by talking out, the teacher says. "Sam, how do we show respect to others in the classroom?" Thus, rule infractions are treated as behavioral errors, not intentions to misbehave.

Making environmental arrangements and providing active supervision. This strategy involves several related practices. One involves having school staff assess locations where problem behavior occurs frequently and to alter physical or interactional aspects of those behavioral contexts. For example, changing traffic patterns in hallways ("walk on the right") can foster positive social behaviors and reduce or prevent inappropriate behavior. Another practice consists primarily of adults providing active supervision, interacting frequently with students (Simonsen, Fairbanks, Briesch, Myers, & Sugai, 2008). Such interactions may include greeting students, delivering instruction, engaging in informal conversations about topics of interest, or using prompts to encourage students to conform to behavioral expectations. Another practice associated with active supervision is for staff to circulate frequently so that the students are aware of an adult's presence. Staff also should visit identified problem areas often but unpredictably, be physically obvious, and scan the setting regularly, especially those areas that are farther away, to check for both appropriate and inappropriate behavior.

Applying consequences to encourage desired behavior and discourage undesired behavior. Guided by the SWPBS leadership team, staff can provide clear and differential responses to students when they engage in expected behavior versus when they exhibit undesirable behavior. All adults are encouraged to acknowledge appropriate student behavior and respond consistently and appropriately when behavior falls short of expectations. A plethora of research has documented the effectiveness of teacher praise on improving student behavior (Simonsen, Fairbanks, et al., 2008). Praise should demonstrate adult approval, immediately follow a specific behavior, and include a description of the behavior (e.g., "I like the way you are showing respect on the playground by taking turns").

Although recognizing appropriate behavior is important, problem behavior should also be addressed and discouraged. A continuum of consequences for inappropriate behavior, ranging from reteaching the rule or expectation to writing an ODR, should exist, and the consequences should be clear, fair, and consistently applied (Darch & Kame'enui, 2004; Simonsen, Sugai et al., 2008). Horner and Sugai (2005) suggest that schools clarify which problem behaviors should be managed in class and which warrant an ODR. Students should be instructed early in the year about the consequences of appropriate and inappropriate behavior. Also, problem behaviors should be addressed consistently.

Error correction is a specific practice that has been shown to be effective across a wide range of schools (Kerr & Nelson, 2010). Like praise, error correction is a statement made by an adult to a student that is immediate and includes a description of a specific behavior. Additionally, when using error correction, the adult indicates the behavior that should have been used instead of the inappropriate behavior, and requires the student to demonstrate the desired behavior. General guidelines for the use of error correction include being brief and specific, using a soft or low voice, and being discrete. The ratio of praise to error correction is an important consideration in using this practice. Although an optimal ratio of praise to reprimands has not been established, authorities recommend a minimum of three praise statements for every error correction to as many as eight for every error correction (Alberto & Troutman, 2009; Sugai & Simonsen, 2007).

Developing school and community links. Linking the school with the community may involve strategies directed at integrating community resources into the instructional program, collaborating with community groups and agencies to enhance the delivery of educational services, or enlisting community resources to promote healthy child development through after-school and parent education programs. The successful integration of educational and community resources may enhance students' achievement by removing barriers to learning, such as poor health care, lack of access to positive peer and adult role models, and the absence of substance abuse counseling for families. Programs and services that support such links include medical, dental, mental health and social services, before- and after-school programs, summer camps, early childhood programs, community celebrations, and other events (Quinn, 2007). Several model programs have the goal of strengthening links between schools and communities by bringing community service providers into the school, establishing connections between local services and the school, or creating a center within or near the school where families can access service providers. Examples of these include community schools, school-linked services, family resource centers, and school-based health services (Briar-Lawson, Lawson, Collier, & Joseph, 1997; Dupper & Poertner, 1997; Dryfoos, 1998a, 1998b; Dryfoos, Brindis, & Kaplan, 1996; Hanson, Jeppson, & Johnson, 1993; Illback & Kalafat, 1995).

Developing school and home links. As with developing links between the school and the community, links between the school and home can be created independent of SWPBS. However, implementing them within the context of SWPBS is likely to improve their effectiveness and also provide an important foundation for Tier 2 and 3 supports. The practices associated with this strategy often focus on increasing family involvement in students' educational process. "Family" is broadly defined to include parents, grandparents, legal guardians, or non–family members living with a student. Family involvement in Tier 1 can range from attending school functions to serving on committees, boards, or councils. Epstein, Coates, Salinas, Sanders, and Simon (1997) identify six types of parental involvement: parenting, communication, volunteering, learning at home, decision making, and collaboration with the community.

Approaches to linking school and home include the following:

- Connecting families with teachers through home visits, phone calls, meals, and other information-sharing sessions
- Connecting families with other families for mutual support and exchange of information
- Increasing the cultural competency of school personnel to address racism and cultural issues that families may encounter (Bye, 2007)

Evidence Base and Future Directions in Tier 1

There is a considerable evidence base for many of the Tier 1 intervention strategies highlighted in this chapter. For example, research supports the use of instructional practices that increase academic engaged time, produce high rates of correct academic responding, and increase content covered (Darch & Kame'enui, 2004; Landrum, Tankersley, & Kauffman, 2003; Lewis, Hudson, Richter, & Johnson, 2004; Mercer & Mercer, 2005; Rosenshine, 2008; Yell, 2009). On the behavioral side, several strategies for supporting desired behavior and preventing or reducing undesired behavior have received empirical support; these include structuring the environment, clarifying expectations, providing active supervision, using contingent praise, giving precision requests, applying corrective feedback, providing direct instruction in social skills, and using group-oriented contingencies and response-contingent punishment procedures such as reprimands, response cost, and time out (Alberto & Troutman, 2009; Kerr & Nelson, 2010; Landrum & Kauffman, 2006; Landrum et al., 2003; Lewis et al., 2004; Simonsen et al., 2008; Sutherland, Wehby, & Copeland, 200; Yell, Meadows, Drascow, & Shriner, 2009). Although the evidence related to school–community and school–home links is less compelling, connecting schools to their surrounding communities has been shown to promote appropriate student social behaviors (Clark, 1988; Eccles, 1999; Hodgkinson, 1989; Vandell & Shumow, 1999). A substantial body of evidence also suggests that children do better behaviorally and academically when their families are involved in the schooling process (Fischer, 2003; Henderson & Mapp, 2002; National Governor's Association Task Force on School Readiness, 2005).

Moreover, the No Child Left Behind Act of 2001 requires schools to involve families in their children's education.

A limitation of this research is that, for the most part, these practices have been studied and applied in isolation from one another. Accumulating evidence from schools that use these practices systematically and cohesively within a system of SWPBS demonstrates them to be effective in reducing problem behavior (Bradshaw, Mitchell, & Leaf, 2009; Horner et al., 2005; Horner et al., 2009; Horner & Sugai, 2009, Sugai & Horner, 2008). Schools that have gathered pre- and postintervention data report a 20% to 60% reduction in ODRs and suspensions when SWPBS is implemented with fidelity. Studies that documented a 2nd year of SWPBS implementation reported that the gains observed during the 1st year were sustained (Horner et al., 2005). Horner et al. (2009) recently completed a study, using a randomized controlled trial, of the implementation and effectiveness of SWPBS in 30 elementary schools in Hawaii and Illinois across a 3-year time frame. Results indicated that state education personnel, operating with available resources, were able to provide the training and technical assistance to enable schools to implement SWPBS systems and practices with fidelity. In addition, statistically significant differences between measures of perceived school safety were obtained, favoring SWPBS schools. Finally, implementation of SWPBS was associated with improved third-grade reading achievement scores, although the authors noted that this finding requires further study. Because ODR data prior to implementation of SWPBS were not available, no causal inferences could be drawn regarding the impact of SWPBS on student problem behavior. Research currently under way involves rigorous experimental analysis to determine the efficacy of SWPBS.

Although these studies are encouraging, the fidelity and effectiveness of SWPBS when implemented in settings without the support of external consultants and funding is less certain. Fortunately, the use of a fidelity measure (the School-wide Evaluation Tool, or SET) and research examining barriers to implementation in school settings are providing local implementers with extremely valuable information (Horner et al., 2004). The SET can be used in documenting the degree of fidelity with which the components of SWPBS are implemented. A SET score of 80% fidelity with evaluation items has been established as the criterion to identify schools that are accurately implementing SWPBS. Schools that implement with 80% or greater fidelity report better student outcomes than those that do not (McIntosh, Horner, & Sugai, 2009). Another tool, the Benchmarks of Quality, has been introduced for SWPBS leadership teams to use in assessing the status of implementation against quality indicators (available at http://www.pbis.org). Recently, Kincaid, Childs, Blase, and Wallace (2007) identified 13 themes that serve as either barriers or facilitators of implementation fidelity. These themes were consistent with the core components for initiating and maintaining SWPBS, such as obtaining administrative and district support, systematically rewarding students and staff, securing staff buy-in prior to implementation, using data, working as teams, and including families and the community in implementation efforts.

Because the fidelity and sustainability of SWPBS practices are critical to positive outcomes, the educational community should intensify research that analyzes barriers and aids to implementation. The effects of alternate strategies to address identified barriers also should be examined. Because general education settings often lack resources or support staff with the requisite skill sets for behavioral consultation, effective assessment, and planning, it is necessary to better understand how these barriers can be overcome. In addition, general education teachers may not have received appropriate training to support secondary and tertiary interventions (MacMillan, Gresham, & Forness, 1996; Walker & Bullis, 1990).

The Role of Support Service Professionals in Implementing Tier 1 Interventions

At the primary prevention level, school psychologists, school social workers, and other support service professionals can provide indirect services to children by addressing the attitudes, beliefs, and behavior of adults (i.e., school faculty and staff). The roles and requisite skills of support service staff at Tier 1 are summarized in Table 2. The overall purpose of activities at Tier 1 is to establish buy-in by creating a shared vision for the school that is based on the principles and key elements of SWPBS. An essential prerequisite to accomplishing such change is articulating how the school climate will be different when an SWPBS approach has been adopted; this is particularly important in the early stages of implementation. Administrative support and competent training of the school leadership team are critical. Support service professionals can be instrumental in developing awareness and buy-in on the part of school administrative leaders, identifying potential members for the leadership team, and facilitating access to training.

Whether support service personnel or an administrator chairs the SWPBS leadership team, that role is critical to successful implementation; the chair can recruit leadership team members, set meeting agendas, facilitate meetings, lead efforts to obtain the necessary staff supports and agreements, and manage data related to implementation fidelity and student outcomes.

Tier 2 Secondary Prevention

Even with effective universal practices in place, up to 20% of students require further supports at either Tier 2 or at Tiers 2 and 3 (Sugai, Sprague, Horner, & Walker, 2000). This group of students is at risk for developing patterns of severe problem behavior for a variety of reasons, including poor peer relations, low academic achievement, or chaotic home environments (Lewis & Sugai, 1999). At Tier 2, SWPBS involves interventions that require little time to implement, incorporate similar features for all targeted students (e.g., systematic social skills instruction, a daily CICO system, or First Steps for Success), and typically involve extra Tier 1 interventions, such as additional monitoring and reinforcement (Fairbanks, Simonsen, & Sugai, 2008).

Table 2. Roles of Support Service Personnel to Support SWPBS and RTI Implementation

Tier 1 Primary Prevention
- Create a vision for the school based on the principles and four key elements of SWPBS and logic of RTI
- Develop awareness and buy-in on the part of school administrative leaders
- Identify and assemble potential members for the leadership team
- Coordinate with and among all school staff, administrators, community agencies, and families
- Facilitate access to training, initially for the leadership team and eventually of all school personnel
- Identify potential Tier 1 interventions to meet the needs of school personnel and students
- Advocate for staff time and resources to improve and sustain effective supports
- Enter, summarize, and present data demonstrating that high-quality universal interventions have been implemented with fidelity and have been effective or ineffective

Requisite skills for fulfilling these Tier 1 roles include expertise in SWPBS and RTI frameworks; group facilitation and consensus-building skills; data entry, analysis, and presentation skills; collaboration and mediation skills; and knowledge of evidence-based Tier 1 interventions.

Tier 2 Secondary Prevention
- Identify potential Tier 2 interventions to meet the needs of school personnel and students
- Provide consultation to the general education teachers who serve on Tier 2 support teams (e.g., student assistance and student support teams) and who deliver targeted interventions
- Identify the training needs of leadership team members, student assistance or student support teams
- Establish a training program or long-range professional development plan to address training needs
- Advocate the reallocation of staff time and resources to improve and sustain effective supports provided by school and district administrators
- Provide coaching and feedback (e.g., praise, encouragement, and error correction) as staff implement the steps involved in an intervention practice or program
- Conduct problem solving with staff, providing direct services as needed
- Coordinate with and among student assistance or student support teams, including family members
- Engage families to establish strong working relationships and develop trust
- Help the student assistance or student support team use data to determine when, and with whom, Tier 3 supports are needed
- Enter, summarize, and present data demonstrating that high-quality Tier 2 interventions have been implemented with fidelity and have been effective or ineffective

Requisite skills for fulfilling these Tier 2 roles include group facilitation and consensus-building skills; data entry, analysis, and presentation skills; collaboration and mediation skills; and knowledge of evidence-based Tier 2 intervention practices.

Tier 3 Tertiary Prevention
- Identify potential Tier 3 interventions to meet the needs of school personnel and students
- Work with students individually (e.g., teaching replacement behaviors)
- Identify and engage participants in a collaborative, participatory process that values buy-in and motivation
- Manage the data that will identify appropriate candidates for this level of support and that may be used to determine whether Tier 3 interventions are effective or ineffective
- Determine and address training needs; suggest reallocation of staff, time, or resources; and consider other systems changes that will improve and sustain the supports being implemented at this level

Table 2. (*continued*)

- Provide training and technical assistance regarding specific intervention procedures
- Facilitate wraparound planning, coordinating and brokering services that are needed but are beyond the ability of the school to provide
- Collect functional behavioral assessment (FBA) data; generate initial hypotheses regarding the function of the child's challenging behavior
- Oversee the initial writing, monitoring, and subsequent revisions of the IEP, BIP, or wraparound plan
- Encourage staff who implement the FBA, BIP, or wraparound plan, and intervene when the plans are not being adequately implemented
- Facilitate meetings to review and revise the plans that are ineffective

Requisite skills for fulfilling these Tier 3 roles include group facilitation and consensus-building skills; data entry, analysis, and presentation skills; collaboration and mediation skills; knowledge of community services; and knowledge and expertise in Tier 3 strategies, particularly FBA, BIP, and wraparound planning.

Guidelines for delivering Tier 2 interventions have become increasingly clear over the past few years. The foremost recommendation is that targeted interventions be administered efficiently and effectively with small groups of students (Filter et al., 2007; Scott & Eber, 2003). The SWPBS literature also suggests that Tier 2 interventions (a) be organized by a school-wide team that serves all at-risk students in the school, such as student assistance teams or student support teams; (b) be conducted in general education settings by general education personnel; (c) require limited time and staff involvement; and (d) be applied to students who have been exposed to but have not responded to high-quality Tier 1 interventions, yet who have not been identified as eligible for special education services (Scott & Eber, 2003).

Identification of Students Who Need Tier 2 Interventions

Consistent with the RTI model, the SWPBS leadership team needs a mechanism to identify *which* students may require Tier 2 interventions. Many elementary schools use ODRs to monitor student behavior and disciplinary action. One of the features of SWPBS is the systematic analysis and use of ODR data as a basis for making decisions regarding whether primary prevention strategies are working, and when, where, and for whom adjustments should be made. If evidence-based Tier 1 strategies are in place, ODR rates are a meaningful metric for identifying students whose lack of response to these supports establishes their eligibility for Tier 2 interventions. The cutoff for determining student eligibility for these interventions will depend on school-wide ODR data. The recommendation is to establish a data decision rule based on the distribution of ODR rates across the entire student population. An 80/20 cutoff is a general guideline; that is, the 20% of students with the highest ODR rates would be considered eligible for Tier 2 prevention supports. Schools create decision rules based on the number of ODRs in a given period, when SWPBS has been in place for a sufficient time to show desired effects. For example, if a school finds that 80% of students have one or fewer ODRs in a given month, a decision might be made that any student who receives more than one ODR in a single month would be eligible for Tier

2 support through targeted interventions. If a substantial proportion of the student body receives multiple ODRs in a given period, primary prevention practices should be examined and revised.

Although ODRs are effective for identifying students who exhibit externalizing (i.e., acting out) behaviors, ODR tracking is not adequate for identifying students with internalizing behavior problems, such as social withdrawal (Clonin, McDougal, Clark, & Davison, 2007; Nelson, Benner, Reid, & Epstein, 2002; Severson, Walker, Hope-Doolittle, Kratochwill, & Gresham, 2007). Sandomierski et al. (2007) recommend that schools using an RTI-based multitiered model also incorporate screening measures to identify *all* students who require support beyond Tier 1 (i.e., those who display internalizing problems as well as those with externalizing behavior problems). They suggest that a nomination process that asks teachers to rank the top externalizing and internalizing students might be useful, such as that used in Walker and Severson's (1990) Systematic Screening for Behavior Disorders (SSBD). Sandomierski et al. also urge intervention teams to assess students' academic proficiency because of the strong correlation between repeated problem behavior and academic deficiencies.

Tier 2 Strategies

Fairbanks et al. (2008) examined the research literature pertaining to Tier 2 interventions. They observed that practices with evidence supporting their use share some of the following features: (a) instruction on targeted skills, (b) self-monitoring strategies, (c) acknowledgement for appropriate behavior, (d) frequent performance feedback concerning target behaviors, and (e) peer tutoring. These features are included in a variety of commercial programs and curricula. The following four strategies illustrate Tier 2 support: social skills instruction, CICO, homework club, and First Step to Success.

Social skills instruction. Of the many types of social skill interventions, most that meet the criteria for a Tier 2 intervention teach discrete social skills using behavioral approaches or use a cognitive social problem–solving model. A variety of social skills curricula exist for elementary students, such as Promoting Alternative Thinking Strategies (PATHS; Kusche & Greenberg, 1994) and the PRePARE curriculum (Goldstein, 1988). Social skills instruction is delivered using direct instruction of discrete skills, modeling, role playing, and provision of feedback to students (Kerr & Nelson, 2010). Cognitive problem-solving models emphasize students' understanding of others' feelings as well as students' ability to use problem-solving strategies to resolve interpersonal problems. Lessons typically include information on the prevalence of violence or conflict and on ways of identifying and expressing feelings, managing anger, using conflict resolution, appreciating diversity, and coping with stress (Frey & Walker, 2007). Some social problem–solving programs involve peer mediation, in which student mediators are taught strategies to help settle disputes among their peers (Maag, 2007). As a result, mediators and disputants learn alternative skills to use when resolving conflicts. The peer mediator serves as an objective third party whose goal is to help peers find a solution that is "win-win" rather than "win-lose." Peer mediation uses an interest-based negotiation procedure along with communication and problem-solving strategies (Fisher & Ury, 1991). Some programs focus on training the entire student population in negotiation procedures; other programs involve training the peer mediators, who in turn train other students as conflicts arise (Peterson & Skiba, 2001).

Check-in/check-out systems. The purpose of a CICO system is to provide students with increased positive feedback and adult attention (Crone, Horner, & Hawken, 2004). There are many types of CICO interventions. For example, a daily behavior report card is a form that the student carries throughout the day for feedback on his or her behavior (Chafouleas, McDougal, Riley-Tillman, Panahon, & Hilt, 2005). Another type of CICO system that has demonstrated good results in recent studies is the Behavior Education Program (BEP; Crone et al., 2004; Hawken, MacLeod, & Rawlings, 2007). Students are referred to the BEP by their teacher, a parent, or other school personnel if increased behavior support is needed, as indicated by ODR or other data (in-school suspensions, time-outs, or SSBD). With the BEP system, students check in with a school staff member before school. The staff member provides the student with a daily progress report form that the student carries with him or her throughout the day. During check-in, students are asked to identify daily goals and are given feedback to encourage success. Students also receive reinforcement (e.g., praise, tokens) for checking in. Throughout the school day they are given feedback on their daily progress report, with specific praise for meeting behavioral expectations and corrective feedback if they are not meeting expectations. At the end of the school day, students return the daily progress report to the staff member to check out. Goals are evaluated and students receive feedback, along with reinforcement through praise and rewards, if they met their daily goals. Students then take their card home to be signed by a parent and bring it to school the following day.

Homework clubs. An emerging Tier 2 academic practice is the homework club, which acknowledges the connection between academic and behavioral difficulties. Students who are identified as having difficulty completing homework are enrolled in a club that meets regularly just before or after the school day. A teacher supervises, tutors, and encourages these students in a small group setting to complete their homework and improve their grades. Although no studies have been completed showing the effects of homework clubs on student academic or behavioral performance, research is under way on this topic (R. Horner, personal communication, August 10, 2007).

First Step to Success. First Step to Success is a Tier 2 early intervention program designed for children K–2 who display emerging externalizing behavior patterns (e.g., aggression toward others, oppositional defiant behavior, tantrumming, rule infractions, escalating confrontations with peers and adults; Walker et al., 1997). The child is the primary focus of the intervention; however, teachers, peers, and parents or caregivers participate in the intervention under the direction and supervision of a school behavioral coach, who has overall responsibility for coordinating the intervention. The First Step intervention requires 2 to 3 months to complete and is applied to individual students in a classroom. First Step consists of three modules, which are designed to be applied in concert with each other: *universal screening*; the *school module*; and the *home module* (Hops & Walker, 1988; Walker & Severson, 1990). The two primary goals of the First Step intervention are to teach the at-risk child to get along with others (teachers and peers) and to engage in assigned schoolwork in an appropriate, successful manner.

Tier 2 Evidence Base and Future Directions

With the exception of First Step to Success, many Tier 2 interventions do not yet have a solid research base to support their effectiveness (Walker et al., 1998; Carter & Horner, 2007). Therefore, schools and districts should closely monitor the implementation and outcomes of these programs (Sandomierski et al., 2007). The placement of some interventions within a multitiered system is somewhat arbitrary, which means that the RTI tenet that high-quality Tier 1 interventions have been applied prior to Tier 2 intervention is rarely met, and the research literature therefore is difficult to interpret. For example, social skills interventions may be applied as Tier 1, Tier 2, or Tier 3 interventions, depending on the context in which they are implemented (i.e., setting and population). Available reviews do not differentiate among applications by tier, and some practices, such as various approaches to social skills instruction (e.g., peer mediation, small group work, and mentoring programs), have been applied and evaluated with students at all tiers. Further complicating the interpretation of the Tier 2 evidence base is the fact that most studies have used teacher perceptions of behavior or standardized rating scales of social skills as the basis for screening participants, so it is unlikely that the screening criteria included non-responsiveness to evidence-based Tier 1 (primary prevention) practices. In fact, Sandomierski et al. (2007) suggest that high-quality Tier 1 practices that include behavioral instruction are rarely evident in schools.

Future research should focus on the development and evaluation of Tier 2 interventions within the context of a multitiered system that includes RTI. For example, little is known specifically about the effectiveness of Tier 2 interventions for students who were unresponsive to high-quality Tier 1 strategies. To evaluate the effectiveness of targeted interventions within the context of SWPBS and RTI, researchers would need to identify the characteristics and proportion of students who do and do not require additional support (Tier 3). Such data would further validate, or refine, the percentages of students served in each of the tiers presented in Figure 2. Other useful data would involve identifying contextual variables that contribute to the effectiveness of Tier 2 interventions, such as school climate or characteristics of the interventionist or student participants, as well as the percentage of students requiring Tier 3 supports. Moreover, researchers should articulate the processes involved in applying the intervention framework at different tiers and suggest how interventions can be modified to fit the needs of students.

The Role of Support Service Professionals in Implementing Tier 2 Interventions

At the secondary prevention level, school psychologists, school social workers, and other support service professionals still primarily offer indirect supports to students by helping school staff work effectively with students for whom universal supports alone are not adequate. The requisite skills and primary roles of support service staff at Tier 2 are summarized in Table 2. One of the main services these personnel can provide at Tier 2 is consultation to the staff who serve on Tier 2 support teams (e.g., student assistance and student support teams) and who deliver targeted interventions. Consultation can be provided in team meetings, which should involve problem solving to ensure that referred students have received high-quality Tier 1 supports and that student data have shown these supports to be ineffective.

At Tier 2, support service personnel begin to take a more direct role, working with teachers who need additional support more intensively and engaging families of children who not only require Tier 2 interventions, but eventually may require Tier 3 supports. Thus, with students for whom Tier 2 interventions prove to be insufficient, this collaboration may mark the informal beginning of the special education identification process.

Tier 3 Tertiary Prevention

Even with effective Tier 1 and Tier 2 supports in place, a small proportion (up to 5%) of students may be expected to need intensive individual supports at the tertiary level. Tier 3 interventions require substantially greater amounts of expertise, time, and other resources (Sugai, Sprague, et al., 2000). Students who have been unresponsive to efforts at Tiers 1 and 2 or those who engage in severe and dangerous behavior are candidates for interventions that involve direct, formalized, and individualized assessment and assessment-based intervention plans (Fairbanks et al., 2008; Scott & Eber, 2003). Although most teachers are committed to serving children with complex needs, they cannot, nor should they be expected to, implement and sustain effective interventions by themselves, especially for those at this tier (Eber et al., 2002). Teams that are constituted for each individual student must guide intensive interventions. These teams include general and special educators, administrators, support service personnel, paraprofessionals, and professionals from other relevant systems, such as mental health, child welfare, and juvenile justice professionals (core professional members may serve on multiple teams). Parents should also be on the team, along with the child, when appropriate (Crone & Horner, 2003; Eber et al., 2002; Lewis & Newcomer, 2002; Scott & Eber, 2003; Scott, Liaupsin, Nelson, & Conroy, 2004).

Identification of Students Who Need Tier 3 Interventions

Monitoring a student's response to interventions at Tier 2, as well as the fidelity with which interventions are applied, determines the need for Tier 3 intervention. Response to intervention clearly is the basis of this decision process, as the data used by the teams to determine the need for Tier 3 intervention come from assessments of individual progress during the application of Tier 2 interventions. As can be seen in Table 1, Tier 2 support strategies may be adjusted to fit individual needs, but to the extent that they depart from the basic protocol and are adapted to suit individual students, they no longer match the key features of Tier 2 interventions (efficiently and effectively delivered to small groups of students) and, in effect, evolve into Tier 3 supports.

Moreover, students who present chronic and intense levels of need should not be required to pass through a prolonged screening process in which they are exposed to less intensive (and probably inadequate) interventions before becoming eligible for Tier 3 support. Thus, since there are no quantitative criteria for deciding which students advance to this level of behavior support, decisions are made on an individual basis. Teams should establish time frames for determining when to consider moving to the most intensive level of intervention planning and delivery. However, as is the case at Tier 2, if a much higher proportion of the student body meets school criteria for Tier 3 supports than would be predicted, Tier 1 and Tier 2 intervention practices should be examined and revised.

Tier 3 Processes and Practices

Practices that illustrate Tier 3 support include behavior intervention and wraparound planning, which are often delivered within the context of special education services, and may actually be part of a child's IEP (Eber et al., 2008). Behavior intervention and wraparound planning are processes rather than discrete practices, and the interventions are more complex, involve more intervention agents, and are likely to span multiple life domains. Therefore, it is prudent to employ more intensive progress monitoring techniques for Tier 3 interventions (Sandomierski et al., 2007).

Behavior intervention planning. An effective BIP begins with a designated leader convening a team established for the student, acknowledging positive contributions and strengths of the child and family, and identifying specific goals and behaviors to be targeted by the plan. Next, the team completes a functional behavioral assessment in which problem behavior is systematically observed and recorded in its various contexts (i.e., settings, antecedent events, and outcomes) to establish how the problem behavior "works" for a student, that is, how it meets his or her needs, such as how to obtain peer or adult attention or to avoid undesired or difficult tasks (Umbreit, Ferro, Liaupsin, & Lane, 2007). Functional assessments are organized around routines the team determines are associated with high levels of problem behavior. The FBA concludes with a summary statement that describes the student's problem behavior; the settings, events, and conditions that typically precede the behavior; and the team's best guess regarding the consequences that maintain the behavior (Horner, Sugai, Todd, & Lewis-Palmer, 2000; O'Neill et al., 1997).

Although there is not one correct way to conduct an FBA, most intervention planning teams use a combination of direct and indirect tools and procedures to determine the function of problem behavior. Examples of direct tools include recording of multiple direct behavioral observations or using an antecedent–behavior–consequence (ABC) matrix to identify the settings in which challenging behaviors occur. Conducting structured teacher and parent interviews and gathering teacher rating scale data from multiple informants are examples of indirect procedures. Sandomierski et al. (2007) suggest that a brief FBA be conducted when a team agrees on the need for Tier 3 intervention, in addition to administering a behavioral or mental health rating scale. A variety of teacher rating scales, such as the SSBD (Walker & Severson, 1990), the Social Skills Improvement System (Gresham & Elliott, 2008), and the Child Behavior Checklist (Achenbach & Rescorla, 2001), can be used for this purpose. Sandomierski et al. also advise that the student's classroom teachers should have a larger role in problem solving at this level, as more in-depth data will be needed regarding daily performance.

Next, data collected by designated team members during the FBA process are evaluated and a BIP is developed. The team then generates a hypothesis regarding the functions of the behavior and the consequences that are maintaining or reinforcing it. After the team agrees on the function of the challenging behavior, they brainstorm prevention strategies, identify additional skills the child needs to learn, and develop new strategies for reinforcing replacement behavior and for discouraging problem behaviors. Horner, Sugai, and Horner (2000) indicate that many school personnel mistakenly believe the purpose of a BIP is to change a child's behavior. Although this is the ultimate outcome, the plan should focus on changing environmental contexts (i.e., physical environment, daily schedule, the timing of interactions with certain individuals) or the behaviors of adults or peers.

The BIPs typically contain the following components: (a) identification of a functionally equivalent and appropriate replacement behavior, (b) instruction necessary to teach this replacement behavior, (c) environmental modifications to bring about and reinforce the replacement behavior and discourage maladaptive challenging behavior, and (d) a systematic plan to monitor and evaluate the effects of the intervention (Crone & Horner, 2003; Kerr & Nelson, 2010; O'Neill et al., 1997; Umbreit et al., 2007). Fairbanks et al. (2008) indicate that most function-based interventions include some combination of the following elements:

- Providing teacher attention
- Teaching self-monitoring skills
- Teaching social skills
- Reducing task duration and breaking down task steps
- Interspersing instruction between preferred activities

The BIP is drafted by a designated team member after the meeting and distributed to all team members. This written plan clearly identifies which team members are responsible for which components of the plan. The team subsequently meets regularly to monitor data on targeted goals and behaviors, review progress, and make adjustments to the plan as needed. If the student has been identified as eligible for special education and related services, the BIP may be incorporated into his or her IEP.

Wraparound planning.   The wraparound planning process is a valuable addition to the orchestration of intervention systems in school and community settings for students with the most challenging behavior problems (Burns & Hoagwood, 2002; Eber et al., 2002, 2008). Although the ultimate goal of the wraparound planning process is to improve child functioning, it is also a tool for building collaborative relationships and support networks among students, their families, teachers, and other caregivers (Eber et al., 2008). A wraparound plan includes not only services provided within the school (e.g., special education, functional behavioral assessments, social skills training, teacher consultation, and parent training) but also those offered in the community (e.g., respite care, mentoring, parent supports, mental health interventions, basic assistance in housing, transportation, job assistance, child care, or healthcare services).

The wraparound planning process is based on two related assumptions. The first is that high-quality community services and supports are often difficult for children and families to access. The second assumption is that any single service delivery system, such as education, child welfare, juvenile justice, or mental health, lacks the perspective, resources, and expertise to effectively intervene as the sole intervention planning and delivery agent with children who exhibit the most challenging behavior problems.

Wraparound planning is structured around values-based elements and guidelines. These values include providing services that are child centered and family focused, community based, and culturally competent (Eber & Keenan, 2004). These elements embrace strengths-based approaches (building on child and family strengths rather than merely targeting deficits), respect the needs and preferences of children and families, and promote strong community collaboration. All these elements are consistent with the principles of SWPBS. According to Eber et al. (2002), effective wraparound plans base services on local community resources, which include community agencies and supports. Plans are individualized for each child and family; plans are based on children's strengths, not just on needs; and services are culturally competent and include families as full and active partners. A key element of wraparound planning is its flexibility in funding and providing services. Agencies collaborating in the wraparound process agree to pool resources (including funds) and to bring services to the child and family rather than relying on traditional office visits for service delivery.

Eber et al. (2002, 2008) also articulated steps involved in wraparound planning. This process begins by engaging a student's family members and members of his or her natural support network (e.g., extended family, friends) to learn about the student's ideas, frustrations, views, values, and hopes. It focuses on strengths in developing a mission statement for the planning team. The team then uses this information to summarize the child's and family's needs across pertinent life domains and prioritize those needs. Next the team identifies necessary actions for meeting these needs, including identifying who is responsible for completing the action. Next, the plan is documented, and subsequent meetings are held to evaluate, refine, and monitor progress toward its goals. Finally, the team plans the steps required to achieve the transition out of the wraparound process. Because wraparound plans encompass life domains beyond the school and involve other agencies or resources, they are not likely to be included in a special education student's IEP, but they do occur simultaneously. Therefore, it is important that IEPs and wraparound plans be coordinated, and that members of each team be familiar with both plans.

Tier 3 Evidence Base and Future Directions

As is true of Tier 2 interventions, consumers of the Tier 3 research base cannot assume that participants in effectiveness studies have been screened for exposure to evidence-based practices at Tier 1 and Tier 2. Despite this uncertainty, the evidence base related to practices at Tier 3 is quite informative.

A substantial body of research has documented the effectiveness of BIPs, when they are applied with adequate fidelity, duration, and intensity (e.g., Blair, Umbreit, & Bos, 1999; Dunlap et al., 1993; Gable, Quinn, Rutherford, & Howell, 1998; Kerr & Nelson, 2010; McEvoy & Welker, 2000; Scott, Liaupsin, & Nelson, 2002; Sugai, Sprague et al., 2000; Todd, Horner, Sugai, & Sprague, 1999; Turnbull et al., 2002). As a result, many leaders in the field of behavior disorders have argued for the use of this process for children exhibiting challenging behavior in school contexts (Dunlap et al. 2006; Fox, Conroy, & Heckaman, 1998; Horner, Sugai, & Horner, 2000). However, the usability and feasibility of behavior intervention planning also has been questioned (Conroy et al., 2002; Van Acker, Boreson, Gable, & Potterton, 2005). Van Acker et al. evaluated the technical adequacy of intervention plans across a statewide initiative and concluded that approximately half of the plans "contained multiple shortcomings that would likely result in poorly designed and ineffective behavior intervention planning" (p. 51). Specifically, 25% of the plans failed to identify the function of the behavior, and 61% indicated no attempt to verify the function prior to the development of a BIP. Simply stated, whether school personnel can realistically lead the process without the assistance of an outside professional is unknown (Scott, Liaupsin, Nelson, & McIntyre, 2005; Scott, McIntyre, Liaupsin, Nelson, & Conroy, 2004).

Only two reviews of the wraparound approach were found. Burchard, Bruns, and Burchard (2002) identified 15 studies evaluating the effectiveness of wraparound planning and concluded that, although the behavioral changes associated with the approach are impressive, the evidence base is inconclusive because of the lack of tools available to measure the fidelity of implementation and the limited rigor of current studies. Ziguras and Stuart (2000) conducted a meta-analysis on 44 studies involving case management interventions in mental health settings and concluded that case management was more effective than usual care and led to small-to-moderate improvements in the effectiveness of mental health services. Unlike behavior intervention planning, research suggests that school-based teams are able to implement the wraparound planning process with high levels of fidelity in schools (Epstein et al., 2005; Nordess, 2005).

Future research efforts should focus on increasing both the intervention options available for school personnel at Tier 3 and the extent to which existing approaches can be implemented efficiently and effectively with existing school resources. Although the research has not been carried out in the context of a multitiered system and RTI framework, a useful knowledge base exists that is related to child characteristics that influence intervention effectiveness for students with the most severe behavior problems. Specifically, research on family interventions at Tier 3 suggests that roughly 40% of families can be classified as nonresponders, some because they never begin and others because they do not complete or engage in the intervention process (Reid, Webster-Stratton, & Hammond, 2003). Beauchaine, Webster-Stratton, and Reid (2005) combined data from six randomized clinical trials to evaluate the moderators, mediators, and predictors of outcomes for interventions to treat early-onset conduct problems. They found that marital adjustment; maternal depression; paternal substance abuse; child comorbid anxiety/depression; and critical, harsh, and ineffective parenting predicted and mediated outcomes. In a related line of research, Patterson and Chamberlain (1994) conducted systematic studies of parental resistance and concluded that parental motivation to change is a critical yet often neglected ingredient in improving parenting practices. Thus, Tier 3 interventions that engage parents and remove the most common barriers to intervention responsiveness have promise and are consistent with the principles of SWPBS.

The Role of Support Service Professionals in Implementing Tier 3 Interventions

Many of the roles that school psychologists, school social workers, and other support service professionals may assume in the implementation of SWPBS at Tier 3 are similar to those in the first two tiers. The main distinction in roles at this tier, however, is that the support worker is now working with a team for which the members are unique to the student and, due to expertise that may not be shared by other personnel in the school, will likely need to provide direct services to the child. The requisite skills and primary roles of support service staff at Tier 3 are summarized in Table 2.

Within the context of wraparound services, support service professionals may serve as service coordinators, coordinating and brokering services that are needed but are beyond the ability of the school to provide. Coordinating services that are available in the community obviously requires not only knowledge of those services, but also the ability to forge positive relationships between the service providers and the school. The flexibility of support service personnel to manage different roles and their knowledge of community agencies and service providers make them logical choices to lead wraparound service coordination.

Support service providers are, in fact, likely to be the school staff responsible for leading behavior support or wraparound planning teams, in addition to chairing special education eligibility and IEP teams. In general, the team leader is the point person whose job is to orchestrate and support a unified and comprehensive intervention plan. It is likely that support service personnel will have membership in FBA, wraparound, and IEP teams. In any case, they may be in the best position to foster communication among teams and to coordinate the actions of these teams.

The support service professional also may be the most appropriate school staff person to provide direct services to students at Tier 3. Although the provider may work directly with students at Tier 2 (e.g., providing social skills instruction to a small group), at Tier 3 he or she may work with students individually (e.g., teaching replacement behaviors), particularly in the early stages of intervention when these skills may be most effectively introduced outside the classroom.

FUTURE DIRECTIONS FOR SWPBS AND RTI APPROACHES

Over the past decade, evidence supporting the effectiveness of SWPBS has been accumulating; at the same time, practical guidance for schools wishing to adopt the approach has increased. Nevertheless, it is still in the early stages of development. In addition to the need to build the knowledge base within each tier, the feasibility and effectiveness of prevention approaches must be examined within the context of SWPBS and RTI frameworks.

Integrating Tier 1, 2, and 3 Supports

Future research efforts should be directed at improving the integration between Tiers 1, 2, and 3. For example, the extent to which the percentages in Figure 2 hold up across schools needs to be examined. Whether these percentages are consistent across varying levels of intervention fidelity in different contexts (e.g., school climate or characteristics of the interventionist or student participants) is not yet known.

Additionally, research on Tier 2 and Tier 3 interventions that are implemented within the context of SWPBS and RTI frameworks would be beneficial. Recent research makes it clear that contextual factors at Tier 1 can either facilitate or inhibit the effectiveness of supports at Tiers 2 and 3 (Eber et al., 2002; Fairbanks et al., 2008; Payne, Scott, & Conroy, 2007; Scott, 2004). For example, it seems likely that the presence or absence of exposure to practices at lower tiers of support would have a measurable impact on overall intervention effectiveness. These lines of research hold promise for the further development of processes and procedures that could help schools determine which students should progress to higher levels of support and which interventions are the most promising at various tiers.

Integrating Behavioral and Academic Domains Into a Unified Framework

Confusion regarding the relationship between SWPBS and RTI has resulted because PBIS is perceived as an approach for promoting students' progress in the social domain and RTI is perceived as a process for identifying students with a specific learning disability through assessments of their response to academic interventions. Recent conceptions have attempted to build a more cohesive model showing that that SWPBS and RTI are closely linked, and in fact the SWPBS model has been expanded to address both behavioral and academic dimensions of student success (Darch & Kame'enui, 2004; Lane, 2004; Sandomierski et al., 2007; Witt, VanDerHeyden, & Gilbertson, 2004). However, to the extent that researchers and practitioners separate SWPBS and RTI, a chasm exists. This chasm is counterproductive and may lead to schools adopting separate systems to address academic and behavioral domains, or to adopt systems that address only one. Although no studies have confirmed this assertion, it seems that a dual domain (e.g., academic and behavioral) system to address student needs would be more effective than a single domain system. It may be that a unified, integrated terminology is necessary to move the field forward and to derive the maximum benefit from multitiered systems of support.

CONCLUSION

School-wide PBIS is a unique approach for supporting students' social and academic success by promoting desired behavior and minimizing or eliminating undesirable behavior. To address social behavior, SWPBS combines effective strategies from applied behavior analysis, cognitive psychology, and social learning theory with strategies for promoting adult learning—such as modeling behaviors, providing choices for self-direction, soliciting buy-in, and assessing motivation and readiness—through systemic or organizational change. When properly executed, the changes associated with the implementation of SWPBS in elementary schools is aptly characterized as building the capacity of the school to support and respond to the full range of student behavior. The ultimate challenge is to sustain these systemic changes and make them an ongoing feature of the school culture.

The SWPBS framework consists of practices and processes that direct attention not only to effective interventions for individuals but also to the contextual factors within schools that promote or discourage their adoption and effective implementation. School-wide PBIS is being embraced by and integrated into a variety of other disciplines, including juvenile justice, mental health, school psychology, and social work (Crone & Horner, 2003; Frey, Lingo, & Nelson, 2008; Horner et al., 2000; Nelson, Sprague, Jolivette, Smith, & Tobin, 2009). Because SWPBS reduces the strain that student misbehavior places on the school system, it allows schools to dedicate more time, energy, and resources to address the needs of individual students and provides an efficient, equitable way to distribute limited resources (Hieneman, Dunlap, & Kincaid, 2005). School-wide PBIS and RTI offer unique opportunities for school support personnel to assume new and expanded roles in adopting, improving, maintaining, and evaluating systemic changes in school climate and procedures. The ultimate goal of such changes, of course, is better academic and social outcomes for all children.

REFERENCES

Achenbach, T. M., & Rescorla, L. A. (2001). *Manual for the Achenbach System of Empirically Based Assessment school age forms and profiles.* Burlington, VT: University of Vermont, Research Center for Children, Youth, and Families. Retrieved from http://www.aseba.org

Alberto, P. A., & Troutman, A. C. (2009). *Applied behavior analysis for teachers* (8th ed.). Upper Saddle River, NJ: Pearson/Merrill/Prentice Hall.

Allen-Meares, P. (2004). An ecological perspective of social work services in the schools. In P. Allen-Meares (Ed.), *Social Work Services in Schools* (4th ed., pp. 71–94). Boston: Allyn and Bacon.

Batsche, G. M., Elliott, J., Graden, J. L., Grimes, J., Kovaleski, J. F., & Prasse, D. (2005). Response to intervention: Policy considerations and implementation. Alexandria, VA: National Association of State Directors of Special Education.

Beauchaine, T. P., Webster-Stratton, C., & Reid, M. J. (2005). Mediators, moderators, and predictors of one-year outcomes among children treated for early-onset conduct problems: a latent growth curve analysis. *Consulting and Clinical Psychology, 73,* 371–388.

Blair, K. C., Umbreit, J., & Bos, C. S. (1999). Using functional behavioral assessment and children's preferences to improve the behavior of young children with behavioral disorders. *Behavioral Disorders, 24,* 151–166.

Bradley, R., Doolittle, J., Lopez, F., Smith, J., & Sugai, G. (2007, January). *Discipline: Improved understanding and implementation.* OSEP Part B Regulations Regional Implementation Meeting: Building the Legacy IDEA 2004. U.S. Department of Education, Washington, DC.

Bradshaw, C., Mitchell, M., & Leaf, P. (2009). Examining the effects of school-wide positive behavioral interventions and supports on student outcomes: Results from a randomized controlled effectiveness trial in elementary schools. *Journal of Positive Behavior Interventions OnLine First.* doi:10.1177/1098300709334798.

Briar-Lawson, K., Lawson, H. A., Collier, C., & Joseph, A. (1997). School-linked comprehensive services: Promising beginnings, lessons learned, and future challenges. *Social Work in Education, 19,* 136–148.

Burchard, J. D., Bruns, E. J., & Burchard, S. N. (2002). The wraparound approach. In B. J. Burns & K. Hoagwood (Eds.), *Community treatment for youth: Evidence-based interventions for severe emotional and behavioral disorders* (pp. 69–90). New York: Oxford University Press.

Burns, B. J., & Hoagwood, K. (2002). *Community treatment for youth: Evidence-based interventions for severe emotional and behavioral disorders.* New York: Oxford University Press.

Bye, L. (2007). School social work with families. In M. A. L. Bye (Ed.), *School social work: theory to practice* (pp. 122–140). Belmont, CA: Thompson Brooks/Cole.

Carter, D. R., & Horner, R. H. (2007). Adding functional behavioral assessment to First Step to Success: A case study. *Journal of Positive Behavior Interventions, 9,* 229–238.

Chafouleas, S. M., McDougal, J. L., Riley-Tillman, T. C., Panahon, C. J., & Hilt, A. M. (2005). What do daily behavior report cards (DBRCs) measure? An initial comparison of DBRCs with direct observation for off-task behavior. *Psychology in the Schools, 42,* 669–676.

Clark, R. M. (1988). *Critical factors in why disadvantaged children succeed or fail in school.* New York: Academy for Educational Development.

Clonin, S. M., McDougal, J. L., Clark, K., & Davison, S. (2007). Use of office discipline referrals in school-wide decision-making: A practical example. *Psychology in the Schools, 44,* 19–27.

Conroy, M., Katsiyannis, A., Clark, D., Gable, D., Gable, R. A., & Fox, J. M. (2002). State Office of Education Practices: Implementing the IDEA disciplinary provisions. *Behavioral Disorders, 27,* 98–108.

Coyne, M., Simonsen, B., & Faggella-Luby, M. (2008). Cooperating initiatives: Supporting behavioral and academic improvement through a systems approach. *Teaching Exceptional Children, 40,* 54–59.

Crone, D. A., & Horner, R. H. (2003). *Building positive behavior support systems in schools: Functional behavioral assessment.* New York: Guilford Press.

Crone, D. A., Horner, R. H., & Hawken, L. S. (2004). *Responding to problem behavior in schools: The Behavior Education Program.* New York: Guilford Press.

Darch, C. B., & Kame'enui, E. J. (2004). *Instructional classroom management: A proactive approach to behavior management* (2nd ed.). Upper Saddle River, NJ: Merrill/Prentice Hall.

Dryfoos, J. G. (1998a). *A look at community schools in 1998.* New York: National Center for Schools and Communities, Fordham University.

Dryfoos, J. G. (1998b). School-based health centers in the context of education reform. *Journal of School Health, 68,* 404–408.

Dryfoos, J. G., Brindis, C., & Kaplan, D. (1996). Research and evaluation in school-based health care. In L. Juszczak & M. Fisher (Eds.), *Adolescent medicine: State of the art health care in schools* (pp. 207–220). Philadelphia: Hanley & Belfus.

Dunlap, G., Kern, L., dePerczel, M., Clarke, S., Wilson, D., Childs, K. E., et al. (1993). Functional analysis of classroom variables for students with emotional and behavioral disorders. *Behavioral Disorders, 18,* 275–291.

Dunlap, G., Strain, P., Fox, L., Carta, J. J., Conroy, J., & Smith, B. J. (2006). Prevention and intervention with young children's challenging behavior: Perspectives regarding current knowledge. *Behavioral Disorders, 32,* 29–45.

Dupper, D. R., & Poertner, J. (1997). Public schools and the revitalization of impoverished communities: School-linked, family resource centers. *Social Work, 42,* 415–422.

Eber, L., Breen, K., Rose, J., Unizycki, R. M., & London, T. H. (2008). Wraparound as a tertiary level intervention for students with emotional/behavioral needs. *Teaching Exceptional Children, 40*(6), 16–22.

Eber, L., & Keenan, S. (2004). Collaboration with other agencies: Wraparound and systems of care for children and youths with emotional and behavioral disorders. In R. B. Rutherford, M. M. Quinn, & S. R. Mathur (Eds.), *Handbook of research in emotional and behavioral disorders* (pp. 502–516). New York: Guilford Press.

Eber, L., Sugai, G., Smith, C., & Scott, T. (2002). Wraparound and positive behavioral interventions and supports in the schools. *Journal of Emotional and Behavioral Disorders, 10,* 171–181.

Eccles, J. S. (1999). The development of children ages 6 to 14. *The Future of Children, 9,* 30–44.

Epstein, J. L., Coates, L., Salinas, K. C., Sanders, M. G., & Simon, B. S. (Eds.). (1997). *School, family and community partnerships*. San Francisco: Corwin Press.

Epstein, M. H., Nordess, P. D., Gallagher, K., Nelson, R. R., Lewis, L., & Scherepf, S. (2005). School as the entry point: Assessing adherence to the basic tenets of the wraparound approach. *Behavioral Disorders, 30,* 85–93.

Fairbanks, S., Simonsen, B., & Sugai, G. (2008). Classwide secondary and tertiary tier practices and systems. *Teaching Exceptional Children, 40*(6), 44–52.

Filter, K. J., McKenna, M. K., Benedict, E. A., Horner, R. H., Todd, A. W., & Watson, J. (2007). Check in/Check out: A post-hoc evaluation of an efficient, secondary-level targeted intervention for reducing problem behaviors in schools. *Education and Treatment of Children, 30,* 69–84.

Fischer, R. L. (2003). School-based family support: Evidence from an exploratory field study. *Families in Society, 84,* 339–348.

Fisher, R. A., & Ury, W. (1991). *Getting to yes* (2nd ed.). New York: Penguin Books.

Fox, J., Conroy, M., & Heckaman, K. (1998). Research issues in functional assessment of the challenging behaviors of students with emotional and behavioral disorders. *Behavioral Disorders, 24,* 26–33.

Frey, A. J., Lingo, A., & Nelson, C. M. (2008). Positive behavior support: A call for leadership. *Children & Schools, 30,* 5–14.

Frey, A. J., & Walker, H. (2007). School social work at the school organization level. In L. Bye & M. Alvarez (Eds.), *School social work: theory to practice* (pp. 82–104). Belmont, CA: Brooks/Cole.

Gable, R. A., Quinn, M. M., Rutherford, R. B., Jr., & Howell, K. (1998). Addressing problem behaviors in schools: Use of functional assessments and behavior intervention plans. *Preventing School Failure, 42,* 106–119.

Goldstein, A. P. (1988). *The Prepare curriculum: Teaching prosocial competencies.* Champaign, IL: Research Press.

Gresham, F. M., & Elliott, S. N. (2008). *Social Skills Improvement System.* Minneapolis, MN: NCS Pearson.

Hanson, J. L., Jeppson, E. S., & Johnson, B. H. (1993). Promoting family-centered services in health care and beyond. *Family Resource Coalition Report, 3,* 12–14.

Hawken, L. S., MacLeod, K. S., & Rawlings, L. (2007). Effects of the Behavior Education Program on problem behavior with elementary school students. *Journal of Positive Behavior Interventions, 9,* 94–101.

Haynes, N. M., Emmons, C. L, Gebreyesus, S., & Ben-Avie, M. (1996). The School Development Program evaluation process. In J. P. Comer, N. M. Haynes, E. T. Joyner, & M. Ben-Avie (Eds.), *Rallying the whole village: The Comer Process for reforming education* (pp. 123–146). New York: Teachers College Press.

Henderson, A. T., & Mapp, K. L. (2002). *A new wave of evidence: The impact of school, family, and community connections on student achievement.* Austin, TX: Southwest Educational Development Laboratory.

Hieneman, M., Dunlap, G., & Kincaid, D. (2005). Positive support strategies for students with behavioral disorders in general education settings. *Psychology in the Schools, 42,* 779–794.

Hodgkinson, H. L. (1989). *The same client: The demographics of education and service delivery systems.* Washington, DC: Institute for Educational Leadership.

Hops, H., & Walker, H. (1988). CLASS: Contingencies for Learning Academic and Social Skills. Seattle, WA: Educational Achievement Systems.

Horner, R. H., & Sugai, G. (2009, July). Is school-wide positive behavior support an evidence-based practice? Retrieved September 27, 2009, from http://www.pbis.org/files/101007evidencebase4pbs.pdf

Horner, R. H., Sugai, G. M., & Horner, H. F. (2000). A school-wide approach to student discipline. *School Administrator, 57,* 20–23.

Horner, R. H., Sugai, G., Smolkowski, K., Todd, A., Nakasato, J., & Esperanza, J. (2009). A randomized control trial of school-wide positive behavior support in elementary schools. *Journal of Positive Behavior Interventions, 11,* 133–144.

Horner, R. H., Sugai, G., Todd, A. W., & Lewis-Palmer, T. (2000). Elements of behavior support plans: A technical brief. *Exceptionality, 8,* 205–215.

Horner, R. H., Sugai, G., Todd, A. W., & Lewis-Palmer, T. (2005). School-wide positive behavior support: An alternative approach to discipline in schools. In L. Bambara & L. Kern (Eds.), *Individualized supports for students with problem behaviors: Designing positive behavior plans* (pp. 359–390). New York: Guilford Press.

Horner, R. H., Todd, A. W., Lewis-Palmer, T., Irvin, L. K., Sugai, G., & Boland, J. (2004). The School-wide Evaluation Tool (SET): A research instrument for assessing school-wide positive behavior support. *Journal of Positive Behavior Interventions, 6,* 3–12.

Illback, R. J., & Kalafat, J. (1995). Initial evaluation of a school-based integrative service program: Kentucky Family Resource and Youth Services Centers. *Special Services in the Schools, 1,* 139–163.

Individuals with Disabilities Education Improvement Act of 2004, P. L. 108-446 § 614 (b)(2)–(3), § 614 (b)(6)(A); 20 U.S.C. § 1400 *et seq.*

Kerr, M. M., & Nelson, C. M. (2010). *Strategies for addressing behavior problems in the classroom* (6th ed.). Upper Saddle River, NJ: Pearson Education.

Kincaid, D., Childs, K., Blase, K. A., & Wallace, F. (2007). Identifying barriers and facilitators in implementing schoolwide positive behavior support. *Journal of Positive Behavior Interventions, 9,* 174–184.

Kusche, C. A. & Greenberg, M. T. (1994). *The PATHS Curriculum.* Seattle, WA: Developmental Research and Programs.

Landrum, T. J., & Kauffman, J. M. (2006). Behavioral approaches to classroom management. In C. M. Evertson & C. S. Weinstein (Eds.), *Handbook of classroom management: Research, practice, and contemporary issues* (pp. 47–71). Mahwah, NJ: Erlbaum.

Landrum, T. J., Tankersley, M., & Kauffman, J. M. (2003). What is special about special education for students with emotional or behavioral disorders? *The Journal of Special Education, 37,* 148–156.

Lane, K. L. (2004). Academic instruction and tutoring interventions for students with emotional and behavioral disorders: 1990 to the present. In R. B. Rutherford, M. M. Quinn, & S. R. Mathur (Eds.), *Handbook of research in emotional and behavioral disorders* (pp. 462–486). New York: Guilford Press.

Lewis, T. J., Hudson, S., Richter, M., & Johnson, N. (2004). Scientifically supported practices in emotional and behavioral disorders: A proposed approach and brief review of current practices. *Behavioral Disorders, 29,* 247–259.

Lewis, T., & Newcomer, L. L. (2002). Examining the efficacy of school-based consultation: Recommendations for improving outcomes. *Child and Family Behavior Therapy, 24,* 165–181.

Lewis, T. J., & Sugai, G. (1999). Effective behavior support: A systems approach to proactive school-wide management. *Focus on Exceptional Children, 31,* 1–24.

Maag, J. W. (2007). Social skills training for students with emotional and behavioral disorders: A review of reviews. *Behavior Disorders, 32,* 5–17.

MacMillan, D. L., Gresham, F. M., & Forness, S. R. (1996). Full inclusion: An empirical perspective. *Behavior Disorders, 21,* 145–159.

McDonald, L., Billingham, S., Conrad, P., Morgan, A., Nina, O., & Payton, E. (1997). Families and Schools Together (FAST): Integrating community development with clinical strategy. *Families in Society, 78,* 140–155.

McEvoy, A., & Welker, R. (2000). Antisocial behavior, academic failure, and school climate: A critical review. *Journal of Emotional Behavioral Disorders, 8,* 130–140.

McIntosh, K., Chard, D. J., Boland, J. B., & Horner, R. H. (2006). Demonstration of combined efforts in schoolwide academic and behavioral systems and incidence of reading and behavior. *Journal of Positive Behavior Interventions, 8,* 146–154.

McIntosh, K., Horner, R. H., & Sugai, G. (2009). Sustainability of systems-level evidence-based practices in schools: Current knowledge and future directions. In W. Sailor, G. Dunlap, G. Sugai, & R. Horner (Eds.), *Handbook of positive behavior support.* New York: Springer.

Mercer, C. D., & Mercer, A. R. (2005). *Teaching students with learning problems* (7th ed.). Upper Saddle River, NJ: Pearson/Merrill/Prentice Hall.

National Governor's Association Task Force on School Readiness. (2005). *Building the foundation for bright futures: Final report of the NGA Task Force on School Readiness; and companion piece, Building the foundation for bright futures: A governor's guide to school readiness.* Retrieved July 28, 2009, from http://www.nga.org/Files/pdf/0501TaskForceReadiness.pdf

Nelson, C. M., Sprague, J. R., Jolivette, K., Smith, C. R., & Tobin, T. J. (2009). Positive behavior support in alternative education, community-based mental health, and juvenile justice settings, In W. Sailor, G. Dunlap, G. Sugai, & R. Horner (Eds.), *Handbook of positive behavior support* (pp. 465–496). New York: Springer.

Nelson, J. R., Benner, G. J., Reid, R. C., & Epstein, M. H. (2002). Convergent validity of office discipline referrals with the CBCL-TRF. *Journal of Emotional and Behavioral Disorders, 10,* 181–188.

No Child Left Behind Act of 2001, 20 U.S.C. § 16301 *et seq.*

Nordess, P. D. (2005). A comparison of school-based and community-based adherence to wraparound during family planning meetings. *Education and the Treatment of Children, 28,* 308–320.

Office of Special Education Programs (OSEP). (2009a). The four key elements of positive behavior support. Retrieved September 27, 2009, from the OSEP Technical Assistance Center on Positive Behavioral Interventions and Supports website: http://www.pbis.org

Office of Special Education Programs (OSEP). (2009b). Academic and behavioral dimensions of school-wide positive behavior support. Retrieved September 27, 2009, from the OSEP Technical Assistance Center on Positive Behavioral Interventions and Supports website: http://www.pbis.org

Office of Special Education Programs (OSEP). (2009c). School-wide positive behavior support. Retrieved September 27, 2009, from the OSEP Technical Assistance Center on Positive Behavioral Interventions and Supports website: http://www.pbis.org

O'Neill, R. E., Horner, R. H., Albin, R. W., Sprague, J. R., Storey, K., & Newton, J. S. (1997). *Functional assessment and program development for problem behavior: A practical handbook* (2nd ed.). Pacific Grove, CA: Brooks/Cole.

Patterson, G. R., & Chamberlain, P. (1994). A functional analysis of resistance during parent training therapy. *Clinical Psychology: Science and Practice, 1,* 53–70.

Payne, L. D., Scott, T. M., & Conroy, M. (2007). A school-based examination of the efficacy of function-based intervention. *Behavioral Disorders, 32,* 158–174.

Peterson, R. L., & Skiba, R. L. (2001). Creating school climates that prevent school violence. *Social Studies, 92,* 167–175.

Quinn, J. (2007). Community schools: New roles for social work practitioners. In M. A. L. Bye (Ed.), *School Social Work: Theory to Practice* (pp. 122–140). Belmont, CA: Thompson Brooks/Cole.

Reid, M. J., Webster-Stratton, C., & Hammond, M. (2003). Follow-up of children who received the Incredible Years intervention for oppositional defiant disorder: Maintenance and prediction of 2-year outcome. *Behavior Therapy, 34,* 471–491.

Rosenshine, B. (2008). Systematic instruction. In T. L. Good (Ed.), *21st century education: A reference handbook: Vol. 1* (pp. 235–243). Thousand Oaks, CA: SAGE.

Sandomierski, T., Kincaid, D., & Algozzine, B. (2007). *Response to intervention and positive behavior support: Brothers from different mothers or sisters with different misters?* Retrieved August 10, 2007, from http://www.pbis.org

Scott, T. M. (2004). Making behavior intervention planning decisions in a school wide system of positive behavior support. *Focus on Exceptional Children, 36,* 1–18.

Scott, T. M., & Eber, L. (2003). Functional assessment and wraparound as systemic school processes: Primary, secondary, and tertiary systems examples. *Journal of Positive Behavior Interventions, 5,* 131–143.

Scott, T. M., Liaupsin, C. J., & Nelson, C. M. (2002). *Behavior intervention planning: Using the functional assessment data.* Longmont, CO: Sopris West.

Scott, T. M., Liaupsin, C., Nelson, C. M., & McIntyre, J. (2005). Team-based functional behavior assessment as a proactive public school process: A descriptive analysis of current barriers. *Journal of Behavioral Education, 14,* 57–71.

Scott, T. M., McIntyre, J., Liaupsin, C., Nelson, C. M., & Conroy, M. (2004). An examination of functional behavior assessment in public school settings: Collaborative teams, experts, and methodology. *Behavioral Disorders, 29,* 384–395.

Scott, T. M., Nelson, C. M., & Liaupsin, C. J. (2001). Effective instruction: The forgotten component in preventing school violence. *Education and Treatment of Children, 24,* 309–322.

Scott, T. M., & Shearer-Lingo, A. (2002).The effects of reading fluency instruction on the academic and behavioral success of middle school students in a self-contained EBD classroom. *Preventing School Failure, 46,* 167–173.

Severson, H. H., Walker, H. W., Hope-Doolittle, J., Kratochwill, T. R., & Gresham, F. M. (2007). Proactive, early screening to detect behaviorally at-risk students: Issues, approaches, emerging innovations, and professional practices. *Journal of School Psychology, 45,* 193–223.

Simonsen, B. (2010). School-wide positive behavior support. In M. M. Kerr & C. M. Nelson, *Strategies for addressing behavior problems in the classroom* (6th ed., pp. 36–68). Upper Saddle River, NJ: Pearson Education.

Simonsen, B., Fairbanks, S., Briesch, A., Myers, D., & Sugai, G. (2008). Evidence-based practices in classroom management: Considerations for research to practice. *Education and Treatment of Children, 31,* 351–380.

Simonsen, B., & Sugai, G. (2007). Using school-wide data systems to make decisions efficiently and effectively. *School Psychology Forum, 1,* 46–58.

Simonsen, B., Sugai, G., & Negron, M. (2008). Schoolwide positive behavior supports: Primary systems and practices. *Teaching Exceptional Children, 40,* 32–42.

Spaulding, S. A., Irving, L. K., Horner, R. H., May, S. L., Emeldi, M., Tobin, T. J., et al. (in press). School-wide social-behavioral climate, student problem behavior, and related administrative decisions: Empirical patterns from 1,510 schools nationwide. *Journal of Positive Behavioral Interventions*.

Sugai, G., & Horner, R. (1999). Discipline and behavioral support: Practices, pitfalls, and promises. *Effective School Practices, 17*(4), 10–22.

Sugai, G., & Horner, R. H. (2002). The evolution of discipline practices: School-wide positive behavior supports. *Child and Family Behavior Therapy, 24,* 23–50.

Sugai, G., & Horner, R. H. (2006). A promising approach for expanding and sustaining school-wide positive behavior support. *School Psychology Review, 35,* 245–259.

Sugai, G., & Horner, R. H. (2007). Is school-wide positive behavior support an evidence-based practice? Retrieved August 14, 2007, from www.pbis.org

Sugai, G., & Horner, R. H. (2008). What we know and need to know about preventing problem behavior in schools. *Exceptionality, 16,* 67–77.

Sugai, G., Horner, R. H., Dunlap, G., Hieneman, M., Lewis, T. J., Nelson, C. M., et al. (2000). Applying positive behavior support and functional behavioral assessment in schools. *Journal of Positive Behavior Interventions, 2,* 131–143.

Sugai, G., Horner, R. H., & Gresham, F. (2002). Behaviorally effective school environments. In M. R. Shinn, H. M. Walker, & G. Stoner (Eds.), *Interventions for academic and behavior problems II: Preventive and remedial approaches* (pp. 315–350). Bethesda, MD: National Association of School Psychologists.

Sugai, G., & Simonsen, B. (2007). *Connecticut school-wide positive behavior support coaches training.* Retrieved June 14, 2007, from http://www.pbis.org

Sugai, G., Sprague, J. R., Horner, R. H., & Walker, H. M. (2000). Preventing school violence: The use of office discipline referrals to assess and monitor school-wide discipline interventions. Special series: School safety: Part 1. *Journal of Emotional and Behavioral Disorders, 8,* 94–101.

Sutherland, K. S., Wehby, J. H., & Copeland, S. R. (2000). Effect of varying rates of behavior-specific praise on the on-task behavior of students with EBD. *Journal of Emotional and Behavioral Disorders, 8,* 2–8

Todd, A. W., Horner, R. H., Sugai, G., & Sprague, J. R. (1999). Effective behavior support: Strengthening school-wide systems through a team-based approach. *Effective School Practices, 17*(4), 23–37.

Turnbull, A., Edmonson, P. G., Sailor, R. F., Guess, D., Lassen, S., McCart, A., et al. (2002). A blueprint for schoolwide positive behavioral support: Implementation of three components. *Exceptional Children, 68,* 377–402.

Umbreit, J., Ferro, J. B., Liaupsin, C. J., & Lane, K. L. (2007). *Functional behavioral assessment and function-based interventions: An effective, practical approach.* Upper Saddle River, NJ: Pearson Education.

Van Acker, R., Boreson, L., Gable, R. A., & Potterton, T. (2005). Are we on the right course? Lessons learned about current FBA/BIP practices in schools. *Journal of Behavioral Education, 14,* 35–56.

Vandell, D. L., & Shumow, L. (1999). After-school childcare programs. *The Future of Children, 9,* 64–80.

Walker, H. M., & Bullis, M. (1990). Behavior disorders and the social context of regular class integration: A conceptual dilemma? In J. W. Lloyd, N. N. Singh, & A. C. Repp (Eds.), *The regular education initiative: Alternative perspectives on concepts, issues, and models* (pp. 75–93). Sycamore, IL: Sycamore Press.

Walker, H. M., Horner, R. H., Sugai, G., Bullis, M., Sprague, J. R., Bricker, D., et al. (1996). Integrated approaches to preventing antisocial behavior patterns among school-age children and youth. *Journal of Emotional and Behavioral Disorders, 4,* 193–256.

Walker, H. M., Kavanagh, K., Stiller, B., Golly, A., Severson, H. H., & Feil, E. G. (1998). First Step to Success: An early intervention approach for preventing antisocial behavior. *Journal of Emotional and Behavioral Disorders, 6,* 66–80.

Walker, H., & Severson, H. H. (1990). *Systematic screening for behavior disorders (SSBD): User's guide and technical manual.* Longmont, CO: Sopris West.

Walker, H. M., Stiller, B., Golly, A., Kavanagh, K., Severson, H. H., & Feil, E. G. (1997). *First Step to Success: Helping young children overcome antisocial behavior* (Vol. 6). Longmont, CO: Sopris West.

Witt, J. C., VanDerHeyden, A. M., & Gilbertson, D. (2004). Instruction and classroom management. In R. B. Rutherford, M. M. Quinn, & S. R. Mathur (Eds.), *Handbook of research in behavior disorders* (pp. 426–445). New York: Guilford Press.

Yell, M. L. (2009). Teaching students with EBD I: Effective teaching. In M. L. Yell, N. B. Meadows, E. Dragow, & J. G. Shriner (Eds.), *Evidence-based practices for educating students with emotional and behavioral disorders* (pp. 320–341). Upper Saddle River, NJ: Pearson Education.

Yell, M. L., Meadows, N. B., Drasgow, E., & Shriner, J. G. (2009). *Evidence-based practices for educating students with emotional and behavioral disorders.* Upper Saddle River, NJ: Pearson Education.

Ziguras, S. J., & Stuart, G. W. (2000). A meta-analysis of the effectiveness of mental health case management over 20 years. *Psychiatric Services, 51,* 1410–1421.

CHAPTER 17

Behavior Prevention and Management in Three Tiers in Secondary Schools

Randall Sprick
Safe & Civil Schools, Eugene, OR

Chris Borgmeier
Portland State University, Portland, OR

INTRODUCTION

Concerns about students who misbehave are not new (reread *Huckleberry Finn*), and both the nature of problem behavior and possible solutions have been discussed regularly since public education began. Throughout this history, the majority of school-based efforts to manage students' behavior have been both *reactive* (e.g., corporal punishment, being made to write "I will not ..." lines, detention) and *exclusionary* (e.g., in-school suspension, out-of-school suspension, shortened day, and expulsion; Sprick, Garrison, & Howard, 2002; Sugai, Horner, & Gresham, 2002). Reactive and exclusionary approaches are especially prevalent in secondary schools for a host of reasons that will be explored later in this chapter. High schools, in particular, have tended to focus on reactive and exclusionary procedures, such as increasing the number of campus security officers and police, performing drug tests and searches, and using metal detectors. Although very appealing and politically popular, these approaches have been particularly ineffective in improving safety or discipline (Elliot, Hamburg, & Williams, 1998; Loeber & Farrington, 1998).

In addition, secondary schools are more likely to use exclusionary procedures than are elementary schools. For example, in the 2005–2006 school year in Florida, more than 16% of middle and high school students received in-school suspensions, compared with only 2% of elementary school students. Percentages of out-of-school suspensions also reveal a marked contrast among the levels: elementary schools reported an out-of-school suspension rate of 3%, middle schools reported 13%, and high schools reported 12% (Florida Department of Education, n.d.).

Although punitive interventions are a popular means of dealing with misbehavior, they have been demonstrably ineffective in dealing with violent behaviors

(Gottfredson, 1997; Lipsey, 1991, 1992; Lipsey & Wilson, 1993; Tolan & Guerra, 1994). When punitive consequences are used without a corresponding effort to support positive behavior, researchers have seen increases in aggression, vandalism, truancy, tardiness, and dropping out (Guess, Helmstetter, Turnbull, & Knowlton, 1987; Sprick, Knight, Reinke, & McKale, 2007). Even when punitive approaches have proved ineffective, school personnel have tended to continue the same ineffective methods with greater frequency and intensity (Mayer, 1995; Mayer & Sulzer-Azaroff, 1990). There is an old adage that may be apt here: "When the horse is dead, it is time to dismount." The growing interest in and dialogue about positive behavior support (PBS) and response to intervention (RTI)—scientifically derived methods that offer evidence-based solutions to the problems of secondary school performance—present an unprecedented opportunity to try something different to reach and teach children with challenging attitudes and behaviors.

The urgency of this need to reform current approaches can be seen in the data on high school graduation rates. Although it is difficult to pin down the exact percentage of students who receive a high school diploma, one current estimate shows that, nationally, the public high school graduation rate remained almost flat over the past decade, going from 72% in 1991 to 71% in 2002. It also shows a wide disparity between the graduation rates of White and minority students. In the class of 2002, about 78% of White students graduated from high school with a regular diploma, compared with 56% of African American students and 52% of Hispanic students (Greene & Winters, 2005).

Graduation rates and dropout percentages given by different organizations vary, owing to methodology, but a look at district or state enrollment numbers can show how many 12th graders a district or state had in any given year and how many freshmen were enrolled 4 years prior to that. For example, in 2004–2005 there were 246,863 12th-grade students in Texas, and 4 years earlier there were 364,270 9th-grade students. What happened to the 32% of 9th graders who seem to have vanished? Yet in the same 2004–2005 school year, the Texas Education Association Academic Excellence Indicator System reported the school-completion rate as 92%, without counting general education development (GED) diplomas. Discrepancies seem to exist between actual enrollment figures and reports (Texas Education Association, 2009).

School districts are now under scrutiny by the general public and by the requirements of the No Child Left Behind Act to make an effort to keep students in school and to educate them successfully. This oversight represents a significant change in what schools are expected to achieve. Americans used to live in an agricultural and industrial society in which the majority of people did not need to be successful in school to survive economically. This is reflected in the graduation rates from years past. By looking at census records, the National Center for Education Statistics has estimated that in 1870 only about 2% of the population achieved a high school diploma. By 1900 it was over 6%, in 1940 it was 51%, and in 2004 it was 75% (U.S. Department of Education, 2005). The point is that, in years past, no one expected the public school system to keep every student in school; unskilled labor was needed for the farms and factories. It is a relatively recent phenomenon that schools are expected to teach every student.

Punishment has rarely changed student behavior in school, but the severe consequences sometimes delivered to students have inadvertently encouraged them to leave the educational system sooner, either by being expelled or by voluntarily dropping out. In addition, schools will never be able to punish students into *wanting* to stay in school. Therefore, America's schools will have to do business differently than they have in the past. They must be serious about educating students who previously would have dropped out, and part of that responsibility lies in creating a supportive environment for students and revising the consequences of misbehavior from punishment to consequences that will encourage these students to stay in school.

Clearly the U.S. educational system has a lot of improvements to make in the 21st century if the goal is to successfully educate all children. People talk about students "falling through the cracks," but if 25–30% of students in school are not graduating, the system does not have cracks—students are falling into vast chasms.

The U.S. educational system can reach and teach all students more effectively. In this chapter, we discuss implementing PBS within a three-tier RTI structure at the secondary school level. We explore the essential elements of PBS and RTI, discuss some of the challenges unique to the implementation of PBS in secondary schools, and suggest methods for overcoming those challenges.

SOLUTIONS TO THE PROBLEM: POSITIVE BEHAVIOR SUPPORT AND RESPONSE TO INTERVENTION

Two converging trends provide a unique opportunity to change the past history of ineffective punitive and reactive approaches. Positive behavior support (PBS) and a response-to-intervention framework that focuses on behavior present a unique opportunity to shape how schools approach students with challenging and chronic behavior problems.

What Is Positive Behavior Support?

Positive behavior support (PBS) has become a popular label that is used in a variety of ways and warrants some clarification. Warger (1999) defines positive behavior support as a long-term, long-view process:

> Unlike traditional behavioral management, which views the individual as the problem and seeks to "fix" him or her by quickly eliminating the challenging behavior, positive behavioral support and functional analysis view systems, settings, and lack of skill as parts of the "problem" and work to change those. As such, these approaches are characterized as long-term strategies to reduce inappropriate behavior, teach more appropriate behavior, and provide contextual supports necessary for successful outcomes. (p. 2)

PBS can involve procedures at the school-wide level, the classroom level, and the individual student level. The essential feature of PBS is the objective of placing more time, effort, staff development, and financial resources on *proactive, positive*, and *instructional* approaches rather than on reactive and exclusionary approaches (Sprick et al., 2007).

PBS, as defined by Warger, can be used to design positive interventions to help the student survive and thrive in the school system. Concurrent with the individual focus, positive system improvements can be designed that will allow more students to thrive without needing individualized intervention. For example, preventive interventions at the system level include enhancing the school climate, providing better supervision, or being more direct in teaching expectations for student behavior in common areas such as cafeterias.

Various models of PBS approaches are being implemented throughout the country. Hundreds of school districts use one of the following specific models: Foundations (Safe & Civil Schools—http://www.safeandcivilschools.com); Positive Behavioral Interventions and Supports (http://www.pbis.org/); Project Achieve (http://www.projectachieve.info/); and Best Behavior (Sprague & Golly, 2005). An essential element of all these PBS models is the schools' use of a leadership team to guide PBS implementation and sustainability; the team's task is to ensure the following:

1. The active involvement of *all* staff in PBS activities
2. The active involvement of students, parents, and community groups in PBS activities that directly affect those stakeholders
3. The establishment of a continuous improvement model in which the behavioral and discipline practices become more effective in successfully reaching more students every year
4. The implementation of a cycle of improvement that involves collecting and analyzing meaningful school-based data to select a manageable number of priorities for improvement, and using data to evaluate the efficacy, or lack thereof, of all improvement efforts
5. For any given priority, the expenditure of more time, effort, and resources on proactive and positive approaches than on reactive, punitive approaches

This team-driven process of continuous improvement means that PBS efforts are ongoing. John Foster Dulles once said, "The measure of success is not whether you have a tough problem to deal with, but whether it's the same problem you had last year." Every year, the team guides all key stakeholders in systems-level improvements and in designing better and more efficient delivery of individualized interventions for high-needs students. The combination of continuously improving the system and concurrently providing extra support for individual students who need it holds great promise for helping students succeed—students who historically would have dropped out or been expelled.

What Is Response to Intervention?

As discussed in many chapters in this volume, RTI is an organized and coordinated prevention and intervention effort, sometimes described as a service delivery system. RTI is a three-tiered process that enables schools to identify the kind of support struggling students need and to provide that support in a timely manner, when and where it is needed. Use of RTI allows struggling students to receive services and interventions at increasing levels of intensity, if earlier efforts have not helped the student achieve success. In other words, the intensity of the intervention is matched to the intensity of the need, based on the student's response to previous interventions. Although RTI originally was associated with academic contexts, there is growing recognition that the concepts of academic and behavioral needs are highly interrelated.

Put simply, RTI is a framework that supports the creation of powerful prevention programs using scientifically based practices that meet the needs of most students. RTI provides a structure to ensure that positive behavior support interventions are delivered at the earliest onset of chronic problems that are resistant to universal interventions. Even in the best circumstances, some students will need "more"; if even more powerful and intensive interventions are provided, some smaller proportion of students will still need "most"—the most powerful and intensive interventions available. Although there is no single widely practiced RTI model that relates specifically to behavior, some patterns are emerging that indicate some important common features. Those features, and a brief description of how each relates to PBS, are discussed in the following sections.

FEATURES OF RTI

When implemented successfully, PBS at the secondary school level will incorporate the same set of standard features as other three-tier approaches. Features include (a) three-tier interventions that are proactive, evidence-based, planful, systematic, and increasingly intensive; (b) screening procedures, either individual or universal, to identify those who need more intervention support; (c) data-based decision making and progress monitoring; and (d) interventions implemented with fidelity.

Three Tiers: Universal, Targeted, and Intensive

The focus of Tier 1 (universal) for secondary school behavior includes all the system-level work that is done as part of a school's PBS efforts to improve safety, climate, discipline, motivation, and school connectedness. The systemic intervention designs associated with PBS—from explicit teaching of agreed-upon behavioral expectations to a system of fair and consistent responses to problem behavior—are available to every student and every staff member in the school (see Table 1). The focus of Tier 2, interventions targeted to students who are more at risk for problematic behavior, are

Table 1. Three-Tier Intervention Model of Suggested Behavioral Interventions Using PBS

Tier	Problem	Solution
Tier 1 – Universal	Many students with discipline referrals and problem behavior; disorderly, negative school climate	Create a more orderly, predictable, and positive school-wide environment through team-led implementation of the following: a. Clearly defined and explicitly taught behavioral expectations b. System for regularly acknowledging student behavior c. Fair and consistent responses to student problem behavior d. Data-based decision making
	High rates of tardiness	School-wide agreements related to the following: a. Explicitly taught hallway expectations (Sprick, 2003) b. Redesign of the environment to prompt effective movement in hallways c. Systemic supervision of hallways d. Procedures to ensure that teachers start class immediately and are not interrupted by students late to class e. Systemic "sweeps" of hallways and escorting of students to their assigned class
	Initial sign of recurring student behavior	a. Planned discussion b. Academic assessment and adaptation c. Goal setting d. Data collection and analysis e. Increased positive interactions
	Limited academic engagement, participation, and success	School-wide agreements related to preliminary individualized interventions delivered by general education teachers: a. Preliminary assessment of academic ability b. Establishment of effective grading practices (Sprick, 2006) c. Self-monitoring or self-evaluation procedures

Table 1. (*continued*)

Tier	Problem	Solution
Tier 2 – Targeted group interventions for students with recurring behavioral concerns	Behavioral concerns due to limited structure, adult attention, and motivation	Use of check-in/check-out, Connections, and other approaches to contribute the following: a. Increased structure b. Increased positive attention from adults c. Explicit teacher prompts for desired behavior d. Increased opportunities for feedback e. Added incentives for positive behavior f. Increased connection between school and home
	Behavioral concerns due to academic deficits or organizational or time management concerns	Academic and instructional supports such as the following: a. Added instructional support b. Support with homework c. Previewing or prereading of challenging text d. Modified assignments e. Course on organizational skills and time management
	Behavioral concerns due to limited social skills	Social skills instructional group: A focus on specific skills with opportunities for practice in an authentic school environment
Tier 3 – Intensive interventions	Chronic, complex problem behavior that is nonresponsive to less individualized interventions	Intensive assessment and individualized behavior support plan: Functional behavioral assessment to inform development and implementation of an individualized behavior support plan
	Contributing concerns outside of school for students exhibiting severe problem behavior	Wraparound supports

more resource intensive in terms of number of personnel involved and the time devoted to problem analysis and intervention design and implementation. The goal of Tier 2 interventions is to use resources efficiently to provide support to at-risk students through group-based interventions whenever possible.

Tier 3 is the most intensive set of interventions and includes increasingly extensive assessments and individualized behavior support plans tailored to meet the specific needs of an individual student. Tier 3 intervention usually consists of a school-based team working to develop and implement a behavioral intervention plan based on a functional behavioral assessment (FBA). In some cases, individual student variables may suggest that additional support beyond the school-based team is needed, so appropriate medical, mental health, community, and other service providers may be included on the intervention team, a support system termed *wraparound support* (Scott & Eber, 2003).

A primary reason that RTI models emphasize the importance of Tier 1 prevention strategies is that no public educational system has the resources to develop and implement individualized plans for 25% to 50% of its students. Beyond the universal interventions that are designed to touch all students and staff on a daily basis, the Safe & Civil Schools model advocates that districts adopt a set of simple, efficient, yet efficacious individualized interventions that *all* teachers are trained to implement. These individualized interventions become a standard protocol for initiating individualized help for any student with behavior or motivation problems (Sprick & Garrison, 2008). The teacher would implement the following Tier 1 individualized interventions for at least 2 weeks:

- Planned Discussion
- Academic Assessment and Adaptation
- Goal Setting
- Data Collection and Analysis
- Increased Positive Interactions

(For more detailed information on the Tier 1 individualized interventions, see Sprick & Garrison, 2008.)

Only when these universal strategies have failed does the teacher ask for assistance from a counselor, problem-solving team, behavior specialist, or other school or district resources. If the intervention has been correctly implemented, the teacher will already have 2 weeks of data that can serve as the baseline for completing a request for assistance.

Individual or Universal Systematic Screening

The second feature of secondary school PBS implementation is a systematic process for the early identification of students who are not responding to the Tier 1 interventions. Most high schools operate reactively—students' needs are identified only after a significant pattern of disruptive behavior is clear or after a major incident. The costs of this referral-driven, one-student-at-a-time practice are staggering in terms of hours spent in meetings. Furthermore, the accuracy of a reactive approach to identifying students in need is questionable. Some students with less severe needs may generate meetings and interventions that other students with more severe needs do not receive.

In terms of efficiency, systematic screening for behavioral needs is clearly a more desirable approach. Schools are faced with two choices—screening applied to individual students as the data suggest (such as frequent disciplinary referrals or chronic absenteeism for any particular student), or universal screening, in which all students are initially considered at the same time. Although universal screening procedures for academic areas are well known and commonly used, such as school-wide testing, formalized universal screening tools for behavioral needs are not as commonplace. However, schools have data sources in place that serve very effectively as screening tools—for example, attendance data is taken for every student every day, which identifies those students who are chronically absent. Schools routinely keep records of detention assignments, and a student who is assigned detention time after time can be identified from the records as someone in need of intervention.

Individual screening for behavioral needs can consist of something as simple as preidentified criteria or decision-making rules that indicate a student may need targeted intervention. These "red flags" might be chronic absenteeism, failing grades in two or more classes in a semester, more than three disciplinary referrals in a semester, or more than six assignments to lunch detention in a semester. When any of these conditions are met for an individual student in a school where these kinds of data are tracked, the situation is brought to the attention of school personnel and the student is identified as someone who may need additional assistance.

Despite the benefits, individual screening on a case-by-case basis can lead personnel to object that they have way too many students who fail two or more classes in a semester to provide targeted or intensive help to all who might appear to need it. However, the systematic presence of some red-flag screening indicators can provide school personnel with program evaluation data regarding their current Tier 1 efforts. Anytime the number of these red flags overwhelms the school's resources, then more work must be done at the prevention level to reduce the prevalence of problems for large numbers of students.

A primary advantage of using these types of red flags warning of the need for further screening is that the data are already being collected in most schools. A valuable step beyond data collection is to have a system in place that can make the data readily accessible to decision-making teams in a user-friendly format for early identification of students. For example, the School-Wide Information System (SWIS; May et al., 2001) can provide teams with up-to-the-minute discipline data, with graphic representation, for quickly identifying red-flagged students.

Often, an impediment to effective behavioral intervention is the length of time schools wait before providing behavioral support to at-risk students. Well-intentioned teachers who are struggling with students with behavioral concerns too often receive support late in the year, after they have tried everything they can think of and "can't take it anymore." When a teacher hits his or her breaking point, the teacher is often less likely to consider implementing another intervention and more likely to suggest that the student be placed in an alternate setting. Early intervention, both across school years and within school years, is a critical element of RTI. Ideally, at-risk students would begin the school year with behavioral supports in place so that they start off successfully and bad habits are less likely to develop or return.

In addition, individual screening using office discipline referrals (ODRs) addresses only one broad type of problem that secondary school students face, that is, externalizing problems such as acting out or disruptive and/or noncompliant behavior. As discussed in chapters 15 and 25 of this book, ODR data often do not identify students at risk for internalizing behavioral problems, such as social withdrawal, depression, or phobias. In response to this problem, Severson and colleagues recommend actively screening all students on both externalizing and internalizing dimensions. The most promising universal screening methodologies have been based on the Systematic Screening for Behavior Disorders (SSBD; Walker et al., 1990, 1994), which has proved to be an effective tool for screening in elementary schools. The SSBD uses a teacher nomination process to identify students at risk for social or behavioral concerns within their classes. Those students identified as at risk are then assessed using a more comprehensive, technically sound, norm-referenced assessment to provide more specific information regarding the extent of student risk as well as the behavioral or social skill deficits of each student. Examples are the Social Skills Rating Scale (Gresham & Elliott, 1990), the Behavioral and Emotional Rating Scale (Epstein & Sharma, 1998), and the Child Behavior Checklist (Achenbach & Rescorla, 2001). Recent studies have shown promise in applying the SSBD or similar models of universal screening at the secondary level (Caldarella, Young, Richardson, Young, & Young, 2008; Nishioka, 2006). One of the difficulties in implementing a more formalized universal screening process similar to the SSBD has been time and feasibility in schools with limited resources (Glover & Albers, 2007).

Data-Based Decision Making and Progress Monitoring

Data-based decision making and progress monitoring is the third feature of PBS implementation in secondary schools. Within a three-tier behavioral intervention system, making Tier 1 prevention effective is a foundation for the subsequent tiers. However, effectiveness must not be judged solely on the basis of teacher satisfaction surveys. Instead, systematic outcome data must be used to evaluate the effectiveness of, and guide decision making for, the implementation of the Tier 1 intervention (see Sprick et al., 2002; Sugai et al., 2000). For example, if data such as number of ODRs suggest that the Tier 1 interventions are not adequately supporting most or all students (at least 80%), the response should be for the school to look at ways to improve the intervention. Alternatively, with regard to examining ODR data at the universal system level, it is suggested that 80% of students have one or fewer ODRs in a school year. Other student data, including attendance, suspension or expulsion, or academic data, can be used to guide decision-making regarding the effectiveness of the universal intervention.

At targeted and intensive levels (Tiers 2 and 3), data must serve two important purposes: (a) to inform selection of interventions for students and (b) to monitor student response to interventions. The predicament posed by student intervention is that there are no certainties that the intervention will work; no intervention works for all students. Intervention selection is critical because selecting the wrong intervention may make the problem behavior worse (more frequent or more severe). A simple example is the commonly used intervention of sending a student to the office. This intervention may be effective in decreasing the future occurrence of a problem behavior for some students; however, other students may see this intervention as an effective means of avoiding the embarrassment of "looking dumb" or failing at an academic task in front of their peers. In such cases, the problem behavior that results in being sent to the office may be functional for the student by providing him or her with the opportunity to avoid the embarrassment related to failing the task, and the behavior is likely to be repeated.

Within a three-tier behavior intervention model, secondary schools must have research-based interventions available at all three tiers of intervention. However, it is equally important that schools use an assessment-based approach to selecting interventions, because success for at-risk students depends on a correct match between student needs and an intervention. In the realm of behavioral intervention, evidence suggests that interventions are best selected based on an understanding of the function of student behavior (Ingram, Lewis-Palmer, & Sugai, 2005; Newcomer & Lewis, 2004). In schools, this form of assessment is often reserved for students with significant behavior problems who require special education services in the form of functional behavioral assessment (FBA). However, there is increasing evidence that function-based assessment can be used proactively to more effectively match students to targeted interventions in the second tier (Freeman et al., 2006). In such cases, a simple FBA is used to identify the function of student behavior and then match students with targeted interventions that address that particular function of behavior.

Use of Research-Based PBS Interventions

All of the interventions used in a three-tier system should include techniques, strategies, and approaches that have been demonstrated in the research literature as being effective. Many studies have documented good results following implementation of Tier 1 positive behavior supports in middle school settings. These results include reduced student disciplinary referrals, increased attendance, improved perceptions of school climate, and improved academic performance (Kartub, Taylor-Greene, March, & Horner, 2000; Lassen, Steele, & Sailor, 2006; Luiselli, Putnam, & Sunderland, 2002; Metzler, Biglan, Rusby, & Sprague, 2001; Oswald, Safran, & Johanson, 2005; Taylor-Greene et al., 1997; Taylor-Greene & Kartub, 2000; Turnbull et al., 2002; Warren et al., 2003). Preliminary evidence is also available on the effectiveness of implementing

Tier 1 PBS systems at the high school level (Bohanon et al., 2006; Bohanon-Edmonson, Fenning, Eber, & Flannery, 2007; Bohanon-Edmonson, Flannery, Eber, & Sugai, 2005; Sprick, 2006).

Tier 2 interventions include targeted group interventions for students who are not sufficiently responding to the Tier 1 intervention. Sprick, Booher, and Garrison (2009) and Sprick, Howard, Wise, Marcum, and Haykin (1998) identify a variety of interventions:

- Student social skills instruction (Brant & Christensen, 2002; Lane et al., 2003)
- Check-in/check-out systems or the daily point card system (Crone, Horner, & Hawken, 2004; Fairchild, 1983; Neyhart & Garrison, 1992 Schumaker, Hovell, & Sherman, 1977; Sprick et al., 2009)
- Mentoring programs (Sinclair, Christenson, Evelo, & Hurley, 1998)
- Creation of meaningful school-based jobs for students
- Academic support

Because of most schools' limited resources, it is likely that they will not be able to have all of the previously mentioned interventions in place simultaneously, so it is important for schools to use data in deciding which interventions will address needs presented by the bulk of at-risk students in their school (Anderson & Borgmeier, in review). Although the targeted interventions identified for Tier 2 (listed above) have research support, they will not be effective if they are not matched to the individual needs of the student. For example, a student who engages in problem behavior to avoid failure with difficult math problems may not benefit from a mentoring program that does not specifically address the student's math deficits. Though having a menu of research-based interventions to choose from is important, individual assessment to guide intervention selection is critical to student success.

Students who do not respond to targeted interventions or students with severe behavioral needs may require more intensive (Tier 3) interventions. Research suggests that individualized behavior support plans should be based on functional behavioral assessment (Crone & Horner, 2003; Sugai et al., 2000). Tier 3 intervention usually consists of a school-based team that includes the administrator, a team member with expertise in behavioral intervention (e.g., the school psychologist), and staff members who regularly work with the student or will be involved in implementing a behavioral intervention. Ongoing data collection is used to monitor plan implementation and student response to the behavioral intervention and to guide planning for ongoing support. The parent, and often the student, also participates on this team, depending on the circumstances. In some cases, individual student variables may suggest that additional supports beyond the school-based team are needed, so appropriate medical, mental health, and community service providers may be included on the intervention team to provide wraparound support (Scott & Eber, 2003).

Monitoring of Students' Response to Intervention

Following any intervention, students must be closely monitored using measures that are sensitive to student progress and behavioral change. Unfortunately, disciplinary referral data are not likely to be sensitive enough for monitoring student progress. The dynamic nature of student behavior adds a further challenge to monitoring student progress for behavioral change. No widely accepted measure exists for monitoring student progress for behavior change. As student behavior becomes more complex, measures must become increasingly individualized to the specific needs of the student. Because schools often have limited resources, data collection in schools must always consider the efficiency and feasibility of approaches.

There are many potential types of data collection for monitoring student response to behavioral interventions. Often, methods for monitoring student behavior will vary to match the qualities of the problem behavior being exhibited. This can be challenging within a system of three-tier interventions because of the extensive time and effort required to come up with individualized data systems for each student. Though individualized data systems may be necessary for students requiring intensive interventions (Tier 3), efficient school-wide data systems can be implemented for Tiers 1 and 2. These systems can be simple but specific and direct measures of behavioral responses, such as frequency counts, along with less direct measures, such as grading systems, points from a check-in/check-out system, or a daily point card system (Riley-Tillman, Chafouleas, & Briesch, 2007).

A daily point card system to monitor student progress may not be as precise as direct data systems because it relies on a subjective staff rating and requires only one score at the end of the time period rather than continuous monitoring. However, it offers the significant advantage of feasibility. A second advantage of point cards is the flexibility offered. Point cards can be used as a more generic data system for initial interventions, and the generic template can be modified to focus on individual student behavioral goals as students in need of Tier 3 interventions are identified. Team members will be encouraged to individualize the point card template only after students' needs have not responded to targeted interventions. By tailoring the existing point card template for individual assessment as needed, the minutes and hours it might take to develop a completely new point card for each student are saved. Another advantage is that a daily behavior point card is already present in some targeted interventions, including check-in/check-out systems, which are among the most commonly implemented of the targeted interventions.

An extension of the point card system may be recommended for monitoring the daily progress of students requiring more intensive interventions and therefore a more individualized point card. As interventions become more intensive, the focus of behaviors being targeted becomes more specific, which may warrant more specific goals and data collection tools. Students who are not responsive to Tier 2 interventions and progress into Tier 3 inevitably exhibit complex and challenging misbehaviors. Unavoidably, more time and resources are necessary to quantify, analyze, and handle these severe misbehaviors.

Fidelity of Intervention Implementation

The final feature of three-tier intervention systems is the use of steps taken to ensure that interventions are implemented with fidelity. To be effective, any evidence-based intervention needs to be implemented the way it was designed. In many cases, a lack of fidelity is the cause of an intervention breaking down. Fidelity of implementation basically means: You can buy a great vacuum cleaner, but you will still have a dirty rug if you don't take it out of the box, plug it in, turn it on, and move it around the rug (and move it the right way, not upside down or sideways). And you need to do this regularly—not just once the day you bought it, but week after week after week. This colloquial example may seem silly, but interventionists often hear, "I tried that but it didn't work," when in fact the intervention was never implemented with the degree of regularity and fidelity needed to change behavior. It is not reasonable to declare that a rug was unresponsive to the intervention of the vacuum cleaner if weeks have passed since anyone has used the device. Studies consistently document the limited implementation of behavioral plans that follow a traditional consultation model, which usually consists of a conversation about the behavior plan with a "specialist" (Codding, Feinberg, Dunn, & Pace, 2005; DiGennaro, Martens, & McIntyre, 2005; Jones, Wickstrom, & Friman, 1997).

At each of the three tiers of intervention, formal steps must be taken to ensure that the interventions are being implemented with fidelity. Implementation of the Tier 1 positive behavior supports can be monitored in several ways. Forms of assessment include observation and teacher or student report, such as the School-wide Evaluation Tool (SET; Sugai, Lewis-Palmer, Todd, & Horner, 2001; Horner et al., 2004), Benchmarks of Quality (BOQ; Cohen, Kincaid, & Childs, 2007), or direct observations of common areas, using a specific observation form (Sprick et al., 2002). Additional data sources include team self-assessments such as the Team Implementation Checklist (Sugai, Horner, & Lewis-Palmer, 2001); perception surveys of staff, students, and parents regarding safety, discipline, motivation, and staff–student and student–student interactions; analysis of injury reports; and occasional focus groups of staff, students, and parents.

When students require individual support at Tier 3, the question of implementation fidelity becomes increasingly important if the team is to make accurate decisions about student response to the intervention. The response to intervention cannot be fairly evaluated if the student didn't actually receive the intervention as it was intended. As a result, implementation of targeted interventions must be routinely evaluated to ensure fidelity. As interventions become more intensive and individualized for students, monitoring the fidelity of implementation becomes increasingly difficult and will require specific planning and resources, including ongoing data collection and performance feedback to maintain high levels of accuracy of implementation (Codding et al., 2005).

Fidelity of implementation will not be achievable without addressing the need for staff development—specifically, how do professionals get personnel in secondary schools to implement PBS (week after week, year after year)? The remainder of the chapter presents the challenges of training staff, along with suggestions for working through those challenges.

STAFF DEVELOPMENT FOR SUCCESSFUL IMPLEMENTATION OF PBS IN SECONDARY SCHOOLS

PBS has the potential to influence how elementary, middle, and high schools go about the business of trying to reach and teach students who exhibit challenging behaviors. However, most people who work in staff development agree that elementary schools are easier to change than middle schools and that high schools tend to present the biggest challenges. The difficulty lies not so much in knowing *what* to do in secondary schools, because the "what" is basically the same as in elementary schools— implementing PBS and RTI well. Although teachers and administrators may not have had extensive training in the pedagogy of PBS, communicating these basics is relatively easy in either preservice or inservice training.

The bigger problem lies in getting secondary school staff, administrators, teachers, counselors, custodians, security staff, food service workers, clerical staff, and others to do what they need to do to help change student behavior. As well intentioned as these people are, they are busy with work, can be distracted by myriad other school issues, and sometimes inadvertently fall into patterns of student correction that are not compatible with PBS. Staff development—teaching people to implement the techniques that research has shown will influence behavior, and to follow through with what they learn—is the keystone of PBS at the secondary school level. A keystone is the topmost stone of an arch that solidifies and holds all the other stones in place. Think about an arch as a metaphor for school efforts involving safety, civility, climate, discipline, and motivation. Now think about RTI and PBS as being two sides of that arch, with staff development being the keystone that holds it all together and makes it strong. Without the keystone, you just have a bunch of loose stones on the ground.

Too often, professional development involves an expert presenting information at a workshop or conference (Lewis, 2001). The participants are then expected to go back and apply the new learning and share the information with the rest of the staff. According to Guskey (1986, 2000), most studies on professional development conclude that this approach fails to have an impact on staff behavior in a way that affects student outcomes. For this reason, the Safe & Civil Schools model of staff development focuses on training *and* implementation. Staff development and feedback are distributed across multiple years and involve the following components:

1. Train district personnel to become trainers and coaches, thus building capacity and creating independent sustainability.
2. Make inservice sessions highly practical, user-friendly, and fun.
3. Encourage individual staff members to be reflective about managing behavior ("What can I learn to do more effectively?").

4. Encourage all staff members in school-wide practices to collectively reflect about managing behavior ("What can *we* learn to do more effectively? And how can we *all* implement with one voice?").

5. Contextualize each aspect of training about behavior (school-wide, classroom, and individual) so participants know how training fits in the bigger picture, how each of these levels is integrally dependent on the others, and how all these levels are integrally dependent on effective instructional practices at all three levels.

6. Emphasize district-level commitment to training and encourage the development of a common language, fidelity of implementation, and sustainability across time and across staff changes.

Building a PBS foundation starts with staff agreements and commitments to work toward and participate in a consistent school-wide vision. Implementing a school-wide effort in secondary schools offers challenges that are not present in most elementary schools. The following sections give examples and suggestions on how to (a) foster staff agreements and commitments that specifically address common challenges faced within secondary schools, and (b) implement the foundational components of PBS in secondary school settings.

Challenge: Secondary Schools' Size and Institutional Nature

A common challenge to attaining school-wide agreements and commitment is often the larger size and increasingly institutional nature of secondary schools compared with elementary schools. For example, one high school implementing Safe & Civil Schools has approximately 5,000 students and approximately 300 professional staff. The size of the professional staff at this school is the size of the student body of many elementary schools. Even a more moderately sized high school of 1,500 students is likely to have more than 100 staff members, compared with an elementary school of 300 that may have 20 professional staff members and 5 to10 noncertified staff. The larger the staff size, the more problematic communication becomes. For example, in a large high school, it is often impossible to have a staff meeting anywhere other than an auditorium.

As communication becomes difficult, factions and subgroups develop that are disenchanted, disengaged, or passively resistant to implementing particular policies or procedures. For example, it is not at all uncommon to find secondary schools in which only part of the staff enforces the school's dress code or helps supervise the halls between classes. This is less likely to be the case in an elementary school, simply because any staff member who is not enforcing a particular policy or procedure is more likely to stand out as noticeably negligent.

PBS can be implemented to help by actively involving the staff in a unified and consistent approach. Although a functional leadership team has been shown to be a key aspect of effective implementation, the team is even more important for creating consistency within a very large staff. The following are some suggestions for forming effective leadership teams to lead school-wide efforts in large secondary schools.

To be most effective, a PBS implementation leadership team will include six to nine staff members, including a school-based administrator and representatives of the entire staff. The suggestion of six to nine members is based solely on group dynamic considerations. If the team gets too large it becomes very difficult for them to sit around a table and discuss issues. The team must meet on a regular basis to maintain the cycle of reviewing data, selecting priorities, and revising policies and procedures they want the staff to adopt and implement. If the team stops meeting (or meets but is not efficient), the process of continuous improvement—a key component of PBS—grinds to a halt.

In large secondary schools, either the principal or an assistant principal will lead a PBS initiative at the school and will be an active, participating team member. However, if the assistant principal is the leader of the initiative, the principal must actively support and participate in communicating to the entire staff the importance of the work the team is doing. The principal must also help ensure fidelity of implementation of any agreed-upon policies and procedures. The staff has to see the principal being directly engaged, or the chance of a faction of the staff being unwilling to follow through increases dramatically.

Representation on the team must mirror, as closely as possible, the population of the staff; because general education teachers make up the largest percentage of the staff, there must be an adequate number of general education teachers on this team. In a high school, this representation of general education teachers might be organized by departments, grade levels, teachers with common planning periods, or professional learning communities, depending on how the lines of organization and communication work within the school. At least one special education teacher should represent the special education staff. Once representation of teaching staff has been ensured, every member of the school staff should be directly connected to a member of this team. Although there may or may not be a custodian on the team, someone on the team must directly represent the custodial staff. Someone must represent counseling staff, clerical staff, food service staff, etc. To limit the team to nine members, some members will have to represent multiple groups. An example of team configuration is shown in Table 2. However, this is only one example, and each school should form the team based on lines of communication and lines of influence and affiliation.

Once the groupings and representation are formed, actual team members can be identified by asking each group to select someone to represent them. In one very successful high school, each group was told to identify someone they respected and "could learn from." In other words, because the team was going to be receiving ongoing training in PBS, each group decided who they wanted to attend the training and bring the information back to them. If the team members are not well respected and influential, there is greater risk that the team may be ineffective, perhaps even creating greater divisions among staff, instead of serving as a unifying force.

Table 2. Possible Team Configurations

Team Members	Represented Group
Principal	Administrative team
9th-grade teacher	9th-grade teachers and clerical staff
10th-grade teacher	10th-grade teachers and counseling staff
11th-grade teacher	11th-grade staff, parent advisory groups, and PTA
12th-grade teacher	12th-grade staff, student council, all other student groups
Special education teacher	Special education staff, psychologist, social worker, mental health liaison
Custodian	Custodial staff and food service staff
Campus security office	Campus security, nursing, and school volunteers

Whenever the team is going to discuss an issue that affects constituents not on the team, the team member representing that constituency should seek input from his or her constituents and should even invite those constituents to the next team meeting. For example, anytime the team is going to discuss any aspect of the cafeteria, food service and custodial personnel should be invited to join the next team meeting, and if they cannot attend, their thoughts and opinions should be brought to the meeting by their representative.

The example does not have a parent or a student on the team; however, all members of the team serve as student and parent representatives. The reason for this is that sometimes the team may need to discuss important internal staff business, such as staff morale or staff inconsistency in implementing a particular policy. It is very difficult to have a frank discussion about important business (which could be viewed as "airing dirty laundry") with a parent or student in attendance. Although involving students and parents in many specific PBS activities is recommended (e.g., collecting and analyzing data, selecting priorities for improvement, and serving on task forces to develop new policies), the team needs the freedom to have frank, open, and even occasionally contentious discussions about internal staff issues.

Once the team is functioning and receiving ongoing training and support, it can take specific actions to guide and unify staff in designing and implementing PBS and a three-tiered model. In the Safe & Civil Schools model, teams are encouraged to develop a team name, along with a logo, to "brand" the team and make it a highly visible force in the school. For example, one high school team became the Triple C Team, for Campus Climate Committee, with a logo that looked like a cattle brand. With a name and brand, the team can put out a staff newsletter or, if less ambitious, at least have a small section of a general staff newsletter. Team members can have the brand visible on general staff meeting agenda items in which the team will discuss PBS issues or tasks. Having the brand be part of any visual displays, memos, or charts creates visibility for the team that comes to exemplify the school's PBS and RTI efforts. By striving to ensure that all staff members have a voice and adequate representation on the team, and by marketing the team's efforts and purpose, the team can unify and motivate staff to actively follow through on all agreed-upon policies and procedures.

Challenge: Secondary Teachers' More Limited Responsibility for Many More Students

Another challenge is the institutional feel common to many larger secondary schools, where a teacher may have limited responsibility for 125 to 200 students compared with the elementary teacher who has broad responsibility for 20 to 30 students. Imagine the daunting task of the English teacher who assigns a weekly writing assignment of two or three pages in each of five classes, each of which has 30 students. As a result, every week during her preparation period and before and after school, this teacher will have to read and provide meaningful feedback on 300 to 450 pages of typewritten text while also managing the grade book, preparing lessons, meeting with individual students, interacting with parents, and serving on building and district committees and teams. That does not even take into account that each day she faces different groups of 30 students at a time for 50 minutes, with only 4 or 5 minutes between each class. And those numbers are not even the extreme. Some teachers in some parts of the country may have six or seven classes per day, and in some cases, more than 40 students per class. Some schools have gone to block or A/B scheduling, which may mean more time with each group and only three groups per day, but over the course of a week, the number of students and the number of minutes will average out to the same overwhelming scenario.

The only upside for the secondary teacher with five classes is that she is only responsible for each student's success in English, and someone else has responsibility for the other aspects of the student's education. This can easily and understandably lead to a "What can I possibly do?" mentality when a student starts to struggle, either academically or behaviorally. This issue is compounded by the fact that most secondary teachers are trained as subject area experts, while elementary teachers are trained as generalists. Typically, if you ask, "What do you teach?" elementary teachers will respond with the grade level of the students they teach—"I teach third grade"— whereas secondary teachers will respond with their subject area—"I teach chemistry." This can result in a lack of ownership or accountability for student success. An extreme example is, "I teach chemistry; some students get it, some do not. What can I do?"

One way PBS can be implemented to help address this problem is to create "schools within schools," or small learning communities in which a group of four to six teachers all share the same group of 120 to 150 students. This can increase the sense of ownership and shared responsibility that a group of teachers feels toward a particular group of students. However, just creating this small learning community (SLC) structure may do little to change the percentage of students who can be successful, unless staff are given training in effective instructional and behavioral practices. Pairing SLCs with implementation of PBS is a logical match, empowering SLC teachers with research-based techniques for improving student behavior and with motivation and procedures to ensure that no students fall through the cracks. If a school is organized around this SLC or some other school-within-school structure, representatives from these groups should form the core of the school-wide behavior support team.

In addition, helping staff to improve the consistency of implementation of school-wide policies (e.g., dress code), procedures (attendance and tardiness reporting), and unity of spirit and school pride can communicate to students a sense of pride and connectedness to something important—"Our school!" Without staff unity and pride, the school may be perceived by students as "just a place with a bunch of adults who try to make you do a bunch of work."

Another benefit of PBS is that staff are trained in the importance of building positive relationships with students in the classroom and in the common areas of the school (Sprick, 2006; Sprick, Knight, et al., 2007). Frequent positive interactions in the halls and classrooms help reduce the degree to which students are viewed as a collective mass and develop a positive climate throughout the entire school.

One example of a creative way to examine whether some students do not have a connection with adults in the school was instituted by a high school in Washington state. The school's behavior leadership team started with a list of the 1,500 students who formed the entire student body. Team members placed their initials next to the name of each student they knew well enough to have a comfortable conversation with. They then passed the marked list around for the entire staff to mark students with whom they had a personal relationship. After completing this activity, many students had lots of marks, some students had only one or two marks, and only 15 students (1%) had no marks. Each of the teachers who had one of those students in class was informed of that student's name and encouraged to build a relationship with any of those 15 students. When the team followed up weeks later with the teachers of those 15 students, several teachers reported that they had built a positive supportive relationship. The only student none of the teachers made a connection with was reported as being difficult to talk to because of her severe speech and articulation difficulties. This was the first anyone in the school knew about the student's speech difficulties, including classroom teachers (since the student said nothing in class), and it was the precursor to getting assistance for the student.

The large number of students that teachers see also presents challenges to multitier interventions in large high schools. If 15% of students may benefit from Tier 2 interventions and 5% from Tier 3 interventions, that could mean that a teacher with 150 students will have up to 30 students, or five per class period, who could be on a check-and-connect system or highly individualized intervention. The good news here is that most high schools have special education personnel who can provide this support for 10% to 15% of the students. Even with help from special education, monitoring and implementing interventions with several students in each class has the potential to be overwhelming. Efficient communication is essential, and problem-solving teams need to be circumspect about when and how they ask teachers to help with students who have targeted and intensive needs—in particular, how many planning and status meetings teachers are asked to attend.

In the planning or implementation phases of a particular intervention for a student, one way to get a lot of information about the student is through the progress report shown in Figure 1. An RTI problem-solving team can route this form to all of the

Figure 1. Example of a student monitoring form.

Progress Report							
Student	Grade						
Please complete performance ratings for this student. The information you provide will be used to help develop an individualized plan of assistance and match the student with appropriate interventions.	**Period or Subject Area**						
	1	2	3	4	5	6	7
Key: Note: 5 = Always *A rating of 3 or below indicates* 4 = Usually *a problem or concern that* 3 = Sometimes *warrants further follow-up.* 2 = Rarely 1 = Never N/A = Not applicable							
Student Performance							

Academic Standing
   List student's current grade using the values assigned on
   the report card (letter grades, ✓/+/−, etc.)							

Attends class regularly							
Punctual							
Cooperative							
Participates in class activities							
Stays on task							
Completes in-class assignments							
Completes homework							
Quality of work is satisfactory							
Passes tests							
Student strengths (list at lease three):							
Goals for improvement:							
Prepared by	Date						

Note. From *Interventions: Evidence-Based Behavior Strategies for Individual Students* (p. 175), by R. S. Sprick and M. Garrison, 2008, Eugene, OR: Pacific Northwest Publishing. Reprinted with permission.

teachers who have a particular student. Thus, without requiring teachers to participate in a meeting, the team has a wealth of data about the student that show strengths and concerns by trait and by teacher and subject. This form can also be used to monitor progress monthly or quarterly.

Challenge: Staff Assumptions of What Students Know About Behavioral Expectations

A related challenge in many secondary schools stems from staff members assuming that students should already know the behaviors that are expected of them and be motivated to behave appropriately. Historically, kindergarten and first-grade teachers have been the best at teaching students expectations because they make no assumptions about what students already know. These primary school teachers know they have to teach all aspects of every expectation. As students get older, many adults assume that students "should know how to behave." However, the older students get, the more teachers they have had. The 10th-grade student has experienced a huge range of classroom procedures. They haven't been taught some standardized pencil-sharpener policy or late-work policy, or even a set of classroom rules. This student has experienced major differences in how teachers enforced their own procedures and policies. Some teachers were very lenient and some were very strict. Others may have varied in their consistency. Sometimes the rules were enforced and other times not.

Assumptions about what behavior expectations students already know can be especially prevalent at the secondary school level. Some secondary teachers tell students their expectations on the first day of school, but then expect students to remember and operate from those expectations from that day forward. Coaching any team sport provides a great model for how to view the teaching of expectations. Effective coaches know that *teaching* is not the same thing as *telling*. Teaching means that you break down expectations into manageable, age-appropriate sets of information that are introduced throughout the first several weeks of practice. For each expectation, play, or pattern, you present how you want it done, verify understanding, and then practice to mastery. Anytime performance is not up to par, more time will be spent during practice on that aspect of performance. Throughout the season, coaching involves teaching expectations and inspiring all team members to strive to do their very best.

Implementing PBS can clarify for teachers what expectations to teach and how and why to teach them. Every classroom is a unique mix of rituals, routines, procedures, and cultural norms that are idiosyncratic to each individual teacher. Therefore, it is important for the classroom teacher to clarify and teach to mastery all the expectations that students need to follow to be successful in their classroom and in school. One way to do this at the high school level is to provide students with a comprehensive behavioral expectation syllabus that clarifies rules, grading procedures, routines for handing things in, late work, and so on. (For an example of such a syllabus, see Sprick, 2006.) This syllabus should also clarify the behavioral expectations for each different type of activity—that is, how the student should behave during lectures, discussions, cooperative groups, tests, independent work periods, and so on. These routines and procedures are what the student must know—just for first period. The student's second-period teacher has different rules, routines, policies, and procedures.

Similarly, schools must focus on how to effectively teach school-wide practices. Each school is also a unique mix of school-wide rituals, routines, procedures, and cultural norms. These school-wide expectations include how to function in the common areas of the school; major policies such as dress code, plagiarism, and other code-of-conduct information; safety information; school pride; and participation in extracurricular activities.

One example of the depth of information that needs to be conveyed is how students are expected to interact in the school cafeteria. In working with hundreds of schools, we have found that, at both middle schools and high schools, the students are calmer and more respectful if they are taught the details of how to behave. This includes teaching students that the food service personnel are valuable members of the school community and deserve to be treated with kindness, dignity, and respect. The vast majority of students will behave appropriately if they are provided with clear, age-appropriate expectations, including an age-appropriate rationale for why those expectations are important.

In many schools, these school-wide expectations are being communicated through school-developed video lessons. If each year students and staff work together to develop video-based lessons on one common area (such as hallways), two major policy or code-of-conduct issues, and one aspect of school pride, then in 4 years the school will have 12 video lessons that can be used at the beginning of the year to orient students to school-wide expectations. Table 3 shows a sample from Safe & Civil Schools training for high schools as a guide to the type of lessons that can be taught school-wide during the first week of each new school year. The section reference for each lesson refers to the section of the lesson-plan notebook that each teacher is given.

When every teacher directly teaches expectations for their unique class, and when the entire staff directly teach expectations for all school-wide areas, policies, routines, rituals, and procedures, most students will strive to behave successfully. This is as true with secondary students as it is for elementary students. The only error teachers can make is not teaching expectations in detail.

Challenge: Frequent Class Changes—Every 50 or 90 Minutes

Another challenge in secondary schools is related to class changes. Passing periods in most secondary schools are vital transitions and somewhat analogous to the circulatory system of the human body. Every 50 or 90 minutes the entire student body is in motion, and if circulation is not healthy, none of the other systems are likely to be healthy. In some schools, passing periods are congested, chaotic, and extremely loud. When the bell rings for classes to begin, there are many students still in the hallway minutes later. The loss of instructional time can be significant if every teacher in every class has three or four students who arrive late—one student a minute late, two students 3 minutes later, and one student 2 minutes after that. As a result, during the first 6 minutes of class the teacher will have had three major interruptions in instruction, costing minutes and resulting in a huge loss of lesson momentum.

Table 3. Safe & Civil Schools Sample Lesson Schedule for the First 5 Days of School

	1st Period	2nd Period	3rd Period	4th Period	5th Period	6th Period
Monday	Section 1 START on Time! #1 Basic Hallway/Restrooms, Expectations	Section 2 START on Time! Tardy Policy/Sweep Procedures	Section 3 Cafeteria Procedures: Teachers of Ninth Graders—Tour	Section 4 START on Time! Locker Logic	Section 5 START on Time! Civility in the Halls and All School Settings	Section 6 Dismissal, Bus Loading, Expectations to and From School, Arrival
Tuesday	Section 7 START on Time! Safety in Halls, Restrooms, and Courtyards	Section 8 Safety Lesson 1: Threats Will Be Taken Seriously	Section 9 Fire Drill, Earthquake, Safety and Lockdown (or "Women and Children First")	Section 10 START on Time! Civil Interactions with Staff and School Pride	Section 11 Safety Lesson 2: Right to Be Safe/Responsibility to Contribute to Safety	Section 12 Campus Environment (or "Loiterers Will Be Prosecuted")
Wednesday	Section 13 Safety Lesson 3: What Is Harassment?	Section 14 Dress Code: Video Broadcast During Last 10 Minutes of Class	Section 15 Safety Lesson 4: Everyone Belongs in This School; This School Belongs to Everyone	Section 16 Grading, Cheating, and Plagiarism (or "Advice from a Sixth Year Senior")	Section 17 Clubs and Service Opportunities at This School	Section 18 Safety Lesson 5: Personal Power and Control, Part 1
Thursday	Section 19 Graduation Requirements—How to Monitor Your Progress	Section 20 Safety Lesson 6: Personal Power and Control, Part 2	Section 21 Athletic Opportunities and Eligibility Requirements	Section 22 Maturity (or "Why 'Yo Mama' is NOT an Appropriate Response")	Section 23 Safety Lesson 7: Teasing and Destructive Humor Can Be an Abuse of Power	Section 24 Personal Conduct/Social Expectations (or "Hey, Don't Say or Touch That!")
Friday	Section 25 Safety Lesson 8: When You Are on the Receiving End of an Abuse of Power (in Foundations)	Section 26 Locker Maintenance and Academic Organization	Section 27 Safety Lesson 9: Everyone Shares Responsibility to Stop Threats, Bullying, Harassment, and Other Abuses	Section 28 Dress Code Redux (or "We've Seen It All Before.")	Section 29 Students' Success Is the Goal: Academic Help Is Available	Section 30 Safety Lesson 10: Help Is Available if You Need It

Note. Teachers of ninth graders allocate at least 10 minutes per lesson; other grade levels use professional judgment. From Safe & Civil Schools, Introduction to Schoolwide Discipline Positive Behavior Support training (http://www.safeandcivilschools.com).

PBS can be implemented to help with passing periods. Although all schools involved in PBS activities should use data to set priorities for improvement, most secondary schools can benefit from a careful look at all procedures and policies that relate to passing periods, including, but not limited to, hallway issues, restroom issues, tardiness, and use of instructional time in classes in the first minutes after the bell has rung. If these interrelated issues are a problem for a school, constructing a comprehensive (school-wide) intervention can ensure that passing times are maximally efficient (Sprick, 2003; Sprick et al., 2002). Staff are encouraged to improve five variables by taking the following steps—structure, teach, observe, interact positively, and correct fluently—which are summarized by the acronym *STOIC* and are described below.

Structure. Are passing times too long, too short, or just right? Would painting lines in the middle of the hall (or particularly, stairway landings) reduce jostling? Would painting "No Parking" in front of bathrooms, drinking fountains, and vending machines improve traffic flow? Would one-way hallways help in extremely crowded hallways? Are clocks and bells coordinated? Perhaps playing music for the first 4 minutes of a 5-minute passing time would be better than having a warning bell and a final bell, so students and staff don't ask, "Was that the real bell or the warning bell?")

Teach. Directly teach students the importance of efficient movement, how to avoid congestion, how to say "Excuse me," how to greet adults, what are appropriate public displays of affection and what are not, and so on. This may seem silly, but teaching "Excuse me" has benefits even at the high school level.

Observe. Are enough staff strategically placed to ensure adult presence in all school settings? Are staff mentally present—that is, actively watching and listening? Are the roles of teachers coordinated with security staff and administrative staff to make it easy for teachers to enforce code-of-conduct issues but not get delayed from starting their own class on time?

Interact positively. Are staff members greeting students and providing positive feedback to all students, not just the charming and popular students? Are staff members greeting each other in a manner that models professional collegial relationships?

Correct fluently (consistently, calmly, and quietly). Do staff correct minor misbehavior immediately and calmly? For example, Fletcher High School in Jacksonville, Florida, trained its staff to use the phrase, "Please honor Fletcher's policy about _____" to correct minor misbehavior such as minor obscenities, minor safety issues, and so on. By mildly but consistently correcting these minor misbehaviors in this way to foster school pride, the staff found that frequency of minor misbehavior diminished, and so did the more major infractions. Are the roles of teachers coordinated with security staff and administrative staff to make it easy for teachers to enforce more serious code-of-conduct issues (e.g., dress code, no ID badge, obscenity directed at someone) without delaying the start of their own class? Can the teachers in each wing of the building be confident that a member of security staff and administrative staff will be present in the hallway to take over for any of these more major infractions? Without this coordination, many teachers would rather turn a blind eye to dress code violations, because if they see it and say anything to the student, the teachers may be delayed and not get their own class started on time.

Although passing period problems are a great challenge for secondary schools, they also provide a great opportunity for powerful demonstration to the staff about what can be accomplished when they all work together. By implementing these types of procedures, schools can reduce tardiness by up to 90% and sustain those gains across multiple years (Sprick, 2003; Sprick & Daniels, 2007). Safe & Civil Schools as an organization has had the opportunity to work with high schools that have reduced disciplinary referrals for serious offenses (such as fighting, drug offenses, and gross insubordination) by as much as 68%, just by developing and implementing a PBS effort related to halls and tardiness (Sprick, 2003), with further reductions in subsequent years as additional priorities are addressed. It is only logical that serious offenses will go down dramatically if students are all in class engaged in instruction, as opposed to whatever they might be engaged in if they are not in class.

Challenge: The Threat to Staff From Student Misbehavior in Secondary Schools

Misbehavior in secondary school can pose a greater threat to adult authority than it does in elementary school. When a teacher asks a student to do something (or to stop doing something disruptive), if the student says, "You can't make me," the teacher realizes the student is right. The highly skilled, experienced teacher knows that you cannot make the student do something, but there are many things you can try that have a reasonable chance to influence the student to make a positive choice. The unskilled teacher gets pulled directly into a power struggle, trying to make the student behave, which, for some students, can actually serve as a positive reinforcer for refusing to follow the teacher's initial direction. If this cycle continues across days or weeks, the teacher begins to resent the student for putting him in this untenable position.

This problem is compounded at the secondary level because of the general tendency of even typical adolescents to test limits and challenge authority. Any 15-year-old may be more likely to challenge authority or test a rule on any given day than a 7-year-old; it is part of growing into adulthood. In addition, a 15-year-old with a history of oppositional behavior has had 8 more years of practice at being oppositional and upsetting adults than a 7-year-old has, and as everyone knows, practice makes perfect.

In addition, secondary students are physically larger, so adults may be more likely to feel physically threatened by misbehavior. Take just one situation for example. You are an elementary school teacher in the hallway 1 minute after the bell rings and you hear a student who you do not know personally utter an obscenity. Because there are lots of adults, and they can be immediately and clearly identified because they are taller than most of the students, you would be very likely to correct this student. Now put the same scenario in a high school. If you need assistance from another adult, it is not as easy to identify them among all the adult-size people in the hall. Or you may be the only adult in that wing of the building who is in the hall. Pair this with an increased chance of meeting with challenging behavior and a student who is 6 inches taller and 30 pounds heavier than you are. Would you correct this student? Even if you would, you would probably feel a bit more trepidation about engaging in this corrective action. It is not uncommon, and very understandable, to find inner-city high schools in which teachers report feeling unsafe in the halls of the school.

PBS can be implemented to help by ensuring more systematic deployment of adults in all school settings. Students are much less likely to misbehave in any setting in which there are more adults rather than fewer adults. An example of this can be seen on the freeways. Most people drive the speed limit when an officer is present but exceed the limit if an officer is not present. In addition, having other staff in the hallway reduces the sense of isolation and anxiety that comes from perceiving that you are the only adult in the hall. Thus, a major focus of Tier 1 prevention needs to be the coordinated and organized deployment of adults. This involves training staff in both the rationale for deployment in halls—"if everybody does a little, then nobody has to do a lot"—and the logistics—who needs to be where at what time.

Another factor is to ensure that adults have the skills to prevent power struggles and deescalate emotionally charged situations, both in common areas and in the classroom. The leadership team can be instrumental in ensuring that training is provided. Through occasional reminders in staff meetings and more formalized inservice activities, staff can get training in how to prevent threatening situations, deescalate emotional situations, and automatically respond to likely behavioral emergencies. The more knowledge you have about how to influence behavior, the less threatening student behavior may seem. If you have no knowledge of how to control a car, being behind the wheel of a car careening down a hill is very frightening, but if you know how to steer and use the brakes to control your descent, it is a much less threatening experience. You can actually enjoy music and the view, as long as you know you have control of at least some of the variables. Staff development, when conducted properly, provides staff with more tools to use—more buttons to press, wheels to turn, and levers to pull—to manage student behavior.

Ensuring that staff have behavior management skills can be accomplished through staff development, but again, it is important that this training be distributed across time. For example, at least once per month at a staff meeting, stage a brainstorming session of a common situation to discuss skillful and unskillful ways of handling that situation. The example in Table 4 is one of a series of 18 mini-inservices from Coaching Classroom Management (Sprick et al., 2007).

Finally, the potential for staff to feel unsafe or threatened can be reduced by establishing and frequently reviewing emergency procedures, that is, what to do in different emergency situations. Most school personnel are not anxious about the possibility of a fire, because there are efficient and well-practiced routines for what everyone should do in the unlikely event of a fire. Most schools are doing a good job of emergency procedures for lockdown drills, but school authorities may not have

Table 4. Sample Brief Staff Development Exercise

Refusal to follow directions

Objectives

To explore intervention options for a student who refuses to work.

To remind staff that responses to misbehavior should treat students with respect and should maintain the flow of the instructional activity.

Situation: In your class, a student of average academic ability is fairly quiet, though she answers any questions you pose directly to her. She has completed all assignments and is achieving average grades. She participates in class if asked to but rarely volunteers answers. During an independent work period, you notice that the student is not working and is staring into space. You go to the student and quietly remind her to get back to work. She looks at you and calmly states, "You can't make me."

Small-group discussion (3 minutes)

With two to four colleagues:

Identify at least two different ways that a teacher might skillfully handle this immediate situation.

Identify at least two different ways that a teacher might be unskillful in responding to this situation.

Large-group debrief (3 minutes)

Groups report what they've identified. The purpose of these discussions is not to identify how best to handle this scenario per se, but to recognize that multiple skillful ways exist for handling other such situations and to remind staff that an unskillful response stands a fair chance of drawing other students off task or coming off as disrespectful.

Optional large-group discussion (3 minutes)

Discuss what a teacher might do if the event with the student repeats itself on each of the next 2 days. Ideas could include how to respond immediately but should also identify other interventions (such as contacting the student's family).

Self-reflection questions: Would your immediate reaction to the situation have been different if the student had been identified as male, or if the student had been identified as being of a particular race or ethnicity? Would your responses or long-term interventions have been different?

Note. From *Coaching Classroom Management: Strategies and Tools for Administrators and Coaches* (p. 24), by R. S. Sprick, J. Knight, W. Reinke, and T. McKale, 2006, Eugene, OR: Pacific Northwest Publishing. Reprinted with permission.

talked to staff and practiced what to do in the event of a fight between two students or a student getting angry and knocking things off shelves. By reviewing how your school has trained for crisis situations (e.g., fire or lockdowns), a school team can use similar methods to develop mini-inservices on how to handle refusal to follow directions or similar types of behavioral events that have occurred with your population of students.

CONCLUSION

A system of positive behavior supports delivered within a three-tier intervention model has great potential to help a large number of students succeed in school—students who historically would not have survived the system. PBS can create the foundation to make the Tier 1 or universal interventions within a school more safe and inviting so the vast majority of students want to come to school and do their best every day. When an individual struggles to thrive in that system, using PBS means that positive and proactive interventions will be implemented to provide individualized support for those students. RTI methods define how service delivery is organized. Tier 1 focuses on prevention and interventions that every professional in the school is trained to implement. Tiers 2 and 3 encompass moving to individualized intervention in a way that tries the easiest, least intrusive, and least costly interventions in the early stages and moves to more staff-intensive and student-intrusive interventions only if less structured interventions have been well implemented but have not been helpful. These features of PBS and RTI are the same in elementary schools as in secondary schools.

What make secondary schools unique are the staff development challenges that the structure of secondary schools create. These challenges include large schools, a staff that deals with large numbers of students, students undergoing massive transitions every 50 or 90 minutes, staff making assumptions about what students already know, and student behavior that may be more threatening and severe. PBS and RTI actually create great opportunities to help staff work through these challenges by making the school an inviting place, where both the needs of the many and the needs of the few are met with professionalism and warmth by a unified school staff.

REFERENCES

Achenbach, T. M., & Rescorla, L. A. (2001). *Manual for ASEBA school-age forms & profiles*. Burlington, VT: University of Vermont, Research Center for Children, Youth, & Families.

Anderson, C. M., & Borgmeier, C. (2009). *Targeted Interventions: Addressing the Social Behavior of Students through Group Interventions*. Manuscript submitted for publication (copy on file with author).

Bohanon, H., Fenning, P., Carney, K. L., Minnis-Kim, M. J., Anderson-Harriss, S., Mortoz, K., et al. (2006). School-wide application of positive behavior support in an urban high school: A case study. *Journal of Positive Behavior Interventions, 8,* 131–145.

Bohanon-Edmonson, H., Fenning, P., Eber, L., & Flannery, B. (2007). Identifying a roadmap of support for secondary students in school-wide positive behavior support applications. *International Journal of Special Education, 22,* 39–52.

Bohanon-Edmonson, H., Flannery, K. B., Eber, L., & Sugai, G. (Eds.). (2005). *Positive behavior support in high schools: Monograph from the 2004 Illinois high school forum of positive behavior interventions and supports*. Retrieved November 2, 2007, from http://www.pbis.org.

Brant, M., & Christensen, R. (2002). *Improving student social skills through the use of cooperative learning, problem solving & direct instruction*. Unpublished master's thesis, Saint Xavier University, School of Education, Chicago.

Caldarella, P., Young, E. L., Richardson, M. J., Young, B. J., & Young, K. R. 2008. Validation of the Systematic Screening for Behavior Disorders in Middle and Junior High School. *Journal of Emotional and Behavioral Disorders, 16,* 105–117.

Codding, R. S., Feinbert, A. B., Dunn, E. K., & Pace, G. M. (2005). Effects of immediate performance feedback on implementation of behavior support plans. *Journal of Applied Behavior Analysis, 38,* 205–219.

Cohen, R., Kincaid, D., & Childs, K. E. (2007). Measuring school-wide positive behavior support implementation: Development and validation of the benchmarks of quality. *Journal of Positive Behavioral Intervention, 9,* 203–213.

Crone, D. A., & Horner, R. H. (2003). *Building positive behavior support systems in schools: Functional behavioral assessment.* New York: Guildford Press.

Crone, D. A., Horner, R. H., & Hawken, L. S. (2004). *Responding to misbehavior in schools: The behavior education program.* New York: Guilford Press.

DiGennaro, F. D., Martens, B. K., & McIntyre, L. L. (2005). Increasing treatment integrity through negative reinforcement: Effects on teacher and student behavior. *School Psychology Review, 34,* 220–231.

Elliot, D. S., Hamburg, B. A., & Williams, K. R. (1998). *Violence in American schools: A new perspective.* New York: Cambridge University Press.

Epstein, M. H., & Sharma, J. M. (1998). *Behavioral and emotional rating scale (BERS): A strength-based approach to assessment – Examiner's manual.* Austin, TX: Pro-Ed.

Fairchild, T. N. (1983). Effects of a daily report card system on an eighth grader exhibiting behavioral and motivational problems. *School Counselor, 31,* 83–86.

Florida Department of Education. (n.d.). *Florida school indicators report* [searchable database]. Retrieved August 10, 2008, from http://www.fldoe.org/eias/eiaspubs/fsir.asp

Freeman, R., Eber, L., Anderson, C., Irvin, L., Horner, R., Bounds, M., et al. (2006). Building inclusive school cultures using school-wide PBS: Designing effective individual support systems for students with significant disabilities. *Research and Practice for Persons with Disabilities, 31,* 4–17.

Glover, T. A., & Albers, C. A. (2007). Considerations for evaluating universal screening assessments. *Journal of School Psychology, 45,* 117–135.

Gottfredson, D. C. (1997). *School-based crime prevention.* In L. Sherman, D. Gottfredson, D. Mackenzie, J. Eck, P. Reuter, & S. Bushway (Eds.), *Preventing crime: What works, what doesn't, what's promising* (pp. 5-1–5-74). College Park: University of Maryland, Department of Criminology and Criminal Justice.

Greene, J. P., & Winters, M. A. (2005). *Public high school graduation and college-readiness rates: 1991–2002* (Education Working Paper No. 8). New York: Manhattan Institute for Policy Research.

Gresham, F. M., & Elliott, S. (1990). *The Social Skills Rating Scale (SSRS).* Circle Pines, MN: American Guidance Service.

Guess, D., Helmstetter, E., Turnbull, H. R., III, & Knowlton, S. (1987). Use of aversive procedures with persons who are disabled: An historical review and critical analysis. *Monograph of the Association for Persons with Severe Handicaps* 2(1). Washington, DC: Association for Persons with Severe Handicaps.

Guskey, T. R. (1986). Staff development and the process of teacher change. *Educational Researcher, 15*(5), 5–12.

Guskey, T. R. (2000). *Evaluating professional development.* Thousand Oaks, CA: Corwin Press.

Horner, R. H., Todd, A. W., Lewis-Palmer, T., Irvin, L. K., Sugai, G., & Boland, J. B. (2004). The School-Wide Evaluation Tool (SET): A Research Instrument for Assessing School-Wide Positive Behavior Support. *Journal of Positive Behavior Interventions, 6,* 3–12.

Ingram, K., Lewis-Palmer, T., & Sugai, G. (2005). Function-based intervention planning: Comparing the effectiveness of FBA indicated and contra-indicated intervention plans. *Journal of Positive Behavior Interventions, 7,* 224–236.

Jones, K. M., Wickstrom, K. F., & Friman, P. C. (1997). The effects of observational feedback on treatment integrity of school-based behavioral consultation. *School Psychology Quarterly, 12,* 316–326.

Kartub, D., Taylor-Greene, S., Horner, R. H., & March, R. (2000). Reducing hallway noise: A systems approach. *Journal of Positive Behavior Interventions, 2,* 179–182.

Lane, K. L., Wehby, J., Menzies, H. M., Doukas, G. L., Munton, S. M., & Gregg, R. M. (2003). Social skills instruction for students at risk for antisocial behavior: The effect of small group instruction. *Behavioral Disorders, 28,* 229–248.

Lassen, S. R., Steele, M. M., & Sailor, W. (2006). The relationship of school-wide positive behavior support to academic achievement in an urban middle school. *Psychology in the Schools, 43,* 701–712.

Lewis, A. (2001). *To create a profession: Supporting teachers as professionals. A report of the AASCU Task Force on Professional Development for Teachers.* Washington, DC: American Association of State Colleges and Universities. (ERIC Document Reproduction Service No. ED 457 146)

Lipsey, M. W. (1991). The effect of treatment on juvenile delinquents: Results from meta-analysis. In F. Losel, D. Bender, &T. Bliesener (Eds.), *Psychology and law* (pp. 131–143). New York: Walter de Gruyter.

Lipsey, M. W. (1992). Juvenile delinquency treatment: A meta-analytic inquiry into the variability of effects. In T. D. Cook (Ed.), *Meta-analysis for explanation: A casebook* (pp. 83–127). New York: Russell Sage Foundation.

Lipsey, M. W., & Wilson, D. B. (1993). The efficacy of psychological, educational, and behavioral treatment: Confirmation from meta-analysis. *American Psychologist, 48,* 1181–1209.

Loeber, R., & Farrington, D. (1998). *Serious and violent juvenile offenders: Risk factors and successful interventions.* Thousand Oaks, CA: SAGE.

Luiselli, J. K., Putnam, R. F., & Sunderland, M. (2002). Longitudinal evaluation of behavior support intervention in a public middle school. *Journal of Positive Behavioral Interventions, 4,* 182–188.

May, S., Ard, B., Todd, A., Horner, R., Sugai, G., & Glasgow, A. (2001). *SWIS User's manual: Learning to use the school-wide information system.* Eugene: University of Oregon, Center on Positive Behavioral Interventions and Supports.

Mayer, G. R. (1995). Preventing antisocial behavior in the schools. *Journal of Applied Behavior Analysis, 28,* 467–478.

Mayer, G. R., & Sulzer-Azaroff, B. (1990). Interventions for vandalism. In G. Stoner, M. R. Shinn, & H. M. Walker (Eds.), *Interventions for achievement and behavior problems* (pp. 559–580). Washington, DC: National Association of School Psychologists.

Metzler, C. W., Biglan, A., Rusby, J. C., & Sprague, J. R. (2001). Evaluation of a comprehensive behavior management program to improve school-wide positive behavior support. *Education & Treatment of Children, 24,* 448–479.

Newcomer, L. L., & Lewis, T. J. (2004). Functional behavioral assessment: An investigation of assessment reliability and effectiveness of function-based interventions. *Journal of Emotional and Behavioral Disorders, 12,* 168–181.

Neyhart, S., & Garrison, M. (2009). Connections: A group-based behavior monitoring plan. In R. S. Sprick, M. Booher, & M. Garrison (Eds.), *Behavioral response to intervention (B-RTI): Creating a continuum of problem-solving and support.* Eugene, OR: Pacific Northwest Publishing.

Nishioka, V. M. (2006). Universal screening: Strategies for assessing and supporting the needs of at-risk students in your school. In *Proceedings of Persistently Safe Schools: The 2006 National Conference of School and Community Violence,* 231–237. Washington, DC: George Washington University, Hamilton Fish Institute.

Oswald, K., Safran, S., & Johanson, G. (2005). Preventing trouble: Making schools safer places using positive behavior support. *Education and Treatment of Children, 28,* 265–278.

Riley-Tillman, T. C., Chafouleas, S. M., & Briesch, A. M. (2007). A school practitioner's guide to using daily behavior report cards to monitor student behavior. *Psychology in the Schools, 44,* 77–89.

Schumaker, J. B., Hovell, M. F., & Sherman, J. A. (1977). An analysis of daily report cards and parent-managed privileges in the improvement of adolescents' classroom performance. *Journal of Applied Behavior Analysis, 10,* 449–464.

Scott, T. M., & Eber, L. (2003). Functional assessment and wraparound as systemic school processes: Primary, secondary, and tertiary systems examples. *Journal of Positive Behavior Interventions, 5,* 131–143.

Sinclair, M. F., Christenson, S. L., Evelo, D. L., & Hurley, C. M. (1998). Dropout prevention for youth with disabilities: Efficacy of a sustained school engagement procedure. *Exceptional Children, 65,* 7–21.

Sprague, J., & Golly, A. (2005). *Best Behavior: Building positive behavior support in schools,* Longmont, CO: Sopris West.

Sprick, R. S. (2003). *START on time! Safe transitions and reduced tardies.* Eugene, OR: Pacific Northwest Publishing.

Sprick, R. S. (2006). *Discipline in the secondary classroom: A positive approach to behavior management* (2nd ed.). San Francisco: Jossey-Bass.

Sprick, R. S., Booher, M., & Garrison, M. (2009). *Behavioral response to intervention (B-RTI): Creating a continuum of problem-solving and support*. Eugene, OR: Pacific Northwest Publishing.

Sprick, R. S., & Daniels, K. (2007). Taming the tardies: Every minute counts. *Middle Ground: The Magazine for Middle Level Education, 11*(2), 21–23.

Sprick, R. S., & Garrison, M. (2008). *Interventions: Evidence-based behavior strategies for individual students*. Eugene, OR: Pacific Northwest Publishing.

Sprick, R. S., Garrison, M., & Howard, L. M. (2002). *Foundations: Developing positive school-wide discipline policies*. Eugene, OR: Pacific Northwest Publishing.

Sprick, R. S., Howard, L., Wise, B. J., Marcum, K., & Haykin, M. (1998). *Administrator's desk reference of behavior management: Meaningful work* (Vol. 3). Eugene, OR: Pacific Northwest Publishing.

Sprick, R. S., Knight, J., Reinke, W., & McKale, T. (2006). *Coaching classroom management: Strategies and tools for administrators and coaches*. Eugene, OR: Pacific Northwest Publishing.

Sugai, G., Horner, R. H., & Gresham, F. M. (2002). Behaviorally effective school environments. In M. Shinn, H. M. Walker, &G. Stoner (Eds.), *Interventions for academic and behavior problems II: Preventive and remedial approaches* (pp. 315–350). Bethesda, MD: National Association of School Psychologists.

Sugai, G., Horner, R. H., & Lewis-Palmer, T. (2001). *Team Implementation Checklist*. Eugene: University of Oregon.

Sugai, G., Lewis-Palmer, T., Todd, A., & Horner, R. H. (2001). *School-wide Evaluation Tool*. Eugene: University of Oregon.

Taylor-Greene, S. J., Brown, D., Nelson, L., Longton, J., Gassman, T., Cohen, J., et al. (1997). School-wide behavioral support: Starting the year off right. *Journal of Behavioral Education, 7,* 99–112.

Taylor-Greene, S. J., & Kartub, D. T. (2000). Durable implementation of school-wide behavior support: The high five program. *Journal of Positive Behavior Interventions, 2,* 233–245.

Texas Education Association, *Academic Excellence Indicator System* [searchable database]. Retrieved August 10, 2008, at Texas Education Association website: http://www.tea.state.tx.us/perfreport/aeis/

Texas Education Agency Department of Assessment, Accountability, and Data Quality, Division of Accountability Research Reports. *Secondary school completion and dropouts in Texas public schools 2004–05* (p.58). Retrieved from http://ritter.tea.state.tx.us/research/pdfs/dropcomp_2004-05.pdf (updated March 20, 2009).

Tolan, P., & Guerra, N. (1994). *What works in reducing adolescent violence: An empirical review of the field*. Boulder: University of Colorado, Center for the Study and Prevention of Violence.

Turnbull, A. P., Edmonson, H., Griggs, P., Wickham, D., Sailor, W., Freeman, R., et al. (2002). Positive behavior support: Implementation of three components. *Exceptional Children, 68,* 377–402.

U.S. Department of Education, IES National Center for Education Statistics. (2005). *Digest of education statistics, 2004*(Table 102). Retrieved November 1, 2007, from http://nces.ed.gov/programs/digest/d04/tables/dt04_102.asp

Walker, H. M., Severson, H. H., Todis, B. J., Block-Pedego, A. E., Williams, G. J., Haring, N. G., et al. (1990). Systematic Screening for Behavior Disorders (SSBD): Further validation, replication, and normative data. *Remedial and Special Education (RASE), 11*(2), 32–46.

Walker, H. M., Severson, H. H., Nicholson, F., Kehle, T., Jenson, W. R., Clark, E. (1994). Replication of the Systematic Screening for Behavior Disorders (SSBD) procedure for the identification of at-risk children. *Journal of Emotional and Behavioral Disorders, 2,* 66–77.

Warger, C. (1999). *Positive behavior support and functional assessment.* Arlington, VA: Council for Exceptional Children. (ERIC Clearinghouse on Disabilities and Gifted Education, ERIC/OSEP Digest E580, No. ED434437)

Warren, J. S., Edmonson, H. M., Griggs, P., Lassen, S., McCart, A., Turnbull, A., et al. (2003). Urban applications of school-wide positive behavior support: Critical issues and lessons learned. *Journal of Positive Behavior Interventions, 5,* 80–91.

CHAPTER 18

Preventing and Remediating Reading Difficulties:
Perspectives From Research

Carolyn A. Denton
University of Texas Health Science Center Houston

Sharon Vaughn
University of Texas at Austin

INTRODUCTION

Large numbers of students in U.S. schools have reading difficulties of varying severity. Although the 2007 results of the National Assessment of Educational Progress reflected small but significant gains in fourth- and eighth-grade reading achievement, about 33% of fourth-grade students and 26% of eighth-grade students still failed to demonstrate even "partial mastery of prerequisite knowledge and skills that are fundamental for proficient work at a given grade" (Lee, Grigg, & Donahue, 2007, p. 6).

For students from poverty-level backgrounds and members of ethnic and linguistic minority groups, these percentages are appreciably higher. Moreover, about 80–90% of students identified as having specific learning disabilities (SLD) have significant reading difficulties (Kavale & Reese, 1992; Lerner, 1989). This situation has significant consequences for individual students, for schools, and for the country. The purpose of this chapter is to provide school psychologists and other practitioners with up-to-date information about evidence-based practices in the prevention and remediation of reading difficulties.

PREVENTION OF READING DIFFICULTIES

Although interventions designed to reduce risk may be provided at any age, the word *prevention* in reading education is commonly used to describe interventions that are provided to young children, usually in the primary grades. As students are just beginning to read at this age, intervention is delivered with the goal of preventing eventual reading difficulties. In this chapter, we refer to reading intervention provided to children in the primary grades as *prevention*, and intervention for older students who have already experienced some degree of reading failure as *remediation*.

Recent educational initiatives have emphasized the critical role of early reading instruction in the prevention of reading difficulties, recognizing that students who do not learn to read adequately in the primary grades typically have persistent reading difficulties throughout their school years (Francis, Shaywitz, Stuebing, Shaywitz, & Fletcher, 1996; Juel, 1988; Torgesen & Burgess, 1998). Over the past 20–30 years, a considerable research base has produced converging findings about critical elements of reading instruction associated with improved outcomes for students. These findings have been synthesized and summarized in several high-profile reports, including the report of the National Research Council in 1998 (Snow, Burns, & Griffin, 1998), the report published 2 years later by the National Reading Panel (2000), and the RAND Reading Study Group report (2001). Since the publication of these documents, several meta-analyses and systematic research syntheses have been published, confirming the knowledge base about the prevention of reading difficulties. Both classroom and tutorial studies have shown that early intervention reduces the number of students at risk for reading difficulties, including those who might eventually be identified as having learning disabilities (Mathes & Denton, 2002; Torgesen, 2000).

This growing research base provides guidelines about factors that need to be in place for preventing reading difficulties in young students. In this section, we will describe these factors, discussing both the content that should be addressed and characteristics of effective instruction for these students. We organize this description within the context of multitiered reading intervention models commonly associated with the implementation of response-to-intervention (RTI) approaches. We begin with a brief overview of RTI models in reading, followed by a description of evidence-based practices in class-wide reading instruction and in small-group reading interventions.

Response to Intervention in Preventive Reading Models

Based on the large body of research related to effective instruction for the prevention of reading difficulties, preventive RTI models for early reading have emerged. In large part, these models were also derived from research on "prereferral intervention," in which teachers provide intervention and adaptations to reduce the overidentification of students with learning and behavioral disabilities when their problems could be addressed within general education.

One widely adopted preventive RTI reading model consists of multiple tiers of intervention of increasing intensity that are delivered as students demonstrate insufficient response to less intensive intervention. These tiered prevention models are delivered using methods of empirically validated reading instruction. Assessment is a cornerstone of RTI models, including assessment for the purposes of screening to identify students at risk for reading difficulties, planning instruction that targets the needs of struggling readers (i.e., diagnostic assessment), monitoring student progress, and measuring outcomes.

Preventive RTI reading models often consist of three tiers of intervention (see, for example, Batsche et al., 2006; Denton, Fletcher, Simos, Papanicolaou, & Anthony, 2007; Denton & Mathes, 2003; Fletcher, Denton, Fuchs, & Vaughn, 2005; Vaughn, Wanzek, Woodruff, & Linan-Thompson, 2007). The first tier consists of high-quality classroom-level reading instruction delivered to all students. This typically includes differentiation of instruction to better address the unique needs of all students, particularly those at risk for reading difficulties. Students with inadequate RTI in Tier 1 receive Tier 2 intervention in addition to quality classroom instruction, provided either by their classroom teachers or by other interventionists. However, even when these two levels of intervention are highly effective, there is a small group of students who receive supplemental intervention but continue to struggle. Under a three-tier model, these students would receive Tier 3 intensive intervention.

Exactly how these Tier 3 interventions are provided differs in implementation. For some schools, this tertiary intervention is provided in "special education" (e.g., Denton & Mathes, 2003). That is, to receive a Tier 3 intervention, the student must be declared eligible for special education services. In other intervention approaches, Tier 3 is considered a general education intervention and is provided to all students who need it. In some school implementation models, only students who require this level of intensive intervention *over an extended period of time* would be candidates for special education (e.g., Batsche et al., 2006). In other models, Tier 3 intervention is provided by special education teachers; however, in these models entitlement to special education is not a requirement for receiving Tier 3 intervention.

Students who are identified as inadequate responders under a tiered intervention model have been found to differ from students with other forms of low achievement in cognitive characteristics and preintervention achievement scores (Stage, Abbott, Jenkins, & Berninger, 2003; Vellutino, Scanlon, & Jaccard, 2003; Vaughn, Linan-Thompson, & Hickman, 2003), as well as in their neurological processing when engaged in reading tasks (Simos et al., 2007a, 2007b). Tiered prevention models hold considerable promise for implementing RTI as a component in the identification of SLDs, while also being a vehicle for providing intervention to all young children who are at risk for reading difficulties, regardless of eligibility for special education services.

Effective Class-Wide Reading Instruction

The first, and arguably the most important, component of effective early reading intervention is the provision of evidence-based high-quality classroom reading instruction to all students in the primary grades. Quality classroom reading instruction can have a large impact. For example, Foorman, Francis, Fletcher, Schatschneider, and Mehta (1998) demonstrated that first grade classroom reading instruction that included explicit, systematic instruction in the alphabetic principle within a print-rich environment brought 75% of at-risk readers to average word reading levels.

Snow and her colleagues in the National Research Council early reading group, concluded that, "Adequate progress in learning to read English beyond the initial level depends on having established a working understanding of how sounds are represented alphabetically, sufficient practice in reading to achieve fluency with different kinds of texts written for different purposes, instruction focused on concept and vocabulary growth, and control over procedures for monitoring comprehension and repairing misunderstandings" (Snow et al., 1998, p. 223). They emphasized the importance of providing (a) explicit instruction in phonemic awareness and phonics, (b) instruction in making meaning from text, and (c) many opportunities to read and write connected text within a literature-rich environment, both with teacher support and feedback and independently. Finally, they identified the need to adapt instruction (including grouping practices and the level of explicitness) to meet the needs of each student.

These recommendations have been echoed in subsequent research syntheses and meta-analyses. The National Reading Panel (2000) described the critical content that should be the focus of reading instruction in the primary grades, identifying phonemic awareness, phonics, fluency, vocabulary, and comprehension. Converging research evidence has demonstrated that effective classroom instruction for most students in kindergarten through Grade 3 includes explicitly and directly teaching phonics or word study and providing opportunities to apply skills in reading and writing connected text (e.g., Ehri, 2003; National Reading Panel, 2000; Rayner, Foorman, Perfetti, Pesetsky, & Seidenberg, 2001; Snow et al., 1998). Effective K–3 instruction also includes integrated instruction in fluency, vocabulary, and comprehension (e.g., Chard, Vaughn, & Tyler, 2002; Jitendra, Edwards, Sacks, & Jacobson, 2004).

Implementation and Adaptation of an Evidence-Based Core Reading Program

Teachers should not be expected to reinvent the wheel in designing classroom reading instruction. A quality, evidence-based published program is the foundation of Tier 1 instruction. To ensure the provision of quality classroom reading instruction, administrators and teachers (a) adopt a published curriculum that has evidence of effectiveness from the converging research base in reading instruction, (b) ensure that teachers have adequate training (and ongoing coaching if possible) to implement the program with confidence and fidelity, and (c) monitor the effective implementation of the curriculum.

Adaptation of Classroom Instruction for At-Risk Readers
Effectively teaching reading to each child in a primary-grade classroom presents substantial challenges, as a typical classroom may include students who are unable to read even at basic levels, along with students who are already proficient readers and need instruction in advanced comprehension and vocabulary strategies. It is common that some students in a primary classroom will have identified disabilities, while others

may have severe learning and behavioral difficulties that have not yet been identified as disabilities. Still others may be identified as having gifts and talents and require specialized instruction. Increasing numbers of students do not speak English as their primary language but receive their reading instruction in English-only classrooms. Meeting the needs of each individual student is a tall order for one teacher, a task that should not be underestimated.

Differentiating instruction. A key characteristic of quality Tier 1 class-wide intervention is *differentiation of instruction*. Differentiation means providing groups of students within the classroom with instruction that is purposefully planned to address their needs. Typically, it involves teachers implementing reading instruction in small groups, as well as whole class and peer partner formats. Differentiated instruction for young students at risk for reading difficulties usually includes the use of diagnostic and progress monitoring assessment (e.g., program placement or mastery tests, inventories of sight word or letter–sound knowledge, repeated measures of reading and reading-related skills) that can provide information to teachers about student strengths and needs. The results of these assessments can be used to form small, flexible groups of students with similar needs and to plan their instruction. Some teachers may need support in designing effective differentiated instruction, managing small-group instruction, and establishing classroom routines that enable students with whom the teacher is not working to engage in independent practice of concepts and skills they have already been taught without direct teacher monitoring.

Although a quality reading curriculum will provide the foundation for effective class-wide instruction, it is typically necessary for teachers to *adapt instruction* for at-risk readers. For example, programs typically introduce skills at a rapid rate and often do not provide enough opportunities for practice for struggling readers. Quality core reading instruction can be adapted for at-risk readers by making it more explicit and systematic and by increasing opportunities for practice with and without teacher feedback and scaffolding. These approaches are described in the following sections.

Increasing explicitness of instruction. A teacher who provides *explicit instruction* (a) plans lessons purposefully with clear objectives in mind, (b) clearly models or demonstrates skills and provides clear descriptions of new concepts (including providing both clear examples and nonexamples), (c) provides guided practice, (d) checks for understanding, (e) provides timely feedback as well as deliberate scaffolding, (f) monitors independent practice, (g) provides opportunities for cumulative practice of previously learned skills and concepts, and (h) monitors student progress, providing reteaching as necessary. When at-risk learners receive clear, explicit instruction, they are not left to infer information. Students who are easily confused are more likely to be successful when teachers demonstrate and clearly explain what they need to learn. On the other hand, if points of confusion are not addressed and foundational skills are not mastered, students will likely fall farther and farther behind their peers.

For example, imagine that Teacher 1 is reading a book aloud to kindergarten students. She comes to the word *pebble* in the book and asks, "Who knows what a pebble is?" Several students answer at once. One calls out, "Part of a flower"; another says, "A rock." The teacher says, "Yes. See the pebbles in the picture?" pointing to the pebbles in the book's illustration, then continues to read the story. Now imagine Teacher 2 reading the same book to her kindergarten class. She has identified in advance three or four words that may be unfamiliar to the students and that are appropriate to teach, and she has written simple, easy-to-understand definitions, as well as more elaborate descriptions, for each word. She selects the word *pebble* because it is important to the understanding of the book she is reading and it appears in traditional stories but is not commonly used in oral conversations. When she comes to the word *pebble*, she says clearly, "A pebble is a little rock. Look at the picture of a pebble here in the book. This big rock is not a pebble [pointing to the illustration], but this little rock is a pebble. Say *pebble*. [Students repeat the word.] Sometimes children like to pick up little pebbles and throw them out into the water." After reading the book, she returns to the word and asks students about times they may have picked up pebbles. She makes sure that students actually use the word *pebble*. She provides feedback or support if students have problems using the word correctly. She will return to the word in future days and use it again to give students multiple exposures to it. Teacher 1 requires students to infer what a pebble is from the picture, and many students may be left confused. Teacher 2 is providing explicit vocabulary instruction.

Providing systematic instruction. Systematic instruction is carefully sequenced, so that easier skills are presented and mastered before more complex skills are introduced, and confusions are minimized. For example, a systematic beginning reading program would introduce new letter–sound correspondences in a sequence designed so that letters are separated from each other if they are potentially visually confusing (e.g., *b* and *d*; *p* and *q*; *v* and *w*) or have similar sounds (e.g., "short" *e* and *i*). Skills and strategies are taught in a predetermined order according to a clear scope and sequence so that "holes" are not left in students' learning. Students' mastery of concepts, skills, and strategies is monitored so that reteaching can occur when needed.

Students with reading difficulties tend to benefit when instruction progresses systematically from simple skills, words, and text to more complex words, higher-level vocabulary, and more challenging comprehension strategies. In most effective reading intervention programs, the pace of introduction of new material is reasonable to ensure mastery by at-risk readers, and the amount of new information introduced at any one lesson is kept to a minimum. Much of the lesson consists of practice of previously introduced skills, strategies, and concepts and the integration of these with the newly taught material. The most important way schools can ensure that teachers provide students with reading difficulties with systematic instruction is by adopting and using curricula developed in this way.

Increasing opportunities for practice. Published core reading programs rarely include enough *practice activities* for at-risk readers to master skills. Students with learning difficulties typically need extended guided, independent, and cumulative practice. During *guided practice*, students practice reading skills in isolation, as well as the application of reading and writing skills in connected text *with teacher feedback*. Students need both positive and corrective feedback. Specific positive feedback calls attention to behaviors and processes the student is implementing well, and also reinforces partially correct responses and attempts, even when they do not result in correct answers. Students also need to know when they have made mistakes. If clear corrective feedback is not provided, students are likely to continue making the same errors, in effect "practicing their mistakes" (Denton & Hocker, 2006, p. 17), forming habits that are difficult to break. Students also need *independent practice*, during which they implement skills and strategies without teacher support (but with close teacher monitoring and reteaching when necessary).

Finally, students at risk for reading difficulties need large amounts of *cumulative practice* over time to learn skills and strategies to the point at which they can apply them automatically, as proficient readers do. In cumulative practice, students practice items they have previously learned integrated with newly learned items, supporting retention of previously learned material. Cumulative practice also provides at-risk readers with the opportunity to *discriminate* between previously and newly learned items such as letter–sound correspondences and high-frequency irregular words. For example, imagine that a student has previously learned to recognize the words *was* and *what*. In a new lesson, the student learns the word *who*. It will be important to provide opportunities to practice quickly and accurately discriminating between these words and other words the student knows in order to integrate new and prior learning.

Two Tier 1 Adaptations

Two broad categories of research-supported classroom-based Tier 1 adaptations have potential for affecting reading performance without requiring major restructuring of the reading program. These are *not* substitutes for the high-fidelity implementation of an evidence-based core reading program or for differentiated instruction for at-risk readers, as described in the previous paragraphs. However, both can be effective in providing additional reinforcement and practice in previously taught concepts, skills, and strategies.

Class-wide peer tutoring. Solid research evidence supports the effectiveness of class-wide peer tutoring models implemented in the early grades to aid in reading development (Fuchs & Fuchs, 2005; Mathes, Torgesen, & Allor, 2001; McMaster, Fuchs, & Fuchs, 2006; Saenz, Fuchs, & Fuchs, 2005; also see chapter 24 in this book). In a typical implementation described by Mathes, Grek, and Howard (1999), low-performing readers are paired with more skilled readers. In these pairs, students engage in highly standardized practice of previously learned elements such as letter–sound correspondences and high-frequency words, followed by paired reading that includes a simple prereading and postreading comprehension routine. It is critical that students are carefully and explicitly taught *routines* to follow when engaging in peer tutoring so that they can implement this format independently with little off-task time.

Computer-assisted instruction. Hall, Hughes, and Filbert (2000) conducted a systematic synthesis of the research on computer-assisted instruction (CAI) for students with learning disabilities, locating experimental, quasi-experimental, and single case studies involving students in kindergarten through high school. They found that most computer applications studied for this population are designed to provide *extra* drill and practice in basic skills. The intensity of CAI provided in these studies varied greatly, with students receiving from 1 to 50 sessions lasting 10–40 minutes each. Hall et al. found evidence of effectiveness of CAI in supporting reading growth for students with learning disabilities, particularly in providing additional opportunities for practice in skills that had been previously taught. It is important to note that *in no case was a computer application suggested as a replacement for teacher-delivered instruction.*

The Hall et al. (2000) review revealed that, in 13 of the 17 studies that met their criteria for inclusion in the synthesis, computer programs were designed to incorporate teaching strategies that have been found effective for students with learning difficulties, and that all of these studies resulted in significant effects favoring the CAI application. Specifically, effective programs included (a) those in which skills and strategies were introduced in a purposeful, systematic way; (b) those that provided elaborated error correction (i.e., correction that included instruction) rather than simply informed the student that he or she had made an error or simply provided the correct response; and (c) those that cycled back through previously missed items, providing additional rehearsal of correct responses (i.e., cumulative practice). Hall and colleagues suggested that educators evaluate computer applications for these and other characteristics associated with effective instruction.

When Class-Wide Instruction Is Not Enough—Tier 2 Intervention

In multitier prevention models, students with an unsatisfactory response to quality class-wide instruction in the primary grades are provided with Tier 2 intervention in addition to their regular classroom reading instruction. This is sometimes referred to as secondary prevention or secondary intervention. The primary goal of Tier 2 intervention is to reduce the performance gap between at-risk readers and their typically developing peers. Given that closing this gap—like catching up in a race— necessitates that at-risk readers learn at a faster rate than their average-performing peers, secondary intervention for these at-risk readers must be both *highly effective* and *efficient.* Unlike traditional "remedial reading" classes, Tier 2 interventions are delivered with a level of intensity that will accelerate the progress of students who have previously demonstrated slow growth on repeated measures of reading skills. Both McMaster, Fuchs, Fuchs, and Compton (2005) and Mathes et al. (2005) found that potentially less than 5% of first-grade students would remain at risk for reading difficulties if high-quality Tier 2 interventions supplemented Tier 1 instruction in first grade.

Characteristics of Effective Intervention

Converging research evidence supports the efficacy of intervening with young students at risk for reading difficulties, both for monolingual English readers and, more recently, for English language learners. (For monolingual, see Blachman et al., 2004; Denton, Fletcher, Anthony, & Francis, 2006; Felton, 1993; Jenkins & O'Connor, 2002; Kamps

& Greenwood, 2005; Lovett, Steinbach, & Frijters, 2000; Mathes et al., 2005; Torgesen et al., 1999; Torgesen, Alexander, et al., 2001; Vellutino et al., 1996. For English language learners, see Vaughn, Cirino et al., 2006; Vaughn, Linan-Thompson et al., 2006.) A recent systematic research synthesis examined implications of studies of long-term, "extensive" early reading interventions, defined as those in which small-group interventions were provided as supplements to regular classroom reading instruction for at least 100 sessions (e.g., daily for about 20 weeks; Wanzek & Vaughn, 2007). Wanzek and Vaughn included studies published in peer-reviewed journals between 1995 and 2005, in which participants were in kindergarten through third grade and were described as having reading difficulties, at risk for reading difficulties, having learning disabilities, and/or having speech–language disorders. They concluded that providing small-group intervention for at least 20 weeks was feasible for schools, that such interventions have resulted in positive outcomes for students, and that interventions with the strongest effects included *both* phonics instruction and text reading. This finding is congruent with that of Snow et al. (1998), discussed previously.

In additional exploratory analyses, Wanzek and Vaughn (2007) found that, regardless of intervention duration, interventions provided in one-on-one formats tended to have higher effects than those provided in small groups of two to eight students. However, they cautioned against overinterpreting these findings; causal inference is not possible because none of the synthesized studies experimentally manipulated intervention duration or group size. Furthermore, it was impossible to contrast, based on the synthesized studies, small-group interventions (i.e., two to four students) with intervention provided in larger group sizes.

Wanzek and Vaughn (2007) also examined research evidence on the effects of scripted interventions and those of less prescriptive interventions, finding no evidence of differences in effects associated with these approaches. This conclusion was based on a relatively small group of studies, but was strengthened by a randomized field trial by Mathes et al. (2005), who compared the effects of two approaches on the reading outcomes of at-risk first-grade readers: one was a fully scripted intervention with a direct instruction approach (the *Proactive* intervention); the other was an intervention in which teachers were provided with a systematic instructional sequence and a menu of fully described activities, from which they designed individualized lessons based on continuous diagnostic assessment (the *Responsive* intervention). Random assignment to one of the two intervention conditions or to a comparison "typical school practice" condition was done within schools. Both the Proactive and Responsive interventions were provided in groups of three to four students by highly trained teachers over 30 weeks, and students in both conditions received explicit instruction in phonemic awareness and phonics, integrated with instruction in fluency and comprehension.

The two interventions differed in that students in the Proactive intervention spent comparably more time practicing skills in isolation and applied them in fully decodable text, whereas those in the Responsive intervention spent more time engaged in reading and writing, with teacher feedback and scaffolding, and read text leveled for difficulty but not designed to be decodable. Students in both intervention groups had significantly higher outcomes than those in the typical practice comparison group on multiple reading measures, but the effects of the two interventions differed significantly on only one measure—the Woodcock-Johnson III Tests of Achievement Word Attack subtest, a test of pseudoword reading, in which the Proactive approach had stronger effects. It is important to note that both interventions had characteristics associated with positive outcomes for students with reading difficulties, including explicit instruction, engaged reading practice with feedback, multiple opportunities for practice, and continuous monitoring of student progress. Differences in the level of standardization versus individualization of the two interventions, and the use of decodable text, did not result in overall significant differences in outcomes.

As shown by these and other studies, outcomes for children at risk for reading difficulties can be significantly affected through the following types of interventions:

- Are provided in addition to regular classroom reading instruction
- Are provided in small-group or one-on-one formats
- Include explicit, well-organized (systematic) instruction as well as opportunities to read connected text
- Are provided for 20–40 minutes at least three to five times per week with extended opportunities for practice, including guided, independent, and cumulative practice with teacher feedback
- Include continuous progress monitoring assessment

What is considered appropriate Tier 2 intervention differs across models of tiered reading intervention that are currently being implemented in various locations. In some, the approaches that are described here as Tier 1 adaptations would be considered Tier 2 interventions. In other implementations, students receive a few weeks of Tier 2 tutoring three or four times per week, while students in some schools receive Tier 2 intervention daily for 20 to 30 weeks. When making decisions regarding the duration of Tier 2 and Tier 3 intervention, it is critical to remember that the hope is to have at-risk readers catch up with their peers , in a relatively brief amount of time. At the same time, it is important to think about the implications of providing intervention for long periods of time without evaluation for special education services.

As educators select or develop instructional programs and curricular materials to implement during Tier 2 or Tier 3 intervention, they should consider whether the program (a) has evidence from research of effectiveness with at-risk readers at the grade level and level of severity of the students in their schools, (b) addresses the specific needs of the students, and (c) is designed to give students many opportunities to actively participate in hands-on activities that provide practice in key skills and in engaged reading practice with teacher feedback.

Implementation of Reading Intervention

Providing quality reading intervention to all students who respond inadequately to Tier 1 classroom instruction can be challenging, given the realities associated with limited time, personnel, and funding in schools. The extent of the resources needed to provide

Tier 2 and Tier 3 intervention will be determined by the number of students at risk for reading problems. If a large percentage of students in a school need Tier 2 intervention, it is advisable to examine Tier 1 classroom reading instruction to determine whether (a) an evidence-based core reading program has been adopted and is being *implemented with high fidelity* by teachers; (b) teachers have been provided with adequate professional development to implement the core reading program competently and confidently; (c) teachers are providing differentiated instruction to meet the needs of diverse learners; and (d) teachers are adapting instruction for at-risk readers by making it more explicit and systematic, increasing opportunities for practice, and providing instruction using appropriate materials, including instructional-level text (text that can be read accurately with teacher support). As a rule of thumb, the more students in a school require Tier 2 intervention, the more critical it is that Tier 1 classroom teachers adapt their instruction as described.

Supplemental intervention can be provided within various formats. Students may receive "push in" intervention, in which the interventionist provides tutoring in the student's regular classroom, or "pull-out" intervention, in which tutoring is provided outside the regular classroom setting. In some schools, intervention is provided before or after school. In others, students in the primary grades leave their classrooms for a few minutes for each intervention lesson. In any case, Tier 2 intervention should be provided *in addition to* Tier 1 classroom reading instruction rather than replacing it. Students who struggle to learn to read need *more* instruction and practice, and, even if their decoding is impaired, they can benefit from grade-level instruction in comprehension and vocabulary.

Interventionists. Tier 2 intervention can be provided by (a) general education classroom teachers who work cooperatively to organize their daily schedules to provide interventions, (b) reading specialists or other certified teachers, including special educators, or (c) carefully selected, highly trained paraprofessionals who receive sustained coaching and supervision from a skilled and experienced teacher. Although having certified teachers provide reading intervention may be ideal, research evidence indicates that Tier 2 intervention provided by well-trained paraprofessionals or tutors who are provided ongoing feedback and support is associated with improved outcomes for students (Elbaum, Vaughn, Hughes, & Moody, 2000; Grek, Mathes, & Torgesen, 2003). If paraprofessionals provide Tier 2 intervention, the following are important considerations: (a) the paraprofessionals should be carefully selected (e.g., able to pass a test of phonemic awareness, experience working positively with children); (b) group sizes should be kept very small (i.e., ratios from 1:1 to 1:3) to facilitate effective instruction and behavior management; (c) published, highly structured reading intervention programs should be implemented, supporting inexperienced tutors; and (d) an experienced full-time teacher should coach the paraprofessionals, spending extended amounts of time observing the tutoring, modeling effective instruction, problem-solving when students fail to make adequate progress, and providing follow-up training sessions. In contrast, Tier 3 intervention should be provided by experienced reading teachers or special educators. Students in Tier 3 are the most challenging to teach, and they need (and deserve) instruction from the most knowledgeable and experienced teachers.

Group size and duration.   Although providing one-on-one instruction to at-risk readers has been associated with positive outcomes, (e.g., Torgesen, Alexander, et al., 2001; Simos et al., 2002; Velutino et al., 1996) this is often not feasible in school settings. In several studies, a large percentage of students have responded positively to Tier 2 intervention delivered in small groups of three to five students (e.g., Mathes et al., 2005; Vaughn & Linan-Thompson, 2003). In general, intervention provided in groups of about three students with one teacher can have comparable effects at Tier 2 to one-on-one interventions (Elbaum, Vaughn, Hughes, & Moody, 2000; Vaughn et al., 2003). Conversely, there is evidence that students benefit significantly less from intervention provided in groups of about 10 students (Vaughn et al., 2003).

Increasing intervention intensity at Tier 3 implies smaller instructional group sizes, longer daily sessions, and intervention over a longer term. A landmark study illustrates what highly intensive intervention can achieve: Torgesen, Alexander, et al. (2001) provided students with severe reading needs in grades 3–5 (all of whom had identified learning disabilities) with intervention for 2 hours per day over an 8-week period in a reading clinic. The intervention was associated with substantial standard score gains in decoding and comprehension, which were maintained for 2 years following intervention. Denton et al. (2006) evaluated the effectiveness of Tier 3 intervention provided in school, rather than in clinical settings. In that study, students who had previously had inadequate RTI in a less intensive intervention, along with a group of teacher-identified students with severe reading difficulties and disabilities, were provided with daily intervention in groups of two students with one teacher over a 16-week period. For the first 8 weeks, intervention was provided for 2 hours per day using a published program that emphasized phonemic awareness and phonemic decoding. Following this phase, students received intervention targeting oral reading fluency for 1 hour per day for an additional 8-week period. Although the results of this study were not as robust as those reported by Torgesen, Alexander, et al., students made significant pre–post growth over the initial decoding-focused phase in basic reading skills (word recognition and phonemic decoding) and in reading comprehension. During the second, fluency-oriented phase, students made significant growth in oral reading fluency. Despite this significant growth in mean standard scores, there was considerable variation in individual students' RTI (Denton, Fletcher, et al., 2007). While some students benefitted considerably from the research intervention, some clearly required either a different type of intervention or intervention provided for a longer duration than the 16 weeks provided in this study.

Although providing intervention for 2 hours per day may not appear feasible in school settings, only a very small percentage of students should require this level of intervention intensity if Tiers 1 and 2 are of high quality. In the implementation of this model in school settings by Denton and her colleagues (2006) the 2-hour intervention block replaced a portion of the Tier 3 students' regular reading instruction (which many received in resource room settings). If Tier 3 intervention is delivered in addition to students' regular classroom reading instruction, somewhat shorter intervention periods may be sufficient. For example, Vaughn, Wanzek, Linan-Thompson, and Murray (2007) described a program of research in which Tier 3 intervention was provided for 50 minutes every day.

Prevention Models and Special Education

For some students who continue to demonstrate inadequate response to intervention of increasing intensity, a full comprehensive evaluation for special education eligibility is indicated. Measures of students' RTI when provided with quality intervention (such as repeated assessments used for monitoring student progress) become a key element of that comprehensive evaluation. For a discussion of the relationship between Tier 3 intervention and special education, and of the nature of the comprehensive evaluation in an RTI model, see Batsche et al. (2006).

REMEDIAL INTERVENTIONS FOR OLDER READERS WITH READING DIFFICULTIES AND DISABILITIES

Considerably more is known about teaching younger students with reading difficulties and disabilities than teaching older students. Early interventions for reading difficulties are typically provided before age 8 and are considered preventive—with instructional goals expressly designed to prevent further reading difficulties and to ensure that students are reading on grade level or above. Interventions for older students typically are remedial, with the goal of enhancing reading performance so students can read for pleasure and to learn.

Three syntheses of studies have recently been conducted examining the effects of reading interventions for older students (Edmonds et al., 2009; Reutebuch, Vaughn, & Scammacca, 2009; Scammacca et al., 2007). Each of these syntheses reviewed relevant research on intervention for older students with reading difficulties but employed different criteria to select the synthesized studies. For example, the synthesis provided by Edmonds et al. summarized interventions for 4th through 12th graders with reading difficulties, with an expressed focus on how the interventions influenced comprehension outcomes, whereas the Scammacca et al. synthesis looked at broader outcomes (e.g., fluency and vocabulary), and the synthesis by Reutebuch et al. focused specifically on students with disabilities.

These syntheses provided the foundation for our analysis and interpretation of effective interventions with older readers. Although the goals of each of these syntheses have a somewhat different focus, many of the outcomes are converging. We have organized the findings from these interventions based on the primary instructional focus of the intervention study: word study, reading fluency, vocabulary, and reading comprehension. We first briefly describe each of these instructional foci with special consideration for what it means for instructing older students with reading difficulties and then summarize the relevant research findings.

Word Study

Many educators wonder whether word study is still a relevant instructional focus for older students. We define word study for older students as explicit instruction in word analysis that allows students to be more proficient word-level readers. For older students this may be a review of some of the phonics rules and skills that were either not acquired or incorrectly applied (e.g., vowel rules, reading digraphs). Word study for older students also frequently involves reading multisyllable words. Older students who read words accurately and fluently, and within two grade levels of their current grade, may not require further word study instruction. However, many students are reaching the upper grades deficient in the skills necessary for them to become competent readers, including the ability to read words accurately.

Fletcher (2007) reported that as many as 60% of older students who have reading difficulties have impaired word reading. An additional percentage can recognize words accurately but read slowly, essentially because of slow and nonautomatic word recognition. Thus, the majority of older students with reading difficulties or disabilities will require additional word study instruction to become proficient word readers so that they can learn effortlessly from the text. These students may have learned ways to compensate for their poor decoding by using listening comprehension to avoid reading. Many of these students have listening comprehension abilities that exceed their reading comprehension, with slow and inaccurate decoding as the likely reason (Shankweiler et al., 1999).

There is evidence that older students who fall behind may benefit considerably from specialized, intensive instruction aimed at improving word reading (e.g., Torgesen, Alexander, et al., 2001). While decoding instruction is typically associated with reading instruction for younger students, age should not be the factor in determining the focus of reading instruction (Moats, 2001); rather, the critical skills students need for success should be the relevant factor. Some older students with reading difficulties are proficient decoders and need instruction in comprehension and vocabulary, but many have reading difficulties that are more comprehensive and require an integrated approach that addresses all aspects of reading, including quick and accurate word reading. For a discussion of the use of assessments to identify students' instructional needs, see Denton, Bryan, et al. (2007).

Word Study Instruction for Older Students

Curtis (2004) indicated that word study interventions with older readers might address one or both of the following: word recognition instruction or word analysis instruction. Word study intervention with older students does not typically include instruction in phonemic awareness, although this domain may be addressed for students with severe word reading difficulties, particularly those with dyslexia.

Word recognition instruction is focused on the phonic elements, syllabication or chunking strategies, and irregular word reading practice needed by many older readers with reading difficulties. This instruction typically occurs through a diagnostic-teaching process that involves identifying those phonic elements students know well and can apply consistently and proficiently and those phonic elements that are either unknown or applied inconsistently. Word study instruction for older students differs from that provided to younger students in that the goal is to move as quickly as possible, teaching the critical and missing phonic elements and applying them to many word types, including multisyllable words and both frequently and infrequently encountered words, spending little or no time reteaching elements the students have mastered. This procedure is necessary because older students have considerably less time to accelerate their reading performance and considerably more complex words to read. As students' reading improves, word study becomes more advanced, addressing application to increasingly complex words.

Word study instruction for older students normally includes instruction in morphology, including affixes, root words, and derivations. The focus is on teaching students practices for gaining access to word reading and meaning by purposely breaking words into meaningful parts such as prefixes, suffixes, root words, and syllables. Students are usually taught to "chunk" words into parts that allow them to quickly read and understand the meanings of the words.

Research on Word Study Interventions

Edmonds et al. (2009) identified three studies of word-level interventions with older students with reading difficulties that had reading comprehension as an outcome, yielding a mean weighted effect size of about 1/3 of a standard deviation. They concluded that word study interventions significantly influenced comprehension. These findings are important because they build a stronger case for the value of teaching word study to older students with reading difficulties, and benefits are evident for comprehension as well as for word reading.

Although there is not an abundance of experimental studies with older readers that specifically focus on word recognition instruction, a study by Bhattacharya and Ehri (2004) provides evidence supporting the use of graphosyllabic analysis to help students read and spell. Bhattacharya and Ehri designed and implemented an intervention that capitalized on the words students knew automatically and accurately (sight words) to teach word parts and components for decoding unknown words to increase word reading accuracy. Students were taught to break words into syllables orally and count their "beats," then map these oral beats or syllables to the words' corresponding graphemic components, and then blend the components into words. Following the intervention, participants performed about 1 standard deviation higher than a similar group of nonparticipants on tasks that required decoding novel words and about 3/4 of a standard deviation better on word reading and spelling.

Intervention research on the benefits of morphological instruction is in the beginning stages and suggests promise rather than proven practice (Ebbers & Denton, 2008). Though morphology does not contribute to word reading at the same level as cognitive ability, vocabulary, and phonology (Deacon & Kirby, 2004; Singson,

Mahony, & Mann, 2000), morphological awareness does contribute about 4–5% of the variance in decoding (Deacon & Kirby, 2004; Mahony, Singson, & Mann, 2000), with a shift in emphasis from phonology to morphology as students encounter more difficult words and text in about fourth grade (Carlisle, 2000; Green et al., 2003).

An experimental study by Abbott and Berninger (1999) provided a rigorous test of the effectiveness of morphology instruction with older students with reading difficulties. Students were randomly assigned to an intervention that focused on structural (morphemic) analysis with training in the alphabetic principle or to an intervention consisting of alphabetic principle training alone. Since both treatment groups received instruction in word recognition using graphophonemic relationships, whatever effects resulted could be attributed to instruction on structural analysis (i.e., morphology). Controlling for instructional time, the students who received the structural analysis intervention along with instruction in the alphabetic principle outperformed the students who received alphabetic principle instruction alone.

Word study is likely to be an important part of reading instruction for older readers with reading difficulties. Although instruction in multisyllable words, complex word types, affixes, prefixes, and root words are all essential elements of word study, providing students with extensive practice reading words in connected text is also necessary to support the development of automatic word recognition.

Reading Fluency

Reading fluency is another important element of reading instruction for older students. Fluency can be described as the ability to read text with appropriate speed, accuracy, and expression (i.e., inflection and phrasing). Fluency can be affected by several factors, particularly the ability to recognize words automatically. For typically developing readers, vocabulary knowledge also appears to influence fluency beyond the contribution of word recognition (Torgesen, Rashotte, and Alexander, 2001). Fluency can also be affected by older students' awareness of the purpose for reading and by their metacognitive monitoring of comprehension. That is, skilled readers slow their reading rate when reading challenging material when the intent is to learn from text, and they slow down or reread sections of text when comprehension breaks down.

For older students with reading difficulties, fluency is primarily affected by the ability to recognize words automatically at sight. Torgesen, Rashotte, Alexander, Alexander, and MacPhee (2003) described the situation faced by older students with word-level reading difficulties: "When they are asked to read material that is close to their grade level in difficulty, these children recognize far fewer words in the passage at a single glance than do children who read in the average range. It is the necessity of slowing down to phonemically decode or guess at words that is the most critical factor in limiting the reading fluency of children with severe reading difficulties" (p. 293). Reading with accuracy and appropriate speed, also known as reading with automaticity, is considered an important element of reading instruction for older students because poor readers typically demonstrate low levels of fluency, and the ability to read correctly, with appropriate speed and inflection, is predictive of reading comprehension (Kuhn & Stahl, 2000; Meyer, & Felton, 1999; Shinn & Good, 1992).

Chall (1983) was one of the first to recognize the role of fluency in skilled reading and included it in her six-stage model of reading. She described fluency as "ungluing from print" by automatically making use of the features in text, such as stress and intonation, while reading. Chall saw fluency as a transition stage promoting comprehension. Support for Chall's interpretation of the relationship between fluency and comprehension can be drawn from evidence that students' scores on brief measures of oral reading fluency are highly predictive of scores on standardized tests of reading comprehension (Fuchs, Fuchs, Hosp, & Jenkins, 2001), although relationships between measures of fluency and comprehension are weaker for middle school students than for younger students (e.g., Denton et al., 2009).

Older students who read effortlessly and successfully typically read between 120 to 170 words correctly per minute, adjusting their reading rate for the text difficulty and the purpose of their reading (Tindal, Hasbrouck, & Jones, 2005). Students with reading difficulties typically read below 100 words correctly per minute and with little expression. There seems to be general consensus that students with reading difficulties read slowly and less accurately than proficient readers. There is considerably less consensus about how to effectively promote fluent reading with older readers with reading difficulties. Little evidence suggests that focusing specifically on those reading fluency activities that are beneficial to younger readers will be associated with the type of reading improvement needed by older readers. More likely, these students will require extensive interventions that also address word study and comprehension.

Fluency Instruction for Older Students

Fluency instruction for younger students typically consists of some variation of repeated reading. There are many ways repeated reading is achieved with elementary-grade children, including partner reading, rereading while listening to a model reader on an audiotape, and rereading through "readers' theatre." Considerably less is known about effective fluency intervention for students at the secondary level. Research has yet to identify the types of fluency activities that are most appropriate for secondary-level readers, particularly whether instructional time with these students is better used by addressing word reading accuracy, fluency, and comprehension through reading of a wide range of different texts rather than rereading the same text multiple times.

What researchers do know is that older readers need many opportunities to read text on their instructional and independent reading levels, whether these opportunities are provided through rereading or continuous reading of text. Closing the gap between the lower reading level of students with reading difficulties and the expected reading level is unlikely to occur without organized opportunities for extensive reading, both with and without teacher feedback.

Research on Fluency Interventions for Older Students

A recent synthesis by Scammacca et al., (2007) reported on the limited available research on fluency interventions for older readers with reading difficulties, showing that such interventions had a very small effect on students' improved reading rate and accuracy ($g = .26$, $n = 4$, 95% CI $= -.08$, .61) and no effect on standardized measures of reading comprehension ($g = -.07$, $n = 2$, 95% CI $= -.54$, .39). This synthesis reflects data from the few available studies that met inclusion criteria for the review ($n = 4$). In all studies the intervention was provided for a limited time, suggesting low intensity. These studies were largely variations of repeated reading. Repeated reading with older students appears to help students' sight-word reading, and therefore gains are generalized to unpracticed passages only when those passages share a large number of the same words as the passages students practiced repeatedly (Rashotte & Torgesen, 1985). This contrasts with the National Reading Panel report (2000), which found support for repeated oral reading with younger children. More experimental research is needed to validate effective practices for supporting fluency development for older students with reading difficulties. It may require a combination of focusing more on word study plus increasing considerably the amount of time students spend reading.

Vocabulary

While vocabulary development is normally considered to be necessary with younger readers, it is often neglected as part of an effective intervention for older students with reading difficulties. This is unfortunate, since many older readers have underdeveloped vocabularies and concept knowledge, which interferes with their understanding and learning from text. The influence of vocabulary on learning and understanding extends beyond reading in English and language arts classes; it also influences learning in social studies, science, and math. It is precisely because of this prevailing influence of vocabulary on learning and comprehension that *all* teachers—not just reading teachers—can aid learning by spending several minutes every day highlighting and explicitly teaching the key vocabulary needed to understand and learn from oral presentations and text reading. Improving reading outcomes requires ongoing support for vocabulary development because text understanding is significantly influenced by word meaning (Graves, 1989; Graves, Brunetti, & Slater, 1982). However, as in other domains, more experimental research on effective vocabulary instruction for older students is warranted. Though research has documented that vocabulary instruction is related to comprehension, the research base shows that vocabulary instruction leads to improved comprehension (Kamil, 2003; Stanovich, 2000).

Although vocabulary instruction is highly valuable and likely necessary for the majority of students with reading difficulties, some students' underdeveloped vocabulary knowledge may be related to their limited reading and the low background knowledge they have acquired. This suggests that, as in the case of word reading instruction, a combination of direct instruction and engaged reading practice in text of appropriate difficulty may be necessary for the remediation of vocabulary difficulties in older students.

Vocabulary Instruction for Older Students

Much like Curtis's (2004) description of word study instruction, vocabulary instruction has two goals: to teach the meanings of specific words and to teach word-learning strategies, that is, strategies students can implement independently to infer meanings of unfamiliar words while reading.

The first step in planning instruction in the meanings of specific words is word selection. In this step, teachers consider the words students need to know to communicate effectively and understand what they hear and read. Particular focus is placed on academic vocabulary, words that students may not know but are likely to encounter frequently in academic settings. Several of these occur frequently in written directions. Some examples are *summarize, initial, represent, survey, conclusion, resolution, bias, similarly,* and *sequence.* In addition, students need to know and understand the academic vocabulary specific to various content areas (e.g., *amoeba, hypotenuse*) as well as words that have different meanings in different content areas (e.g., chemical *solutions* and *suspensions* contrasted with *solutions* to problems and *suspension* of reality, a *sine wave* and an *ocean wave*).

The second step in planning instruction considers the depth of knowledge students need to have for specific words. There is a big difference between *knowing* a word on a superficial level (e.g., enough to match it with a memorized definition on a weekly quiz) and being able to *use* a word effectively in communication. More than 40 years ago vocabulary learning was described by Dale (1965) based on four stages of "knowing" a word:

- Stage 1: No knowledge of the word—never saw it or heard it before
- Stage 2: Heard or read the word before but doesn't know the meaning
- Stage 3: Knows something about the word when it is seen or heard in context
- Stage 4: Knows and understands the meaning(s) of the word and can use it in speaking and writing.

Ideally, students should have as many words in Stage 4 as possible and will increase considerably their number of words in Stage 3.

There is evidence from research that we can effectively teach students the meanings of specific words, but, due to the sheer number of words students encounter, there is interest in also teaching word-learning strategies that enable students to infer word meanings independently. Two word-learning strategies, *morphemic analysis* and *contextual analysis*, are typically thought to be highly valuable practices for improving vocabulary acquisition. Two studies of vocabulary instruction conducted with fifth graders provide evidence that instruction in morphemic and contextual analysis, either in combination or alone, can improve students' vocabulary but not necessarily their comprehension (Baumann et al., 2002; Baumann, Edwards, Boland, Olejnik, & Kame'enui, 2003).

Researchers have also explored the benefits of fostering *word consciousness* (Graves & Watts-Taffe, 2002; Nagy & Scott, 2000), but the relationship of this construct to improved comprehension has not been established. Word consciousness is a kind of metalinguistic awareness, or awareness of language (Nagy, 2007; Nagy & Scott). Students with high levels of word consciousness are responsive to words they see and hear. For example, they notice the similarities between words that share common roots (e.g., import, portable). Another promising area in vocabulary learning is the learning of new words and their meanings incidentally through reading of content, such as history or science (Carlisle, Fleming, & Gudbrandsen, 2000).

Research on Vocabulary Interventions for Older Students

Several reviews and syntheses identify practices that are associated with improved vocabulary knowledge (Bryant, Goodwin, Bryant, & Higgins, 2003; Ebbers & Denton, 2008; Jitendra et al. 2004). The following are some of the research-supported practices:

- Using key words and mnemonic devices to build associations between words and meanings
- Providing understandable, clear definitions and descriptions of what words mean and do not mean, including examples and nonexamples of words and allowing students sufficient practice with feedback to learn and use new words accurately
- Illustrating what words mean and how they are related through semantic mapping, graphic organizers, and other concept-enhancement procedures

The meta-analysis by Scammacca et al. (2007) examined the effectiveness of vocabulary interventions for older students with reading difficulties. The researchers identified six vocabulary intervention studies that met their criteria for inclusion. Vocabulary interventions were associated with the overall highest effect sizes, compared with word study, fluency, and comprehension. However, this finding is mitigated by the fact that none of the six intervention studies used standardized outcome measures, and researcher-developed outcome measures typically lead to higher effects. The report indicated that the overall effect size for these research-developed measures was $ES = 1.62$ (very large effect) that differed significantly from 0 (95% CI = 1.13, 2.10). Largely, these studies measured only whether students learned the words that were taught in the research interventions and did not examine effects on students' general word knowledge. Whether these interventions had an impact on reading comprehension could not be determined.

Reading Comprehension

Word study, fluency, and vocabulary are promoted as a means of improving the reading comprehension of students; however, most older students need instruction that specifically addresses reading comprehension. Many older readers are not given instructional opportunities designed specifically to improve their understanding and processing of text in later grades. There are several possible explanations (RAND, 2002) for this, including the following:

- Teaching students how to read is frequently not considered the role of secondary teachers.
- Teachers may assume if students can read the words, they can understand the text.
- Teachers may not have the knowledge and skills to promote reading comprehension.

For example, the RAND report highlighted that most upper-grade teachers lack adequate preparation for teaching the components of reading. Thus, if effective reading comprehension instruction for older students with reading difficulties is to occur, additional professional development for teachers will be required.

Comprehension Instruction for Older Students

Many students with reading difficulties have significant challenges understanding and learning from text even when they are able to decode adequately. Reading comprehension is a process of determining an author's intent and constructing meaning by coordinating a number of complex processes (Jenkins, Larson, & Fleischer, 1983; O'Shea, Sindelar, & O'Shea, 1987). Reading for understanding and learning requires the ability to successfully apply complex inferential and analytical skills (Duke & Pearson, 2002; Pressley, 2000). It can be hindered by inaccurate word reading, inadequate knowledge of word meanings, insufficient understanding or background knowledge related to the topic, failure to actively monitor understanding while reading, failure to effectively apply comprehension strategies, and undeveloped verbal reasoning (Biancarosa & Snow, 2004; Carlisle & Rice, 2002; Kamil, 2003; RAND, 2002).

Perhaps one of the most complete models of comprehension is provided by Kintsch (1998), in which he differentiates between garnering text-based information through word-level reading and *learning* from text by actively constructing meaning during reading and connecting new information with prior knowledge (Kintsch & Kintsch, 2004). Applying this complex level of processing and connecting within and across text and ideas is challenging for many older readers.

Research on Comprehension Interventions for Older Students

The National Reading Panel report (2000) evaluated empirical comprehension research conducted with students in grades 1–11, with most studies including students in grades 3–8. The panel highlighted effective comprehension instructional practices, including the following:

- Teaching students to monitor their understanding while reading and to adjust reading practices for different text types
- Participating in cooperative learning practices that provide interaction with peers about text understanding in the context of reading

- Developing and interacting with graphic and semantic organizers to help students make meaningful connections within and across texts
- Engaging students in developing and answering questions about text and about the author's intent, interacting and obtaining feedback from students, and developing and responding to questions about text types
- Modeling and providing practice with feedback to teach students to write summaries of text
- Providing students with adequate information prior to reading to understand the text
- Teaching students to integrate and apply selected and purposively taught comprehension strategies

Perhaps one of the most consistent findings from syntheses of intervention research on older students with reading difficulties is the effectiveness of *directly teaching comprehension strategies*, or plans of action that students can learn to apply independently to help them make sense of text, monitor their own reading for sense-making, organize information, extract key ideas, and remember key information. When students are taught to use cognitive and metacognitive strategies within an instructional framework that provides explicit and systematic instruction with modeling, feedback, and practice, older readers demonstrate improved reading comprehension (Edmonds et al., 2009; Gersten, Fuchs, Williams, & Baker, 2001; Scammacca et al., 2007; Swanson, 1999).

Scammacca et al. (2007) conducted a meta-analysis of 23 intervention studies with older students with reading difficulties or disabilities that included one or more measures of reading comprehension. Because studies that used a standardized measure of reading represented 8 of those 23 studies, these studies were considered separately, as they typically reflect a more rigorous test of the efficacy of the intervention. Overall, effect sizes from these interventions were quite high, and Scammacca et al. reported an effect size of 0.97 across all 23 intervention studies for comprehension. This is almost a full standard deviation improvement in favor of the treatment group over the comparison group. However, the overall estimate of effect sizes for the eight studies that used a norm-referenced measure of comprehension was 0.35. This estimate of improvement based on standardized measures is considerably lower than the overall effect for all comprehension outcomes. There was enough variation between effects from various studies to warrant further examination of possible explanations for this difference.

Considering the type of each intervention and its effects on comprehension resulted in the following findings: (a) outcomes were largest for interventions that implemented comprehension strategy instruction, with an overall effect size of 1.35 and an effect size of 0.54 for those studies that used standardized measures; and (b) multicomponent interventions that included instruction in two or more reading domains (e.g., word reading and comprehension) also demonstrated high outcomes in comprehension, with an overall effect size of 0.80 and, for interventions using standardized measures, 0.59.

Intervention for Secondary Students With Severe and Persistent Reading Difficulties

As illustrated in the previous discussion, there is an emerging, but still limited, research base on effective reading intervention for older students. There is an even greater need for intervention research that specifically evaluates intervention for students in secondary schools with severe and persistent reading difficulties (i.e., Tier 3 students).

In one such study Denton, Wexler, Vaughn, and Bryan (2008) provided a multicomponent reading intervention to middle school students with severe reading difficulties. Most of these students were Spanish-speaking English language learners, and nearly all of them had severe vocabulary deficits. Most bilingual students displayed these problems in both languages. Students were randomly assigned to receive the researcher-developed intervention, consisting of daily explicit and systematic small-group instruction for 40 minutes over 13 weeks, provided in groups of two to four students, or their regularly assigned special education or remedial reading classes. Despite the provision of explicit small-group instruction in the research intervention, there were no significant differences in reading outcomes between the treatment and comparison groups, and neither group made significant standard-score growth over the course of the study. Denton et al. hypothesized that students needed intervention over a longer period of time, or intervention with a different approach or focus. This is an area that merits further study.

CONCLUSION

It has become increasingly clear that if students do not learn to read adequately in the primary grades, it is likely that they will continue to struggle with reading unless they are provided with intensive intervention (Francis et al., 1996; Juel, 1988; Torgesen & Burgess, 1998). As illustrated in the research we have described, remediation of reading difficulties for older students is possible, but remediating severe reading problems in secondary-level students is highly challenging. A prevention model is designed to "catch them before they fall" (Torgesen, 1998, p. 1).

At the same time, the need to provide reading intervention to older students is not likely to disappear. Unless high-quality prevention models are universally employed, there will be students in Grade 4 and above who have reading difficulties of different types and levels of severity. Moreover, some students will need continued support throughout their school careers. In particular, some students with attention and behavior difficulties will need consistent classroom-based intervention, and often more intensive intervention.

As illustrated in our description of the current research base, much more needs to be learned about reading intervention for students beyond the primary grades, particularly those with severe reading challenges. The best-researched domain is comprehension strategy instruction, and evidence supports the effectiveness of this kind of instruction. However, recent research has indicated that many middle school students who fail high-stakes tests of reading comprehension have problems with decoding or fluency or both (Fletcher, 2007). Much less is known about how to address these deficits. Finally, more effective tools are needed to instruct older students who have seriously impaired oral vocabularies as well as impairments in decoding, fluency, and comprehension.

Multitiered intervention models are designed to provide all students with the instruction they need to learn to read adequately. Although schools will always face the challenges associated with inadequate funding, time, and personnel, implementation of tiered intervention is feasible. It is a matter of setting priorities in the use of existing resources—and sometimes thinking creatively about obtaining additional resources. Implementing a tiered intervention model within an RTI framework has the potential to address the needs of all students, regardless of the reasons underlying their reading difficulties, and it can provide important data to inform decisions related to the presence of a learning disability and special education eligibility.

We suggest that educators should feel a sense of urgency with respect to providing effective preventive and remedial reading interventions. For individual students, time is short. Without effective intervention, weak readers tend to fall farther and farther behind until they exhibit generalized deficit patterns (Stanovich, 1986). If students' reading difficulties are addressed, they will be better able to learn from content-area textbooks, supporting achievement across subject areas and the ability to think and reason about text, certainly an important goal of our educational system.

REFERENCES

Abbott, S. P., & Berninger, V. W. (1999). It's never too late to remediate: Teaching word recognition to students with reading disabilities in grades 4–7. *Annals of Dyslexia, 49,* 223–250.

Batsche, G., Elliott, J., Graden, J. L., Grimes, J., Kovaleski, J. F., Prasse, D., et al. (2006). *Response to intervention: Policy considerations and implementation.* Alexandria, VA: National Association of State Directors of Special Education.

Baumann, J. F., Edwards, E. C., Boland, E., Olejnik, S., & Kame'enui, E. J. (2003). Vocabulary tricks: Effects of instruction in morphology and context on fifth-grade students ability to derive and infer word meaning. *American Educational Research Journal, 40,* 447–494.

Baumann, J. F., Edwards, E. C., Font, G., Tereshinski, C. A., Kame'enui, E. J., & Olejnik, S. (2002). Teaching morphemic and contextual analysis to fifth grade students. *Reading Research Quarterly, 37,* 150–176.

Bhattacharya, A., & Ehri, L. C. (2004). Graphosyllabic analysis helps adolescent struggling readers read and spell words. *Journal of Learning Disabilities, 37,* 331–348.

Biancarosa, G., & Snow, C. E. (2004). *Reading next—A vision for action and research in middle and high school literacy: A report from Carnegie of New York.* Washington, DC: Alliance for Excellence in Education.

Blachman, B. A., Schatschneider, C., Fletcher, J. M., Francis, D. J., Clonan, S., Shaywitz, B., et al. (2004). Effects of intensive reading remediation for second and third graders. *Journal of Educational Psychology, 96,* 444–461.

Bryant, D. P., Goodwin, M., Bryant, B. R., & Higgins, K. (2003). Vocabulary instruction for students with learning disabilities: A review of the research. *Learning Disability Quarterly, 26,* 117–128.

Carlisle, J. F. (2000). Awareness of the structure and meaning of morphologically complex words: Impact on reading. *Reading and Writing, 12,* 169–190.

Carlisle, J. F., Fleming, J. E., & Gudbrandsen, B. (2000). Incidental word learning in science classes. *Contemporary Educational Psychology, 25,* 184–211.

Carlisle, J. F., & Rice, M. S. (2002). *Improving reading comprehension: Research-based principles and practices.* Baltimore: York Press.

Chall, J. S. (1983). *Stages of reading development.* New York: McGraw-Hill.

Chard, D. J., Vaughn, S., & Tyler, B. (2002). A synthesis of research on effective interventions for building reading fluency with elementary students with learning disabilities. *Journal of Learning Disabilities, 35,* 386–406.

Curtis, M. (2004). Adolescents who struggle with word identification: Research and practice. In T. L. Jetton & J. A. Dole (Eds.), *Adolescent literacy research and practice* (pp. 119–134). New York: Guilford Press.

Dale, E. (1965). Vocabulary measurement: Technique and major findings. *Elementary English, 42,* 82–88.

Deacon, S. H., & Kirby, J. R. (2004). Morphological awareness: Just "more phonological"? The roles of morphological and phonological awareness in reading development. *Applied Psycholinguistics, 25*(2), 223–228.

Denton, C. A., Barth, A., Fletcher, J. M., Wexler, J., Vaughn, S., Cirino, P. T., et al. (2009). *The Relations among oral and silent reading fluency and comprehension in middle school: Implications for identification and instruction of students with reading difficulties.* Manuscript submitted for publication

Denton, C. A., Bryan, D., Wexler, J., Reed, D., & Vaughn, S. (2007). *Effective instruction for middle school students with reading difficulties: The reading teacher's sourcebook.* Austin, TX: Texas Education Agency and the University of Texas System. Retrieved July 31, 2008, from http://www.texasreading.org/utcrla/materials/middle_school_instruction.asp

Denton, C. A., Fletcher, J. M., Anthony, J. L., & Francis, D. J. (2006). An evaluation of intensive intervention for students with persistent reading difficulties. *Journal of Learning Disabilities, 39,* 447–466.

Denton, C. A., Fletcher, J. M., Simos, P. C., Papanicolaou, A. C., & Anthony, J. L. (2007). An implementation of a tiered intervention model: Reading outcomes and neural correlates. In D. Haager, J. Klingner, & S. Vaughn (Eds.), *Evidence-based reading practices for response to intervention* (pp. 107–137). Baltimore: Brookes.

Denton, C. A., & Hocker, J. L. (2006). *Responsive reading instruction: Flexible intervention for struggling readers in the early grades.* Longmont, CO: Sopris West.

Denton, C. A., & Mathes, P. G. (2003). Intervention for struggling readers: Possibilities and challenges. In B. R. Foorman (Ed.), *Preventing and remediating reading difficulties: Bringing science to scale* (pp. 229–251). Timonium, MD: York Press.

Denton, C. A., Wexler, J., Vaughn, S., & Bryan, D. (2008). Intervention provided to middle school students with severe reading difficulties. *Learning Disabilities Research and Practice, 23,* 79–89.

Duke, N. K., & Pearson, P. D. (2002). Effective practices for developing reading comprehension. In A. E. Farstrup & S. J. Samuels (Eds.), *What research has to say about reading instruction* (3rd ed., pp. 205–242). Newark, DE: International Reading Association.

Ebbers, S., & Denton, C. A. (2008). A Root awakening: Effective vocabulary instruction for older students with reading difficulties. *Learning Disabilities Research and Practice, 23,* 90–102.

Edmonds, M. S., Vaughn, S., Wexler, J., Reutebuch, C., Cable, A., Tackett, K., et al. (2009). A synthesis of reading interventions and effects on reading outcomes for older struggling readers. *Review of Educational Research, 79*(1), 262–301.

Ehri, L. C. (2003, March). *Systematic phonics instruction: Findings of the National Reading Panel.* Paper presented to the Standards and Effectiveness Unit, Department for Education and Skills, British Government, London.

Elbaum, B., Vaughn, S., Hughes, M. T., & Moody, S. W. (2000). How effective are one-to-one tutoring programs in reading for elementary students at risk for reading failure? *Journal of Educational Psychology, 92,* 605–619.

Felton, R. (1993). Effects of instruction on the decoding skills of children with phonological-processing problems. *Journal of Learning Disabilities, 26,* 583–589.

Fletcher, J. M. (2007, February). *Overview of the Texas Center for Learning Disabilities.* Pacific Coast Research Conference, San Diego, CA.

Fletcher, J. M., Denton, C. A., Fuchs, L., & Vaughn, S. R. (2005). Multi-tiered reading instruction: Linking general education and special education. In International Reading Association, S. O. Richardson, & J. W. Gilger (Eds.), *Research-based education and intervention: What we need to know* (pp. 21–43). Baltimore: International Reading Association.

Foorman, B. R., Francis, D. J., Fletcher, J. M., Schatschneider, C., & Mehta, P. (1998). The role of instruction in learning to read: Preventing reading disabilities in at-risk children. *Journal of Educational Psychology, 90,* 37–55.

Francis, D. J., Shaywitz, S. E., Stuebing, K. K., Shaywitz, B. A., & Fletcher, J. M. (1996). Developmental lag versus deficit models of reading disability: A longitudinal, individual growth curves analysis. *Journal of Educational Psychology, 88,* 3–17.

Fuchs, D., & Fuchs, L. (2005). Peer-assisted learning strategies: Promoting word recognition, fluency, and reading comprehension in young children. *Journal of Special Education, 39,* 34–44.

Fuchs, L. S., Fuchs, D., Hosp, M. K., & Jenkins, J. R. (2001). Oral reading fluency as an indicator of reading competence: A theoretical, empirical, and historical analysis. *Scientific Studies of Reading, 5,* 239–256.

Gersten, R., Fuchs, L., Williams, J., & Baker, S. (2001). Teaching reading comprehension strategies to students with learning disabilities: A review of research. *Review of Educational Research, 71,* 279–320.

Graves, M. F. (1989). A quantitative and qualitative study of elementary school children's vocabularies. *Journal of Educational Research, 82*(4), 203–209.

Graves, M. F., Brunetti, G. J., & Slater, W. H. (1982). The reading vocabularies of primary grade children of varying geographic and social backgrounds. In J. A. Harris & L. A. Harris (Eds.), *New inquiries in reading research and instruction* (pp. 99–104). Rochester, NY: National Reading Conference.

Graves, M. F., & Watts-Taffe, S. M. (2002). The place of word consciousness in a research-based vocabulary program. In A. E. Farstrup & S. J. Samuels (Eds.), *What research has to say about reading instruction* (3rd ed., pp. 140–165). Newark, DE: International Reading Association.

Green, L., McCutchen, D., Schwiebert, C., Quinlan, T., Eva-Wood, A, & Juelis, J. (2003). Morphological development in children's writing. *Journal of Educational Psychology, 95,* 752–761.

Grek, M. L., Mathes, P. G., & Torgesen, J. K. (2003). Similarities and differences between experienced teachers and trained paraprofessionals. In S. Vaughn & K. L. Briggs (Eds.), *Reading in the classroom: Systems for the observation of teaching and learning* (pp. 267–296). Baltimore: Brookes.

Hall, T. E., Hughes, C. A., & Filbert, M. (2000). Computer assisted instruction in reading for students with learning disabilities: A research synthesis. *Education and Treatment of Children, 23,* 173–193.

Jenkins, J. R., Larson, K., & Fleischer, L. (1983). Effects of error correction on word recognition and reading comprehension. *Learning Disability Quarterly, 6,* 139–145.

Jenkins, J. R., & O'Connor, R. E. (2002). Early identification and intervention for young children with reading/learning disabilities. In R. Bradley, L. Danielson, & D. P. Hallahan (Eds.), *Identification of learning disabilities: Research to practice* (pp. 99–149). Mahwah, NJ: Erlbaum.

Jitendra, A., Edwards, L., Sacks, G., & Jacobson, L. (2004). What research says about vocabulary instruction for students with learning disabilities. *Exceptional Children, 70,* 299–311.

Juel, C. (1988). Learning to read and write: A longitudinal study of 54 children from first through fourth grades. *Journal of Educational Psychology, 80,* 437–447.

Kamil, M. L. (2003). Adolescents and literacy: Reading for the 21st century. Washington, DC: Alliance for Excellent Education.

Kamps, D. M., & Greenwood, C. R. (2005). Formulating secondary-level reading interventions. *Journal of Learning Disabilities, 38,* 500–509.

Kavale, K. A., & Reese, J. H. (1992). The character of learning disabilities: An Iowa profile. *Learning Disability Quarterly, 15,* 74–94.

Kintsch, W. (1998). Comprehension: A paradigm for cognition. New York: Cambridge University Press.

Kintsch, W., & Kintsch, E. (2004). Comprehension. In S. G. Paris & S. A. Stahl (Eds.), *Children's reading comprehension and assessment* (pp. 71–92). Mahwah, NJ: Erlbaum.

Kuhn, M. R., & Stahl, S. A. (2000). *Fluency: A review of developmental and remedial practices* (Rep. No. 2-008). Ann Arbor, MI: Center for the Improvement of Early Reading Achievement.

Lee, J., Grigg, W. S., & Donahue, P. L. (2007). *The nation's report card: Reading 2007: National assessment of educational progress at grades 4 and 8* (NCES No. 2007-496). Washington, DC: National Center for Education Statistics. Retrieved November 5, 2007, from http://nationsreportcard.gov/reading_2007

Lerner, J. W. (1989). Educational interventions in learning disabilities. *Journal of the American Academy of Child & Adolescent Psychiatry, 28,* 326–331.

Lovett, M. W., Steinbach, K. A., & Frijters, J. C. (2000). Remediating the core deficits of developmental reading disability: A double-deficit perspective. *Journal of Learning Disabilities, 33,* 334–358.

Mahony, D., Singson, M., & Mann, V. (2000). Reading ability and sensitivity to morphological relations. *Reading and Writing: An Interdisciplinary Journal, 12,* 191–218.

Mathes, P. G., & Denton, C. A. (2002). The prevention and identification of reading disability. *Seminars in Pediatric Neurology, 9*(3), 185–191.

Mathes, P. G., Denton, C. A., Fletcher, J. M., Anthony, J. L., Francis, D. J., & Schatschneider, C. (2005). The effects of theoretically different instruction and student characteristics on the skills of struggling readers. *Reading Research Quarterly, 40,* 148–182.

Mathes, P. G., Grek, M. L., & Howard, J. K. (1999). Peer-assisted learning strategies for first-grade readers: A tool for preventing early reading failure. *Learning Disabilities Research and Practice, 14,* 50–60.

Mathes, P. G., Torgesen, J. K., & Allor, J. H. (2001). The effects of peer-assisted literacy strategies for first-grade readers with and without additional computer-assisted instruction in phonological awareness. *American Educational Research Journal, 38,* 371–410.

McMaster, K. L., Fuchs, D., & Fuchs, L. S. (2006). Research on peer-assisted learning strategies: The promise and limitations of peer-mediated instruction. *Reading & Writing Quarterly, 22,* 5–25.

McMaster, K. L., Fuchs, D., Fuchs, L. S., & Compton, D. L. (2005). Responding to nonresponders: An experimental field trial of identification and intervention methods. *Exceptional Children, 71,* 445–463.

Meyer, M. S., & Felton, R. H. (1999). Repeated reading to enhance fluency: Old approaches and new directions. *Annals of Dyslexia, 49,* 283–306.

Moats, L. C. (2001). When older students can't read [Electronic version]. *Educational Leadership, 58.* http://www.cdl.org/resources/reading_room/older_read.html

Nagy, W. E. (2007). Metalinguistic awareness and the vocabulary-comprehension connection. In R. K. Wagner, A. E Muse, & K. R. Tannenbaum (Eds.), *Vocabulary acquisition: Implications for reading comprehension* (pp. 52–77). New York: Guilford Press.

Nagy, W. E., & Scott, R. S. (2000). Vocabulary processes. In M. L. Kamil, P. B. Mosenthal, P. D. Pearson, & R. Barr (Eds.), *Handbook of reading research* (Vol. 3, pp. 269–284). Mahwah, NJ: Erlbaum.

National Reading Panel. (2000). *Teaching children to read: An evidence-based assessment of the scientific research literature on reading and its implications for reading instruction.* Washington, DC: U.S. Government Printing Office.

O'Shea, L. J., Sindelar, P., & O'Shea, D. J. (1987). Effects of repeated readings and attentional cues on the reading fluency and comprehension of learning disabled readers. *Learning Disabilities Research, 2,* 103–109.

Pressley, M. (2000). What should comprehension instruction be the instruction of? In M. Kamil, P. Mosenthal, P. Pearson, & R. Barr (Eds.), *Handbook of reading research* (Vol. 3, pp. 545–562). Mahwah, NJ: Erlbaum.

RAND Reading Study Group. (2002). *Reading for understanding: Toward an R&D program in reading comprehension.* Santa Monica, CA: RAND.

Rashotte, C. A., & Torgesen, J. K. (1985). Repeated reading and reading fluency in learning disabled children. *Reading Research Quarterly, 20,* 180–188.

Rayner, K., Foorman, B. R., Perfetti, C. A., Pesetsky, D., & Seidenberg, M. S. (2001). How psychological science informs the teaching of reading. *Psychological Science in the Public Interest 2,* 31–74.

Reutebuch, C. K., Vaughn, S., & Scammacca, N. (2009). *Reading intervention research for secondary students with learning disabilities: An effect size and multivocal synthesis.* Manuscript submitted for publication.

Saenz, L. M., Fuchs, L. S., & Fuchs, D. (2005). Peer-assisted learning strategies for English language learners with learning disabilities. *Exceptional Children, 71,* 231–247.

Scammacca, N., Roberts, G., Vaughn, S., Edmonds, M., Wexler, J., Reutebuch, C. K., et al. (2007). *Interventions for adolescent struggling readers: A meta-analysis with implications for practice.* Portsmouth, NH: RMC Research Corporation, Center on Instruction. Available for download from http://www.centeroninstruction.org/index.cfm

Shankweiler, D., Lundquist, E., Katz, L., Stuebing, K. K., Fletcher, J. M., Brady, S. M., et al. (1999). Comprehension and decoding: Patterns of association in children with reading difficulties. *Scientific Studies of Reading, 3,* 69–94.

Shinn, M. R., & Good, R. H. (1992). Curriculum-based measurement of oral reading fluency: A confirmatory analysis of its relation to reading. *School Psychology Review, 21,* 459–479.

Simos, P. G., Fletcher, J. M., Bergman, E., Breier, J. I., Foorman, B. R., Castillo, E. M., et al. (2002). Dyslexia-specific brain activation profile becomes normal following successful remedial training. *Neurology, 58,* 1203–1213.

Simos, P. G., Fletcher, J. M., Sarkari, S., Billingsley, R. L., Denton, C., & Papanicolaou, A. C. (2007a). Altering the brain circuits for reading through intervention: A magnetic source imaging study. *Neuropsychology, 21,* 485–496.

Simos, P. G., Fletcher, J. M., Sarkari, S., Billingsley-Marshall, R., Denton, C., & Papanicolaou, A. C. (2007b). Intensive instruction affects brain magnetic activity associated with reading fluency in children with persistent reading disabilities. *Journal of Learning Disabilities, 40,* 37–48.

Singson, M., Mahony, D., & Mann, V. (2000). The relation between reading ability and morphological skills: Evidence from derivational suffixes. *Reading and Writing: An Interdisciplinary Journal, 12,* 219–252.

Snow, C. E., Burns, M. S., & Griffin, P. (Eds.). (1998). *Preventing reading difficulties in young children.* Washington, DC: National Academy Press.

Stage, S. A., Abbott, R. D., Jenkins, J. R., & Berninger, V. W. (2003). Predicting response to early reading intervention from verbal IQ, reading-related language abilities, attention ratings, and verbal IQ-word reading discrepancy: Failure to validate discrepancy method. *Journal of Learning Disabilities, 36,* 24–33.

Stanovich, K. E. (1986). Matthew effects in reading: Some consequences of individual differences in the acquisition of literacy. *Reading Research Quarterly, 21,* 360–407.

Stanovich, K. (2000). *Progress in understanding reading: Scientific foundations and new frontiers.* New York: Guilford Press.

Swanson, H. L. (1999). Instructional components that predict treatment outcomes for students with learning disabilities: Support for a combined strategy and direct instruction model. *Learning Disabilities Research and Practice, 14*(3), 129–140.

Tindal, G., Hasbrouck, J., & Jones, C. (2005). *Oral reading fluency: 90 years of measurement* (Behavioral Research and Teaching Technical Report No. 33). Eugene: University of Oregon.

Torgesen, J. K. (1998). Catch them before they fall: Identification and assessment to prevent reading failure in young children. American Educator, *22,* 1–8. Retrieved November 7, 2007, from http://www.aft.org/pubs-reports/american_educator/spring_sum98/torgesen.pdf

Torgesen, J. K. (2000). Individual differences in response to early interventions in reading: The lingering problem of treatment resisters. *Learning Disabilities Research and Practice, 15,* 55–64.

Torgesen, J. K., Alexander, A. W., Wagner, R. K., Rashotte, C. A., Voeller, K., Conway, T., et al. (2001). Intensive remedial instruction for children with severe reading disabilities: Immediate and long-term outcomes from two instructional approaches. *Journal of Learning Disabilities, 34,* 33–58.

Torgesen, J. K., & Burgess, S. R. (1998). Consistency of reading-related phonological processes throughout early childhood: Evidence from longitudinal-correlational and instructional studies. In J. Metsala & L. Ehri (Eds.), *Word Recognition in Beginning Reading.* Hillsdale, NJ: Erlbaum.

Torgesen, J. K., Rashotte, C. A., & Alexander, A. W. (2001). Principles of fluency instruction in reading: Relationships with established empirical outcomes. In M. Wolf (Ed.), *Dyslexia, fluency, and the brain* (pp. 333–355). Timonium, MD: York Press.

Torgesen, J. K., Rashotte, C. A., Alexander, A., Alexander, J., & MacPhee, K. (2003). Progress toward understanding the instructional conditions necessary for remediating reading difficulties in older children. In B. R. Foorman (Ed.), *Preventing and remediating reading difficulties: Bringing science to scale* (pp. 275–297). Timonium, MD: York Press.

Torgesen, J. K., Wagner, R. K., Rashotte, C. A., Rose, E., Lindamood, P., Conway, T., et al. (1999). Preventing reading failure in your children with phonological processing disabilities: Group and individual responses to instruction. *Journal of Educational Psychology, 91,* 579–593.

Vaughn, S., Cirino, P. T., Linan-Thompson, S., Mathes, P. G., Carlson, C. D., Cardenas-Hagan, E., et al. (2006). Effectiveness of a Spanish intervention and an English intervention for English language learners at risk for reading problems. *American Educational Research Journal, 43,* 449–487.

Vaughn, S., & Linan-Thompson, S. (2003). Group size and time allotted to intervention: Effects for students with reading difficulties. In B. Foorman (Ed.), *Preventing and remediating reading difficulties: Bringing science to scale* (pp. 275–298). Timonium, MD: York Press.

Vaughn, S., Linan-Thompson, S., & Hickman, P. (2003). Response to instruction as a means of identifying students with reading/learning disabilities. *Exceptional Children, 69,* 391–409.

Vaughn, S., Linan-Thompson, S., Mathes, P. G., Cirino, P. T., Carlson, C. D., Pollard-Durodola, S. D., et al. (2006). Effectiveness of Spanish intervention for first-grade English language learners at risk for reading difficulties. *Journal of Learning Disabilities, 39,* 56–73.

Vaughn, S., Wanzek, J., Linan-Thompson, S., & Murray, C. S. (2007). Monitoring response to supplemental services for students at risk for reading difficulties: High and low responders. In S. R. Jimerson, M. K. Burns, & A. M. Van Der Heyden (Eds.), *Handbook of response to intervention: The science and practice of assessment and intervention* (pp. 234–243). New York: Springer.

Vaughn, S., Wanzek, J., Woodruff, A. L., & Linan-Thompson, S. (2007). A three-tier model for preventing reading difficulties and early identification of students with reading disabilities. In D. Haager, J. Klingner, & S. Vaughn (Eds.), *Evidence-based reading practices for response to intervention* (pp. 11–28). Baltimore: Brookes.

Vellutino, F. R., Scanlon, D. M., & Jaccard, J. (2003). Toward distinguishing between cognitive and experiential deficits as primary sources of difficulty in learning to read: A two year follow-up to difficult to remediate and readily remediated poor readers. In B. R. Foorman (Ed.), *Preventing and remediating reading difficulties: Bringing science to scale* (pp. 73–120). Timonium, MD: York Press.

Vellutino, F. R., Scanlon, D. M., Sipay, E. R., Small, S. G., Pratt, A., Chen, R., et al. (1996). Cognitive profiles of difficult-to-remediate and readily remediated poor readers: Early intervention as a vehicle for distinguishing between cognitive and experiential deficits as basic causes of specific reading disability. *Journal of Educational Psychology, 88,* 601–638.

Wanzek, J., & Vaughn, S. (2007). Research-based implications from extensive early reading interventions. *School Psychology Review, 36,* 541–561.

CHAPTER 19

Early Reading Instruction and Intervention With English Learners:
Key Considerations in a Multitiered Approach

Scott K. Baker
Pacific Institutes for Research/University of Oregon

Russell Gersten
Instructional Research Group

Sylvia Linan-Thompson
University of Texas at Austin

INTRODUCTION

This chapter presents evidence-based recommendations for teaching reading, language arts, and English language development to English learners in the primary grades in schools that use multiple tiers of instructional support.[1] The most extensive scientific knowledge pertains to the primary grades (Gersten, Baker, et al., 2007; Shanahan & August, 2007). However, many of the principles and examples we provide are relevant for older English learners.

We limit this chapter to Tier 1 and Tier 2 interventions for a number of reasons. First, Tier 1 and Tier 2 instructional support systems are designed to meet the needs of a majority of English learners. Second, this focus allows us to address instruction designed for students who are at or above grade level, as well as students who are below grade level. In addition, the current research base addresses only Tier 1 and Tier 2 interventions. Important distinctions exist between instruction for students in Tier 2

---

[1] We use the term *English learners* in this chapter to refer to students (a) whose native or home language is not English and (b) who have not yet achieved a level of proficiency in English—particularly academic or formal English—that enables them to make satisfactory progress in classes taught in English without ongoing language support from the teacher. Many terms have been used in education to describe these students: *English language learners, second language learners* or students, and *language minority students*. The official designation still used by the federal government is *limited English proficient*. English learners or English language learners is more accepted currently because it is considered a more accurate description of these students and less pejorative than many other terms. We use English learners rather than English language learners because *language* seems redundant.

and Tier 3; however, there is insufficient research to say with assurance how these tiers differ for English learners, who face the double demands of learning academic material while mastering the conventions of a new language (Gersten, 1996).

In making recommendations about instructional support for English learners in the primary grades, we try to be clear about the strengths and weaknesses of the evidence supporting recommended practice. In areas where the evidence base is very weak or nonexistent, our recommendations are based on consensus in the field. Because practitioners in a district or school with multitiered instructional support systems often need to take action even when there is insufficient scientific evidence for guidance, we include some recommendations that are based only on expert opinion. Whenever possible, practitioners should use valid formative and summative assessment data to carefully evaluate the effectiveness of *any* intervention, particularly interventions that are not supported by previous scientific evidence. Given the limited research on effective practices with English learners, however, an array of modifications and adaptations should be considered to successfully meet the needs of these students.

This chapter does not address issues related to the language of instruction because there is little evidence to suggest that academic instruction in the native language or in English is superior for students entering school. Articles and book chapters have asserted that native language instruction is superior to instruction in English (e.g., Green, 1997; August & Shanahan, 2006), or that students should be taught to read simultaneously in both English and Spanish (Cheung & Slavin, 2005). However, our review of the individual studies found serious design flaws or irrelevant studies (e.g., relying on only one teacher per condition, or having students spend part of the day learning a heritage language, that is, a language spoken by their ancestors). Because of the ambiguity of the evidence on this topic, we focus on instructional features that are likely to enhance English learners' achievement.

WHY A MULTITIERED LITERACY FRAMEWORK MAKES SENSE FOR ENGLISH LEARNERS

An instruction and intervention framework structured around multiple tiers of support can be an effective way to organize instruction for English learners. Furthermore, schools and districts that organize instruction using multiple tiers for their fluent English speakers do not need a separate system for their English learners (Baker & Baker, 2008; Gersten et al., 2008; Haager, Klingner, & Vaughn, 2007).

In terms of early literacy and language development, schools do not need separate goals and practices for English learners and fluent English speakers (Baker & Baker, 2008). In some ways effective instruction will look similar for English learners and native English speakers, and in other ways instruction will have to be adjusted for English learners to effectively address some of their specific learning needs. Inherent in a multitiered approach is both the flexibility (e.g., differentiated instruction in Tier 1) and structure (e.g., the same reading goals) necessary for schools to provide instructional supports so that all English learners have the opportunity to achieve at high levels.

Currently, in many districts, more English learners than non–English learners will require instructional support in Tiers 2 and 3 if they are to reach desired early literacy goals (Baker & Baker, 2008). The basis of this tiered support is determined using universal screening data along with progress monitoring data and, when appropriate, subsequent diagnostic testing (see chapters 11 and 18 in this book). For example, schools that screen students for decoding problems at the beginning of the year in first grade will likely find, on average, that more English learners than native English speakers demonstrate some degree of decoding difficulty that places them at higher risk for long-term reading problems (Chiappe, Siegel, & Wade-Woolley, 2002; Fien et al., in press).

Learning to read early in school helps set the stage for academic success. However, English learners must work over many years to master academic content and become proficient in a second language. Early and strong instruction in *academic language*—that is, the language of the classroom, of academic disciplines (science, history, literary analysis, etc.), of texts and literature, and of reasoned discourse—is essential in terms of long-term educational outcomes (Scarcella, 2003). Unfortunately, there is little empirical support to guide how academic language instruction should be conceptualized, organized, and delivered (Gersten, Baker, et al., 2007). Despite the limited scientific research on this topic, we recommend that schools provide extensive, high-quality language and vocabulary instruction for English learners beginning in kindergarten (and earlier if possible). The structure for this instruction, at least conceptually, fits well within the context of a multitiered framework. For example, throughout the early grades (e.g., K–3), district policy might be that English learners must receive the extensive academic language and vocabulary instruction they need as part of their Tier 1 reading instruction. The scope and intensity of this Tier 1 foundation could be differentiated from the instruction provided to native English speakers, even if formative reading measures indicate that some English learners are at low risk for reading problems.

Comprehensive Assessment System

A fundamental element of a multitiered intervention approach is a comprehensive assessment system that consists of universal screening to identify students with reading problems and frequent progress monitoring assessments to determine if students are making sufficient reading progress over time. A comprehensive assessment system also includes diagnostic measures that can pinpoint more precisely the possible causes of reading difficulty when students are not making progress, even following intense and effective instructional interventions in Tiers 2 and above. Also, a comprehensive system includes measures that can be used to determine when students are reaching important content milestones and are either reading at grade level or higher or appear to be on track for grade-level reading proficiency.

The four primary aspects of early reading assessments in multitiered approaches are (a) performing universal screening of all students to identify reading problems, (b) systematically and regularly monitoring reading progress of students experiencing reading difficulties, (c) determining if students have reached grade-level reading goals, and (d) gathering diagnostic information on students in Tiers 2 and above who are not making satisfactory reading progress. Determining how well English learners respond to instruction in Tier 1, plus how well they respond to interventions in Tier 2 and above—that is, measuring the progress students make in response to increasingly intense instructional interventions—requires a goal against which the adequacy of progress can be evaluated.

Formative Assessments for Screening and Progress Monitoring

Although an extensive data base exists regarding the science of progress monitoring and universal screening in reading for native speakers (Miura Wayman, Wallace, Ives Wiley, Ticha, & Espin, 2007), far fewer studies have been conducted with English learners (Shanahan & August, 2007). The assessment tools with the most evidence are derived from research and practice regarding curriculum-based measurement (CBM; Deno, 1985; Shinn, 1998). The primary CBM measure in reading is a short oral reading test in which students read grade-level passages aloud and the tester counts the number of words read correctly. One CBM measure is oral reading fluency. Oral reading fluency measures are useful in multitiered approaches because they are psychometrically strong, can be implemented in school settings, and are constructed specifically to monitor student progress on a regular basis (Baker et al., 2008; Fuchs & Fuchs, 1994; Fuchs, Fuchs, Hosp, & Jenkins, 2001). This research has demonstrated that the number of words students read correctly in 1 minute (passage reading fluency or oral reading fluency) is associated with criterion measures of overall reading, including comprehension.

With English learners specifically, a handful of studies that focus on oral reading fluency have been conducted (Baker & Good, 1995; Dominguez de Ramirez & Shapiro, 2006; Fien et al., 2008; Leafstedt, Richards, & Gerber, 2004; Wiley & Deno, 2005). These studies have supported the use of oral reading fluency measures with English learners. For example, Baker and Good found that the criterion-related validity of oral reading and the reading comprehension subtest of the Stanford Diagnostic Reading Test were not statistically different for English learners and native English speakers. In terms of monitoring progress over time, slope of improvement over 10 weeks on oral reading was significant and reliable with English learners specifically, indicating that the measure was sensitive to small improvements in reading proficiency over time.

Research-Based Predictors of Reading Achievement

The best predictors of reading achievement for English learners are phonological awareness, print awareness, and alphabetic knowledge (Chiappe et al., 2002;

Durgunoglu, Nagy, & Hancin-Bhatt, 1993; Lesaux & Siegel, 2003; Oh, Haager, & Windmueller, 2004). *Oral* language proficiency is a comparatively poor predictor of how well children will develop early reading skills. For example, Chiappe et al. found that in kindergarten, English learners showed weaker performance on measures requiring greater vocabulary and memory demands (e.g., oral cloze test, memory for sentences), but performed as well as native English speakers on phonological awareness measures such as syllable and phoneme identification, and phoneme deletion. Although the performance of English learners was below the performance of native English speakers on phonological awareness tasks at the beginning of the study, by the end of first grade, their performance was comparable on skills requiring phonological processing.

Lesaux and Siegel (2003) obtained similar results in their longitudinal study with English learners from kindergarten to second grade. Phonological awareness instruction in kindergarten (e.g., syllable and phoneme identification, phoneme deletion, and phoneme segmentation and blending) was as effective for English learners as for native English speakers. And, although English learners had more difficulty in kindergarten with tasks related to language skills and memory, phonological processing was the single best predictor of word reading and comprehension in second grade. Moreover, by second grade, English learners performed *better* than native English speakers on word reading tasks, rapid naming, and real and pseudoword spelling, indicating that language and memory skills were developing simultaneously with other reading skills. However, performance on language tasks did not account for a significant percentage of the variance in word reading proficiency.

Similarly, the ability to read simple material fluently (e.g., fluent reading of words students have learned to decode accurately) does *not* appear to depend on strong language proficiency skills. Geva and Yaghoub–Zadeh (2006) found that although language proficiency levels differed between English learners and native English speakers in second grade, scores on tasks involving word recognition, word reading accuracy, and word attack did not differ. In fact, English learners read isolated words significantly faster than native English speakers. They also read simple texts at or slightly below the level of their oral proficiency with the same efficiency as native English speakers, indicating that oral proficiency in the second language contributed only marginally to word or simple text reading efficiency. However, when reading materials were more demanding in terms of vocabulary and syntactic structures, oral language proficiency played a stronger role in text comprehension. These findings reinforce the importance of *not* requiring English learners to have strongly developed oral language skills *before* teaching them to read in English. The findings also highlight the importance of providing strong vocabulary and academic language instruction in English from the beginning of kindergarten.

Contemporary Research on Formative Assessments

In a contemporary study addressing the predictive validity of CBM oral reading, Wiley and Deno (2005) studied students in Grades 3 and 5 who were struggling with reading comprehension. Hmong was the primary home language for 80% of the third-grade sample and 100% of the fifth-grade sample. These English learners and native English speakers were administered passage reading measures from *Standard Reading Passages* and the Minnesota Comprehensive Assessment in reading (Children's Educational Services, 1987). For the English learners, words read correctly (WRC) on the passages predicted reading performance on the state assessment in both Grades 3 and 5 ($r = .61$ vs. .69). The data suggest the WRC in the fall was a moderate predictor of end-of-year reading performance. Results were virtually identical for native English speakers.

Two studies have investigated the use of nonsense word fluency (NWF) with English learners (Fien et al., in press; Leafstedt et al., 2004). NWF is a measure of alphabetic understanding and can be used in kindergarten and early in first grade. Fien et al. examined NWF with English learners and native English speakers in Grades K–2 who were being taught in schools using a multitiered framework. On 19 of 24 comparisons (79%), the correlations were statistically equivalent for English learners and native English speakers, indicating that the measure appeared to function similarly for both groups. The other five correlations were significantly higher for the native English speakers. Most of the largest differences involved the initial administration of NWF, which occurred in the winter of kindergarten. This finding suggests that perhaps for English learners, administration early in kindergarten is complicated by the fact that these students fail to understand the directions and are having a hard time learning how to pronounce each sound appropriately early in kindergarten. Therefore, this type of measure may not reflect underlying reading skills until the end of kindergarten for English learners.

In the second study examining NWF with English learners, Leafstedt et al. (2004) implemented a phonological awareness intervention in kindergarten that was effective in improving performance on phonological awareness and reading tasks. Outcome measures were subtests of the *Woodcock-Johnson Tests of Achievement III*, targeting word reading and pseudoword reading, that is, word attack (Woodcock, McGrew, & Mather, 2001). Progress monitoring measures for phonological awareness (phonemic segmentation fluency) and nonsense word fluency were administered biweekly to the intervention group during the 10-week study (Good & Kaminski, 2002). Performance on a single 1-minute administration of phonemic segmentation fluency and NWF, as well as multiple administrations over time, corresponded to ability-grouping decisions established on the basis of pretest word reading scores and teacher recommendations. Also, performance scores increased consistently over the 10-week intervention, demonstrating sensitivity to small changes in performance, an important issue in a science-based progress monitoring tool. These data suggest that measures such as NWF can be valid as progress monitoring measures in the context of intense instruction in phonics and phonemic awareness, but still seem problematic for use as screening measures in kindergarten.

In summary, a cornerstone of multitiered instruction models is a comprehensive assessment system that effectively screens all students for reading problems and measures reading progress over time. Important evidence is accumulating that early reading measures of fluency and alphabetic understanding that are used with native speakers can be used for similar purposes with English learners. This information, coupled with evidence that English learners can make the same progress in learning to read as native English speakers when provided with effective instruction, suggests that a *common* multitiered system of early reading can be used with English learners and non–English learners. An important message from this is that districts and schools should be able to teach English learners in a way that ensures that the vast majority reach grade-level reading goals by the time instruction shifts substantially from teaching students how to read, to teaching content area subjects through reading and other means. This shift occurs in Grades 3 and 4.

TIER 1 CONSIDERATIONS IN READING FOR ENGLISH LEARNERS

Formative assessment approaches in multitiered instructional contexts can provide the structure needed for helping to ensure that English learners receive the instruction they need to succeed in school. However, the progress English learners make in developing essential skills and knowledge depends on the quality of instruction they receive in the classroom on a regular, daily basis. The following section addresses major elements of effective core instruction for English learners.

Foundational Aspects of Reading for English Learners

Research has shown that early, systematic instruction in phonemic awareness and decoding has the greatest impact on students' reading outcomes in Grades 1–3 (Graves, Gersten, & Haager, 2004; Haager, Gersten, Baker, & Graves, 2003). An important, hitherto largely unknown research finding is that English learners who receive reading instruction in the foundational skills of phonemic awareness and phonics acquire these reading skills *as quickly and proficiently* as English-only students (Chiappe et al., 2002; Geva, Yaghoub-Zadeh, & Schuster, 2000; Lesaux, Rupp, & Siegel, 2007). These studies have been conducted with English learners in the primary grades who receive their instruction exclusively in general education classrooms with other students. Much of this evidence comes from research conducted in Canadian schools that provide explicit and systematic instruction for all children. In these contexts, English learners have been able to develop comparable word reading, word attack, and spelling skills in kindergarten through the second grade (Gersten, Baker, et al., 2007; Chiappe & Siegel, 1999; Chiappe et al., 2002; Lesaux & Siegel, 2003; Limbos & Geva, 2001; Verhoeven, 1990, 2000).

Other evidence shows that English learners are able to develop equivalent degrees of fluency in reading both word lists and connected text by second grade (Geva & Yaghoub-Zadeh, 2006; Lesaux & Siegel, 2003). Some limited evidence also shows that English learners can develop equivalency with native English speakers in reading comprehension (Chiappe, Glaeser, & Ferko, 2007; Lesaux, Lipka, & Siegel, 2006; Lesaux & Siegel, 2003).

Several research studies indicate that components of early reading, such as phonological awareness and aspects of phonics can be taught without language comprehension being a necessary condition for learning these tasks (Chiappe et al., 2002; Geva & Yaghoub-Zadeh, 2006; Lesaux & Siegel, 2003). For example, an English learner as young as 5 years old can segment and blend sounds in the word *lip*, a phonemic awareness task, without necessarily understanding the meaning of the word. Also, a child whose native language is based on the alphabetic system, such as Spanish, can recognize letter sounds that are similar in English and Spanish (i.e., almost all consonants) without speaking English (Bialystok, Luk, & Kwan, 2005).

This parity in growth in phonemic awareness and decoding can be explained as follows: students can learn English sounds, and the various ways in which sounds can be combined to make words, without understanding the precise meaning of the words formed when the sounds are combined (Baker & Baker, 2008). In addition, learning to read early is likely to increase students' comprehension of English in that they work with the words they can read in an array of meaningful contexts.

This finding does not mean, however, that the other components of reading (i.e., fluency, vocabulary, and comprehension) are not necessary, only that their impact may not be as evident in the earliest stages of reading acquisition. Vocabulary instruction is essential for comprehension, and if English learners are not making good progress in developing vocabulary knowledge in the earliest grades, by the time they reach Grades 3 and 4 they may have sufficient skills for decoding but insufficient knowledge of word meanings to understand what they are reading.

Thus, an essential component of Tier 1 instruction for English learners is frequent and intense vocabulary and comprehension instruction (both reading and listening). In particular, Tier 1 instruction not only must include phonics and decoding instruction but also must emphasize the relationship between and among words and must teach comprehension strategies explicitly. That is, English learners should be taught the meanings of words they are learning to decode, receive extensive practice in using these words in several media (i.e., reading, listening, and speaking), and also receive instruction in additional words and phrases they are not yet able to read on their own, all of which are the foundations of academic language. Given the difficulty some students have in developing strong decoding skills, educators might be tempted to narrow the focus of early instruction to teaching decoding or other isolated basic components, but this narrowly focused instruction is less effective than instruction that addresses the full range of essential reading components and provides students with many opportunities to read (Gersten, Baker, et al., 2007).

Newer versions of foundational reading programs, frequently used in districts and schools as Tier 1 core reading programs, typically do a better job of addressing these essential reading components than the programs of the past. In fact, the recently adopted California standards for core reading series provide numerous specific guidelines for textbook developers to use for their 2008–2009 versions of their texts. More attention is given to phonemic awareness and explicit phonics instruction, for example, and more guidance is given to teachers in terms of how to teach the program effectively and with fidelity. Core programs still provide insufficient practice and frequently overlook the importance of application and practice for English learners. Despite these shortcomings, however, core programs still provide an important structure for Tier 1 instruction. In the absence of a core program constructed according to principles of science-based reading research, classroom teachers bear a huge burden of responsibility for ensuring that appropriate materials are being used for instruction.

In terms of comprehension instruction, Tier 1, or core programs, should focus on repeated use of a limited number of strategies before, during, and after reading. These strategies should be used with enough frequency that they become semiautomatic to students. For example, *before reading* a story each day, teachers can routinely establish an explicit purpose for reading, briefly discuss the previous reading to activate prior knowledge, and ask English learners to make predictions about the content. Also, teachers should provide student-friendly definitions of essential words the students will encounter in the story (Beck & McKeown, 1991). The predictions and words can be written on a white board during instruction so that students will be mindful of them. These activities clearly indicate the comprehension objective. Activities after reading the story also reinforce comprehension, giving teachers and students an opportunity to review important story events and elements, and to engage in important overall summary activities. For example, the students' predictions made before or during the reading of the story are subsequently evaluated by the class as to their alignment with actual outcomes in the story.

During reading instruction, teachers should teach English learners comprehension strategies by explicitly modeling or demonstrating for students how good readers monitor their own comprehension during reading, probing the meanings of important vocabulary, and asking the students questions about the content. After reading, students are taught to use skills such as story retell, sequencing, and summarizing. Partner activities such as Think–Pair–Share and peer-assisted learning are recommended for these activities (McMaster, Kung, Han, & Cao, 2008).

Clearly, many of these practices that are effective with English learners will also be effective with native English speakers. However, instruction with English learners incorporates more language activities to build oral language. In studies, the types of language tasks that have resulted in positive student outcomes have been explicit instruction in English language use and clarification of the meaning of words used in directions, in phonics activities, and in stories (Vaughn, Cirino, et al., 2006; Vaughn, Mathes, et al., 2006). Additionally, because the lessons were interactive, students were taught to use consistent language during lessons. The language use ranged from very basic phonemic awareness activities to story retell. Additional instructional time, approximately 7–10 minutes per day, can be spent on language activities involving reading expository text aloud. The use of informational text contributes to the development of students' content area knowledge and vocabulary (Pearson, Hiebert, & Kamil, 2007).

Although these studies had a strong focus on oral language, benefits to English learners also occurred in reading, including reading comprehension (Vaughn, Cirino, et al., 2006; Vaughn, Mathes, et al., 2006). The opportunities to use language may have improved students' ability to understand and participate in the lessons.

Enhancement of Tier 1 Instruction for English Learners

The next two sections, on vocabulary and academic language, address major aspects of instruction that should be fundamental for all English learners. Many features of instruction that emphasize vocabulary and academic language development also would be an excellent instructional framework for native English speakers, particularly for students who are at risk for reading-related difficulties. The extensive vocabulary and academic language instruction we discuss in these sections also might be considered particularly appropriate for Tier 2 interventions for English learners who are at higher levels of risk or who are not making sufficient progress in these areas. Whether at Tier 1 or Tier 2, this instruction centers on the following fundamental instructional ideas:

- Extensive time devoted to vocabulary and academic language instruction
- Intense instructional formats—for example, instruction provided in small groups led by experienced teachers
- Extended and extensive opportunities for English learners to practice vocabulary and academic language with direct supervision and feedback by the teacher
- Structured peer learning activities

Vocabulary

For English learners, widespread vocabulary instruction that supports the development of reading comprehension should be considered an essential component of Tier 1 instruction. In terms of duration and intensity, vocabulary instruction should go beyond what might typically constitute Tier 1 instruction for students who are native English speakers, particularly those students who are from middle-class backgrounds or who enter school with strong vocabulary skills. Tier 1 instruction should focus on teaching essential content words in depth (e.g., energy, anarchy, synergy, cosmic, antagonism), as well as the meanings of common words and phrases (e.g., toothache, partner, select) and colloquial expressions (e.g., "Heads up" or "Eyes on me") that English learners have not yet learned.

Research findings. Given the obvious importance of vocabulary instruction for English learners, it is surprising how little relevant research has been conducted on this topic. Although the research base involving English learners is limited, the research on explicit vocabulary instruction with native English speakers is extensive and has important instructional implications for English learners (National Institute of Child Health and Human Development, 2000).

Vocabulary research with English learners demonstrates that explicit and intensive vocabulary instruction helps English learners learn word meanings and has the potential to enhance reading comprehension (Carlo et al., 2004; Perez, 1981; Rousseau, Tam, &

Ramnarain, 1993). These findings are largely compatible with findings from research conducted with native English speakers. Effective vocabulary instruction includes *multiple* exposures to target words over several days and across reading, writing, and speaking opportunities. Intervention research suggests that English learners benefit most from rich, intensive vocabulary instruction that emphasizes "student-friendly" definitions, engages students in the meaningful use of word definitions across different types of language activities, and provides regular review (Carlo et al., 2004; Perez, 1981; Rousseau et al., 1993).

For example, the teacher could ask: "Did the woman *saunter* down the stairs when she saw the fire? Would someone *saunter* around the park if they loved the trees and flowers there? Why?" The goal of this instruction is for students to use target words, and related words, in their communication and as a basis for further learning (Carlo et al., 2004; Perez, 1981). In its most complete form, vocabulary instruction for English learners also should be emphasized in other parts of the academic curriculum, including reading, writing, science, history, and geography. Applying this comprehensive approach to vocabulary instruction is an essential part of Tier 1 instruction for English learners that should be consistently applied throughout K–12.

Which words to teach. English learners need to learn many words to reach levels of vocabulary knowledge comparable to native English speakers (Umbel, Pearson, Fernández, & Oller, 1992; Verhallen & Schoonen, 1993). Although eliminating this gap through explicit vocabulary instruction alone will be impossible, an essential component of Tier 1 instruction is directly teaching word meanings and providing students with a wide array of activities requiring meaningful word use. A core reading program is a reasonable place to begin selecting words for instruction, although core programs rarely provide adequate guidelines for vocabulary instruction for English learners. Even core reading programs developed according to principles of scientific research may not emphasize the words that are critical to understanding a story or that are most useful for the child's language development (Hiebert, 2005). The instructional procedures in core programs also may stress decoding skills rather than comprehension of the text. For English learners, teachers will need to identify additional words for their instructional attention, and teaching procedures will need to be much richer and more extensive than instruction usually recommended within core reading programs (August, Carlo, Dressler, & Snow, 2005; Blachowicz, Fisher, Ogle, & Watts-Taffe, 2006).

To specify the words that should be taught, districts should develop core vocabulary lists for English learners. These lists ensure that essential words are receiving the proper focus and that there is no unnecessary duplication of effort across classrooms. A district's core vocabulary list does not prevent teachers or students from adding words that are used in the classroom; in fact, a good vocabulary program will encourage the inclusion of additional words.

Words for explicit instruction should be selected carefully. Long lists of words cannot be taught in depth because rich vocabulary instruction is time-intensive. Only a handful of words should be taught intensively at any one time. Recommendations for this type of instruction typically involve teaching about 8 to 15 words per week (Beck, Perfetti, & McKeown, 1982; Biemiller, 1999). A key aspect of the approach is for teachers to have these core vocabulary lists as they teach reading, social studies, and science units, so they know in advance which words to teach in depth.

Vocabulary instruction for English learners also should emphasize the acquisition of meanings of everyday words that native English speakers know and that are not necessarily part of the academic curriculum (August et al., 2005). These words include relatively simple words or conversational words that native English speakers acquire before they enter school or learn in school without explicit teaching. Many of these words are crucial for understanding text and other academic content. For example, words such as *bank, take, can,* or *sink* may not be known by an English learner, and textbooks typically do not target these words for vocabulary instruction. Textbooks also typically do not provide recommendations for how to teach these types of words if students do not know them. English learners can learn these words easily if teachers provide them with brief explanations during lessons, accompanied by visual aids downloaded from a website or from a reading series. This instruction can include models and examples demonstrated by the teacher, and opportunities for students to engage in rapid practice activities. This type of instruction is most effective if it is interspersed throughout the day.

Only three empirical studies to date have directly investigated the impact of systematic and explicit vocabulary instruction with English learners (Carlo et al., 2004; Perez, 1981; Rousseau et al., 1993). All three resulted in improvements in reading comprehension, and in the one study that assessed impact on vocabulary specifically, the effect was positive. In the study by Carlo et al., 16 classrooms were randomly assigned to treatment and control conditions (*n* = 10 and *n* = 6). The classroom teachers then implemented intervention or control instruction that lasted 15 weeks. In the intervention condition, 10 to 12 target words were taught each week. Intervention activities included reading in both the students' native language and English, vocabulary discussions with the teacher, and homogeneous groups of students working on vocabulary analysis activities. In this study, not only was there a positive outcome on language measures (as expected), but there was also an impact on reading comprehension. The positive finding on reading comprehension helps highlight the important causal connection between learning word meanings and reading comprehension.

Academic Language

Even when English learners know word meanings, they may be uncertain how to use new words appropriately. Words have to be used with the appropriate number (*goose, geese*), tense (*is, are, was*), and word form (*fun, funnier, funny*). Systematic instruction in usage and language conventions needs to be a Tier 1 feature of language development for native English speakers as well as English learners, and many of the words used should be the same words students are working with during their reading lesson.

Academic language is the language of the classroom; of academic disciplines such as science, history, and literary analysis; and of extended, reasoned discourse. It is more abstract than conversational English, and adapted to specific contexts. For example, some words used in everyday conversation take on special meanings when they are used in scientific or other discourse. Unfortunately, little research has been done on the teaching of academic English. Two studies reviewed by the What Works Clearinghouse (Institute of Education Sciences, 2006, 2007) demonstrated a positive intervention impact on two narrow areas of academic English: quality of oral narrative and syntax (Scientific Learning Corporation, 2004; Uchikoshi, 2005). However, these studies only indirectly addressed classroom instruction.

Preliminary frameworks and guidelines developed by researchers list topics teachers should address when focusing on academic English, but these guidelines are not designed for regular use by teachers in the classroom or as a daily instructional manual (Diaz-Rico & Weed, 2002; Dutro & Moran, 2003; Feldman & Kinsella, 2005; Fillmore & Snow, 2000; Girard, 2005; Scarcella, 2003).

Despite the lack of research on how best to help English learners develop academic English, there is strong consensus among experts that English learners require considerable *explicit* and *deliberate* instruction to learn the features of formal English used in the schools and in academic discourse. When instruction in academic English is given early, consistently, and simultaneously across content areas, it can make a difference in English learners' ability to access the core curriculum, according to most scholars (August & Hakuta, 1997; August & Shanahan, 2006; Bailey, 2006; Callahan, 2005; Diaz-Rico & Weed, 2002; Fillmore, 2004; Fillmore & Snow, 2000; Francis, Rivera, Lesaux, Kieffer, & Rivera, 2006; Genesee, Lindholm-Leary, Saunders, & Christian, 2006; Goldenberg, 2006; Meltzer & Haman, 2005; Saunders, Foorman, & Carlson, 2006; Scarcella, 2003; Schleppegrell, 2001, 2004).

Focused instruction in academic English should begin in the earliest grades, not wait until students are able to read and write in English. Before English learners are reading, the development of age-appropriate academic English—morphology, syntax, vocabulary, etc.—can be accelerated orally through daily planned and deliberate instruction (Francis et al., 2006; Gibbons, 2002). This importance increases as children enter the upper grades (August & Hakuta, 1997; Bailey, 2006; Fillmore & Snow, 2000; Francis et al.; Genesee et al., 2006; Goldenberg, 2006; Scarcella, 2003; Schleppegrell, 2001, 2004).

Focused instruction in academic English also can build on students' work with expository text. For example, when English learners read expository text that includes academic language, teachers should discuss the text and the language in structured ways (Goldenberg, 2006). Instruction should also focus on teaching English learners to use specific aspects of academic language related to language features such as tense agreement, plurals, and proper use of adjectives and adverbs (Celce-Murcia, 2002). Students need practice using these features in the context of meaningful oral and written communication (Fillmore & Snow, 2000; Francis et al., 2006). They also must learn to use language accurately in a range of situations—for instance, to tell stories, describe events, define words and concepts, explain problems, retell actions, summarize content, and question intentions (Bailey, 2006; Gibbons, 2002; Schleppegrell, 2004).

Instructional focus on the development of academic English can come after a challenging text has been read and discussed, so that the vocabulary and meaning are clear. Then the teacher can come back to the story and focus on the particular aspects of language that may be problematic for English learners, such as sentence construction, word usage, and prepositions, using the familiar text. Language-focused activities will have more meaning for English learners if they already have a general understanding of the material in the text.

For English learners, many features of academic English should be taught *during* the block of time devoted to reading instruction. Instruction in academic English will help students gain perspective on what they read, understand relationships, and follow logical lines of thought. Knowledge of academic English also helps students in writing—developing topic sentences, providing smooth transitions between ideas, and editing their writing effectively. Reading, discussing, and writing about text needs to be a central part of the instruction in English language development that is dispersed throughout the day (August & Hakuta, 1997; Callahan, 2005; Fillmore & Snow, 2000; Francis et al., 2006; Genesee et al., 2006; Goldenberg, 2006; Meltzer & Haman, 2005; Scarcella, 2003). When integrated effectively, English language development, specifically during reading instruction, can help emphasize the importance of comprehension in early reading and the strong role regular oral language use can have in helping students engage in text-based, academic discussions.

District Leadership in Promoting Effective Language Instruction

Providing effective vocabulary and academic language instruction can be difficult, particularly as it requires common and consistent approaches across teachers, subject areas, and grade levels. Because this type of instruction is not common in classrooms, teachers may struggle with learning how to implement it (Baker, Gersten, Haager, & Dingle, 2006; Gersten, Baker, Smith-Johnson, Dimino, & Peterson, 2006). Therefore, concerted professional development and coaching will be necessary to ensure that all teachers learn to provide effective Tier 1 language instruction for English learners.

Given the importance of this instruction and the challenges schools and teachers will face in learning to provide effective Tier 1 language instruction for English learners, we recommend that districts play a strong role by adopting sound *frameworks* and *expectations* for vocabulary and academic language instruction. These frameworks should be evidence-based when possible (e.g., vocabulary instruction methods) and provide teachers with extensive professional development, tools, and strategies that can be used in the classroom. Frameworks should include sufficient detail for daily vocabulary and academic language instruction that are both an integrated part of reading instruction and an essential component of English language development.

One method of high-quality professional development is teacher study groups, which can be used to engage teachers in planning effective vocabulary and academic language instruction (Gersten, Dimino, Jayanthi, Kim, & Santoro, 2007; Umbel et al., 1992; Verhallen & Schoonen, 1993). These groups are best facilitated by an expert in vocabulary and academic language instruction, and should include extensive hands-on activities for teachers, such as transforming textbook definitions into student-friendly definitions, identifying crucial words from the texts students will read, and developing daily lesson plans for intensive vocabulary instruction (Gersten et al., 2006).

Another method for preparing teachers for effective classroom instruction in vocabulary and academic language includes a strong classroom coaching component. For the vast majority of teachers, these instruction routines will best be learned in the classroom, with coaches providing immediate feedback, modeling lessons, and demonstrating methods.

Opportunities for English Learners to Process Content Through Structured Practice

Students learn from structured opportunities to process academic content and apply what they have been taught. English learners in particular may benefit when these opportunities involve verbal engagement with academic content. A number of studies have demonstrated positive learning impacts in their English language development when English learners work with a partner on academic tasks or in small cooperative groups (Calderón, Hertz-Lazarowitz, & Slavin, 1998; Calhoon, Al Otaiba, Cihak, King, & Avalos, 2006; Klingner & Vaughn, 1996; McMaster et al., 2008; Saenz, Fuchs, & Fuchs, 2005). These peer-assisted learning interactions can include practice activities involving correct and incorrect responses, as well as complex student responses and elaborated explanations, in which interactions focus on reading comprehension. For example, Saenz et al. (2005) implemented peer-assisted instruction with English learners in Grades 3–6. Each student assumed the role of tutor and tutee, engaging in reading comprehension activities involving retelling stories, summarizing text, and generating predictions. These interactions resulted in a positive impact on reading comprehension.

Other studies involving peer-assisted learning have resulted in similar improve-ments in complex knowledge and skills, as well as more basic skills such as decoding and reading fluency (e.g., see chapter 24 in this book). Despite the lack of empirical evidence that peer-assisted learning has a positive impact on *language development*, we recommend this practice for vocabulary and academic language instruction because of the opportunities present for frequent and meaningful language-based activities. During part of the day normally reserved for English language development, peers working together in ways similar to the Saez et al. study can engage in vocabulary and academic language that can build on teacher-directed instruction, and reinforce other, more traditional types of instruction for English language development directed by language teachers and other specialists.

Peer-assisted learning cannot replace teacher-led instruction. In fact, high-quality teacher-led instruction is a necessary precursor to peer-assisted learning because English learners must have a solid understanding of the content, and use their work with peers to practice what has been taught rather than engage in new learning activities. Peer-assisted instructional routines can replace some of the independent seatwork or round-robin reading that students do, for example, when the overt intention of the teacher is to provide practice and extended learning opportunities for students.

Preparing classrooms for peer-assisted learning is not easy. Very clear roles and routines are required of students if implementation is going to mirror the procedures used in empirical studies. In most cases, students need explicit prompt cards and other procedural aids if they are to take on the roles of tutors and tutees (Baker, Gersten, & Scanlon, 2002). In most examples of peer-assisted learning formats, role reciprocity is the norm; that is, students assume roles of both tutors and tutees during the lesson. Typically, student pairs differ in skill levels in either reading or English language proficiency, and the more advanced child typically assumes the role of tutor first and tutee second in the lesson.

However, all students in the classroom can participate in peer-assisted instruction, thus giving the teacher a consistent routine that can be used with everyone in the classroom. Consequently, teachers do not have to plan additional activities for separate groups of students in the class. Not only does this type of partner work give teachers a way to structure learning opportunities that address some of the unique learning needs of English learners, but it also provides a meaningful learning experience for other students in the class. Once students have learned peer-assisted instruction routines, the format can be used in a number of different content areas across grade levels.

The U.S. Department of Education's Institute of Education Sciences (IES) practice guide on English learners recommends that the peer-assisted learning approach be used for at least 90 minutes per week and that districts encourage or require schools to use this approach with their English learners (IES, 2007). Given the importance of following clear structures, the approach works best when districts provide strong training for schools to follow a consistent peer-assisted approach. This helps ensure that peer-assisted instructional routines are used in the same way across classrooms and schools, increasing fidelity. English learners also benefit from the consistent implementation because they can learn a common instructional routine quickly and know what is expected of them. District training should be provided early in the school year so that teachers can practice immediately with their own students and teach the peer-assisted instructional routine as they would many other routines early in the school year. If possible, district or school coaches should observe teachers using this routine early in the year and provide feedback as they get started, to help teachers during the more difficult early phases.

TIER 2 CONSIDERATIONS IN READING FOR ENGLISH LEARNERS

When screening data or other sources of information indicate that the reading skills of English learners are below grade level, small group instruction is one of the most powerful, instructionally intense, and efficient ways of providing the instruction English learners need to reach grade-level goals. Putting English learners in small group formats with well-trained personnel and quality curriculum gives them frequent opportunities to use academic language—to explain content, provide answers, and build on the responses of their peers and teacher. Because the group is small, teachers can expertly reinforce students' language use, extend it, provide highly specific feedback, and engage in extended academic discussions with students centered on specific instructional objectives and content.

Homogeneous groups of three to five students provide a setting in which teachers can focus instruction, provide corrective feedback, provide multiple practice opportunities, and review essential content as needed. Although most Tier 2 sessions tend to be about 30 minutes, effective Tier 2 interventions for English learners should be *longer*, at least 40–50 minutes, so that language tasks can be included (Vaughn, Mathes, et al., 2006). Some of this time—perhaps a 7–10 minute block—can be dedicated to having students read aloud using expository texts, which will help English learners acquire content-area knowledge, practice recently learned vocabulary, and learn comprehension strategies.

When these small groups include students with homogeneous reading skills but heterogeneous English language skills, teachers can provide focused reading instruction as well as extended language instruction because of the diversity of language skills. That is, when teachers ask group participants to summarize story content or make a prediction, they can tailor their expectations to meet the language skills of the English learners in the group. For students with less proficient language skills, the same cognitively engaging questions might elicit less extensive English responses; for more English proficient children, the same question might be expected to elicit a more extended verbal response. The children who are more verbally proficient benefit from more advanced expectations in terms of English language use; those who are less verbally proficient benefit from hearing how more verbally proficient students use language.

The amount of time a student spends in small group instruction and the intensity of this instruction should reflect the degree of risk students face for long-term reading and academic difficulties. Interventions, particularly in the early grades, should focus on the five core elements of reading—that is, phonological awareness, phonics, reading fluency, vocabulary, and comprehension (NRP, 2001). Therefore we recommend that teachers stress both reading and listening comprehension during these sessions.

A good deal of high-quality experimental research supports the use of small group formats, and other approaches to increase the amount or intensity of instruction, as a means for increasing both decoding ability and reading comprehension. In the past several years, four high-quality randomized controlled trials of reading interventions for struggling English learners have been conducted (Denton, Anthony, Parker, & Hasbrouck, 2004; Gunn, Smolkowski, Biglan, & Black, 2002; Vaughn, Cirino, et al., 2006; Vaughn, Mathes, et al., 2006). These studies are presented under the Intervention Reports section on the What Works Clearinghouse website (http://ies.ed.gov/ncee/wwc/reports/topic.aspx?tid=10).

Participants in these research studies were English learners in Grades 1–5 with serious reading problems (i.e., reading at least 1 year below grade level or scoring in the lowest quartile on standardized tests). Reading achievement was assessed on a wide range of measures, including word reading, comprehension, and vocabulary. Across these intervention studies, reading instruction was delivered daily in small groups for 30–50 minutes per day. Different curricula, constructed according to research-based principles that build on the tradition of direct instruction, demonstrated a positive impact on reading achievement (Gersten, Baker, Pugach, Scanlon, & Chard, 2001). Two of the studies demonstrated a positive impact on reading performance that lasted well beyond the intervention. In one of these studies, the intervention was implemented in first grade, where there was a positive effect, and this effect was maintained through second grade (Cirino et al., 2009). In the second study, the positive reading effect was maintained 2 years after the intervention ended (Gunn et al., 2002).

Programs that follow the principles of direct and explicit instruction to teach core reading elements in small groups are likely to produce the beneficial effects demonstrated in the preceding studies. Interventions that district and school personnel consider should provide sufficient coverage of the five core elements of reading—that is, phonological awareness, phonics, reading fluency, vocabulary, and both reading and listening comprehension (August & Siegel, 2006; Quiroga, Lemos-Britton, Mostafapour, Abbott, & Berninger, 2002; Shanahan & Beck, 2006). The major instructional principles that characterize the intervention are (a) multiple opportunities for students to respond to questions; (b) multiple opportunities for students to practice reading both words and sentences, either in a small group or with a peer; (c) clear feedback from the teacher when students make errors; (d) an instructional pace that is both brisk and clear; and (e) explicit instruction in all areas of reading, including explicit comprehension and vocabulary instruction.

Training for teachers and other school personnel who provide small group instruction should focus on how to deliver instruction effectively, independent of the particular program the teacher will use. Although it is important that the training cover the use of the specific program materials, it should also emphasize that these instructional techniques can be used in other programs and across other subject areas (Vaughn, Cirino, et al., 2006; Vaughn, Mathes, et al., 2006; Gunn et al., 2002).

Each of the four research studies that resulted in a positive impact on reading achievement involved *extensive training* of the teachers and interventionists. This training is most effective when all personnel who work with English learners participate in the same professional development activities (Haager & Windmueller, 2001). For many teachers, this type of fast-paced interactive instruction will be unfamiliar, and coaching support in the classroom will be critical for these teachers to be effective. "Master" teachers who have experience in the specific program being used should provide this essential training and coaching support in the classroom.

SUMMARY AND CONCLUSION

In this chapter, we attempted to distill the research on early screening and identification of English learners who are likely to require additional support. We briefly addressed types of classroom reading and language development instruction (Tier 1 instruction) that are likely to be most effective for these students. Although in many critical academic areas there is no solid basis of empirical evidence, in general the quantity and quality of research has dramatically improved over the past decade.

We also presented valid measures for screening and assessing the progress of English learners as they learn to read and for helping teachers identify which students require additional instruction to succeed. Increasingly, these measures are used in American schools. We caution that some students may need additional assistance in the areas of vocabulary and English language development. Unfortunately, assessments are in their infancy in these areas. There are promising practices in terms of interventions to enhance vocabulary and knowledge of academic language. However, these are based solely on expert opinion, not on solid scientific evidence.

We envision the expansion of research to create valid and reliable measures of language development and means to monitor vocabulary growth. Even more important are the development and validation of interventions that contribute to language development, listening comprehension, and ultimately reading comprehension and language facility. The effective integration of multiple literacy strands is a new and critical frontier for psychologists and teachers to explore to serve English learners experiencing difficulty in learning to read.

REFERENCES

August, D., Carlo, M., Dressler, C., & Snow, C. (2005). The critical role of vocabulary development for English language learners. *Learning Disabilities Research and Practice, 20*(1), 50–57.

August, D., & Hakuta, K. (1997). *Improving schooling for language-minority children: A research agenda.* Washington, DC: National Academy Press.

August, D., & Shanahan, L. (2006). *Developing literacy in second-language learners: Report of the National Literacy Panel on Language Minority Children and Youth.* Washington, DC: National Literacy Panel on Language-Minority Children and Youth (US).

August, D., & Siegel, L. (2006). Literacy instruction for language-minority children in special education settings. In D. August & T. Shanahan (Eds.), *Developing literacy in second-language learners: Report of the National Literacy Panel on Language Minority Children and Youth* (pp. 523–554). Mahwah, NJ: Erlbaum.

Bailey, A. (2006). From lambie to lambaste: The conceptualization, operationalization and use of academic language in assessment of ELL students. In K. Rolstad (Ed.), *Rethinking school language.* Mahwah, NJ: Erlbaum.

Baker, S. K., & Baker, D. L. (2008). English learners and response to intervention: Improving quality of instruction in general and special education. In E. L. Grigorenko (Ed.), *Educating individuals with disabilities: IDEA 2004 and beyond* (pp. 249–273). New York: Springer.

Baker, S. K., Gersten, R., Haager, D., & Dingle, M. (2006). Teaching practice and the reading growth of first-grade English learners: Validation of an observation instrument. *Elementary School Journal, 107*(2), 200–219.

Baker, S., Gersten, R., & Scanlon, D. (2002). Procedural facilitators and cognitive strategies: Tools for unraveling the mysteries of comprehension and the writing process, and for providing meaningful access to the general curriculum. *Learning Disabilities Research and Practice, 17*(1), 65–77.

Baker, S., & Good, R. (1995). Curriculum-based measurement of English reading with bilingual Hispanic students: A validation study with second-grade students. *School Psychology Review, 24,* 561–579.

Baker, S., Smolkowski, K., Katz, R., Fien, H., Seeley, J., Kame'enui, E., et al. (2008). Reading fluency as a predictor of reading proficiency in low-performing high poverty schools. *School Psychology Review, 37,* 18–37.

Beck, I. L., & McKeown, M. (1991). Conditions of vocabulary acquisition. In R. Barr, M. Kamil, P. Mosenthal, & P. D. Pearson (Eds.), *Handbook of reading research* (Vol. 2, pp. 789–814). New York: Longman.

Beck, I. L., Perfetti, C. A., & McKeown, M. G. (1982). Effects of long-term vocabulary instruction on lexical access and reading comprehension. *Journal of Educational Psychology, 74,* 506–521.

Bialystok, E., Luk, G., & Kwan, E. (2005). Bilingualism, biliteracy, and learning to read: Interactions among languages and writing systems. *Scientific Studies of Reading 9*(1), 43–61.

Biemiller, A. (1999, April). *Estimating vocabulary growth for ESL children with and without listening comprehension instruction.* Paper presented at the Annual Conference of the American Educational Research Association, Montreal, Quebec, Canada

Blachowicz, C., Fisher, P., Ogle, D., & Watts-Taffe, S. (2006). Vocabulary: Questions from the classroom. *Reading Research Quarterly, 41,* 524–539.

Calderón, M., Hertz-Lazarowitz, R., & Slavin, R. (1998). Effects of bilingual cooperative integrated reading and composition on students making the transition from Spanish to English reading. *Elementary School Journal, 99,* 153–165.

Calhoon, M. B., Al Otaiba, S., Cihak, D., King, A., & Avalos, A. C. (2006). *Effects of peer-mediated program on reading skill acquisition for two-way bilingual first grade classrooms.* Unpublished manuscript.

Callahan, R. M. (2005). Tracking and high school English learners: Limiting opportunity to learn. *American Educational Research Journal, 42,* 305–328.

Carlo, M. S., August, D., McLaughlin, B., Snow, C. E., Dressler, C., Lippman, D. N., et al. (2004). Closing the gap: Addressing the vocabulary needs of English-language learners in bilingual and mainstream classrooms. *Reading Research Quarterly, 39,* 188–215.

Celce-Murcia, M. (2002). On the use of selected grammatical features in academic writing. In M. Schleppergrell & M. C. Colombi (Eds.), *Developing advanced literacy in first and second languages* (pp. 143–158). Mahwah, NJ: Erlbaum.

Cheung, A., & Slavin, R. E. (2005). Effective reading programs for English language learners and other language-minority students. *Bilingual Research Journal, 29,* 241–267.

Chiappe, P., Glaeser, B., & Ferko, D. (2007). Speech perception, vocabulary, and the development of reading skills in English among Korean- and English-speaking children. *Journal of Educational Psychology, 99,* 154–166.

Chiappe, P., & Siegel, L. (1999). Phonological awareness and reading acquisition in English- and Punjabi-speaking Canadian children. *Journal of Educational Psychology, 91,* 20–29.

Chiappe, P., Siegel, L., & Wade-Woolley, L. (2002). Linguistic diversity and the development of reading skills: A longitudinal study. *Scientific Studies of Reading, 6*(4), 369–400.

Cirino, P. T., Vaughn, S., Linan-Thompson, S., Cardenas-Hagan, E., Fletcher, J. M., & Francis, D. J. (2009). One-year follow-up outcomes of Spanish and English interventions for English language learners at risk for reading problems. *American Educational Research Journal, 46,* 744–781. doi:10.3102/0002831208330214

Deno, S. L. (1985). Curriculum-based measurement: The emerging alternative. *Exceptional Children, 52,* 219–232.

Denton, C. A., Anthony, J. L., Parker, R., & Hasbrouck, J. E. (2004). Effects of two tutoring programs on the English reading development of Spanish–English bilingual students. *Elementary School Journal, 104*(4), 289.

Diaz-Rico, L. T., & Weed, K. Z. (2002). *The crosscultural, language, and academic development handbook: A complete K–12 reference guide.* Boston: Allyn & Bacon.

Dominguez de Ramirez, R., & Shapiro, E. (2006). Curriculum-based measurement and the evaluation of reading skills of Spanish-speaking English language learners in bilingual education classrooms. *School Psychology Review, 35,* 356–369.

Durgunoglu, A. Y., Nagy, W. E., & Hancin-Bhatt, B. J. (1993). Cross-language transfer of phonological awareness. *Journal of Educational Psychology, 85,* 453–465.

Dutro, S., & Moran, C. (2003). Rethinking English language instruction: An architectural approach. In G. Garcia (Ed.), *English learners: Reaching the highest level of English literacy* (pp. 227–258). Newark, DE: International Reading Association.

Feldman, K., & Kinsella, K. (2005). Create an active participation classroom. The CORE Reading Expert. Retrieved January 17, 2008, from http://corelearn.com/pdfs/Newsletters/CORE%202005%20Spring%20Newsletter.pdf

Fien, H., Baker, S. K., Smolkowski, K., Smith, J. M., Kame'enui, E. J., & Thomas Beck, C. (2008). Using nonsense word fluency to measure reading proficiency in K–2 for English learners and native English speakers. *School Psychology Review 37,* 391–408.

Fillmore, L. W. (2004). The role of language in academic development. In *Excerpts from a presentation by Lily Wong Fillmore at the Closing the Achievement Gap for EL Students conference.* Retrieved January 18, 2008, from http://www.scoe.k12.ca.us/aiming_high/docs/AH_language.pdf

Fillmore, L. W., & Snow, C. E. (2000). *What teachers need to know about language: Clearinghouse on languages and linguistics* [Electronic version]. http://www.cal.org/ericcll/teachers/teacher.pdf

Francis, D., Rivera, M., Lesaux, N. K., Kieffer, M., & Rivera, H. (2006). *Research-based recommendations for the use of accommodations in large-scale assessments.* Retrieved January 17, 2008, from http://www.centeroninstruction.org/files/ELL3-Assessments.pdf

Fuchs, L. S., & Fuchs, D. (1994). Academic assessment and instrumentation. In S. Vaughn & C. Bos (Eds.), *Research issues in learning disabilities: Theory, methodology, assessment, and ethics* (pp. 233–242). New York: Springer-Verlag.

Fuchs, L. S., Fuchs, D., Hosp, M. K., & Jenkins, J. R. (2001). Oral reading fluency as an indicator of reading competence: A theoretical, empirical, and historical analysis. *Scientific Studies of Reading, 5,* 239–256.

Genesee, F., Lindholm-Leary, K., Saunders, W., & Christian, D. (2006). *Educating English language learners: A synthesis of research evidence.* New York: Cambridge University Press.

Gersten, R. (1996). The double demands of teaching English language learners. *Educational Leadership, 53*(5), 18–22.

Gersten, R., Baker, S., Pugach, M. C., Scanlon, D., & Chard, D. (2001). Contemporary research on special education teaching. In V. Richardson (Ed.), *Handbook for research on teaching* (4th ed., pp. 695–722). Washington, DC: American Educational Research Association.

Gersten, R., Baker, S. K., Shanahan, T., Linan-Thompson, S., Collins, P., & Scarcella, R. (2007). *IES practice guide: Effective literacy and English language instruction for English learners in the elementary grades* (Report No. NCEE 2007–4011). Washington, DC: National Center for Education Evaluation and Regional Assistance, Institute of Educational Sciences, U.S. Department of Education.

Gersten, R., Baker, S., Smith-Johnson, J., Dimino, J., & Peterson, A. (2006). Eyes on the prize: Teaching complex historical content to middle school students with learning disabilities. *Exceptional Children, 72,* 264–280.

Gersten, R., Dimino, J., Jayanthi, M., Kim, J., & Santoro, L. (2007). *Teacher study groups as a means to improve reading comprehension and vocabulary instruction for English learners: Results of randomized controlled trials.* Signal Hill, CA: Instructional Research Group.

Gersten, R., Compton, D., Connor, C. M., Dimino, J., Santoro, L., Linan-Thompson, S., et al. (2008). *Assisting students struggling with reading: Response to intervention and multi-tier intervention for reading in the primary grades. A practice guide* (NCEE 2009-4045). Washington, DC: National Center for Education Evaluation and Regional Assistance, Institute of Education Sciences, U.S. Department of Education.

Geva, E., & Yaghoub-Zadeh, Z. (2006). Reading efficiency in native English-speaking and English-as-a-second-language children: The role of oral proficiency and underlying cognitive-linguistic processes. *Scientific Studies of Reading, 10*(1), 31–57.

Geva, E., Yaghoub-Zadeh, Z., & Schuster, B. (2000). Part IV: Reading and foreign language learning: Individual differences in word recognition skills of ESL children. *Annals of Dyslexia, 50,* 121–154.

Gibbons, P. (2002). *Scaffolding language, scaffolding learning: Teaching second language learners in the mainstream classroom.* Portsmouth, NH: Heinemann.

Girard, V. (2005). *English learners and the language arts.* Retrieved May 5, 2008, from http://www.schoolsmovingup.net/cs/wested/view/e/313

Goldenberg, C. (2006). Improving achievement for English-learners: What the research tells us. *Education Week, 25*(43), 34–36.

Good, R. H., & Kaminski, R. A. (2002). Nonsense word fluency. In R. H. Good & R. A. Kaminski (Eds.), *Dynamic Indicators of Basic Early Literacy Skills* (6th ed.). Eugene, OR: Institute for the Development of Educational Achievement.

Graves, A., Gersten, R., & Haager, D. (2004). Literacy instruction in multiple-language first-grade classrooms: Linking student outcomes to observed instructional practice. *Learning Disabilities Research and Practice, 19*(4), 262–272.

Green, E. J. (1997). Guidelines for serving linguistically and culturally diverse young children. *Early Childhood Education Journal, 24*(3), 147–154.

Gunn, B., Smolkowski, K., Biglan, A., & Black, C. (2002). Supplemental instruction in decoding skills for Hispanic and non-Hispanic students in early elementary school: A follow-up. *Journal of Special Education, 36,* 69–79.

Haager, D., Gersten, R., Baker, S. K., & Graves, A. (2003). The English-language learner classroom observation instrument: Observations of beginning reading instruction in urban schools. In S. R. Vaughn & K. L. Briggs (Eds.), *Reading in the classroom: Systems for observing teaching and learning* (pp. 111–114). Baltimore: Brookes.

Haager, D., Klinger, J. K., & Vaughn, S. (2007). *Validated reading practices for three tiers of intervention.* Baltimore: Brookes.

Haager, D., & Windmueller, M. (2001). Early reading intervention for English language learners at-risk for learning disabilities: Student and teacher outcomes in an urban school. *Learning Disabilities Quarterly, 24,* 235–249.

Hiebert, E. H. (2005). State reform policies and the task textbooks pose for first-grade readers. *Elementary School Journal, 105*(3), 245–267.

Institute of Education Sciences (IES), U.S. Department of Education. (2006, September 16). WWC Intervention Report: *Arthur.* Retrieved September 20, 2009, from the What Works Clearinghouse: http://ies.ed.gov/ncee/wwc/reports/english_lang/arthur/research.asp

Institute of Education Sciences (IES), U.S. Department of Education. (2007, July 9). WWC Intervention Report: Fast ForWord. Retrieved September 20, 2009, from the What Works Clearinghouse: http://ies.ed.gov/ncee/wwc/reports/beginning_reading/fastfw/research.asp

Institute of Education Sciences (IES), U.S. Department of Education. (2007). *Effective literacy and English language instruction for English learners in the elementary grades.* IES Practice Guide. Retrieved September 30, 2009, from the What Works Clearinghouse website: http://ies.ed.gov/ncee/wwc/

Klingner, J. K., & Vaughn, S. (1996). Reciprocal teaching of reading comprehension strategies for students with learning disabilities who use English as a second language. *Elementary School Journal, 96*(3), 275–293.

Leafstedt, J., Richards, C., & Gerber, M. (2004). Effectiveness of explicit phonological-awareness instruction for at-risk English learners. *Learning Disabilities Research and Practice, 19*(4), 252–261.

Lesaux, N., Lipka, O., & Siegel, L. (2006). Investigating cognitive and linguistic abilities that influence the reading comprehension skills of children from diverse linguistic backgrounds. *Reading and Writing, 19*(1), 99–131.

Lesaux, N. K., Rupp, A. A., & Siegel, L. S. (2007). Growth in reading skills of children from diverse linguistic backgrounds: Findings from a 5-year longitudinal study. *Journal of Educational Psychology, 99*, 821–834.

Lesaux, N., & Siegel, L. (2003). The development of reading in children who speak English as a second language. *Developmental Psychology, 39*, 1005–1020.

Limbos, M., & Geva, E. (2001). Accuracy of teacher assessments of second-language students at risk for reading disability. *Journal of Learning Disabilities, 34*, 136–152.

McMaster, K. L., Kung, S.-H., Han, I., & Cao, M. (2008). Peer-assisted learning strategies: A "Tier 1" approach to promoting English learners' response to intervention. *Exceptional Children, 74*, 194–214.

Meltzer, J., & Haman, E. T. (2005). *Meeting the literacy development needs of adolescent English language learners through content-area learning, Part two: Focus on classroom teaching and learning strategies.* Retrieved January 17, 2008, from http://www.alliance.brown.edu/pubs/aslit/adell_litdv2.pdf

Miura Wayman, M., Wallace, T., Ives Wiley, H., Ticha, R., & Espin, C. (2007). Literature synthesis on curriculum-based measurement in reading. *Journal of Special Education, 41*, 85–120.

National Institute of Child Health and Human Development (NICHD). (2000). *Report of the National Reading Panel: An evidence-based assessment of scientific research literature on reading and its implications for reading instruction* (NIH Pub. No. 00-4769). Bethesda, MD: Author.

National Reading Panel. (2001). *Put reading first: The research building blocks for teaching children to read. Kindergarten through grade 3.* Washington, DC: National Institute for Literacy.

Oh, D., Haager, D., & Windmueller, M. (2004). *Assembling the puzzle of predictability: Validity of the Dynamic Indicators of Basic Early Literacy Skills assessment with English learners in kindergarten.* Unpublished manuscript.

Pearson, P. D., Hiebert, E. H., & Kamil, M. L. (2007). Vocabulary assessment: What we know and what we need to know. *Reading Research Quarterly, 42*, 282–296.

Perez, S. A. (1981). Effective approaches for improving the reading comprehension of problem readers. *Reading Horizons, 22*(1), 59–65.

Quiroga, T., Lemos-Britton, Z., Mostafapour, E., Abbott, R. D., & Berninger, V. W. (2002). Phonological awareness and beginning reading in Spanish-speaking ESL first graders: Research into practice. *Journal of School Psychology, 40*, 85–111.

Rousseau, M. K., Tam, B. K. Y., & Ramnarain, R. (1993). Increasing reading proficiency of language-minority students with speech and language impairments. *Education and Treatment of Children, 16*(3), 254–271.

Saenz, L., Fuchs, L., & Fuchs, D. (2005). Peer-assisted learning strategies for English language learners with learning disabilities. *Exceptional Children, 71,* 231–247.

Saunders, W., Foorman, B., & Carlson, C. (2006). Is a separate block of time for oral English language development in programs for English learners needed? *Elementary School Journal, 107*(2), 181–198.

Scarcella, R. (2003). *Accelerating academic English: A focus on the English learner.* Oakland, CA: Regents of the University of California.

Schleppegrell, M. J. (2001). Linguistic features of the language of schooling. *Linguistics and Education, 12,* 431–459.

Schleppegrell, M. J. (2004). *The language of schooling: A functional linguistics perspective.* Mahwah, NJ: Erlbaum.

Scientific Learning Corporation. (2004). *Improved language skills by children with low reading performance who used Fast ForWord language.* MAPS for Learning: Product Report 3(1): 1–13. Retrieved September 30, 2009, from http://www.scilearn. com/results/main=abstract/pdf=30052FFWLanguageProdRpt.pdf

Shanahan, T., & August, D. (2007). *Developing reading and writing in second language learners: Lessons from the report of the National Literacy Panel on language-minority children and youth.* New York: National Literacy Panel on Language-Minority Children and Youth.

Shanahan, T., & Beck, I. (2006). Effective literacy teaching for English-language learners. In D. L. August & T. Shanahan (Eds.), *Developing literacy in a second language: Report of the National Literacy Panel* (pp. 415–488). Mahwah, NJ: Erlbaum.

Shinn, M. R. (1998). *Advanced applications of curriculum-based measurement.* New York: Guilford Press.

Uchikoshi, Y. (2005). Narrative development in bilingual kindergarteners: Can *Arthur* help? *Developmental Psychology, 41,* 464–478.

Umbel, V. M., Pearson, B. Z., Fernández, M. C., & Oller, D. K. (1992). Measuring bilingual children's receptive vocabularies. *Child Development, 63,* 1012–1020.

Vaughn, S., Cirino, P. T., Linan-Thompson, S., Mathes, P. G., Carlson, C. D., Hagan, E. C., et al. (2006). Section on teaching, learning, and human development— Effectiveness of a Spanish intervention and an English intervention for English-language learners at risk for reading problems. *American Educational Research Journal, 43,* 449–489.

Vaughn, S., Mathes, P., Linan-Thompson, S., Cirino, P., Carlson, C., Pollard-Durodola, S., et al. (2006). Effectiveness of an English intervention for first-grade English language learners at risk for reading problems. *Elementary School Journal, 107*(2), 154–180.

Verhallen, M., & Schoonen, R. (1993). Lexical knowledge of monolingual and bilingual children. *Applied Linguistics, 14*(4), 344–363.

Verhoeven, L. (1990). Acquisition of reading in a second language. *Reading Research Quarterly, 25,* 90–114.

Verhoeven, L. (2000). Components in early second language reading and spelling. *Scientific Studies of Reading, 4,* 313–330.

Wiley, H. I., & Deno, S. L. (2005). Oral reading and maze measures as predictors of success for English learners on a state standards assessment. *Remedial and Special Education, 26,* 207–214.

Woodcock, R. W., McGrew, K. S., & Mather, N. (2001). *Woodcock-Johnson III tests of achievement standard test book.* Itasca, IL: Riverside Publishing Company.

CHAPTER 20

Promoting Positive Math Outcomes

Marcy Stein
Diane Kinder
Kathy Zapp
Laura Feuerborn
University of Washington, Tacoma

INTRODUCTION

The poor performance of U.S. students in the area of mathematics has been well documented throughout the past decade. International and national assessments of mathematics performance, including the Trends in International Mathematics and Science Study (TIMSS), the Programme for International Student Assessment (PISA), and the National Assessment of Educational Progress (NAEP), all suggest the need for an overhaul of mathematics education. *What* we teach (math standards), *how* we teach (explicitly or indirectly), and *how* we measure student progress (continuously or annually) have emerged as important topics of interest to the education community at large as well as to the general public.

TIMSS is a comprehensive cross-country comparative study of mathematics and science. TIMSS data have been collected every 4 years since 1995, but at the time this chapter was written, the 2007 TIMSS data were not available. Therefore, our comments are based on the 2003 study. In 2003, 46 countries participated in TIMSS at either the fourth-grade or eighth-grade level or both. In that study, only 7% of U.S. eighth-grade students scored at the advanced level, whereas 33% of the students from the highest-performing countries scored at the advanced level (Mullis, Martin, Gonzales, & Chrostowski, 2004). Although the mathematics performance of U.S. eighth graders improved between 1995 and 2003, most of that progress occurred between 1995 and 1999.

Another international assessment, the Programme for International Student Assessment, provided even fewer positive results than TIMSS (Organisation for

Address all correspondence and feedback on this chapter to Marcy Stein at mstein@u.washington.edu.

Economic Co-operation and Development, 2004). PISA is a standardized assessment developed jointly by 41 participating countries. The assessment includes areas of mathematics that 15-year-olds need for life skills and as a basis for further study of mathematics. In the 2000 assessment, U.S. students' performance in overall mathematics literacy and problem solving was lower than the average performance of students in most countries. The 2003 PISA also showed that about two-thirds of the students in participating countries outperformed the U.S. students. In 2003, more U.S. students scored at or below the lowest level of proficiency in problem solving compared with the international average.

Although the math portion of the 2006 PISA was less in-depth than the 2003 assessment, results were similar, with American students performing significantly below the international average, just behind Azerbaijan and the Russian Federation (Organisation for Economic Co-operation and Development, 2007). Of additional concern is that the United States has a below-average proportion of high-performing students compared with the other participating countries.

The math performance of U.S. students as measured by the National Assessment of Educational Progress (NAEP) appears to be consistent with findings from the international studies. Data from the 2003 NAEP showed that only 29% of eighth-grade students scored at the *proficient* level; 32% scored below the *basic* level, demonstrating only partial mastery of the prerequisite knowledge and skills that are fundamental for proficient work (National Center for Educational Statistics [NCES], 2003). For example, only 10% of eighth graders could demonstrate three ways to divide an L-shaped figure in order to determine its area.

Results of the 2007 NAEP for Grades 4 and 8 suggest that both fourth and eighth graders are scoring higher than in earlier assessments, with steady increases in scores since 1990 (NCES, 2007). However, when disaggregated, the data show that students in fourth and eighth grade who were eligible for free and reduced lunch scored lower than those who were not eligible (9% and 19%, compared with 30% and 45%, respectively). Regardless of the reported increases, the performance of students who may be considered most at risk for academic failure is clearly unacceptable by any standard.

Performance of Students With Math Learning Disability

The reports of poor math performance of general education students briefly summarized to this point suggest that the problems facing students with math learning disabilities (MLD) may be even more daunting. Although the etiology of MLD is still unknown, and no diagnostic tool is available for reliably identifying students with MLD, Geary (2004) estimated that 5–8% of school-age children have been identified as having MLD. Available research in special education has documented that the performance of students identified as having a math disability lags significantly behind the performance of their nondisabled peers; however, the performance of MLD students is quite variable (Cawley, Parmar, Foley, Salmon, & Roy, 2001; Gersten,

Jordan, & Flojo, 2005; Harris, Miller, & Mercer, 1995; Miller, Butler, & Lee, 1998; Montague & Applegate, 2000). More specifically, students with MLD tend to struggle with fluency of computational skills (including arithmetic fact retrieval), which is believed to be associated with poor working memory or other associated deficits in cognition (Geary, 2004; Mabbott & Bisanz, 2008).

Addressing the needs of struggling students, whether they receive math instruction in general or special education, is a particular focus of this chapter on promoting positive math outcomes.

Current Reform Efforts in Mathematics Instruction

The recent demand for mathematics instruction reform and the corresponding math debates are comparable to the reading reform efforts of the 1980s and 1990s. The debates on reading during those times centered on the relative merits of using an *explicit phonics approach* versus a more *implicit whole language approach* to teaching beginning reading. In math, the debate centers on using *explicit strategy instruction* versus more implicit approaches such as *guided discovery* to teach computation and problem solving. As the research community continues to generate and investigate questions of both theoretical and practical importance, the impact of these debates on classroom instruction remains considerable. These unresolved debates affect the development of state standards, state assessments, and subsequently curricula for both academically successful and academically challenged students.

To resolve the reading instruction debates between explicit phonics and implicit whole language, the National Reading Panel was convened by Congress in 1997 and produced a research report called *Teaching Children to Read* (National Institute of Child Health and Human Development, 2000). Similarly, to resolve the explicit strategy versus implicit guided discovery debates in math, in 2006 Congress created the National Mathematics Advisory Panel (NMP) and charged it with providing the Department of Education with advice on the use of scientifically based research in mathematics. The NMP report *Foundations for Success* was completed in 2008.

One striking difference between the reading and math reform efforts is the difference in the volume of high-quality research available for review in each area. Though the reading research community has been actively conducting research for decades, a major theme running through the NMP report is the need for more math research. Despite this low research volume, the NMP does make research-based recommendations throughout its report.

A PROBLEM-SOLVING APPROACH TO MATH IMPROVEMENT

Reform initiatives like those in reading and math arise when a discrepancy between actual and expected levels of performance becomes apparent (Deno, 2002). Addressing these performance discrepancies requires educators to engage in some form of problem solving, regardless of where the discrepancy is observed: within general education (e.g., the poor performance of U.S. students compared with students from other countries), compensatory education (e.g., the performance gap between students eligible for free and reduced lunch and those not eligible), or special education (e.g., the underperformance of students with MLD compared with their nondisabled peers).

Problem-solving approaches to educational challenges are not new (Bransford & Stein, 1984; Deno & Mirkin, 1977). Fuchs and Deshler (2007) observed that the term *problem solving* is currently used in three distinct ways. First, problem solving is used to describe how general education teachers prepare to differentiate instruction for individual students within their classrooms. Second, the term refers to the careful planning and preparation required to address the more serious academic and social–emotional challenges that students with disabilities face. Third, problem solving is often used to describe the school-wide decision-making process that guides the improvement of the academic performance of students most at risk for failure.

Response to intervention (RTI) is a multitiered problem-solving approach predicated on the assumption that high-quality instruction in the general education classroom can prevent significant academic failure for most students. Students in the general education classroom who perform at grade level are considered to be Tier 1 students. Students who respond poorly to instruction in the general education classroom become candidates for more intensive interventions (Tier 2 students) and may be eligible for special education services (Tier 3 students). Research suggests that using this type of problem-solving approach may not only reduce the prevalence of MLD but also improve the performance of students with MLD (Fuchs et al., 2005; Shapiro, Edwards, & Zigmond, 2005).

Collaboration among teachers and other school personnel (including school psychologists and principals) appears to be central to the implementation of most successful school-wide problem-solving approaches, including RTI (Ephraim, 2008; Gersten, Chard, & Baker, 2000). However, even in schools where mutual accountability is inherent in the school culture, coordinating the efforts of all school personnel to implement early-intervening services remains a challenge. Recent research suggests that the use of instructional coaches may be an effective and efficient way to organize and implement the activities associated with the multitiered problem-solving approaches needed to improve student performance in math (Gersten, Morvant, & Brengelman, 1995; Knight, 2005).

Instructional coaches have been used in classrooms to improve literacy instruction for many years. Most recently, the implementation of Reading First, the federally funded literacy component of No Child Left Behind, required the use of literacy coaches (Deussen, Coskie, Robinson, & Autio, 2007). In their discussion of Reading First literacy coaches, Deussen et al. identified five categories of literacy coaches based on the amount of time they spend on specific activities. *Data-oriented* coaches spend most of their school time coordinating assessments and managing student performance data. *Student-oriented* coaches spend more of their time providing interventions directly to small groups of students. *Managerial* coaches are responsible for facilitating and planning team meetings and coordinating inservice activities. The final two categories are *teacher-oriented* coaches; those who spend most of their time in individual classrooms and those who work directly with teachers in small groups.

This chapter describes a problem-solving approach in which the math coach plays a central role, one that incorporates the responsibilities identified in each of the coaching categories outlined above. In our conceptualization, the primary responsibilities of the math coach are organized into two major areas: (a) evaluation of mathematics instruction, and (b) math action planning. These areas include the central features of problem-solving approaches, including RTI, that are grounded in data-based decision making (Deno, 2002; Fuchs & Deshler, 2007; Walker & Shinn, 2002). The coaching-based approach described in this chapter expands on most other problem-solving approaches by more explicitly linking needs-based evaluation to professional development activities.

NEEDS-BASED EVALUATION FOR MATHEMATICS INSTRUCTION

To assist math coaches in working with teachers engaged in academic problem solving, we developed the Mathematics Problem Solving Inventory (MPSI), a needs-based evaluation tool. The inventory is divided into three distinct sections. The first section relates to evaluation of student performance measures. The second section focuses on the evaluation of curriculum and instruction needs. The third section addresses the evaluation of professional development needs. The purpose of the MPSI is to assist math coaches in identifying and prioritizing areas for math action planning. Though most problem-solving models include an analysis of student performance data, math coaches using this inventory also collect information about curriculum materials and organization, along with professional development needs, including inservice training and math coaching needs. Although the inventory itself is too lengthy to be reproduced here, Figure 1 gives examples of the kinds of questions that appear in each of the three sections of the inventory. The entire MPSI is available from the authors upon request.

To help the math coach organize the information that is collected, we developed a corresponding MPSI summary form (see Figure 2). Using data from the MPSI, the math coach indicates on the summary form those areas for which an action may be needed. This form helps the math coach consolidate a large amount of information so it can be more easily shared with teachers and other school personnel.

Inventory of Student Performance Measurement Needs

The MPSI section on student performance includes four different types of student performance measures that teachers and coaches should consider as they make critical instructional decisions: benchmark assessment, progress monitoring, program-specific assessment, and assessment of content coverage. The questions on the inventory guide math coaches in recording information about the assessments given to students in each

Figure 1. Examples of questions from the Mathematics Problem Solving Inventory (MPSI).

I. **Evaluation of Student Performance Measurement Needs**

Benchmark Assessment
Are benchmark assessments being administered consistently throughout grade levels?

Progress Monitoring
Are progress monitoring assessments administered during the school year, and are these assessments administered frequently enough to discover when students are not making satisfactory progress?

Program-Specific Assessment
Are placement assessments administered at the beginning of the school year to determine starting points for students in Tiers 2 and 3 in all materials?

Assessment of Content Coverage
Have content coverage goals (pacing guides) been established for Tier 1 students in the core program?

II. **Evaluation of Curriculum and Instruction Needs**

Materials and Organization
Are materials and instruction structured sufficiently to meet the needs of Tier 1 students?

Organizational Variables: Time and Grouping
Is sufficient time for instruction in math allocated to Tier 3 students?

III. **Evaluation of Professional Development Needs**

Inservice Training Needs
Are teachers receiving sufficient support to reliably administer and score progress monitoring assessments?

In-Class Coaching Needs
Are all teachers and assistants receiving high-quality in-class instructional coaching on newly adopted curriculum materials?

of the three tiers so they can better determine whether more or different types of measures are needed to inform the math action planning process.

Benchmark Assessment
Benchmark measures help determine the extent to which students are meeting grade-level expectations. This type of assessment, also known as universal screening, provides data to help identify early those students who may need additional support. For many school systems, benchmark assessments are administered three times a year: in the fall, winter, and spring. The first assessment of the school year not only helps identify which students are starting the year below expected levels but also provides teachers with a

Figure 2. Mathematics Problem Solving Inventory (MPSI) summary form.

MATH PROBLEM SOLVING INVENTORY (MPSI) SUMMARY FORM

Name_____ School_____   Date_____

Directions: Using data from the MPSI, check all topics in each area where an action may be needed.

I. Student Performance Measurment Needs
A. Benchmark Assessment ☐
B. Progress Monitoring ☐
C. Program-Specific Assessment ☐
D. Assessment of Content Coverage ☐

II. CURRICULUM AND INSTRUCTION NEEDS	**III. PROFESSIONAL DEVELOPMENT NEEDS**
A. Materials	A. Inservice Training
A.1 Curriculum Materials for Each Tier ☐	A.1 Inservice: Assessment and Data Utilization ☐
A.2 Curriculum Adoption Needed ☐	A.2 Inservice: Curriculum and Instruction ☐
B. Organizational Variables	B. In-Class Coaching
B.1 Instructional Time ☐	B.1 In-Class Instructional Coaching ☐
B.2 Instructional Grouping ☐	B.2 In-Class Behavioral Coaching ☐

general sense of the instructional levels of the students in the class. The winter and spring assessments provide data on student progress toward end-of-year goals and state standards. Schools currently using benchmark assessments for reading are increasingly aware of the benefits of this type of assessment and will find its application to math fairly easy.

Students performing slightly below expected levels on benchmark assessment may require strategic intervention and more frequent progress monitoring. Students performing significantly below expected levels and students failing to respond to interventions will require more intensive intervention and weekly progress monitoring. If a majority of the students in a class or grade are falling below benchmark standards, the next step may be evaluating the core curriculum to see how well it aligns with the district or state math standards.

Progress Monitoring

If a student has been identified as needing additional support (i.e., Tier 2) based on benchmark testing, then more frequent progress monitoring is recommended. Whereas benchmark measures compare an individual student's performance with the average performance of other students, progress monitoring allows for an analysis of an individual student's performance over time relative to an expected rate of progress. If scientifically based assessment tools are used, students' responses can be analyzed and individual strengths and weaknesses identified through careful examination of students errors.

Several progress monitoring systems are commercially available to help teachers and math coaches monitor students' mathematics performance. One example is AIMSweb, which includes both measures for early math skills (e.g., early numeracy and quantity discrimination) and mixed-skill computation (Pearson Education, Inc., 2008). Other similar commercially developed curriculum-based measurement systems include Monitoring Basic Skills Progress (MBSP) Concepts/Applications and Computation (Fuchs, Hamlett, & Fuchs, 1999) and Yearly Progress Pro (CTB/McGraw-Hill, 2008).

These systems are typically linked to a data management system that is designed for ease of use. Most of these systems provide comprehensive data to show student performance, including whether students are mastering the material and which skills need additional review. The systems save teachers considerable time on summarizing student data and constructing student and class reports. The reports help teachers communicate with parents and guardians about student performance levels. Many of these commercial programs can be used for both reading and mathematics.

Program-Specific Assessment

Program-specific assessments are those tests that accompany a published math curriculum. The tests fall into two categories: (a) placement testing and (b) mastery monitoring or criterion-referenced assessment. How well these assessments are designed is addressed later in this chapter. The MPSI's questions about program-specific assessment are designed to show how frequently and how effectively teachers are using the assessments to guide their instruction. Responses may reveal a need to increase professional development in interpreting assessment results or in conducting error analyses.

Assessment of Content Coverage

To ensure that struggling students make sufficient progress toward mathematics proficiency, teachers must be able to balance *content mastery* with *content coverage*. That is, teachers need to be able to predict whether their students will have covered the essential content during the time allocated. Content mastery at the expense of content coverage will preclude many students from acquiring new skills necessary for advanced math topics. Likewise, covering content without requiring students to perform adequately does little to help students meet their academic goals. For example, introducing decimals to students who have not mastered basic fraction concepts will confuse some students and delay mastery of the newly introduced material. Teachers often feel pressure from their schools or districts to introduce topics too fast for student mastery of even the most basic concepts. Because finding the right balance between mastery of content and coverage of content is difficult, too many disconnected concepts are not taught to mastery in many core mathematics programs. As a result, students with severe math deficiencies never "get good at anything," including critical prerequisites for later mathematics success. Not unexpectedly, students learn to hate and avoid math. Improving mathematics performance requires attention to *both* content coverage and content mastery.

Inventory of Curriculum and Instruction Needs

On the MPSI, questions in the curriculum and instruction section address both *curriculum materials* and the *organizational variables* of time allocation and instructional grouping. In a three-tier model, students may require different or additional curriculum materials, depending on their performance level. Core curriculum materials that are used primarily in general education classrooms may need to be modified or supplemented for students in Tier 2 and Tier 3 instruction. Often, the core curriculum is not appropriate for use with Tier 3 students, and a replacement core program must be adopted.

The organizational variables of time allocation and instructional grouping may need to be altered for students not performing at grade level. Math coaches can use the inventory to summarize how time is currently allocated, how that time is spent, and how students are grouped for instruction.

Inventory of Professional Development Needs

The final section on the inventory addresses professional development needs. The questions in this section focus on two topics: inservice training and in-class coaching. The inventory records how much and what types of inservice training teachers have received related to assessment and data utilization, and curriculum and instruction. These questions are designed to highlight areas for which teachers may need additional support or training. Other questions determine whether procedures for conducting grade-level team meetings are in place, and whether procedures for designing action plans have been developed.

Professional development questions also help determine whether teachers are receiving in-class coaching as they deliver math instruction. Math coaches can use the information recorded on the inventory to help them differentially allocate their coaching time to teachers in the classroom. For example, some teachers may need more demonstration teaching than others to effectively implement a newly adopted instructional program.

MATH ACTION PLANNING

Action planning refers to the design of instructional changes for *all* students based on assessments that have been given. Figure 3 illustrates the relationship between the three areas of the MPSI: I. Student Performance Measures, II. Curriculum and Instruction, and III. Professional Development. These three areas are part of an iterative process. Although information on student performance usually precedes action planning, and professional development usually follows curriculum decisions (e.g., adopting new curricula), educators need to be aware that action planning can include revisiting any of the three areas. Given the extensive discussion of student performance

Figure 3. Math action planning relationships.

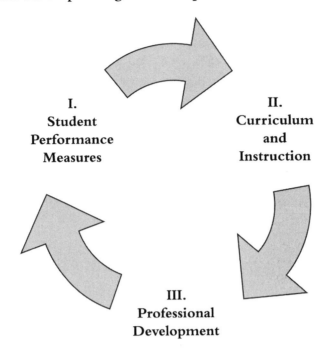

I.
Student
Performance
Measures

II.
Curriculum
and
Instruction

III.
Professional
Development

measures up to this point, the focus in the remainder of this chapter is on areas 2 and 3: curriculum and instruction, and professional development.

We use the term *action planning* rather than intervention planning to encourage both general and special educators to work collaboratively to prevent math failure of students in Tier 1 and Tier 2 and to accelerate the math performance of students in Tier 3. Action planning can involve various participants, but planning among grade-level teams has become more common (Johnston, Knight, & Miller, 2007). The team meeting provides teachers with a structured opportunity to learn about research-based instructional practices and to obtain support for implementing these practices in their classrooms (Gersten & Dimino, 2001). Math coaches are typically responsible for scheduling grade-level team meetings, generating the meeting agendas, and facilitating the action planning discussion.

Curriculum and Instruction

This section integrates available research with specific recommendations to help math coaches implement research-based instructional actions related to two aspects of curriculum and instruction: (a) evaluating, selecting, and modifying math curriculum materials; and (b) implementing interventions that focus on organizational variables, such as increasing instructional time and using appropriate instructional grouping.

Curriculum Materials

Mathematics curriculum materials should offer well-designed content, develop ideas in depth, and clarify relationships among topics; that is, they should reflect a high degree of instructional integrity. Commenting on the role that curriculum likely played in the results from the 2002 TIMSS research, Schmidt, Houang, and Cogan (2002) stated, "The curriculum itself—what is taught—makes a huge difference" (p. 12), and they observed that the United States and Australia were the only TIMSS countries that lacked a national mathematics curriculum.

In the United States, many educators consider the widely used commercial mathematics programs approved by state and district adoption committees as the de facto national curriculum (Cai, Watanabe, & Lo, 2002). Although the term *curriculum* is not technically synonymous with *program*, in this chapter, we use the terms *curriculum materials* and *instructional programs* interchangeably when referring to those commercially developed mathematics programs used by both general education and special education teachers. Often educators are surprised to learn that most publishers do not routinely evaluate the effectiveness of their programs, either during development or once the programs are in classrooms (Reys, Reys, & Chavez, 2004). Because research is costly, publishers tend not to engage in extensive research on their programs. Given the limited scientific evidence on the effectiveness of math instructional programs, educators need to examine the programs carefully prior to purchasing and implementing them in their classrooms.

Because curriculum materials are integral to the overall implementation of effective mathematics instruction, we recommend that educators use a carefully designed selection process when acquiring those materials. Stein, Stuen, Carnine, and Long (2001) described a systematic adoption process for the selection of reading programs that can easily be applied to math programs. We briefly discuss three critical features of the process: time allocation, committee responsibilities, and curriculum evaluation training.

A school district's curriculum adoption committee often includes the math coach, general and special education teachers, and administrators. A thorough examination of math instructional programs requires a significant amount of time and training. Adequate time needs to be allocated for committee members to perform critical activities such as reviewing relevant research in math, designing screening and evaluation criteria based on that research, performing the initial screening of submitted programs, and then thoroughly evaluating those programs that pass the screening.

The committee members are in the best position to make informed decisions on curriculum adoption. However, in most cases, a committee does not select the programs that will be adopted by an entire school or district; instead, all teachers vote on the program options. Teachers in a school or district will feel more comfortable with a committee decision if the school's math coach on the committee communicates regularly and effectively with the groups they represent as they participate in the adoption process (see Stein et al., 2001, for more details).

As mentioned above, objectively evaluating curriculum materials is complex and requires extensive training. The following recommendations serve only as an introduction to the curriculum evaluation process. Figure 4 contains a set of questions derived from both instructional research in math and instructional design that is useful in evaluating curriculum materials (Engelmann & Carnine, 1991; Przychodzin, Marchand-Martella, Martella, & Azim, 2004; Snider & Crawford, 2004). We have organized these questions into three categories: general program design, instructional strategies, and assessment (for more detailed information, see Kinder & Stein, 2006). These evaluation questions also can be used when evaluating existing programs for modification.

General program design includes questions related to instructional objectives and program coherence. In order to get a better sense of general program design, evaluators must examine both the scope and sequence of the program and a series of sample lessons from selected levels.

Examining program objectives may provide the first indication of how systematically a program is designed. Ideally, the objectives should contain a statement of a measurable behavior. However, evaluators may find that many recently published programs contain objectives that describe *teacher behavior* rather than student behavior. For example, in our curriculum evaluation work, we found objectives similar to this one: "Introduce subtraction with regrouping." That objective identifies what the teacher is to do but not what the students are expected to learn. In contrast, an example of a well-designed student objective specifies exactly what the student will be able to

Figure 4. **Mathematics curriculum evaluation.**

I. General Program Design
    A. Do the lessons include objectives with measureable student behaviors?
    B. Are newly taught strategies integrated with those previously taught?
    C. Is there a balance between computation instruction and problem-solving instruction?
    D. Is the program organized using a spiral or strand design?

II. Instructional Strategies
    A. Are strategies explicitly taught in the program?
    B. Are the strategies appropriately generalizable—neither too narrow nor too broad?
    C. Are critical component skills taught prior to the strategy?
    D. Are there adequate examples provided for instruction?
    E. Are discrimination examples included?
    F. Are examples included for cumulative review?

III. Assessment
    A. Does the program include a placement test with options for various starting points?
    B. Do in-program assessments include recommendations for acceleration or remediation?
    C. Are the in-program assessments carefully aligned with instruction?

do as a result of instruction. For example, "Students will accurately regroup from the tens column to the ones column when given a set of mixed problems."

To develop competence in mathematics, students must understand the relationships inherent in the critical math content taught in their instructional programs. Therefore, another question under general program design addresses *program coherence* and focuses on the organization and integration of the content within the curriculum materials. One way to determine the extent of program coherence is to look for evidence that a newly taught strategy has been integrated with previously taught content. Another way of determining program coherence is by examining how well the program integrates instruction in computation with instruction in problem solving.

A more comprehensive way of establishing the degree of program coherence is by identifying whether the program is organized using a *spiral* or a *strand* design. In programs using a spiral design, many topics are introduced at each level and repeated across many levels within and across grades. Spiral mathematics programs are the most common in the United States. Typically, programs using a spiral design lack adequate initial instruction and review to promote student mastery. Lessons in these programs usually cover a different topic each day. Schmidt et al. (2002) referred to programs organized using a spiral design as "a mile wide and inch deep" (p. 12).

Recently, more instructional programs are being organized using a strand design (Snider, 2004). These programs present fewer topics over a longer period of time and have a definite focus on student mastery. A unique feature of strand design is that lessons are organized around multiple topics. For example, a single lesson at the fourth-grade level might include some work on multiplication facts, some work on subtraction with regrouping, some work on fraction analysis, and some work on measurement.

Program coherence has been identified as a common characteristic of the curricula used in the top-performing countries participating in international assessments such as the TIMSS. As a result, one of the recommendations of the National Mathematics Advisory Panel (2008) directly addresses program coherence:

> A focused, coherent progression of mathematics learning, with an emphasis on proficiency with key topics, should become the norm in elementary and middle school mathematics curricula. Any approach that continually revisits topics year after year without closure is to be avoided. (p. 22)

The second category of curriculum evaluation questions addresses how well the *instructional strategies* within a program are designed (see Figure 4). Research reviewed by the Instructional Practices Group of the NMP supports the use of *explicit strategy instruction* for low-achieving students and for those with MLD (Baker, Gersten, & Lee, 2002; Gersten, Chard, Jayanthi, Baker, & Lee, 2006; Ketterlin-Geller, Chard, & Fien, 2008; Kroesbergen & Van Luit, 2003; National Mathematics Advisory Panel, 2008). For example, according to the research literature, students are more likely to be successful if teachers teach students how and when to apply specific algorithms to word problems, rather than relying on students to generate their own problem-solving strategies. Therefore, the first question in this category directs evaluators to determine the degree to which the strategies in the instructional programs are explicit. We recommend that evaluators locate the point at which a strategy is first introduced and examine whether the steps in that strategy are clearly outlined at that point. Usually, the strongest instructional support for students is provided when a new strategy is first introduced.

The second question about instructional strategies addresses how *generalizable* the strategy is. In his discussion of generalizability, Prawat (1989) suggests that efficient strategies would be of intermediate generality. Strategies that are too narrow or of limited generality only apply to a small number of examples yet often require a great amount of instructional time. Strategies that are too broad are usually less explicit. For example, the common problem-solving strategy "guess and check" is far too broad to be of use to young students who are struggling to solve complex word problems involving comparisons (e.g., Jane is 5 ft. 6 in. tall. If Mary is 6 inches taller than Jane, how tall is Mary?). Determining the level of generality is often quite difficult. Evaluators need to inspect the examples that accompany the strategies to determine if the strategy can easily be applied to a sufficient number of different examples.

Efficient strategy instruction requires that background knowledge and requisite component skills be identified and taught before the introduction of the strategy. Many programs either fail to identify critical component skills or they introduce the component skills simultaneously with the strategy. Having to master both a new component skill *and* the new strategy increases the instructional demands placed on students. For example, students may be introduced to the concept of "least common multiple" at the same time they are taught the strategy for "adding fractions with unlike denominators." Requiring that students learn both skills during the same lessons will likely cause confusion for some students. When examining instructional strategies, evaluators need to determine the critical component skills for each strategy and determine where and when those component skills are taught.

Once evaluators have carefully examined the quality of the instructional strategies, they can then compare programs with respect to the *number of examples* provided for the strategies being taught. When selecting programs for students in Tier 2 and Tier 3, evaluators may want to err in selecting programs with *more* rather than fewer examples. For many teachers, eliminating some of the examples used during instruction is far easier than generating more examples.

In addition to the number of practice examples, evaluators need to examine the type of practice provided. *Discrimination practice* refers to a presenting set of examples that requires students to determine not only how but also when to apply a strategy. For example, after the introduction of addition of fractions with unlike denominators, the program should provide practice on a mixed set of problems in which some fractions have like denominators and others have unlike denominators. Discrimination practice increases the likelihood that students will consistently be successful when independently applying strategies to similar problems.

Research strongly supports certain types of review (Dempster, 1988). Well-designed programs include review that is *sufficient* (i.e., adequate for students to initially learn the content), *distributed* (i.e., practiced over time so that students do not forget what they have learned), and *cumulative* (i.e., integrated with previously related content). By examining the practice examples available for several newly introduced strategies, evaluators can determine the extent to which a program provides appropriate types of review.

The final category of questions we recommend for the curriculum evaluation address the *assessment* options that accompany commercial math programs. Evaluators need to examine the teacher manuals as well as any supplementary student assessment materials to answer the questions on this topic. Though the program-specific questions on the MPSI focus on whether and how teachers use program-specific assessments, the questions from the curriculum evaluation guidelines concern the quality and usefulness of those assessments.

First, evaluators need to determine whether a program contains a placement test and placement options that allow students to be placed according to their current mathematical skill levels. Having multiple options for placement in a given program is particularly important for students who lack critical skills and have limited time to acquire them. These students and their teachers do not have the time to review those skills they have already mastered. Reviewing skills that have been previously learned should be included during independent work.

Next, evaluators should determine if recommendations for acceleration and remediation (i.e., "skip lessons 14–16 if not needed," or "reteach lessons 14–16") are based on the program's assessment results. Again, these recommendations should help ensure that the math instruction is efficient and effective. Finally, evaluators need to establish the extent to which the program's assessments are aligned with instruction. This alignment is necessary for teachers to use the program's assessments to make informed instructional decisions regarding students' progress and mastery of the content.

Our experience has shown that the design of the instructional strategies in a math curriculum should be given greater consideration than the other components when evaluating instructional programs (see Mathematics Curriculum Evaluation in Figure 4). Instructional strategies are the most difficult for teachers to modify, and few teachers have adequate mathematical knowledge, instructional design expertise, and time to design new instructional strategies or to field test those strategies to determine if they are effective.

Modifying specific features of strategy instruction may be far less complicated for some teachers, however. In some instructional programs, the problem-solving strategies may be well designed but the programs may lack sufficient practice and review opportunities. Teachers can supplement these programs by first adding more practice examples during initial instruction, then building in more systematic review throughout. Although easier than designing strategies, adding practice and review can be extremely time-consuming, especially when attempting to carefully integrate new and previously introduced content. The difficulty of modifying curriculum demonstrates the necessity of performing a thorough, systematic review of instructional programs prior to selecting them for use. Although no individual instructional program will meet the needs of all students, programs that require less modification are undoubtedly preferable (for more on program modification, see Stein, Kinder, Silbert, & Carnine, 2006).

Organizational Variables

In their review of the teacher effectiveness literature in the 1980s, Rosenshine and Stevens (1986) called attention to the importance of both allocating sufficient time for instruction and ensuring that students are engaged during that time. As a result of that early work, more recent research has focused on ways of increasing allocated and engaged time through structural changes within a classroom or school. This section gives examples of the kinds of changes that can be made through action planning, such as several research-based practices that are designed to increase the amount of high-quality instructional time students receive, These practices include double dosing, the strategic use of work checks, peer tutoring, and instructional grouping.

Double dosing, an increasingly popular way to augment instructional time for math, usually involves adding a second session of math instruction during the regular school day (Cavanagh, 2006; Wanzek & Vaughn, 2008). The instruction in the second session may entail preteaching or reteaching content from the adopted curriculum materials or supplementing those materials with additional content (Lalley & Miller, 2006; Peele, 1998).

Adding a *work check* to the instructional schedule is, in some ways, similar to double dosing. A work check is a 15- to 20-minute teacher-directed activity, preferably scheduled in addition to the time typically allocated for math instruction. During a work check, the teacher provides specific feedback to students and helps them identify errors on their independent work (Stein, Kinder, Silbert, & Carnine, 2006). The sooner student errors can be identified and remedied, the greater the probability of preventing serious deficiencies that would require more intensive intervention. Put another way, the longer a student practices completing a problem the wrong way, the more difficult that practice is to correct.

Cooperative learning and class-wide *peer tutoring*, both of which can occur within or outside of the school day, have consistently been shown to have positive effects on student performance in math, perhaps because of the likelihood that students are more engaged during those activities (Baker et al., 2002; National Mathematics Advisory Panel, 2008; Slavin & Karweit, 1985; also see chapter 24 in this book). In the Classwide Peer Tutoring intervention, for example, all students serve as both tutors and tutees, inevitably resulting in increased time and attention to math activities (Fuchs, Fuchs, Yazdian, & Powell, 2002; Greenwood, 1991).

As with cooperative learning and peer tutoring, long-standing support exists for the use of flexible, homogeneous *instructional grouping* (i.e., based on skill level) to address student needs more efficiently (Lou et al., 1996; Slavin, 1987). An interesting comparison can be made between instructional grouping and academic engagement time. What makes instructional grouping an effective strategy is less about *where* the students receive instruction (e.g., in a whole class, small group, resource room) and more about *how* and *what* they are taught. Similarly, academic engaged time is less about the minutes that are allocated for instruction and more about students being engaged during those minutes. Attempting to teach a small group of low-performing students using curriculum materials that are too difficult will not likely improve their math performance. Likewise, allocating a double dose of a poorly designed instructional program to struggling students is not likely to yield positive results. Although evidence suggests that it is a good practice to take time and grouping into account during action planning, educators need to always remember to integrate that information with information from other areas of the MPSI.

Professional Development

A primary goal of professional development is to help teachers effectively implement research-based practices as part of their classroom routines. Professional development activities that have a clearly identified purpose, are concrete and practical, and are tied directly to a school's overall efforts toward improvement are most likely to lead to lasting change (Gersten, Chard, & Baker, 2000; Gersten, Morvant, & Brengelman, 1995; Little & Houston, 2003). Although research on effective instruction is limited in the area of mathematics, even less research is available on how best to prepare teachers to deliver high-quality math instruction (Ball, Lubienski, & Mewborn, 2001; Ma, 1999). However, the reviews of the existing math professional development literature have led us to conclude that effective professional development must also focus on relevant and research-based content and provide opportunities for teachers to engage in active learning (Cohen & Hill, 2000; Garet, Porter, Desimone, Binnan, & Yoon, 2001; National Mathematics Advisory Panel, 2008).

We have organized our discussion of professional development around two distinct but related types of activities: (a) inservice training, and (b) in-class coaching. Inservice training refers to any training that occurs outside of the classroom and can range from a 2-hour meeting after school with an individual teacher to a 5-day workshop during summer break for an entire school faculty. In-class coaching, on the other hand, is more often highly individualized and occurs within a teacher's classroom. Ideally, the math coach designs professional development to promote a seamless integration between inservice training and in-class coaching. For example, once new instructional programs have been adopted, the math coach would schedule inservice training opportunities that target specific program features (e.g., error correction procedures), followed closely by in-class coaching on the implementation of those program features. The following sections describe how a math coach might use the MPS summary form to guide professional development using both inservice training and in-class coaching.

Inservice Training

The professional development area of the MPSI is designed to direct math coaches to those topics for which teachers demonstrate greatest need. As indicated on the MPS summary form, inservice training topics include assessment, curriculum and instruction, and data utilization (see Figure 2). Regardless of the topic, inservice training should focus on specific research-based content with an emphasis on helping teachers understand how that content can be applied to their classrooms.

In a three-tier model designed to promote positive math performance, inservice training related to various assessment types is critical. Teachers need to understand how to (a) choose assessments that will best inform their instruction, and (b) accurately and reliably administer, score, and interpret information from those assessments. For example, some teachers will need considerable practice before they are able to reliably score the math–curriculum-based measurement (M-CBM) probes that involve counting correct digits per minute. Another important assessment topic that lends itself to inservice training is the correct use of program-specific assessment. Although information on these assessments is usually shared during initial inservice training on newly adopted programs, teachers may require more extensive and review opportunities to explore how and when to use the assessments.

The need for a coherent, focused curriculum is, in part, related to research documenting that many U.S. teachers are simply unprepared to teach mathematics (Ball, Hill, & Bass, 2005; Ball et al., 2001; Ma, 1999; Schmidt et al., 2002). Although no curriculum materials will meet the needs of every student, giving teachers access to well-designed instructional programs may play an important role in improving students' math performance (Schmidt et al.). However, teachers need extensive preparation and ongoing support in implementing instructional programs. Before attributing a lack of student progress to the instructional program, the math coach, along with grade-level teams, should feel confident that the program is being implemented the way the program authors intended, that is, with fidelity. Additional inservice training in the area of curriculum and instruction includes practice in strategic program modification and modification of organizational variables such as scheduling and grouping.

The final area designated under inservice training is data utilization. In many ways, this area is the most complex. Teachers need to understand if and when their students have learned mathematical content. Many teachers are not explicitly taught in their teacher preparation programs how to use objective measures to evaluate student learning. Moreover, teachers are not often taught how to link assessment data to instructional decision making. Therefore, inservice training targeted at how to use data to make instructional decisions is essential (Baker, Gersten, Dimino, & Griffiths, 2004; Little and Houston, 2003).

Grade-level team meetings may be the most appropriate and convenient means of reporting data and engaging in shared decision making. To that end, many teachers will need professional development on the procedures that make grade-level team meetings and action planning efficient and productive. In the area of data utilization, professional development should include inservice activities related to both the implementation of grade-level team meetings and the use of data within the team meeting to make instructional decisions and design action plans. In addition, we strongly recommend that those persons who are knowledgeable and who have experience using both formative assessment data and diagnostic information, such as school psychologists, be included as members of the grade-level team.

In-Class Coaching

From their work with peer coaching, Joyce and Showers (2002) estimated that 90% of teachers receiving in-class peer coaching were likely to implement newly learned teaching practices, compared with 60% of teachers receiving demonstrations and practice, and just 10% of teachers receiving demonstrations alone. Whereas inservice training provides a context for understanding new instructional practices, in-class coaching provides direct support to teachers as they implement those new practices.

The purpose of in-class coaching is to improve the teacher's delivery of mathematics lessons. That delivery can be divided into two broad areas: instructional and behavioral. The in-class coaching needs of teachers will vary depending on teacher skills and student needs in both areas. Teachers with many students who are struggling academically will undoubtedly need greater instructional support, whereas teachers who have weaker classroom management skills may need in-class coaching on implementing positive behavior support.

In-class coaching sessions provide different levels of support, ranging from less intrusive to more intrusive. An example of less-intrusive in-class coaching involves the math coach observing the delivery of a math lesson. In contrast, during more-intrusive in-class coaching sessions, math coaches model specific math lessons or demonstrate the use of a reward system that reinforces effort and attention. Because in-class coaching can be anxiety-producing for many teachers, we suggest that math coaches establish well-defined objectives and communication procedures to foster a productive collaboration.

Professional development that integrates data-based decision making and research-based instructional practice provides the basis for a problem-solving model that is more likely to promote positive math outcomes for all students. The more teachers can experience firsthand an association between problem solving and student progress, the more likely they will be to sustain their successful teaching practices over time (Gersten & Dimino, 2001; Moss, Jacob, Boulay, Horst, & Poulos, 2006).

CONCLUSION

The title of this chapter, Promoting Positive Math Outcomes, is intentionally general with a broad scope. Our purpose was to introduce readers to a comprehensive problem-solving approach to improving student performance in mathematics. We have drawn from the literature in school psychology, general education, special education, and education policy. We have taken into account large-scale reform initiatives such as

Reading First and response to intervention (RTI), which are essentially problem-solving models for areas in which student performance does not match expectations.

In this chapter, we designated the math coach as the central figure of the problem-solving approach so that readers would be able to concentrate on the *what* rather than the *who* as they were introduced to various activities. The math coach has been assigned the leadership role, with the responsibilities of coordinating research-based assessment and action planning activities. Historically, classroom support in the form of consulting teachers, behavior specialists, or instructional coaches has been shown to increase the likelihood that teachers will acquire the skills necessary for successful implementation of the research-based activities (Gersten, Darch, Davis, & George, 1990; Metzler, Biglan, Rusby, & Sprague, 2001; Moss et al., 2006). Consequently, the math coach also is responsible for coordinating the professional development necessary to ensure that all of the activities are implemented with fidelity. Having mastered the activities, the teachers are then more likely to sustain their use (Gersten, Chard, & Baker, 2000).

Can the problem-solving approach we propose here for providing multitiered, early-intervening services be implemented without a math coach? Of course it can. Although the math coach is clearly an appropriate designee for the role of coordinator, the responsibilities of the math coach most certainly can be distributed among those with suitable expertise. For example, given the training that school psychologists receive in measurement and testing, they are often the best prepared to coordinate the assessment, data utilization, and error analysis activities for a district, school, or individual teacher. As a member of a grade-level team and collaborator, school psychologists can contribute to action planning by introducing teams to research-based activities drawn from the school psychology literature.

The participation of school principals and other administrators also are integral to the successful implementation of a comprehensive problem-solving approach (Lau et al., 2006). The responsibility for coordinating professional development activities frequently lies with the school principal, who has the most control over budget and scheduling. Moreover, principals are essential participants in critical placement decisions, especially when those decisions involve students with disabilities.

Just as a championship basketball team may be carried by a star player, so is it possible for schools and teachers to be carried by a star math coach. However, most championships are won through the contributions of all team members. All of the members of the team must be engaged in deliberate, focused decision making and a commitment to the implementation of research-based instructional practices in order to achieve the desired results.

REFERENCES

Baker, S., Gersten, R., Dimino, J. A., & Griffiths, R. (2004). The sustained use of research-based instructional practice: A case study of peer-assisted learning strategies in mathematics. *Remedial and Special Education, 25,* 5–24.

Baker, S., Gersten, R., & Lee, D. (2002). A synthesis of empirical research on teaching mathematics to low-achieving students. *Elementary School Journal, 103,* 51–73.

Ball, D. L., Hill, H. C., & Bass, H. (2005). *Developing measures of mathematics knowledge for teaching.* Ann Arbor: University of Michigan Press.

Ball, D. L., Lubienski, S., & Mewborn, D. (2001). Research on teaching mathematics: The unsolved problem of teachers' mathematics knowledge. In V. Richardson (Ed.), *Handbook of research on teaching* (4th ed., pp. 433–456). New York: Macmillan.

Bransford, J. D., & Stein, B. S. (1984). *The ideal problem solver.* New York: Freeman.

Cai, J., Watanabe, T., & Lo, J. J. (2002). Intended treatments of arithmetic averages in U.S. and Asian school mathematics textbooks. *School Science and Mathematics, 102,* 391–404.

Cavanagh, S. (2006). Students double-dosing on reading and math. *Education Week, 25*(40), 1, 12–13.

Cawley, J., Parmar, R., Foley, T. E., Salmon, S., & Roy, S. (2001). Arithmetic performance of students: Implications for standards and programming. *Exceptional Children, 67,* 311–328.

Cohen, D. K., & Hill, H. C. (2000). Instructional policy and classroom performance: The mathematics reform in California. *Teachers College Record, 102,* 294–343.

CTB/McGraw-Hill. (2008). Yearly ProgressPro [Computer software]. Monterey, CA: CTB/McGraw Hill.

Dempster, F. (1988). The spacing effect: A case study in the failure to apply results to psychological research. *American Psychologist, 43,* 627–634.

Deno, S. L. (2002). Problem-solving as best practice. In A. Thomas & J. Grimes (Eds.), *Best practices in school psychology IV* (pp. 1–17). Bethesda, MD: National Association of School Psychologists.

Deno, S. L., & Mirkin, P. K. (1977). *Data-based program modification: A manual.* Rustin, VA: Council for Exceptional Children.

Deussen, T., Coskie, T., Robinson, L., & Autio, E. (2007, June). *"Coach" can mean many things: Five categories of literacy coaches in Reading First* (Issues & Answers Report, REL 2007-No. 005). Washington, DC: U.S. Department of Education, Regional Educational Laboratory Program. Retrieved from http://ies.ed.gov/ncee/edlabs

Engelmann, S., & Carnine, D. (1991). *Theory of instruction: Principles and applications.* Eugene, OR: ADI Press.

Ephraim, R. (2008, April). *Knowledge and skillful leadership.* Presentation at Math Leadership Conference, Seattle, WA.

Fuchs, L. S., Compton, D. L., Fuchs, D., Paulsen, K., Bryant, J. D., & Hamlett, C. L. (2005). The prevention, identification, and cognitive determinants of math difficulty. *Journal of Educational Psychology, 97,* 493–513.

Fuchs, D., & Deschler, D. (2007). What we need to know about responsiveness to intervention (And shouldn't be afraid to ask). *Learning Disabilities Research and Practice, 22,* 129–136.

Fuchs, L. S., Fuchs, D., Yazdian, L., & Powell, S. (2002). Enhancing first-grade children's mathematical development with peer-assisted learning strategies. *School Psychology Review, 31,* 569–583.

Fuchs, L. S., Hamlett, B., & Fuchs, D. (1999). Monitoring Basic Skills Progress (2nd ed.) [Computer software]. Austin, TX: Pro-Ed.

Garet, M. S., Porter, A. C., Desimone, L., Binnan, B. F., & Yoon, K. S. (2001).What makes professional development effective? Results from a national sample of teachers. *American Educational Research Journal, 38,* 915–945.

Geary, D. (2004). Mathematics and learning disabilities. *Journal of Learning Disabilities, 37,* 4–15.

Gersten, R., Chard, D., & Baker, S. (2000). Factors enhancing sustained use of research-based instructional practices. *Journal of Learning Disabilities, 33,* 445–457.

Gersten, R. H., Chard, D. J., Jayanthi, M., Baker, S., & Lee, D. (2006). A meta-analysis of research on mathematics interventions for elementary students with learning disabilities. Manuscript in preparation

Gersten, R., Darch, C., Davis, G., & George, N. (1990). Apprenticeship and intensive training of consulting teachers: A naturalistic study. *Exceptional Children, 57,* 226–237.

Gersten, R., & Dimino, J. A. (2001). The realities of translating research into classroom practice. *Learning Disabilities Research and Practice, 16,* 120–130.

Gersten, R., Jordan, N. C., & Flojo, J. R. (2005). Early identification and interventions for students with mathematics difficulties. *Journal of Learning Disabilities, 38,* 293–304.

Gersten, R., Morvant, M., & Brengelman, S. (1995). Close to the classroom is close to the bone: Coaching as a means to translate research into classroom practice. *Exceptional Children, 62,* 52–66.

Greenwood, C. R. (1991). Longitudinal analysis of time, engagement, and achievement in at-risk versus non-risk students. *Exceptional Children, 57,* 521–535.

Harris, C. A., Miller, S. P., & Mercer, C. D. (1995). Teaching initial multiplication skills to students with disabilities in general education classrooms. *Learning Disabilities Research and Practice, 10,* 180–195.

Hill, H. C., Rowan, B., & Ball, D. L. (2005). Effects of teachers' mathematical knowledge for teaching on student achievement. *American Educational Research Journal, 42*(2), 371–406.

Johnston, J., Knight, M., & Miller, L. (2007). Finding time for teams. *Journal of Staff Development, 28*(2), 14–18.

Joyce, B. R., & Showers, B. (2002). *Student achievement through staff development.* Alexandria, VA: Association for Supervision and Curriculum Development.

Ketterlin-Geller, L. R., Chard, D. J., & Fien, H. (2008). Making connections in mathematics: Conceptual mathematics intervention for low-performing students. *Remedial and Special Education, 29,* 33–45.

Kinder, D., & Stein, M. (2006). Quality mathematics programs for students with disabilities. In M. Montague & A. K. Jitendra (Eds.), *Teaching mathematics to middle school students with learning disabilities* (pp. 133–153). New York: Guilford Press.

Knight, J. (2005). A primer on instructional coaches. *Principal Leadership, 5*(9), 16–21.

Kroesbergen, E. H., & Van Luit, J. E. H. (2003). Mathematics interventions for students with special educational needs: A meta-analysis. *Remedial and Special Education, 24,* 97–114.

Lalley, J. P., & Miller, R. H. (2006). Effects of pre-teaching and re-teaching on math achievement and academic self-concept of students with low achievement in math. *Education, 126,* 747–755.

Lau, M. Y., Sieler, J. D., Muyskens, P., Canter, A., VanKeuren, B., & Marston, D. (2006). Perspectives on the use of the problem-solving model from the view point of a school psychologist, administrator, and teacher from a large Midwest, urban school district. *Psychology in the Schools, 43,* 117–127.

Little, M. E., & Houston, D. (2003). Research into practice through professional development. *Remedial and Special Education, 24,* 75–87.

Lou, Y., Abrami, P. C., Spence, J. C., Poulsen, C., Chambers, B., & D'Apollonia, S. (1996). Within-class grouping: A meta-analysis. *Review of Educational Research, 66,* 423–458.

Ma, L. (1999). *Knowing and teaching elementary mathematics.* Mahwah, NJ: Erlbaum.

Mabbott, D., & Bisanz, J. (2008). Computational skills, working memory, and conceptual knowledge in older children with mathematics learning disabilities. *Journal of Learning Disabilities, 41*(1), 15–28.

Metzler, C. W., Biglan, A., Rusby, J. C., & Sprague, J. R. (2001). Evaluation of a comprehensive behavior management program to improve school-wide positive behavior support. *Education and Treatment of Children, 24,* 448–479.

Miller, S. P., Butler, F. M., & Lee, K. (1998). Validated practices for teaching mathematics to students with learning disabilities: A review of the literature. *Focus on Exceptional Children, 31*(1), 1–24.

Montague, M., & Applegate, B. (2000). Middle school students' perceptions, persistence, and performance in mathematical problem solving. *Learning Disability Quarterly, 23,* 215–227.

Moss, M., Jacob, R., Boulay, B., Horst, M., & Poulos, J. (2006). Reading First implementation evaluation: Interim report. Washington, DC: U.S. Department of Education Office of Planning and Program Studies Service.

Mullis, I. V. S, Martin, M. O., Gonzalez, E. J., & Chrostowski, S. J. (2004). *TIMSS 2003 international mathematics report: Findings from IEA's trends in international mathematics and science study at fourth and eighth grade.* Boston, MA: International Association for the Evaluation of Educational Achievement. Retrieved from http://timss.bc.edu/PDF/t03_download/T03INTLMATRPT.pdf

National Center for Educational Statistics (NCES). (2003). *The nation's report card: Mathematics highlights 2003. National Assessment of Educational Progress.* Washington, DC: U.S. Department of Education. Retrieved from http://nces.ed.gov/pubsearch/pubsinfo.asp?pubid=2004451

National Center for Educational Statistics. (2007). *The nation's report card: Mathematics highlights 2007. National Assessment of Educational Progress.* Washington, DC: U.S. Department of Education. Retrieved from http://nces.ed.gov/pubsearch/pubsinfo.asp?pubid=2007494

National Institute of Child Health and Human Development. (2000). *Report of the National Reading Panel. Teaching children to read: An evidence-based assessment of the scientific research literature on reading and its implications for reading instruction* (NIH Publication No. 00-4769). Washington, DC: U.S. Government Printing Office.

National Mathematics Advisory Panel. (2008). *Foundations for Success: The Final Report of the National Mathematics Advisory Panel.* Washington, DC: U.S. Department of Education. Retrieved from http://www.ed.gov/about/bdscomm/list/mathpanel/report/final-report.pdf

Organisation for Economic Co-operation and Development. (2004). *Learning for tomorrow's world – First results from PISA 2003.* Retrieved from http://www.pisa.oecd.org/document/55/0,3343,en_32252351_32236173_33917303_1_1_1_1,00.html

Organisation for Economic Co-operation and Development. (2007). *Executive summary. PISA 2006: Science competencies for tomorrow's world.* Retrieved from http://www.pisa.oecd.org/document/2/0,3343,en_32252351_32236191_39718850_1_1_1_1,00.html

Pearson Education Inc. (2008). AIMSweb Progress Monitoring and Response to Intervention System [Computer software]. Upper Saddle River, NJ: Pearson.

Peele, L. L. (1998). Double-dose: A viable instructional alternative. *NASSP Bulletin, 82,* 111–114.

Prawat. R. S. (1989). Promoting access to knowledge, strategy, and disposition in students: A research synthesis. *Review of Educational Research, 59*(1), 1–41.

Prychodzin, A. M., Marchand-Martella, N. E., Martella, R. C., & Azim, D. (2004). Direct instruction mathematics programs: An overview and research summary. *Journal of Direct Instruction, 4*(1), 53–84.

Reys, B. J., Reys, R. E., & Chavez, O. (2004). Why mathematics textbooks matter. *Educational Leadership, 61*(5), 61–66.

Rosenshine, B., & Stevens, R. Teaching functions. (1986). In M. C. Wittrock (Ed.), *Handbook of research on teaching* (3rd ed., pp. 376–391). New York: Macmillan.

Schmidt, W., Houang, R., & Cogan, L. (2002). A coherent curriculum: The case of mathematics. *American Educator, 26*(2), 10–26.

Schmidt, W. H., Tatto, M. T., Bankov, K., Blomeke, S., Cedillo, T., Cogan, L., et al. (2007). *The preparation gap: Teacher education for middle school mathematics in six countries.* East Lansing, MI: MSU Center for Research in Mathematics and Science Education. Retrieved from http://usteds.msu.edu

Shapiro, E., Edwards, L., & Zigmond, N. (2005). Progress monitoring of mathematics among students with learning disabilities. *Assessment for Effective Intervention, 30*(2), 15–32.

Slavin, R. E. (1987). Ability grouping and student achievement in elementary schools: A best evidence synthesis. *Review of Educational Research, 57,* 293–336.

Slavin, R. E., & Karweit, N. L. (1985). Effects of whole class, ability grouped, and individualized instruction on mathematics achievement. *American Educational Research Journal, 22*, 351–367.

Snider, V. E. (2004). A comparison of spiral versus strand curriculum. *Journal of Direct Instruction, 4*, 29–40.

Snider, V. E., & Crawford, D. (2004). Mathematics. In N. E. Marchand-Martella, T. A. Slocum, &R. C. Martella (Eds.), *Introduction to direct instruction* (pp. 206–245). Boston: Pearson/Allyn & Bacon.

Stein, M., Kinder, D., Silbert, J., & Carnine, D. W. (2006). *Designing effective mathematics instruction: A direct instruction approach.* Upper Saddle River, NJ: Pearson/Merrill/Prentice Hall.

Stein, M. L., Stuen, C., Carnine, D., & Long, R. M. (2001). Textbook evaluation and adoption practices. *Reading and Writing Quarterly, 17*(1), 5–23.

Walker, H. M., & Shinn, M. R. (2002). Structuring school-based interventions to achieve integrated primary, secondary, and tertiary prevention goals for safe and effective schools. In M. R. Shinn, H. M. Walker, & G. Stoner (Eds.), *Interventions for academic and behavior problems: Preventive and remedial approaches* (pp. 1–27). Bethesda, MD: National Association of School Psychologists.

Wanzek, J., & Vaughn, S. (2008). Response to varying amounts of time in reading intervention for students with low response to intervention. *Journal of Learning Disabilities, 41*, 126–142.

INTERVENTIONS

for Achievement and Behavior Problems in a Three-Tier Model Including RTI

CHAPTER 21

Evidence-Based Writing Practices for Tiers 1, 2, and 3

Natalie G. Olinghouse
University of Connecticut, Storrs

Steve Graham
Karen R. Harris
Vanderbilt University, Nashville, TN

INTRODUCTION

Today's society requires people to write for multiple purposes in and outside of school. Academic writing has become an essential part of schooling, as students write to demonstrate, support, refine, and extend their learning and knowledge. Students who do not learn to write well are at a disadvantage. Weaker writers are less likely than their more skilled classmates to use writing to support and extend content learning. Their grades are likely to suffer, especially in classes where writing is the primary means for assessing progress (Graham, 2006b). Poor writing skills reduce a student's chance of attending college, as universities increasingly use writing to evaluate applicants' qualifications. Likewise, postsecondary and workplace environments expect proficient writing skills from high school graduates (e.g., National Commission on Writing, 2003, 2004, 2005), with writing becoming a gateway for employment and promotion, especially in salaried positions. Employees in many sectors are expected to produce written documentation, visual presentations, memoranda, technical reports, and electronic messages, among others. However, writing is an essential skill for jobs other than salaried positions; it also is necessary for jobs requiring a high school education or less (Essential Skills, n.d.).

Outside of work, writing is deeply integrated into the school and personal lives of today's generation, where electronic communication (e.g., e-mailing, blogging, instant messaging, and social networking) is becoming more prevalent in teens' lives (National Commission on Writing, 2008). In the community at large, as e-mail has progressively replaced the telephone for communication, those who are not able to communicate in writing may be unable to participate fully in civic life.

Despite the importance of writing for success in school, work, and community, many students do not learn the writing skills needed to meet the demands of these environments. For example, the most recent National Assessment of Educational Progress revealed that many students are not developing the writing competence needed at their grade level (Persky, Daane, & Jin, 2003). Despite small improvements since the previous assessment in 1998, two thirds or more of students writing in 4th, 8th, and 12th grade were below grade-level proficiency (Greenwald, Persky, Ambell, & Mazzeo, 1999). In its 2003 report, the National Commission on Writing bluntly stated that the writing of students in the United States "is not what it should be" (p. 7). Poor writing performance extends into postsecondary environments too, as college instructors estimate that 50% of high school graduates are not prepared for college-level writing demands (Achieve Incorporated, 2005), and American businesses spend $3.1 billion annually for writing remediation (National Commission on Writing, 2005).

One obvious reason why students' writing is "not what it should be" is because schools are not doing an adequate job of teaching writing. According to the National Commission on Writing (2003), this skill is the most neglected of the "three Rs" in the American classroom. One immediate priority in making writing instruction more effective for all students, including those with disabilities and those at risk for developing disabilities, is to identify effective writing practices appropriate for the general education classroom. The National Commission on Writing (2003) provided several instructional recommendations, including increasing the amount of writing students do within and outside of school, assessing students' progress in writing, using technology to advance the learning and teaching of writing, and improving teacher preparation to teach writing. Although each of these ideas has merit, they provide only a broad outline of how to improve writing instruction, and they ignore the unique needs of students who fail to respond to general education instruction.

EVIDENCE-BASED WRITING INSTRUCTION FOR THREE TIERS

This chapter draws on scientific studies of writing interventions to identify effective instructional procedures for use in general education classrooms (Tier 1), as well as effective remedial practices that can be applied at Tiers 2 and 3 for students who do not respond to general education instruction. In a response-to-intervention (RTI) framework, Tier 1 interventions are scientifically validated practices that have been shown to be effective for many children, although no instructional program works for all children or all the time (Cronbach, 1975; Fuchs & Deshler, 2007). Tier 2 interventions are provided for students who fail to respond to Tier 1 instruction, whereas Tier 3 interventions are provided to students who do not successfully respond to small-group, high-intensity Tier 2 interventions (Fuchs, Mock, Morgan, & Young, 2003). An evidence-based approach may also combine Tier 1 and Tier 2 interventions for a student with greater instructional needs, without waiting for the student to demonstrate a failure to benefit from Tier 1 instruction. At this point, the research base in writing is not advanced enough to distinguish between Tier 2 and Tier 3 writing interventions; therefore, we combined the recommendations for students who require more intensive instruction.

The lack of commercial writing programs often means that educators are responsible for designing their own writing program. Advice and suggestions to assist in this process come from many sources. One source of advice on teaching writing comes from professional writers who draw on their own experiences and insights to make recommendations (see for example King, 2000, or Saltzman, 1993). Another source of advice comes from teachers of writing who recommend the use of instructional procedures they find effective in their classroom (see Atwell, 1987). A third source comes from those who observe writing teachers in action and promote the use of teacher practices they view as worthwhile (see Graves, 1983). Although professional writers and teachers of writing surely possess considerable wisdom about writing instruction, there may be no empirical evidence that a recommended procedure actually produces the desired effects across a larger population. Thus, developing a writing program solely on the basis of recommendations from skilled writers, teachers, or experts is risky, as the reliability, validity, and generalizability of their recommendations are typically unknown.

A more trustworthy approach for identifying effective teaching practices can be drawn from scientific studies examining the effectiveness of specific intervention techniques. Such studies provide evidence on whether the instructional procedure resulted in the desired impact, whether the observed effects are representative, and how much confidence can be placed in the results. Because these studies quantify the observed impact of an intervention on writing performance, the findings from individual studies can be converted into a common metric (i.e., effect size), making it possible to determine the strength of an intervention's impact across investigations.

This chapter draws on several recent meta-analyses to identify specific evidence-based writing instruction practices for Tier 1 and Tiers 2 and 3, a purpose to which meta-analytic techniques are ideally suited. Meta-analysis is used to summarize the magnitude and direction of the effects obtained in a set of empirical research studies examining the same basic phenomena (Lipsey & Wilson, 2001). One of these meta-analyses involved all experimental and quasi-experimental writing intervention studies (published studies and dissertations) conducted with students in Grades 4 to 12 (Graham & Perin, 2007a, 2007c). Another meta-analysis of single-subject dissertations and published studies summarized the effects for intervention studies with students in Grades 1 to 12 (Rogers & Graham, 2008). A third paper provided a single additional meta-analysis of the impact of handwriting, spelling, and typing instruction (Graham, in press). To broaden the possible writing instruction techniques available to teachers, we also drew on a research synthesis of five qualitative studies (Graham & Perin, 2007b). This synthesis identified recurring patterns in the instructional practices of teachers and schools that produced exceptional literacy achievement. Such an analysis cannot establish that a particular practice is responsible (i.e., attribution of cause and effect) for students' improved writing performance; however, it is reasonable to assume that writing practices employed by the majority of teachers or schools in the studies provide important insights into effective writing practices.

Findings that apply primarily to the full range of students in the general education classroom are presented as Tier 1 evidence-based practices; those that apply primarily to students who struggle with writing, including students with disabilities are presented as Tier 2 and 3 practices combined.

When available, we indicate the strength of the effects for each of the evidence-based treatments by including the *direction* (positive or negative) and *strength* (small, moderate, or large) of the effect size. When the effect size was calculated for group experimental studies, a *small* effect corresponds to an effect size (Cohen's *d*) of .20 to .49, a *moderate* effect size to .50 to .79, and a *large* effect of .80 or greater (Lipsey & Wilson, 2001). Effect sizes for single-subject studies were calculated using the percent of non-overlapping data (PND; Scruggs, Mastropieri, & Casto, 1987), which is the percentage of data points in the treatment phase that show improvement over the highest baseline score. When the effect sizes are calculated for single-subject design studies, a *small* effect corresponds to a PND of 50.1% to 70%, a *moderate* effect size corresponds to a PND of 70.1% to 90%, and a *large* effect size corresponds to a PND of 90.1% and higher (Scruggs & Mastropieri, 1998). It is important to note that the findings across different types of studies (i.e., group, single-subject design, and qualitative) generally support one another, but this is not always the case. This lack of agreement will be seen in the section on grammar instruction, for example.

EVIDENCE-BASED PRACTICES FOR TIER 1

Before presenting evidence-based writing practices for Tier 1, it is important first to consider how writing is currently taught in schools. If several recent national surveys are representative (Cutler & Graham, 2008; Graham, Harris, MacArthur, & Fink-Chorzempa, 2003), writing instruction at the elementary level is mostly driven by a combination of the process writing approach (which places considerable emphasis on developing a supportive writing environment; engaging in cycles of planning, drafting, and revising writing; personalized assistance and instruction; writing for real purposes; as well as students' ownership and responsibility for their writings) and basic skills instruction involving spelling, usage, handwriting, and grammar. These surveys also indicate a surprisingly small amount of the school day devoted to the actual writing of text, and relatively little emphasis placed on directly teaching important processes such as planning and revising (Cutler & Graham, 2008). At the secondary level, Kiuhara, Graham, and Hawken (2008) report that writing instruction is relatively infrequent (although teachers report using many of the evidence-based practices described in this chapter), and most of the writing that students are asked to do involves brief responses and little critical interpretation of sophisticated concepts. Among the most common writing activities is writing short-answer responses to homework, completing worksheets, writing a list, and summarizing material read. Thus, although some of the evidence-based practices presented in this paper are applied by teachers in today's schools (e.g., process writing approach, handwriting instruction, and spelling instruction), others are used infrequently or are never used.

Findings From Quantitative Meta-Analyses

The first set of recommendations at Tier 1 is drawn from *Writing Next: Effective Strategies to Improve Writing of Adolescents in Middle and High Schools* (Graham & Perin, 2007a, 2007c). The report involved a meta-analysis of all experimental and quasi-experimental intervention studies conducted with students in Grades 4 to 12, including peer-reviewed articles, dissertations, theses, and reports. The *Writing Next* recommendations are based on studies that met the following criteria:

1. The performance of the treatment group was compared with that of another group that received an alternative treatment or no treatment, ensuring that the impact of the treatment was not due to factors such as students' maturation. Treatment-group-only studies were excluded.
2. The meta-analysis verified that writing was measured reliably in each study, limiting the role of error in assessing the impact of the treatment.
3. At least four studies in the meta-analysis investigated the effectiveness of the treatment, providing evidence that the findings could be reasonably replicated.

In addition, the following recommendations are based only on studies in which the *overall quality* of students' writing was assessed. Though discrete elements of writing are important and merit an instructional emphasis (e.g., spelling, writing vocabulary, or sentence structure), interventions that improve the overall quality of students' writing address the necessary coordination of multiple aspects of writing. This coordination is especially difficult for young writers, and students with disabilities continue to struggle with this aspect into later years.

1. Explicitly teach students strategies for planning, revising, and editing their compositions *(strong positive impact)*.

In many general education classrooms, writing instruction incorporates implicit instruction, in which writing strategies are demonstrated without direct identification of the purpose and application of the writing strategies (Graham & Harris, 1997). In contrast, explicit instruction includes a clear presentation of the strategies, scaffolded learning, immediate feedback, and practice at every step. Additionally, effective strategy instruction involves the teacher modeling how to use the target strategies and providing students with assistance in applying them, until they can use them independently. Writing strategies can range from more general processes, such as brainstorming and peer revising strategies, which can be applied across genres. Strategies also have been developed for specific types of writing, such as writing an explanation or writing to persuade. An example of the latter would include teaching students how to plan in advance by thoroughly considering every side of an argument, choosing a position, deciding which ideas will be used to support this position, and how arguments for the other position(s) will be handled.

2. Explicitly teach students strategies and procedures for summarizing reading material, as this improves their ability to concisely and accurately present this information in writing *(strong positive impact)*.

Summarization is an important academic skill that is used from early school years through postsecondary education. To effectively summarize, the student must distinguish the important information from the unimportant information in a passage. This skill allows the reader to effectively condense and remember information that was read. Written summarization solidifies content learning, requiring the writer to slow down thinking, access background knowledge, and organize thoughts in a way that is different from speaking or reading.

Summarization instruction ranges from explicitly teaching strategies for summarizing written materials to teaching summarization by providing students with models of good summaries and progressively fading the models as they practice writing summaries.

3. Develop instructional arrangements in which students work cooperatively to plan, draft, revise, and edit their compositions *(moderate to strong positive impact)*.

Collaborative writing arrangements include developing a structure for students' collaborative efforts. It is important to note that students need to be taught how to work collaboratively in pairs, along with the specific focus of the peer cooperation. This includes teaching a specific structure for providing feedback. In some cases, students are provided with checklists that guide their collaboration.

An example of peer collaboration is collaborative revising, in which one student (the author) reads a draft of a paper to another student (the reviewer). The reviewer then tells the author several things they like about the paper and provides specific feedback on selected aspects of it. This could include noting places that are unclear, where more detail or explanation is needed, or other targeted skills. The author then decides which feedback to use when revising his or her paper.

4. Use word processing as a primary tool for writing, as it has a positive influence on what students write *(moderate positive impact)*.

The effective use of word processing involves a variety of different arrangements, ranging from collaborative student assignments using laptop computers to word processing under teacher guidance. It also includes the use of word-processing programs that have other features, such as spell checkers, bundled together as part of the software package.

5. Explicitly teach students how to write increasingly more complex sentences. Provide instruction in combining simpler sentences into more sophisticated ones to enhance the quality of writing *(moderate positive impact)*.

Sentence combining typically involves the teacher modeling how to combine two or more sentences into a more complex one. Students practice combining similar sentences following the teacher's model. Students then apply the sentence combining skill they are learning while revising one or more of their papers.

6. Implement a process writing approach *(small positive impact)*.

A process writing approach involves crafting writing opportunities in classrooms that mimic real-world writing experiences. The teacher is involved in students' writing throughout every aspect of the process. A process writing approach includes extended opportunities for writing; writing for real audiences; engaging in cycles of planning, translating, and reviewing; personal responsibility and ownership of writing projects; high levels of student interactions; creation of a supportive writing environment; self-reflection and evaluation; and personalized individual assistance and instruction. This is a very complex writing program, and how it is accomplished varies from one class to the next. It must be noted that its effectiveness depends on how much preparation teachers have received in how to implement it. Teachers who have not been taught how to formerly implement this program are likely to have little or no impact on improving their students' writing.

7. Involve students in writing activities designed to sharpen their inquiry skills *(small positive impact)*.

Inquiry activities help students engage in activities to develop ideas and content for a writing task by analyzing immediate data. These activities are characterized by a clearly specified goal (e.g., describe the actions of peers), analysis of concrete and immediate data (e.g., observe one or more peers during specific activities), use of specific strategies to conduct the analysis (e.g., retrospectively ask the peer being observed the reason for their action), and applying what was learned (e.g., write a story where the insights from the inquiry are incorporated into the composition).

8. Engage students in activities that help them gather and organize ideas for their composition before they write a first draft *(small positive impact)*.

Prewriting activities include gathering possible information for a paper by reading, developing a visual representation of ideas (e.g., graphic organizers) before writing, and organizing prewriting ideas.

9. Provide students with good models for each type of writing that is the focus of instruction *(small positive impact)*.

Teachers provide good models of specific writing types and discuss the features of the models with the students. Students analyze the models and are encouraged to imitate the critical elements embodied in the models in their own writing.

10. Avoid teaching grammar using formal methods, such as studying parts of speech, sentence diagramming, and so forth *(formal grammar instruction had a small negative impact)*.

Explicit and systematic grammar instruction does not improve students' grammar skills (Andrews et al., 2006) or writing quality (Graham & Perin, 2007a, 2007c). When compared with other teaching approaches, traditional school grammar instruction is also less effective in improving the overall quality of students' writing (Graham & Perin, 2007a, 2007c). Classic examples of traditional grammar instruction include the teacher describing a rule, with students applying it through multiple-choice or fill-in-the blank sentence activities. Thus, teachers should not assume that time spent teaching students about parts of speech, exercises diagramming sentences, or decontextualized activities (such as those described above) in which students choose the correct grammar response, will have a positive impact on reducing grammar errors in text or improving how well students write.

Findings From a Qualitative Metasynthesis

The next set of recommendations for Tier 1 instruction is drawn from a qualitative metasynthesis of five qualitative studies that examined the nature of effective writing instruction (Graham & Perin, 2007b). The five studies were located through literature searches conducted for *Writing Next*, and all provided observations and descriptions of effective writing teachers or schools (Graham & Perin, 2007a, 2007c). Themes evident in the majority of the studies were included in these findings. Graham and Perin (2007b) identified 10 writing practices that were consistently applied in most of the qualitative studies examining exceptional teachers and schools at the elementary and middle school levels. These recommendations must be treated cautiously, as the evidence supporting them is more tenuous than the evidence for the first 10 recommendations. Because the studies were qualitative, it was not possible to determine the overall strength of the effect (i.e., small, moderate, or strong). Many of these recommendations are consistent with the first 10 recommendations presented above.

11. Dedicate time to writing and writing instruction, with writing occurring across the curriculum.
12. Involve students in various forms of writing over time.
13. Encourage students to treat writing as a process in which they plan, draft, revise, edit, and share their work.
14. Keep students engaged and on task by involving them in thoughtful activities (such as planning their composition) rather than activities that do not require

thoughtfulness (such as completing a workbook page that can be finished quickly, leaving many students off task).

15. Mix teaching the whole class with teaching small groups and have one-on-one interactions with students; this includes teaching students how to plan, draft, and revise, as well as teaching more basic writing skills.

16. Model, explain, and provide guided assistance when teaching.

17. Provide just enough support that students can make progress or carry out writing tasks and processes, but encourage students to act in a self-regulated fashion, doing as much as they can on their own.

18. Be enthusiastic about writing and create a positive environment where students are constantly encouraged to try hard, believe that the skills and strategies they are learning will permit them to write well, and attribute success to effort and the tactics they are learning.

19. Set high expectations for students, encouraging them to surpass their previous efforts or accomplishments.

20. Adapt writing assignments and instruction to better meet the needs of individual students.

Summary of Evidence-Based Practices for Tier 1

Results from the quantitative meta-analyses and the qualitative metasynthesis provide guidelines for designing effective writing practices in a general education setting. First, teachers should create a positive writing environment in which they set high expectations for all students. The writing program should include dedicated time devoted to writing a wide variety of text types, including writing across the curriculum. Planned writing activities should be thoughtful, encouraging students to stay on task and engaged. These activities could include a process-based approach, inquiry-based activities, or examining models of good writing. In addition, teachers should attend to the instructional arrangements of writing instruction, such as teaching to varying group sizes, adapting writing instruction and assignments to meet the needs of individual students, and including opportunities for collaborative work among students. Students should be explicitly and systematically taught specific writing skills and strategies designed to improve their abilities to plan, write, edit, revise, summarize, and use complex sentences. Teachers should model and scaffold their instruction, providing just enough assistance to allow students to complete the task. Finally, students should use word processing as a primary writing tool (at least by fourth grade).

EVIDENCE-BASED PRACTICES FOR TIERS 2 AND 3

Although several recent surveys provide information about typical writing instruction practices, few evidence-based practices exist for providing additional or specialized writing instruction for students who are not progressing adequately in the regular classroom. The surveys indicate that a sizable proportion of teachers provide few or no adaptations for these students (Graham et al., 2003; Graham et al., 2008; Kiuhara et al., 2009). On the basis of this evidence and our own experience in schools, we suspect that the Tier 2 and Tier 3 evidence-based practices presented here are applied in schools infrequently.

In this section, we present evidence-based practices that can be used with students who are not making adequate writing progress in the general education classroom. In the multitiered early intervention model, including RTI, Tier 2 interventions target students who (a) are below their peers in writing achievement and may be at risk for writing failure, (b) do not respond to general classroom instruction, or (c) are making slower-than-expected progress. Interventions in Tier 2 typically involve several features that differentiate it from Tier 1, including explicit instruction; small-group, high-intensity instruction; and increased duration. Tier 2 instruction can be received either in the general education classroom or outside the classroom using a special education-like instructional model (McMaster, Fuchs, Fuchs, & Compton, 2005). Students who then continue to demonstrate slower-than-expected growth rates while receiving Tier 2 interventions are moved to Tier 3, which may involve placement in special education, depending on the model.

The Tier 2 and Tier 3 recommendations in this section also are drawn from *Writing Next* (Graham & Perin, 2007a, 2007c), Graham (in press), and a meta-analysis of single-subject design writing intervention studies (Rogers & Graham, 2008). Although these recommendations are appropriate for students needing Tier 2 or Tier 3 interventions, they also may be effective for the general education classroom. As noted earlier, the research base is not sufficiently developed to make distinctions between interventions that work best at Tier 2 and those that work best at Tier 3. Also, all have been validated in at least four studies with struggling writers (typically in settings outside the general education classroom).

Experimental Interventions

The first three recommendations are based just on experimental or quasi-experimental research. Recommendations 21 and 23 were drawn from *Writing Next* (Graham & Perin, 2007a, 2007b) and recommendation 22 is from Graham (in press). Each of these interventions resulted in improved writing quality for students who were struggling with writing skills.

21. Set clear and specific goals for what struggling writers are to accomplish in their writing *(moderate to strong positive impact)*.

Goal setting involves identifying the purpose of the assignment as well as characteristics of the final product. For example, when writing a persuasive letter, the purpose of the assignment might include writing a letter that leads the audience to agree with a position. Students then set goals to have their letter contain a statement that tells their belief, two or three reasons for this belief, examples or supporting detail for each reason, two or three reasons why others might disagree, and why those reasons are incorrect.

22. Explicitly teach handwriting, spelling, and typing to students who experience difficulty acquiring these skills *(moderate positive impact)*.

Handwriting, spelling, and typing instruction provide support for those with low-level writing skills, and translate into improved writing quality for students who struggle with these skills. Such instruction goes beyond what is typically offered in the general education classroom, either by increasing the amount of time devoted to teaching these skills or by providing specific instructional activities not typically applied in this setting. For example, handwriting competency might be addressed by having a child repeatedly copy a short passage over a series of days with a goal of copying the passage about 10% faster each time (see Graham, 1999).

23. Explicitly teach students strategies for planning and revising their compositions using the self-regulated strategy development model *(strong positive impact)*.

This recommendation involves a particularly effective approach for teaching writing skills. The self-regulated strategy development (SRSD) model (Harris & Graham, 1996) is one of the best researched evidence-based practices for students who are struggling writers, including students with disabilities. In *Writing Next*, this model of instruction resulted in the largest effect size of all treatments (effect size = 1.14) based on improvement in the quality of students' writing. SRSD also demonstrated the largest effect size in the single-subject design meta-analysis based on improvements in the schematic structure of students' writing (Rogers & Graham, 2008). Though this approach is effective as a primary intervention tool, it has been especially effective with struggling writers (Graham, 2006a; Graham & Harris, 2003).

SRSD embeds writing strategy instruction in a model that emphasizes criterion-based learning, individualization, and direct teaching of self-regulation procedures to manage the writing strategies, the writing process, and students' behavior. The model includes the following six steps to teach a writing strategy:

1. Develop background knowledge. Students are taught any background knowledge needed to use the strategy successfully.
2. Describe it. The strategy as well as its purpose and benefits are described and discussed; a mnemonic for remembering the steps of the strategy may be introduced.
3. Model it. The teacher models how to use the strategy.
4. Memorize it. The students memorize the steps of the strategy and any accompanying mnemonic.

5. Support it. The teacher supports or scaffolds students' mastery of the strategy.
6. Independent use. Students use the strategy with little or no supports.

SRSD can be used to teach a number of writing strategies, such as PLAN (*P*ay attention to the prompt, *L*ist the main idea, *A*dd supporting details, *N*umber your ideas) or POW (*P*ick a topic, *O*rganize ideas (or plan) in advance of writing, and *W*rite and say more while writing). For more detailed information, see Harris, Graham, Mason, and Friedlander (2008).

Single-Subject Design Studies

The remaining recommendations are based on the meta-analysis of single-subject design studies (Rogers & Graham, 2008). Studies were included in the meta-analysis if they evaluated the effectiveness of a writing intervention using a valid single-subject design, included graphed and interpretable data needed to calculate effect sizes and demonstrate experimental control, and had at least one outcome measure related to writing.

Single-subject studies evaluate the effectiveness of interventions at the individual level, although the studies typically involve more than one participant. Writing single-subject studies involves repeatedly measuring a student's writing performance before as well as during and/or after instruction to establish a stable baseline and treatment effect (assuming that treatment has a positive impact on performance). The researcher also controls when the treatment is presented to a student or several students to rule out counter-explanations of the findings (e.g., the student's performance improved because of something that happened outside of the intervention period). For example, a pattern of findings that show stable or improved writing performance of students who receive the treatment, versus findings showing a stable lack of improvement of students who have yet to receive the treatment, provides evidence that the treatment caused the positive change in writing performance. When this pattern is repeated successively across multiple students, the claim of treatment effectiveness is strengthened (Horner et al., 2005).

Effect sizes for single-subject design studies are computed from data presented visually on a graph or in an accompanying table. Researchers do not typically graph every measure they administer repeatedly to students (often they only graph one). In the case of single-subject studies on writing, this measure frequently did not involve writing *quality*, the outcome measure in the meta-analyses with experimental and quasi-experimental studies. More common outcome measures in the single-subject design investigations focused on schematic structure of a composition (e.g., number of basic story elements) or productivity measures, like number of words written. Rogers and Graham (2008) only computed a summary effect size (percent of non-overlapping data, PND) for a treatment assessed using single-subject design where there were four or more studies using the same basic measure (e.g., paragraph structure or number of errors corrected). Therefore, the recommendations below include the type of writing outcome measure to which the findings apply.

Although the majority of single-subject studies did not include writing quality as a primary outcome measure, it should be noted that there were some single-subject studies that graphed writing quality results. These studies supported the effectiveness of the following previous recommendations: using word processing (recommendation 4), using prewriting activities (recommendation 8), and teaching planning, revision, and editing strategies using the SRSD model (recommendation 23). The single-subject studies yielded results similar to those of the experimental or quasi-experimental studies for general education instruction (recommendations 4 and 8) and struggling writers (recommendation 23).

Single-subject studies also examined another previously recommended instructional technique, setting assignment goals (recommendation 21), although the outcome measure in the single-subject studies were graphs showing writing output (i.e., how much writing students produced). Similar to the group studies examining impact on writing quality, setting assignment goals had a moderate impact on increasing written output. To avoid repetition, recommendations 4, 8, 21, and 23 are not repeated in the following recommendations; however, they have been shown to be effective for struggling writers or students with learning disabilities.

The recommendations from single-subject design studies for Tier 2 and Tier 3 interventions listed below are ordered in terms of strength of effect size. It should be noted that recommendations 25 through 27 primarily involve strategies developed at the University of Kansas as part of the Learning Strategies curriculum (Schumaker, Deshler, Alley, & Warner, 1983).

24. Reinforce positive aspects of struggling writers' compositions *(strong positive impact on writing output)*.

Reinforcement involves providing social praise, tangible rewards, or both, as a means of increasing specific writing behaviors. For instance, weaker writers might be provided tokens contingent upon increases in the number of sentences written in each composition. Tokens could then be traded for desirable rewards at the end of each week.

25. Explicitly teach students strategies for constructing paragraphs *(strong positive impact on schematic structure of paragraphs)*.

The explicit teaching of paragraph construction strategies ranges from teaching students how to write descriptive paragraphs to teaching strategies for organizing expository paragraphs. For example, students are taught a five-step basic strategy for writing paragraphs:

1. Show the type of paragraph (e.g., describe, show sequence, compare and contrast, and cause and effect) they will write in the first sentence.
2. List details they plan to use.
3. Order the details.

4. Write the details in complete sentences.

5. Finish the paragraph with a concluding, passing, or summary sentence.

26. Explicitly teach students strategies for editing their compositions *(moderate positive effect on number of errors corrected).*

Students are taught a strategy for monitoring and correcting errors. Examples include the use of spell checkers while editing compositions or the use of specific error monitoring strategies, such as COPS. The mnemonic provides students a prompt to check the Capitalization, Overall appearance, Punctuation, and Spelling of their composition (Schumaker et al., 1982).

27. Explicitly teach students formulas for constructing sentences *(moderate positive effect on writing complete sentences).*

Instruction in sentence construction involves teaching students formulas for writing simple, compound, complex, and compound-complex sentences. For instance, the student first picks the formula he or she want to use, then explores words that fit the formula. Once a set of appropriate words is chosen, the student writes the words down using the formula, and the sentence is checked to see if it is complete and makes sense.

28. Explicitly and directly teach struggling writers basic writing skills, such as capitalization, punctuation, sentence construction, and so forth *(moderate positive impact on grammar skills).*

Basic writing skill instruction involves the teacher modeling how to use the skill correctly, coupled with student practice applying it. In addition, taught skills are reviewed periodically. For example, a teacher could focus on instructing students to properly use capitalization skills or subject-verb agreements within sentences. It is not clear if these procedures for teaching grammar and usage skills are effective with children in general, as they have only been tested with struggling writers.

29. Encourage struggling writers to monitor one or more aspects of their writing performance to determine how well they are doing *(small positive impact on writing output).*

Self-monitoring procedures range from students monitoring the number of words or sentences written to monitoring their on-task behavior. Many times, students graph their performance as part of the self-monitoring procedure. For example, students might be asked to count how many words they generate each time they write, or determine if specific genre traits or elements (e.g., story parts such as setting, plot, action, and resolution) are included in their papers. After writing, the students graph the total number of words or specific genre traits, providing a visual representation of their progress.

Summary of Evidence-Based Practices for Tier 2 or Tier 3

Results from the quantitative and single-subject meta-analyses provide guidelines for designing effective writing practices for students requiring more intensive writing instruction. Priority should be given to writing instruction techniques that improve overall writing quality, such as using the SRSD model; teaching handwriting, spelling, or typing to students who struggle with these skills; and setting clear and specific goals for writing. Other writing instruction recommendations address more discrete writing skills and should be embedded within a larger writing curriculum for struggling writers. These include teaching paragraph and sentence construction skills, editing strategies, and basic writing skills (e.g., capitalization or punctuation skills). In contrast to the experimental and quasi-experimental results, the single-subject meta-analysis indicated that teaching grammar and usage skills resulted in a small improvement in students' correct use of these skills. Finally, struggling writers benefit from reinforcement and self-monitoring strategies to improve writing output.

CONCLUSION

Although the evidence-based recommendations presented in this chapter provide a basic foundation for developing effective writing instruction programs for general education and special education students, there is still much that is unknown. For example, the research does not provide guidance on how much or what combination of the recommendations is most beneficial for students receiving Tier 1, Tier 2, or Tier 3 interventions. The research does not provide clear direction on how the increased use of technological tools, such as work prediction, speech synthesis, or multimedia writing programs, might benefit struggling writers. Additionally, the recommendations also do not address several areas of writing typically included in writing curricula, such as enhancing writing vocabulary, using writing assessment as a tool for instruction, and using reading and writing to support each other.

In some cases, instructional practices such as the teaching of vocabulary as a means of enhancing writing, or parental involvement in the writing program, have some preliminary evidence to suggest these practices are effective, but the findings have not been replicated sufficiently to ensure that they are reliable (Graham & Perin, 2007a). The findings for other instructional procedures, such as providing students with feedback on their written products, teaching the different text structures, and increasing the amount of time students spend writing, have been so variable that no reasonable conclusion can be drawn about their effectiveness (Graham & Perin).

Finally, as previously stated, it is important to realize that evidence-based practices do not ensure that the instructional technique will work under all conditions and in all classrooms. Progress monitoring, an essential component of RTI (Vaughn & Fuchs, 2003), provides data for teachers to determine the impact of the instructional program within each level of instruction. In writing, traditional curriculum-based writing measures used for progress monitoring include total words written, number or percentage of correctly spelled words, and correct word sequences or correct minus incorrect word sequences (McMaster & Espin, 2007). However, educators are cautioned in their use and interpretation of these measures, as research still needs to determine the most effective method of progress monitoring in writing across grade levels. Although a procedure should not be abandoned if effects are not immediately evident, teachers should evaluate available data from progress monitoring and employ common sense to decide when instruction needs reworking or needs to be changed completely.

Despite these limitations, the 29 recommendations give teachers evidence-based ideas for providing effective writing instruction to students with varying writing abilities. Many challenges remain for teachers of writing, and a commitment to improving writing skills in all students is necessary. Students with effective writing skills have a better chance of success in school, along with increased access to higher education, chances for promotion at work, and likelihood of participating in civic society.

REFERENCES

Achieve Incorporated. (2005). *Rising to the challenge: Are high school graduates prepared for college and work?* Washington, DC: Author.

Andrews, R., Torgerson, C., Beverton, S., Freeman, A., Locke, T., Low, G., et al. (2006). The effects of grammar teaching on writing development. *British Educational Research Journal, 32,* 39–55.

Atwell, N. (1987). In the middle: Reading, writing, and learning from adolescents. Portsmouth, NH: Heinemann.

Essential Skills. (n.d.). Human Resources and Skills Development Canada. Retrieved October 4, 2009, from http://www.hrsdc.gc.ca/eng/workplaceskills/essential_skills/general/home.shtml

Cronbach, L. J. (1975). The two disciplines of scientific psychology. *The American Psychologist, 30,* 116–127.

Cutler, L., & Graham, S. (2008). Primary grade writing instruction: A national survey. *Journal of Educational Psychology, 100,* 907–919.

Fuchs, D., & Deshler, D. D. (2007). What we need to know about responsiveness to intervention (and shouldn't be afraid to ask). *Learning Disabilities Research and Practice, 22,* 129–136.

Fuchs, D., Mock, D., Morgan, P. L., & Young, C. L. (2003). Responsiveness-to-intervention: Definitions, evidence, and implications for the learning disabilities construct. *Learning Disabilities Research and Practice, 18,* 157–171.

Graham, S. (1999). Handwriting and spelling instruction for students with learning disabilities. *Learning Disabilities Quarterly. 22,* 78–98.

Graham, S. (2006a). Strategy instruction and the teaching of writing: A meta-analysis. In C. MacArthur, S. Graham, & J. Fitzgerald (Eds.), *Handbook of writing research* (pp. 187–207). New York: Guilford Press.

Graham, S. (2006b). Writing. In P. Alexander & P. Wine (Eds.), *Handbook of educational psychology* (pp. 457–477). Mahwah, NJ: Erlbaum.

Graham, S. (in press). Teaching writing. In P. Hogan (Ed.), *Cambridge encyclopedia of language sciences*. Cambridge, U.K.: Cambridge University Press.

Graham, S., & Harris, K. R. (1997). It can be taught, but it does not develop naturally: Myths and realities in writing instruction. *School Psychology Review, 26,* 414–424.

Graham, S., & Harris, K. R. (2003). Students with learning disabilities and the process of writing: A meta-analysis of SRSD studies. In L. Swanson, K. R. Harris, & S. Graham (Eds.), *Handbook of research on learning disabilities* (pp. 383–402). New York: Guilford Press.

Graham, S., Harris, K. R., MacArthur, C., & Fink-Chorzempa, B. (2003). Primary grade teachers' instructional adaptations for weaker writers: A national survey. *Journal of Educational Psychology, 95,* 279–293.

Graham, S., Morphy, P., Harris, K., Fink-Chorzempa, B., Saddler, B., Moran, S., et al. (2008). Teaching spelling in the primary grades: A national survey of instructional practices and adaptations. *American Educational Research Journal, 45,* 796–825.

Graham, S., & Perin, D. (2007a). A meta-analysis of writing instruction for adolescent students. *Journal of Educational Psychology, 99,* 445–476.

Graham, S., & Perin, D. (2007b). What we know, what we still need to know: Teaching adolescents to write. *Scientific Studies in Reading, 11,* 313–336.

Graham, S., & Perin, D. (2007c). *Writing next: Effective strategies to improve writing of adolescents in middle and high schools.* New York: Carnegie Corporation.

Graves, D. (1983). *Writing: Teachers and children at work.* Exeter, NH: Heinemann.

Greenwald, E., Persky, H., Ambell, J., & Mazzeo, J. (1999). *National assessment of educational progress: 1998 report card for the nation and the states.* Washington, DC: U.S. Department of Education.

Harris, K. R., & Graham, S. (1996). *Making the writing process work: Strategies for composition and self-regulation* (2nd ed.). Cambridge, MA: Brookline Books.

Harris, K. R., Graham, S., Mason, L., & Friedlander, B. (2008). *Powerful writing strategies for all students.* Baltimore: Brookes.

Horner, R. H., Carr, E. G., Halle, J., McGee, G., Odom, S., & Wolery, M. (2005). The use of single subject research to identify evidence-based practices in special education. *Exceptional Children, 71,* 165–179.

King, S. (2000). *A memoir of the craft: On writing.* New York: Pocket Books.

Kiuhara, S., Graham, S., & Hawken, L. (2009). Teaching writing to high school students: A national survey. *Journal of Educational Psychology, 101,* 136–160.

Lipsey, M., & Wilson, D. (2001). Practical meta-analysis. Thousand Oaks, CA: SAGE.

McMaster, K. L., & Espin, C. A. (2007). Technical features of curriculum-based measurement in writing: A literature review. *Journal of Special Education, 41,* 68–84.

McMaster, K. L., Fuchs, D., Fuchs, L. S., & Compton, D. L. (2005). Responding to nonresponders: An experimental field trial of identification and intervention methods. *Exceptional Children, 71,* 445–463.

National Commission on Writing. (2003, April). *The neglected R: The need for a writing revolution.* Retrieved from http://www.collegeboard.com

National Commission on Writing. (2004, September). *Writing: A ticket to work... or a ticket out: A survey of business leaders.* Retrieved from http://www.collegeboard.com

National Commission on Writing. (2005, July). *Writing: A powerful message from State government.* Retrieved from http://www.collegeboard.com

National Commission on Writing. (2008, April). *Writing, technology and teens.* Retrieved from http://www.collegeboard.com

Persky, H. R., Daane, M. C. Jin, Y. (2003). *The nation's report card: Writing 2002* (NCES 2003–529). National Center for Education Statistics, U.S. Dept. of Education. Washington, DC: U.S. Government Printing Office.

Rogers, L., & Graham, S. (2008). A meta-analysis of single subject design writing intervention research. *Journal of Educational Psychology, 100,* 879–906.

Saltzman, J. (1993). *If you can talk, you can write.* New York: Warner Books.

Schumaker, J., Deshler, D., Alley, G., & Warner, M. (1983). Towards the development of an intervention model for learning disabled adolescents: The University of Kansas Institute. *Exceptional Education Quarterly, 4,* 45–74.

Schumaker, J. B., Deshler, D. D., Alley, G. R., Warner, M. M., Clark, F. L., & Nolan, S. (1982). Error monitoring: A learning strategy for improving adolescent academic performance. In W. M. Cruickshank & J. W. Lerner (Eds.), *Coming of age: Vol. 3. The best of ACLD* (pp. 170–183). Syracuse, NY: Syracuse University Press.

Scruggs, T., & Mastropieri, M. (1998). Summarizing single-subject research: Issues and applications. *Behavior Modification, 22,* 221–242.

Scruggs, T. E., Mastropieri, M. A., & Casto, G. (1987). The quantitative synthesis of single-subject research: Methodology and validation. *Remedial and Special Education, 8,* 24–33.

Vaughn, S., & Fuchs, L. S. (2003). Redefining LD as inadequate response to instruction: The promise and potential problems. *Learning Disabilities Research and Practice, 18,* 137–146.

CHAPTER 22

Study Skills: Making the Invisible Visible

Mary M. Gleason
Educational Consultant, Eugene, OR

Anita L. Archer
Educational Consultant, Portland, OR

Geoff Colvin
Educational Consultant, Eugene, OR

INTRODUCTION

It is widely acknowledged that many students who have difficulty learning also lack the study and organizational skills of successful learners. Deficits in these skills are particularly evident in students found eligible for special education. Unfortunately for many of these students, the curriculum that teaches study and organizational skills is *invisible* to them (Gleason, Archer, & Colvin, 2002; Gleason, Colvin, & Archer, 1991). That is, teachers embed the task demands that require these skills in a variety of school tasks, from kindergarten (e.g., "Hang your coat up;" "Put your crayons away") to high school ("Your assignment is due Tuesday"; "Tomorrow we'll have a discussion on chapter 23"). Yet too often these important skills are not taught explicitly, actively, or continuously. In addition, using these required skills is rarely explicitly rewarded outside of the task itself. For example, a student may improve his or her grade to a C on a quiz, but the improvement in note-taking skills that led to the increased performance is not usually acknowledged.

Successful students had no trouble learning the invisible curriculum of study and organizational skills even when instruction was implicit or was learned with the support of parents, many of whom had learned these secrets on their own. Too many students do not learn these secrets, and a sizable proportion struggle with school success. At the elementary school level, the lack of study and organizational skills is usually attributed

Address all correspondence regarding this chapter to Mary M. Gleason, PhD maryglearick@aol.com.

to some characteristic of the student. It is the student that is "sloppy" or "unmotivated" or "disorganized." These within-the-child deficits are then tolerated until middle school when the student faces many different teachers, each teaching their own content-area course such as science, history, or mathematics. The lack of study and organizational skills is more obvious in multiple contexts, thus making the relationship clearer between the absence of skills such as completing homework and school outcomes (e.g., failing on tests).

Often by the time a student's study and organizational problems are acknowledged, the pattern of school failure has been established. Historically, failing students in middle school and high school content classes are then pulled out for remedial programs or special education. Ironically, it is in these types of programs where study and organizational skills are finally addressed. And as happens with other efforts designed to remediate problems related to school success, such as basic reading skills, the study and organizational skill interventions are provided (a) to too few students, (b) too late, (c) too informally, and (d) in environments far from where they need to be used, from which such skills are not easily generalized.

With respect to such remedial efforts reaching too few students, a sizable proportion of students have difficulty with study and organization skills. For example, Bryan and Burstein (2004) reported that more than 50% of students identified with specific learning disabilities (SLD) have problems completing homework, although almost one student in three (28%) of nonidentified students has the same problem. With respect to being taught these skills too late, when study and organizational skill interventions are provided only to students with severe and chronic problems, it is too late to meaningfully influence school success. Unfortunately, the prevailing "wait to fail" approach is compounded by the lack of systematic and explicit instruction in study and organizational skills using evidence-based practices (Vaughn & Fuchs, 2003). Too often, intervention consists of informal solutions provided by teachers in the context of help with homework (Conderman & Pedersen, 2007). Finally, more than 25 years of research have shown that the likelihood of any study and organizational skill generalizing from special education or remedial classes to general education is very low (e.g., Ellis, Lenz, & Sabornie, 1987; Garner, 1990; Wong, 1994). A student who learns a specific note-taking strategy may not use it if general education teachers do not support or reward the use of the strategy learned.

STUDY AND ORGANIZATIONAL SKILLS IN A MULTITIER MODEL

Study and organizational skills need to be delivered to more than a few students, early, and in the environments where and when they are needed most. Because of RTI, today's schools make it easier to deliver interventions where they will do the most good with the most students. Study and organizational skills can be delivered to all students and made visible by general education teachers in a multitiered approach, with the assumption that, if skills are taught and maintained well, very few students will need Tier 2 and Tier 3 interventions.

The focus of this chapter is on equipping general education teachers with a set of *specific learning strategies* for Tier 1 instruction that will help them meet the embedded study and organizational skill demands of content-area subjects, whether those subjects are taught by the same teacher in the same classroom, or across teachers and classrooms. Learning strategies are not new, and in fact were part of a plan supported by federal research begun in 1978 to support students in content-area instruction that continues today (Deshler, Lowrey, & Alley, 1979). Much work in the area of learning strategies, now best represented by the Strategic Instruction Model, was conducted by Schumaker, Deshler, and their colleagues at the University of Kansas (Tralli, Colombo, Deshler, & Schumaker, 1996) and is reported in this book (see chapter 23). Consequently, we have refrained from citing much of their work and encourage you to read their chapter. Other researchers have also found evidence that many students can learn to be more successful in the context of general education classes if teachers explain directly, demonstrate, and provide opportunities to practice the various strategies described in this chapter. The chapter is divided into two major parts: general procedures for teaching study and organizational strategies, and specific study and organizational strategies for commonly observed problem areas.

GENERAL PROCEDURES FOR TEACHING STUDY STRATEGIES

One of the major goals of a multitier model is to ensure that all teachers have a translatable body of knowledge about effective teaching that promotes positive development and prevents learning and behavior problems in as many students as possible. Students' independent use of study and organizational strategies will be tied directly to the degree to which teachers systematically engage in explicit strategy instruction (e.g., Dickson, Collins, Simmons, & Kame'enui, 1998; Duffy, 2003; Nokes & Dole, 2004; Rosenshine, 2008). To provide effective instruction for study and organizational skills, teachers can use the following general procedures.

When teaching any new strategy, including study and organizational skills, teachers should first discuss the rationale for its use. This rationale should center on how the new strategy will contribute to success in school and how it will make learning easier for students (Day & Elksnin, 1994). Although providing students with a rationale may seem trivial, when delivered in a consistent, positive tone by multiple teachers, the rationale can create a positive vision for success.

Next, the teacher should use all the design principles that would be used to teach and generalize any new cognitive skill, whether it is how to organize a paper or how to do multiple-step tasks such as long division (Engelmann & Carnine, 1982). In a meta-analysis, H. L. Swanson (1999) found that these design principles are enhanced by what is known to *enhance* strategy instruction. Swanson's meta-analysis determined that combining direct instruction and strategy instruction was more effective than either type of instruction alone.

Explicit Instruction in Study Strategies

Explicit instruction of study strategies requires teachers to (a) overtly and explicitly *model* (i.e., demonstrate and explain) each strategy, (b) *prompt* or *guide* students in the use of the strategy with an appropriate amount of *scaffolding* or assistance, and (c) *check* students' use of the strategy by having students *practice* without the teacher's assistance (Duffy, 2002; Hunter, 1982; Larkin, 2001; Rosenshine, 2008). Across these three steps, the selection and juxtaposition of teacher examples are critical, because no single example can teach a strategy, and inappropriate examples can confuse many students. Examples should be varied and cognitively complex (Vaughn, Gersten, & Chard, 2000). In addition, the modeling and guiding opportunities should demonstrate self-questioning or self-monitoring methods and then have students use them during the independent practice (Graham & Harris, 2003; Malone & Mastropieri, 1992; Wong & Jones, 1982). Students using these methods will keep themselves on track by asking themselves questions about or checking off statements related to each step in the strategy, thus leading to a greater likelihood of using the new strategy successfully.

For some study strategies, it is useful for the teacher to engage in a basic task analysis. Teachers must break the strategy down into its component parts and use the *model, prompt,* and *check* steps on separate components of the strategy before incorporating them into an entire strategy. For example, when students are to write answers to questions at the end of a textbook chapter, they must be taught separate strategies for turning the question into part of the answer, for finding the answer in the text material, for writing the complete answer to the question, and for proofreading their answers. Likewise, when studying for and taking tests, students must be taught a strategy for anticipating what will be on the test, a strategy for studying and memorizing the necessary information, and a strategy for responding to specific formats (e.g., multiple choice, true–false). Learning to perform each step in the strategy before attempting to use the entire strategy will provide students with more immediate success and will result in more efficient learning of the strategy. The model, prompt, and check series of steps are explained below as they apply to instruction in study strategies.

Modeling the Strategy

Teaching any strategy requires teachers to present an initial demonstration of the strategy. At the same time that teachers are demonstrating, they should *exaggerate* the critical steps in the strategy and describe exactly what they are doing. Stating explicitly what they are thinking (i.e., "thinking aloud") is an instructional component associated with positive achievement outcomes (H. L. Swanson, Hoskyn, & Lee, 1999; Nokes & Dole, 2004). For example, when teaching students how to use an index, the instructor opens a book to the index and demonstrates how to run a finger down the page until the correct letter of the alphabet is located and then until the desired topic is located. At the same time, they talk about what they are doing and what they are looking for.

Then they demonstrate and talk about how to determine the pages to look at within the textbook to find the desired information.

Guiding Students Through the Strategy

Using new examples, teachers then guide students through the strategy, at the same time continuing to think aloud and modeling the questions students should be asking themselves. This time, however, teachers have the students answer the questions, and teachers listen to determine if students are learning to use the strategy. If errors are made or misunderstandings become apparent, then teachers provide corrective feedback. Ongoing and systematic feedback is a critical component of effective interventions (Konold, Miller, & Konold, 2004; Vaughn et al., 2000). Several practice opportunities (at least three) should be provided, and scaffolding or prompting should be removed gradually across successive examples. For each practice opportunity a new example would be used.

By providing a range of examples, the teacher is showing the students that the steps in the strategy remain the same even though the examples are different. For instance, when teaching how to use an index, teachers should provide several different textbooks, each with an index that looks different and is organized differently. Students learn that although indexes are often structured differently, the purpose of an index and the way it is used remains the same. By the third guided practice, teachers decrease the scaffolding, allowing students to employ more of the strategy on their own. At the same time, teachers monitor whether students are ready for independence. If students continue to be successful even when receiving less prompting, teachers move on to testing whether students can in fact use the strategy independently.

Checking Student Performance of the Strategy

After three or four sessions of guided practice, the teacher gives students the opportunity to use the strategy independently. Only when students can independently use the strategy in a particular context or content area with a range of examples will they be ready to *transfer* or *generalize* that knowledge—that is, use the skills they learned in a new setting or with a new set of materials (transfer), or use the new skills in a new way but maybe in the same setting (generalize).

The importance of giving students enough practice with feedback so they can transfer and generalize new skills cannot be overstated. In a meta-analysis of intervention studies involving adolescents with learning disabilities, H. L. Swanson (1999) found that extended practice with feedback was the *only* instructional component that contributed independently to the variance of the effect sizes when teaching complex material and skills.

Transfer and Generalization

One of the major assumptions underlying interventions with any student, and with students who have learning problems in particular, is that eventually students will be able to transfer the skills and behaviors they have learned in one setting into another setting. The other setting might be another general education classroom, a social situation, or an employment situation. However, transfer is not at all easy to accomplish. Teachers must *expect* and *tell* students to use their newly learned skills in another setting, make sure the way the strategy was taught matches how it will be used in the new setting, and make sure students have mastered and maintained the strategy in the original setting and over time.

Generalizing a skill or strategy to use it in new ways is even more difficult than transferring a skill from one setting to another. To use a strategy in a new way, students must have had the opportunity to use the strategy on a *range* of examples. A comparison of two learning situations involving the same students demonstrates the benefits. In one scenario, students attending a special education resource center part of the day are taught to identify the main idea in a paragraph. The examples used in the original teaching set are on a worksheet with multiple choice items asking about the main idea, each paragraph is composed of three or four sentences, and one of the possible answers matches several key words presented in the first sentence of the paragraph. Students do not have to ascertain the gist of a whole paragraph in order to identify the main idea. They merely look at the key words in the first sentence. In the second scenario, the same students are participating in a general education classroom, where students are presented with a textbook chapter and asked to identify the main idea in the third paragraph, which happens to be seven sentences long. In addition, the main idea is not stated in the first sentence, so students must consider all seven sentences at once to determine what the paragraph is about. It would not be surprising if most students in the second scenario would be unable to complete the task; the range of examples they were initially taught in the resource center did not include the type they are now encountering in the general education classroom (Engelmann & Carnine, 1982; Horner, Bellamy, & Colvin, 1984).

Although teaching students to transfer or generalize can be difficult, there are many things teachers can do to increase the likelihood that students will transfer or generalize their new skills and strategies. First and foremost, teachers must systematically plan for transfer or generalization *before* instruction occurs. Lenz, Ellis, and Scanlon (1996) found that students of various abilities learned to generalize Strategic Instruction Model (SIM) strategies when generalization was included as a phase of strategy teaching.

Because generalization is more difficult to achieve than transfer, the remainder of this section emphasizes generalization although transfer is still mentioned. Teachers can organize generalization planning using three time frames: before strategy instruction, during, and after. Not all of the suggestions in the following section need to be used for each strategy taught, but they can serve as an outline for teachers' planning.

Generalization Planning Before Instruction
Teachers should carry out two major procedures *before* instruction to increase the probability that students will use their new skills. The first step is to carefully select

study skills that are relevant to the students; the second step involves following two basic rules in choosing the examples to be used for instruction.

Carefully select relevant study skills. Because the major purpose for teaching study skills is to empower students and promote successful and independent learning, the strategies taught must be relevant to the students (e.g., Nokes & Dole, 2004; Pressley et al, 1995). For example, if students attend three classes in which the teacher lectures, learning a strategy for taking notes from lectures would meet an immediate need. In addition, teachers must select skills that can be applied in a variety of settings, have proven effectiveness, and have a specific outcome that can be observed by the teacher. If the study skills taught are relevant to the students' success in school, students are more likely to use the skills (Lenz et al., 1996).

Follow two basic rules. To promote generalization, teachers should apply the following two rules in choosing examples for instruction of a particular strategy or skill. First, teachers should select teaching examples for that strategy or skill that cover the *range* that students will likely encounter. To identify the potential range, teachers should examine the contexts in which that particular strategy or skill is likely to be needed or applied. For example, if the teacher decides to teach comprehension strategies, and specifically, to teach the paragraph rule that each paragraph has one main idea, the first step would be to identify the various contexts in which the students are likely to be required to read paragraphs at school. These contexts could include worksheets, overhead transparencies, workbooks, textbooks, novels, periodicals, newspapers, letters, and magazines of various lengths, all of which state the main idea with various levels of explicitness. Examples should then be selected to adequately represent the range of paragraph types included in these contexts (Horner et al., 1984).

Once the teacher has selected a range of examples that communicates a breadth of application to students, instruction is more likely to be effective if the teaching examples are then sequenced so that successive examples are maximally different, not minimally different; that is, one example from the end or near the end of the continuum is considered right after an example from the opposite end of the continuum (Engelmann & Carnine, 1982). The assumption is that by studying the examples that represent the whole continuum, the student would be able to apply the strategy or skill to all examples along the continuum. For instance, the first example used in teaching the paragraph rule about one main idea could be a short excerpt on an overhead transparency. The successive examples could be paragraphs from a textbook, a worksheet, and a newspaper. Similarly, examples could be sequenced on the basis of length of the paragraph (e.g., overhead, three sentences; textbook, seven sentences; worksheet, two sentences; newspaper, five sentences). In addition, the explicitness of the main idea could be varied, from paragraphs in which the main idea is matched by key words in the first sentence to paragraphs in which the main idea must be gleaned from all sentences in the paragraph. In effect these successive examples are sequenced to show maximum variation across the possible variables. But, in each case, every paragraph is about one main idea.

The second rule for choosing examples for instruction requires the teacher to go beyond the examples used in the initial instruction. To test for the possibility of generalization, the teacher should produce a second set of examples (Engelmann & Carnine, 1982). For example, once students show they have mastered the skill of identifying the main idea in a paragraph, as demonstrated on the first sequence of teaching examples, the teacher should now introduce a new set of examples that were *not* used in the initial teaching (e.g., text on an Internet site or paragraphs of 10 or more sentences in a three-column format).

Generalization Planning During Instruction

While teachers are demonstrating and guiding students through a new study strategy, they can take several steps *during* instruction to promote generalization and transfer of those skills.

Provide rationale for use of the strategy. Teachers can help students understand the relevance of learning a particular strategy by explaining what is to be gained by its use. In particular, teachers should emphasize the increased success that students will experience after learning a new study skill. Presenting the benefits of using a particular strategy has been found to be one of the instructional components that predicts greater outcomes (H. L. Swanson, 1999).

Discuss when and where the strategy can be used. In addition to discussing why students should learn the strategy, teachers should discuss when and where students might use the strategy (Gersten et al., 2001; P. N. Swanson & De La Paz, 1998). Teachers also might ask students to name other settings and other sets of materials in which they could use their new study strategy.

Ensure that students achieve mastery of the new strategy. In all cases, systematic instruction must be provided that ensures that students become proficient in the use of a particular study skill. If students cannot perform the skill at a high level of success in the training setting, then they probably will not transfer use of the skill to another setting or another part of the school day.

Teach students effective self-monitoring or self-evaluation procedures. In addition to receiving instruction on using a learning strategy independently, students benefit from acquiring self-regulation strategies or self-management skills such as self-questioning, self-monitoring, self-evaluation, or self-recording skills (e.g., Gersten & Baker, 2001; Reid & Lienemann, 2006; H. L. Swanson, 1999; Wong & Jones, 1982). A meta-analysis of the effects of teaching students to use self-questioning strategies found such interventions to be successful (Huang, 1992). Later, students can use these strategies or skills to monitor their progress in other settings.

Generalization Planning After Instruction

Students in the initial stages of learning, students at risk for failure, and students with disabilities forget what they have learned if it is no longer reviewed or maintained. Therefore it is important for teachers to address generalization *after* instruction, as well as *before* and *during* instruction.

Inform others of new strategies. It would be ideal if all teachers that students encounter would teach and require the use of learning strategies; however, such skills more often are taught in just one setting, such as language arts, with the teacher's expectation that these study skills will transfer or generalize to another setting, such as science. Therefore, the language arts teacher should tell the science teacher about the strategy and encourage the science teacher to review the new strategy, employ a scaffold (e.g., a poster listing the steps in the strategy), and reinforce the use of the strategy on a consistent basis. The science teacher might review the steps in the strategy with everyone and then pair more successful students with less successful students until they are independently using the new strategy in this transfer setting. Review of strategies and reminders to use strategies have been found to be important to achieving high strategy use (H. L. Swanson, 1999).

Tell students to use the strategy in other settings. Although this procedure may seem obvious, many teachers do not routinely tell students to use new strategies in other settings. At the end of a lesson or at the end of the day, teachers should remind students that new strategies are to be used in other classes throughout the school day (Borkowski, Estrada, Milstead, & Hale, 1989). This reminder can be as simple as one sentence that tells students to remember to use this strategy in your next class. Or the reminder can be slightly more involved, such as having a discussion with students about when they will use the strategy and how they will remember to use it.

Ask students to verbalize their success with strategies in other settings. Many students with problems learning find it difficult to associate their skills and knowledge with their success in school. To strengthen this association, teachers should encourage students to report their use of new strategies in other settings and discuss their success. If students do not make the association between their use of study strategies and improved learning, then teachers should point out the connection (Borkowski, Carr, Rellinger, & Pressley, 1990). In a number of experiments, Schunk and Rice found that students who received strategy–value feedback that connected strategy use to success demonstrated higher skill and higher self-efficacy than students in strategy-only or control conditions. Subsequently, students in the strategy–value feedback condition also maintained strategy use (as cited in Schunk and Zimmerman, 2007).

Discuss cues that signal use of the strategy in other settings or across different parts of the school day. Generalization of study and organizational skills is particularly difficult when the skills are not associated with specific subjects or classroom tasks, especially when the skills are first taught in a content-free setting such as a resource room center. For this reason, it is important for the teacher who provides the initial instruction to discuss with students the similarities and differences between the response demands and cues of the initial setting and those of the transfer setting (Deshler & Schumaker, 1986; Gelzheiser, Sheperd, & Wozniak, 1986). For example, the cue for taking notes in the instructional setting of language arts might be the teacher announcing that students should take out notebook paper and begin taking notes. In the science class, the cue might be the teacher announcing that students are going to have a test on Friday on the current day's lesson or the teacher writing an outline on the blackboard while talking about a particular topic.

Similarly, during one part of the school day the cue for students to spell correctly might be the teacher announcing a spelling test, but the cue during another part of the day might be invisible because teachers usually expect students to spell correctly when working on a written composition even if the teacher doesn't mention the expectation. In both examples, this dissimilarity in cues could hinder generalization. Teachers will be more apt to see students using the strategy in another setting or later in the day if the teacher of the initial instruction provides a strategy cue card that students can reference (Jitendra, Hoppes, & Xin, 2000).

Use role-playing to practice transfer of skills to other settings. Helping students role-play the transfer of skills to other settings is especially beneficial if the response demands and cues of the other settings are considerably different from those used during the training. For example, students could practice responding to various cues that indicate "it is time to listen to the teacher and take notes." The teacher who is presenting study strategies to the students might mix up a variety of cues to see if the students can choose which study strategy to use. Students need many opportunities to practice and review all the strategies they have learned.

STUDY AND ORGANIZATIONAL STRATEGIES IN TIER 1

For more than a decade, Archer and Gleason field-tested and revised strategies for early instruction at the elementary level (Grades 3–6) so that study and organizational behaviors might be firmly established by the time students reach the challenges of middle or junior high school or of high school. These specific strategies have seen widespread use for the past two decades, have been revised twice, and are the basis for this chapter (Archer & Gleason, 2002). These learning strategies include, among many others, skimming through textbook material to find information needed for answering a particular question, reading textbook material and deciding which information is important and which is not, and using the identified relevant information to take notes and study the material.

Many students, including students with learning disabilities, are passive in their approach to learning (Hallahan, Kauffman, & Lloyd, 1999; Torgesen, 1982). Teachers face the challenge of transforming these passive learners into learners who are involved more actively. *All* teachers can help students meet classroom expectations by equipping all students with specific and effective learning strategies for gathering or gaining information, responding to information, and organizing information. Although these strategies can be taught in isolation, they are best taught in the context of learning new information in one or more subject areas (Pressley, 2000). That is, instead of teaching a learning strategy outside of a particular subject, it is best to teach the strategy as part of a particular subject, such as teaching students to gather information from the history textbook.

Gathering Information From Content-Area Textbooks

A major goal in general education content-area classes is that of gaining knowledge by gathering information from textbooks and other text sources. Students will find that using study skills to gather information can be difficult if students are left to their own strategies. Archer and Gleason (2002, 2003c, 2003d) determined that for students to gather information from text they must be directly and explicitly taught strategies for the following five tasks:

1. Decoding longer words
2. Surveying the chapter and forming a general impression of the important information to be emphasized in the chapter
3. Reading the text and attending to the main ideas and important details
4. Verbally rehearsing the main ideas and details and/or completing written notes on the main ideas and details
5. Attending to the content of maps and graphics that accompany the text

Archer and Gleason (2002, 2003c) and Archer, Gleason, and Vachon (2005) use the explicit strategy instruction that was discussed in the first part of this chapter to teach these five components and the remaining strategies presented in this chapter. In addition, they follow the design principles discussed earlier in the chapter that support transfer and generalization. Each strategy is described with enough detail that school psychologists or other readers could teach the strategy themselves or could coach a teacher to teach the strategy provided that they embed the strategy in an explicit instructional cycle and plan for generalization.

Further information on content-area reading strategies can be found in reviews and compilations by Beers (2003); Boyle and Yeager (1997); Bryant, Ugel, Thompson, and Hamff (1999); Buehl (2001); De La Paz (1999); Gersten (1998); Mastropieri and Scruggs (1997); Munk, Bruckert, Call, Stoehrmann, and Radandt (1998); Nokes and Dole (2004); P. N. Swanson and De La Paz (1998); Vaughn et al. (2000); and Vaughn, Klingner, and Bryant (2001), as well as many others. In the interest of space, this chapter does not include background knowledge or vocabulary strategies; however, these strategies are very important in helping students gain information from text (Blachowicz & Fisher, 2000; Marzano, 2004). Background knowledge strategies, which help students build reservoirs of knowledge they can access mentally while trying to comprehend new material, and vocabulary strategies each require a separate chapter. And in fact, each has been the subject of at least one book (e.g., Beck, McKeown, & Kucan, 2002; Marzano, 2004).

Decoding Longer Words
One of the major challenges that students face when reading content-area textbooks is the number of "long" words. Poor readers tend to skip or guess at these multisyllabic words. Nagy and Andersen (1984) determined that beginning in fifth grade, each year

students encounter approximately 10,000 words they have never encountered in print before. Most of these new words are longer words having two or more syllables (Cunningham, 1998). In content-area passages, multisyllabic words such as *evaporation, precipitation,* and *transpiration* generally carry most of the passage's meaning. Unfortunately, too many students, especially poor readers, have a difficult time with multisyllabic words (Just & Carpenter, 1987; Samuels, LaBerge, & Bremer, 1978). The presumption that a student can read *all* words because he or she can read short words or single-syllable words proficiently is false.

Several studies have shown that teaching students *strategies* for decoding longer words improves their general reading ability and therefore their ability to gain information from content-area textbooks. Shefelbine (1990) taught fourth and sixth graders having difficulty decoding multisyllabic words to use a strategy for pronouncing longer words. When compared with a control group, the students who learned the strategy made significant gains in their ability to pronounce long words. Similarly, Lenz and Hughes (1990) were able to reduce oral reading errors and increase students' comprehension at reading level by teaching seventh, eighth, and ninth graders a multisyllabic word decoding strategy.

Archer, Gleason, Vachon, and Hollenbeck (2009) reported that students who were taught a research-validated decoding strategy that was later incorporated into the *REWARDS* program (Archer et al., 2005/2000) made significant gains in decoding longer words presented in isolation and within passages. The success of this strategy was replicated by Shippen, Houchins, Steventon, and Sartor (2005), who also found significant gains when they used the REWARDS program to assist struggling seventh graders.

The REWARDS strategy reflects two important patterns in multisyllabic words: (a) the presence of *affixes* in about 80% of multisyllabic words, and (b) the presence of a *vowel grapheme* (i.e., letter or letters that map a vowel sound) in all decodable "chunks" or word parts. When examining the word *entertainment*, for example, a student will see one affix at the beginning of the word (*en*), one affix at the end of the word (*ment*), and vowel graphemes in the remaining decodable chunks (*er* in *ter* and *ai* in *tain*). When learning to use the REWARDS strategy, the student does not have to learn to segment a word into perfect dictionary syllables but rather into manageable chunks or word parts that can be decoded. For example, once students have learned to recognize the affix *ism* at the end of words, the word *astigmatism* can be divided into the chunks *a stig mat ism* rather than *a stig ma tism* as it would be found in the dictionary. Also, the student does not have to emerge with the exact pronunciation of the word on the first attempt. Instead, the student achieves a close approximation of the word's pronunciation and corrects it using his or her knowledge of language and the context in which the word appears. Thus, students learn a flexible strategy rather than a rule-bound strategy.

As seen in Figure 1, students are first taught an overt strategy in which they physically circle affixes at the beginning and end of words and underline vowel graphemes in the rest of the word. Later, students transition to a covert strategy in which they look for affixes and vowel graphemes and note them mentally before saying the word parts and then the whole word.

Figure 1. Strategies for reading long words.

Overt Strategy

1. Circle the prefixes.

2. Circle the suffixes.

3. Underline the vowels.

4. Say the parts of the word.

5. Say the whole word.

6. Make it a real word.

EXAMPLE

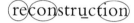

Covert Strategy

1. Look for prefixes, suffixes, and vowels.

2. Say the parts of the word.

3. Say the whole word.

4. Make it a real word.

Surveying the Chapter

Too many students, especially those with achievement problems, read a textbook chapter without a framework for sorting the *important* information from the *less important* information. This lack of discrimination frequently leads to poor comprehension of the chapter. Students comprehend content-area chapters more successfully when they first learn a *surveying* or *previewing strategy* to use before reading the chapter. The purposes of the preview are to (a) learn as much as possible in a small amount of time, (b) activate their background knowledge concerning the subjects covered, (c) and make predictions about the content (Klingner & Vaughn, 1998). In the survey or preview strategy, students are taught to examine chapter headings and subheadings, key graphics, chapter summaries, questions at the end of the chapter, and any other features that might help them focus on certain aspects of the chapter. Additionally, students determine how the chapter is organized, which helps them in selecting appropriate strategies for reading the chapter.

An evidence-based strategy can help ameliorate the problem of discriminating more important from less important information. For example, in a strategy called *Warm-Up*, Archer and Gleason (2002, 2003c) taught students previewing skills for content-area chapters so that students would determine and emphasize important information and develop an organizational framework for the information. Before showing students the strategy, teachers discussed the rationale for the strategy, telling students that warming up for reading is just like warming up for an athletic event. Students were to warm up for reading by accomplishing two goals: (a) finding out what the chapter was about, and (b) making predictions about what was to be learned from the chapter.

To teach the Warm-Up strategy, the teacher asks students to examine the *beginning* of the chapter (the title of the chapter and the introduction), the *middle* (the headings and subheadings), and the *end* (the summary and the questions at the end of the chapter). While students examine different parts of the chapter, they practice making predictions about what is to be learned from the chapter. The steps for warming up are presented on a poster or on a document camera for all students to see, and the teacher covers the steps and provides students an opportunity for verbal rehearsal. Students then *practice* the Warm-Up strategy with several textbook chapters, verbally reporting their predictions to the teacher or to a peer. Students then complete a written worksheet that demonstrates their predictions about the chapter content and share the content with the teacher.

In addition to the Warm-Up strategy, a number of similar evidence-validated preview strategies are available. As part of Collaborative Strategic Reading, students quickly preview passages by looking at the chapter headings; words that are bolded or underlined; and pictures, tables, graphs, and other key information to help them brainstorm what they already know about the topic and to predict what they will learn (Klingner & Vaughn, 1998; Vaughn & Klingner, 1999; Vaughn et al., 2001). The students are then given about 6 minutes to discuss among themselves what they have learned, predictions they have formulated, and any connections they can make between what they already know and what they will read.

Another strategy used to activate students' background knowledge is *KWL* (Know, Want, Learn). Before reading a selection, students record on a KWL table what they *know*, and what they *want* to learn (Ogle, 1986/1992). After reading the selection, students record what they have *learned*.

Reading the Text and Verbally Rehearsing Information

After students have previewed the chapter sufficiently, they must read the chapter. As they read, they attend to the main ideas and important details that are worth remembering and will help them answer questions at the end of the chapter. The strategy that will work best for a particular group of students depends on their reading skill level and their experience with reading content-area material. Dozens of study strategies for reading expository materials have been developed and tested with elementary and secondary school students (e.g., Archer & Gleason, 2002, 2003c; Bakken, Mastropieri, & Scruggs, 1997; Englert & Mariage, 1991; Fuchs, Fuchs, & Burish, 2000; Gajria, Jitendra, Sood, & Sacks, 2007; Scanlon, Duran, Reyes, & Gallego, 1992; Wong, Wong, Perry, & Sawatsky, 1986).

Although each of these strategies is unique, they all have several similarities (Archer & Gleason, 2003d). First, they all attempt to *engage students more actively* in the reading process. Students are asked to formulate questions, take notes on content, or verbally paraphrase the critical information. Second, the strategies attempt to *direct students' attention to the most important ideas and details*. Third, the strategies *engage the students in rehearsal* by asking them to recite or write down critical information. Four strategies that appear to exemplify these key steps are outlined here.

The first strategy, a *self-questioning summarization strategy* developed by Wong et al. (1986), teaches students to ask themselves a series of six questions as they proceed paragraph by paragraph and section by section to read and summarize a chapter.

1. In this paragraph, is there anything I don't understand?
2. In this paragraph, what's the most important sentence (main idea sentence)? Let me underline it.
3. Let me summarize the paragraph. To summarize, I rewrite the main idea sentence and add important details.
4. Now, does my summary sentence link up with the subheading?
5. When I have written summary statements for whole subsection:

    a. Let me review my summary statements for the whole subsection. (A subsection is one with several paragraphs under the same subheading.)
    b. Do my summary statements link up with one another?
    c. Do they all link up with the subheading?

6. At the end of the assigned reading section: Can I see all the themes here? If yes, let me predict the teacher's test question on this section. If no let me go back to Step 4 (pp. 24–26).

Active Reading is a second strategy for reading text and for verbally rehearsing the important information. Active Reading is based on a strategy for memorizing material called RCRC that assists students in memorizing by having them *read, cover, recite,* and *check* material such as spelling words, math facts, or vocabulary meanings (Archer & Gleason, 2000, 2003b, 2003c). When using RCRC with spelling words, for example, students apply the *read, cover, recite,* and *check* steps one word at a time. When using

Active Reading, students use the same steps but with connected text, one paragraph at a time. First the teacher and then the students *read* a paragraph and tell themselves the topic and details. They *cover* the paragraph and *recite* the important information in their own words. Then they uncover the paragraph and *check* their recitation by examining the paragraph again.

Before learning the Active Reading strategy, students first must be taught some component preparatory skills. With several short paragraphs the teacher demonstrates *naming the topic* of the paragraph, then asks students to practice naming the topics of several more paragraphs. Once students can name the topic of a paragraph, they are taught to *identify critical details* in the paragraph and to *retell the topic and details* in their own words with the topic already given. During additional practice, with either the teacher or peers, students practice saying and checking off on an Active Reading checklist that they have (a) said the topic, (b) noted the important details, and (c) used their own words. When students can retell paragraph content accurately and with ease, the teacher demonstrates how to put all the steps of the Active Reading strategy together.

As in the other study and organizational learning strategies, the content-area teacher discusses the rationale for the strategy. Students are told that using this strategy will help them remember more information from a chapter. The teacher then models the steps of the Active Reading strategy, provides guided practice, and prepares the students for independent practice. As a class, students verbally rehearse the RCRC steps as used in the Active Reading strategy (see Figure 2 for the steps) and practice using the strategy with several paragraphs, verbally reporting their topics and details to a teacher or peer. Finally, they complete a written worksheet in which the peer checks on the Active Reading checklist whether the recitation included topic and details and was in the student's own words.

The third strategy for engaging students in reading content-area textbooks is to have them take notes on the important information. Archer and Gleason (2002, 2003c) developed a system of note taking, called *Indentation Notes*, that is appropriate for upper elementary and secondary school students. A critical error made in many classrooms is to allow students to take notes without guidance or instruction. The results too often are haphazard. Some students will use a transcription approach. Others will take no notes at all. Still others write what they believe is important to remember without a clear process that differentiates *important* from *unimportant* information or shows relationships among levels of information. Once students learn to take notes in a more systematic way, the notes can be used more effectively in studying for tests, writing summaries of what was read, answering chapter questions, or writing a report.

As with the Active Reading strategy, the Indentation Notes method of note taking depends on the single paragraph as the unit for reading and writing notes and requires students to attend to the topic and important details. Students should demonstrate mastery of the Active Reading strategy before attempting the note-taking strategy. As with all teacher-directed strategies, the teacher provides a rationale, demonstrates use of the strategy, and guides students through the steps. The teacher tells students that taking notes will help them concentrate better on what the author is saying and that their notes

Figure 2. A verbal rehearsal strategy referred to as Active Reading.

Active Reading

R = READ

Read a paragraph.

Think about the topic and the important details.

C = COVER

Cover the paragraph with your hand.

R = RECITE

Tell yourself what you have read.
• Say the topic.
• Say the important details.
• Say it in your own words.

C = CHECK

Lift your hand and check.

If you forget something important, begin again.

Note. From *Advanced Skills for School Success: Module 3* (Rev. ed., p. 94), by A. Archer and M. Gleason, 2003, North Billerica, MA: Curriculum Associates. Copyright 2003 by Curriculum Associates. Reprinted by permission.

can be used for other purposes, such as studying for tests. Students are told why notes should be written briefly and in their own words. Students record headings or subheadings in the center of the paper, followed by the corresponding page numbers. Then they take notes on each paragraph, using an indenting style (see Figure 3 for an example).

To produce notes such as those in Figure 3, students read each paragraph and record the topic for the paragraph. Then they indent and record the important details, using abbreviations and symbols when possible, and indenting again when recording subordinate details. When notes have been completed, the students check them for clarity. Next to each paragraph section of notes the students write a question in the left-hand margin that could be asked about those notes.

Any note-taking strategy will benefit students *only* if they are provided with opportunities to *use* the notes. If students take notes but do not look at them again, then they will likely remember less information than if they were to review the notes to remember the information for class discussions or for written tests. To remember the information contained in the notes, students can use a verbal rehearsal strategy such as RCRC (read the question, cover, recite the answer, check the answer). They can participate in a class study session in which the teacher asks questions about the content; students answer the questions, then quickly show where the information can be located in their notes. Students also can conduct similar sessions with their peers, thus giving them practice in the use of their notes, feedback on the adequacy of their notes, and experience participating in study teams.

As an alternative to the indentation style, students can *map* the topics and important details. Having students create various types of graphic organizers, including cognitive maps, concept maps, and cognitive organizers, helps students see relationships among

Figure 3. Example of using Indentation Notes strategy.

Indentation Notes

	Internal Structure of Earth (p. 25)
How many layers does the earth have?	*Model of earth* *-developed by scientists from bits of info.* *-3 layers*
What is the crust like?	*Crust* *-thin layer of solid rock* *-covered w/rock, soil, sand, oceans, seas*
How does the thickness of the crust vary?	*Thickness of crust* *-different thicknesses* *-thinner under oceans and seas*

Hints for Taking Good Notes
1. Write your notes in your own words.
2. Make your notes brief.
3. Use abbreviations and symbols.
4. Be sure you understood your notes.

Note. From *Advanced Skills for School Success: Module 3* (p. 83), by A. Archer and M. Gleason, 1992, North Billerica, MA: Curriculum Associates. Copyright 1992 by Curriculum Associates. Reprinted by permission.

ideas and between the ideas and a main concept, resulting in increased comprehension and recall (Boyle, 1996; DiCecco & Gleason, 2002; Nesbit & Adesope, 2006).

When teaching students to generate concept maps, Archer and Gleason (2002, 2003c) taught students first to prepare a preliminary map by drawing circles and recording the headings and subheadings. Next, the authors directed students to read each paragraph under a particular subheading, draw another circle for each new topic, and record important details on lines extending from the topic circle. Students then linked headings, subheadings, topics, and details to show the semantic relationships among the ideas, that is, "grasslands of Australia," "short front legs," "long hind legs," and "tail balances" are all phrases that refer to "information about kangaroos" (see Figure 4 for an example of mapping information about pouched mammals).

To assist students in creating cognitive maps, Boyle and Yeager (1997) taught students the following steps using the acronym *TRAVEL*:

1. *T*opic: Students write down the topic and circle it.
2. *R*ead: Students carefully read the first paragraph.
3. *A*sk: Students covertly ask themselves what the main idea and three details are and then write them down in as few words as possible.
4. *V*erify: Students verify the written main idea by placing a circle around it and then draw a line from the main idea to each detail.
5. *E*xamine: Students repeat the Read, Ask, and Verify steps on each successive paragraph.
6. *L*ink: Students link together all of the main ideas that are related to one another. (p. 30)

Attending to Content of Maps and Graphics That Accompany Text

The study and organizational strategies that all teachers should be able to provide to all students have concentrated up to this point on reading the text portion of content-area textbooks. However, nearly all content-area textbooks also provide students with a lot of information through visual aids, including graphics, pictures, and maps that accompany the text. The information contained in the visual aids often is not described nor repeated in the text. If these aids only added or embellished the text-based information, lack of student skill in gaining information from them would not be a problem. But too often, this is not the case, as these aids contain information vital to student understanding and success. For example, the questions at the end of a social studies chapter or the questions on tests may require answers that can be found *only* in these aids. For most content-area teachers, again, an assumption is that students would know how to read and use the aids. As a result, explicit instruction in the interpretation of these aids typically is lacking.

As part of schools' efforts to improve academic success for all students, school psychologists may want to examine the textbooks used and determine the types of visual aids that are required for gathering and responding to information. Efforts can then be directed to staff development or coaching to ensure that teachers have active strategies for teaching students to learn from these textbooks. Archer and Gleason

Figure 4. **Example of a chapter map.**

Mapping Written Material

1. Draw circles for the heading and subheadings.
2. Take notes on each paragraph.
   a. Write the topic in the circle.
   b. Write an important detail on each line.

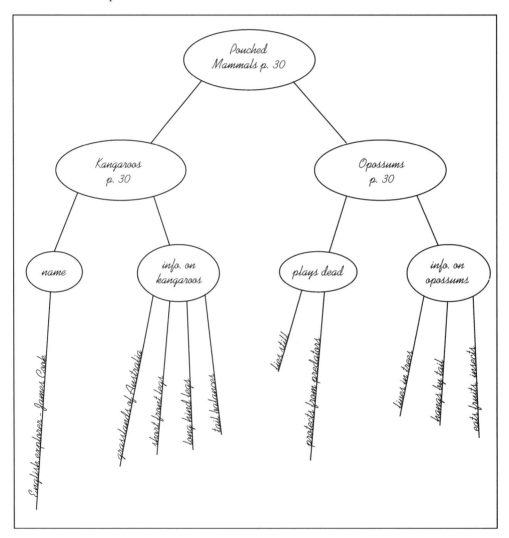

Note. From *Advanced Skills for School Success: Module 3* (p. 84), by A. Archer and M. Gleason, 1992, North Billerica, MA: Curriculum Associates. Copyright 1992 by Curriculum Associates. Reprinted by permission.

(2002) found that directly teaching students how to interpret mathematics tables and graphics, such as pie graphs, pictographs, bar graphs, and line graphs, was particularly efficient. In a few short days, students could answer math questions above a 90% level based on explicit teaching of strategies to all students.

Archer and Gleason taught their strategy by *demonstrating* and *guiding* students through a series of steps. First, the teacher and students determined the topic of the graphic material by interpreting the title or caption. Then they looked at the numbers or words across the bottom or top and on the left side to understand the organization of the graphic. The students located information in the graphic and answered literal questions about the information, questions that could easily be answered because information was right there; no inferences were required. Students also compared the visual (nonnumerical) information in the graph (e.g., size of the pie pieces, height of the bars) as well as the numerical information. The teacher guided the students in calculating answers to questions by adding, subtracting, or multiplying information in the graphs. Finally, students made inferences based on the information.

In some lessons, students learned to compare information from two graphs. The teacher provided relevant information, demonstrated how the comparison of two graphs works, and asked a set of questions specifically structured to require students to look at and compare two graphs. The series of questions might sound like this:

- What are the titles of the two graphs we're going to compare?
- Notice how the numbers of miners in Virginia and Utah have declined over the years. Why might the number of miners have declined?
- What do the numbers across the bottom of each graph refer to?
- What do the numbers on the left side of each graph refer to?
- In which year were the most miners employed in Virginia?
- In which year were the fewest miners employed in Virginia?
- How many more miners worked in Utah than in Virginia in 1925?
- Figure out the difference between the numbers of miners in the two states in 1945.
- What was the total number of people employed in the mines for the two highest employment years in Virginia?

In addition to learning how to interpret visual aids, students also must be taught *when* to refer to the visual aids and *how* to move from reading the text to examining the aid and back again. Typically, various cues are embedded in text to let the reader know when to refer to a visual aid. Some cues may take the form of explicit directions (such as "see diagram"), but this is not standard practice. Texts often have cues that are only implicit, such as a general discussion of a subject that is supplemented with a visual aid but includes no explicit reference to it. As part of instruction in learning strategies, students can be taught to read in the text up to the point where a proximate visual aid is referred to or up to the point where the text implies there might be a visual aid (e.g., "In the past decade, the number of known moons orbiting some planets in our solar system has changed dramatically"). Students would place a finger at that place in the text, refer to the visual aid, examine the information, and then resume reading where the finger was keeping the place. Teachers must emphasize to students that they must not neglect the visual aids while reading a textbook.

Responding to Information Learned From Content-Area Textbooks

The previous section presented strategies that students can be taught for gathering information from textbooks. A second major goal in content-area classes is to lead students to *respond* to the information they learned. Using study skills to respond to information learned is difficult for students who must create their own strategies without explicit instruction from teachers. High-performing students, students who have successfully navigated the invisible curriculum—those study skills not explicitly taught—already have considerable experience in generating their own responses to information. Many students are able to design their own strategies ad hoc, but at best these strategies are time consuming, and at worst they are ineffective. Low-performing or at-risk students lack ready, consistent, and effective strategies for responding to information, which only adds to the challenges they face to achieve success.

For example, a student might decide that to do well on content-area tests he or she must memorize every sentence of an assigned chapter. This is not a practical strategy. Clearly, the student must be introduced to a more efficient strategy. Three efficient and effective study and organizational strategies can be taught to all students to cover many of the task demands they will encounter in content classes: (a) answering questions at the end of a chapter or on worksheets, (b) writing summaries of what they read, and (c) performing well on tests and quizzes.

Answering Questions About an Assigned Chapter

One common expectation across content-area classrooms is that students will answer questions on teacher-prepared worksheets or at the end of textbook chapters. To be able to accomplish these activities successfully, students must turn the question into part of the answer, find the answer in the text material, and write the complete answer to the question. Archer and Gleason (2002, 2003b) embed these in a strategy called *Answering Chapter Questions*.

Before learning the strategy for answering chapter questions, students are taught explicitly to read the question carefully, turn the question into part of the answer, and then write that part down. This initial step is beneficial to students because it gives them two things: (a) a way to focus on the content of the question, and (b) a written referent *while* they are looking back in the chapter for the answer. It also helps students write a complete sentence for the answer and ensures that they will answer the question that was asked. For example, when students are answering the question "What are three ways to recycle natural resources?" if they first write down "Three ways to recycle natural resources are," then they are much more likely to look back in the chapter and find three ways to recycle natural resources and to write a complete answer to the question.

Practicing the preparatory skill of turning the question into part of the answer may take many sessions before students are ready to learn the Answering Chapter Questions strategy. When students have mastered this skill, teachers *demonstrate* and *guide* students through the whole strategy. Teachers begin by having students preview and then read a chapter or part of a chapter. Then, on their own, students read a question carefully and change the question into part of the answer and write that part down. After writing down part of the answer, students locate headings or subheadings in the section of the chapter that addresses the topic indicated by the question. They read that section until they find the answer, and then write the rest of the answer in a complete sentence that answers the question. After repeated practice with the teacher's feedback, students use this strategy independently, by following the steps contained in Figure 5.

Another strategy for answering questions on expository and narrative material is the QAR, or Question–Answer Relationship strategy (Raphael, 1986; Raphael & Au, 2005; Raphael & Pearson, 1985). This strategy stresses the relationships among the question, the text to which it refers, and the background knowledge of the reader. When using this strategy, students are taught to read the question and determine if the source of the answer is the text material ("in the text") or their own background knowledge ("in my head").

Writing Summaries of Materials Read

Learning how to write a summary of what has been read can help students comprehend and remember text material (Gajria & Salvia, 1992; Nelson, Smith, & Dodd, 1992). This strategy can also provide a type of writing practice that can be used to write reports or research papers.

Figure 5. Strategy for answering written questions.

Answering Written Questions

(Note: Read the textbook material <u>before</u> attempting to answer the questions.)

Step 1: **Read the question carefully.**

Step 2: **Change the question into part of the answer and write it down.**

Step 3: **Locate the section of the chapter that talks about the topic.**

Use the headings and subheadings.

Step 4: **Read the section until you find the answer.**

Step 5: **Complete your answer.**

Note. From *Advanced Skills for School Success: Module 2* (Rev. ed., p. 77), by A. Archer and M. Gleason, 2003, North Billerica, MA: Curriculum Associates. Copyright 2003 by Curriculum Associates. Reprinted by permission.

Because writing summaries is a frequent and common expectation across content-area classes (e.g., English and science) and across grades, the assumption is that all students know how to do so effectively and efficiently. Despite this common expectation and the benefits of developing successful strategies, summarization skills are taken for granted, and if they are taught at all, they are often undertaught. It is well established that cursory instruction in summarizing strategies is insufficient (Brown & Day, 1983; Hare & Borchardt, 1984). Summarizing is a difficult skill to develop to proficiency. Trabasso and Bouchard (2002) reviewed 18 studies on summarizing and concluded that students must be *taught* to identify main ideas and remove redundancies to achieve quality. In addition, *Writing NEXT* concluded that "teaching adolescents to summarize text had a consistent, strong, positive effect on their ability to write good summaries" (Graham & Perin, 2007, p. 16).

Any strategy that teaches all students to write summaries requires core components: students must determine the information to include and *exclude*, as well as reorganize and reword the information so it results in a concise summary. Although a variety of summarization strategies are available (e.g., Bean & Steenwyk, 1984; Rinehart, Stahl, & Erickson, 1986), one of the most explicit strategies found in the literature was developed by Sheinker and Sheinker (1989). Their strategy guides students in summarizing content-area material by teaching students to skim a passage and list key points, combine related points into single statements, cross out the least important points, reread the list, and combine and cross out some statements to condense the points. Finally, the student numbers the remaining points in a logical order and translates the points in that order into a paragraph (p. 135).

Taking Tests

When studying for and taking tests, students benefit from being taught a set of three strategies: anticipating what will be on the test, studying and memorizing the necessary information, and responding to specific test formats, such as multiple choice or true–false. The first strategy can be taught through either the self-questioning summarization strategy developed by Wong et al. (1986) or the note-taking strategy designed by Archer and Gleason (2002, 2003c). Both strategies were described previously in this chapter.

The second strategy, studying and memorizing the necessary information, can be accomplished with the RCRC strategy, also described earlier (Archer & Gleason, 2002, 2003b), or with any number of *mnemonic strategies* reported in the literature (e.g., Bulgren, Schumaker, & Deshler, 1994; Mastropieri, Sweda, & Scruggs, 2000).

The third strategy, responding to specific test formats (e.g., multiple choice, true–false), should be taught in several forms. Students should be taught one form for each testing format that they will be faced with. The following example illustrates a procedure for teaching students how to take a multiple-choice test (Archer & Gleason, 2002).

Multiple-choice items are composed of two parts: the stem, worded as a statement or a question, and the answer choices. First, teachers model how students would read an entire item. Then teachers think aloud while considering each answer choice to determine whether it might be the best answer. Finally, teachers justify their selection of the best answer. They then guide students in applying the test-taking steps to several multiple-choice items, some with "All of the above" and some with "None of the above" as one of the choices. Students complete some items independently, then check their answers with the teacher. Teachers provide several opportunities for practice, and students use the strategy each time they complete a multiple-choice test.

Many studies have demonstrated the benefits of teaching students explicit test-taking skills. For example, Scruggs, Mastropieri, and Tolfa-Veit (1986) found that fourth-, fifth-, and sixth-grade students with mild disabilities who received training on test-taking skills like those required for the Stanford Achievement Test (SAT) scored significantly higher on tests of reading decoding and math concepts. They concluded that the results of this and other investigations suggest that students with mild disabilities or at-risk students know more than they are able to demonstrate on published tests. Furthermore, according to Scruggs et al., training in test-taking skills should be undertaken not only to add to the strategy repertoire of these students but also to promote generalization and transfer of learned information.

Once teachers have taught students a strategy for taking a particular type of test, they should not take it for granted that students will remember that strategy without review or that a strategy for one test format would generalize to another test format. Students should learn strategies for and practice *each* test format throughout the school year. Students will benefit most from distributed practice rather than a concentrated period of test preparation shortly before taking a single test, particularly a high-stakes test such as a state test. Langer (2001) found that high-achieving classrooms and schools integrated test preparation into ongoing lessons. In Langer's study, each content-area teacher reviewed multiple-choice decision-making at the end of every unit. Many textbook publishers provide banks of test questions to schools that request them so that teachers do not have to create their own test questions.

Organizing Information

Managing the use of time for school tasks and managing materials used in completion of school tasks are important parts of being successful students. These management skills become more critical to students' success around Grade 3 and continue to increase in importance as students move to higher grades. Students with problems learning too often have difficulty (a) locating homework, (b) coming to class with materials, and (c) tracking when assignments are due. Generally, the academic performance of most students is enhanced when these skills are taught to all students.

To help resolve time and materials management problems, teachers must introduce three general organizational skills. The use of these skills must be (a) actively and explicitly modeled and taught by teachers, (b) practiced by students, and (c) rewarded as often as possible (e.g., on a daily basis). The first skill is the organization of materials in a notebook or set of folders for easy retrieval and for study. The second skill is the organization of time through the use of an assignment calendar that helps students to record assignments, determine nightly homework activities, and remember important events. The third skill is the completion of neat, well-organized papers so that the appearance meets the standards usually expected of successful students.

Notebook Organization

In a preventive model like response to intervention, students would be taught very early in their academic careers to build an organizational system that allows them to store papers, retrieve necessary materials, and transport materials between the classroom and home. In a classic study of organizational skills with students with learning disabilities, Lobay (1993) found a strong relationship between students' use of notebooks and their grade point averages.

Archer and Gleason (2002, 2003a) employ a variation of a standard organization protocol that can be taught to all intermediate and secondary students. They teach students to use a three-ring notebook with standard components, including a pen and pencil pouch, pocket dividers for each subject area, and notebook paper. Students place the pen and pencil pouch at the front of the notebook. Then, students label several dividers with the names of subject areas they will study, one divider labeled "Take Home" for finished work or notices to take home to parents, and one divider labeled "Extra Paper" for blank notebook paper to be stored at the back of the notebook. Contrary to the common practice of putting paper in each section so that students have paper for each subject area, putting all the paper in one section gives students only one place to check each day to make sure they have paper for the next day regardless of which class requires it. A simpler variation of this notebook organization is taught to younger students. Instead of a binder, primary school students use two folders: one for in-class use and one for taking things home. The pockets of the in-class folder are labeled "Paper" and "Work," and the take-home folder pockets are labeled "Leave at Home" and "Bring Back to School."

Regardless of the system, whether notebooks or folders, general education teachers must use the same effective pedagogical practices discussed earlier in this chapter. That is, their instruction of organizational skills must include demonstrating *how* to use the system, providing frequent (e.g., daily) opportunities for students to *practice* storing and retrieving materials and keeping materials organized, and reward students for their use, including keeping their materials organized. If students' materials become unorganized, they should be required to reorganize materials.

Often, a standard materials organization process is taught only once, at the beginning of the year. Although this teaching can work for successful students who have mastered the invisible curriculum, most students need consistent and ongoing support for maintaining organization. Teachers can encourage students to maintain their organizational systems through a variety of activities. Teachers might give frequent whole-class feedback regarding notebook organization. They might help students place papers behind the correct divider in the notebook when a paper is handed back, which also provides an opportunity for positive student–teacher interaction and reinforcement of organizational skills. Teachers might show students how to use a checklist to give themselves feedback about their organization, including such features as *all papers are stored in the correct sections* and *blank paper is in the section in the back*. Finally, teachers can praise students who remember to take notebooks home, bring them back, and take them to other classes, and they can invite students to show their organized notebooks to significant school personnel (e.g., the principal).

Assignment Calendars

Students typically begin to assume responsibility for longer assignments and for bringing various materials home in Grades 3 and above. For those students, educational achievement is improved when they are explicitly taught basic time management skills in their general education classes. One of these skills involves keeping a monthly assignment calendar that students use to record when assignments are due or when special events will occur (Archer & Gleason, 2002, 2003a). Students also can learn to use their calendars to determine nightly study activities, such as reading several pages in their textbook, studying notes for a test on Friday, or beginning to collect samples of objects that demonstrate earth science principles.

Teaching the assignment calendar skills requires teaching a number of component skills first. Many teachers, even those with considerable experience with students who have problems learning, underestimate the skills required to use an assignment calendar. For example, even older students benefit from learning how to locate "today's date" on a monthly calendar, what the definition of *due date* is and how to locate certain due dates on the calendar given a variety of directions (e.g., due a week from Thursday, due the Wednesday after next), how to write abbreviations for subject areas and for assignments, and how to record appropriate calendar entries. Failing to teach these component skills has serious consequences for many students. However, once they have learned these component skills for using assignment calendars, they will have the foundation for planning for nightly homework activities, that is, breaking homework assignments into small parts and using calendar entries to determine homework assignments that should be completed. Teachers should teach the component skills separately and provide many opportunities for practice.

After these preliminary skills have been demonstrated and practiced, teachers can give assignments and ask students to record them on their calendars, then follow through by asking students to turn in their assignments on the date due. Teachers support students in *daily* use of the calendars by providing time each day for them to consult their calendars and prepare materials to take home with their homework. In addition, students can be encouraged to show their assignment calendars to their parents and tell them about homework assignments and special events.

Teaching students to maintain the use of the assignment calendars throughout the school year is a challenging task. One solution for this challenge is to maintain a class master calendar, either physically, by locating it in a prominent place in the room, visually, through the use of a document camera or interactive whiteboard, or electronically, by maintaining the master calendar on a class or teacher Web page. This master calendar can be made for each month, with assignments that students should have included in their individual calendars. Thus, teachers are not only providing visible cues for maintaining individual calendars but also modeling these skills for their students.

Results of studies on assignment calendar use provide a strong basis for actively teaching these skills. For example, in a study with middle school students, Hughes, Ruhl, Schumaker, and Deshler (2002) found that students could be taught to independently record and complete assignments and maintain these self-management skills even after instruction was discontinued. However, they warned that students would not have performed as well without explicit instruction or generalization instruction, topics addressed earlier in this chapter.

Neatness of Work

A third organizational skill is that of organizing and presenting written papers that have a neat appearance. Students frequently hear teachers ask them to make their papers neater, but most students do not know the attributes of a neat, well-organized paper. In a strategy called *HOW*, Archer and Gleason (2002, 2003a) break down the features *heading, organized,* and *written neatly* into specific attributes that are introduced to students (see Figure 6).

Figure 6. Checklist indicating the standards to be applied in the HOW strategy.

HOW Should Your Papers Look?

H = Heading

1. First and last name
2. Today's date
3. Subject/period
4. Page number if needed

O = Organized

1. On the front side of the paper
2. Left margin
3. Right margin
4. At least one blank line at the top
5. At least one blank line at the bottom
6. Uniform spacing

W = Written neatly

1. Words and numbers on the lines
2. Words and numbers written neatly
3. Neat erasing or crossing out

Note. From *Advanced Skills for School Success: Module 1* (Rev. ed., p. 68), by A. Archer and M. Gleason, 2003, North Billerica, MA: Curriculum Associates. Copyright 2003 by Curriculum Associates. Reprinted by permission.

The attributes for neat, well-organized papers with a heading are again best taught through demonstration and guided practice. Teachers should present *positive examples* that show what is wanted in a neat paper and *negative examples* that illustrate what is *not* wanted in a student paper. The purpose for showing both positive and negative examples is to demonstrate the difference to students so that they can determine for themselves when their papers have a neat appearance and when their papers do not look acceptable. Students should *practice* evaluating other people's papers until they understand what makes a paper attractive, and then they should begin evaluating their own papers.

Teachers can assist students in maintaining use of this skill by following up with a number of activities. For example, teachers might make two large posters, one that lists the attributes of an attractive paper and one that displays an example of an attractive paper, and post them in the front of the room. Or they can reproduce positive and negative examples of student papers with identifying information removed. These examples can be posted on webpages or provided as samples for inclusion in students' notebooks. Teachers also might provide a checklist so students can evaluate their papers' appearance before submitting them to the teacher. Papers that are well done can be displayed publicly on a bulletin board or in the hallway. Alternately, excellent papers can be shared with parents at conference time. To encourage constant attention to producing neat papers, teachers can ask students to redo papers if they do not meet the established standards.

STUDY SKILLS AND ORGANIZATIONAL STRATEGIES IN TIERS 2 AND 3

As noted early in the chapter, teaching students strategies for studying and organization has been the purview of remedial programs and especially special education. Only a small subset of students is taught critical skills, and any strategies taught are usually taught too informally and too late. Even if such skills are taught in general education classes, the likelihood of students generalizing those skills in their classes would be remote, especially if their other general education teachers lacked knowledge of a particular strategy and did not expect and support its use. Instead, the chapter focus has been on providing explicit study and organizational strategies to all students in Tier 1, the environment where these skills should be used and rewarded most often and where the most students would benefit.

At Tier 1, the emphasis has been on general and specific teaching strategies that are closely tied to content and can be applied across content areas. Some students need more intensive instruction in study and organizational skills. In these instances, two approaches have been shown to be effective. In the first approach, students receive instruction using very specific techniques such as in the Strategic Instruction Model, delivered by a SIM-certified teacher. In the second approach, a research-based study and organizational program, such as Skills for School Success should be considered. Either approach includes what study and organizational strategies to teach, how to teach them, and how to support students; their use of strategies is not left to chance.

The least effective approach is to have teachers invent and deliver their own programs. More than 30 years of this type of intervention has shown that this approach becomes "help with homework" or "study hall," with limited effects on achievement.

WHAT SCHOOL PSYCHOLOGISTS CAN DO TO HELP

Although direct teaching of study skills at any tier would not be practical for school psychologists, they should serve as advocates for *all* students to learn study skills as early as possible. School psychologists also can support institutional systems that sustain the use of these skills across grades; for example, Sprick (2006, and chapter 17 in this book) builds the use of study skills into the grading system. The only way to build such institutional systems is to expand general education teachers' abilities to explicitly, consistently, and continuously teach a targeted set of study and organizational skills. School psychologists could serve as advocates for abandoning the weak system in which study and organizational skills interventions are provided in remedial programs or special education but not used in general education settings. The literature is replete with cases in which students with learning problems and identified disabilities struggle to learn in general education settings (e.g., McIntosh, Vaughn, Schumm, Haager, & Lee, 1994; Vaughn et al., 2001; Zigmond & Baker, 1996). Lacking study skills might be one of the reasons. School psychologists can play an important role in encouraging the transformation of an invisible curriculum to one that is visible.

1. School psychologists should advocate for the inclusion of study and organizational strategy interventions in the school improvement plan being created as schools build multitiered systems and implement a response-to-intervention (RTI) model.
2. Content-area classrooms and courses could be evaluated as to the degree to which teachers use and support evidence-based practices for developing students' study and organizational skills. Staff development or coaching could follow for those classrooms that could be improved.
3. School psychologists could acquire the knowledge and skills to coach teachers' instruction of study and organizational skills (e.g., by using the Strategic Instruction Model or a program such as Skills for School Success).
4. School psychologists could advocate for presentations on study and organizational skills to be offered at national and state conferences for school psychologists, and assist in soliciting articles on these types of interventions for the school psychology journals such as *School Psychology Review*.

CONCLUSION

Many students struggle in school because they lack the specific learning strategies—for example, their study and organizational skills—that would help them be more successful. In a multitier model, the problem is best addressed not by developing and implementing more Tier 2 and Tier 3 interventions for the subset of students with chronic achievement problems. Instead, the emphasis should be on equipping general education teachers to provide study and organizational strategies for all their students. By making good study and organizational skills part of all students' repertoires, they will be more accomplished in gaining, responding to, and organizing information. By supporting the use of those strategies within and across content areas and grades, schools can ensure that students will have consistent and sustained use of these skills for school success. Instead of study skills being the invisible curriculum, known to only a few students, they can be "seen" by all.

REFERENCES

Archer, A., & Gleason, M. (2003a/1992). *Advanced skills for school success, Module 1: School behaviors and organization skills.* North Billerica, MA: Curriculum Associates.

Archer, A., & Gleason, M. (2003b/1993). *Advanced skills for school success, Module 2: Completing daily assignments.* North Billerica, MA: Curriculum Associates.

Archer, A., & Gleason, M. (2003c/1992). *Advanced skills for school success, Module 3: Effective reading of textbooks.* North Billerica, MA: Curriculum Associates.

Archer, A., & Gleason, M. (2003d). Direct instruction in content area reading. In D. W. Carnine, J. Silbert, E. J. Kame'enui, & S. G. Tarver (Eds.), *Direct instruction reading* (4th ed.). Upper Saddle River, NJ: Prentice-Hall.

Archer, A., & Gleason, M. (2002/1994/1989). *Skills for school success* (teacher guides and student workbooks, grades 3–6). North Billerica, MA: Curriculum Associates.

Archer, A. L., Gleason, M. M., & Vachon, V. (2005/2000). *REWARDS Reading excellence: Word attack and rate development strategies.* Longmont, CO: Sopris West.

Archer, A. L., Gleason, M. M., Vachon, V., & Hollenbeck, K. (2009). *Instructional strategies for teaching struggling fourth and fifth-grade students to read long words.* Manuscript in preparation

Bakken, J. P., Mastropieri, M. A., & Scruggs, T. E. (1997). Reading comprehension of expository science material and students with learning disabilities: A comparison of strategies. *The Journal of Special Education, 31,* 300–324.

Bean, T. W., & Steenwyk, F. L. (1984). The effect of three forms of summarization instruction on sixth graders' summary writing and comprehension. *Journal of Reading Behavior, 16*(4), 297–306.

Beck, I. L., McKeown, M. G., & Kucan, L. (2002). *Bringing words to life: Robust vocabulary instruction.* New York: Guilford Press.

Beers, K. (2003). *When kids can't read: What teachers can do.* Portsmouth, NH: Heinemann.

Blachowicz, C. L. Z., & Fisher, P. (2000). Vocabulary instruction. In M. L. Kamil, P. B. Mosenthal, P. D. Pearson, & R. Barr (Eds.), *Handbook of reading research* (Vol. 3, pp. 503–524). White Plains, NY: Longman.

Borkowski, J. G., Carr, M., Rellinger, E. A., Pressley, M. (1990). Self-regulated strategy use: Interdependence of metacognition, attributions, and self-esteem. In B. F. Jones (Eds.), *Dimensions of thinking: Review of research* (pp. 53–92). Hillsdale, NJ: Erlbaum.

Borkowski, J. G., Estrada, M. T., Milstead, M., & Hale, C. A. (1989). General problem-solving skills: Relations between metacognition and strategic processing. *Learning Disabilities Quarterly, 12,* 57–70.

Boyle, J. R. (1996). The effects of a cognitive mapping strategy on the literal and inferential comprehension of students with mild disabilities. *Learning Disability Quarterly, 19,* 86–98.

Boyle, J. R., & Yeager, N. (1997). Blueprints for learning: Using cognitive frameworks for understanding. *Teaching Exceptional Children, 29*(4), 26–31.

Brown, A. L., & Day, J. D. (1983) Macro-rules for summarizing texts: The development of expertise. *Journal of Verbal Learning and Verbal Behavior, 22,* 1–14.

Bryant, D. P., Ugel, N., Thompson, S., & Hamff, A. (1999). Instructional strategies for content-area reading instruction. *Intervention in School and Clinic, 34,* 293–302.

Bryan, T., & Burstein, K. (2004). Improving homework completion and academic performance: Lessons from special education. *Theory Into Practice, 43,* 213–219.

Buehl, D. (2001). *Classroom strategies for interactive learning.* Newark, DE: International Reading Association.

Bulgren, J. A., Schumaker, J. B., & Deshler, D. D. (1994). The effects of a recall enhancement routine on the test performance of secondary students with and without learning disabilities. *Learning Disabilities Research & Practice, 9*(1), 2–11.

Conderman, G., & Pedersen, T. (2007). Avoid the tutoring trap. *Intervention in School and Clinic, 42*(4), 234–238.

Cunningham, P. (1998). The multisyllabic word dilemma: Helping students build meaning, spell, and read "big" words. *Reading and Writing Quarterly: Overcoming Learning Disabilities, 14*(2), 189–219.

Day, V. P., & Elksnin, L. K. (1994). Promoting strategic learning. *Intervention in School and Clinic, 29,* 262–270.

De La Paz, S. (1999). Teaching writing strategies and self-regulation procedures to middle school students with learning disabilities. *Focus on Exceptional Children, 31*(5), 1–16.

Deshler, D. D., Lowrey, N., & Alley, G. R. (1979). Programing alternatives for learning-disabled adolescents. *Education Digest, 45*(1), 5–62.

Deshler, D. D., & Schumaker, J. B. (1986). Learning strategies: An instructional alternative for low-achieving adolescents. *Exceptional Children, 52,* 583–590.

DiCecco, V. M., & Gleason, M. M. (2002). Using graphic organizers to attain relational knowledge from expository text. *Journal of Learning Disabilities, 35*(4), 306–320.

Dickson, S. V., Collins, V. L., Simmons, D. C., & Kame'enui, E. J. (1998). Metacognitive strategies: Research bases. In D. C. Simmons & E. J. Kame'enui (Eds.), *What reading research tells us about children with diverse learning needs: Bases and basics.* Mahwah, NJ: Erlbaum.

Duffy, G. G. (2002). The case for direct explanation of strategies. In C. C. Block & M. Pressley (Eds.), *Comprehension instruction: Research-based best practices* (pp. 28–41). New York: Guilford Press.

Duffy, G. G. (2003). Explaining *reading: A resource for teaching concepts, skills, and strategies*. New York: Guilford Press.

Ellis, E. S., Lenz, B. K., & Sabornie, E. J. (1987). Generalization and adaptation of learning strategies to natural environments: Part 2. Research into practice. *Remedial and Special Education, 8*(2), 6–23.

Engelmann, S., & Carnine, D. (1982). *Theory of instruction: Principles and applications*. New York: Irvington.

Englert, C. S., & Mariage, T. V. (1991). Making students partners in the comprehension process: Organizing the reading "POSSE". *Learning Disability Quarterly, 14,* 123–138.

Fuchs, D., Fuchs, L. S., & Burish, P. (2000). Peer-assisted learning strategies: An evidence-based practice to promote reading achievement. *Learning Disabilities Research & Practice, 15*(2), 85–91.

Gajria, M., Jitendra, A. K., Sood, S., & Sacks, G. (2007). Improving comprehension of expository text in students with LD: A research synthesis. *Journal of Learning Disabilities, 40,* 210–225.

Gajria, M., & Salvia, J. (1992). The effects of summarization instruction on text comprehension of students with learning disabilities. *Exceptional Children, 58,* 508–516.

Garner, R. (1990). When children and adults do not use learning strategies: Toward a theory of settings. *Review of Educational Research, 60,* 517–529.

Gelzheiser, L. M., Shepherd, M. J., & Wozniak, R. H. (1986). The development of instruction to induce skill transfer. *Exceptional Children, 53,* 125–129.

Gersten, R. (1998). Recent advances in instructional research for students with learning disabilities: An overview. *Learning Disabilities Research & Practice, 13*(3), 162–170.

Gersten, R., Fuchs, L. S., Williams, J. P., & Baker, S. (2001). Teaching reading comprehension strategies to students with learning disabilities: A review of research. *Review of Educational Research, 71,* 279–320.

Gersten, R., & Baker, S. (2001). Teaching expressive writing to students with learning disabilities: A meta-analysis. *The Elementary School Journal, 101*(3), 251–272.

Gleason, M. M., Archer, A. L., & Colvin, G. (2002). Interventions for improving study skills. In M. R. Shinn, H. M. Walker, & G. Stoner (Eds.), *Interventions for academic and behavior problems II: Preventive and remedial approaches* (pp. 651–680). Bethesda, MD: National Association of School Psychologists.

Gleason, M. M., Colvin, G., & Archer, A. L. (1991). Interventions for improving study skills. In G. Stoner, M. R. Shinn, & H. M. Walker (Eds.), *Interventions for achievement and behavior problems* (pp. 137–160). Silver Spring, MD: National Association of School Psychologists.

Graham, S., & Harris, K. R. (2003). Students with learning disabilities and the process of writing: A meta-analysis of SRSD studies. In H. L. Swanson, K. R. Harris, & S. Graham (Eds.), *Handbook of learning disabilities* (pp. 323–344). New York: Guilford Press.

Graham, S., & Perin, D. (2007). *Writing next: Effective strategies to improve writing of adolescents in middle and high schools – A report to Carnegie Corporation of New York.* Washington, DC: Alliance for Excellent Education.

Hallahan, D. P., Kauffman, J. M., & Lloyd, J. W. (1999). *Introduction to learning disabilities* (2nd ed.). Needham Heights, MA: Allyn & Bacon.

Hare, V. C., & Borchardt, K. M. (1984). Direct instruction of summarization skills. *Reading Research Quarterly, 20,* 62–78.

Horner, R. H., Bellamy, G. T., & Colvin, G. T. (1984). Responding in the presence of nontrained stimuli: Implications of generalization error patterns. *Journal of the Association for Persons with Severe Handicaps, 9*(4), 287–295.

Huang, Z. (1992). A meta-analysis of student self-questioning strategies. *Dissertation Abstracts International, 52*(11), 3874A

Hughes, C. A., Ruhl, K. L., Schumaker, J. B., & Deshler, D. D. (2002). Effects of instruction in an assignment completion strategy on the homework performance of students with learning disabilities in general education classes. *Learning Disabilities Research & Practice, 17*(1), 1–18.

Hunter, M. (1982). *Mastery teaching.* El Segundo, CA: TIP Publications.

Jitendra, A. K., Hoppes, M. K., & Xin, Y. P. (2000). Enhancing main idea comprehension for students with learning problems: The role of a summarization strategy and self-monitoring instruction. *Journal of Special Education, 34,* 127–139.

Just, M. A., & Carpenter, P. A. (1987). *The psychology of reading and language comprehension.* Boston: Allyn & Bacon.

Klingner, J. K., & Vaughn, S. (1998). Using collaborative strategic reading. *Teaching Exceptional Children, 30*(6), 32–37.

Konold, K. E., Miller, S. P., & Konold, K. B. (2004). Using teacher feedback to enhance student learning. *Teaching Exceptional Children, 36*(6), 64–69.

Langer, J. A. (2001). Beating the odds: Teaching middle and high school students to read and write well. *American Educational Research Journal, 38,* 837–880.

Larkin, M. J. (2001). Providing support for student independence through scaffolded instruction. *Teaching Exceptional Children, 34*(1), 30–34.

Lenz, B. K, Ellis, E. S., & Scanlon, D. (1996). *Teaching learning strategies to adolescents and adults with learning disabilities.* Austin, TX: PRO-ED.

Lenz, B. K., & Hughes, C. A. (1990). A word identification strategy for adolescents with learning disabilities. *Journal of Learning Disabilities, 23,* 149–158, 163.

Lobay, E. E. (1993). *Middle school study skills: The correlation between binder skills and academic achievement.* Unpublished Master's thesis. San Jose State University.

Malone, L. D., & Mastropieri, M. A. (1992). Reading comprehension instruction: Summarization and self-monitoring training for students with learning disabilities. *Exceptional Children, 58,* 270–279.

Marzano, R. J. (2004). *Building background knowledge for academic achievement: Research on what works in schools*. Alexandria, VA: Association for Supervision and Curriculum Development.

Mastropieri, M. A., & Scruggs, T. E. (1997). Best practices in promoting reading comprehension in students with learning disabilities 1976–1996, *Remedial and Special Education, 18,* 197–213.

Mastropieri, M. A., Sweda, J., & Scruggs, T. E. (2000). Putting mnemonic strategies to work in an inclusive classroom. *Learning Disabilities Research & Practice, 15*(2), 69–74.

McIntosh, R., Vaughn, S., Schumm, J. S., Haager, D., & Lee, O. (1994). Observations of students with learning disabilities in general education classrooms. *Exceptional Children, 60,* 249–261.

Munk, D. D., Bruckert, J., Call, D. T., Stoehrmann, T., & Radandt, E. (1998). Strategies for enhancing the performance of students with LD in inclusive science classes. *Intervention in School and Clinic, 34,* 73–78.

Nagy, W. E., & Anderson, R. C. (1984). How many words are there in printed school English? *Reading Research Quarterly, 19,* 304–330.

Nelson, J. R., Smith, D. J., & Dodd, J. M. (1992). The effects of teaching a summary skills strategy to students identified as learning disabled on their comprehension of science text. *Education and Treatment of Children, 15,* 228–243.

Nesbit, J. C., & Adesope, O. O. (2006). Learning with concept and knowledge maps: A meta-analysis. *Review of Educational Research, 76,* 413–448.

Nokes, J. D., & Dole, J. A. (2004). Helping adolescent readers through explicit strategy instruction. In T. L. Jetton & J. A. Dole (Eds.), *Adolescent literacy research and practice* (pp. 162–182). New York: Guilford Press.

Ogle, D. M. (1986). K-W-L: A teaching model that develops active reading of expository text. *The Reading Teacher, 39,* 564–570.

Ogle, D. M. (1992). KWL in action: Secondary teachers find applications that work. In E. K. Dishner, T. W. Bean, J. E. Readence, & D. W. Moore (Eds.), *Content area reading: Improving classroom instruction* (3rd ed., pp. 270–282). Dubuque, IA: Kendall/Hunt.

Pressley, M. (2000). What should comprehension instruction be the instruction of? In M. L. Kamil, P. B. Mosenthal, P. D. Pearson, & R. Barr (Eds.), *Handbook of reading research* (Vol. III, pp. 546–561). Mahwah, NJ: Erlbaum.

Pressley, M., Woloshyn, V., Burkell, J., Cariglia-Bull, T., Lysynchuk, L., McGoldrick, J. A., Schneider, B., Snyder, B., & Symons, S. (1995). *Cognitive strategy instruction that really improves children's academic performance* (2nd ed.). Cambridge, MA: Brookline Books.

Raphael, T. E. (1986). Teaching question answer relationships, revisited. *The Reading Teacher, 39,* 516–522.

Raphael, T. E., & Au, K. H. (2005). QAR: Enhancing comprehension and test taking across grades and content areas. *The Reading Teacher, 59,* 206–221.

Raphael, T. E., & Pearson, P. D. (1985). Increasing students' awareness of sources of information for answering questions. *American Educational Research Journal, 22,* 217–235.

Reid, R., & Lienemann, T. O. (2006). *Strategy instruction for students with learning disabilities.* New York: Guilford Press.

Rinehart, S. D., Stahl, S. A., & Erickson, L. G. (1986). Some effects of summarization training on reading and studying, *Reading Research Quarterly, 21,* 422–438.

Rosenshine, B. (2008). Systematic instruction. In T. L. Good (Ed.), *21st century education: A reference handbook* (pp. 235–243). Thousand Oaks, CA: SAGE.

Samuels, S. J., LaBerge, D., & Bremer, C. D. (1978). Units of word recognition: Evidence for developmental changes. *Journal of Verbal Learning and Verbal Behavior, 17,* 715–720.

Scanlon, D. J., Duran, G. Z., Reyes, E I., & Gallego, M. A. (1992). Interactive semantic mapping: An interactive approach to enhancing LD students' content area comprehension. *Learning Disabilities Research & Practice, 7*(3), 142–146.

Schunk, D. H., & Zimmerman, B. J. (2007). Influencing children's self-efficacy and self-regulation of reading and writing through modeling. *Reading & Writing Quarterly: Overcoming Learning Difficulties, 23*(1), 7–25.

Scruggs, T. E., Mastropieri, M. A., & Tolfa-Veit, D. (1986). The effects of coaching on the standardized test performance of learning disabled and behaviorally disordered students. *Remedial and Special Education, 7,* 37–41.

Shefelbine, J. (1990). A syllabic-unit approach to teaching decoding of polysyllabic words to fourth- and sixth-grade disabled readers. In J. Zutell & S. McCormick (Eds.), *Literacy theory and research: Analysis from multiple paradigms. Thirty-ninth yearbook of the National Reading Conference* (pp. 223–229). Fort Worth, TX: Texas Christian University Press.

Sheinker, J., & Sheinker, A. (1989). *Metacognitive approach to study strategies.* Rockville, MD: Aspen.

Shippen, M. E., Houchins, D. E., Steventon, C., & Sartor, D. (2005). A comparison of two direct instruction reading programs for urban middle school students. *Remedial and Special Education, 26,* 175–182.

Sprick, R. S. (2006). *Discipline in the secondary classroom* (2nd ed.). San Francisco, CA: Jossey–Bass.

Swanson, H. L. (1999). Instructional components that predict treatment outcomes for students with learning disabilities: Support for a combined strategy and direct instruction model. *Learning Disabilities Research & Practice, 14*(3), 129–140.

Swanson, H. L., Hoskyn, M., & Lee, C. (1999). *Interventions for students with learning disabilities: A meta-analysis of treatment outcomes.* New York: Guilford Press.

Swanson, P. N., & De La Paz, S. (1998). Teaching effective comprehension strategies to students with learning and reading disabilities. *Intervention in School and Clinic, 33,* 209–218.

Torgesen, J. K. (1982). The learning disabled child as an inactive learner: Educational implications. *Topics in Learning and Learning Disabilities, 2*(1), 45–52.

Trabasso, T., & Bouchard, E. (2002). Teaching readers how to comprehend text strategically. In C. C. Block & M. Pressley (Eds.), *Comprehension instruction: Research-based best practices* (pp. 176–200). New York: Guilford Press.

Tralli, R., Colombo, B., Deshler, D. D., & Schumaker, J. B. (1996). The Strategies Intervention Model: A model for supported inclusion at the secondary level. *Remedial and Special Education, 17,* 204–216.

Vaughn, S., & Fuchs, L. S. (2003). Redefining learning disabilities as inadequate response to instruction: The promise and potential problems. *Learning Disabilities Research & Practice, 18*(3), 137–146.

Vaughn, S., Gersten, R., & Chard, D. J. (2000). The underlying message in LD intervention research: Findings from research syntheses. *Exceptional Children, 67,* 99–114.

Vaughn, S., & Klingner, J. K. (1999). Teaching reading comprehension through collaborative strategic reading. *Intervention in School and Clinic, 34,* 284–292.

Vaughn, S., Klingner, J. K., & Bryant, D. P. (2001). Collaborative strategic reading as a means to enhance peer-mediated instruction for reading comprehension and content-area learning. *Remedial and Special Education, 22,* 66–74.

Wong, B. Y. L. (1994). Instructional parameters promoting transfer of learned strategies in students with learning disabilities. *Learning Disability Quarterly, 17,* 110–120.

Wong, B. Y. L., & Jones, W. (1982). Increasing meta-comprehension in learning disabled and normally achieving students through self-questioning training. *Learning Disability Quarterly, 5,* 228–240.

Wong, B. Y. L., Wong, R., Perry, N., & Sawatsky, D. (1986). The efficacy of a self-questioning summarization strategy for use by underachievers and learning disabled adolescents in social studies. *Learning Disabilities Focus, 2*(1), 20–35.

Zigmond, N., & Baker, J. M. (1996). Full inclusion for students with learning disabilities; too much of a good thing? *Theory Into Practice, 35,* 26–34.

INTERVENTIONS

for Achievement and Behavior Problems in a Three-Tier Model Including RTI

CHAPTER 23

Using a Tiered Intervention Model in Secondary Schools to Improve
Academic Outcomes in Subject-Area Courses

Jean B. Schumaker
Donald D. Deshler
University of Kansas

INTRODUCTION

During the early part of the 21st century, educators are facing a growing number of challenges. Two of the most significant ones involve implementing policies and practices that (a) raise the bar for all students so they will be adequately prepared to successfully compete in the global economy, where increasingly complex skill sets are required to obtain jobs that provide adequate compensation and quality of life; and (b) close the achievement gap for growing numbers of adolescents who are performing markedly below grade level and who lack the necessary skills and work habits to enable them to successfully respond to rigorous academic demands. To address these challenges, school leaders often need to determine how very limited financial, staffing, and professional-development resources will be allocated. How school leaders make decisions to address these two challenges can have important ramifications for adolescents in middle and high school settings.

The purpose of this chapter is to discuss how to implement an array of evidence-based interventions within a school-wide framework designed to improve academic outcomes in subject-area courses for *all* secondary students (high, average, and low achievers, including those with disabilities) in a coordinated, synergistic manner. The framework described in this chapter is a multitiered intervention system that provides increasingly intense instruction across the tiers and outlines the important role that every secondary teacher should play relative to academic outcomes. Although the roles played by various teachers within this framework are often unique, they also must be complementary. Prior to addressing these roles and the various components of this

Address all correspondence regarding this chapter to Jean B. Schumaker, PhD, at jschumak@ku.edu.

framework, the two challenges mentioned above will be described in detail to portray the context within which the different tiers of the model and intervention practices associated with each must be embedded. The second section of this chapter will explain the rationale for, importance of, and unique challenges in implementing a multitiered framework for instruction in secondary schools. The third section provides a detailed description of the tiered intervention framework (i.e., the Content Literacy Continuum), as well as sample interventions found at the various tiers. Finally, the last section provides a brief description of those factors that experience has indicated are important in supporting reform initiatives in middle and high school settings.

Critical Challenges Facing School Leaders and Teachers

In 2006, the National Academy of Sciences released a report—*Rising Above the Gathering Storm: Energizing and Employing America for a Brighter Economic Future*—to explain more clearly America's current economic standing within the world and to make recommendations for steps to be taken to ensure a vibrant economy in the future. The conclusion was that, to prevent other nations from surpassing the United States economically, the performance of America's youth must be markedly improved, particularly in the STEM areas (science, technology, engineering, and math). For example, in this report, a representative of Intel Corporation was quoted as saying: "We go where the smart people are. Now our business operations are 2/3 in the U.S. and 1/3 overseas. But that ratio will flip over the next 10 years." To counter such predictions and to increase U.S. competitiveness, the report concluded that schools must increase expectations for all students. As a result, school personnel are feeling considerable pressure to respond to the calls for raising the bar on student achievement (Deshler, Palincsar, Biancarosa, & Nair, 2007).

The number of reports detailing the poor performance of struggling adolescent learners, including those with disabilities, is voluminous (e.g., Deshler & Schumaker, 2006; Kamil, 2003; Wagner, Newman, Cameto, & Levine, 2006). Almost without exception, these reports underscore the magnitude of the achievement gap that these students face, between their actual level of performance and the demands they are expected to meet, both in skill areas and in subject-area classes. An example of the significant size of the gap is found in the most recent National Assessment of Educational Progress report, in which 68% of all eighth graders were found to be performing *below proficiency*, and 26% of eighth graders were performing at the *below-basic* level (National Center for Education Statistics, 2005). To illustrate the significance of these large achievement gaps, consider those Grade 9 students who are performing at the fourth-grade level in terms of skill achievement. In order to be performing at grade level at the time of graduation, these students will need to make 2 years of gain *per year* in school for each of their 4 years of high school. The challenge of closing this gap in a 4-year period is very daunting.

Thus, educators in secondary schools are confronted with a very difficult instructional assignment: simultaneously raising the bar to make students more competitive while closing the achievement gap so that a large percentage of adolescents are not marginalized or, in the most extreme circumstance, eliminated from school altogether because they choose to drop out.

Use of a Tiered Framework to Improve Academic Outcomes in Secondary Schools

One of the greatest barriers to student growth and achievement in secondary schools (especially high schools) is the issue of *fragmentation*. That is, students have multiple teachers throughout each day, and these teachers rarely, if ever, coordinate what or how they teach students. Unlike elementary students, secondary students who struggle with learning do not get the necessary reinforcement of critical skills, strategies, and subject-area information. Hence, the often disjointed, uncoordinated educational programs that secondary students experience rarely lead to the type of instructional synergy that is required for students to make dramatic achievement gains. One strategy for counteracting this dynamic is to implement a tiered instructional framework throughout a school. The overriding goals of a tiered system are to (a) minimize fragmentation for students, (b) facilitate coordination of instruction across teachers, (c) engage all teachers in assuming responsibility for improving academic outcomes, and (d) differentiate instruction through increased levels of intensity of instruction across tiers, with higher tiers involving more and more intensive instruction.

Experience in implementing tiered instructional models in secondary schools underscores the importance of providing high-quality instruction at each tier in the model. The success of a tiered model of instruction is dependent on the commitment of a large majority of the members of a school staff and a willingness on the part of different staff members to provide the type of instruction that is expected at the tier in which they are involved. That is, if teachers provide instruction at higher tiers, the instruction they provide must be individualized, intensive, explicit, and relentless. If unique, high-quality instruction is not offered at each tier in the model, eventually the model will become weak and ineffective. In short, tiered models of instruction depend on a broad level of support from teachers and administrators and a commitment to developing strength at each tier, so student needs are optimally met.

A TIERED INSTRUCTIONAL MODEL FOR SECONDARY STUDENTS

To provide some background information on the new instructional model to be described in this section, in 1978, the University of Kansas Institute for Research on Learning Disabilities was founded to develop an intervention model for secondary students who have learning disabilities. The early work of institute staff members focused on developing instructional tools that could be used in resource rooms to enhance the learning of these students. The resulting instructional model was called the Strategic Instruction Model and focused on teaching students how to be good learners by teaching them learning strategies in an intensive way (Deshler & Schumaker, 1988).

As the emphasis on mainstreaming and then full inclusion grew, institute staff members also began to develop instructional methods that could be used by secondary general educators to enhance the learning of at-risk students in their courses. Meanwhile, the name of the institute changed to the University of Kansas Center for Research on Learning (KU-CRL) so that the population served could be broadened to all learners. Nevertheless, the emphasis of KU-CRL work remained the student who is at-risk for failure. After a number of effective interventions had been developed, KU-CRL staff members began investigating ways that these interventions might be combined within whole-school reform efforts.

As a result, these staff members have designed a tiered intervention model for at-risk secondary students that takes into account these students' need to learn how to succeed independently in subject-area classes, as well as their instructional needs within these environments. Called the Content Literacy Continuum (CLC; Lenz, Ehren, & Deshler, 2005), the model is necessarily an adaptation of a response-to-intervention (RTI) logic model (Sugai, 2007). Such an adaptation was necessary because the emphasis within secondary environments is not on *early* identification of learning disabilities, but on the support of students with specific learning disabilities (SLD) and other at-risk students within these environments. In essence, the CLC is one way that schools can operationalize the Strategic Instruction Model to provide instruction across the curriculum in strategic learning skills.

Within the CLC, which is a framework that cuts across classes and departments within a secondary school, special education teachers and general education teachers maintain different roles as they work cooperatively to improve the performance of low-achieving students in general education classes. Both types of teachers take on the role of a "learning specialist," one who teaches students *how to learn and how to succeed* in response to academic demands in required general education classes.

Within the context of the "learning apprenticeship" (Hock, Deshler, & Schumaker, 1993, 1999) that takes place within the CLC framework, the major roles of the general education teacher are to (a) teach students how to learn the particular type of content that is the focus of the course, and (b) teach them critical content that is fundamental to understanding core concepts in the subject area. The role of the special education teacher and others in support roles (e.g., teachers in after-school programs, reading instructors, and speech and language therapists) is to teach the students the skills and strategies they need to succeed in the required subject-area courses. The partnership between the two types of teachers comes through their communication about (a) the demands related to succeeding in particular subject-area classes, (b) the skills needed by particular students, (c) students' progress, and (d) techniques that can be used to help at-risk students within required subject-area classes.

Features of the CLC Model

The CLC model combines important features of assessment and instruction to promote literacy and learning. Although some of these features have been empirically validated, others still need to be developed and tested. The features include the following.

Universal Screening

All of the students enrolled in required secondary subject-area classes are initially tested to determine their knowledge and skill levels prior to instruction. Some of the tests are general; others are course specific. For an example of a general test, all students entering middle school are tested to determine their basic reading and math skills. In addition, for each required course, the teacher(s) teaching that course develop and administer a test to measure students' content knowledge and prerequisite skills required in the discipline (e.g., dictionary usage, report writing). Specific criteria are set and applied by the school and by each teacher for identifying those students who might need closer monitoring or immediate intervention.

Progress Monitoring

Each student's performance is monitored throughout the instruction using assessments that are matched with the instructional targets. During skill-based instruction, progress monitoring can be conducted using criterion-based measures specially designed for each type of skill being taught (Duffy, 2007). With regard to subject-area courses, assessments are most often in the form of unit tests or activities that measure student acquisition of content that all students must learn, some students must learn, and only a few students must learn. Instructional decisions for groups of students and individual students are made based on individual student performance on these unit tests. These data may be used as part of the set of information needed to make referral decisions, which may lead to categorical as well as noncategorical placement decisions for students with disabilities and other at-risk students. For example, the data may be used to refer students to additional levels of the CLC model or for additional evaluation to determine eligibility for disability status.

Levels of Intervention

There are several tiers, or levels, of instruction and intervention within the CLC model. The first level, or the primary intervention, involves whole-group instruction of all the students enrolled in a required subject-area class by the general education teacher who utilizes research-based instructional methods (e.g., high rates of academic responding, modeling, graphic organizers, behavioral management) to deliver the course content. Subsequent levels of the model involve increasingly more intensive instruction by altering the content of the instruction, the teacher–student ratio, the type of feedback and additional instruction given, and the duration and frequency of instruction. Teacher use of, and student placement in, subsequent levels is based on the results of administering progress-monitoring measures.

Fidelity of Instruction

CLC teachers, including general educators and special educators, are trained to deliver the initial tier of instruction as well as more intensive levels of intervention. The teachers' implementation is observed and recorded by administrators, and they receive additional coaching and instruction in the classroom as needed until they reach (and continue to maintain) a level of quality of instruction above 95% of the specified behaviors according to fidelity checklists.

Standard Treatment Protocols

Written protocols for instructional delivery are used by CLC teachers across the tiers of intervention to help ensure that the tiers are implemented with fidelity.

Levels of Intervention Within the CLC Model

Although schools and other agencies (e.g., McPeak & Trygg, 2007) have adapted the CLC model in a variety of ways, the original CLC as described by Lenz et al. (2005) has five levels of intervention (see Table 1). These levels are briefly introduced here; more detailed information follows in later sections. At Level 1, teachers of general education courses use research-based methods, called Content Enhancement Routines, to enhance their delivery of content information (Bulgren & Schumaker, 2006). At Level 2, these same general education teachers embed the instruction of learning strategies (Deshler, Schumaker, & Woodruff, 2004) within their course curriculum as needed. Such strategies are specially selected to correspond to the content of the course. At Level 3, students are given intensive instruction in learning strategies. At Level 4, students are given intensive instruction in basic skills (e.g., reading and math skills). At Level 5, students are involved in clinical services related to particular needs (e.g., speech and hearing services). Upon entry into a CLC school, students are assessed and placed in as many levels as needed in order to meet their needs. Through progress monitoring, additional decisions can be made with regard to level placements.

In Level 1 of the CLC, general education teachers use Content Enhancement Routines to identify the most important content of their courses, corresponding to state and district standards. They also use these routines to organize that content and communicate that organization to students, present the content, and ensure that students learn the content. In other words, they present the content in learner-friendly

Table 1. The Content Literacy Continuum: A Continuum of Action for Educators

Level 1: Enhanced Content-Area Instruction
 General education teacher's role: Use content enhancement routines to teach the content.
Level 2: Embedded Learning Strategy Instruction
 General education teacher's role: Teach or prompt use of learning strategies, coordinated with subject-area content delivery.
Level 3: Intensive Learning Strategy Instruction
 Support teacher's role: Teach learning strategies to mastery levels.
Level 4: Intensive Basic Skills Instruction
 Support teacher's role: Teach basic skills (e.g., math facts, phonics) to mastery.
Level 5: Clinical Interventions
 Clinician's role: Teach the language skills needed for participation in the other levels.

ways. Each routine is a set of instructional procedures with a specific purpose. For example, the Concept Mastery Routine is a set of methods for teaching students the meaning of a key concept like "democracy" (Bulgren, Deshler, & Schumaker, 1993; Bulgren, Schumaker, & Deshler, 1988).

If general education teachers find that a large group of students in a class are not mastering the content that has been identified for all students to learn, they can implement research-based instructional methods for embedding learning strategy instruction within their content instruction to implement Level 2. For example, if students are required to learn vocabulary words each week and take a vocabulary test, the teacher might teach them a learning strategy for learning the meaning of vocabulary words. This learning strategy instruction is necessarily brief because of the demand that certain amounts of content be taught in each course. Nevertheless, this instruction is content specific and provides students with the necessary strategy or strategies that will enable them to succeed in the given course.

If students are continuing to have difficulty learning, they can be referred to the remaining three levels of intervention. In the third level, support teachers (e.g., special education teachers, teachers in before- and after-school programs, teachers of learning strategy courses, teachers of special courses) teach small groups of students how to apply learning strategies to succeed in their courses. The instruction is intensive and focused, and research-based instructional methods are used.

In the fourth level of the CLC model, support teachers (e.g., special education teachers, reading specialists) teach basic skills such as basic reading skills (e.g., phonics) or math skills (e.g., math facts) to small groups of students with severe deficits, using research-based curricula. Again, the instruction is intensive and focused, and the emphasis is on learning the skills as quickly as possible, so students can progress to the third level of intervention, where they can learn strategies. Finally, the CLC offers a fifth level of intervention for those students who have severe language deficits and who need one-on-one or one-on-two attention from a clinical specialist such as a speech-and-language clinician.

The various levels of CLC intervention might occur together or in pairs for an individual student, based on that student's needs. For example, a student might be enrolled in a required English course (Levels 1 and 2), might be enrolled in a learning strategy course (Level 3) to learn how to study for tests, might attend an after-school program to learn a strategy for completing assignments (Level 3), might take part in an intensive reading program (Level 4), and might have weekly speech-and-language sessions (Level 5). The following sections describe the intervention options that might be available within the different levels and the research that has been completed related to these options.

LEVEL 1: ENHANCED CONTENT-AREA INSTRUCTION

As described earlier, the role of the content-area teacher within the CLC framework is not only to teach a prescribed subject matter to students but to do so in a way that aids students' understanding and recall of that content and helps them learn how to learn that particular type of content. These additional aspects of the role of content-area teachers are particularly pertinent in light of the increasingly intense challenge that they are expected to meet with respect to teaching not only large amounts of content but also more advanced and complex content (Powell, Farrar, & Cohen, 1985). These increased pressures have surfaced in recent years as a result of the Excellence in Education movement (Spady & Marx, 1984) and the adoption of high-stakes assessment tests (Erickson, Ysseldyke, Thurlow, & Elliott, 1998).

In order to fulfill these aspects of their role, general education teachers must use a variety of routines, devices, and instructional arrangements to promote performance gains by students. Several criteria have been applied by researchers at the KU-CRL when designing and researching teaching routines for use in content-area courses. First, such teaching routines must be straightforward and easy to master in a relatively short time. Second, the routines must be perceived by teachers as practical and easy to use. Third, teachers must be able to teach similar amounts of content through the use of these routines versus having to sacrifice large amounts of their content because they are using the routines. Fourth, the routines must be perceived by teachers as being effective for normal-achieving and high-achieving students, as well as for at-risk students and students with disabilities. Similarly, typically achieving and high-achieving students must perceive the teacher's use of the routines as facilitative, not as "extra baggage" that gets in the way of learning. Fifth, the routines must be sufficiently powerful to improve the performance of students with disabilities and other at-risk learners in required general education classes in which heterogeneous groupings of students are enrolled. Furthermore, their performance must be improved to a level where they are at least passing classes, and hopefully to a level where they can feel good about their progress (i.e., they earn grades of C and above). Finally, the routines must lend themselves to easy integration with current teaching practices.

The routines that have been developed by KU-CRL researchers and associates that fulfill these criteria are called Content Enhancement Routines because they enable teachers to enhance the learning of content by all the students in their classes (Lenz & Bulgren, 1995; Bulgren & Lenz, 1996; also see Schumaker, Deshler, & McKnight, 2002, and Bulgren & Schumaker, 2006, for reviews of the content enhancement interventions not described in detail here). In general, through the use of Content Enhancement Routines, teachers think deeply about the content that students need to learn, organize and manipulate that content in a way that makes the content learner friendly, and deliver that content to students in a way that keeps them active in the learning process and enhances their retention of the content.

The design of the routines is based on several principles, such as the following: (a) students learn more when they are actively involved; (b) students learn abstract content easier if it is presented in concrete form; (c) students learn more information when the structure or organization of that information is presented to them first and when relationships among pieces of information are explicitly taught; (d) students are more likely to learn new information if it is tied to information they already know; and

(e) students learn more important information if that information is distinguished from unimportant information (Deshler, Schumaker, Lenz, et al., 2001).

A total of 16 Content Enhancement Routines have been developed and empirically validated within three categories: *organizing* routines, *understanding* routines, and *recall* routines. Organizing routines are used to show students how the information related to a course is organized and related. Understanding routines are used to teach students about the major concepts and main ideas in a course. Recall routines are used to help students understand and remember important details related to a course.

Organizing Routines

Several organizing routines have been developed. Teachers can use the Course Organizer Routine to introduce a whole course to students and to review progress through the course (Lenz, Schumaker, Deshler, & Bulgren, 1998). They can use the Unit Organizer Routine to introduce and review progress through a unit of study (Lenz, Bulgren, Schumaker, Deshler, & Boudah, 1994). They can use the Lesson Organizer Routine as an advance organizer for a lesson or a small group of lessons within a unit (Lenz, Marrs, Schumaker, & Deshler, 1993).

Indeed, all three of these routines serve as advance organizers, that is, information that is delivered "in advance of and at a higher level of generality, inclusiveness, and abstraction than the learning task itself" (Ausubel & Robinson, 1969, p. 606). The purpose of an advance organizer is to strengthen a student's cognitive structures, which are defined by Ausubel (1963) as the student's knowledge of a given subject matter at a given time with regard to its organization, clarity, and stability. For students with little background knowledge or an inability to organize information so it can be easily retrieved, and for those with poor motivation or inactive learning styles, advance organizers take on special roles. They can serve as vehicles for presenting background knowledge that is required for understanding a lesson, for highlighting organizational patterns about which the students should be aware, for motivating students to learn, and for communicating to students expectations about what they should be doing during instructional activities.

In one of the studies that has been conducted on organizing routines, Lenz, Alley, and Schumaker (1987) designed a Lesson Organizer Routine consisting of 12 components and evaluated its effectiveness in terms of students' learning in general education classrooms. These 12 components can be used to inform the learner about (a) the purpose of the advance organizer for the lesson, (b) the actions to be taken by the teacher and the students during the lesson, (c) the topic and subtopics to be covered in the lesson, (d) background knowledge related to the lesson, (e) concepts to be learned, (f) reasons for learning the information, (g) new vocabulary, (h) organizational frameworks, and (i) desired lesson outcomes.

In the Lenz et al. (1987) study, teachers were trained to design and deliver lesson organizers containing the 12 components in their secondary content classes (e.g., history, English, physical sciences) at the beginning of each class period. The researchers monitored the effects of the routine on students' acquisition of the information presented in the class period by interviewing the students after each class. They found that teachers who used few of the lesson organizer components at the start of their lessons could be trained in less than one hour to use them at mastery levels in the classroom. When students with disabilities were specifically taught to attend to the teacher's use of the routine, the number of relevant statements they made about the content of the lesson after the lesson increased substantially compared with the number of statements they made after lessons when they had not been informed about how to attend to the lesson organizer. A multiple-baseline across–students design showed that the improvement occurred only after students had been instructed to attend to the lesson organizer.

Understanding Routines

The purpose of routines in this category is to deliver information about complex, abstract concepts (e.g., democracy, thesis, equation) in such a way that students' understanding and memory of the information will be enhanced. The Concept Mastery Routine involves teaching students about the basic information related to a major concept using a graphic organizer called the Concept Diagram and interactive discussion (Bulgren et al., 1988; Bulgren et al., 1993). Basic information includes the characteristics that are always, sometimes, and never present in examples of the concept. The Concept Anchoring Routine involves teaching students about a new concept, such as *white blood cell*, by "anchoring" it to or relating it to a concept that they already understand, such as *army* (Bulgren, Deshler, Schumaker, & Lenz, 2000; Bulgren, Schumaker, & Deshler, 1994a; Deshler, Schumaker, Bulgren, et al., 2001). The Concept Comparison Routine involves comparing and contrasting two or more related concepts, such as socialism, capitalism, and communism (Bulgren, Schumaker, Deshler, Lenz, & Marquis, 2002).

Empirical support for the effectiveness of Understanding Routines is exemplified by a study conducted by Bulgren and colleagues (2002), in which 107 students in Grades 7–12 participated. For this study, a Comparison Table, a graphic display showing how two or more concepts are alike and how they are different, was drafted. A counterbalanced design with randomly assigned stratified subgroups of students was used, with a researcher delivering the instruction. In selected classes, a researcher used the Concept Comparison Routine to lead an interactive discussion to help the students create a Comparison Table. The final product of the lesson was a graphic device constructed by the teacher or researcher and students working together. Other classes participated in a traditional lecture or discussion about the same information covered in the graphic device. Thus, the subject-area content was controlled across the classes.

When the Concept Comparison Routine was used, all subgroups of students, including students with SLD and high-, medium-, and low-achieving students, recalled significantly more information on written tests than when it was not used. Students with SLD in the control group earned a mean test score of 57%, whereas students with SLD in the experimental group earned a mean test score of 71%. Other low-achieving students in the control group earned a mean test score of 63%, and low-achieving students in the experimental group earned a mean test score of 86%. Similarly, typically achieving students in the control group earned a mean test score of 76% and in the experimental group earned a mean test score of 84%. Thus, all types of students benefited from the use of the routine, and students with SLD earned passing scores when the routine was used and failing scores when it was not. Large effect sizes were achieved.

Similar positive outcomes have been achieved in other studies as well. For example, Bulgren et al. (2002) conducted a study with 10 secondary subject-area teachers. Through the use of a multiple-baseline design, these researchers showed that teachers could be trained to use the Concept Comparison Routine in their classrooms at mastery levels after 3 hours of training. These results were replicated by Schumaker, Fisher, and Walsh (2009), who also demonstrated that teachers could learn to use the routine at high levels of fidelity through a virtual workshop on a CD-Rom and that the results these teachers achieved with students were equivalent to the results achieved by teachers who delivered live instruction. Students with and without disabilities ($N = 292$) in the classes of both groups of teachers made significant gains on concept tests ($p < .0001$).

Recall Routines

A third category of routines that have been used by general education teachers and that produce gains in the performance of students with learning problems is the recall routines. One of these routines, the Recall Enhancement Routine (Schumaker, Bulgren, Deshler, & Lenz, 1998), has been the focus of two experimental studies. This routine involves the construction of mnemonic devices (i.e., memory tools) by the teacher and students to help the students remember information. For example, if students are required to remember that Joseph Swan developed an early form of the light bulb, they might make a mental picture of a swan holding a light bulb that shines weakly. To use the routine, the teacher cues students that certain information is important to remember and explains why, helps the students construct a mnemonic device for remembering the information, and supervises student review of the information. The first study showed that students with SLD scored significantly higher on content tests when this routine was used as opposed to when it was not used (71% vs. 42%; Bulgren, Schumaker, & Deshler, 1994b). The second study showed that students whose teachers used the routine scored significantly higher on a test that measured their ability to construct mnemonic devices than students of teachers who did not use the routine (Bulgren, Deshler, & Schumaker, 1997).

Integration of Routines

Certainly, additional research is required to further study the usefulness of the notion that general education teachers can enhance the understanding and recall of information by all students, including those with disabilities or who are at risk for failure. Some of the routines need further study in isolation to determine under what conditions they are most effective. Additionally, the effects of the integration of the routines should be studied as well. For example, the Course Organizer Routine might be used to introduce a course, the Unit Organizer Routine might be used to introduce each unit in the course, the Concept Mastery Routine might be used to present information related to a major concept in each unit, the Lesson Organizer Routine might be used to enhance difficult lessons, and the Recall Enhancement Routine might be used to highlight information as it is presented in each lesson. Conceivably, such an integrated sequence might have an even greater effect on students' performance than can be created when the teaching routines are used in isolation.

LEVEL 2: EMBEDDED LEARNING STRATEGY INSTRUCTION

For Level 2 of the CLC model, general education teachers embed learning strategy instruction within their subject-matter instruction. Either they select learning strategies that are particularly pertinent to their courses, or, through cooperative planning with other teachers in their departments and across departments, they select a strategy or strategies within a sequence of strategies that are to be taught to all students at the school.

Learning strategy instruction is instruction in a set of steps or behaviors that students can use to complete a learning task. It has been validated as one of the most effective types of instruction for students with SLD (Swanson, 1999). When provided effectively, learning strategy instruction typically involves (a) describing the strategy, (b) modeling the strategy, (c) giving students opportunities to practice the strategy starting with easy tasks and progressing to more and more difficult ones, (d) requiring mastery, and (e) providing individual feedback to students about their performance (Schumaker & Deshler, 2006).

However, because of the conditions of secondary subject-area classes (i.e., large numbers of students, heterogeneous classes) and the enormous demands associated with covering certain amounts of content (Schumaker, Deshler, Bui, & Vernon, 2006), the implementation of embedded learning strategy instruction in these environments requires the sacrifice of some of these validated methods. For example, individual feedback for every student just is not possible. However, adaptations have been made in learning strategy instruction for these types of classes, and teachers have been successful in promoting the acquisition of learning strategies in these environments.

Empirical investigations provide evidence of improved outcomes when learning strategy instruction is employed in large classes. For example, Faggella-Luby, Schumaker, and Deshler (2007) randomly assigned 79 ninth graders with and without disabilities to six literature classes. The students in the three experimental classes were taught three strategies related to story grammar: (a) self-questioning about story grammar elements as a prereading activity, (b) story structure analysis through creation of a story grammar diagram during reading, and (c) summarizing of the story in writing based on story grammar elements after reading. Students in the three control classes were taught three comprehension skills: (a) the LINCS vocabulary strategy, to use prior to reading (Ellis, 1992); (b) Question–Answer Relationships, to use during reading (Raphael, 1982, 1986); and (c) semantic summary mapping, to use after reading (Englert, Mariage, Garmon, & Tarrant, 1998).

The interventions were embedded within the instruction of a unit consisting of eight short stories. The strategy and skill instruction consisted of five introductory lessons and four additional lessons in which the strategies and skills were taught across a sequence, during which the teacher first described and modeled the strategies and skills in relation to stories, then the teacher conducted guided-practice and cooperative-practice activities in relation to stories, and finally the students practiced independently with stories. The final lesson consisted of review activities. The same teacher taught all six classes.

Students in the experimental classes earned significantly higher scores than students in the control classes on measures of story-structure strategy use, story-structure knowledge, and retention of information about the eight stories. No differences were found related to the gains made by students with and without disabilities in the experimental classes. Thus, this study shows that strategies can be taught in a subject-area class in such a way that student learning of the subject matter of the course is enhanced. Moreover, all types of students can benefit.

Another study conducted by Harris, Schumaker, & Deshler (2009) supports the contention that learning strategies can be learned in general education classes. These researchers conducted a study in nine English classes in which 230 ninth graders were enrolled. Six of the classes were randomly assigned to one of two intervention groups. In one group, students were taught the Word Mapping Strategy (WM, a morphological analysis strategy; Harris, Schumaker, & Deshler, 2008); students in the other group (LV) were taught the LINCS Vocabulary Strategy, a mnemonic strategy (Ellis, 1992). The remaining three intact classes established a baseline comparison for knowledge of targeted words.

The WM and LV strategy groups were taught their targeted strategy in four introductory class periods by the same teacher. The same 20 new vocabulary words were targeted for instruction for both groups. The teacher described and modeled the strategy and involved the students in guided-practice and independent-practice activities using a few example words. In the next three lessons, the students practiced using the strategy in whole-group guided-practice activities for the first 10 targeted words. In the following three lessons, the students practiced using the strategy in pairs for the final 10 targeted words.

Results showed that both the WM and LV groups mastered their targeted strategy; that is, both groups earned mean scores of 87% on a test of strategy use. Both groups also learned the meaning of the targeted vocabulary words, and their scores were significantly higher than the scores of the comparison group. The WM group earned significantly higher scores than the other two groups on a test measuring their ability to predict the meaning of new words. On average, they predicted the meaning of about 50% of the new words presented to them. There were no differences between the posttest scores of the students with and without disabilities in the two strategy groups on the test of word knowledge, showing that students with disabilities were able to learn a vocabulary strategy within the context of a general education class. Again, this study showed that students can learn strategies when the instruction is embedded within a subject-area course (Harris, 2007).

In both of the studies reviewed here, the strategies were relatively simple, the instruction was limited to a few introductory lessons and then a few more days of practice, and the teacher provided primarily group feedback. Some students who were having difficulty were given individual feedback as the teacher circulated through the room, but this was not done systematically or regularly.

LEVEL 3: INTENSIVE LEARNING STRATEGY INSTRUCTION

Level 3 of the CLC model is for students who need more intensive learning strategy instruction than what can take place in subject-area classes. This instruction might focus on strategies that are or are not the target of instruction in those subject-area classes. In the former case, a student might not be mastering a strategy that her English teacher is teaching in class, so the English teacher might refer the student for more intensive instruction. In the latter case, the ninth-grade English teacher might be teaching the entire class a vocabulary strategy, but the student is reading at the sixth-grade level, so the student is also enrolled in an intensive reading comprehension strategy class.

The venues within which intensive strategy instruction can take place vary. Traditionally, learning strategies have been taught in resource room programs across the nation. Since the early 1980s, more than 100,000 special education teachers have learned to teach learning strategies through workshops in their districts and states and in college courses. In some schools, students are enrolled in resource programs that focus on learning strategy instruction as a part of their special education services. Some school districts and even some states (e.g., Florida) have designed required learning strategy courses as a part of their curricula. Some schools have set up special courses focusing on a particular type of strategy, such as reading strategies or writing strategies. Students are enrolled in these courses based on their scores on universally administered tests. Some schools have created before- or after-school programs in which learning strategies are taught using a specially designed instructional methodology, called Strategic Tutoring (Hock, Deshler, & Schumaker, 2000), whereby students acquire learning strategies while they are helped to complete their assignments.

Regardless of the venue, teachers teach the learning strategies contained within the *Learning Strategies Curriculum* using validated instructional methods (Ellis, Deshler, Lenz, Schumaker, & Clark, 1991; Schumaker & Deshler, 2006). These strategies are organized in three groups, according to whether they help students acquire information from written materials; store information in their brains or in notes; or express information on tests, in discussions, or in writing. When learning strategies are taught within Level 3 of the CLC, the teacher–student ratio is low, with students typically taught in small groups. The teacher has extensive training in how to teach the strategies to students who have difficulty learning. The frequency of the instruction is high (e.g., daily), and the duration is longer than can be accommodated in general education classes.

When a strategy is taught intensively, the teacher gives a pretest to determine students' skills, describes and models the strategy, leads students in verbal practice of the strategy steps, and provides many scaffolded practice opportunities for students. Each practice attempt is followed by individual and elaborated feedback (Kline, Schumaker, & Deshler, 1991), and the teacher monitors student progress until the student has mastered the skills. Finally, the teacher teaches the students how to use the strategy in other settings on typical learning tasks that they might encounter in subject-area classes. A modified version of this sequence of instruction occurs within Strategic Tutoring sessions, because the tutor is teaching the student how to complete a current assignment while simultaneously teaching the strategy (Hock et al., 2000).

One evidence-based learning strategy is the Word Identification Strategy, which enables students to decode the multisyllabic words they encounter in secondary content-area classes (Lenz & Hughes, 1990; Lenz, Schumaker, Deshler, & Beals, 1984). Because large numbers of low-achieving students and students with disabilities reach high school reading below grade level and earn scores averaging at the fourth- or fifth-grade level (Warner, Schumaker, Alley, & Deshler, 1980), some schools have created a short-term course for these students to teach them the Word Identification Strategy. For example, at Muskegon High School in Michigan, entering ninth-grade students are tested to determine their decoding skills. Students who score 2 or more years below grade level in decoding skills are enrolled in small groups in a short-term course to learn the strategy for a period of 4 to 8 weeks, depending on each student's progress. They are given credit in their English course for the work they complete in the short reading course.

The results of such courses are promising. When Deshler, Schumaker, and Woodruff (2004) evaluated the effects of this short Muskegon High School course, they found that the strategy course produced strong, positive gains in decoding skills. Their study used a comparison design in which 68 entering ninth graders at Muskegon High were matched to a comparison group of students who had the same level of decoding deficits and who were enrolled at a nearby high school. African American, Hispanic, and Caucasian students; female and male students; and students with and without learning disabilities at Muskegon High all showed similar gains. All of the 68 students in the experimental group at Muskegon High had gained at least one grade level in decoding skills (mean gain = 3.4 grade levels), compared with an average improvement of 0.2 grade levels for the students with whom they were matched.

Numerous studies have been conducted during the past three decades on individual interventions within the Learning Strategies Curriculum with small groups of students with SLD in secondary resource room programs (see Schumaker & Deshler,

2006, for a review). One example is a study conducted by Schmidt, Deshler, Schumaker, and Alley (1988/89), which involved seven students with learning disabilities in Grades 10 through 12, who were taught at least two of four writing strategies: the Sentence Writing Strategy (Schumaker & Sheldon, 1999), the Paragraph Writing Strategy (Schumaker & Lyerla, 1991), the Error Monitoring Strategy (Schumaker, Nolan, & Deshler, 1985), and the Theme Writing Strategy (Schumaker, 2003). For each student, a multiple-baseline across-strategies design was employed to show the effects of instruction in each strategy on assignments written in the special education class and in English and history general education classes before, during, and after instruction and in the following school year.

On all of the products written in the special education classroom immediately following instruction on a given strategy, all of the students exceeded the strategy mastery criteria. When the students' general education writing products were analyzed, the results were mixed. Students generalized their use of the writing strategies to some extent. Although their scores improved, they were not at the same level that they had achieved in their special education classroom. The teachers then used a variety of instructional procedures to promote generalization across classes. By the end of the school year, six of the seven students wrote as well in general education classes as they had in their special education resource room.

At the beginning of the study, the students' grade point average (GPA) was 2.1 in English and social studies courses taught in the resource room by a special education teacher; after strategy instruction, their GPA was 2.7 in English and social studies general education courses. Before the study, none of the students had earned GPAs of 3.0. After the study, four of the students did. On the written language subtest of the Woodcock-Johnson Psychoeducational Battery, the students earned a grade-level score of 6.2 at the beginning of the study and 8.2 at the end of the study. This outcome was higher than the predicted grade-level score of 7.0 based on the students' previous rate of improvement on the Woodcock-Johnson. Students who learned the Theme Writing Strategy performed significantly better on the district's writing competency exam compared to the district's average for all 11th graders (they earned a mean score of 3.5 versus 2.5). Students in the study who did not learn the Theme Writing Strategy earned a mean score of 2.4 on the district exam.

Learning strategy instruction can take place within before- and after-school programs, as well. In fact, learning strategy instruction is an important ingredient in these types of programs, since the outcomes of traditional tutoring programs are poor (e.g., Chicago Public Schools, 2005; Hock, Deshler, & Schumaker, 1999). As mentioned above, a special type of learning strategy instruction, called Strategic Tutoring (Hock, Schumaker, & Deshler, 2000), has been designed for the purpose of teaching students strategies while also helping them complete their current assignments. To do this, the strategic tutor first assesses the assignment to be completed, the student's current success level with that type of task, and the strategy the student is already using for that type of task. For example, the tutor might determine that the student needs to complete a worksheet using information in the textbook and that the student is currently not turning in these types of worksheet assignments. Next, the strategic tutor selects a strategy to be taught or constructs a strategy with the student that includes elements of what the student is already doing. Then the tutor models the strategy while helping the student complete the task. For example, the tutor shows the student how she would read each question focusing on key words in the question, look for a heading or subheading in the text that corresponds to words in the question, skim the section for the answer, and translate the answer into her own words while writing it on the worksheet. Next, the tutor has the student practice using the strategy and provides feedback on each attempt to answer a question.

Over time and over the course of several additional similar assignments, the tutor fades out support and feedback until the student becomes independent in completing the task. The same student may receive other types of assignments, and similar procedures are used by the tutor to teach the student strategic ways to approach those tasks as well. As a result, the student not only completes assignments but also learns a process for completing similar assignments independently in the future.

Again, empirical studies provide evidence of effectiveness for Strategic Tutoring. In one study by Hock (1998), Strategic Tutoring was used to teach 28 underprepared student athletes enrolled in English 101 college courses to use the Theme Writing Strategy to complete their essay-writing assignments. These students had earned average scores of 17.7 on the ACT college admissions test and a mean grade point average of 2.8 in high school. Their grades at the end of the college English course were compared to the grades of 28 other student athletes who had earned average scores of 28.2 on the ACT, had a mean grade point average of 3.3 in high school, and who received traditional tutoring in the same English 101 course. Hock found that the students who received Strategic Tutoring earned an average English grade of 2.5, versus an average English grade of 2.6 earned by the comparison students. Moreover, the grade point average for their first freshman semester for the Strategic Tutoring group was 2.50 and for the comparison group was 2.54. Thus, the underprepared students who received Strategic Tutoring earned grades similar to those of a group of students who were more adequately prepared for college.

In a second research effort, Hock, Pulvers, Deshler, and Schumaker (2001) employed a multiple-baseline across-students design in two studies with nine junior-high students to evaluate the effects of Strategic Tutoring on the students' class test scores and report-card grades in general education math and biology courses. They found that the students learned the strategies they were taught, and also important, their test scores and grades improved substantially. For example, on average, before Strategic Tutoring, the three students in the first study were earning average algebra test scores during baseline of 46%, 54%, and 59%; after strategic tutoring, they earned average test scores of 70%, 86%, and 87%, respectively.

Finally, Lancaster and Lancaster (2006) conducted a study with 14 strategic tutors and 14 traditional tutors who were each randomly assigned one student with SLD. Strategic tutors taught their assigned students a strategy for paraphrasing textbook content while helping them complete their assignments. Traditional tutors only helped the students to do their assignments. At the end of the study, the posttest scores of the two groups of students on a strategy knowledge test and a strategy use test were significantly different, with large effect sizes in both cases in favor of the students who had received Strategic Tutoring.

LEVEL 4: INTENSIVE BASIC SKILLS INSTRUCTION

Students are referred to Level 4 interventions if they have large deficits in basic skills. Typically, they are reading below the third-grade level. These students often do not have the skills needed to benefit from learning strategy instruction and from participation in the secondary general education curriculum. For example, they might be decoding words at the first- or second-grade level, and as a result, do not have the prerequisite skills needed for instruction in the Word Identification Strategy or any of the reading comprehension strategies. Students typically need to be reading at the fourth-grade level to benefit from this instruction. Thus, students with severe skill deficits need to be identified as they enter the secondary program and immediately enrolled in interventions in which they can learn the needed skills quickly.

Example Level 4 interventions that have been used in schools include the SRA Corrective Reading Series and the SRA Corrective Math Series (Adams & Engelmann, 1996; Borman, Hewes, Overman, & Brown, 2003). For these programs, students are assigned to small classes for daily instruction, and their progress is monitored each day.

LEVEL 5: CLINICAL INTERVENTIONS

Level 5 is designed for those students who have not mastered the underlying language competencies that enable them to effectively process text or express information orally. They often are identified as having a specific disability or a unique manner of processing information. The skills required to meet the needs of these students generally are possessed by professionals such as speech-language pathologists and reading specialists. These professionals can work individually with students and with their teachers to ensure that their work is directly tied to the information that students are expected to learn in their general education courses. For example, a speech-language pathologist can work with a student individually to help her learn how to "talk through" and explain a Unit Organizer or a Concept Diagram. In this way, the student can learn not only language skills but also the content of the subject-area course.

OTHER IMPORTANT FACTORS FOR IMPROVING ACADEMIC OUTCOMES

The preceding sections of this chapter have addressed one of the most essential factors for improving student achievement: a well-designed, coordinated framework within which evidence-based interventions can be embedded. This framework, called the Content Literacy Continuum (CLC), might be thought of as the centerpiece of a school's instructional core. Other components of the instructional core that need to be developed and cultivated on an ongoing basis would be (a) motivational and behavioral supports to promote a school culture of orderliness and self-directed productivity (e.g., Sprick, 2008); (b) formative assessments to guide instructional decision making, including moving students within and across tiers; and (c) an array of engaging and diverse materials to provide students ample opportunities to practice targeted strategies and to build vocabulary and background knowledge.

Instruction that is scaffolded and coordinated across teachers and settings is found in those secondary schools that have in place a critical set of infrastructure supports (e.g., Coyne, Kame'enui, & Carnine, 2007; Lenz, Deshler, & Kissam, 2003.) The purpose of these supports is to provide the necessary conditions that will allow effective instruction to take root and be sustained over time. Important components of the infrastructure support system in secondary schools include a system of instructional coaching (Knight, 2007) that provides job-embedded professional development, flexible course scheduling options that enable students to move among the various instructional tiers, a mechanism for ongoing teacher planning that enables teachers to coordinate and reinforce key points of learning across classes, a system that works toward curriculum coherence and logic from both a knowledge and a skill-acquisition standpoint, and a literacy leadership team made up of key teachers and administrators who assume responsibility through a distributed leadership model for overseeing and driving literacy improvement efforts within the school.

Finally, undertaking efforts to improve student achievement in secondary schools is very difficult. It requires a long-term vision, hard work, strong leadership, and a commitment to the continuous growth and improvement of individual professionals and the school staff as a whole. According to Elmore (2004), continuous growth takes place when the school's leadership team creates the kinds of conditions that enable them to practice key leadership behaviors, such as the following: organizing work around important instructional activities and supervising that work; observing, describing, and analyzing instructional practice; creating and using internal accountability mechanisms; and building a common language and set of expectations. Additionally, Elmore contends that continuous growth is dependent on teachers practicing key instructional behaviors, including these behaviors: observing models of practice; developing protocols for observing practice; focusing on observing, describing, and analyzing instructional practice; and building a common language and set of expectations.

SUMMARY

In summary, empirical evidence supports the notion that the academic performance of students who are at risk for failure in today's secondary schools can be improved through the use of instructional methods that are embedded throughout the curriculum. Specifically, Content Enhancement Routines can be used in general education courses to improve the level of performance of all of the students enrolled in these courses, much like a rising tide raises the level of all of the boats. Learning strategies can be taught in intensive and less intensive ways to ensure that students have the necessary skills to complete learning tasks in their courses. Additionally, students who need specialized instruction in basic skills and other areas can be provided with that instruction. By coordinating these methods across teachers and departments through the use of a tiered framework like the CLC, a great deal can be accomplished with regard to creating positive outcomes for at-risk students.

REFERENCES

Adams, G., & Engelmann, S. (1996). *Research on direct instruction: 25 years beyond DISTAR.* Seattle, WA: Educational Achievement Systems.

Ausubel, D. P. (1963). *The psychology of meaningful verbal learning.* New York: Grune & Stratton.

Ausubel, D. P., & Robinson, F. G. (1969). *School learning: An introduction to educational psychology.* New York: Holt, Rinehart & Winston.

Borman, G. D., Hewes, G. M., Overman, L. T., & Brown, S. (2003). Comprehensive school reform and achievement: A meta-analysis. *Review of Educational Research, 73*(2), 125–230.

Bulgren, J. A., Deshler, D. D., & Schumaker, J. B. (1993). *The Concept Mastery Routine: Instructor's manual.* Lawrence, KS: Edge Enterprises.

Bulgren, J. A., Deshler, D. D., & Schumaker, J. B. (1997). Use of a recall enhancement routine and strategies in inclusive secondary classes. *Learning Disabilities Research and Practice, 12*(4), 198–208.

Bulgren, J. A., Deshler, D. D., Schumaker, J. B., & Lenz, B. K. (2000). The use and effectiveness of analogical instruction in diverse secondary content classrooms. *Journal of Educational Psychology, 92,* 426–441.

Bulgren, J. A., & Lenz, B. K. (1996). Strategic instruction in the content areas. In D. D. Deshler, E. S. Ellis, & B. K. Lenz (Eds.), *Teaching Adolescents with Learning Disabilities: Strategies and Methods.* (2nd ed., pp. 409–473). Denver, CO: Love Publishing.

Bulgren, J. A., & Schumaker, J. B. (2006). Teaching practices that optimize curriculum access. In D. D. Deshler & J. B. Schumaker (Eds.), *High school students with disabilities: Strategies for accessing the curriculum* (pp. 79–120). Thousand Oaks, CA: Corwin Press.

Bulgren, J., Schumaker, J. B., & Deshler, D. D. (1988). Effectiveness of a concept teaching routine in enhancing the performance of LD students in secondary-level mainstream classes. *Learning Disability Quarterly, 11*(1), 3–17.

Bulgren, J. A., Schumaker, J. B. & Deshler, D. D. (1994a). *The Concept Anchoring Routine: Instructor's manual.* Lawrence, KS: Edge Enterprises.

Bulgren, J. A., Schumaker, J. B., & Deshler, D. D. (1994b). The effects of a recall enhancement routine on the test performance of secondary students with and without learning disabilities. *Learning Disabilities Research and Practice, 9*(1), 2–11.

Bulgren, J. A., Schumaker, J. B., Deshler, D. D., Lenz, B. K., & Marquis, J. (2002). The use and effectiveness of a comparison routine in diverse secondary content classes. *Journal of Educational Psychology, 94,* 357–371.

Chicago Public Schools. (2005). *SES Tutoring Programs: An evaluation of the second year—Part one of a two-part report.* Chicago: Office of Research, Evaluation and Accountability, Chicago Public Schools.

Coyne, M. D., Kame'enui, E. J., & Carnine, D. W. (2007). *Effective teaching strategies that accommodate diverse learners* (3rd ed.). Upper Saddle River, NJ: Pearson/Merrill Prentice Hall.

Deshler, D. D., Palincsar, A. S., Biancarosa, G., & Nair, M. (2007). *Informed choices: Principles and programs for adolescent literacy.* Newark, DE: International Reading Association.

Deshler, D. D. & Schumaker, J. B. (1988). An instructional model for teaching students how to learn. In J. L. Graden, J. E. Zins, & M. L. Curtis (Eds.), *Alternative education delivery systems: Enhancing instructional options for all students* (pp. 391–411). Washington, DC: National Association of School Psychologists.

Deshler, D. D., & Schumaker, J. B. (2006). *High school students with disabilities: Strategies for accessing the curriculum.* Thousand Oaks, CA: Corwin Press.

Deshler, D. D. Schumaker, J. B., Bulgren, J. A., Lenz, B. K., Jantzen, J. E., Adams, G., et al. (2001). Making learning easier: Connecting new knowledge to things students already know. *Teaching Exceptional Children, 33*(4), 82–85.

Deshler, D. D., Schumaker, J. B., Lenz, B. K., Bulgren, J. A., Hock, M. F., Knight, J., et al. (2001). Ensuring content-area learning by secondary students with learning disabilities. *Learning Disabilities Research and Practice, 16*(2), 96–108.

Deshler, D. D., Schumaker, J. B., & Woodruff, S. (2004). Improving literacy skills of at-risk adolescents: A school-wide response. In D. S. Strickland & D. E. Alvermann (Eds.), *Bridging the literacy achievement gap: Grades 4–12.* New York: Teachers College Press.

Duffy, H. (2007). *Meeting the needs of significantly struggling learners in high school: A look at approaches to tiered interventions.* Washington, DC: National High School Center.

Ellis, E. S. (1992). *The vocabulary strategy: LINCS.* Lawrence, KS: Edge Enterprises.

Ellis, E. S., Deshler, D. D., Lenz, B. K., Schumaker, J. B., & Clark, F. L. (1991). An instructional model for teaching learning strategies. *Focus on Exceptional Children, 23*(6), 1–24.

Elmore, R. (2004). *School reform from the inside out.* Cambridge, MA: Harvard University Press.

Englert, C. S., Mariage, T. V., Garmon, M. A., & Tarrant, K. L. (1998). Accelerating reading progress in early literacy project classrooms: Three exploratory studies. *Remedial and Special Education, 19,* 142–159.

Erickson, R. N., Ysseldyke, J. E., Thurlow, M. L., & Elliott, J. L. (1998). Inclusive assessment and accountability systems: Tools of the trade in educational reform. *Teaching Exceptional Children, 31*(2), 4–9.

Faggella-Luby, M. N., Schumaker, J. B., & Deshler, D. D. (2007). Embedded learning strategy instruction: Story-structure pedagogy in heterogeneous secondary literature classes. *Learning Disability Quarterly, 30,* 131–147.

Harris, M. L., Schumaker, J. B., & Deshler, D. D. (2008). *The Word Mapping Strategy: Instructor's manual.* Lawrence, KS: Edge Enterprises.

Harris, M. (2007). *Effects of strategic morphological analysis instruction on the vocabulary performance of secondary students with and without learning disabilities.* Unpublished doctoral dissertation. Lawrence, KS: University of Kansas.

Hock, M. F. (1998). *The effectiveness of an instructional tutoring model and tutor training on the academic performance of underprepared college student athletes.* Unpublished doctoral dissertation. Lawrence, KS: University of Kansas.

Hock, M. F., Deshler, D. D., & Schumaker, J. B. (1993). Learning strategy instruction for at-risk and learning disabled adults: The development of strategic learners through apprenticeship. *Preventing School Failure, 38*(1), 43–49.

Hock, M. F., Deshler, D. D., & Schumaker, J. B. (1999). Tutoring programs for academically underprepared college students: A review of the literature. *Journal of College Reading and Learning, 29*(2), 101–122.

Hock, M. F., Deshler, D. D., & Schumaker, J. B. (2000). *Strategic Tutoring.* Lawrence, KS: Edge Enterprises.

Hock, M. F., Pulvers, K. A., Deshler, D. D., & Schumaker, J. B. (2001). The effects of an after-school tutoring program on the academic performance of at-risk and students with learning disabilities. *Remedial and Special Education, 22,* 172–186.

Hock, M. F., Schumaker, J. B., & Deshler, D. D. (1999). Closing the gap to success in secondary schools: A model for cognitive apprenticeship. In D. D. Deshler, J. B. Schumaker, K. R. Harris, & S. Graham (Eds.), *Teaching every adolescent every day: Learning in diverse schools and classrooms* (pp. 1–52). Cambridge, MA: Brookline.

Kamil, M. L. (2003). *Adolescents and literacy: Reading for the 21st century.* Washington, DC: Alliance for Excellent Education.

Kline, F. M., Schumaker, J. B., & Deshler, D. D. (1991). Development and validation of feedback routines for instructing students with learning disabilities. *Learning Disability Quarterly, 14,* 191–207.

Knight, J. (2007). *Instructional coaching: A partnership approach to improving instruction.* New York: Corwin Press.

Lenz, B. K., Alley, G. R., & Schumaker, J. B. (1987). Activating the inactive learner through the presentation of advance organizers. *Learning Disability Quarterly, 10,* 53–67.

Lenz, B. K., & Bulgren, J. A. (1995). Promoting learning in content classes. In P. T. Cegelka & W. H. Berdine (Eds.), *Effective instruction for students with learning disabilities* (pp. 385–417). Boston: Allyn and Bacon.

Lenz, B. K., Bulgren, J. A., Schumaker, J. B., Deshler, D. D., & Boudah, D. A. (1994). *The Unit Organizer Routine.* Lawrence, KS: Edge Enterprises.

Lenz, B. K., Deshler, D. D., & Kissam, B. R. (2003). *Teaching content to all: Evidence-based inclusive practices in middle and secondary schools.* Boston: Allyn & Bacon.

Lenz, B. K., Ehren, B. J., Deshler, D. D. (2005). The Content Literacy Continuum: A school-reform framework for improving adolescent literacy for all students. *Teaching Exceptional Children, 37*(6), 60–63.

Lenz, B. K., & Hughes, C. A. (1990). A word identification strategy for adolescents with disabilities. *Journal of Learning Disabilities, 23*(3), *149*–158, 163.

Lenz, B. K., Marrs, R. W., Schumaker, J. B., & Deshler, D. D. (1993). *The Lesson Organizer Routine.* Lawrence, KS: Edge Enterprises.

Lenz, B. K., Schumaker, J. B., Deshler, D. D., & Beals, V. L. (1984). *The Word Identification Strategy: Instructor's manual.* Lawrence, KS: University of Kansas Center for Research on Learning.

Lenz, B. K., with Schumaker, J. B., Deshler, D. D., & Bulgren, J. A. (1998). *The Course Organizer Routine.* Lawrence, KS: Edge Enterprises.

McPeak, L. & Trygg, L. (2007). *The secondary literacy instruction and intervention guide: Helping school districts transform into systems that produce life-changing results for all children.* Mill Valley, CA: The Stupski Foundation.

National Academy of Sciences. (2006). *Rising above the gathering storm: Energizing and employing America for a brighter economic future.* Washington, DC: Author.

National Center for Education Statistics. (2005). *Mapping 2005 state proficiency standards onto the NAEP scales* (NCES Report 2007–482). Washington, DC: U.S. Government Printing Office.

Powell, A. G., Farrar, E., & Cohen, D. K. (1985). *The shopping mall high school: Winners and losers in the educational marketplace.* Boston: Houghton Mifflin.

Raphael, T. (1982). Question-answering strategies for children. *Reading Teacher, 36,* 186–190.

Raphael, T. (1986). Teaching question-answer relationships, revisited. *Reading Teacher, 39,* 516–522.

Schmidt, J. L., Deshler, D. D., Schumaker, J. B., & Alley, G. R. (1988/89). Effects of generalization instruction on the written language performance of adolescents with learning disabilities in the mainstream classroom. *Reading, Writing, and Learning Disabilities, 4*(4), 291–309.

Schumaker, J. B. (2003). *The Theme Writing Strategy: Instructor's manual.* Lawrence, KS: Edge Enterprises.

Schumaker, J. B., Bulgren, J. A., Deshler, D. D., & Lenz, B. K. (1998). *The Recall Enhancement Routine.* Lawrence, KS: University of Kansas Center for Research on Learning.

Schumaker, J. B., & Deshler, D. D. (2006). Teaching adolescents to be strategic learners. In D. D. Deshler & J. B. Schumaker (Eds.), *Teaching adolescents with disabilities: Accessing the general education curriculum* (pp. 121–156). New York: Corwin Press.

Schumaker, J. B., Deshler, D. D., Bui, Y., & Vernon, S. (2006). High schools and adolescents with disabilities: Challenges at every turn. In D. D. Deshler & J. B. Schumaker (Eds.), *Teaching adolescents with disabilities: Accessing the general education curriculum* (pp. 1–34). New York: Corwin Press.

Schumaker, J. B., Deshler, D. D., & McKnight, P. (2002). Ensuring success in the secondary general education curriculum through the use of teaching routines. In M. R. Shinn, H. M. Walker, & G. Stoner (Eds.), *Interventions for achievement and behavior problems II: Preventive and remedial approaches* (pp. 791–824). Bethesda, MD: National Association of School Psychologists.

Schumaker, J. B., Fisher, J., & Walsh, L. (2009). *The effects of e-learning on teachers' knowledge and behavior and students' resulting knowledge of concepts.* Unpublished manuscript. Lawrence, KS: Edge Enterprises.

Schumaker, J. B., & Lyerla, K. D. (1991). *The Paragraph Writing Strategy: Instructor's manual.* Lawrence, KS: University of Kansas Institute for Research in Learning Disabilities.

Schumaker, J. B., Nolan, S. M., & Deshler, D. D. (1985). *The Error Monitoring Strategy: Instructor's manual.* Lawrence, KS: University of Kansas Institute for Research in Learning Disabilities.

Schumaker, J. B., & Sheldon, J. A. (1999). *Proficiency in the Sentence Writing Strategy: Instructor's manual.* Lawrence, KS: University of Kansas Center for Research on Learning.

Spady, W. G., & Marx, G. (1984). *Excellence in our schools: Making it happen.* San Francisco: Far West Laboratory.

Sprick, R. S. (2008). *Discipline in the secondary classroom* (2nd ed.). San Francisco: Jossey-Bass.

Sugai, G. (2007, December). *RTI: Reasons, practices, systems, and considerations.* Keynote speech delivered at the RTI Summit sponsored by the Office of Special Education Programs, Washington, DC.

Swanson, H. L. (1999). Instructional components that predict treatment outcomes for students with learning disabilities: Support for a combined strategy and direct instruction model. *Learning Disabilities Research and Practice, 14*(3), 129–140.

Wagner, M., Newman, L., Cameto, R., & Levine, P. (2006). The academic achievement and functional performance of youth with disabilities: A report from the national longitudinal transition study-2. Berkeley, CA: SRI International.

Warner, M. M., Schumaker, J. B., Alley, G. R., & Deshler, D. D. (1980). Learning disabled adolescents in the public schools: Are they different from other low achievers? *Exceptional Education Quarterly, 1*(2), 27–35. Reprinted in the *Mainstreamed Library: Issues, Ideas, Innovations* (American Library Association), 1982.

CHAPTER 24

Peer Teaching Interventions for Multiple Levels of Support

Charles R. Greenwood
Karen Seals
Debra Kamps
Juniper Gardens Children's Project, University of Kansas

INTRODUCTION

In 1991, when this chapter was first published, peer teaching methods for academic instruction, such as Classwide Peer Tutoring (CWPT) and Peer-Assisted Learning Strategies (PALS), were described as promising new techniques (Greenwood, Maheady, & Carta, 1991). Ten years later, they had become evidence-based practices as a result of the findings of several key experimental studies. Now, almost 20 years later, research syntheses have summarized the numerous experimental studies describing peer methods of instruction and their effects on student learning outcomes (Rohrbeck, Ginsberg-Block, Fantuzzo, & Miller, 2003). Effect sizes reported for these methods have averaged in the moderate range for academic outcomes (Rohrbeck et al., 2003) and large range for enabling behavior classroom measures such as engagement in academic responding (Greenwood, Kamps, Terry, & Linebarger, 2006). Today, CWPT, among other peer teaching methods such as Kindergarten PALS (K-PALS), are cited in the U.S. Department of Education's What Works Clearinghouse website as promising and effective practices based on rigorous empirical evidence (see appendix). However, there are still areas in need of research, including peer teaching with English language learners (ELLs) and applications in both secondary and higher education, to name just three.

In the majority of these studies and syntheses, CWPT or PALS was used in elementary general education classrooms to strengthen the effectiveness of the general education reading or math curriculum provided for all students, including students with disabilities. Additionally, many of these studies took place in inner-city, Title 1 schools in which low-socioeconomic-status students were the majority of the population (often greater than 50%, but ranging up to 75%). The effectiveness of

CWPT and of PALS, which was based on the CWPT framework, within these settings yielded early glimpses of its potential utility for addressing learning needs of students with delays and disabilities in general education settings. Many studies of CWPT in the past two decades were funded by the Office of Special Education Programs of the U.S. Department of Education. The objective was to rigorously test the hypothesized, potentially strong benefit to students with learning disabilities and other disabilities. As described later in this chapter, using peer teaching to differentiate Tier 1 instruction for all students has been shown to benefit both struggling learners as well as students with disabilities in the general education curricula (Greenwood et al., 2006). Research also has shown that peer tutors benefit in terms of increased achievement because of having taught others (Elbaum, Vaughn, Hughes, & Moody, 2000).

While fewer applications are reported in the secondary school literature, peer teaching methods have been shown to be effective in middle and high school. Stenhoff and Lignugaris-Kraft (2007) reported that peer teaching was moderately effective at improving the academic performance of students with disabilities based on the synthesis of 20 group and single case experimental studies. Outcomes in these studies included reading and math measures, as well as content subject matter knowledge, as measured by chapter and unit tests, among others (e.g., science vocabulary learned). They also noted that better outcomes were obtained in programs in which the tutors were trained to tutor compared with those who were not. Finally, research has shown that peer tutoring methods are capable of improving social and language outcomes of students who have increased opportunities to learn and communicate with others (Ginsberg-Block, Rohrbeck, & Fantuzzo, 2006).

Historically, peer tutoring methods have had wide use in schools because of their feasibility, relatively low cost, and acceptability to learners, peer teachers, and classroom teachers (Allen, 1976; Topping & Ehly, 1998). In a wide range of instances in which resources are limited, such as one-room schools and locations in the United States with few qualified teachers, as well as in developing countries seeking to establish formal schooling for their children and youth, peer teaching is a feasible approach to educating a large number of learners. Evidence now supports its effectiveness.

To many, peer tutoring is simply having one student informally tutor another student with the presumption that the tutor has a higher level of skill or knowledge that qualifies him or her to teach others who lack the same skill or knowledge. To others, peer tutoring is synonymous with "peer pairing." Simply put, advanced learners are the teachers of younger, same age, or less-skilled students. Tutors are left to their own devices with respect to how they teach and interact with their student tutee. This informal view of peer tutoring requires only knowing who should tutor another, then scheduling it.

We use the terms *peer tutoring* and *peer teaching* synonymously to refer to the fact that a student–peer is serving in some of the roles of the teacher or instructor. Aspects of these roles include presenting learning tasks, modeling correct responding, observing and charting tutee progress, and providing correction and feedback. In peer teaching, students are taught by their peers, who are *trained* and *supervised* by the classroom teacher. These peers may be the same age or cross age (e.g., younger or older than the tutee) and at different skill levels (e.g., higher, same, or lower than the tutee), and with or without a disability.

Although systematic forms of peer tutoring such as evidence-based CWPT or PALS often include variations in peer pairing strategies, they differ in many other respects as well. Systematic peer tutoring practices typically are exacting in the specific procedures and materials used, and in most cases, tutors and tutees are taught how to carry out their roles. Some of the differences include the use of curriculum materials specifically designed for evidence-based peer teaching, specific roles for both tutors and tutees to guide their responding to ensure correct item presentation, written and oral responding of the tutor, and feedback from the tutor regarding accuracy, and practicing correct responding following an error, etc. Commercially available training, tutoring materials, and software can be used for some of these procedures, and do not have to be developed from scratch (see appendix). Also, it is not uncommon in some forms of tutoring for students who are equally skilled to function in both tutor and tutee roles by trading roles during tutoring sessions.

Whereas in earlier years peer tutoring was just a promising intervention, it now has the potential to be part of a system that differentiates instruction as a part of the multiple tiers of support. This chapter is designed to spark a discussion of peer teaching methods with respect to how they might be used to support the three tiers of instruction. Though peer tutoring strategies are increasingly evidence based in general education core curriculum, the potential of peer tutoring in the delivery of Tier 2 and Tier 3 levels of instruction has less empirical support, and more research and development are needed in the next decade to address these applications.

In this chapter, we first describe the application of peer tutoring as a means of strengthening the effectiveness of Tier 1 instruction. Next, we review specific peer tutoring practices and the evidence supporting those practices within each tier, followed by an examination of constraints and design factors related to the implementation of Tier 2 and Tier 3 peer tutoring services. For example, should peer tutoring be considered a primary method of delivering Tier 2 and Tier 3 services, or is it best used as a supplement to boost effectiveness of teacher-led or other forms of small-group or one-on-one instruction? Following that discussion we consider the knowledge and training school psychologists need to implement these programs and train others to implement them. We conclude with a discussion of implications for both general and special education.

ADVANTAGES OF PEER TEACHING, COMPARED WITH TEACHER-LED INSTRUCTION

The relative advantages of peer tutoring reported in the literature, versus traditional whole-class, teacher-led instruction, are profiled in Table 1. As can be seen, peer tutoring can be viewed as superior to teacher-led instruction across 14 factors, ranging

Table 1. Comparison of Teacher–Led Instruction Versus Peer Tutoring

	Instructor	
Factors	**Teacher**	**Peer**
Advantages		
Pupil–teacher ratio	High	Low
Engaged time	Variable	High
Opportunities to respond	Low	High
Opportunities for error correction	Low	High
Immediacy of error correction	Delayed	Immediate
Opportunities for help and encouragement	Few	Many
Opportunities for both competitive and cooperative learning experiences	Few	Many
Motivation	Teacher	Teacher and peer
Learn to teach others	No	Yes
Learn peer social skills	No	Yes
Increased engagement	No	Yes
Skill mastery	Good	Better
Achievement test results	Good	Better
Reading fluency	Good	Better
Disadvantages		
Tutor training requirements	Few	Many
Quality control requirement	Few	Many
Content coverage	Good	Variable
Tutor selection	None	Required
Curriculum adaptations	Few	Many
Costs	Low	High
Ethical concerns	Few	Increased

Note. From C. R. Greenwood, J. J. Carta, & D. Kamps. (1990). "Teacher- Versus Peer-Mediated Instruction. A Review of Educational Advantages and Disadvantages." In H. Foot, M. Morgan, & R. Shute (Eds.), *Children Helping Children* (p. 191). Chichester, U.K.: Wiley. Adapted with permission.

from pupil–teacher ratio to reading fluency. The advantages reflect many aspects of instruction known to promote and accelerate learning. For example, teachers can arrange one peer teacher for every student, a pupil–teacher ratio of 1:1, using peer tutoring for a portion of daily instructional time (King-Sears & Cummings, 1996). Research reports comparing peer tutoring to teacher-led instruction indicated that with peer tutoring students are more engaged; are afforded more opportunities to respond to the curriculum; receive more frequent error correction, help, and encouragement; and experience both competitive and cooperative learning (Greenwood, 1991; Simmons, Fuchs, Fuchs, Hodge, & Mathes, 1994). Because of a range of possible reward structures and contingencies of reinforcement, students in peer tutoring, compared with teacher-led instruction, are more motivated by and satisfied with their experiences (Kohler & Greenwood, 1986, 1990). Compared with traditional instruction, students using peer tutoring learn the social skills necessary to teach others (Strayhorn, Strain, & Walker, 1993). Research comparisons report that peer tutoring promotes consistently greater learning across a range of subject matter and ages of students (Greenwood, 1996).

With respect to the seven disadvantages, ranging from training requirements through ethical concerns, peer tutoring was rated behind teacher-led instruction. The disadvantages compared with traditional instruction reflect an increased cost in time and effort to establish and sustain peer tutoring programs. Teachers and peer tutors need to be trained, and the quality of the students' tutoring needs to be monitored, both of which add to the level of effort. If planning steps are not carefully undertaken to integrate peer tutoring instruction with the existing curriculum, what is taught in peer tutoring may be misaligned with mandated goals and standardized tests. An increasing number of "out of the box" curricula are now ready made for use by peer tutors (see appendix). However, curriculum adaptations may be needed, depending on specific contexts, particularly in a build-your-own program or a context in which peer teaching is being integrated with and supporting an existing curriculum. Thus, start-up costs of peer tutoring programs might initially be higher than for teacher-led instruction, given issues like extra planning time, teacher training, material development, and monitoring of implementation. However, once under way, costs may approach levels that are similar or possibly less than those of teacher-led programs (Armstrong, Conlon, Pierson, & Stahlbrand, 1979).

To address questions and ethical concerns regarding the effectiveness of peer tutoring programs as a replacement for teacher-led instruction, coordinators and teachers need to adequately address up front the decision to use the approach. First, schools should use only peer tutoring programs with an evidence base. Second, parents and other consumers need to know that peer tutoring is an evidence-based practice and that tutors and tutees have been shown to benefit from participating in peer tutoring programs. Third, parents and other consumers need to be informed about how peer tutoring programs will be monitored by the teacher for fidelity of implementation and for students' progress in learning the subject matter taught. Only with this knowledge is peer tutoring defensible as a substitute for the provision of instruction directly by the classroom teacher.

DESIGN ASPECTS OF PEER TUTORING PROGRAMS

Effective peer tutoring programs vary across a number of design factors that affect utility, scale, outcomes, sustainability, and participant satisfaction. Among these factors are (a) ways of overcoming tutor obsolescence; (b) decisions about who may tutor whom, (c) informal versus structured and explicit instructional procedures; (d) tutoring arrangements, such as pairs, triads, or teams; (e) contingencies, rewards, and consequences; (f) specially designed materials and tasks, and implications for training; (g) indirect benefits of peer tutoring; and (h) progress monitoring.

Ways of Overcoming Tutor Obsolescence

All tutoring programs must address the fact that any single tutor–tutee partnership becomes "obsolete" as soon as the tutee has mastered the skills the tutor originally was assigned to teach. This problem is particularly true of informal programs that depend solely on the superior knowledge of the peer tutor as the key ingredient affecting tutee progress, and relatively less on materials, evidence-based curricula, and explicit peer teaching procedures and training for tutors and tutees. A traditional design point in informal peer tutoring programs is achieving a "good fit" between a tutor and tutee. In informal applications, it is commonly believed that all that is required is (a) a tutor with the knowledge needed (cross-ability or cross-skill-level matching), and (b) a matching and rematching process for tutors and tutees when obsolescence is reached.

Informal programs are also largely incidental; that is, they are used temporarily to meet one or two students' needs when the teacher or other teaching staff are unable to provide this instruction. When used temporarily, higher-skilled tutors for these students will always be in good supply. Tutor obsolescence has frequently limited the duration and scale of peer tutoring to just a handful of students in one classroom for only a few weeks. Thus, informal peer tutoring has always been considered a patch, to be used only in those few cases in which a student needed to catch up and be ready to learn using conventional instructional methods. However, when used as a systematic approach to instruction, programs that pair students solely based on cross-skill or cross-ability matching are ill-founded, because the supply of higher-skilled tutors needed in any one classroom will often be less than needed for all students. The teacher's workload associated with continually assessing and reassigning well-matched, cross-skill pairs is too high.

We know now that obsolescence may be eliminated using instructional strategies that *anticipate* and *overcome* it. For example, different strategies for pairing partners may be used, some based on cross-skill pairings and others based on random pairing. Other strategies provide tutors with materials that help them give accurate error corrections (so they do not have to rely on memory alone) and regularly refresh the content to be taught during each session. Another procedure is to introduce both tutors and tutees to new material by calling on their background knowledge and by providing examples and rehearsals prior to tutoring sessions. These and other strategies discussed below help overcome obsolescence and promote content coverage, scale, and sustainability of use.

Decisions About Who May Tutor Whom

Conventional wisdom is that the ideal tutor is the student who has both the social and academic skills necessary to tutor and who needs a minimum amount of training, teacher planning, and teacher assistance. In school-wide programs, this goal is often achieved by assigning upper-grade students to tutor lower-grade students (cross-age and cross-grade tutoring). In any one classroom or grade level within a school, the number of higher-skilled tutors is always in short supply. One of the systematic means of ability (or skill-level) matching is the "rank and divide" approach. The teacher first rank orders the class (or grade level) from highest to lowest based on the skills to be taught. Second, matching occurs by identifying the student who is one below the middle of the class and aligning the lower half of the list to the higher half of the list.

Given that students are in rank order, this matching ensures that all or nearly all students are taught by a higher-skilled tutor. As often happens in classrooms, because of an odd number of students or daily absences, there is nearly always one student lacking a tutor, or vice versa. In this case, a triad can be formed. In this approach, tutors have been upper-grade or higher-skilled students who spend a portion of the day working one on one with students who are lower skilled, in a lower grade, or in a self-contained, special education classroom (e.g., Jenkins & Jenkins, 1985).

However, additional methods of peer pairing have been shown to be both feasible and effective. For example, we know that peer pairs with equal or unmatched academic skills are able to provide effective tutoring services given specific procedures, training, materials, monitoring, and support. CWPT is a case in point. In this class-wide approach, tutor–tutee pairs may be formed randomly each week. Students form their own partner pairs by drawing names from a box. Each student serves as the tutor for half the session, and then the students switch roles in the second half. This style of peer tutoring is called *reciprocal* peer tutoring. These partners, when provided with answer sheets and assistance from the teacher, are able to provide relatively accurate tutoring and corrective feedback when serving in the tutor's role.

Random pairing of students each week in CWPT has additional advantages. The weekly reconfiguration of pairs reduces boredom and increases excitement about who will be working with whom, particularly in elementary school applications with younger students. Such factors help sustain the program over time and increase students' satisfaction. Not frequently changing tutors and tutoring pairs can lead to boredom and student complaints. Not allowing lower-skilled students to tutor (so they always have to be the learner taught by others) has the effect of stigmatizing these students as low functioning in the eyes of the peer group. The lack of variation in tutoring partners risks students becoming reluctant participants, or even refusing to engage in tutoring activities (e.g., Greenwood, Carta, & Hall, 1988).

Designating lower-skilled students to be the tutors throughout a session (reverse ability matching, or reverse-role tutoring) has also been shown to have beneficial effects. Reverse-role peer tutoring has its roots in special education, where the term is used to refer to a student with a disability teaching a student without a disability (Brown, 1993a, 1993b; Osguthorpe & Scruggs, 1986; Top & Osguthorpe, 1987). However, it can also mean assigning lower-skilled students to tutor higher-skilled students. Evidence of the effectiveness of this approach is not yet well documented, but reverse-role peer tutoring does take advantage of established knowledge that students benefit academically as much from serving in the tutoring role as in the role of the learner. For some students, including ELLs, the interaction of teacher and learner roles in peer tutoring has important effects that require more research.

Informal Versus Structured and Explicit Teaching Procedures

Historically, tutoring programs have differed in the extent to which peer tutors are left to devise their own instructional tactics rather than using scripted roles designed for them by their teachers or instructional design experts. Informal tutoring methods typically do not equip tutors with formal teaching procedures. Instead, tutors are given broad responsibility for determining how to work with their tutees. In contrast, structured, explicit peer teaching methods provide scripts, materials, training, and teacher feedback that supports what is being taught by tutors, how it is corrected, and what the tutors and tutees need to know and do to carry out their roles in the program.

Most systematic tutoring programs today use structured, explicit strategies because of reports that tutors trained to use specific instructional techniques (e.g., using task presentation with response feedback) produce better achievement outcomes compared with no training (Niedermeyer, 1970; Stenhoff & Lignugaris-Kraft, 2007). Explicit instruction by tutors is designed to guide a student's learning using prompting, scaffolding, and feedback. For example, the explicit instructional designs and materials in direct instruction have been successfully adapted for use in class-wide peer tutoring for teaching phonemic segmentation in beginning reading (Mathes, Howard, Allen, & Fuchs, 1998). Thus, most programs equip tutors with explicit peer teaching strategies, including routines for task presentation, error correction, and provision of feedback and reinforcement (i.e., scripted interactions).

Once peer teaching strategies are identified and shown to work, they can be taught to many or most of the students in a classroom. Because peer teaching strategies are explicit, the performance of individual tutors can be monitored for implementation fidelity and quality (Van Keer, 2004; Van Keer & Vanheghe, 2005). Consequently, use of structured peer teaching procedures support effectiveness, quality, scale, and sustainability.

Tutoring Arrangements: Pairs, Triads, and Teams

Although pairs are the typical tutoring unit, some tutoring programs accommodate triads (i.e., one tutor and two tutees) and small-group, team arrangements (Maheady, Sacca, & Harper, 1987; 1988; Pigott, Fantuzzo, & Clement, 1986). Either by design, or when an uneven number of students are present in class, one tutor can teach two tutees simultaneously. Other programs may employ teams composed of small student groups in which any team member may tutor any other member. For example, in Classwide Student Tutoring Teams (CSTT), the tutoring role is rotated among four to six students of heterogeneous ability on each of four or five teams (Harper & Maheady, 1999).

Other programs employ *both* pairs and teams within a class-wide peer tutoring program (Heward, Heron, Ellis, & Cooke, 1986). As in CSTT, tutor–tutee pairs are assigned to heterogeneous teams. Teams meet before and after tutoring sessions to introduce new material and correct completed work. The teams, or "tutor huddles," are supervised by the highest-skilled student on the team, who introduces new material, clarifies instructions, supervises, and corrects. During tutoring sessions, the tutoring pairs work independently through the material to be learned (Heron, Heward, Cooke, and Hill, 1983).

Contingencies, Rewards, and Consequences

Reinforcement boosts motivation and maintains enthusiasm (Greenwood & Hops, 1981; Lo, 2004). Where points are used, they may be traded for pencils, notepaper, other desired objects, or special activities. However, because tutoring procedures' use of reinforcement varies, the beneficial effects may not be fully exploited. In many cases, forms of social reinforcement such as being on a winning team or receiving teacher recognition may be sufficient. Social consequences for tutoring performance (e.g., praise versus criticism) are thought to operate naturally in the context of the moment-to-moment give-and-take between tutor and tutee. These contingencies are naturally determined by the tutor and tutee while they work together. Tutors and tutees provide one another with prompts for responses, feedback, and forms of approval or disapproval as they work together with the subject matter. However, where issues of behavior management or behavior problems are of concern, combining point systems with backup reinforcement contingencies and peer tutoring is often highly effective (Bell, Young, Blair, & Nelson, 1990).

In many tutoring programs, the tutor is taught to use prompts, feedback, and especially approval as positive reinforcement for correct responding. In CWPT, for example, use of these tutoring skills is monitored by the classroom teacher and praised. Prompts, feedback, and approval are used by tutors in conjunction with different forms of instruction, such as discrete task trials (e.g., Kohler, Richardson, Mina, Dinwiddie, & Greenwood, 1985), or conceptual discussions of mathematics rules and principles (Fuchs, Fuchs, Hamlett, et al., 1997), or work with phonemic awareness activities (McMaster, Kung, Han, & Cao, 2008).

Both individual and group reinforcement contingencies may be effectively used in peer tutoring programs. Individual reinforcement contingencies are those in which the behavior of the individual student results in individual consequences, either positive or negative. Group-oriented contingencies of reinforcement are those in which the collective behavior of the group determines the consequences for a group member, whether they be positive or negative. Group reinforcement contingences in peer tutoring programs are those focused on the collective performance of teams or of the entire class. In a CWPT study, for example, at the individual level, tutees earned points for responding to the tutor or the tutoring materials and reported these point scores to the teacher so they could be posted publicly (Greenwood, Delquadri, et al., 1997). Additionally, each tutor–tutee pair was a member of one of two teams competing for the highest point total (group level). At the group reinforcement level, each pair contributed its individual point total toward a team total. At the end of each session, individual pair points were summed for each team, and the team with the highest point total was announced as the winner.

Specially Designed Materials, Tasks, and Training Implications

Subject matter content and learning tasks used in class-wide peer tutoring, compared with those used in conventional teacher-led instruction, often require specialized materials. These are needed to guide learners and ensure that students' success rates and satisfaction remain high. For example, if the tutoring program is based on a mastery learning approach, learning tasks need to be organized into short units sequenced hierarchically by difficulty level.

When students with moderate to severe disabilities are included in the general education instruction, separate curricula linked to students' individual education plans and Tier 3 instruction may be necessary. For example, while the majority of the class is engaged in reading tutoring, low-performing students may engage in peer tutoring on color discrimination tasks or learn survival and safety vocabulary (e.g., Reddy et al., 1999). Additionally, for students with severe disabilities who have a paraprofessional assigned to assist them, it is possible to include the paraprofessional in the peer tutoring framework. For example, children with significant hearing loss may participate directly in peer tutoring through the help of the paraprofessional's translation of tutor–tutee interactions. The peer tutor may present a word to be spelled; the paraprofessional may then sign the word, observe the tutee's signed spelling of the word, and then translate it to spoken English.

If peer tutoring is organized around developing a class product or completing a project, task individualization based on skill levels can be accomplished by differentiating students' contributions. For example, when painting a picture depicting the Westward migration in the 1870s, a tutee with fine motor difficulties might paint the sky, and the tutor, who does not have fine motor disabilities, might sketch the covered wagons.

Tutoring materials are often designed to fit interactive formats of tutor presentation and tutee response (e.g., Greenwood et al., 2006; Heron, Heward, Cook, & Hill, 1983). For example, flashcards are often used in a format in which the tutor presents a word written on a card to the tutee and says, "Read this word." If the word is read correctly, it is stacked in a pile of cards that received correct responses; if read incorrectly, it is corrected by the tutor, who might say, "No, it's cat. What is it?" to which the tutee responds, "Cat." The card is then placed back into the deck for an additional trial (Heward, 1996, p. 66). Or the tutor might look at a list of spelling words and ask the tutee to spell the word "cat." The tutee then may attempt to spell "cat," orally while also writing it on a response sheet. When complete, the tutor then checks the word against the spelling list and awards points if correct or provides correction when an error is made. Similar peer teaching curricula may include vocabulary words or sentences read orally from text passages, with each sentence counted as a response opportunity. Alternately, students learn to identify the main ideas in the material they read, known as paragraph shrinking (Fuchs, Fuchs, Mathes, & Simmons, 1997). Tutors ask tutees to identify the main idea, using prompts such as: "Identify the 'who or what' in this story," and "What was the most important thing about the 'who or what'?" Thus, peer teaching materials and tasks are quite different from the often open-ended study tasks or worksheets used during independent study or seatwork activities.

Spelling and vocabulary materials for use with ELLs have been developed with special attention placed on critical factors in ELL learning, such as students' active engagement in learning tasks, opportunities to respond, interactive teaching, extended discourse in English, and respect for cultural diversity (e.g., Linan-Thompson, Vaughn, Prater, & Cirino, 2006; Prater & Bermudez, 1993; Wright, Cavanaugh, Sainato, & Heward, 1995). For example, first graders were taught sight words as part of a needed English vocabulary base to foster their language and literacy skills (Greenwood, Arreaga-Mayer, et al., 2001). Prior to the week's session, the teacher introduced new sight vocabulary words using bilingual flashcards and modeling procedures within a whole-class discussion format. First, the teacher pronounced each word in Spanish and the students repeated the word in Spanish. Second, the teacher pronounced each word in English and the students repeated the word in English. Third, the teacher spelled each word aloud in English and the students spelled the words in English. In addition, the teacher used scaffolding strategies and mediation/feedback techniques to expand the students' understanding of the vocabulary words.

Flashcards were made using sight words from the Dolch word lists and first-grade readers. Flashcards were placed in the center of an 8 1/2 × 11 placemat with a "smiley face" on the left side and a question mark on the right side (Greenwood et al., 2006). Students were paired into tutor and tutee roles by the teacher based on their level of English proficiency. The tutor was then instructed to show the flashcard to the tutee and ask the tutee to say the word. If the word was pronounced correctly, the tutor placed the flashcard on the smiley face. For every correct response, the tutor awarded the tutee two points. If the tutee did not pronounce the word correctly, the tutor supplied the correct response. The tutee pronounced the word once. Following this response, the tutee was awarded one point. The flashcard was then placed on the question mark. If the tutor and tutee did not know the word, the tutor raised his or her hand, holding up the help card for teacher assistance.

Researchers have developed evidence-based beginning reading curricula for use in peer tutoring and reported its effectiveness with ELLs (McMaster et al., 2008; Sáenz, Fuchs, & Fuchs, 2005). Conventional curriculum materials also may be employed directly in class-wide peer tutoring programs. One example is using basal textbook stories in each day's tutoring sessions. When divided into 100-word passages that are short enough to be read and reread several times during peer tutoring, the basal text may be used to build students' reading accuracy and fluency (e.g., Greenwood, Delquadri, & Hall, 1989). Based on reading these passages, tutors may also ask comprehension questions framed around "who, what, where, when, and why," providing formal opportunities for students to recall, apply, and extend the knowledge acquired through their reading. A prediction–relay task, in which tutees are prompted by their tutor through the task of predicting (before reading) and then confirming actual outcomes (after reading) in a passage is another example (Fuchs, Fuchs, Thompson, et al., 2001). In this task, students use what they have learned while reading earlier paragraphs to predict what might happen next. By then confirming predictions after reading, the students' use and understanding of what they are reading is improved.

Materials and procedures that enable the tutor to *accurately correct* the tutee's responses are a highly desired component of effective peer tutoring materials. These may include answer lists, words spelled phonetically to prompt correct pronunciation by tutors, and correction routines. Additionally, procedures that make it possible to chart and monitor tutees' performance over time frequently are employed. Sheets designed for recording points earned or graphing the number of correctly spelled words also are typical components in effective peer tutoring programs.

Typically, four to eight sessions are needed to train tutors in CWPT. However, the amount of training, follow-up, and retraining provided to teach tutors and their tutees to use tutoring procedures varies widely, depending on the complexity of the program and the social skills of the tutors. If tutors need to learn specific methods of task presentation and error correction and the uses of consequences (e.g., points, tokens, praise), tutor training requires advanced planning. In some class-wide peer tutoring programs with very young students or students with disabilities, it may be necessary to teach tutors the correct academic responses that they then must teach to their tutees. For example, Kohler (1987) reported that preschool-age tutors had to be trained first in color names prior to tutoring their peers in the same skills. Brown, Fenrick, and Klemme (1971) used similar preteaching procedures with students with moderate to severe disabilities.

Indirect Benefits of Peer Tutoring

Beyond the improved academic learning for tutees, the indirect effects of peer tutoring are several. First, reports have indicated that the tutors benefit academically as much or more than their tutees (e.g., Polirstok & Greer, 1986). However, this outcome has not always been the case and likely depends on the learning requirements of tutors in the program. For example, tutors who are required to teach skills that they have mastered only recently may have the opportunity to improve these skills as a result of tutoring others. While tutoring, peer teachers may have new opportunities to review or generalize uses of academic skills that they acquired previously during teacher-led instruction.

Second, tutoring programs implemented primarily to improve students' academic skills also have been linked to increases in the sociometric status of tutored students (Maheady & Sainato, 1985), increases in peer social interactions between students with and without disabilities (Kamps, Barbetta, Leonard, & Delquadri, 1994), and improved relationships between minority group and majority group students (Greenwood, Delquadri, & Hall, 1989).

Third, being a tutor in cross-age/grade programs often means time away from a student's classroom program of instruction, with potential negative consequences, including the perception that this might not be the best use of this student's time. Knowledge that tutoring improves achievement as a direct effect is a key point here. However, the trade-off between time away and time tutoring is a consideration that should be made relative to the potential benefits for both tutor and tutee.

Progress Monitoring

Peer tutoring programs vary in the extent to which data on student learning are collected and used to monitor progress, differentiate instruction based on students' response to intervention (RTI), and improve the effectiveness of the program. Most of the peer programs reviewed in this chapter employed either unit-mastery monitoring or fluency-based curriculum-based measurement.

Mastery monitoring can measure exactly what has been taught that day, that week, or in a subject-matter unit. One example is the use of weekly pre- and posttest gains in spelling accuracy to indicate mastery before and after peer tutoring. This form of measurement is helpful in establishing growth in specific skills taught and learned using peer tutoring. It also helps in identifying the skills that still need to be taught. Fluency-based curriculum measures are particularly helpful in monitoring students' rates of growth in a curriculum domain of interest (e.g., oral reading fluency). Another example of assessing the effect of tutoring is using curriculum-based measurement to assess students' weekly growth in the number of correctly written digits on a math test. Both mastery and fluency methods address the issue of students' response to intervention and the success or failure of the instruction provided them (Deno, 1997). Software has been developed supporting this measurement for specific peer tutoring programs (Fuchs, Fuchs, & Hamlett, 1994; Fuchs, Hamlett, & Fuchs, 1999; Greenwood, Delquadri, Hou, et al., 2001). AIMSweb (http://www.aimsweb.com/) is one website that supports fluency-based curriculum measurement and can be used to monitor progress associated with peer tutoring programs.

Peer tutoring programs also vary in the extent that measures are available for assessing fidelity of implementation. For example, Maheady and Harper (1987) and Greenwood, Dinwiddie, et al. (1987) employed observational checklists to assess the presence of the necessary materials, correct sequence of teacher behaviors, and students' tutoring behaviors. Similarly, Greenwood, Dinwiddie, et al. (1987) used implementation data to certify teachers as trained in a class-wide tutoring program and to monitor the quality of teachers' continued implementation over time. Programs that employ point systems to reward tutoring behaviors may use point-earning data to track tutees' academic responding in daily tutoring sessions (e.g., Maheady & Harper, 1987). If a student's academic responding is low, based on the number of points earned relative to the number earned the previous day or compared to peers' scores, adaptations in the program can be made to improve student responding in terms of the number of spelling words attempted or sentences read (Greenwood, Hou, et al., 2001). Computerized analyses and advice provided by computer software is increasingly capable of reporting the quality of implementation and advising teachers in specific strategies for altering curricula.

PEER TEACHING ACROSS THE THREE TIERS

Most multitier models use evidence-based practices within each tier to achieve the largest learning effect size possible (Chard, Harn, et al., 2008). Thus, instruction is differentiated by methods and curriculum that increase the probability of improving learning at each tier. Table 2 illustrates this intensification of instruction based on evidence-based peer tutoring methods. Tier 1 instruction is designed to serve all students. Tier 2 instruction uses different methods and techniques designed to strengthen or intensify instruction received by children who are not achieving a benchmark level of expectation with only Tier 1. Tier 3 instruction is intensified further to promote the progress of students not meeting benchmarks with Tier 1 and Tier 2.

A number of these factors are similar to those seen in teacher-led or teacher-directed instruction across tiers. Examples include intensification of session time and group size, as well as explicitness of instruction. However, several unique considerations in peer tutoring designs for the three tiers emerge from this comparison. One is the peer teaching method. CWPT and PALS, for example, are appropriate to an entire class application (Tier 1). At Tiers 2 and 3, however, cross-age, reciprocal, and reverse-role peer tutoring may provide a better fit. Cross-age tutoring ensures that a higher-skilled student is always providing instruction, modeling correct responding, and accurately correcting errors. Reciprocal- and reverse-role peer tutoring enable the tutee at Tier 3 to learn from "being the teacher," as well as from being taught. Similarly, the classroom teacher's role is extended in the higher tiers to include paraprofessionals or specialist teachers who are managing and supervising tutors. The tutor (peer teacher) and the tutee (learner) roles also are changed to increase opportunities to respond and to receive correction and feedback.

TIER 1: CLASSWIDE PEER TUTORING USED TO PROMOTE STUDENTS' RESPONSE TO INSTRUCTION

This section reviews four forms of peer tutoring that typically are employed with Tier 1: Classwide Peer Tutoring (CWPT), two Peer-Assisted Learning Strategies (PALS and K-PALS), and Classwide Student Tutoring Teams (CSTT).

Classwide Peer Tutoring (CWPT)

CWPT originated in the 1980s as a means of improving the spelling accuracy of low-achieving students or with LD. Because teachers did not want to base student groups on differing abilities, they used CWPT as a way of including *all* students in classroom spelling instruction at the same time. To include all students in instruction, the subsequent design of CWPT sought to take full advantage of a number of effective components, including one-on-one peer teaching and group contingencies of reinforcement. Other components of the tutor modeling included scripted tutor task presentations, tutor-led response opportunities, tutor monitoring of tutee performance, an error correction strategy, and recording of points earned by the tutee (Greenwood, Delquadri, & Carta, 1997). Additional instructional components were taken from the

Table 2. Peer Tutoring Features Linked to Three Tiers of Support

Peer Tutoring Aspects	Conceptualization of Multiple Levels of Instructional Intensity and Support		
	Tier 1	Tier 2	Tier 3
1. Time to learn	Daily dedicated time	Supplemental to Tier 1, 15–30 minute daily addition	Supplemental or alternative to Tier 1, 15–30 minute daily allocation
2. Opportunities to respond and engagement in academic responding	Same as conventional instruction	Two times greater than conventional instruction	Five times greater than conventional instruction
3. Group size (teacher–pupil ratio)	1:1 within class	1:1 within small groups	1:1 individual
4. Curriculum focus	Grade-level appropriate, evidence-based skills, universal curriculum	Targeted, precursor skills in the universal curriculum	Individualized scope and sequence based on individually assessed need
5. Specificity (explicitness) of peer-assisted instruction	Core skills curricula with an annual scope and sequence using large and small group instruction in a literacy– or numeracy-rich classroom with assessment used for planning and evaluating outcomes	Moderate to high specificity of instructional design on targeted core curriculum skills, immediate feedback	Highly scripted lessons, direct teaching, teaching to mastery, immediate feedback, and positive reinforcement
6. Learner's (tutee's) role	Reciprocal: learner and peer teacher	Learner only or reciprocal: learner and peer teacher	Learner only and/or reverse-role tutoring
7. Peer teacher (tutor's) role	Reciprocal: learner and peer teacher	Tutor only, or reciprocal: peer teacher and learner	Higher skilled, same-aged peer; or cross-aged peer
8. Teacher's or other professional's role	Design, monitor, and support daily tutoring implementation; monitor progress over time	Design and monitor Paraprofessional or reading specialist: train tutors, support daily implementation, monitor progress over time	Teacher or team: design and monitor Reading specialist or special education teacher: train tutors, support daily implementation, monitor progress over time
9. Illustrative PALS procedures	CWPT/K-PALS	Reciprocal peer tutoring (RPT), cross-age peer tutoring	Cross-age peer tutoring, reverse-role peer tutoring

Note. Other factors also are included, and each is designed to intensify instruction from one tier to the next. For example, time to learn is increased by as much as 30 minutes per day in Tier 2. Similarly, opportunities to respond are more frequent in the higher tiers, as are other factors listed, such as group size, explicitness of instruction, learner's role, teacher's role, and the tutoring procedures used.

available research on effective instruction. They included (a) frequent opportunities to respond and practice, (b) reciprocal tutor–tutee roles, (c) immediate error correction, (d) frequent testing (e.g., weekly), (e) teaching to mastery with content coverage, and (f) feedback on progress (Greenwood, Terry, Delquadri, Elliot, & Arreaga-Mayer, 1995).

These core procedures in CWPT today include the following:

- Review and introduction of new material to be learned
- Unit content materials to be tutored (e.g., reading passages, spelling word lists, math fact lists)
- New partners each week
- Partner-pairing strategies
- Reciprocal roles in each session
- Teams competing for the highest team point total
- Contingent individual tutee point earning
- Tutors providing immediate error correction
- Verbal tutor acknowledgement of tutee correct responses
- Public posting of individual and team scores
- Social rewards for the winning team

Added to these core procedures are subject-matter-specific procedures that support peer teaching. At the elementary level, CWPT is designed to supplement traditional instruction in basic academic skills and to replace seatwork, lecture, and oral reading group activities. The teacher's role during CWPT sessions is to supervise and monitor responding of both tutors and tutees. Teachers are concerned with the quality of tutoring and award bonus points to tutors for using correct teaching behaviors. The teacher ensures that tutees are working quickly and are spelling words aloud as they write them. Teachers evaluate the general outcomes of the program, such as oral reading fluency and mastery of content tutored.

At the middle and high school levels, CWPT focuses on practice, skill building, application, and review of subject-matter content such as science, social studies, or history. Building on the work of Maheady, Sacca, and Harper (1988), we included teacher-developed study guides as a means of structuring tutor–tutee interactions around details of the subject matter in the CWPT format. Like traditional study guides that help students locate important information, CWPT study guides organize the interaction between the tutor and tutee in ways that teach the content. The interaction between tutors and tutees is similar to that described earlier for spelling, math, and reading at the elementary level, as can be seen in this interaction focused on Ancient Greece.

> Tutor: "On what continent is Greece located?"
> Tutee: [Saying and then writing] "Europe."
> Tutor: "Correct! Two points."

Tutor: "What two effects did the mountainous geography of Greece have during ancient times?"

Tutee: "Travel and communication were difficult, and they protected Greece from invasion."

Tutor: "Yes, two points."

Using the study guide, the tutor reads a question. The tutee responds orally and in writing, and the tutor checks for accuracy and awards points. Questions and tutees' responses continue during the teacher's allotted time for peer tutoring, with the game's goal being to earn as many points as possible for the team.

A week's tutoring using a study guide is organized as follows: The teacher introduces new content on Monday using a lecture format. Tutoring on new material occurs on Tuesday and Wednesday. A tutoring review is conducted on Thursday, and testing of progress is completed on Friday, along with a pretest on the next week's planned material. Weekly study guides are organized as smaller units within larger units or chapters from textbooks (Greenwood, Delquadri, Hou, Terry, & Arreaga-Mayer, 2001).

In the context of beginning reading, a peer tutoring curriculum and teacher support tools are available for teaching phonemic awareness and other early skills (Greenwood et al., 2007). For elementary school, the focus is on reading fluency and comprehension of connected text. For middle school and subject-matter instruction, the focus is on comprehension using peer taught study guides prepared by the teacher. An information technology approach to Classwide Peer Tutoring (CWPT) is also available. This approach, called the Classwide Peer Tutoring–Learning Management System (CWPT-LMS) is a system of peer tutoring instruction with computer software supports designed to help teachers implement effective instruction, monitor progress, and sustain use of the program over time (Buzhardt, Abbott, Greenwood, & Tapia, 2005). The CWPT-LMS is distributed by the Juniper Gardens Children's Project, University of Kansas.

Perhaps the most persuasive outcomes supporting CWPT have come from a 12-year experimental, longitudinal study (Greenwood & Delquadri, 1995). Results indicated that in comparison with an at-risk control group and a nonrisk comparison group that did not receive CWPT, the CWPT intervention (a) increased engagement during instruction for students in Grades 1 through 3; (b) increased growth in student achievement at Grades 2, 3, 4, and 6; (c) reduced the number of CWPT students needing special education services by Grade 7; and (d) reduced the number of CWPT students dropping out of school by the end of Grade 11 (Greenwood, 1991; Greenwood & Delquadri, 1995; Greenwood, Delquadri, & Hall, 1989; Greenwood, Terry, et al., 1993).

CWPT has successfully been used to integrate students with disabilities into the general education curriculum (Mortweet et al., 1999; Sideridis et al., 1997). For example, Kamps et al. (1994) reported that CWPT improved the reading skills and peer interactions of students with autism and general education peers in an integrated setting. These students were a subgroup of high-functioning students with autism. They were children of normal cognitive ability but with serious deficits in social competence (e.g., rigid adherence to structure and schedules; a socially perceived general disinterest in others, especially peers; and perseveration on objects or topics, or both). DuPaul and Henningson (1993) reported that CWPT was effective for students with attention deficit hyperactivity disorder (ADHD) in general education classrooms. Harper, Mallette, Maheady, Bentley, and Moore (1995) demonstrated improvements in spelling for students with mild disabilities, including improved retention of words learned during CWPT and generalization to writing tasks in the absence of specific training. Wright, Cavanaugh, Sainato, and Heward (1995) reported improvements in the academic, language learning, and social outcomes of ELLs. Similar findings have been reported by Arreaga-Mayer (1998a; 1998b) and Greenwood, Arreaga-Mayer, et al. (2001).

Bell, Young, Blair, and Nelson (1990) reported improvements in the behavior and achievement of secondary level students with behavioral disorders in a history class. Similar findings were reported for secondary-level applications by Maheady, Harper, and Sacca (1988) and Maheady, Sacca, and Harper (1987, 1988). CWPT also has been extended to physical education settings with positive results (Block, Oberweiser, & Bain, 1995; Ward, Crouch, & Patrick, 1998). Compared with alternative teaching practice, CWPT produced superior results in the teaching of cardiopulmonary resuscitation to physical education majors (Ward & Ward, 1996).

In one of the larger and longest investigations, involving 975 middle school students in 52 classrooms in Grades 6 through 8 over a 3-year period, Kamps, Greenwood, Arreaga-Mayer, et al., (2007) reported that effect sizes favored CWPT compared with teacher-led instruction ($M_{effect\ size}$ = 1.11). Across individual classrooms, effect sizes ranged from moderate to large based on teacher-administered weekly quizzes on the content taught.

Types of Peer-Assisted Learning Strategies (PALS)

Developed in the early 1990s, PALS was an effort to provide elementary-grade teachers with an effective, feasible, and acceptable intervention for an entire class in which students with LD were included (Mathes & Fuchs, 1993; Simmons, Fuchs, Fuchs, Hodge, & Mathes, 1994). PALS was built around CWPT, but it includes a number of different effective peer teaching strategies, and it can be linked to computerized formative evaluation systems using CBM (Fuchs, Fuchs, Phillips, & Karns, 1994). Thus, like CWPT, PALS combines effective class-wide peer tutoring components with specific instructional tasks and peer teaching strategies.

PALS Math, for example, provides teachers with group and individual CBM reports on students' learning of specific math skills. These data enable teachers to gear instruction to the group as well as to the needs of specific students. PALS Math sessions typically are 40 minutes in duration and may be implemented at least twice a week. Higher-performing students are paired with lower-performing students by rank ordering class members on math performance, splitting the list at the median, and then pairing the first student in the upper half with the first student in the lower half, etc. This step may be performed by the teacher or by the computer program accompanying the program. This strategy creates 13 to 15 unique pairings (or triads) capable of working together at the same time on individually tailored learning tasks, instead of receiving instruction through a conventional whole-class, teacher-directed activity that may address the instructional needs of only a few students. PALS math tutoring is reciprocal, like CWPT, in that each student serves as a "player" and a "coach" during the session. The stronger student serves first as coach, to be a model and accuracy checker, followed by the weaker student. Student pairings are changed every 2 weeks.

General PALS Math strategies consist of skill coaching followed by practice. During coaching, the player solves assigned problems. The coach guides the player's responding by presenting a series of questions read from a prompt card. The questions break down the problem into its component parts (e.g., "Look at the [mathematical sign]. What kind of problem is this?"). The coach corrects responses and awards points much like tutors in CWPT. Midway through the sheet of assigned problems, coaches and players trade roles and continue. Practice follows after 15–20 minutes of coaching. During practice, each student completes a problem sheet that contains easier problems combined with the problem type that was coached. After 10–15 minutes, students exchange papers and correct the answers. The pair of students with the highest point total wins applause and the opportunity to collect the PALS folder from their classmates, ending the session.

PALS Reading is designed to be implemented two to three times per week during 35-minute sessions. Sessions are divided into 10-minute class-wide activities that include (a) partner reading, (b) story retell after partner reading, (c) paragraph shrinking, and (d) prediction relays. The remaining few minutes are devoted to cleanup and transitional activities. As with PALS Math, pairs are formed to include heterogeneous pairs of higher-performing and lower-performing readers. Classroom textbook materials are used and teachers may individualize the difficulty of the reading materials for each pair, with a specific emphasis on the needs of the weaker reader. Like CWPT, both coaches and players read the assigned material.

During partner reading and story retell the coach reads first as a model for 4 minutes. The player then reads for the next 4 minutes. The player lists out in conversation the major events from the material read for about 1–2 minutes. During paragraph shrinking, for the next 4 minutes the coach resumes reading new text and stops after each paragraph to summarize the material. Then the player continues reading new material and summarizes each paragraph. Prompt cards are used to direct readers to answer comprehension questions (e.g., who, what, where, when, and why) in 10 or fewer words. During prediction relays, students continue reading new textbook material; the coach reads aloud for 5 minutes, stopping after each page to summarize information and make a prediction about what will happen next. The player then follows the same procedure for the next 5 minutes. Players earn points from the coaches for reading each sentence correctly, for summarizing what they read, for making reasonable predictions, and for working cooperatively with their partner.

Kindergarten PALS is a program developed to teach the beginning reading skills identified by the National Reading Panel in 2000: phonemic awareness, letter–sound recognition, decoding, and fluency. K-PALS uses the procedures previously described using the materials and games (e.g., rhyme game, sound game) developed for this purpose.

Research on the effectiveness of PALS has provided convincing support for the program's superiority compared with conventional general education instruction in reading and math. Reviews in the Department of Education's What Works Clearinghouse have indicated that all students, regardless of whether they have LD, made greater progress on test scores in the same amount of time. Social validity also was high. Teachers and students both reported high levels of satisfaction with PALS instruction. In addition, the authors reported that students with LD were better liked, made more friends, and were better known by peers during PALS instruction than in conventional teacher-led instruction (Mathes, Fuchs, Fuchs, Henley, & Sanders, 1994). As in CWPT, these findings also have been extended to students with behavior disorders (e.g, Locke & Fuchs, 1995) and English language learners (e.g., McMaster et al., 2008; Saenz, Fuchs, & Fuchs, 2005). Reports also support its effectiveness in middle and high school applications (e.g., Calhoun, 2005; Fuchs, Fuchs, Thompson, et al., 2001; Nyman, 2001).

Classwide Student Tutoring Teams (CSTT)

CSTT, another variation of CWPT, is designed specifically to support content-area instruction at the secondary level (Harper & Maheady, 1999; Maheady, Harper, & Mallette, 2001; Maheady, Mallette, & Harper, 2006). CSTT activities incorporate content-related discussions and content review to supplement teacher-led mathematics, social studies, science, and history instruction. It has been used as a means of improving students' mastery of skills and concepts that the teacher has previously introduced. Developed during the late 1980s (Maheady, Sacca, & Harper, 1988), CSTT combined the peer teaching procedures of CWPT with specific facets of Teams-Games-Tournaments, or TGT (DeVries & Slavin, 1978; Harper, Mallette, Maheady, & Brennan, 1993). TGT combines heterogeneously skilled teams of students in a classroom with competition among teams. In contrast to CWPT and PALS, CSTT uses four to five heterogeneous learning teams consisting of at least one high-performing, one average-performing, and one low-performing student to increase the probability and accuracy of peer teaching, help, and correction.

As noted in the CSTT instructor's manual, a major antecedent requirement of CSTT is the development of study guides for use by the student teams (Maheady, Harper, Sacca, & Mallette, 1991). Development of these study guides involves identifying important units of instruction that correspond to weekly subject matter. Each study guide consists of questions that evoke student responses of practice, recall, and application, and that reflect content instructional goals. Tutors use the study guides to prompt their teaching. Short exams are developed based on the guides and administered as pretest and posttest indicators of unit learning outcomes. It is essential that CSTT be used in the context of clear classroom behavior rules and that students be fully taught how to work within the class-wide student tutoring teams and fulfill the roles of a CSTT member.

In most secondary classrooms, CSTT is relatively easy to implement. After new subject matter is introduced, CSTT is used. CSTT is typically incorporated into a teacher's instructional program twice a week, allowing 30 minutes per session (Harper, Mallette, Maheady, & Brennan, 1993; Harper, Maheady, & Mallette, 1994; Maheady, Harper, Mallette, & Winstanley, 1991). The peer teachers in each team use the study guides to focus student attention and eliminate guesswork about what must be learned.

During a CSTT session, each team is given a folder containing the study guide for the week, paper and pencils, and a small deck of cards. The cards are numbered to correspond with items in the study guide. Students' roles rotate within each team, so that each student "takes turns" as the teacher during each session. The peer teacher draws a card from the deck of cards and reads the corresponding item to the teams (e.g., "What does empiricism mean?"). Each student writes his or her answer. The peer teacher then checks each teammate's response against the answer guide, awarding five points if correct or supplying the correct answer if in error. A student may receive two points if he or she corrects the error and successfully writes the correct response three times. When all answers have been corrected, the study guide is passed to the next student to the left and the top card is selected, thereby designating the next study question for the group's tutor to read. The team continues working. If time remains after completing 30 items, students reshuffle the deck and continue the activity to earn additional points.

Like CWPT and PALS, the teacher's role in CSTT is one of (a) monitoring team teaching; and (b) awarding bonus points for implementation of teaching steps, good manners, and constructive, supporting comments between and among team members. The teacher times the sessions, answers questions, collects team points, and posts winning point totals on the board. The noncompetitive reward system in CSTT ensures that (a) all teams that meet a minimum standard are recognized by the teacher, (b) the most improved team is recognized, and (c) the most outstanding team members (according to point totals) are recognized. Maheady, Sacca, and Harper (1988) compared the effects of CSTT to conventional teacher-led instruction on the math performance of six classes of low-achieving ninth- and 10th-grade students enrolled in a program for potential high school dropouts. These classrooms contained 28 students with mild disabilities and 63 peers without disabilities. During CSTT instruction, all students' weekly math quiz scores increased by approximately 20 percentage points. The academic gains of the students with mild disabilities closely paralleled those of their nondisabled peers. Students with and without disabilities were able to identify important content material and become better listeners. Furthermore, all students reported that because of CSTT they had developed new friends and increased their self-esteem.

TIER 2: PEER TUTORING AS A MEANS OF STRENGTHENING SECONDARY INSTRUCTION

As described above, peer teaching has been a successful means of strengthening Tier 1 instruction in the general education classroom. This approach seeks to include all students, and tutoring roles are often reciprocal. The peer tutoring approaches we discuss next may be used either in general education or in special-education-like pullout applications. More research is needed to support the effectiveness of these approaches when used in Tiers 2 and 3 for students not responsive to Tier 1.

In a recent study using PALS Reading, McMaster, Fuchs, Fuchs, and Compton (2005) implemented the following interventions in three tiers as follows: PALS Reading (Tier 1), Modified PALS (Tier 2), and individual pullout tutoring (Tier 3). These differences in procedures were designed to intensify instructional experiences in ways previously discussed.

Modified PALS (Tier 2) differed from Tier 1 PALS in that (a) "Coaches were used that could read the lessons independently, (b) fewer sounds and words were introduced at one time and Readers (the tutee) worked on lessons that matched their skill level, (c) the coach (the tutor) modeled the sounds and words for the reader before providing the reader with opportunities to read without a model, and (d) greater emphasis was placed on phonological awareness and decoding skill" (McMasters et al., 2005, p. 450). Students who were not progressing in Tier 1 were provided with these experiences in the regular classroom three times per week for 35 minutes in the context of ongoing PALS instruction for all.

Individual pullout tutoring (Tier 3) was provided by a trained adult three times per week for 35 minutes to students not progressing with Tier 2 experiences. Unlike PALS and Modified PALS, individual tutoring was not reciprocal. Tutoring focused on phonemic awareness using a direct instruction approach. The material was organized in short units and new material was not presented until mastery of prior material had occurred. With the tutors' help, tutees charted their daily progress relative to an overall goal of learning all the material. This was considered a motivational component. Student outcomes in this study were not statistically significant between intervention groups, however. The small sample size and low power were cited as limitations. Regardless, this is an excellent example of tutoring designed in ways known to boost intensity in a full three-tier system.

Using peer tutoring in Tier 2 instruction is another step toward increasing intensity, in contrast to the more frequently discussed teacher-led small-group instruction approach without peer tutoring components (Kamps & Greenwood, 2005). Adding peer tutoring experiences to Tier 2 provides students with access to one-on-one peer teaching and its benefits. Depending on the peer teaching design, Tier 2 students may also have the opportunity to tutor as well as be tutored (reciprocal peer tutoring). Illustrative procedures discussed in this chapter for Tier 2 include reciprocal peer tutoring (RPT; Fantuzzo & Ginsburg-Block, 1998) and cross-age peer tutoring (Medcalf, Glynn, & Moore, 2004; Topping & Bryce, 2004).

Reciprocal Peer Tutoring (RPT)

Developed in the late 1980s, RPT was initially used as a pullout program to serve low-achieving, high-risk students in urban elementary schools (Fantuzzo, King, & Heller, 1992; Fantuzzo & Ginsburg-Block, 1998), and hence it is considered relevant to Tier 2. RPT's record shows measurably superior results in improving the math achievement of students who typically tested within the 20th and 50th percentile range prior to RPT. RPT also was designed to take advantage of effective CWPT components, including peer teaching and the interdependence of pairs of learners produced by group reward systems. In RPT, as in CWPT, PALS, and CSTT, students serve as both teachers and students during tutoring sessions, and they follow a structured format of interacting and teaching each other. As in PALS Math, in RPT an initial 20-minute session of reciprocal coaching is followed by a 7-minute worksheet-testing session. Peers select rewards and performance goals from a list prepared by the teacher. Peers monitor and evaluate their own individual performance (Fantuzzo, King, & Heller, 1992). Unlike in PALS, students in RPT are paired randomly in same-age dyads.

Tutee responding in RPT is structured by four standard-response opportunities for each problem: Try 1, Try 2, Help, and Try 3 (Fantuzzo & Ginsburg-Block, 1998). The peer tutor presents the tutee with a problem to solve, using a flashcard with the answer on the back. The student solves the problem by writing the answer on a structured worksheet similar to that used in CWPT math or spelling. If the tutee's first try is correct, the peer tutor praises the student and presents the next problem. If incorrect, the peer tutor provides structured help, as described on the answer side of the flashcard, and coaching. The tutee then attempts the problem at Try 2. If the answer is still wrong, a teacher aide is called to coach the tutee in finding the correct solution, with another effort by the tutee to solve it (i.e., the Help step). The tutee is provided an additional opportunity to solve the problem independently in Try 3. Following the first 10 minutes of RPT, the tutor and tutee switch roles and continue for another 10 minutes. After 20 minutes, the learning of both is assessed using a 16-problem quiz covering the material taught. Following this testing session, the individual accomplishments of each student are combined and compared with the students' predetermined goal. If the student exceeds that goal, he or she scores a "win" for the day. After five wins, the pair is permitted to obtain the previously selected reward.

Early RPT evaluations demonstrated significant academic gains in achievement, better social interactions, and less disruptive behavior for participating students (Pigot, Fantuzzo, & Clement, 1986). Subsequent replications and applications also indicated significantly improved math achievement with RPT students for low-income minority and nonminority groups in urban schools (Fantuzzo, Polite, & Grayson, 1990). In an investigation of the component procedures of RPT, Fantuzzo, King, and Heller (1992) reported that students did best when the RPT program combined structured peer tutoring with the group reward component. The structured peer tutoring component provided tutors training in the use of a script defining their instructional interactions with each other. The group reward component provided students with rewards contingent on the combined average performance of each partner pair, rather than on individual performance (Ginsburg-Block & Fantuzzo, 1997). Students significantly increased their academic gains compared to students in structure-only, group-reward-only, and no-structure and no-reward comparison groups.

These component research findings confirmed the importance of using an explicit, well-designed peer teaching procedure (i.e., a script). Furthermore, creating interdependence through the group reward system was shown to make an important contribution to the overall effects of RPT in terms of increasing the concern, help, and support of the partner's progress during tutoring. A combination of RPT at school with parent home tutoring also has been reported to be effective (Heller & Fantuzzo 1993; Fantuzzo, Davis, & Ginsburg, 1995). African American fourth- and fifth-grade students who had experienced both components produced superior performance on math CBM measures and standardized tests. RPT is an interesting approach because it has been used in a pullout approach for lower-performing students, and when combined with parent home tutoring, it enables yet another degree of intensity.

Peer and Cross-Age Tutoring Combination

Cross-age tutoring is another format with implications for Tier 2 services. It has many of the advantages of prior methods but adds greater assurance that the tutors will have mastery of the material they teach. For example, 10- and 11-year-old students tutored 6-year-old students in writing during 20-minute sessions four times per week in the younger students' regular classes during their usual writing time (Medcalf, Glynn, & Moore, 2004). Tutors were trained to help tutees (a) produce a writing plan, (b) use the plan to develop a piece of writing with assistance, (c) proofread for meaning and accuracy, and (d) make editing changes by prompting tutees with appropriate questions. Tutors learned to provide responsive feedback to tutees and used a problem-solving approach rather than a constrained linear methodology in their interactions with tutees. Results indicated gains in writing rate, accuracy, and audience ratings of clarity of message and enjoyment of writing for both tutors and tutees.

Another interesting application used with at-risk second graders involved twice weekly peer tutoring sessions with repeated readings, combined with once per week tutoring by a college student (Green, Alderman, & Liechty, 2004). The college student focused on teaching onsets and reducing the rhyme errors made by the second graders recorded earlier by their peer tutors. Tutored students who completed the 10-week program attained a median gain of 30 words read correctly, compared to 20 words read correctly by a comparison group. Peer tutors and tutees consistently reported satisfaction with their experiences.

These examples of Tier 2 application reflect several interesting dimensions. The first is that peer tutoring was provided to students who had not been successful with Tier 1 instruction (Green, Alderman, & Liechty, 2004). The second is that the Tier 2 experience was provided as either a pullout experience or in the general education classroom (Medcalf, Glynn, & Moore, 2004). The third is that peer tutoring was arranged to support learning of different subject matter, and tutors were selected, trained, and supervised to provide accurate and competent instruction at high levels of fidelity. The fourth is the combination of peer tutoring with parent home tutoring (RPT), illustrating additional ways of strengthening instructional intensity.

TIER 3: TUTORING AS A MEANS OF STRENGTHENING INSTRUCTION

As with Tier 2, Tier 3 applications of peer tutoring have a basis in educational research. However, they remain to be systematically evaluated within a three-tier framework. Perhaps the most interesting aspect that peer tutoring brings to Tier 3 is as a feasible means of providing individual students with highly focused, one-on-one instruction by a highly skilled tutor. Comparing the effects of alternate forms of instruction, Bloom (1984) reported that the largest learning effect sizes then in the literature belonged to "one-on-one instruction by a highly skilled teacher/tutor." This finding is particularly relevant because students served by Tier 3 instruction are those most unresponsive to Tiers 1 and 2, and many will be eligible for special education services involving special education teachers and Tier 3 resources. The potential benefit of one-on-one teaching at Tier 3 follows from the (a) greater knowledge and skill of the tutor compared to Tiers 2 and 1, and (b) greater assurance of high fidelity of implementation of the planned teaching role (e.g., greater accuracy of error correction). If provided by an adult (i.e., special education teacher, reading specialist, student teacher, or paraprofessional) or perhaps a volunteer like a college student, Tier 3 instruction can achieve the quality and precision needed to support the most struggling learners (Green, Alderman, & Liechty, 2004).

Reverse-role peer tutoring is a potential Tier 3 application, but it needs additional study and evaluation. It differs from reciprocal peer tutoring primarily in that the lower-functioning student assumes the tutoring role for longer periods of time, not just half the session. As noted earlier, its rationale stems from both the academic learning benefits associated with performing the tutor's role and the social benefits that have been observed and reported (e.g., Brown, 1993a). Thus, reverse-role peer tutoring may be used at Tier 3 as another means of providing students with learning or intellectual disabilities new opportunities to use what skills they have or that they are learning by teaching someone else. Teaching a new skill to someone else can be thought of as a form of generalizing new skills to a similar but different situation. For example, an older student with a reading delay may generalize and strengthen new skills as a result of teaching a much younger student the same concept, skill, or task.

A key aspect in using reverse-role peer tutoring to teach new skills is that the tutors will need to be taught what it is they are being asked to teach, prior to teaching it. Tutors also need to be taught to tutor (i.e., how to engage the learner, present tasks, and respond with feedback and positive reinforcement) and perhaps how to measure progress of the learner. For students with behavior disorders in particular, reverse-role tutoring has been used in a context in which they may learn academic and prosocial skills associated with being a teacher or tutor (Shisler, Top, & Osguthorpe, 1986). Research on reverse-role peer tutoring appears promising, but further research is needed with Tier 3 instruction.

KNOWLEDGE AND TRAINING REQUIRED OF THE SCHOOL PSYCHOLOGIST

School psychologists are in a position to play a substantial role in bringing peer tutoring strategies to scale in local schools as policy makers, trainers, interventionists, team members, supervisors, and evaluators. As we have shown, peer tutoring programs are excellent options for differentiating instruction in Tier 1 and for carrying out the systematic implementation of Tier 2 and 3 interventions. School psychologists support this logical first step in the context of RTI problem solving with students at risk for poor academic performance. In the case of CWPT at least, evidence indicates that use of peer tutoring interventions in the early grades may preclude the need for special education for some students by middle school (Greenwood et al., 2006). Early use of peer tutoring with students at risk in the elementary grades may promote resiliency and success in the secondary grades.

Background Knowledge

Knowledge of response to intervention (RTI), progress monitoring, and data-based decision making are prerequisites for using peer tutoring for multiple levels of support. School psychologists, as members of a school's leadership team responsible for its school-wide three-tier model, may design, develop, evaluate, and improve the evidence-based practices used.

Firsthand experience in establishing and maintaining school- and classroom-based interventions is necessary for school psychologists and is essential to promoting student progress. Implementing interventions differs greatly from just making diagnostic recommendations based on test results and advising teachers on alternative approaches to solving a particularly troublesome problem. Because peer tutoring programs are specific practices, they must be established in classrooms with a high degree of fidelity to avoid diluting their beneficial effects on student learning. School psychologists must know how to directly provide one-on-one classroom assistance, as well as prepare a cadre of peer tutoring coaches to assist new teachers through their first implementation of evidence-based practices when going to scale. School psychologists also should be experienced in the use of formative assessment (e.g., CBM, mastery monitoring) because formative assessments are needed to track student progress and plan changes for future lessons. This knowledge is particularly useful in demonstrating the effects of peer tutoring. Because of school psychologists' training in measurement and standards of evidence for educational decision making, they are in a position to recommend and defend peer tutoring programs based on evidence. They also are able to point out limitations and lack of evidence.

Implementation Support

School psychologists need to know and use current information from implementation research to guide peer tutoring efforts. Fixsen, Naoom, Blase, Friedman, and Wallace (2005) concluded that successful implementation is always a 2- to 4-year process. The first step is *exploration,* in which districts or schools search for programs and curricula. This step includes obtaining administration and teacher buy-in, which are necessary for actual implementation and sustainability (Chard, Harn, Sugai, Horner, et al., 2008).

Step 2 is *installation.* In this phase, structural supports that include outcome expectations, a framework of operation (e.g., data collection), and material selection are put in place. Step 3, *initial implementation*, is marked by wide-scale change at every level, from the school administration down to teachers and to students. This change is imposed from outside the system. During step 4, *full implementation*, the system internally assumes responsibility for the programs and curricula and accepts the implementation as "best practice." Step 5, *innovation*, moves beyond the first generation of implementers as new practitioners move into the system and are trained by successive generations of practitioners and administrative staff. The last step is *sustainability*, in which the new practices are now mainstream, and every aspect of implementation continues to be maintained by future generations.

School psychologists need to know about the barriers and challenges to reaching successful implementation and how to avoid and solve these problems. For example, the time elementary schools take to fully implement CWPT varies widely (Abbott, Greenwood, Buzhardt, & Tapia, 2006). Starting from the initial training of local school leaders (on-site trainers of teachers) in an August training institute, the duration to full implementation was reported to range from 30 to 52 weeks, with an average of 3 weeks required to complete each of 12 major implementation steps (Buzhardt, Greenwood, Abbott, & Tapia, 2006). Schools with more than four identified barriers (e.g., late start, limited support, change in site coordinator, overburdened coordinator) had the most difficulty reaching full implementation. Two schools encountered six barriers, including no coordinator, a coordinator who had not received initial training, and a coordinator overburdened by too many other duties. The most frequently observed barriers were minor technology problems (e.g., network connections needed to access training and technical assistance communications). The second most observed barrier was starting too late in the school year.

In addition to using peer tutoring in RTI applications, school psychologists may recommend them to teachers having problems with instruction or problem behavior. Used in the early grades, peer tutoring may prevent behavior problems by helping students eliminate the attention seeking or escape functions of problem behavior. Peer tutoring interventions are particularly attractive options because teachers and students can implement the programs, and the interventions' powerful effects are almost immediately obvious in the classroom. Peer tutoring programs also support inclusion of students with disabilities and ELLs in the general education curricula.

School psychologists should be able to directly train teachers as well as related personnel (i.e., principals and special education teachers, volunteers) in the use of peer tutoring. In addition, school psychologists will need to provide the designs and measures for summarizing and correctly interpreting peer tutoring results. They should be able to assist teachers in solving the academic and behavioral problems presented by individual students. They also should provide important checks on teachers' implementation of peer tutoring and the feedback necessary to maintain a high level of program fidelity.

CONCLUSION

Teachers require effective and sustainable strategies for meeting the wide range of academic and social needs of individual students. Peer tutoring programs discussed in this chapter provide an additional, reasonable means to this end in the development of three tiers of support. Peer tutoring extends the range of options by which schools can provide effective, interesting, and satisfying learning experiences to students beyond teacher-led or computer-assisted instruction. Substantial evidence supports CWPT and PALS use in Tier 1 instruction as a means of differentiating instruction in ways that benefit many students, including those with disabilities and ELLs. In the past decade, these programs have become sophisticated instructional systems that are supported and improved by research findings. They also are accompanied by curriculum materials, software, and training needed for wide-scale applications. These Tier 1 peer tutoring programs should be considered as research-based components of a school's comprehensive curricula. However, not all students are responsive to these approaches and do not make adequate gains.

Fuchs and Fuchs (2006) reported that 20% of nondisabled, low-achieving students and 50% of students with disabilities did not make adequate progress. Students not making expected rates of progress were those with lower skill levels, lower levels of attention, less behavioral control, and lower cognitive development. Thus, decision making that increases the intensity of intervention for students struggling to learn has the prospect of improving progress and preventing early delays from becoming disabilities later.

The RTI approach must use evidence-based strategies such as CWPT and PALS. In this regard, the case for peer tutoring is strong. However, relatively few studies exist that demonstrate the effectiveness of peer teaching used in all three tiers, particularly in Tiers 2 or 3. Although Table 2 illustrates how peer tutoring methods may fit the RTI framework and a three-tier approach, more research and practice experiences are needed to support their use with Tiers 2 and 3. This chapter has shown how peer teaching techniques can be embedded systematically into Tier 2 by combining peer tutoring components with nontutoring components to increase intensity. One-on-one teaching or tutoring at Tier 3 is clearly a strong option, as indicated by research. Much less is known about the value of reverse-role peer tutoring in Tier 3. Research is needed on the extent to which peer tutors are effective choices for Tier 3 applications, compared with adult teachers providing one-on-one instruction. Such research deserves serious consideration by those in a position to fund and support it.

Peer tutoring programs are a means of accelerating the learning of students with and without learning risks and disabilities. Peer tutoring experiences provide the opportunity for increased practice, high levels of student engagement, immediate error correction with feedback, and the integration of students with heterogeneous abilities, including disabilities. They also blend evidence-based teaching roles with strong curricula features, allowing much greater individualization and differentiation in ways that are acceptable to students and teachers, sustainable over time, and cost-efficient relative to alternate practices. This chapter has shown the advantages of peer teaching strategies for the many students who could benefit from them and the important role school psychologists can play in implementing and evaluating those strategies in the schools.

REFERENCES

Abbott, M., Greenwood, C. R., Buzhardt, J., & Tapia, Y. (2006). Using technology-based teacher support tools to scale up the Classwide Peer Tutoring program. *Reading and Writing Quarterly, 22*(1), 47–64.

Abbott, M., Walton, C., Tapia, Y., & Greenwood, C. R. (1999). Research to practice: A blueprint for closing the gap in local schools. *Exceptional Children, 65,* 339–352.

Abbott, M., Wills, H., Kamps, D., Greenwood, C. R., Dawson-Bannister, H., Kaufman, J., et al. (2008). The Kansas Reading and Behavior Center Prevention Model. In C. R. Greenwood, T. Kratochwill, & M. Clements (Eds.), *School-wide prevention models: Lessons learned in elementary schools* (pp. 215–268). New York: Guilford Press.

Algozzine, B., Cooke, N. L., White, R. B., Helf, S., Algozzine, K., & McClanahan, T. (2008). The North Carolina Reading and Behavior Center's K–3 Prevention Model: Eastside Elementary School case study. In C. Greenwood, T. R. Kratochwill, & M. Clements (Eds.), Schoolwide prevention models: Lessons learned in elementary schools (pp. 173–214). New York: Guilford Press.

Allen, V. L. (1976). Children as teachers: Theory and research on tutoring. New York: Academic Press.

Armstrong, S. B., Conlon, M. F., Pierson, P. M., & Stahlbrand, K. (1979, May). *The cost effectiveness of peer and cross-age tutoring.* Paper presented at the Annual Meeting of the Council for Exceptional Children, Dallas TX.

Arreaga-Mayer, C. (1998a). Increasing active student responding and improving academic performance through class-wide peer tutoring. *Intervention in School and Clinic, 34,* 89–94.

Arreaga-Mayer, C. (1998b). Language sensitive peer-mediated instruction for culturally and linguistically diverse learners in the intermediate elementary grades. In R. M. Gersten & R. T. Jimenez (Eds.), *Promoting learning for culturally and linguistically diverse students* (pp. 73–90). Belmont, CA: Wadsworth.

Arreaga-Mayer, C., Terry, B., & Greenwood, C. R. (1998). Class-wide peer tutoring. In K. Topping & S. Ehly (Eds.), *Peer-mediated instruction* (pp. 105–119). Mahwah, NY: Erlbaum.

Bell, K., Young, K. R., Blair, M., & Nelson, R. (1990). Facilitating mainstreaming of students with behavior disorders using classwide peer tutoring. *School Psychology Review, 19,* 564–573.

Bennett, W. J. (1986). Tutoring. In *What works: Research about teaching and learning* (p. 36). Washington, DC: U.S. Department of Education.

Block, M. E., Oberweiser, B., & Bain, M. (1995). Using classwide peer tutoring to facilitate inclusion of students with disabilities in regular physical education. *Physical Educator, 52,* 47–56.

Bloom, B. S. (1984). The 2 sigma problem: The search for methods of group instruction as effective as one-to-one tutoring. *Educational Researcher, 13,* 4–16.

Bowman, L., Greenwood, C. R., & Tapia, Y. (2007). The efficacy of CWPT used in secondary alternative school classrooms with small teacher/pupil ratios and students with emotional and behavioral disorders. *Education and Treatment of Children, 30,* 65–88.

Brown, J. A. (1993a). Reverse-role tutoring: An alternative intervention for learning disabled students. *British Columbia Journal of Special Education, 17*(3), 238–243.

Brown, J. A. (1993b). Reverse-role tutoring: An alternative intervention for learning disabled students. *Canadian Journal of Special Education, 9*(2), 154–159.

Brown, L., Fenrick, N., & Klemme, H. (1971). Trainable pupils learn to teach each other. *Teaching Exceptional Children, 4,* 18–24.

Buzhardt, J., Abbott, M., Greenwood, C. R., & Tapia, Y. (2005). Usability testing of the Classwide Peer Tutoring Learning Management System. *Journal of Special Education Technology, 20*(1), 19–31.

Buzhardt, J., Greenwood, C. R., Abbott, M., & Tapia, Y. (2006). Research on scaling up effective instructional intervention practice: Developing a measure of the rate of implementation. *Educational Technology Research and Development, 54*(5), 467–492.

Calhoon, M. B. (2005). Effects of a peer-mediated phonological skill and reading comprehension program on reading skill acquisition for middle school students with reading disabilities. *Journal of Learning Disabilities, 38,* 424–433.

Chard, D. J., & Harn, B. A. (2008). Project CIRCUITS: Center for improving reading competence using intensive treatments schoolwide. In C. R. Greenwood, T. Kratchowill, & M. Clements (Eds.), *School-wide prevention models: Lessons learned in elementary schools* (pp. 143–172). New York: Guilford Press.

Chard, D. J., Harn, B., Sugai, G., Horner, R., et al. (2008). Core features of multi-tier systems of reading and behavioral support. In C. R. Greenwood, T. Kratochwill, & M. Clement (Eds.), *School-wide prevention models: Lessons learned in elementary schools* (pp. 31–60). New York: Guilford Press.

Chard, D., Vaughn, S., & Tyler, B. J. (2002). A synthesis of research on effective interventions for building reading fluency. *Journal of Learning Disabilities, 35,* 386–406.

Cooke, N. L., Heron, T. E., & Heward, W. L. (1983). Peer tutoring: Implementing classwide programs in the primary grades. Columbus, OH: Special Press.

Council for Exceptional Children. (1994). Statistics profile of special education in the United States, 1994. *Teaching Exceptional Children, 26*(Suppl.), 1–4.

Custer, J. D., & Osguthorpe, R. T. (1983). Improving social acceptance by training handicapped students to tutor their non-handicapped peers. *Exceptional Children, 50,* 175.

Delquadri, J., Greenwood, C. R., Stretton, K., & Hall, R. V. (1983). The peer tutoring game: A classroom procedure for increasing opportunity to respond and spelling performance. *Education and Treatment of Children, 6,* 225–239.

Delquadri, J., Greenwood, C. R., Whorton, D., Carta, J. J., & Hall, R. V. (1986). Classwide peer tutoring. *Exceptional Children, 52,* 535–542.

Deno, S. L. (1997). Whether thou goest...Perspectives on progress monitoring. In J. W. Lloyd, E. J. Kame'enui, & D. Chard (Eds.), *Issues in educating students with disabilities* (pp. 77–99). Mahwah, NJ: Erlbaum.

DeVries, D. L., & Slavin, R. E. (1978). Teams-Games-Tournaments (TGT): Review of ten classroom experiments. *Journal of Research and Development in Education, 12*(1), 28–38.

DuPaul, G. J., & Henningson, P. N. (1993). Peer tutoring effects on the classroom performance of children with attention deficit hyperactivity disorder. *School Psychology Review, 22,* 134–143.

Elbaum, B., Vaughn, S., Hughes, M. T., & Moody, S. W. (2000). How effective are one-to one tutoring programs in reading for elementary students at risk for reading failure? A meta-analysis of the intervention research. *Journal of Educational Psychology, 92,* 605–619.

Fantuzzo, J. W., Davis, G. Y., & Ginsburg, M. D. (1995). Effects of parent involvement in isolation or in combination with peer tutoring on student self-concept and mathematics achievement. *Journal of Educational Psychology, 87,* 272–281.

Fantuzzo, J., & Ginsburg-Block, M. (1998). Reciprocal peer tutoring: Developing and testing effective peer collaborations for elementary school students. In K. Topping & S. Ehly (Eds.), *Peer assisted learning* (pp. 121–144). Mahwah, NJ: Erlbaum.

Fantuzzo, J. W., King, J. A., & Heller, L. R. (1992). Effects of reciprocal peer tutoring on mathematics and school adjustment: A component analysis. *Journal of Educational Psychology, 84,* 331–339.

Fantuzzo, J., Polite, K., & Grayson, N. (1990). An evaluation of reciprocal peer tutoring across elementary school settings. *Journal of School Psychology, 21,* 255–263.

Fixsen, D. L., Naoom, S. F., Blase, K. A., Friedman, R. M., & Wallace, F. (2005). Implementation research: A synthesis of the literature. Tampa, FL: University of South Florida.

Fuchs, D., Fuchs, L. S., & Mathes, P. G. (1994). Importance of instructional complexity and role reciprocity to classwide peer tutoring. *Learning Disabilities Research and Practice, 9,* 203–212.

Fuchs, D., Fuchs, L. S., Mathes, P. G., & Simmons, D. C. (1997). Peer-assisted learning strategies: Making classrooms more responsive to diversity. *American Educational Research Journal, 34,* 174–206.

Fuchs, D., Fuchs, L. S., Thompson, A., Svenson, E., Yen, L., Al Otaiba, S., et al. (2001). Peer-assisted learning strategies: Extensions downward into kindergarten/ first grade and upward into high school. *Remedial and Special Education, 22,* 15–21.

Fuchs, L. S., & Fuchs, D. (1998). General educators' instructional adaptation for students with learning disabilities. *Learning Disability Quarterly, 21,* 23–33.

Fuchs, L. S., Fuchs, D., & Hamlett, C. L. (1994). Strengthening the connection between assessment and instructional planning with expert systems. *Exceptional Children, 61,* 138–147.

Fuchs, L. S., Fuchs, D., Hamlett, C. L., & Bentz, J. (1994). Classwide curriculum-based measurement: Helping general educators meet the challenge of student diversity. *Exceptional Children, 60,* 518–537.

Fuchs, L. S., Fuchs, D., Hamlett, C. L., Phillips, N. B., Karns, K., & Dutka, S. (1997). Enhancing students' helping behavior during peer-mediated instruction with conceptual mathematical explanations. *The Elementary School Journal, 97,* 223–229.

Fuchs, L. S., Fuchs, D., Phillips, N. B., & Karns, K. (1994). Peer-mediated mathematics instruction: A manual. Nashville, TN: Vanderbilt University, Peabody College.

Fuchs, L. S., Hamlett, C. L., & Fuchs, D. (1999). Monitoring basic skills progress (MBSP) (2nd ed.). Austin, TX: ProEd.

Gerber, M., & Kauffman, J. M. (1981). Peer tutoring in academic settings. In P. Strain (Ed.), *The utilization of peers as behavior change agents* (pp. 155–188). New York: Plenum Press.

Ginsburg-Block, M., & Fantuzzo, J. (1997). Reciprocal Peer Tutoring: An analysis of "teacher" and "student" interaction as a function of training and experience. *School Psychology Quarterly, 12,* 134–149.

Ginsburg-Block, M. D., Rohrbeck, C. A., & Fantuzzo, J. W. (2006). A meta-analytic review of the social, self-concept and behavioral conduct outcomes of peer assisted learning. *Journal of Educational Psychology, 98,* 732–749.

Green, S. K., Alderman, G., & Liechty, A. (2004). Peer tutoring, individualized intervention, and progress monitoring with at-risk second-grade readers. *Preventing School Failure, 49*(1), 11–17.

Greenberg, P. (1998). Warmly and calmly teaching young children to read, write, and spell: Thoughts about the first four of twelve well-known principles: Part 2. *Young Children, 53*(5), 68–82.

Greenwood, C. R. (1981). Peer-oriented behavioral technology and ethical issues. In P. Strain (Ed.), *The utilization of peers as behavior change agents* (pp. 327–360). New York: Plenum Press.

Greenwood, C. R. (1991). A longitudinal analysis of time to learn, engagement, and academic achievement in urban versus suburban schools. *Exceptional Children, 57,* 521–535.

Greenwood, C. R. (1996). Research on the practices and behavior of effective teachers at the Juniper Gardens Children's Project: Implications for diverse learners. In D. L. Speece & B. K. Keogh (Eds.), *Research on classroom ecologies: Implications for inclusion of children with learning disabilities* (pp. 39–68). Mahwah, NJ: Erlbaum.

Greenwood, C. R. (1997). Classwide Peer Tutoring. *Behavior and Social Issues, 7,* 11–18.

Greenwood, C. R. (2008). Social and academic achievement of children and youth in urban, poverty neighborhoods. In S. B. Neuman (Ed.), *Educating the other America: Top experts tackle poverty, literacy, and achievement in our schools* (pp. 113–136). Baltimore: Brookes.

Greenwood, C. R., Arreaga-Mayer, C., Utley, C. A., Gavin, K., & Terry, B. J. (2001). Classwide Peer Tutoring Learning Management System: Applications with elementary-level English language learners. *Remedial and Special Education, 22,* 34–47.

Greenwood, C. R., Carta, J. J., & Hall, R. V. (1988). The use of tutoring strategies in classroom management and educational instruction. *School Psychology Review, 17,* 258–275.

Greenwood, C. R., Carta, J. J., & Kamps, D. (1990). Teacher- versus peer–mediated instruction. A review of educational advantages and disadvantages. In H. Foot, M. Morgan, & R. Shute (Eds.), *Children helping children* (pp. 177–205). Chichester, U.K.: Wiley.

Greenwood, C. R., & Delquadri, J. (1995). Classwide Peer Tutoring and the prevention of school failure. *Preventing School Failure, 39*(4), 21–25.

Greenwood, C. R., Delquadri, J., & Bulgren, J. (1993). Current challenges to behavioral technology in the reform of schooling: Large-scale, high-quality implementation and sustained use of effective educational practices. *Education and Treatment of Children, 16,* 401–440.

Greenwood, C. R., Delquadri, J., & Carta, J. J. (1997). Together we can! Classwide Peer Tutoring for basic academic skills. Longmont, CO: Sopris West.

Greenwood, C. R., Delquadri, J., & Hall, R. V. (1984). Opportunity to respond and student academic performance. In W. L. Heward, T. E. Heron, J. Trap-Porter & D. S. Hill (Eds.), *Focus on behavior analysis in education* (pp. 58–88). Columbus, OH: Merrill.

Greenwood, C. R., Delquadri, J., & Hall, R. V. (1989). Longitudinal analysis of the effects of classwide peer tutoring. *Journal of Educational Psychology, 81,* 371–383.

Greenwood, C. R., Delquadri, J., Hou, L. S., Terry, B., & Arreaga-Mayer, C. (2001). Together we can! Classwide Peer Tutoring Learning Management System (CWPT-LMS): Teacher's manual. Kansas City: University of Kansas, Juniper Gardens Children's Project.

Greenwood, C. R., Delquadri, J., & Terry, B. (1998). Classwide Peer Tutoring: CD-Interactive. Kansas City: University of Kansas, Juniper Gardens Children's Project.

Greenwood, C. R., Dinwiddie, G., Bailey, V., Carta, J. J., Dorsey, D., Kohler, F. W., et al. (1987). Field replication of classwide peer tutoring. *Journal of Applied Behavior Analysis, 20,* 151–160.

Greenwood, C. R., Dinwiddie, G., Terry, B., Wade, L., Thibadeau, S., & Delquadri, J. (1984). Teacher- vs. peer-mediated instruction. *Journal of Applied Behavior Analysis, 17,* 521–538.

Greenwood, C. R., Finney, R., Terry, B., Arreaga-Mayer, C., Carta, J. J., Delquadri, J., et al. (1993). Monitoring, improving, and maintaining quality implementation of the Classwide Peer Tutoring Program using behavioral and computer technology. *Education and Treatment of Children, 16,* 19–47.

Greenwood, C. R., & Hops, H. (1981). Group contingencies and peer behavior change. In P. Strain (Ed.), *The utilization of classroom peers as behavior change agents* (pp. 189–259). New York: Plenum Press.

Greenwood, C. R., Horner, R., Kratochwill, T., & Clements, M. (2008). Introduction. In C. R. Greenwood, T. Kratchowill, & M. Clements (Eds.), *School-wide prevention models: Lessons learned in elementary schools* (pp. 3–50). New York: Guilford Press.

Greenwood, C. R., & Hou, L. S. (1997). *The Classwide Peer Tutoring Learning Management System (CWPT-LMS): User's Guide.* Kansas City: University of Kansas, Juniper Gardens Children's Project.

Greenwood, C. R., Hou, L. S., Delquadri, J., Terry, B. J., & Arreaga-Mayer, C. (2001). Classwide Peer Tutoring Program: A learning management system. In J. Woodward & L. Cuban (Eds.), *Technology, curriculum, and professional development: Adapting schools to meet the needs of students with disabilities* (pp. 61–86). Thousand Oaks, CA: Corwin Press.

Greenwood, C. R., Kamps, D., Terry, B., & Linebarger, D. (2006). Primary Intervention: A means of preventing special education? In S. Vaughn, C. Haager, & J. Klingner (Eds.), *Validated Reading Practices for Three Tiers of Intervention.* New York: Brookes.

Greenwood, C. R., Kratchowill, T., & Clements, M. (Eds.). (2008). School-wide prevention models: Lessons learned in elementary schools. New York: Guilford.

Greenwood, C. R., Maheady, L., & Carta, J. J. (1991). Peer tutoring programs in the regular education classroom. In G. Stoner, M. R. Shinn, & H. M. Walker (Eds.), *Interventions for achievement and behavior problems* (1st ed., pp. 179–200). Washington, DC: National Association of School Psychologists.

Greenwood, C. R., Maheady, L., & Delquadri, J. C. (2002). Classwide peer tutoring programs. In M. R. Shinn, H. M. Walker, & G. Stoner (Eds.), *Interventions for academic and behavior problems II: Preventive and remedial approaches.* (pp. 611–650). Bethesda, MD: National Association of School Psychologists.

Greenwood, C. R., Terry, B., Arreaga-Mayer, C., & Finney, D. (1992). The classwide peer tutoring program: Implementation factors that moderate students' achievement. *Journal of Applied Behavior Analysis, 25,* 101–116.

Greenwood, C. R., Terry, B., Delquadri, J., Elliott, M., & Arreaga-Mayer, C. (1995). Classwide Peer Tutoring (CWPT): Effective teaching and research review. Kansas City: University of Kansas, Juniper Gardens Children's Project.

Greenwood, C. R., Terry, B., & Sparks, C. (1997). *Accommodating students with special needs: Classwide Peer Tutoring* [Satellite broadcast and video tape]. Athens, GA: University of Georgia, Interactive Teaching Network (ITN).

Greenwood, C. R., Terry, B., Utley, C. A., Montagna, D., & Walker, D. (1993). Achievement placement and services: Middle school benefits of Classwide Peer Tutoring used at the elementary school. *School Psychology Review, 22,* 497–516.

Greer, R. D., & Polirstok, S. R. (1982). Collateral gains and short-term maintenance in reading and ontask responses by some inner-city adolescents as a function of their use of social reinforcement while tutoring. *Journal of Applied Behavior Analysis, 15,* 123–139.

Harper, G. F., & Maheady, L. (1999). Classwide Student Tutoring Teams: Aligning course objectives, student practice, and testing. *Proven Practice: Prevention and Remediation of School Problems, 1,* 55–59.

Harper, G. F., Maheady, L., & Mallette, B. (1994). The power of peer-mediated instruction: Why and how does it promote success for all students? In J. S. Thousand, R. A. Villa, & A. I. Nevin (Eds.), *Creativity and collaborative learning: A practical guide to empowering students* (pp. 229–241). Baltimore: Brookes.

Harper, G. F., Mallette, B., Maheady, L., Bentley, A. E., & Moore, J. (1995). Retention and treatment failure in Classwide Peer Tutoring: Implications for further research. *Journal of Behavioral Education, 5,* 399–414.

Harper, G. F., Mallette, B., Maheady, L., & Brennan, G. (1993). Classwide Student Tutoring Teams and Direct Instruction as combined instructional program to teacher generalizable strategies for mathematics word problems. *Education and Treatment of Children, 16,* 115–134.

Harper, G. F., Mallette, B., Maheady, L., Parkes, V., & Moore, J. (1993). Retention and generalization of spelling words acquired using peer-mediated instructional procedure by children with mild handicapping conditions. *Journal of Behavioral Education, 3*(1), 25–38.

Hashimoto, K., Utley, C., Greenwood, C. R., & Pitchlyn, C. L. (2007). The effects of modified Classwide Peer Tutoring procedures on the generalization of spelling skills of urban third-grade elementary students. *Learning Disabilities: A Contemporary Journal, 5*(2), 1–29.

Heller, L. R., & Fantuzzo, J. W. (1993). Reciprocal peer tutoring and parent partnership: Does parent involvement make a difference? *School Psychology Review, 22,* 517–534.

Heron, T. E., Heward, W. L., Cooke, N. L., & Hill, D. S. (1983). Evaluation of classwide peer tutoring systems: First graders teach each other sight words. *Education and Treatment of Children, 6,* 137–152.

Heward, W. L. (1996). Exceptional children: An introduction to special education (5th Ed.). Columbus, OH: Merrill.

Heward, W. L., Heron, T. E., & Cooke, N. L. (1982). Tutor huddle: Key element in a classwide peer tutoring system. *Elementary Education Journal, 82,* 115–123.

Heward, W. L., Heron, T. E., Ellis, D. E., & Cooke, N. L. (1986). Teaching first grade peer tutors to use praise on an intermittent schedule. *Education and Treatment of Children, 9,* 5–15.

Jenkins, J., & Jenkins, L. (1985). Peer tutoring in elementary and secondary programs. *Focus on Exceptional Children, 17*(6), 1–12.

Johnson, M., & Bailey, J. S. (1974). Cross-age tutoring: Fifth graders as arithmetic tutors for kindergarten children. *Journal of Applied Behavior Analysis, 7,* 223–232.

Kamps, D., Abbott, M., Greenwood, C. R., Arreaga-Mayer, C., Wills, H., Longstaff, J., et al. (2007). Use of evidence-based, small group reading instruction in high risk English language learners in primary elementary grades: Second tier intervention. *Journal of Learning Disabilities, 30,* 153–168.

Kamps, D., Abbott, M., Greenwood, C. R., Wills, H., Veerkamp, M., & Kaufman, J. (2008). Effects of small-group reading instruction and curriculum differences for students most at risk in kindergarten: Two-year results for secondary and tertiary-level interventions. *Journal of Learning Disabilities, 41,* 101–114.

Kamps, D., Barbetta, P. M., Leonard, B. R., & Delquadri, J. (1994). Classwide peer tutoring: An integration strategy to improve and promote peer interactions among students with autism and general education peers. *Journal of Applied Behavior Analysis, 27,* 49–61.

Kamps, D., & Greenwood, C. R. (2005). Formulating secondary-level reading interventions. *Journal of Learning Disabilities, 38,* 500–509.

Kamps, D., Greenwood, C., Arreaga-Mayer, C., Veerkamp, M. B., Utley, C., Tapia, Y., et al. (2008). The efficacy of Classwide Peer Tutoring in middle schools. *Education and Treatment of Children, 31,* 119–152.

King-Sears, M. E., & Cummings, C. S. (1996). Inclusive practices for classroom teachers. *Remedial and Special Education, 17,* 217–225.

Kohler, F. (1987, May). *Peer mediation in the integrated classroom: A presentation of research at the LEAP preschool.* Symposium presented at the 13th Annual Convention of the Association for Behavior Analysis, Nashville, TN.

Kohler, F., & Greenwood, C. R. (1986). Toward a technology of generalization: The identification of natural contingencies of reinforcement. *The Behavior Analyst, 9,* 19–26.

Kohler, F. W., & Greenwood, C. R. (1990). Effects of collateral peer supportive behaviors within the classwide peer tutoring program. *Journal of Applied Behavior Analysis, 23,* 307–322.

Kohler, F. W., Richardson, T., Mina, C., Dinwiddie, G., & Greenwood, C. R. (1985). Establishing cooperative peer relations in the classroom. *The Pointer, 29,* 12–16.

Levin, H., Glass, G., & Meister, G. (1984). *Cost effectiveness of four educational interventions* (Report No. 84–A11). Stanford, CA: Institute for Research in Educational Finance and Governance, Stanford University.

Linan-Thompson, S., Vaughn, S., Prater, K., & Cirino, P. (2006). The response to intervention of English language learners at risk for reading problems. *Journal of Learning Disabilities, 39,* 390–398.

Lo, Ya-Yu. (2004). Total class peer tutoring and interdependent group oriented contingency: Improving the academic and task related behaviors of fourth-grade urban students. *Education and Treatment of Children, 27,* 235–262.

Locke, W. R., & Fuchs, L. S. (1995). Effects of peer-mediated reading instruction on the on-task and social interaction of children with behavior disorders. *Journal of Emotional and Behavioral Disorders, 3,* 92–99.

Maheady, L. (1998). Advantages and disadvantages of peer-assisted learning strategies. In K. Topping & S. Ehly (Eds.), *Peer assisted learning* (pp. 45–65). Mahwah, NJ: Erlbaum.

Maheady, L., & Harper, G. (1987). A classwide peer tutoring program to improve the spelling test performance of low-income, third- and fourth-grade students. *Education and Treatment of Children, 10,* 120–133.

Maheady, L., Harper, G., Mallette, B., & Winstanley, N. (1991). Training and implementation requirements associated with the use of a classwide peer tutoring system. *Education and Treatment of Children, 14,* 177–198.

Maheady, L., Harper, G. F., & Mallette, B. (2001). Peer-mediated instruction and interventions and students with mild disabilities. *Remedial and Special Education, 22,* 4–15.

Maheady, L., Harper, G. F., & Sacca, M. K. (1988). Classwide peer tutoring programs in secondary self-contained programs for the mildly handicapped. *Journal of Research and Development in Education, 21*(3), 76–83.

Maheady, L., Harper, G. F., Sacca, M. K., & Mallette, B. (1991). *Classwide Student Tutoring Teams (CSTT): Instructor's manual and video package.* Fredonia, NY: School of Education, SUNY College at Fredonia.

Maheady, L., Mallette, B., & Harper, G. (2006). Four classwide peer tutoring models: Similarities, differences, and implications. *Reading & Writing Quarterly, 22,* 65–89.

Maheady, L., Sacca, M. K., & Harper, G. F. (1987). Classwide peer tutoring teams: Effects on the academic performance of secondary students. *Journal of Special Education, 21,* 107–121.

Maheady, L., Sacca, M. K., & Harper, G. F. (1988). The effects of a classwide peer tutoring program on the academic performance of mildly handicapped students enrolled in 10th grade social studies classes. *Exceptional Children, 55,* 52–59.

Maheady, L., & Sainato, D. (1985). The effects of peer tutoring upon the social status and social interaction patterns of high and low status elementary students. *Education and Treatment of Children, 8,* 51–65.

Maheady, L., Winstanley, N., Mallette, B., & Harper, G. F. (1989). *Training requirements in the use of classwide peer tutoring.* East Lansing: Michigan State University, Department of Counseling, Educational Psychology, and Special Education.

Mallette, B., Harper, G. F., Maheady, L., & Dempsy, M. (1991). Retention of spelling words acquired using a peer-mediated instructional strategy. *Education and Training in Mental Retardation,* June, 156–164.

Mathes, P., & Fuchs, L. S. (1993). Peer-mediated reading instruction in special education resource rooms. *Learning Disabilities Research and Practice, 8*(4), 233–243.

Mathes, P., Fuchs, D., & Fuchs, L. S. (1998). Enhancing teachers' ability to accommodate diversity through Peabody Classwide Peer Tutoring. *Interventions in School and Clinic, 31,* 46–50.

Mathes, P., Fuchs, D., Fuchs, L. S., Henley, A. M., & Sanders, A. (1994). Increasing strategic reading practice with Peabody classwide peer tutoring. *Learning Disabilities Research and Practice, 8*(4), 233–243.

Mathes, P., Howard, J. K., Allen, S. H., & Fuchs, D. (1998). Peer-assisted learning strategies for first-grade readers: Responding to the needs of diverse learners. *Reading Research Quarterly, 33,* 62–94.

Mathes, P., Howard, J., Torgesen, J., Edwards, B., & Allen, S. (1997–1998). Peer-assisted learning strategies for beginning readers. Tallahassee: Florida State University.

McMaster, K. L., Fuchs, D., Fuchs, L. S., & Compton, D. (2005). Responding to nonresponders: An experimental field trial of identification and intervention methods. *Exceptional Children, 71,* 445–463.

McMaster, K. L., Kung, S., Han, I., & Cao, M. (2008). Peer-Assisted Learning Strategies: A tier 1 approach to promoting English learners' response to intervention. *Exceptional Children, 74,* 194–214.

Medcalf, J., Glynn, T., & Moore, D. (2004). Peer tutoring in writing: A school systems approach. *Educational Psychology in Practice, 20*(2), 157–178.

Moody, S. W., Vaughn, S., & Schumm, J. S. (1997). Instructional grouping for reading: Teachers' views. *Remedial and Special Education, 18,* 347–356.

Mortweet, S. L., Utley, C. A., Walker, D., Dawson, H. L., Delquadri, J. C., Reddy, S. S., et al. (1999). Classwide peer tutoring: Teaching students with mild mental retardation in inclusive classrooms. *Exceptional Children, 65*(4), 425–536.

Niedermeyer, F. C. (1970). Effects of training on the instructional behaviors of student tutors. *Journal of Educational Research, 64,* 119–123.

Nyman, K. (2001). Peer-assisted learning strategies: Extensions downward into kindergarten/first grade and upward into high school. *Remedial and Special Education, 22,* 15–21.

Osguthorpe, R. T., & Scruggs, T. E. (1986). Special education students as tutors: A review and analysis. *Remedial and Special Education, 7,* 15–26.

Perrott, L. B., Greenwood, C. R., & Tapia, Y. (2007). Classwide Peer Tutoring as an intervention for students with emotional and behavioral disorders in secondary alternative school classrooms. *Education and Treatment of Children, 30,* 65–87.

Pigott, H. E., Fantuzzo, J. W., & Clement, P. W. (1986). The effects of reciprocal peer tutoring and group contingencies on the academic performance of elementary school children. *Journal of Applied Behavior Analysis, 19,* 93–98.

Polirstok, S. R., & Greer, R. D. (1986). A replication of collateral effects and a component analysis of a successful tutoring package for inner-city adolescents. *Education and Treatment of Children, 9,* 101–121.

Prater, D. L., & Bermudez, A. B. (1993). Using peer response groups with limited English proficient writers. *Bilingual Research Journal, 17*(1/2), 99–116.

Reddy, S. S., Utley, C. A., Delquadri, J. C., Mortweet, S. L., Greenwood, C. R., & Bowman, V. (1999). Peer tutoring for health and safety. *TEACHING Exceptional Children, 31*(3), 44–52.

Rohrbeck, C. A., Ginsberg-Block, M. D., Fantuzzo, J. W., & Miller, T. R. (2003). Peer-assisted learning interventions with elementary school students: A meta-analytic review. *Journal of Educational Psychology, 95,* 240–257.

Sáenz, L. M., Fuchs, L. S., & Fuchs, D. (2005). Peer-Assisted Learning Strategies for English language learners with learning disabilities. *Exceptional Children, 71,* 231–247.

Shisler, L., et al. (1987). The effects of reverse-role tutoring on the social acceptance of students with behavioral disorders. *Behavioral Disorders, 13,* 35–44.

Shisler, L., Top, B.L., & Osguthorpe, R.T. (1986). Behaviorally disordered students as reverse-role tutors: Increasing social acceptance and reading skills. *B.C. Journal of Special Education, 10,* 101–119.

Sideridis, G. D., Utley, C., Greenwood, C. R., Delquadri, J., Dawson, H., Palmer, P., et al. (1997). Classwide peer tutoring: Effects on the spelling performance and social interactions of students with mild disabilities and their typical peers in an integrated instructional setting. *Journal of Behavioral Education, 7,* 435–462.

Simmons, D. C., Fuchs, D., Fuchs, L.S., Hodge, J. P., & Mathes, P. G. (1994). Importance of instructional complexity and role reciprocity to classwide peer tutoring. *Learning Disabilities Research and Practice, 9*(4), 203–212.

Simmons, D. C., Kame'enui, E. J., & Chard, D. J. (1998). General education teachers' assumptions about learning and students with learning disabilities: Design of instruction analysis. *Journal of Learning Disabilities, 21,* 6–21.

Stenhoff, D. M., & Lignugaris-Kraft, B. (2007). A review of the effects of peer tutoring on students with mild disabilities in secondary settings. *Exceptional Children, 74,* 8–30.

Strayhorn, J. M., Strain, P. S., & Walker, H. M. (1993). The case for interaction skills training in the context of tutoring as a preventive mental health intervention in schools. *Behavior Disorders, 19,* 11–26.

Top, B. L., & Osguthorpe, R. T. (1987). Reverse-role tutoring: The effects of handicapped students tutoring regular class students. *The Elementary School Journal, 87*(4), 413–423.

Topping, K., & Bryce, A. (2004). Cross-age peer tutoring of reading and thinking: Influence on thinking skills. *Educational Psychology, 24*(5), 595–621.

Topping, K., & Ehly, S. (1998). *Peer-assisted learning.* Mahwah, NJ: Erlbaum.

Utley, C. A., Mortweet, S. L., & Greenwood, C. R. (1997). Peer-mediated instruction and interventions. *Focus on Exceptional Children, 29*(5), 1–23.

Van Keer, H. (2004). Fostering reading comprehension in fifth grade by explicit instruction in reading strategies and peer tutoring. *British Journal of Educational Psychology, 74*(1), 37–70.

Van Keer, H., & Verhaeghe, J. P. (2005). Effects of explicit reading strategies instruction and peer tutoring on second and fifth graders' reading comprehension and self-efficacy perceptions. *The Journal of Experimental Education, 73*(4), 291–329.

Vaughn, S., Hughes, M. T., Schumm, J. S., & Klingner, J. (1998). A collaborative effort to enhance reading and writing instruction in inclusion classrooms. *Learning Disability Quarterly. 21,* 57–74.

Veerkamp, M. B., Kamps, D. M., & Cooper, L. (2007). The effects of Classwide Peer Tutoring on the reading achievement of urban middle school students. *Education and Treatment of Children, 30,* 21–51.

Walker, H. M., Colvin, G., & Ramsey, E. (1995). Antisocial behavior in school: Strategies and best practices. Pacific Grove, CA: Brooks/Cole.

Ward, P., Crouch, D. W., & Patrick, C. A. (1998). Effects of peer-mediated accountability on opportunities to respond and correct skill performance by elementary school children in physical education. *Journal of Behavioral Education, 8,* 103–114.

Ward, P., & Ward, M. C. (1996). The effects of classwide peer tutoring on correct cardiopulmonary resuscitation performance in physical education majors. *Journal of Behavioral Education, 6,* 331–342.

Wright, J. E., Cavanaugh, R. A., Sainato, D. M., & Heward, W. L. (1995). Somos todos ayudantes y estudiantes: A demonstration of a classwide peer tutoring program for modified Spanish class for secondary students identified as learning disabled and academically at risk. *Education and Treatment of Children, 18,* 33–52.

APPENDIX. PEER TUTORING PROGRAM MATERIALS AND RESOURCES LIST

Research Syntheses and Conceptual Articles

Barley, Z., Lauer, P. A., Arens, S. A., Apthorp, H. S., Englert, K. S., Snow, D., et al. (2002). *Helping at-risk students meet standards: A synthesis of evidence-based classroom practices*. Mid-Continent Research for Education and Learning. Retrieved December 14, 2008, from http://www.nichcy.org/Research/Summaries/pages/Abstract6.aspx

Foot, H., Morgan, M. J., & Shute, R. H. (Eds.). (1990). *Children helping children*. Chichester, England: Wiley.

Fuchs, D., Fuchs, L. S., Mathes, P. G., & Simmons, D. C. (1997). Peer-assisted learning strategies: Making classrooms more responsive to diversity. *American Educational Research Journal, 34*(1), 174–206.

Gardner, R., III, Nobel, M. M., Hessler, T., Yawn, C. D., & Heron, T. E. (2007). Tutoring system innovations: Past practice to future prototypes. *Intervention in school and clinic, 43*(2), 71–81.

Ginsburg-Block, M. D., Rohrbeck, C. A., & Fantuzzo, J. W. (2006). A meta-analytic review of the social, self-concept and behavioral conduct outcomes of peer assisted learning. *Journal of Educational Psychology, 98,* 732–749.

Heron, T. E., Villareal, D. M., Yao, M., Christianson, R. J., & Heron, K. M. (2006). Applications in classroom and specialized environments. *Reading and Writing Quarterly, 22*(1), 27–45.

Kunsch, C. A., Jitendra, A. K., & Sood, S. (2007). The effects of peer-mediated instruction in mathematics for students with learning problems: A research synthesis. *Learning Disabilities Research and Practice, 22*(1), 1–12.

Maheady, L., Mallette, B., & Harper, G. F. (2006). Four classwide peer tutoring models: Similarities, difference, and implications for research and practice. *Reading and Writing Quarterly, 22*(1), 65–89.

McMaster, K. L., Fuchs, D., & Fuchs, L. S. (2006). Research on peer-assisted learning strategies: The promise and limitations of peer-mediated instruction. *Reading and Writing Quarterly, 22*(1), 5–25.

Morgan, S. A. (Ed.). (2006). Four Classwide peer tutoring programs–Research, recommendations for implementation, and future directions: Thematic Issue. *Reading & Writing Quarterly, 22*(1), 1–4.

Rohrbeck, C. A., Ginsberg-Block, M. D., Fantuzzo, J. W., & Miller, T. R. (2003). Peer-assisted learning interventions with elementary school students: A meta-analytic review. *Journal of Educational Psychology, 95,* 240–257.

Topping, K. (2005). Trends in peer learning. *Journal of Educational Psychology, 25,* 631–645.

Topping, K., & Ehly, S. (Eds.). (1998). *Peer-assisted learning*. Mahwah, NJ: Erlbaum.

Utley, C. A. (Ed.). (2001). Peer-mediated instruction and interventions (Part 1). *Remedial and Special Education, 22,* 1–34.

Utley, C. A., Mortweet, S. L., & Greenwood, C. R. (1997). Peer-mediated instruction and interventions. *Focus on Exceptional Children, 29*(5), 1–23.

Websites

Special Connections. http://www.specialconnections.ku.edu/cgi-bin/cgiwrap/specconn/main.php?cat=instruction&section=main&subsection=cwpt/materialsneeded

National Center on Response to Intervention, American Institutes for Research (AIR). http://www.rti4success.org/index.php?option=com_frontpage&Itemid=1

Peer Assisted Learning Strategies (PALS). http://kc.vanderbilt.edu/pals/

AIMSweb: Progress Monitoring and RTI System. http://www.aimsweb.com/

What Works Clearinghouse Research Syntheses

Bilingual Cooperative Integrated Reading and Composition. (February 15, 2007). http://ies.ed.gov/ncee/wwc/pdf/WWC_BCIRC_021507.pdf

Classwide Peer Tutoring (CWPT). (July 9, 2007). http://ies.ed.gov/ncee/wwc/reports/beginning_reading/cwpt/info.asp

Cooperative Integrated Reading and Composition. (July 16, 2007). http://ies.ed.gov/ncee/wwc/reports/beginning_reading/circ/

Peer-Assisted Learning Strategies (PALS). (May 14, 2007). http://ies.ed.gov/ncee/wwc/reports/english_lang/pals/ http://ies.ed.gov/ncee/wwc/pdf/WWC_PALS_051407.pdf http://ies.ed.gov/ncee/wwc/reports/beginning_reading/pals/info.asp

Peer Tutoring and Response Groups. (July 9, 2007). http://ies.ed.gov/ncee/wwc/pdf/WWC_Peer_Tutoring_070907.pdf

Peer Teaching Curricula and Materials

Fuchs, D., & Fuchs, L. S. (n.d.). Peer-Assisted Learning Strategies (PALS): Reading and Math Teacher Manuals and Videos. Retrieved December 13, 2009, from http://kc.vanderbilt.edu/pals

Greenwood, C. R., Delquadri, J., & Carta, J. J. (1997). Together We Can! Classwide Peer Tutoring for Basic Academic Skills. Longmont, CO: Sopris West. http://www.sopriswest.com

Greenwood, C. R., Delquadri, J., Hou, L. S., Terry, B., & Arreaga-Mayer, C. (2001). Together We Can! Classwide Peer Tutoring Learning Management System (CWPT-LMS): Teacher's manual. Kansas City: University of Kansas, Juniper Gardens Children's Project.

Greenwood, C. R., Kamps, D., Terry, B., & Linebarger, D. (2007). Beginning Reading CWPT [Curriculum manual, lesson chart, CD-ROM, and software]. Kansas City: University of Kansas, Juniper Gardens Children's Project.

Heron, T., & Heward, W. (2005). *Total tutoring procedures manual.* Columbus: Ohio State University, School of Physical Activity and Education Services.

Maheady, L., Harper, G., & Mallette, B. (1993). *Classwide peer tutoring teams: A teachers manual and video.* Fredonia, NY: SUNY Fredonia, School of Education.

Mathes, P., Allor, J. H. Allen, S. H., & Torgesen, J. K. (2001). Teacher-directed PALS (Paths to Achieving Literacy Success). Longmont, CO: Sopris West. http://www.sopriswest.com

Mathes, P., Clancy-Menchetti, J., & Torgesen, J. K. (2003). K-PALS (Kindergarten Peer-Assisted Literacy Strategies). Longmont, CO: Sopris West. http://www.sopriswest.com

Mathes, P., Torgesen, J. K., Allen, S. H., Allor, J. H. & (2002). First grade PALS (Peer-Assisted Literacy Strategies). Longmont, CO: Sopris West. http://www.sopriswest.com

INTERVENTIONS

for Achievement and Behavior Problems in a Three-Tier Model Including RTI

CHAPTER 25

Universal, School-Based Screening for the Early Detection of Behavioral Problems Contributing to Later Destructive Outcomes

Hill M. Walker
Herbert H. Severson
John R. Seeley
University of Oregon and Oregon Research Institute, Eugene, OR

INTRODUCTION

America's public school system is charged with the mass processing and accommodation of all students who enter the schoolhouse door, and schools are expected to effectively foster their academic and social development. However, as student populations have become increasingly diverse along ethnic, linguistic, social, economic, and cultural dimensions, educators have encountered severe challenges in realizing this goal. Further, their task in this regard has been exacerbated by factors such as the following:

- The public's rising demand for a more tangible impact of the huge investment in federally funded research, particularly psychological research
- Concerns about the safety and security of the school setting, resulting from gang activity and school violence
- Federal legislative mandates (e.g., No Child Left Behind Act, or NCLB) for increased accountability as reflected in high-stakes testing and sanctions for schools not achieving at benchmark levels

Within this context, at-risk students coming from chaotic home environments, who are difficult to teach and manage, have become increasingly marginalized and are viewed by many school personnel as impediments to their effective responses to these external accountability pressures.

Address all correspondence and feedback on this chapter to Hill M. Walker at hwalker@uoregon.edu.

Public schools provide an ideal setting for the early application of universal screening procedures, tied to evidence-based interventions, services, and supports that can disrupt the negative trajectories of at-risk students and increase the likelihood of their achieving success in school (Hoagwood et al., 2007). School success, in turn, serves as an important protective or buffering influence against a host of negative outcomes in adolescence and young adulthood (see Hawkins, Catalano, Kosterman, Abbott, & Hill, 1999). Recent advances in the field of school-based mental health services—relating to both methods of screening and the delivery of promising early interventions within behavioral domains—hold the potential to achieve true prevention outcomes in the context of schooling (see Albers, Glover, & Kratochwill, 2007; Gresham, 2004; Levitt, Saka, Hunter-Romanelli, & Hoagwood, 2007; Walker, 2004; Watson, 2007). However, this outcome is heavily dependent upon the implementation of (a) technically adequate, (b) minimally disruptive, and (c) cost-effective screening procedures that are correlated with access to appropriate intervention or placement services. These three dimensions are essential for realizing a true prevention agenda within school settings that enables the appropriate matching of early intervention strategies with identified needs and problems of at-risk students.

This chapter builds the case for implementing proactive, universal screening procedures in school settings that can do the following:

- Identify, early in their school careers, those students who are at risk for school failure and dropout due to maladaptive forms of behavior they bring to the schooling process.
- Connect identified students to appropriate services, both within and outside the school setting, that are matched to the intensity or severity of the at-risk student's problems.
- Allocate and use school resources cost-effectively in addressing these challenges.

The field of school-based mental health contains the expertise and provides the infrastructure to deliver these critical services through collaborative partnerships with schools, families, and community agencies (see Adelman & Taylor, 2004). For this to occur, however, school mental health services need to be embedded within and integrated into the normal routines and processes of schooling (Atkins, Graczyk, Frazier, & Abdul-Adil, 2003; Burns & Hoagwood, 2002; VanDerHeyden & Witt, 2005). Currently, a number of competing forces present barriers to achieving this goal, such as academic accountability pressures, fiscal constraints, resistance to being responsible for (or "owning") the mental health problems of at-risk students, and philosophical differences.

An array of successful approaches to universal screening within behavioral domains has emerged over the past two decades, but their adoption and implementation, accompanied by the necessary levels of fidelity, are comparatively limited at present (see Albers et al., 2007). However, as educators grow more aware of the benefits of early intervention, resistance to the necessity for such screening has lessened to some degree (Hoagwood et al., 2007; Levitt et al., 2007).

The remainder of this chapter discusses the following: (a) risk factors and prevalence of students having mental health problems in today's schools; (b) schools' traditional accommodation of at-risk students; (c) the case for proactive, universal screening of all students for behavioral problems; (d) barriers to early detection and screening efforts; (e) sample models of screening for use in behavioral domains, along with their characteristics and outcomes; (f) procedures for integrating screening procedures and results with prevention approaches involving universal, selected, and indicated interventions; (g) technical issues related to early screening and detection of at-risk students; (h) usability and consumer satisfaction issues; (i) recommendations for practice; and (j) current state of the science and some needed future research.

RISK FACTORS AND PREVALENCE OF STUDENTS WITH MENTAL HEALTH PROBLEMS IN SCHOOLS

The deteriorating social and economic conditions of society, accompanied by increasing fragmentation and cultural alienation, have resulted in increased risk factors—such as dysfunctional parenting practices, substance abuse by caregivers, neglect, impoverished language environments, and poverty—and placed increased numbers of American youth at risk for school failure and later destructive outcomes (Reid, Patterson, & Snyder, 2002; Walker, Ramsey, & Gresham, 2004). These outcomes include poor academic achievement, school failure and dropout; rejection by teachers, peers, and sometimes primary caregivers; grade retention; mental health referrals; juvenile delinquency; substance abuse; and suspension or expulsion from school (see Crews et al., 2007; Loeber & Farrington, 1998; chapters 5, 10, and 11 in this book). Exposure to risk factors in family, community, and school contexts has been associated with these outcomes across a range of empirical studies (Biglan, Wang, & Walberg, 2003; Crews et al., 2007).

A large proportion of these risk factors are external rather than internal to the school setting, they are difficult to influence directly, and they often spill over into the school setting in destructive ways. These external risk conditions can affect school performance through the cross-setting pathways of behavioral histories, attitudes, beliefs, and prior deviancy training in coercive processes that substantial numbers of today's students are bringing to the schooling process (Reid et al., 2002). The dysfunctional conditions that at-risk youth experience in these contexts outside of school can severely disrupt their learning and achievement, result in social rejection and isolation by teachers and peers, and place them at substantial developmental risk (Burns & Hoagwood, 2002). Often these unfortunate influences result in untreated psychiatric disorders that not only impair school functioning but also are associated with longer-term negative outcomes. For example, Vander Stoep, Weiss, Kuo, Cheney, and Cohen (2003) calculated an attributable risk index to estimate the extent to which adolescents' failure to complete secondary schooling in the United States was associated with adolescent psychiatric disorder. Their longitudinal findings revealed that over half of U.S. adolescents who failed to complete their high school experience had a diagnosable psychiatric disorder. Vander Stoep et al. (2003) estimated the proportion of student failure to complete secondary school that was attributable to a specific psychiatric disorder in 46% of cases.

The average proportion of students with a diagnosable mental disorder in U.S. schools is about 20% (Costello, Mustillo, Erkanli, Keeler, & Angold, 2003; Hoagwood & Erwin, 1997; Levitt et al., 2007). Between 1% and 16% of the youth enrolled in schools are believed by experts to have serious problems that warrant evaluation, referral, intervention, and/or specialized accommodation and placement (Horwitz, Leaf, Leventhal, Forsyth, & Speechley, 1992). Currently, however, only about 1% of the total public school population are identified as having an emotional or behavioral disability (EBD) and served under the aegis of the Individuals with Disabilities Education Improvement Act of 2004 (IDEA reauthorization).

The vast majority of behaviorally at-risk students are not given access to services and supports through any sort of systematic screening and identification process. Instead, over 75% of such referrals are made by general education classroom teachers (Lloyd, Kauffman, Landrum, & Roe, 1992). In an analysis of federal data relating to the proportion of students who are served in the EBD category, Walker, Nishioka, Zeller, Severson, and Feil (2000) found no change in these rates between 1993 and 1998, with EBD referrals peaking at Grade 9, while academic teacher referrals peaked at Grade 2. Studies continue to show a significant underidentification of young children who are exhibiting serious behavioral disorders in school and could be diagnosed with mental health disorders. Even when students are identified, the EBD referral often comes *after* their problems have reached intractable, crisis levels.

SCHOOLS' TRADITIONAL ACCOMMODATION OF AT-RISK STUDENTS

At-risk students often tax the behavior management and instructional skills of general education teachers because of the severity of their skill–performance deficits and behavioral adjustment problems, particularly in the context of peer relations and teacher–student conflicts (Walker, Ramsey, & Gresham, 2004). Prior to the IDEA reauthorization in 2004, schools had been constrained to a "wait to fail" model, wherein such students only had access to specialized services through special education referral by their teacher *after* the teacher had decided that the at-risk student's challenging behavior was intolerable or their academic or behavioral problems exceeded the teacher's expertise (Gerber & Semmel, 1984). In such cases, the teacher would typically lobby school personnel, such as related services specialists or school-wide assistance teams, to assume responsibility for managing the student's problems. This sequence of events often resulted in a *refer-test-place* option that removed a difficult student from the general education classroom, increased the overall homogeneity of the classroom, and improved the teaching environment.

Several problems can be seen in this referral-driven approach to serving the needs of at-risk students in schools. For example, teachers are often insensitive to or unaware of students with internalizing problems, such as anxiety or depression, compared with students who have externalizing problems, such as disruption or noncompliance. Teacher referrals can be highly idiosyncratic and subjective, thus contributing to their inaccuracy. Referrals of at-risk students are likely to be the result of a complex interaction of teachers' behavioral tolerance levels, their standards and expectations for student performance, their perception of the likely dispensation of referrals, and the at-risk student's behavioral characteristics (Walker, 1986). Adoption of structured universal and proactive screening procedures that utilize and integrate differing types of measures (e.g., nominations, informant ratings, direct observations, archival school records), are much more likely to (a) address the problem of teacher underreferral of at-risk students, (b) create a more equitable balance between externalizing (teacher-owned) and internalizing (student-owned) problems, and (c) improve the accuracy of teacher referrals (Albers et al., 2007).

THE CASE FOR SYSTEMATIC UNIVERSAL SCREENING OF ALL STUDENTS AT RISK FOR BEHAVIORAL PROBLEMS

School-wide and district-wide screening to identify students at risk for school failure or for behavioral problems has become recognized as an important professional practice (Glover & Albers, 2007). For example, both the President's Commission on Excellence in Special Education (U.S. Department of Education, 2002) and the No Child Left Behind Act of 2001 strongly endorsed the approach. In a 2002 report on minority and gifted students in special education, the National Research Council (NRC) recommended that states adopt a universal screening and multitiered intervention strategy to address the needs of these school populations (see Donovan & Cross, 2002). Also, in the 2004 reauthorization of IDEA, up to 15% of the program's available funds can be used for early screening, intervention, and prevention to reduce referrals to special education and related services.

The U.S. Public Health Service (2000) recommended that early indicators of mental health problems be identified within existing preschool, child-care, education, health, welfare, juvenile justice, and substance abuse treatment systems. Hoagwood et al. have been especially articulate and persuasive in public discussions of the need to address the mental health problems of at-risk children within school contexts (Burns & Hoagwood, 2002; Hoagwood & Erwin, 1997; Hoagwood et al., 2007). Their work supports implementation of early universal screening procedures integrated with appropriate intervention strategies that can lead to highly valued prevention outcomes (Burns & Hoagwood, 2002; Levitt et al., 2007).

BARRIERS TO EARLY DETECTION AND SCREENING EFFORTS

One of the criticisms of systematic universal screening approaches is that they may reduce teacher flexibility and discretion in the process of identifying and referring students. In some cases, this restriction can lead to teacher resistance to class-wide and school-wide screening procedures. In other cases, teachers have complained about the need for certain components of universal screening systems. For example, Elliott, Huai, and Roach (2007) reported that a significant number of teachers favored only two out of the three phases of their multistage Brief Academic Competence Evaluation Scales System (BACESS), a universal screening system for evaluating students' academic competence. The basis for the teachers' objections was that they were already sufficiently knowledgeable of and familiar with students' characteristics and thus a mass screening phase was not necessary. Another commonly mentioned barrier to universal screening methods concerns the perception of extra work involved in implementation, adding another burden to already-overburdened teachers. Levitt et al. (2007) and Albers, Glover, and Kratochwill (2007) have cautioned that the benefits of such universal screening have to be perceived as "worth it" to school personnel who are gatekeepers of this process (e.g., school psychologists, teachers, administrators). Thus, universal screening procedures, especially those involving multiple stages, must be brief, must be technically adequate, and must produce valued outcomes in order to be acceptable to educational consumers.

As a rule, students are not perceived as being stigmatized by screening initiatives that identify them as in need of academic support and specialized instruction; however, at-risk students who are identified as having potential mental health needs are another matter. Some fear that, once identified, these students may be inappropriately referred for counseling, therapy, or drug regimens (Levitt et al., 2007). Many parents and some educators are understandably opposed to school-based initiatives that identify students as needing intervention services and treatments for social–emotional or behavioral problems. A recent initiative in Congress that would have mandated broad-based mental health screening in schools drew considerable resistance from a range of stakeholders.

Although social–emotional screening is important, we believe it should be accompanied by appropriate safeguards, if possible, to address the concerns described above. For example, parents should be contacted in advance whenever any such screening initiatives are being planned and should be provided with transparent and detailed information about the initiatives' purpose and methods. The wishes of parents who object to their child's inclusion in such efforts should be respected. The goals and design of these initiatives should be targeted to relatively narrow and specific purposes, such as (a) improving school success for struggling students, (b) preventing bullying and student harassment, (c) improving teacher and peer relationships, (d) increasing school safety and security, and (e) teaching students to regulate and control their behavior.

Systematic screening for behavioral deficits and problems is, on balance, cost-effective and, in our view, well worth the effort involved. We believe that these methods have the potential to improve the effectiveness of schooling and that universal, proactive screening for behavioral problems should be a regular part of schools' routine operations (much like screening for hearing, vision, and early reading problems have become accepted school practice).

SCREENING MODELS FOR USE IN BEHAVIORAL AND SOCIAL–EMOTIONAL DOMAINS

The major approaches to the screening and identification of at-risk students in schools can be classified under three general types: teacher nomination and referral; systematic, universal screening; and intervention-based screening and identification. Table 1 compares these approaches across the dimensions of methods and tools, accuracy, cost, and problems or obstacles. This comparison generally favors universal screening methods and intervention-based screening systems over the traditional teacher nomination and referral practices employed by most educators over the past 30 years. However, a comparative evaluation of the current acceptability of these approaches would still likely favor the traditional practice of teacher referral of at-risk students. In this regard, the multiple-gating methods of universal screening and identification, as well as intervention-based approaches, are rapidly gaining acceptance and are being adopted by educators as best and preferred practices (see Albers et al., 2007; Levitt et al., 2007).

Table 1. Major Approaches to the Screening and Identification of At-Risk Students in School Contexts

Major Approaches	Teacher Referral	Proactive Universal Screening	Intervention-Based Identification
Primary Verification Methods and Tools	Confirmation by expert judgment Interventions, direct observations, ratings by informants, functional behavioral assessment, direct and indirect academic assessments	Multiple-gating methods Nominations, rank-ordering on key dimensions, ratings and checklists, direct observations, archival school records, normative comparisons	Unresponsive to treatment Academic and behavioral progress monitoring, expert judgment, detect failing and/or unresponsive students, assign to a more intensive level of instruction or intervention
Accuracy	Medium to high	High	Low to medium
Cost	Low to medium	Medium	Low
Problems	Bias, teacher subjectivity	Linkage of screening-identification outcomes to available intervention services and supports	Insensitivity

Two examples of universal screening models illustrate intervention-based screening and multiple-gating approaches used within the social–emotional and behavioral domain. The School-Wide Positive Behavior Support (SWPBS) model, developed by Horner, Sugai, Lewis-Palmer, and Todd (2001), is profiled as an exemplary intervention-based approach to universal screening and intervention. The Systematic Screening for Behavior Disorders (SSBD) procedure, developed by Walker and Severson (1990), is profiled as a multiple-gating approach to universal screening and identification of students having serious behavior problems and disorders in the primary and intermediate elementary grades.

The SWPBS Model

The SWPBS model was developed as a systemic intervention to create a positive school climate and culture of competence in which all students receive the supports they need to achieve school success (Sugai, Horner, & Gresham, 2002). It also functions as an intervention-based, universal screening approach. SWPBS consists of three tiers in which universal, selected, and indicated interventions are implemented concurrently but are coordinated with one another. In Tier 1, the school commits to teaching and reinforcing three core values: be respectful, be safe, and be responsible. School staff directly teach, recognize, and reinforce the behavioral expression of these core values across all school settings (e.g., classrooms, hallways, gym, lunchroom, playground).

The SWPBS program consists of six major components:

- Statement of purpose (mission)
- List of positively stated behavioral expectations or rules
- Procedures for directly teaching these expectations to all students
- Continuum of strategies for encouraging these expectations
- Continuum of strategies for discouraging rule violations
- Procedures for monitoring and record keeping

Implementing SWPBS requires buy-in support by 80% of school staff over a 2-year period. Office disciplinary referrals are the primary criterion for evaluating the efficacy of the SWPBS program. Typically, full implementation of the SWPBS model is associated with a substantial reduction in office disciplinary referrals.

The performance of all students is monitored carefully by SWPBS implementers during the universal intervention phase of the program. Students who are unresponsive or are judged to be weak responders are selected for exposure to more intensive intervention procedures in Tier 2. These target students may be included in small group interventions or have an individualized support plan developed for them that is accompanied by a functional behavioral assessment (O'Neill, Horner, Albin, Sprague, Newton, & Storey, 2002). The small number of students who are unresponsive to Tier 2 procedures move on to Tier 3, in which extra school services, such as case management or wraparound services, are investigated as possible resources. At this level, collaborative partnerships involving families, schools, and community agencies are typically involved to address the severity of the students' problems.

The SWPBS model has been adopted by over 9,000 schools across the United States to date. It is an effective, well-researched intervention and universal screening approach that has achieved broad acceptance among school personnel at all levels—from classroom teachers to school district administrators. SWPBS is a highly recommended best practice for addressing both school intervention and universal screening priorities. A significant advantage of SWPBS is that it has the potential to form a foundation or base that enhances the efficacy of selected and indicated intervention approaches. Although this is a logical and likely outcome of SWPBS implementation, empirical research has not been reported as yet that clearly validates this observation.

The SSBD Model

The Systematic Screening for Behavior Disorders (SSBD) program is a research-validated, universal screening system to identify school-related externalizing or internalizing behavior problems for students in the elementary grades. Recent work has suggested that this screening system is also promising at the middle school level (Caldarella, Young, Richardson, Young, & Young, 2008). The SSBD was developed over a 5-year period by Walker and Severson and published in 1990. It consists of three integrated screening stages. In Stage 1, general education teachers are provided with standardized behavioral descriptions and examples of externalizing and internalizing behavior disorders. The general education teacher creates a rank-order listing of students whose behavioral characteristics most closely match the externalizing and internalizing behavioral descriptions. The three highest-ranked students on each list move to screening Stage 2, where they are evaluated by their teacher on two brief frequency-based rating scales and a "critical events" checklist of high-intensity but low-frequency forms of behavior (e.g., attacking others, exposing oneself, experiencing hallucinations).

Students who exceed normative decision criteria (i.e., cutoff points) on the Stage 2 measures move on to Stage 3. Target students in this final screening stage are observed directly in the classroom, using a stopwatch measure of academic engaged time, and in playground settings, using the peer social behavior (PSB) playground observation code (see a review of the PSB code by Leff and Lakin, 2005). Although classroom observations of academic engaged time are recorded using a stopwatch, when measured on the playground, partial interval coding procedures using the PSB code are implemented to record and assess how the target student interacts with peers (frequency and quality), as well as how the student allocates his or her time across playground activities. The targeted students who exceed the behavioral criteria of Stage 3, as determined by normative comparisons regarding either academic engagement or peer social behavior, are referred for further evaluation and diagnostic assessments and available school-based services. As a rule, an archival (historical) school records search is conducted for the target students as a final step in the screening identification process.

In the Leff and Lakin (2005) review of 45 behavioral coding systems, the PSB code emerged as one of only three recommended coding systems that met their selection criteria of being long-standing, empirically based, and well-established. To be included in the review, coding systems had to have the following features: (a) the goal of the system is to measure specific, targeted behaviors; (b) the behaviors being observed are operationally defined a priori; (c) observations are conducted using highly objective, standardized procedures; (d) the times and places of the observations are carefully selected; (e) the scoring and summation of recorded data are standardized; and (f) the system has a training and procedural manual that is available for critique by the code's authors. The PSB code was characterized in the Leff and Lakin review as "having great utility as a component of the larger SSBD system and that its main strength is to identify high-risk externalizing and internalizing elementary students" (p. 482).

The SSBD program has a national normative base of over 4,400 cases representing schools in eight states distributed across the United States. Norms for the two observational codes in screening Stage 3 were based on 1,300 cases drawn from these same participating schools. It is rare to have observational codes with a national normative database available for evaluating the behavior of target students. When combined with local school playground and/or classroom norms, this feature provides a powerful means for decision making about students.

The SSBD model was well researched during its development, and its technical manual describes extensive psychometric studies and normative procedures. The SSBD Stage 2 and 3 instruments have been popular measures in research on behavioral disorders conducted by other investigators in school settings. The SSBD model is broadly regarded as a best practice in the domain of systematic, universal screening for school-based behavior problems and disorders.

The SSBD was designed originally to carefully screen at-risk students having either externalizing or internalizing behavior problems and disorders. As such, it is considered a narrow-band screening instrument that contains expensive assessments of increasing precision and as one progresses through the successive screening stages. It is likely that target students who are rank ordered and nominated by their teachers for movement on to screening Stage 2, but who do not meet cutoff points for exiting out of Stage 2 and into Stage 3, would be good candidates for selected intervention approaches designed to achieve prevention goals and outcomes with behaviorally at-risk students. Similarly, those students who do not meet cutoff points for exiting Stage 3 would likely benefit from school-based, indicated interventions. However, this remains an untested hypothesis.

The two promising screening models described in this section represent but a relatively small segment of the growth in screening systems for the early detection of at-risk students who manifest serious adjustment problems in schooling contexts. In the past two decades, substantial progress has been achieved in this area, particularly within preschool and elementary settings. The adoption and use of best practices in screening, and early detection within school settings, lag well behind the development and validation of promising methods for doing so. (See chapter 10 in this book for descriptions of additional approaches to the cost-effective behavioral screening of at-risk students.)

INTEGRATION OF SCREENING PROCEDURES WITH THREE-TIERED INTERVENTIONS

Figure 1 illustrates a response-to-intervention (RTI) model that adapts the U.S. Public Health Service classification of prevention types to school settings (Gresham, 1991; Sugai, Horner, & Gresham, 2002; Walker et al., 1996). In this model, the two halves of the triangle represent all students in a school and their distribution across the three levels of intervention (universal, or Tier 1; selected, or Tier 2; indicated, or Tier 3) as they relate to academic and behavioral domains. Interventions are implemented to achieve prevention for all students. Selected Tier 2 intervention approaches are then implemented for those students who prove unresponsive to universal interventions, with the intent of achieving secondary prevention outcomes. The small subset of students within the Tier 2 group who do not respond to selected interventions move on to Tier 3, in which comprehensive, indicated intervention approaches are implemented to achieve tertiary prevention outcomes. The goals of the three intervention tiers are to prevent harm, to reverse harm, and to reduce harm. These linked intervention approaches focus on all, some, and a few students within a school, respectively.

Horner and his associates have established a research and development process for validating an RTI model for use with behavioral systems (Horner, Sugai, Lewis-Palmer, & Todd, 2005). Currently, they have implemented their behavioral RTI model in approximately 9,000 K–12 schools. Other investigators have accomplished a similar process for academic systems (Kame'enui, Good, & Harn, 2005; also chapter 18 in this book). These contributions provide an excellent conceptual framework for addressing the issue of reading difficulty. Their primary prevention component consists of a core reading program to minimize and reduce student reading failure. Students who prove unresponsive to the core reading curriculum are targeted for secondary prevention efforts that include supplemental reading instruction in small groups. Those students who continue to have reading difficulties are earmarked for intensive, individualized instruction and support in reading. As with the behavioral systems of the RTI model, these authors align their reading instruction to ensure that at-risk students receive the level of instruction that matches their deficits and overall needs (Musti-Rao & Cartledge, 2007). The proportions of students in Figure 1 who are distributed across these three levels are approximations. However, SWPBS research that has and is currently being conducted in a large number of U.S. schools closely validates these distribution estimates.

Figure 1. A model of prevention for addressing academic and behavior problems in the context of schooling.

Designing School-Wide Systems for Student Success

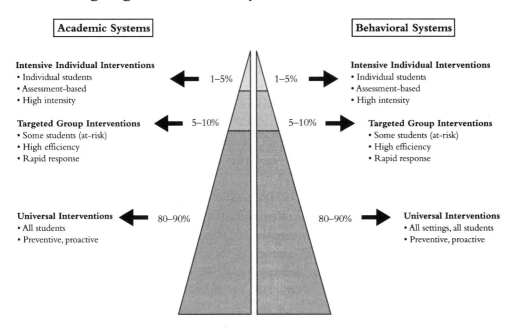

Note. From "Behaviorally Effective School Environments," by G. Sugai, R. H. Horner, & F. Gresham, 2002, in *Interventions for Academic and Behavior Problems II: Preventive and Remedial Approaches,*" by M. R. Shinn, H. M. Walker, & G. Stoner (Eds.), p. 320, Bethesda, MD: National Association of School Psychologists. Adapted with permission.

Considerable research remains to be conducted on how to establish behavioral and academic criteria within SWPBS approaches for moving students from one intervention stage to another in a cost-effective manner. In the academic domain, it is essential that both teacher judgment and direct curriculum-based assessments of student performance be included in a progress monitoring regimen. Similarly, in the behavioral domain, measures such as direct observations and teacher Likert ratings of adaptive and maladaptive behaviors can be combined to sensitively monitor student progress to inform decisions that involve moving a target student from one intervention stage to another. Social–behavioral monitoring systems similar to progress monitoring procedures also have been used successfully with academic performance (see chapter 14 in this book). Finally, universal screening systems such as the SSBD could be used as part of a progress monitoring process to identify the number and characteristics of target students whose behavioral profiles remain within the at-risk range and who are candidates for more intensive supports and services.

The SSBD screening system parallels the multitier approach to intervention in that the students who remain following the sequential screening stages are likely to have more serious behavioral and emotional challenges. The SSBD's potential applications within an RTI context involving multitier intervention approaches have not been extensively explored to date. Two areas in which this system could be useful would be (a) screening and identifying at-risk students who are likely candidates for Tier 2 and 3 interventions, and (b) regularly monitoring Tier 1, 2, and 3 interventions to determine their efficacy and establish benchmarks for moving from a less intensive intervention approach to a more intensive one.

Naquin and her associates at the University of New Orleans are currently using the SSBD system within a pupil assistance model being implemented in the Jefferson Parish Public Schools System. The pupil assistance model is also the implementation vehicle for a corrective action plan (CAP) that resulted from district monitoring provided by the Louisiana Department of Education. The CAP requires that a systematic process be developed to identify unserved and underserved students having emotional and behavioral problems and that staff development efforts be implemented to assist school staffs in more effectively serving this student subpopulation (see Walker et al., in press).

The SSBD was the screening instrument used for meeting the child identification portion of the CAP mandate and the *adaptive* and *maladaptive* rating scales in SSBD screening Stage 2 provided the behavioral content for use by school-based SWPBS teams in meeting the needs of participating schools and individual teachers and students regarding key areas and domains of behavioral concern. This work provides an important example of how universal screening and SWPBS technologies can be integrated to achieve more positive outcomes for the EBD school population.

TECHNICAL ISSUES FOR EARLY SCREENING AND DETECTION OF AT-RISK STUDENTS

Guidelines for evaluating the technical adequacy of assessment instruments are described by the *Standards for Educational and Psychological Testing* (American Educational Research Association et al., 1999). Glover and Albers (2007) reviewed these guidelines as they pertain to universal screening, including the following aspects:

- Adequacy of the normative sample, such as sample size and representativeness to the target population.
- Reliability of the instrument (e.g., internal consistency, test–retest, and inter-rater reliability).
- Validity (i.e., content, construct, and criterion related). Criterion-related validity, including both concurrent and predictive validity, is particularly important for evaluating the technical adequacy of a screening instrument.

The following section provides a brief overview of diagnostic methods for evaluating the predictive validity and technical adequacy of screening instruments.

Diagnostic methods were initially developed from statistical decision theory in the context of signal detection (Tanner & Swets, 1954). They have since been applied in medicine, public health, and psychology (see Kraemer, 1992, and Pepe, 2003, for medicine; Fleiss, 1981, and Katz & Foxman, 1993, for public health; Roberts, Lewinsohn, & Seeley, 1991; Seeley, Stice, & Rohde, 2007; and Swets, Dawes, & Monahan, 2000, for psychology). Recently, diagnostic methods have also begun to appear in educational research (Hintze, Ryan, & Stoner, 2003; Silberglitt & Hintze, 2005). The main purpose of diagnostic decision methods is to improve accuracy and simplify the decision processes that lead to correct identification of at-risk students who warrant intervention. For example, a decision maker, such as a reading teacher, must choose between two options: (a) to provide additional reading support for a student, or (b) to not provide the support. The decision maker also may need to choose between two interventions, one being more intensive than the other, or between further testing or not. Accurate diagnostic decisions lead to the efficient allocation of available resources to the students who need them. In addition, brief screening procedures that are technically adequate may help to conserve resources for intervention and minimize negative impacts on students than more intensive diagnostic assessments.

Assuming that a screening instrument is psychometrically sound, diagnostic decision making involves a number of important considerations. First, the researcher needs to determine the criterion measures, also called "the gold standard" or reference test, used to validate the screening instrument. Second, the decision rules for the evaluation of a classification test need to be established. A final consideration includes the diagnostic methods and statistics used to evaluate the decision rules and overall performance of the screening procedures.

Criterion Measures

Ideally, each measure used for diagnostic screening would have been evaluated against a perfect reference test. However, criterion measures are seldom perfect, even in medicine (Pepe, 2003). For example, comprehensive measures of reading, such as the Stanford Achievement Test, are assumed to more accurately gauge reading performance than brief curriculum-based measures (CBM) and should lead to more accurate cutoff scores over the use of benchmarks on CBM assessments as reference tests (Silberglitt & Hintze, 2005). Similarly, structured clinical diagnostic interviews (e.g., the Diagnostic Interview Schedule for Children) are assumed to be more accurate in diagnosing emotional and behavioral disorders than elevated scores on symptom or behavior checklists such as the Child Behavior Checklist (Achenbach, 1991; Shaffer, Fisher, Lucas, Dulcan, & Schwab-Stone, 2000). Criterion measures may also include key outcomes such as referral to special education or mental health services, school failure and dropout, and suspension or expulsion from school. Hence, the validity of the criterion measure or outcome is a key consideration when evaluating the diagnostic accuracy of the screening instrument.

Another important consideration for evaluating the performance of a screening instrument, or screener, includes decisions about the types of misclassification errors that may result from the screener's use. For example, some students may get incorrectly classified with reading difficulties by the screener while others "pass" the screener but still fail to obtain the expected score on the criterion measure. Decision rules involve choices about how to measure these errors and which type of error is more costly. In addition, serial screening strategies may be employed to minimize misclassification errors such as the multiple-gating procedures used in the SSBD universal screening system. Because no screeners are perfect, minimizing one type of error generally involves inflating another type of error. For example, employing a screening strategy to decrease the false positive rate, such as a multiple-gating procedure, will usually increase the false negative rate.

Diagnostic Methods

Given accurate criterion measures and assumptions about misclassification errors and their costs, the statistical methods used to determine the optimal cutoff scores for a diagnostic test involve the use of contingency table analyses. An example of a contingency table is provided in Table 2. Contingency tables involve a number of indexes that can be used to select and evaluate a cutoff score on a screening instrument. These screening indexes measure the accuracy of the screener with respect to the outcome prediction (Pepe, 2003) and include sensitivity, specificity, positive predictive value (PPV), and negative predictive value (NPV). Sensitivity refers to the proportion of students with a poor outcome who are correctly classified as at risk by the screening instrument (i.e., true positive / true positive + false negative). Specificity refers to the proportion of students with an adequate outcome who are correctly classified as not at risk by the screener (i.e., true negative / true negative + false positive). PPV refers to the proportion of students who are correctly classified as at risk by the screening instrument among students who screen positive (i.e., true positive / true positive + false positive). NPV refers to the proportion of students who are correctly screened as not at risk among students who screen negative (i.e., true negative / true negative + false negative). As summarized by Glover and Albers (2007), the diagnostic utility of screening instruments with sensitivity and specificity rates below .75 should be questioned.

Because screening instruments often employ continuous-type scales (e.g., SSBD screening Stage 2), determining the cutoff score to identify at-risk students is an important diagnostic decision. To examine each cutoff score requires the computation

Table 2. Contingency Table of Screening Performance

Screening Classification	Criterion Measure Classification	
	Adequate outcome	Poor outcome
Not at risk	True negative	False negative
At risk	False positive	True positive

of a contingency table. Thus, to fully evaluate the screening properties of a measure as part of the instrument selection process, a series of contingency tables needs to be computed to select a measure. An efficient method for evaluating the efficacy of a screening measure, or screener, is through a receiver operating characteristic (ROC) analysis. ROC analysis is a useful technique for examining the sensitivity and specificity of different cut points on the screening measure (Hsiao, Bartko, & Potter, 1989; Murphy et al., 1987). From a ROC curve, one can choose a cutoff score on a screener by selecting the point closest to the top left-hand corner of the plot, which balances sensitivity and specificity. These procedures, however, assume that the costs associated with false positive errors are similar in magnitude to those associated with false negative errors. Costs, in this context, include financial costs, such as time and resources, as well as the cost associated with missing an at-risk student; that is, failing to provide needed services, or mislabeling an adequately achieving student as being at risk. Assuming equivalent costs associated with false positives and false negatives may represent poor judgment. Depending on the objectives of the interventionist, one may choose to maximize sensitivity (e.g., the intervention is inexpensive and missing an at-risk student is costly) or to maximize specificity (e.g., the intervention is expensive and resources should be targeted to those students at greatest risk).

The ROC curve also provides a useful summary of overall screener performance (i.e., the area under the curve, or AUC; Pepe, 2003). The AUC ranges from .5 to 1.0 and can be obtained directly from logistic regression procedures (Peng & So, 2002). A ROC curve for a poorly performing screener will cover half of the area—the AUC would be .5. This represents selection at random, with no discrimination between at-risk students and those not at risk. The plot of a perfect screener will cover the entire area—the AUC would reach 1.0. Although precise criterion values for the AUC have not been established, generally speaking, AUC values above .95 indicate an excellent screener, .90 or above indicate a very good screener, and .75 and above, an acceptable screener (Swets, 1996). Values below .75 represent relatively poor diagnostic utility. Fan, Upadhye, and Worster (2006) characterized tests with an AUC below .75 as not clinically meaningful, but such a screener may still allow for more efficient allocation of resources than chance alone, depending on the costs of the classification test—among other factors.

Educational Research Example

As mentioned earlier, educational research outcomes regarding diagnostic decision methods have begun to emerge. For example, Silberglitt and Hintze (2005) evaluated CBM reading probes in Grades 1–3 to predict grade-level performance on a statewide reading achievement test administered in Grade 3. Based on ROC analyses, the optimal cutoff score on the CBM reading probe (maximizing sensitivity and specificity) achieved screening indexes of .70–.82 for sensitivity and specificity across the three grade levels. Hence, according to this ROC analysis, CBM probes would appear to have diagnostic utility as a universal screening instrument for identifying students who are at risk for reading difficulties. Similar analyses could be conducted and would likely have substantial utility within the behavioral domain.

Acceptance and Satisfaction

Instituting a universal screening system in schools to enable early detection and prevention clearly has a number of potential benefits. Yet many school-age children and youth are at risk or show clear signs of mental health disorders that have not been identified; these students are not receiving urgently needed services. Despite these recognized needs, some substantial obstacles remain to implementing a systematic screening system in school settings. Although the sample screening systems described earlier meet criteria for accuracy and positive predictive value, significant barriers exist to the acceptability of conducting either universal or selected screening procedures in schools.

Given current realities of the financial and public accountability pressures on school systems, educators sometimes express a number of reservations about implementing a system that will result in detection of significantly more students identified as qualifying for and needing specialized services. The potential for lawsuits by parents who perceive their children's needs as not being adequately addressed is an ongoing concern for educators.

Although there is a general call by federal agencies and task forces for investing in early intervention and preventive interventions, it is often difficult to get schools and staff to commit to this goal. It is quite reasonable, and desirable, for parents and school staff to express concerns and to demand a clear justification for school-based screening processes and explanations of the sort of outcomes that will be derived from the screening. Therefore, before any screening is implemented, a process must be in place to obtain full buy-in by parents and school staff on the value of such screening.

At present, additional research is needed to determine what forms of screening might be considered appropriate and applicable in school settings. Educators are more accepting of generic approaches that are cost-effective, solve a high-priority problem, do not require extensive effort, and are central to the core mission of schooling. This last point is especially relevant, as educators need to see the relationship between the screening process and improvement in academic performance. We find that parents may initially be wary of screening procedures that may identify their child as in need of specialized services. However, after meeting with a counselor, instructional specialist, or behavioral coach, and learning of the direct benefits such screening may provide for the success of their child in school, they are usually more supportive.

Because mental health services are often seen by educators as peripheral to the school's core mission, it is critical that the relationship of mental health services to academic outcomes be demonstrated (Adelman & Taylor, 2004). Efforts to clearly delineate educationally relevant outcomes for the early screening and intervention of mental health problems would aid substantially in building the acceptability of such best practices among school personnel and parents. Hoagwood et al. (2007) has forcefully advocated for mainstreaming mental health services into the broader mission of schools. To this end, special attention needs to be given to creating opportunities in schools that can provide entry points for mental health services and professionals.

An additional challenge for conducting screening in schools is soliciting the full cooperation and support of parents. For the school to conduct universal screening in the behavioral domain, key school personnel have to make special efforts to obtain the support and agreement of parents in the district. Ideally, this should be achieved with the full cooperation of parents who have given their voluntary, active, and informed consent. Often, parents and caregivers of the most at-risk students are the least likely to provide consent (Severson & Ary, 1983; Severson & Biglan, 1989). This resistance is generally not the case with academic and achievement screening or assessments; standard practice in this regard usually involves simple notification of parents.

Although Levitt et al. (2007) advocate using only positive consent procedures, we have been able to use passive consent for implementation of the SSBD screening Stages 1 and 2 because we are not singling out any one student for any special assessments or programs. A strong effort is made to inform parents, either through letters to the home or in school newsletters. Parents are informed that the school is engaging in school-wide screening and that if their child is identified through this procedure, we would be in direct contact with them and they would have the right to accept or refuse any further assessments or interventions with their child. A key consideration is how the screening process is presented to the parents. For example, the SSBD is presented to parents as a procedure in which teachers are asked to rank order and rate students on behavioral criteria (i.e., externalizing versus internalizing), and it is explained that the school is trying to identify students who may need extra assistance and/or are having problems adjusting to the demands of the classroom. A framing that relates the screening to the receipt of extra assistance and to enhanced success in the classroom is more acceptable to parents in general. Many school districts have been open to this explanation of screening procedures, in which the earliest stages of screening are conducted using a passive consent format.

An important issue involving the use of screening in schools is the potential for the violation of a student's privacy and the possible labeling of identified students that can be perceived as pejorative or stigmatizing. Schools must carefully consider the extent to which they can protect a student's privacy and ensure confidentiality of the data collected. It is also crucial to educate the school staff about both the purpose of screening and the reciprocal nature of the relationship of social and emotional problems and school success. A process in which teachers and other school staff are educated about the importance of screening and early intervention to help at-risk students can clear the way for implementing proactive screening procedures as a standard practice. If school-based early identification procedures can be coordinated with both school support and community resources, it is more likely that the at-risk student will receive appropriate services and not be pejoratively labeled or socially punished by peers.

One obstacle often cited in the educational literature regarding screening and early detection is the perception that there will be a high cost for both the screening and the recommended interventions that may result from the assessment (Kauffman, 2005a, 2005b). Though the cost of such screening is usually quite modest, the cost in terms of teaching staff time and of professionals who can carry out the screening procedures has to be openly dealt with as a possible increased cost for the school. A particular concern in this regard is that implementation of a universal screening procedure will identify more students who are at risk for mental health problems than can be served by clinical services offered by the school district or community. A commonly heard lament among educators is that it is not appropriate to identify students for whom no services exist. On the other hand, such services are not likely to be provided as long as schools tolerate huge levels of underreferral for the behaviorally at-risk student population (see Levitt et al., 2007).

In our experience, when screening is carried out systematically in the early elementary grades, most of the children identified through the screening process can be accommodated within the existing school and community systems. However, this may not hold true when screening is conducted in middle or high schools, as there may not be adequate services to address the complex problems of adolescents identified as needing them. This further highlights the crucial task of educating school staff and parents about the importance of providing mental health services and instructional interventions to promote academic and behavioral success in school. This educational process would also need to help parents see the direct connections between high-risk behaviors and the detrimental effects on their child's future, both in and outside of school.

In sum, if schools are to implement universal screening in a cost-effective and efficient manner, a number of key issues need to be confronted. Educators and related services personnel now have much broader experience with the implementation of screening procedures in schools and are aware of schools' and parents' need for information about these procedures (Glover & Albers, 2007; Levitt et al., 2007). In our experience with universal screening over the past two decades, schools and school systems that have implemented these procedures and have a system in place for using the information appropriately have been very positive about the benefits to both students and the schooling process. A recent survey of SWPBS schools in five states regarding the need for an electronic version of the SSBD confirms these findings (Walker, Severson, & Seeley, 2009).

RECOMMENDATIONS FOR IMPROVED PRACTICES

The goal of systematic screening for identifying students at risk should resonate with the educators who control school operations, such as administrators, related services personnel, and classroom teachers. As a rule, educators are extremely reluctant to invest time, effort, and resources in screening initiatives for social–emotional and behavioral problems (such as anxiety disorders or substance abuse) that they do not view as appropriate responsibilities for schools. For example, on this point, Adelman and Taylor (2004) argued that school mental health practices should be anchored in the forms of student behavior that disrupt the teaching-learning process and impair school success. Although this perspective poses some constraints in the application of mental health expertise in schools, in our view it is realistic, given the values and current attitudes of most educators. Typically, school personnel will assume responsibility of student mental health problems only to the extent that they are perceived as impairing academic performance and closely related forms of behavior (such as task engagement).

The following recommendations of best practices are designed to improve student access to support and services that aid in prevention through early intervention. These practices make schools more responsive to the challenges and recurring problems faced by students at risk for failure in academic and/or behavioral domains.

First, systematic universal screening using proven methods as described in this chapter are necessary to effectively address the underreferral of students with externalizing and internalizing disorders. Left to their own devices, teachers are unlikely to refer students at the levels needed to match the rates of occurrence for these disorders, especially internalizing problems. A tragic consequence of underreferral is a broad-based failure of schools to detect and interrupt destructive trajectories for at-risk youth early in their development.

Second, the lack of integration of mental health services and supports in the routine operation of schools also continues to be a pervasive problem. Hoagwood et al. (2007) and Adelman and Taylor (2004) have made persuasive cases as to the added value of making such a structural change. We strongly endorse their arguments and believe that students and parents are not well served when up to approximately 20% of students are in need of services but are denied access to them.

Third, assessments for screening and identification differ in form and substance from those needed to design or select appropriate instructional and behavioral interventions. Elliott, Gresham, Frank, and Beddow (2007) have contributed an excellent analysis of the assessment forms and key features of measurement instruments that can be used for conducting screening and for linking the results of screening to proven and promising interventions. Elliott, Gresham, et al. argue that assessment instruments of this type should be evaluated in terms of their intervention validity.

Currently, there is an urgent need to integrate systematic screening efforts with RTI service delivery models so at-risk students can have access to evidence-based interventions at primary, secondary, and tertiary prevention levels. Mass screening assessments that are appropriately scheduled in conjunction with RTI implementation could be of particular value in informing decisions regarding which students require a more intensive level of intervention. To date, very few demonstrations of this sort of integration have been reported in the professional literature.

We recommend that universal screening approaches apply the more rigorous diagnostic criteria and methods used in the ROC system described in this chapter. This has long been the case in medicine and psychology but is only now being adopted by educators. We believe it would result in much-improved decision making in regard to the schools' handling of cases involving at-risk students.

There is an ongoing need to restructure the roles of school psychologists and other school-based assessment specialists so they can work effectively in collaboration with school and district-level personnel in screening, identification, and progress monitoring, and in the domains of intervention design, delivery, and supervision. At present, there is considerable duplication of effort and poor use of resources in this regard within large numbers of school districts.

STATE OF THE SCIENCE AND NEEDED RESEARCH

In the past decade an emerging interest in systematic screening and early detection has driven the development of a number of approaches and instruments. These approaches have improved our collective ability in screening, particularly within the 2- to 5-year-old age range (see Bricker, Squires, & Mounts, 1995, in press; Walker, Severson, & Feil, 1995). In addition, better standards for judging promising assessments and technological advances have resulted in improved screening outcomes and in greater correlation of those outcomes with intervention services and supports. However, many issues remain to be addressed. The areas below are in urgent need of additional research and investment:

- Social marketing of the value and benefits of systematic screening in developing school success for all students. Marketing efforts should highlight the critically important role of the classroom teacher as an initiator of the early intervention process.
- Research to determine the acceptability and utility of different approaches to screening among school personnel who must decide whether and how screening is implemented. In this context, there is a need to evaluate the efficacy of different strategies for persuading schools to adopt universal screening procedures.
- Additional research on the predictive validity of early screening-identification efforts (Albers, Glover, & Kratochwill, 2007). This is one of the most important issues facing the field and is crucial to making the case for the value of early screening efforts across a range of educational and noneducational contexts.
- Research to develop usable assessments of risk and protective factors operating in the lives of students who fail Tier 2 or Tier 3 interventions. Such assessments need to be both brief and relevant; they should inform the clinical diagnostic process, as well as wraparound case management treatment plans that are ultimately developed.
- Differentiation of the roles of national norms and local norms in decision making regarding at-risk students in screening, identification, and intervention-related assessments.
- Research on the comparative accuracy of different screening systems on representative and diverse samples of school children to evaluate the positive predictive value of each screening system and to determine which outcomes are best predicted for subgroups of students.

CONCLUSION

Schools provide the best setting in which to conduct universal screening efforts to detect those youth who may be at risk for behavior problems and to begin the process of early intervention. Schools also are the best setting for establishing *prevention* initiatives that foster collaboration among families, community-based professionals, and key educational decision makers. Recent advances in the conceptual models, tools, and interventions and knowledge of such systems now enable schools to begin addressing the complex needs of school-age children and youth who are experiencing serious behavior problems, disorders, and associated impairments (see Detrich, Keyworth, & States, 2007; Glover & Albers, 2007; Hoagwood et al., 2007; Levitt et al., 2007). Currently available universal screening approaches have substantial efficacy and proven viability and can help make this vision an effective reality for tomorrow's schools. By combining universal screening approaches with evidence-based approaches such as SWPBS, schools can significantly increase the potential for successfully influencing this historically intractable problem in schools.

REFERENCES

Achenbach, T. M. (1991). *Manual for the child behavior checklist/4–18 and the 1991 profile.* Burlington: University of Vermont, Department of Psychiatry.

Adelman, H., & Taylor, L. (2004). Promoting mental health in schools in the midst of school reform. *Journal of School Health, 70,* 171–178.

Albers, C., Glover, T., & Kratochwill, T. (2007). Introduction to the special issue: How can universal screening enhance educational and mental health outcomes? *Journal of School Psychology, 45,* 113–116.

American Educational Research Association (AERA), American Psychological Association, & National Council on Measurement in Education. (1999). *Standards for educational and psychological testing.* Washington, DC: AERA.

Atkins, M., Frazier, S., Adil, J., & Talbot, E. (2003). School-based mental health services in urban communities. In M. Weist, S. Evans, & N. Tashman (Eds.), *Handbook of school mental health: Advancing practice and research* (pp. 165–178). New York: Kluwer Academic/Plenum Publishers.

Atkins, M. S., Graczyk, P. A., Frazier, S. L., & Abdul-Adil, J. (2003), Toward a new model for promoting urban children's mental health: Accessible, effective, and sustainable school-based mental health services. *School Psychology Review, 32,* 503–519.

Biglan, T., Wang, M., & Walberg, H. (2003). Preventing youth problems. New York: Kluwer Academic/Plenum Publishers.

Bricker, D., Squires, J., & Mounts, L. (1995). *Ages and stages questionnaires: A parent-completed, child-monitoring system.* Baltimore: Brookes.

Bricker, D., Squires, J., & Mounts, L. (in press). *Ages and stages questionnaires: A parent-completed, child-monitoring system* (3rd ed.). Baltimore: Brookes.

Burns, B., & Hoagwood, K. (2002). Community treatment for youth: Evidence-based interventions for severe emotional and behavioral disorders. New York: Oxford University Press.

Caldarella, P., Young, E. L., Richardson, M. J., Young, B. J., & Young, R. (2008). Validation of the systematic screening for behavior disorders in middle and junior high school. *Journal of Emotional and Behavioral Disorders, 16* 105–117

Costello, J., Mustillo, S., Erkanli, A., Keeler, G., & Angold, A. (2003). Prevalence and development of psychiatric disorders in childhood and adolescence. *Archives of General Psychiatry, 60,* 837–844.

Crews, S., Bender, H., Cook, C., Gresham, F., Kern, L., & Vanderwood, M. (2007). Risk and protective factors of emotional and/or behavioral disorders in children and adolescents: A mega-analytic synthesis. *Behavioral Disorders, 32,* 64–77.

Detrich, R., Keyworth, R., & States, J. (2007). A roadmap to evidence-based education: Building an evidence-based culture. *Journal of Evidence-Based Practices for Schools, 8,* 26–44.

Donovan, M., & Cross, C. (2002). *Minority students in gifted and special education.* Washington, DC: National Academy Press.

Elliott, S., Gresham, F., Frank, J., & Beddow, P. (2007). Intervention validity of social behavior rating scales: Features of assessments that link results to treatment plans. Manuscript submitted for publication.

Elliott, S., Huai, N., & Roach, A. (2007). Universal and early screening for educational difficulties: Current and future approaches. *Journal of School Psychology, 45,* 137–161.

Fan, J., Upadhye, S., & Worster, A. (2006). Understanding receiver operating characteristic (ROC) curves. *Canadian Journal of Emergency Medicine, 8*(1), 19–20.

Fleiss, J. L. (1981). Statistical methods for rates and proportions (2nd ed.). New York: Wiley.

Gerber, M., & Semmel, M. (1984). Teacher as imperfect test: Reconceptualizing the referral process. *Educational Psychologist, 19,* 137–148.

Glover, T., & Albers, C. (2007). Considerations for evaluating universal screening assessments. *Journal of School Psychology, 45,* 117–136.

Gresham, F. (1991). Conceptualizing behavior disorders in terms of resistance to intervention. *School Psychology Review, 20,* 23–36.

Gresham, F. (2004). Current status and future directions of school-based behavioral interventions. *School Psychology Review, 33,* 326–343.

Hawkins, D., Catalano, R., Kosterman, R., Abbott, R., & Hill, K. (1999). Preventing adolescent health-risk behaviors by strengthening protection during childhood. *Archives of Pediatrics and Adolescent Medicine, 153,* 226–234.

Hintze, J. M., Ryan, A. L., & Stoner, G. (2003). Concurrent validity and diagnostic accuracy of the dynamic indicators of basic early literacy skills and the comprehensive test of phonological processing. *School Psychology Review, 32,* 541–556.

Hoagwood, K. & Erwin, H. (1997). Effectiveness of school-based mental health services for children: A 10-year research review. *Journal of Child and Family Studies, 6,* 435–451.

Hoagwood, K., Olin, S. S., Kerker, B., Kratochwill, T., Crowe, M., & Saka, N. (2007). Empirically based school interventions targeted at academic and mental health functioning. *Journal of Emotional and Behavioral Disorders, 15,* 66–92.

Horner, R., Sugai, G., Lewis-Palmer, T., & Todd, A. (2001). Teaching school-wide behavioral expectations. *Report on Emotional and Behavioral Disorders in Youth, 1*(4), 77–80.

Horowitz, S., Leaf, P., Leventhal, J., Forsyth, B., & Speechley, K. (1992). Identification and management of psychosocial and developmental problems in community-based, primary care pediatric practices. *Pediatrics, 89,* 480–485.

Hsiao, J. K., Bartko, J. J., & Potter, W. Z. (1989). Diagnosing diagnoses: Receiver operating characteristic methods and psychiatry. *Archives of General Psychiatry, 46,* 664–667.

Individuals with Disabilities Education Improvement Act of 2004, Pub. Law No. 108-446, 118 Stat. 2647 (2004).

Kame'enui, E., Good, R., & Harn, B. (2005). Beginning reading failure and the quantification of risk: Reading behavior as the supreme index. In W. Heward, T. Heron, N. Neef, S. Peterson, D. Sainato, G. Cartledge, et al. (Eds.), *Focus on behavior analysis in education: Achievements, challenges, and opportunities* (pp. 88–89). Upper Saddle River, NJ: Merrill/Prentice Hall.

Katz, D., & Foxman, B. (1993). How well do prediction equations predict? Using receiver operating characteristic curves and accuracy curves to compare validity and generalizability. *Epidemiology, 4,* 319–326.

Kauffman, J. (2005a). *Characteristics of emotional and behavioral disorders of children and youth.* (8th ed.). Upper Saddle River, NJ: Merrill/Prentice Hall.

Kauffman, J. (2005b). How we prevent the prevention of emotional and behavioral difficulties in education. In P. Clough, P. Garner, J. T. Pardeck, & F. K. O. Yuen (Eds.), *Handbook of emotional and behavioral difficulties in education* (pp. 429–440). London: SAGE.

Kraemer, H. (1992). Evaluating medical tests: Objective and quantitative guidelines. Newbury Park, CA: SAGE.

Leff, S., & Lakin, R. (2005). Playground-based observational systems: A review and implications for practitioners and researchers. *School Psychology Review, 34,* 475–489.

Levitt, J., Saka, N., Hunter-Romanelli, L., & Hoagwood, K. (2007). Early identification of mental health problems in schools: The status of instrumentation. *Journal of School Psychology, 45,* 163–192.

Lloyd, J., Kauffman, J., Landrum, T., & Roe, D. (1992). Why do teachers refer students for special education? An analysis of referral records. *Exceptionality, 2,* 115–126.

Loeber, R., & Farrington, D. (Eds.). (1998). *Serious and violent juvenile offenders: Risk factors and successful interventions.* Thousand Oaks, CA: SAGE.

Murphy, J. M., Burwick, D. M., Weinstein, M. C., Boris, J. F., Budman, S. H., & Klerman, G. L. (1987). Performance of screening and diagnostic tests: Application of receiver operating characteristics analysis. *Archives of General Psychiatry, 44,* 550–555.

Musti-Rao, S., & Cartledge, G. (2007). Effects of a supplemental early reading intervention with at-risk urban learners. *Topics in Early Childhood Special Education, 27,* 70–85.

O'Neill, R., Horner, R., Albin, R., Sprague, J., Newton, S., & Storey, K. (2002). Functional assessment and program development for problem behavior: A practical handbook. (2nd ed.). Pacific Grove, CA: Brooks/Cole.

Peng, C.-Y. J., & So, T.-S. H. (2002). Logistic regression analysis and reporting: A primer. *Understanding Statistics, 1,* 31–70.

Pepe, M. S. (2003). *The statistical evaluation of medical tests for classification and prediction.* New York: Oxford University Press.

Reid, J., Patterson, G., & Snyder, J. (Eds.). (2002). Antisocial behavior in children and adolescents: A developmental analysis and the Oregon Model for Intervention. Washington, DC: American Psychological Association.

Roberts, R. E., Lewinsohn, P. M., & Seeley, J. R. (1991). Screening for adolescent depression: A comparison of depression scales. *Journal of the American Academy of Child and Adolescent Psychiatry, 30,* 58–66.

Seeley, J. R., Stice, E., & Rohde, P. (2007). Screening for depression prevention: Identifying adolescent girls at high risk for future depression. Manuscript submitted for publication.

Severson, H., & Biglan, A. (1989). Rationale for the use of passive consent in smoking prevention research: Politics, policy, and pragmatics. *Preventive Medicine, 18,* 267–279.

Severson, H. H., & Ary, D. V. (1983). Sampling bias due to consent procedures with adolescents. *Addictive Behaviors, 8,* 433–437.

Severson, H. H., Walker, H. M., Hope-Doolittle, J., Kratochwill, T. R., & Gresham, F. (2007). Proactive early screening to detect behaviorally at-risk students: Issues, approaches, emerging innovations, and professional practices. *Journal of School Psychology, 45,* 193–223.

Shaffer, D., Fisher, P., Lucas, C. P., Dulcan, M. K., & Schwab-Stone, M. E. (2000). NIMH Diagnostic Interview Schedule for Children Version IV (NIMH DISC-IV): Description, differences from previous versions, and reliability of some common diagnoses. *Journal of the American Academy of Child and Adolescent Psychiatry, 39* 28–38.

Silberglitt, B., & Hintze, J. (2005). Formative assessment using CBM-R cut scores to track progress toward success on state-mandated achievement tests: A comparison of methods. *Journal of Psychoeducational Assessment, 23,* 304–325.

Sugai, G., Horner, R., & Gresham, F. (2002). Behaviorally effective school environments. In M. Shinn, H. Walker, & G. Stoner (Eds.). *Interventions for academic and behavior problems II: Preventive and remedial approaches.* (pp. 315–350). Bethesda, MD: National Association of School Psychologists.

Swets, J. A. (1996). *Signal detection theory and ROC analysis in psychology and diagnostics: Collected papers.* Hillsdale, NJ: Erlbaum.

Swets, J. A., Dawes, R. M., & Monahan, J. (2000). Psychological science can improve diagnostic decisions. *Psychological Science in the Public Interest, 1,* 1–26.

Tanner, W. P., & Swets, J. A. (1954). A decision-making theory of signal detection. *Psychological Review, 61*(6), 401–409.

U.S. Department of Education Office of Special Education and Rehabilitative Services. (2002). *A new era: Revitalizing special education for children and their families.* Washington, DC: Author.

U.S. Public Health Service. (2000). *Report of the Surgeon General's Conference on Children's Mental Health: A national action agenda.* Washington, DC: U.S. Department of Health and Human Services.

VanDerHeyden, A., & Witt, J. (2005). Quantifying the context of assessment: Capturing the effects of base rates on teacher referral and a problem-solving model of identification. *School Psychology Review, 34,* 161–183.

Vander Stoep, A., Weiss, N., Kuo, E., Cheney, D., & Cohen, P. (2003). What proportion of failure to complete secondary school in the U.S. population is attributable to adolescent psychiatric disorder? *Journal of Behavioral Health Services & Research, 30,* 119–124.

Walker, H. M. (2004). Commentary: Use of evidence-based intervention in schools: Where we've been, where we are, and where we need to go. *School Psychology Review, 33,* 398–407.

Walker, H. M., Horner, R., Sugai, G., Bullis, M., Sprague, J., Bricker, D., et al. (1996). Integrated approaches to preventing antisocial behavior patterns among school-age children and youth. *Journal of Emotional and Behavioral Disorders, 4,* 194–209.

Walker, H. M., Nishioka, V., Zeller, R., Severson, H., & Feil, E. (2000). Causal factors and partial solutions for the persistent under-identification of students having emotional and behavioral disorders in the context of schooling. *Assessment for Effective Intervention, 26,* 29–40.

Walker, H. M., Ramsey, E., & Gresham, F. (2004). *Antisocial behavior in school: Strategies and best practices* (2nd ed.). Belmont, CA: Wadsworth.

Walker, H. M., & Severson, H. H. (1990). *Systematic screening for behavior disorders.* Longmont, CO: Sopris West.

Walker, H. M., Severson, H., & Feil, E. (1995). *The early screening project.* Longmont, CO: Sopris West.

Walker, H. M, Severson, H., Naquin, G., D'Atrio, C., Feil, E., Hawken, L., et al. (in press). Implementing universal screening systems within an RTI-PBS context. In B. Doll, W. Pfohl, & J. Yoon (Eds.), *Handbook of youth prevention science.* New York: Routledge.

Walker, H. M., Severson, H., & Seeley, J. (2009). *Survey to determine the need for development of an electronic version of the SSBD screening-identification procedure.* Eugene, OR: Deschutes Research.

Watson, T. (2007). Introduction to the special issue: From the Wing Institute. *Journal of Evidence-Based Practices for Schools, 8,* 2–3.

CHAPTER 26

Social Development in Preschool Classrooms: Promoting Engagement, Competence, and School Readiness

Robin L. Hojnoski
Lehigh University

Kristen N. Missall
University of Iowa

INTRODUCTION

For many practitioners and researchers, school readiness is an entirely academic construct that encompasses areas such as study skills, beginning literacy, early mathematics, and emergent writing skills (DiPerna & Elliott, 2002). To others, school readiness is primarily about mastery of school-related social–emotional skills, including communication, self-regulation, and the development of social support networks among peers (Graue, 2006; Raver, 2002). This either/or perspective regarding school readiness fails to consider the complex interactions that occur between the development of academic and social–emotional skills (Zins, Bloodworth, Weissberg, & Walberg, 2004). Skills and knowledge in these two domains do not develop in isolation but emerge together within a transactional process that connects experiences in a variety of contexts. As a result, skills and competence gained in one domain are generally linked to development in the other (Raver & Knitzer, 2002). Furthermore, a child-centered perspective of school readiness (i.e., the child is or is not ready for school) fails to consider the importance of appropriately preparing the classroom environment so that classrooms are ready to actively support development of academic and social–emotional skills and competency in *all* children.

Although recent research has provided clear evidence on the importance of early academic skills to later school success, learning is also a social phenomenon (Duncan et al., 2007; Zins et al., 2004). Particularly at the preschool level, children's knowledge

---

Address all correspondence regarding the manuscript to Robin Hojnoski, PhD at roh206@lehigh.edu.

and skills typically develop through ongoing social relationships with peers and adults. Through their meaningful interactions with the social (e.g., teachers, peers, routines, instruction) and physical (e.g., materials, space, arrangements) environment, young children develop the academic and social skills necessary for achieving school success (McConnell & Missall, 2004). For example, a child who is actively engaged in shared story reading develops concepts about print and phonological awareness; similarly, a child who plays with peers learns negotiation skills, social reciprocity, role taking, and sharing. Children who are not actively engaged miss opportunities to learn crucial skills that are precursors to achieving academic and social competence levels that are both expected and necessary for school success (Coolahan, Fantuzzo, Mendez, & McDermott, 2000; Fantuzzo, Perry, & McDermott, 2004). Thus, we view engagement as an overarching construct that has the potential to conceptually integrate academic and social–emotional perspectives on school readiness. Engagement is required for the development of academic and social competencies and thus serves as an important target outcome in efforts to facilitate school readiness.

In McFall's (1982) classic conceptualization of the relationship between skills and competence, skills are viewed as the specific strategies and tactics used by an individual to address a particular social task. Competency refers to the judgment of parents, teachers, and peers as to the child's ability to effectively use academic and social skills to achieve a target goal.

Figure 1 illustrates the relationship between development of specific skills, engagement, and academic and social competency as foundations for school readiness. As the figure shows, skill development in preschool classrooms centers on learning-related social skills (e.g., listening, following directions, task persistence) and interpersonal social skills (e.g., initiating and maintaining interactions, sharing, communicating). Although presented as two separate skill areas, development in one area influences development in the other. Moreover, these skills contribute to a child's ability to actively engage in learning opportunities within her or his environment, which in turn leads to both academic and social competence. The appropriate and effective application of learning-related and interpersonal social skills becomes a key determinant of a child's overall competence, as judged by significant individuals in the child's life, and may be viewed as an indicator of school readiness. Effectively arranged classrooms play a critical role in supporting engagement and the development and mastery of the specific skills that lead to competency.

The child's development of specific skills, level of engagement, and overall perceived competencies are influenced by many variables, including age, developmental level, gender, and other biological characteristics, factors that are sometimes referred to as "inside-out" influences (Odom, McConnell, & Brown, 2007; Whitehurst & Lonigan, 1998). Two important inside-out influences are self-regulation and behavioral self-control. "Outside-in" influences include culture and early experiences within the family, community, and classroom, and are equally important to understanding a child's journey toward achieving school success (Odom et al., 2007). Physical (e.g., materials, classroom layout), programmatic (e.g., curriculum,

Figure 1. Relationship between social and academic skills, engagement, competency, and school readiness.

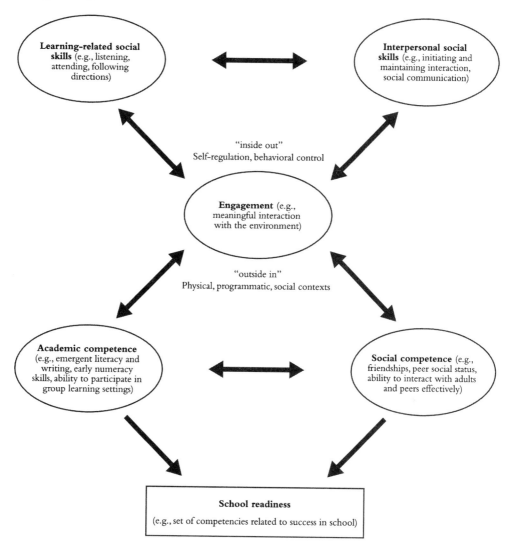

instruction), and social (interactions with peers and adults) contexts, shown in Figure 1, are important outside-in variables. The dynamic exchanges between individuals and their environments are critical to the development of skills, engagement, and competency. In preschool classrooms, the physical, programmatic, and social contexts offer opportunities to create conditions that maximize children's engagement. Thus, it is important to focus on whether and how the preschool classroom environment promotes specific skill development through active engagement as a means of preparing children for school success.

Outcomes associated with academic and social competence for preschool-age children are not directly addressed in this chapter—for example, early literacy, early number sense (numeracy), and emergent writing (academic competence), and peer acceptance, friendships, and successful social interactions (social competence). Instead, the chapter focuses on how the preschool classroom can be strategically arranged to promote the development of learning-related and interpersonal social skills, thereby increasing engagement as a means of promoting competence and, ultimately, school readiness.

TARGET SKILLS FOR PREPARING YOUNG CHILDREN FOR SCHOOL

A substantial body of research evidence suggests that social behaviors important to school readiness are (a) learning-related social skills, and (b) peer-related social skills (Bronson, 1994; Cooper & Farran, 1988; McClelland & Morrison, 2003; McClelland, Morrison, & Holmes, 2000). Learning-related social skills have also been called approaches to learning and are defined as observable behaviors that children use to engage in learning and social activities (Fantuzzo et al., 2007; Fantuzzo et al., 2004; McDermott et al., 2002). Because children's interactions with adults are as important to school readiness as their interactions with their peers are (Clark & Ladd, 2000; DeMulder, Denham, Schmidt, & Mitchell, 2000), we use the term *interpersonal social skills* to include all social relationships. Both skill sets support a child's ability to participate successfully in classroom activities and engage with peers, adults, and materials.

Learning-Related Social Skills

Learning-related social skills can be defined as verbal and physical behaviors that are goal oriented and consistent with the demands of the situation. Learning-related social skills include such things as listening, following directions, participating in group activities, attending to a task, and organizing and using task-related materials (Agostin & Bain, 1997; Foulks & Morrow, 1989; McClelland & Morrison, 2003; McClelland et al., 2000). For example, if the class is engaged in a large group activity, learning-related social skills might include having one's body and eyes oriented toward the source of instruction, answering questions verbally, or moving together in rhythm with a song.

Learning-related social skills are also part of children's approaches to learning that involve problem solving, task persistence, motivation, and attitudes toward learning (National Education Goals Panel, 1997). These types of skills appear to be uniquely related to children's academic success (Cooper & Farran, 1988; Cooper & Speece, 1988; Fantuzzo et al., 2007; McClelland et al., 2000; McWayne, Fantuzzo, & McDermott, 2004) and are valued by educators as essential skills for academic survival and for satisfactory adjustment to and participation in the classroom (Foulks & Morrow, 1989).

Children who demonstrate learning-related social skills are likely to be more engaged in classroom activities and learning interactions with peers and adults in the classroom. They are likely to benefit more from their early education experiences and have less difficulty responding to the specific task demands of routine instruction. The link between these skills and the development of academic skills in the areas of language, emergent literacy, early mathematics, and emergent writing is both intuitive and logical (Missall & Hojnoski, 2007).

Interpersonal Social Skills

Interpersonal social skills include initiating and maintaining positive interactions, sharing, taking turns, and engaging in cooperative play (Bronson, 1994; McClelland & Morrison, 2003). Because much incidental learning occurs through peer interactions, developing solid peer relationships is an important part of the early education experience and influences overall adjustment to school (Ladd, 1990; Ladd & Coleman, 1997). Children's peer-related social skills are essential for developing a larger network of friends and achieving greater acceptance among peers. Also, children with strong skills are more likely to participate in classroom activities and demonstrate active engagement, which can lead to higher levels of academic achievement (Ladd, Birch, & Buhs, 1999). Finally, peer-related social skills have substantial face validity. In a survey of 470 early childhood educators, social–emotional skills and abilities were rated as more important than language and literacy or early math skills and abilities (Kowalski, Pretti-Frontczak, & Johnson, 2001).

Children also need to interact effectively with adults in their environment. Although some of these interactions are characterized by learning-related social skills, such as listening to the teacher and following directions, children also need to be able to engage interpersonally with adults in general. Many of the social skills required for social interactions with peers may be applied to interactions with adults; however, children need to learn flexibility in their use of skills, as adult–child interactions obviously differ from peer interactions. For example, communication skills may be more important in adult–child interactions, whereas play skills may be more important in peer interactions. Children who are able to regulate their emotions and independently navigate their classroom are more likely to establish appropriate relationships with their teachers (Pianta, Nimetz, & Bennett, 1997). Relationships characterized by positive reciprocal interactions can further support exploration of and engagement with the learning environment, fostering continued growth and development.

Learning-related and interpersonal social skills appear to operate in concert. That is, research shows that children who have positive peer interaction skills also display positive engagement in the classroom (Coolahan et al., 2000; Fantuzzo, Bulotsky-Shearer, Fusco, & McWayne, 2005; Fantuzzo et al., 2004). Furthermore, indicators of effective peer-related social skills, such as having friends or being accepted by peers, have been linked to positive school adjustment (Ladd, 1990; Ladd & Coleman, 1997). Conversely, children who display negative peer interactions, or children who are nonsocial and withdrawn from peer interactions, display conduct problems and maladaptive learning, inattention, low motivation, and lower affective engagement (Coolahan et al., 2000; Fantuzzo, Bulotsky-Shearer, et al., 2005). In addition, children who have responsive relationships with their teachers benefit more from learning opportunities and tend to have more success in developing academic skills, being accepted by peers, and establishing reciprocal, mutually satisfying friendships (Clark & Ladd, 2000; Howes & Smith, 1995; Pianta & Stuhlman, 2004).

Engagement

In the early education field, engagement has been defined as "the amount of time children spend interacting with the environment (i.e., with adults, children, materials) in a manner that is developmentally appropriate" (McWilliam, Trivette, & Dunst, 1985, p. 60). Research on engagement led to empirically validated levels that form a continuum of behavioral complexity, from no engagement to sophisticated engagement (McWilliam & Casey, 2008). Engagement has been used by researchers as an indicator of the quality of the classroom environment (McCormick, Noonan, & Heck, 1998; Ridley, McWilliam, & Oates, 2000) and is emerging as a potential target that can be used in a tiered model of assessment and intervention; for example, engagement may be used as a behavioral indicator of response to an intervention (Barnett, Daly, Jones, & Lentz, 2004; VanDerHeyden, Witt, & Barnett, 2005). Furthermore, research with school-age children suggests that engagement is an important indicator of academic success and achievement, thereby strengthening its potential as a target for intervention (Greenwood, 1991; Rosenshine, 1981).

Within this chapter, engagement is defined broadly as active and meaningful interaction with the physical (classroom setting and materials), programmatic (curriculum and instruction), and social environment (child–teacher and peer interactions), and it incorporates both learning-related and interpersonal social skills. In the continuum of engagement noted above, we focus on behaviors consistent with sophisticated engagement, including active manipulation of materials in a goal-directed manner, social communication, symbolic play, and problem solving (McWilliam & Casey, 2008). Although focused attention represents a more passive form of engagement, it is also included because it indirectly facilitates academic and social competence through the learning process.

Assessment and intervention designed to increase engagement in preschool classrooms can target both learning-related and interpersonal social skills. Young children are likely to display considerable variation in their skill development in these areas, and as a result may need varying levels of support to engage in classroom activities and social interactions. Accordingly, a tiered model of assessment and intervention that offers differing levels of support to match children's needs provides a valuable framework for supporting skill development that will increase all children's engagement in early learning and improve their social interactions.

ASSESSMENT IN A TIERED MODEL OF SERVICE DELIVERY

A critical component of intervention is effective assessment. Prevention and early intervention with behavioral or developmental difficulties are essential in maximizing opportunities to benefit from meaningful interaction. In a tiered model of intervention, child performance data (e.g., behavioral indicators and early academic indicators) are central to decision making about the support or intervention warranted (VanDerHeyden & Snyder, 2006). Data from universal screening procedures can be used initially to determine levels of performance and the need for additional support or intervention. Progress monitoring data collected over time can be used to inform continued instructional decision making (VanDerHeyden & Snyder). Data can be gathered through a variety of means, including direct assessment, rating scales, permanent products, and observation. Effective systems of assessment should be driven by careful consideration of the purpose of assessment and by linking of data to instruction and intervention (National Research Council, 2008).

Generic Developmental Screening

As depicted in Figure 1, a number of "inside out" factors can influence a child's level of engagement and subsequent skill development. A major obstacle to the timely delivery of early intervention services is failure to identify, early and accurately, infants, toddlers, and young children who have developmental delays or disorders. Obtaining needed services for such children and their families requires the establishment of comprehensive, first-level screening programs. The goal of comprehensive screening programs is to accurately detect and separate the few infants and young children who require more extensive evaluation from those who do not. To be useful, first-level screening programs need to assess large numbers of children; therefore they require screening measures or procedures that are easy to administer, low-cost, efficient, accurate, and appropriate for diverse populations.

Ages and Stages Questionnaires, Third Edition: A Parent-Completed, Child-Monitoring System (ASQ; Squires & Bricker, 2009), meets these criteria for a first-level comprehensive screening program. The ASQ screening system is composed of 21 questionnaires designed to be completed by parents or primary caregivers. Each questionnaire is divided into five areas: communication, gross motor, fine motor, problem solving, and personal–social and contains 30 developmental items written in simple, straightforward language. Another section addresses general parental concerns. Questionnaire intervals include 2, 4, 6, 8, 9, 10, 12, 14, 16, 18, 20, 22, 24, 27, 30, 33, 36, 42, 48, 54, and 60 months of age. In most cases, the ASQ questionnaires can accurately identify infants or young children who are in need of further evaluation to determine whether they are eligible for early intervention services.

The ASQ questionnaires can be used for two important purposes. First, they can accomplish comprehensive, first-level screening of large groups of infants and young children. For example, parents can complete questionnaires about their child prior to a kindergarten roundup or at well-baby checkups. Providing information at these junctures can be important in monitoring *all* children's development to ensure that children are making adequate progress and to inform additional assessment and timely intervention in the event there are developmental concerns. Second, the questionnaires can be used to monitor the status of children who are at risk for developmental disabilities or delays resulting from medical factors such as low birth weight, prematurity, seizures, or serious illness, or from environmental factors such as poverty, parents with mental impairments, history of abuse and/or neglect in the home, or teenage parents. In this way, information is provided on an ongoing and formative basis that can be used for program planning purposes. In the context of engagement, systematic use of the ASQ may provide early educators with information about a child's skills across developmental domains that may interfere with levels of engagement. Such information allows teachers to use appropriate strategies and supports to increase levels of engagement for individual children.

Preschool Social–Emotional Screening

Squires, Bricker, and Twombly (2002) developed the ASQ:SE system (Ages and Stages Questionnaire: Social Emotional) to complement the ASQ by specifically addressing the social and emotional status of young children in the 3 to 66 months age range and to provide early childhood educators and preschool professionals with a tool for screening social–emotional problems. Like the ASQ, the ASQ:SE has strong psychometrics and receives consistently positive ratings from a broad range of users. This instrument can be used as a reliable, valid, and acceptable resource for identifying early those young children who have weak social–emotional repertoires and whose later school success is at risk. Squires and Bricker (2007) also created an activity-based approach to developing young children's social–emotional competence that serves as a companion guide to the ASQ:SE screening tool. This combined assessment-intervention package provides early childhood educators with a powerful tool for enhancing young children's developmental mastery in the two critical domains of social and emotional competence so important for school success (see chapter 12 in this book for more complete details on the ASQ:SE and its companion intervention-curriculum guide).

A tiered approach to assessment, the Early Screening Project (ESP; Walker, Severson, & Feil, 1995) was designed, trial tested, normed, and validated in a series of studies by Feil, Severson, and Walker (1995, 1998) and Walker et al. (1998). The ESP is a multiple-gating approach to identifying 3- to 5-year-olds who are at risk for developing either externalizing or internalizing behavior problems and disorders. The ESP is a validated adaptation of the Systematic Screening for Behavior Disorders (SSBD) screening procedure (Walker & Severson, 1990), and like the ASQ:SE, it was developed in response to professionals' requests for a preschool version. The ESP accomplishes universal screening within preschool classrooms, meaning that each enrolled child has an equal chance to be nominated and identified as being at risk for externalizing or internalizing problems and disorders. The ESP process consists of three interconnected and sequential screening stages. In Stage 1 the preschool teacher nominates and rank orders children in relation to externalizing and internalizing behavioral criteria. In Stage 2 the highest ranked children from Stage 1 are rated on a series of brief scales that assess adaptive and maladaptive forms of behavior. In Stage 3, children exceeding Stage 2 cutoff points are observed in structured and unstructured preschool settings using a specially designed observation code. Those children demonstrating significant levels of problem behavior in Stage 3 are then referred for appropriate intervention and/or further assessment. The ESP has excellent psychometric features and has been extensively investigated in a series of preschool studies.

Assessing Engagement

In addition to universal screening and procedures specific to social–emotional development, child data may be generated through assessment specifically focused on engagement. Data on both group and individual child levels of engagement may be collected through structured observational systems, or teacher rating scales (McWilliam & Casey, 2008). For example, if classroom levels of engagement are of interest, an observer may count the number of children in the classroom at a given time, and then note the number of children actively engaged. The proportion of children actively engaged to total number of children can provide an indicator of the extent to which the classroom promotes active engagement and thus inform classroom changes. If individual child engagement is the focus, observational procedures can be used to track the total amount of time a child is engaged. Additionally, teacher rating scales may be used to provide an estimate of the child's level of engagement. Observational and rating scale data may be collected frequently over time to provide an indicator of behavioral change in response to changes in instructional strategies or supports. (See McWilliam & Casey for a more detailed discussion of methods to measure engagement.)

Assessing the Environment

To promote an ecological perspective of child behavior, effective systems should include systematic and regular assessment of the instructional environment. Given the impact that environmental arrangements can have on children's engagement in the classroom (Nordquist & Twardosz, 1990), routine evaluation of the extent to which the classroom supports such behavior is critical. There are an increasing number of tools available to assist educators with classroom evaluation (see National Research Council, 2008, for a detailed review of tools). Global assessment of the classroom environment can be accomplished using the Early Childhood Environment Rating Scale–Revised (ECERS-R; Harms, Clifford, & Cryer, 1998) and the Classroom Assessment Scoring System (CLASS; Pianta, La Paro, & Hamre, 2007). Some curricula commonly used in classrooms, such as the Creative Curriculum (Trister Dodge, Colker, & Heroman, 2002), also include a classroom environment evaluation component. Finally, the Early Language and Literacy Classroom Observation Tool Pre-K (ELLCO; Smith, Brady, &

Anastasopoulos, 2008) offers a means of evaluating the environment specifically as it relates to elements that support language and literacy development, and the Preschool Classroom Mathematics Inventory (PCMI: National Institute for Early Education Research, 2007) is designed to assess the quality of mathematics instruction in the preschool classroom.

Implementing a tiered approach to intervention requires a systematic approach to assessment, and the assessments described here may be used as part of such an approach. Regardless of the specific tool selected, assessment should be grounded in a problem-solving approach to identifying and evaluating instructional strategies. Consideration should be given to the instructional environment as well as to individual child characteristics and performance. Finally, assessment should be part of an integrated data collection system that is used to monitor child progress and guide decision making (National Research Council, 2008). The success of tiered models of intervention is largely influenced by the effective collection and use of assessment data.

THREE-TIERED APPROACH TO INTERVENTION

A number of multitiered intervention models have been described in the early childhood education literature (Brown, Odom, & Conroy, 2001; Fox, Dunlap, Hemmeter, Joseph, & Strain, 2003; Sandall & Schwartz, 2008). Consistent across all these models is the emphasis on interventions that progressively increase in intensity as the child's needs and problems dictate. Several key principles are reflected in these models:

- Minimizing the development of behavior problems by creating environments that teach, encourage, and support desired social behaviors
- Using interventions that are instructional and that may be directed toward children, individually or in groups, who have not responded to an intervention implemented at the previous level
- Using explicit, specialized, and individualized interventions for children who have greater needs and more severe problems

In the following sections, more attention is given to Tier 1 strategies than to Tiers 2 and 3 for several reasons. First, Tier 1 strategies constitute a universal approach designed to prevent problems from emerging and to reduce the need for more intensive interventions. They represent the broadest effort to provide all children with effective, empirically based practices that promote positive development. Second, Tier 1 strategies minimize potential stigma that may be associated with delivery of specialized instruction or intervention in preschool classrooms. Furthermore, these strategies have intuitive and logical appeal—when more effort is dedicated to promoting meaningful engagement, less effort has to be expended on addressing problem behaviors in the classroom. Finally, if tiered models of intervention are to be used in conjunction with tiered models of assessment and decision making, such as response to intervention, known as RTI (e.g., Recognition & Response; Buysse, Winton, & Zimmerman, 2007), strategies used at Tier 1 must be of the highest quality to ensure accurate decision making if the intensity of services needs to be increased.

Early education programs face particular challenges in implementing Tier 1 strategies, given the lack of consensus about appropriate programming; the limited availability of empirically supported, universal programming for preschoolers; and the variability of factors such as attendance, setting, and curricular approach (National Research Council, 2001). For example, children might be in half-day, part-time, or full-time preschools; they might be in state-funded preschools, private programs, Head Start, or for-profit child care; and the school's approach might be Montessori, art-based, or developmentally appropriate practices. These variations make it imperative that early childhood education professionals identify core elements of high-quality preschool programming and ensure that those elements are implemented with integrity for all young children.

Some features of quality preschool programs have been broadly identified as small class size, low adult–child ratios, and rich discourse (National Research Council, 2001). In addition, the specific elements necessary for establishing effective classroom environments using multitiered models of intervention have been outlined (Brown et al., 2001; Fox et al., 2003). This chapter presents research on environmental arrangements in preschool classrooms to support social competence by promoting learning-related and interpersonal social skills specifically, and engagement more broadly. Environmental arrangements—physical, programmatic, and social features of classrooms—are consistent with Tier 1 approaches in that they are applied with all children and represent an important consideration in designing effective learning environments. Tier 1 strategies based on careful consideration, deliberate planning, and intentional behavior produce positive outcomes and reduce the need for more intensive interventions. A classroom that is strategically arranged to promote desired behavior is essential in a tiered intervention model because it provides a foundation for implementing interventions that are more intensive and individualized.

Tier 1 Environmental Arrangements

A primary goal of Tier 1 strategies is to promote positive development by creating environments that teach, encourage, and support desired behaviors through intentional use of prompts and cues for positive behavior (Sugai & Horner, 2002). Environmental arrangements refer to the physical, programmatic, and social features of classrooms, all of which may be manipulated to obtain and support desired outcomes (Nordquist & Twardosz, 1990). The environmental arrangements for preschool classrooms discussed below have empirical support and are viewed as features of quality early education environments; that is, they contribute to the development of learning-related and interpersonal social skills and engagement.

Physical Classroom Environment

Strategies that target changing the classroom environment, such as arrangement of the classroom and materials available, offer a means of creating classrooms that promote and support engagement and the development of essential skills. In addition to developmentally appropriate practice, the environment can be strategically arranged to produce desired changes in child behavior, whether to address a particular problem behavior, achieve a specific goal, or promote a targeted skill (McEvoy, Fox, & Rosenberg, 1991; Nash, 1981). Two primary considerations with regard to learning-related and peer-related or interpersonal social skills are the physical layout of activity areas and the materials available in the classroom. Changing these can create opportunities for developing targeted skills and increasing engagement.

Activity areas can be arranged to promote problem solving, task persistence, and social interaction (Field, 1980). Areas should incorporate children's natural interests, with the goal of increasing and sustaining their motivation to actively engage in academic and social tasks. In addition, the compatibility of adjoining areas can be considered (Hart, 1978); for example, an area can be set up so it is free from other distractions, allowing the children to become deeply engaged in their work and develop task persistence. Placing the block area near high-traffic areas such as by the bathroom or in front of shelves may interfere with the children's sustained engagement with blocks. Adjoining areas can be strategically arranged to encourage spillover of play or to increase social interaction (Kinsman & Berk, 1979; Nash, 1981). Additionally, the size of the play area can allow for different types of peer interaction and positively affect levels of on-task behavior (Brown, Fox, & Brady, 1987; Krantz & Risley, 1977). The number of activity areas open at any one time can promote or inhibit interaction. If only a few activity areas are available to children, they have more opportunities to interact with one another. Certainly, some classroom areas are more intrinsically social than others, such as the dramatic play area. Finally, ensuring adequate space in each activity area fosters active, uninterrupted engagement (Hart, 1978).

Similar considerations should be given to the materials in the preschool classroom, to ensure that they are interesting and stimulating. (Brown et al., 1987). Children are more likely to use materials if they are simply made available; for example, if books are in the classroom, children are likely to read them (Adams, 1990; Schirrmacher, 1993). Young children also may be more likely to engage with materials when the materials are rotated to provide novelty (Nordquist & Twardosz, 1990). Furthermore, materials should be selected that are appealing to children and support specific skill development. For example, materials such as gears may stimulate interactive problem solving as children attempt to build a working model or structure. Materials used in creative play may help children practice negotiating roles and sharing materials. The use of social materials, such as puppets and dramatic play props, in appropriate classroom areas is likely to increase peer interaction in general (Ivory & McCollum, 1999; Montes & Risley, 1975; Poresky & Hooper, 1984; Quiltich & Risley, 1973; Rettig, Kallam, & McCarthy-Salm, 1993). Materials also can be distributed intentionally to encourage interaction between peers. For example, if two children are painting, one child may be given two colors and the other child two different colors. If the children want to create a more colorful picture, they will need to communicate and share colors. Finally, allowing children to pick out materials on their own and requiring them to return the materials to the appropriate place when they are finished fosters independence and responsibility.

Physical classroom arrangements and availability of materials may seem like simple strategies to address learning-related and interpersonal social skills. We propose that engagement is not influenced just by the arrangement or materials themselves; it is influenced by the intention behind those arrangements. Therefore, to maximize the effectiveness of environmental arrangements, educators must articulate the goals for skill development and identify the link between the goals and the strategies. In addition, attention must be given to whether the intervention is having its intended effect, or whether other strategies are necessary.

Programmatic Environment

Deliberation and intentionality should also characterize curriculum and instruction, the major components of the programmatic environment. Child development is supported when specific goals for learning-related and interpersonal social skills are defined and when these goals are considered in designing, adopting, and implementing curriculum and instruction. Identification of targeted behaviors or skills is particularly critical given the range of curriculum and instruction across early education classrooms, the variability in skill development, and the importance of specific skills in later educational outcomes. Furthermore, although goals can be effectively supported through naturalistic or incidental teaching, it is important to identify intentional strategies to address stated goals and identified behaviors.

Tier 1 programmatic strategies can address learning-related and interpersonal social skills, such as direction following, attention, and social interaction, through formally published curricula used with an entire classroom (Serna, Nielsen, Lambros, & Forness, 2000). In supporting skill development, curricula may focus on teaching social problem-solving strategies, techniques for recognizing and labeling emotions, and friendship skills and anger management strategies (Domitrovich, Cortes, & Greenberg, 2007; Izard, Trentacosta, King, & Mostow, 2004; Shure, 1992; Vaughn, Ridley, & Levine, 1986; Webster-Stratton, 1990; Webster-Stratton, Reid, & Stoolmiller, 2008). A review of social–emotional curricula by Joseph and Strain (2003a) may be helpful in selecting curricula that are supported by empirical evidence. Aligning curricula content with targeted social skills and examining the feasibility of implementation are critical in choosing a program that can be used with integrity and help children meet selected goals. Even without structured curricula, specific skills can be taught through everyday activities and interactions. Bricker and her associates have developed a highly recommended approach, called activity-based instruction, to address this topic (see Bricker, Pretti-Frontczak, & McComas, 1998; Pretti-Frontczak & Bricker, 2004). More direct instruction also might occur through special activities, such as morning check-ins in which children indicate their emotional state, or indirectly, through naturally occurring situations in which teachers can help children recognize their emotions (Joseph & Strain, 2003b). These types of activities can assist teachers to be more in tune with children's emotions and adjust their interactions to better support children's individual needs.

In addition to structured curricula and instruction, other aspects of the instructional environment or classroom routines can support the development of specific social skills. Strategies can be used during teacher-directed, whole-group activities. For example, during large group instruction, choral responding and response cards can be used to increase active responding and on-task behavior, while decreasing inappropriate behavior (Godfrey, Grisham-Brown, Schuster, & Hemmeter, 2003). Having materials available for all children during large group instruction helps keep children actively engaged (Doke & Risley, 1972). Encouraging children to take leadership roles in the classroom by assigning them responsibilities can promote listening, following directions, organizing, and attending to a task, in addition to increasing opportunities for structured social interaction (Sainato, Maheady, & Shook, 1986).

Skill development may also be supported through child-directed activities, by making strategic use of children's interests and motivation. Allowing children to rotate through activity areas independently is likely to increase their motivation to engage in activities (Doke, 1975; McEvoy & Brady, 1988). In addition, creating opportunities for children to initiate their own learning and playing activities can support the development of self-regulation as children learn to plan, make choices, and maintain sustained engagement (National Research Council, 2000). Allowing sufficient time for children to become engaged in tasks can encourage task persistence and lead to more complex social interactions (Christie, 1988; Nordquist, Twardosz, & McEvoy, 1991; Tegano & Burdette, 1991; Wien, 1996).

Other programmatic tactics include scheduling that provides a balance between the types of activities and the compatibility of the sequence of activities. For example, sustained attention and engagement in large group activities may be increased if the preceding activity is quiet, rather than active (Krantz & Risley, 1977). Using photos to illustrate the activities on the schedule has helped increase engagement for children with autism and could be used as a visual cue for an entire classroom (MacDuff, Krantz, & McClannahan, 1993; Massey & Wheeler, 2000). In addition, staffing patterns can affect behavior during transitions and activities. Zone approaches to teacher supervision allow children to move more independently, reducing wait time and increasing on-task behavior (Casey & McWilliam, 2005; LeLaurin & Risley, 1972). Finally, using posted rules that are reviewed periodically and referred to during daily activities help children understand expectations (see Paine, Radicchi, Rosellini, Deutchman, & Darch, 1983; Rosenberg, 1986). These strategies can be used to teach targeted skills as well as help children develop self-regulation by providing external cues for behavior.

Social Environment

Although classroom arrangement and programmatic strategies are useful in supporting skill development, perhaps the most essential component of environmental arrangements is the social environment. Specifically, the relationships and interactions that occur between children and teachers are critical in providing children with opportunities to develop both learning-related and peer-related social skills. Through skillful and sensitive interactions, teachers can demonstrate that they are attuned to the child's developmental needs. Teachers can build on (or scaffold) learning experiences in a way that supports a child's development slightly beyond what she or he is currently capable of doing independently (Vygotsky, 1962). Teachers may support the important skills of independence and task persistence by providing just the right amount of assistance, but not too much, to complete a task. Teachers may also embed activities into existing routines that will extend skill development, such as providing more complex directions during cleanup or transition times as children become more competent in following directions. Peer-related social skills may be developed through teacher assistance with entering, negotiating, and maintaining interactions; that assistance is gradually faded as children become more competent in their use of such skills.

Teachers also can use prompting, modeling, and positive attention to support the development of important social skills. In addition, offering positive attention, providing suggestions and information, and modeling effective strategies foster motivation, which will enhance children's engagement in learning interactions (Fagot, 1973; Hamilton & Gordon, 1978). Teacher–child interactions characterized by explicit expectations, the use of positive consequences, instruction in expected behaviors, and clear directions are likely to enhance teacher–child relationships, support learning, and increase a child's school success (National Research Council, 2001). Learning is a social process, and the outcomes are highly dependent on the quality of the interactions in which the learning occurs (Zins et al., 2004). The importance of the classroom emotional climate cannot be understated. Positive teacher–child relationships contribute to active engagement and support the development of learning-related and interpersonal social skills by reducing levels of problem behavior, increasing opportunities for learning and peer interaction (National Research Council, 2001). Without quality interactions, much of the learning that happens in preschool classrooms would not occur.

In sum, Tier 1 strategies can be used together to ensure conditions that support the skills necessary for school readiness. Strategically arranged classroom environments set the stage for giving children opportunities to learn and use skills. Curricula and instructional efforts provide a foundation for skill development; and skillful, nurturing teacher interactions support continued skill growth. To prepare children to learn, educators must be aware of the experiences children gain from the environment—how opportunities to develop learning-related skills are provided, how social interaction is fostered, and ultimately, how engagement is supported. Tier 1 strategies, when intentionally selected and correctly implemented, can be effective for a large percentage of preschool children. Environmental arrangements considered as elements of Tier 1 strategies increase the quality of the overall classroom environment and provide the foundation educators need in order to consider more intensive interventions for those children who need additional support to develop skills and competency.

Tier 2 Interventions and Environmental Arrangements

Tier 2 interventions are typically directed toward children who need more support than Tier 1 strategies provide. The distinguishing features of Tier 2 interventions include a higher degree of intensity and structure. Furthermore, interventions are seen as supplements to what is already in place, or modifications and adaptations to existing efforts. Some curricula and instructional strategies used as Tier 1 strategies may also be used as Tier 2 interventions to teach specific skills to identified children who are having difficulty acquiring or consistently using learning-related and interpersonal social skills (e.g., following directions, persisting with tasks, or interacting with peers). Some children might benefit more from small group instruction and increased opportunities to practice skills and receive individualized feedback and reinforcement. Similarly, although positive attention might be used with all children, some children might benefit from structured systems of positive attention. One system, the Behavior Education Program (BEP; Crone, Horner, & Hawken, 2003), has components such as social contacts, clearly defined behavioral goals, and performance monitoring, which can be adapted for use with preschoolers. For example, some children might benefit from a morning check-in procedure that proactively prompts them about a desired behavior or classroom expectations, and an afternoon check-out procedure that provides them with positive attention for meeting expectations.

The preschool version of the First Step Early Intervention Program (Walker et al., 1998, 2001) was developed as a companion intervention to the ESP screening procedure. First Step is a selected intervention designed to address Tier 2 goals and outcomes for behaviorally at-risk young children whose school success and adjustment are jeopardized by their challenging behavior. It is appropriate for use with those students who exceed ESP screening-stage cutoff points and, in most cases, those who exceed Stage 3 cutoff points.

Peers may also act as agents in Tier 2 interventions to promote learning-related and interpersonal social skill development. Socially skilled peers may be paired with children lacking specific social skills to model successful social interactions in supportive and strategic settings (Fantuzzo, Manz, Atkins, & Meyers, 2005). Experienced peers may also be used to assist target children with transitioning between activities (Sainato, Strain, Lefebvre, & Rapp, 1987). Finally, peer tutoring, with appropriate modifications, may have utility in a preschool setting. For example, peers may be strategically paired for hands-on constructive learning experiences that focus on problem solving, organization of materials, and cooperation to achieve a goal (Brady, 1997). Peer-mediated interventions may require additional effort on the part of educators in terms of the student training and supervision that may be needed. However, the use of peers as intervention agents may be less stigmatizing than teacher-mediated or individualized interventions, and may fit well within the existing classroom structure (Odom et al., 1999).

Tier 3

Although Tier 2 interventions can provide needed additional supports to increase engagement and promote the development of learning-related and interpersonal social skills, a small percentage of children are likely to need more intensive and individualized interventions. Tier 3 interventions are typically developed from more intensive assessment procedures, such as functional behavioral assessment (FBA), and are used with individual children rather than large or small groups. Distinguishing features of Tier 3 interventions involve the application of principles of applied behavior analysis, with a dual goal of increasing a child's ability to participate in his or her daily environment and reducing problematic behaviors and altering conditions that maintain problem behavior. FBA can be used to promote learning-related and interpersonal social skills by reducing behavior that interferes with child's ability to learn and interact with others and by maximizing a child's development and use of learning-related and interpersonal social skills (Hojnoski & Missall, 2006).

In selecting alternative desired behaviors as part of the FBA process, interventions should target keystone behaviors, that is, behaviors that are related to successful engagement in the classroom. For example, interventions may involve individualized direct instruction and support in attending to instruction during group activities; one-on-one instruction in peer social skills, supplemented by prompting and modeling during interactions; instruction in alternative communication skills to indicate wants and needs; or frequent positive reinforcement coupled with tangible rewards. Given the individualized nature of interventions at this level, the reader is referred to more detailed discussion of individualized positive behavior support and the use of FBA procedures in Bambara and Kern (2004) and Crone and Horner (2003).

Systems of Support

The three levels of intervention described above can be part of a systemic and comprehensive approach to supporting social development, commonly referred to as school-wide positive behavior support (Horner & Sugai, 2000). Although the school-wide positive behavior support literature typically has focused on applications with older children, the basic principles and procedures can be adapted and applied effectively to early education. Central components of a school-wide approach include defining behavioral expectations and instructing students in behavioral expectations, and delivering positive attention for appropriate behavior and corrective feedback for inappropriate behavior (Bambara & Kern, 2004). These components can be modified to reflect developmentally appropriate considerations for young children (see Fox & Little, 2001; Stormont, Lewis, & Beckner, 2005).

In the context of learning-related and interpersonal social skills, behavioral expectations might focus on listening, following directions, or playing gently with friends. In addition to general behavioral expectations, context-specific expectations may be created as well. For example, "walking feet" may be an expectation for moving through hallways; "eyes up front, hands and feet still" may be an expectation for large groups during instructional times. These expectations can be expressed through verbal and visual cues, thereby increasing the input children receive regarding appropriate behavior. Instruction may occur in large or small groups in a structured fashion, or more informally through teacher–child interactions embedded in ongoing activities (Fox & Little, 2001). Acknowledging and reinforcing children's use of learning-related and interpersonal social skills may be best accomplished through interactions with teachers characterized by positive attention that is specific and genuine. Children's meaningful relationships with caregivers increase the value, and thus the effectiveness, of this kind of reinforcement.

CONCLUSION

This chapter has promoted environmental arrangements as a key Tier 1 strategy in providing a positive and effective setting that supports the development of learning-related and interpersonal skills and fosters engagement. Classrooms are dynamic; environmental arrangements—the physical, programmatic, and social features of classrooms—interact with other contextual variables, including child and teacher characteristics, in a complex transactional process (see Hojnoski et al., 2008; Kontos, Burchinal, Howes, Wisseh, & Galinsky, 2002; Powell, Burchinal, File, & Kontos, 2008). Thus, social development is a product of what individuals bring to the learning environment, as well as what the learning environment provides. A transactional perspective by Bagnato (2006) emphasizes both the skill sets and competencies that children bring to schooling, and what schools do to support further development of skills and competencies.

> Most young children do not naturally wait, share, take turns, follow directions, use words instead of actions, or communicate their needs; most children can learn these things through guided daily experiences and discovery; some children require more individual guidance and structure to reach their potential. (p. 617)

In a preschool environment characterized by careful, strategic, and deliberate arrangement of the environment, the goal of early education is less focused on preparing children to learn and more focused on designing instruction and programming that actively engages all children in the learning process (National Research Council, 2000). A tiered intervention model is, in a way, preparing schools for children as much as preparing children for schools, by allowing educators to implement strategies that match children's skill levels and needs, thus enabling all children to receive the support necessary to be successful in school.

REFERENCES

Adams, M. (1990). *Learning to read: Thinking and learning about print.* Cambridge, MA: MIT Press.

Agostin, T. M., & Bain, S. K. (1997). Predicting early school success with developmental and social skills screeners. *Psychology in the Schools, 34,* 219–228.

Bagnato, S. J. (2006). Of helping and measuring for early childhood intervention: Reflections on issues and school psychology's role. *School Psychology Review, 35,* 615–620.

Bambara, L. M., & Kern, L. (2004). *Individualized supports for students with behavior problems: Designing positive behavior plans.* New York: Guilford Press.

Barnett, D. W., Daly, E. J., III, Jones, K. M., & Lentz, F. E., Jr. (2004). Response to intervention: Empirically based special service decisions from single-case designs of increasing and decreasing intensity. *Journal of Special Education, 38,* 66–79.

Brady, N. C. (1997). The teaching game: A reciprocal peer tutoring program for preschool children. *Education and Treatment of Children, 20,* 123–149.

Bricker, D., Pretti-Frontczak, K., & McComas, N. (1998). *An activity-based approach to early intervention.* Baltimore: Brookes.

Bronson, M. B. (1994). The usefulness of an observational measure of young children's social and mastery behaviors in early childhood classrooms. *Early Childhood Research Quarterly, 9,* 19–43.

Brown, W. H., Fox, J. J., & Brady, M. P. (1987). Effects of spatial density on 3- and 4-year-old children's socially directed behavior during freeplay: An investigation of a setting factor. *Education and Treatment of Children, 10,* 247–258.

Brown, W. H., Odom, S. L., & Conroy, M. A. (2001). An intervention hierarchy for promoting preschool children's peer interactions in natural environments. *Topics in Early Childhood Special Education, 21,* 162–175.

Buysse, V., Winton, P., & Zimmerman, T. (2007). RTI goes to pre-K: An early intervening system called recognition and response. *Early Developments, 11,* 6–10.

Casey, A. M., & McWilliam, R. A., (2005). Where is everybody? Organizing adults to promote child engagement. *Young Exceptional Children, 8*(2), 2–10.

Christie, J. F. (1988). The effect of play period duration on children's play patterns. *Journal of Research in Childhood Education, 3*(2), 123–131.

Clark, K. E., & Ladd, G. W. (2000). Connectedness and autonomy support in parent-child relationships: Links to children's socioemotional orientation and peer relationships. *Developmental Psychology, 36,* 485–498.

Coolahan, K., Fantuzzo, J., Mendez, J., & McDermott, P. (2000). Preschool peer interactions and readiness to learn: Relationships between classroom peer play and learning behaviors and conduct. *Journal of Educational Psychology, 92,* 458–465.

Cooper, D. H., & Farran, D. C. (1988). Behavioral risk factors in kindergarten. *Early Childhood Research Quarterly, 3*, 1–19.

Cooper, D. H., & Speece, D. L. (1988). A novel methodology for the study of children at risk for school failure. *Journal of Special Education, 22*, 186–198.

Crone, D. A., & Horner, R. H. (2003). *Building positive behavior support systems in schools: Functional behavioral assessment.* New York: Guilford Press.

Crone, D. A., Horner, R. H., & Hawken, L. S. (2003). *Responding to problem behavior in schools: The Behavior Education Program.* New York: Guilford Press.

DeMulder, E. K., Denham, S., Schmidt, M., & Mitchell, J. (2000). Q-Sort assessment of attachment security during the preschool years: Links for home to school. *Developmental Psychology, 36*, 274–282.

DiPerna, J., & Elliott, S. (Eds.). (2002). Promoting academic enablers to improve student performance: Considerations for research and practice. [Special issue.] *School Psychology Review, 31*(3).

Doke, L. A. (1975). The organization of day care environments: Formal versus informal activities. *Child Care Quarterly, 4*(3), 216–222.

Doke, L. A., & Risley, T. R. (1972). The organization of day-care environments: Required versus optional activities. *Journal of Applied Behavior Analysis, 5*, 405–420.

Domitrovich, C. E., Cortes, R. C., & Greenberg, M. T. (2007). Improving young children's social and emotional competence: A randomized trial of the preschool "PATHS" curriculum. *Journal of Primary Prevention, 28*(2), 67–91.

Duncan, G. J., Claessens, A., Huston, A. C., Pagani, L. S., Engel, M., Sexton, H., et al. (2007). School readiness and later achievement. *Developmental Psychology, 43*, 1428–1446.

Fagot, B. (1973). Influence of teacher behavior in preschool. *Developmental Psychology, 9*, 198–206.

Fantuzzo, J., Bulotsky-Shearer, R., Fusco, R., & McWayne, C. (2005). An investigation of preschool classroom behavioral adjustment problems and social-emotional school readiness competencies. *Early Childhood Research Quarterly, 20*, 259–275.

Fantuzzo, J., Bulotsky-Shearer, R., McDermott, P. A., McWayne, C., Frye, D., & Perlman, S. (2007). Investigation of dimensions of social-emotional classroom behavior and school readiness for low-income urban preschool children. *School Psychology Review, 36*, 44–62.

Fantuzzo, J., Manz, P., Atkins, M., & Meyers, R. (2005). Peer-mediated treatment of socially withdrawn maltreated preschool children: Cultivating natural community resources. *Journal of Clinical Child and Adolescent Psychology, 34*, 320–325.

Fantuzzo, J., Perry, M. A., & McDermott, P. (2004). Preschool approaches to learning and their relationship to other relevant classroom competencies for low-income children. *School Psychology Quarterly, 19*, 212–230.

Feil, E. G., Severson, H. H., & Walker, H. M. (1995). The early screening project for young children with behavior problems. *Journal of Emotional and Behavioral Disorders, 3*, 194–202.

Feil, E. G., Severson, H. H., & Walker, H. M. (1998). Screening for emotional and behavioral delays: The early screening project. *Journal of Early Intervention, 21,* 252–266.

Field, T. M. (1980). Preschool play: Effects of teacher/child ratios and organization of classroom space. *Child Study Journal, 10*(3), 191–205.

Foulks, B., & Morrow, R. D. (1989). Academic survival skills for the young child at risk for school failure. *Journal of Educational Research, 82*(3), 158–165.

Fox, L., Dunlap, G., Hemmeter, M. L., Joseph, G. E., & Strain, P. (2003). The teaching pyramid: A model for supporting social competence and preventing challenging behavior in young children. *Young Children, 58*(4), 48–53.

Fox, L., & Little, N. (2001). Starting early: Developing school-wide behavior support in a community preschool. *Journal of Positive Behavior Interventions, 3,* 251–254.

Godfrey, S. A., Grisham-Brown, J., Schuster, J. W., & Hemmeter, M. L. (2003). The effects of three techniques on student participation with preschool children with attending problems. *Education and Treatment of Children, 26,* 255–272.

Graue, E. (2006). The answer is readiness—Now what is the question? *Early Education and Development, 17*(1), 43–56.

Greenwood, C. R. (1991). Longitudinal analysis of time, engagement, and achievement in at-risk versus non-risk students. *Exceptional Children, 57,* 521–535.

Hamilton, H., & Gordon, D. (1978). Teacher child interactions in preschool and task persistence. *American Educational Research Journal, 15,* 459–466.

Harms, T., Clifford, R., & Cryer, D. (1998). *Early childhood environment ratings scale* (Rev. ed.). New York: Teachers College Press.

Hart, B. (1978). Organizing program implementation. In K. E. Allen, V. A. Holm, & R. L. Schiefelbusch (Eds.), *Early intervention—A team approach* (pp. 309–330). Baltimore: University Park Press.

Hojnoski, R. L., Margulies, A. S., Barry, A., Bose-Deakins, J., Sumara, K., & Harman, J. (2008). Analysis of two early childhood education settings: Classroom variables and peer verbal interaction. *Journal of Research in Childhood Education, 23*(2), 193–209.

Hojnoski, R. L., & Missall, K. N. (2006). Addressing school readiness: Expanding school psychology in early education. *School Psychology Review, 35,* 602–614.

Horner, R. H., & Sugai, G. (2000). School-wide behavior support: An emerging initiative. *Journal of Positive Behavior Interventions, 2,* 231–232.

Howes, C., & Smith, E. W. (1995). Relations among child care quality, teacher behavior, children's play activities, emotional security, and cognitive activity in child care. *Early Childhood Research Quarterly, 10,* 381–404.

Ivory, J. J., & McCollum, J. A. (1999). Effects of social and isolate toys on social play in an inclusive setting. *Journal of Special Education, 32*(4), 238–243.

Izard, C. E., Trentacosta, C. J., King, K. A., & Mostow, A. J. (2004). An emotion-based prevention program for Head Start children. *Early Education and Development, 15*(4), 407–422.

Joseph, G. E., & Strain, P. S. (2003a). Comprehensive evidence-based social-emotional curricula for young children: An analysis of efficacious adoption potential. *Topics in Early Childhood Special Education, 23,* 65–76.

Joseph, G. E., & Strain, P. S. (2003b). Enhancing emotional vocabulary in young children. *Young Exceptional Children, 6*(4), 18–27.

Kinsman, C. A., & Berk, L. E. (1979). Joining the block and housekeeping areas: Changes in play and social behavior. *Young Children, 39,* 66–75.

Kontos, S., Burchinal, M., Howes, C., Wisseh, S., & Galinsky, E. (2002). An ecobehavioral approach to examining the contextual effects of early childhood classrooms. *Early Childhood Research Quarterly, 17,* 239–258.

Kowalski, K., Pretti-Frontczak, K., & Johnson, L. (2001). Preschool teacher's beliefs concerning the importance of various developmental skills and abilities. *Journal of Research in Childhood Education, 16*(1), 5–14.

Krantz, P. J., & Risley, T. R. (1977). Behavioral ecology in the classroom. In K. D. O'Leary & S. G. O'Leary (Eds.), *Classroom management: The successful use of behavior modification* (2nd ed.). New York: Pergamon Press.

Ladd, G. W. (1990). Having friends, keeping friends, making friends, and being liked by peers in the classroom: Predictors of children's early school adjustment? *Child Development, 61,* 1081–1100.

Ladd, G. W., Birch, S. H., & Buhs, E. (1999). Children's social and scholastic lives in kindergarten: Related spheres of influence? *Child Development, 70,* 1373–1400.

Ladd, G. W., & Coleman, C. C. (1997). Children's classroom peer relationships and early school attitudes: Concurrent and longitudinal associations. *Early Education and Development, 8*(1), 51–66.

LeLaurin, K., & Risley, T. (1972). The organization of day-care environments: "Zone" versus "man-to-man" staff assignments. *Journal of Applied Behavior Analysis, 5,* 225–232.

MacDuff, G. S., Krantz, P. J., & McClannahan, L. E. (1993). Teaching children with autism to use photographic activity schedules: Maintenance and generalization of complex response chains. *Journal of Applied Behavior Analysis, 26,* 89–97.

Massey, N. G., & Wheeler, J. J. (2000). Acquisition and generalization of activity schedules and their effects on task engagement in a young child with autism in an inclusive pre-school classroom. *Education and Training in Mental Retardation and Developmental Disabilities, 35*(3), 326–335.

McClelland, M. M., & Morrison, F. J. (2003). The emergence of learning-related social skills in preschool children. *Early Childhood Research Quarterly, 18,* 206–224.

McClelland, M. M., Morrison, F. J., & Holmes, D. L. (2000). Children at risk for early academic problems: The role of learning-related social skills. *Early Childhood Research Quarterly, 15,* 307–329.

McConnell, S. R, & Missall, K. N. (2004). Defining "school readiness." *NHSA Dialog: A Research-to-Practice Journal for the Early Intervention Field, 7*(1), 10–12.

McCormick, L., Noonan, M. J., & Heck, R. (1998). Variables affecting engagement in inclusive preschool classrooms. *Journal of Early Intervention, 21,* 160–176.

McEvoy, M. A., Fox, J. J., & Rosenberg, M. S. (1991). Organizing preschool environments: Suggestions for enhancing the development/learning of preschool children with handicaps. *Topics in Early Childhood Special Education, 11,* 18–28.

McFall, R. (1982). A review and reformulation of the concept of social skills. *Behavioral Assessment, 4,* 1–35.

McWayne, C. M., Fantuzzo, J. W., & McDermott, P. A. (2004). Preschool competency in context: An investigation of the unique contribution of child competencies to early academic success. *Developmental Psychology, 40,* 633–645.

McWilliam, R. A., & Casey, A. C. (2008). *Engagement of every child in the preschool classroom.* Baltimore: Brookes.

McWilliam, R. A., Tivette, C. M., & Dunst, C. J. (1985). Behavior engagement as a measure of the efficacy of early intervention. *Analysis and Intervention in Developmental Disabilities, 5,* 59–71.

Missall, K. N., & Hojnoski, R. L. (2007). The critical nature of young children's emerging peer-related social competence for transition to school. In W. Brown, S. Odom, & S. McConnell (Eds.), *Social competence of young children: Risk, disability and intervention* (pp. 117–137). Baltimore: Brookes.

Montes, F., & Risley, T. R. (1975). Evaluating traditional day care practice: An empirical approach. *Child Care Quarterly, 13,* 274–287.

Nash, B. C. (1981). The effects of classroom spatial organization on four- and five-year old children's learning. *British Journal of Educational Psychology, 51,* 144–155.

National Education Goals Panel. (1997). *Getting a good start in school.* Washington, DC: National Education Goals Panel.

National Institute for Early Education Research. (2007). *Preschool classroom mathematics inventory.* Rutgers, NJ: Author.

National Research Council. (2000). *From neurons to neighborhoods: The science of early childhood development.* Washington, DC: National Academy Press.

National Research Council. (2001). *Eager to learn: Educating our preschoolers.* Washington, DC: National Academy Press.

National Research Council. (2008). *Early childhood assessment: Why, what and how.* Washington, DC: National Academy Press.

Nordquist, V. M., & Twardosz, S. (1990). Preventing behavior problems in early childhood special education classrooms through environmental organization. *Education and Treatment of Children, 13,* 274–287.

Nordquist, V. M., Twardosz, S., & McEvoy, M. A. (1991). Effects of environmental reorganization in classrooms for children with autism. *Journal of Early Intervention, 15,* 135–152.

Odom, S. L., McConnell, S. R., & Brown, W. H. (2007). Social competence of young children: Conceptualization, assessment, and influences. In W. Brown, S. Odom, & S. McConnell (Eds.), *Social competence of young children: Risk, disability, and intervention* (pp. 3–29). Baltimore: Brookes.

Odom, S. L., McConnell, S. R., McEvoy, M. A., Peterson, C., Ostrosky, M., Chandler, L., et al. (1999). Relative effects of interventions supporting the social competence of young children with disabilities. *Topics in Early Childhood Special Education, 19,* 75–91.

Paine, S. C., Radicchi, J. A., Rosellini, L. C., Deutchman, L., & Darch, C. B. (1983). *Structuring your classroom for academic success.* Champaign, IL: Research Press.

Pianta, R. C., La Paro, K. M., & Hamre, B. K. (2007). *Classroom assessment scoring system.* Baltimore: Brookes.

Pianta, R. C., Nimetz, S. L., & Bennett, E. (1997). Mother-child relationships, teacher-child relationships, and school outcomes in preschool and kindergarten. *Early Childhood Research Quarterly, 12,* 263–280.

Pianta, R. C., & Stuhlman, M. W. (2004). Teacher-child relationships and children's success in the first years of school. *School Psychology Review, 33,* 444–458.

Poresky, R. H., & Hooper, D. J. (1984). Enhancing prosocial play between handicapped and nonhandicapped preschool children. *Psychological Reports, 54,* 391–402.

Powell, D. R., Burchinal, M. R., File, M., & Kontos, S. (2008). An eco-behavioral analysis of engagement in urban public school preschool classrooms. *Early Childhood Research Quarterly, 23,* 108–123.

Pretti-Frontczak, K., & Bricker, D. (2004). *An activity-based approach to early intervention* (2nd ed.). Baltimore: Brookes.

Quilitch, H. R., & Risley, T. R. (1973). The effects of play materials on social play. *Journal of Applied Behavior Analysis, 6,* 573–578.

Raver, C. C. (2002). Emotions matter: Making the case for the role of young children's emotional development for early school readiness. *Society for Research in Child Development Social Policy Report, 16*(3).

Raver, C., & Knitzer, J. (2002). *Ready to enter: What research tells policymakers about strategies to promote social and emotional readiness among three- and four-year old children.* New York: National Center for Children in Poverty.

Rettig, M., Kallam, M., & McCarthy-Salm, K. (1993). The effect of social and isolate toys on the social interactions of preschool-aged children. *Education and Training in Mental Retardation, 28,* 252–256.

Ridley, S. M., McWilliam, R. A., & Oates, C. S. (2000). Observed engagement as an indicator of child care program quality. *Early Education and Development, 11,* 133–146.

Rosenberg, M. S. (1986). Maximizing the effectiveness of structured management programs: Implementing rule-review procedures with disruptive and distractible students. *Behavioral Disorders, 11,* 239–248.

Rosenshine, R. V. (1981). Academic engaged time, content covered, and direct instruction. *Journal of Education, 3,* 38–66.

Sainato, D. M., Maheady, L., & Shook, G. L. (1986). The effects of a classroom manager role on the social interaction patterns and social status of withdrawn kindergarten students. *Journal of Applied Behavior Analysis, 19,* 187–195.

Sainato, D. M., Strain, P. S., Lefebvre, D., & Rapp, N. (1987). Facilitating transition times with handicapped preschool children: A comparison between peer-mediated and antecedent prompt procedures. *Journal of Applied Behavior Analysis, 20,* 285–291.

Sandall, S. R., & Schwartz, I. S., (2008). *Building blocks for teaching preschoolers with special needs* (2nd ed.). Baltimore: Brookes.

Schirrmacher, R. (1993). *Art and creative development for young children.* Albany, NY: Delmar.

Serna, L., Nielsen, E., Lambros, K., & Forness, S. (2000). Primary prevention with children at risk for emotional or behavioral disorders: Data on a universal intervention for Head Start classrooms. *Behavioral Disorders, 26,* 70–84.

Shure, M. B. (1992). *I can problem solve: An interpersonal cognitive problem-solving program.* Champaign, IL: Research Press.

Smith, M. W., Brady, J. P., & Anastasopoulos, L. (2008). *Early language and literacy classroom observation tool.* Baltimore: Brookes.

Squires, J., & Bricker, D. (2007). *An activity-based approach to developing young children's social-emotional competence.* Baltimore: Brookes.

Squires, J., & Bricker, D. (2009). *The ages and stages questionnaires* (3rd ed.). Baltimore: Brookes.

Squires, J., Bricker, D., & Twombly, E. (2002). *The ages and stages questionnaires: Social-emotional.* Baltimore: Brookes.

Stormont, M., Lewis, T. J., & Beckner, R. (2005). Positive behavior support systems; Applying key features in preschool settings. *TEACHING Exceptional Children, 37,* 42–49.

Sugai, G., & Horner, R. (2002). The evolution of discipline practices: School-wide positive behavior supports. *Child and Family Behavior Therapy, 24,* 23–50.

Tegano, D. W., & Burdette, M. P. (1991). Length of activity periods and play behaviors of preschool children. *Journal of Research in Childhood Education, 5*(5), 93–99.

Trister Dodge, D., Colker L., J., Heroman, C. (2002). *The Creative Curriculum for Preschool* (4th ed.). Washington, DC: Teaching Strategies, Inc.

VanDerHeyden, A. M., & Snyder, P. (2006). Integrating frameworks from early childhood intervention and school psychology to accelerate growth for all young children. *School Psychology Review, 35,* 519–534.

VanDerHeyden, A. M., Witt, J. C., & Barnett, D. A. (2005). The emergence and possible futures of response to intervention. *Journal of Psychoeducational Assessment, 23,* 339–361.

Vaughn, S. R., Ridley, C. R., & Levine, L. (1986). *PALS: Developing social skills through language.* Chicago: Science Research Associates.

Vygotsky, L. S. (1962). *Thought and language.* Cambridge, MA: MIT Press.

Walker, H. M., Kavanaugh, K., Stiller, B., Golly, A., Severson, H. H., Feil, E. G. (1998). First step to success: An early intervention approach for preventing school antisocial behavior. *Journal of Emotional and Behavioral Disorders, 6,* 66–80.

Walker, H. M., Kavanaugh, K., Stiller, B., Golly, A., Severson, H. H., Feil, E. G. (2001). First step to success: An early intervention approach for preventing school antisocial behavior. In H. M. Walker & M. H. Epstein (Eds.), *Making school safer and violence free: Critical issues, solutions, and recommended practices* (pp. 73–87). Austin, TX: Pro-Ed.

Walker, H. M., & Severson, H. (1990). *Systematic screening for behavior disorders (SSBD).* Longmont, CA: Sopris West.

Walker, H. M., Severson, H., & Feil, E. (1995). *The early screening project (ESP).* Available through Applied Behavior Science Press, Deschutes Research, Inc., 261 E. 12th Ave., Eugene, OR 97403.

Webster-Stratton, C. (1990). *The teachers and children's videotape series: Dina Dinosaur's social skills and problem-solving curriculum.* Seattle, WA: University of Washington Press.

Webster-Stratton, C., Reid, J., & Stoolmiller, M. (2008). Preventing conduct problems and improving school readiness: Evaluation of the incredible years teacher and child training programs in high-risk schools. *Journal of Child Psychology and Psychiatry, 49,* 471–488.

Wien, C. A. (1996). Time, work, and developmentally appropriate practice. *Early Childhood Research Quarterly, 11,* 377–393.

Whitehurst, G. J., & Lonigan, C. J. (1998). Child development and emergent literacy. *Child Development, 69,* 848–872.

Zins, J. E., Bloodworth, M. R, Weissberg, R. P., & Walberg, H. J. (2004). The scientific base linking social and emotional learning to school success. In J. E. Zins, R. P. Weissberg, M. C. Wang, & H. J. Walberg (Eds.), *Building academic success on social and emotional learning: What does the research say?* (pp. 3–22). New York: Teachers College Press.

CHAPTER 27

Bullying and Peer Harassment

Dorothy L. Espelage
University of Illinois at Urbana–Champaign

Susan M. Swearer
University of Nebraska–Lincoln

INTRODUCTION

Both suicidal and homicidal behaviors have heightened awareness of and increased research on bullying and victimization among school-age youth worldwide. In the early 1980s in Norway, three suicides were linked to the youth being bullied, which led the Norwegian government to launch a national campaign to investigate bullying and victimization problems (Olweus, 1993). In the United States, an investigation was commissioned in 2000 by the Secret Service; family and friends of students involved in 37 incidents of targeted school shootings and school attacks between 1974 and 2000 were interviewed. Researchers discovered that 71% of the perpetrators had been victims of bullying (Vossekuil, Fein, Reddy, Borum, & Modzeleski, 2002). Over the past three decades, increasingly larger and more complex investigations of the etiology and consequences of bullying have been conducted in several countries (e.g., Australia, Canada, and Japan).

Research in U.S. schools has only been conducted within the past 15 years. Studies consistently find bullying to be prevalent among children and adolescents (Batsche & Knoff, 2004). Worldwide incidence rates for bullying among school-age youth range from 10% of secondary students to 27% of middle school students who report being bullied often (Whitney & Smith, 1993). Studies in the United States have yielded slightly higher rates of bullying, ranging from a low of 10% for "extreme victims" of bullying (Perry, Kusel, & Perry, 1988) to a high of 75% who reported being bullied at least one time during their school years (Hoover, Oliver, & Hazler, 1992). In a nationally representative study of American students in Grades 6 through 10, Nansel

---

Address all correspondence and feedback on this chapter to Dorothy L. Espelage at espelage@uiuc.edu.

and colleagues (2001) reported that 17% had been bullied with some regularity (several times or more within the semester) and 19% had bullied others.

Bullying is not a part of normative development for children and adolescents and should be considered a precursor to more serious aggressive behaviors (Nansel et al., 2001). It is consistently linked to negative social, academic, and interpersonal disruptions (Espelage & Swearer, 2003). Involvement in bullying has serious detrimental consequences for bullies, bully–victims (those who both bully others and are bullied), victims, and bystanders (active and passive observers). The majority of the research to date has focused on identifying the correlates, both of bullying perpetration and of victimization, to identify critical components in the design of bullying prevention and intervention programs. Taken together, the literature supports a social–ecological framework for understanding how bullying emerges in schools (Swearer & Espelage, 2004; Espelage & Horne, 2008). This social–ecological framework argues that bullying emerges from the intersection of individual risk factors such as anger, empathy, and attitudes supportive of aggression with other contexts such as family, peers, school, and neighborhood factors. Peer factors, such as popularity, friendship, peer norms, or a need for control and dominance in peer relations, provide a platform for bullying perpetration. Family influences, such as communication, cohesion, sibling bullying, or family violence, increase the likelihood of bullying perpetration. School factors, such as school climate and school leaders' response to bullying, and neighborhood factors, such as safety and supervision, are also important predictors of bullying perpetration. These characteristics are thought to contribute to the cumulative risk of bullying perpetration and victimization.

Programs to address school violence use two basic approaches: *universal* and *targeted*. A universal approach, also called primary prevention, is used with all people involved in the school and promotes awareness and the skills necessary to prevent problems. Such programs can be offered through classroom psychoeducational groups or school-wide presentations. A targeted or more intensive intervention (a secondary or tertiary intervention) involves groups of students identified as aggressive or involved in bullying situations as a bully or victim. These students are often identified by school personnel after a bullying incident. Up till now the only established tertiary interventions in U.S. schools have consisted of punitive approaches or zero-tolerance policies (policies that require punishment, regardless of the basis of the problem behavior), including suspension and expulsion. What has been learned to date is that zero-tolerance policies are not effective in curbing aggressive behaviors, and expulsion appears to be equally ineffective (Casella, 2003; Morrison, Redding, Fisher, & Peterson, 2006).

Whole-school or primary preventive interventions for bullying have slowly been introduced over the past few decades, following the introduction of the Norway-based Olweus Bullying Prevention Program (OBPP; Olweus, Limber, & Mihalic, 2000), which at this time has yet to produce a single peer-reviewed article on its effectiveness with children in the United States. However, the introduction of this program in the United States in 1993 was a hallmark development. Since then, the U.S. Department of Health and Human Services has launched its Stop Bullying Now: Take a Stand, Lend a

Hand campaign and provided schools and administrators with information on best practices in bullying prevention and intervention, which is available from its website (http://www.stopbullyingnow.hrsa.gov/kids/).

Although the extant literature on correlates of bullying supports the inclusion of certain components (e.g., anger management, peer norms) in school-based prevention programs, most school-based bullying reduction programs lack effectiveness studies or efficacy data. Although some evaluation efforts have offered promising findings, results of recent meta-analysis of 14 whole-school antibullying programs provided a more modest assessment of the prevention programs' effectiveness (Smith, Schneider, Smith, & Ananiadou, 2004). These programs were all based on the Olweus Bullying Prevention Program (Olweus, 1993). Results yielded moderate effect sizes on self-reported victimization that students experienced from bullies (e.g., being teased, called names, shoved or hit) and small to negligible effects on self-reported bullying perpetration (e.g., teasing, name-calling, or hitting or pushing others). Smith et al. concluded that significant caution should be observed when implementing school-wide programs.

A more recent meta-analytic investigation of 16 studies published between 1980 and 2004 yielded similarly disappointing results regarding the impact of antibullying programs (Merrell, Gueldner, Ross, & Isava, 2008). This meta-analysis included data from over 15,000 students (kindergarten to Grade 12) in Europe, Canada, and the United States. Positive effect sizes were found for only one third of the study variables, which primarily reflected favorable changes in knowledge, attitudes, and perceptions of bullying. No changes were found for bullying behaviors.

Despite the rather disheartening results of these two meta-analyses, a third meta-analysis by Ttofi, Farrington, and Baldry (2008) has yielded mixed results. In a report for the Swedish National Council for Crime Prevention, they evaluated 30 bullying intervention studies, of which 13 were based on the Olweus program. This meta-analysis was noteworthy because of the rigorous study selection procedures used. Results indicated that bullying and victimization were reduced by 17–23% in experimental schools compared to control schools. Ttofi and colleagues found a dosage effect; the more elements included in a program, the greater likelihood of reducing bullying. The researchers also noted that antibullying programs were more efficacious in smaller-scale European studies and less effective in the United States. Interestingly, Ttofi and colleagues' review suggests that greater success was achieved with older (i.e., coded age 11 and older) students.

So, what do these findings mean for school-based bullying programming in North America? These mixed results suggest that, although school-based and school-wide bullying prevention efforts *can* be effective, success in one school or context is no guarantee of success in another. Indeed, given the pioneering work that Dan Olweus has done in the area of bullying (e.g., Olweus, 1993), it is not surprising that almost half of the programs included in the meta-analyses above were based on the Olweus Bullying Prevention Program (Olweus, 1993), which despite many successful trials in Scandinavian countries, has not yet demonstrated consistent efficacy within schools in

North America (Bauer et al., 2007). Researchers are only beginning to understand the factors that contribute to this variation in outcomes.

Furthermore, the majority of programs are designed for use with elementary school–age children, a few are designed for middle school students, and none are designed for high school students. Most of these programs focus on primary prevention, and all students in the school receive the same instruction. Thus, more programs need to be developed for middle and high school students, and programs need to engage in secondary and tertiary prevention. Developing these programs should incorporate the extant literature on the developmental aspects of bullying and aggression and on the causes of these behavior patterns. In this chapter we offer research findings from studies of early childhood through adolescence to guide the development of bullying and harassment prevention programs.

PREVALENCE OF BULLYING IN SCHOOL-AGE CHILDREN

Although many investigations report prevalence rates of bullying and victimization, these rates vary widely across studies because of methodological differences in the assessment of these behaviors. The sections that follow examine the prevalence of bullying, peer harassment, and victimization across the school years to demonstrate the need to adopt prevention and intervention strategies that are developmentally appropriate.

Elementary School Bullying and Peer Harassment

For many reasons, research on bullying and victimization has rarely been conducted with elementary-age populations. A primary reason is that the available methodologies make research on this age group particularly difficult. For example, some critics do not support the use of self-reporting measures of bullying for younger students and have instead endorsed the use of direct observation (in which researchers observe children or adolescents) or peer nomination (children report on who is the bully or victim) to assess bullying and victimization in elementary-age students (Craig, Pepler, & Rona, 2000; Perry, Kusel, & Perry, 1988). Some advocates of alternative methodologies have instead focused their research on aggressive childhood behavior and not necessarily on bullying. They argue that labeling children of this age as "bullies" or "victims" is problematic because their intent to harm others is unclear, and a power differential (based on differences in physical size, social status, or age) among younger children is difficult to assess (Hanish, Kochenderfer-Ladd, Fabes, Martin, & Denning, 2004).

Despite these criticisms, existing research using self-reported data has indicated that as many as 34% of U.S. elementary school students may be frequently (defined as two or more times in the past month) victimized by their peers (Bradshaw, Sawyer, & O'Brennan, 2007). Similarly, Kochenderfer and Ladd (1996) found that among kindergarten students, nearly 20% reported being victimized frequently. Additionally, a self-reporting study by Pellegrini, Bartini, and Brooks (1999) estimated that 18% of their fifth-grade sample had been victimized, 14% reported bullying others, and 5% both bullied others and were victimized (bully–victims). Orpinas and colleagues (2003) found that among the early elementary grades, some studies of student populations have reported different rates of victimization based on the type of bullying the youngsters experienced. For example, 25% of 6- and 8-year-old students from a U.K. sample reported that they had experienced direct bullying (i.e., physical and/or verbal), and 46% of the same sample indicated that they had been relationally victimized (i.e., victimization centered around damaging relationships; Woods & Wolke, 2004). A cross-national study of U.K. and German youth found that 24% of British youth were victimized weekly, compared with only 8% of German youth. In contrast, about 3–5% of British boys engaged in bullying on a weekly basis, and 8% of German boys bullied others weekly (Wolke, Woods, Stanford, & Schulz, 2001).

Overall, at best we can conclude that bullying occurs among elementary school youth, with prevalence rates between 5% and 25%, depending on the methods used to assess bullying and what is considered bullying across cultures. We also know that children who are bullies and victims during elementary school can vary from year to year. Rather, individuals assessed across time have shown that movement among groups (i.e., bullies to victims to bully–victims) is a fairly common phenomenon (Dempsey, Fireman, & Wang, 2006). However, despite moving among the bully and victim roles, students who displayed highly aggressive behavior in early elementary school tended to exhibit aggressive behavior during middle school (Harachi et al., 2006).

Transition From Elementary to Middle School

Educational theorists and researchers have long recognized that the transition from elementary school to middle or junior high school is a potential stressor for students (Feldlaufer, Midgley, & Eccles, 1988; Hirsch & Rapkin, 1987; Wigfield, Eccles, MacIver, Reuman, & Midgley, 1991). For many years, Eccles and colleagues have proposed and tested a model of stage–environment fit to guide research on the impact of school transitions on social and emotional development among adolescents (Eccles, 2004; Eccles & Midgley, 1989; Eccles et al., 2003; Eccles & Roeser, 1999). Stage–environment fit refers to the appropriateness of the environment to meet the needs of individuals at their particular stage of development; it is not synonymous with person–environment fit, which refers to the interaction between individual and personality characteristics with environmental factors. The transition from elementary to middle school is considered a stressor because it requires an adjustment to a new classroom environment and school culture and necessitates changes in peer groups, all of which are potentially associated with negative emotional and psychological responses for some students, such as a decrease in self-esteem or an increase in symptoms of depression (Hankin et al., 1998).

Fifth graders identify bullying as one of their primary concerns about starting sixth grade (Akos, 2002; Pellegrini, 2002). Evidence indicates that bullying behaviors increase for both boys and girls following the transition from elementary to middle school (Nansel et al., 2001; Pellegrini & Long, 2002; Solberg, Olweus, & Endresen, 2007). Students' fears of having increased involvement in aggression as perpetrators may exacerbate stress that occurs as a result of the elementary to middle school transition. In a recent study examining factors that predicted bullying during the transition from elementary school to middle school, Poteat, Espelage, Holt, and VanBoven (2009) found that teacher attachment in fifth grade was a strong predictor of lower levels of bullying for students during their sixth-grade year, even when considering those students' level of bullying during their fifth-grade year. This finding provides additional support for targeting this transition in programs to prevent bullying and violence. Programs should prepare students for the transition and specifically address their adjustment to the many changes during this period.

Middle School Bullying and Peer Harassment

Aggression and antisocial behavior among children transitioning from elementary to middle schools is a particularly visible problem among U.S. students (National Center for Educational Statistics, 1995). Correspondingly, a great number of research studies have investigated the prevalence of bullying and victimization among middle school students. The largest U.S. study conducted to date included 15,686 students in 6th through 10th grade who completed self-reported measures of bullying and victimization (Nansel et al., 2001). The results of the study showed that 30% of students reported moderate to frequent involvement in bullying. Of those students, 13% identified themselves as bullies, about 11% reported being victimized on a frequent basis, and over 6% reported that they had been bullied and victimized.

A large study of bullying and victimization among Norwegian middle school students included more than 14,000 participants and indicated that approximately 10% of students were frequently victimized, while about 5% engaged in frequent bullying behaviors. The same study reported that 2% of students were bully–victims (Solberg, Olweus, & Endresen, 2007). These findings correspond with previous European investigations, in which 7–10% of middle school students exhibited frequent bullying behaviors, and 5–10% of students were victimized on a regular basis (Salmivalli, Lappalainen, & Lagerspetz, 1998; Solberg & Olweus, 2003). Research in the United States over the past decade reported that among middle school students, about 8–13% frequently (defined consistently as several times in past month) bullied others, 11–21% of students were victimized, and 1–13% of students both bullied others and were victimized themselves (Batsche & Knoff, 1994; Cunningham, 2007; Demaray & Malecki, 2003; Kauffman et al., 1998; Nansel et al., 2001; Seals & Young, 2003; Unnever, 2005; Wenxin, 2002).

Additionally, males are more likely than females both to bully others and to be victimized, and they tend to engage in reciprocal physical aggression, in which both parties are aggressive (McNeilly-Choque, Hart, Robinson, Nelson, & Olsen, 1996; Nansel et al., 2001; Solberg et al., 2007). Some studies indicate that female bullies are more likely than males to act from relational aggression; that is, the aggression is directed at damaging another's reputation or at damaging friendships (Borg, 1999; Crick & Grotpeter, 1995; Crick & Nelson, 2002; Whitney & Smith, 1993).

High School Bullying and Peer Harassment

Although bullying seems to increase during students' transition from elementary to middle school, the same increase does not appear to hold true for the transition between middle and high school (Nansel et al., 2001). Empirical studies have found that physical aggression may give way to multiple forms of harassment during the later teen years. Specifically, sexual harassment becomes significantly more common for female students during the high school years than during middle school (Gruber & Fineran, 2007). The American Association of University Women conducted two large-scale studies of sexual harassment in U.S. schools, each finding similar results (AAUW, 1993, 2001). Approximately 81% of all students experienced sexual harassment during their school years. In comparison, 54% of students reported having sexually harassed another student during their school years. Prevalence rates increased as students aged, with 55% of 8th and 9th graders and 61% of 10th and 11th graders reporting being physically sexually harassed, from being brushed against to being forced to do something sexual with someone when they did not want to. The reports also indicated that female students experienced sexual harassment at higher frequencies than male students. Research has indicated that when male students are harassed, it most often is verbal (Timmerman, 2005). Additional research has indicated that high school males who were harassed by being called "gay" or "wimp" were more likely to suffer psychosocial difficulties than their counterparts who were harassed for other reasons (Swearer, Babl, Givens, & Turner, 2007). However, as Timmerman noted, males who were victims of verbal harassment showed much less psychological and somatic impairment than females who were physically sexually harassed.

Bradshaw and colleagues (2007) surveyed both staff and students at 14 high schools in the Northeast. They wanted to determine how well high school teachers predicted the amount of bullying and harassment that occurred at their school. Unfortunately, only 9% of school staff correctly predicted that approximately 28% of high school students reported being victimized, and more than 57% predicted that less than 10% of the students at their school had been victimized during the past month. It is clear that high school personnel are not clued into the victimization experiences of their students, which means that they cannot intervene. Both elementary and middle school personnel predicted victimization of their students more accurately than high school personnel. This could be because high schools are larger and lack familiarity among students and teachers. Thus, although overall rates of bullying and victimization have been shown to decrease during high school (Nansel et al., 2001), this phenomenon continues and is confounded by sexual harassment and staff underestimation of the prevalence of bullying, victimization, and harassment.

ELEMENTARY, MIDDLE, AND HIGH SCHOOL BULLYING: EVIDENCE FOR A THREE-TIER MODEL

Clearly, bullying, victimization, and peer harassment are behavioral phenomena that occur across the elementary, middle, and high school years. Although prevalence rates vary greatly, the evidence suggests that bullying that occurs among young children peaks during the middle school years and then becomes more sexual in nature during the high school years. To be effective, programs to prevent bullying must be based on developmental needs across school years.

Effective programs to curb youth violence, bullying, and peer harassment need to include primary, secondary, and tertiary systems of intervention (Walker & Shinn, 2002). In this three-tier approach, primary prevention strategies (e.g., skills training) focus on 80% of students of a school population that do not have serious behavior problems. Secondary intervention strategies, such as mentoring programs, target the 5% to 15% of students in a school that are at risk for behavior problems. Tertiary strategies (e.g., wraparound services) are directed at the 1% to 7% of students who have intense and chronic problems. A common approach schools use to plan bullying prevention and intervention involves adopting a whole-school or primary prevention program (Smith, Pepler, & Rigby, 2004). However, differences in staff support, implementation efforts, and student and staff factors affect the schools' success with such programs (Smith, Schneider, Smith, & Ananiadou, 2004). This section describes a framework for a three-tier approach for preventing and responding to bullying across elementary, middle, and high schools and gives examples of programs that have solid research evidence and can be augmented with tertiary programs to address specific developmental needs.

Steps to Respect: A Bullying Prevention Program

Steps to Respect: A Bullying Prevention Program is designed to help students build supportive relationships with one another (Committee for Children, 2001). The Steps to Respect program promotes a whole-school primary- and secondary-level approach to bullying prevention by addressing factors at four levels: school staff, peer group membership or friendships, individual child, and family. Intervening at multiple levels, the program developers believe, is the most effective way to reduce school bullying. Empirical support has shown reductions in playground bullying, acceptance of bullying behavior, and argumentative behavior. At the same time, the program has demonstrated increases in agreeable interactions and perceptions that adults will be responsive to bullying incidents, in comparison with control schools (Frey et al., 2005). More recently, it has demonstrated reductions in observed aggression and destructive bystander behavior (bystanders assisting the bully by directing aggression toward the victim) and higher teacher ratings of peer social skills (Hirschtein & Frey, 2006; Hirschtein, Van Schoiack, Frey, Snell, & MacKenzie, 2007). Steps to Respect relies heavily on adults to deliver structured and systemized training from a curriculum and to continually emphasize those lessons throughout the school year. The Steps to Respect prevention program is specifically respected for its well-established empirical support.

Knowing that approximately 80% of students will benefit from a primary-level intervention encourages school officials and stakeholders to invest time and effort into programs that systemically change the school climate in a comprehensive fashion. For example, the first component of the Steps to Respect program is staff training for "all adults" in the school building, emphasizing that the term includes janitors, bus drivers, mentors, receptionists, school nurses, volunteers, licensed staff, administrators, teachers, assistants, and other adults at school who are involved in the daily lives of students. Training meetings include a scripted session that provides basic information on the Steps to Respect program, information on bullying, and training on how to receive bullying reports from students. Administrators, teachers, or counselors who will work directly with student victims or bullies receive additional training.

Steps to Respect includes lessons to increase students' social–emotional competence and positive social values. Specifically, the program addresses three general skills. First, students learn the skills of perspective taking and empathy as well as learn how to manage their emotions. Second, academic skills are also encouraged by incorporating themes of friendship and bullying into literature unit activities such as oral expression, writing composition, and analytical reasoning. Third, the curriculum addresses students' social values by encouraging students' sense of fairness, and attempts to instill a desire for rewarding friendships. Also, literature units are included that integrate previously learned components of Steps to Respect for activities such as writing activities, spelling lists, and reading books (Committee for Children, 2005).

The program also recognizes research findings that bullying becomes sexualized during early adolescence. Thus, it defines sexual bullying as one student targeting another with unwanted words, actions, or media images about sex. The program offers two ways of teaching about this issue. One option discusses sexual bullying behaviors in general bullying terms without using the term "sexual harassment." A second, supplementary, section defines sexual harassment and specifically links bullying and sexual harassment.

The universal design of the Steps to Respect program makes it an easy fit for implementation in elementary schools. It relies mostly on teachers and adults, who assist students in modifying the school climate or environment by encouraging positive friendships and reducing bullying behaviors. As a universal intervention, it does not ignore the potential contribution of all students. These bystanders play a critical role in reducing and eliminating bullying from a school environment. As Frey and colleagues demonstrated (2005), reducing the acceptability of bullying behaviors and increasing perceived adult responsiveness are key components to building a positive school community.

In research by Frey and colleagues (2005), six elementary schools were randomly assigned to either receive the intervention or be a control group. Playground observations were collected in the fall and spring, along with surveys of student skills and attitudes identified as factors in bullying and victimization. Following staff training, intervention schools created bullying policies and implemented the classroom curricula twice a week for approximately 12 weeks. Positive outcomes included a 25% reduction in playground bullying incidents, compared with a control group, and a decrease in bystanders to bullying episodes who encouraged the aggression. Furthermore, the effects of the Steps to Respect program were most pronounced among students who were observed to do the most bullying before program implementation.

A more recent study examined the level of teacher implementation related to the effectiveness of Steps to Respect (Hirschstein, Edstrom, Frey, Snell, & MacKenzie, 2007). Specifically, the study examined the effects of teachers "walking the talk"—that is, teachers who wove support for positive behaviors into daily interactions with students and coached those involved in bullying. After 1 year of the program, high levels of "walking the talk" were linked to less aggression and victimization among fifth- and sixth-grade students. The program also resulted in less observed victimization of all children who had previously been victimized and less destructive bystander behavior among all children who had previously been observed contributing to bullying as bystanders.

Bully Busters

Bully Busters is a program that can be implemented by schools with fewer resources and can be used at the primary, secondary, or tertiary intervention levels. The program is designed as "a collaborative effort in which teachers, support staff (counselors, social workers, psychologists, and others), and administrators can become more aware of the bullying problem and develop the knowledge base and skills to deal with the problem confidently" (Newman et al., 2000, p. 1). The program is in two parts—Grades K–5 and 6–8—and contains seven learning modules on how to increase awareness, how to recognize the bully and victims, interventions for bullies and victims, classroom prevention, and coping skills, along with corresponding classroom activities.

Bully Busters is the most complete curriculum we have reviewed to date, and solid data support this program. Teachers receiving Bully Busters training reported significantly higher levels of self-efficacy for managing bullying behavior, demonstrated greater knowledge of classroom behavior management, and had fewer classroom behavior problems and office referrals than comparison teachers (Newman-Carlson & Horne, 2004). The first of the seven modules is designed to increase teachers' and students' awareness of bullying. Teachers are encouraged to develop a definition of bullying by working collaboratively with students. Exercises facilitate a conversation among students about who is a bully, what bullying is, and where it takes place. Students then participate in several activities to recognize how their words and actions can be hurtful, and they role-play more constructive ways of interacting. The second module includes a discussion with students about how bullying develops and the forms it can take. Activities in this module include viewing movies in which characters are victims or bullies. Students discuss both aggressive and passive forms of bullying. This second module ends with a focus on misconceptions about bullying.

In the third module, students discuss the effects of victimization and challenge myths about victims. Students are encouraged to recognize different types of victims, including individuals who are passive or provocative, as well as bystanders. The majority of students do not engage directly in bullying, but their reluctance to intervene when bullying occurs can promote this behavior in others. Thus, students are encouraged to break the "code of silence" and create a safer climate for all students. The fourth module includes specific strategies for teachers to create a bully-free classroom. Similar to the classroom-level interventions of the Olweus Bullying Prevention Program, teachers are given specific strategies (e.g., setting rules, acting quickly), along with empathy skills training, social skills training, and anger management training.

The fifth module expands on these skills by providing specific strategies for working with victims. Several activities are used to help victims become aware of their strengths, view themselves in a positive manner, and build skills and confidence in joining groups. The sixth module includes a discussion of the role of prevention. Activities in the sixth module are designed to educate teachers about the need for prevention and to introduce prevention theory. Teachers are encouraged to identify how their attitudes and behaviors influence student behavior and how school-level factors relate to bullying. The final module focuses on teaching relaxation and coping skills to teachers, because it is important that teachers manage their own stress to prevent aggression within their classrooms.

Bullyproof

Bullyproof provides a framework for teachers and students to understand bullying, identify the differences between bullying and teasing, be able to define sexual harassment, and develop appropriate responses to such behaviors (Sjostrom & Stein, 1996). This guide includes 11 sequential core lessons for fourth and fifth graders, consisting of writing activities, reading assignments, class discussions, role-playing, case studies, and homework assignments intended to encourage children to think about the distinctions between teasing and bullying. These activities help children focus on the boundaries between appropriate and inappropriate, and playful and hurtful behavior.

Before implementation of the lessons, time must be spent creating a safe environment. The program explicitly discusses topics including showing respect, reserving judgment, dealing with disclosure issues, preparing ground rules, and dealing with diversity issues and language. Bullyproof is flexible regarding how the lessons are taught, but it suggests that the lessons take place within a period of consecutive days, rather than over a period of many weeks. A 3-year evaluation, funded by the U.S. Centers for Disease Control and Prevention (CDC), provided independent research into the curriculum's effectiveness with fifth-grade students and their teachers in Austin, Texas (Rosenbluth, Whitaker, Sanchez, & Valle, 2004; Whitaker, Rosenbluth, Sanchez, & Valle, 2004). Results from the study showed that students in the intervention schools (those that used Bullyproof), when compared with the control schools, showed greater accuracy over time in identifying behaviors that constituted sexual harassment. In addition, the intervention may have influenced girls' attitudes about bullies. The use of Bullyproof as an intervention tool was successful in increasing student and staff knowledge about sexual harassment. Although students in the intervention schools did not demonstrate an increase in their knowledge of bullying behaviors, the intervention group reported bullying at school and on the bus more frequently following the program.

For middle and high school students, the developers of Bullyproof designed Flirting or Hurting? for Grades 6–12 (Stein & Sjostrom, 1994). This curriculum guide includes introductory comments for teachers for preparing and teaching the lessons and for using it across the curriculum. Six core lessons, supplemental activities, additional resources, and relevant readings are included. Activities include in-class writings, interviews, case studies, and role-playing.

Bully-Proofing Your School (BPYS): Working With Victims and Bullies

The Bully-Proofing Your School (BPYS) program first encourages adoption of a school-wide campaign to prevent bullying, including creating a mission statement and philosophy around bullying prevention and intervention (Garrity, Jens, Porter, Sager, & Short-Camilli, 1997, 2004). An assessment of the school climate must be conducted by administering surveys to students and teachers. BPYS requires six sessions of staff training. Upon adoption of the program, teachers implement the lesson plans according to their students' grade level (from preschool through middle school). Additionally, teachers or social workers implement individualized training for victims and perpetrators.

The program facilitators begin the BPYS training for teachers and administrators by discussing the program authors' definition of bullying. The next section outlines techniques for teachers to address bullying situations within their classrooms, followed by a discussion of how to provide individual support for the victim. Within this chapter, teachers and social workers receive general information on victimization and potential intervention strategies. Additionally, the facilitators are provided with six sessions for helping the victims make friends, increase self-esteem, and increase communication skills. The final section in the manual encourages giving individual support to the bully, including individual understanding, peer understanding, and ways of solving social problems. Teachers and social workers are provided with research findings and general information about interventions with bullies.

Although the BPYS has yet to be the subject of a large-scale clinical trial, several studies suggest that it is a promising program. For example, Epstein and colleagues (2002) reported significant decreases in bullying behaviors and improved school safety perceptions in a longitudinal study of the impact of BPYS in a suburban elementary school. However, there were no control schools in this study. A study by Beran and Tutty (2002) did include both an intervention school (an adaptation of BPYS) and a comparison school, and they found decreased reports of witnessed bullying in the intervention school compared with no changes in the comparison school.

CONSIDERATION OF DEVELOPMENTALLY APPROPRIATE INTERVENTION STRATEGIES

Managing bullying and aggression problems within a school setting requires that school administrators determine which developmentally appropriate intervention strategies are best for their school. School administrators also must consider allocating resources (e.g., money, staff, and time) for these strategies. We suggest that incorporating research on the prevalence of bullying across ages into the management of three-tier intervention models will assist in the management of bullying and harassment in schools. For example, research has shown that bullying incidents and involvement peak in early middle school (Nansel et al., 2001; National Center for Educational Statistics, 1995). This knowledge should be utilized from a resource management perspective by preparing middle schools for the use of targeted intervention strategies. Although it would likely be unwise to abandon universal school-wide strategies to reduce bullying in middle and high schools, it is important to identify effective targeted intervention strategies. Interventions for aggressive behaviors in schools have most recently been found in individualized cognitive behavioral therapy (CBT), a well-established method of cognitive restructuring that has shown positive utility in school settings (Lochman & Wells, 2003; Smith, Lochman, & Daunic, 2005). Programs such as The Coping Power Program (Lochman & Wells, 1996) has been effective for aggressive children in Grades 4–6 and has specifically been found to help students during the transition to middle school (Lochman & Wells, 2002). Program components include anger management skills, problem-solving skills, and social skills. Involving professionals with appropriate training to provide targeted therapies for bullying and aggressive behaviors appears to be a wise investment.

Prevalence estimates have also indicated that elementary school is a period of development in which comparatively few instances of bullying and aggression occur (Pellegrini & Long, 2002). Therefore schools should focus first on implementing universal interventions that will have the greatest impact on the school climate and students. Using the Steps to Respect program or other school-wide interventions to encourage antibullying attitudes and to make schools safer will have long-term benefits for students.

Making effective changes to prevent bullying and harassment in high school is slightly different than in both elementary and middle school. Research demonstrates that although bullying and harassment occur less frequently in high school than in middle school, when bullying and harassment do occur, they occur with more consistency, such as dating violence or stalking. For example, with the knowledge that high school students commonly experience verbal and sexual harassment, school personnel should actively address these behaviors (AAUW, 1993, 2001). Using a universal prevention strategy for harassment will encourage all students to think about their behavior and how sexual harassment might affect others. In addition to implementing universal strategies, schools should also adopt targeted interventions for those students who do not respond to universal strategies. These targeted interventions may include group or individual interventions. In these cases, individual risk factors should be evaluated, and secondary or tertiary interventions should be chosen that address those factors.

SUMMARY AND CONCLUSIONS

Despite almost three decades of bullying research, as well as prevention and intervention efforts worldwide, remarkably little progress has been made in developing empirically supported primary, secondary, and tertiary school-based prevention programs. Most school districts in the United States continue to rely on zero-tolerance policies, in-school and out-of-school suspensions, and expulsions. These are not best practices; even the zero-tolerance programs that are endorsed by state and federal agencies have not yielded consistent and convincing data showing their efficacy.

In this chapter, we argued that future bullying prevention programs need to consider a developmental approach which acknowledges that children's bullying behaviors may have different motivations and typology than adolescents' bullying behaviors. This developmental approach has virtually been ignored in the extant literature. Research has shown that aggression and bullying are expressed differently across the elementary, middle, and high school years. Whereas aggression is largely physical in preschool, it becomes verbal, subtle, and social (e.g., group exclusion and rumor spreading) through the early and middle elementary school years. The transition from elementary to middle school finds an increase in bullying, and bullying and sexual harassment become closely intertwined throughout the high school years. Given these empirical findings, it is vitally important to tailor prevention and intervention efforts and to use universal, selected, and targeted interventions that are developmentally sensitive and that address the typology of bullying in a particular school and community.

REFERENCES

Akos, P. (2002). Student perceptions of the transition to middle school. *Professional School Counseling, 5,* 339–345.

American Association of University Women. (1993). *Hostile hallways: The AAUW survey on sexual harassment in America's schools* (Research Rep. No. 923012). Washington, DC: Harris/Scholastic Research.

American Association of University Women. (2001). *Hostile hallways: Bullying, teasing and sexual harassment in school.* Washington, DC: Author.

Batsche, G. M., & Knoff, H. M. (1994). Bullies and their victims: Understanding a pervasive problem in the schools. *School Psychology Review, 23,* 165–174.

Bauer, N. S., Lozano, P., & Rivara, F. P. (2007). The effectiveness of the Olweus Bullying Prevention Program in public middle schools: A controlled trial. *Journal of Adolescent Health, 40,* 266–274.

Beran, T. N., & Tutty, L. (2002). *An evaluation of the Dare to Care: Bully Proofing Your School Program.* Unpublished research report to the University of Calgary, RESOLVE Alberta.

Borg, M. G. (1999). The extent and nature of bullying among primary and secondary schoolchildren. *Educational Research, 41,* 137–153.

Bradshaw, C. P., Sawyer, A. L., & O'Brenna, L. M. (2007). Bullying and peer victimization at school: Perceptual differences between students and school staff. *School Psychology Review, 36,* 361–382.

Casella, R. (2003). Zero tolerance policy in schools: Rationale, consequences, and alternatives. *Teachers College Record, 105,* 872–892.

Committee for Children. (2001). *Steps to Respect: A Bullying Prevention Program.* Seattle, WA: Author.

Committee for Children. (2005). *Steps to Respect program guide.* Retrieved February 27, 2008, from http://www.cfchildren.org/media/files/str_research_foundations.pdf

Craig, W. M., Pepler, D., & Rona, A. (2000). Observations of bullying in the playground and in the classroom. *School Psychology International, 21,* 22–36.

Crick, N. R., & Grotpeter, J. K. (1995). Relational aggression, gender, and social-psychological adjustment. *Child Development, 66,* 710–722.

Crick, N. R., & Nelson, D. A. (2002). Relational and physical victimization within friendships: Nobody told me there'd be friends like this. *Journal of Abnormal Child Psychology, 32,* 599–607.

Cunningham, N. J. (2007). Level of bonding to school and perception of the school environment by bullies, victims, and bully victims. *Journal of Early Adolescence, 27,* 457–478.

Demaray, T. R., & Malecki, M. K. (2003). Perceptions of the frequency and importance of social support by students classified as victims, bullies, and bully/victims in an urban middle school. *School Psychology Review, 32,* 471–489.

Dempsey, J. P., Fireman, G. D., & Wang, E. M. (2006). Transitioning out of peer victimization in school children: Gender and behavioral characteristics. *Journal of Psychopathology and Behavioral Assessment, 28,* 271–280.

Eccles, J. S. (2004). Schools, academic motivation, and stage-environment fit. In R. M. Lerner & L. Sternberg (Eds.), *Handbook of Adolescent Psychology* (2nd ed., pp. 125–153). Hoboken, NJ: Wiley.

Eccles, J. S., & Midgley, C. (1989). Stage/environment fit: Developmentally appropriate classrooms for early adolescents. In R. Ames & C. Ames (Eds.), *Research on motivation in education* (Vol. 3, pp. 139–181). New York: Academic Press.

Eccles, J. S., Midgley, C., Wigfield, A., Miller-Buchanan, C., Reuman, D., Flanagan, C., et al. (2003). Development during adolescence: The impact of stage-environment fit on young adolescents' experiences in schools and in families. *American Psychologist, 48,* 90–101.

Eccles, J. S., & Roeser, R. (1999). School and community influences on human development. In M. Bornstein & M. Lamb (Eds.), *Developmental psychology: An advanced textbook* (4th ed., pp. 503–554). Mahwah, NJ: Erlbaum.

Epstein, L., Plog, A., & Porter, W. (2002). Bully-Proofing your school: Results of a four-year intervention. *Emotional and Behavior Disorders in Youth,* Summer, 55–78.

Espelage, D., & Horne, A. (2008). School violence and bullying prevention: From research-based explanations to empirically based solutions. In S. Brown & R. Lent (Eds.), *Handbook of counseling psychology* (4th ed., pp. 588–606). Hoboken, NJ: Wiley.

Espelage, D. L., & Swearer, S. M. (2003). Research on school bullying and victimization: What have we learned and where do we need to go? In S. M. Swearer & D. L. Espelage (Eds.), Bullying prevention and intervention: Integrating research and evaluation findings [Special issue]. *School Psychology Review, 32,* 365–383.

Feldlaufer, H., Midgley, C., & Eccles, J. S. (1988). Student, teacher, and observer perceptions of the classroom environment before and after the transition to junior high school. *Journal of Early Adolescence, 8,* 133–156.

Frey, K. S., Hirschstein, M. K., Snell, J. L., Edstrom, L. V., MacKenzie, E. P., & Broderick, C. J. (2005). Reducing playground bullying and supporting beliefs: An experimental trial of the Steps to Respect program. *Developmental Psychology, 41,* 479–491.

Garrity, C., Jens, K., Porter, W, Sager, N., & Short-Camilli, C. (1997). Bully proofing your school: Creating a positive climate. *Intervention in School & Clinic, 32,* 235–243.

Garrity, C., Jens, K., Porter, W., Sager, N., & Short-Camilli, C. (2004). *Bully proofing your school: A comprehensive approach for elementary schools.* Longmont, CO: Sopris West.

Gruber, J. E., & Fineran, S. (2007). The impact of bullying and sexual harassment on middle and high school girls. *Violence Against Women, 13,* 627–643.

Hanish, L. D., Kochenderfer-Ladd, B., Fabes, R. A., Martin, C. L., & Denning, D. (2004). Bullying among young children: The influence of peers and teachers. In D. Espelage & S. Swearer (Eds.), *Bullying in American schools: A social-ecological perspective on prevention and intervention* (pp. 141–159). Mahwah, NJ: Erlbaum.

Hankin, B. L., Abramson, L. Y., Moffitt, T. E., Silva, P. A., McGee, R., & Angell, K. E. (1998). Development of depression from preadolescence to young adulthood: Emerging gender differences in a 10-year longitudinal study. *Journal of Abnormal Psychology, 107,* 128–140.

Harachi, T. W., Fleming, C. B., White, H. R., Ensminger, M. E., Abbott, R. D., Catalano, R. F., & Haggerty, K. P. (2006). Aggressive behavior among girls and boys during middle childhood: Predictors and sequelae of trajectory group membership. *Aggressive Behavior, 32,* 279–293.

Hirsch, B. J., & Rapkin, B. D. (1987). The transition to junior high school: A longitudinal study of self esteem, psychological symptomatology, school life, and social support. *Child Development, 58,* 1235–1243.

Hirschstein, M. K., Edstrom, L. V. S., Frey, K. S., Snell, J. L., & MacKenzie, E. P. (2007). Walking the talk in bullying prevention: Teacher implementation variables related to initial impact of the Steps to Respect program. *School Psychology Review, 36,* 3–21.

Hirschstein, M. K., & Frey, K. S. (2006). Promoting behavior and beliefs that reduce bullying: The Steps to Respect program. In S. Jimerson & M. Furlong (Eds.), *The handbook of school violence and school safety: From research to practice* (pp. 309–323). Mahwah, NJ: Erlbaum.

Hoover, J., Oliver, R., & Hazler, R. (1992). *Causal attributions: From cognitive processes to collective beliefs.* Oxford, UK: Basil Blackwell.

Kaufman, P., Chen, X., Chandler, S. P., Chapman, K. A., Rand, C. D., & Ringel, M. R. (1998). *Indicators of school crime and safety* (NCES 98–251/NCJ-172215). Washington, DC: Government Printing Office.

Kochenderfer, B. J., & Ladd, G. W. (1996). Peer victimization: Manifestations and relations to school adjustment in kindergarten. *Journal of School Psychology, 34,* 267–283.

Lochman, J. E., & Wells, K. C. (1996). A social-cognitive intervention with aggressive children: Prevention effects and contextual implementation issues. In R. Dev. Peters & R. J. McMahon (Eds.), *Prevention and early intervention: Childhood disorders, substance use, and delinquency* (pp. 111–143). Newbury Park, CA: SAGE.

Lochman, J. E., & Wells, K. C. (2002). The Coping Power program at the middle school transition: Universal and indicated prevention effects. *Psychology of Addictive Behaviors, 16,* S40–S54.

Lochman, J. E., & Wells, K. C. (2003). Effectiveness of the Coping Power program and of classroom intervention with aggressive children: Outcomes at a one-year follow-up. *Behavior Therapy, 34,* 493–515.

McNeilly-Choque, M. K., Hart, C. H., Robinson, C. C., Nelson, L. J., & Olsen, S. F. (1996). Overt and relational aggression on the playground: Correspondence among different informants. *Journal of Research in Childhood Education, 11,* 47–67.

Merrell, K. W., Gueldner, B. A., Ross, S. W., & Isava, D. M. (2008). How effective are school bullying intervention programs? A meta-analysis of intervention research. *School Psychology Quarterly, 23,* 26–42.

Morrison, G. M., Redding, M., Fisher, E., & Peterson, R. (2006). Assessing school discipline. In S. R. Jimerson & M. Furlong (Eds.), *Handbook of school violence and school safety: From research to practice* (pp. 211–220). Mahwah, NJ: Erlbaum.

Nansel, T. R., Overpeck, M., Pilla, R. S., Ruan, W. J., Simons-Morton, B., & Scheidt, P. (2001). Bullying behaviors among U.S. youth. *Journal of the American Medical Association, 285,* 2094–2100.

National Center for Educational Statistics. (1995). *Student victimization in schools.* Washington, DC: U.S. Department of Education.

Newman-Carlson, D., & Horne, A. (2004). Bully-Busters: A psychoeducational intervention for reducing bullying behavior in middle school students. *Journal of Counseling and Development, 82,* 259−267.

Newman, D. A., Horne, A. M., & Bartolomucci, C. L. (2000). *Bully Busters: A teacher's manual for helping bullies, victims, and bystanders.* Champaign, IL: Research Press.

Olweus, D. (1993). *Bullying at school.* Oxford, UK: Blackwell Publishing.

Olweus, D., Limber, S. P., & Mihalic, S. (2000). *The Bullying Prevention Program: Blueprints for violence prevention* (Vol. 10). Boulder, CO: Center for the Study and Prevention of Violence.

Orpinas, P., Horne, A. M., & Staniszewski, D. (2003). School bullying: Changing the problem by changing the school. *School Psychology Review, 23,* 431–444.

Pellegrini, A. D. (2002). Bullying, victimization, and sexual harassment during the transition to middle school. *Educational Psychologist, 37,* 151–163.

Pellegrini, A. D., Bartini, M., & Brooks, F. (1999). School bullies, victims, and aggressive victims: Factors relating to group affiliation and victimization in early adolescence. *Journal of Educational Psychology, 91,* 216–224.

Pellegrini, A. D., & Long, J. D. (2002). A longitudinal study of bullying, dominance, and victimization during the transition from primary school through secondary school. *British Journal of Developmental Psychology, 20,* 259–280.

Perry, D. G., Kusel, S. J., & Perry, L. C. (1988). Victims of peer aggression. *Developmental Psychology, 24,* 807–814.

Poteat, V. P., Espelage, D. L., Holt, M., & VanBoven, A. (2009). *Bullying perpetration and victimization across the transition to middle school: exploring peer, teacher, and parental influences.* Manuscript in preparation.

Rosenbluth, B., Whitaker, D. J., Sanchez, E., & Valle, L. A. (2004). The Expect Respect project: Preventing bullying and sexual harassment in U.S. elementary schools. In P. K. Smith, D. Pepler, & K. Rigby (Eds.), *Bullying in schools: How successful can interventions be?* (pp. 211–233). Cambridge, UK: Cambridge University Press.

Salmivalli, C., Lappalainen, M., & Lagerspetz, K. M. J. (1998). Stability and change of behavior in connection with bullying in schools: A two-year follow up. *Aggressive Behavior, 24,* 205–218.

Seals, D., & Young, J. (2003). Bullying and victimization: Prevalence and relationship to gender, grade level, ethnicity, self-esteem, and depression. *Adolescence, 38,* 735–747.

Sjostrom, L., & Stein, N. (1996). *Bullyproof: A teacher's guide on teasing and bullying in school (grades 4 and 5).* Boston: Wellesley College Center for Research on Women and the National Education Association Professional Library.

Smith, J. D., Schneider, B. H., Smith, P. K., & Ananiadou, K. (2004). The effectiveness of whole-school antibullying programs: A synthesis of evaluation research. *School Psychology Review, 33,* 547–560.

Smith, P. K., Pepler, D., & Rigby, K. (Eds.). (2004). *Bullying in schools: How successful can interventions be?* New York: Cambridge University Press.

Smith, S. W., Lochman, J. E., & Daunic, A. P. (2005). Managing aggression using cognitive-behavioral interventions: State of practice and future decisions. *Behavioral Disorders, 30,* 227–240.

Solberg, M. E., & Olweus, D. (2003). Prevalence estimation of school bullying with the Olweus bully/victim questionnaire. *Aggressive Behavior, 29,* 239–268.

Solberg, M. E., Olweus, D., & Endresen, I. M. (2007). Bullies and victims at school: Are they the same pupils? *British Journal of Educational Psychology, 77,* 441–464.

Stein, N., & Sjostrom, L. (1994). *Flirting or hurting? A teacher's guide on student to student sexual harassment in grades 6–12.* Washington, DC: National Education Association Professional Library.

Swearer, S. M., Babl, J. P., Givens, J., & Turner, R. (2007, August). *Homophobic bullying and psychological well-being.* Paper presented at the American Psychological Association, San Francisco.

Swearer, S. M., & Espelage, D. L. (2004). Introduction: A social-ecological framework of bullying among youth. In D. L. Espelage & S. M. Swearer (Eds.), *Bullying in American schools: A social-ecological perspective on prevention and intervention* (pp. 1–12). Mahwah, NJ: Erlbaum.

Timmerman, G. (2005). A comparison between girls' and boys' experiences of unwanted sexual behaviour in secondary schools. *Educational Research, 47,* 291–306.

Ttofi, M. M., Farrington, D. P., & Baldry, A. C. (2008). *Effectiveness of programmes to reduce school bullying.* Stockholm: Swedish Council for Crime Prevention, Information, and Publications.

Unnever, J. (2005). Bullies, aggressive victims and victims: Are they distinct groups? *Aggressive Behavior, 31,* 153–171.

Vossekuil, B., Fein, R. A., Reddy, M., Borum, R., & Modzeleski, W. (2002). *The final report and findings of the Safe School Initiative: Implications for the prevention of school attacks in the United States.* Washington, DC: U.S. Secret Service and U.S. Department of Education.

Walker, H. M., & Shinn, M. R. (2002). Structuring school-based interventions to achieve integrated primary, secondary, and tertiary prevention goals for safe and effective schools. In M. R. Shinn, H. M. Walker, & G. Stoner (Eds.), *Interventions for academic and behavior problems: Preventive and remedial approaches* (pp. 1–26). Bethesda, MD: National Association of School Psychologists.

Wenxin, Z. (2002). Prevalence and major characteristics of bullying/victimization among primary and junior middle school students. *Acta Psychologica Sinica, 34,* 387–394.

Whitaker, D., Rosenbluth, B., Valle, L. A., & Sanchez, E. (2004). Expect Respect: A school-based intervention to promote awareness and effective responses to bullying and sexual harassment. In D. L. Espelage & S. M. Swearer (Eds.), *Bullying in American schools: A social-ecological perspective on prevention and intervention* (pp. 327–350). Mahwah, NJ: Erlbaum.

Whitney, L., & Smith, P. K. (1993). A survey of the nature and extent of bullying in junior/middle and secondary school. *Educational Research, 35,* 3–25.

Wigfield, A., Eccles, J. S., MacIver, D., Reuman, D., & Midgley, C. (1991). Transitions during early adolescence: Changes in children's domain-specific self-perceptions and general self-esteem across the transition to junior high school. *Developmental Psychology, 27*(4), 552–565.

Wolke, D., Woods, S., Standford, K., & Schulz, H. (2001). Bullying and victimization of primary school children in England and Germany: Prevalence and school factors. *British Journal of Psychology, 92,* 673–696.

Woods, S., & Wolke, D. (2004). Direct and relational bullying among primary school children and academic achievement. *Journal of School Psychology, 42,* 135–155.

CHAPTER 28

Deviant Peer Clustering and Influence Within Public School Settings:
Inadvertent Negative Outcomes From Traditional Professional Practices

Jennifer E. Lansford
Duke University

Thomas J. Dishion
University of Oregon

Kenneth A. Dodge
Duke University

INTRODUCTION

Youth with behavior problems are vulnerable to becoming more deviant when they associate with deviant peers. This problem, known as deviant peer contagion, is recognized by parents of teenagers, teachers, school psychologists, and social policy makers. A well-replicated finding in the developmental literature is that a group of peers acting together is much more likely to engage in deviant behavior than is a single adolescent acting alone (e.g., Dishion, Andrews, & Crosby, 1995; Thornberry & Krohn, 1997; Warr, 1996). In fact, the strongest correlate of adolescents' delinquency is the delinquency of their peers (Akers, Krohn, Lanza-Kaduce, & Radosevich, 1979; Pratt & Cullen, 2000; Warr, 1993). A number of studies have found that youth who engage in deviant behaviors select friends who engage in similar behaviors (e.g., McPherson & Smith-Lovin, 1987). However, evidence from methodologically sophisticated studies that partial out the effects of peer selection show that once deviant peers are in a group together, they incrementally increase one another's engagement in deviant behaviors (Aseltine, 1995; Dishion & Owen, 2002; Fisher & Bauman, 1988; Matsueda & Anderson, 1998). Furthermore, peers influence one another across a diverse set of behaviors, including early and high-risk sexual behavior,

Address all correspondence and feedback on this chapter to Jennifer E. Lansford at lansford@duke.edu.

violent offenses, and substance use (Dishion, 2000; Dishion & Skaggs, 2000; Elliott & Menard, 1996).

Deviant peer influences can be found not only in naturally occurring groups and settings, but also in contexts created by well-meaning adults and social policies. Many school programs, practices, and policies wind up segregating deviant students from their mainstream peers and aggregating them in settings with other deviant students, with the result that problem behaviors among these youth are exacerbated. In fact, the most common and expensive (because it is used the most frequently) public policy response to problem behaviors is that of placing youth in groups with other deviant youth (Dodge, Lansford, & Dishion, 2006). Financial and logistical constraints sometimes dictate these placements, and public opinion is often in favor of separating deviant youth to minimize the disruptions and dangers they may otherwise pose for their mainstream peers. Nevertheless, such practices are not necessarily in the best interests of the deviant youth, and depending on the nature of the problem behavior and how it is managed within a mainstreamed setting, segregating the deviant youth may not notably benefit the nondeviant youth (Cook & Ludwig, 2006). For example, the governor of Illinois recently signed legislation requiring that all high-risk students in Chicago schools participate in the Scared Straight intervention, which involves aggregation of those students and is known to have detrimental effects (Sherman & Strang, 2004). This legally mandated practice was expensive and appears not to have been in the best interests of the deviant youth.

How extensive is the problem of deviant peer aggregation in school settings, and is this policy scientifically supported? This chapter explores the potential effects of school practices and policies on the likelihood that deviant peer clustering will occur (thereby exacerbating problem behaviors and posing challenges to the successful management of such behaviors by school staff). We first discuss deviant peer clustering in school settings, with particular emphasis on universal practices that are implemented across entire schools or classrooms and on selected practices that are implemented with at-risk students only. We then discuss mechanisms of deviant peer contagion and present a general model for addressing deviant peer effects in interventions and policies. Finally, we offer empirically supported solutions and alternatives to these school practices that address problem behavior and improve students' academic progress.

DEVIANT PEER CLUSTERING IN SCHOOL SETTINGS

There are two primary ways that deviant peers may end up being clustered in school settings. The first of these involves practices that affect all students within a school, such as grouping children according to their abilities or providing school choice options. The second of these involves practices that affect only selected groups of at-risk students, such as grouping children with behavior problems in special resource rooms or alternative schools.

Universal Practices

Universal practices are those that affect all students within a school. Just being within the school system increases child and adolescent clustering and the behavior that emerges from such contact. For example, violent crime is 28% higher on days when school is in session than on days when school is not in session. Jacob and Lefgren (2003) attribute these findings to peer influences that occur when deviant youth interact with one another in contexts that school practices and policies have helped to create. In unruly classrooms, as well as outside the classroom in relatively unsupervised places such as restrooms, the cafeteria, the playground, and hallways, students victimize and intimidate one another. Adults have a difficult time controlling bullying and other negative behaviors that occur naturally in school settings (Espalage & Swearer, 2003). In addition, students sometimes become friends with peers in school who draw them into gangs and groups that engage in drug use, delinquency, and other problem behaviors outside of school (Reid, Patterson, & Snyder, 2002).

Although the policy of academic tracking, or grouping students based on academic performance, is intended to be a proactive universal-level practice, it has the most notable implications for the aggregation of deviant youth (Kellam, Ling, Merisca, Brown, & Ialongo, 1998; Warren, Schoppelrey, Moberg, & McDonald, 2005). Academic problems are often accompanied by behavior problems in school. As a result, youth with behavior problems may end up being concentrated in the lower academic tracks. Children in these lower tracks spend more time together, are more likely to form friendships with one another, and are likely to have less in common over time with students in higher academic tracks (Kubitschek & Hallinan, 1998). If these youth, who are struggling academically and behaviorally in school, come to collectively define their identity in terms of disengagement from school, deviant behavior may become contagious.

Crosnoe (2002) found that high school students who were not in college preparatory classes had higher levels of self-reported delinquency, as well as delinquency among their friends, than did students in college preparatory courses. More important, the delinquency of students not in the college preparatory class was significantly related to increases in their friends' delinquency over time, but no increase was seen for those in the college preparatory track. The students not in the college preparatory track appeared to be more susceptible to deviant peer influences because they were less bonded to the school as an institution and less committed to academic achievement.

School-choice policies function similarly by permitting higher-performing students with more proactive and educated parents to attend higher-performing schools. Lower-performing students, who may have less-involved and less-educated parents, are then left behind in more homogeneously low-performing schools, putting them at even higher risk for engendering academic and behavioral difficulties (Reinke & Walker, 2006).

Selected Interventions

Despite the potential for universal-level policies and programs to enhance the risk for deviant peer contagion, most of the school policies that raise concerns are at the selected and indicated levels. That is, they are programs for youth who are identified as being at risk for school difficulties, or who meet criteria for mental health or special education services (those with conduct disorders or who are socially and emotionally disturbed). Such targeted programs are common in public schools. Their strategies vary widely and are often not based on practices that have been shown to work in rigorous scientific evaluations (Silver & Eddy, 2006). Most of the programs discussed in the following sections could be described as indicated because they are implemented with students who have already engaged in problem behaviors.

Grade retention, which has become more common because of the No Child Left Behind Act of 2001, is an example of an intensive effort in which a small subset of the most at-risk students are held back in school rather than advanced to the next grade level. This policy segregates deviant youth from peers of the same age, increases the likelihood that retained students will form bonds with other retained youth, and may serve to connect high-risk students who may not have associated with one another in different circumstances (Jimerson, 2001). As with academic tracking, students who have been retained may come to identify with one another and define their similarities in terms of their perceived failure in school. Students who have been retained are more likely to eventually drop out of school than are students who achieve at similarly low levels but receive social promotions (Jimerson, Anderson, & Whipple, 2002).

In addition to grade retention, referrals to special education programs constitute another practice that often functions to aggregate students with conduct problems, or students diagnosed as "seriously emotionally disturbed" or "behaviorally or emotionally handicapped." Once in the special education system, children with conduct disorders often are put in groups in self-contained classrooms or resource rooms for part of the day. These settings afford opportunities for deviant peer contagion and deprive children of opportunities to be positively influenced by well-behaving peers. Even though federal legislation prohibits special education students from being suspended for offenses that may be a manifestation of their disability, special education students are still more frequently suspended and expelled than are students who are not in special education classes (Kingery, 2000; Morrison & D'Incau, 1997). Furthermore, placement into special education appears to increase rather than decrease students' conduct problems. Within these self-contained classrooms, students may be motivated to misbehave in order to fit in with other misbehaving peers, thereby gaining peer status and acceptance, or in order to avoid being victimized by aggressive peers (Reinke & Walker, 2006).

Because of the potential for such peer contagion, many educators and parents have advocated mainstreaming special education children into traditional classrooms whenever possible. However, students with serious conduct problems often have a negative effect on the climate of traditional classrooms, so mainstreaming them may not be a viable option, especially without behavior management plans in place to minimize their defiance and disruptiveness. Yet only 11% of emotionally disturbed children who were served in regular classrooms had a behavior management plan in place, according to the National Longitudinal Transition Study (Wagner, 1995).

Several policies related to school suspensions and expulsions may have the inadvertent effect of aggregating deviant peers. The Gun-Free Schools Act of 1994 and cases of school violence have prompted federally mandated zero-tolerance policies that have resulted in an unprecedented increase in the use of long-term suspensions and expulsion from school (Kingery, 2000). In the 2005–2006 school year alone, 830,700 serious disciplinary actions were taken, involving suspensions for 5 days or more, transfers to alternative schools, or expulsions without services for the remainder of the school year (U.S. Department of Education, 2009). There has been increasing concern that suspended or expelled students mingle in the community without supervision when they are barred from school, increasing their exposure to deviant peers and limiting their exposure to well-behaved peers at school. Past suspensions are the best predictors of future suspensions (Tobin, Sugai, & Colvin, 1996), and repeat offenders account for approximately 40% of suspensions (Bowditch, 1993), suggesting that suspensions may be of limited effectiveness in preventing future misbehavior. Incarceration rates are 2.2 times higher for adults with a history of school suspension than for adults with no suspension history, even after controlling for other risk factors such as family characteristics, socioeconomic status, prior delinquency, and years of education (Arum & Beattie, 1999).

The schools that are the most likely to suspend and expel students are those characterized by the highest levels of antisocial behavior and lowest academic achievement (Le Blanc, Vallieres, & McDuff, 1992; McEvoy & Welker, 2000). If the overall school culture is one that allows deviant behavior and low academic achievement, then removing individual students through suspension or expulsion is not likely to result in improvements in students' behavior or change the overall level of school safety. These findings have spawned efforts to find programs for youth who are prohibited from attending traditional schools with mainstream peers.

The most common school policies that occur at an intensive level may also promote deviant peer contagion. These policies involve the use of self-contained classrooms for students with emotional or behavioral problems and alternative schools for youth who have been suspended or expelled from traditional schools. In self-contained classrooms and alternative schools, students with high levels of problem behaviors are segregated from mainstream peers and isolated in a context in which deviance is the norm. Very little systematic research has been conducted to measure the impact of self-contained classrooms on student outcomes, including behavioral and emotional adjustment and academic progress. Research using randomized intervention trials with selected youth revealed that, despite gains in specific skills, the inadvertent collateral effects can be profound with respect to long-term development of the student. Increases in student drug use and problem behavior can foreshadow future involvement in deviant peer groups, leading to even more serious levels of problem behavior and potentially school failure and dropping out, which in turn sets the stage for adult developmental dysfunction (Dishion, McCord, & Poulin, 1999).

Even seemingly benign classroom assignments that attempt to engage unmotivated students can have potentially negative effects. For example, Cho, Hallfors, and Sanchez (2005) found that creating a special classroom for disaffected high school students was of dubious value. Despite training teachers to implement an empirically supported program, the outcomes were less than optimal. It was apparent that some high school classrooms were more effective than others; in the less effective ones, teachers tended to try to "connect" with students by telling stories of their own past deviance, undermining possible benefits of the program (Hallfors, Cho, Dishion, Cuffee, & Hartman, 2009).

Alternative schools were originally developed for nondeviant youth who were struggling to learn in traditional school settings. Over time these schools have changed to accommodate deviant youth (Raywid, 1994). Raywid reviewed the evidence for the effectiveness of educational programs that attempt to manage behavior problems in group settings; the author found little to no evidence that these programs are effective and found some evidence that such programs may cause harm. For example, a review of alternative education programs by officials in Oklahoma found some positive effects, such as lower rates of school dropout, but also found that programs that emphasized discipline had negative effects on student outcomes, such as delinquency (Raywid).

Few studies use designs incorporating random assignment to examine the effects of different school practices and policies on students' academic achievement and behavior. A rare exception addresses several limitations of much of the extant research. Cox (1999) randomly assigned 83 students in sixth through eighth grades who had been referred by school officials to alternative school placements, and instead either sent them to an alternative school for one semester or had them remain in their traditional school. At the end of the semester, students who were assigned to the alternative school did not differ on academic achievement or attitudes toward school when compared with students in the traditional school. The students who were assigned to the alternative school had better attendance, higher grade-point averages, and higher self-esteem at the end of the semester than the students who remained in their traditional school. However, these effects disappeared after the alternative school students returned to their traditional school. The self-reported delinquency scores did not significantly differ between the groups, but the means were in directions that would be predicted if deviant peer contagion effects occurred. Mean levels of self-reported delinquency were 2.90, 3.07, and 3.20 for the students randomly assigned to the alternative school before the program, immediately after the program, and at 1-year follow-up, respectively. The comparable means for the students randomly assigned to remain in their traditional school were 2.83, 2.71, and 2.83 at these same time points.

Additional research using true experimental designs is needed to help determine the extent to which deviant peer contagion may be operating in a variety of school settings and programs. Research will have to focus on outcomes such as problem behavior and emotional well-being when considering the long-term impact of these types of school programs, because benefits might be seen in some domains (attendance, grades), but at the expense of serious, unintended side effects (drug use, delinquent behavior).

Of the approximately 47 million public school K–12 students in the United States in 2000, more than 613,000 students (1.3%) were enrolled in alternative schools or group programs for deviant youth (Kleiner, Porch, & Farris, 2002). This number does not include the aggregation of deviant youth that occurs within schools through low academic tracking or grade retention. By 2001, 39% of public school districts had alternative schools or similar programs, which amounts to 10,900 public alternative schools and programs for at-risk students. For 54% of these programs, the recent demand has exceeded the available spaces (Kleiner et al., 2002). The practice continues to grow. For example, in North Carolina, an alternative school placement option must be available for deviant youth in every school district. These figures suggest that if space in these programs was not so limited, the practice of aggregating deviant students would be even more prevalent.

In 2003–2004, $501.3 billion in tax dollars were budgeted to be spent on K–12 education in the United States (U.S. Department of Education, 2004). The costs of programs that aggregate deviant youth are substantial, although the exact amount spent on such programs is difficult to determine because they are funded jointly from federal, state, and local sources that are not reported uniformly across districts. One state estimates that nationally, more than $15 billion dollars are spent each year on alternative schools and programs for deviant students (Public Schools of North Carolina, 2003).

DEVIANT PEER CONTAGION MECHANISMS

Peer contagion describes a process of mutual influence that is not intentional, purposeful, or planned, but is initiated and maintained by social dynamics. The term is analogous to a contagious disease process as is the focus in epidemiology (Anthony, 2006). In general, peer contagion is the often rapid disinhibition of behavior patterns within a group of children, involving peers, friends, or siblings. The primary focus to date has been on peer contagion as it relates to problem behavior, and less frequently, the underlying emotion that accompanies problem behavior.

The literature suggests several mechanisms that could account for deviant peer contagion effects in school programs that aggregate youth who demonstrate problem behaviors; the same mechanisms may explain the success of programs that do not involve the aggregation of deviant youth (Dishion & Dodge, 2006). A key principle is that peer contagion is amplified by the powerful learning capabilities inherent in human language (Hayes, Barnes-Holmes, & Roche, 2001). Thus, the various mechanisms identified to date are not likely to be mutually exclusive, but perhaps differences of emphasis in different academic disciplines or theoretical perspectives. One mechanism involves labeling effects. When a youth is placed in a group composed of deviant youth, both the individual child and the entire group may be labeled by themselves and others as being deviant. Once an individual has been labeled as being deviant, self-fulfilling prophecies may be set in motion. These processes have been well documented in school settings. Teachers and school staff change how they interact with students labeled as deviant, and conversely, student reactions to school staff become more deviant (Rosenthal, 1994). Labeling often occurs unconsciously (Harris, 1994), but such thoughts eventually culminate in overt actions and reactions that exacerbate the deviance and undermine academic engagement. The majority of labeling research focuses on adult–student interactions, but labeling effects may extend to peer–peer interactions, as described below.

A second mechanism involves increased opportunities for deviant behavior that are created by contact with peers. For example, the peers may provide drugs or weapons, communicate information that can be used for committing crimes (e.g., promising targets for robbery), foster enmity against rival gangs, and be the team for engaging in deviant behavior. In addition to these opportunities, peer groups may also influence a youth's perception that deviant behavior is the norm, positively reinforcing a youth's engagement in deviant behaviors (Jussim & Osgood, 1989).

Yet another mechanism is described in Dishion's theory of deviancy training (Dishion, Spracklen, & Patterson, 1996). Deviancy training is a process that is set in motion when a peer engages in or discusses antisocial behavior and other peers reinforce that behavior by smiling, providing verbal approval, or granting high status to the initiator. The process is mutual and dynamic and becomes increasingly sophisticated over time. Youth who become polished in their abilities to connect with other deviant youth by the age of 13 are much more likely to engage in high levels of antisocial behavior and drug use in young adulthood (Dishion, Nelson, Winter, & Bullock, 2004; Dishion & Owen, 2002).

It is not surprising that students with problem behaviors are often rejected by their well-functioning peers (Coie & Kupersmidt, 1983; Dodge, 1983). For some time, developmental researchers have been interested in the social and emotional sequelae of peer rejection (Parker & Asher, 1987). They have found that one consequence of peer rejection is the child's increasing involvement in a deviant peer group (Dishion, Patterson, Stoolmiller, & Skinner, 1991). By early adolescence, the same deviant behavior can be a source of both popularity and rejection, as indicated by the work of Rodkin, Farmer, Pearl, and Van Acker (2000). Dishion, Piehler, and Myers (2008) have proposed a process of "social augmentation" to describe how some students are pushed into deviant peer groups after being rejected by their peers. Students marginalized by others in their school are more susceptible to peer reinforcement, and therefore more vulnerable to deviant peer influence. In an ethnically diverse sample of young adolescents, it was found that peer rejection or peer liking, academic failure, and antisocial behavior all predicted gang involvement by the eighth grade of public middle school. As predicted from the social augmentation hypothesis, peer rejection and liking were positive predictors of future gang involvement. Ethnic differences in the rate of gang involvement were completely accounted for in males and females by the sixth-grade predictors (Dishion, Nelson, & Yasui, 2005).

Thus, marginalized students in the public school system are more likely to organize into groups and to use their deviance as the currency of their emerging friendships. As students move into adolescence, they tend to remain in these groups and to spend their free time with peers, unsupervised by adults, which is the best predictor of long-term academic failure and increased problem behavior (Dishion, Nelson, & Bullock, 2004; Granic & Dishion, 2003).

A GENERAL MODEL OF DEVIANT PEER EFFECTS IN INTERVENTIONS AND POLICIES

Research in diverse domains, including mental health, juvenile justice, and community programs, in addition to education, indicates that at least four different effects, or factors, simultaneously exert influence during interventions and programs for deviant youth (Dishion, Dodge, & Lansford, 2006). These factors can be either positive or negative and may exacerbate or mitigate one another's effects. Taken together, these four factors act jointly to determine the effectiveness of a program or practice. The first factor involves the desired positive effects that accrue from individual administration of the program (Weisz, Weiss, Han, Granger, & Morton, 1995). The second factor involves the decreased effectiveness of the program if it is administered in a group rather than individually. This decrease of the positive effect of the program may occur, for example, if the teacher has less time to spend with each individual student if she is working with a group rather than in one-on-one tutoring. The third factor involves the negative effects of a program that places a deviant youth with deviant peers. Mechanisms of labeling, exposure to deviant group norms, opportunities to offend, and deviancy training almost always result in program effects that are marginally negative. The fourth factor involves the set of moderating characteristics (e.g., child's age, teacher's experience) that can mitigate or magnify the adverse impact of being placed with deviant peers.

This model leads to two main hypotheses that are supported by the empirical literature. First, placement with deviant peers reduces an otherwise positive effect of programs and practices designed to help deviant youth. Second, characteristics of the individual youth, the group, and the group leader can mitigate or magnify the adverse impact of deviant peer aggregation.

Cultural Norms

Clearly, deviancy training depends on a shift in individual norms for deviance. However, it is important to consider the norms of the group with respect to the long-term viability of deviant norms. Group norms that promote deviant behavior exacerbate the effects of placing an individual with deviant peers. Groups, like cultures, tend to have norms for behavior that are established within the group. These norms can be difficult to change because they perpetuate themselves within the group over time, even when the individual members change. For example, the behavioral norms of a school can remain, even though there is a complete turnover of students over the course of a few years. Research on how classroom cultures are related to individual students' behavior suggests that students are likely to behave in ways consistent with the classroom cultural norm. For example, in classrooms in which aggression is the norm, individual children are more likely to behave aggressively, and aggression is related to higher peer status than in classrooms in which aggression is not the norm (Stormshak et al., 1999). Barth, Dunlap, Dane, Lochman, and Wells (2004) found that fourth graders who were rated by teachers as being high in aggression and poor in academic focus demonstrated greater increases in these problem behaviors if their fifth-grade classroom had a climate characterized by aggression and poor academic focus than if their fifth-grade classroom had less of these negative characteristics, suggesting that negative classroom cultures have a particularly adverse impact on behaviorally at-risk students. Similarly, Kellam et al. (1998) showed that aggressive boys whose first-grade classrooms were poorly managed and chaotic were at increased risk of being aggressive in middle school when compared with aggressive boys whose first-grade classrooms were managed well. In another longitudinal investigation, collective levels of aggression in school classrooms were predictive of students' aggression outside the classroom when rated by their parents 2 years later (Warren et al., 2005). Taken together, these findings suggest the long-term impacts of classroom contexts on students' behavior, as well as the malleability of students' behavior, which can change with classroom cultural norms.

Moderating Characteristics of Individual Children

Characteristics of individual children, such as age, propensity toward problem behavior, and ability to regulate one's own behavior, have all been found to moderate the effects of being placed in a deviant peer group (Dishion et al., 2006). Most important, early adolescence is a developmental period in which youth are more susceptible to deviant peer influences than they are earlier in childhood or later in adolescence. In addition, children are most likely to be influenced by peers who are slightly older than they are.

The particular problem behaviors that are most susceptible to deviant peer influences vary depending on the youth's developmental stage, which helps to define the behaviors that are of highest interest and most salience. For example, physical aggression is most salient during elementary school, whereas delinquency, substance use, and sexual behavior are more salient during adolescence. Peer contagion effects are influenced by youth's state of readiness for the behaviors involved, suggesting that grouping deviant youth to discuss topics that are especially salient during their particular developmental stage should be avoided (e.g., aggregating early adolescents who have demonstrated problem behavior to discuss delinquency, substance use, and risky sexual behavior). Deviant peer influence is also highest for behaviors such as violence, delinquency, and substance use because these types of behaviors are most often acquired through social processes.

Furthermore, youth who are placed in a program with deviant peers after experiencing a brief period of their own behavior problems are at greatest risk for experiencing deviant peer contagion (Feldman, Caplinger, & Wodarski, 1983). For youth who are already highly deviant, placement with other deviant youth may not add substantially to their negative outcomes. Institutions such as juvenile correctional facilities that are designed for severely deviant youth may be needed to put the safety of the community first, and the added risk to deviant youth from aggregation with their peers may be relatively small in the face of their other serious difficulties. At the other end of the spectrum, youth who are well-adjusted and well-supported in their environments do not appear to have an increase in deviant behavior through exposure to moderately deviant peers in classroom settings, suggesting that leaving moderately deviant youth in traditional school settings will not adversely affect the nondeviant youth (Silver & Eddy, 2006). Thus, for the most extreme groups, aggregation does not necessarily confer substantially greater risk; and for youth who are not deviant, placement with those who are does not convert them into deviant youth. However, aggregation with deviant peers can catalyze antisocial development among youth who are initially moderately deviant, especially if these youth are placed with peers who are slightly more deviant than they are (Boxer, Guerra, Huesmann, & Morales, 2005; Lavallee, Bierman, Nix, & Conduct Problems Prevention Research Group, 2005). These findings suggest that targeted programs that are designed for at-risk youth who are still in traditional education settings (e.g., dropout prevention programs for high-risk youth, in-school suspensions) may be most susceptible to deviant peer contagion effects.

Other individual differences among children may affect their susceptibility to deviant peer influences. For example, particular life experiences such as rejection by parents or weak family ties may make children more susceptible to peer influence. Children's personality characteristics may also have an impact. For example, highly impulsive children may be more susceptible to deviant peer influences than children who are better able to self-regulate. Several studies suggest that youth high in self-regulation are less vulnerable to influence even when exposed to deviant peers (Dishion & Connell, 2006; Goodnight, Bates, Newman, Dodge, & Pettit, 2006). These findings suggest that efforts in early childhood to develop children's school readiness in areas such as self-regulation, may pay off in early adolescence by reducing vulnerability to deviant peer influences.

Ratio of Deviant to Nondeviant Youth, Leadership, and Program Structure as Moderating Factors

Several characteristics of programs or interventions might also moderate deviant peer group effects (Feldman et al., 1983). For example, the ratio of deviant to nondeviant youth in the group is important. Deviant peer contagion effects appear not to occur when only one deviant youth is included in a group, especially if the teacher or group leader is skilled and experienced. On the other end of the spectrum, groups composed only of deviant youth are particularly conducive to deviant peer contagion effects. Between these two extremes one would expect a higher ratio of deviant to nondeviant youth to result in greater risk for deviant peer contagion. However, some teachers or group leaders are especially skilled at managing the behavior of deviant youth and may be able to prevent deviant peer contagion effects even when the ratio of deviant to nondeviant youth in the group is relatively high. Other teachers or group leaders may be able to manage only groups with fewer deviant youth. Experienced teachers or group leaders are often more skilled than novice ones at respecting yet controlling students, diverting attention when misbehavior occurs (e.g., by engaging other students in the classroom in a different activity rather than letting them reward disruptions with laughter or other attention that could be interpreted by the disruptive student as encouragement for future misbehavior), and reestablishing prosocial norms after disruptions.

A second factor is whether the program is highly structured or whether the youth have many opportunities to "hang out" in unstructured activities. Deviant peer contagion is much more likely to occur in unstructured situations where peers have the opportunity to positively reinforce one another's deviant talk and behavior. Even when programs themselves are highly structured, caution is needed to prevent unstructured contact from occurring before or after the structured program. For example, youth might participate in a highly structured and well-managed program at an alternative school, but if they are bused together to the school, they may have unstructured time together before and after school.

SOLUTIONS TO DEVIANT PEER EFFECTS IN EDUCATION

The following sections describe promising strategies at the universal, selected, and indicated levels that have been demonstrated to minimize risks of deviant peer contagion in school settings.

Universal-Level Strategies

Although most of the concerns related to school policies that may promote deviant peer contagion are at the selected or indicated level, a majority of the most promising solutions are at the universal level, because at this level there is no grouping of deviant youth or unwitting promotion of their collective identity in terms of deviance. To the extent possible, the practices of tracking youth with low academic achievement into isolated classrooms, mandatory grade retention, self-contained classrooms for students with behavioral problems, alternative schools, and suspensions and expulsions should be eliminated. Instead, universal programs and policies that focus on improving school-wide behavior should be encouraged. For example, the Good Behavior Game (a program in which teachers assign both deviant and prosocial students to teams that are rewarded for adhering to specified behavioral standards) and school-wide positive behavior support strategies stress behavior management practices for the entire school and apply to all students, in every situation, without selecting youth with behavior problems for any special treatment.

Problem behavior rates in schools have been improved by the implementation of universal, environment-focused programs (Ialongo, Poduska, Werthamer, & Kellam, 2001; Sugai & Horner, 2002). These successful universal programs share several important features, including promoting consistent, proactive discipline strategies; monitoring "hot spots" (e.g., hallways, restrooms, playgrounds, parking lots, cafeterias) to reduce antisocial behavior during unstructured and unsupervised time; enhancing systems to monitor students' achievement and behavior (e.g., evaluation of academic achievement, office visits for discipline referrals); and presenting clear, detailed expectations of how students and teachers will behave (Silver & Eddy, 2006).

An alternative or complement to using universal approaches with students is intervening with teachers. Effective behavior management practices and reduction of school-wide levels of problem behaviors can be promoted through training, incentives, and supports for teachers (Hoglund & Leadbeater, 2004). The most effective classroom management strategies identified through meta-analysis included group contingencies such as evaluation of the behavior of a group of students to determine whether the whole group receives a reward, self-management techniques, and differential reinforcement of positive and negative behaviors (Stage & Quiroz, 1997). One example of this is the Incredible Years Teacher Training Program (Webster-Stratton, Reid, & Hammond, 2004). Aggregating misbehaving students and segregating them from the mainstream did not emerge as an effective behavior management practice for teachers. Instead, teachers who are clear about their expectations for students' behavior, who reinforce positive behaviors, and who consistently use appropriate consequences for negative behaviors will reduce disruptive behaviors and increase prosocial behaviors within their classrooms (Bear, Webster-Stratton, Furlong, & Rhee, 2000; Brophy, 1996; Reinke & Herman, 2002; Walker, Colvin, & Ramsey, 1995).

The frequency and severity of students' behavior problems in school can be reduced by working with teachers to develop behavior support plans that target the needs of individual youth (O'Neil et al., 1997). Students may be unnecessarily moved to more restrictive settings such as self-contained special education classrooms or alternative schools if they do not have individual behavior support plans in place. More students could remain in traditional classrooms (thereby avoiding the potential harms of aggregating deviant peers) if they had appropriate behavior support plans. The school curriculum can also be expanded to include programs such as Responding in Peaceful and Positive Ways (RIPP; Farrell, Meyer, Sullivan, & Kung, 2003) and Providing Alternative Thinking Strategies (PATHS; Greenberg, Kusche, Cook, & Quamma, 1995), which have been found to enhance students' social competence and reduce rates of problem behaviors.

Group norms also can be manipulated to promote a prosocial rather than deviant peer culture within a school. For example, building on the model used by the Montessori program with young children, new children can be integrated into the group gradually, with each new child added only after a prosocial peer culture has already been established with the existing group members. In the Montessori program, 3-, 4-, and 5-year-olds often stay in the same classroom for these 3 years. At the beginning of a new school year, the previous year's 3- and 4-year-olds (who are now 4 and 5) are brought back to school. The older children are reminded of the group's norms for sharing, cooperation, and other prosocial behaviors. Once these prosocial norms are reestablished, the 3-year-olds are added to the class one at a time. A new 3-year-old is added only after the prosocial norms are clear to everyone (including the new 3-year-olds) already in the class. Thus, the teachers play a key role in engineering the prosocial norms within the group.

Selected and Indicated Strategies

In addition to these universal strategies, targeted or intensive strategies that do not aggregate deviant youth also hold promise. Many of these strategies can be implemented with students within the school context. Brain Power (Hudley et al., 1998), the Peer Coping Skills Training Program (Prinz, Blechman, & Dumas, 1994), and the Montreal Longitudinal Project (Vitaro, Brendgen, & Tremblay, 1999) are examples of coaching programs that have paired one deviant child with one nondeviant child to develop the skills of the deviant child and promote cooperative learning. There is evidence that these programs are beneficial for deviant children without being detrimental to nondeviant children.

One of the most effective intervention strategies for youth with behavior problems is to intervene with parents, with a specific focus on motivating and supporting behavior management (Kazdin, 1993, 2002; Spoth, Kavanagh, & Dishion, 2002). Early research on family centered interventions revealed that working with parents improved the child's behavior in school (Patterson, 1974), especially when there were efforts to coordinate the parenting intervention with those in the school (Blechman, Taylor, & Schrader, 1981). Recently, scientists who study the prevention of behavior problems designed cost-effective, parent-focused interventions to be delivered within the school context, including the Adolescent Transitions Program (e.g., Dishion, Andrews, Kavanagh, & Soberman, 1996; Dishion, Kavanagh, Schneiger, Nelson, & Kaufman, 2002), Linking the Interests of Families and Teachers (LIFT; Eddy, Reid, & Fetrow, 2000), and the Seattle Social Development Project (Hawkins, Catalano, Kosterman, Abbott, & Hill, 1999). These family-centered interventions suggest that selected programs for at-risk youth can be integrated with universal programs implemented with all students in a school. Interventions that offer these coordinated efforts can keep high-risk youth in mainstream public education and promote long-term improvements in problem behavior and school retention (see chapter 5 in this book).

RECOMMENDATIONS FOR PROGRAMS AND POLICIES IN SCHOOL SETTINGS

The research evidence suggests two main sets of recommendations for programs and policies related to deviant youth in school settings. The first set of recommendations includes, when possible, implementing empirically validated programs that do not aggregate deviant youth. For example, universal programs that are integrated into the behavior management practices of the entire school can reduce the overall rate of problem behavior in schools. For youth whose behavior is more problematic, programs that support teachers' behaviorally based classroom management practices can reduce disruptive behavior and prevent escalations. Including social skill lessons in the school curriculum can also reduce problem behaviors at school. Finally, for high-risk youth, targeted family-based interventions can be paired with school-based efforts to manage children's behavior.

The second set of recommendations applies to reducing the risk of deviant peer contagion within student groups when it is not possible to avoid aggregating deviant youth. First, because early adolescence is a time of high susceptibility to peer influence and because modestly deviant youth are most vulnerable to deviant peer influences, these youth should not be placed in group settings with older or more deviant youth. Second, because more time spent with deviant peers is related to more problem behaviors, the amount of time deviant youth are grouped together should be minimized. The dose–response relation between time spent with deviant peers and negative peer influences applies both to effects that occur within a day (e.g., alternative schools would be expected to have worse effects than programs that pull students out of regular classrooms for just part of the day) and across days (e.g., long-term suspensions likely have worse effects than short-term suspensions). These dose-response effects are likely the joint result of deviancy training that occurs in the group and reduced opportunities for socialization by prosocial peers outside of the deviant group. Third, when deviant youth are in a group, activities should be highly structured to minimize opportunities for deviant peers to interact without the supervision and careful monitoring by adults. This would include minimizing informal interactions before and after school and during breaks between classes. Fourth, the ratio of deviant to nondeviant youth in a group should be minimized, and the ratio of adults to youth should be maximized. Fifth, adults should work to create and maintain a prosocial group culture and introduce new members only after establishing a prosocial culture with the existing members. Sixth, teachers or other group leaders should be trained in behavior management practices and taught to keep the group highly structured, avoiding activities such as nondirective, open discussions.

CONCLUSIONS, IMPLICATIONS, AND FUTURE DIRECTIONS

The practice of removing youth with behavioral problems from traditional education settings and aggregating them with other similar youth is most often justified by citing the need to protect nondeviant students and school personnel, save costs, and treat deviant youth in a targeted way. However, protection for nondeviant students and school personnel is generally short-lived; except in extreme cases in which risks to society necessitate that a violent youth be incarcerated, deviant students eventually return to school or cause problems in the larger community. Although it may initially be less expensive to place a deviant student in a setting with similar students than to treat that student individually, this strategy may be more expensive in the long run. Over the course of a lifetime, criminals cost society more than $2 million each, suggesting that the long-term costs of not socializing youth to prepare them for an adulthood that does not involve crime may be high. Finally, the empirical evidence suggests that youth with behavioral problems tend to fare better when they are not treated in a targeted manner but rather when they are allowed to remain in their original peer group while receiving either individual or family based services. The potential for long-term drawbacks of placements in deviant peer groups should be weighed against the immediate effects.

Given that the most common response to problem behavior of youth is to separate deviant youth from their mainstream peers and segregate them in groups with other deviant youth, it is important to be concerned about the risk of deviant peer contagion. However, it is also important to remain cautious about instituting major changes in policies or practices. Of particular note is the issue that youth without behavior problems in traditional schools may benefit from the removal of deviant youth from these settings, even if the deviant youth do not benefit. When the safety of well-behaving students is put in jeopardy by including deviant students in regular classrooms or schools, and their learning environments are affected, removing the problem youth from traditional education settings may be necessary.

The competing demands on school systems are complex. All parents want what is best for their children, and what is best for a deviant child may not be what is best for his or her mainstream peers. A system-level approach is needed within individual school districts, schools, and classrooms to evaluate the perspectives of the diverse stakeholders in a school system and decide what policies and practices will result in the best system for all or most students. Good intentions from well-meaning adults are not enough; in the past these have resulted in the creation of programs with harmful effects, such as increasing rather than decreasing youths' problem behaviors. Instead, empirical evaluations of programs and policies are needed to determine the system-level impact of these interventions before they are placed into practice or policy.

AUTHOR NOTE

This chapter draws on the work of the Duke University Executive Sessions Panel on Deviant Peer Contagion, which assembled six times over a 3-year period to complete a comprehensive analysis of the problem of deviant peer influence in interventions in education, mental health, juvenile justice, and community programs. The complete report of the group and an executive summary are found in Dodge, Dishion, and Lansford (2006a, 2006b). The authors are grateful for funding for these efforts from the Duke University Provost's Office and the W. T. Grant Foundation.

REFERENCES

Akers, R. L., Krohn, M. D., Lanza-Kaduce, L., & Radosevich, M. (1979). Social learning and deviant behavior: A specific test of a general theory. *American Sociological Review, 44,* 636–655.

Anthony, J. C. (2006). Deviant peer effects: Perspectives of an epidemiologist. In Dodge, Dishion, & Lansford (2006b), pp. 44–66.

Arum, R., & Beattie, I. (1999). High school experience and the risk of adult incarceration. *Criminology, 37,* 515–537.

Aseltine, R., Jr. (1995). A reconsideration of parental and peer influences on adolescent deviance. *Journal of Health and Social Behavior, 36,* 103–121.

Barth, J., Dunlap, S., Dane, H., Lochman, J., & Wells, K. (2004). Classroom environment influences on aggression, peer relations, and academic focus. *Journal of School Psychology, 42,* 115–133.

Bear, G. G., Webster-Stratton, C., Furlong, M. J., & Rhee, S. (2000). Preventing aggression and violence. In K. M. Minke & G. G. Bear (Eds.), *Preventing school problems – promoting school success: Strategies and programs that work* (pp. 1–69). Bethesda, MD: National Association of School Psychologists.

Blechman, E. A., Taylor, C. J., & Schrader, S. M. (1981). Family problem solving versus home notes as early intervention with high-risk children. *Journal of Consulting and Clinical Psychology, 49,* 919–926.

Bowditch, C. (1993). Getting rid of troublemakers: High school disciplinary procedures and the production of dropouts. *Social Problems, 40,* 493–507.

Boxer, P., Guerra, N. G., Huesmann, L. R., & Morales, J. (2005). Proximal peer-level effects of a small-group selected prevention on aggression in elementary school children: An investigation of the peer contagion hypothesis. *Journal of Abnormal Child Psychology, 33,* 325–338.

Brophy, J. (1996). *Teaching problem students.* New York: Guilford Press.

Cho, H., Hallfors, D., & Sanchez, V. (2005). Evaluation of a high school peer group intervention for at-risk youth. *Journal of Abnormal Child Psychology, 33,* 363–374.

Coie, J. D., & Kupersmidt, J. B. (1983). A behavioral analysis of emerging social status in boys' groups. *Child Development, 54,* 1400–1416.

Cook, P. J., & Ludwig, J. (2006). Assigning youths to minimize total harm. In Dodge, Dishion, & Lansford (2006b), pp. 67–89.

Cox, S. M. (1999). An assessment of alternative education programs for at-risk delinquent youth. *Journal of Research in Crime and Delinquency, 36,* 323–336.

Crosnoe, R. (2002). High school curriculum track and adolescent association with delinquent friends. *Journal of Adolescent Research, 17,* 143–167.

Dishion, T. J. (2000). Cross-setting consistency in early adolescent psychopathology: Deviant friendships and problem behavior sequelae. *Journal of Personality, 68,* 1109–1126.

Dishion, T. J., Andrews, D., & Crosby, L. (1995). Antisocial boys and their friends in early adolescence: Relationship characteristics, quality, and interactional process. *Child Development, 66,* 139–151.

Dishion, T. J., Andrews, D. W., Kavanagh, K., & Soberman, L. H. (1996). Preventive interventions for high-risk youth: The Adolescent Transitions Program. In R. D. Peters & R. J. McMahon (Eds.), *Preventing childhood disorders, substance abuse, and delinquency* (pp. 184–214). Thousand Oaks, CA: SAGE.

Dishion, T. J., & Connell, A. (2006). Adolescents' resilience as a self-regulatory process: Promising themes for linking intervention with developmental science. *Annals of the New York Academy of Sciences, 1094,* 125–138.

Dishion, T. J., & Dodge, K. A. (2006). Deviant peer contagion in intervention and programs: An ecological framework for understanding influence mechanisms. In K. A. Dodge, T. J. Dishion, & J. E. Lansford (Eds.), *Deviant peer influences in programs for youth: Problems and solutions* (pp. 14–43). New York: Guilford Press.

Dishion, T. J., Dodge, K. A., & Lansford, J. E. (2006). Findings and recommendations: A blueprint to minimize deviant peer influence in youth interventions and programs. In K. A. Dodge, T. J. Dishion, & J. E. Lansford (Eds.), *Deviant peer influences in programs for youth: Problems and solutions* (pp. 366–394). New York: Guilford Press.

Dishion, T. J., Kavanagh, K., Schneiger, A., Nelson, S., & Kaufman, N. K. (2002). Preventing early adolescent substance use: A family-centered strategy for the public middle school. *Prevention Science, 3,* 191–201.

Dishion, T. J., McCord, J., & Poulin, F. (1999). When interventions harm: Peer groups and problem behavior. *American Psychologist, 54,* 755–764.

Dishion, T. J., Nelson, S. E., & Bullock, B. M. (2004). Premature adolescent autonomy: Parent disengagement and deviant peer process in the amplification of problem behavior. *Journal of Adolescence, 27,* 515–530.

Dishion, T. J., Nelson, S. E., Winter, C. E., & Bullock, B. M. (2004). Adolescent friendship as a dynamic system: Entropy and deviance in the etiology and course of male antisocial behavior. *Journal of Abnormal Child Psychology, 32,* 651–663.

Dishion, T. J., Nelson, S. E., & Yasui, M. (2005). Predicting early adolescent gang involvement from middle school adaptation. *Journal of Clinical Child and Adolescent Psychology, 34,* 62–73.

Dishion, T. J., & Owen, L. D. (2002). A longitudinal analysis of friendships and substance use: Bidirectional influence from adolescence to adulthood. *Developmental Psychology, 38,* 480–491.

Dishion, T. J., Patterson, G. R., Stoolmiller, M., & Skinner, M. L. (1991). Family, school, and behavioral antecedents to early adolescent involvement with antisocial peers. *Developmental Psychology, 27,* 172–180.

Dishion, T. J., Piehler, T. F., & Myers, M. W. (2008). Dynamics and ecology of adolescent peer influences. In M. J. Prinstein & K. A. Dodge (Eds.), *Understanding peer influence in children and adolescents* (pp. 72–93). New York: Guilford Press.

Dishion, T. J., & Skaggs, N. (2000). An ecological analysis of monthly "bursts" in early adolescent substance use. *Applied Developmental Science, 4,* 89–97.

Dishion, T. J., Spracklen, K. M., & Patterson, G. R. (1996). Deviancy training in male adolescent friendships. *Behavior Therapy, 27,* 373–390.

Dodge, K. A. (1983). Behavioral antecedents of peer social status. *Child Development, 54,* 1386–1389.

Dodge, K. A., Dishion, T. J., & Lansford, J. E. (2006a). Deviant peer influences in intervention and public policy for youth. *Social Policy Report, 20,* 1–19.

Dodge, K. A., Dishion, T. J., & Lansford, J. E. (Eds.). (2006b). *Deviant peer influences in programs for youth: Problems and solutions.* New York: Guilford Press.

Dodge, K. A., Lansford, J. E., & Dishion, T. J. (2006). The problem of deviant peer influences in intervention programs. In K. A. Dodge, T. J. Dishion, & J. E. Lansford (Eds.), *Deviant peer influences in programs for youth: Problems and solutions* (pp. 3–13). New York: Guilford Press.

Eddy, J. M., Reid, J. B., & Fetrow, R. A. (2000). An elementary school-based prevention program targeting modifiable antecedents of youth delinquency and violence: Linking the Interests of Families and Teachers (LIFT). *Journal of Emotional and Behavioral Disorders, 8,* 165–176.

Elliott, D., & Menard, S. (1996). Delinquent friends and delinquent behavior: Temporal and developmental patterns. In J. D. Hawkins (Ed.), *Delinquency and crime: Current theories. Cambridge criminology series* (pp. 28–67). New York: Cambridge University Press.

Espalage, D., & Swearer, S. (2003). Mini-series: Bullying prevention and intervention: Integrating research and evaluation findings: Research on school bullying and victimization: What have we learned and where do we go from here? *School Psychology Review, 32,* 365–384.

Farrell, A. D., Meyer, A. L., Sullivan, T. N., & Kung, E. M. (2003). Evaluation of the Responding in Peaceful and Positive Ways (RIPP) seventh grade violence prevention curriculum. *Journal of Child and Family Studies, 12,* 101–120.

Feldman, R. A., Caplinger, T. E., & Wodarski, J. S. (1983). *The Saint Louis conundrum: The effective treatment of antisocial youth.* Englewood Cliffs, NJ: Prentice Hall.

Fisher, L. A., & Bauman, K. E. (1988). Influence and selection in the friend-adolescent relationship: Findings from studies of adolescent smoking and drinking. *Journal of Applied Social Psychology, 18,* 289–314.

Goodnight, J. A., Bates, J. E., Newman, J. P., Dodge, K. A., & Pettit, G. S. (2006). The interactive influences of friend deviance and reward dominance on the development of externalizing behavior during middle adolescence. *Journal of Abnormal Child Psychology, 34,* 573–583.

Granic, I., & Dishion, T. J. (2003). Deviant talk in adolescent friendships: A step toward measuring a pathogenic attractor process. *Social Development, 12,* 314–334.

Greenberg, M. T., Kusche, C. A., Cook, E. T., & Quamma, J. P. (1995). Promoting emotional competence in school-aged children: The effects of the PATHS curriculum. *Development and Psychopathology, 7,* 117–136.

Hallfors, D., Cho, H., Dishion, T. J., Cuffee, J., & Hartman, S. (2009). The role of teachers in school-based interventions for high risk adolescents: An alternative paradigm for predicting deviancy training. Manuscript submitted for publication.

Harris, M. J. (1994). Self-fulfilling prophesies in the clinical context: Review and implications for clinical practice. *Applied and Preventative Psychology, 3,* 145–158.

Hawkins, J. D., Catalano, R. F., Kosterman, R., Abbott, R., & Hill, K. G. (1999). Preventing adolescent health-risk behaviors by strengthening protection during childhood. *Archives of Pediatric and Adolescent Medicine, 153,* 226–234.

Hayes, S. C., Barnes-Holmes, D., & Roche, B. (Eds.). (2001). *Relational frame theory: A post-Skinnerian account of human language and cognition.* New York: Kluwer Academic/Plenum Publishers.

Hoglund, W. L., & Leadbeater, B. J. (2004). The effects of family, school, and classroom ecologies on changes in children's social competence and emotional and behavioral problems in first grade. *Developmental Psychology, 40,* 533–544.

Hudley, C., Britsch, B., Wakefield, W. D., Smith, T., Demorat, M., & Cho, S. (1998). An attributional retraining program to reduce aggression in elementary school students. *Psychology in the Schools, 35,* 271–282.

Ialongo, N. S., Poduska, J., Werthamer, L., & Kellam, S. G. (2001). The distal impact of two first-grade preventive interventions on conduct problems and disorder in early adolescence. *Journal of Emotional and Behavioral Disorders, 9,* 146–190.

Jacob, B., & Lefgren, L. (2003). *Are idle hands the devil's workshop? Incapacitation, concentration, and juvenile crime* (NBER Paper No. 9653). Washington, DC: National Bureau of Economic Research.

Jimerson, S. R. (2001). Meta-analysis of grade retention research: Implications for practice in the 21st century. *School Psychology Review, 30,* 420–437.

Jimerson, S. R., Anderson, G., & Whipple, A. (2002). Winning the battle and losing the war: Examining the relation between grade retention and dropping out of high school. *Psychology in the Schools, 39,* 441–457.

Jussim, L., & Osgood, D. W. (1989). Influence and similarity among friends: An integrative model applied to incarcerated adolescents. *Social Psychology Quarterly, 52,* 98–112.

Kazdin, A. E. (1993). Treatment of conduct disorder: Progress and directions in psychotherapy research. *Development and Psychopathology, 5,* 277–310.

Kazdin, A. E. (2002). Psychosocial treatments for conduct disorder in children and adolescents. In P. E. Nathan & J. M. Gorman (Eds.), *A guide to treatments that work* (2nd ed., pp. 57–85). London: Oxford University Press.

Kellam, S. G., Ling, X., Merisca, R., Brown, C. H., & Ialongo, N. (1998). The effect of the level of aggression in the first grade classroom on the course and malleability of aggressive behavior into middle school. *Development and Psychopathology, 10,* 165–185.

Kingery, P. (2000). *Zero tolerance: The alternative is education.* Washington, DC: George Washington University, Hamilton Fish Institute.

Kleiner, B., Porch, R., & Farris, E. (2002). *Public alternative schools and programs for students at risk of education failure: 2000–01* (NCES 2002–004). Washington, DC: U.S. Department of Education, National Center for Education Statistics.

Kubitscheck, W., & Hallinan, M. (1998). Tracking and students' friendships. *Social Psychology Quarterly, 61,* 1–15.

Lavallee, K. L., Bierman, K. L., Nix, R. L., & Conduct Problems Prevention Research Group. (2005). The impact of first-grade "friendship group" experiences on child social outcomes in the Fast Track program. *Journal of Abnormal Child Psychology, 33,* 307–324.

Le Blanc, M., Vallieres, E., & McDuff, P. (1992). Adolescents' school experience and self-reported offending: An empirical elaboration of an interactional and developmental- school social control theory. *International Journal of Adolescence and Youth, 3,* 197–247.

Matsueda, R. L., & Anderson, K. (1998). The dynamics of delinquent peers and delinquent behavior. *Criminology, 36,* 269–308.

McEvoy, A., & Welker, R. (2000). Antisocial behavior, academic failure, and school climate: A critical review. *Journal of Emotional and Behavioral Disorders, 8,* 130–140.

McPherson, J. M., & Smith-Lovin, L. (1987). Homophily in voluntary organizations: Status distance and the composition of face-to-face groups. *American Sociological Review, 52,* 370–379.

Morrison, G. M., & D'Incau, B. (1997). The web of zero tolerance: Characteristics of students who are recommended for expulsion from school. *Education and Treatment of Children, 20,* 316–335.

O'Neil, R., Horner, R., Albin, R., Sprague, J., Storey, K., & Newton, J. S. (1997). *Functional assessment and program development for problem behavior: A practical handbook* (2nd ed.). New York: Brooks/Cole Publishing Company.

Parker, J. G., & Asher, S. R. (1987). Peer relations and later personal adjustment: Are low-accepted children at risk? *Psychological Bulletin, 102,* 357–389.

Patterson, G. R. (1974). Interventions for boys with conduct problems: Multiple settings, treatments, and criteria. *Journal of Consulting and Clinical Psychology, 42,* 471–481.

Pratt, T. C., & Cullen, F. T. (2000). The empirical status of Gottfredson and Hirschi's General Theory of Crime: A meta-analysis. *Criminology, 38,* 931–964.

Prinz, R. J., Blechman, E. A., & Dumas, J. E. (1994). An evaluation of peer coping-skills training for childhood aggression. *Journal of Clinical Child Psychology, 23,* 193–203.

Public Schools of North Carolina. (2003). *Alternative learning programs evaluation: 2001– 2002.* Raleigh: North Carolina State Board of Education/Department of Public Instruction.

Raywid, M. A. (1994). Alternative schools: The state of the art. *Educational Leadership, 52,* 26–34.

Reid, J. B., Patterson, G. R., & Snyder, J. J. (2002). *Antisocial behavior in children and adolescents: A developmental analysis and the Oregon model for intervention*. Washington, DC: American Psychological Association.

Reinke, W. M., & Herman, K. C. (2002). Creating school environments that deter antisocial behaviors in youth. *Psychology in the Schools, 39,* 549–559.

Reinke, W. M., & Walker, H. M. (2006). Deviant peer effects in education. In K. A. Dodge, T. J. Dishion, & J. E. Lansford (Eds.), *Deviant peer influences in programs for youth: Problems and solutions* (pp. 122–140). New York: Guilford Press.

Rodkin, P. C., Farmer, T. W., Pearl, R., & Van Acker, R. (2000). Heterogeneity of popular boys: Antisocial and prosocial configurations. *Developmental Psychology, 36,* 14–24.

Rosenthal, R. (1994). Interpersonal expectancy effects: A 30-year perspective. *Current Directions in Psychological Science, 3,* 176–179.

Sherman, L. W., & Strang, H. (2004). Verdicts or inventions? Interpreting results from randomized controlled experiments in criminology. *American Behavioral Scientist, 47,* 575–607.

Silver, R. B., & Eddy, J. M. (2006). Research-based prevention programs and practices for delivery in schools that decrease the risk of deviant peer influence. In K. A. Dodge, T. J. Dishion, & J. E. Lansford (Eds.), *Deviant peer influences in programs for youth: Problems and solutions* (pp. 253–277). New York: Guilford Press.

Spoth, R. L., Kavanagh, K. A., & Dishion, T. J. (2002). Family-centered preventive intervention science: Towards benefits to larger populations of children, youth, and families. *Prevention Science, 3,* 145–152.

Stage, S. A., & Quiroz, D. R. (1997). A meta-analysis of interventions to decrease disruptive classroom behavior in public education settings. *School Psychology Review, 26,* 333–368.

Stormshak, E. A., Bierman, K. L., Bruschi, C., Dodge, K. A., Coie, J. D., & Conduct Problems Prevention Research Group. (1999). The relation between behavior problems and peer preference in different classroom contexts. *Child Development, 70,* 169–182.

Sugai, G., & Horner, R. (2002). The evolution of discipline practices: School-wide positive behavior supports. *Child and Family Behavior Therapy, 24,* 23–50.

Thornberry, T. P., & Krohn, M. D. (1997). Peers, drug use, and delinquency. In D. Stoff, J. Breiling, & J. Maser (Eds.), *Handbook of antisocial behavior* (pp. 218–233). New York: Wiley.

Tobin, T., Sugai, G., & Colvin, G. (1996). Patterns in middle school discipline records. *Journal of Emotional and Behavioral Disorders, 4,* 82–94.

U.S. Department of Education. (2004). *10 facts about K–12 education funding*. Washington, DC: National Center for Education Statistics.

U.S. Department of Education. (2009). *Indicators of school crime and safety: 2008*. Washington, DC: National Center for Education Statistics.

Vitaro, F., Brendgen, M., & Tremblay, R. E. (1999). Prevention of school dropout through the reduction of disruptive behaviors and school failure in elementary school. *Journal of School Psychology, 37,* 205–226.

Wagner, M. (1995). Outcomes for youths with serious emotional disturbance in secondary school and early adulthood. *The Future of Children: Critical Issues for Children and Youths, 5,* 90–112.

Walker, H. M., Colvin, G., & Ramsey, E. (1995). *Antisocial behavior in school: Strategies and best practices.* Pacific Grove, CA: Brooks/Cole Publishing Co.

Warr, M. (1993). Age, peers, & delinquency. *Criminology, 31,* 17–40.

Warr, M. (1996). Organization and instigation in delinquent groups. *Criminology, 34,* 11–37.

Warren, K., Schoppelrey, S., Moberg, D., & McDonald, M. (2005). A model of contagion through competition in the aggressive behaviors of elementary school students. *Journal of Abnormal Child Psychology, 33,* 283–292.

Webster-Stratton, C., Reid, M. J., & Hammond, M. (2004). Treating children with early-onset conduct problems: Intervention outcomes for parent, child, and teacher training. *Journal of Clinical Child and Adolescent Psychology, 33,* 105–124.

Weisz, J. R., Weiss, B., Han, S. S., Granger, D. A., & Morton, T. (1995). Effects of psychotherapy with children and adolescents: A meta-analysis of treatment outcome studies. *Psychological Bulletin, 117,* 450–468.

INTERVENTIONS
for Achievement and Behavior Problems in a Three-Tier Model Including RTI

CHAPTER 29

Gang Prevention Strategies for Schools

G. Roy Mayer
California State University, Los Angeles

INTRODUCTION

The No Child Left Behind Act of 2001 asks schools to focus on the importance of addressing student behavior and providing a school environment that is safe and conducive to learning. It also requires that any program supported by legislatively appropriated Title IV funds have research evidence showing that the program is effective in reducing violent and problem behavior in schools. Furthermore, all students from the ages of 6 to 18 have a legal right to a quality public education in a safe environment, including gang members, because belonging to a gang is not illegal. Yet school safety is threatened by the presence of youth street gangs, whose members are frequently involved in drugs and violence. To make matters worse, gangs are spreading from ghettos and major urban areas to suburban and rural communities. In the past, gangs consisted mainly of teenagers and young adults, but they are now recruiting elementary school-age members. Now no school appears safe from gangs. It is imperative, then, that educators understand and help prevent gang membership and gang-related activities. This chapter describes youth gangs, their characteristics and impact on schools, and the gang members themselves; it also reviews the preventive strategies that have been tried; and suggests approaches that seem to hold promise in preventing and reducing gang membership and gang activities on school campuses.

HOW GANGS AFFECT YOUTH AND SCHOOLS

A street gang is a group of three or more individuals (adult or juvenile, male or female) who associate with one another, commit crimes (whether it be a misdemeanor or felony), and have some type of identifier, such as a name, sign, symbol, or color (California Attorney General's Office, 2003).

Crimes typically committed by gangs generally include the following: (a) assault with a deadly weapon or use of force that is likely to produce great bodily injury; (b) homicide or manslaughter; (c) robbery; (d) shooting directed at an inhabited dwelling or occupied motor vehicle; (e) the sale, possession for sale, transportation, manufacture, offer for sale, or offer to manufacture of controlled substances; (f) arson; (g) the intimidation of witnesses and victims; and (h) grand theft of any vehicle, trailer, or vessel. This list is by no means exhaustive, but experts on gangs agree that these offenses characterize the crimes committed by gangs generally.

Typical Characteristics of Gang Members

Typical gang member characteristics include (a) having identifying tattoos, hand signs, graffiti, and clothing, such as baggy pants, identifying belt buckles, particular color of clothing, bandanas, shoelaces, hats, jewelry, or insignias (however, some members are now beginning to disguise their gang affiliation); (b) using a new nickname; and (c) selling various drugs. Some gang members also scar their bodies by burning skin patterns with a cigarette, such as three or five dots. Others use a knife or a razor blade to etch a design or marks on their bodies. Members of some gangs, such as skinheads, engage in racially motivated crimes and violence.

However, gang member characteristics vary somewhat from gang to gang and area to area and change over time (see Mayer and Ybarra, 2006). Therefore, the first step in addressing gang activity is to talk directly with individual gang members in a target area to discover a specific gang's current characteristics, values, and behavior.

Characteristics of Schools Having Gangs

Schools that have identified gang members on their campus experience several characteristics in common when compared with schools without gangs:

- More students report knowing another student who has brought a gun to campus, or seeing a gun on campus. The threatening environment guns create makes teaching and learning difficult. Approximately 1 in 16 seniors report carrying a gun to school (U.S. Department of Justice, 1999).
- More students report that drugs, such as marijuana, cocaine (coke or crack), methamphetamines (speed, uppers), and MDMA (Ecstasy), are readily available at school.
- Numerous security measures are enacted on campus.
- The hours that the school is open are reduced, making teachers less available to students and parents after regular school hours.
- Violent victimization at school more than doubles.
- Higher rates of truancies, suspensions, and expulsions are recorded.
- Higher costs of vandalism are incurred, including removing graffiti.

This profile of schools having gang problems shows how the safety and security of a school can be severely compromised not to mention the disruption of school climate and reduced teaching and learning that result.

Consequences of Being a Gang Member

Gang members are highly likely to experience the following risk factors: (a) substance abuse, (b) manipulation by older gang members to commit more serious offenses, (c) a criminal record that can hamper future job opportunities, (d) exposure of the individual and family members to bodily injury and death, and (e) truancy, school failure, and dropout. This lack of formal education and skills deficits typically handicap a gang member's ability to access viable employment, thereby increasing dependence on the gang for economic survival that provides a powerful disincentive to withdraw from gang membership.

Signs of Gang Involvement

A variety of signs can indicate *possible* gang involvement. However, observing one or more of the following signs does not mean that the child is involved in a gang. For example, a number of students who are not in gangs copy gang apparel. However, if one or more of the following signs are present, parents and teachers should communicate with the child to determine if he or she is involved in a gang. Possible indicators of gang involvement include the following:

- Wearing excessively large shirts and baggy pants.
- Having to wear a particular color of clothing or a particular logo.
- Changing demeanor, becoming distant from family.
- Seeking privacy and being secretive about whereabouts, friends, etc.
- Constantly listening to or viewing gangster-influenced music, videos, and movies.
- Associating with other gang members and using hand signs.
- Practicing using hand signs at home.
- Breaking rules at home.
- Having unexplained cash or goods.
- Coming home with physical injuries and lying about the events surrounding them.
- Using alcohol and drugs with attitude change.
- Making peculiar drawings or writings on books, book bags, shoes, etc.

Gangs are obviously a very serious issue, not only for schools but also for gang members themselves, for the youth who are victimized by them, for families, and for the larger community and its quality of life. A sense of safety and well-being is obviously impossible when gangs have a strong presence within a community.

PREVENTION AND INTERVENTION STRATEGIES FOR SCHOOLS: WHAT WORKS?

The following sections examine strategies and programs that have been tried in attempts to prevent, reduce, and stop gang activities within the context of schooling.

Traditional Gang Prevention Research

A variety of gang prevention programs have been developed, applied, and evaluated over the past several decades as gangs have had an increased impact on schools (see a review by Mayer & Ybarra, 2006). Such programs include the Gang Resistance Education and Training (G.R.E.A.T.) Program, Gang Alternatives Program (GAP), Gang Risk Intervention Program of Los Angeles County (GRIP), and Weapons Are Removed Now (WARN). These programs have focused on incorporating gang prevention lessons into schools' curricula, providing presentations on gangs and weapons by experts, and increasing the number of trained security officers in schools. Studies of these programs have shown small constructive changes in attitudes toward gangs but have not demonstrated any appreciable impact on youth's antisocial behavior or school gang problems. Furthermore, most of these evaluation studies did not have a control group condition (Esbensen & Osgood, 1999; Palumbo & Ferguson, 1995; U.S. Department of Justice, 1999), making it difficult to conclude whether the modest results that were actually achieved were due to the implemented program or to extraneous factors. For example, when the G.R.E.A.T. program was evaluated using a comparison group, the results showed an increase in gang-resistant attitudes for *both* groups, with almost no differences between the two groups (Ramsey, Rust, & Sobel, 2003). Thus, outcomes achieved by these programs have not demonstrated a measurable impact on preventing or reducing adolescent gang involvement and antisocial behavior in schools.

An Alternative Approach to Gang Prevention and Reduction

Delinquent or antisocial behavior has been shown to be linked to drug use, cigarette smoking, and risky sexual behavior (Biglan, Brennan, Foster, & Holder, 2005). In addition, most youth who join gangs engage in a variety of antisocial behaviors, such as aggression, vandalism, and defiance, and often do poorly academically prior to joining a gang (Mayer & Ybarra, 2006). The logical conclusion from these findings is that if schools and communities can prevent antisocial behavior, they might be able to reduce gang involvement and a variety of other problem behaviors.

The behavioral research conducted to date on preventing antisocial behavior is most promising. These experimental studies have addressed contextual factors and incorporated a team approach that has focused on making the school environment more positive and reinforcing for students and staff members (Mayer & Butterworth,

1979, 1981; Mayer, Butterworth, Nafpaktitis, & Sulzer-Azaroff, 1983; Mayer & Sulzer-Azaroff, 1991; Mayer et al., 1993; Metzler, Biglan, Rusby, & Sprague, 2001; Sprague et al., 2001). These studies reported meaningful reductions in school antisocial behavior rates that received interventions, compared with control schools that did not. Substantial reductions occurred in rates of vandalism, office referrals, classroom disruptions (e.g., fights, yelling out, swearing), attendance problems, suspensions, and dropout. In the intervention schools, increases were also obtained in the amount of time students spent on assigned tasks, their perceptions of school safety, cooperation and positive feelings among students and staff, and enhanced feelings of being connected to schooling. A low sense of being connected to school personnel and a failure to engage in schooling have been found to be related to a range of adolescent health risk behavioral outcomes, including substance abuse, early sexual activity, heavy drinking, school infractions, delinquency, and violence (Hawkins, Catalano, Kosterman, Abbott, & Hill, 1999; Lonczak, Abbott, Hawkins, Kosterman, & Catalano, 2002; McNeely, Nonnemaker, & Blum, 2002).

Contextual Factors

Successful programs address school contexts that contribute to violence, vandalism, various other problem behaviors, and gang involvement, including a punitive or aversive environment in the school, a large number of students with repeated academic failure combined with social skills deficits, unclear rules governing student behavior, lack of positive consequences for desired student performance, students who do not respect individual differences, and other factors. Studies have found that these contextual factors of schools are predictive of higher rates of school vandalism, reduced school safety, and lower academic achievement (Mayer, 1995; Mayer et al., 1983; West, Taylor, Wheatley, & West, 2007). In fact, West and colleagues found that measures of various contextual factors within schools were better predictors of achievement and safety than measures of community risk were, such as economic status, language used at home, family bonding, academic status, community affiliation, neighborhood stability, and peer associations. Problem behaviors that co–occur and appear to be interrelated probably have similar contextual factors. Thus, a major strategy that educators can use for creating safe, positive school environments conducive to learning is to address the school contextual factors that are known to promote antisocial behavior and lead to students joining gangs. School administrators and related services personnel should carefully review each of the following factors to see which are present and need to be addressed in the school setting.

A Punitive School Environment

One important contextual factor is the overuse of punitive methods of control that lead to the creation of a punitive or aversive school environment. Punitive environments have long been known to be a major cause of aggression, vandalism, violence, and escape- or avoidance-related behaviors, such as tuning out, noncompliance or defiance, tardiness or truancy, and dropping out (Azrin, Hake, Holz, & Hutchinson, 1965; Azrin & Holz, 1966; Berkowitz, 1983; Carr, Newsom, & Binkoff, 1976; Hutchinson, 1977; Mayer, 1995; Mayer et al., 1983). However, many educators continue to emphasize punishment, and the presence of this factor permeates many other identified contextual factors.

In schools with this contextual factor, punishment and exclusion are the most common responses teachers resort to when they must deal with students who are at risk of developing delinquent lifestyles or who already are immersed in patterns of antisocial behavior (Sugai & Horner, 1999). Also, in such schools, educators spend more time and energy in implementing punitive rather than positive or preventive measures (Brodinsky, 1980). Colvin and Sugai (1988) point out that, whereas proactive strategies are generally used to remediate academic problems, reactive punitive strategies tend to be used by educators in an attempt to contain behavior problems. Yet both academic and behavior problems are learned, and both respond to similar teaching and management strategies.

To determine if an overuse of punishment might be a factor contributing to gangs, aggression, and other problem behaviors in a school, educators should answer the following questions. Those not receiving a "yes" response should be systematically addressed.

1. Do teachers and administrators emphasize teaching students how to behave appropriately rather than emphasizing punishment or exclusion for dealing with infractions?
2. Are suspensions minimized and not used disproportionately with certain groups of students?
3. Do teacher approval statements outnumber disapproval statements made to students or certain groups of students?
4. Are penalties appropriate and not humiliating and/or disproportionate to the offense?
5. Is there an emphasis on implementing preventive or positive measures, rather than on reactive, punitive measures?
6. Is there a strong, supportive, and reinforcing environment that uses positive behavioral interventions to reduce and prevent infractions rather than a school-wide reliance on punitive discipline and/or security arrangements such as guards, metal detection, locked doors, and so forth?

With regard to number 2, there is no evidence that suspensions are effective in preventing or reducing infractions. However, there is some evidence that their use can communicate rejection, lower connectedness, and evoke aggression (DeRidder, 1991; Dupper, 1994; McNeely et al., 2002; Williams & Falkenberg, 2002; also see Mayer & Ybarra, 2003, for a discussion of the use of expulsion and suspension and their effects on students).

Academic Failure

Repeated academic failure experiences are punishing to students and result in more behavior problems. Poor scholastic experiences appear to contribute to behaving in a delinquent and disruptive manner, dropping out of school, and joining gangs (Berlin & Sum, 1988; Gold & Mann, 1982; Lee, Sugai, & Horner, 1999; Mayer & Ybarra, 2006). Similarly, Ysseldyke et al. (1997) point out that problem behaviors are often due to a "mismatch between the characteristics of the learner and those of the instructional environment or the broader home/school context" (p. 5).

Interestingly, empirical findings suggest that youth are more likely to complete tasks, to engage in fewer problem behaviors, and to choose to do more work when the work is at their functional level and when easier items or activities have been interspersed within their assignments (e.g., Cates et al., 1999; Johns, Skinner, & Nail, 2000; Logan & Skinner, 1998). This holds true even when the length of the task is increased. Not only do individuals usually *prefer* tasks composed of both difficult and easy tasks, but they also tend to accomplish more and remain on task longer, probably owing to heightened rates of gaining immediate reinforcement for completing problems. Also, because this technique of interspersing tasks of varying difficulty provides more practice opportunities, students demonstrate higher retention and fluency levels.

Teachers should beware of assigning overly easy tasks exclusively because this practice has been associated with increases in problem behaviors. Umbreit, Lane, and Dejud (2004) addressed 10-year-old Jason's excessive talking and wandering around the classroom by assigning him more challenging material. When Jason was permitted to work ahead on his assignments and workbooks until he reached one in which he was unable to answer all questions correctly within 10 minutes of continuous work, that assignment was deemed to be more challenging. At that point his behavior improved, and both the student and his teacher gave the intervention a very positive acceptability rating. Again, this study points out the importance of adjusting task assignments to the functional levels (neither too high nor too low) of each individual student.

To help determine if this factor may be contributing to antisocial behavior and gang membership in the school setting, the following questions should be posed. Those questions not answered positively indicate that poor instruction or inappropriate curriculum might be contributing to academic failure and associated challenging behavior.

1. Are accommodations made for learners' diverse characteristics?
2. Are instructional and curriculum materials appropriate for each student's functional level?
3. Is instruction designed to produce frequent success for each student?
4. Do teachers assume the responsibility for teaching without relying on out-of-school resources, such as tutoring?

Unclear Rules for Student Behavior

When students are not given a clear idea of which behaviors are acceptable and unacceptable in school, a lack of compliance and an increase in problem behavior are likely to occur. This lack of compliance often prompts an increased use of more punitive sanctions. Communicating clear classroom and school-wide discipline policies or rules for student behavior is a major step in setting up effective classrooms as well as school-wide discipline programs (see Mayer & Ybarra, 2003, for illustrative rules). The following questions that are not answered positively may indicate that unclear rules are a factor contributing to school behavior problems.

1. Are students involved in the development of the rules?
2. Are rules stated positively to help teach students how to behave?
3. Are rules simple and short (about three to seven rules)?
4. Are conflicts between school policies and classroom rules avoided?
5. Are students taught the rules?
6. Are students the recipients of frequent reinforcement for following the rules?
7. Are parents informed of the rules and are their help and support solicited?
8. Are the rules periodically reviewed and revised as necessary?
9. Are there clear and consistent consequences for meeting or not meeting expectations between administrators and teachers?

Regarding number 9, administrators need to know the specific steps teachers took before they decided to send a student to the office. Similarly, teachers must know that disciplinary action will be taken consistently by the administration when a student is sent to the office. It is important to have a clear policy as to which behaviors are to be handled by teachers and which infractions should cause students to be sent to the office.

Lack of Positive Consequences

Almost all student populations benefit from reinforcing environments. The findings cited below give several examples of the importance of providing a reinforcing or positive school environment that acknowledges and rewards behavior and performance contributing to school success and healthy social development.

- Favell et al. (1982) found that simply making toys available for children with autism resulted in less self-injury than keeping them in sterile surroundings.
- Nevin (1988) demonstrated that high rates of reinforcement helped to maintain prosocial behavior and to prevent the occurrence of problem behavior.
- Zanolli and Daggett (1998) found that the spontaneous social initiations of preschoolers increased when higher rates of noncontingent reinforcement were provided, compared with lower rates.
- Van Camp et al. (2000) found that reinforcing environments for children with autism helped prevent the stereotypic and self-abusive behavior so characteristic of many of these children.

- Todd et al. (2002) simply increased specific feedback to students to a ratio of 4:1 positive to corrective comments, resulting in both decreases in problem behavior and increases in staff satisfaction.
- O'Reilly et al. (2006) found that aggression was much more likely to occur when extinction (i.e., withdrawal or withholding of adult attention) was used immediately after the problem behavior as a consequence than when reinforcement was readily available for other alternative behaviors. Depriving individuals of reinforcement appears to evoke aggression in many instances.

A lack of positive feedback and other positive consequences has an adverse effect on students and contributes to student misbehavior. Also, when students do not receive positive recognition for their appropriate behavior, they often tend to misbehave, because negative recognition is better than no recognition for many students. Children who crave attention often misbehave because it is one of the easiest ways for them to get attention from their parents and teachers. Not only will appropriate positive recognition strengthen the appropriate behavior, but it will also decrease the need to misbehave. To help determine if appropriate positive consequences are being provided, questions similar to the following could be asked and answered (all should receive yes answers):

1. Are students positively recognized for exceptional behavior and accomplishments occurring in their classrooms and throughout the school setting?
2. Do students receive positive recognition for behaving appropriately as a general practice (e.g., attending to work, taking pride in their campus, and following classroom rules)?
3. Is the frequency of positive feedback provided to students by staff higher than disapproving and critical feedback?

Numerous illustrations of providing various types of positive recognition can be found in Mayer, Ybarra, Pegadiotes, Fogliatti, and Pines (2000), and Sulzer-Azaroff and Mayer (1991).

Students Lacking Critical Social Skills

Too often, students who lack critical social skills that would enable them to do well academically or to relate positively to others are punished by their teachers or school administrators for their "misbehavior." That is, they are punished for *not* paying attention or *not* complying with instructions—rather than being taught the necessary social skills that enable school success. As a result, a punitive school environment is created that inadvertently fosters student misbehavior—particularly among at-risk student populations. For example, most children learn to pay attention when they are read to and when they participate in family discussions. However, many children come from family contexts in which they do not have these experiences and do not learn to pay attention effectively. As a result, their lack of paying attention in class often results in punishment from their teachers. Similarly, some students might not have learned to persist on a task, comply with requests, negotiate differences, resist peer pressure, handle criticism from adults and teasing from peers, or make appropriate decisions. The following questions will help determine whether social skills should be targeted for identification and intervention and whether they should be focused on individual, small group, or universal instructional contexts:

1. Is the emphasis by teachers and administrators on teaching students how to behave and not on punishment for misbehavior?
2. Are peer conflicts, bullying, and harassment problems in your school?
3. Is there a system that identifies youth who need social skills training?
4. Are there trained staff members who can or do provide social skills training?
5. Is social skills training offered as a part of the regular school curriculum or is it reserved for targeted students having identified social skills deficits?
6. Are school resources available for teaching social skills to individual students or in small instructional groups?

A variety of social skills training programs are available, some of which are summarized in Mayer and Ybarra (2003). (See chapter 14 in this book for a comprehensive treatment of the topic of social skills in school contexts.)

Lack of Respect for Individual Differences

Some behavioral problems are a result of students', teachers', and others' lack of understanding and sensitivity toward students from different cultures or with different physical attributes. One reason why some bullying and attacks by gang members occur is lack of acceptance, valuing, or appreciation of individual differences. For example, bullying more frequently occurs when the victim does not act or appear "normal" to the bully (according to particular social norms). The bullying victim may be very short; of a different race, ethnicity, or sexual orientation; wear a hearing aid; have poor coordination; speak a different language; cry or become emotionally distraught easily; lack "appropriate" social skills; have difficulty picking up social cues; wear different clothes; or have other atypical physical or behavioral attributes or some specific developmental disability. Thus, students *must* be taught respect, acceptance, and understanding of individual differences if schools and communities are to reduce antisocial forms of behavior, including bullying and violence. The following questions might be asked to help determine if intolerance of differences is a contributing factor to antisocial behavior in the school setting:

1. Are "different" students included rather than being isolated or bullied by peers?
2. Are ethnic or racial and sexual slurs avoided and discouraged by students generally?

3. Are students disciplined and reinforced consistently regardless of gender, race, ethnicity, or sexual orientation?

4. Do behavioral interventions address only the behavior's purpose or function rather than being primarily reactive to the challenging behavior and the situation in which it occurs?

Other Factors Contributing to Joining Gangs

Other factors (many related to the school contextual factors discussed above) contribute specifically to an individual's decision to become a gang member. These diverse factors include (a) family tradition—in some families becoming a gang member is a tradition; (b) the desire to secure protection from other gang members; (c) for financial gain, to buy personal items and to make dating possible; (d) lack of employment opportunities; (e) lack of positive consequences and access to sources of support, including respect, bonding, friendship, and positive recognition; (f) a sense of identity and success tied to gang activities, while school and home experiences involve failure and a lack of success; (g) a sense of family and belonging (child comes from a dysfunctional family and does not fit in with other peers); and (h) lack of critical social skills and corresponding low rates of positive feedback from adults and peers.

For a discussion of other factors that might contribute to antisocial behavior and gang membership—such as parents and teachers giving up on students, lack of support and training for staff and parents, lack of student involvement, and school size—plus an instrument to assist in identifying and correcting all these factors within the school, see Mayer and Ybarra (2006).

Contextual Factors in the Home and School

A number of the school contextual factors described above are similar to factors in the home that research has identified as promoting antisocial behavior. These include a reliance on coercive or punitive discipline, lack of positive consequences, inconsistencies in setting of rules and delivery of consequences, and rejection (Dishion & Stormshak, 2007; Patterson, Reid, & Dishion, 1992; Reid, Patterson, & Snyder, 2002).

Several critical contextual factors within schools appear to contribute to a wide variety of problem behaviors and gang membership. These factors include (a) overly punitive attempts to enforce rules, dress codes, hair styles, and so forth; (b) poor monitoring of school areas that receive reduced adult supervision (e.g., playgrounds); and (c) discrimination by students and staff against certain target student groups based on race, ethnicity, cultural values, sexual orientation, and so forth. These school factors can have a considerable impact on student behavior as evidenced by the reviewed research (American Psychological Association, 1993). Once the predisposing factors that might exist in a school have been identified, they should be rank ordered according to the importance and ease with which they can be altered. It is recommended that change efforts focus initially on important factors that can be altered easily through administrative actions, with the remainder addressed over the long term through more intensive intervention approaches that involve school staff with the required expertise.

One particularly important but complex factor in this regard, school organization, is discussed in the next section. The U.S. Department of Education (2000) reported that the problems of "approximately four of every five disruptive students can be traced to some dysfunction in the way schools are organized, staff members are trained, or schools are run" (p. 10). A related finding is that high levels of victimization in the schools are not necessarily also seen in the community, suggesting "that the school environment makes a unique contribution to the criminal victimization of adolescents" (Curry, Maxson, & Howell, 2001, p. 6).

SCHOOL AND DISTRICT ORGANIZATION

Organizational issues need to be addressed to promote sustained prevention of student problems. Delivering and maintaining prevention strategies in school is a greater challenge than identifying and developing those strategies (Sugai & Horner, 1999). The district and school must be committed to institutionalizing a preventive approach to addressing antisocial behavior and gang membership so that the resulting long-term efforts and positive outcomes can be sustained, independent of leadership changes. Gang prevention activities need to be an ongoing, integrated part of the school discipline program, not reactive programs that are employed when serious incidents occur, such as students being assaulted or killed in a school violence incident. The organizational structure below, which incorporates a positive behavioral support approach involving creation of two school-wide teams, can help achieve such lasting prevention only if institutionalized so that it becomes a part of the school's enduring culture.

Organization of School-Wide Teams

Seldom can one individual in a school (e.g., the principal or school security officer) protect students from victimization by gangs, prevent them from joining gangs, or prevent other antisocial behaviors. Whole-school response capability is needed to address these goals. Establishing two school teams appears to be an effective alternative for addressing primary, secondary, and tertiary prevention goals and outcomes: the Positive Behavior Support Team (PBST) and the Student Success Team (SST). The functions of each are described below.

The Positive Behavior Support Team focuses on primary prevention (i.e., a universal approach that provides programming and monitoring for all students in order to prevent problem behaviors). The team may be incorporated within the school's staff council or the school safety planning committee. The PBST has the responsibility of addressing and preventing discipline problems that are of campus-wide concern, including those presented by gangs. PBST programs that are implemented effectively usually solve, prevent, or address the problem behaviors of about 80% of the students on a campus.

The Student Success Team has the responsibility of addressing and preventing problems exhibited by the remaining 20% or so of the school population who are at risk for severe academic or behavioral problems or for joining gangs. These problems are addressed using secondary prevention strategies that often involve small group activities such as tutoring and social skills training. The SST also can work with students who are at high risk, such as those already involved in gangs or who demonstrate severe behavioral or academic problems. Tertiary prevention strategies often include individual programs such as functional assessment and wraparound services. The SST's focus, then, is on providing small group and individualized intensive interventions for a relatively limited number of students.

The school-wide programs developed by the PBST are helpful but insufficient for those students who may also need small group and/or individual interventions. It takes coordination of all three prevention strategies to have a meaningful school-wide impact on student behavior. The school's PBST addresses the contextual factors that are known to contribute to student problems, enabling the school to make progress in preventing serious behavior problems and gang activities on campus. However, the SST also should help identify and target students at higher risk for problem behavior and academic failure. Table 1 displays the two teams' respective responsibilities.

PBST and SST Membership

The PBST must include all stakeholders. Membership in the team usually consists of two to five teachers (depending on the size of the school), the school principal, a school counselor or psychologist who has skills as a behavior intervention case manager, two or three students who represent the various groups on campus (not just the grade A students), at least two parents, a school custodian, a school secretary, and, if possible, community members. Others can be added temporarily, depending on the student problem areas and school contexts targeted. For example, when gangs are being addressed, a gang expert from a law enforcement agency should be invited to serve as a team member. In other situations, lunchroom or playground supervisors, bus drivers, street crossing guards, or others may need to be involved, depending on the nature of the program.

At least one member of the SST should overlap with the school PBST to help coordinate and share knowledge and information. The SST needs to have access to individuals possessing expertise in the following areas:

- Diagnosing mental health problems.
- Evaluating academic difficulties.

Table 1. Comparison of Responsibilities of School-Wide Positive Behavior Support Teams and Student Success Teams

Positive Behavior Support Team (PBST)	Student Success Team (SST)
Addresses 100% of the students and prevents problem behaviors for about 80% of the students.	Designs intensive and early intervention programs for about 20% of the students who are at risk for, or are experiencing, serious academic or behavioral problems.
Determines the areas of need within a school, including contextual factors that need to be addressed.	Conducts proactive, regular student screenings to determine those who may need services, particularly those who have been referred to the office for harassment or fighting, and coordinates and shares information with the PBST.
Determines priorities within school.	Supports specific students' mental health and academic growth; requests school and community specialized assessments as needed.
Identifies needed strategies, staff training, and resources to address identified contextual factors that contribute to student problem behaviors.	Conducts social skills assessment and provides needed social skills training for identified students.
Designs classroom and school-wide positive behavioral interventions and supports.	Designs positive behavioral interventions and supports for individual students, small groups, and specific classrooms needing intensive help.
Provides ongoing support for teachers and other staff members implementing positive behavior support programs.	Consults with and provides ongoing support for school staff and parents who have a student with serious behavior problems, including a student at risk for joining a gang or who is a member of a gang.
Shares school-wide outcomes with staff, parents, and students, and makes program modifications as necessary.	Shares student outcomes with the student, his or her parents, and teachers, and makes program modifications as necessary.
Coordinates school and community services.	Coordinates school and community wraparound services for a student with serious problems, including gang membership.
Monitors and evaluates the progress and procedures in place for school-wide programs to ensure fidelity of program implementation, continued support, and program effectiveness.	Monitors and evaluates the progress and procedures in place for students to ensure fidelity of program implementation, continued support, and program effectiveness.

Note. For more information on establishing a PBST and SST, see Mayer and Ybarra (2003).

- Conducting ongoing proactive student screening to identify those at risk for gang membership and severe academic or behavioral problems.
- Conducting a functional assessment of student behavior to determine why a behavior problem or incident occurs. For complex or severe problem behaviors, the

functional assessment should be conducted by a board-certified behavior analyst or by someone under the supervision of a certified analyst.

- Designing positive behavioral interventions based on the behavior's identified function.
- Developing social skills lessons.
- Training other staff in positive behavioral interventions and social skills.
- Consulting with and supporting school staff, students, and families.
- Coordinating school and community services.

What Else Can the PBST Do?

The PBST can recommend that staff members follow suggestions presented by Sakamoto (2001). The following can be useful to almost anyone attempting to work effectively with and assist gang members and other youth at risk for behavior or academic failure:

- Treat gang-involved students with the same respect shown to other students.
- Keep current on words or activities that are gang related—dress, music, hair styles, slang, etc.—but do not allow students to use words or engage in activities that are gang related on campus.
- Have an open-door policy for extra assistance.
- Provide gang prevention curricula within the instructional framework.
- Provide a school environment that truly accepts diversity and values all students and staff.
- Provide student assistance programs and support.

Other suggestions provided by Mayer and Ybarra (2006) include the following:

- Develop a purpose statement. For example: "We the staff, students and parents of _____ school are committed to helping all students acquire the academic, social, and behavioral skills necessary to become productive citizens now and in the future. All students have the right to learn these skills in a safe, caring, and respectful environment" (Sprague, Sugai, & Walker, 1998, p. 455).
- Learn what the local gang situation is and design lessons with the assistance of law enforcement and other appropriate community agencies or organizations that address the situation.
- Develop and implement curriculum with law enforcement on nonviolent conflict resolution that discourages gang participation and substance abuse while providing alternatives.
- Draw on the expertise of gang specialists from local law enforcement agencies and probation departments for training parents, staff, and school administrators in effective roles they can play to address school-based gang problems and develop and coordinate prevention and intervention efforts.
- Encourage parent involvement in assisting with various school activities, allowing their children to see their interest and commitment.

- Invite community merchants, business representatives, and social service providers to become more knowledgeable about issues of gangs and drugs and how they can support efforts of the school and community to address them.
- Consult with community members about developing ways to integrate community services, such as mentoring programs for at-risk students, adopt-a-youth or adopt-a-school programs, and Big Brothers/Big Sisters programs into school planning efforts to address gang problems.
- Assess security needs with the school administration. Consider temporarily contracting with security guards, school police, or local law enforcement officers as needed.
- Establish a formal memorandum and spell out the policies and relationships with juvenile justice and other agencies that serve youth.

What Else Can the SST Do?

Mayer and Ybarra (2006) suggest that each school's SST do the following:

- Educate staff and families in the role and function of the SST.
- Inform staff and families that the SST is the proper channel to bring concerns regarding a student who may be exhibiting early warning signs.
- Educate staff and families of early warning signs of antisocial behavior or potential gang membership, such as the following:

  ○ Expression of violence in writing and drawings
  ○ Social withdrawal and excessive feelings of isolation
  ○ Excessive feelings of rejection
  ○ Being a victim of violence
  ○ Patterns of impulsive and chronic hitting, intimidating, and bullying behaviors
  ○ Low school interest and poor academic performance
  ○ Uncontrolled anger
  ○ Feelings of being picked on and persecuted
  ○ History of discipline problems
  ○ History of violent and aggressive behavior
  ○ Intolerance for differences and prejudicial attitudes
  ○ Drug and/or alcohol use
  ○ Affiliation with gangs (wearing gang-style apparel, using hand signs, listening to gangster rap, using gang language, possessing unexplained cash or goods, having gang symbols and/or gang graffiti on backpacks, shoes, etc.)
  ○ Defiance of authority
  ○ Attendance problems, including frequent truancy

The above signs, or risk factors, suggest that a student might become involved or may already be involved in gangs or engage in antisocial behavior. The student may need individual or small-group intervention, positive behavior support, mentoring or some other intervention from the SST. Once the student is referred to the SST, the SST will make the determination of what, if any, services might be beneficial for the student.

District and Community Support for PBST and SST

Policies and programs of other agencies and professionals within the school, district, and community can help the teams promote and execute long-term violence prevention and gang-related prevention efforts.

How Can School Boards Help Prevent Gang Activity?

District-wide policies established by the school board can help promote long-term violence prevention efforts. The following actions to develop and support those policies have been suggested by Mayer and Yabarra (2006):

- Develop a policy statement, an action plan, and an evaluation plan for district administrators to follow to help prevent antisocial behavior problems and gang membership.
- Include in the policy statement that the PBST at each school will establish and maintain school-wide discipline and gang prevention programs and policies. These policies and programs will continue even when a new principal is assigned to the school. Any changes in a school's policies and programs must be approved by the school's PBST and be in agreement with district policy.
- Assure all school district personnel that their calls for assistance in preventing or intervening in gang activity will not adversely affect their career. Clearly communicate that attempts to secure and promote gang prevention measures will be rewarded.
- Develop policies forbidding weapons on school property, and make it clear that each school has an obligation to ensure an environment that is conducive to learning and free of assaults and intimidation.
- Consider the use of a dress code to ban the wearing of gang attire and colors.

What Can School District Personnel Do?

Active support from the district's central office is critical if long-term prevention of gangs and antisocial behaviors is to be successful. District office personnel can:

- Commit to institutionalizing a preventive approach (a combination of primary, secondary, and tertiary prevention) to antisocial behavior and gang membership so that the necessary long-term effort can be sustained independent of leadership changes.
- Encourage and implement school board policy on antisocial behavior and gang prevention. See above and Mayer and Ybarra (2006) for illustrative board policies.
- Provide resources (e.g., curriculum materials) and training to school site administrators to help them with training their staff.

- Positively recognize school administrators who take a leadership role in preventing antisocial behavior, vandalism, and gangs on campus.
- Establish guidelines for school personnel to follow regarding search and seizure. Because gang activity is connected with drugs and weapons, school personnel need to have a policy regarding search of lockers, desks, school property, and students' property, such as book bags, purses, and vehicles (see Mayer and Ybarra, 2006, for illustrative policies).

What Can School Administrators Do?

School administrators must follow through on a number of important responsibilities to help promote a successful program:

- Actively support the PBST by attending meetings and facilitating program implementations.
- Actively support and honor individual staff members who assume leadership in preventing gangs, and those who implement classroom or school-wide programs, by recognizing their efforts publicly, providing release time, reducing other responsibilities on campus, etc.
- Work with law enforcement and community organizations and agencies to develop the necessary programs to educate staff and parents on gangs and to provide workshops on parenting skills related to preventing gang membership.
- Keep a good record system to monitor office referrals, crimes, vandalism frequency and cost, fights, etc. Data collection will assist in the evaluation of any program.
- When a student is identified as engaging in gang conduct, notify parents and the SST.

What Can Support Personnel Do?

Adequately trained support personnel such as school psychologists and school counselors have considerable skills to offer gang prevention efforts:

- Attend or conduct SST meetings.
- Provide social skills training for those who need them.
- Collaborate and provide assistance to the SST-identified students, teachers, and parents.
- Teach students to monitor their own behavior, recognize its purpose or function, and understand the possible chain of events that leads to the escalation of their antisocial behavior.
- Teach students more adaptive ways of achieving the purpose or function of their behavior. For example, if they use profanity when they encounter a difficult assignment, teach them how to ask for assistance; if they might seek out gangs for support, friendship, or a feeling of success, involve them in after-school activities, provide a mentor and tutor, or help them obtain employment.

- Offer parental skills classes including incentives such as snacks, baby-sitting, and transportation. Free materials are often needed to encourage attendance by parents who might benefit most from the class.

As part of the parental skills class, parents need to be taught how their child's gang membership can ruin lives, expose their children and family members to bodily injury and death, or lead to criminal records or prison. Parents also need to be taught the signs indicating that their child may be involved in a gang.

What Can Students Do?

Dr. Martin Luther King Jr. said: "It is not the malicious acts that will do us in, but the appalling silence and indifference of good people." Students can be taught and encouraged to intervene in the following ways:

- Request friends to stop gang activities.
- Take the offender, if a friend, aside and see if he or she will "cool it."
- Report (in confidence) rumors of attacks or gang fights about to occur.
- Support the school being a safe place and neutral zone.
- Report (in confidence) those who bring weapons on campus.
- Avoid calling names, acting aggressively against the offender, or getting others to gang up on the offender.
- Show respect to others; do not put another student down.
- Show consideration for one another by listening and helping, and stressing with peers the importance of an education.

ORGANIZATIONAL SELF-EVALUATION QUESTIONS

The following sample questions are presented to help you determine what might need to be done organizationally to address gangs and antisocial behavior on your campus:

1. What does the school have in place, and what needs to be done to establish a quality PBST and SST at its site?
2. What is the PBST doing to address the contextual factors within the school that might contribute to various problem behaviors, including school violence and gang activity?
3. What is being done to educate staff and parents in early warning signs for gang-related or antisocial behavior and potential gang membership?
4. Is adequate support and training being provided for teachers and parents in dealing with gang-related behavior and other antisocial behavior?
5. What type of organized early-identification system does the school need in order to identify gang members and students at risk for joining gangs, academic failure, and problem behaviors?

6. What types of campus intervention programs exist, and what programs are needed to help prevent gang involvement?

7. What has been done, and needs to be done, to establish a positive, consistent working relationship with local law enforcement officials?

8. What district and school policies and supports are in place or are needed for prevention of gang-related and antisocial behavior?

9. Is a systematic evaluation program in place for monitoring and assessing program progress?

The following indicator variables are often measured to determine program progress: reductions in fights, guns on campus, reported drugs on campus, office referrals, assessment referrals for possible special education placement, vandalism cost and frequency, graffiti, suspensions, expulsions, dropouts, and truancies; and improvements in achievement, on-task behavior, student and staff perceptions of school safety, school attendance, cooperation, and positive feelings among students and staff. A combination of archival records, incident reports, self-report measures, and observational data are typically used to evaluate these variables.

CONCLUSION

Prior to addressing contextual factors for reducing gangs and various problem behaviors on campus, schools must put in place an organizational structure that will provide long-term support for program implementation and sustainability, independent of school leadership changes. As noted previously, gang prevention must not be an add-on program; it should be institutionalized as part of the school's disciplinary program, in which administrators, educators, students, and parents all have important roles.

Much can be done in schools to prevent youth from joining gangs. This chapter has reviewed a variety of contextual factors within schools that appear to contribute to various problem behaviors and gang membership and influence academic achievement. Primary among these is a punitive environment for the student. An intervention approach was presented that addresses these factors and is likely to reduce the probability of students joining gangs. The approach would reduce the occurrence of academic failure and antisocial behaviors (e.g., aggression, vandalism, and cutting school), which are precursor behaviors students are likely to engage in prior to joining a gang. When gang prevention programs have been implemented without addressing such factors, little change can be expected, as the factors that promote violence, vandalism, and gang involvement still exist in the school environment. When contextual factors are addressed, schools provide more tutoring, social skills training, mentoring, successful student experiences, reinforcement, after-school activities, clearly stated rules for student conduct, and teaching of acceptance and appreciation of individual differences. In addition, such schools develop an organizational structure that promotes program implementation and sustainability.

Schools and communities *can* win the war on gangs by implementing sustainable programs that *prevent* at-risk behaviors. Otherwise, there will be a continuous supply of at-risk youth who are likely to join gangs, engage in antisocial behavior, and fail or drop out of school. Schools can focus on the same prevention activities to help students who have become gang members leave their gangs—for example, help them find jobs, experience success, and develop positive relationships. Contrary to popular belief, gang membership does not have to be permanent for most students. In fact, about one half to two thirds of the youth who join gangs are members for a year or less (Mayer & Ybarra, 2006). However, if a gang member violates the law, he or she obviously needs to be referred to law enforcement. Similarly, if a gang member violates important school rules, then the established school consequences should apply. It is hoped that the approaches described in this chapter will assist school personnel to substantially reduce gangs and produce and maintain secure, positively reinforcing, and orderly educational environments in which teachers can teach and students can learn.

REFERENCES

American Psychological Association. (1993). *Violence and youth: Psychology's response. Volume I: Summary report of the American Psychological Association Commission on Violence and Youth.* Washington, DC: Author.

Azrin, N. H., Hake, D. G., Holz, W. C., & Hutchinson, R. R. (1965). Motivational aspects of escape from punishment. *Journal of Experimental Analysis of Behavior, 8,* 31–34.

Azrin, N. H., & Holz, W. C. (1966). Punishment. In W. A. Honig (Ed.), *Operant behavior: Areas of research and application* (pp. 380–447). New York: Appleton.

Berkowitz, L. (1983). Aversively stimulated aggression: Some parallels and differences in research with animals and humans. *American Psychologist, 38,* 1135–1144.

Berlin, J. A., & Sum, A. (1988). *Toward more perfect union: Basic skills, poor families, and our economic future.* New York: The Ford Foundation.

Biglan, A., Brennan, P. A., Foster, S. L., & Holder, H. D. (2005). *Helping adolescents at risk: Prevention of multiple problem behaviors.* New York: Guilford Press.

Brodinsky, B. (1980). *AASA critical issues report: Student discipline, problems, and solutions* (Report No. 021 00334). Arlington, VA: American Association of School Administrators.

California Attorney General's Office, Crime and Violence Prevention Center. (2003). *Gangs: A community response.* Sacramento, CA: Author.

Carr, E. G., Newsom, C. D., & Binkoff, J. S. (1976). Stimulus control of self-destructive behavior in a psychotic child. *Journal of Abnormal Child Psychology, 4,* 139–153.

Cates, G. L., Skinner, C. H., Watkins, C. E., Rhymer, K. N., McNeill, S. L., & McCurdy, M. (1999). Effects of interspersing additional brief math problems on student performance and perception of math assignments: Getting students to prefer to do more work. *Journal of Behavioral Education, 9,* 177–192.

Colvin, G., & Sugai, G. (1988). Proactive strategies for managing social behavior problems: An instructional approach. *Education and Treatment of Children, 11,* 341–348.

Curry, D., Maxson, C. L., & Howell, J. C. (2001, March). *Youth gang homicides in the 1990's* (OJJDP Fact Sheet #FS-200103). Washington, DC: U.S. Department of Justice.

DeRidder, L. M. (1991). How suspension and expulsion contribute to dropping out. *Education Digest, 56*(6), 44–47.

Dishion, T., & Stormshak, E. (2007). *Intervening in children's lives: An ecological, family-centered approach to mental health care.* Washington, DC: APA Books.

Dupper, D. R. (1994). Reducing out-of-school suspensions: A survey of attitudes and barriers. *Social Work in Education, 16*(2), 115–124.

Esbensen, F., & Osgood, D. W. (1999). Gang Resistance Education and Training (G.R.E.A.T.): Results from the national evaluation. *Journal of Research in Crime and Delinquency, 36,* 194–225.

Favell, J. E., Azrin, N. H., Baumeister, A. A., Carr, E. G., Dorsey, M. F., Forehand, R., et al. (1982). The treatment of self-injurious behavior. *Behavior Therapy, 13,* 529–554.

Gang Alternatives Program. (1983). *Gang Alternatives Program.* San Pedro, CA: Author. http://www.gangfree.org/programs_index.html

Gold, M., & Mann, D. W. (1982). Alternative schools for troublesome secondary students. *Urban Review, 14,* 305–316.

Hawkins, J. D., Catalano, R. F., Kosterman, R., Abbott, R., & Hill, K. G. (1999). Preventing adolescent health-risk behaviors by strengthening protection during childhood. *Archives of Pediatrics & Adolescent Medicine, 153,* 226–234.

Hutchinson, R. R. (1977). By-products of aversive control. In W. K. Honig & J. E. R. Staddon (Eds.), *Handbook of operant behavior* (pp. 415–431). Englewood Cliffs, NJ: Prentice Hall.

Johns, G. A., Skinner, C. H., & Nail, G. L. (2000). Effects of interspersing briefer mathematics problems on assignment choice in students with learning disabilities. *Journal of Behavioral Education, 10,* 95–106.

Lee, Y., Sugai, G., & Horner, R. H. (1999). Using an instructional intervention to reduce problem and off-task behaviors. *Journal of Positive Behavior Interventions, 1,* 195–204.

Logan, P., & Skinner, C. H. (1998). Improving students' perceptions of a mathematics assignment by increasing problem completion rates: Is problem completion a reinforcing event? *School Psychology Quarterly, 13,* 322–331.

Lonczak, H. S., Abbott, R. D., Hawkins, J. D., Kosterman, R., & Catalano, R. F. (2002). Effects of the Seattle social development project on sexual behavior, pregnancy, birth, and sexually transmitted disease outcomes by age 21 years. *Archives of Pediatric Adolescent Medicine, 156,* May, 438–447.

Mayer, G. R. (1995). Preventing antisocial behavior in the schools. *Journal of Applied Behavior Analysis, 28,* 436–441.

Mayer, G. R., & Butterworth, T. (1979). A preventive approach to school violence and vandalism: An experimental study. *Personnel and Guidance Journal, 57,* 436–441.

Mayer, G. R., & Butterworth, T. W. (1981). Evaluating a preventive approach to reducing school vandalism. *Phi Delta Kappan, 62,* 498–499.

Mayer, G. R., Butterworth, T., Nafpaktitis, M., & Sulzer-Azaroff, B. (1983). Preventing school vandalism and improving discipline: A three-year study. *Journal of Applied Behavior Analysis, 16,* 355–369.

Mayer, G. R., Mitchell, L., Clementi, T., Clement-Robertson, E., Myatt, R., & Bullara, D. T. (1993). A dropout prevention program for at-risk high school students: Emphasizing consulting to promote positive classroom climates. *Education and Treatment of Children, 16,* 135–146.

Mayer, G. R., & Sulzer-Azaroff, B. (1991). Interventions for vandalism. In G. Stoner, M. K. Shinn, & H. M. Walker (Eds.), *Interventions for achievement and behavior problems* (pp. 559–580). Bethesda, MD: National Association of School Psychologists.

Mayer, G. R., & Ybarra, W. J. (2003). *Teaching alternative behaviors schoolwide: A resource guide to prevent discipline problems.* Downey, CA: Los Angeles County Office of Education.

Mayer, G. R., & Ybarra, W. J. (2006). *Gang violence: Prevention and intervention strategies for schools.* Downey, CA: Los Angeles County Office of Education, Safe Schools Center.

Mayer, G. R., Ybarra, W. J., Pegadiotes, D., Fogliatti, H., & Pines, M. (2000). *Classroom management: A California resource guide.* Sacramento, CA: California Department of Education; Downey, CA: Los Angeles County Office of Education, Safe Schools Center.

McNeely, C. A., Nonnemaker, J. M., & Blum, R. W. (2002). Promoting school connectedness: Evidence from the national longitudinal study of adolescent health. *Journal of School Health, 72,* 138–146.

Metzler, C. W., Biglan, A., Rusby, J. D., & Sprague, J. R. (2001). Evaluation of a comprehensive behavior management program to improve school-wide positive behavior support. *Education and Treatment of Children, 24,* 448–479.

Nevin, J. A. (1988). Behavioral momentum and the partial reinforcement effect. *Psychological Bulletin, 103,* 44–56.

O'Reilly, M. F., Sigafoos, J., Edrisinha, C., Lancioni, G., Cannella, H., Choi, H. Y., et al. (2006). A preliminary examination of the evocative effects of the establishing operation. *Journal of Applied Behavior Analysis, 39,* 239–242.

Palumbo, D. J., & Ferguson, J. L. (1995). Evaluating Gang Resistance Education and Training (GREAT): Is the impact the same as that of Drug Abuse Resistance Education (DARE)? *Evaluation Review, 19,* 591–619.

Patterson, G. R., Reid, J. B., & Dishion, T. J. (1992). *Antisocial boys.* Eugene, OR: Castalia.

Ramsey, A. L., Rust, J. O., Sobel, S. M. (2003). Evaluation of the Gang Resistance Education and Training (GREAT) program: A school-based prevention program. *Education, 124,* 297–310.

Reid, J. B., Patterson, G. R., & Snyder, J. J. (Eds.). (2002). *Antisocial behavior in children and adolescents: A developmental analysis and the Oregon Model for Intervention.* Washington, DC: American Psychological Association.

Sakamoto, W. (2001, June). *Gangs: School-based strategies.* Paper presented at the California School Resource Officers' Association 4th Annual Conference, San Diego, CA.

Sprague, J., Sugai, G., & Walker, H. (1998). Behavior in schools. In H. Watson & F. Gresham (Eds.), *Handbook of child behavior therapy* (pp. 451–474). New York: Plenum Press.

Sprague, J., Walker, H., Golly, A., White, K., Myers, D., & Shannon, T. (2001). Translating research into effective practice: The effects of a universal staff and student intervention on indicators of discipline and school safety. *Education and Treatment of Children, 24,* 495–511.

Sugai, G., & Horner, R. H. (1999). Discipline and behavioral support: Preferred processes and practices. *Effective School Practices, 17*(4), 10–22.

Sulzer-Azaroff, B., & Mayer, G. R. (1991). *Behavior analysis for lasting change.* Fort Worth, TX: Harcourt, Brace & Jovanovich.

Todd, A., Haugen, L., Anderson, K., & Spriggs, M. (2002). Teaching recess: Low-cost efforts producing effective results. *Journal of Positive Behavior Interventions, 4,* 56–52.

Umbreit, J., Lane, K. L., & Dejud, C. (2004). Improving classroom behavior by modifying task difficulty: Effects of increasing the difficulty of too-easy tasks. *Journal of Positive Behavior Interventions, 6,* 13–20.

U.S. Department of Education. (2000). Effective Alternative Strategies: Grant competition to reduce student suspensions and expulsions and ensure educational progress of suspended and expelled students (OMB# 1810-0551). Washington, DC: Safe and Drug-Free Schools Program.

U.S. Department of Justice. (1999). Promising strategies to reduce gun violence. Washington, DC: Office of Juvenile Justice and Delinquency Prevention.

Van Camp, C. M., Lerman, D. C., Kelley, M. E., Contrucci, S. A., & Vorndran, C. M. (2000). Variable-time reinforcement schedules in the treatment of socially maintained problem behavior. *Journal of Applied Behavior Analysis, 33,* 545–557.

West, R. P., Taylor, M. J., Wheatley, R. K., & West, J. H. (2007, February). *Indicators of behavior support: Relationships to academic achievement and school safety.* Poster session presented at the annual meeting of the California Association for Behavior Analysis, San Francisco.

Williams, C. J., & Falkenberg, P. (2002, April 27). German teen kills 17, self in shooting spree at school. *Los Angeles Times,* A-1, 5.

Ysseldyke, J., Dawson, P., Lehr, C., Reschly, D., Reynolds, M., & Telzrow, C. (1997). *School psychology: A blueprint for training and practice II*. Bethesda, MD: National Association of School Psychologists.

Zanolli, K., & Daggett, J. (1998). The effects of reinforcement rate on the spontaneous social initiations of socially withdrawn preschoolers. *The Journal of Applied Behavior Analysis, 31,* 117–125.

INTERVENTIONS

for Achievement and Behavior Problems in a Three-Tier Model Including RTI

CHAPTER 30

Preventive Interventions for Students With Internalizing Disorders:
Effective Strategies for Promoting Mental Health in Schools

Kenneth W. Merrell
University of Oregon

Barbara A. Gueldner
The Children's Hospital, Aurora, CO

INTRODUCTION

Frequently overlooked and often misunderstood by educators and school-based mental health providers, *internalizing disorders*—including depression, anxiety, social withdrawal, and the physical and cognitive states that may accompany these problems—constitute a distinct class of emotional and behavioral problems. At the broadest level, internalizing disorders consist of problems that are thought to be based on *overcontrol* of symptoms (Cicchetti & Toth, 1991; Merrell, 2008a), meaning they are manifested when individuals attempt to maintain control of or regulate their internal emotional and cognitive states in a manner that is maladaptive or otherwise ineffective. In other words, internalizing disorders may be elicited and maintained by the way individuals think about their feelings, thoughts, and related physical symptoms, and the way in which they try to cope with unpleasant events.

The term *internalizing* also indicates that these problems are developed and maintained to a great extent *within* the individual, rather than being directed at other people or to the external social environment. Certainly, individuals' biological predispositions and the environment in which they must function are key influences in the development and maintenance of internalizing problems. However, the manifestation of specific symptoms reflecting internal affective and cognitive states may not be easily interpreted by others. For this reason, one expert in the area of children's internalizing disorders has referred to this constellation of symptoms as *secret illnesses* (Reynolds, 1992). "Secret" is an appropriate label because symptoms can be quite difficult for others to detect through observation. As a result, it is not uncommon for teachers and other school personnel to be in situations where some of the students they must educate and support are experiencing moderate or even great distress related to internalizing symptoms, and the educators in question may not have a clue as to what is going on.

This chapter begins by providing some background on internalizing disorders and on the use of a three-tier model. The chapter then focuses on interventions designed to address prevention goals and outcomes, beginning with a comprehensive overview of primary prevention for internalizing disorders, with a particular emphasis on the use of universal social and emotional learning strategies to promote mental health in schools. We give examples from our Strong Kids affective instructional programs illustrating how primary prevention may specifically address the issue of wellness and early intervention within the internalizing domain (Merrell, Carrizales, Feuerborn, Gueldner, & Tran, 2007).

The chapter then explores secondary prevention strategies, with a review of structured curricula to promote mental health. These curricula are more in-depth and narrowly focused on the internalizing domain in school contexts and may be used to help students who need more support than is possible through a primary prevention or universal approach. Although the major focus of the chapter is on primary and secondary prevention approaches, a section on tertiary prevention approaches gives examples of how they may be used in supporting students who have serious internalizing disorders. The chapter concludes with some recommendations for helping schools make preventive interventions for internalizing disorders a mainstream practice within education.

UNDERSTANDING INTERNALIZING PROBLEMS

This section provides some context aimed at helping readers better understand internalizing problems. Issues related to recognition, classification, prevalence, and the stability of internalizing problems are discussed.

Recognition of Internalizing Problems

The secretive and somewhat obscure way in which internalizing disorders may be manifested has contributed to the long history of misunderstanding and failure to provide appropriate support for children and adolescents who experience these disorders. Practitioners new to the profession may be surprised to learn that it was not until about the 1980s that the mental health community began to recognize that depression and other internalizing problems had the potential to exist in children. Earlier in the 20th century, the idea that depression could exist in children was widely rejected because of the notion that children theoretically lacked the "ego strength" to experience the inner conflicts that resulted in depression (Merrell, 2008b). This notion is one of many ideas promoted by psychiatry in that era that is now considered to be absurd. Fortunately, both practitioners' understanding of internalizing disorders in youth and the professional tools available to support students who experience these problems have advanced greatly in the past three decades.

Classification: The "Shape" of Internalizing Problems

It is worth taking a moment to consider how internalizing disorders fit into the broader realm of children's behavioral, social, and emotional problems, and how the field has come to understand the "shape" of things in this area. From about 1980 to 2000, extensive research efforts were undertaken by several investigators to examine the distribution and patterns of children's psychopathology symptoms. The findings consistently demonstrated that the vast majority of these problems could be divided into two general areas: *internalizing* or *externalizing* domains (see Merrell, 2008a, for a review of this research). These two domains differ with respect to whether their characteristic symptoms are inner directed or outer directed, the latter form of which is quite easy to observe because the characteristic symptoms are disruptive and involve acting out behavior.

The problems experienced across the two domains can be easily differentiated with respect to the acting-out versus self-directed natures of the behavioral characteristics (see Table 1). Furthermore, the externalizing domain can be more easily detected through simple observation. One notion to consider is that there is less overlap between the behavioral characteristics of individuals with externalizing disorders and "normal" individuals than there is between the characteristics of individuals who have internalizing disorders and those who do not. However, it is a mistake to think that the two domains—no matter how statistically robust—are mutually exclusive. In fact, there is a moderate amount of overlap between the two domains when it comes to how they are actually experienced by children and adolescents. Practitioners should keep in mind that even children with the most aggressive and disruptive behavior may also experience mental health concerns such as depression and anxiety, and that such a pattern of symptom overlap is not particularly unusual (Merrell & Walker, 2004).

With respect to multivariate analyses of the internalizing domain, researchers have also identified some common subtypes of characteristics or symptom clusters. Table 2 includes the four general clusters of problems that have frequently been identified within the internalizing domain—depression, anxiety, social withdrawal, and somatic problems (physical symptoms associated with emotional distress)—each with characteristic behavioral, cognitive, and affective presentations. Internalizing disorder subtypes that have been most commonly identified through multivariate statistical analyses are somewhat different from the symptom lists in the *Diagnostic and Statistical*

Table 1. Breakdown of the Externalizing and Internalizing Domains of Children

Externalizing	Internalizing
Aggressive behavior	Depression
Conduct problems	Anxiety
Disruptive behavior	Social withdrawal
Hyperactivity–impulsivity	Somatic (physical) complaints
"Acting-out" problems	"Self-directed" problems

Table 2. Examples of Narrow-Band Clusters of Symptoms of Internalizing Problems

Depression
- Depressed mood, excessive sadness
- Loss of interest in activities that were previously enjoyable
- Feelings of low self-esteem or inferiority
- Cries frequently

Anxiety
- Excessive worrying
- Anxious, fearful, tense
- Self-conscious, easily embarrassed
- Distorted thoughts or cognitive appraisal of anxiety-provoking situations

Social Withdrawal
- Withdraws from company of others
- Aloof
- Does not seek social support
- Shy, timid, bashful

Somatic Problems
- Physiologic hyperarousal
- Excessive vigilance in noticing physical symptoms
- Reports physical distress, particularly in stomach area, neck, head, and back
- Lethargic, tired, or physically exhausted

Manual of Mental Disorders, Fourth Edition (*DSM-IV-TR*; American Psychiatric Association, 2000). This disparity brings into question the accuracy and utility of current diagnostic systems for use with children (Merrell, 2008a). Of course, *DSM-IV-TR* advocates would likely argue that this approach is more valid and useful with children than the behavioral dimensions approach or related empirically based approaches, but the evidence in support of this notion is not very compelling, particularly when anxiety disorders are considered (e.g., van Lang, Ferdinand, Oldehinkel, Ormel, & Verhulst, 2005).

Prevalence and Stability

In addition to considering the nature of internalizing disorders, it is also critical to understand that many of these problems are far more serious than simply a brief passing phase that a child is going through. It is also worth noting that internalizing disorders are not uncommon in children and adolescents. On the contrary, symptoms of internalizing problem are among the most frequently experienced mental health concerns, and they can produce severe distress that may interfere greatly with the ability to enjoy life and to be successful in school, to make friends, and to pursue avocational interests. As many as 4–6% of school-age youth may experience internalizing disorders at any point in time ("point prevalence"), which equates to one or two students out of a typical general education classroom of about 30 students (Merrell, 2008b).

Because internalizing problem episodes are cumulative over the course of child and adolescent development, the percentages of affected youth are much higher. For example, in a longitudinal study of major depression among randomly selected youth, Seeley, Rohde, Lewinsohn, and Clarke (2002) identified the "lifetime" prevalence rather than the point prevalence of depression in young people, and presented the alarming results that by age 18, about one in five boys and one in three girls will have experienced one or more episodes of major depression (also see chapter 15 in this book). When depression is combined with conduct disorders, this rate increases substantially. With respect to the number and intensity of episodes experienced during a child's development, current theory and research support efforts to promote early identification and intervention, as each additional episode tends to increase the probability of further episodes and greater intensity of symptoms. These ideas are incorporated in the "kindling hypothesis" developed by Post and colleagues (e.g., Post, 1992), which asserts that repeated episodes of affective disorders may result in neurobiological changes that increase vulnerability to additional serious episodes at the slightest provocation.

Focus on Preventive Interventions

A major thematic emphasis of this book is on the use of the three-tier model for developing and implementing preventive interventions for various achievement and behavior problems in schools (see Figure 1). Although the key ideas of the three-tier model were articulated by the editors in chapter 1, a few additional comments in this regard may be useful to help readers understand how interventions for internalizing disorders may be optimally delivered in schools. The three-tier model has been successfully adapted from the public health field for use in the field of education, and it has been a significant influence in U.S. schools (Merrell & Buchanan, 2006). With respect to the recognition and treatment of internalizing disorders, the public health framework is not new; the mental health prevention and community psychology fields have been promoting interventions for depression using these methods for many years. We believe that *all schools* should develop the capacity to deliver universal, targeted, and intensive mental health interventions within a comprehensive program of positive behavioral and instructional supports. The delivery of services for this constellation of problems surrounding internalizing disorders should be embedded in a comprehensive approach to promoting the success and wellness of all students, and not a separate add-on program that is implemented infrequently and for only targeted individuals.

PRIMARY PREVENTION THROUGH SOCIAL AND EMOTIONAL LEARNING

Delivery of mental health services is trending toward using the school as the primary setting in which students can have access to treatment (Kutash, Duchnowski, & Lynn, 2006). Not only are many schools providing mental health treatment, but the notion of

Figure 1. Modified flow chart of recommended preventive interventions for internalizing disorders within a three-tier model.

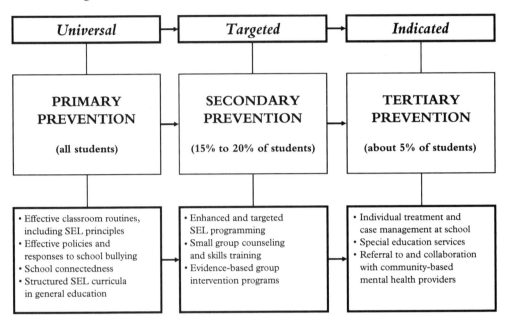

Tier 1 universal prevention efforts (that is, applicable to *all* students), much like vaccination programs found in public health, are gaining acceptance as a more cost-effective means to buffer students from developing more serious mental health problems. By definition, Tier 1 prevention is "the prevention of the occurrence, or at least the expression" of a disability or disorder (Kauffman, 1997, p. 138). Although there are a wide range of contexts in which Tier 1 prevention is conceptualized and delivered (Kutash) the field of mental health promotion is focused on a common goal—the well-being of children. We contend that school-based primary prevention efforts are a critical way of addressing internalizing disorders, among other important mental health problems.

In our experience, many school administrators and researchers have looked at education and mental health as two independent systems, each with its own goals (i.e., academic outcomes and mental health outcomes). Viewing or organizing school systems in this manner may present some significant challenges to the adoption of effective mental health practices in schools. Adelman and Taylor (e.g., 2000a, 2000b, 2005) have argued forcefully that to be effective and gain acceptance from educators, school mental health efforts must address barriers to academic learning and achievement. A preferable way to promote school mental health efforts would be to view the school system as a single complex system with multiple goals and problems that must be addressed in a unified manner. For example, seamlessly infusing activities to promote mental health into academic learning activities, such as social and emotional learning, helps to remove the arbitrary separation of the two areas, and may promote greater acceptance of mental health efforts in schools.

The gap between academic and mental health services in schools may be closing as educators discover the effects of one area on the other and as evidence builds that demonstrates the effectiveness of prevention programs. Greenberg and colleagues (2003) described strategies focusing on the child, social relationships, and systems-level factors to promote successful implementation. More specifically, they recommend teaching students social and emotional skills; facilitating respect and support in peer and student-to-adult relationships; developing school, home, and community relationships where positive behaviors are promoted; and planning and implementing programs that continue across the academic tenure of a student. With respect to the primary prevention of internalizing disorders such as depression and anxiety, implementation of some of the above strategies may help start closing the academic and mental health services gap.

Introduction to Social and Emotional Learning

In addition to the general preventive strategies noted above, the area of social and emotional learning has emerged as an important construct that uses these ideas, and has major implications for the prevention of internalizing disorders and related mental health problems. The term *social and emotional learning* (SEL) was initially coined in 1994, during an era in which many prevention-oriented programs were being widely implemented in the school setting, but their use was short term and fragmented, with very little follow-up to determine whether they had any effect, positive or negative (Greenberg et al., 2003). Certainly, many school professionals implemented such programs in good faith and with the expectation that success would be assured. Recent ideological and technological advances have broadened the profession's understanding of systems issues that can unintentionally thwart the success of theoretically sound SEL implementation efforts. To improve the state of service delivery for all students of preschool through high school age, the Collaborative for Academic, Social, and Emotional Learning (CASEL; http://www.casel.org) was organized in 1994 to address demands for thoughtful and strategic coordination of SEL implementation, including ongoing examination of outcomes through quantitative and qualitative methods (Greenberg et al., 2003). Extensive efforts have been made by the CASEL group and others to study SEL strategies and programs, the barriers to desired success, and the best methods to provide a framework from which SEL can be optimally delivered.

Social and emotional learning instruction teaches students about human emotions, how to recognize different emotions in themselves and others, methods for identifying and practicing strategies to cope with uncomfortable feelings, ways to solve intra- and interpersonal difficulties, and methods to set and achieve goals that lead to responsible decision making (CASEL, 2003). A major premise of SEL is that *these skills can be taught and learned*, much like academic skills in such areas as mathematics and language arts. When applied to everyday living situations, SEL opens up a broad new dimension of understanding for all students that can support them through their inevitable life challenges.

The prevailing goal of SEL instruction is to aid students in their academic, social, and emotional growth and to give them a desire to participate in their community (Payton et al., 2000). Acquisition and application of SEL skills not only strengthens students' social and emotional well-being but also directly affects their academic performance (Wang, Haertel, & Walberg, 1997). For example, a student who is paralyzed with worry about making a mistake on a writing assignment might fail to complete the work, receive a grade of incomplete, and begin a pattern that will continue until the student fails the class. The student may be seen as lacking the motivation to complete work at the expected level of performance. However, had this student learned how to manage stress and find ways to set and accomplish realistic goals, he or she might not only feel more relaxed but also experience academic success instead of failure. Zins, Weissberg, Wang, and Walberg (2004) thoroughly explored this notion and made a strong case for including SEL programming in everyday academic operations. Schools could enhance students' academic performance by improving problem-solving and organizational skills, teaching them to make responsible decisions, and boosting their self-awareness and confidence. In essence, a powerful transaction occurs when students understand and use self-regulation strategies, manage stress effectively, set goals, and use interpersonal management skills—benefits that can positively affect students' social, emotional, *and* academic lives.

Expecting that schools would encounter barriers to implementing social and emotional learning interventions, Elias, Bruene-Butler, Blum, and Schuyler (2000) reviewed potential problems and suggested ways to address them within the context of schools. A frequently encountered barrier is the frustration and concern some educators express that schools are providing this type of instruction to begin with, that this really is a job for families, and that teachers are not prepared to deliver such material. Despite these concerns, our own research has shown that teachers can deliver quality SEL interventions with successful outcomes (Gueldner & Merrell, in press; Merrell, 2010; Merrell, Juskelis, Tran, & Buchanan, 2008; Tran, 2007). Finding ways to make families a part of this instruction in SEL concepts would benefit families.

In addition, the United States is currently experiencing a period when improving academic standards and addressing school violence are among the top priorities for schools. Setting aside resources and time for SEL programming may seem unrealistic for some school districts; however, our experiences consistently reinforce the notion that many schools are strongly interested and deeply committed to SEL instruction. Schools in the 21st century must provide more than academic instruction in order to address the social and emotional needs of students that are undeniably linked with academic performance (Greenberg et al., 2003). Addressing barriers to SEL implementation includes consideration of feasibility and cost for school districts, for individual schools, and for classrooms (Elias et al., 2000). Academicians and practitioners must listen to the needs of the personnel charged with service delivery and consider and share the experiences of those who have incorporated SEL to use strategies that worked well and be cautious of those strategies that should not be repeated.

SEL programming is most effective when its implementation is planned, is strategic, occurs over the duration of students' academic tenure, and assessment processes are used to guide adjustments in the activities and monitor success (Greenberg et al., 2003). Payton and colleagues (2000) reviewed the features most important for implementing SEL programming and found that, in addition to these strategies, the following were also useful:

- Instructional materials are based on a conceptual framework and are easy to implement.
- Students have opportunities to actively participate in relevant experiences.
- Teachers receive additional training support.
- Technical assistance is available on-site.
- SEL concepts are implemented throughout the course of a school day.
- There is a focus on developing school–family and school–community partnerships.
- Ongoing research efforts study the extent to which SEL programs have been successful and have been implemented as intended.

More work is needed to refine program implementation, but this work *is* being conducted and exciting findings are sure to be documented that can be used to best support school personnel to give *all* students a chance at building their social and emotional strengths.

Strong Kids: SEL Delivered Through Structured Curriculum

An increasingly popular method of delivering SEL instruction is through the use of structured curricula, often targeting topics such as social skills training, violence prevention, and bullying prevention and intervention. Many practitioners have found these curricula to be an efficient means for delivering SEL content because they are specifically designed for classroom use and have been field-tested for effectiveness. At the University of Oregon, we and our colleagues developed an SEL program titled Strong Kids: A Social and Emotional Learning Curriculum to promote resiliency and coping skills for students in kindergarten through 12th grade (Merrell, Carrizales, Feuerborn, Gueldner, & Tran, 2007). The curriculum series consists of five volumes to deliver the content in a way that is sensitive to students' development: Strong Start: Pre–K (Merrell, Whitcomb, & Parisi, 2009); Strong Start: Grades K–2 (Merrell, Parisi, & Whitcomb, 2007); Strong Kids: Grades 3–5; Strong Kids: Grades 6–8; and Strong Teens: Grades 9–12. The Strong Kids curricula may be used in general education classrooms as well as outside the classroom, such as in self-contained special education classes or residential facilities (Feuerborn, 2004; Isava, 2006; Merrell, in press; Merrell et al., 2007). These curricula were designed as low-cost options that consumers could implement without the help of mental health professionals such as school counselors and school psychologists. The content is scripted to decrease the time spent in preparation, to ensure that foundational design elements and content are delivered, and to increase the ease with which the program is implemented in general.

Conceptually, Strong Kids is based on Cowen's (1994) concept of the five pathways to promoting wellness:

- Experiencing healthy attachment
- Developing age-appropriate competencies
- Coping with stress
- Having exposure to settings that promote wellness
- Experiencing a sense of empowerment regarding one's own fate

In Strong Kids, students participate in instruction and learn emotion identification as experienced by themselves and others, learn to understand the link between emotions and thoughts, identify irrational thoughts and replace them with adaptive thoughts that are more appropriate, learn optimistic styles of perceiving the present and future, learn relaxation techniques and ways to manage stress, and learn problem-solving and goal-setting skills. Cross-cultural adaptations can be made by understanding variations in students' backgrounds, communities, and current life situations; promoting tolerance in the classroom; and soliciting feedback from students and school personnel regarding the appropriateness of these adaptations.

The two versions of Strong Start each consist of 10 lessons, whereas the Strong Kids/Strong Teens programs each contain 12 lessons. Each day's lessons follow the same general instructional format and are organized as follows: describe the purpose of the lesson; introduce the objectives of the lesson; provide a list of materials that will be needed; review concepts from the previous lesson and introduce new content and instruction; finish the lesson by briefly reviewing the content covered that day; and hand out homework to students. Throughout the lesson, students participate in activities specifically designed to help students apply the lessons to real life and help them retain the concepts. Small- and large-group discussions and role-playing activities are a major focus, as well as precorrecting, reminding, and reinforcing the concepts and skills during the course of a typical school day and in between lessons.

An example of this process is taken from Lesson Six: Clear Thinking 1. The instructor reviews the content from Lesson 5: Understanding Other People's Feelings and introduces the new content about how emotions vary in terms of intensity (a little or a lot), and students learn to identify maladaptive thoughts and thinking errors. The students then participate in an activity where they identify an emotion, rate the emotion on an "intensity thermometer," and begin to discuss the idea that emotions and thoughts can coexist. The following is a sample script that introduces this idea and can be adapted as necessary:

> When we feel strong emotions, we have thoughts that go with those emotions that happen at about the same time. It's important to pay attention to both our feelings and our thoughts.

Students are led through an activity, using an overhead transparency, to learn about six thinking errors that can occur when experiencing uncomfortable emotions and thoughts. Figure 2 includes the student handout and instructor overhead from the manual that is used to teach these common thinking errors. Students review these thinking errors and discuss six scenarios that could elicit these thoughts. For example:

> Michael's parents are getting a divorce. He thinks that this is all his fault because he has been getting into trouble lately.

A thinking error that is occurring in this scenario is "making it personal." The class reviews this concept and potentially brainstorms about other situations that they may find themselves in that would elicit any of the six thinking errors. The class wraps up with a review of the concepts that were covered and a homework assignment is distributed.

The lessons can be naturally included in a language arts, social studies, or health curriculum. Table 3 includes the lesson names, primary focus, and content aims for each of the 12 lessons in the Strong Kids and Strong Teens curricula. Our experience with these programs has taught us that they may be conducted by individual classroom teachers, but teachers also may find it helpful to coteach the curriculum with another teacher or mental health specialist, such as a school psychologist. Typical classroom management strategies should continue, with the addition of extra reinforcement for participation using individual or group rewards. The use of assessment is recommended to not only monitor student outcomes and adjust instructional variables as appropriate, but also measure the fidelity of implementation and the technical assistance that practitioners may need in order to deliver the curriculum. Of course, cultural adaptations must be considered as well as any community climate issues, where persons may be unfamiliar with social and emotional learning and have concerns with its content.

General Strategies for Promoting Tier 1 Universal Approaches

In addition to structured SEL curricula, there are general strategies that teachers and administrators can use to promote mental health in their schools and give students the opportunity to learn SEL concepts, rules, and principles. Such general steps are a natural first choice in the universal promotion of social–emotional assets and wellness. Administrators are charged with finding and allocating resources, financial and otherwise, and are in a key position to make the prevention of mental health problems among the school's top priorities. Training can be made available to staff, making use of in-house mental health specialists or accessing community resources, and using evidence-based programs that fit with the school's culture and goals for students. Educators are encouraged to consider long-term planning and sustainability to avoid using programs on a short-term basis, which is a long-standing problem that often does not lead to desired outcomes. Policies should be reviewed and revised to address

Figure 2. Common thinking errors student handout from the Strong Kids social–emotional learning program.

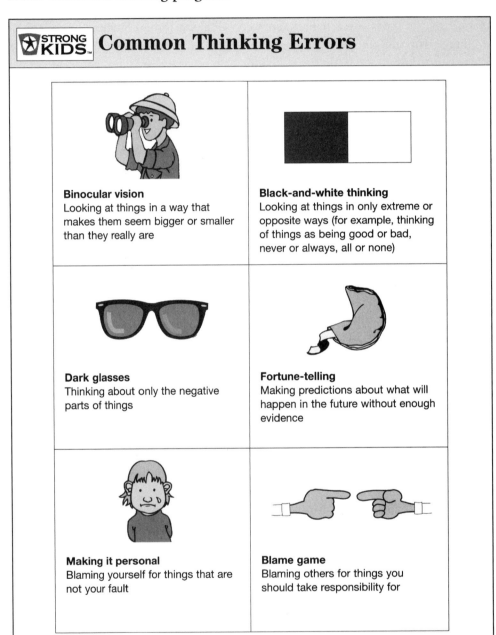

Note. From the curriculum *Strong Kids: A Social and Emotional Learning Curriculum* (p. 94), by K. W. Merrell, D. Carrizales, L. Feuerborn, B. A. Gueldner, and O. K. Tran, 2007, Baltimore: Brookes. Reprinted with permission.

Table 3. Program Structure and Lesson Content of the Strong Kids and Strong Teens Social–Emotional Learning Curricula

Lesson	Title	Description
1	About Strong Kids: Emotional Strength Training	Overview of the curriculum
2	Understanding Your Feelings: Part 1	Introduction to emotions Identify emotions as comfortable or uncomfortable
3	Understanding Your Feelings: Part 2	Discussion of appropriate and inappropriate ways of expressing emotions
4	Dealing With Anger	Recognizing triggers to anger Practice ways to change inappropriate responses
5	Understanding Other People's Feelings	Identifying others' emotions by using clues
6	Clear Thinking: Part 1	Recognizing negative thought patterns
7	Clear Thinking: Part 2	Challenging these thought patterns to think more positively
8	The Power of Positive Thinking	Promoting optimistic thinking
9	Solving People Problems	Conflict resolution strategies
10	Letting Go of Stress	Stress reduction and relaxation exercises
11	Behavior Change: Setting Goals and Staying Active	Increasing time spent in enjoyable activities and in meeting goals
12	Finishing Up!	Review of the lessons

procedures that should be taken when students are in crisis. The school climate also should be evaluated regularly to determine areas that need to be addressed to make conditions amenable to proactive prevention efforts, so that school staff are not always just responding to crises.

Teachers can immediately implement prevention strategies in their classrooms by providing a safe place for students to learn and express themselves. Effective policies and actions must be implemented in response to the seemingly ubiquitous problems of bullying, peer harassment, and relational aggression in schools, which have been linked to the development of internalizing problems in some students (see Espelage & Swearer, 2004; Merrell, Buchanan, & Tran, 2006). Teachers also engage in effective instruction when they model intra- and interpersonal problem-solving skills that are more formally taught in class. Finally, mental health specialists are a valuable resource to all school staff, and although their time may be limited, these personnel are strongly encouraged to continue to maintain an ongoing dialogue with administrators to support the use of SEL in the classroom and find ways in which these efforts can be maintained over time. Specialists such as school psychologists, school counselors, school social workers, and behavior support personnel may be in the best position to understand current research and practice and act as ambassadors on behalf of children's mental health.

SECONDARY PREVENTION STRATEGIES

Effective Tier 1 intervention efforts aimed at promoting mental health, such as SEL, have the potential to diminish the development of internalizing disorders in students. The goal of such efforts is to provide other students with needed skills and tools so that episodes of depression, anxiety, or related internalizing problems that develop may be less intense or may be overcome more quickly. It is this second group—those who may be at heightened risk for mental health problems—that constitute the focus of Tier 2 efforts. The aim of secondary prevention is to prevent an existing disorder from growing worse and "to minimize the stress experienced by the family, teachers, and peers of a youngster who exhibits disordered emotions or behavior and to minimize the complications or worsening of the disorder itself" (Kauffman, 1997, p. 138).

The line between primary prevention and secondary prevention efforts in schools is often blurred. Efforts that constitute primary prevention for one student may in part constitute a secondary prevention strategy for another. However, generally the different aims of primary and secondary prevention reflect the difference between efforts that target all students and efforts that target a smaller percentage of students who are at increased risk for particular problems, and may be exhibiting the early stages of these problems.

General Strategies for Secondary Prevention in Classrooms

General SEL programs used for primary prevention, such as Strong Kids or similar efforts that are delivered in general education classrooms, may also be fine-tuned or enriched to promote secondary prevention within the same group. This dual-purpose goal is accomplished by adapting the general program to focus on relevant areas for those students who need "a little more" than what can be accomplished through a primary prevention program. Our experience in developing and refining the Strong Kids programs included monitoring the delivery of the programs in settings with several students who were in the early stages of developing internalizing problems or disorders. We found that the following adaptations of standard SEL programs may be particularly useful in helping to support at-risk students for secondary prevention efforts:

- Take extra time to cover critical concepts in SEL content, such as dividing a single lesson into two lessons.
- Increase the range of examples that are provided to illustrate particular concepts or applications.
- Increase the opportunities for practicing new skills, including providing modeling and corrective feedback as appropriate.
- Broaden the range of practice applications of new skills that are taught, such as through the use of homework assignments or exercises that are to occur outside of the classroom setting, and include accountability and feedback mechanisms in the

process, so students are more likely to generalize the learning of new skills into various settings.

- Conduct frequent cumulative reviews during the course of the curriculum of critical concepts that were previously taught.
- Provide "booster session" reviews of these critical concepts several weeks after completion of the curriculum.
- Infuse the content and examples from the SEL program curriculum into the daily routine of the classroom, and model the use of these strategies for targeted students using "think-aloud" processes.

Secondary Prevention Outside of General Classroom Settings

Secondary prevention activities to address early signs of internalizing problems are not limited to a specific location or setting. Although the general education classroom may be a good location for such activities, and the general education teacher an important first line of secondary prevention efforts, there are times when such efforts need to be expanded and specialized. In this vein, students who require supports that are not available through primary prevention sometimes need to receive services outside of the general classroom, provided by school personnel other than the general classroom teacher.

Within the schedule and constraints of the typical school day, the most likely school personnel to provide the more specialized preventive interventions include school counselors, school psychologists, school social workers, behavior specialists, and consulting teachers. We have also observed some principals who take an active role in supporting at-risk students. In most cases, preventive interventions at the secondary level are most efficiently and economically delivered in small groups, with individual follow-up and monitoring as needed. For students at risk for developing internalizing problems, some of the most common methods of delivering secondary interventions outside of the general classroom include the following:

- Small group and individual counseling sessions, focused specifically on mental health and internalizing problems
- Skills training instruction, including structured SEL programs
- Behavioral contracting, goal-setting, and progress monitoring
- Psychoeducational approaches to educating students about mental health and internalizing problems
- Bibliotherapy activities (using age-appropriate literature and pamphlets) that are focused on the particular concerns of internalizing problems, and with follow-up discussions
- Home–school communication and parent education regarding the particular concerns of internalizing problems

Evidence-Based Tier 2 Programs for Internalizing Disorders

Educators and school-based mental health professionals who need to provide secondary interventions should consider the evidence-based psychoeducational programs that are available. Several programs have been developed and researched specifically for reducing symptoms and minimizing the impact of mild and moderate internalizing problems, particularly depression and anxiety (see Merrell, 2008b, for a comprehensive review and discussion of many of these programs). Four of the best of these interventions are discussed here. These programs all have all been used successfully in school settings, they have step-by-step treatment manuals, and they use a psychoeducational approach that is much like regular instruction in a classroom setting. Table 4 includes a summary of the main features of these four programs, including information on where they may be obtained.

For school practitioners working with students who are at high risk for depression, or who have mild to moderate levels of depression symptoms, we recommend the Coping with Adolescent Depression course and the Taking Action program. Coping with Adolescent Depression, which is aimed at adolescents of high school age, consists of 16 highly structured lessons, and the group leader's manual is tightly scripted. An optional parent education manual is included with the program, and an excellent student workbook with activities for each of the 16 lessons is available. This program is based on a comprehensive cognitive–behavioral therapy approach to depression, with activities designed to increase students' knowledge of depression, change overly pessimistic and negative thinking styles that trigger and maintain depression, and increase students' participation in positive activities.

Taking Action is for middle and high school students and includes 30 lessons that require approximately 1 hour each to deliver. The implementation manual includes

Table 4. Secondary Prevention: Some Evidence-Based Programs for Children and Adolescents With Internalizing Disorders

Intervention Program and Authors	Content Target and Age Focus	Program Structure and Characteristics
Coping with Adolescent Depression (Clark, Lewinsohn, & Hops, 1990)	Depression, ages 14–18	16 lessons, 2 hours each; includes group leader's manual, student workbooks, and parent education program
Taking Action (Stark & Kendall, 1996)	Depression, ages 12–18	30 lessons, 1 hour each; includes group leader's manual and student workbook
Coping Cat (Kendall & Hedtke, 2006)	Anxiety, ages 8–13	16 lessons, 1 hour each; includes treatment manual, group leader's manual, and student workbooks
C.A.T. for Adolescents (Kendall, Choudhury, Hudson, & Webb, 2002)	Anxiety, ages 14–17	16 lessons, 1 hour each; includes treatment manual, group leader's manual, and student workbooks

outlines for each lesson, but the manual is not scripted, allowing some adaptability in implementation. However, it also requires group leaders to have a fair amount of knowledge and skill for optimal delivery. Like the Coping with Adolescent Depression course, Taking Action is based on a comprehensive cognitive–behavioral approach to change, focusing on a student's affect, thoughts, and behaviors. Taking Action is designed for use in groups, but it can also be implemented individually or supplemented with individual or family sessions as needed.

For students who are beginning to experience anxiety-related problems (ranging from generalized anxiety disorders to specific fears and phobias and panic disorders), we particularly recommend the excellent Coping Cat programs, including the Coping Cat program for anxious children (Kendall & Hedtke, 2006) and C.A.T. for adolescents (Kendall, Choudhury, Hudson, & Webb, 2002). Both of these programs include detailed manuals for group leaders, workbooks for students, and ancillary materials. The Coping Cat program is for children ages 8–13, and the C.A.T. program is for adolescents ages 14–17. These programs include a systematic combination of plans for treatment sessions based on empirically supported premises of cognitive–behavioral therapies. The individual and family treatment components of the Coping Cat program include 16 sessions each, whereas the group component includes 18 sessions. The guidelines for Coping Cat and C.A.T. treatment sessions are general and fairly flexible, but it should be assumed that each session would require approximately 1 hour for completion.

Group leaders who are using either of these programs as a secondary prevention tool in schools may opt to cover the group lessons and individual workbook activities but forgo the family and individual therapy components. Although these treatment programs are flexible and not scripted with word-by-word treatment directions, they generally follow two distinct phases, whether delivered to individuals, groups, or families. The first phase of treatment (about eight sessions) involves a psychoeducational process to teach students to identify the somatic, cognitive, and behavioral components of anxiety. The second phase involves application of the new skills in real-life situations tailored to the specifics of the student's anxiety problems. A combination of cognitive and behavioral techniques is used to accomplish the treatment goals. For example, self-monitoring, identification of distorted and unrealistic thoughts, evaluation of physiological symptoms, disputing of irrational thoughts, relaxation training, self-instruction, and self-reinforcement are all used to some extent.

Several other tools, techniques, and programs also are available that might be appropriate for secondary prevention support with students who have internalizing disorders (see Merrell, 2008b, for a more detailed overview). The four exemplary programs described in this section were selected because of their empirical support, ease of implementation, user-friendly manuals, and reliance on a structured psychoeducational approach that is not intimidating to students and can be used in groups rather than strictly in individual therapy sessions. One final issue that is worth considering with regard to using these or other structured programs for secondary prevention efforts in schools is the time that may be required for successful implementation. These four programs require anywhere from 16 to 30 lessons of 1 to 2 hours each. Successful implementation of secondary prevention efforts of this type require considerable planning and time, and because of that they may not be feasible in some school settings; however, they are well worth the investment.

TERTIARY EFFORTS FOR INTERNALIZING DISORDERS

Although our main emphasis for this chapter is primary and secondary prevention of internalizing problems, attention must also be given to issues pertaining to students who experience severe symptoms of depression and anxiety. Many students are in need of immediate and often long-term attention because of serious mental health problems. After a student has experienced a severe episode of depression or anxiety, it is highly advisable to continue to use many of the strategies that we have described for prevention efforts, such as stress reduction, goal setting, and engagement in enjoyable activities. By definition, tertiary or Tier 3 prevention involves the care of an individual who has a well-established disorder or disability, with the intent of restoring their highest level of functioning, minimizing the negative effects of the disorder, and preventing complications. For children and adolescents who have developed significant internalizing disorders, variations on the strategies used to manage major symptoms are used to maintain functional mental health as well as prevent future occurrences of severe symptoms.

Necessity of Tier 3 Efforts in Schools

Although a legitimate argument can be made that tertiary prevention of mental health disorders is not the primary responsibility or mission of schools, the somewhat stark reality of the situation is that schools have become de facto mental health service providers. Many youth who have significant emotional and behavioral problems will receive mental health services either in the schools or not at all. For example, Hoagwood and Johnson (2003) have stated that 75% of all mental health services received by children and youth occur in schools. Even in communities that have ample resources available for mental health services outside of the school setting, the initial impetus for seeking such services may need to come from school personnel, and these educators will usually need to be involved in some way in follow-up care or monitoring after outside treatment. Thus, educators and school-based mental health specialists should become as knowledgeable and skilled as possible in tertiary approaches to internalizing disorders and related mental health issues, especially in approaches that involve collaborating with community-based mental health providers. Refusing to acknowledge or address the problem is shortsighted and unhelpful at best, and it is unethical and potentially harmful to children at worst.

School personnel interact every day with children and adolescents who are experiencing highly uncomfortable emotions. School resources are challenged and probably overwhelmed by the need to respond in a way that meets the needs of these students and the school. For example, an elementary-age student who has experienced traumatic life events, such as community violence, may not have the skills to cope with escalating fear and worry. This student may consequently develop panic symptoms that can interfere with everyday living skills, such as riding a bus to school. What appears to be an issue of school avoidance or truancy may have started with internalizing symptoms (i.e., fear and worry) that were not addressed. School personnel are often deeply frustrated by attempting to balance an anxious student's needs against enforcing attendance policies and communicating with parents who desperately want help for their child. Also, some students, particularly at the high school level, can experience severe depression symptoms characterized by suicidal ideation, and at times, associated psychotic features. In these cases, swift and expert care is of paramount importance and school personnel must be prepared to take appropriate action.

Schools are in a strategic position to assist students with their internalizing problems. Acknowledging and responding to serious symptoms of anxiety and depression are essential school responsibilities; moreover, the available interventions for internalizing problems that can be delivered in school settings may be highly effective for many struggling students and their families. However, this is a challenging task that is often filled with significant obstacles and barriers. For example, Weist (2005) described today's three-tier school mental health movement as a "young and tenuous" system (p. 735), in which evaluation, consultation, and treatment services—an invaluable part of supporting students—are commonly in short supply. Our own work in schools regarding these issues has shown us how many teachers generally believe that the mental health of students is absolutely essential to their academic and overall success. However, most schools have limited trained personnel and resources sufficient to realize these outcomes, or the resources cannot be committed because of competing administrative priorities (Buchanan, Gueldner, Tran, & Merrell, 2009).

Access to Tertiary Services

As the importance of mental health prevention and intervention for children gains recognition, respect, and support among educators, dedicated professionals have made progress in developing and offering such services. Research grants and research-supported initiatives provide some schools with the financial resources to train and support school personnel in implementing interventions and finding ways to maintain these services over time (Weist, 2005). School-based health clinics are a typical venue for students to obtain immediate and ongoing treatment from professionals with medical and mental health training, such as nurse practitioners, social workers, psychologists, and psychiatrists. The challenge is that many schools experience multiple obstacles that limit their capacity to acquire funding for mental health services that would assist children and families with acute and chronic problems. Additionally, many of the problems that students experience fall outside the scope of school-based clinicians' practice. As a result, students and their families typically are encouraged to access mental health services in the community, and the road from identifying the problem to finding appropriate and timely care is often marked by wrong turns and frequent delays.

There are ways school personnel can respond to students experiencing significant mental health problems outside of the one or two professionals in the school who are trained to respond to mental health problems, including crises. Responding might have to include referring students to community-based professionals who are trained in and have the capacity to provide appropriate services. However, because many schools are located in areas with very limited access to community mental health programs and services, especially psychiatric services, school professionals must find creative ways in which they can provide some kind of tertiary-level service to students that addresses their mental health concerns within those limited resources. In places where community resources are more abundant, school professionals can initiate and foster ongoing relationships with community agencies such as family medicine clinics, hospitals that provide psychiatric services, social services agencies, and community-based mental health programs.

These school–community connections can provide a rich array of resources to students, enhance the efficiency with which community-based services are accessed, and foster collaborative partnerships among school, community, and home that promote an ecological approach to assessment and intervention. Through these collaborative relationships, school personnel glean a better understanding of community approaches to mental health care (e.g., medication use and management, therapeutic intervention techniques), exchange observations and impressions, and educate community agency personnel and medical professionals such as primary practice physicians regarding school-based resources and expectations. Of course, school districts have a variety of policies guiding their decisions to refer students with mental health problems to personnel at community agencies, and school personnel will have to familiarize themselves with the specific guidelines in their individual school district prior to contacting outside services.

Generally, referrals are appropriate when students experience severe or chronic problems, their daily functioning is impaired, the safety of the student or others is of concern (e.g., suicidal ideation, hallucinations commanding a student to harm someone), interventions provided at school do not appear to be effective, or it has been determined that the student would benefit from a therapy regimen not provided at school (Merrell, 2008b). Primary care clinics and hospital emergency departments are often the first community facilities that families visit when they need additional services. In the event of an urgent mental health problem, such as acute psychosis and suicidal and/or homicidal ideation and behavior, school-based professionals must arrange for an immediate emergency evaluation, typically conducted in the hospital emergency department.

Physiological factors are also considered when assessing mental health status. Although uncommon, viral and bacterial infections can produce severe psychological symptoms, such as disorientation and psychosis. More commonly, families seek the advice of their primary care physician to obtain a referral to a mental health agency, and sometimes an evaluation to determine whether medication could be helpful. Many primary care physicians have had some exposure to mental health assessment and consultation but need additional training and support to provide optimal care for their patients. As a result, referrals are often made directly to psychiatrists for medication evaluations and management, as well as to psychotherapists for individual and family therapy. Of course, there are many rural communities in which access to a psychiatrist, particularly one who is skilled with children and adolescents, is very difficult to obtain. An exciting new development in primary care medicine is the increasing support available to physicians in developmental, mental health, and behavioral domains.

An example of this type of effort is Project CLIMB: Consultation and Liaison in Mental Health and Behavior, at The Children's Hospital in Denver, Colorado (A. Talmi, personal communication, August 30, 2007). In this project, pediatric residents and attending physicians work as a team with psychologists and psychology interns, psychiatrists and psychiatry fellows, and additional clinic support staff to participate in well- and sick-child visits to address typical developmental issues as well as concerns with a child's mental health and behavioral functioning. Project CLIMB also includes an additional service for families with children from birth to age 3 called Healthy Steps. This program provides support regarding postpartum issues, promotes healthy development, and offers screening to address any areas of development and behavior that are of concern to parents and clinicians. These services, and others that follow similar formats, give underserved children and families access to care in a multidisciplinary context. In addition, medical practitioners are able to improve their skills in early detection and intervention of mental health problems and better understand how to access community resources for their patients.

The assistance that a school-based practitioner can provide during a time of transition from school-based support to community-based service is unquestionably valuable. It cannot be overemphasized that the school-based practitioner must have some form of direct communication with community-based providers. Many families attend a medical appointment unsure of how to describe the extent or complexity of the problems they are experiencing. A brief letter written by the school-based mental health practitioner can support the student and family through the referral process, help the physician better understand the problem and its impact on home and school functioning, and initiate a collaborative process between education and medicine that ultimately benefits the student in improving mental health. Phone conversations with community mental health providers, such as family therapists, can provide similar benefits. Of course, legal and ethical confidentiality and privacy requirements must be observed when communicating with nonschool professionals. However, most students and families welcome the opportunity to work with their schools to share information with community treatment providers, with the intention of coordinating services in both settings.

CONCLUSION

This chapter has provided a foundation for understanding internalizing disorders and for proactively identifying and responding to students' mental health needs within school contexts. At each level of prevention, there are effective and realistic strategies that educators and school-based mental health specialists can implement to help support students who have mental health concerns. We are especially optimistic regarding the potential of the social and emotional learning approach in promoting the mental health of students. Although we addressed SEL as being a primary and secondary approach to prevention—something that could be used a great deal at Tier 1 and Tier 2, the reality is that it can be used in different settings and for problems of varying severity. Even at the Tier 3 or tertiary level of need, SEL strategies may be an important part of an overall effort to support students who are experiencing significant levels of depression, anxiety, and related internalizing disorders.

Although many school systems take their responsibility as de facto mental health providers seriously, and they have ambitiously embraced the three-tier model of prevention and intervention, such enthusiasm and support is not universal and may not even be typical. In fact, there are cultural, ideological, political, and logistical impediments that still exist which prevent schools moving toward this direction. In a sense, we need to mainstream mental health promotion from its historically marginalized position into the very fabric of our schools, so that it becomes an integral, systemic, and necessary aspect of what we do in education (Adelman & Taylor, 2000a, 2000b; Taylor & Adelman, 2000). Such an accomplishment will require a great deal of sustained effort, but the road map to getting there is now clear, the tools are currently available, and the costs for failing to do so are too high for our society to absorb.

REFERENCES

Adelman, H. S., & Taylor, L. (2000a). Moving prevention from the fringes into the fabric of school improvement. *Journal of Educational and Psychological Consultation, 11,* 7–36.

Adelman, H. S., & Taylor, L. (2000b). Shaping the future of mental health in schools. *Psychology in the Schools, 37,* 49–60.

Adelman, H. S., & Taylor, L. (2005). *The school leader's guide to student learning supports.* Thousand Oaks, CA: Corwin Press.

American Psychiatric Association. (2000). *Diagnostic and statistical manual of mental disorders* (4th ed., text rev.). Washington, DC: Author.

Buchanan, R., Gueldner, B. A., Tran, O. K., & Merrell, K. W. (2009). Social and emotional learning in classrooms: A survey of teachers' knowledge, perceptions, and practices. *Journal of Applied School Psychology, 25,* 1–17.

Cicchetti, D., & Toth, S. L. (Eds.). (1991). *Internalizing and externalizing expressions of dysfunction.* Hillsdale, NJ: Erlbaum.

Clarke, G., Lewinsohn, P., & Hops, H. (1990). *Coping with adolescent depression course: Leader's manual for adolescent groups*. Eugene, OR: Castalia. Available as a free download from the Kaiser Permanente Center for Health Research website: http://www.kpchr.org/public/acwd/acwd.html

Collaborative for Academic, Social, and Emotional Learning. (2003). *Safe and sound: An educational leader's guide to evidence-based social and emotional learning programs*. Retrieved July 1, 2005, from http://www.casel.com

Cowen, E. L. (1994). The enhancement of psychological wellness: Challenges and opportunities. *American Journal of Community Psychology, 22,* 149–179.

Elias, M. J., Bruene-Butler, L., Blum, L., & Schuyler, T. (2000). Voices from the field: Identifying and overcoming roadblocks to carrying out programs in social and emotional learning/emotional intelligence. *Journal of Educational and Psychological Consultation, 11,* 253–272.

Espelage, D. L., & Swearer, S. M. (2004). *Bullying in American schools: A social-ecological perspective on prevention and intervention*. Mahwah, NJ: Erlbaum.

Feuerborn, L. L. (2004). *Promoting emotional resiliency through classroom instruction: The effects of a classroom-based prevention program*. Unpublished doctoral dissertation, University of Oregon, Eugene.

Greenberg, M. T., Weissberg, R. P, Utne O'Brien, M., Zins, J. E., Redericks, L., Resnik, H., et al. (2003). Enhancing school-based prevention and youth development through coordinated social, emotional, and academic learning. *American Psychologist, 58,* 466–474.

Gueldner, B. A., & Merrell, K. W. (in press). Evaluation of a social–emotional learning intervention using performance feedback to teachers in a structured consultation model. *Journal of Educational and Psychological Consultation.*

Hoagwood, K., & Johnson, J. (2003). School psychology: A public health framework I. *Journal of School Psychology, 41,* 3–21.

Isava, D. M. (2006). *An investigation of the impact of a social–emotional learning curriculum on problem symptoms and knowledge gains among adolescents in a residential treatment center*. Unpublished doctoral dissertation, University of Oregon, Eugene.

Kauffman, J. M. (1997). *Characteristics of emotional and behavioral disorders of children and youth* (6th ed.). Upper Saddle River, NJ: Merrill/Prentice Hall.

Kendall, P. C., Choudhury, M., Hudson, J., & Webb, A. (2002). *The C.A.T. project workbook for the cognitive behavioral treatment of anxious adolescents*. Llanfair, PA: Workbook Publishing.

Kendall, P. C., & Hedtke, K. A. (2006). *Cognitive–behavioral therapy for anxious children: Therapist manual* (3rd ed.). Llanfair, PA: Workbook Publishing.

Kutash, K., Duchnowski, A. J., & Lynn, N. (2006). *School-based mental health: An empirical guide for decision-makers*. Retrieved August 29, 2007, from the University of South Florida, Research and Training Center for Children's Mental Health website: http://rtckids.fmhi.usf.edu

Merrell, K. W. (2010). Linking prevention science and social and emotional learning: The Oregon Resiliency Project. *Psychology in the Schools, 47,* 55–70.

Merrell, K. W. (2008a). *Behavioral, social, and emotional assessment of children and adolescents* (3rd ed.). New York: Erlbaum/Taylor & Francis Group.

Merrell, K. W. (2008b). *Helping students overcome depression and anxiety: A practical guide* (2nd ed.). New York: Guilford Press.

Merrell, K. W., & Buchanan, R. S. (2006). Intervention selection in school-based practice: Using public health models to enhance systems capacity of schools. *School Psychology Review, 35,* 167–180.

Merrell, K. W., Buchanan, R. S., & Tran, O. K. (2006). Relational aggression in children and adolescents: A review with implications for school settings. *Psychology in the Schools, 43,* 345–360.

Merrell, K. W., Carrizales, D., Feuerborn, L., Gueldner, B. A., & Tran, O. K. (2007). *Strong Kids: A Social and Emotional Learning Curriculum.* Baltimore: Brookes.

Merrell, K. W., Juskelis, M. P., Tran, O. K., & Buchanan, R. (2008). Social and emotional learning in the classroom: Evaluation of Strong Kids and Strong Teens on students' social–emotional knowledge and symptoms. *Journal of Applied School Psychology, 24,* 209–224

Merrell, K. W., Parisi, D., & Whitcomb, S. (2007). *Strong Start—Grades K-2: A social and emotional learning curriculum.* Baltimore: Brookes.

Merrell, K. W., & Walker, H. M. (2004). Deconstructing a definition: Emotionally disturbed versus socially maladjusted, and moving the EBD field forward. *Psychology in the Schools, 41,* 899–910.

Merrell, K. W., Whitcomb, S. A., & Parisi, D. (2009). *Strong Start—Pre-K: A social and emotional learning curriculum.* Baltimore: Brookes.

Payton, J. W., Wardlaw, D. M., Graczyk, P. A., Bloodworth, M. R., Tompsett, C. J., & Weissberg, R. P. (2000). Social and emotional learning: A framework for promoting mental health and reducing risk behaviors in children and youth. *Journal of School Health, 70,* 179–185.

Post, R. M. (1992). Transduction of psychosocial stress into the neurobiology of recurrent affective disorder. *American Journal of Psychiatry, 149,* 999–1010.

Reynolds, W. M. (Ed.). (1992). *Internalizing disorders in children and adolescents.* New York: Wiley.

Seeley, J. R., Rohde, P., Lewinsohn, P. M., & Clarke, G. N. (2002). Depression in youth: Epidemiology, identification, and intervention. In M. R. Shinn, H. M. Walker, & G. Stoner (Eds.), *Interventions for academic and behavior problems II: Preventative and remedial approaches* (pp. 885–911). Bethesda, MD: National Association of School Psychologists.

Stark, K. D., & Kendall, P. C. (1996). *Treating depressed children: Therapist manual for Taking Action.* Ardmore, PA: Workbook Publishing.

Taylor, L., & Adelman, H. S. (2000). Toward ending the marginalization of mental health in schools. *Journal of School Health, 70,* 210–215.

Tran, O. K. (2007). *Promoting social and emotional learning in schools: An investigation of massed versus distributed practice schedules and social validity of the Strong Kids curriculum in late elementary aged students.* Unpublished doctoral dissertation, University of Oregon, Eugene.

Van Lang, N. D. J., Ferdinand, R. F., Oldehinkel, A. J., Ormel, J., & Verhulst, F. C. (2005). Concurrent validity of the DSM-IV scales: Affective problems and anxiety problems of the youth self-report. *Behavior Research and Therapy, 43,* 1485–1494.

Wang, M. C., Haertel, G. D., & Walberg, H. J. (1997). Learning influences. In H. J. Walberg & G. D. Haertel (Eds.), *Psychology and educational practice* (pp. 199–211). Berkeley, CA: McCatchan.

Weist, M. D. (2005). Fulfilling the promise of school-based mental health: Moving toward a public mental health promotion approach. *Journal of Abnormal Child Psychology, 33,* 735–741.

Zins, J. E., Weissberg, R. P., Wang, M. C., & Walberg, H. J. (Eds.). (2004). *Building academic success on social and emotional learning: What does the research say?* New York: Teacher's College Press.

INTERVENTIONS

for Achievement and Behavior Problems in a Three-Tier Model Including RTI

CHAPTER 31

Interventions for Attention Deficit Hyperactivity Disorder

George J. DuPaul
Lehigh University

Gary Stoner
University of Rhode Island

INTRODUCTION

Among the most frequent behavior difficulties exhibited by children in classroom settings are problems with attention, impulse control, and activity level (Barkley, 2006). In fact, approximately 3–5% of elementary school children in the United States are diagnosed with attention deficit hyperactivity disorder (ADHD), a psychiatric condition of individuals who exhibit developmentally inappropriate levels of inattention, impulsivity, or overactivity (American Psychiatric Association, 2000). Boys with ADHD outnumber girls with this disorder at ratios between 2:1 and 5:1 (Barkley, 2006). Given that most public school classrooms have 20 to 30 students, teachers will likely have to address the needs of at least one student with ADHD per school year. Furthermore, ADHD symptoms typically persist from early childhood through at least adolescence for a majority of individuals (Barkley, Murphy, & Fischer, 2008; Weiss & Hechtman, 1993). Thus, attention and behavioral difficulties are likely to affect a child's school functioning throughout his or her educational career.

Children with attention problems related to ADHD are at higher-than-average risk for a variety of behavioral difficulties, including defiance toward authority figures, poor relationships with peers, and antisocial acts such as lying, stealing, and fighting (American Psychiatric Association, 2000; Barkley, 2006). In addition, students with ADHD frequently struggle scholastically, presumably because of their low academic engagement rates and inconsistent work productivity (DuPaul & Stoner, 2003). The results of prospective follow-up studies of children with ADHD into adolescence and adulthood indicate significantly higher rates of grade retention, placement in special education classrooms, and school dropout relative to their peers, as well as significantly lower high school grade point averages, enrollment in college degree programs, and socioeconomic status (Barkley et al., 2008). These students tend to complete less classroom work than expected, which may in part account for the association of ADHD with academic underachievement, because up to 80% of students with this disorder have been found to exhibit academic performance problems (Cantwell & Baker, 1991). Furthermore, a significant minority (i.e., 20–30%) of children with ADHD are classified as having learning disabilities because of deficits in the acquisition of specific academic skills (DuPaul & Stoner, 2003; Knivsberg, Reichelt, & Nodland, 1999; Semrud-Clikeman et al., 1992). Additionally, students with ADHD may receive special education services as a result of being classified as "other health impaired." In fact, "other health impaired" is one of the fastest growing special education categories, increasing from 0.1% of the school population in 1992 to 0.6% of the population in 2002, presumably owing to an increased identification of students with ADHD (U.S. Department of Education, 2005).

Given the strong risk for poor academic outcomes, school professionals must design and implement interventions to address not only the attention problems and behavioral difficulties associated with ADHD, but also the academic achievement problems accompanying this disorder. The two primary interventions for ADHD are psychostimulant medication (e.g., methylphenidate) and contingency management programs (e.g., praise, reinforcement using tokens). These intervention strategies have been found to enhance rates of academic productivity and accuracy for most study participants (Barkley, 2006; DuPaul & Eckert, 1997). The most comprehensive, large-scale treatment outcome study to date, referred to as the Multimodal Treatment Study of Children with ADHD (MTA), found that pharmacotherapy was superior to behavioral interventions in reducing ADHD symptoms and related disruptive behaviors (MTA Cooperative Group, 1999, 2004); however, these two treatments did not differ with respect to their effects on academic achievement. Furthermore, some children may require the combination of stimulant medication and behavioral intervention to show improvements in academic functioning (MTA Cooperative Group, 1999).

Nevertheless, despite their positive effects, these interventions do not comprehensively address all of the academic deficits that may be exhibited by students with ADHD. For example, 47% of children treated with methylphenidate will either show no change or show declines in academic performance when compared with those receiving a placebo (Rapport, Denney, DuPaul, & Gardner, 1994). Effect sizes for academic outcome measures typically are lower than for measures of behavioral outcome for both stimulant medication (Jensen et al., 2007) and behavioral interventions (DuPaul & Eckert, 1997). For example, the MTA study found small effect sizes (0.1 to 0.2) for within-group change in reading achievement for carefully titrated medication, behavioral intervention, and their combination (Jensen et al., 2007). Thus, although necessary for many students with ADHD, these interventions *are not sufficient* for ameliorating academic performance problems.

The purpose of this chapter is to describe empirically supported school-based interventions that address the attention problems, behavior difficulties, and academic performance of children exhibiting behaviors related to ADHD. It reviews conceptual issues underlying the design and implementation of interventions and describes them in the context of a three-tiered service delivery model that involves universal, selected, and indicated strategies. The chapter also discusses interventions that are useful for elementary and secondary school students. The use of psychotropic medication to treat ADHD is described briefly.

Throughout, this chapter emphasizes several overarching points regarding school-based interventions for students with ADHD. First, for interventions to be effective, they must be linked to baseline and ongoing assessment data to monitor progress. Second, children with attention problems related to ADHD are a heterogeneous group. Therefore, for those students requiring more intensive treatment, strategies must be individually tailored to meet both student needs and the specific environmental context. Finally, a balanced approach to treatment planning should be adopted wherein both proactive (antecedent-based) and reactive (consequent-based) intervention strategies are implemented.

CONCEPTUAL FOUNDATIONS OF INTERVENTION

School psychologists and other professionals are guided by numerous approaches to intervention design, implementation, and evaluation; for example, intervention strategies are linked to functional analysis of problem behavior. A three-tiered response-to-intervention (RTI) model can be used to plan service delivery to students with ADHD. This model includes universal, selected, and indicated intervention strategies that are implemented based on students' response to treatment (Jimerson, Burns, & VanDerHeyden, 2007). Universal strategies are delivered to all students on a class-wide or school-wide basis. Although universal approaches will be helpful for some students with ADHD, most individuals will require more intensive interventions at the selected or indicated levels.

In designing interventions for students with ADHD, particularly at the selected and indicated levels, practitioners should focus on five guiding principles. Intervention effectiveness can be enhanced by attending to these five principles, which involve the use of (a) assessment of data for progress monitoring and other purposes, (b) multiple intervention agents or mediators, (c) both proactive and reactive intervention strategies, (d) individualized strategies, and (e) interventions in proximity to the behavior of concern. Each principle is described briefly in the following sections and illustrated throughout the chapter using examples of ADHD intervention strategies.

Linking Assessment Data to Interventions

Interventions are more effective when they include ongoing assessment data, such as baseline data and functional assessment data. Assessment data can be used in many ways to guide interventions. For example, functional assessment data can inform professionals as to when and under what conditions problem behavior is most likely to occur, such as during math instruction, and least likely to occur, such as during nonacademic times (Touchette, MacDonald, & Langer, 1985). In addition, these data can be used to generate hypotheses about what function a certain behavior might serve, such as producing social attention, or escaping or avoiding an aversive task (Nelson, Roberts, & Smith, 1998; O'Neill et al., 1997). These data can help guide decisions pertaining to when and where interventions are most needed. In addition, these data might suggest what could be done to prevent problem behavior through changes in instruction or classroom structure (e.g., moving the student's desk closer to the teacher), and what strategies are likely to be effective in managing the behaviors of concern (e.g., teaching or strengthening appropriate behaviors for obtaining social attention).

In addition, once interventions are put in place, treatment integrity data (i.e., information regarding the degree to which interventions have been implemented as intended) can be used both for refining intervention strategies so they can be implemented by individual teachers and for evaluating treatment outcomes (Gresham, MacMillan, Beebe-Frankenberger, & Bocian, 2000). A weak treatment effect could mean the treatment was well implemented yet might be considered a failure in this instance. Or outcome data could show that the intervention was not implemented with enough integrity to produce an acceptable effect, prompting a redesign of the intervention.

Finally, outcome data are collected to help practitioners draw conclusions about the intervention's overall effectiveness, the students' need for more intensive interventions across tiers, satisfaction with treatment outcomes, and the magnitude of treatment effects relative to baseline data and treatment goals. These conclusions allow practitioners to decide whether to continue, discontinue, revise, or supplement the current intervention strategy or to move to a more intensive level.

These uses of assessment data thus improve the link between assessment and intervention, enhance understanding of treatment integrity and feasibility, and promote accountability in treatment implementation. Ultimately, these data can enhance treatment effectiveness by prompting the continuation of only the effective strategies and determining the most appropriate level of service delivery, thereby making the best use of available resources.

Using Multiple Intervention Agents

The second guiding principle is that interventions for students with ADHD are more effective when multiple intervention agents are used. This principle is consistent with the notion that when psychotropic medication is used to treat students with ADHD, it should not be the sole intervention strategy. Physicians treating ADHD most often recommend that medication be accompanied by individualized behavioral and academic support strategies. The intervention agents involved would likely be a physician, a teacher, and parents.

Table 1 shows the different types of interventions, by intervention agent, by the student's age. In general, interventions that involve the use of multiple intervention agents and intervention strategies will prevent overreliance on one strategy.

Combining Proactive and Reactive Strategies

A third guiding principle for designing effective interventions for students with ADHD is that treatment should combine proactive and reactive support strategies. Proactive strategies are instructional or behavioral management strategies designed to prevent problem behavior from occurring in the first place by changing antecedent events (i.e., those events preceding a specific behavior of interest). For example, reviews of classroom rules and expectations at the start of an activity could reduce the likelihood of problem behavior occurring. Also, reviewing and clarifying assignment directions prior to beginning an academic task would be considered a proactive strategy.

Reactive strategies, on the other hand, are designed to effectively manage problem behavior when it takes place by changing the consequences (i.e., events that follow the behavior of interest). For example, under a token economy, removing a token from a student for exhibiting a problem behavior calls the student's attention to both expectations and consequences, as well as reduces the likelihood of future problems. Combinations of proactive and reactive strategies are more effective at engendering well-regulated behavior, compared with either approach alone. However, this observation has yet to be examined empirically.

Table 1. **ADHD Academic and Behavior Support Strategies, by Intervention Agent and Age**

Intervention Agent	Preschool	Elementary	Secondary
Teacher-mediated	Behavior management, instructional strategies	Behavior management, instructional strategies	Study skills, contracting
Parent-mediated	Behavior management, communication with teachers	Goal-setting, contracting, daily report card, parent tutoring	Negotiating, contracting, home based, reinforcement
Peer-mediated		Peer tutoring	Peer coaching, peer mediation
Computer-assisted		Instruction, drill and practice	Instruction, word processing
Self-directed		Self-monitoring	Self-monitoring, self-evaluation
Other-directed (e.g., physician or counselor)	Medication and monitoring (behavioral outcomes)	Medication and monitoring (academic and behavioral outcomes)	Medication and monitoring (including self-report)

Note. From "Interventions for Attention Problems" by G. J. DuPaul and G. Stoner, 2002, in *Interventions for Academic and Behavior Problems II: Preventive and Remedial Approaches*, by M. R. Shinn, H. M. Walker, and G. Stoner (Eds.), p. 917, Bethesda, MD: National Association of School Psychologists. Reprinted with permission.

Individualizing Intervention Strategies

Although students may share a common diagnosis of ADHD, they are a heterogeneous group that varies widely with respect to the type and magnitude of difficulties, and to the variables causing or maintaining their challenging behaviors (DuPaul, Eckert, & McGoey, 1997). As a result, interventions will be more effective when they are individualized to accommodate these different characteristics. Although this fourth guiding principle may seem self-evident, it is not uncommon for professionals in schools and communities to use a similar approach for all students with ADHD.

To avoid a one-size-fits-all approach, planning for such individualization needs to take into account (a) the child's current level of academic functioning, (b) current problem behaviors, (c) the possible environmental functions of the child's inattentive behavior (i.e., the maintaining consequences), (d) the target behaviors of greatest concern to the teacher or student, and (e) the elements of the classroom environment or teaching approach that might limit the effectiveness of some interventions. Individualized interventions should be developed through a consultative problem-solving process using assessment data and collaborative interactions among teachers, parents, and other school professionals (DuPaul et al., 2006).

Delivering Interventions at the Point of Performance

A final guiding principle in designing effective interventions for students with ADHD is to intervene at the point of performance (Goldstein & Goldstein, 1998). This principle suggests that to be optimally effective, strategies must be implemented as close in time and place as possible to the target behaviors. For example, if the behavior of concern is lack of attention to math work, then using strategies intended to address the behavior must occur in math class, at the time when the student is expected to complete math work, rather than at another time and place. The further removed the intervention is from the occurrence of the target behavior, the less effective that strategy is likely to be. This principle is based on evidence that impulsiveness is the primary deficit underlying the attention difficulties and other symptoms of ADHD (Barkley, 2006). Thus, to be effective at changing and managing impulsive behavior, selected and indicated interventions need to be implemented at the point of performance of those behaviors.

INTERVENTIONS FOR ELEMENTARY AND SECONDARY SCHOOL STUDENTS

Planning interventions for students with ADHD begins with teacher-mediated strategies. That is, teachers who are working with students throughout the school day are always at the point of performance, whether academic or behavioral. In addition to teachers, the classroom-based strategies described here would be used by other adults working in classrooms, such as teacher aides, parents, grandparents, or community volunteers.

Teacher-mediated strategies can be proactive or reactive. Proactive strategies often involve the entire class (i.e., universal level) and are intended to prevent academic and behavioral difficulties by altering the classroom conditions that allow problems to arise (e.g., moving a student's desk closer to teacher and away from classmates). In comparison, reactive strategies can be used to respond to both appropriate and problem behavior as part of an overall selected or indicated intervention program. Together, the goal of these strategies is to promote the monitoring and improvement of student performance using clearly communicated expectations and the provision of both positive and corrective feedback.

Universal Interventions

Intervention strategies delivered on a school- or class-wide basis are designed to prevent academic and behavioral difficulties by explicitly teaching expectations, supporting students in meeting their academic demands, and actively recognizing and reinforcing appropriate behavior. In an RTI model, primary prevention of problem behavior includes giving students instruction in the social skills they need for school success (Horner, Sugai, Lewis-Palmer, & Todd, 2001). Identifying, teaching, and reinforcing behavior consistent with school-wide or class-wide expectations can in turn give teachers more instructional time by reducing the time spent coping with behavioral crises. Using effective strategies as part of a well-designed educational support program can allow a teacher to deliver instruction and evaluate student learning without the continual distractions and interruptions that occur in poorly managed schools or classrooms.

Universal educational support requires the active participation of all staff, including teachers, administrators, paraprofessionals, cafeteria workers, playground supervisors, bus drivers, and other school support staff. When new students arrive at the school, they may be unprepared or unable to act in accordance with the school and class social and behavioral expectations, but with a universal program in place, students are given multiple opportunities to learn and practice appropriate behaviors, rather than simply being punished for inappropriate behaviors (March, Hawken, & Green, 2003).

Universal Interventions to Increase Prosocial Behavior

An example of a universal-level intervention program is the effective behavior support (EBS) model, which provides a primary level of behavioral instruction for all students (Lewis & Sugai, 1999; Todd, Horner, Sugai, & Sprague, 1999). The focus of teachers' effort in EBS is on teaching three to five positively stated expectations (e.g., students raise hands before speaking), along with the routines and behaviors that actively promote and demonstrate those expectations. The explicit teaching of routines benefits all students, while also providing important opportunities for the rehearsal of positive social behaviors for students with ADHD. Because the act of teaching expectations is not enough to ensure learning, a school-wide or classroom reinforcement system, such as the use of cues and prompts, is also critical and increases the likelihood of creating a behaviorally effective school and classroom environment (Lewis & Sugai, 1999).

The degree to which teachers provide students with cues, prompts, or signals to follow classroom rules ultimately determines the effectiveness of those rules in maintaining appropriate student behavior (Paine, Radicchi, Rosellini, Deutchman, & Darch, 1983). Unfortunately, many elementary school children, including those with attention problems and ADHD, have difficulty following classroom rules, presumably because these rules have not been learned well. Behavioral coaching by the teacher and other classroom staff can greatly enhance this process.

All teachers have classroom rules, which they typically teach at the beginning of the school year. However, actively teaching these rules throughout the school year can be an effective deterrent for problem behavior, as well as a support for appropriate behavior. Active teaching of classroom rules involves the following procedures: (a) developing four or five clearly stated rules—these should be "positively" stated, that is, conveying information about what to do or how to behave, rather than what not to do in the classroom; (b) teaching the rules initially, and giving examples of behaviors that follow the rules and behaviors that do not follow the rules; and (c) periodically reteaching or discussing one or two of the rules. This last procedure could involve reviewing one rule by spending 2 minutes stating and discussing the rule and its importance. This reteaching might be done one or two times per week at the beginning of a class or day; in addition, acknowledgement of one or two examples of students following the rules could be done each class period or three or four times throughout the day (e.g., "Sharon, that was polite of you to let Ramon use the pencil sharpener before you").

In addition to active teaching of classroom rules, teachers working with children who exhibit significant attention difficulties and ADHD-related behaviors should consider altering the classroom environment to allow for more careful monitoring of student activities. For example, placing a student's desk near the teacher's may allow easier observation of the student's behaviors and enhance the probability that the student will understand the teacher's directives (Paine et al., 1983). Teachers also should be encouraged to arrange the classroom so that students with ADHD are more likely to participate in class activities. For example, students with ADHD may sometimes be placed in isolated parts of the classroom to decrease potential distractions for the child. Although such environmental arrangements may be successful in some ways, it is important that the student remain accessible to teacher instruction, to appropriate peer interaction, and to important class activities.

Transitions from one area of the school to another, such as from one classroom to another, often can be the antecedent or trigger for problem behavior. Allowing time to teach, model, and practice efficient transition processes may prevent problem behaviors from occurring. It is particularly important for children with ADHD to have an opportunity to review expectations and consequences when moving to a new setting, or to a setting that typically is challenging (Pfiffner, Barkley, & DuPaul, 2006). Transitions into and out of areas that include a lot of students, such as the cafeteria and hallways, often are particularly problematic and a source of many disciplinary referrals. Active supervision by adults (e.g., patrolling the area, looking for potentially problematic interactions before they occur, and interacting briefly and positively with students) has been shown to decrease problem behaviors in common areas (Colvin, Sugai, Good, & Lee, 1997).

Universal Interventions to Enhance Academic Performance

Children with ADHD are likely to benefit from class-wide instructional strategies that provide a direct, teacher-mediated link between assessment and intervention. Such strategies may include flexible grouping for academic instruction, continuous progress monitoring of basic academic skills, and explicit instruction in strategies for studying and organization. Universally applied programs that include assessment and intervention, such as the School-wide Reading Improvement Model (Kame'enui, Simmons, & Coyne, 2000) integrate well with behavioral strategies that allow staff to be proactive in preventing academic and social problems. Programs based on this model use dynamic repeated measures of early literacy and reading skill fluency to monitor progress over time and provide a close connection between assessment and intervention to develop reading skills. An important factor for students with ADHD is the focus on continuous assessment to decide what and how to teach children who may be at risk for reading problems. That is, the model's use of early and repeated screening of critical prereading skills allows for early identification and tracking of the effectiveness of interventions. Frequent progress monitoring allows teachers to target instruction more closely to student needs. Given that children with ADHD are at risk for problems with academic skills, programs based on this model can be particularly helpful in either preventing or managing such problems.

Explicit instruction in study and organizational skills is another universal strategy that can help to prevent the problem of poor grades due to lost work or lack of planning for tests and projects. Study strategies are skills that are critical to the success of children and adolescents with ADHD. These organizational and metacognitive strategies often are embedded in classroom curriculum and instruction; however, students with ADHD may need more explicit or individualized instruction that teaches the strategy through modeling and demonstration and allows for practice and rehearsal. Many students need instruction in basic skills, modifications in the delivery of instruction, and instruction in specific learning strategies (see chapter 22 in this book). For students with ADHD, specific strategies that can be taught include notebook or binder organization, the use of planners or assignment calendars, and explicit instruction in the organization of written work. Teaching memorization strategies and specific test-taking and study strategies to older children and adolescents with ADHD also may help promote academic success (Robin, 1998).

The program such as Skills for School Success curriculum (Archer & Gleason, 2002) has great potential for students with ADHD in that it provides consistent, direct instruction in a range of study and organizational skills across elementary and secondary grade levels. For example, the program provides multiple strategies that teach effective study skills, such as active reading of textbooks, efficient survey and review strategies, and verbal and written rehearsal focused on comprehension of the main ideas and supporting information. One useful tool is the HOW strategy (Heading, Organized, and Written neatly), which teaches students how to plan appropriate headings, margins, and spacing when completing written work. Many students also benefit from explicit instruction in reading comprehension strategies. Students who struggle with reading comprehension need direct instruction in strategies to separate critical information or big ideas from less important information.

Universal strategies such as those described in this section promote the development of positive behavior and academic skills have the potential to benefit all students and are an important component of an overall support plan for students with ADHD.

Selected Intervention Strategies

Interventions at the selected level of service delivery are directed toward students who are at risk for more significant behavioral or academic difficulties as a function of their ADHD symptoms. Selected interventions are considered for students who experience only limited success with universal strategies. Both proactive and reactive strategies should be considered when developing a balanced treatment plan.

Proactive intervention strategies typically involve arranging the conditions of the classroom environment before the problem behavior can occur and in a way that prevents that undesirable behavior. That is, if the teacher is able to accurately identify situations and antecedent events that are reliably followed by inattentive and disruptive behavior by a particular student, the most efficient way to improve the situation is to do something beforehand, rather than waiting to react to the problem behavior. For many children with attention problems associated with ADHD, the two classroom situations that prompt inattentive behavior are primarily teacher-directed instruction and independent academic work. Inattentive behaviors can lead to academic difficulties, behavior problems, or both. Proactively selecting a classroom strategy for an individual student involves identifying antecedent conditions—that is, the task, person, time, or setting—that are associated with that student's academic or behavioral difficulty. Several proactive interventions have been identified that can improve the academic performance of students with ADHD. These include providing peer tutoring, arranging for students to have and make choices in their academic tasks, and providing for directed note-taking activities.

Students with ADHD have been shown to respond positively to peer tutoring strategies. Peer tutoring is defined as any instructional strategy in which two students work together on an academic activity, with one student providing assistance, instruction, and feedback to the other (see chapter 24 in this book). Various peer tutoring models have been developed that differ as to instructional focus (acquisition versus practice), structure (reciprocal versus nonreciprocal), and procedural components (e.g., number of sessions per week, methods of pairing students, type of reward system used). However, the different peer tutoring models share a number of instructional characteristics that are known to enhance the task-related attention of students with ADHD, including the following: (a) one-on-one work with another individual; (b) instructional pace that is determined by learner; (c) continuous prompting of academic responses; and (d) frequent, immediate feedback about quality of performance (Pfiffner, Barkley, & DuPaul, 2006).

One widely used peer tutoring program is the Classwide Peer Tutoring program. CWPT has been implemented in general education classrooms to enhance the mathematics, reading, and spelling skills of students of all achievement levels. The primary procedures of CWPT include the following steps. First, the class is divided into two groups, identified as teams. Within each team, classmates form tutoring pairs. Students take turns tutoring each other using academic scripts, such as math problems with answers. Students who answer correctly can receive praise and points. Errors are corrected immediately by peers, and the pair is given an opportunity to practice the correct answer. The classroom teacher monitors the tutoring pairs and provides bonus points for pairs that are carefully following the CWPT procedures. Finally, students tally their own points at the conclusion of each session.

CWPT tutoring sessions typically last 20 minutes, with an additional 5 minutes for charting progress and putting materials away. At week's end, the team with the most points is recognized by applause and praise from the other team. CWPT has been found to enhance the on-task behavior and academic performance of nonmedicated students with ADHD in general education classrooms. In a study by DuPaul et al., typically achieving students also showed improvements in attention and academic performance when participating in CWPT activities (DuPaul, Ervin, Hook, & McGoey, 1998). Thus, peer tutoring is an intervention that can help *all* students. As such, it has the potential to be seen by teachers as both a practical and time-efficient strategy for meeting the needs of children with ADHD.

A variant of peer tutoring is peer coaching, an approach that pairs a student with ADHD with a classmate or older student who can provide ongoing support in the school setting. Dawson and Guare (1998) developed a model for coaching students with ADHD that has the potential for successful implementation by peers. The coaching process involves five steps: (a) identifying the need for a coach, (b) obtaining the target student's commitment to coaching, (c) matching the student with a coach, (d) setting up the first meeting with the coach, and (e) implementing daily coaching sessions. During the initial daily sessions (about 5 minutes), the coach helps the student set long-term goals, determine the steps to achieve these goals, identify potential obstacles, brainstorm ways to circumvent obstacles, identify ways to enhance the probability of success, and ensure that the plan is realistic. Once goals and plans are formulated, daily sessions include reviewing progress since the last session, evaluating the relative success of the plan, anticipating what needs to be done next, and planning what to do before the next session. Dawson and Guare state that adult supervision (e.g., a school psychologist or special educator) is necessary to ensure that disagreements are handled in a proactive and effective fashion. In addition, controlled empirical studies are needed to support the efficacy of peer coaching for students with ADHD.

Another proactive strategy is choice making, in which students are allowed to choose from two or more concurrent activities. Several studies have demonstrated the value of providing task-related choices to students with behavior difficulties, including ADHD, because on-task behavior and work productivity can increase when choice is offered (e.g., Dunlap et al., 1994). Choice making typically is implemented by providing students with a menu of tasks in a particular academic subject area from which they can choose. For example, if students are having difficulty completing independent math assignments, they could select from several possible math assignments. The students would be expected to choose and complete one of the tasks listed on the menu during the allotted time. Thus, while the teacher retains control over the general nature of the assigned work, students are provided with some control over the specific assignment.

Adolescents with ADHD may exhibit inferior organizational and study skills, thereby increasing the risk for poor scholastic achievement (Barkley, 2006). Thus, secondary school students with ADHD may benefit from instruction and support in taking organized notes for later study. For example, the Directed Notetaking Activity (DNA; Spires & Stone, 1989) involves lectures and prompts in an attempt to increase students' on-task behavior, improve comprehension of classroom materials, and reduce the frequency of disruptive behaviors. Specifically, the teacher models the note-taking process by illustrating how to outline notes based on main ideas and details. The number of teacher prompts is slowly faded until students are able to independently form an outline based on the presented lecture material. The DNA program has been found to increase the quality of notes and the recording of instructional details by adolescents diagnosed with ADHD (Evans, Pelham, & Grudberg, 1995).

The Challenging Horizons program includes a comprehensive school-based protocol for addressing both academic and social relationship difficulties encountered by middle school students with ADHD (Evans, Langberg, Raggi, Allen, & Buvinger, 2005). Interventions are delivered over 15 sessions and target academic skills such as assignment tracking, note taking, and organization of school materials. Social skills such as social problem-solving skills and conversation skills also are addressed. Preliminary findings indicate improvement in parent-rated ADHD symptoms and social skills after 3 years of training relative to a group that did not receive training (Evans, Serpell, Schultz, & Pastor, 2007). No cumulative academic benefits have been found; however, within-year analyses indicate benefits in student grades.

Indicated Intervention Strategies

For those students with ADHD who do not respond successfully to universal or selected intervention strategies, more intensive, individualized approaches may be necessary. Indicated interventions include computer-assisted instruction (CAI), contingency management systems, school–home notes, and self-management.

CAI is a proactive, antecedent-based approach that can deliver instructional support for elementary school–age students. Specifically, computers are used to teach initial academic skills using instructional technology and to enhance the mastery of already acquired skills using drill-and-practice software. Several recent studies have demonstrated the efficacy of CAI in promoting the reading and math achievement of students with ADHD (Clarfield & Stoner, 2005; Mautone, DuPaul, & Jitendra, 2005; Ota & DuPaul, 2002). CAI also was found to increase on-task behavior when compared with typical classwork conditions in all three studies. The instructional features of CAI help students to focus their attention on academic stimuli. Although not all programs have every feature listed here, the following instructional design features of CAI are shown to be beneficial: (a) specific instructional objectives are readily presented alongside activities; (b) highlighting of essential material (e.g., through large print and color) is provided; (c) multiple sensory modalities are used; (d) content material is divided into manageable bits of information; and (e) immediate feedback about response accuracy is provided. In addition, CAI can readily limit the presentation of nonessential features that may be distracting (e.g., sound effects, animation). More research is needed, but it is clear that classroom use of CAI has the potential to enhance the academic behavior and performance of students with attention problems.

Reactive intervention strategies typically focus on providing feedback or consequences to students. These strategies are usually developed to focus on individual students, but they can also be implemented class-wide. Individually tailored strategies can help to minimize the impact of disruptive behavior on a classroom, reduce the frequency of negative interactions between a student and teacher, and teach the child a more appropriate way to have his or her needs meet (e.g., gaining teacher attention). Thus, the goal of reactive strategies is to provide information and support to enhance the student's ability to focus on learning and minimize the likelihood that disruptive behavior will be reinforced. This latter goal in particular is aided by the use of functional assessment to assist in understanding which variables maintain problem behaviors among students with ADHD.

Functional Assessment Strategies

Functional assessment strategies include interviews, observations, and environmental manipulation to identify setting variables that reliably precede or follow problem behaviors of concern. Hypotheses are then formed about what conditions prompt the occurrence of the problem behavior, called *preceding variables*, and what conditions reinforce or maintain problem behaviors, called *following variables* (see Nelson, Roberts, & Smith, 1998).

Understanding the factors that maintain problem behaviors, along with the situations that appear to set the stage for those behaviors, is an essential first step in planning successful interventions (DuPaul & Stoner, 2003). For example, a target student's disruptive classroom behavior (e.g., verbal disruptions, speaking out of turn) may be consistently prompted by the teacher's instructional presentation of new math material. A possible intervention in this case could involve the teacher providing assistance at the beginning of that activity to ensure that the student understands rules and expectations, has all the materials needed to participate in the instruction, and is able to clearly see and hear the teacher's presentation. Alternatively, if the student's disruptive behavior reliably results in teacher attention, the hypothesis might be that Michael's disruptive behavior is being reinforced through teacher-delivered social attention ("Michael, please stop disrupting the lesson! Don't you remember the class rules?").

At least one component of a functional approach to intervention would include behavior management strategies intended to strengthen an alternative behavior that would produce the same type and likelihood of reinforcement—in this case teacher attention. For example, the teacher might use a strategy that includes providing attention contingent upon Michael responding appropriately to a question posed by the teacher, or otherwise maintaining appropriate attention to the lesson, and withholding attention when disruptive behavior occurs.

Ervin et al. conducted a study using functional assessment strategies to develop classroom-based interventions for four adolescents diagnosed with ADHD (Ervin, DuPaul, Kern, & Friman, 1998). For example, the interventions were linked to the problem hypothesized to serve the function of escape from written tasks for one student, and access to peer attention for the second student. The student who was escaping from written tasks was allowed to complete written assignments using a computer rather than writing by hand. The second student's intervention provided peer attention if the student displayed on-task behavior. The results of this study suggest that classroom interventions based on functional assessment strategies resulted in significant improvements in the behavior of both students.

Response Cost

One strategy that combines proactive and reactive approaches to behavior management is known as response cost, a form of a token economy. Reinforcement using tokens is a commonly used strategy in which students earn points for meeting behavioral expectations, and the points can be exchanged for privileges. With response cost, students earn tokens based on positive classroom behavior and lose them for inappropriate behavior. Response-cost systems require planning and clear communication from the outset. The rules of the system should be taught and reviewed on an ongoing basis. The student should understand when the system will be used, how points may be gained or lost, what privileges are available in exchange for points, and when points may be turned in for privileges. It may be useful for the teacher to check which privilege a student is working toward on a daily basis before beginning an activity, and to intermittently change the available privileges in order to maintain student interest.

For these systems to be effective, the students should be involved in creating the menu of possible privileges, and be able to receive their earned privileges on a regular basis. Electronic versions of response cost, such as the Attention Training System (ATS; Rapport, 1987), allow the teacher to respond to inappropriate behavior on the part of one child while continuing to work with other children or the whole class. This electronic system is made up of a student module, which sits on the student's desk, and a teacher module. The student automatically accumulates points as he or she works independently or in a group. When the teacher notices off-task or disruptive behavior, student points can be readily deducted by pushing a button on the teacher module. Thus, immediate feedback on student behavior is provided without interrupting classroom activities or instruction.

A manual version of the response-cost system uses numbered cards held together by a binder ring. The teacher adds and subtracts points by changing the top card on her set of cards as the child demonstrates appropriate or inappropriate behavior. As the teacher changes her cards, the student changes the number of points on his or her set of cards to match the teacher's set. These strategies provide the student with frequent and immediate feedback on performance, which is an important factor in helping children with ADHD meet the behavioral expectations of the classroom. This immediate communication of positive or corrective feedback helps to improve student outcomes in the areas of behavior and classroom achievement. Several studies have supported the use of response-cost strategies for children with attention problems associated with ADHD (see Pfiffner, Barkley, & DuPaul, 2006).

Several cautions regarding the use of response cost should be noted. First, some teachers might object to the punishing features of response cost, while others might see the delivery of reinforcement via an electronic console as unacceptably mechanical. Second, the loss of points may prompt behavioral outbursts by highly agitated students. Finally, the use of response cost should never lead to a situation in which the student can "go in the hole" or accumulate negative points, as this would significantly affect student motivation to cooperate with the program.

Contingency Contracting

Contingency contracting involves the negotiation of an agreement between a student and teacher that stipulates (a) what is expected of the student (responsibilities), (b) what will happen if responsibilities are fulfilled (privileges), and (c) what will happen if responsibilities are not met or if major rule violations are committed (penalties). This contract is a more abstract version of the token reinforcement approach used with younger children.

Several factors should be considered when designing a contract for a student with ADHD (DuPaul & Stoner, 2003). First, the length of time between the required behavior and the contingent reinforcement should be as brief as possible. Daily and weekly reinforcement is preferred over longer delays, because students with ADHD often engage in impulsive actions that require relatively immediate consequences. Second, attainable goals should be set for the student so that immediate success can be achieved. The probability of success is further enhanced by the inclusion of a small number of goals or responsibilities at a time. Third, students should have a voice in determining the privileges toward which they are working. This may necessitate including the parents in the negotiation process, as home-based activities (e.g., access to driving privileges) may be necessary to motivate secondary school students. Finally, the contract should be renegotiated on a regular basis (at least monthly), as a student's progress often will require changes to goals and privileges over time.

Parents as Intervention Agents

Educators can provide an important service to parents of a child with ADHD by clearly communicating school expectations and by teaching strategies that parents can use to promote academic success. Systematic ongoing communication is needed between the parents and teachers in order for parents to effectively support their children's academic performance. Designing a system to support ongoing communication is important, whether it consists of notes sent home on a daily or weekly basis (school–home notes), weekly check-in phone calls or e-mails, brief conversations when a child is picked up after school, or some other system that fits the particular family and school. Maintaining communication allows parents to hear about their child's struggles and successes in school, to communicate about home issues that may be influencing classroom performance, and to build a partnership with teachers with a goal of improving their child's ability to succeed in school.

Home-based reinforcement programs can help strengthen school-based behavior management systems by allowing the child to earn privileges at home for displaying positive behavior at school. Effective home-based programs require ongoing communication between the teacher and parents; this can be accomplished through the use of a daily note or report that is sent home with the student (e.g., Fabiano et al., 2007). Parents and teachers can negotiate a contingency contract, which specifies the academic outcomes and classroom behaviors that are expected and the privileges that can be earned at home if the child successfully demonstrates the behaviors. This type of contract is most likely to be successful if privileges can be earned each day, rather than weekly. Long-term success is built on small successes right from the start, so choosing criteria that the child is easily able to meet at the beginning, while slowly building up to more challenging goals, is an important feature of the school–home note system.

Fabiano and colleagues (2007) incorporated daily and weekly school–home notes as part of a comprehensive classroom management system for 48 children with ADHD attending a summer treatment program. Children were also randomly assigned to stimulant medication and nonmedication conditions. The study found that high-intensity classroom intervention (including daily school–home notes) was equivalent or superior to two doses of methylphenidate in reducing disruptive behavior and increasing classwork productivity (see Figure 1). Thus, school–home notes may be particularly effective when combined with other classroom-based contingency systems.

Figure 1. Graphs of classroom behavior measures.

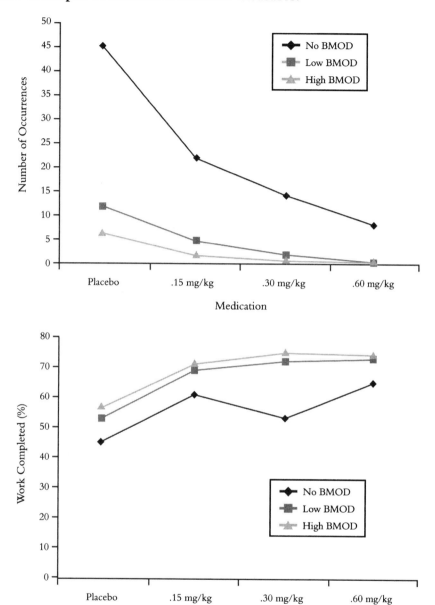

Note. The top panel illustrates frequency of classroom rule violations at each level of behavior modification and medication; the bottom panel represents the percentage of assigned seatwork completed at each level of behavior modification and medication. BMOD = behavior modification. From "The Single and Combined Effects of Multiple Intensities of Behavior Modification and Methylphenidate for Children With ADHD in a Classroom Setting," by G. A. Fabiano et al., 2007, *School Psychology Review, 36,* p. 206. Copyright 2007 by National Association of School Psychologists. Reprinted with permission.

Self-Management

Self-management interventions include self-monitoring and self-evaluation. Strategies that include one or both self-management components have been associated with moderate to large effects on classroom behavior and academic productivity (Reid, Trout, & Schartz, 2005).

Self-monitoring strategies involve training students to recognize and report whether they have engaged in a specific behavior or sequence of behaviors during an identified time period. For example, Gureasko-Moore, DuPaul, and White (2006) investigated the effectiveness of a self-monitoring program in helping three middle school boys with ADHD be better prepared for class. The boys received brief training from a school psychologist in how to monitor their classroom preparedness behaviors using a checklist describing the range of student classroom behavior, from very consistent with classroom rules and expectations to very inconsistent with them. Students also were taught to evaluate their performance against goals they had set with the school psychologist (i.e., self-reinforcement). As they exhibited success with the procedures, the involvement of the school psychologist was faded so that procedures were eventually entirely self-managed. Each of the three students consistently improved in being prepared for class, and these improvements were maintained over time, even in the absence of external support. These findings were replicated in a separate sample of six middle school students with ADHD, and effects were extended to self-monitoring of homework performance (Gureasko-Moore, DuPaul, & White, 2007).

Self-evaluation strategies incorporate a gradual shift from external to self-reinforcement. They have been found to enhance the attention and behavior of students with ADHD and related behavior disorders (e.g., Hoff & DuPaul, 1998; Rhode, Morgan, & Young, 1983). Prior to the first stage of self-management, students are trained by teachers to recognize target behaviors associated with ratings from 0 to 5, with 5 being all work completed, of excellent quality, and 0 being little or no work completed, quality of work poor. These behaviors are modeled for the students, and the students also role-play target behaviors while stating the rating associated with the behavior. During the first stage of self-management, students and teachers independently rate student performance during one academic period. Ratings are then compared: (a) if the student's rating is within one point of the teacher's, the student keeps the points he or she gave himself or herself; (b) if the student's rating matches the teacher's exactly, the student receives the points given by the teacher, plus one bonus point; and (c) if student and teacher ratings deviate by more than one point, no points are awarded. As with a token reinforcement system, points are exchanged for preferred activities on a daily or weekly basis.

During successive stages of the self-evaluation program, the frequency of teacher–student matches is gradually reduced to 0%. For example, during the 50% match stage, a coin is flipped following each rating period wherein the student is required to match the teacher an average of 50% of the time. Given that the outcome is random and unpredictable, the student cannot assume prior to the coin flip that he or she does not have to match the teacher's rating. On the occasions in which he or she does not have to match, the student automatically keeps the points awarded. In the investigation by Hoff and DuPaul (1998), student behavior was evaluated across these self-management phases. Generalization across settings was programmed for and systematically evaluated. Data showed that the student was able to maintain behavioral improvements initially elicited under token reinforcement despite the fading of teacher feedback. It is important to note that throughout the study, the student continued to provide written ratings of performance and continued to receive backup contingencies (i.e., access to classroom privileges such as playing educational games with peers). The ideal outcome would be for written ratings to be faded to oral ratings while backup contingencies are phased out.

MEDICATION TREATMENT OF STUDENTS WITH ADHD

Elementary school-age students with ADHD are considered by pediatricians, psychologists, psychiatrists, and others to be good candidates for treatment with psychotropic medications, particularly psychostimulants. The discussion of the use of medications with these children is limited in this chapter, but a few points need to be made (for more detail, see Connor, 2006, and DuPaul and Stoner, 2003). First, when students with ADHD are treated with psychostimulants, medication should be considered one component of a treatment package that also includes behavioral and educational supports. In fact, the use of carefully designed behavioral interventions can reduce the need for or the dosage of stimulant medication for some children (see Figure 1; Fabiano et al., 2007; MTA Cooperative Group, 2004). Second, school psychologists and other school personnel, such as school nurses and teachers, can play a crucial role in monitoring medication response, including the effects of medication dose on academic performance and behavior. Third, these professionals also can play a critical role in ongoing monitoring of medication effects, including the presence or absence of potentially adverse side effects. Finally, through careful and professional collaboration and communication with the medical professionals responsible for medication treatments, school-based personnel can enhance the experiences and functioning of children with ADHD and their parents and teachers.

As is the case for younger children, a variety of psychotropic medications (especially stimulants) can be helpful for adolescents with ADHD. Approximately 50–60% of teenagers with this disorder will respond positively to methylphenidate or other stimulants (Connor, 2006; Evans et al., 2001). Care must be taken to monitor not only the behavioral effects of these medications, but also their impact on academic performance at school and home. Furthermore, students should be instructed to participate in the evaluation of their response by reporting changes in their behavior and possible adverse side effects (DuPaul et al., 1998). Because some of the side effects of stimulant medications may not be overt (e.g., dysphoric mood), students can report a greater number of these emergent effects than teachers or parents. Finally, even when medication is effective, it should be supplemented with behavioral and educational interventions to optimize functioning in these areas.

CONCLUSION

Students identified with ADHD are likely to be difficult to teach and difficult to manage in classroom settings. Because these students are a heterogeneous group, in some cases these difficulties will occur across settings, and in other cases they will be confined to specific academic areas or particular situations. However, most of these students are capable of functioning quite well in school—behaving and performing academically in ways that are similar to their typical peers. The strategies described in this chapter, as mediated by teachers, parents, peers, computers, and the students themselves, and tailored to each student and setting, hold great promise for ensuring that students with ADHD are given the support they need to succeed in school.

AUTHOR NOTE

Preparation of this chapter was supported, in part, by National Institute of Mental Health grants R01- MH62941 and R01-61563. Correspondence regarding this chapter should be directed to George J. DuPaul, PhD, College of Education, Lehigh University, 111 Research Drive, Bethlehem, PA 18015; e-mail: gjd3@lehigh.edu.

REFERENCES

American Psychiatric Association. (2000). *Diagnostic and statistical manual of mental disorders* (4th ed., Text rev.). Washington, DC: Author.

Archer, A., & Gleason, M. (2002). *Skills for school success.* North Billerica, MA: Curriculum Associates.

Barkley, R. A. (Ed.). (2006). *Attention-deficit hyperactivity disorder: A handbook for diagnosis and treatment* (3rd ed.). New York: Guilford Press.

Barkley, R. A., Murphy, K., & Fischer, M. (2008). *ADHD in adults: What the science says.* New York: Guilford Press.

Cantwell, D. P., & Baker, L. (1991). Association between attention–deficit hyperactivity disorder and learning disorders. *Journal of Learning Disabilities, 24,* 88–95.

Clarfield, J., & Stoner, G. (2005). The effects of computerized reading instruction on the academic performance of students identified with ADHD. *School Psychology Review, 34,* 246–254.

Colvin, G., Sugai, G., Good, R. H., III, & Lee, Y. (1997). Using active supervision and precorrection to improve transition behaviors in elementary school. *School Psychology Quarterly, 12,* 344–363.

Connor, D. F. (2006). Stimulants. In R. A. Barkley (Ed.), *Attention-deficit hyperactivity disorder: A handbook for diagnosis and treatment* (3rd ed., pp. 608–647). New York: Guilford Press.

Dawson, P., & Guare, R. (1998). *Coaching the ADHD student.* North Tonawanda, NY: Multi-Health Systems.

Dunlap, G., dePerczel, M., Clarke, S., Wilson, D., Wright, S., White, R., et al. (1994). Choice making to promote adaptive behavior for students with emotional and behavioral challenges. *Journal of Applied Behavior Analysis, 27,* 505–518.

DuPaul, G. J., Anastopoulos, A. D., Kwasnik, D., Barkley, R. A., & McMurray, M. B. (1996). Methylphenidate effects on children with attention deficit hyperactivity disorder: Self-report of symptoms, side effects, and self-esteem. *Journal of Attention Disorders, 1,* 3–15.

DuPaul, G. J., & Eckert, T. L. (1997). The effects of school-based interventions with attention deficit hyperactivity disorder: A meta-analysis. *School Psychology Review, 26,* 5–27.

DuPaul, G. J., Eckert, T. L., & McGoey, K. E. (1997). Interventions for students with attention-deficit/hyperactivity disorder: One size does not fit all. *School Psychology Review, 26,* 369–381.

DuPaul, G. J., Ervin, R. A., Hook, C. L., & McGoey, K. E. (1998). Peer tutoring for children with attention deficit hyperactivity disorder: Effects on classroom behavior and academic performance. *Journal of Applied Behavior Analysis, 31,* 579–592.

DuPaul, G. J., Jitendra, A. K., Volpe, R. J., Tresco, K. E., Lutz, J. G., Vile Junod, R. E., et al. (2006). Consultation-based academic interventions for children with ADHD: Effects on reading and mathematics achievement. *Journal of Abnormal Child Psychology, 34,* 633–646.

DuPaul, G. J., & Stoner, G. (2002). Interventions for attention problems. In M. R. Shinn, H. M. Walker, & G. Stoner (Eds.), *Interventions for academic and behavior problems II: Preventive and remedial approaches* (pp. 913–938). Bethesda, MD: National Association of School Psychologists.

DuPaul, G. J., & Stoner, G. (2003). *ADHD in the schools: Assessment and intervention strategies* (2nd ed.). New York: Guilford Press.

Ervin, R. A., DuPaul, G. J., Kern, L., & Friman, P. C. (1998). Classroom-based functional and adjunctive assessments: Proactive approaches to intervention selection for adolescents with attention deficit hyperactivity disorder. *Journal of Applied Behavior Analysis, 31,* 65–78.

Evans, S. W., Langberg, J., Raggi, V., Allen, J., & Buvinger, E. C. (2005). Development of a school-based treatment program for middle school youth with ADHD. *Journal of Attention Disorders, 9,* 343–353.

Evans, S. W., Pelham, W., & Grudberg, M. V. (1995). The efficacy of notetaking to improve behavior and comprehension of adolescents with attention deficit hyperactivity disorder. *Exceptionality, 5,* 1–17.

Evans, S. W., Pelham, W. E., Smith, B. H., Bukstein, O., Gnagy, E. M., Greiner, A. R., et al. (2001). Dose-response effects of methylphenidate on ecologically valid measures of academic performance and classroom behavior in adolescents with ADHD. *Experimental and Clinical Psychopharmacology, 9,* 163–175.

Evans, S. W., Serpell, Z. N., Schultz, B. K., & Pastor, D. A. (2007). Cumulative benefits of secondary school-based treatment of students with attention-deficit hyperactivity disorder. *School Psychology Review, 36,* 256–273.

Fabiano, G. A., Pelham, W. E., Jr., Gnagy, E. M., Burrows-Maclean, L., Coles, E. K., Chacko, A., et al. (2007). The single and combined effects of multiple intensities of behavior modification and methylphenidate for children with attention deficit hyperactivity disorder in a classroom setting. *School Psychology Review, 36,* 195–216.

Goldstein, S., & Goldstein, M. (1998). *Managing attention disorders in children.* New York: Wiley.

Gresham, F. M., MacMillan, D. L., Beebe-Frankenberger, M. E., & Bocian, K. M. (2000). Treatment integrity in learning disabilities intervention research: Do we really know how treatments are implemented? *Learning Disabilities Research & Practice, 15,* 198–205.

Gureasko-Moore, S., DuPaul, G. J., & White, G. P. (2006). The effects of self-management in general education classrooms on the organizational skills of adolescents with ADHD. *Behavior Modification, 30,* 159–183.

Gureasko-Moore, S., DuPaul, G. J., & White, G. P. (2007). Self-management of classroom preparedness and homework: Effects on school functioning of adolescents with attention deficit hyperactivity disorder. *School Psychology Review, 36,* 647–664.

Hoff, K., & DuPaul, G. J. (1998). Reducing disruptive behavior in general education classrooms: The use of self-management strategies. *School Psychology Review, 27,* 290–303.

Horner, R. H., Sugai, G., Lewis-Palmer, T., & Todd, A. W. (2001). Teaching school-wide behavior expectations. *Report on Emotional and Behavioral Disorders in Youth, 1*(4), 77–79, 93–96.

Jensen, P. S., Arnold, L. E., Swanson, J. M., Vitiello, B., Abikoff, H. B., Greenhill, L. L. et al. (2007). Three-year follow-up of the NIMH MTA study. *Journal of the American Academy of Child and Adolescent Psychiatry, 46,* 989–1002.

Jimerson, S. R., Burns, M. K., & VanDerHeyden, A. M. (Eds.). (2007). *Handbook of response to intervention: The science and practice of assessment and intervention.* New York: Springer.

Kame'enui, E., & Carnine, D. (1998). *Effective teaching strategies that accommodate diverse learners.* Upper Saddle River, NJ: Prentice Hall.

Kame'enui, E. J., Simmons, D. C., & Coyne, M. D. (2000). Schools as host environments: Toward a schoolwide reading improvement model. *Annals of Dyslexia, 50*(1), 33–51.

Knivsberg, A., Reichelt, K. L., & Nodland, M. (1999). Comorbidity, or coexistence, between dyslexia and attention deficit hyperactivity disorder. *British Journal of Special Education, 26,* 42–47.

Lewis, T. J., & Sugai, G. (1999). Effective behavior support: A systems approach to proactive school-wide management. *Focus on Exceptional Children, 31*(6), 1–24.

March, R., Hawken, L., & Green, J. (2003). School-wide behavior support: Creating urban schools that accommodate diverse learners. *Journal of Special Education Leadership, 16*(1), 15–22.

Mautone, J. A., DuPaul, G. J., & Jitendra, A. K. (2005). The effects of computer-assisted instruction on the mathematics performance and classroom behavior of children with attention-deficit/hyperactivity disorder. *Journal of Attention Disorders, 8,* 301–312.

MTA (Multimodal Treatment Study of Children with ADHD) Cooperative Group. (1999). A 14-month randomized clinical trial of treatment strategies for attention-deficit/hyperactivity disorder. *Archives of General Psychiatry, 56,* 1073–1086.

MTA Cooperative Group. (2004). National Institute of Mental Health multimodal treatment study of ADHD follow-up: 24-month outcomes of treatment strategies for attention-deficit/hyperactivity disorder. *Pediatrics, 113,* 754–761.

Nelson, J. R., Roberts, M. L., & Smith, D. J. (1998). *Conducting functional behavioral assessments: A practical guide.* Longmont, CO: Sopris-West.

O'Neill, R. E., Horner, R. H., Albin, R. W., Sprague, J., Storey, K., & Newton, J. S. (1997). *Functional analysis and program development for problem behavior: A practical handbook.* Pacific Grove, CA: Brooks/Cole.

Ota, K. R., & DuPaul, G. J. (2002). Task engagement and mathematics performance in children with attention deficit hyperactivity disorder: Effects of supplemental computer instruction. *School Psychology Quarterly, 17,* 242–257.

Paine, S. C., Radicchi, J., Rosellini, L. C., Deutchman, L., & Darch, C. B. (1983). *Structuring your classroom for academic success.* Champaign, IL: Research Press.

Pfiffner, L. J., Barkley, R. A., & DuPaul, G. J. (2006). Treatment of ADHD in school settings. In R. A. Barkley (Ed.), *Attention-deficit hyperactivity disorder: A handbook for diagnosis and treatment* (3rd ed., pp. 547–589). New York: Guilford Press.

Rapport, M. D. (1987). *The Attention Training System: User's manual.* DeWitt, NY: Gordon Systems.

Rapport, M. D., Denney, C. B., DuPaul, G. J., & Gardner, M. J. (1994). Attention deficit disorder and methylphenidate: Normalization rates, clinical effectiveness, and response prediction in 76 children. *Journal of the American Academy of Child and Adolescent Psychiatry, 33,* 882–893.

Reid, R., Trout, A. L., & Schartz, M. (2005). Self-regulation interventions for children with attention-deficit/hyperactivity disorder. *Exceptional Children, 71,* 361–377.

Rhode, G., Morgan, D. P., & Young, K. R. (1983). Generalization and maintenance of treatment gains of behaviorally handicapped students from resource rooms to regular classrooms using self-evaluation procedures. *Journal of Applied Behavior Analysis, 16,* 171–188.

Robin, A. L. (1998). ADHD in adolescents: Diagnosis and treatment. New York: Guilford Press.

Semrud-Clikeman, M., Biederman, J., Sprich-Buckminster, S., Lehman, B. K., Faraone, S. V., & Norman, D. (1992). Comorbidity between ADDH and learning disability: A review and report in a clinically referred sample. *Journal of the American Academy of Child and Adolescent Psychiatry, 31,* 439–448.

Spires, H. A., & Stone, D. P. (1989). The directed note taking activity: A self-questioning approach. *Journal of Reading, 33,* 36–39.

Todd, A. W., Horner, R. H., Sugai, G., & Sprague, J. R. (1999). Effective behavior support: Strengthening school-wide systems through a team-based approach. *Effective School Practices, 17*(4), 23–27.

Touchette, P. E., MacDonald, R. F., & Langer, S. N. (1985). A scatter plot for identifying stimulus control of problem behavior. *Journal of Applied Behavior Analysis, 18,* 343–351.

U.S. Department of Education, Office of Special Education and Rehabilitative Services, Office of Special Education Programs. (2005). *26th annual (2004) report to Congress on the implementation of the Individuals with Disabilities Education Act* (vol. 1). Washington, DC: Author.

Weiss, G., & Hechtman, L. (1993). *Hyperactive children grown up* (2nd ed.). New York: Guilford Press.

INDEX

E

.